Microsoft® Office 365™
EXCEL® 2016

COMPREHENSIVE

D1448699

Microsoft® Office 365™
EXCEL® 2016

COMPREHENSIVE

Steven M. Freund

Joy L. Starks
Indiana University Purdue
University Indianapolis

Eric J. Schmieder

CENGAGE
Learning®

SHELLY CASHMAN SERIES®

Australia • Brazil • Japan • Korea • Mexico • Singapore • Spain • United Kingdom • United States

Microsoft® Excel® 2016: Comprehensive
Steven M. Freund, Joy L. Starks and
Eric J. Schmieder

SVP, General Manager: Balraj S. Kalsi

Product Director: Kathleen McMahon

Senior Product Team Manager: Lauren Murphy

Product Team Manager: Andrea Topping

Senior Director, Development: Julia Caballero

Product Development Manager: Leigh Hefferon

Managing Content Developer: Emma F. Newsom

Developmental Editor: Karen Stevens

Product Assistant: Erica Chapman

Manuscript Quality Assurance: Jeffrey Schwartz, John Freitas, Serge Palladino, Susan Pedicini, Danielle Shaw, Chris Scriver

Production Director: Patty Stephan

Senior Content Project Manager: Stacey Lamodi

Manufacturing Planner: Julio Esperas

Designer: Diana Graham

Vice President, Marketing: Brian Joyner

Marketing Director: Michele McTighe

Marketing Manager: Stephanie Albracht

Cover image(s): Piotr Zajc/Shutterstock.com; Mrs. Opossum/Shutterstock.com

Compositor: Lumina Datamatics, Inc.

For product information and technology assistance, contact us at
Cengage Learning Customer & Sales Support, 1-800-354-9706

For permission to use material from this text or product,
submit all requests online at **www.cengage.com/permissions**.
Further permissions questions can be e-mailed to
permissionrequest@cengage.com

Library of Congress Control Number: 2016941570

Soft-cover Edition ISBN: 978-1-305-87072-7

Loose-leaf Edition ISBN: 978-1-337-25105-1

Cengage Learning
20 Channel Center Street
Boston, MA 02210
USA

Cengage Learning is a leading provider of customized learning solutions with employees residing in nearly 40 different countries and sales in more than 125 countries around the world. Find your local representative at **www.cengage.com.**

Cengage Learning products are represented in Canada by Nelson Education, Ltd.

To learn more about Cengage Learning, visit **www.cengage.com**

Purchase any of our products at your local college store or at our preferred online store **www.cengagebrain.com**

Printed in the United States of America
Print Number: 01   Print Year: 2016

Microsoft® Office 365™
EXCEL® 2016

COMPREHENSIVE

Contents

Microsoft **Excel 2016**

MODULE ONE
Creating a Worksheet and a Chart

MODULE TWO
Formulas, Functions, and Formatting

Productivity Apps for School and Work

Corinne Hoisington

Lochlan keeps track of his class notes, football plays, and internship meetings with OneNote.

Zoe is using the annotation features of Microsoft Edge to take and save web notes for her research paper.

Nori is creating a Sway site to highlight this year's activities for the Student Government Association.

Hunter is adding interactive videos and screen recordings to his PowerPoint resume.

© Rawpixel/Shutterstock.com

Being computer literate no longer means mastery of only Word, Excel, PowerPoint, Outlook, and Access. To become technology power users, Hunter, Nori, Zoe, and Lochlan are exploring Microsoft OneNote, Sway, Mix, and Edge in Office 2016 and Windows 10.

In this Module

Learn to use productivity apps!
Links to companion **Sways**, featuring **videos** with hands-on instructions, are located on www.cengagebrain.com.

Introduction to OneNote 2016

notebook | section tab | To Do tag | screen clipping | note | template | Microsoft OneNote Mobile app | sync | drawing canvas | inked handwriting | Ink to Text

As you glance around any classroom, you invariably see paper notebooks and notepads on each desk. Because deciphering and sharing handwritten notes can be a challenge, Microsoft OneNote 2016 replaces physical notebooks, binders, and paper notes with a searchable, digital notebook. OneNote captures your ideas and schoolwork on any device so you can stay organized, share notes, and work with others on projects. Whether you are a student taking class notes as shown in **Figure 1** or an employee taking notes in company meetings, OneNote is the one place to keep notes for all of your projects.

Figure 1: OneNote 2016 notebook

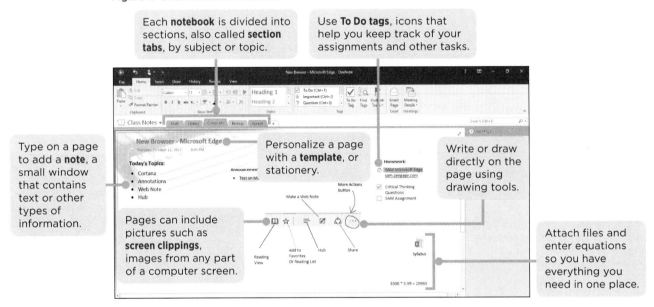

Each **notebook** is divided into sections, also called **section tabs**, by subject or topic.

Use **To Do tags**, icons that help you keep track of your assignments and other tasks.

Type on a page to add a **note**, a small window that contains text or other types of information.

Personalize a page with a **template**, or stationery.

Write or draw directly on the page using drawing tools.

Pages can include pictures such as **screen clippings**, images from any part of a computer screen.

Attach files and enter equations so you have everything you need in one place.

Creating a OneNote Notebook

OneNote is divided into sections similar to those in a spiral-bound notebook. Each OneNote notebook contains sections, pages, and other notebooks. You can use One-Note for school, business, and personal projects. Store information for each type of project in different notebooks to keep your tasks separate, or use any other organization that suits you. OneNote is flexible enough to adapt to the way you want to work.

When you create a notebook, it contains a blank page with a plain white background by default, though you can use templates, or stationery, to apply designs in categories such as Academic, Business, Decorative, and Planners. Start typing or use the buttons on the Insert tab to insert notes, which are small resizable windows that can contain text, equations, tables, on-screen writing, images, audio and video recordings, to-do lists, file attachments, and file printouts. Add as many notes as you need to each page.

Syncing a Notebook to the Cloud

OneNote saves your notes every time you make a change in a notebook. To make sure you can access your notebooks with a laptop, tablet, or smartphone wherever you are, OneNote uses cloud-based storage, such as OneDrive or SharePoint. **Microsoft OneNote Mobile app**, a lightweight version of OneNote 2016 shown in **Figure 2**, is available for free in the Windows Store, Google Play for Android devices, and the AppStore for iOS devices.

If you have a Microsoft account, OneNote saves your notes on OneDrive automatically for all your mobile devices and computers, which is called **syncing**. For example, you can use OneNote to take notes on your laptop during class, and then open OneNote on your phone to study later. To use a notebook stored on your computer with your OneNote Mobile app, move the notebook to OneDrive. You can quickly share notebook content with other people using OneDrive.

Figure 2: Microsoft OneNote Mobile app

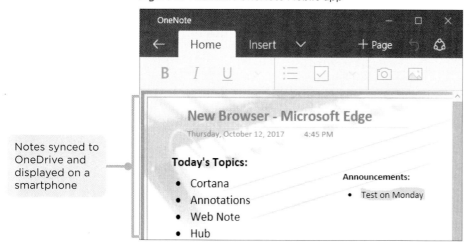

Notes synced to OneDrive and displayed on a smartphone

Taking Notes

Use OneNote pages to organize your notes by class and topic or lecture. Beyond simple typed notes, OneNote stores drawings, converts handwriting to searchable text and mathematical sketches to equations, and records audio and video.

OneNote includes drawing tools that let you sketch freehand drawings such as biological cell diagrams and financial supply-and-demand charts. As shown in **Figure 3**, the Draw tab on the ribbon provides these drawing tools along with shapes so you can insert diagrams and other illustrations to represent your ideas. When you draw on a page, OneNote creates a **drawing canvas**, which is a container for shapes and lines.

On the Job Now

OneNote is ideal for taking notes during meetings, whether you are recording minutes, documenting a discussion, sketching product diagrams, or listing follow-up items. Use a meeting template to add pages with content appropriate for meetings.

Figure 3: Tools on the Draw tab

Draw tab

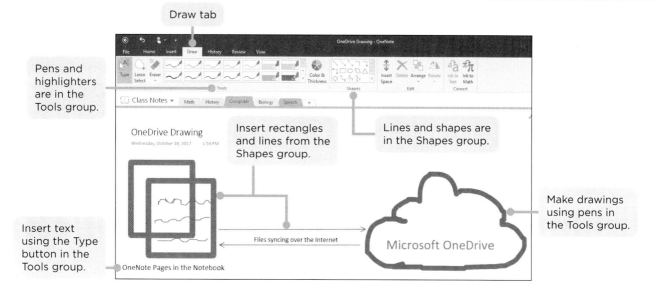

Pens and highlighters are in the Tools group.

Insert rectangles and lines from the Shapes group.

Lines and shapes are in the Shapes group.

Make drawings using pens in the Tools group.

Insert text using the Type button in the Tools group.

Files syncing over the Internet

Microsoft OneDrive

OneNote Pages in the Notebook

Converting Handwriting to Text

When you use a pen tool to write on a notebook page, the text you enter is called **inked handwriting**. OneNote can convert inked handwriting to typed text when you use the **Ink to Text** button in the Convert group on the Draw tab, as shown in **Figure 4**. After OneNote converts the handwriting to text, you can use the Search box to find terms in the converted text or any other note in your notebooks.

Figure 4: Converting handwriting to text

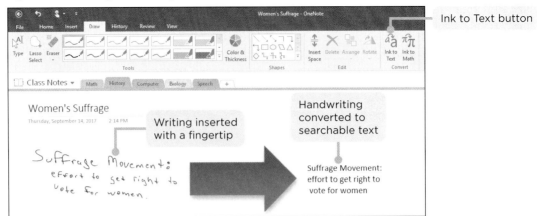

Ink to Text button

Writing inserted with a fingertip

Handwriting converted to searchable text

On the Job Now

Use OneNote as a place to brainstorm ongoing work projects. If a notebook contains sensitive material, you can password-protect some or all of the notebook so that only certain people can open it.

Recording a Lecture

If your computer or mobile device has a microphone or camera, OneNote can record the audio or video from a lecture or business meeting as shown in **Figure 5**. When you record a lecture (with your instructor's permission), you can follow along, take regular notes at your own pace, and review the video recording later. You can control the start, pause, and stop motions of the recording when you play back the recording of your notes.

Figure 5: Video inserted in a notebook

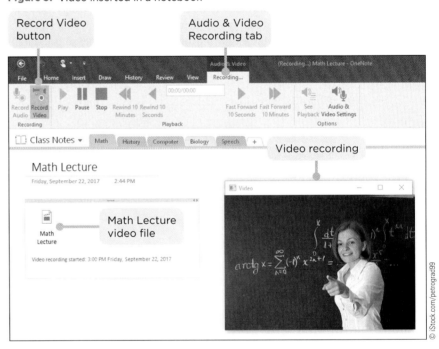

Record Video button

Audio & Video Recording tab

Video recording

Math Lecture video file

Try This Now

Learn to use OneNote!

Links to companion **Sways**, featuring **videos** with hands-on instructions, are located on www.cengagebrain.com.

1: Taking Notes for a Week

As a student, you can get organized by using OneNote to take detailed notes in your classes. Perform the following tasks:

   a. Create a new OneNote notebook on your Microsoft OneDrive account (the default location for new notebooks). Name the notebook with your first name followed by "Notes," as in **Caleb Notes**.
   b. Create four section tabs, each with a different class name.
   c. Take detailed notes in those classes for one week. Be sure to include notes, drawings, and other types of content.
   d. Sync your notes with your OneDrive. Submit your assignment in the format specified by your instructor.

2: Using OneNote to Organize a Research Paper

You have a research paper due on the topic of three habits of successful students. Use OneNote to organize your research. Perform the following tasks:

   a. Create a new OneNote notebook on your Microsoft OneDrive account. Name the notebook **Success Research**.
   b. Create three section tabs with the following names:

   - **Take Detailed Notes**
   - **Be Respectful in Class**
   - **Come to Class Prepared**

   c. On the web, research the topics and find three sources for each section. Copy a sentence from each source and paste the sentence into the appropriate section. When you paste the sentence, OneNote inserts it in a note with a link to the source.
   d. Sync your notes with your OneDrive. Submit your assignment in the format specified by your instructor.

3: Planning Your Career

Note: This activity requires a webcam or built-in video camera on any type of device.

Consider an occupation that interests you. Using OneNote, examine the responsibilities, education requirements, potential salary, and employment outlook of a specific career. Perform the following tasks:

   a. Create a new OneNote notebook on your Microsoft OneDrive account. Name the notebook with your first name followed by a career title, such as **Kara - App Developer**.
   b. Create four section tabs with the names **Responsibilities, Education Requirements, Median Salary**, and **Employment Outlook**.
   c. Research the responsibilities of your career path. Using OneNote, record a short video (approximately 30 seconds) of yourself explaining the responsibilities of your career path. Place the video in the Responsibilities section.
   d. On the web, research the educational requirements for your career path and find two appropriate sources. Copy a paragraph from each source and paste them into the appropriate section. When you paste a paragraph, OneNote inserts it in a note with a link to the source.
   e. Research the median salary for a single year for this career. Create a mathematical equation in the Median Salary section that multiplies the amount of the median salary times 20 years to calculate how much you will possibly earn.
   f. For the Employment Outlook section, research the outlook for your career path. Take at least four notes about what you find when researching the topic.
   g. Sync your notes with your OneDrive. Submit your assignment in the format specified by your instructor.

Introduction to Sway

Sway site | responsive design | Storyline | card | Creative Commons license | animation emphasis effects | Docs.com

Expressing your ideas in a presentation typically means creating PowerPoint slides or a Word document. Microsoft Sway gives you another way to engage an audience. Sway is a free Microsoft tool available at Sway.com or as an app in Office 365. Using Sway, you can combine text, images, videos, and social media in a website called a **Sway site** that you can share and display on any device. To get started, you create a digital story on a web-based canvas without borders, slides, cells, or page breaks. A Sway site organizes the text, images, and video into a **responsive design**, which means your content adapts perfectly to any screen size as shown in **Figure 6**. You store a Sway site in the cloud on OneDrive using a free Microsoft account.

Figure 6: Sway site with responsive design

You can display a Sway presentation in a web browser.

Sway uses responsive design to make sure pages fit perfectly on any device.

© iStock.com/marinello, © iStock.com/marekulasz

Creating a Sway Presentation

You can use Sway to build a digital flyer, a club newsletter, a vacation blog, an informational site, a digital art portfolio, or a new product rollout. After you select your topic and sign into Sway with your Microsoft account, a **Storyline** opens, providing tools and a work area for composing your digital story. See **Figure 7**. Each story can include text, images, and videos. You create a Sway by adding text and media content into a Storyline section, or **card**. To add pictures, videos, or documents, select a card in the left pane and then select the Insert Content button. The first card in a Sway presentation contains a title and background image.

Figure 7: Creating a Sway site

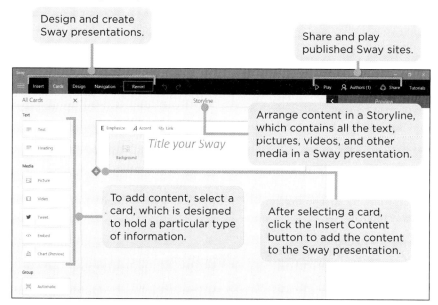

Design and create Sway presentations.

Share and play published Sway sites.

Arrange content in a Storyline, which contains all the text, pictures, videos, and other media in a Sway presentation.

To add content, select a card, which is designed to hold a particular type of information.

After selecting a card, click the Insert Content button to add the content to the Sway presentation.

Adding Content to Build a Story

As you work, Sway searches the Internet to help you find relevant images, videos, tweets, and other content from online sources such as Bing, YouTube, Twitter, and Facebook. You can drag content from the search results right into the Storyline. In addition, you can upload your own images and videos directly in the presentation. For example, if you are creating a Sway presentation about the market for commercial drones, Sway suggests content to incorporate into the presentation by displaying it in the left pane as search results. The search results include drone images tagged with a **Creative Commons license** at online sources as shown in **Figure 8**. A Creative Commons license is a public copyright license that allows the free distribution of an otherwise copyrighted work. In addition, you can specify the source of the media. For example, you can add your own Facebook or OneNote pictures and videos in Sway without leaving the app.

On the Job Now

If you have a Microsoft Word document containing an outline of your business content, drag the outline into Sway to create a card for each topic.

Figure 8: Images in Sway search results

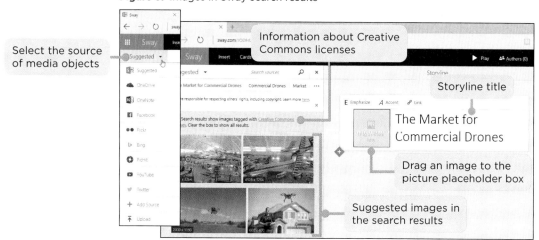

Select the source of media objects

Information about Creative Commons licenses

Storyline title

The Market for Commercial Drones

Drag an image to the picture placeholder box

Suggested images in the search results

Designing a Sway

Sway professionally designs your Storyline content by resizing background images and fonts to fit your display, and by floating text, animating media, embedding video, and removing images as a page scrolls out of view. Sway also evaluates the images in your Storyline and suggests a color palette based on colors that appear in your photos. Use the Design button to display tools including color palettes, font choices, **animation emphasis effects**, and style templates to provide a personality for a Sway presentation. Instead of creating your own design, you can click the Remix button, which randomly selects unique designs for your Sway site.

Publishing a Sway

Use the Play button to display your finished Sway presentation as a website. The Address bar includes a unique web address where others can view your Sway site. As the author, you can edit a published Sway site by clicking the Edit button (pencil icon) on the Sway toolbar.

Sharing a Sway

When you are ready to share your Sway website, you have several options as shown in **Figure 9**. Use the Share slider button to share the Sway site publically or keep it private. If you add the Sway site to the Microsoft **Docs.com** public gallery, anyone worldwide can use Bing, Google, or other search engines to find, view, and share your Sway site. You can also share your Sway site using Facebook, Twitter, Google+, Yammer, and other social media sites. Link your presentation to any webpage or email the link to your audience. Sway can also generate a code for embedding the link within another webpage.

Figure 9: Sharing a Sway site

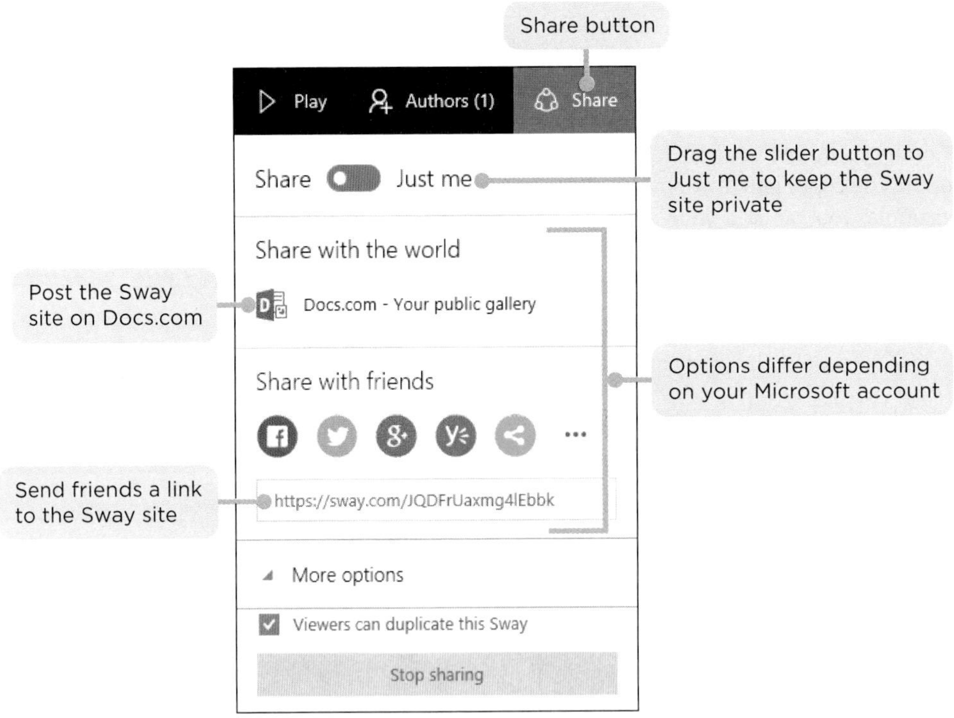

Share button

Drag the slider button to Just me to keep the Sway site private

Post the Sway site on Docs.com

Options differ depending on your Microsoft account

Send friends a link to the Sway site

Try This Now

Learn to use Sway!
Links to companion **Sways**, featuring **videos** with hands-on instructions, are located on www.cengagebrain.com.

1: Creating a Sway Resume

Sway is a digital storytelling app. Create a Sway resume to share the skills, job experiences, and achievements you have that match the requirements of a future job interest. Perform the following tasks:

   a. Create a new presentation in Sway to use as a digital resume. Title the Sway Storyline with your full name and then select a background image.
   b. Create three separate sections titled **Academic Background, Work Experience**, and **Skills**, and insert text, a picture, and a paragraph or bulleted points in each section. Be sure to include your own picture.
   c. Add a fourth section that includes a video about your school that you find online.
   d. Customize the design of your presentation.
   e. Submit your assignment link in the format specified by your instructor.

2: Creating an Online Sway Newsletter

Newsletters are designed to capture the attention of their target audience. Using Sway, create a newsletter for a club, organization, or your favorite music group. Perform the following tasks:

   a. Create a new presentation in Sway to use as a digital newsletter for a club, organization, or your favorite music group. Provide a title for the Sway Storyline and select an appropriate background image.
   b. Select three separate sections with appropriate titles, such as Upcoming Events. In each section, insert text, a picture, and a paragraph or bulleted points.
   c. Add a fourth section that includes a video about your selected topic.
   d. Customize the design of your presentation.
   e. Submit your assignment link in the format specified by your instructor.

3: Creating and Sharing a Technology Presentation

To place a Sway presentation in the hands of your entire audience, you can share a link to the Sway presentation. Create a Sway presentation on a new technology and share it with your class. Perform the following tasks:

   a. Create a new presentation in Sway about a cutting-edge technology topic. Provide a title for the Sway Storyline and select a background image.
   b. Create four separate sections about your topic, and include text, a picture, and a paragraph in each section.
   c. Add a fifth section that includes a video about your topic.
   d. Customize the design of your presentation.
   e. Share the link to your Sway with your classmates and submit your assignment link in the format specified by your instructor.

Introduction to Office Mix

add-in | clip | slide recording | Slide Notes | screen recording | free-response quiz

Bottom Line
- Office Mix is a free PowerPoint add-in from Microsoft that adds features to PowerPoint.
- The Mix tab on the PowerPoint ribbon provides tools for creating screen recordings, videos, interactive quizzes, and live webpages.

To enliven business meetings and lectures, Microsoft adds a new dimension to presentations with a powerful toolset called Office Mix, a free add-in for PowerPoint. (An **add-in** is software that works with an installed app to extend its features.) Using Office Mix, you can record yourself on video, capture still and moving images on your desktop, and insert interactive elements such as quizzes and live webpages directly into PowerPoint slides. When you post the finished presentation to OneDrive, Office Mix provides a link you can share with friends and colleagues. Anyone with an Internet connection and a web browser can watch a published Office Mix presentation, such as the one in **Figure 10**, on a computer or mobile device.

Figure 10: Office Mix presentation

Adding Office Mix to PowerPoint

Learn to use Office Mix!
Links to companion **Sways**, featuring **videos** with hands-on instructions, are located on www.cengagebrain.com.

To get started, you create an Office Mix account at the website mix.office.com using an email address or a Facebook or Google account. Next, you download and install the Office Mix add-in (see **Figure 11**). Office Mix appears as a new tab named Mix on the PowerPoint ribbon in versions of Office 2013 and Office 2016 running on personal computers (PCs).

Figure 11: Getting started with Office Mix

Capturing Video Clips

A **clip** is a short segment of audio, such as music, or video. After finishing the content on a PowerPoint slide, you can use Office Mix to add a video clip to animate or illustrate the content. Office Mix creates video clips in two ways: by recording live action on a webcam and by capturing screen images and movements. If your computer has a webcam, you can record yourself and annotate the slide to create a **slide recording** as shown in **Figure 12**.

On the Job Now

Companies are using Office Mix to train employees about new products, to explain benefit packages to new workers, and to educate interns about office procedures.

Figure 12: Making a slide recording

When you are making a slide recording, you can record your spoken narration at the same time. The **Slide Notes** feature works like a teleprompter to help you focus on your presentation content instead of memorizing your narration. Use the Inking tools to make annotations or add highlighting using different pen types and colors. After finishing a recording, edit the video in PowerPoint to trim the length or set playback options.

The second way to create a video is to capture on-screen images and actions with or without a voiceover. This method is ideal if you want to show how to use your favorite website or demonstrate an app such as OneNote. To share your screen with an audience, select the part of the screen you want to show in the video. Office Mix captures everything that happens in that area to create a **screen recording**, as shown in **Figure 13**. Office Mix inserts the screen recording as a video in the slide.

On the Job Now

To make your video recordings accessible to people with hearing impairments, use the Office Mix closed-captioning tools. You can also use closed captions to supplement audio that is difficult to understand and to provide an aid for those learning to read.

Figure 13: Making a screen recording

Inserting Quizzes, Live Webpages, and Apps

To enhance and assess audience understanding, make your slides interactive by adding quizzes, live webpages, and apps. Quizzes give immediate feedback to the user as shown in **Figure 14**. Office Mix supports several quiz formats, including a **free-response quiz** similar to a short answer quiz, and true/false, multiple-choice, and multiple-response formats.

Figure 14: Creating an interactive quiz

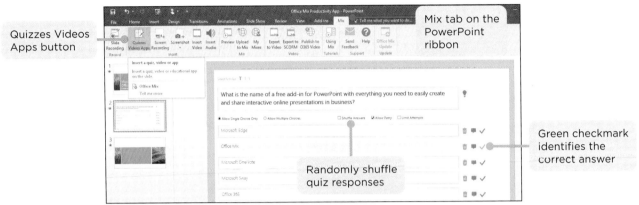

Quizzes Videos Apps button

Mix tab on the PowerPoint ribbon

Green checkmark identifies the correct answer

Randomly shuffle quiz responses

Sharing an Office Mix Presentation

When you complete your work with Office Mix, upload the presentation to your personal Office Mix dashboard as shown in **Figure 15**. Users of PCs, Macs, iOS devices, and Android devices can access and play Office Mix presentations. The Office Mix dashboard displays built-in analytics that include the quiz results and how much time viewers spent on each slide. You can play completed Office Mix presentations online or download them as movies.

Figure 15: Sharing an Office Mix presentation

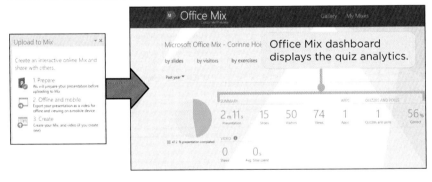

Office Mix dashboard displays the quiz analytics.

Try This Now

1: Creating an Office Mix Tutorial for OneNote

Note: This activity requires a microphone on your computer.

Office Mix makes it easy to record screens and their contents. Create PowerPoint slides with an Office Mix screen recording to show OneNote 2016 features. Perform the following tasks:

a. Create a PowerPoint presentation with the Ion Boardroom template. Create an opening slide with the title **My Favorite OneNote Features** and enter your name in the subtitle.
b. Create three additional slides, each titled with a new feature of OneNote. Open OneNote and use the Mix tab in PowerPoint to capture three separate screen recordings that teach your favorite features.
c. Add a fifth slide that quizzes the user with a multiple-choice question about OneNote and includes four responses. Be sure to insert a checkmark indicating the correct response.
d. Upload the completed presentation to your Office Mix dashboard and share the link with your instructor.
e. Submit your assignment link in the format specified by your instructor.

Learn to use Office Mix!
Links to companion **Sways**, featuring **videos** with hands-on instructions, are located on www.cengagebrain.com.

2: Teaching Augmented Reality with Office Mix

Note: This activity requires a webcam or built-in video camera on your computer.

A local elementary school has asked you to teach augmented reality to its students using Office Mix. Perform the following tasks:

a. Research augmented reality using your favorite online search tools.
b. Create a PowerPoint presentation with the Frame template. Create an opening slide with the title **Augmented Reality** and enter your name in the subtitle.
c. Create a slide with four bullets summarizing your research of augmented reality. Create a 20-second slide recording of yourself providing a quick overview of augmented reality.
d. Create another slide with a 30-second screen recording of a video about augmented reality from a site such as YouTube or another video-sharing site.
e. Add a final slide that quizzes the user with a true/false question about augmented reality. Be sure to insert a checkmark indicating the correct response.
f. Upload the completed presentation to your Office Mix dashboard and share the link with your instructor.
g. Submit your assignment link in the format specified by your instructor.

3: Marketing a Travel Destination with Office Mix

Note: This activity requires a webcam or built-in video camera on your computer.

To convince your audience to travel to a particular city, create a slide presentation marketing any city in the world using a slide recording, screen recording, and a quiz. Perform the following tasks:

a. Create a PowerPoint presentation with any template. Create an opening slide with the title of the city you are marketing as a travel destination and your name in the subtitle.
b. Create a slide with four bullets about the featured city. Create a 30-second slide recording of yourself explaining why this city is the perfect vacation destination.
c. Create another slide with a 20-second screen recording of a travel video about the city from a site such as YouTube or another video-sharing site.
d. Add a final slide that quizzes the user with a multiple-choice question about the featured city with five responses. Be sure to include a checkmark indicating the correct response.
e. Upload the completed presentation to your Office Mix dashboard and share your link with your instructor.
f. Submit your assignment link in the format specified by your instructor.

Introduction to Microsoft Edge

Reading view | Hub | Cortana | Web Note | Inking | sandbox

Bottom Line
- Microsoft Edge is the name of the new web browser built into Windows 10.
- Microsoft Edge allows you to search the web faster, take web notes, read webpages without distractions, and get instant assistance from Cortana.

Microsoft Edge is the default web browser developed for the Windows 10 operating system as a replacement for Internet Explorer. Unlike its predecessor, Edge lets you write on webpages, read webpages without advertisements and other distractions, and search for information using a virtual personal assistant. The Edge interface is clean and basic, as shown in **Figure 16**, meaning you can pay more attention to the webpage content.

Figure 16: Microsoft Edge tools

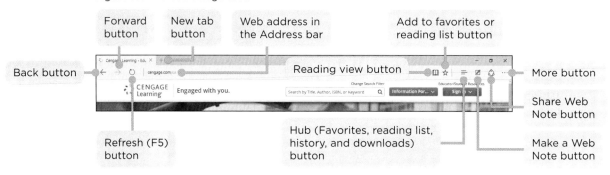

Browsing the Web with Microsoft Edge

One of the fastest browsers available, Edge allows you to type search text directly in the Address bar. As you view the resulting webpage, you can switch to **Reading view**, which is available for most news and research sites, to eliminate distracting advertisements. For example, if you are catching up on technology news online, the webpage might be difficult to read due to a busy layout cluttered with ads. Switch to Reading view to refresh the page and remove the original page formatting, ads, and menu sidebars to read the article distraction-free.

Consider the **Hub** in Microsoft Edge as providing one-stop access to all the things you collect on the web, such as your favorite websites, reading list, surfing history, and downloaded files.

Locating Information with Cortana

Cortana, the Windows 10 virtual assistant, plays an important role in Microsoft Edge. After you turn on Cortana, it appears as an animated circle in the Address bar when you might need assistance, as shown in the restaurant website in **Figure 17**. When you click the Cortana icon, a pane slides in from the right of the browser window to display detailed information about the restaurant, including maps and reviews. Cortana can also assist you in defining words, finding the weather, suggesting coupons for shopping, updating stock market information, and calculating math.

Learn to use Edge!
Links to companion **Sways**, featuring **videos** with hands-on instructions, are located on www.cengagebrain.com.

On the Job Now

Businesses started adopting Internet Explorer more than 20 years ago simply to view webpages. Today, Microsoft Edge has a different purpose: to promote interaction with the web and share its contents with colleagues.

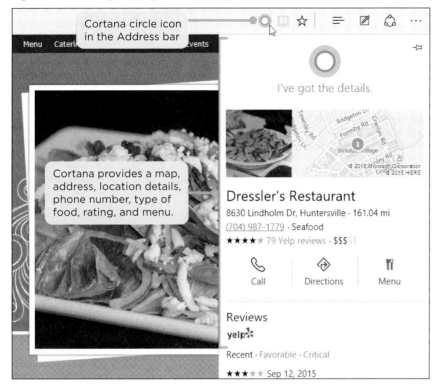

Annotating Webpages

One of the most impressive Microsoft Edge features are the **Web Note** tools, which you use to write on a webpage or to highlight text. When you click the Make a Web Note button, an **Inking** toolbar appears, as shown in **Figure 18**, that provides writing and drawing tools. These tools include an eraser, a pen, and a highlighter with different colors. You can also insert a typed note and copy a screen image (called a screen clipping). You can draw with a pointing device, fingertip, or stylus using different pen colors. Whether you add notes to a recipe, annotate sources for a research paper, or select a product while shopping online, the Web Note tools can enhance your productivity. After you complete your notes, click the Save button to save the annotations to OneNote, your Favorites list, or your Reading list. You can share the inked page with others using the Share Web Note button.

On the Job Now

To enhance security, Microsoft Edge runs in a partial sandbox, an arrangement that prevents attackers from gaining control of your computer. Browsing within the **sandbox** protects computer resources and information from hackers.

Figure 18: Web Note tools in Microsoft Edge

Inking toolbar with Web Note tools for making annotations

Writing and drawing created with the Pen tool

Highlighted text

Save a copy of the webpage with annotations

Typed note

Try This Now

1: Using Cortana in Microsoft Edge

Note: This activity requires using Microsoft Edge on a Windows 10 computer.

Cortana can assist you in finding information on a webpage in Microsoft Edge. Perform the following tasks:

a. Create a Word document using the Word Screen Clipping tool to capture the following screenshots.

- Screenshot A—Using Microsoft Edge, open a webpage with a technology news article. Right-click a term in the article and ask Cortana to define it.
- Screenshot B—Using Microsoft Edge, open the website of a fancy restaurant in a city near you. Make sure the Cortana circle icon is displayed in the Address bar. (If it's not displayed, find a different restaurant website.) Click the Cortana circle icon to display a pane with information about the restaurant.
- Screenshot C—Using Microsoft Edge, type **10 USD to Euros** in the Address bar without pressing the Enter key. Cortana converts the U.S. dollars to Euros.
- Screenshot D—Using Microsoft Edge, type **Apple stock** in the Address bar without pressing the Enter key. Cortana displays the current stock quote.

b. Submit your assignment in the format specified by your instructor.

2: Viewing Online News with Reading View

Note: This activity requires using Microsoft Edge on a Windows 10 computer.

Reading view in Microsoft Edge can make a webpage less cluttered with ads and other distractions. Perform the following tasks:

a. Create a Word document using the Word Screen Clipping tool to capture the following screenshots.

- Screenshot A—Using Microsoft Edge, open the website **mashable.com**. Open a technology article. Click the Reading view button to display an ad-free page that uses only basic text formatting.
- Screenshot B—Using Microsoft Edge, open the website **bbc.com**. Open any news article. Click the Reading view button to display an ad-free page that uses only basic text formatting.
- Screenshot C—Make three types of annotations (Pen, Highlighter, and Add a typed note) on the BBC article page displayed in Reading view.

b. Submit your assignment in the format specified by your instructor.

3: Inking with Microsoft Edge

Note: This activity requires using Microsoft Edge on a Windows 10 computer.

Microsoft Edge provides many annotation options to record your ideas. Perform the following tasks:

a. Open the website **wolframalpha.com** in the Microsoft Edge browser. Wolfram Alpha is a well-respected academic search engine. Type **US$100 1965 dollars in 2015** in the Wolfram Alpha search text box and press the Enter key.

b. Click the Make a Web Note button to display the Web Note tools. Using the Pen tool, draw a circle around the result on the webpage. Save the page to OneNote.

c. In the Wolfram Alpha search text box, type the name of the city closest to where you live and press the Enter key. Using the Highlighter tool, highlight at least three interesting results. Add a note and then type a sentence about what you learned about this city. Save the page to OneNote. Share your OneNote notebook with your instructor.

d. Submit your assignment link in the format specified by your instructor.

Office 2016 and Windows 10: Essential Concepts and Skills

Objectives

You will have mastered the material in this module when you can:

- Use a touch screen
- Perform basic mouse operations
- Start Windows and sign in to an account
- Identify the objects on the Windows 10 desktop
- Identify the apps in and versions of Microsoft Office 2016
- Run an app
- Identify the components of the Microsoft Office ribbon

- Create folders
- Save files
- Change screen resolution
- Perform basic tasks in Microsoft Office apps
- Manage files
- Use Microsoft Office Help and Windows Help

This introductory module uses Excel 2016 to cover features and functions common to Office 2016 apps, as well as the basics of Windows 10.

Roadmap

In this module, you will learn how to perform basic tasks in Windows and Excel. The following roadmap identifies general activities you will perform as you progress through this module:

1. SIGN IN to an account
2. USE WINDOWS
3. USE Features in Excel that are Common across Office APPS
4. FILE and Folder MANAGEMENT
5. SWITCH between APPS
6. SAVE and Manage FILES

7. CHANGE SCREEN RESOLUTION

8. EXIT APPS

9. USE ADDITIONAL Office APP FEATURES

10. USE Office and Windows HELP

At the beginning of the step instructions throughout each module, you will see an abbreviated form of this roadmap. The abbreviated roadmap uses colors to indicate module progress: gray means the module is beyond that activity, blue means the task being shown is covered in that activity, and black means that activity is yet to be covered. For example, the following abbreviated roadmap indicates the module would be showing a task in the USE APPS activity.

1 SIGN IN | 2 USE WINDOWS | 3 USE APPS | 4 FILE MANAGEMENT | 5 SWITCH APPS | 6 SAVE FILES
7 CHANGE SCREEN RESOLUTION | 8 EXIT APPS | 9 USE ADDITIONAL APP FEATURES | 10 USE HELP

Use the abbreviated roadmap as a progress guide while you read or step through the instructions in this module.

Introduction to the Windows 10 Operating System

Windows 10 is the newest version of Microsoft Windows, which is a popular and widely used operating system (Figure 1). An **operating system (OS)** is a set of programs that coordinate all the activities among computer or mobile device hardware.

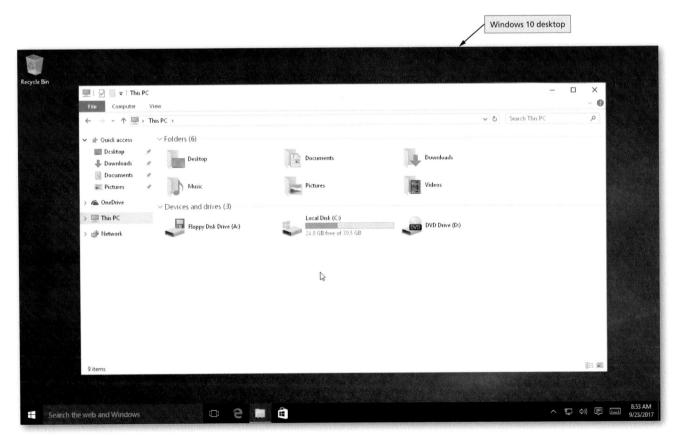

Windows 10 desktop

Figure 1

The Windows operating system simplifies the process of working with documents and apps by organizing the manner in which you interact with the computer. Windows is used to run apps. An application, or **app**, consists of programs designed to make users more productive and/or assist them with personal tasks, such as using spreadsheets or browsing the web.

Using a Touch Screen and a Mouse

Windows users who have computers or devices with touch screen capability can interact with the screen using gestures. A **gesture** is a motion you make on a touch screen with the tip of one or more fingers or your hand. Touch screens are convenient because they do not require a separate device for input. Table 1 presents common ways to interact with a touch screen.

If you are using your finger on a touch screen and are having difficulty completing the steps in this module, consider using a stylus. Many people find it easier to be precise with a stylus than with a finger. In addition, with a stylus you see the pointer. If you still are having trouble completing the steps with a stylus, try using a mouse.

Table 1 Touch Screen Gestures

Motion	Description	Common Uses	Equivalent Mouse Operation
Tap	Quickly touch and release one finger one time.	Activate a link (built-in connection). Press a button. Run a program or an app.	Click
Double-tap	Quickly touch and release one finger two times.	Run a program or an app. Zoom in (show a smaller area on the screen, so that contents appear larger) at the location of the double-tap.	Double-click
Press and hold	Press and hold one finger to cause an action to occur, or until an action occurs.	Display a shortcut menu (immediate access to allowable actions). Activate a mode enabling you to move an item with one finger to a new location.	Right-click
Drag, or slide	Press and hold one finger on an object and then move the finger to the new location.	Move an item around the screen. Scroll.	Drag
Swipe	Press and hold one finger and then move the finger horizontally or vertically on the screen.	Select an object. Swipe from edge to display a bar such as the Action Center, Apps bar, and Navigation bar (all discussed later).	Drag
Stretch	Move two fingers apart.	Zoom in (show a smaller area on the screen, so that contents appear larger).	None
Pinch	Move two fingers together.	Zoom out (show a larger area on the screen, so that contents appear smaller).	None

Will your screen look different if you are using a touch screen?

The Windows and Microsoft Office interface varies slightly if you are using a touch screen. For this reason, you might notice that your Windows or Excel screens looks slightly different from the screens in this book.

CONSIDER THIS

BTW
Pointer
If you are using a touch screen, the pointer may not appear on the screen as you perform touch gestures. The pointer will reappear when you begin using the mouse.

Windows users who do not have touch screen capabilities typically work with a mouse that has at least two buttons. For a right-handed user, the left button usually is the primary mouse button, and the right mouse button is the secondary mouse button. Left-handed people, however, can reverse the function of these buttons.

Table 2 explains how to perform a variety of mouse operations. Some apps also use keys in combination with the mouse to perform certain actions. For example, when you hold down the CTRL key while rolling the mouse wheel, text on the screen may become larger or smaller based on the direction you roll the wheel. The function of the mouse buttons and the wheel varies depending on the app.

Table 2 Mouse Operations

Operation	Mouse Action	Example*	Equivalent Touch Gesture
Point	Move the mouse until the pointer on the desktop is positioned on the item of choice.	Position the pointer on the screen.	None
Click	Press and release the primary mouse button, which usually is the left mouse button.	Select or deselect items on the screen or run an app or app feature.	Tap
Right-click	Press and release the secondary mouse button, which usually is the right mouse button.	Display a shortcut menu.	Press and hold
Double-click	Quickly press and release the primary mouse button twice without moving the mouse.	Run an app or app feature.	Double-tap
Triple-click	Quickly press and release the primary mouse button three times without moving the mouse.	Select a paragraph.	Triple-tap
Drag	Point to an item, hold down the primary mouse button, move the item to the desired location on the screen, and then release the mouse button.	Move an object from one location to another or draw pictures.	Drag or slide
Right-drag	Point to an item, hold down the secondary mouse button, move the item to the desired location on the screen, and then release the mouse button.	Display a shortcut menu after moving an object from one location to another.	Press and hold, then drag
Rotate wheel	Roll the wheel forward or backward.	Scroll vertically (up and down).	Swipe
Free-spin wheel	Whirl the wheel forward or backward so that it spins freely on its own.	Scroll through many pages in seconds.	Swipe
Press wheel	Press the wheel button while moving the mouse.	Scroll continuously.	None
Tilt wheel	Press the wheel toward the right or left.	Scroll horizontally (left and right).	None
Press thumb button	Press the button on the side of the mouse with your thumb.	Move forward or backward through webpages and/or control media, games, etc.	None

*Note: The examples presented in this column are discussed as they are demonstrated in this module.

Scrolling

A **scroll bar** is a horizontal or vertical bar that appears when the contents of an area may not be visible completely on the screen (Figure 2). A scroll bar contains **scroll arrows** and a **scroll box** that enable you to view areas that currently cannot be seen on the screen. Clicking the up and down scroll arrows moves the screen content up or down one line. You also can click above or below the scroll box to move up or down a section, or drag the scroll box up or down to move to a specific location.

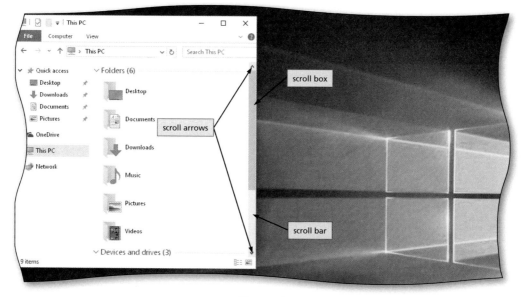

Figure 2

Keyboard Shortcuts

In many cases, you can use the keyboard instead of the mouse to accomplish a task. To perform tasks using the keyboard, you press one or more keyboard keys, sometimes identified as a **keyboard shortcut**. Some keyboard shortcuts consist of a single key, such as the F1 key. For example, to obtain help in many apps, you can press the F1 key. Other keyboard shortcuts consist of multiple keys, in which case a plus sign separates the key names, such as CTRL+ESC. This notation means to press and hold down the first key listed, press one or more additional keys, and then release all keys. For example, to display the Start menu, press CTRL+ESC, that is, hold down the CTRL key, press the ESC key, and then release both keys.

Starting Windows

It is not unusual for multiple people to use the same computer in a work, educational, recreational, or home setting. Windows enables each user to establish a **user account**, which identifies to Windows the resources, such as apps and storage locations, a user can access when working with the computer.

Each user account has a user name and may have a password and an icon, as well. A **user name** is a unique combination of letters or numbers that identifies a specific user to Windows. A **password** is a private combination of letters, numbers, and special characters associated with the user name that allows access to a user's account resources. An icon is a small image that represents an object; thus, a **user icon** is a picture associated with a user name.

When you turn on a computer, Windows starts and displays a **lock screen** consisting of the time and date (Figure 3). To unlock the screen, click the lock screen. Depending on your computer's settings, Windows may or may not display a sign-in screen that shows the user names and user icons for users who have accounts on the computer. This **sign-in screen** enables you to sign in to your user account and makes the computer available for use. Clicking the user icon begins the process of signing in, also called logging on, to your user account.

BTW
Minimize Wrist Injury
Computer users frequently switch between the keyboard and the mouse during a spreadsheet session; such switching strains the wrist. To help prevent wrist injury, minimize switching. For instance, if your fingers already are on the keyboard, use keyboard keys to scroll. If your hand already is on the mouse, use the mouse to scroll. If your hand is on the touch screen, use touch gestures to scroll.

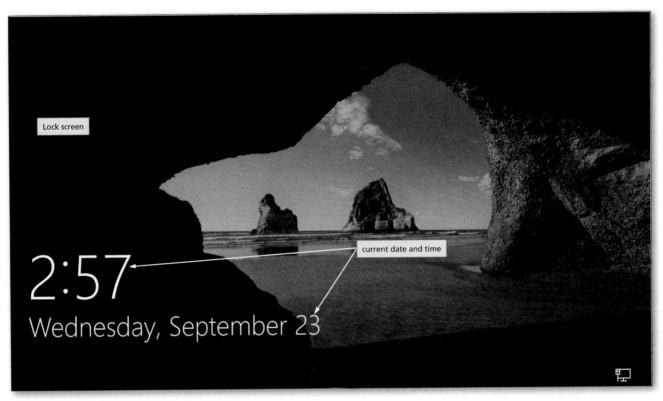

Lock screen

2:57

Wednesday, September 23

current date and time

Figure 3

At the bottom of the sign-in screen is the 'Connect to Internet' button, 'Ease of access' button, and a Shut down button. Clicking the 'Connect to Internet' button displays a list of each network connection and its status. You also can connect to or disconnect from a network. Clicking the 'Ease of access' button displays the Ease of access menu, which provides tools to optimize a computer to accommodate the needs of the mobility, hearing, and vision impaired users. Clicking the Shut down button displays a menu containing commands related to putting the computer or mobile device in a low-power state, shutting it down, and restarting the computer or mobile device. The commands available on your computer or mobile device may differ.

- The Sleep command saves your work, turns off the computer fans and hard drive, and places the computer in a lower-power state. To wake the computer from sleep mode, press the power button or lift a laptop's cover, and sign in to your account.

- The Shut down command exits running apps, shuts down Windows, and then turns off the computer.

- The Restart command exits running apps, shuts down Windows, and then restarts Windows.

1 SIGN IN | 2 USE WINDOWS | 3 USE APPS | 4 FILE MANAGEMENT | 5 SWITCH APPS | 6 SAVE FILES
7 CHANGE SCREEN RESOLUTION | 8 EXIT APPS | 9 USE ADDITIONAL APP FEATURES | 10 USE HELP

To Sign In to an Account

The following steps, which use SCSeries as the user name, sign in to an account based on a typical Windows installation. ***Why?*** *After starting Windows, you might be required to sign in to an account to access the computer or mobile device's resources.* You may need to ask your instructor how to sign in to your account.

1

- Click the lock screen (shown in Figure 3) to display a sign-in screen.

- Click the user icon (for SCSeries, in this case) on the sign-in screen, which depending on settings, either will display a second sign-in screen that contains a Password text box (Figure 4) or will display the Windows desktop (Figure 5).

Q&A Why do I not see a user icon?
Your computer may require you to type a user name instead of clicking an icon.

What is a text box?
A text box is a rectangular box in which you type text.

Why does my screen not show a Password text box?
Your account does not require a password.

- If Windows displays a sign-in screen with a Password text box, type your password in the text box.

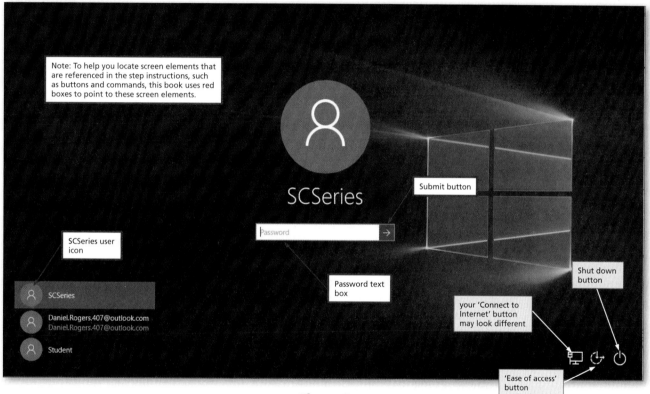

Figure 4

2

- Click the Submit button (shown in Figure 4) to sign in to your account and display the Windows desktop (Figure 5).

Q&A Why does my desktop look different from the one in Figure 5?
The Windows desktop is customizable, and your school or employer may have modified the desktop to meet its needs. Also, your screen resolution, which affects the size of the elements on the screen, may differ from the screen resolution used in this book. Later in this module, you learn how to change screen resolution.

How do I type if my tablet has no keyboard?
You can use your fingers to press keys on a keyboard that appears on the screen, called an on-screen keyboard, or you can purchase a separate physical keyboard that attaches to or wirelessly communicates with the tablet.

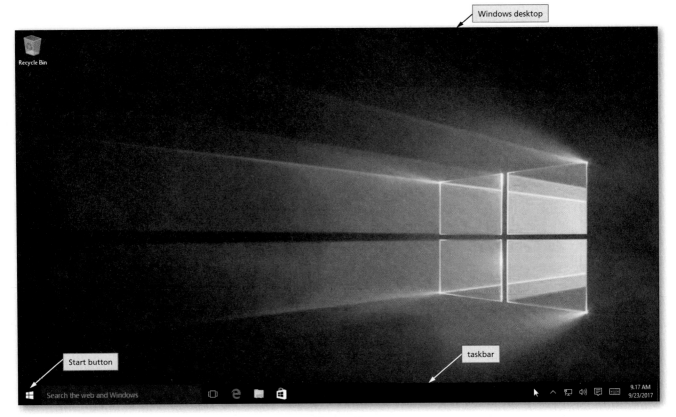

Figure 5

The Windows Desktop

The Windows 10 desktop (Figure 5) and the objects on the desktop emulate a work area in an office. Think of the Windows desktop as an electronic version of the top of your desk. You can perform tasks such as placing objects on the desktop, moving the objects around the desktop, and removing items from the desktop.

When you run an app in Windows 10, it appears on the desktop. Some icons also may be displayed on the desktop. For instance, the icon for the **Recycle Bin**, the location of files that have been deleted, appears on the desktop by default. A **file** is a named unit of storage. Files can contain text, images, audio, and video. You can customize your desktop so that icons representing programs and files you use often appear on your desktop.

Introduction to Microsoft Office 2016

Microsoft Office 2016 is the newest version of Microsoft Office, offering features that provide users with better functionality and easier ways to work with the various files they create. This version of Office also is designed to work more optimally on mobile devices and online.

Microsoft Office 2016 Apps

Microsoft Office 2016 includes a wide variety of apps, such as Word, PowerPoint, Excel, Access, Outlook, Publisher, and OneNote:

- **Microsoft Word 2016**, or Word, is a full-featured word processing app that allows you to create professional-looking documents and revise them easily.

- **Microsoft PowerPoint 2016**, or PowerPoint, is a complete presentation app that enables you to produce professional-looking presentations and then deliver them to an audience.

- **Microsoft Excel 2016**, or Excel, is a powerful spreadsheet app that allows you to organize data, complete calculations, make decisions, graph data, develop professional-looking reports, publish organized data to the web, and access real-time data from websites.

- **Microsoft Access 2016**, or Access, is a database management system that enables you to create a database; add, change, and delete data in the database; ask questions concerning the data in the database; and create forms and reports using the data in the database.

- **Microsoft Outlook 2016**, or Outlook, is a communications and scheduling app that allows you to manage email accounts, calendars, contacts, and access to other Internet content.

- **Microsoft Publisher 2016**, or Publisher, is a desktop publishing app that helps you create professional-quality publications and marketing materials that can be shared easily.

- **Microsoft OneNote 2016**, or OneNote, is a note taking app that allows you to store and share information in notebooks with other people.

Microsoft Office 2016 Suites

A **suite** is a collection of individual apps available together as a unit. Microsoft offers a variety of Office suites, including a stand-alone desktop app, Microsoft Office 365, and Microsoft Office Online. **Microsoft Office 365**, or Office 365, provides plans that allow organizations to use Office in a mobile setting while also being able to communicate and share files, depending upon the type of plan selected by the organization. **Microsoft Office Online** includes apps that allow you to edit and share files on the web using the familiar Office interface.

During the Office 365 installation, you select a plan, and depending on your plan, you receive different apps and services. Office Online apps do not require a local installation and can be accessed through OneDrive and your browser. **OneDrive** is a cloud storage service that provides storage and other services, such as Office Online, to computer and mobile device users.

How do you sign up for a OneDrive account?

- Use your browser to navigate to onedrive.live.com.

- Create a Microsoft account by clicking the Sign up button and then entering your information to create the account.

- Sign in to OneDrive using your new account or use it in Excel to save your files on OneDrive.

CONSIDER THIS

Apps in a suite, such as Microsoft Office, typically use a similar interface and share features. Once you are comfortable working with the elements and the interface and performing tasks in one app, the similarity can help you apply the knowledge and skills you have learned to another app(s) in the suite. For example, the process for saving a file in Excel is the same in Word, PowerPoint, and some of the other Office apps. While briefly showing how to use Excel, this module illustrates some of the common functions across the Office apps and identifies the characteristics unique to Excel.

Running and Using an App

To use an app, you must instruct the operating system to run the app. Windows provides many different ways to run an app, one of which is presented in this section (other ways to run an app are presented throughout this module). After an app is running, you can use it to perform a variety of tasks. The following pages use Excel to discuss some elements of the Office interface and to perform tasks that are common to other Office apps.

Excel

Excel is a powerful spreadsheet app that allows users to organize data, complete calculations, make decisions, graph data, develop professional-looking reports, publish organized data to the web, and access real-time data from websites (Figure 6). The four major parts of Excel are:

- **Workbooks and Worksheets:** A workbook is like a notebook. Inside the workbook are sheets, each of which is called a worksheet. Thus, a workbook is a collection of worksheets. Worksheets allow users to enter, calculate, manipulate, and analyze data, such as numbers and text. The terms worksheet and spreadsheet are interchangeable.

- **Charts:** Excel can draw a variety of charts, such as column charts and pie charts.

- **Tables:** Tables organize and store data within worksheets. For example, once a user enters data into a worksheet, an Excel table can sort the data, search for specific data, and select data that satisfies defined criteria.

- **Web Support:** Web support allows users to save Excel worksheets or parts of a worksheet in a format that a user can view in a browser, so that a user can view and manipulate the worksheet using a browser. Excel web support also provides access to real-time data, such as stock quotes, using web queries.

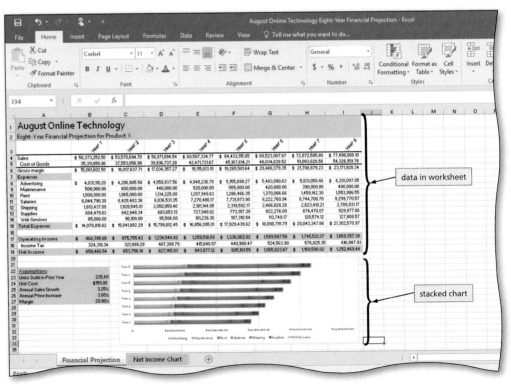

Figure 6

To Run an App Using the Start Menu and Create a Blank Document

Across the bottom of the Windows 10 desktop is the taskbar. The taskbar contains the **Start button**, which you use to access apps, files, folders, and settings. A **folder** is a named location on a storage medium that usually contains related documents.

Clicking the Start button displays the Start menu. The **Start menu** allows you to access programs, folders, and files on the computer or mobile device and contains commands that allow you to start programs, store and search for documents, customize the computer or mobile device, and sign out of a user account or shut down the computer or mobile device. A **menu** is a list of related items, including folders, programs, and commands. Each **command** on a menu performs a specific action, such as saving a file or obtaining help. *Why? When you install an app, for example, the app's name will be added to the All apps list on the Start menu.*

The following steps, which assume Windows is running, use the Start menu to run Excel and create a blank workbook based on a typical installation. You may need to ask your instructor how to run Excel on your computer. Although the steps illustrate running the Excel app, the steps to run any Office app are similar.

- Click the Start button on the Windows 10 taskbar to display the Start menu (Figure 7).

Figure 7

2

- Click All apps at the bottom of the left pane of the Start menu to display a list of apps installed on the computer or mobile device. If necessary, scroll to display the app you wish to run, Excel 2016, in this case (Figure 8).

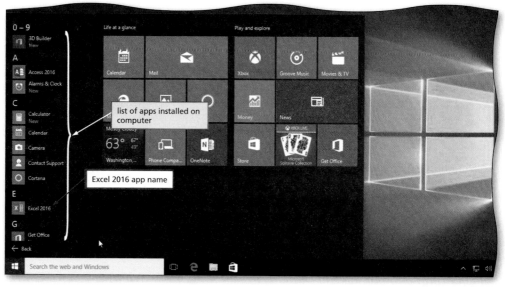

Figure 8

❸

- If the app you wish to run is located in a folder, click or scroll to and then click the folder in the All apps list to display a list of the folder's contents.

- Click, or scroll to and then click, the app name (Excel 2016, in this case) in the list to run the selected app (Figure 9).

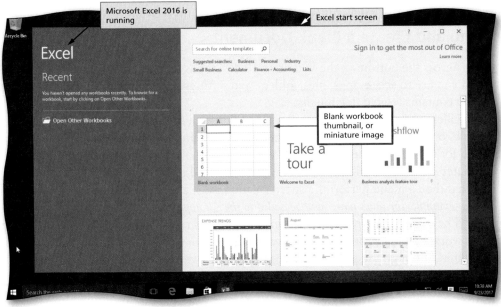

Figure 9

❹

- Click the Blank workbook thumbnail on the Excel start screen to create a blank Excel workbook in the Excel window (Figure 10).

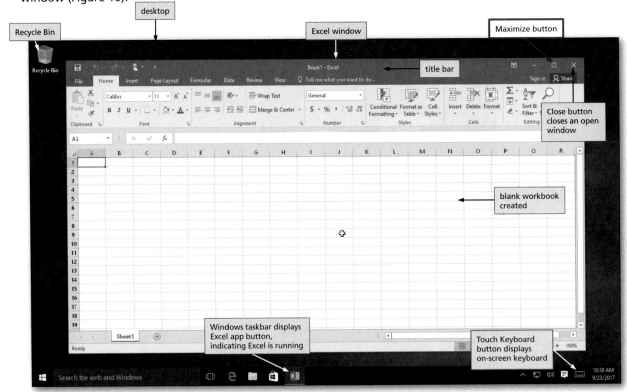

Figure 10

Q&A What happens when you run an app?

Some apps provide a means for you to create a blank document, as shown in Figure 9; others immediately display a blank document in an app window, such as the Excel window shown in Figure 10. A **window** is a rectangular area that displays data and information. The top of a window has a **title bar**, which is a horizontal space that contains the window's name.

Other Ways

1. Type app name in search box, click app name in results list
2. Double-click file created in app you want to run

To Maximize a Window

Sometimes content is not visible completely in a window. One method of displaying the entire contents of a window is to **maximize** it, or enlarge the window so that it fills the entire screen. The following step maximizes the Excel window; however, any Office app's window can be maximized using this step. *Why? A maximized window provides the most space available for using the app.*

- If the Excel window is not maximized already, click the Maximize button (shown in Figure 10) next to the Close button on the Excel window's title bar to maximize the window (Figure 11).

Q&A

What happened to the Maximize button?
It changed to a Restore Down button, which you can use to return a window to its size and location before you maximized it.

How do I know whether a window is maximized?
A window is maximized if it fills the entire display area and the Restore Down button is displayed on the title bar.

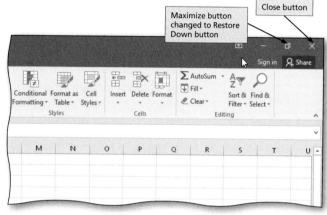

Figure 11

Other Ways

1. Double-click title bar

2. Drag title bar to top of screen

Excel Workbook Window, Ribbon, and Elements Common to Office Apps

The Excel window consists of a variety of components to make your work more efficient and worksheets more professional. These include the worksheet window, ribbon, Tell Me box, mini toolbar and shortcut menus, Quick Access Toolbar, and Microsoft Account area. Some of these components are common to other Office apps; others are unique to Excel.

Excel opens a new workbook with one worksheet. If necessary, you can add additional worksheets. Each worksheet has a sheet name that appears on a **sheet tab** at the bottom of the workbook. For example, Sheet1 is the name of the active worksheet displayed in the blank workbook shown in Figure 12. You can add more sheets to the workbook by clicking the New sheet button.

Worksheet   The worksheet is organized into a rectangular grid containing vertical columns and horizontal rows. A column letter above the grid, called the **column heading**, identifies each column. A row number on the left side of the grid, called the **row heading**, identifies each row.

The intersection of each column and row is a cell. A **cell** is the basic unit of a worksheet into which you enter data. Each worksheet in a workbook has 16,384 columns and 1,048,576 rows for a total of 17,179,869,184 cells. Only a small fraction of the active worksheet appears on the screen at one time.

A cell is referred to by its unique address, or **cell reference**, which is the coordinates of the intersection of a column and a row. To identify a cell, specify the

BTW

Touch Keyboard
To display the on-screen touch keyboard, click the Touch Keyboard button on the Windows taskbar. When finished using the touch keyboard, click the X button on the touch keyboard to close the keyboard.

BTW

The Worksheet Size and Window
The 16,384 columns and 1,048,576 rows in Excel make for a huge worksheet that — if you could imagine — takes up the entire side of a building to display in its entirety. Your computer screen, by comparison, is a small window that allows you to view only a minute area of the worksheet at one time. While you cannot see the entire worksheet, you can move the window over the worksheet to view any part of it.

column letter first, followed by the row number. For example, cell reference C6 refers to the cell located at the intersection of column C and row 6 (Figure 12).

One cell on the worksheet, designated the **active cell**, is the one into which you can enter data. The active cell in Figure 12 is A1. The active cell is identified in three ways. First, a heavy border surrounds the cell; second, the active cell reference shows immediately above column A in the Name box; and third, the column heading A and row heading 1 are highlighted so that it is easy to see which cell is active (Figure 12).

The horizontal and vertical lines on the worksheet itself are called **gridlines**. Gridlines make it easier to see and identify each cell in the worksheet. If desired, you can turn the gridlines off so that they do not show on the worksheet. While learning Excel, gridlines help you to understand the structure of the worksheet.

The pointer in Figure 12 has the shape of a block plus sign. The pointer appears as a block plus sign whenever it is located in a cell on the worksheet. Another common shape of the pointer is the block arrow. The pointer turns into the block arrow when you move it outside the worksheet or when you drag cell contents between rows or columns.

Scroll Bars   You use a scroll bar to display different portions of a document in the document window. At the right edge of the document window is a vertical scroll bar. If a document is too wide to fit in the document window, a horizontal scroll bar also appears at the bottom of the document window. On a scroll bar, the position of the scroll box reflects the location of the portion of the document that is displayed in the document window.

Status Bar   The **status bar**, located at the bottom of the document window above the Windows taskbar, presents information about the document, the progress of current tasks, and the status of certain commands and keys; it also provides controls for viewing the document. As you type text or perform certain tasks, various indicators and buttons may appear on the status bar. The right side of the status bar includes buttons and controls you can use to change the view of a document and adjust the size of the displayed document.

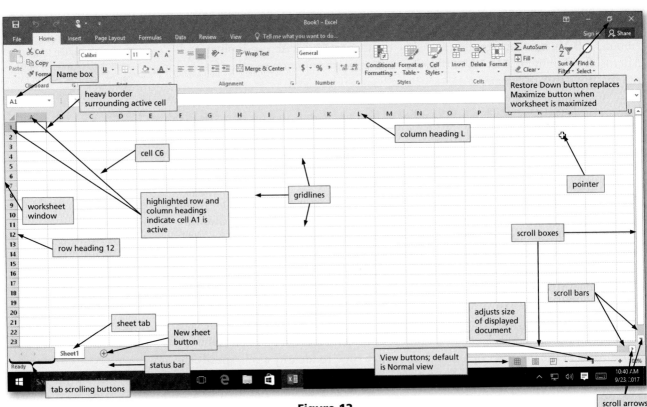

Figure 12

Ribbon   The ribbon, located near the top of the window below the title bar, is the control center in Excel and other Office apps (Figure 13). The ribbon provides easy, central access to the tasks you perform while creating a document. The ribbon consists of tabs, groups, and commands. Each **tab** contains a collection of groups, and each **group** contains related commands. When you run an Office app, such as Excel, it initially displays several main tabs, also called default or top-level tabs. All Office apps have a Home tab, which contains the more frequently used commands. When you run Excel, the ribbon displays eight main tabs: File, Home, Insert, Page Layout, Formulas, Data, Review, and View. The Formulas and Data tabs are specific to Excel. The Formulas tab allows you to work with Excel formulas, and the Data tab allows you to work with data processing features such as importing and sorting data.

BTW

Customizing the Ribbon

In addition to customizing the Quick Access Toolbar, you can add items to and remove items from the ribbon. To customize the ribbon, click File on the ribbon to open the Backstage view, click the Options tab in the Backstage view, and then click Customize Ribbon in the left pane of the Options dialog box. More information about customizing the ribbon is presented in a later module.

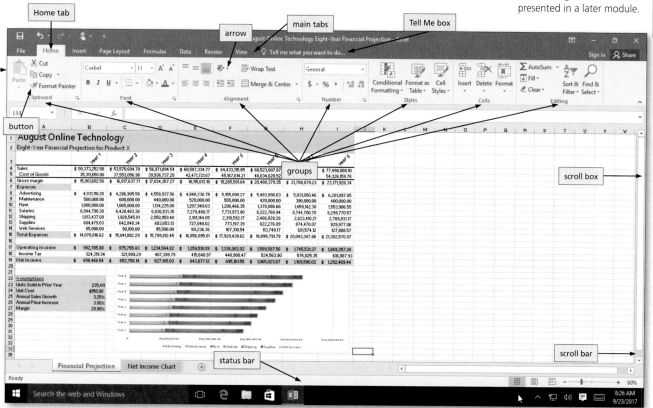

Figure 13

In addition to the main tabs, the Office apps display **tool tabs**, also called contextual tabs (Figure 14), when you perform certain tasks or work with objects such as pictures or tables. If you insert a chart in an Excel workbook, for example, the Chart Tools tab and its related subordinate Design and Format tabs appear, collectively referred to as the Chart Tools Design tab or Chart Tools Format tab. When you are finished working with the chart, the Chart Tools tab disappears from the ribbon. Excel and other Office apps determine when tool tabs should appear and disappear based on tasks you perform.

Items on the ribbon include buttons, boxes, and galleries (shown in Figures 13 and 14). A **gallery** is a set of choices, often graphical, arranged in a grid or in a list. You can scroll through choices in an in-ribbon gallery by clicking the gallery's scroll arrows. Or, you can click a gallery's More button to view more gallery options on the screen at a time.

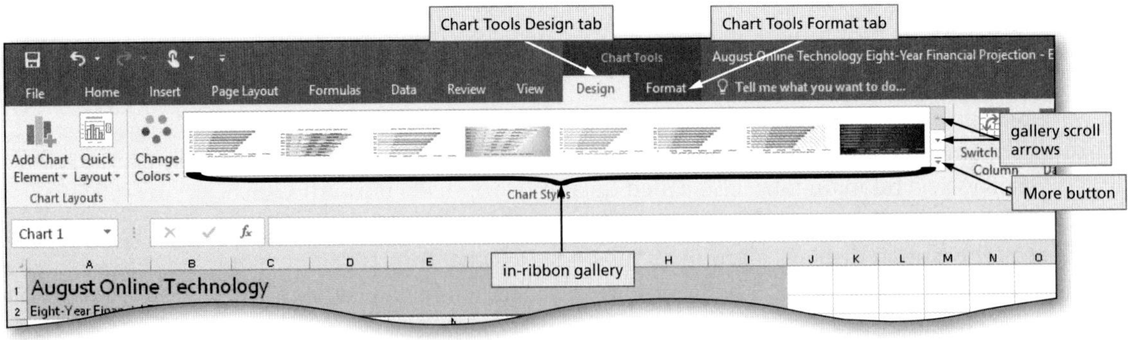

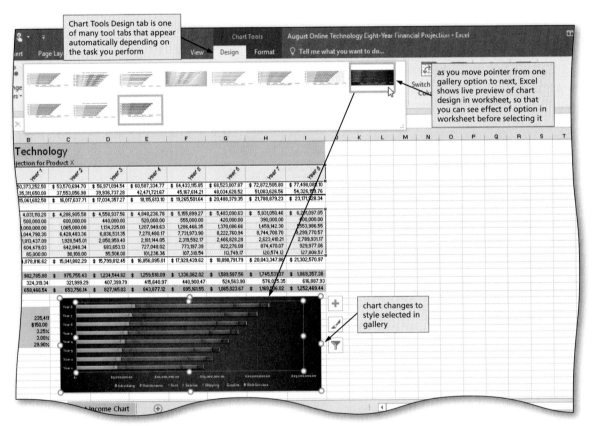

Figure 14

Some buttons and boxes have arrows that, when clicked, also display a gallery; others always cause a gallery to be displayed when clicked. Most galleries support **live preview**, which is a feature that allows you to point to a gallery choice and see its effect in the document — without actually selecting the choice (Figure 15). Live preview works only if you are using a mouse; if you are using a touch screen, you will not be able to view live previews.

Figure 15

Some commands on the ribbon display an image to help you remember their function. When you point to a command on the ribbon, all or part of the command glows in a darker shade of gray, and a ScreenTip appears on the screen. A **ScreenTip** is an on-screen note that provides the name of the command, available keyboard shortcut(s), a description of the command, and sometimes instructions for how to obtain help about the command (Figure 16).

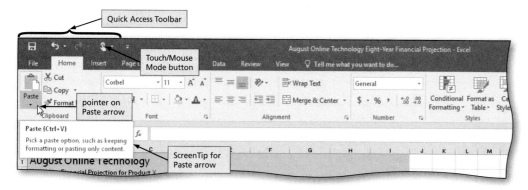

Figure 16

Some groups on the ribbon have a small arrow in the lower-right corner, called a **Dialog Box Launcher**, that when clicked, displays a dialog box or a task pane with additional options for the group (Figure 17). When presented with a dialog box, you make selections and must close the dialog box before returning to the document. A **task pane**, in contrast to a dialog box, is a window that can remain open and visible while you work in the document.

BTW
Touch Mode
The Office and Windows interfaces may vary if you are using touch mode. For this reason, you might notice that the function or appearance of your touch screen differs slightly from this module's presentation.

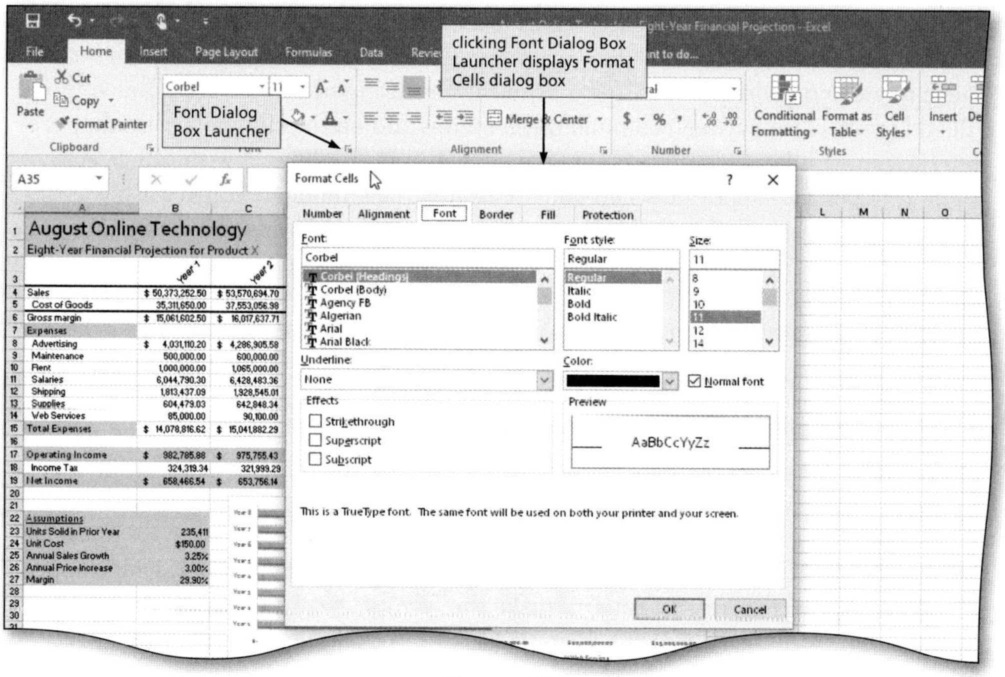

Figure 17

Mini Toolbar The **mini toolbar**, which appears automatically based on tasks you perform, contains commands related to changing the appearance of text in a document (Figure 18). If you do not use the mini toolbar, it disappears from the screen. The buttons, arrows, and boxes on the mini toolbar vary, depending on whether you are using Touch mode versus Mouse mode. If you right-click an item in the document window, Excel displays both the mini toolbar and a shortcut menu, which is discussed in a later section in this module.

BTW
Turning Off the Mini Toolbar
If you do not want the mini toolbar to appear, click File on the ribbon to open the Backstage view, click the Options tab in the Backstage view, if necessary, click General (Options dialog box), remove the check mark from the 'Show Mini Toolbar on selection' check box, and then click the OK button.

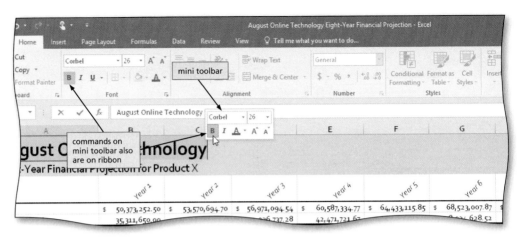

Figure 18

All commands on the mini toolbar also exist on the ribbon. The purpose of the mini toolbar is to minimize hand or mouse movement.

Quick Access Toolbar The **Quick Access Toolbar**, located initially (by default) above the ribbon at the left edge of the title bar, provides convenient, one-click access to frequently used commands (shown in Figure 16). The commands on the Quick Access Toolbar always are available, regardless of the task you are performing. The Touch/Mouse Mode button on the Quick Access Toolbar allows you to switch between Touch mode and Mouse mode. If you primarily are using touch gestures, Touch mode will add more space between commands on menus and on the ribbon so that they are easier to tap. While touch gestures are convenient ways to interact with Office apps, not all features are supported when you are using Touch mode. If you are using a mouse, Mouse mode will not add the extra space between buttons and commands. The Quick Access Toolbar is discussed in more depth later in the module.

KeyTips If you prefer using the keyboard instead of the mouse, you can press the ALT key on the keyboard to display **KeyTips**, or keyboard code icons, for certain commands (Figure 19). To select a command using the keyboard, press the letter or number displayed in the KeyTip, which may cause additional KeyTips related to the selected command to appear. To remove KeyTips from the screen, press the ALT key or the ESC key until all KeyTips disappear, or click anywhere in the app window.

Formula Bar As you type, Excel displays the entry in the **formula bar**, which appears below the ribbon (Figure 19). You can make the formula bar larger by dragging the sizing handle at the bottom of the formula bar or clicking the expand button to the right of the formula bar. Excel also displays the active cell reference in the **Name box** on the left side of the formula bar.

Tell Me Box The **Tell Me box**, which appears to the right of the tabs on the ribbon, is a type of search box that helps you to perform specific tasks in an Office app (Figure 19). As you type in the Tell Me box, the word-wheeling feature displays search results that are refined as you type. For example, if you want to center text in a document, you can type "center" in the Tell Me box and then select the appropriate command. The Tell Me box also lists the last five commands accessed from the box.

Microsoft Account Area In this area, you can use the Sign in link to sign in to your Microsoft account (Figure 19). Once signed in, you will see your account information, as well as a picture if you have included one in your Microsoft account.

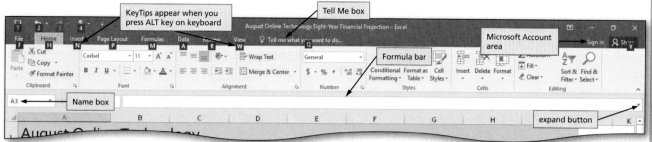

Figure 19

To Display a Different Tab on the Ribbon

1 SIGN IN | 2 USE WINDOWS | 3 USE APPS | 4 FILE MANAGEMENT | 5 SWITCH APPS | 6 SAVE FILES
7 CHANGE SCREEN RESOLUTION | 8 EXIT APPS | 9 USE ADDITIONAL APP FEATURES | 10 USE HELP

The tab currently displayed is called the **active tab**. The following step displays the Insert tab, that is, makes it the active tab. *Why? When working with an Office app, you may need to switch tabs to access other options for working with a document.*

- Click Insert on the ribbon to display the Insert tab (Figure 20).

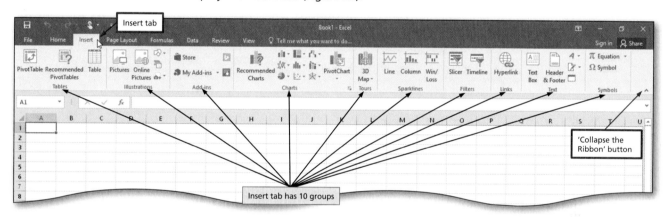

Figure 20

Experiment

- Click the other tabs on the ribbon to view their contents. When you are finished, click Insert on the ribbon to redisplay the Insert tab.

Other Ways

1. Press ALT, press letter corresponding to tab to display

To Collapse and Expand the Ribbon and Use Full Screen Mode

1 SIGN IN | 2 USE WINDOWS | 3 USE APPS | 4 FILE MANAGEMENT | 5 SWITCH APPS | 6 SAVE FILES
7 CHANGE SCREEN RESOLUTION | 8 EXIT APPS | 9 USE ADDITIONAL APP FEATURES | 10 USE HELP

To display more of a document or other item in the window of an Office app, some users prefer to collapse the ribbon, which hides the groups on the ribbon and displays only the main tabs, or to use **Full Screen mode**, which hides all the commands and just displays the document. Each time you run an Office app, such as Excel, the ribbon appears the same way it did the last time you used that Office app. The modules in this book, however, begin with the ribbon appearing as it did at the initial installation of Office or Excel.

The following steps collapse, expand, and restore the ribbon in Excel and then switch to Full Screen mode. *Why? If you need more space on the screen to work with your document, you may consider collapsing the ribbon or switching to Full Screen mode to gain additional workspace.*

- Click the 'Collapse the Ribbon' button on the ribbon (shown in Figure 20) to collapse the ribbon (Figure 21).

Figure 21

Q&A | What happened to the 'Collapse the Ribbon' button?
The 'Pin the ribbon' button replaces the 'Collapse the Ribbon' button when the ribbon is collapsed. You will see the 'Pin the ribbon' button only when you expand a ribbon by clicking a tab.

- Click Home on the ribbon to expand the Home tab (Figure 22).

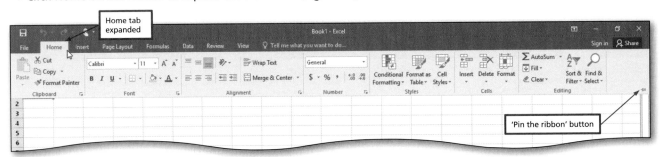

Figure 22

Q&A | Why would I click the Home tab?
If you want to use a command on a collapsed ribbon, click the main tab to display the groups for that tab. After you select a command on the ribbon and resume working in the document, the groups will be collapsed once again. If you decide not to use a command on the ribbon, you can collapse the groups by clicking the same main tab or clicking in the app window.

Experiment

- Click Home on the ribbon to collapse the groups again. Click Home on the ribbon to expand the Home tab.

- Click the 'Pin the ribbon' button on the expanded Home tab to restore the ribbon.
- Click the 'Ribbon Display Options' button to display the Ribbon Display Options menu (Figure 23).

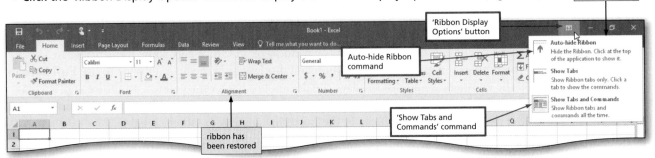

Figure 23

❹

- Click Auto-hide Ribbon to use Full Screen mode, which hides all the commands from the screen (Figure 24).
- Click the ellipsis to display the ribbon temporarily.
- Click the 'Ribbon Display Options' button to display the Ribbon Display Options menu (shown in Figure 23).
- Click 'Show Tabs and Commands' on the Ribbon Display Options menu to exit Full Screen mode.

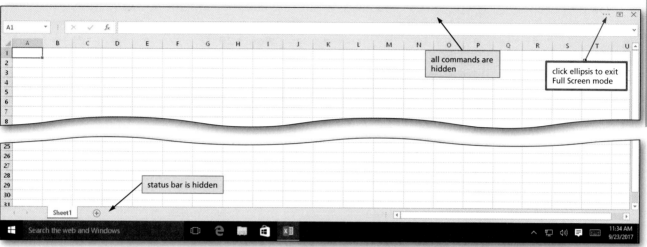

Figure 24

Other Ways
1. Double-click tab on ribbon

To Use a Shortcut Menu to Relocate the Quick Access Toolbar

1 SIGN IN | 2 USE WINDOWS | 3 USE APPS | 4 FILE MANAGEMENT | 5 SWITCH APPS | 6 SAVE FILES
7 CHANGE SCREEN RESOLUTION | 8 EXIT APPS | 9 USE ADDITIONAL APP FEATURES | 10 USE HELP

When you right-click certain areas of the Excel and other Office app windows, a shortcut menu will appear. A **shortcut menu** is a list of frequently used commands that relate to an object. *Why? You can use shortcut menus to access common commands quickly.* When you right-click the status bar, for example, a shortcut menu appears with commands related to the status bar. When you right-click the Quick Access Toolbar, a shortcut menu appears with commands related to the Quick Access Toolbar. The following steps use a shortcut menu to move the Quick Access Toolbar, which by default is located on the title bar.

❶

- Right-click the Quick Access Toolbar to display a shortcut menu that presents a list of commands related to the Quick Access Toolbar (Figure 25).

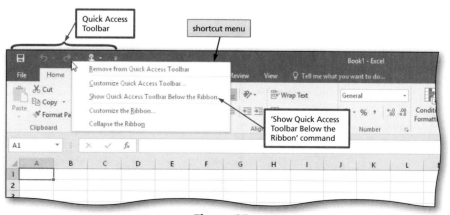

Figure 25

- Click 'Show Quick Access Toolbar Below the Ribbon' on the shortcut menu to display the Quick Access Toolbar below the ribbon (Figure 26).

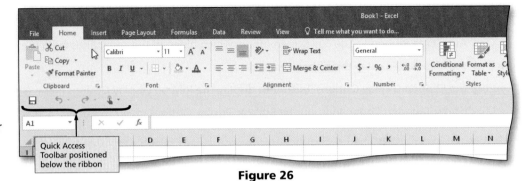

Figure 26

 ...

- Right-click the Quick Access Toolbar to display a shortcut menu (Figure 27).

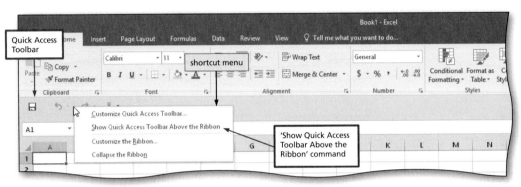

Figure 27

- Click 'Show Quick Access Toolbar Above the Ribbon' on the shortcut menu to return the Quick Access Toolbar to its original position (shown in Figure 25).

Other Ways

1. Click 'Customize Quick Access Toolbar' button on Quick Access Toolbar, click 'Show Below the Ribbon' or 'Show Above the Ribbon'

To Customize the Quick Access Toolbar

1 SIGN IN | 2 USE WINDOWS | 3 USE APPS | 4 FILE MANAGEMENT | 5 SWITCH APPS | 6 SAVE FILES
7 CHANGE SCREEN RESOLUTION | 8 EXIT APPS | 9 USE ADDITIONAL APP FEATURES | 10 USE HELP

The Quick Access Toolbar provides easy access to some of the more frequently used commands in the Office apps. By default, the Quick Access Toolbar contains buttons for the Save, Undo, and Redo commands. If your computer or mobile device has a touch screen, the Quick Access Toolbar also might display the Touch/Mouse Mode button. You can customize the Quick Access Toolbar by changing its location in the window, as shown in the previous steps, and by adding more buttons to reflect commands you would like to access easily. The following steps add the Quick Print button to the Quick Access Toolbar in the Excel window. *Why? Adding the Quick Print button to the Quick Access Toolbar speeds up the process of printing.*

- Click the 'Customize Quick Access Toolbar' button to display the Customize Quick Access Toolbar menu (Figure 28).

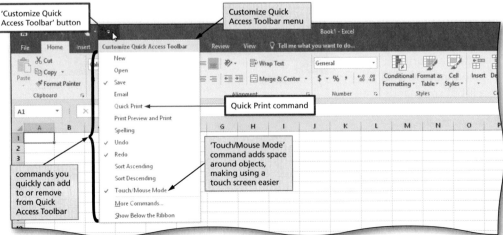

Figure 28

2

- Click Quick Print on the Customize Quick Access Toolbar menu to add the Quick Print button to the Quick Access Toolbar (Figure 29).

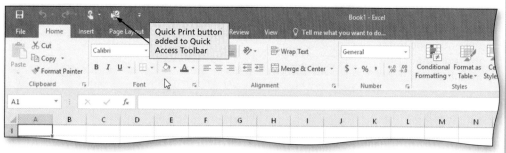

Figure 29

Q&A How would I remove a button from the Quick Access Toolbar?
You would right-click the button you wish to remove and then click 'Remove from Quick Access Toolbar' on the shortcut menu or click the 'Customize Quick Access Toolbar' button on the Quick Access Toolbar and then click the button name in the Customize Quick Access Toolbar menu to remove the check mark.

To Enter a Worksheet Title

1 SIGN IN | 2 USE WINDOWS | 3 USE APPS | 4 FILE MANAGEMENT | 5 SWITCH APPS | 6 SAVE FILES
7 CHANGE SCREEN RESOLUTION | 8 EXIT APPS | 9 USE ADDITIONAL APP FEATURES | 10 USE HELP

To enter data into a cell, you first must select it. The easiest way to select a cell (make it active) is to use the mouse to move the block plus sign pointer to the cell and then click. An alternative method is to use the arrow keys that are located just to the right of the typewriter keys on the keyboard. An arrow key selects the cell adjacent to the active cell in the direction of the arrow on the key.

In Excel, any set of characters containing a letter, hyphen (as in a telephone number), or space is considered text. **Text** is used to place titles, such as worksheet titles, column titles, and row titles, on the worksheet. The following steps enter the worksheet title in cell A1. **Why?** *A title informs others as to the contents of the worksheet.*

1

- If it is not already the active cell, click cell A1 to make it the active cell.

- Type **Silver Sky Hardware** in cell A1 (Figure 30).

Q&A What is the blinking vertical bar to the right of the text?
The blinking bar is the insertion point, which indicates where text will be inserted in the worksheet.

What if I make an error while typing?
You can press the BACKSPACE key until you have deleted the text in error and then retype the text correctly.

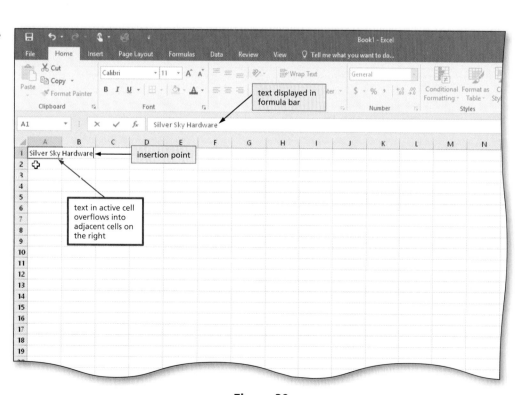

Figure 30

2

- Click the Enter button to complete the entry and enter the worksheet title in cell A1 (Figure 31).

Why do some commands on the ribbon appear dimmed?
Excel dims the commands that cannot be used at the current time.

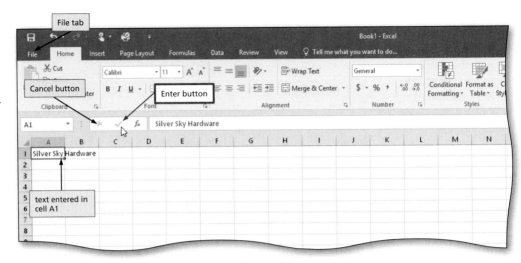

Figure 31

Document Properties

You can organize and identify your files by using **document properties**, which are the details about a file, such as the project author, title, and subject. For example, a class name or workbook topic can describe the file's purpose or content.

CONSIDER THIS

Why would you want to assign document properties to a document?
Document properties are valuable for a variety of reasons:

- Users can save time locating a particular file because they can view a file's document properties without opening the file.

- By creating consistent properties for files having similar content, users can better organize their files.

- Some organizations require users to add document properties so that other employees can view details about these files.

To Change Document Properties

1 SIGN IN | 2 USE WINDOWS | 3 USE APPS | 4 FILE MANAGEMENT | 5 SWITCH APPS | 6 SAVE FILES
7 CHANGE SCREEN RESOLUTION | 8 EXIT APPS | 9 USE ADDITIONAL APP FEATURES | 10 USE HELP

You can change the document properties while working with the file in an Office app. When you save the file, the Office app (Excel, in this case) will save the document properties with the file. The following steps change document properties. *Why? Adding document properties will help you identify characteristics of the file without opening it.*

1

- Click File on the ribbon (shown in Figure 31) to open the Backstage view and then, if necessary, click the Info tab in the Backstage view to display the Info gallery.

Q&A
What is the purpose of the File tab on the ribbon and what is the Backstage view?
The File tab opens the Backstage view for each Office app, including Excel. The **Backstage view** contains a set of commands that enable you to manage documents (opening, saving, sharing, and printing) and provides data about the documents.

What is the purpose of the Info gallery in the Backstage view?
The Info tab, which is selected by default when you click File on the ribbon, displays the Info gallery, where you can protect a document, inspect a document, and manage versions of a document as well as view all the file properties, such as when the file was created.

- Click to the right of the Title property in the Properties list and then type `CIS 101 Assignment` in the text box (Figure 32).

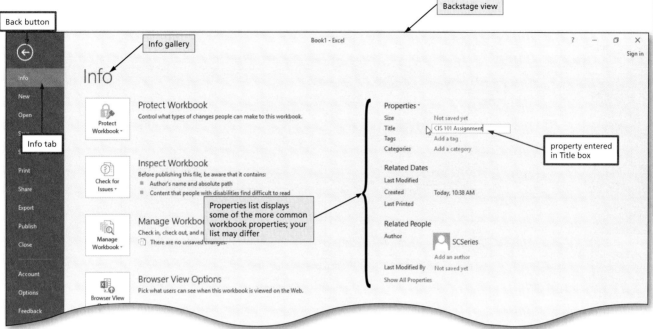

Figure 32

- Click the Back button in the upper-left corner of the Backstage view to return to the document window.

Printing, Saving, and Organizing Files

While you are creating a document, the computer or mobile device stores it in memory. When you save a document, the computer or mobile device places it on a storage medium, such as a hard disk, solid state drive (SSD), USB flash drive, or optical disc. The storage medium can be permanent in your computer, may be portable where you remove it from your computer, or may be on a web server you access through a network or the Internet.

A saved document is referred to as a file. A **file name** is the name assigned to a file when it is saved. When saving files, you should organize them so that you easily can find them later. Windows provides tools to help you organize files.

BTW
File Type
Depending on your Windows settings, the file type .xlsx may be displayed immediately to the right of the file name after you save the file. The file type .xlsx identifies an Excel 2016 workbook.

Printing a Document

After creating a document, you may want to print it. Printing a document enables you to distribute it to others in a form that can be read or viewed but typically not edited.

To Print a Document

1 SIGN IN | 2 USE WINDOWS | 3 USE APPS | 4 FILE MANAGEMENT | **5 SWITCH APPS** | 6 SAVE FILES
7 CHANGE SCREEN RESOLUTION | 8 EXIT APPS | 9 USE ADDITIONAL APP FEATURES | 10 USE HELP

With the document opened, you may want to print it. ***Why?*** *Because you want to see how the text will appear on paper; you want to print a hard copy on a printer.* The following steps print a hard copy of the contents of the document.

- Click File on the ribbon to open the Backstage view.
- Click the Print tab in the Backstage view to display the Print gallery (Figure 33).

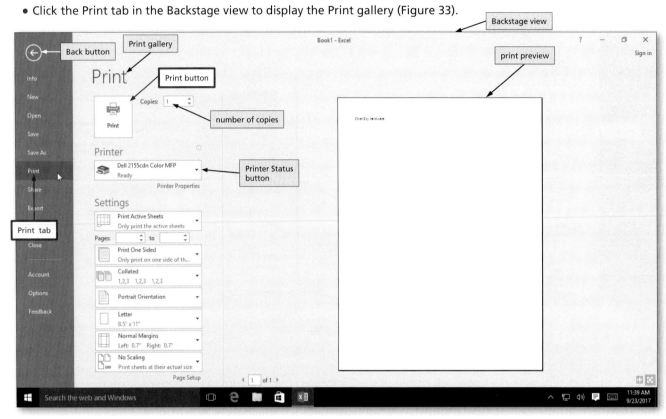

Figure 33

Q&A | How can I print multiple copies of my document?
Increase the number in the Copies box in the Print gallery.

What if I decide not to print the document at this time?
Click the Back button in the upper-left corner of the Backstage view to return to the document window.

- Verify that the selected printer will print a hard copy of the document. If necessary, click the Printer Status button to display a list of available printer options and then click the desired printer to change the currently selected printer.

- Click the Print button in the Print gallery to print the document on the currently selected printer.
- When the printer stops, retrieve the hard copy (Figure 34).

Silver Sky Hardware

Figure 34

Q&A | What if I want to print an electronic image of a document instead of a hard copy?
You would click the Printer Status button in the Print gallery and then select the desired electronic image option, such as Microsoft Print to PDF, which would create a PDF file.

Other Ways

1. Press CTRL+P

Organizing Files and Folders

A file contains data. This data can range from an inventory list to an accounting spreadsheet to an electronic math quiz. You should organize and store files in folders to avoid misplacing a file and to help you find a file quickly.

If you are taking an introductory computer class (CIS 101, for example), you may want to design a series of folders for the different subjects covered in the class. To accomplish this, you can arrange the folders in a hierarchy for the class, as shown in Figure 35. The hierarchy contains three levels. The first level contains the storage medium, such as a hard drive. The second level contains the class folder (CIS 101, in this case), and the third level contains seven folders, one each for a different Office app (Word, PowerPoint, Excel, Access, Outlook, Publisher, and OneNote).

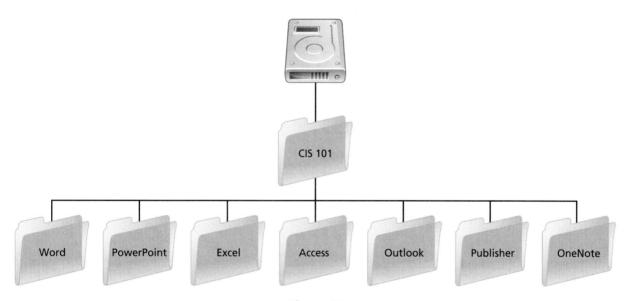

Figure 35

When the hierarchy in Figure 35 is created, the storage medium is said to contain the CIS 101 folder, and the CIS 101 folder is said to contain the separate Office folders (i.e., Word, PowerPoint, Excel, etc.). In addition, this hierarchy easily can be expanded to include folders from other classes taken during additional semesters.

The vertical and horizontal lines in Figure 35 form a pathway that allows you to navigate to a drive or folder on a computer or network. A **path** consists of a drive letter (preceded by a drive name when necessary) and colon, to identify the storage device, and one or more folder names. A hard drive typically has a drive letter of C. Each drive or folder in the hierarchy has a corresponding path.

By default, Windows saves documents in the Documents folder, music in the Music folder, photos in the Pictures folder, videos in the Videos folder, and downloads in the Downloads folder.

The following pages illustrate the steps to organize the folders for this class and save a file in a folder:

1. Create the folder identifying your class.
2. Create the Excel folder in the folder identifying your class.
3. Save a file in the Excel folder.
4. Verify the location of the saved file.

To Create a Folder

When you create a folder, such as the CIS 101 folder shown in Figure 35, you must name the folder. A folder name should describe the folder and its contents. A folder name can contain spaces and any uppercase or lowercase characters, except a backslash (\), slash (/), colon (:), asterisk (*), question mark (?), quotation marks ("), less than symbol (<), greater than symbol (>), or vertical bar (|). Folder names cannot be CON, AUX, COM1, COM2, COM3, COM4, LPT1, LPT2, LPT3, PRN, or NUL. The same rules for naming folders also apply to naming files.

The following steps create a class folder (CIS 101, in this case) in the Documents folder. *Why? When storing files, you should organize the files so that it will be easier to find them later.*

- Click the File Explorer button on the taskbar to run File Explorer.

- If necessary, double-click This PC in the navigation pane to expand the contents of your computer.

- Click the Documents folder in the navigation pane to display the contents of the Documents folder in the file list (Figure 36).

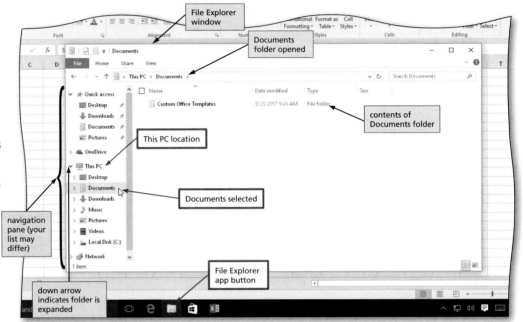

Figure 36

- Click the New folder button on the Quick Access Toolbar to create a new folder with the name, New folder, selected in a text box (Figure 37).

Q&A

Why is the folder icon displayed differently on my computer or mobile device?

Windows might be configured to display contents differently on your computer or mobile device.

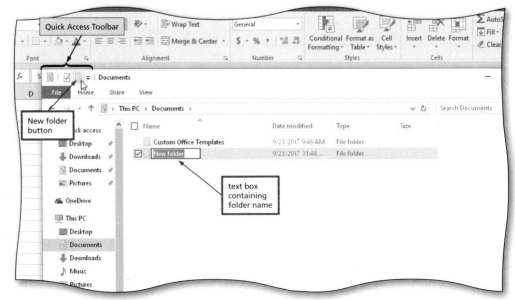

Figure 37

❸

- Type **CIS 101** (or your class code) in the text box as the new folder name.

  If requested by your instructor, add your last name to the end of the folder name.

- Press the ENTER key to change the folder name from New folder to a folder name identifying your class (Figure 38).

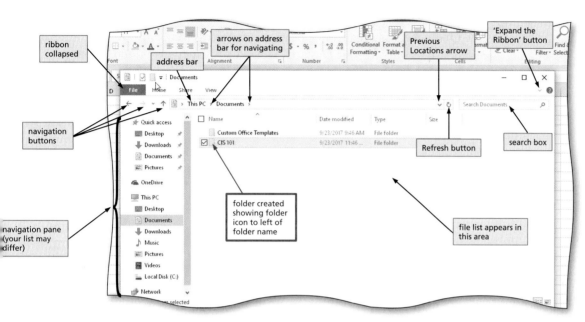

Figure 38

Q&A

What happens when I press the ENTER key?

The class folder (CIS 101, in this case) is displayed in the file list, which contains the folder name, date modified, type, and size.

Other Ways

1. Press CTRL+SHIFT+N   2. Click New folder button (Home tab | New group)

Folder Windows

The File Explorer window (shown in Figure 38) is called a folder window. Recall that a folder is a specific named location on a storage medium that contains related files. Most users rely on **folder windows** for finding, viewing, and managing information on their computers. Folder windows have common design elements, including the following (shown in Figure 38):

- The **address bar** provides quick navigation options. The arrows on the address bar allow you to visit different locations on the computer or mobile device.

- The buttons to the left of the address bar allow you to navigate the contents of the navigation pane and view recent pages.

- The **Previous Locations arrow** displays the locations you have visited.

- The **Refresh button** on the right side of the address bar refreshes the contents of the folder list.

- The **Search box** contains the dimmed words, Search Documents. You can type a term in the search box for a list of files, folders, shortcuts, and elements containing that term within the location you are searching.
- The **ribbon** contains four tabs used to accomplish various tasks on the computer or mobile device related to organizing and managing the contents of the open window. This ribbon works similarly to the ribbon in the Office apps.
- The **navigation pane** on the left contains the Quick access area, the OneDrive area, the This PC area, and the Network area.
- The **Quick Access area** shows locations you access frequently. By default, this list contains links only to your Desktop, Downloads, Documents, and Pictures.

To Create a Folder within a Folder

With the class folder created, you can create folders that will store the files you create using Excel. The following step creates an Excel folder in the CIS 101 folder (or the folder identifying your class). *Why? To be able to organize your files, you should create a folder structure.*

- Double-click the icon or folder name for the CIS 101 folder (or the folder identifying your class) in the file list to open the folder.
- Click the New folder button on the Quick Access Toolbar to create a new folder with the name, New folder, selected in a text box folder.
- Type **Excel** in the text box as the new folder name.
- Press the ENTER key to rename the folder (Figure 39).

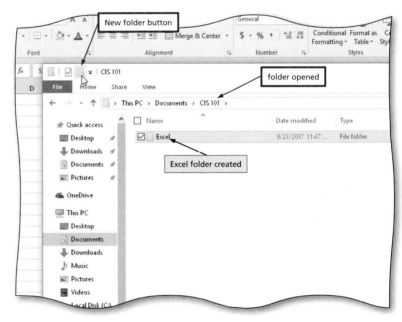

Figure 39

Other Ways

1. Press CTRL+SHIFT+N

2. Click New folder button (Home tab | New group)

To Expand a Folder, Scroll through Folder Contents, and Collapse a Folder

Folder windows display the hierarchy of items and the contents of drives and folders in the file list. You might want to expand a folder in the navigation pane to view its contents, scroll through its contents, and collapse it when you are finished viewing its contents. *Why? When a folder is expanded, you can see all the folders it contains. By contrast, a collapsed folder hides the folders it contains.* The following steps expand, scroll through, and then collapse the folder identifying your class (CIS 101, in this case).

- Double-click the Documents folder in the This PC area of the navigation pane, which expands the folder to display its contents, indicated by a down arrow to the left of the Documents folder icon (Figure 40).

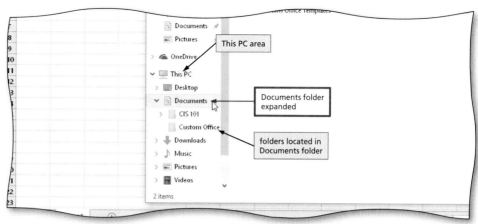

Figure 40

- Double-click the CIS 101 folder, which expands the folder to display its contents, indicated by a down arrow to the left of the folder icon (Figure 41).

Experiment

- Drag the scroll box down or click the down scroll arrow on the vertical scroll bar to display additional folders at the bottom of the navigation pane. Drag the scroll box up or click the scroll bar above the scroll box to move the scroll box to the top of the navigation pane. Drag the scroll box down the scroll bar until the scroll box is halfway down the scroll bar.

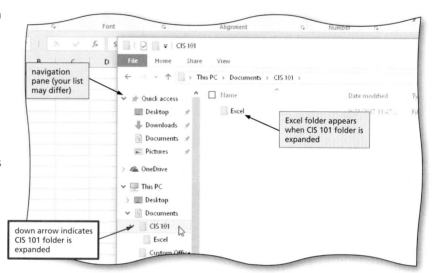

Figure 41

- Double-click the folder identifying your class (CIS 101, in this case) in the navigation pane to collapse the folder (Figure 42).

Q&A
Why are some folders indented below others?
A folder contains the indented folders below it.

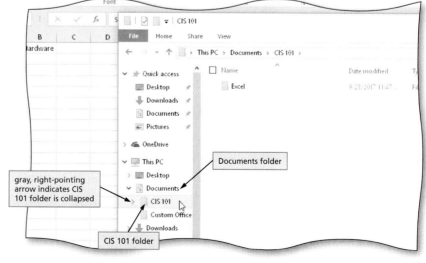

Figure 42

Other Ways

1. Point to display arrows in navigation pane, click arrow to expand or collapse

2. Select folder to expand or collapse using arrow keys, press RIGHT ARROW to expand; press LEFT ARROW to collapse

To Switch from One App to Another

The next step is to save the Excel file containing the title you typed earlier. However, Excel is not the active window. You can use the button on the taskbar and live preview to switch to Excel and then save the document in the Excel workbook window.

Why? *By clicking the appropriate app button on the taskbar, you can switch to the open app you want to use.* The steps below switch to the Excel window; however, the steps are the same for any active Office app currently displayed as a button on the taskbar.

- Point to the Excel app button on the taskbar to see a live preview of the open workbook(s) or the window title(s) of the open workbook(s), depending on your computer's configuration (Figure 43).

Q&A

What if I am using a touch screen?
Live preview will not work if you are using a touch screen. If you are using a touch screen and do not have a mouse, proceed to Step 2.

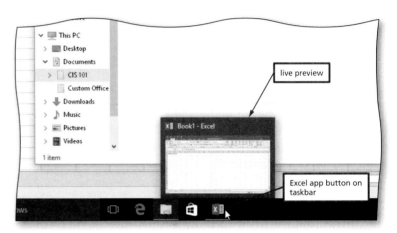

Figure 43

- Click the Excel app button or the live preview to make the app associated with the app button the active window (Figure 44).

Q&A

What if multiple documents are open in an app?
Click the desired live preview to switch to the window you want to use.

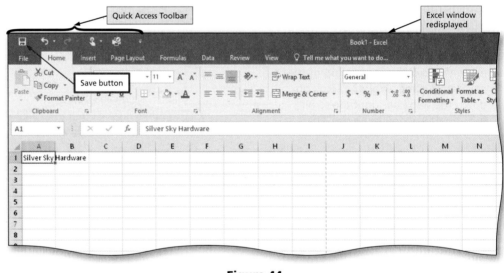

Figure 44

Other Ways

1. Press ALT + TAB until app you wish to display is selected

To Save a File in a Folder

With the Excel folder created, you can save the Excel workbooks shown in the Excel window in the Excel folder. **Why?** *Without saving a file, you may lose all the work you have completed and will be unable to reuse or share it with others later.* The following steps save a file in the Excel folder contained in your class folder (CIS 101, in this case) using the file name, Silver Sky Hardware.

- Click the Save button (shown in Figure 44) on the Quick Access Toolbar, which depending on settings, will display either the Save As gallery in the Backstage view (Figure 45) or the Save As dialog box (Figure 46).

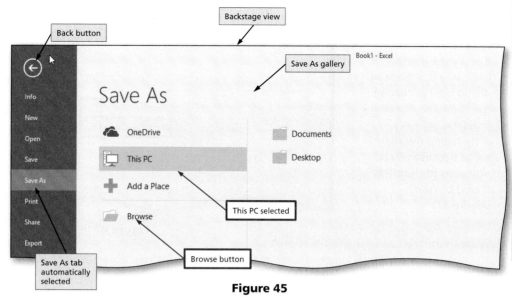

Figure 45

Q&A What if the Save As gallery is not displayed in the Backstage view?
Click the Save As tab to display the Save As gallery.

How do I close the Backstage view?
Click the Back button in the upper-left corner of the Backstage view to return to the Excel window.

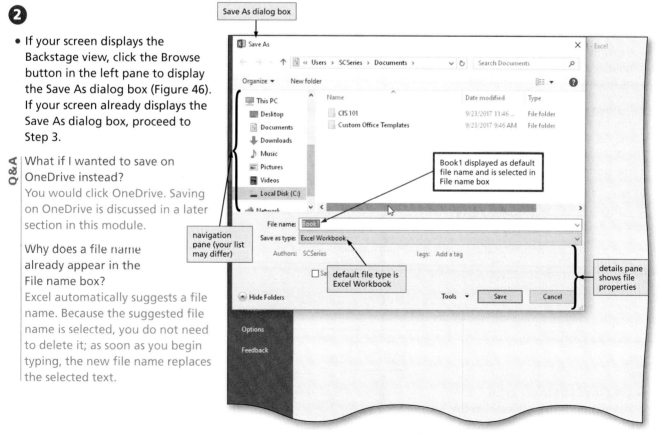

- If your screen displays the Backstage view, click the Browse button in the left pane to display the Save As dialog box (Figure 46). If your screen already displays the Save As dialog box, proceed to Step 3.

Q&A What if I wanted to save on OneDrive instead?
You would click OneDrive. Saving on OneDrive is discussed in a later section in this module.

Why does a file name already appear in the File name box?
Excel automatically suggests a file name. Because the suggested file name is selected, you do not need to delete it; as soon as you begin typing, the new file name replaces the selected text.

Figure 46

- Type **Silver Sky Hardware** in the File name box (Save As dialog box) to change the file name. Do not press the ENTER key after typing the file name because you do not want to close the dialog box yet (Figure 47).

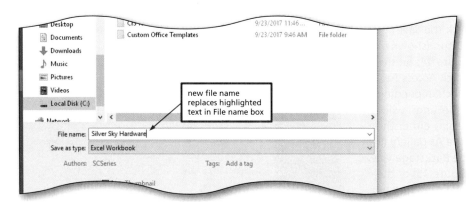

Figure 47

Q&A What characters can I use in a file name?

The only invalid characters are the same as those for folder names: the backslash (\), slash (/), colon (:), asterisk (*), question mark (?), quotation mark ("), less than symbol (<), greater than symbol (>), and vertical bar (|).

- Navigate to the desired save location (in this case, the Excel folder in the CIS 101 folder [or your class folder] in the Documents folder) by performing the tasks in Steps 4a and 4b.

- If the Documents folder is not displayed in the navigation pane, drag the scroll bar in the navigation pane until Documents appears.

- If the Documents folder is not expanded in the navigation pane, double-click Documents to display its folders in the navigation pane.

- If your class folder (CIS 101, in this case) is not expanded, double-click the CIS 101 folder to select the folder and display its contents in the navigation pane (Figure 48).

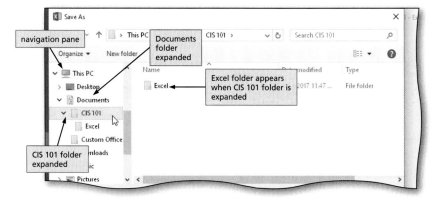

Figure 48

Q&A What if I do not want to save in a folder?

Although storing files in folders is an effective technique for organizing files, some users prefer not to store files in folders. If you prefer not to save this file in a folder, select the storage device on which you wish to save the file and then proceed to Step 5.

- Click the Excel folder in the navigation pane to select it as the new save location and display its contents in the file list (Figure 49).

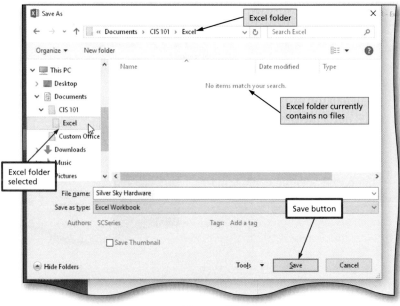

Figure 49

5

- Click the Save button (Save As dialog box) to save the document in the selected folder in the selected location with the entered file name (Figure 50).

Q&A How do I know that the file is saved?

While an Office app such as Excel is saving a file, it briefly displays a message on the status bar indicating the amount of the file saved. In addition, the file name appears on the title bar.

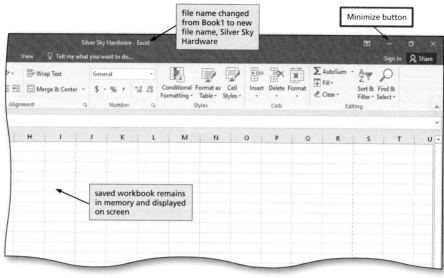

file name changed from Book1 to new file name, Silver Sky Hardware

Minimize button

saved workbook remains in memory and displayed on screen

Figure 50

Other Ways

1. Click File on ribbon, click Save As in Backstage view, click Browse button, type file name (Save As dialog box), navigate to desired save location, click Save button

2. Press F12, type file name (Save As dialog box), navigate to desired save location, click Save button

How often should you save a document?

It is important to save a document frequently for the following reasons:

- The document in memory might be lost if the computer is turned off or you lose electrical power while an app is running.

- If you run out of time before completing a project, you may finish it at a future time without starting over.

Navigating in Dialog Boxes

Navigating is the process of finding a location on a storage device. While saving the Silver Sky Hardware file, for example, Steps 4a and 4b navigated to the Excel folder located in the CIS 101 folder in the Documents folder. When performing certain functions in Windows apps, such as saving a file, opening a file, or inserting a picture in an existing workbook, you most likely will have to navigate to the location where you want to save the file or to the folder containing the file you want to open or insert. Most dialog boxes in Windows apps requiring navigation follow a similar procedure; that is, the way you navigate to a folder in one dialog box, such as the Save As dialog box, is similar to how you might navigate in another dialog box, such as the Open dialog box. If you chose to navigate to a specific location in a dialog box, you would follow the instructions in Steps 4a and 4b.

To Minimize and Restore a Window

1 SIGN IN | **2 USE WINDOWS** | 3 USE APPS | 4 FILE MANAGEMENT | 5 SWITCH APPS | 6 SAVE FILES
7 CHANGE SCREEN RESOLUTION | 8 EXIT APPS | 9 USE ADDITIONAL APP FEATURES | 10 USE HELP

Before continuing, you can verify that the Excel file was saved properly. To do this, you will minimize the Excel window and then open the CIS 101 window so that you can verify the file is stored in the CIS 101 folder on the hard drive. A **minimized window** is an open window that is hidden from view but can be displayed quickly by clicking the window's button on the taskbar.

In the following example, Excel is used to illustrate minimizing and restoring windows; however, you would follow the same steps regardless of the Office app you are using. *Why? Before closing an app, you should make sure your file saved correctly so that you can find it later.* The following steps minimize the Excel window, verify that the file is saved, and then restore the minimized window.

- Click the Minimize button on the Excel window title bar (shown in Figure 50) to minimize the window (Figure 51).

Q&A
Is the minimized window still available?
The minimized window, Excel in this case, remains available but no longer is the active window. It is minimized as a button on the taskbar.

- If the File Explorer window is not open on the screen, click the File Explorer button on the taskbar to make the File Explorer window the active window.

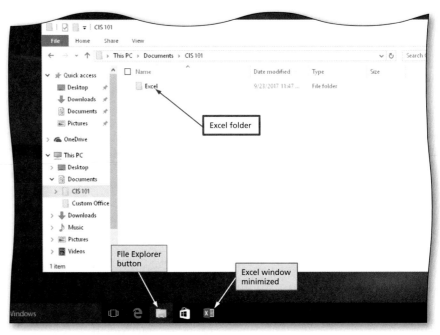

Figure 51

- Double-click the Excel folder in the file list to select the folder and display its contents (Figure 52).

Q&A
Why does the File Explorer button on the taskbar change?
A selected app button indicates that the app is active on the screen. When the button is not selected, the app is running but not active.

- After viewing the contents of the selected folder, click the Excel button on the taskbar to restore the minimized window (as shown in Figure 50).

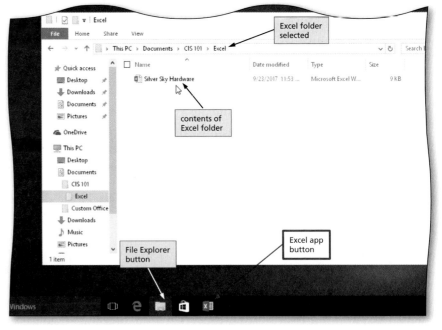

Figure 52

Other Ways

1. Right-click title bar, click Minimize on shortcut menu, click taskbar button in taskbar button area
2. Press WINDOWS + M, press WINDOWS + SHIFT + M
3. Click Excel app button on taskbar to minimize window. Click Excel app button again to restore window.

To Save a File on OneDrive

One of the features of Office is the capability to save files on OneDrive so that you can use the files on multiple computers or mobile devices without having to use an external storage device, such as a USB flash drive. Storing files on OneDrive also enables you to share files more efficiently with others, such as when using Office Online and Office 365.

In the following example, Excel is used to save a file on OneDrive. *Why? Storing files on OneDrive provides more portability options than are available from storing files in the Documents folder.*

You can save files directly on OneDrive from within an Office app. The following steps save the current Excel file on OneDrive. These steps require you have a Microsoft account and an Internet connection.

- Click File on the ribbon to open the Backstage view.

- Click the Save As tab in the Backstage view to display the Save As gallery.

- Click OneDrive in the left pane to display OneDrive saving options or a Sign In button, if you are not signed in already to your Microsoft account (Figure 53).

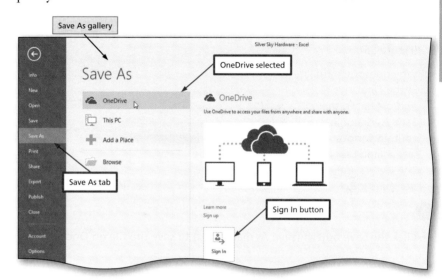

Figure 53

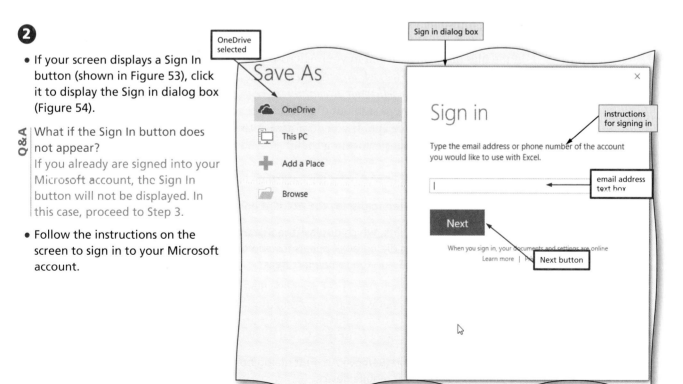

- If your screen displays a Sign In button (shown in Figure 53), click it to display the Sign in dialog box (Figure 54).

Q&A

What if the Sign In button does not appear?

If you already are signed into your Microsoft account, the Sign In button will not be displayed. In this case, proceed to Step 3.

- Follow the instructions on the screen to sign in to your Microsoft account.

Figure 54

- If necessary, in the Backstage view, click OneDrive in the left pane in the Save As gallery to select OneDrive as the save location.

- Click the Documents folder in the right pane to display the Save As dialog box (Figure 55).

Q&A Why does the path in the OneDrive address bar in the Save As dialog box contain various letters and numbers?
The letters and numbers in the address bar uniquely identify the location of your OneDrive files and folders.

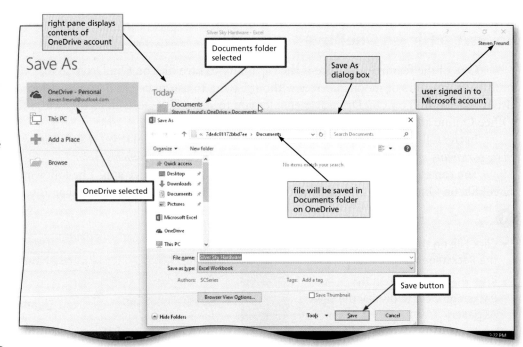

Figure 55

- Click the Save button (Save As dialog box) to save the file on OneDrive.

To Sign Out of a Microsoft Account

If you are using a public computer or otherwise wish to sign out of your Microsoft account, you should sign out of the account from the Accounts gallery in the Backstage view. Signing out of the account is the safest way to make sure that nobody else can access online files or settings stored in your Microsoft account. *Why? For security reasons, you should sign out of your Microsoft account when you are finished using a public or shared computer. Staying signed in to your Microsoft account might enable others to access your files.*

The following steps sign out of a Microsoft account from Excel. You would use the same steps in any Office app. If you do not wish to sign out of your Microsoft account, read these steps without performing them.

1 Click File on the ribbon to open the Backstage view.

2 Click the Account tab to display the Account gallery (Figure 56).

3 Click the Sign out link, which displays the Remove Account dialog box. If a Can't remove Windows accounts dialog box appears instead of the Remove Account dialog box, click the OK button and skip the remaining steps.

Q&A Why does a Can't remove Windows accounts dialog box appear?
If you signed in to Windows using your Microsoft account, then you also must sign out from Windows, rather than signing out from within Excel. When you are finished using Windows, be sure to sign out at that time.

4 Click the Yes button (Remove Account dialog box) to sign out of your Microsoft account on this computer or mobile device.

Q&A Should I sign out of Windows after removing my Microsoft account?
When you are finished using the computer, you should sign out of Windows for maximum security.

5 Click the Back button in the upper-left corner of the Backstage view to return to the document.

Figure 56

Screen Resolution

Screen resolution indicates the number of pixels (dots) that the computer uses to display the letters, numbers, graphics, and background you see on the screen. When you increase the screen resolution, Windows displays more information on the screen, but the information decreases in size. The reverse also is true: as you decrease the screen resolution, Windows displays less information on the screen, but the information increases in size.

Screen resolution usually is stated as the product of two numbers, such as 1366 × 768 (pronounced "thirteen sixty-six by seven sixty-eight"). A 1366 × 768 screen resolution results in a display of 1366 distinct pixels on each of 768 lines, or about 1,049,088 pixels. Changing the screen resolution affects how the ribbon appears in Office apps and some Windows dialog boxes. Figure 57, for example, shows the Excel ribbon at screen resolutions of 1366 × 768 and 1024 × 768. All of the same commands are available regardless of screen resolution. The app (Excel, in this case), however, makes changes to the groups and the buttons within the groups to accommodate the various screen resolutions. The result is that certain commands may need to be accessed differently depending on the resolution chosen. A command that is visible on the ribbon and available by clicking a button at one resolution may not be visible and may need to be accessed using its Dialog Box Launcher at a different resolution.

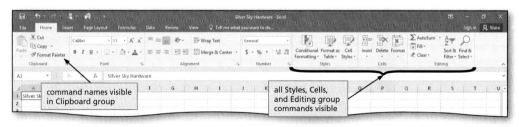

Figure 57(a) Ribbon at 1366 × 768 Resolution

Figure 57(b) Ribbon at 1024 × 768 Resolution

Comparing the two ribbons in Figure 57, notice the changes in content and layout of the groups and galleries. In some cases, the content of a group is the same in each resolution, but the layout of the group differs. For example, the same gallery and buttons appear in the Styles groups in the two resolutions, but the layouts differ. In other cases, the content and layout are the same across the resolution, but the level of detail differs with the resolution.

To Change the Screen Resolution

1 SIGN IN | 2 USE WINDOWS | 3 USE APPS | 4 FILE MANAGEMENT | 5 SWITCH APPS | 6 SAVE FILES
7 CHANGE SCREEN RESOLUTION | 8 EXIT APPS | 9 USE ADDITIONAL APP FEATURES | 10 USE HELP

If you are using a computer to step through the modules in this book and you want your screen to match the figures, you may need to change your screen's resolution. *Why? The figures in this book use a screen resolution of 1366 × 768.* The following steps change the screen resolution to 1366 × 768. Your computer already may be set to 1366 × 768. Keep in mind that many computer labs prevent users from changing the screen resolution; in that case, read the following steps for illustration purposes.

- Click the Show desktop button, which is located at the far-right edge of the taskbar, to display the Windows desktop.

- Right-click an empty area on the Windows desktop to display a shortcut menu that contains a list of commands related to the desktop (Figure 58).

Q&A Why does my shortcut menu display different commands?
Depending on your computer's hardware and configuration, different commands might appear on the shortcut menu.

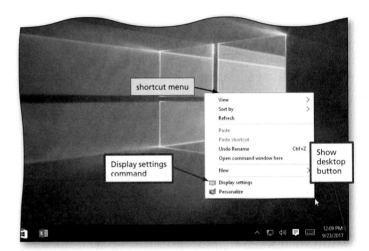

Figure 58

2

- Click Display settings on the shortcut menu to open the Settings app window. If necessary, scroll in the right pane to display the 'Advanced display settings' link (Figure 59).

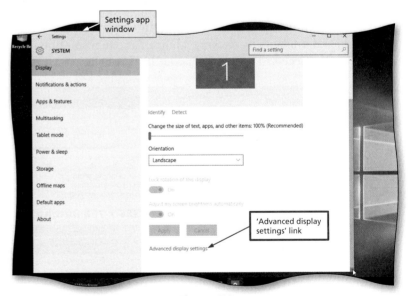

Figure 59

3

- Click 'Advanced display settings' in the Settings app window to display the advanced display settings.

- If necessary, scroll to display the Resolution box (Figure 60).

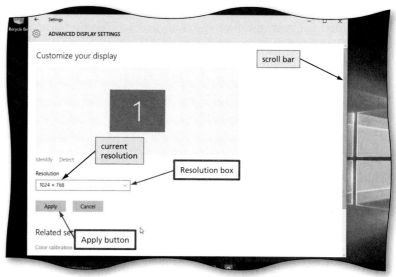

Figure 60

4

- Click the Resolution box to display a list of available screen resolutions (Figure 61).

- If necessary, scroll to and then click 1366 × 768 to select the screen resolution. If your screen resolution already is set to 1366 × 768, click the Close button to close the Settings app window and then skip Step 5.

Q&A What if my computer does not support the 1366 × 768 resolution?
If your computer does not support the recommended resolution, select a resolution that is close to 1366 × 768.

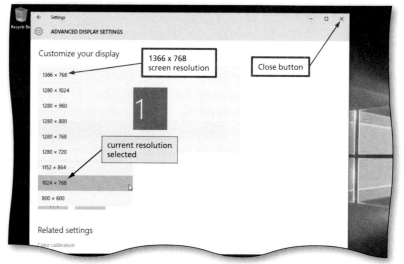

Figure 61

5

- Click the Apply button (shown in Figure 60) to change the screen resolution and display a confirmation message (Figure 62).

- Click the Keep changes button to accept the new screen resolution.

- Click the Close button (shown in Figure 61) to close the Settings app window.

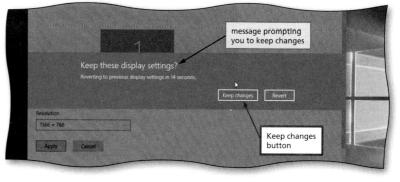

Figure 62

Other Ways

1. Click Start button, click Settings, click System, click Display (if necessary), click 'Advanced display settings,' select desired resolution in Resolution box, click Apply button, click Keep changes button

2. Type **screen resolution** in search box, click 'Change the screen resolution,' select desired resolution in Resolution box, click Apply, click Keep changes

To Exit an App with One Document Open

When you exit an Office app, such as Excel, if you have made changes to a file since the last time the file was saved, the app displays a dialog box asking if you want to save the changes you made to the file before it closes the app window. *Why? The dialog box contains three buttons with these resulting actions: the Save button saves the changes and then exits the app, the Don't Save button exits the app without saving changes, and the Cancel button closes the dialog box and redisplays the file without exiting the app.*

If no changes have been made to an open document since the last time the file was saved, the app will close the window without displaying a dialog box. The following steps exit Excel. You would follow similar steps in other Office apps.

- If necessary, click the Excel app button on the taskbar to display the Excel window on the desktop. If the Backstage view is displayed, click the Back button to return to the worksheet (Figure 63).

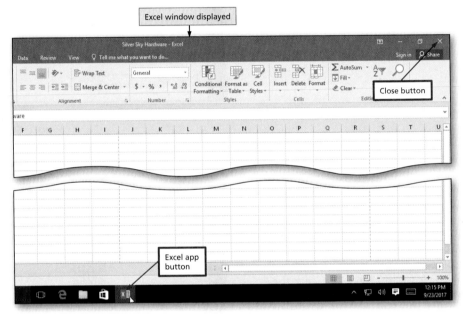

Figure 63

- Click the Close button on the right side of the Excel window title bar to close the document and exit Excel. If a Microsoft Excel dialog box appears, click the Save button to save any changes made to the document since the last save.

Q&A
What if I have more than one document open in Excel?
You could click the Close button for each open document. When you click the last open document's Close button, you also exit Excel. As an alternative that is more efficient, you could right-click the Excel app button on the taskbar and then click 'Close all windows' on the shortcut menu to close all open documents and exit Excel.

Other Ways

1. Right-click Excel app button on Windows taskbar, click 'Close window' on shortcut menu   2. Press ALT + F4

To Copy a Folder to OneDrive

To back up your files or easily make them available on another computer or mobile device, you can copy them to OneDrive. The following steps copy your CIS 101 folder to OneDrive. If you do not have access to a OneDrive account, read the following steps without performing them. *Why? It often is good practice to have a backup of your files so that they are available in case something happens to your original copies.*

1

- Click the File Explorer button on the taskbar to make the folder window the active window.

- Navigate to the CIS 101 folder [or your class folder] in the Documents folder.

- Click Documents in the This PC area of the navigation pane to display the CIS 101 folder in the file list.

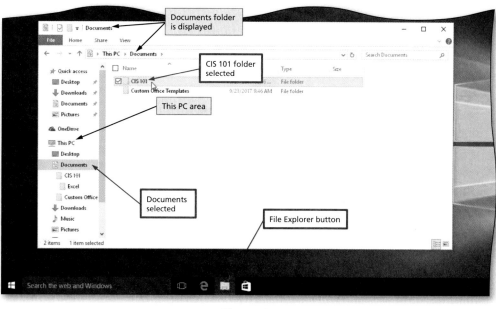

Figure 64

Q&A
What if my CIS 101 folder is stored in a different location?
Use the navigation pane to navigate to the location of your CIS 101 folder. The CIS 101 folder should be displayed in the file list once you have located it.

- Click the CIS 101 folder in the file list to select it (Figure 64).

2

- Click Home on the ribbon to display the Home tab.

- Click the Copy to button (Home tab | Organize group) to display the Copy to menu (Figure 65).

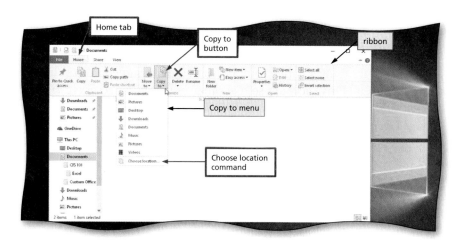

Figure 65

3

- Click Choose location on the Copy to menu to display the Copy Items dialog box.

- Click OneDrive (Copy Items dialog box) to select it (Figure 66).

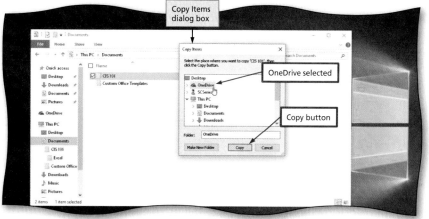

Figure 66

- Click the Copy button (Copy Items dialog box) to copy the selected folder to OneDrive.

- Click OneDrive in the navigation pane to verify the CIS 101 folder displays in the file list (Figure 67).

Q&A
Why does a Microsoft OneDrive dialog box display when I click OneDrive in the navigation pane?
If you are not currently signed in to Windows using a Microsoft account, you will manually need to sign in to a Microsoft account to save files to OneDrive. Follow the instructions on the screen to sign in to your Microsoft account. If the Microsoft Excel window indicates you are signed in to your Microsoft account, that does not necessarily mean you are signed in to Windows with a Microsoft account.

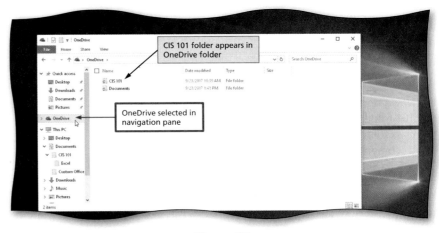

Figure 67

Other Ways

1. In File Explorer, select folder to copy, click Copy button (Home tab | Clipboard group), display contents of OneDrive in file list, click Paste button (Home tab | Clipboard group)

2. In File Explorer, select folder to copy, press CTRL+C, display contents of OneDrive in file list, press CTRL+V

3. Drag folder to copy to OneDrive in navigation pane

To Unlink a OneDrive Account

1 SIGN IN | 2 USE WINDOWS | 3 USE APPS | 4 FILE MANAGEMENT | 5 SWITCH APPS | 6 SAVE FILES
7 CHANGE SCREEN RESOLUTION | 8 EXIT APPS | 9 USE ADDITIONAL APP FEATURES | 10 USE HELP

If you are using a public computer and are not signed in to Windows with a Microsoft account, you should unlink your OneDrive account so that other users cannot access it. *Why? If you do not unlink your OneDrive account, other people accessing the same user account on the computer will be able to view, remove, and add to files stored in your OneDrive account.* The following steps unlink your OneDrive account. If you do not wish to unlink your OneDrive account, read these steps without performing them.

- Click the 'Show hidden icons' button on the Windows taskbar to show a menu of hidden icons (Figure 68).

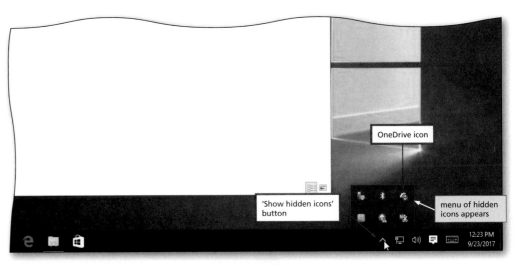

Figure 68

2

- Right click the OneDrive icon (shown in Figure 68) to display a shortcut menu (Figure 69).

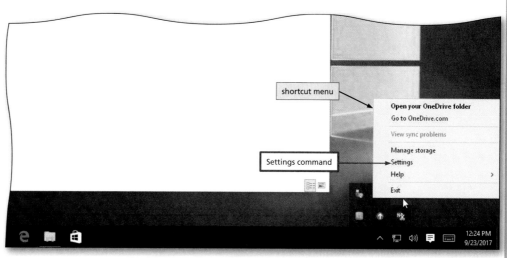

Figure 69

3

- Click Settings on the shortcut menu to display the Microsoft OneDrive dialog box (Figure 70).

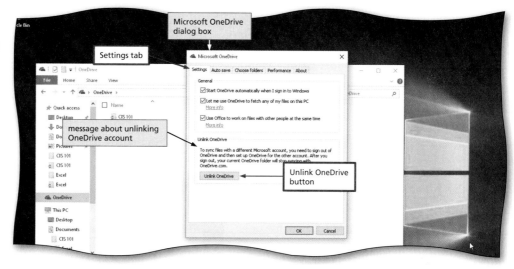

Figure 70

4

- If necessary, click the Settings tab.

- Click the Unlink OneDrive button (Microsoft OneDrive dialog box) to unlink the OneDrive account (Figure 71).

- When the Microsoft OneDrive dialog box appears with a Welcome to OneDrive message, click the Close button.

- Minimize the File Explorer window.

Figure 71

Break Point: If you wish to take a break, this is a good place to do so. To resume at a later time, continue to follow the steps from this location forward.

Additional Common Features of Office Apps

The previous section used Excel to illustrate common features of Office and some basic elements unique to Excel. The following sections continue to use Excel to present additional common features of Office.

In the following pages, you will learn how to do the following:

1. Run Excel using the search box.
2. Open a document in Excel.
3. Close the document.
4. Reopen the document just closed.
5. Create a blank Excel document from File Explorer and then open the file.
6. Save a document with a new file name.

To Run an App Using the Search Box

1 SIGN IN | **2 USE WINDOWS** | 3 USE APPS | 4 FILE MANAGEMENT | 5 SWITCH APPS | 6 SAVE FILES

7 CHANGE SCREEN RESOLUTION | 8 EXIT APPS | **9 USE ADDITIONAL APP FEATURES** | 10 USE HELP

The following steps, which assume Windows is running, use the search box to run Excel based on a typical installation; however, you would follow similar steps to run any app. *Why? Some people prefer to use the search box to locate and run an app, as opposed to searching through a list of all apps on the Start menu.* You may need to ask your instructor how to run Excel on your computer.

- Type **Excel 2016** as the search text in the search box and watch the search results appear in the search results (Figure 72).

Q&A

Do I need to type the complete app name or use correct capitalization?
No, you need to type just enough characters of the app name for it to appear in the search results. For example, you may be able to type Excel or excel, instead of Excel 2016.

What if the search does not locate the Excel app on my computer?
You may need to adjust the Windows search settings. Search for the word, index; click 'Indexing Options Control Panel'; click the Modify button (Indexing Options dialog box); expand the Local Disk, if necessary; place a check mark beside all Program Files entries; and then click the OK button. It may take a few minutes for the index to rebuild. If it still does not work, you may need to click the Advanced button (Indexing Options dialog box) and then click the Rebuild button (Advanced Options dialog box).

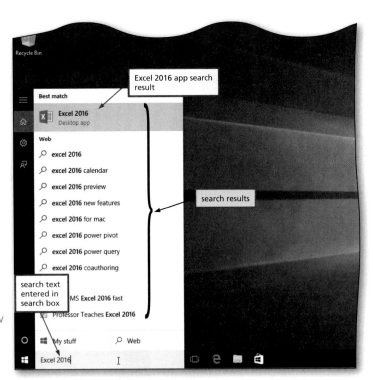

Figure 72

2

- Click the app name, Excel 2016, in the search results to run Excel and display the Excel start screen.

- Click the Blank workbook thumbnail on the Excel start screen (shown earlier in this module in Figure 9) to create a blank workbook and display it in the Excel window.

- If the Excel window is not maximized, click the Maximize button on its title bar to maximize the window (Figure 73).

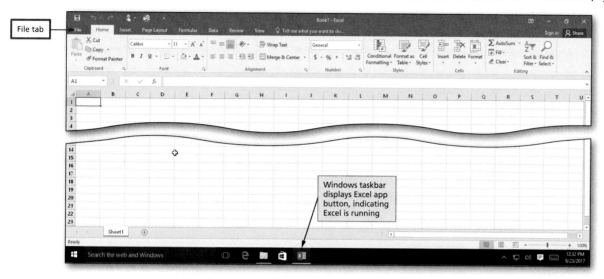

Figure 73

To Open an Existing File

1 SIGN IN | 2 USE WINDOWS | 3 USE APPS | 4 FILE MANAGEMENT | 5 SWITCH APPS | 6 SAVE FILES
7 CHANGE SCREEN RESOLUTION | 8 EXIT APPS | 9 USE ADDITIONAL APP FEATURES | 10 USE HELP

As discussed earlier, the Backstage view contains a set of commands that enable you to manage documents and data about the documents. *Why? From the Backstage view in Excel, for example, you can create, open, print, and save documents. You also can share documents, manage versions, set permissions, and modify document properties. In other Office apps, the Backstage view may contain features specific to those apps.* The following steps open a saved file, specifically the Silver Sky Hardware file.

- Click File on the ribbon (shown in Figure 73) to open the Backstage view and then if necessary, click the Open tab in the Backstage view to display the Open gallery in the Backstage view.

- Click the Browse button in the right pane to display the Open dialog box.

- If necessary, navigate to the location of the file to open (Excel folder in the CIS 101 folder).

- Click the file to open, Silver Sky Hardware in this case, to select the file (Figure 74).

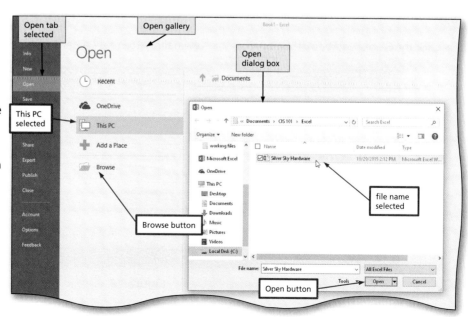

Figure 74

- Click the Open button (Open dialog box) to open the file (shown earlier in the module in Figure 50). If necessary, click the Enable Content button.

Q&A Why did a Security Warning appear?
The Security Warning appears when you open an Office file that might contain harmful content. The files you create in this module are not harmful, but you should be cautious when opening files from other people.

Other Ways

1. Press CTRL+O, browse for file | 2. Navigate to file in File Explorer window, double-click file name | 3. Click Recent in Backstage view, click file name

To Create a New Document from the Backstage View

1 SIGN IN | 2 USE WINDOWS | 3 USE APPS | 4 FILE MANAGEMENT | 5 SWITCH APPS | 6 SAVE FILES
7 CHANGE SCREEN RESOLUTION | 8 EXIT APPS | 9 USE ADDITIONAL APP FEATURES | 10 USE HELP

You can open multiple documents in an Office program, such as Excel, so that you can work on the documents at the same time. The following steps create a file, a blank workbook in this case, from the Backstage view. **Why?** *You want to create a new document while keeping the current document open.*

- Click File on the ribbon to open the Backstage view.

- Click the New tab in the Backstage view to display the New gallery (Figure 75).

Q&A Can I create documents through the Backstage view in other Office apps?
Yes. If the Office app has a New tab in the Backstage view, the New gallery displays various options for creating a new file.

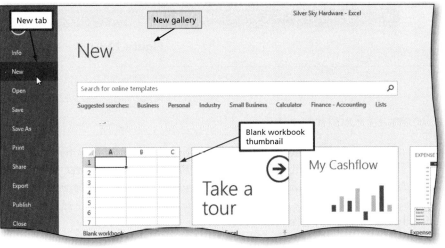

Figure 75

- Click the Blank workbook thumbnail in the New gallery to create a new document (Figure 76).

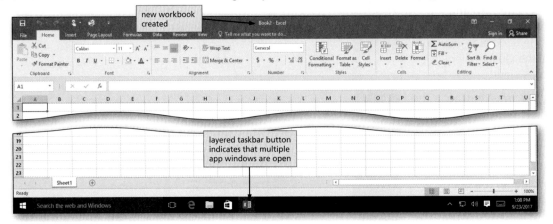

Figure 76

Other Ways

1. Press CTRL+N

To Enter a Worksheet Title

The new Excel workbook will contain a sales analysis. The following steps enter a worksheet title.

1 If it is not already the active cell, click cell A1 to make it the active cell.

2 Type **Silver Sky Hardware Sales Analysis** in cell A1.

3 Click the Enter button to complete the entry and enter the worksheet title in cell A1 (Figure 77).

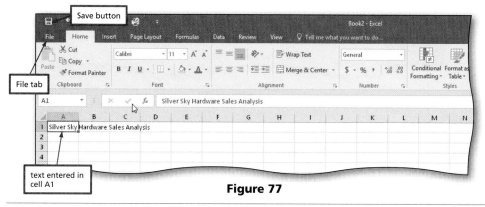

Figure 77

To Save a File

The following steps save the second document in the Excel folder in the class folder (CIS 101, in this case) in the Documents folder using the file name, SSH Sales Analysis.

1 Click the Save button on the Quick Access Toolbar, which depending on settings will display either the Save As gallery in the Backstage view or the Save As dialog box.

2 If your screen displays the Backstage view, click the Browse button in the right pane to display the Save As dialog box.

3 If necessary, type **SSH Sales Analysis** in the File name box (Save As dialog box) to change the file name. Do not press the ENTER key after typing the file name because you do not want to close the dialog box at this time.

4 If necessary, navigate to the desired save location (in this case, the Excel folder in the CIS 101 folder [or your class folder] in the Documents folder). For specific instructions, perform the tasks in Steps 4a and 4b in the previous section in this module titled To Save a File in a Folder.

5 Click the Save button (Save As dialog box) to save the document in the selected folder on the selected drive with the entered file name.

To Close a File Using the Backstage View

1 SIGN IN | 2 USE WINDOWS | 3 USE APPS | 4 FILE MANAGEMENT | 5 SWITCH APPS | 6 SAVE FILES
7 CHANGE SCREEN RESOLUTION | 8 EXIT APPS | 9 USE ADDITIONAL APP FEATURES | **10 USE HELP**

Sometimes, you may want to close an Office file, such as an Excel workbook, and start over with a new file. **Why?** *You should close a file when you are done working with it so that you do not make inadvertent changes to it.* The following steps close the current active Excel file, that is, the SSH Sales Analysis document, without exiting Excel.

- Click File on the ribbon to open the Backstage view (Figure 78).

- Click Close in the Backstage view to close the open file (SSH Sales Analysis, in this case) without exiting the active app (Excel).

Q&A What if Excel displays a dialog box about saving?
Click the Save button if you want to save the changes, click the Don't Save button if you want to ignore the changes since the last time you saved, and click the Cancel button if you do not want to close the workbook.

Can I use the Backstage view to close an open file in other Office apps, such as Word and PowerPoint?
Yes.

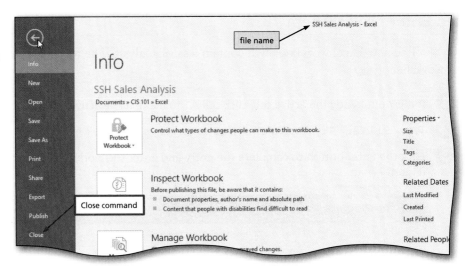

Figure 78

Other Ways

1. Press CTRL+F4

To Open a Recent File Using the Backstage View

1 SIGN IN | 2 USE WINDOWS | 3 USE APPS | 4 FILE MANAGEMENT | 5 SWITCH APPS | 6 SAVE FILES
7 CHANGE SCREEN RESOLUTION | 8 EXIT APPS | 9 USE ADDITIONAL APP FEATURES | **10 USE HELP**

You sometimes need to open a file that you recently modified. *Why? You may have more changes to make, such as adding more content or correcting errors.* The Backstage view allows you to access recent files easily. The following steps reopen the SSH Sales Analysis file just closed.

- Click File on the ribbon to open the Backstage view.
- If necessary, click the Open tab in the Backstage view to display the Open gallery (Figure 79).

- Click the desired file name in the Recent list, SSH Sales Analysis in this case, to open the file.

Q&A Can I use the Backstage view to open a recent file in other Office apps, such as Word and PowerPoint?
Yes, as long as the file name appears in the list of recent files.

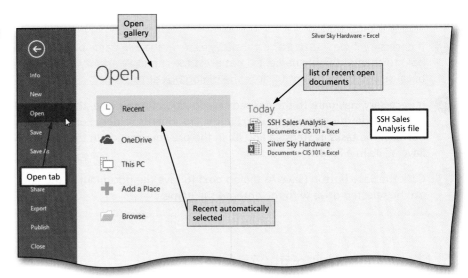

Figure 79

Other Ways

1. Click File on ribbon, click Open in Backstage view, click Browse button, navigate to file (Open dialog box), click Open button

To Create a New Blank Workbook from File Explorer

File Explorer provides a means to create a blank Office document without first running an Office app. The following steps use File Explorer to create a blank Excel workbook. *Why? Sometimes you might need to create a blank workbook and then return to it later for editing.*

- Click the File Explorer button on the taskbar to make the folder window the active window.

- If necessary, double-click the Documents folder in the navigation pane to expand the Documents folder.

- If necessary, double-click your class folder (CIS 101, in this case) in the navigation pane to expand the folder.

- Click the Excel folder in the navigation pane to display its contents in the file list.

- With the Excel folder selected, right-click an open area in the file list to display a shortcut menu.

- Point to New on the shortcut menu to display the New submenu (Figure 80).

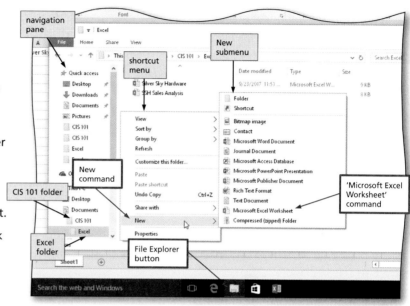

Figure 80

- Click 'Microsoft Excel Worksheet' on the New submenu to display an icon and text box for a new file in the current folder window with the file name, New Microsoft Excel Worksheet, selected (Figure 81).

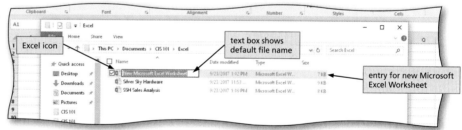

Figure 81

- Type **SSH Expenditures** in the text box and then press the ENTER key to assign a new file name to the new file in the current folder (Figure 82).

Figure 82

To Open a File Using File Explorer

Previously in this module, you learned how to run Excel using the Start menu and the search box. The following steps, which assume Windows is running, open a file using File Explorer. If the app you used to create the file (Microsoft Excel, in this case) is not running, Windows will run the app and open the file. *Why? Another way to open a file is from File Explorer, which causes the app in which the file was created to run, if necessary, and then open the selected file.*

- If necessary, display the file to open in the folder window in File Explorer (shown in Figure 82).

- Right-click the file icon or file name you want to open (SSH Expenditures, in this case) to display a shortcut menu (Figure 83).

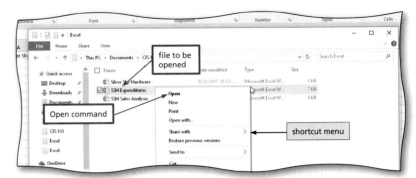

Figure 83

- Click Open on the shortcut menu to open the selected file in the app used to create the file, Excel in this case (shown in Figure 84).

- If the window is not maximized, click the Maximize button on the title bar to maximize the window.

Other Ways

1. Double-click file name in file list

To Enter a Worksheet Title

The next step is to enter a worksheet title in the blank Excel worksheet. The following steps enter a worksheet title.

1 If it is not already the active cell, click cell A1 to make it the active cell.

2 Type **Silver Sky Hardware Expenditures** in cell A1.

3 Click the Enter button to complete the entry and enter the worksheet title in cell A1.

To Save an Existing Office File with the Same File Name

1 SIGN IN | 2 USE WINDOWS | 3 USE APPS | 4 FILE MANAGEMENT | 5 SWITCH APPS | 6 SAVE FILES
7 CHANGE SCREEN RESOLUTION | 8 EXIT APPS | 9 USE ADDITIONAL APP FEATURES | 10 USE HELP

Saving frequently cannot be overemphasized. *Why? You have made modifications to the file since you created it. Thus, you should save again. Similarly, you should continue saving files frequently so that you do not lose the changes you have made since the time you last saved the file.* You can use the same file name, such as SSH Expenditures, to save the changes made to the workbook. The following step saves a file again with the same file name.

- Click the Save button on the Quick Access Toolbar to overwrite the previously saved file (SSH Expenditures, in this case) in the Excel folder (Figure 84).

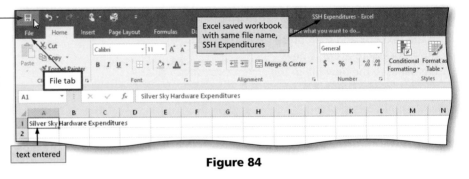

Figure 84

Other Ways

1. Press CTRL+S

2. Press SHIFT+F12

To Save a File with a New File Name

You might want to save a file with a different file name or to a different location. For example, you might start a homework assignment with a data file and then save it with a final file name for submission to your instructor, saving it to a location designated by your instructor. The following steps save a file with a different file name.

① Click the File tab to open the Backstage view.

② Click the Save As tab to display the Save As gallery.

③ Click the Browse button in the left pane to display the Save As dialog box.

④ Type `SSH Income and Expenses` in the File name box (Save As dialog box) to change the file name. Do not press the ENTER key after typing the file name because you do not want to close the dialog box at this time.

⑤ If necessary, navigate to the desired save location (in this case, the Excel folder in the CIS 101 folder [or your class folder] in the Documents folder). For specific instructions, perform the tasks in Steps 4a and 4b in the previous section titled To Save a File in a Folder.

⑥ Click the Save button (Save As dialog box) to save the document in the selected folder on the selected drive with the entered file name.

To Exit an Office App

You are finished using Excel. The following steps exit Excel.

① Because you have multiple Excel workbooks open, right-click the Excel app button on the taskbar and then click 'Close all windows' on the shortcut menu to close all open workbooks and exit Excel.

② If a dialog box appears, click the Save button to save any changes made to the file since the last save.

Renaming, Moving, and Deleting Files

Earlier in this module, you learned how to organize files in folders, which is part of a process known as **file management**. The following sections cover additional file management topics including renaming, moving, and deleting files.

To Rename a File

1 SIGN IN | 2 USE WINDOWS | 3 USE APPS | 4 FILE MANAGEMENT | 5 SWITCH APPS | 6 SAVE FILES
7 CHANGE SCREEN RESOLUTION | 8 EXIT APPS | 9 USE ADDITIONAL APP FEATURES | 10 USE HELP

In some circumstances, you may want to change the name of, or rename, a file or a folder. *Why? You may want to distinguish a file in one folder or drive from a copy of a similar file, or you may decide to rename a file to better identify its contents.* The following steps change the name of the Silver Sky Hardware file in the Excel folder to Silver Sky Hardware Workbook.

①

- If necessary, click the File Explorer button on the taskbar to make the folder window the active window.

- If necessary, navigate to the location of the file to be renamed (in this case, the Excel folder in the CIS 101 [or your class folder] folder in the Documents folder) to display the file(s) it contains in the file list.

- Click the file to be renamed, the Silver Sky Hardware icon or file name in the file list in this case, to select it.

- Right-click the selected file to display a shortcut menu that presents a list of commands related to files (Figure 85).

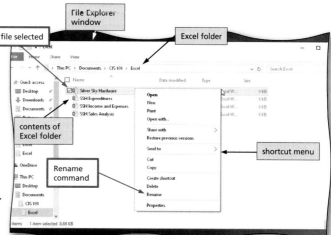

Figure 85

- Click Rename on the shortcut menu to place the current file name in a text box.

- Type `Silver Sky Hardware Workbook` in the text box and then press the ENTER key (Figure 86).

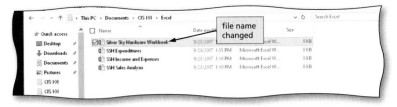

Figure 86

Q&A

Are any risks involved in renaming files that are located on a hard drive?
If you inadvertently change a file extension (the three letter or four letters following the period) while renaming a file, the app that created the file might not be able to recognize and open the file.

Can I rename a file when it is open?
No, a file must be closed to change the file name.

Other Ways

1. Select file, press F2, type new file name, press ENTER
2. Select file, click Rename (Home tab | Organize group), type new file name, press ENTER

To Move a File

1 SIGN IN | 2 USE WINDOWS | 3 USE APPS | **4 FILE MANAGEMENT** | 5 SWITCH APPS | 6 SAVE FILES
7 CHANGE SCREEN RESOLUTION | 8 EXIT APPS | 9 USE ADDITIONAL APP FEATURES | **10 USE HELP**

Why? *You may want to move a file from one folder, called the source folder, to another, called the destination folder. When you move a file, it no longer appears in the original folder. If the destination and the source folders are on the same media, you can move a file by dragging it. If the folders are on different media, you will need to right-drag the file and then click Move here on the shortcut menu. The following step moves the SSH Income and Expenses file from the Excel folder to the CIS 101 folder.*

- If necessary, in File Explorer, navigate to the location of the file to be moved (in this case, the Excel folder in the CIS 101 folder [or your class folder] in the Documents folder).

- If necessary, click the Excel folder in the navigation pane to display the files it contains in the right pane.

- Drag the file to be moved, the SSH Income and Expenses file in the right pane, to the CIS 101 folder in the navigation pane (Figure 87).

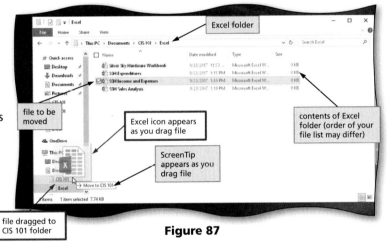

Figure 87

Experiment

- Click the CIS 101 folder in the navigation pane to verify that the file was moved. When you have finished, return to the Excel folder.

Other Ways

1. Right-click file to move, click Cut on shortcut menu, right-click destination folder, click Paste on shortcut menu
2. Select file to move, press CTRL+X, select destination folder, press CTRL+V

To Delete a File

1 SIGN IN | 2 USE WINDOWS | 3 USE APPS | **4 FILE MANAGEMENT** | 5 SWITCH APPS | 6 SAVE FILES
7 CHANGE SCREEN RESOLUTION | 8 EXIT APPS | 9 USE ADDITIONAL APP FEATURES | **10 USE HELP**

A final task you may want to perform is to delete a file. Exercise caution when deleting a file or files. When you delete a file from a hard drive, the deleted file is stored in the Recycle Bin where you can recover it until you empty the Recycle Bin. If you delete a file from removable media, such as a USB flash drive, the file is deleted permanently. The next steps delete the SSH Income and Expenses file from the CIS 101 folder. *Why?* *When a file no longer is needed, you can delete it to conserve space on your storage location.*

1

- If necessary, in File Explorer, navigate to the location of the file to be deleted (in this case, the CIS 101 folder [or your class folder] in the Documents folder).

- Click the file to be deleted, the SSH Income and Expenses icon or file name in the right pane in this case, to select the file.

- Right-click the selected file to display a shortcut menu (Figure 88).

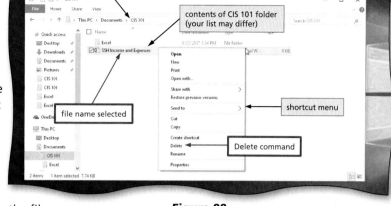

Figure 88

2

- Click Delete on the shortcut menu to delete the file.

- If a dialog box appears, click the Yes button to delete the file.

Q&A

Can I use this same technique to delete a folder?

Yes. Right-click the folder and then click Delete on the shortcut menu. When you delete a folder, all of the files and folders contained in the folder are deleted as well. For example, if you delete the CIS 101 folder, you will delete all folders and files inside the CIS 101 folder.

Other Ways

1. Select file, press DELETE

Microsoft Office and Windows Help

At any time while you are using one of the Office apps, such as Excel, you can use Office Help to display information about all topics associated with the app. Help in other Office apps operates in a similar fashion.

In Office, Help is presented in a window that has browser-style navigation buttons. Each Office app has its own Help home page, which is the starting Help page that is displayed in the Help window. If your computer is connected to the Internet, the contents of the Help page reflect both the local help files installed on the computer and material from Microsoft's website.

To Open the Help Window in an Office App

1 SIGN IN | 2 USE WINDOWS | 3 USE APPS | 4 FILE MANAGEMENT | 5 SWITCH APPS | 6 SAVE FILES
7 CHANGE SCREEN RESOLUTION | 8 EXIT APPS | 9 USE ADDITIONAL APP FEATURES | 10 USE HELP

The following step opens the Excel 2016 Help window. *Why? You might not understand how certain commands or operations work in Excel, so you can obtain the necessary information using help.*

1

- Run Excel.

- Click the Blank workbook thumbnail to display a blank workbook.

- Press F1 to open the Excel 2016 Help window (Figure 89).

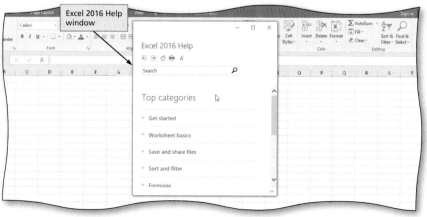

Figure 89

Moving and Resizing Windows

At times, it is useful, or even necessary, to have more than one window open and visible on the screen at the same time. You can resize and move these open windows so that you can view different areas of and elements in the window. In the case of the Help window, for example, it could be covering document text in the Excel window that you need to see.

To Move a Window by Dragging

1 SIGN IN | **2 USE WINDOWS** | 3 USE APPS | 4 FILE MANAGEMENT | 5 SWITCH APPS | 6 SAVE FILES
7 CHANGE SCREEN RESOLUTION | 8 EXIT APPS | 9 USE ADDITIONAL APP FEATURES | 10 USE HELP

You can move any open window that is not maximized to another location on the desktop by dragging the title bar of the window. **Why?** *You might need to have a better view of what is behind the window or just want to move the window so that you can see it better.* The following step drags the Excel 2016 Help window to the upper-left corner of the desktop.

- Drag the window title bar (the Excel 2016 Help window title bar, in this case) so that the window moves to the upper-left corner of the desktop, as shown in Figure 90.

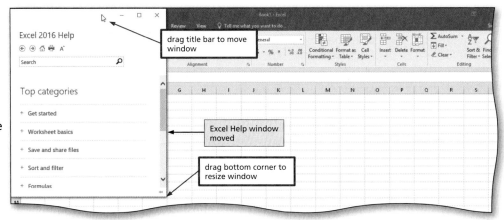

Figure 90

To Resize a Window by Dragging

1 SIGN IN | **2 USE WINDOWS** | 3 USE APPS | 4 FILE MANAGEMENT | 5 SWITCH APPS | 6 SAVE FILES
7 CHANGE SCREEN RESOLUTION | 8 EXIT APPS | 9 USE ADDITIONAL APP FEATURES | 10 USE HELP

A method used to change the size of the window is to drag the window borders. The following step changes the size of the Excel 2016 Help window by dragging its borders. **Why?** *Sometimes, information is not visible completely in a window, and you want to increase the size of the window.*

- Point to the lower-right corner of the window (the Excel 2016 Help window, in this case) until the pointer changes to a two-headed arrow.

- Drag the bottom border downward to display more of the active window (Figure 91).

Q&A

Can I drag other borders on the window to enlarge or shrink the window?
Yes, you can drag the left, right, and top borders and any window corner to resize a window.

Will Windows remember the new size of the window after I close it?
Yes. When you reopen the window, Windows will display it at the same size it was when you closed it.

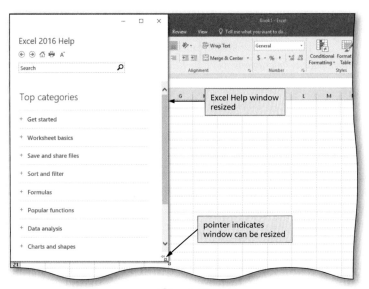

Figure 91

Using Office Help

Once an Office app's Help window is open, several methods exist for navigating Help. You can search for help by entering search text in the Search text box or by clicking the links in the Help window.

To Obtain Help Using the Search Text Box

1 SIGN IN | 2 USE WINDOWS | 3 USE APPS | 4 FILE MANAGEMENT | 5 SWITCH APPS | 6 SAVE FILES
7 CHANGE SCREEN RESOLUTION | 8 EXIT APPS | 9 USE ADDITIONAL APP FEATURES | 10 USE HELP

Assume for the following example that you want to know more about fonts. The following steps use the Search text box to obtain useful information about fonts by entering the word, fonts, as search text. *Why? You may not know the exact help topic you are looking to find, so using keywords can help narrow your search.*

- Type **fonts** in the Search text box at the top of the Excel 2016 Help window to enter the search text.

- Press the ENTER key to display the search results (Figure 92).

Q&A

Why do my search results differ?
If you do not have an Internet connection, your results will reflect only the content of the Help files on your computer. When searching for help online, results also can change as content is added, deleted, and updated on the online Help webpages maintained by Microsoft.

Why were my search results not very helpful?
When initiating a search, be sure to check the spelling of the search text; also, keep your search specific to return the most accurate results.

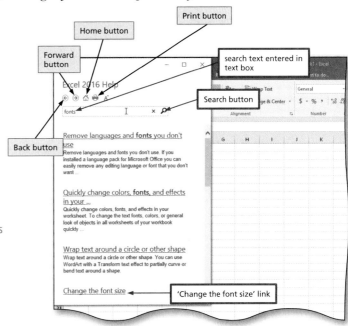

Figure 92

- Click the 'Change the font size', or similar, link to display the Help information associated with the selected topic (Figure 93).

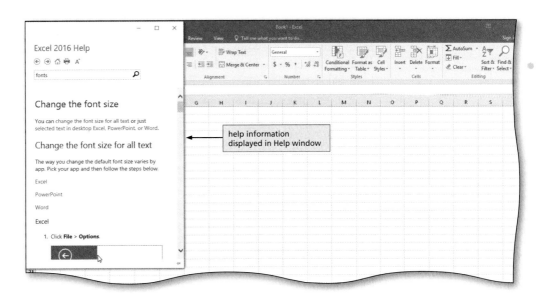

Figure 93

- Click the Home button in the Help window to clear the search results and redisplay the Help home page (Figure 94).

- Click the Close button in the Excel 2016 Help window to close the window.

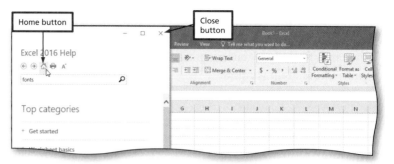

Figure 94

Obtaining Help while Working in an Office App

You also can access the Help functionality without first opening the Help window and initiating a search. For example, you may be confused about how a particular command works, or you may be presented with a dialog box that you are not sure how to use.

If you want to learn more about a command, point to its button and wait for the ScreenTip to appear, as shown in Figure 95. If the Help icon and 'Tell me more' link appear in the ScreenTip, click the 'Tell me more' link (or press the F1 key while pointing to the button) to open the Help window associated with that command.

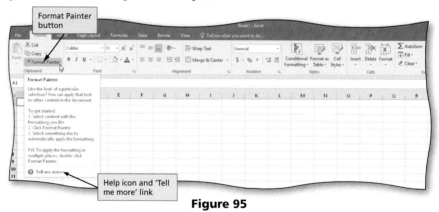

Figure 95

Dialog boxes also contain Help buttons, as shown in Figure 96. Clicking the Help button (or pressing the F1 key) while the dialog box is displayed opens a Help window, which will display help contents specific to the dialog box, if available. If no help file is available for that particular dialog box, then the window will display the Help home page.

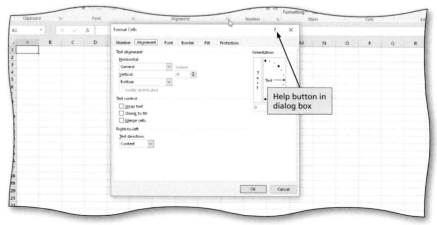

Figure 96

As mentioned previously, the Tell Me box is integrated into the ribbon in most Office apps and can perform a variety of functions, including providing easy access to commands and help content as you type.

To Obtain Help Using the Tell Me Box

1 SIGN IN | 2 USE WINDOWS | 3 USE APPS | 4 FILE MANAGEMENT | 5 SWITCH APPS | 6 SAVE FILES
7 CHANGE SCREEN RESOLUTION | 8 EXIT APPS | 9 USE ADDITIONAL APP FEATURES | 10 USE HELP

If you are having trouble finding a command in an Office app, you can use the Tell Me box to search for the function you are trying to perform. As you type, the Tell Me box will suggest commands that match the search text you are entering. *Why? You can use the Tell Me box to access commands quickly you otherwise may be unable to find on the ribbon.* The following steps find information about margins.

- Type **margins** in the Tell Me box and watch the search results appear.

- Click Adjust Margins, or another active link, to display a submenu displaying the various margin settings (Figure 97).

- Click an empty area of the document window to close the search results.

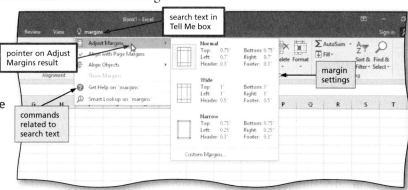

Figure 97

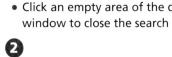

- Exit Microsoft Excel.

Using the Windows Search Box

One of the more powerful Windows features is the Windows search box. The search box is a central location from where you can enter search text and quickly access related Windows commands or web search results. In addition, **Cortana** is a new search tool in Windows that you can access using the search box. It can act as a personal assistant by performing functions such as providing ideas; searching for apps, files, and folders; and setting reminders. In addition to typing search text in the search box, you also can use your computer or mobile device's microphone to give verbal commands.

To Use the Windows Search Box

1 SIGN IN | 2 USE WINDOWS | 3 USE APPS | 4 FILE MANAGEMENT | 5 SWITCH APPS | 6 SAVE FILES
7 CHANGE SCREEN RESOLUTION | 8 EXIT APPS | 9 USE ADDITIONAL APP FEATURES | 10 USE HELP

The following step uses the Windows search box to search for a Windows command. *Why? Using the search box to locate apps, settings, folders, and files can be faster than navigating windows and dialog boxes to search for the desired content.*

- Type **notification** in the search box in the Windows taskbar to display the search results. The search results include related Windows settings, Windows Store apps, and web search results (Figure 98).

- Click an empty area of the desktop to close the search results.

- Close the File Explorer window.

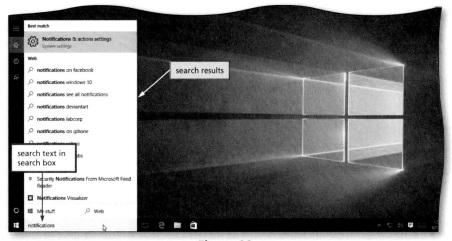

Figure 98

Summary

In this module, you learned how to use the Windows interface, several touch screen and mouse operations, and file and folder management. You also learned some basic features of Excel and discovered the common elements that exist among Microsoft Office apps. Topics covered included signing in, using Windows, using apps, file management, switching between apps, saving files, changing screen resolution, exiting apps, using additional app features, and using help.

CONSIDER THIS: PLAN AHEAD

What guidelines should you follow to plan your projects?

The process of communicating specific information is a learned, rational skill. Computers and software, especially Microsoft Office 2016, can help you develop ideas and present detailed information to a particular audience and minimize much of the laborious work of drafting and revising projects. No matter what method you use to plan a project, it is beneficial to follow some specific guidelines from the onset to arrive at a final product that is informative, relevant, and effective. Use some aspects of these guidelines every time you undertake a project, and others as needed in specific instances.

1. Determine the project's purpose.

    a) Clearly define why you are undertaking this assignment.

    b) Begin to draft ideas of how best to communicate information by handwriting ideas on paper; composing directly on a laptop, tablet, or mobile device; or developing a strategy that fits your particular thinking and writing style.

2. Analyze your audience.

    a) Learn about the people who will read, analyze, or view your work.

    b) Determine their interests and needs so that you can present the information they need to know and omit the information they already possess.

    c) Form a mental picture of these people or find photos of people who fit this profile so that you can develop a project with the audience in mind.

3. Gather possible content.

    a) Locate existing information that may reside in spreadsheets, databases, or other files.

    b) Conduct a web search to find relevant websites.

    c) Read pamphlets, magazine and newspaper articles, and books to gain insights of how others have approached your topic.

4. Determine what content to present to your audience.

    a) Write three or four major ideas you want audience members to remember after reading or viewing your project.

    b) Envision your project's endpoint, the key fact you wish to emphasize, so that all project elements lead to this final element.

    c) Determine relevant time factors, such as the length of time necessary to develop the project, how long readers will spend reviewing your project, or the amount of time allocated for your speaking engagement.

    d) Decide whether a graph, photo, or artistic element can express or enhance a particular concept.

    e) Be mindful of the order in which you plan to present the content, and place the most important material at the top of the worksheet. Readers and audience members generally remember the first and last pieces of information they see and hear.

How should you submit solutions to questions in the assignments identified with a symbol?

Every assignment in this book contains one or more questions with a symbol. These questions require you to think beyond the assigned file. Present your solutions to the question in the format required by your instructor. Possible formats may include one or more of these options: write the answer; create a document that contains the answer; present your answer to the class; discuss your answer in a group; record the answer as audio or video using a webcam, smartphone, or portable media player; or post answers on a blog, wiki, or website.

Apply Your Knowledge

Reinforce the skills and apply the concepts you learned in this module.

Creating a Folder and a Workbook

Instructions: You will create an Excel Assignments folder and then create an Excel workbook and save it in the folder.

Perform the following tasks:

1. Open the File Explorer window and then double-click to open the Documents folder.
2. Click the New folder button on the Quick Access Toolbar to display a new folder icon and text box for the folder name.
3. Type **Excel Assignments** in the text box to name the folder. Press the ENTER key to create the folder in the Documents folder.
4. Run Excel and create a new blank workbook.
5. Enter the text shown in Figure 99.

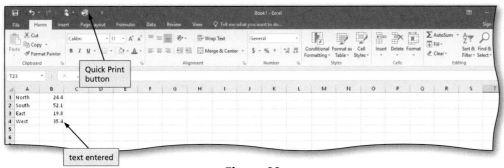

Figure 99

6. If requested by your instructor, enter your name in the Excel workbook.
7. Click the Save button on the Quick Access Toolbar. Navigate to the Excel Assignments folder in the Documents folder and then save the document using the file name, Apply 1 Workbook.
8. If your Quick Access Toolbar does not show the Quick Print button, add the Quick Print button to the Quick Access Toolbar. Print the document using the Quick Print button on the Quick Access Toolbar. When you are finished printing, remove the Quick Print button from the Quick Access Toolbar.
9. Submit the printout to your instructor.
10. Close the File Explorer window.
11. Exit Excel.
12. What other commands might you find useful to include on the Quick Access Toolbar?

Extend Your Knowledge

Extend the skills you learned in this module and experiment with new skills. You will use Help to complete the assignment.

Using Help

Instructions: Use Excel Help to perform the following tasks.

Perform the following tasks:
1. Run Excel.
2. Press F1 to open the Excel 2016 Help window (shown in Figure 89).
3. Search Excel Help to answer the following questions and type the answers in a new blank Excel workbook.

   a. What are three new features to Excel 2016?
   b. What type of training is available through Excel Help for Excel 2016?
   c. What are the steps to customize the ribbon?
   d. What is the purpose of the Office Clipboard?
   e. What is the Name box?
   f. What is a sparkline?
   g. How do you insert charts?
   h. How do you change the size of text?
   i. What are the steps to zoom in and out of a workbook?
   j. What is the purpose of the Insights pane? How do you display it?

4. If requested by your instructor, enter your name it the Excel workbook.
5. Save the workbook with a new file name and then submit it in the format specified by your instructor.
6. Exit Excel.
7. ✳ What search text did you use to perform the searches above? Did it take multiple attempts to search and locate the exact information for which you were searching?

Expand Your World

Create a solution that uses cloud or web technologies by learning and investigating on your own from general guidance.

Creating Folders on OneDrive and Using the Excel Online App

Instructions: You will create the folders shown in Figure 100 on OneDrive. Then, you will use the Excel Online app to create a small file and save it in a folder on OneDrive.

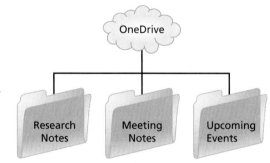

Figure 100

Perform the following tasks:
1. Sign in to OneDrive in your browser.
2. Use the New button to create the folder structure shown in Figure 100.
3. In the Upcoming Events folder, create an Excel workbook with the file name, Extend 1 Task List, that contains the text, Prepare itinerary for upcoming trip, in cell A1.
4. If requested by your instructor, add your name to the Excel workbook.
5. Save the workbook in the Upcoming Events folder and then exit the Excel Online app.

6. Submit the assignment in the format specified by your instructor.

7. ✳ Based on your current knowledge of OneDrive, do you think you will use it? What about the Excel Online app?

In the Labs

Design, create, modify, and/or use files following the guidelines, concepts, and skills presented in this module. Labs 1 and 2, which increase in difficulty, require you to create solutions based on what you learned in the module; Lab 3 requires you to apply your creative thinking and problem-solving skills to design and implement a solution.

Lab 1: **Creating Folders for a Bookstore**

Problem: Your friend works for a local bookstore. He would like to organize his files in relation to the types of books available in the store. He has seven main categories: fiction, biography, children, humor, social science, nonfiction, and medical. You are to create a folder structure similar to Figure 101.

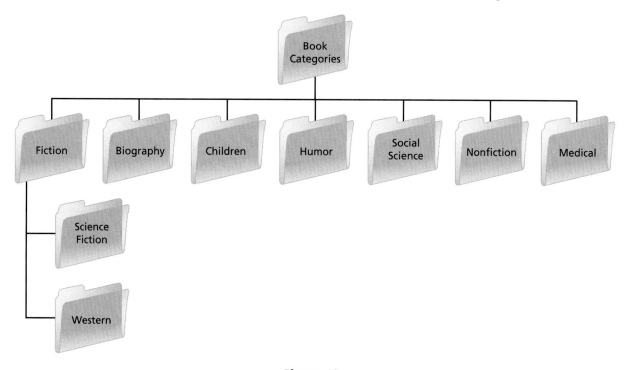

Figure 101

Perform the following tasks:

1. Click the File Explorer button on the taskbar and display the contents of the Documents folder.

2. In the Documents folder, create the main folder and name it Book Categories.

3. Navigate to the Book Categories folder.

4. Within the Book Categories folder, create a folder for each of the following: Fiction, Biography, Children, Humor, Social Science, Nonfiction, and Medical.

5. Within the Fiction folder, create two additional folders, one for Science Fiction and the second for Western.

Continued >

In the Labs continued

6. If requested by your instructor, add another folder using your last name as the folder name.

7. Submit the assignment in the format specified by your instructor.

8. ✳ Think about how you use your computer for various tasks (consider personal, professional, and academic reasons). What folders do you think will be required on your computer to store the files you save?

Lab 2: Creating Excel Workbooks and Saving Them in Appropriate Folders

Problem: You are taking a class that requires you to complete three Excel modules. You will save the work completed in each module in a different folder (Figure 102).

Perform the following tasks:

1. Create the folders shown in Figure 102.

2. Create an Excel workbook containing the text, Module 1 Notes, in cell A1.

3. In the Backstage view, click Save As.

4. Click the Browse button to display the Save As dialog box. Click Documents to open the Documents folder. Navigate to the Module 1 folder and then save the file using the file name, Lab 2 Module 1 Notes.

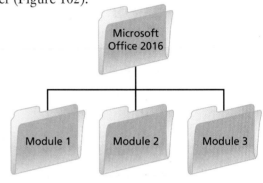

Figure 102

5. Create another Excel workbook containing the text, Module 2 Notes, in cell A1, and then save it in the Module 2 folder using the file name, Lab 2 Module 2 Notes.

6. Create a third Excel workbook containing the text, Module 3 Notes, in cell A1, and then save it in the Module 3 folder using the file name, Lab 2 Module 3 Notes.

7. If requested by your instructor, add your name to each of the three Excel workbooks.

8. Submit the assignment in the format specified by your instructor.

9. ✳ Based on your current knowledge of Windows and Excel, how will you organize folders for assignments in this class? Why?

Lab 3: Consider This: Your Turn

Researching Malware

Problem: You have just purchased a new computer running the Windows operating system. Because you want to be sure that it is protected from malware, you decide to research malware, malware protection, and removing malware.

Part 1: Research the following three topics: malware, malware protection, and removing malware. Use the concepts and techniques presented in this module to use the search box on the Windows taskbar to find information regarding these topics. Create an Excel workbook that contains steps to safeguard a computer properly from malware, three ways to prevent malware, as well as at least two different methods to remove malware or a virus should your computer become infected (include one tip per row). Submit your assignment and the answers to the following critical thinking questions in the format specified by your instructor.

Part 2: ✳ What decisions did you make while researching malware for this assignment? What was the rationale behind these decisions? How did you locate the required information about malware?

1 Creating a Worksheet and a Chart

Objectives

You will have mastered the material in this module when you can:

- Describe the Excel worksheet
- Enter text and numbers
- Use the Sum button to sum a range of cells
- Enter a simple function
- Copy the contents of a cell to a range of cells using the fill handle
- Apply cell styles
- Format cells in a worksheet

- Create a 3-D pie chart
- Change a worksheet name and sheet tab color
- Change document properties
- Preview and print a worksheet
- Use the AutoCalculate area to display statistics
- Correct errors on a worksheet

Introduction

Almost every organization collects vast amounts of data. Often, data is consolidated into a summary so that people in the organization better understand the meaning of the data. An Excel worksheet allows data to be summarized and charted easily. A **chart** conveys a visual representation of data. In this module, you will create a worksheet that includes a chart. The data in the worksheet and chart comprise a personal budget that contains monthly estimates for each income and expense category.

Project — Personal Budget Worksheet and Chart

The project in this module follows proper design guidelines and uses Excel to create the worksheet and chart shown in Figure 1–1a and Figure 1–1b. The worksheet contains budget data for Linda Fox. She has compiled a list of her expenses and sources of income and wants to use this information to create an easy-to-read worksheet to see how much she will be ahead or behind each month. In addition, she would like a 3-D pie chart to show her estimated expenses by category for each of the 12 months.

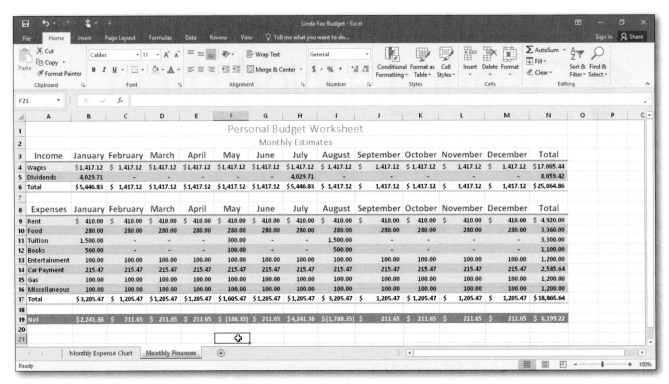

Figure 1–1(a) Personal Budget Worksheet

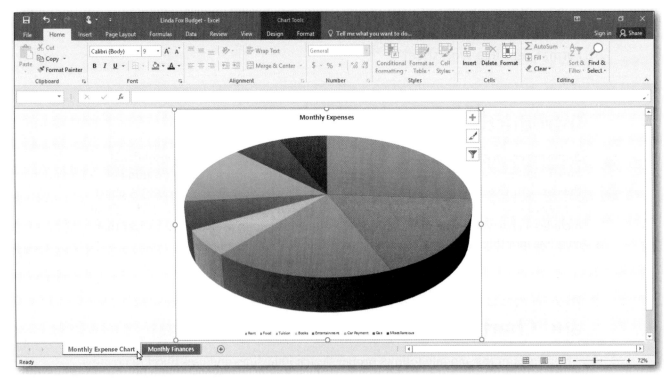

Figure 1–1(b) Pie Chart Showing Monthly Expenses by Category

The first step in creating an effective worksheet is to make sure you understand what is required. The person or persons requesting the worksheet may supply their requirements in a requirements document, or you can create one. A requirements document includes a needs statement, a source of data, a summary of calculations, and any other special requirements for the worksheet, such as charting and web support. Figure 1–2 shows the requirements document for the new workbook to be created in this module.

Worksheet Title	Personal Budget Worksheet
Word	A yearly projection of Linda Fox's personal budget
Source of data	Data supplied by Linda Fox includes monthly estimates for income and expenses
Calculations	The following calculations must be made: 1. For each month, a total for income and expenses 2. For each budget item, a total for the item 3. For the year, total all income and expenses 4. Net = income − expenses

Figure 1–2

In this module, you will learn how to perform basic workbook tasks using Excel. The following roadmap identifies general activities you will perform as you progress through this module:

1. ENTER TEXT in a blank worksheet.
2. CALCULATE SUMS AND USE FORMULAS in the worksheet.
3. FORMAT TEXT in the worksheet.
4. INSERT a pie CHART into the worksheet.
5. Assign a NAME to the sheet TAB.
6. PREVIEW AND PRINT the WORKSHEET.

For an introduction to Windows and instructions about how to perform basic Windows tasks, read the Office and Windows module at the beginning of this book, where you can learn how to resize windows, change screen resolution, create folders, move and rename files, use Windows Help, and much more.

CONSIDER THIS

Why is it important to plan a worksheet?

The key to developing a useful worksheet is careful planning. Careful planning can reduce your effort significantly and result in a worksheet that is accurate, easy to read, flexible, and useful. When analyzing a problem and designing a worksheet solution, what steps should you follow?

• Define the problem, including need, source of data, calculations, charting, and web or special requirements.

• Design the worksheet.

• Enter the data and formulas.

• Test the worksheet.

After carefully reviewing the requirements document (Figure 1–2) and making the necessary decisions, the next step is to design a solution or draw a sketch of the worksheet based on the requirements, including titles, column and row headings, the location of data values, and the 3-D pie chart, as shown in Figure 1–3. The dollar signs and commas that you see in the sketch of the worksheet indicate formatted numeric values.

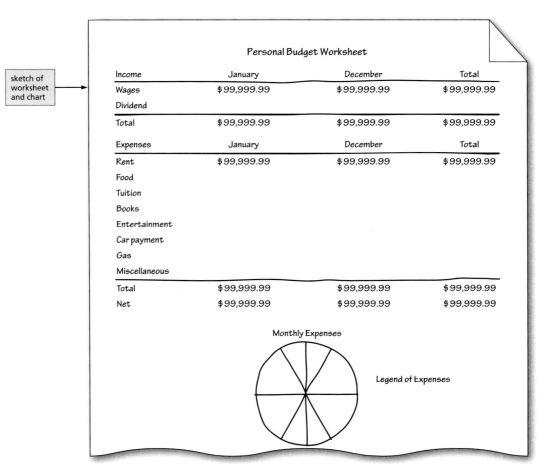

sketch of worksheet and chart

Figure 1–3

With a good understanding of the requirements document, an understanding of the necessary decisions, and a sketch of the worksheet, the next step is to use Excel to create the worksheet and chart.

Selecting a Cell

To enter data into a cell, you first must select it. The easiest way to **select** a cell (make it active) is to use the mouse to move the block plus sign pointer to the cell and then click.

An alternative method is to use the arrow keys that are located just to the right of the alphanumeric keys on a standard keyboard. An arrow key selects the cell adjacent to the active cell in the direction of the arrow on the key.

You know a cell is selected, or active, when a heavy border surrounds the cell and the active cell reference appears in the Name box on the left side of the formula bar. Excel also changes the color of the active cell's column and row headings to a darker shade.

Entering Text

In Excel, any set of characters containing a letter, hyphen (as in a telephone number), or space is considered **text**. Text is used for titles, such as column and row titles, on the worksheet.

Worksheet titles and subtitles should be as brief and meaningful as possible. A worksheet title could include the name of the organization, department, or a description of the content of the worksheet. A worksheet subtitle, if included, could include a more detailed description of the content of the worksheet. Examples of worksheet titles are January 2018 Payroll and Year 2018 Projected Budget, and examples of subtitles are Finance Department and Monthly Projections, respectively.

As shown in Figure 1–4, data in a worksheet is identified by row and column titles so that the meaning of each entry is clear. Rows typically contain information such as categories of data. Columns typically describe how data is grouped in the worksheet, such as by month or by department.

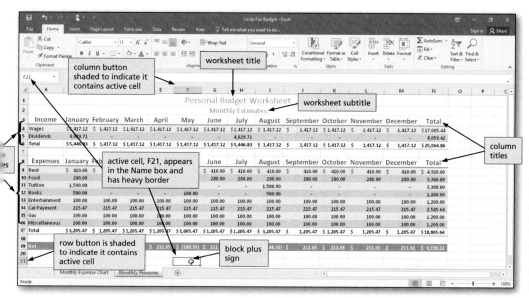

BTW

Excel Screen Resolution

If you are using a computer to step through the project in this module and you want your screens to match the figures in this book, you should change your screen's resolution to 1366 x 768. For information about how to change a computer's resolution, refer to the Office and Windows module at the beginning of this book.

Figure 1–4

To Enter the Worksheet Titles

1 ENTER TEXT | 2 CALCULATE SUMS & USE FORMULAS | 3 FORMAT TEXT
4 INSERT CHART | 5 NAME TAB | 6 PREVIEW & PRINT WORKSHEET

As shown in Figure 1–4, the worksheet title, Personal Budget Worksheet, identifies the purpose of the worksheet. The worksheet subtitle, Monthly Estimates, identifies the type of data contained in the worksheet. *Why?* *A title and subtitle help the reader to understand clearly what the worksheet contains.* The following steps enter the worksheet titles in cells A1 and A2. Later in this module, the worksheet titles will be formatted so that they appear as shown in Figure 1–4.

1

- Run Excel and create a blank workbook in the Excel window.

- If necessary, click cell A1 to make cell A1 the active cell (Figure 1–5).

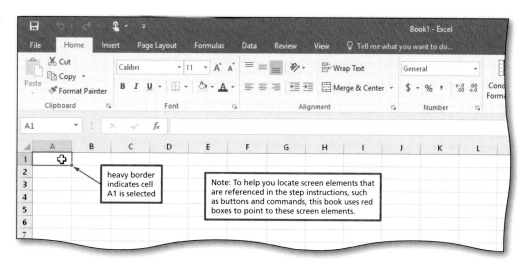

Figure 1–5

- Type **Personal Budget Worksheet** in cell A1 (Figure 1–6).

Q&A Why did the appearance of the formula bar change?
Excel displays the title in the formula bar and in cell A1. When you begin typing a cell entry, Excel enables two additional boxes in the formula bar: the Cancel button and the Enter button. Clicking the Enter button completes an entry. Clicking the Cancel button cancels an entry.

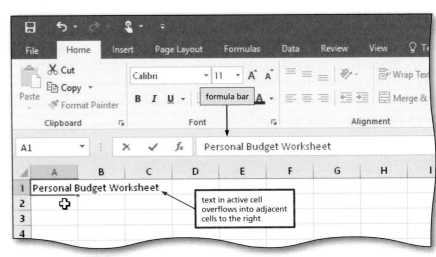

Figure 1–6

- Click the Enter button to complete the entry and enter the worksheet title (Figure 1–7).

Q&A Why does the entered text appear in three cells?
When the text is longer than the width of a cell, Excel displays the overflow characters in adjacent cells to the right as long as those adjacent cells contain no data. If the adjacent cells contain data, Excel hides the overflow characters. The overflow characters are visible in the formula bar whenever that cell is active.

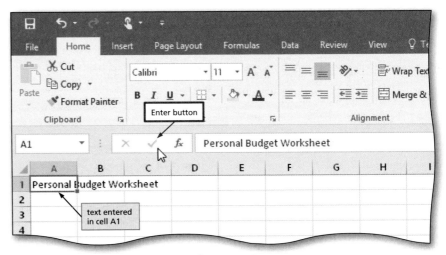

Figure 1–7

- Click cell A2 to select it.

- Type **Monthly Estimates** as the cell entry.

- Click the Enter button to complete the entry and enter the worksheet subtitle (Figure 1–8).

Q&A What happens when I click the Enter button?
When you complete an entry by clicking the Enter button, the insertion point disappears and the cell in which the text is entered remains the active cell.

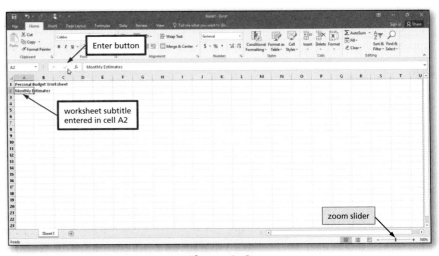

Figure 1–8

Other Ways

1. To complete entry, click any cell other than active cell

2. To complete entry, press ENTER

3. To complete entry, press HOME, PAGE UP, PAGE DOWN, END, UP ARROW, DOWN ARROW, LEFT ARROW, or RIGHT ARROW

CONSIDER THIS

Why is it difficult to read the text on my screen?

If you are having trouble reading the cell values in your spreadsheet, you can zoom in to make the cells larger. When you zoom in, fewer columns and rows display on your screen, and you might have to scroll more often. To zoom in, drag the zoom slider on the right of the status bar, or click the plus button on the zoom slider, until you reach your desired zoom level. In addition to the zoom slider, you also can zoom by clicking the Zoom button (View tab | Zoom group), selecting a desired zoom percentage (Zoom dialog box), and then clicking the OK button (Zoom dialog box).

AutoCorrect

The **AutoCorrect** feature of Excel works behind the scenes, correcting common mistakes when you complete a text entry in a cell. AutoCorrect makes three types of corrections for you:

1. Corrects two initial uppercase letters by changing the second letter to lowercase.
2. Capitalizes the first letter in the names of days.
3. Replaces commonly misspelled words with their correct spelling. For example, it will change the misspelled word *recieve* to *receive* when you complete the entry. AutoCorrect will correct the spelling of hundreds of commonly misspelled words automatically.

BTW

The Ribbon and Screen Resolution

Excel may change how the groups and buttons within the groups appear on the ribbon, depending on the computer's screen resolution. Thus, your ribbon may look different from the ones in this book if you are using a screen resolution other than 1366 x 768.

To Enter Column Titles

1 ENTER TEXT | 2 CALCULATE SUMS & USE FORMULAS | 3 FORMAT TEXT
4 INSERT CHART | 5 NAME TAB | 6 PREVIEW & PRINT WORKSHEET

The worksheet is divided into two parts, income and expense, as shown in Figure 1–4. Grouping income and expense data by month is a common method for organizing budget data. The column titles shown in row 3 identify the income section of the worksheet and indicate that the income values will be grouped by month. Likewise, row 8 is clearly identified as the expense section and similarly indicates that the expense values will be estimated on a per month basis. The following steps enter the column titles in row 3. **Why?** *Data entered in columns should be identified using column titles to identify what the column contains.*

1

- Click cell A3 to make it the active cell.

- Type **Income** to begin entry of a column title in the active cell (Figure 1–9).

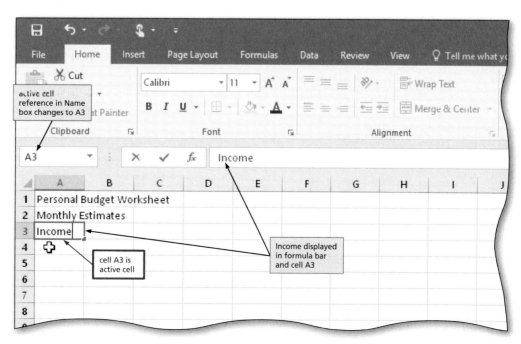

Figure 1–9

2

- Press the RIGHT ARROW key to enter the column title and make the cell to the right the active cell (Figure 1–10).

Q&A

◄ Why is the RIGHT ARROW key used to complete the entry in the cell?

Pressing an arrow key to complete an entry makes the adjacent cell in the direction of the arrow (up, down, left, or right) the next active cell. However, if your next entry is in a nonadjacent cell, you can complete your current entry by clicking the next cell in which you plan to enter data. You also can press the ENTER key and then click the appropriate cell for the next entry.

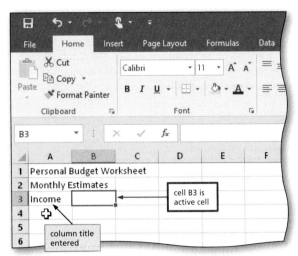

Figure 1–10

3

- Repeat Steps 1 and 2 to enter the remaining column titles; that is, enter **January** in cell B3, **February** in cell C3, **March** in cell D3, **April** in cell E3, **May** in cell F3, **June** in cell G3, **July** in cell H3, **August** in cell I3, **September** in cell J3, **October** in cell K3, **November** in cell L3, **December** in cell M3, and **Total** in cell N3 (complete the last entry in cell N3 by clicking the Enter button in the formula bar).

- Click cell A8 to select it.

- Repeat Steps 1 and 2 to enter the remaining column titles; that is, enter **Expenses** in cell A8, **January** in cell B8, **February** in cell C8, **March** in cell D8, **April** in cell E8, **May** in cell F8, **June** in cell G8, **July** in cell H8, **August** in cell I8, **September** in cell J8, **October** in cell K8, **November** in cell L8, **December** in cell M8, and **Total** in cell N8 (complete the last entry in cell N8 by clicking the Enter button in the formula bar) (Figure 1–11).

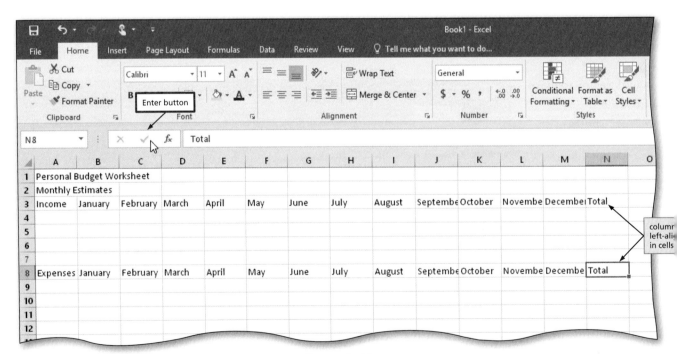

Figure 1–11

To Enter Row Titles

The next step in developing the worksheet for this project is to enter the row titles in column A. For the Personal Budget Worksheet data, the row titles contain a list of income types and expense types. Each income or expense item should be placed in its own row. *Why? Entering one item per row allows for maximum flexibility, in case more income or expense items are added in the future.* The following steps enter the row titles in the worksheet.

- Click cell A4 to select it.

- Type **Wages** and then click cell A5 or press the DOWN ARROW key to enter a row title (Figure 1–12).

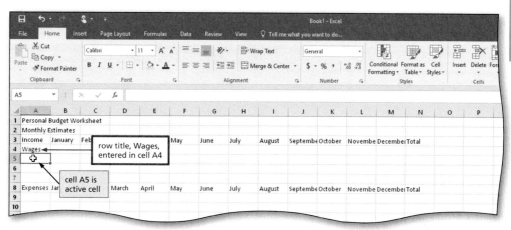

Figure 1–12

- Repeat Step 1 to enter the remaining row titles in column A; that is, enter **Dividends** in cell A5, **Total** in cell A6, **Rent** in cell A9, **Food** in cell A10, **Tuition** in cell A11, **Books** in cell A12, **Entertainment** in cell A13, **Car Payment** in cell A14, **Gas** in cell A15, **Miscellaneous** in cell A16, **Total** in cell A17, and **Net** in cell A19 (Figure 1–13).

Q&A
Why is the text left-aligned in the cells?
Excel automatically left-aligns the text in the cell. Excel treats any combination of numbers, spaces, and nonnumeric characters as text. For example, Excel would recognize the following entries as text: 401AX21, 921–231, 619 321, 883XTY. How to change the text alignment in a cell is discussed later in this module.

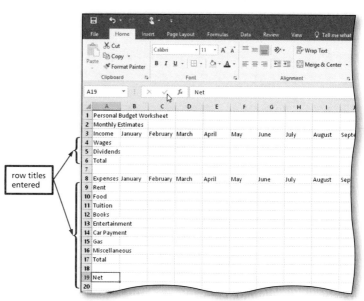

Figure 1–13

Entering Numbers

In Excel, you enter a **number** into a cell to represent an amount or value. A number can contain only the following characters:

0 1 2 3 4 5 6 7 8 9 + – ( ) , / . $ % E e

If a cell entry contains any other keyboard character (including spaces), Excel interprets the entry as text and treats it accordingly. The use of special characters is explained when they are used in this book.

To Enter Numbers

The Personal Budget Worksheet numbers used in Module 1 are summarized in Table 1–1. These numbers, which represent yearly income and expense amounts, are entered in rows 4–5 and 9–16. *Why?* *One of the most powerful features of Excel is the ability to perform calculations on numeric data. Before you can perform calculations, you first must enter the data.* The following steps enter the numbers in Table 1–1 one row at a time.

Table 1–1 Personal Budget Worksheet

Income	January	February	March	April	May	June	July	August	September	October	November	December
Wages	1417.12	1417.12	1417.12	1417.12	1417.12	1417.12	1417.12	1417.12	1417.12	1417.12	1417.12	1417.12
Dividends	4029.71	0	0	0	0	0	4029.71	0	0	0	0	0

Expenses	January	February	March	April	May	June	July	August	September	October	November	December
Rent	410	410	410	410	410	410	410	410	410	410	410	410
Food	280	280	280	280	280	280	280	280	280	280	280	280
Tuition	1500	0	0	0	300	0	0	1500	0	0	0	0
Books	500	0	0	0	100	0	0	500	0	0	0	0
Entertainment	100	100	100	100	100	100	100	100	100	100	100	100
Car Payment	215.47	215.47	215.47	215.47	215.47	215.47	215.47	215.47	215.47	215.47	215.47	215.47
Gas	100	100	100	100	100	100	100	100	100	100	100	100
Miscellaneous	100	100	100	100	100	100	100	100	100	100	100	100

1

- Click cell B4 to select it.

- Type `1417.12` and then press the RIGHT ARROW key to enter the data in the selected cell and make the cell to the right (cell C4) the active cell (Figure 1–14).

Q&A Do I need to enter dollar signs, commas, or trailing zeros for the amounts?

You are not required to type dollar signs, commas, or trailing zeros. When you enter a dollar value that has cents, however, you must add the decimal point and the numbers representing the cents. Later in this module, you will learn how to format numbers with dollar signs, commas, and trailing zeros to improve their appearance and readability.

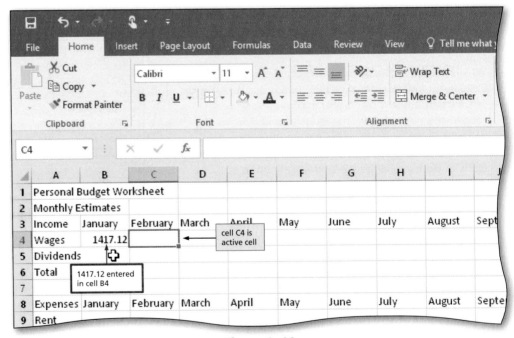

Figure 1–14

• Enter   `1417.12`   in cells C4, D4, E4, F4, G4, H4, I4, J4, K4, L4, and M4 to complete the first row of numbers in the worksheet (Figure 1–15).

Q&A

Why are the numbers right-aligned?

When you enter numeric data in a cell, Excel recognizes the values as numbers and automatically right-aligns the values in order to vertically align decimal and integer values.

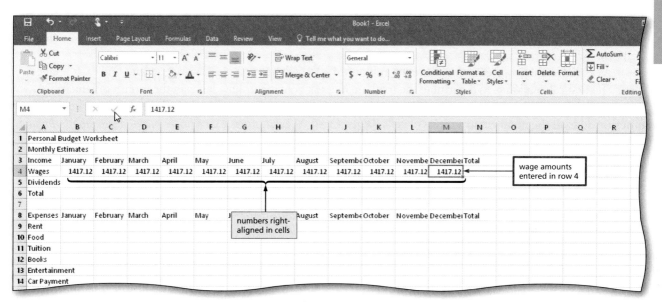

Figure 1–15

• Click cell B5 to select it and complete the entry in the previously selected cell.

• Enter the remaining numbers provided in Table 1–1 for each of the nine remaining budget items in row 5 and rows 9–16 (Figure 1–16).

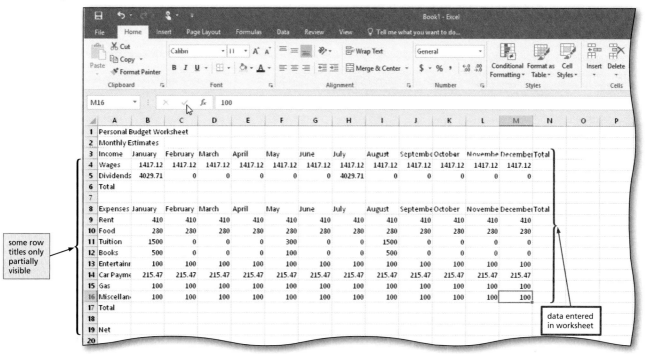

Figure 1–16

Calculating a Sum

The next step in creating the worksheet is to perform any necessary calculations, such as calculating the column and row totals. In Excel, you easily can perform calculations using a **function**, or a predefined formula. When you use functions, Excel performs the calculations for you, which helps to prevent errors and allows you to work more efficiently.

To Sum a Column of Numbers

1 ENTER TEXT | 2 CALCULATE SUMS & USE FORMULAS | 3 FORMAT TEXT
4 INSERT CHART | 5 NAME TAB | 6 PREVIEW & PRINT WORKSHEET

As stated in the requirements document in Figure 1–2, totals are required for each month and each budget item. The first calculation is to determine the total income for Wages and Dividends in the month of January (column B). To calculate this value in cell B6, Excel must add, or sum, the numbers in cells B4 and B5. The **SUM function** adds all the numbers in a range of cells. *Why? Excel's SUM function is an efficient means to accomplish this task.*

A **range** is a series of two or more adjacent cells in a column, row or rectangular group of cells. For example, the group of adjacent cells B4 and B5 is a range. Many Excel operations are performed on a range of cells.

After calculating the total income for January, the monthly totals for income and expenses and the yearly total for each budget item will be calculated. The following steps sum the numbers in column B.

- Click cell B6 to make it the active cell.

- Click the Sum button (Home tab | Editing group) to enter a formula in the formula bar and in the active cell (Figure 1–17).

Q&A

What if my screen displays the Sum menu?
If you are using a touch screen, you may not have a separate Sum button and Sum arrow. In this case, select the desired option (Sum) on the Sum menu.

How does Excel know which cells to sum?
Excel automatically selects what it considers to be your choice of the range to sum. When proposing the range, Excel first looks for a range of cells with numbers above the active cell and then to the left. If Excel proposes the wrong range, you can correct it by dragging through the correct range before pressing the ENTER key. You also can enter the correct range by typing the beginning cell reference, a colon (:), and the ending cell reference.

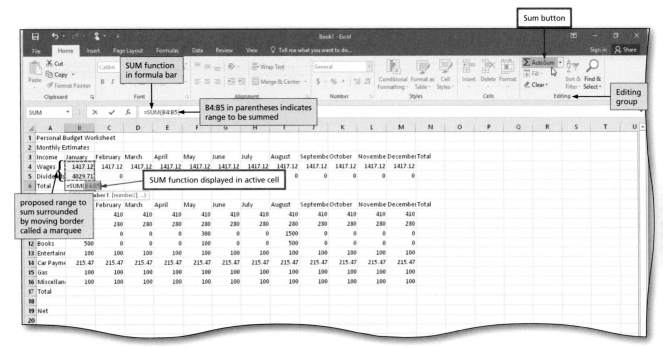

Figure 1–17

2

- Click the Enter button in the formula bar to enter the sum in the active cell.

Q&A What is the purpose of the arrow next to the Sum button on the ribbon?

The Sum arrow (shown in Figure 1–17) displays a list of functions that allow you to easily determine the average of a range of numbers, the number of items in a selected range, or the maximum or minimum value of a range.

3

- Repeat Steps 1 and 2 to enter the SUM function in cell B17 (Figure 1–18).

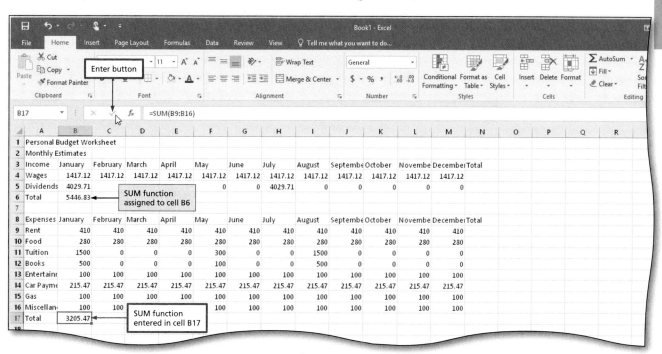

Figure 1–18

Other Ways

1. Click Insert Function button in formula bar, select SUM in Select a function list, click OK button (Insert Function dialog box), click OK button

    (Function Arguments dialog box)

2. Click Sum arrow (Home tab | Editing group), click More Functions in list, scroll to and

    then click SUM (Insert Function dialog box), click OK button, select range (Function Arguments dialog box), click OK button

3. Type **=S** in cell, select SUM in list, select range, click Enter button

4. Press ALT+EQUAL SIGN (=) twice

Using the Fill Handle to Copy a Cell to Adjacent Cells

You want to calculate the totals for income during each month in cells C6:M6. Table 1–2 illustrates the similarities between the function and range used in cell B6 and the function and ranges required to sum the totals in cells C6, D6, E6, F6, G6, H6, I6, J6, K6, L6, and M6.

To calculate each total for each range across the worksheet, you could follow the same steps shown previously in Figure 1–17 and Figure 1–18. A more efficient method, however, would be to copy the SUM function from cell B6 to the range C6:M6. The cell being copied is called the **source area** or **copy area**. The range of cells receiving the copy is called the **destination area** or **paste area**.

Table 1–2 Sum Function Entries in Row 6		
Cell	**SUM Function Entries**	**Result**
B6	=SUM(B4:B5)	Sums cells B4 and B5
C6	=SUM(C4:C5)	Sums cells C4 and C5
D6	=SUM(D4:D5)	Sums cells D4 and D5
E6	=SUM(E4:E5)	Sums cells E4 and E5
F6	=SUM(F4:F5)	Sums cells F4 and F5
G6	=SUM(G4:G5)	Sums cells G4 and G5
H6	=SUM(H4:H5)	Sums cells H4 and H5
I6	=SUM(I4:I5)	Sums cells I4 and I5
J6	=SUM(J4:J5)	Sums cells J4 and J5
K6	=SUM(K4:K5)	Sums cells K4 and K5
L6	=SUM(L4:L5)	Sums cells L4 and L5
M6	=SUM(M4:M5)	Sums cells M4 and M5

Although the SUM function entries in Table 1–2 are similar to each other, they are not exact copies. The range in each SUM function entry uses cell references that are one column to the right of the previous column. When you copy formulas that include cell references, Excel automatically adjusts them for each new position, resulting in the SUM function entries illustrated in Table 1–2. Each adjusted cell reference is called a **relative reference**.

To Copy a Cell to Adjacent Cells in a Row

1 ENTER TEXT | 2 CALCULATE SUMS & USE FORMULAS | 3 **FORMAT TEXT**

4 **INSERT CHART** | 5 **NAME TAB** | 6 **PREVIEW & PRINT WORKSHEET**

The easiest way to copy the SUM formula from cell B6 to cells C6:M6 is to use the fill handle. *Why?* *Using the fill handle copies content to adjacent cells more efficiently.* The **fill handle** is the small green square located in the lower-right corner of the heavy border around the active cell. The following steps use the fill handle to copy cell B6 to the adjacent cells C6:M6.

1

• With cell B6 active, point to the fill handle to activate it. Your pointer changes to a crosshair (Figure 1–19).

Q&A Why is my fill handle not a green square?
If you are using a touch screen, the fill handle appears as a black and white rectangle with a blue down arrow in it.

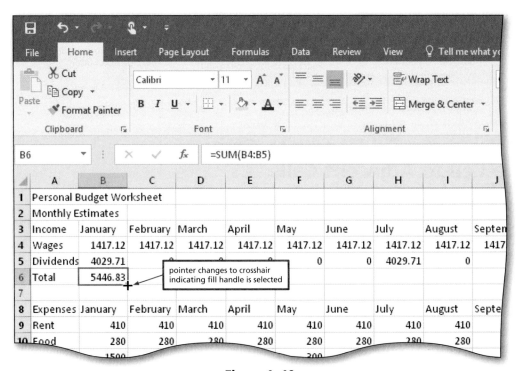

Figure 1–19

2

- Drag the fill handle to select the destination area, range C6:M6, which will draw a heavy green border around the source area and the destination area (Figure 1–20). Do not release the mouse button.

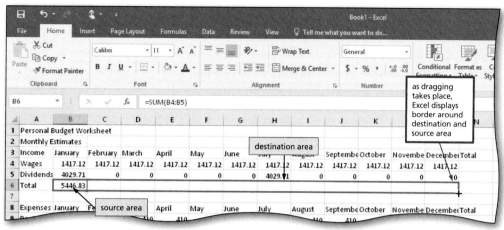

Figure 1–20

3

- Release the mouse button to copy the SUM function from the active cell to the destination area and calculate the sums (Figure 1–21).

Q&A

What is the purpose of the 'Auto Fill Options' button? The 'Auto Fill Options' button allows you to choose whether you want to copy the values from the source area to the destination area with the existing formatting, without the formatting, or with the formatting but without the functions.

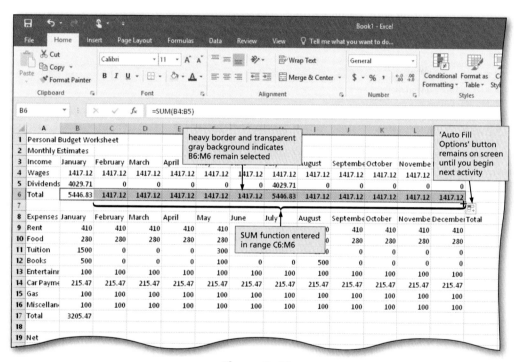

Figure 1–21

4

- Repeat Steps 1–3 to copy the SUM function from cell B17 to the range C17:M17 (Figure 1–22).

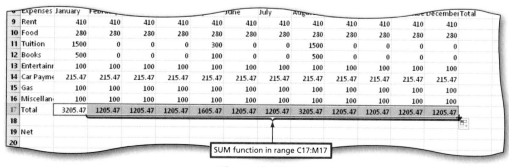

Figure 1–22

Other Ways

1. Select source area, click Copy button (Home tab | Clipboard group), select destination area, click Paste button (Home tab | Clipboard group)

2. Right-click source area, click Copy on shortcut menu, select and right-click destination area, click Paste on shortcut menu

To Calculate Multiple Totals at the Same Time

The next step in building the worksheet is to determine the total income, total expenses, and total for each budget item in column N. To calculate these totals, you use the SUM function similar to how you used it to total the income and expenses for each month in rows 6 and 17.

In this example, however, Excel will determine totals for all of the rows at the same time. *Why? By determining multiple totals at the same time, the number of steps to add totals is reduced.* The following steps sum multiple totals at once.

1
• Click cell N4 to make it the active cell (Figure 1–23).

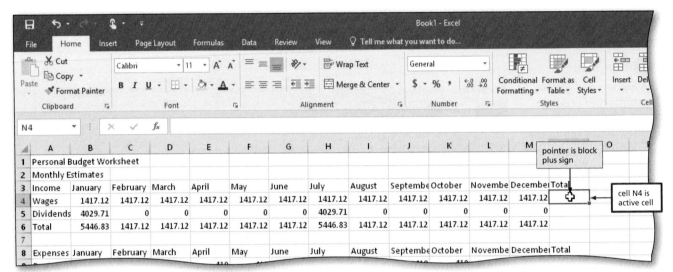

Figure 1–23

2
• With the pointer in cell N4 and in the shape of a block plus sign, drag the pointer down to cell N6 to highlight the range with a transparent view (Figure 1–24).

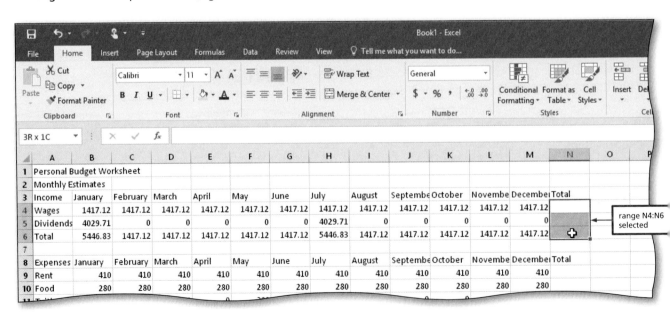

Figure 1–24

3

- Click the Sum button (Home tab | Editing group) to calculate the sums of the corresponding rows (Figure 1–25).

Q&A How does Excel create unique totals for each row?

If each cell in a selected range is adjacent to a row of numbers, Excel assigns the SUM function to each cell when you click the Sum button.

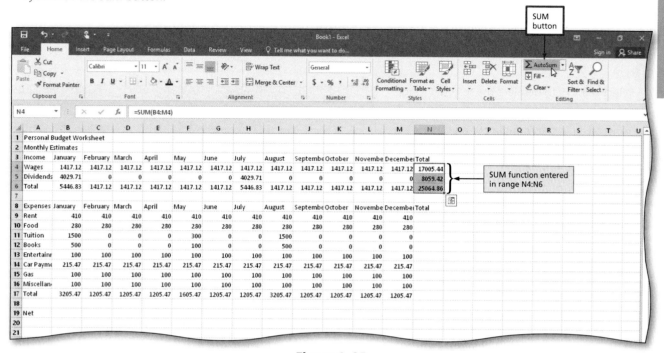

Figure 1–25

4

- Repeat Steps 1–3 to select cells N9 to N17 and calculate the sums of the corresponding rows (Figure 1–26).

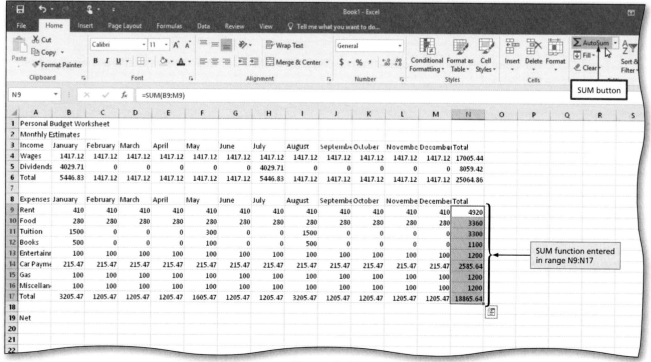

Figure 1–26

To Enter a Formula Using the Keyboard

The net for each month, which will appear in row 19, is equal to the income total in row 6 minus the expense total in row 17. The formula needed in the worksheet is noted in the requirements document as follows:

Net (row 19) = Income (row 6) – Expenses (row 17)

The following steps enter the net formula in cell B19 using the keyboard. *Why? Sometimes a predefined function does not fit your needs; therefore, you enter a formula of your own.*

1

- Select cell B19 to deselect the selected range.

- Type `=b6-b17` in the cell. The formula is displayed in the formula bar and the current cell, and colored borders are drawn around the cells referenced in the formula (Figure 1–27).

Q&A

What occurs on the worksheet as I enter the formula?

The equal sign (=) preceding b6–b17 in the formula alerts Excel that you are entering a formula or function and not text. Because the most common error when entering a formula is to reference the wrong cell, Excel highlights the cell references in the formula in color, and uses same colors to highlight the borders of the cells to help you ensure that your cell references are correct. The minus sign (–) following b6 in the formula is the arithmetic operator that directs Excel to perform the subtraction operation.

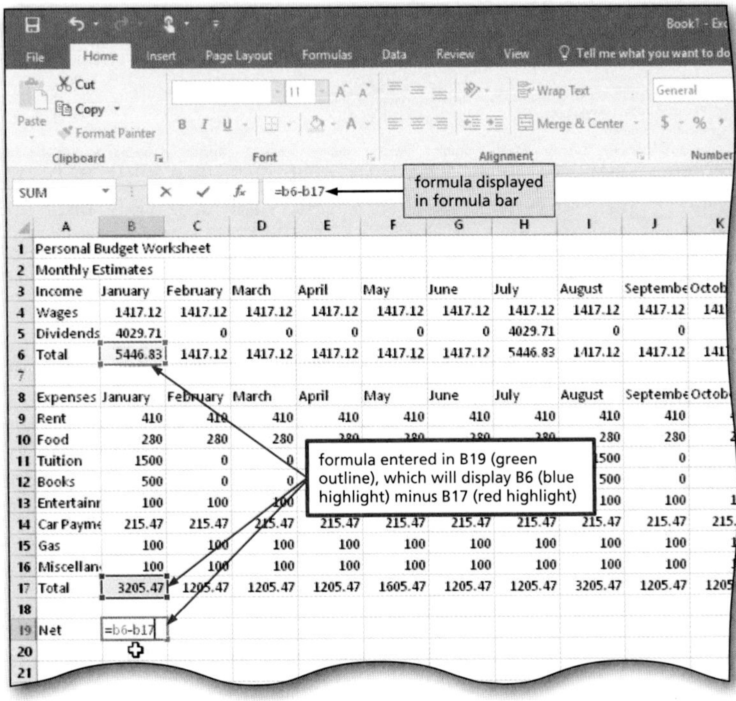

Figure 1–27

2

- Click cell C19 to complete the arithmetic operation, display the result in the worksheet, and select the cell to the right (Figure 1–28).

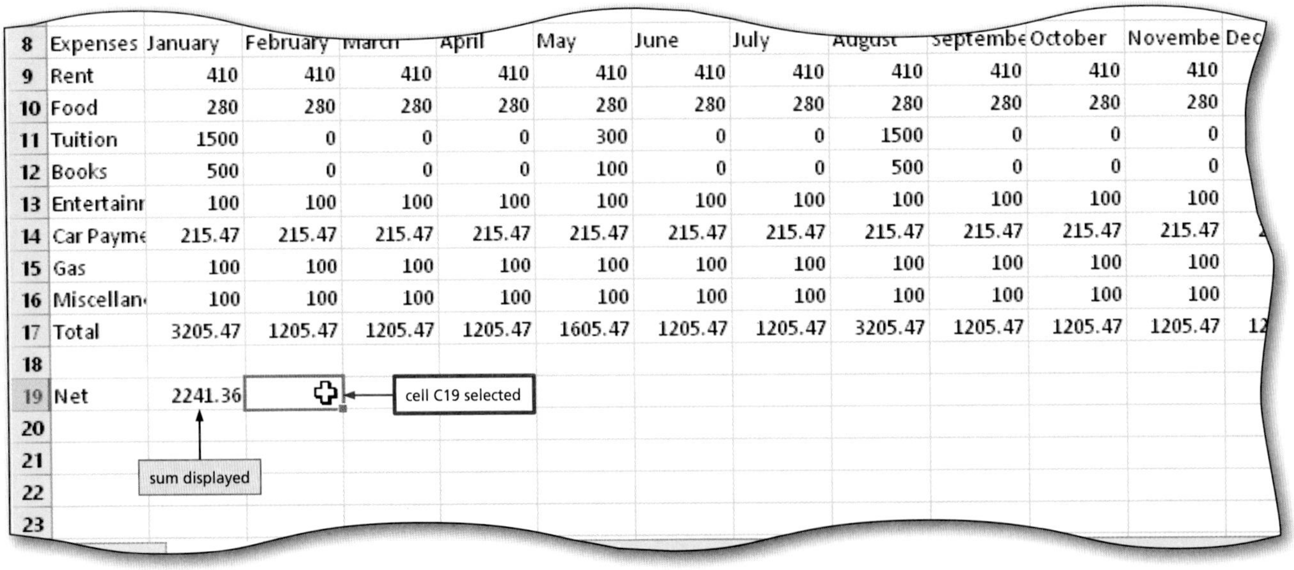

Figure 1–28

To Copy a Cell to Adjacent Cells in a Row

The easiest way to copy the SUM formula from cell B19 to cells C19, D19, E19, F19, G19, H19, I19, J19, K19, L19, M19, and N19 is to use the fill handle. The following steps use the fill handle to copy the formula in cell B19 to the adjacent cells C19:N19.

1 Select cell B19.

2 Drag the fill handle to select the destination area, range C19:N19, which draws a shaded border around the source area and the destination area. Release the mouse button to copy the simple formula function from the active cell to the destination area and calculate the results.

3 Save the worksheet on your hard drive, OneDrive, or other storage location using Linda Fox Budget as the file name.

Q&A | Why should I save the workbook at this time?
You have performed many tasks while creating this workbook and do not want to risk losing work completed thus far.

Break Point: If you wish to take a break, this is a good place to do so. You can exit Excel. To resume at a later time, run Excel, open the file called Linda Fox Budget, and continue following the steps from this location forward.

Formatting the Worksheet

The text, numeric entries, and functions for the worksheet now are complete. The next step is to format the worksheet. You **format** a worksheet to emphasize certain entries and make the worksheet easier to read and understand.

Figure 1–29a shows the worksheet before formatting. Figure 1–29b shows the worksheet after formatting. As you can see from the two figures, a worksheet that is formatted not only is easier to read but also looks more professional.

To change the unformatted worksheet in Figure 1–29a so that it looks like the formatted worksheet in Figure 1–29b, the following tasks must be completed:

BTW
Organizing Files and Folders
You should organize and store files in folders so that you easily can find the files later. For example, if you are taking an introductory technology class called CIS 101, a good practice would be to save all Excel files in an Excel folder in a CIS 101 folder. For a discussion of folders and detailed examples of creating folders, refer to the Office and Windows module at the beginning of this book.

CONSIDER THIS

What steps should I consider when formatting a worksheet?
The key to formatting a worksheet is to consider the ways you can enhance the worksheet so that it appears professional. When formatting a worksheet, consider the following steps:

• Identify in what ways you want to emphasize various elements of the worksheet.

• Increase the font size of cells.

• Change the font color of cells.

• Center the worksheet titles, subtitles, and column headings.

• Modify column widths to best fit text in cells.

• Change the font style of cells.

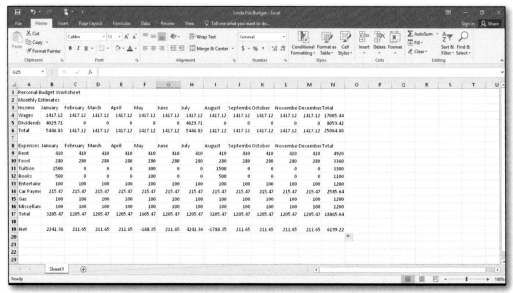

(a) Unformatted Worksheet

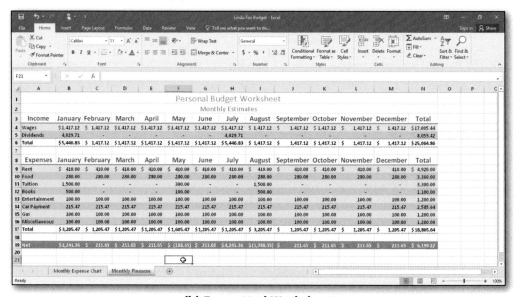

(b) Formatted Worksheet

Figure 1–29

1. Change the font, change the font style, increase the font size, and change the font color of the worksheet titles in cells A1 and A2.

2. Center the worksheet titles in cells A1 and A2 across columns A through N.

3. Format the body of the worksheet. The body of the worksheet, range A3:N19, includes the column titles, row titles, and numbers. Formatting the body of the worksheet changes the numbers to use a dollars-and-cents format, with dollar signs in rows 4 and 9 and in the total rows (row 6 and 17); changes the styles of some rows; adds underlining that emphasizes portions of the worksheet; and modifies the column widths to fit the text in the columns and make the text and numbers readable.

Although the formatting procedures are explained in the order described above, you could make these format changes in any order. Modifying the column widths, however, usually is done last because other formatting changes may affect the size of data in the cells in the column.

Font Style, Size, and Color

The characters that Excel displays on the screen are a specific font, style, size, and color. The **font**, or font face, defines the appearance and shape of the letters, numbers, and special characters. Examples of fonts include Calibri, Cambria, Times New Roman, Arial, and Courier. **Font style** indicates how the characters are emphasized. Common font styles include regular, bold, underline, and italic. The **font size** specifies the size of the characters. Font size is gauged by a measurement system called points. A single point is 1/72 of one inch in height. Thus, a character with a **point size** of 10 is 10/72 of one inch in height. Finally, Excel has a wide variety of **font colors** from which to choose to define the color of the characters.

When Excel first runs, the default font for the entire workbook is Calibri, with a font size, font style, and font color of 11-point regular black. You can change the font characteristics in a single cell, a range of cells, the entire worksheet, or the entire workbook.

To Change a Cell Style

1 ENTER TEXT | 2 CALCULATE SUMS & USE FORMULAS | 3 FORMAT TEXT
4 INSERT CHART | 5 NAME TAB | 6 PREVIEW & PRINT WORKSHEET

You can change several characteristics of a cell, such as the font, font size, and font color, all at once by assigning a predefined cell style to a cell. A **cell style** is a predefined font, font size, and font color that you can apply to a cell. *Why? Using the predefined styles provides a consistent appearance to common portions of your worksheets, such as worksheet titles, worksheet subtitles, column headings, and total rows.* The following steps assign the Title cell style to the worksheet title in cell A1.

- Click cell A1 to make cell A1 the active cell.
- Click the Cell Styles button (Home tab | Styles group) to display the Cell Styles gallery (Figure 1–30).

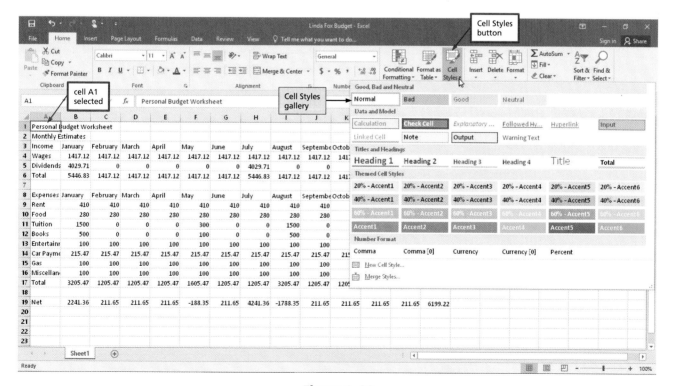

Figure 1–30

2

• Point to the Title cell style in the Titles and Headings area of the Cell Styles gallery to see a live preview of the cell style in the active cell (Figure 1–31).

Q&A Can I use live preview on a touch screen?
Live preview is not available on a touch screen.

Experiment

• Point to other cell styles in the Cell Styles gallery to see a live preview of those cell styles in cell A1.

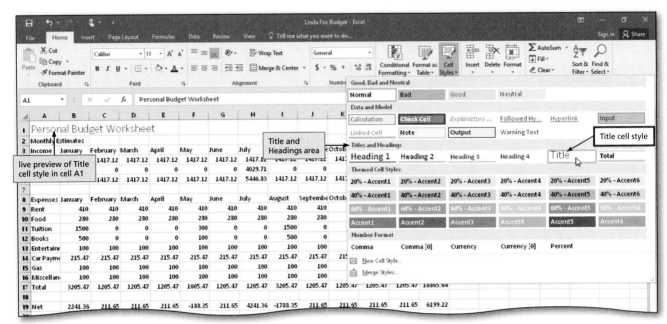

Figure 1–31

3

• Click the Title cell style to apply the cell style to the active cell (Figure 1–32).

Q&A Why do settings in the Font group on the ribbon change? The font and font size change to reflect the font changes applied to the active cell, cell A1, as a result of applying the Title cell style.

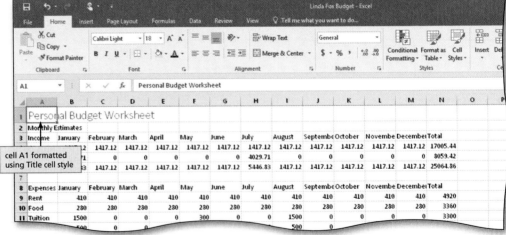

Figure 1–32

1 ENTER TEXT | 2 CALCULATE SUMS & USE FORMULAS | 3 FORMAT TEXT
4 INSERT CHART | 5 NAME TAB | 6 PREVIEW & PRINT WORKSHEET

To Change the Font

Why? *Different fonts often are used in a worksheet to make it more appealing to the reader and to relate or distinguish data in the worksheet.* The following steps change the worksheet subtitle's font to Calibri Light.

1

- Click cell A2 to make it the active cell.

- Click the Font arrow (Home tab | Font group) to display the Font gallery. If necessary, scroll to Calibri Light.

- Point to Calibri Light in the Font gallery to see a live preview of the selected font in the active cell (Figure 1–33).

Experiment

- Point to several other fonts in the Font gallery to see a live preview of the other fonts in the selected cell.

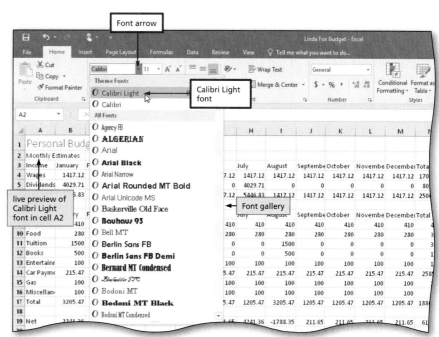

Figure 1–33

2

- Click Calibri Light in the Font gallery to change the font of the worksheet subtitle to Calibri Light (Figure 1–34).

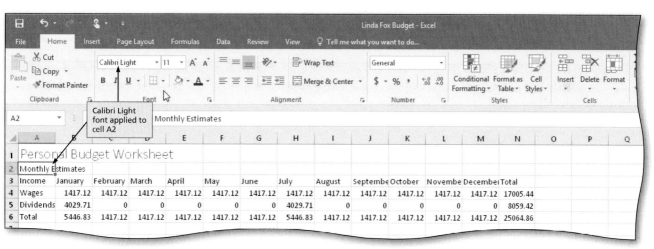

Figure 1–34

Other Ways

1. Click Font Settings Dialog Box Launcher, click Font tab (Format Cells dialog box), click desired font in Font list, click OK button

2. Right-click cell to display mini toolbar, click Font box arrow on mini toolbar, click desired font in Font gallery

3. Right-click selected cell, click Format Cells on shortcut menu, click Font tab (Format Cells dialog box), click desired font, click OK button

---

1 ENTER TEXT | 2 CALCULATE SUMS & USE FORMULAS | 3 FORMAT TEXT
4 INSERT CHART | 5 NAME TAB | 6 PREVIEW & PRINT WORKSHEET

To Apply Bold Style to a Cell

Bold, or boldface, text has a darker appearance than normal text. ***Why?** You apply bold style to a cell to emphasize it or make it stand out from the rest of the worksheet.* The following steps apply bold style to the worksheet title and subtitle.

1

- Click cell A1 to make it active and then click the Bold button (Home tab | Font group) to change the font style of the active cell to bold (Figure 1–35).

What if a cell already has the bold style applied?
If the active cell contains bold text, then Excel displays the Bold button with a darker gray background.

How do I remove the bold style from a cell?
Clicking the Bold button (Home tab | Font group) a second time removes the bold style.

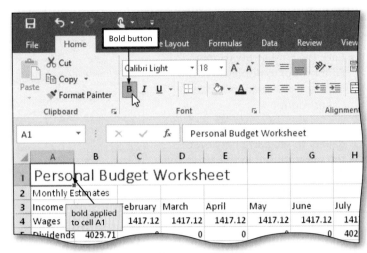

Figure 1–35

2

- Repeat Step 1 to bold cell A2.

Other Ways

1. Click Font Settings Dialog Box Launcher, click Font tab (Format Cells dialog box), click Bold in Font style list, click OK button

2. Right-click selected cell, click Bold button on mini toolbar

3. Right-click selected cell, click Format Cells on shortcut menu, click Font tab (Format Cells dialog box), click Bold, click OK button

4. Press CTRL+B

To Increase the Font Size of a Cell Entry

1 ENTER TEXT | 2 CALCULATE SUMS & USE FORMULAS | 3 FORMAT TEXT
4 INSERT CHART | 5 NAME TAB | 6 PREVIEW & PRINT WORKSHEET

Increasing the font size is the next step in formatting the worksheet subtitle. **Why?** *You increase the font size of a cell so that the entry stands out and is easier to read.* The following steps increase the font size of the worksheet subtitle in cell A2.

1

- With cell A2 selected, click the Font Size arrow (Home tab | Font group) to display the Font Size gallery.

- Point to 14 in the Font Size gallery to see a live preview of the active cell with the selected font size (Figure 1–36).

Experiment

- If you are using a mouse, point to several other font sizes in the Font Size list to see a live preview of those font sizes in the selected cell.

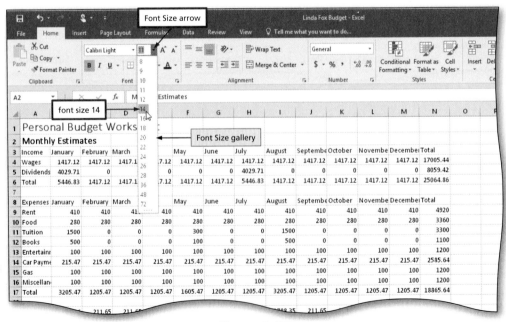

Figure 1–36

1

- Click 14 in the Font Size gallery to change the font size in the active cell (Figure 1–37).

Q&A

Can I choose a font size that is not in the Font Size gallery?
Yes. An alternative to selecting a font size in the Font Size gallery is to click the Font Size box (Home tab | Font group), type the font size you want, and then press the ENTER key.

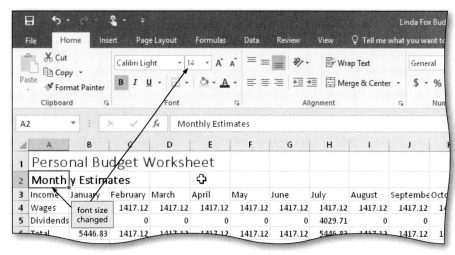

Figure 1–37

Other Ways

1. Click 'Increase Font Size' button (Home tab | Font group) or 'Decrease Font Size' button (Home tab | Font group)

2. Click Font Settings Dialog box Launcher, click Font tab (Format Cells dialog box), click desired size in Size list, click OK button

3. Right-click cell to display mini toolbar, click Font Size arrow on mini toolbar, click desired font size in Font Size gallery

4. Right-click selected cell, click Format Cells on shortcut menu, click Font tab (Format Cells dialog box), select font size in Size box, click OK button

---

1 ENTER TEXT | 2 CALCULATE SUMS & USE FORMULAS | 3 FORMAT TEXT
4 INSERT CHART | 5 NAME TAB | 6 PREVIEW & PRINT WORKSHEET

To Change the Font Color of a Cell Entry

The next step is to change the color of the font in cells A1 and A2 to orange. *Why? Changing the font color of cell entries can help the text stand out more. You also can change the font colors to match the company or product's brand colors.* The following steps change the font color of a cell entry.

1

- Click cell A1 and then click the Font Color arrow (Home tab | Font group) to display the Font Color gallery.

- Point to 'Orange, Accent 2' (column 6, row 1) in the Theme Colors area of the Font Color gallery to see a live preview of the font color in the active cell (Figure 1–38).

Experiment

- Point to several other colors in the Font Color gallery to see a live preview of other font colors in the active cell.

Q&A

How many colors are in the Font Color gallery?
You can choose from approximately 70 different font colors in the Font Color gallery. Your Font Color gallery may have more or fewer colors, depending on the color settings of your operating system. The Theme Colors area contains colors that are included in the current workbook's theme.

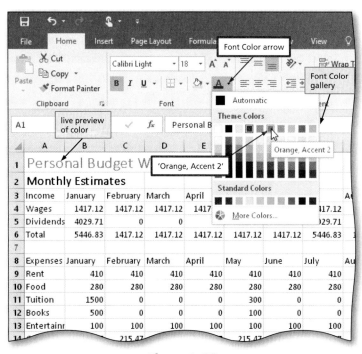

Figure 1–38

2

• Click 'Orange, Accent 2' (column 6, row 1) in the Font Color gallery to change the font color of the worksheet title in the active cell (Figure 1–39).

Q&A | Why does the Font Color button change after I select the new font color?
When you choose a color on the Font Color gallery, Excel changes the Font Color button (Home tab | Font group) to your chosen color. Then when you want to change the font color of another cell to the same color, you need only to select the cell and then click the Font Color button (Home tab | Font group).

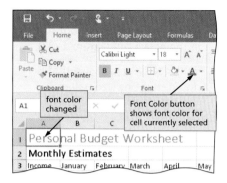

Figure 1–39

3

• Click the Font Color button to apply Orange, Accent 2 (column 6, row 1) to cell A2.

Other Ways

1. Click Font Settings Dialog Box Launcher, click Font tab (Format Cells dialog box), click desired color in Color list, click OK button

2. Right-click the cell to display mini toolbar, click Font Color arrow on mini toolbar, click desired font color in Font Color gallery

3. Right-click selected cell, click Format Cells on shortcut menu, click Font tab (Format Cells dialog box), select color in Font Color gallery, click OK button

---

To Center Cell Entries across Columns by Merging Cells

1 ENTER TEXT | 2 CALCULATE SUMS & USE FORMULAS | 3 FORMAT TEXT
4 INSERT CHART | 5 NAME TAB | 6 PREVIEW & PRINT WORKSHEET

The final step in formatting the worksheet title and subtitle is to center them across columns A through N. **Why?** *Centering a title across the columns used in the body of the worksheet improves the worksheet's appearance.* To do this, the 14 cells in the range A1:N1 are combined, or merged, into a single cell that is the width of the columns in the body of the worksheet. The 14 cells in the range A2:N2 are merged in a similar manner. **Merging cell**s involves creating a single cell by combining two or more selected cells. The following steps center the worksheet title and subtitle across columns by merging cells.

1

• Select cell A1 and then drag to cell N1 to highlight the range to be merged and centered (Figure 1–40).

Q&A | What if a cell in the range B1:N1 contains data?
For the 'Merge & Center' button (Home tab | Alignment group) to work properly, all the cells except the leftmost cell in the selected range must be empty.

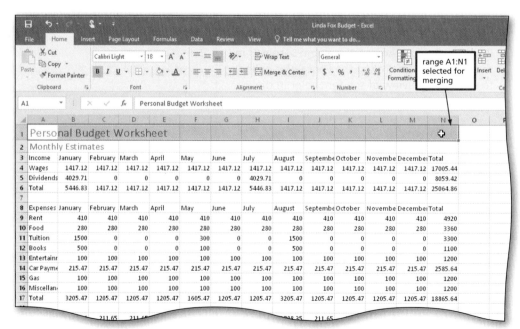

Figure 1–40

2

- Click the 'Merge & Center' button (Home tab | Alignment group) to merge cells A1 through N1 and center the contents of the leftmost cell across the selected columns (Figure 1–41).

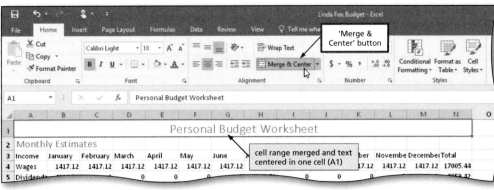

Figure 1– 41

Q&A What if my screen displays a Merge & Center menu?

Select the desired option on the Merge & Center menu if you do not have a separate 'Merge & Center' button and 'Merge & Center' arrow.

What happened to cells B1 through N1?

After the merge, cells B1 through N1 no longer exist. The new cell A1 now extends across columns A through N.

3

- Repeat Steps 1 and 2 to merge and center the worksheet subtitle across cells A2 through N2 (Figure 1–42).

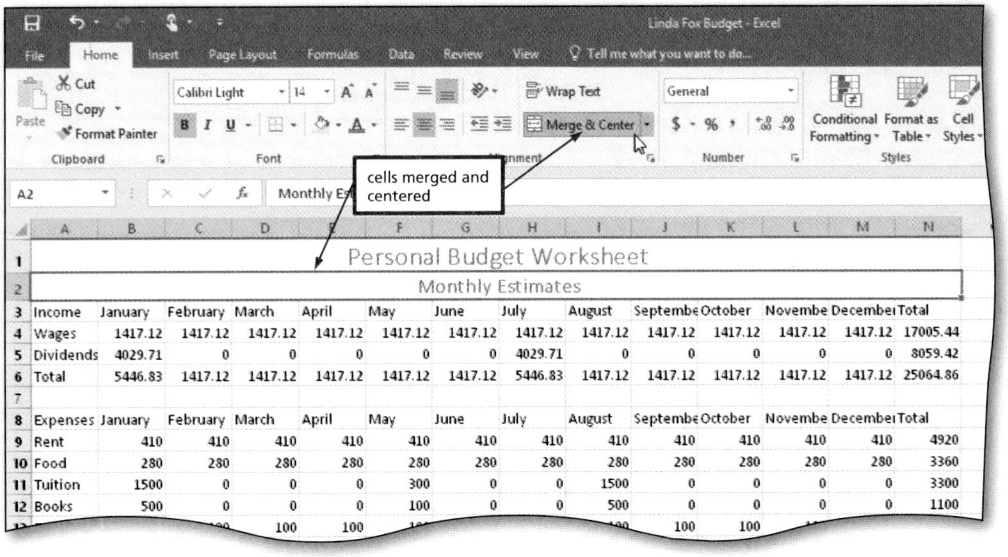

Q&A Are cells B1 through N1 and B2 through N2 lost forever?

No. The opposite of merging cells is **splitting** a merged cell. After you have merged multiple cells into one cell, you can unmerge, or split, the cell to display the original range of cells. You

Figure 1–42

split a merged cell by selecting it and clicking the 'Merge & Center' button. For example, if you click the 'Merge & Center' button a second time in Step 2, it will split the merged cell A1 into cells A1, B1, C1, D1, E1, F1, G1, H1, I1, J1, K1, L1, M1, and N1, and move the title to it's original location in cell A1.

Other Ways

1. Right-click selection, click 'Merge & Center' button on mini toolbar

2. Right-click selected cell, click Format Cells on shortcut menu, click Alignment tab (Format Cells dialog box), select 'Center Across Selection' in Horizontal list, click OK button

1 ENTER TEXT | 2 CALCULATE SUMS & USE FORMULAS | 3 FORMAT TEXT
4 INSERT CHART | 5 NAME TAB | 6 PREVIEW & PRINT WORKSHEET

To Format Rows Using Cell Styles

The next step to format the worksheet is to format the rows. **Why?** *Row titles and the total row should be formatted so that the column titles and total row can be distinguished from the data in the body of the worksheet. Data rows can be formatted to make them easier to read as well.* The following steps format the column titles and total row using cell styles in the default worksheet theme.

- Click cell A3 and then drag to cell N3 to select the range.
- Click the Cell Styles button (Home tab | Styles group) to display the Cell Styles gallery.
- Point to the Heading 1 cell style in the Titles and Headings area of the Cell Styles gallery to see a live preview of the cell style in the selected range (Figure 1–43).

Experiment

- Point to other cell styles in the Titles and Headings area of the Cell Styles gallery to see a live preview of other styles.

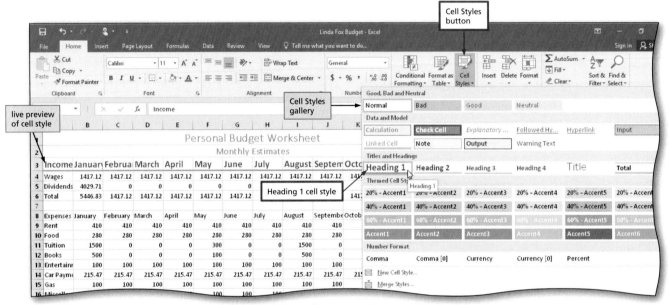

Figure 1–43

- Click the Heading 1 cell style to apply the cell style to the selected range.
- Click the Center button (Home tab | Alignment group) to center the column headings in the selected range.
- Select the range A8 to N8 (Figure 1–44).

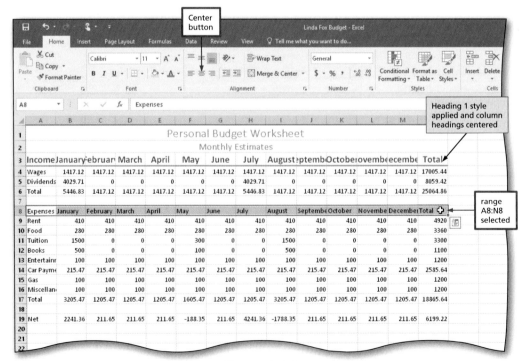

Figure 1–44

3

- Apply the Heading 1 cell style format and then center the headings (Figure 1–45).

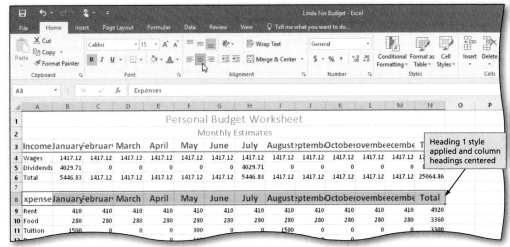

Figure 1–45

4

- Format the range A6:N6 and A17:N17 with the Total cell style format.

- Format the range A19:N19 with the Accent2 cell style format.

- Format the range A4:N4, A9:N9, A11:N11, A13:N13, A15:N15 with the 20% - Accent2 cell style format.

- Format the range A5:N5, A10:N10, A12:N12, A14:N14, A16:N16 with the 40% - Accent2 cell style format. Deselect the selected ranges

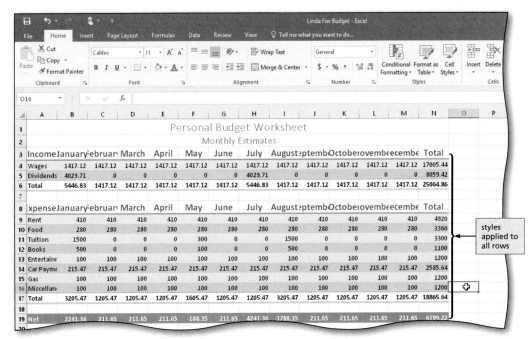

Figure 1–46

1 ENTER TEXT | 2 CALCULATE SUMS & USE FORMULAS | 3 FORMAT TEXT
4 INSERT CHART | 5 NAME TAB | 6 PREVIEW & PRINT WORKSHEET

To Format Numbers in the Worksheet

The requirements document requested that numbers in the first row and last row of each section should be formatted to use a dollar-and-cents format, while other numbers receive a comma format. *Why? Using a dollar-and-cents format for selected cells makes it clear to users of the worksheet that the numbers represent dollar values without cluttering the entire worksheet with dollar signs, and applying the comma format makes larger numbers easier to read.* Excel allows you to apply various number formats, many of which are discussed in later modules. The following steps use buttons on the ribbon to format the numbers in the worksheet.

1

- Select the range B4:N4.

- Click the 'Accounting Number Format' button (Home tab | Number group) to apply the accounting number format to the cells in the selected range.

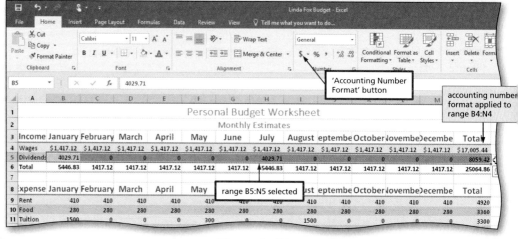

Q&A What if my screen displays an Accounting Number Format menu?

If you are using a touch screen, you may not

Figure 1–47

have a separate 'Accounting Number Format' button and 'Accounting Number Format' arrow. In this case, select the desired option on the Accounting Number Format menu.

What effect does the accounting number format have on the selected cells?

The accounting number format causes numbers to be displayed with two decimal places and to align vertically. Cell widths are adjusted automatically to accommodate the new formatting.

- Select the range B5:N5 (Figure 1–47).

2

- Click the Comma Style button (Home tab | Number group) to apply the comma style format to the selected range.

Q&A What effect does the comma style format have on the selected cells?

The comma style format formats numbers to have two decimal places and commas as thousands separators.

- Select the range B6:N6 to make it the active range (Figure 1–48).

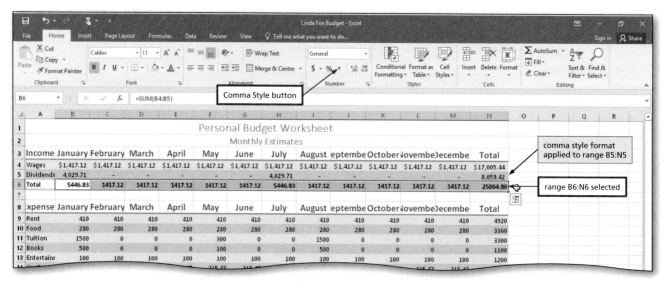

Figure 1–48

3

- Click the 'Accounting Number Format' button (Home tab | Number group) to apply the accounting number format to the cells in the selected range.

4

- Format the ranges B9:N9, B17:N17, and B19:N19 with the accounting number format.

- Format the range B10:N16 with the comma style format. Click cell A1 to deselect the selected ranges (Figure 1–49).

Q&A

How do I select the range B10:N16?

Select this range the same way as you select a range of cells in a column or row; that is, click the first cell in the range (B10, in this case) and drag to the last cell in the range (N16, in this case).

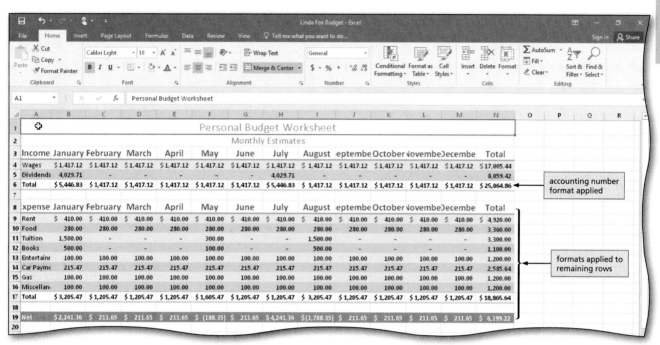

Figure 1–49

Other Ways

1. Click 'Accounting Number Format' or Comma Style button on mini toolbar

2. Right-click selected cell, click Format Cells on shortcut menu, click Number tab (Format Cells dialog box), select Accounting in Category list or select Number and click 'Use 1000 Separator', click OK button

To Adjust the Column Width

1 ENTER TEXT | 2 CALCULATE SUMS & USE FORMULAS | 3 FORMAT TEXT
4 INSERT CHART | 5 NAME TAB | 6 PREVIEW & PRINT WORKSHEET

The last step in formatting the worksheet is to adjust the width of the columns so that each title is visible. **Why?** *To make a worksheet easy to read, the column widths should be adjusted appropriately.* Excel offers other methods for adjusting cell widths and row heights, which are discussed later in this book. The following steps adjust the width of columns A through N so that the contents of the columns are visible.

1

- Point to the boundary on the right side of the column A heading above row 1 to change the pointer to a split double arrow (Figure 1–50).

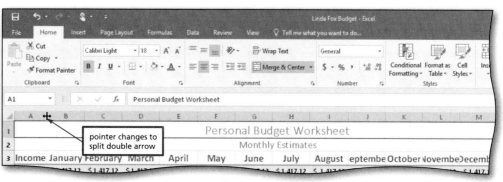

Figure 1–50

2

• Double-click the boundary to adjust the width of the column to accommodate the width of the longest item in the column (Figure 1–51).

Q&A What if all of the items in the column are already visible?
If all of the items are shorter in length than the width of the column and you double-click the column boundary, Excel will reduce the width of the column.

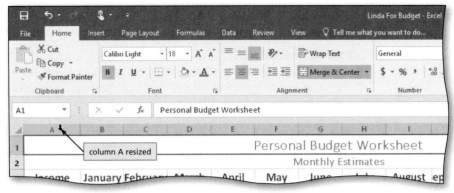

Figure 1–51

3

• Repeat Steps 1 and 2 to adjust the column width of columns B through N (Figure 1–52).

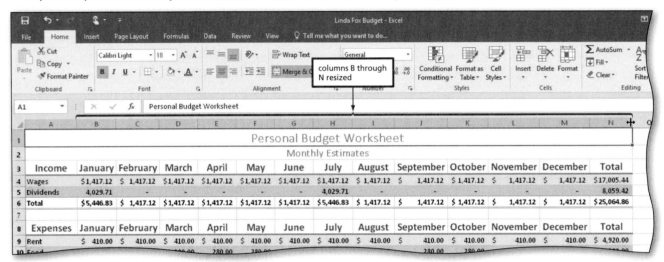

Figure 1–52

To Use the Name Box to Select a Cell

1 ENTER TEXT | 2 CALCULATE SUMS & USE FORMULAS | 3 FORMAT TEXT
4 INSERT CHART | 5 NAME TAB | 6 PREVIEW & PRINT WORKSHEET

The next step is to chart the monthly expenses. To create the chart, you need to identify the range of the data you want to feature on the chart and then select it. In this case you want to start with cell A3. Rather than clicking cell A3 to select it, you will select the cell by using the Name box, which is located to the left of the formula bar. **Why?** *You might want to use the Name box to select a cell if you are working with a large worksheet and it is faster to type the cell name rather than scrolling to and clicking it.* The following steps select cell A3 using the Name box.

1

• Click the Name box in the formula bar and then type **a3** as the cell you want to select (Figure 1–53).

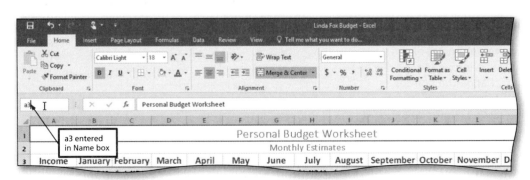

Figure 1–53

2

- Press the ENTER key to change the active cell in the Name box and make cell A3 the active cell (Figure 1–54).

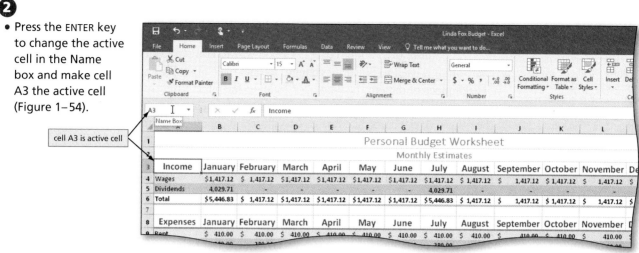

cell A3 is active cell

Figure 1–54

Other Ways to Select Cells

As you will see in later modules, in addition to using the Name box to select any cell in a worksheet, you also can use it to assign names to a cell or range of cells. Excel supports several additional ways to select a cell, as summarized in Table 1–3.

Table 1–3 Selecting Cells in Excel

Key, Box, or Command	Function
ALT+PAGE DOWN	Selects the cell one worksheet window to the right and moves the worksheet window accordingly.
ALT+PAGE UP	Selects the cell one worksheet window to the left and moves the worksheet window accordingly.
ARROW	Selects the adjacent cell in the direction of the arrow on the key.
CTRL+ARROW	Selects the border cell of the worksheet in combination with the arrow keys and moves the worksheet window accordingly. For example, to select the rightmost cell in the row that contains the active cell, press CTRL+RIGHT ARROW. You also can press the END key, release it, and then press the appropriate arrow key to accomplish the same task.
CTRL+HOME	Selects cell A1 or the cell one column and one row below and to the right of frozen titles and moves the worksheet window accordingly.
Find command on Find & Select menu (Home tab | Editing group) or SHIFT+F5	Finds and selects a cell that contains specific contents that you enter in the Find and Replace dialog box. If necessary, Excel moves the worksheet window to display the cell. You also can press CTRL+F to display the Find and Replace dialog box.
Go To command on Find & Select menu (Home tab | Editing group) or F5	Selects the cell that corresponds to the cell reference you enter in the Go To dialog box and moves the worksheet window accordingly. You also can press CTRL+G to display the Go To dialog box.
HOME	Selects the cell at the beginning of the row that contains the active cell and moves the worksheet window accordingly.
Name box	Selects the cell in the workbook that corresponds to the cell reference you enter in the Name box.
PAGE DOWN	Selects the cell down one worksheet window from the active cell and moves the worksheet window accordingly.
PAGE UP	Selects the cell up one worksheet window from the active cell and moves the worksheet window accordingly.

Break Point: If you wish to take a break, this is a good place to do so. Be sure to save the Linda Fox Budget file again and then you can exit Excel. To resume at a later time, run Excel, open the file called Linda Fox Budget, and continue following the steps from this location forward.

Adding a Pie Chart to the Worksheet

Excel includes 15 chart types from which you can choose, including column, line, pie, bar, area, X Y (scatter), stock, surface, radar, treemap, sunburst, histogram, box & whisker, waterfall, and combo. The type of chart you choose depends on the type and quantity of data you have and the message or analysis you want to convey.

A column or cylinder chart is a good way to compare values side by side. A line chart often is used to illustrate changes in data over time. Pie charts show the contribution of each piece of data to the whole, or total, of the data. A pie chart can go even further in comparing values across categories by showing each pie piece in comparison with the others. Area charts, like line charts, illustrate changes over time, but often are used to compare more than one set of data, and the area below the lines is filled in with a different color for each set of data. An X Y (scatter) chart is used much like a line chart, but each piece of data is represented by a dot and is not connected with a line. Scatter charts are typically used for viewing scientific, statistical, and engineering data. A stock chart provides a number of methods commonly used in the financial industry to show fluctuations in stock market data. A surface chart compares data from three columns and/or rows in a 3-D manner. A radar chart can compare aggregate values of several sets of data in a manner that resembles a radar screen, with each set of data represented by a different color. A combo chart allows you to combine multiple types of charts.

Excel 2016 includes five new charts. Treemap and sunburst charts are hierarchy charts, used to compare parts to a whole. A treemap chart uses nested rectangles to show data in a hierarchy. A sunburst chart stacks multiple pie charts on one another to illustrate related data. New statistical charts include histogram and box & whisker charts. A histogram chart shows the distribution of data. A box & whisker chart, or box plot, is used to display variation within a set of data. The new waterfall chart is used to visualize increases and decreases within a set of data and is grouped with stock charts.

As outlined in the requirements document in Figure 1–2, the budget worksheet should include a pie chart to graphically represent the yearly expense totals for each item in Linda Fox's budget. The pie chart shown in Figure 1–55 is on its own sheet in the workbook. The pie chart resides on a separate sheet, called a **chart sheet**, which contains only the chart.

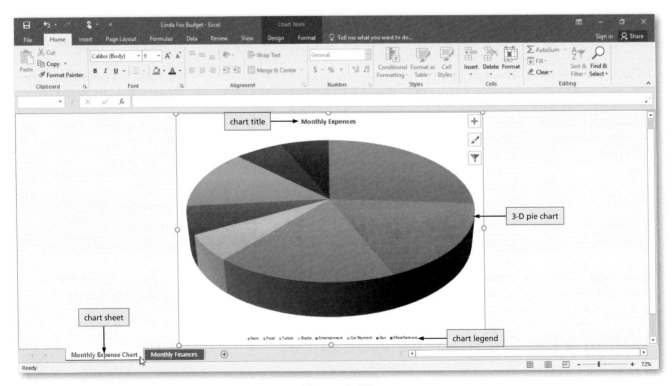

Figure 1–55

In this worksheet, the ranges you want to chart are the nonadjacent ranges A9:A16 (expense titles) and N9:N16 (yearly expense totals). The expense titles in the range A9:A16 will identify the slices of the pie chart; these entries are called category names. The range N9:N16 contains the data that determines the size of the slices in the pie; these entries are called the **data series**. Because eight budget items are being charted, the 3-D pie chart contains eight slices.

To Add a 3-D Pie Chart

1 ENTER TEXT | 2 CALCULATE SUMS & USE FORMULAS | 3 FORMAT TEXT
4 INSERT CHART | **5 NAME TAB** | **6 PREVIEW & PRINT WORKSHEET**

Why? When you want to see how each part relates to the whole, you use a pie chart. The following steps draw the 3-D pie chart.

- Select the range A9:A16 to identify the range of the category names for the 3-D pie chart.

- While holding down the CTRL key, select the nonadjacent range N9:N16.

- Click Insert on the ribbon to display the Insert tab.

- Click the 'Insert Pie or Doughnut Chart' button (Insert tab | Charts group) to display the Insert Pie or Doughnut Chart gallery (Figure 1–56).

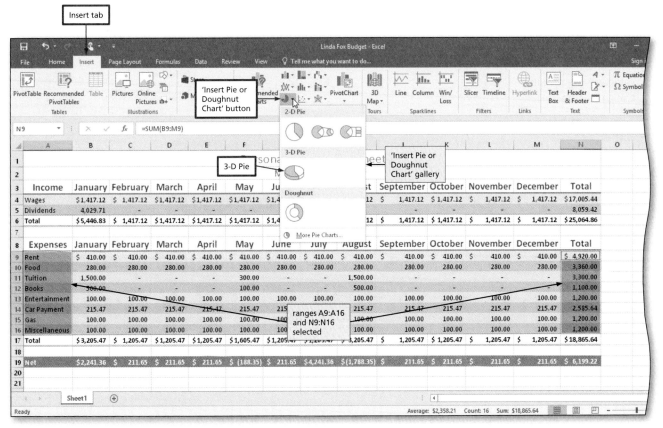

Figure 1–56

2

- Click 3-D Pie in the Insert Pie or Doughnut Chart gallery to insert the chart in the worksheet (Figure 1–57).

Q&A Why have new tabs appeared on the ribbon?
The new tabs provide additional options and functionality when you are working with certain objects, such as charts, and only display when you are working with those objects.

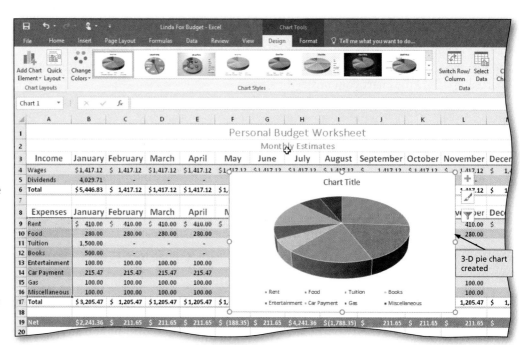

Figure 1–57

3

- Click and drag to select all the text in the chart title.
- Type **Monthly Expenses** to specify the title.
- Deselect the chart title to view the new title (Figure 1–58).

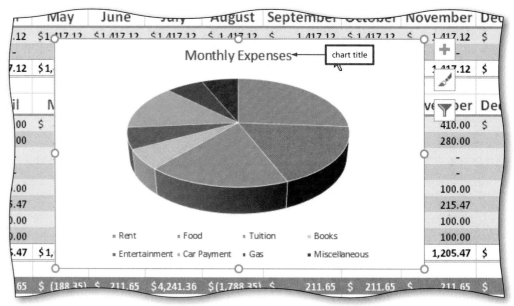

Figure 1–58

To Apply a Style to a Chart

1 ENTER TEXT | 2 CALCULATE SUMS & USE FORMULAS | 3 FORMAT TEXT
4 INSERT CHART | 5 NAME TAB | 6 PREVIEW & PRINT WORKSHEET

Why? *If you want to enhance the appearance of a chart, you can apply a chart style.* The following steps apply Style 5 to the 3-D pie chart.

1

- Click the Chart Styles button to display the Chart Styles gallery.
- Scroll in the Chart Style gallery to display the Style 5 chart style (Figure 1–59).

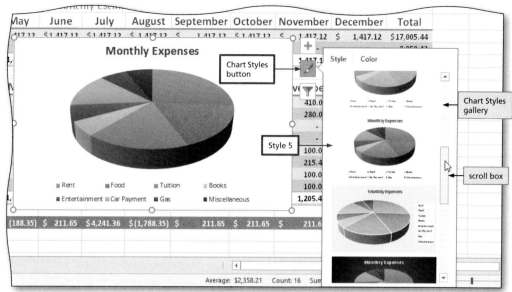

Figure 1–59

2

- Click Style 5 in the Chart Styles gallery to change the chart style to Style 5 (Figure 1–60).

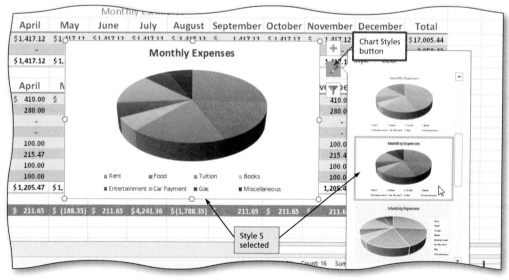

Figure 1–60

3

- Click the Chart Styles button to close the Chart Styles gallery.

Changing the Sheet Tab Names

The sheet tabs at the bottom of the window allow you to navigate between any worksheet in the workbook. You click the sheet tab of the worksheet you want to view in the Excel window. By default, the worksheets are named Sheet1, Sheet2, and so on. The worksheet names become increasingly important as you move toward more sophisticated workbooks, especially workbooks in which you reference cells between worksheets.

BTW
Exploding a Pie Chart
If you want to draw attention to a particular slice in a pie chart, you can offset the slice so that it stands out from the rest. A pie chart with one or more slices offset is referred to as an exploded pie chart. To offset a slice, click the slice two times to select it (do not double-click) and then drag the slice outward.

To Move a Chart to a New Sheet

Why? By moving a chart to its own sheet, the size of the chart will increase, which can improve readability. The following steps move the 3-D pie chart to a chart sheet named, Monthly Expenses.

- Click the Move Chart button (Chart Tools Design tab | Location group) to display the Move Chart dialog box (Figure 1–61).

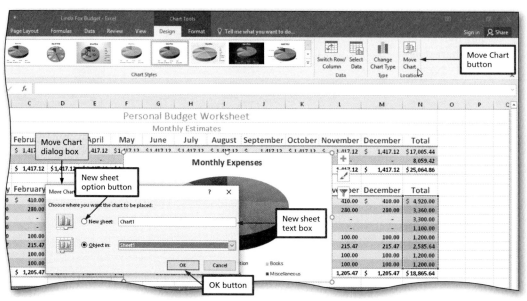

Figure 1–61

2

- Click New sheet to select it (Move Chart dialog box) and then type **Monthly Expense Chart** in the New sheet text box to enter a sheet tab name for the worksheet that will contain the chart.

- Click the OK button (Move Chart dialog box) to move the chart to a new chart sheet with the sheet tab name, Monthly Expense Chart (Figure 1–62).

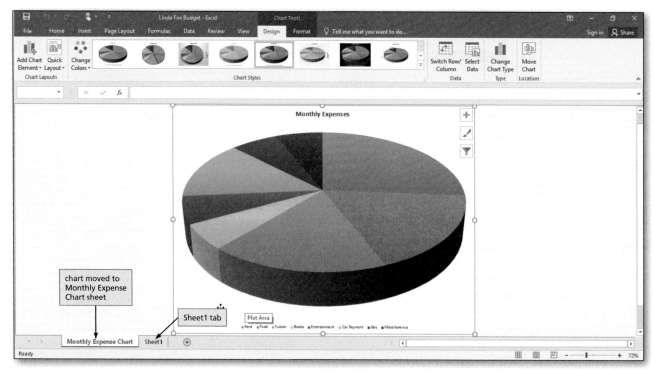

Figure 1–62

Creating a Worksheet and a Chart   **Excel Module 1**   **EX** 39

1 ENTER TEXT | 2 CALCULATE SUMS & USE FORMULAS | 3 FORMAT TEXT
4 INSERT CHART | 5 NAME TAB | 6 PREVIEW & PRINT WORKSHEET

Excel Module 1

To Change the Sheet Tab Name

You decide to change the name of the Sheet1 tab to Monthly Finances. **Why?** *Use simple, meaningful names for each sheet tab. Sheet tab names often match the worksheet title. If a worksheet includes multiple titles in multiple sections of the worksheet, use a sheet tab name that encompasses the meaning of all of the sections.* The following steps rename the sheet tab.

- Double-click the sheet tab labeled Sheet1 in the lower-left corner of the window.

- Type **Monthly Finances** as the sheet tab name and then press the ENTER key to assign the new name to the sheet tab (Figure 1–63).

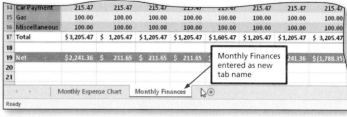

Figure 1–63

Q&A | What is the maximum length for a sheet tab name?
Sheet tab names can be up to 31 characters (including spaces) in length. Longer worksheet names, however, mean that fewer sheet tabs will display on your screen. If you have multiple worksheets with long sheet tab names, you may have to scroll through sheet tabs.

- Right-click the sheet tab labeled, Monthly Finances, in the lower-left corner of the window to display a shortcut menu.

- Point to Tab Color on the shortcut menu to display the Tab Color gallery (Figure 1–64).

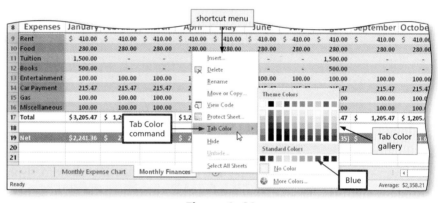

Figure 1–64

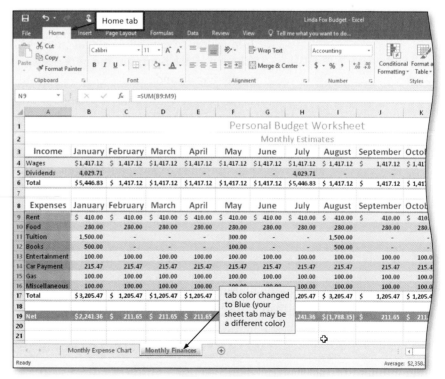

- Click a color that matches your shirt in the Theme Colors area to change the color of the tab (Figure 1–65).

- If necessary, click Home on the ribbon to display the Home tab.

- Save the workbook again on the same storage location with the same file name.

Q&A | Why should I save the workbook again?
You have made several modifications to the workbook since you last saved it. Thus, you should save it again.

Figure 1–65

Document Properties

Excel helps you organize and identify your files by using **document properties**, which are the details about a file such as the project author, title, and subject. For example, you could use the class name or topic to describe the workbook's purpose or content in the document properties.

CONSIDER THIS

Why would you want to assign document properties to a workbook?
Document properties are valuable for a variety of reasons:

• Users can save time locating a particular file because they can view a file's document properties without opening the workbook.

• By creating consistent properties for files having similar content, users can better organize their workbooks.

• Some organizations require Excel users to add document properties so that other employees can view details about these files.

Common document properties include standard properties and those that are automatically updated. **Standard properties** are associated with all Microsoft Office files and include author, title, and subject. **Automatically updated properties** include file system properties, such as the date you create or change a file, and statistics, such as the file size.

TO CHANGE DOCUMENT PROPERTIES

To change document properties, you would follow these steps.

1. Click File on the ribbon to open the Backstage view and then, if necessary, click the Info tab in the Backstage view to display the Info gallery. The Properties list is found in the right pane of the Info gallery.

2. If the property you wish to change is in the Properties list, click to the right of the property category to display a text box. (Note that not all properties are editable.) Type the desired text for the property and then click anywhere in the Info gallery to enter the data, or press TAB to navigate to the next property. Click the Back button in the upper-left corner of the Backstage view to return to the Excel window.

3. If the property you wish to change is not in the Properties list or you cannot edit it, click the Properties button to display the Properties menu, and then click Advanced Properties to display the Summary tab in the Properties dialog box. Type your desired text in the appropriate property text boxes. Click the OK button (Properties dialog box) to close the dialog box and then click the Back button in the upper-left corner of the Backstage view to return to the workbook.

Q&A   Why do some of the document properties in my Properties dialog box contain data?
Depending on where you are using Office 2016, your school, university, or place of employment may have customized the properties.

Printing a Worksheet

After creating a worksheet, you may want to print it. Printing a worksheet enables you to distribute the worksheet to others in a form that can be read or viewed but not edited. It is a good practice to save a workbook before printing a worksheet, in the event you experience difficulties printing.

CONSIDER THIS

What is the best method for distributing a workbook?

The traditional method of distributing a workbook uses a printer to produce a hard copy. A **hard copy** or **printout** is information that exists on paper. Hard copies can be useful for the following reasons:

- Some people prefer proofreading a hard copy of a workbook rather than viewing it on the screen to check for errors and readability.

- Hard copies can serve as a backup reference if your storage medium is lost or becomes corrupted and you need to recreate the workbook.

Instead of distributing a hard copy of a workbook, users can distribute the workbook as an electronic image that mirrors the original workbook's appearance. An electronic image of a workbook is not an editable file; it simply displays a picture of the workbook. The electronic image of the workbook can be sent as an email attachment, posted on a website, or copied to a portable storage medium such as a USB flash drive. Two popular electronic image formats, sometimes called fixed formats, are PDF by Adobe Systems and XPS by Microsoft. In Excel, you can create electronic image files through the Save As dialog box and the Export, Share, and Print tabs in the Backstage view. Electronic images of workbooks, such as PDF and XPS, can be useful for the following reasons:

- Users can view electronic images of workbooks without the software that created the original workbook (e.g., Excel). Specifically, to view a PDF file, you use a program called Adobe Reader, which can be downloaded free from Adobe's website. Similarly, to view an XPS file, you use a program called XPS Viewer, which is included in the latest version of Windows.

- Sending electronic workbooks saves paper and printer supplies. Society encourages users to contribute to **green computing**, which involves reducing the electricity consumed and environmental waste generated when using computers, mobile devices, and related technologies.

To Preview and Print a Worksheet in Landscape Orientation

1 ENTER TEXT | 2 CALCULATE SUMS & USE FORMULAS | 3 FORMAT TEXT
4 INSERT CHART | 5 NAME TAB | 6 PREVIEW & PRINT WORKSHEET

Pages printed in **portrait orientation** have the short (8½") edge at the top of the printout; the printed page is taller than it is wide. **Landscape orientation** prints the long (11") edge at the top of the paper; the printed page is wider than it is tall. With the completed workbook saved, you may want to print it. *Why? Because the worksheet is included in a report delivered in person, you will print a hard copy on a printer.* The following steps print a hard copy of the contents of the worksheet.

1

- Click File on the ribbon to open the Backstage view.

- Click the Print tab in the Backstage view to display the Print gallery (Figure 1–66).

 Q&A How can I print multiple copies of my worksheet?
Increase the number in the Copies box in the Print gallery.

What if I decide not to print the worksheet at this time?
Click the Back button in the upper-left corner of the Backstage view to return to the workbook window.

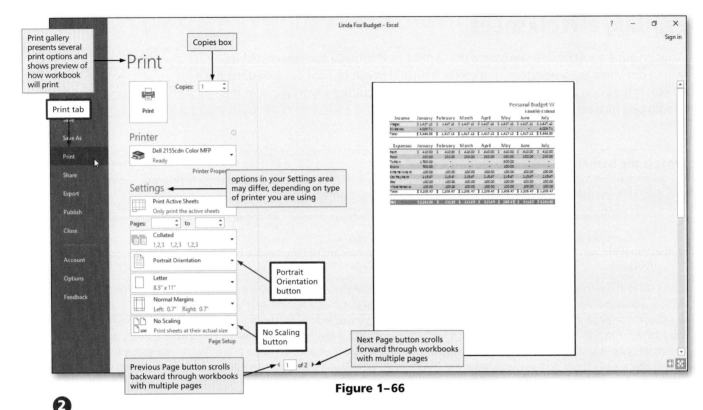

Figure 1–66

②

- Verify that the printer listed on the Printer Status button will print a hard copy of the workbook. If necessary, click the Printer Status button to display a list of available printer options and then click the desired printer to change the currently selected printer.

③

- Click the Portrait Orientation button in the Settings area and then select Landscape Orientation to change the orientation of the page to landscape.

- Click the No Scaling button and then select 'Fit Sheet on One Page' to print the entire worksheet on one page (Figure 1–67).

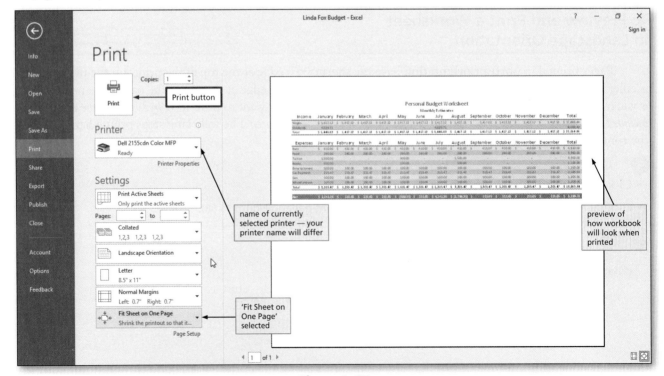

Figure 1–67

4

- Click the Print button in the Print gallery to print the worksheet in landscape orientation on the currently selected printer.

- When the printer stops, retrieve the hard copy (Figure 1–68).

Q&A Do I have to wait until my worksheet is complete to print it?
No, you can print a document at any time while you are creating it.

Personal Budget Worksheet
Monthly Estimates

Income	January	February	March	April	May	June	July	August	September	October	November	December	Total
Wages	$ 1,417.12	$ 1,417.12	$ 1,417.12	$ 1,417.12	$ 1,417.12	$ 1,417.12	$ 1,417.12	$ 1,417.12	$ 1,417.12	$ 1,417.12	$ 1,417.12	$ 1,417.12	$ 17,005.44
Dividends	4,029.71	-	-	-	-	-	4,029.71	-	-	-	-	-	8,059.42
Total	$ 5,446.83	$ 1,417.12	$ 1,417.12	$ 1,417.12	$ 1,417.12	$ 1,417.12	$ 5,446.83	$ 1,417.12	$ 1,417.12	$ 1,417.12	$ 1,417.12	$ 1,417.12	$ 25,064.86

Expenses	January	February	March	April	May	June	July	August	September	October	November	December	Total
Rent	$ 410.00	$ 410.00	$ 410.00	$ 410.00	$ 410.00	$ 410.00	$ 410.00	$ 410.00	$ 410.00	$ 410.00	$ 410.00	$ 410.00	$ 4,920.00
Food	280.00	280.00	280.00	280.00	280.00	280.00	280.00	280.00	280.00	280.00	280.00	280.00	3,360.00
Tuition	1,500.00	-	-	-	300.00	-	-	1,500.00	-	-	-	-	3,300.00
Books	500.00	-	-	-	100.00	-	-	500.00	-	-	-	-	1,100.00
Entertainment	100.00	100.00	100.00	100.00	100.00	100.00	100.00	100.00	100.00	100.00	100.00	100.00	1,200.00
Car Payment	215.47	215.47	215.47	215.47	215.47	215.47	215.47	215.47	215.47	215.47	215.47	215.47	2,585.64
Gas	100.00	100.00	100.00	100.00	100.00	100.00	100.00	100.00	100.00	100.00	100.00	100.00	1,200.00
Miscellaneous	100.00	100.00	100.00	100.00	100.00	100.00	100.00	100.00	100.00	100.00	100.00	100.00	1,200.00
Total	$ 3,205.47	$ 1,205.47	$ 1,205.47	$ 1,205.47	$ 1,605.47	$ 1,205.47	$ 1,205.47	$ 3,205.47	$ 1,205.47	$ 1,205.47	$ 1,205.47	$ 1,205.47	$ 18,865.64

| Net | $ 2,241.36 | $ 211.65 | $ 211.65 | $ 211.65 | $ (188.35) | $ 211.65 | $ 4,241.36 | $ (1,788.35) | $ 211.65 | $ 211.65 | $ 211.65 | $ 211.65 | $ 6,199.22 |

Figure 1–68

Other Ways

1. Press CTRL+P to open Print Gallery, press ENTER

Autocalculate

You easily can obtain a total, an average, or other information about the numbers in a range by using the **AutoCalculate area** on the status bar. First, select the range of cells containing the numbers you want to check. Next, right-click the AutoCalculate area to display the Customize Status Bar shortcut menu (Figure 1–69). The check marks indicate that the calculations are displayed in the status bar; more than one may be selected. The functions of the AutoCalculate commands on the Customize Status Bar shortcut menu are described in Table 1–4.

Table 1–4 Commonly Used Status Bar Commands

Command	Function
Average	AutoCalculate area displays the average of the numbers in the selected range
Count	AutoCalculate area displays the number of non-empty cells in the selected range
Numerical Count	AutoCalculate area displays the number of cells containing numbers in the selected range
Minimum	AutoCalculate area displays the lowest value in the selected range
Maximum	AutoCalculate area displays the highest value in the selected range
Sum	AutoCalculate area displays the sum of the numbers in the selected range

BTW

Distributing a Workbook
Instead of printing and distributing a hard copy of a workbook, you can distribute the workbook electronically. Options include sending the workbook via email; posting it on cloud storage (such as OneDrive) and sharing the file with others; posting it on social media, a blog, or other website; and sharing a link associated with an online location of the workbook. You also can create and share a PDF or XPS image of the workbook, so that users can view the file in Acrobat Reader or XPS Viewer instead of in Excel.

To Use the AutoCalculate Area to Determine a Maximum

The following steps determine the largest monthly total in the budget. *Why? Sometimes, you want a quick analysis, which can be especially helpful when your worksheet contains a lot of data.*

• Select the range B19:M19. Right-click the status bar to display the Customize Status Bar shortcut menu (Figure 1–69).

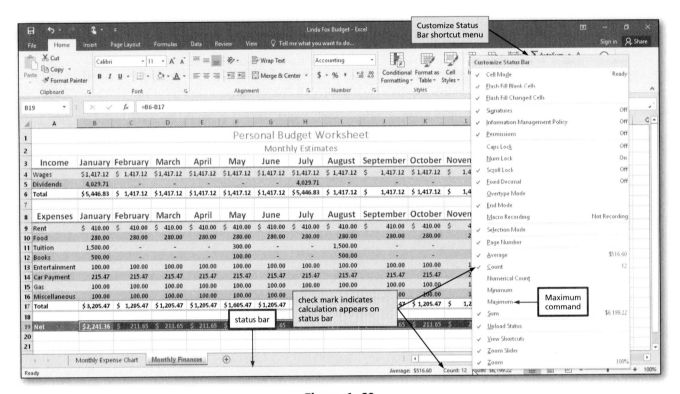

Figure 1–69

• Click Maximum on the shortcut menu to display the Maximum value in the range B19:M19 in the AutoCalculate area of the status bar.

• Click anywhere on the worksheet to close the shortcut menu (Figure 1–70).

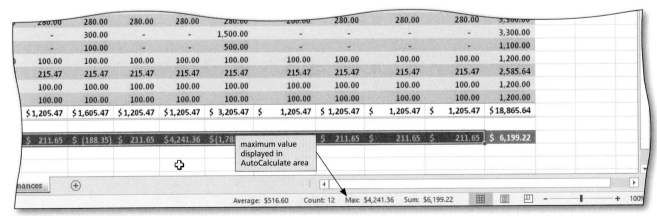

Figure 1–70

- Right-click the AutoCalculate area and then click Maximum on the shortcut menu to deselect it. The Maximum value will no longer appear on the status bar.

- Close the shortcut menu.

- Save the workbook using the same file name in the same storage location.

- If desired, sign out of your Microsoft account.

- Exit Excel.

Correcting Errors

You can correct data entry errors on a worksheet using one of several methods. The method you choose will depend on the extent of the error and whether you notice it while entering the data or after you have entered the incorrect data into the cell.

Correcting Errors while Entering Data into a Cell

If you notice an error while you are entering data into a cell, press the BACKSPACE key to erase the incorrect character(s) and then enter the correct character(s). If the error is a major one, click the Cancel box in the formula bar or press the ESC key to erase the entire entry and then reenter the data.

Correcting Errors after Entering Data into a Cell

If you find an error in the worksheet after entering the data, you can correct the error in one of two ways:

1. If the entry is short, select the cell, retype the entry correctly, and then click the Enter button or press the ENTER key. The new entry will replace the old entry.

2. If the entry in the cell is long and the errors are minor, using Edit mode may be a better choice than retyping the cell entry. In **Edit mode**, Excel displays the active cell entry in the formula bar and a flashing insertion point in the active cell, and you can edit the contents directly in the cell — a procedure called **in-cell editing**.

   a. Double-click the cell containing the error to switch Excel to Edit mode (Figure 1–71).

   b. Make corrections using the following in-cell editing methods.

      (1) To insert new characters between two characters, place the insertion point between the two characters and begin typing. Excel inserts the new characters to the left of the insertion point.

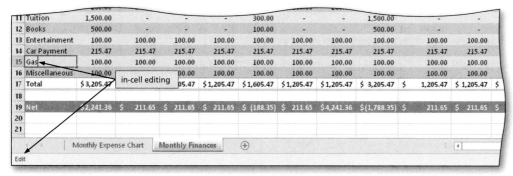

Figure 1–71

(2) To delete a character in the cell, move the insertion point to the left of the character you want to delete and then press the DELETE key, or place the insertion point to the right of the character you want to delete and then press the BACKSPACE key. You also can drag to select the character or adjacent characters you want to delete and then press the DELETE key or CTRL+X, or click the Cut button (Home tab | Clipboard group).

(3) When you are finished editing an entry, click the Enter button or press the ENTER key.

There are two ways for entering data in Edit mode: Insert mode and Overtype mode. In the default **Insert mode**, as you type a character, Excel inserts the character and moves all characters to the right of the typed character one position to the right. You can change to Overtype mode by pressing the INSERT key. In **Overtype mode**, Excel replaces, or overtypes, the character to the right of the insertion point. The INSERT key toggles the keyboard between Insert mode and Overtype mode.

While in Edit mode, you may have reason to move the insertion point to various points in the cell, select portions of the data in the cell, or switch from inserting characters to overtyping characters. Table 1–5 summarizes the more common tasks performed during in-cell editing.

Table 1–5 Summary of In-Cell Editing Tasks			
	Task	**Mouse Operation**	**Keyboard**
1.	Move the insertion point to the beginning of data in a cell.	Point to the left of the first character and click.	Press HOME
2.	Move the insertion point to the end of data in a cell.	Point to the right of the last character and click.	Press END
3.	Move the insertion point anywhere in a cell.	Point to the appropriate position and click the character.	Press RIGHT ARROW or LEFT ARROW
4.	Highlight one or more adjacent characters.	Drag through adjacent characters.	Press SHIFT+RIGHT ARROW or SHIFT+LEFT ARROW
5.	Select all data in a cell.	Double-click the cell with the insertion point in the cell if the data in the cell contains no spaces.	
6.	Delete selected characters.	Click the Cut button (Home tab | Clipboard group).	Press DELETE
7.	Delete characters to the left of the insertion point.		Press BACKSPACE
8.	Delete characters to the right of the insertion point.		Press DELETE
9.	Toggle between Insert and Overtype modes.		Press INSERT

Undoing the Last Cell Entry

The Undo button on the Quick Access Toolbar (Figure 1–72) allows you to erase recent cell entries. Thus, if you enter incorrect data in a cell and notice it immediately, click the Undo button and Excel changes the cell entry to what it was prior to the incorrect data entry.

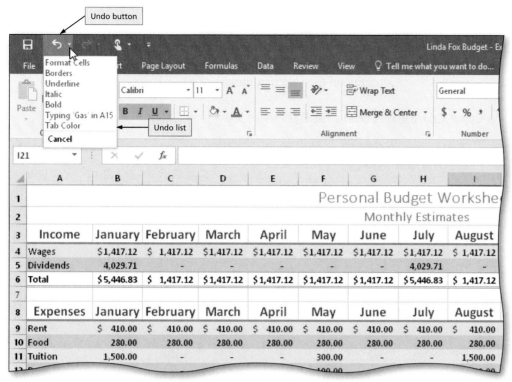

Figure 1–72

Excel remembers the last 100 actions you have completed. Thus, you can undo up to 100 previous actions by clicking the Undo arrow to display the Undo list and then clicking the action to be undone (Figure 1–72). You can drag through several actions in the Undo list to undo all of them at once. If no actions are available for Excel to undo, then the dimmed appearance of the Undo button indicates that it is unavailable.

The Redo button, next to the Undo button on the Quick Access Toolbar, allows you to repeat previous actions; that is, if you accidentally undo an action, you can use the Redo button to perform the action again.

Clearing a Cell or Range of Cells

If you enter data into the wrong cell or range of cells, you can erase, or clear, the data using one of the first four methods listed below. The fifth method clears the formatting from the selected cells. To clear a cell or range of cells, you would perform the following steps:

TO CLEAR CELL ENTRIES USING THE FILL HANDLE

1. Select the cell or range of cells and then point to the fill handle so that the pointer changes to a crosshair.
2. Drag the fill handle back into the selected cell or range until a shadow covers the cell or cells you want to erase.

To Clear Cell Entries Using the Shortcut Menu

1. Select the cell or range of cells to be cleared.
2. Right-click the selection.
3. Click Clear Contents on the shortcut menu.

To Clear Cell Entries Using the Backspace Key

1. Select the cell or range of cells to be cleared.
2. Press the BACKSPACE key.

To Clear Cell Entries and Formatting Using the Clear Button

1. Select the cell or range of cells to be cleared.
2. Click the Clear button (Home tab | Editing group).
3. Click Clear Contents on the Clear menu.

Note that the Clear All command on the Clear menu is the only command that clears both the cell entry and the cell formatting.

To Clear Formatting Using the Cell Styles Button

1. Select the cell or range of cells from which you want to remove the formatting.
2. Click the Cell Styles button (Home tab | Styles group) and then click Normal in the Cell Styles gallery.

As you are clearing cell entries, always remember that you should *never press the SPACEBAR to clear a cell*. Pressing the SPACEBAR enters a blank character. A blank character is interpreted by Excel as text and is different from an empty cell, even though the cell may appear empty.

Clearing the Entire Worksheet

If the required worksheet edits are extremely extensive or if the requirements drastically change, you may want to clear the entire worksheet and start over. To clear the worksheet or delete an embedded chart, you would use the following steps.

To Clear the Entire Worksheet

1. Click the Select All button on the worksheet. The Select All button is located above the row 1 identifier and to the left of the column A heading.
2. Click the Clear button (Home tab | Editing group) and then click Clear All on the menu to delete both the entries and formats.

The Select All button selects the entire worksheet. Instead of clicking the Select All button, you can press CTRL+A. To clear an unsaved workbook, click the Close Window button on the workbook's title bar or click the Close button in the Backstage view. Click the No button if the Microsoft Excel dialog box asks if you want to save changes. To start a new, blank workbook, click the New button in the Backstage view.

Summary

In this module you have learned how to create a personal budget worksheet and chart. Topics covered included selecting a cell, entering text, entering numbers, calculating a sum, using the fill handle, formatting a worksheet, adding a pie chart, changing sheet tab names, printing a worksheet, AutoCalculate, and correcting errors.

CONSIDER THIS: PLAN AHEAD

What decisions will you need to make when creating workbooks and charts in the future?

1. Determine the workbook structure.

   a) Determine the data you will need for your workbook.

   b) Sketch a layout of your data and your chart.

2. Create the worksheet.

   a) Enter titles, subtitles, and headings.

   b) Enter data, functions, and formulas.

3. Format the worksheet.

   a) Format the titles, subtitles, and headings using styles.

   b) Format the totals.

   c) Format the numbers.

   d) Format the text.

   e) Adjust column widths.

4. Create the chart.

   a) Determine the type of chart to use.

   b) Determine the chart title and data.

   c) Format the chart.

Apply Your Knowledge

Reinforce the skills and apply the concepts you learned in this module.

Changing the Values in a Worksheet

Note: To complete this assignment, you will be required to use the Data Files. Please contact your instructor for information about accessing the required files.

Instructions: Run Excel. Open the workbook Apply 1–1 Lima Wholesale (Figure 1–73a). The workbook you open contains sales data for Lima Wholesale. You are to apply formatting to the worksheet and move the chart to a new sheet tab.

Table 1–6 New Worksheet Data	
Cell	**Change Cell Contents To**
A2	Monthly Departmental Sales
B5	15242.36
C7	114538.23
D5	25747.85
E6	39851.44
F7	29663.77
G6	19885.41

Perform the following tasks:
1. Make the changes to the worksheet described in Table 1–6 so that the worksheet appears as shown in Figure 1–73b. As you edit the values in the cells containing numeric data, watch the totals in row 8, the totals in column H, and the chart change.
2. Change the worksheet title in cell A1 to the Title cell style and then merge and center it across columns A through H.
3. Use buttons in the Font group on the Home tab on the ribbon to change the worksheet subtitle in cell A2 to 16-point font and then center it across columns A through H. Change the font color of cell A2 to Dark Blue, Text 2, Darker 25%.
4. Apply the worksheet name, Monthly Sales, and the Dark Blue, Text 2, Darker 25% color to the sheet tab.
5. Move the chart to a new sheet called Sales Analysis Chart (Figure 1–73c). Change the chart title to SALES TOTALS.
6. If requested by your instructor, replace Lima in cell A1 with your last name.
7. Save the workbook using the file name, Apply 1–1 Lima Wholesale Sales Analysis.
8. Submit the revised workbook as specified by your instructor and exit Excel.
9. ✵ Besides the styles used in the worksheet, what other changes could you make to enhance the worksheet?

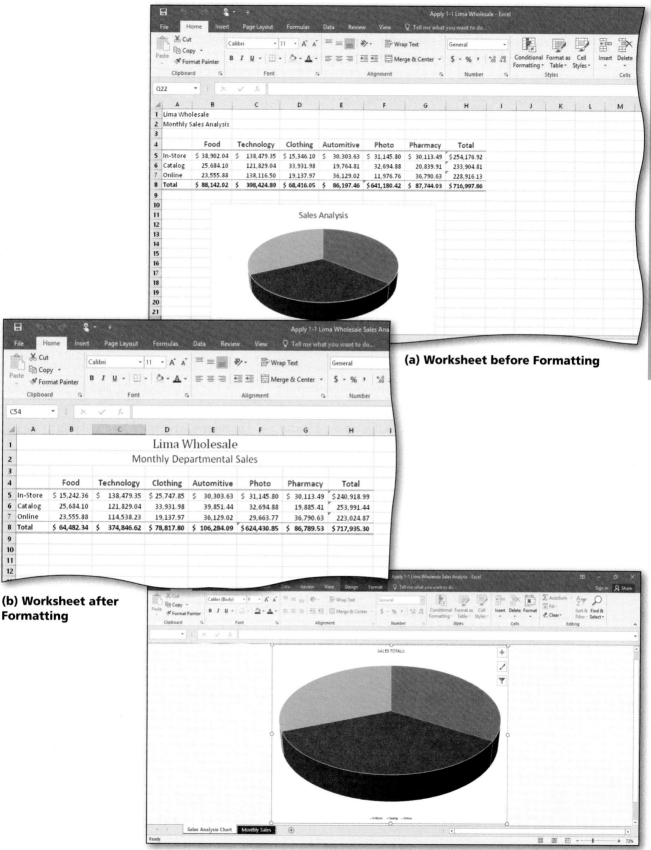

(a) Worksheet before Formatting

(b) Worksheet after Formatting

(c) 3-D Pie Chart on Separate Sheet

Figure 1–73

Extend Your Knowledge

Extend the skills you learned in this module and experiment with new skills. You may need to use Help to complete the assignment.

Creating Styles and Formatting a Worksheet

Note: To complete this assignment, you will be required to use the Data Files. Please contact your instructor for information about accessing the required files.

Instructions: Run Excel. Open the workbook Extend 1–1 Dasminne Grocery (Figure 1–74). The workbook you open contains sales data for Dasminne Grocery. You are to create styles and format a worksheet using them.

Perform the following tasks:

1. Select cell A4. Use the New Cell Style command in the Cell Styles gallery to create a style that uses the Blue, Accent 1, Darker 50% font color (row 6, column 5). Name the style, MyHeadings.

2. Select cell A5. Use the New Cell style dialog box to create a style that uses the Blue, Accent 1, Darker 25% (row 5, column 5) font color. Name the style, MyRows.

3. Select cell ranges B4:G4 and A5:A8. Apply the MyHeadings style to the cell ranges.

4. Select the cell range B5:G7. Apply the MyRows style to the cell range.

5. Apply a worksheet name to the sheet tab and apply a color of your choice to the sheet tab.

6. If requested by your instructor, change the font color for the text in cells A1 and A2 to the color of your eyes, if available.

7. Save the workbook using the file name, Extend 1–1 Dasminne Grocery Third Quarter.

8. Submit the revised workbook as specified by your instructor and exit Excel.

9. ✷ What other styles would you create to improve the worksheet's appearance?

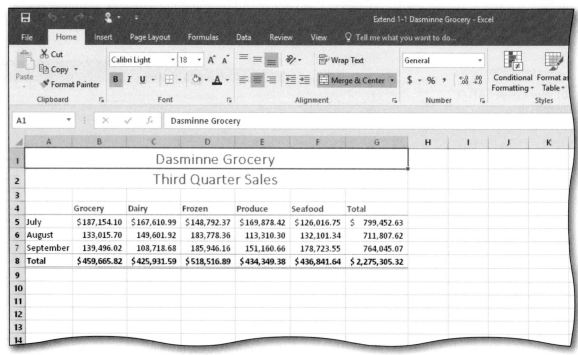

Figure 1–74

Expand Your World

Create a solution that uses cloud or web technologies by learning and investigating on your own from general guidance.

College Loan Calculator

Instructions: You are tasked with determining how long it will take you to pay back your college loans. You decide to download and use one of Excel's templates to create your worksheet.

Perform the following tasks:
1. Click the New tab in the Backstage view and then search for and click the College loan calculator template to download it.
2. Enter data for your estimated salary after graduation, the date you will begin paying back loans, as well as fictitious (but realistic) information for four loans, including loan number, lender, loan amount, annual interest rate, beginning date, and length (in years).
3. Save the file as Expand 1-1: College Loans. Print the worksheet.
4. Submit the assignment as specified by your instructor.
5. ✳ Which template would you use if you wanted to plan and keep track of a budget for a wedding?

In the Labs

Design, create, modify, and/or use a workbook following the guidelines, concepts, and skills presented in this module. Labs 1 and 2, which increase in difficulty, require you to create solutions based on what you learned in the module; Lab 3 requires you to apply your creative thinking and problem-solving skills to design and implement a solution.

Lab 1: First Quarter Revenue Analysis Worksheet

Problem: You work as a spreadsheet specialist for Katie's Kicks, which has four regional shops in the state of Florida. Your manager has asked you to develop a first quarter revenue analysis similar to the one shown in Figure 1–75.

Perform the following tasks:
1. Run Excel and create a new blank workbook. Enter the worksheet title, Katie's Kicks, in cell A1 and the worksheet subtitle, First Quarter Revenue Analysis, in cell A2. Beginning in row 4, enter the region data shown in Table 1–7.

Table 1–7 Katie's Kicks

	North	South	East	West
Sneakers	72714.58	77627.29	76607.31	49008.32
Shoes	45052.23	69165.66	76243.41	84844.01
Sandals	77630.94	78684.24	56601.25	72716.68
Accessories	65423.73	77690.69	58383.67	54433.07
Miscellaneous	55666.92	78618.97	47317.09	68594.40

2. Create totals for each region, product, and company grand total.
3. Format the worksheet title with the Title cell style. Center the title across columns A through F.

Continued >

In the Labs continued

4. Format the worksheet subtitle to 16-point Calibri Light, and change the font color to Blue-Gray, Text 2. Center the subtitle across columns A through F.

5. Use Cell Styles to format the range A4:F4 with the Heading 3 cell style, the range B4:F4 with the Accent1 cell style, and the range A10:F10 with the Total cell style.

6. Center the column titles in row 4. Apply the accounting number format to the ranges B5:F5 and B10:F10. Apply the comma style format to the range B6:F9. Adjust any column widths to the widest text entry in each column.

7. Select the ranges B4:E4 and B10:E10 and then insert a 3-D pie chart. Apply the Style 3 chart style to the chart. Move the chart to a new worksheet named Revenue Analysis Chart. Change the chart title to First Quarter Revenue Analysis.

8. Rename the Sheet1 tab, First Quarter, and apply the Green color to the sheet tab.

9. If requested by your instructor, change the font color of the text in cells A1 and A2 to the color of the shirt you currently are wearing.

10. Save the workbook using the file name, Lab 1-1 Katie's Kicks.

11. Preview and print the worksheet in landscape orientation.

12. ☀ If you wanted to chart the item totals instead of the regions, which ranges would you use to create the chart?

13. Submit the assignment as specified by your instructor.

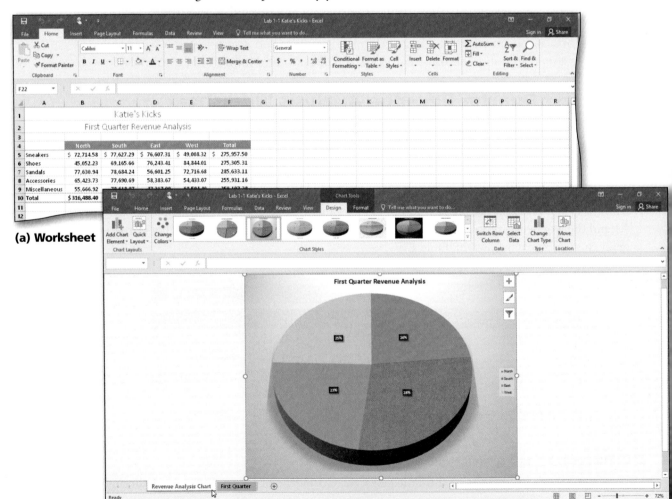

(a) Worksheet

(b) Pie Chart

Figure 1–75

Lab 2: **Sales Analysis Worksheet**

Problem: As the chief accountant for Davis Mobile Concepts, a leading car audio dealer serving four states, you have been asked by the vice president to create a worksheet to analyze the yearly sales for each state (Figure 1–76). The packages and corresponding sales by state for the year are shown in Table 1–8.

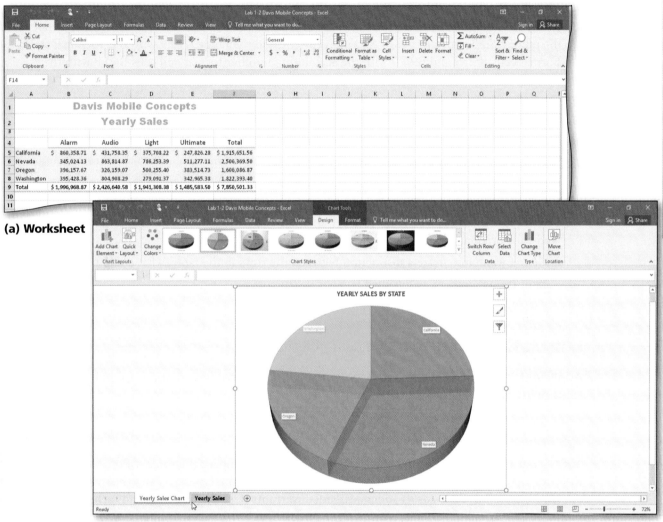

(a) Worksheet

(b) Pie Chart

Figure 1–76

Perform the following tasks:

1. Create the worksheet shown in Figure 1–76a using the data in Table 1–8.

Table 1–8 Davis Mobile Concepts				
	Alarm	**Audio**	**Light**	**Ultimate**
California	860358.71	431758.35	375708.22	247826.28
Nevada	345024.13	863814.87	786253.39	511277.11
Oregon	396157.67	326159.07	500255.40	383514.73
Washington	395428.36	804908.29	279091.37	342965.38

Continued >

In the Labs *continued*

2. Use the SUM function to determine total revenue for each of the four packages, the totals for each state, and the company total. Add column and row headings for the totals row and totals column, as appropriate.

3. Format the worksheet title and subtitle with the Title cell style and center them across columns A through F. Use the Font group on the ribbon to format the worksheet title and subtitle as 18-point Arial Black. Format the title and subtitle with Green, Accent 6 font color. Center the titles across columns A through F.

4. Format the range B4:F4 with the Heading 2 cell style and center the text in the cells. Format the range A5:F8 with the 20% - Accent6 cell style and the range A9:F9 with the Total cell style. Format cells B5:F5 and B9:F9 with the accounting number format and cells B6:F8 with the comma style format. If necessary, resize all columns to fit the data.

5. Create a 3-D pie chart on its own sheet that shows the total sales contributions of each state. Chart the state names (A5:A8) and corresponding totals (F5:F8). Use the sheet tab name, Yearly Sales Chart. Apply a chart style of your choosing. Change the chart title to Yearly Sales by State.

6. Change the Sheet1 tab name to Yearly Sales and apply the Orange color to the sheet tab.

7. If requested by your instructor, change the state in cell A8 to the state in which you were born. If your state already is listed in the spreadsheet, choose a different state.

8. Save the workbook using the file name, Lab 1-2 Davis Mobile Concepts. Print the worksheet in landscape orientation.

9. ✳ If you wanted to make a distinction between the rows in the table, what could you do?

10. Submit the assignment as specified by your instructor.

Lab 3: **Consider This: Your Turn**

Apply your creative thinking and problem-solving skills to design and implement a solution.

✳ Comparing Televisions

Part 1: You are shopping for a new television and want to compare the prices of three televisions. Research new televisions. Create a worksheet that compares the type, size, and the price for each television, as well as the costs to add an extended warranty. Use the concepts and techniques presented in this module to calculate the average price of a television and average cost of an extended warranty and to format the worksheet. Submit your assignment in the format specified by your instructor.

Part 2: Based upon the data you found, how could you chart the information to show the comparisons? Which chart would be the best to use? Include a chart to compare the different television costs.

2 Formulas, Functions, and Formatting

Objectives

You will have mastered the material in this module when you can:

- Use Flash Fill
- Enter formulas using the keyboard
- Enter formulas using Point mode
- Apply the MAX, MIN, and AVERAGE functions
- Verify a formula using Range Finder
- Apply a theme to a workbook
- Apply a date format to a cell or range

- Add conditional formatting to cells
- Change column width and row height
- Check the spelling on a worksheet
- Change margins and headers in Page Layout view
- Preview and print versions and sections of a worksheet

Introduction

In Module 1, you learned how to enter data, sum values, format a worksheet to make it easier to read, and draw a chart. This module continues to illustrate these topics and presents some new ones.

The new topics covered in this module include using formulas and functions to create a worksheet. Recall from Module 1 that a function is a prewritten formula that is built into Excel. Other new topics include using option buttons, verifying formulas, applying a theme to a worksheet, adding borders, formatting numbers and text, using conditional formatting, changing the widths of columns and heights of rows, checking spelling, generating alternative worksheet displays and printouts, and adding page headers and footers to a worksheet. One alternative worksheet display and printout shows the formulas in the worksheet instead of the values. When you display the formulas in the worksheet, you see exactly what text, data, formulas, and functions you have entered into it.

Project — Worksheet with Formulas and Functions

The project in this module follows proper design guidelines and uses Excel to create the worksheet shown in Figure 2–1. Every two weeks, the owners of Olivia's Art Supply create a salary report by hand, where they keep track of employee payroll data. Before paying employees, the owners must summarize the hours worked, pay rate, and tax information for each employee to ensure that the business properly compensates its employees. This report also includes the following information for each employee: name, email address, number of dependents, hours worked, hourly pay rate, tax information, net pay, and hire date. As the complexity of creating the salary report increases, the owners want to use Excel to make the process easier.

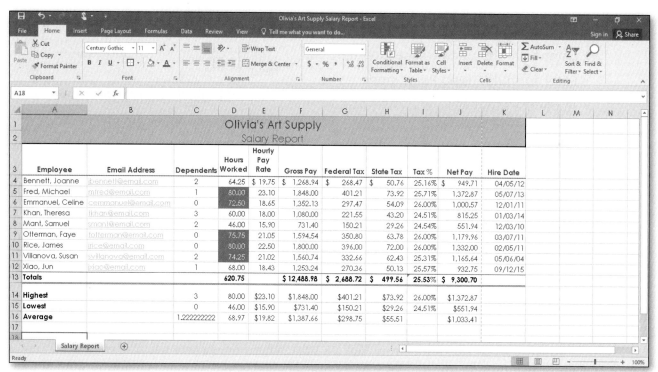

Figure 2–1

Recall that the first step in creating an effective worksheet is to make sure you understand what is required. The people who request the worksheet usually provide the requirements. The requirements document for the Olivia's Art Supply Salary Report worksheet includes the following needs: source of data, summary of calculations, and other facts about its development (Figure 2–2).

Worksheet Title	Olivia's Art Supply Salary Report
Needs	An easy-to-read worksheet that summarizes the company's salary report (Figure 2–3). For each employee, the worksheet is to include the employee's name, email address, number of dependents, hours worked, hourly pay rate, gross pay, federal tax, state tax, total tax percent, net pay, and hire date. The worksheet also should include the total pay for all employees, as well as the highest value, lowest value, and average for each category of data.
Source of Data	Supplied data includes employee names, number of dependents, hours worked, hourly pay rate, and hire dates.
Calculations	The following calculations must be made for each of the employees: 1. Gross Pay = Hours Worked * Hourly Pay Rate 2. Federal Tax = 0.22 * (Gross Pay * Number of Dependents * 24.32) 3. State Tax = 0.04 * Gross Pay 4. Tax % = (Federal Tax + State Tax) / Gross Pay 5. Net Pay = Gross Pay * (Federal Tax + State Tax) 6. Compute the totals for hours worked, gross pay, federal tax, state tax, and net pay 7. Compute the total tax percent 8. Use the MAX and MIN functions to determine the highest and lowest values for number of dependents, hours worked, hourly pay rate, gross pay, federal tax, state tax, total tax percent, and net pay 9. Use the AVERAGE function to determine the average for hours worked, number of dependents, hourly pay rate, gross pay, federal tax, state tax, and net pay

Figure 2–2

In addition, using a sketch of the worksheet can help you visualize its design. The sketch for the Olivia's Art Supply Salary Report worksheet includes a title, a subtitle, column and row headings, and the location of data values (Figure 2–3). It also uses specific characters to define the desired formatting for the worksheet, as follows:

1. The row of Xs below the leftmost column heading defines the cell entries as text, such as employee names.

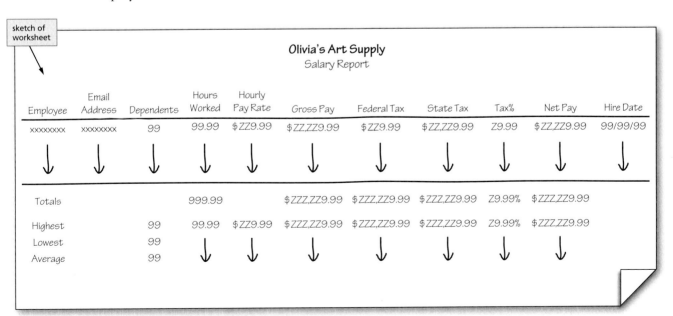

Figure 2–3

For an introduction to Windows and instructions about how to perform basic Windows tasks, read the Office and Windows module at the beginning of this book, where you can learn how to resize windows, change screen resolution, create folders, move and rename files, use Windows Help, and much more.

For an introduction to Office and instructions about how to perform basic tasks in Office apps, read the Office and Windows module at the beginning of this book, where you can learn how to run an application, use the ribbon, save a file, open a file, print a file, exit an application, use Help, and much more.

2. The rows of Zs and 9s with slashes, dollar signs, decimal points, commas, and percent signs in the remaining columns define the cell entries as numbers. The Zs indicate that the selected format should instruct Excel to suppress leading 0s. The 9s indicate that the selected format should instruct Excel to display any digits, including 0s.

3. The decimal point means that a decimal point should appear in the cell entry and indicates the number of decimal places to use.

4. The slashes in the last column identify the cell entry as a date.

5. The dollar signs that are adjacent to the Zs below the totals row signify a floating dollar sign, or one that appears next to the first significant digit.

6. The commas indicate that the selected format should instruct Excel to display a comma separator only if the number has sufficient digits (values in the thousandths) to the left of the decimal point.

7. The percent sign (%) in the Tax % column indicates a percent sign should appear after the number.

In this module, you will learn how to use functions and create formulas. The following roadmap identifies general activities you will perform as you progress through this module:

1. ENTER FORMULAS in the worksheet.

2. ENTER FUNCTIONS in the worksheet.

3. VERIFY FORMULAS in the worksheet.

4. FORMAT the WORKSHEET.

5. CHECK SPELLING.

6. PRINT the WORKSHEET.

What is the function of an Excel worksheet?

The function, or purpose, of a worksheet is to provide a user with direct ways to accomplish tasks. In designing a worksheet, functional considerations should supersede visual aesthetics. Consider the following when designing your worksheet:

• Avoid the temptation to use flashy or confusing visual elements within the worksheet.

• Understand the requirements document.

• Choose the proper functions and formulas.

• Build the worksheet.

BTW
Touch Screen Differences
The Office and Windows interfaces may vary if you are using a touch screen. For this reason, you might notice that the function or appearance of your touch screen differs slightly from this module's presentation.

Entering the Titles and Numbers into the Worksheet

The first step in creating the worksheet is to enter the titles and numbers into the worksheet. The following sets of steps enter the worksheet title and subtitle and then the salary report data shown in Table 2–1.

To Enter the Worksheet Title and Subtitle

With a good comprehension of the requirements document, an understanding of the necessary decisions, and a sketch of the worksheet, the next step is to use Excel to create the worksheet. The following steps enter the worksheet title and subtitle into cells A1 and A2.

1 Run Excel and create a blank workbook in the Excel window.

2 If necessary, select cell A1. Type **Olivia's Art Supply** in the selected cell and then press the DOWN ARROW key to enter the worksheet title.

3 Type **Salary Report** in cell A2 and then press the DOWN ARROW key to enter the worksheet subtitle.

To Enter the Column Titles

The column titles in row 3 begin in cell A3 and extend through cell K3. The employee names and the row titles begin in cell A4 and continue down to cell A16. The employee data is entered into rows 4 through 12 of the worksheet. The remainder of this section explains the steps required to enter the column titles, payroll data, and row titles, as shown in Figure 2–4, and then to save the workbook. The following steps enter the column titles.

1 With cell A3 selected, type **Employee** and then press the RIGHT ARROW key to enter the column heading.

2 Type **Email Address** in cell B3 and then press the RIGHT ARROW key.

3 In cell C3, type **Dependents** and then press the RIGHT ARROW key.

4 In cell D3, type **Hours** and then press the ALT+ENTER keys to enter the first line of the column heading. Type **Worked** and then press the RIGHT ARROW key to enter the column heading.

Q&A Why do I use the ALT+ENTER keys?
You press ALT+ENTER in order to start a new line in a cell. The final line can be completed by clicking the Enter button, pressing the ENTER key, or pressing one of the arrow keys. When you see ALT+ENTER in a step, press the ENTER key while holding down the ALT key and then release both keys.

5 Type **Hourly** in cell E3, press the ALT+ENTER keys, type **Pay Rate,** and then press the RIGHT ARROW key.

6 Type **Gross Pay** in cell F3 and then press the RIGHT ARROW key.

7 Type **Federal Tax** in cell G3 and then press the RIGHT ARROW key.

8 Type **State Tax** in cell H3 and then press the RIGHT ARROW key.

9 Type **Tax %** in cell I3 and then press the RIGHT ARROW key.

10 Type **Net Pay** in cell J3 and then press the RIGHT ARROW key.

11 Type **Hire Date** in cell K3 and then press the RIGHT ARROW key.

BTW

Screen Resolution
If you are using a computer or mobile device to step through the project in this module and you want your screens to match the figures in this book, you should change your screen's resolution to 1366 x 768. For information about how to change a computer's resolution, refer to the Office and Windows module at the beginning of this book.

BTW

Wrapping Text
If you have a long text entry, such as a paragraph, you can instruct Excel to wrap the text in a cell. This method is easier than your pressing ALT+ENTER to end each line of text within the paragraph. To wrap text, right-click in the cell, click Format Cells on a shortcut menu, click the Alignment tab, and then click Wrap text. Excel will increase the height of the cell automatically so that the additional lines will fit. If you want to control where each line ends in the cell, rather than letting Excel wrap the text based on the cell width, you must end each line with ALT+ENTER.

To Enter the Salary Data

The salary data in Table 2-1 includes a hire date for each employee. Excel considers a date to be a number and, therefore, it displays the date right-aligned in the cell. The following steps enter the data for each employee, except their email addresses, which will be entered later in this module.

BTW
Two-Digit Years
When you enter a two-digit year value (xx) that is less than 30, Excel changes that value to 20xx; when you enter a value that is 30 or greater (zz), Excel changes the value to 19zz. Use four-digit years, if necessary, to ensure that Excel interprets year values the way you intend.

1 Select cell A4. Type **Bennett, Joanne** and then press the RIGHT ARROW key two times to enter the employee name and make cell C4 the active cell.

2 Type **2** in cell C4 and then press the RIGHT ARROW key.

3 Type **64.25** in cell D4 and then press the RIGHT ARROW key.

4 Type **19.75** in cell E4.

5 Click cell K4 and then type **4/5/12**.

6 Enter the payroll data in Table 2–1 for the eight remaining employees in rows 5 through 12.

Q&A In Step 5, why did the date change from 4/5/12 to 4/5/2012?
When Excel recognizes a date in mm/dd/yy format, it formats the date as mm/dd/yyyy. Most professionals prefer to view dates in mm/dd/yyyy format as opposed to mm/dd/yy format to avoid confusion regarding the intended year. For example, a date displayed as 3/3/50 could imply a date of 3/3/1950 or 3/3/2050.

Table 2–1 Olivia's Art Supply Salary Report Data

Employee	Email Address	Dependents	Hours Worked	Hourly Pay Rate	Hire Date
Bennett, Joanne		2	64.25	19.75	4/5/12
Fred, Michael		1	80.00	23.10	5/7/13
Emmanuel, Celine		0	72.50	18.65	12/1/11
Khan, Theresa		3	60.00	18.00	1/3/14
Mant, Samuel		2	46.00	15.90	12/3/10
Otterman, Faye		0	75.75	21.05	3/7/11
Rice, James		0	80.00	22.50	2/5/11
Villanova, Susan		2	74.25	21.02	5/6/04
Xiao, Jun		1	68.00	18.43	9/12/15

BTW
The Ribbon and Screen Resolution
Excel may change how the groups and buttons within the groups appear on the ribbon, depending on the computer or mobile device's screen resolution. Thus, your ribbon may look different from the ones in this book if you are using a screen resolution other than 1366 x 768.

Flash Fill

When you are entering data in a spreadsheet, occasionally Excel will recognize a pattern in the data you are entering. **Flash Fill** is an Excel feature that looks for patterns in the data and automatically fills or formats data in remaining cells. For example if column A contains a list of 10 phone numbers without parentheses around the area code or dashes after the prefix, Flash Fill can help create formatted phone numbers with relative ease. To use Flash Fill, simply start entering formatted phone numbers in cells next to the unformatted numbers. After entering a few formatted phone numbers, Flash Fill will suggest similarly formatted phone numbers for the remaining cells in the column. If you do not want to wait for Excel to offer suggestions, type one or two examples and then click the Flash Fill button (Data tab | Data Tools group). Flash fill will autocomplete the remaining cells. If Flash Fill makes a mistake, simply click the Undo button, enter a few more examples, and try again. In addition to formatting data, Flash Fill can perform tasks such as concatenating data from multiple cells and separating data from one cell into multiple cells.

To Use Flash Fill

1 ENTER FORMULAS | 2 ENTER FUNCTIONS | 3 VERIFY FORMULAS
4 FORMAT WORKSHEET | 5 CHECK SPELLING | 6 PRINT WORKSHEET

In the Olivia's Art Supply Salary Report worksheet, you can use Flash Fill to generate email addresses using first and last names from another column in the worksheet. *Why? The Flash Fill feature is a convenient way to avoid entering a lot of data manually.* The following steps use Flash Fill to generate employee email addresses using the names entered in column A.

- Click cell B4 to select it.
- Type **jbennett@ email.com** and then press the DOWN ARROW key to select cell B5.
- Type **mfred@ email.com** and then click the Enter button to enter Michael Fred's email address in cell B5 (Figure 2–4).

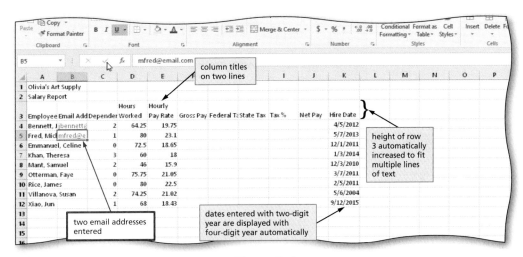

Figure 2–4

- Click Data on the ribbon to select the Data tab.
- Click Flash Fill (Data tab | Data Tools group) to enter similarly formatted email addresses in the range B6:B12.
- Remove the entries from cells B1 and B2 (Figure 2–5).

Q&A
Why was I unable to click the Flash Fill button after entering the first email address?
One entry might not have been enough for Excel to recognize a pattern. For instance, Flash Fill might have used the letter *j* before each last name in the email address, instead of using the first initial and last name.

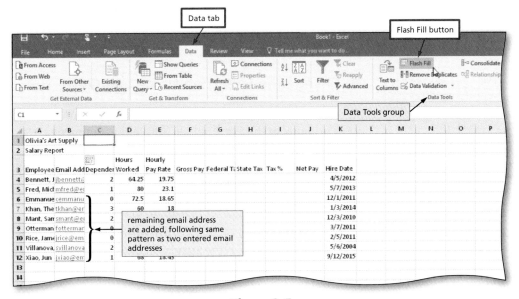

Figure 2–5

What would have happened if I kept typing examples without clicking the Flash Fill button?
As soon as Excel recognized a pattern, it would have displayed suggestions for the remaining cells. Pressing the ENTER key when the suggestions appear will populate the remaining cells.

BTW
Formatting Worksheets
With early worksheet programs, users often skipped rows to improve the appearance of the worksheet. With Excel it is not necessary to skip rows because you can increase row heights to add white space between information.

To Enter the Row Titles

The following steps add row titles for the rows that will contain the totals, highest, lowest, and average amounts.

1 Select cell A13. Type **Totals** and then press the DOWN ARROW key to enter a row header.

2 Type **Highest** in cell A14 and then press the DOWN ARROW key.

3 Type **Lowest** in cell A15 and then press the DOWN ARROW key.

4 Type **Average** in cell A16 and then press the DOWN ARROW key (Figure 2–6).

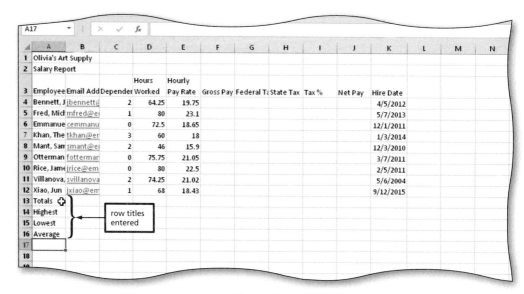

Figure 2–6

BTW
Organizing Files and Folders
You should organize and store files in folders so that you easily can find the files later. For example, if you are taking an introductory technology class called CIS 101, a good practice would be to save all Excel files in an Excel folder in a CIS 101 folder. For a discussion of folders and detailed examples of creating folders, refer to the Office and Windows module at the beginning of this book.

To Change the Sheet Tab Name and Color

The following steps change the sheet tab name, change the tab color, and save the workbook in the Excel folder (for your assignments).

1 Double-click the Sheet1 tab and then enter **Salary Report** as the sheet tab name and then press the ENTER key.

2 Right-click the sheet tab to display the shortcut menu.

3 Point to Tab Color on the shortcut menu to display the Tab Color gallery. Click Green (column 6, row 7) in the Standard Colors area to apply the color to the sheet tab.

4 Save the workbook in your hard drive, OneDrive, or other storage location using Olivia's Art Supply Salary Report as the file name.

Q&A Why should I save the workbook at this time?
You have performed many tasks while creating this workbook and do not want to risk losing work completed thus far.

Entering Formulas

One of the reasons Excel is such a valuable tool is that you can assign a formula to a cell, and Excel will calculate the result. A **formula** consists of cell references, numbers, and arithmetic operators that instruct Excel to perform a calculation. Consider, for example, what would happen if you had to multiply 64.25 by 19.75 and then manually enter the product for Gross Pay, 1,268.94, in cell F4. Every time the values in cells D4 or E4 changed, you would have to recalculate the product and enter the new value in cell F4. By contrast, if you enter a formula in cell F4 to multiply the values in cells D4 and E4, Excel recalculates the product whenever new values are entered into those cells and displays the result in cell F4.

A formula in a cell that contains a reference back to itself is called a **circular reference**. Excel warns you when you create circular references. In almost all cases, circular references are the result of an incorrect formula. A circular reference can be direct or indirect. For example, placing the formula =A1 in cell A1 results in a direct circular reference. A **direct circular reference** occurs when a formula refers to the same cell in which it is entered. An **indirect circular reference** occurs when a formula in a cell refers to another cell or cells that include a formula that refers back to the original cell.

BTW

Entering Numbers in a Range
An efficient way to enter data into a range of cells is to select a range and then enter the first number in the upper-left cell of the range. Excel responds by accepting the value and moving the active cell selection down one cell. When you enter the last value in the first column, Excel moves the active cell selection to the top of the next column.

To Enter a Formula Using the Keyboard

1 ENTER FORMULAS | 2 ENTER FUNCTIONS | 3 VERIFY FORMULAS
4 FORMAT WORKSHEET | 5 CHECK SPELLING | 6 PRINT WORKSHEET

The formulas needed in the worksheet are noted in the requirements document as follows:

1. Gross Pay (column F) = Hours Worked × Hourly Pay Rate
2. Federal Tax (column G) = 0.22 × (Gross Pay − Dependents × 24.32)
3. State Tax (column H) = 0.04 × Gross Pay
4. Tax % (column I) = (Federal Tax + State Tax) / Gross Pay
5. Net Pay (column J) = Gross Pay − (Federal Tax + State Tax)

The gross pay for each employee, which appears in column F, is equal to hours worked in column D times hourly pay rate in column E. Thus, the gross pay for Joanne Bennett in cell F4 is obtained by multiplying 64.25 (cell D4) by 19.75 (cell E4) or = D4 × E4. The following steps enter the initial gross pay formula in cell F4 using the keyboard. **Why?** *In order for Excel to perform the calculations, you must first enter the formulas.*

❶
- With cell F4 selected, type **=d4*e4** in the cell to display the formula in the formula bar and the current cell and to display colored borders around the cells referenced in the formula (Figure 2–7).

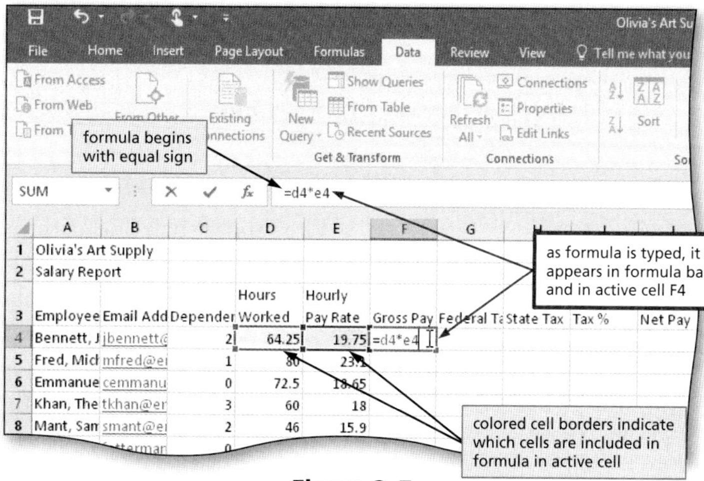

Q&A

What happens when I enter the formula?
The **equal sign** (=) preceding d4*e4 alerts Excel that you are entering a formula or function — not text. Because the most common error when entering a formula is to reference the wrong cell, Excel colors the cells referenced in the formula. The colored cells help you determine whether the cell references are correct. The asterisk (*) following d4 is the arithmetic operator for multiplication.

Is there a function, similar to the SUM function, that calculates the product of two or more numbers?
Yes. The **PRODUCT function** calculates the product of two or more numbers. For example, the function, =PRODUCT(D4,E4) will calculate the product of cells D4 and E4.

Figure 2–7

• Press the RIGHT ARROW key to complete the arithmetic operation indicated by the formula, display the result in the worksheet, and select the cell to the right (Figure 2–8). The number of decimal places on your screen may be different than shown in Figure 2–8, but these values will be adjusted later in this module.

Figure 2–8

BTW
Automatic Recalculation
Every time you enter a value into a cell in the worksheet, Excel automatically recalculates all formulas. You can change to manual recalculation by clicking the Calculation Options button (Formulas tab | Calculation group) and then clicking Manual. In manual calculation mode, pressing the F9 key instructs Excel to recalculate all formulas.

Arithmetic Operations

Excel provides powerful functions and capabilities that allow you to perform arithmetic operations easily and efficiently. Table 2–2 describes multiplication and other valid Excel arithmetic operators.

Table 2–2 Arithmetic Operations Listed in Order of Operations			
Arithmetic Operator	**Meaning**	**Example of Usage**	**Result**
–	Negation	–78	Negative 78
%	Percentage	=23%	Multiplies 23 by 0.01
^	Exponentiation	=3 ^ 4	Raises 3 to the fourth power
*	Multiplication	=61.5 * C5	Multiplies the contents of cell C5 by 61.5
/	Division	=H3 / H11	Divides the contents of cell H3 by the contents of cell H11
+	Addition	=11 + 9	Adds 11 and 9
–	Subtraction	=22 – F15	Subtracts the contents of cell F15 from 22

BTW
Troubling Formulas
If Excel does not accept a formula, remove the equal sign from the left side and complete the entry as text. Later, after you have entered additional data in the cells reliant on the formula or determined the error, reinsert the equal sign to change the text back to a formula and edit the formula as needed.

Order of Operations

When more than one arithmetic operator is involved in a formula, Excel follows the same basic order of operations that you use in algebra. The **order of operations** is the collection of rules that define which mathematical operations take precedence over the others in expressions with multiple operations. Moving from left to right in a formula, the order of operations is as follows: first negation (–), then all percentages (%), then all exponentiations (^), then all multiplications (*) and divisions (/), and, finally, all additions (+) and subtractions (–).

As in algebra, you can use parentheses to override the order of operations. For example, if Excel follows the order of operations, 8 * 3 + 2 equals 26. If you use parentheses, however, to change the formula to 8 * (3 + 2), the result is 40, because the parentheses instruct Excel to add 3 and 2 before multiplying by 8. Table 2–3 illustrates several examples of valid Excel formulas and explains the order of operations.

Table 2–3 Examples of Excel Formulas	
Formula	**Result**
=G15	Assigns the value in cell G15 to the active cell.
=2^4 + 7	Assigns the sum of 16 + 7 (or 23) to the active cell.
=100 + D2 or =D2 +100 or =(100 + D2)	Assigns 100 plus the contents of cell D2 to the active cell.
=25% * 40	Assigns the product of 0.25 times 40 (or 10) to the active cell.
– (K15 * X45)	Assigns the negative value of the product of the values contained in cells K15 and X45 to the active cell. *Tip:* You do not need to type an equal sign before an expression that begins with a minus sign, which indicates a negation.
=(U8 – B8) * 6	Assigns the difference between the values contained in cells U8 and B8 times 6 to the active cell.
=J7 / A5 + G9 * M6 – Z2 ^ L7	Completes the following operations, from left to right: exponentiation (Z2 ^ L7), then division (J7 / A5), then multiplication (G9 * M6), then addition (J7 / A5) + (G9 * M6), and finally subtraction (J7 / A5 + G9 * M6) – (Z2 ^ L7). If cells A5 = 6, G9 = 2, J7 = 6, L7 = 4, M6 = 5, and Z2 = 2, then Excel assigns the active cell the value –5; that is, 6 / 6 + 2 * 5 – 2 ^ 4 = –5.

BTW

Parentheses
Remember that you can use parentheses to override the order of operations. You cannot use brackets or braces in place of parentheses in arithmetic operations.

To Enter Formulas Using Point Mode

1 ENTER FORMULAS | 2 ENTER FUNCTIONS | 3 VERIFY FORMULAS
4 FORMAT WORKSHEET | 5 CHECK SPELLING | 6 PRINT WORKSHEET

The sketch of the worksheet in Figure 2–3 calls for the federal tax, state tax, tax percentage, and net pay for each employee to appear in columns G, H, I, and J, respectively. All four of these values are calculated using formulas in row 4:

Federal Tax (cell G4) = 0.22 × (Gross Pay − Dependents × 24.32) or = 0.22 * (F4 − C4 * 24.32)
State Tax (cell H4) = 0.04 × Gross Pay or = 0.04 * F4
Tax % (cell I4) = (Federal Tax + State Tax) / Gross Pay or = (G4 + H4) / F4
Net Pay (cell J4) = Gross Pay − (Federal Tax + State Tax) or = F4 − (G4 + H4)

An alternative to entering the formulas in cells G4, H4, I4, and J4 using the keyboard is to enter the formulas using the pointer and Point mode. **Point mode** allows you to select cells for use in a formula by using the pointer. The following steps enter formulas using Point mode. ***Why?*** *Using Point mode makes it easier to create formulas without worrying about typographical errors when entering cell references.*

• With cell G4 selected, type =0.22* (to begin the formula and then click cell F4 to add a cell reference in the formula (Figure 2–9).

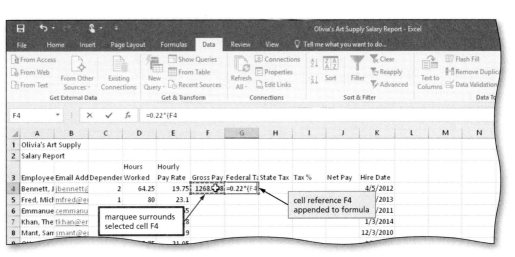

Figure 2–9

- Type – (minus sign) and then click cell C4 to add a subtraction operator and a reference to another cell to the formula.

- Type ***24.32)** to complete the formula (Figure 2–10).

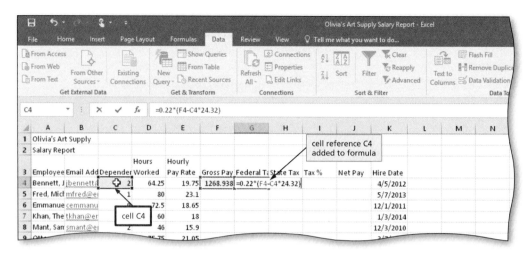

Figure 2–10

❸

- Click the Enter button in the formula bar and then select cell H4 to prepare to enter the next formula.

- Type **=0.04*** and then click cell F4 to add a cell reference to the formula (Figure 2–11).

Q&A Why should I use Point mode to enter formulas?

Using Point mode to enter formulas often is faster and more accurate than using the keyboard, but only when the cell you want to select does not require you to scroll. In many instances, as in these steps, you may want to use both the keyboard and pointer when entering a formula in a cell. You can use the keyboard to begin the formula, for example, and then use the pointer to select a range of cells.

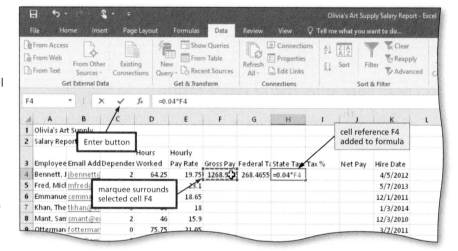

Figure 2–11

❹

- Click the Enter button in the formula bar to enter the formula in cell H4.

- Select cell I4. Type **= (** (equal sign followed by an open parenthesis) and then click cell G4 to add a reference to the formula.

- Type **+** (plus sign) and then click cell H4 to add a cell reference to the formula.

- Type **) /** (close parenthesis followed by a forward slash), and then click cell F4 to add a cell reference to the formula.

- Click the Enter button in the formula bar to enter the formula in cell I4 (Figure 2–12).

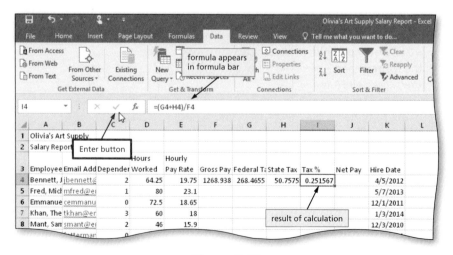

Figure 2–12

5

- Click cell J4, type = (equal sign) and then click cell F4.

- Type – ((minus sign followed by an open parenthesis) and then click cell G4.

- Type + (plus sign), click cell H4, and then type) (close parenthesis) to complete the formula (Figure 2–13).

- Click the Enter button.

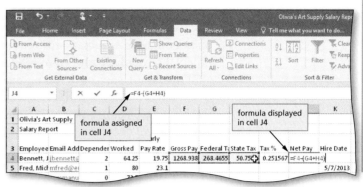

Figure 2–13

To Copy Formulas Using the Fill Handle

The five formulas for Joanne Bennett in cells F4, G4, H4, I4, and J4 now are complete. The next step is to copy them to the range F5:J12. When copying formulas in Excel, the source area is the cell, or range, from which data or formulas are being copied. When a range is used as a source, it sometimes is called the **source range**. The destination area is the cell, or range, to which data or formulas are being copied. When a range is used as a destination, it sometimes is called the **destination range**. Recall from Module 1 that the fill handle is a small square in the lower-right corner of the active cell or active range. The following steps copy the formulas using the fill handle.

1 Select the source range, F4:J4 in this case, activate the fill handle, drag the fill handle down through cell J12, and then continue to hold the mouse button to select the destination range.

2 Release the mouse button to copy the formulas to the destination range (Figure 2–14).

Q&A | How does Excel adjust the cell references in the formulas in the destination area?
Recall that when you copy a formula, Excel adjusts the cell references so that the new formulas contain new cell references corresponding to the new locations and perform calculations using the appropriate values. Thus, if you copy downward, Excel adjusts the row portion of cell references relative to the source cell. If you copy across, then Excel adjusts the column portion of cell references relative to the source cell. Cell references that adjust relative to the location of the source cell are called **relative cell references**.

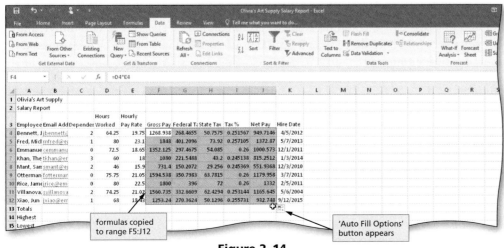

Figure 2–14

Option Buttons

Excel displays option buttons in a worksheet to indicate that you can complete an operation using automatic features such as AutoCorrect, Auto Fill, error checking, and others. For example, the 'Auto Fill Options' button shown in Figure 2–14 appears after a fill operation, such as dragging the fill handle. When an error occurs in a formula in a cell, Excel displays the Trace Error button next to the cell and identifies the cell with the error by placing a green triangle in the upper left of the cell.

Table 2–4 summarizes the option buttons available in Excel. When one of these buttons appears on your worksheet, click its arrow to produce the list of options for modifying the operation or to obtain additional information.

Table 2–4 Option Buttons in Excel	
Name	**Menu Function**
Auto Fill Options	Provides options for how to fill cells following a fill operation, such as dragging the fill handle
AutoCorrect Options	Undoes an automatic correction, stops future automatic corrections of this type, or causes Excel to display the AutoCorrect Options dialog box
Insert Options	Lists formatting options following an insertion of cells, rows, or columns
Paste Options	Specifies how moved or pasted items should appear (for example, with original formatting, without formatting, or with different formatting)
Trace Error	Lists error-checking options following the assignment of an invalid formula to a cell

CONSIDER THIS

Why is the Paste Options button important?
The Paste Options button provides powerful functionality. When performing copy and paste operations, the button allows you great freedom in specifying what it is you want to paste. You can choose from the following options:

- Paste an exact copy of what you copied, including the cell contents and formatting.
- Copy only formulas.
- Copy only formatting.
- Copy only values.
- Copy a combination of these options.
- Copy a picture of what you copied.

BTW
Selecting a Range
You can select a range using the keyboard. Press the F8 key and then use the arrow keys to select the desired range. After you are finished, make sure to press the F8 key to turn off the selection process or you will continue to select ranges.

To Determine Totals Using the Sum Button

The next step is to determine the totals in row 13 for the hours worked in column D, gross pay in column F, federal tax in column G, state tax in column H, and net pay in column J. To determine the total hours worked in column D, the values in the range D4 through D12 must be summed using the SUM function. Recall that a function is a prewritten formula that is built into Excel. Similar SUM functions can be used in cells F13, G13, H13, and J13 to total gross pay, federal tax, state tax, and net pay, respectively. The following steps determine totals in cell D13, the range F13:H13, and cell J13.

1 Select the cell to contain the sum, cell D13 in this case. Click the Sum button (Home tab | Editing group) to sum the contents of the range D4:D12 in cell D13 and then click the Enter button to display a total in the selected cell.

2 Select the range to contain the sums, range F13:H13 in this case. Click the Sum button (Home tab | Editing group) to display totals in the selected range.

3 Select the cell to contain the sum, cell J13 in this case. Click the Sum button (Home tab | Editing group) to sum the contents of the range J4:J12 in cell J13 and then click the Enter button to display a total in the selected cell (Figure 2–15).

Q&A Why did I have to click the Enter button?
When calculating a sum for a single column, you click the Enter button. If you are calculating the sum for multiple ranges, you click the Sum button.

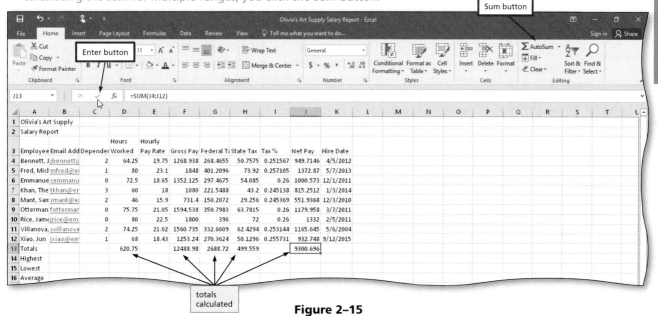

totals calculated

Figure 2–15

To Determine the Total Tax Percentage

With the totals in row 13 determined, the next step is to copy the tax percentage formula in cell I12 to cell I13. The following step copies the tax percentage formula.

1 Select the cell to be copied, I12 in this case, and then drag the fill handle down through cell I13 to copy the formula (Figure 2–16).

Q&A Why was the SUM function not used for tax percentage in I13?
The total tax percentage is calculated using the totals of the Gross Pay, Federal Tax and State Tax columns, not by summing the tax percentage column.

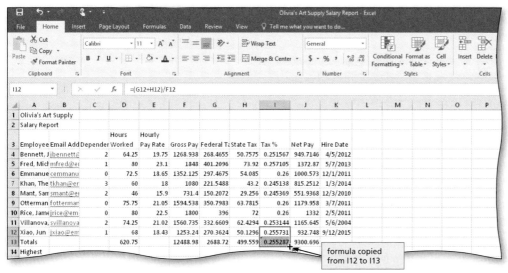

formula copied from I12 to I13

Figure 2–16

BTW
Statistical Functions
Excel usually considers a blank cell to be equal to 0. The statistical functions, however, ignore blank cells. Excel thus calculates the average of three cells with values of 10, blank, and 8 to be 9 [(10 + 8) / 2] and not 6 [(10 + 0 + 8) / 3].

Using the AVERAGE, MAX, and MIN Functions

The next step in creating the Olivia's Art Supply Salary Report worksheet is to compute the highest value, lowest value, and average value for the number of dependents listed in the range C4:C12 using the MAX, MIN, and AVERAGE functions in the range C14:C16. Once the values are determined for column C, the entries can be copied across to the other columns.

With Excel, you can enter functions using one of five methods: (1) keyboard, touch gesture, or pointer; (2) the Insert Function button in the formula bar; (3) the Sum menu; (4) the Sum button (Formulas tab | Function Library group); and (5) the Name box area in the formula bar. The method you choose will depend on your typing skills and whether you can recall the function name and required arguments.

In the following sections, three of these methods will be used. The Insert Function button in the formula bar method will be used to determine the highest number of dependents (cell C14). The Sum menu will be used to determine the lowest number of dependents (cell C15). The keyboard and pointer will be used to determine the average number of dependents (cell C16).

To Determine the Highest Number in a Range of Numbers Using the Insert Function Dialog Box

1 ENTER FORMULAS | 2 ENTER FUNCTIONS | 3 VERIFY FORMULAS
4 FORMAT WORKSHEET | 5 CHECK SPELLING | 6 PRINT WORKSHEET

The next step is to select cell C14 and determine the highest (maximum) number in the range C4:C12. Excel includes a function called the **MAX function** that displays the highest value in a range. The following steps use the Insert Function dialog box to enter the MAX function. *Why? Although you could enter the MAX function using the keyboard and Point mode as described previously, an alternative method to entering the function is to use the Insert Function button in the formula bar to open the Insert Function dialog box. The Insert Function dialog box is helpful if you do not remember the name of a function or need to search for a particular function by what it does.*

- Select the cell to contain the maximum number, cell C14 in this case.

- Click the Insert Function button in the formula bar to display the Insert Function dialog box.

- Click MAX in the Select a function list (Insert Function dialog box; Figure 2–17). You may need to scroll.

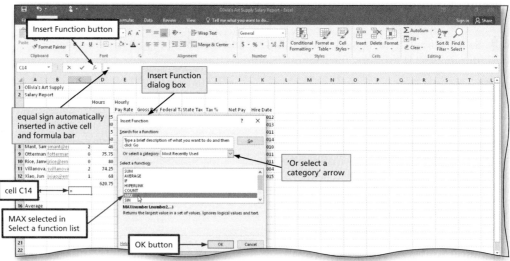

Figure 2–17

Q&A What if the MAX function is not in the Select a function list?
Click the 'Or select a category' arrow to display the list of function categories, select All, and then scroll down and select the MAX function in the Select a function list.

How can I learn about other functions?
Excel has more than 400 functions that perform nearly every type of calculation you can imagine. These functions are categorized in the Insert Function dialog box shown in Figure 2–17. To view the categories, click the 'Or select a category' arrow. Click the name of a function in the Select a function list to display a description of the function.

2

- Click the OK button (Insert Function dialog box) to display the Function Arguments dialog box.

- Replace the text in the Number1 box with the text, **c4:c12** (Function Arguments dialog box) to enter the first argument of the function (Figure 2–18).

|What are the numbers that appear to the right of the Number1 box in the Function Arguments dialog box?
The numbers shown to the right of the Number1 box are the values in the selected range (or if the range is large, the first few numbers only). Excel also displays the value the MAX function will return to cell C14 in the Function Arguments dialog box, shown in Figure 2–18.

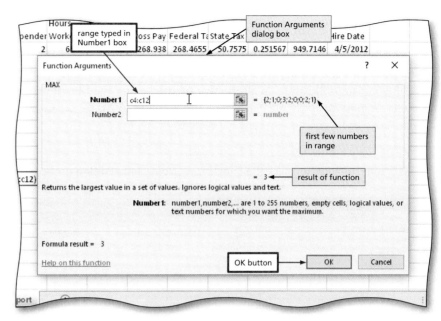

Figure 2–18

3

- Click the OK button (Function Arguments dialog box) to display the highest value in the chosen range in cell C14 (Figure 2–19).

|Why should I not just enter the highest value that I see in the range C4:C12 in cell C14?
In this example, rather than entering the MAX function, you could examine the range C4:C12, determine that the highest number of dependents is 3, and manually enter the number 3 as a constant in cell C14. Excel would display the number similar to how it appears in Figure 2–19. However, because C14 would then contain a constant, Excel would continue to display 3 in cell C14 even if the values in the range change. If you use the MAX function, Excel will recalculate the highest value in the range each time a new value is entered.

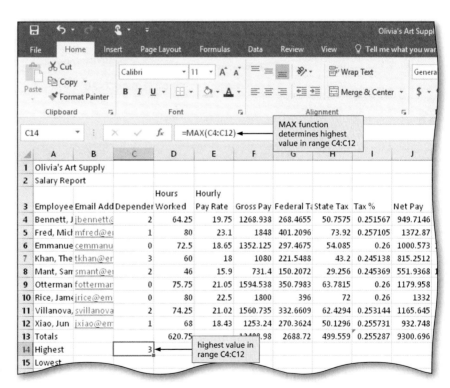

Figure 2–19

Other Ways

1. Click Sum arrow (Home tab | Editing group), click Max

2. Click Sum arrow (Formulas tab | Function Library group), click Max

3. Type `=MAX(` in cell, specify range, type)

To Determine the Lowest Number in a Range of Numbers Using the Sum Menu

The next step is to enter the **MIN function** in cell C15 to determine the lowest (minimum) number in the range C4:C12. Although you can enter the MIN function using the method used to enter the MAX function, the following steps illustrate an alternative method using the Sum button (Home tab | Editing group). *Why? Using the Sum menu allows you quick access to five commonly used functions, without having to memorize their names or required arguments.*

- Select cell C15 and then click the Sum arrow (Home tab | Editing group) to display the Sum menu (Figure 2–20).

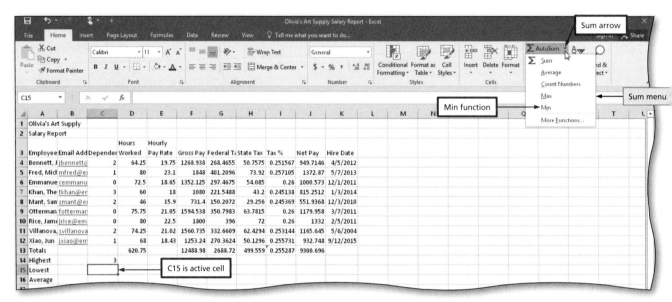

Figure 2–20

- Click Min to display the MIN function in the formula bar and in the active cell (Figure 2–21).

Q&A

Why does Excel select the incorrect range?

The range selected by Excel is not always the right one. Excel attempts to guess which cells you want to include in the function by looking for ranges containing numeric data that are adjacent to the selected cell.

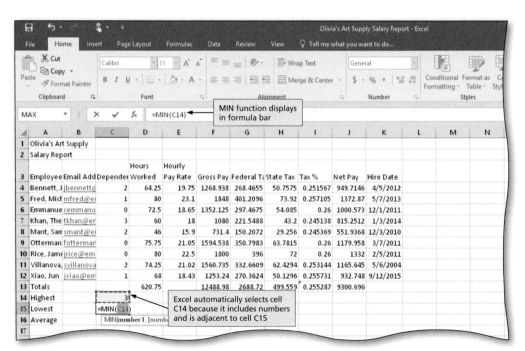

Figure 2–21

3

- Click cell C4 and then drag through cell C12 to update the function with the new range (Figure 2–22).

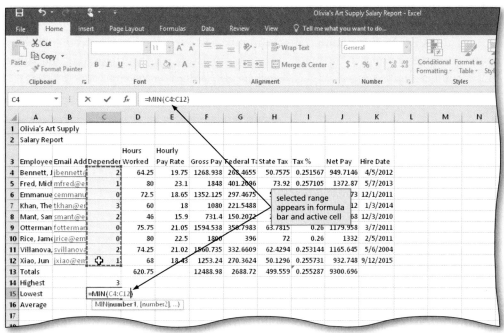

Figure 2–22

4

- Click the Enter button to determine the lowest value in the range C4:C12 and display the result in cell C15 (Figure 2–23).

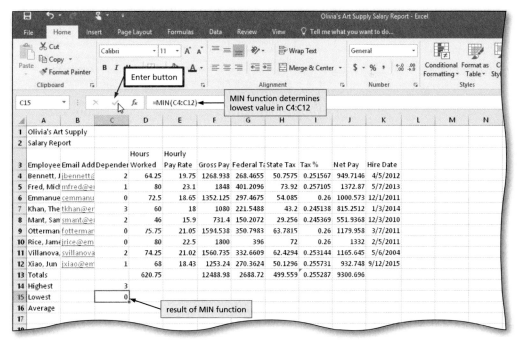

Figure 2–23

Other Ways

1. Click Insert Function button in formula bar, select Statistical category if necessary, click MIN, specify arguments
2. Click Sum arrow (Formulas tab | Function Library group), click Min
3. Type `=MIN(` in cell, fill in arguments, type `)`

To Determine the Average of a Range of Numbers Using the Keyboard

The **AVERAGE function** sums the numbers in a specified range and then divides the sum by the number of cells with numeric values in the range. The following steps use the AVERAGE function to determine the average of the numbers in the range C4:C12. *Why? The AVERAGE function calculates the average of a range of numbers.*

- Select the cell to contain the average, cell C16 in this case.

- Type =av in the cell to display the Formula AutoComplete list. Press the DOWN ARROW key to highlight the AVERAGE function (Figure 2–24).

Q&A What is happening as I type?
As you type the equal sign followed by the characters in the name of a function, Excel displays the Formula AutoComplete list. This list contains those functions whose names match the letters you have typed.

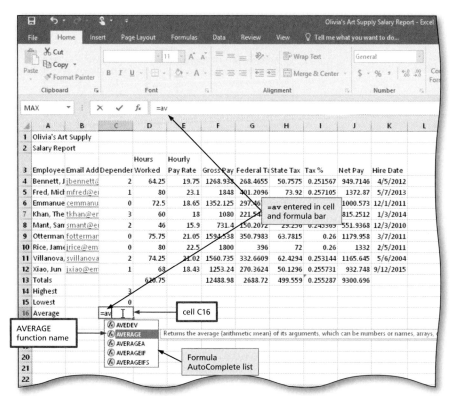

Figure 2–24

- Double-click AVERAGE in the Formula AutoComplete list to select the function.

- Select the range to be averaged, C4:C12 in this case, to insert the range as the argument to the function (Figure 2–25).

Q&A As I drag, why does the function in cell C16 change?
When you click cell C4, Excel surrounds cell C4 with a marquee and appends C4 to the left parenthesis in the formula bar. When you begin dragging, Excel appends to the argument a colon (:) and the cell reference of the cell where the pointer is located.

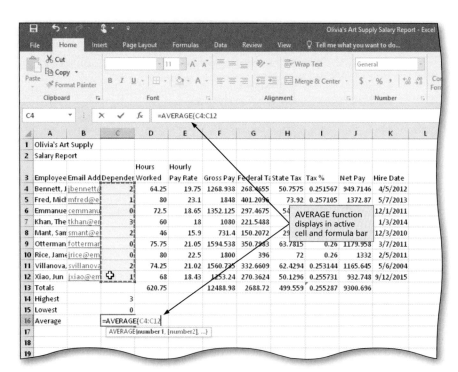

Figure 2–25

3

- Click the Enter button to compute the average of the numbers in the selected range and display the result in the selected cell (Figure 2–26).

Q&A

Can I use the arrow keys to complete the entry instead?

No. While in Point mode, the arrow keys change the selected cell reference in the range you are selecting instead of completing the entry.

What is the purpose of the parentheses in the function?

Most Excel functions require that the argument (in this case, the range C4:C12) be included within parentheses following the function name. In this case, Excel appended the right parenthesis to complete the AVERAGE function when you clicked the Enter button.

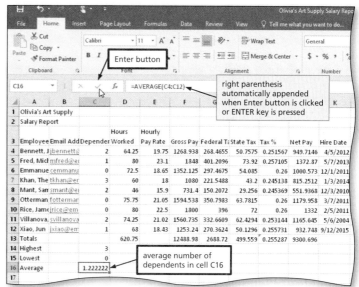

Figure 2–26

To Copy a Range of Cells across Columns to an Adjacent Range Using the Fill Handle

The next step is to copy the AVERAGE, MAX, and MIN functions in the range C14:C16 to the adjacent range D14:J16. The following steps use the fill handle to copy the functions.

1 Select the source range from which to copy the functions, in this case C14:C16.

2 Drag the fill handle in the lower-right corner of the selected range through cell J16 to copy the three functions to the selected range.

3 Select cell I16 and then press the DELETE key to delete the average of the Tax % (Figure 2–27).

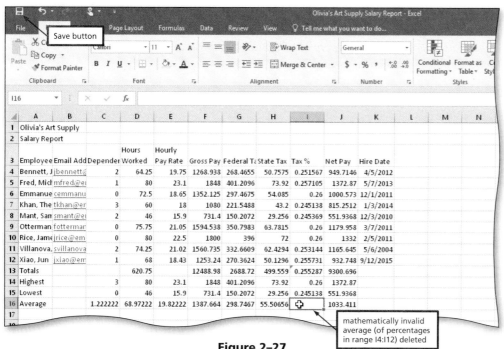

Figure 2–27

4 Save the workbook again on the same storage location with the same file name.

Q&A Why delete the formula in cell I16?
You deleted the average in cell I16 because averaging this type of percentage is mathematically invalid.

How can I be sure that the function arguments are correct for the cells in range D14:J16?
Remember that Excel adjusts the cell references in the copied functions so that each function refers to the range of numbers above it in the same column. Review the functions in rows 14 through 16 by clicking on individual cells and examining the function as it appears in the formula bar. You should see that the functions in each column reference the appropriate ranges.

Other Ways

1. Select source area, click Copy button (Home tab | Clipboard group), select destination area, click Paste button (Home tab | Clipboard group)

2. Right-click source area, click Copy on shortcut menu; right-click destination area, click Paste icon on shortcut menu

3. Select source area and then point to border of range; while holding down CTRL, drag source area to destination area

4. Select source area, press CTRL+C, select destination area, press CTRL+V

Break Point: If you wish to take a break, this is a good place to do so. You can exit Excel now. To resume at a later time, run Excel, open the file called Olivia's Art Supply Salary Report, and continue following the steps from this location forward.

Verifying Formulas Using Range Finder

One of the more common mistakes made with Excel is to include an incorrect cell reference in a formula. An easy way to verify that a formula references the cells you want it to reference is to use Range Finder. **Range Finder** checks which cells are referenced in the formula assigned to the active cell.

To use Range Finder to verify that a formula contains the intended cell references, double-click the cell with the formula you want to check. Excel responds by highlighting the cells referenced in the formula so that you can verify that the cell references are correct.

To Verify a Formula Using Range Finder

1 ENTER FORMULAS | 2 ENTER FUNCTIONS | **3 VERIFY FORMULAS**
4 FORMAT WORKSHEET | 5 CHECK SPELLING | 6 PRINT WORKSHEET

Why? *Range Finder allows you to correct mistakes by making immediate changes to the cells referenced in a formula.* The following steps use Range Finder to check the formula in cell I4.

1
• Double-click cell I4 to activate Range Finder (Figure 2–28).

2
• Press the ESC key to quit Range Finder and then click anywhere in the worksheet, such as cell A18, to deselect the current cell.

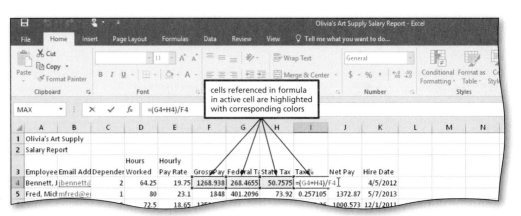

Figure 2–28

Formatting the Worksheet

Although the worksheet contains the appropriate data, formulas, and functions, the text and numbers need to be formatted to improve their appearance and readability.

In Module 1, cell styles were used to format much of the worksheet. This section describes how to change the unformatted worksheet in Figure 2–29a to the formatted worksheet in Figure 2–29b using a theme and other commands on the ribbon. A **theme** formats a worksheet by applying a collection of fonts, font styles, colors, and effects to give it a consistent appearance.

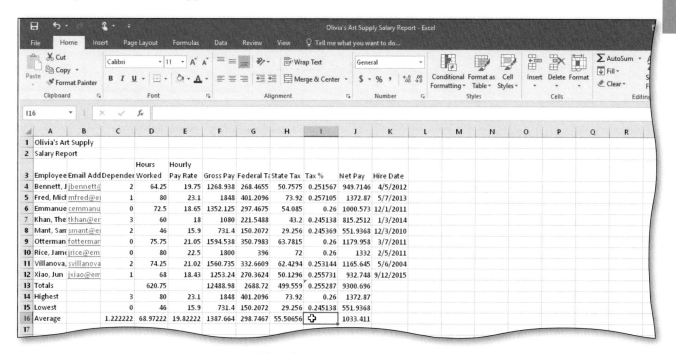

(a) Unformatted Worksheet

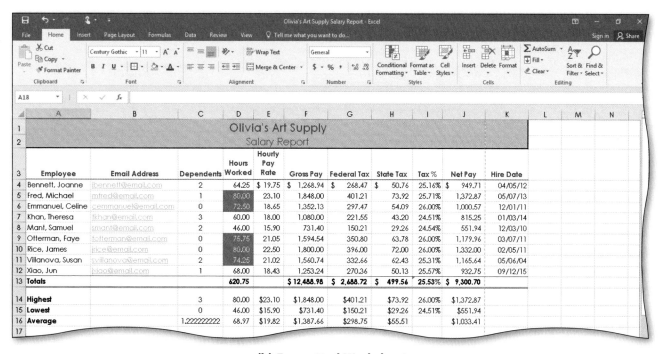

(b) Formatted Worksheet

Figure 2–29

To Change the Workbook Theme

Why? *A company or department may choose a specific theme as their standard theme so that all of their documents have a similar appearance. Similarly, you may want to have a theme that sets your work apart from the work of others. Other Office programs, such as Word and PowerPoint, include the same themes so that all of your Microsoft Office documents can share a common look.* The following steps change the workbook theme to the Ion theme.

1

- Click Page Layout to display the Page Layout tab.

- Click the Themes button (Page Layout tab | Themes group) to display the Themes gallery (Figure 2–30).

Experiment

- Point to several themes in the Themes gallery to preview the themes.

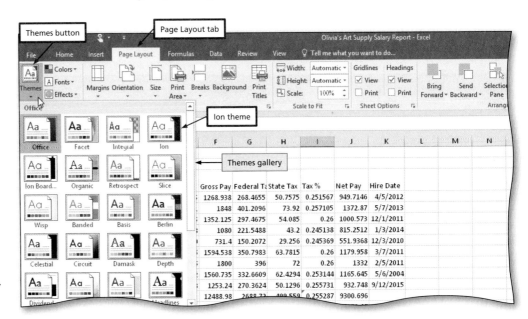

Figure 2–30

2

- Click Ion in the Themes gallery to change the workbook theme (Figure 2–31).

Q&A Why did the cells in the worksheet change?

Originally, the cells in the worksheet were formatted with the default font of the default Office theme. The Ion theme has a different default font than the Office theme, so when you changed the theme, the font changed. If you had modified the font for any cells, those cells would not have changed to the default font of the Ion theme.

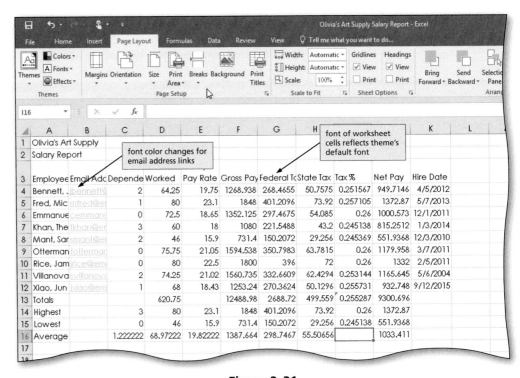

Figure 2–31

To Format the Worksheet Titles

The following steps merge and center the worksheet titles, apply the Title cells style to the worksheet titles, and decrease the font of the worksheet subtitle.

1 Display the Home tab.

2 Select the range to be merged, A1:K1 in this case, and then click the 'Merge & Center' button (Home tab | Alignment group) to merge and center the text in the selected range.

3 Select the range A2:K2 and then click the 'Merge & Center' button (Home tab | Alignment group) to merge and center the text.

4 Select the range to contain the Title cell style, in this case A1:A2, click the Cell Styles button (Home tab | Styles group) to display the Cell Styles gallery, and then click the Title cell style in the Cell Styles gallery to apply the Title cell style to the selected range.

5 Select cell A2 and then click the 'Decrease Font Size' button (Home tab | Font group) to decrease the font size of the selected cell to the next lower font size (Figure 2–32).

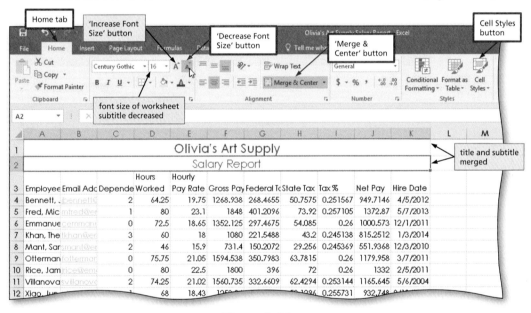

Figure 2–32

Q&A What happens when I click the 'Decrease Font Size' button?

When you click the 'Decrease Font Size' button, Excel assigns the next smaller font size in the Font Size gallery to the selected range. The 'Increase Font Size' button works in a similar manner, assigning the next larger font size in the Font Size gallery to the selected range.

CONSIDER THIS

Which colors work best when formatting your worksheet?

Knowing how people perceive colors can help you focus attention on parts of your worksheet. Warmer colors (red and orange) tend to reach toward the reader. Cooler colors (blue, green, and violet) tend to pull away from the reader.

To Change the Background Color and Apply a Box Border to the Worksheet Title and Subtitle

Why? *A background color and border can draw attention to the title of a worksheet.* The final formats assigned to the worksheet title and subtitle are the blue-gray background color and thick outside border. The following steps complete the formatting of the worksheet titles.

• Select the range A1:A2 and then click the Fill Color arrow (Home tab | Font group) to display the Fill Color gallery (Figure 2–33).

Experiment

• Point to a variety of colors in the Fill Color gallery to preview the selected colors in the range A1:A2.

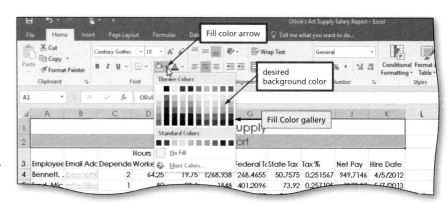

Figure 2–33

❷

• Click Blue-Gray, Accent 5, Lighter 60% (column 9, row 3) in the Theme Colors area to change the background color of the range of cells (Figure 2–34).

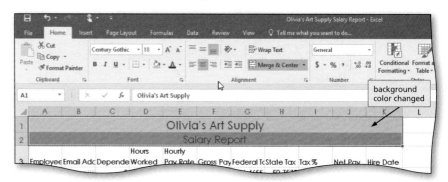

Figure 2–34

❸

• Click the Borders arrow (Home tab | Font group) to display the Borders gallery (Figure 2–35).

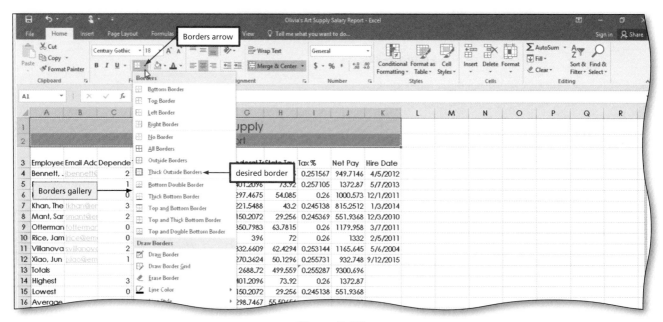

Figure 2–35

4

- Click 'Thick Outside Borders' in the Borders gallery to create a thick outside border around the selected range.

- Click anywhere in the worksheet, such as cell A18, to deselect the current range (Figure 2–36).

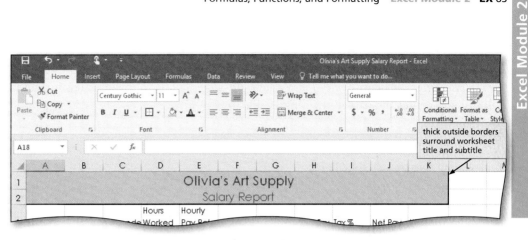

Figure 2–36

Other Ways

1. Click Font Settings Dialog Box Launcher (Home tab | Font group), click Fill tab (Format Cells dialog box), click desired fill, click OK button

2. Right-click range, click Format Cells on shortcut menu, click Fill tab (Format Cells dialog box), click desired fill, click OK button

3. Press CTRL+1, click Fill tab (Format Cells dialog box), click desired fill, click OK button

To Apply a Cell Style to the Column Headings and Format the Total Rows

As shown in Figure 2–29b, the column titles (row 3) should have the Heading 3 cell style and the totals row (row 13) should have the Total cell style. The headings in the range A14:A16 should be bold. The following steps assign these styles and formats to row 3, row 13, and the range A14:A16.

1 Select the range to be formatted, cells A3:K3 in this case.

2 Use the Cell Styles gallery to apply the Heading 3 cell style to the range A3:K3.

3 Click the Center button (Home tab | Alignment group) to center the column headings.

4 Apply the Total cell style to the range A13:K13.

5 Bold the range A14:A16 (Figure 2–37).

BTW

Color Selection
Bright colors jump out of a dark background and are easiest to see. White or yellow text on a dark blue, green, purple, or black background is ideal for highlighting.

BTW

Background Colors
The most popular background color is blue. Research shows that the color blue is used most often because this color connotes serenity, reflection, and proficiency. Use color in spreadsheets to highlight data or to format worksheet elements such as titles. In most cases, colors should not be used for data presentation.

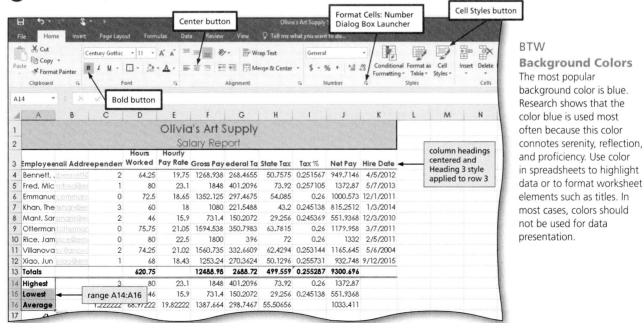

Figure 2–37

To Format Dates and Center Data in Cells

Why? *You may want to change the format of the dates to better suit your needs. In addition, numbers that are not used in calculations often are centered instead of right-aligned.* The following steps format the dates in the range K4:K12 and center the data in the range C4:C16.

- Select the range to contain the new date format, cells K4:K12 in this case.

- Click the Format Cells: Number Format Dialog Box Launcher (Home tab | Number group) (shown in Figure 2–37) to display the Format Cells dialog box.

- If necessary, click the Number tab (Format Cells dialog box), click Date in the Category list, and then click 03/14/12 in the Type list to choose the format for the selected range (Figure 2–38).

- Click the OK button (Format Cells dialog box) to format the dates in the current column using the selected date format style.

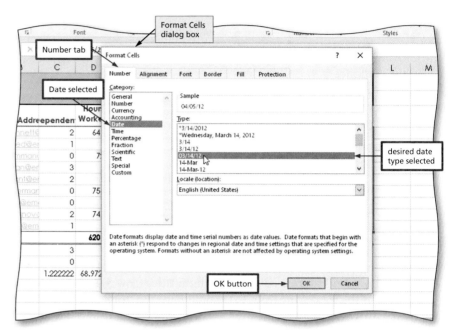

Figure 2–38

- Select the range C4:C16 and then click the Center button (Home tab | Alignment group) to center the data in the selected range.

- Select cell E4 to deselect the selected range (Figure 2–39).

Q&A How can I format an entire column at once?
Instead of selecting the range C4:C16 in Step 3, you could have clicked the column C heading immediately above cell C1, and then clicked the Center button (Home tab | Alignment group). In this case, all cells in column C down to the last cell in the worksheet would have been formatted to use center alignment. This same procedure could have been used to format the dates in column K.

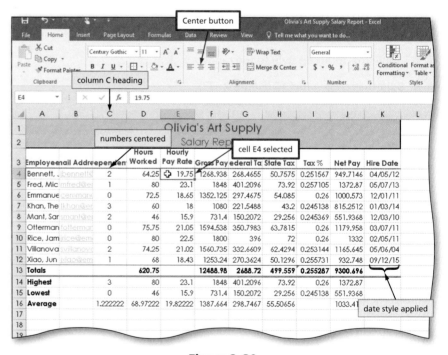

Figure 2–39

Other Ways

1. Right-click range, click Format Cells on shortcut menu, click Number tab (Format Cells dialog box), click desired number format, click OK button

2. Press CTRL+1, click Number tab (Format Cells dialog box), click desired number format, click OK button

To Apply an Accounting Number Format and Comma Style Format Using the Ribbon

As shown in Figure 2–29b, the worksheet is formatted to resemble an accounting report. In columns E through H and J, the numbers in the first row (row 4), the totals row (row 13), and the rows below the totals (rows 14 through 16) have dollar signs, while the remaining numbers (rows 5 through 12) in columns E through H and column J do not. The following steps assign formats using the 'Accounting Number Format' button and the Comma Style button. **Why?** *This gives the worksheet a more professional look.*

1 Select the range to contain the accounting number format, cells E4:H4 in this case.

2 While holding down the CTRL key, select cell J4, the range F13:H13, and cell J13 to select the nonadjacent ranges and cells.

3 Click the 'Accounting Number Format' button (Home tab | Number group) to apply the accounting number format with fixed dollar signs to the selected nonadjacent ranges.

Q&A What is the effect of applying the accounting number format?

The 'Accounting Number Format' button assigns a fixed dollar sign to the numbers in the ranges and rounds the figure to the nearest 100th. A fixed dollar sign is one that appears to the far left of the cell, with multiple spaces between it and the first digit in the cell.

4 Select the ranges to contain the comma style format, cells E5:H12 and J5:J12 in this case.

5 Click the Comma Style button (Home tab | Number group) to assign the comma style format to the selected ranges.

6 Select the range D4:D16 and then click the Comma Style button (Home tab | Number group) to assign the comma style format to the selected range (Figure 2–40).

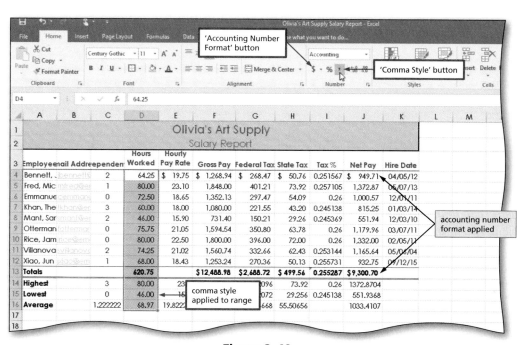

Figure 2–40

To Apply a Currency Style Format with a Floating Dollar Sign Using the Format Cells Dialog Box

Why? *The Currency format places dollar signs immediately to the left of the number (known as floating dollar signs, as they change position depending on the number of digits in the cell) and displays a zero for cells that have a value of zero.* The following steps use the Format Cells dialog box to apply the currency style format with a floating dollar sign to the numbers in the ranges E14:H16 and J14:J16.

- Select the ranges (E14:H16 and J14:J16) and then click the Number Format Dialog Box Launcher (Home tab | Number group) to display the Format Cells dialog box.

- If necessary, click the Number tab to display the Number sheet (Format Cells dialog box).

- Click Currency in the Category list to select the necessary number format category and then click the third style ($1,234.10) in the Negative numbers list to select the desired currency format for negative numbers (Figure 2–41).

Q&A How do I decide which number format to use?
Excel offers many ways to format numbers. Once you select a number category, you can select the number of decimal places, whether to include a dollar sign (or a symbol of another currency), and how negative numbers should appear. Selecting the appropriate negative numbers format is important, because some formats add a space to the right of the number in order to align numbers in the worksheet on the decimal points and some do not.

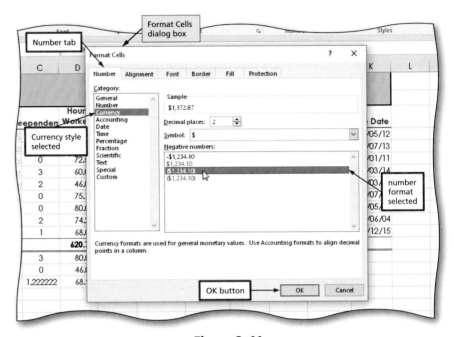

Figure 2–41

- Click the OK button (Format Cells dialog box) to assign the currency style format with a floating dollar sign to the selected ranges (Figure 2–42).

Q&A What is the difference between using the accounting number style and currency style?
When using the currency style, recall that a floating dollar sign always appears immediately to the left of the first digit. With the accounting number style, the fixed dollar sign always appears on the left side of the cell.

									268.47	$	50.7	
5	Fred, Mic	mfred@e	1	80.00	23.10	1,848.00	401.21	73.92	0.257105	1,372.87	05/07/13
6	Emmanue	cemman	0	72.50	18.65	1,352.13	297.47	54.09	0.26	1,000.57	12/01/11
7	Khan, The	tkhan@e	3	60.00	18.00	1,080.00	221.55	43.20	0.245138	815.25	01/03/14
8	Mant, Sar	smant@e	2	46.00	15.90	731.40	150.21	29.26	0.245369	551.94	12/03/10
9	Otterman	fotterma	0	75.75	21.05	1,594.54	350.80	63.78	0.26	1,179.96	03/07/11
10	Rice, Jam	jrice@em	0	80.00	22.50	1,800.00	396.00	72.00	0.26	1,332.00	02/05/11
11	Villanova	svillanova	2	74.25	21.02	1,560.74	332.66	62.43	0.253144	1,165.64	05/06/04
12	Xiao, Jun	jxiao@em	1	68.00	18.43	1,253.24	270.36	50.13	0.255731	932.75	09/12/15
13	**Totals**			**620.75**			**$12,488.98**	**$2,688.72**	**$ 499.56**	0.255287	**$9,300.70**
14	**Highest**		3	80.00	$23.10	$1,848.00	$401.21	$73.92	0.26	$1,372.87
15	**Lowest**		0	46.00	$15.90	$731.40	$150.21	$29.26	0.245138	$551.94
16	**Average**		1.222222	68.97	$19.82	$1,387.66	$298.75	$55.51		$1,033.41
17										
18										
19										

Figure 2–42

Other Ways

1. Press CTRL+1, click Number tab (Format Cells dialog box), click Currency in Category list, select format, click OK button

2. Press CTRL+SHIFT+DOLLAR SIGN ($)

To Apply a Percent Style Format and Use the Increase Decimal Button

The next step is to format the tax percentage in column I. *Why? Currently, Excel displays the numbers as decimal fractions when they should appear as percentages.* The following steps format the range I4:I15 to the percent style format with two decimal places.

- Select the range to format, cells I4:I15 in this case.

- Click the Percent Style button (Home tab | Number group) to display the numbers in the selected range as a rounded whole percent.

Q&A

What is the result of clicking the Percent Style button?

The Percent Style button instructs Excel to display a value as a percentage, which is determined by multiplying the cell entry by 100, rounding the result to the nearest percentage, and adding a percent sign. For example, when cell I4 is formatted using the Percent Style buttons, Excel displays the actual value 0.251567 as 25%.

- Click the Increase Decimal button (Home tab | Number group) two times to display the numbers in the selected range with two decimal places (Figure 2–43).

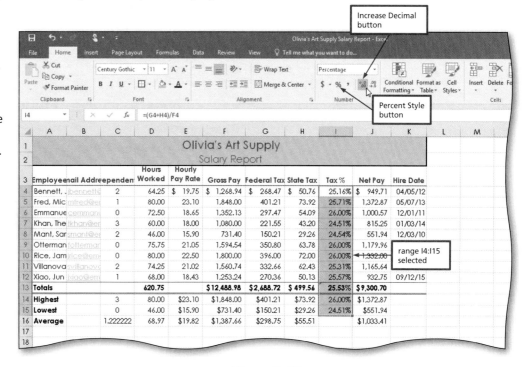

Figure 2–43

Other Ways

1. Right-click selected range, click Format Cells on shortcut menu, click Number tab (Format Cells dialog box), click Percentage in Category list, select format, click OK button

2. Press CTRL+1, click Number tab (Format Cells dialog box), click Percentage in Category list, select format, click OK button

3. Press CTRL+SHIFT+PERCENT SIGN (%)

Conditional Formatting

Conditional formatting offers you the ability to automatically change how a cell appears — the font, font color, background fill, and other options — based on the value in the cell. Excel offers a variety of commonly used conditional formatting rules, along with the ability to create your own custom rules and formatting. The next step is to emphasize the values greater than 72 in column D by formatting them to appear with a blue background and white font color (Figure 2–44).

BTW

Conditional Formatting

You can assign any format to a cell, a range of cells, a worksheet, or an entire workbook conditionally. If the value of the cell changes and no longer meets the specified condition, Excel suppresses the conditional formatting.

To Apply Conditional Formatting

The following steps assign conditional formatting to the range D4:D12. *Why? After formatting, any cell with a value greater than 72 in column D will appear with a blue background and a white font.*

- Select the range D4:D12.

- Click the Conditional Formatting button (Home tab | Styles group) to display the Conditional Formatting menu (Figure 2–44).

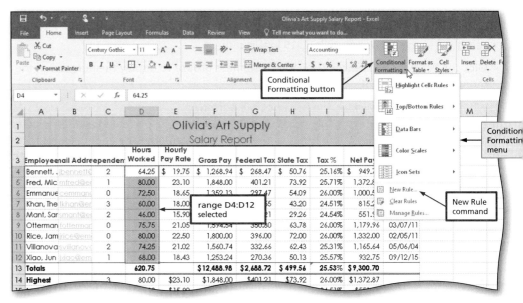

Figure 2–44

- Click New Rule on the Conditional Formatting menu to display the New Formatting Rule dialog box.

- Click 'Format only cells that contain' in the Select a Rule Type area (New Formatting Rule dialog box) to change the Edit the Rule Description area.

- In the Edit the Rule Description area, click the arrow in the relational operator box (second box) to display a list of relational operators, and then select greater than to select the desired operator.

- Select the rightmost box, and then type 72 to enter the value of the rule description (Figure 2–45).

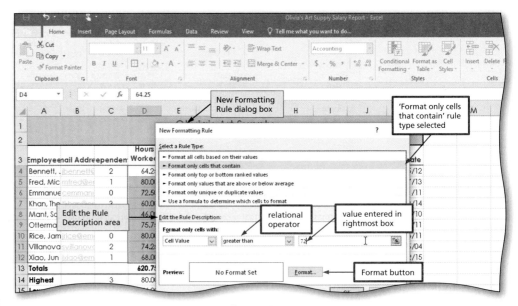

Figure 2–45

Q&A

What do the changes in the Edit the Rule Description area indicate?

The Edit the Rule Description area allows you to view and edit the rules for the conditional format. In this case, the rule indicates that Excel should format only those cells with cell values greater than 72.

❸

- Click the Format button (New Formatting Rule dialog box) to display the Format Cells dialog box.

- If necessary, click the Font tab (Format Cells dialog box) to display the Font sheet. Click the Color arrow to display the Color gallery and then click White, Background 1 (column 1, row 1) in the Color gallery to select the font color (Figure 2–46).

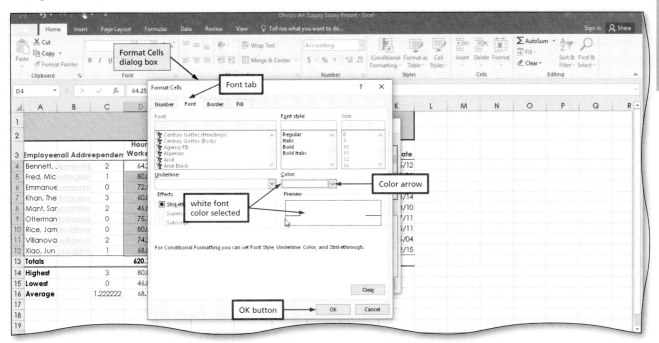

Figure 2–46

❹

- Click the Fill tab (Format Cells dialog box) to display the Fill sheet and then click the blue color in column 9, row 1 to select the background color (Figure 2–47).

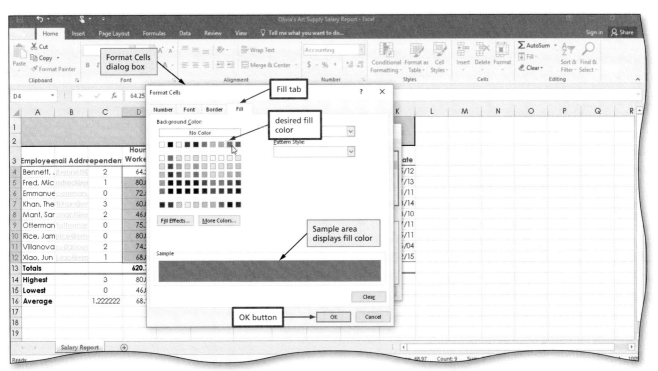

Figure 2–47

• Click the OK button (Format Cells dialog box) to close the Format Cells dialog box and display the New Formatting Rule dialog box with the desired font and background colors displayed in the Preview area (Figure 2–48).

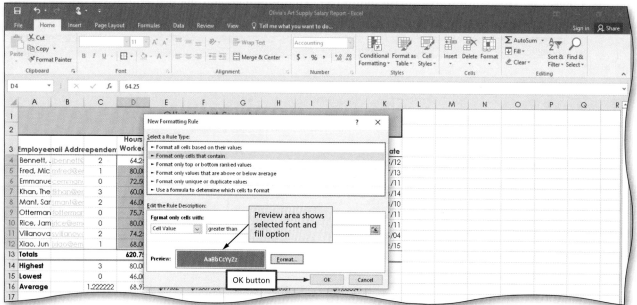

Figure 2–48

• Click the OK button (New Formatting Rule dialog box) to assign the conditional format to the selected range.

• Click anywhere in the worksheet, such as cell A18, to deselect the current range (Figure 2–49).

Q&A What should I do if I make a mistake setting up a rule?

If after you have applied the conditional formatting you realize you made a mistake when creating a rule, select the cell(s) with the rule you want to edit, click the Conditional Formatting button (Home tab | Styles group), select the rule you want to edit, and then click either the Edit Rule button (to edit the selected rule) or the Delete Rule button (to delete the selected rule).

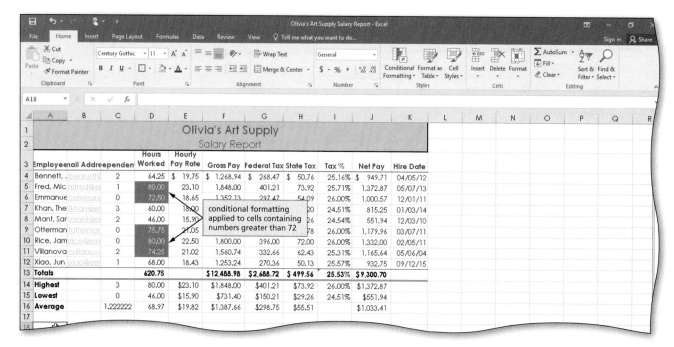

Figure 2–49

Conditional Formatting Operators

As shown in the New Formatting Rule dialog box, when the selected rule type is "Format only the cells that contain," the second text box in the Edit the Rule Description area allows you to select a relational operator, such as greater than, to use in the condition. The eight different relational operators from which you can choose for conditional formatting are summarized in Table 2–5.

Table 2–5 Summary of Conditional Formatting Relational Operators	
Relational Operator	**Formatting will be applied if...**
between	cell value is between two numbers
not between	cell value is not between two numbers
equal to	cell value is equal to a number
not equal to	cell value is not equal to a number
greater than	cell value is greater than a number
less than	cell value is less than a number
greater than or equal to	cell value is greater than or equal to a number
less than or equal to	cell value is less than or equal to a number

BTW

Excel Help
At any time while using Excel, you can find answers to questions and display information about various topics through Excel Help. Used properly, this form of assistance can increase your productivity and reduce your frustrations by minimizing the time you spend learning how to use Excel. For instructions about Excel Help and exercises that will help you gain confidence in using it, read the Office and Windows module at the beginning of this book.

Changing Column Width and Row Height

You can change the width of the columns or height of the rows at any time to make the worksheet easier to read or to ensure that an entry fits properly in a cell. By default, all of the columns in a blank worksheet have a width of 8.43 characters, or 64 pixels. This value may change depending on the theme applied to the workbook. For example, when the Ion theme was applied to the workbook in this module, the default width of the columns changed to 8.38 characters. A **character** is defined as a letter, number, symbol, or punctuation mark. An average of 8.43 characters in 11-point Calibri font (the default font used by Excel) will fit in a cell.

The default row height in a blank worksheet is 15 points (or 20 pixels), which easily fits the 11-point default font. Recall from Module 1 that a point is equal to 1/72 of an inch. Thus, 15 points is equal to about 1/5 of an inch.

Another measure of the height and width of cells is pixels. A **pixel**, which is short for picture element, is a dot on the screen that contains a color. The size of the dot is based on your screen's resolution. At the resolution of 1366 × 768 used in this book, 1366 pixels appear across the screen and 768 pixels appear down the screen for a total of 1,049,088 pixels. It is these 1,049,088 pixels that form the font and other items you see on the screen.

BTW

Hidden Rows and Columns
For some people, trying to unhide a range of columns using the mouse can be frustrating. An alternative is to use the keyboard: select the columns to the right and left of the hidden columns and then press CTRL+SHIFT+) (RIGHT PARENTHESIS). To use the keyboard to hide a range of columns, press CTRL+0 (zero). You also can use the keyboard to unhide a range of rows by selecting the rows immediately above and below the hidden rows and then pressing CTRL+SHIFT+ ((LEFT PARENTHESIS). To use the keyboard to hide a range of rows, press CTRL+9.

To Change Column Width

1 ENTER FORMULAS | 2 ENTER FUNCTIONS | 3 VERIFY FORMULAS
4 FORMAT WORKSHEET | 5 CHECK SPELLING | 6 PRINT WORKSHEET

When changing the column width, you can set the width manually or you can instruct Excel to size the column to best fit. **Best fit** means that the width of the column will be increased or decreased so that the widest entry will fit in the column. *Why? Sometimes, you may prefer more or less white space in a column than best fit provides. To change the white space, Excel allows you to change column widths manually.*

When the format you assign to a cell causes the entry to exceed the width of a column, Excel changes the column width to best fit. If you do not assign a format to a cell or cells in a column, the column width will remain 8.43 characters. Recall from Module 1 that to set a column width to best fit, double-click the right boundary of the column heading above row 1. The following steps change the column widths.

1

- Drag through column headings A, B, and C above row 1 to select the columns.

- Point to the boundary on the right side of column heading C to cause the pointer to become a split double arrow (Figure 2–50).

Q&A What if I want to make a large change to the column width?
If you want to increase or decrease column width significantly, you can right-click a column heading and then use the Column Width command on the shortcut menu to change the column's width. To use this command, however, you must select one or more entire columns.

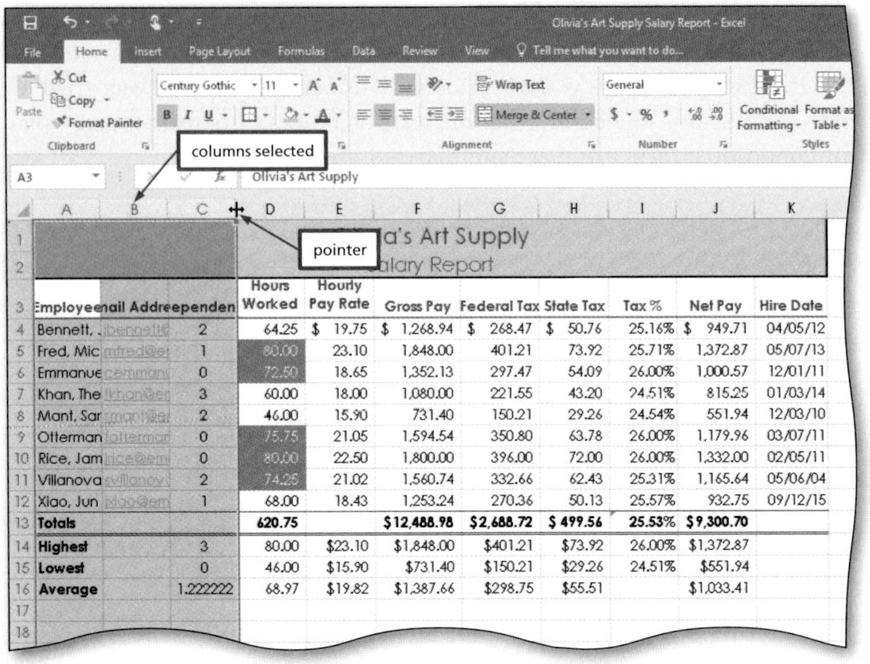

Figure 2–50

2

- Double-click the right boundary of column heading C to change the width of the selected columns to best fit.

- Point to the right boundary of the column H heading above row 1.

- When the pointer changes to a split double arrow, drag until the ScreenTip indicates Width: 10.25 (87 pixels). Do not release the mouse button (Figure 2–51).

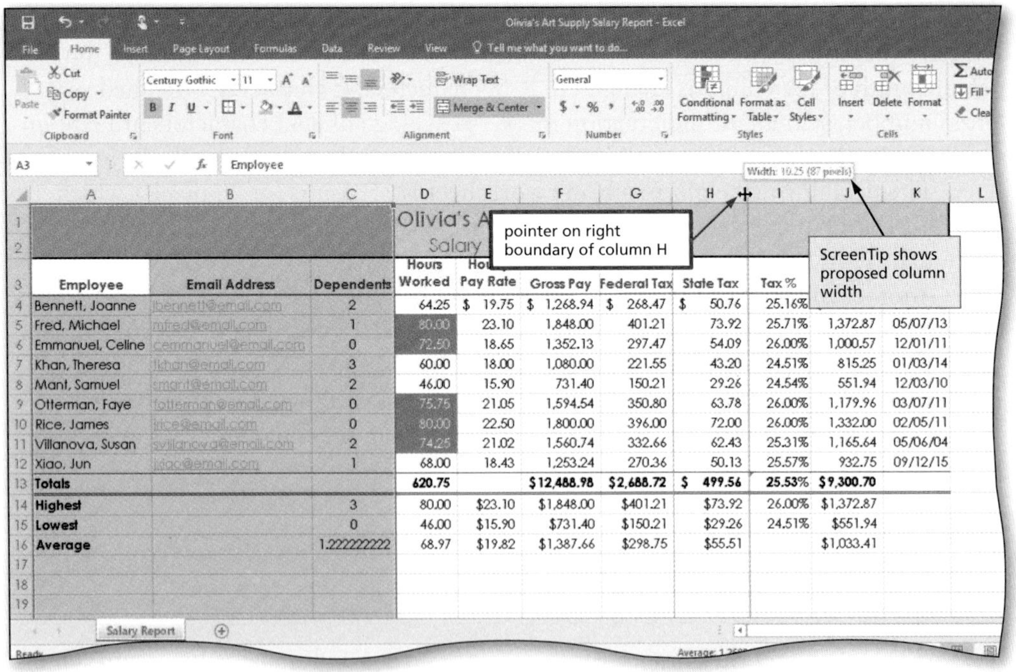

Q&A What happens if I change the column width to zero (0)?
If you decrease the column width to 0, the column is hidden. Hiding cells is a technique you can use to hide data that might not be relevant to a particular report. To instruct Excel to display a hidden column, position the mouse pointer to the right of the column heading boundary where the hidden column is located and then drag to the right.

Figure 2–51

3

- Release the mouse button to change the column width.

- Click the column D heading above row 1 to select the column.

- While holding down the CTRL key, click the column E heading and then the column I heading above row 1 so that nonadjacent columns are selected.

- Point to the boundary on the right side of the column I heading above row 1.

- Drag until the ScreenTip indicates Width: 7.50 (65 pixels). Do not release the mouse button (Figure 2–52).

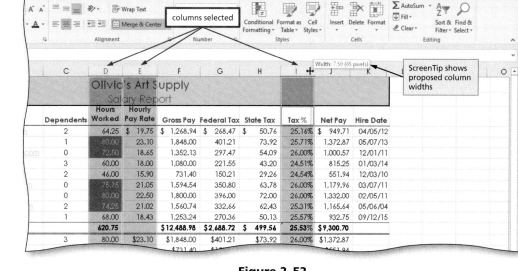

Figure 2–52

4

- Release the mouse button to change the column widths.

- Click the column F heading and drag to select the column G heading.

- While holding down the CTRL key, click the column J heading and drag to select the column K heading above row 1 so that nonadjacent columns are selected.

- Drag the right boundary of column G until the ScreenTip indicates Width: 11.00 (93 pixels). Release the mouse button to change the column widths.

- Click anywhere in the worksheet, such as cell A18, to deselect the columns (Figure 2–53).

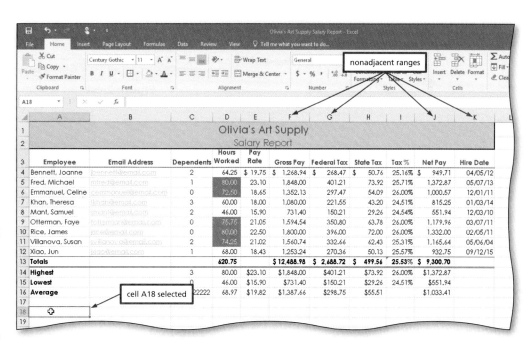

Figure 2–53

Other Ways

1. Click column heading or drag through multiple column headings, right-click selected column, click Column Width on shortcut menu, enter desired column width, click OK button

To Change Row Height

Why? *You also can increase or decrease the height of a row manually to improve the appearance of the worksheet.* When you increase the font size of a cell entry, such as the title in cell A1, Excel increases the row height to best fit so that it can display the characters properly. Recall that Excel did this earlier when multiple lines were entered in a cell in row 3, and when the cell style of the worksheet title and subtitle was changed. The following steps improve the appearance of the worksheet by increasing the height of row 3 to 48.00 points and increasing the height of row 14 to 27.00 points.

- Point to the boundary below row heading 3 until the pointer becomes a split double arrow.

- Drag down until the ScreenTip indicates Height: 48.00 (64 pixels). Do not release the mouse button (Figure 2–54).

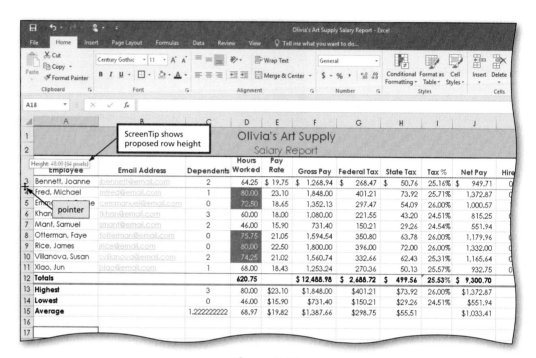

Figure 2–54

- Release the mouse button to change the row height.

- Point to the boundary below row heading 14 until the pointer becomes a split double arrow and then drag downward until the ScreenTip indicates Height: 27.00 (36 pixels). Do not release the mouse button (Figure 2–55).

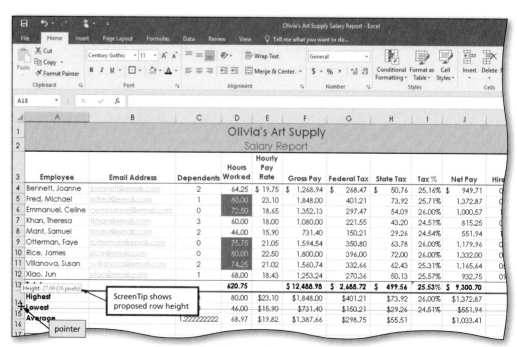

Figure 2–55

3

- Release the mouse button to change the row height.
- Click anywhere in the worksheet, such as cell A18, to deselect the current cell (Figure 2–56).

Q&A

Can I hide a row?

Yes. As with column widths, when you decrease the row height to 0, the row is hidden. To instruct Excel to display a hidden row, position the pointer just below the row heading boundary where the row is hidden and then drag downward. To set a row height to best fit, double-click the bottom boundary of the row heading. You also can hide and unhide rows by right-clicking the row or column heading and selecting the option to hide or unhide the cells.

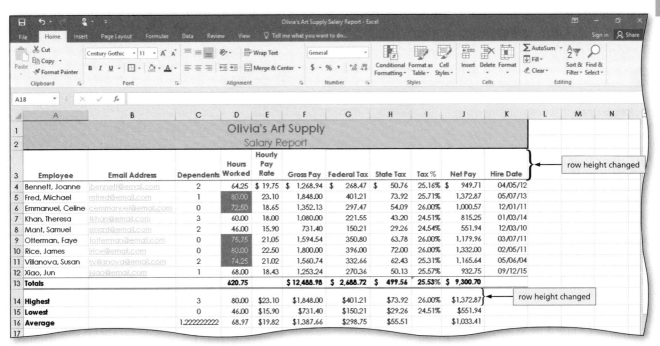

Figure 2–56

Other Ways

1. Right-click row heading or drag through multiple row headings, right-click selected heading, click Row Height on shortcut menu, enter desired row height, click OK button

Break Point: If you wish to take a break, this is a good place to do so. Be sure to save the Olivia's Art Supply Salary Report file again and then you can exit Excel. To resume at a later time, run Excel, open the file called Olivia's Art Supply Salary Report, and continue following the steps from this location forward.

Checking Spelling

Excel includes a **spelling checker** you can use to check a worksheet for spelling errors. The spelling checker looks for spelling errors by comparing words on the worksheet against words contained in its standard dictionary. If you often use specialized terms that are not in the standard dictionary, you may want to add them to a custom dictionary using the Spelling dialog box. When the spelling checker finds a word that is not in either dictionary, it displays the word in the Spelling dialog box. You then can correct it if it is misspelled.

BTW

Spell Checking

While Excel's spell checker is a valuable tool, it is not infallible. You should proofread your workbook carefully by pointing to each word and saying it aloud as you point to it. Be mindful of misused words such as its and it's, through and though, and to and too. Nothing undermines a good impression more than a professional looking report with misspelled words.

CONSIDER THIS

Does the spelling checker catch all spelling mistakes?

While Excel's spelling checker is a valuable tool, it is not infallible. You should proofread your workbook carefully by pointing to each word and saying it aloud as you point to it. Be mindful of misused words such as its and it's, through and though, your and you're, and to and too. Nothing undermines a good impression more than a professional report with misspelled words.

To Check Spelling on the Worksheet

1 ENTER FORMULAS | 2 ENTER FUNCTIONS | 3 VERIFY FORMULAS
4 FORMAT WORKSHEET | 5 CHECK SPELLING | 6 PRINT WORKSHEET

Why? *Everything in a worksheet should be checked to make sure there are no spelling errors.* To illustrate how Excel responds to a misspelled word, the following steps purposely misspell the word, Employee, in cell A3 as the word, Empolyee, as shown in Figure 2–57.

1

- Click cell A3 and then type **Empolyee** to misspell the word, Employee.

- Select cell A2 so that the spelling checker begins checking at the selected cell.

- Click Review on the ribbon to display the Review tab.

- Click the Spelling button (Review tab | Proofing group) to use the spelling checker to display the misspelled word in the Spelling dialog box (Figure 2–57).

Q&A What happens when the spelling checker finds a misspelled word?
When the spelling checker identifies that a cell contains a word not in its standard or custom dictionary, it selects that cell as the active cell and displays the Spelling dialog box. The Spelling dialog box displays the word that was not found in the dictionary and offers a list of suggested corrections (Figure 2–58).

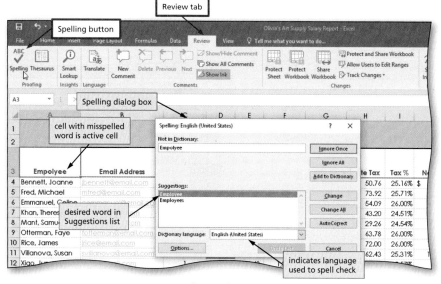

Figure 2–57

2

- Verify that the word highlighted in the Suggestion area is correct.

- Click the Change button (Spelling dialog box) to change the misspelled word to the correct word (Figure 2–58).

- Click the Close button to close the Spelling dialog box.

- If a Microsoft Excel dialog box is displayed, click the OK button.

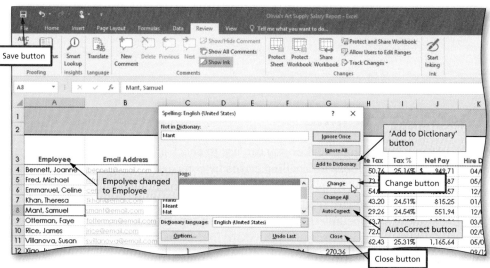

Figure 2–58

❸

- Click anywhere in the worksheet, such as cell A18, to deselect the current cell.

- Display the Home tab.

- Save the workbook again on the same storage location with the same file name.

Q&A | What other actions can I take in the Spelling dialog box?
If one of the words in the Suggestions list is correct, select it and then click the Change button. If none of the suggested words are correct, type the correct word in the 'Not in Dictionary' text box and then click the Change button. To change the word throughout the worksheet, click the Change All button instead of the Change button. To skip correcting the word, click the Ignore Once button. To have Excel ignore the word for the remainder of the worksheet, click the Ignore All button.

Other Ways

1. Press F7

Additional Spelling Checker Considerations

Consider these additional guidelines when using the spelling checker:

- To check the spelling of the text in a single cell, double-click the cell to make the formula bar active and then click the Spelling button (Review tab | Proofing group).

- If you select a single cell so that the formula bar is not active and then start the spelling checker, Excel checks the remainder of the worksheet, including notes and embedded charts.

- If you select a cell other than cell A1 before you start the spelling checker, Excel will display a dialog box when the spelling checker reaches the end of the worksheet, asking if you want to continue checking at the beginning.

- If you select a range of cells before starting the spelling checker, Excel checks the spelling of the words only in the selected range.

- To check the spelling of all the sheets in a workbook, right-click any sheet tab, click 'Select All Sheets' on the sheet tab shortcut menu, and then start the spelling checker.

- To add words to the dictionary, such as your last name, click the 'Add to Dictionary' button in the Spelling dialog box (shown in Figure 2–58) when Excel flags the word as not being in the dictionary.

- Click the AutoCorrect button (shown in Figure 2–58) to add the misspelled word and the correct version of the word to the AutoCorrect list. For example, suppose that you misspell the word, do, as the word, dox. When the spelling checker displays the Spelling dialog box with the correct word, do, in the Suggestions list, click the AutoCorrect button. Then, anytime in the future that you type the word, dox, Excel will change it to the word, do.

Printing the Worksheet

Excel allows for a great deal of customization in how a worksheet appears when printed. For example, the margins on the page can be adjusted. A header or footer can be added to each printed page as well. A **header** is text and graphics that print at the

BTW
Error Checking
Always take the time to check the formulas of a worksheet before submitting it to your supervisor. You can check formulas by clicking the Error Checking button (Formulas tab | Formula Auditing group). You also should test the formulas by employing data that tests the limits of formulas. Experienced spreadsheet specialists spend as much time testing a workbook as they do creating it, and they do so before placing the workbook into production.

BTW
Distributing a Workbook
Instead of printing and distributing a hard copy of a workbook, you can distribute the workbook electronically. Options include sending the workbook via email; posting it on cloud storage (such as OneDrive) and sharing the file with others; posting it on social media, a blog, or other website; and sharing a link associated with an online location of the workbook. You also can create and share a PDF or XPS image of the workbook, so that users can view the file in Acrobat Reader or XPS Viewer instead of in Excel.

top of each page. Similarly, a **footer** is text and graphics that print at the bottom of each page. Excel also has the capability to alter the worksheet in Page Layout view. Page Layout view allows you to create or modify a worksheet while viewing how it will look in printed format. The default view that you have worked in up until this point in the book is called Normal view.

To Change the Worksheet's Margins, Header, and Orientation in Page Layout View

1 ENTER FORMULAS | 2 ENTER FUNCTIONS | 3 VERIFY FORMULAS
4 FORMAT WORKSHEET | 5 CHECK SPELLING | 6 PRINT WORKSHEET

The following steps change to Page Layout view, narrow the margins of the worksheet, change the header of the worksheet, and set the orientation of the worksheet to landscape. *Why? You may want the printed worksheet to fit on one page. You can do that by reducing the page margins and changing the page orientation to fit wider printouts across a sheet of paper. You can use the header to identify the content on each page.* **Margins** are those portions of a printed page outside the main body of the printed document and always are blank when printed. The current worksheet is too wide for a single page and requires landscape orientation to fit on one page in a readable manner.

- Click the Page Layout button on the status bar to view the worksheet in Page Layout view (Figure 2–59).

Q&A What are the features of Page Layout view?

Page Layout view shows the worksheet divided into pages. A gray background separates each page. The white areas surrounding each page indicate the print margins. The top of each page includes a Header area, and the bottom of each page includes a Footer area. Page Layout view also includes rulers at the top and left margin of the page that assists you in placing objects on the page, such as charts and pictures.

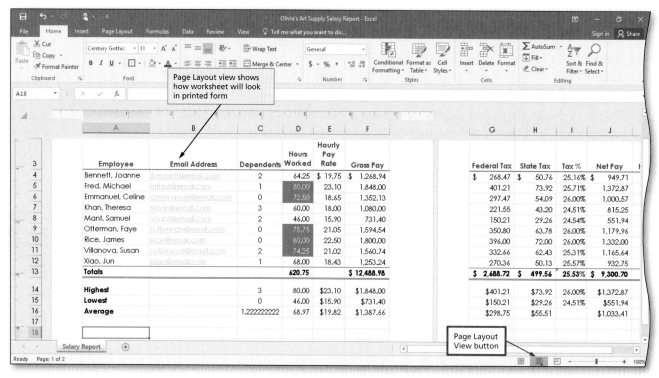

Figure 2–59

2

- Display the Page Layout tab.

- Click the Adjust Margins button (Page Layout tab | Page Setup group) to display the Margins gallery (Figure 2–60).

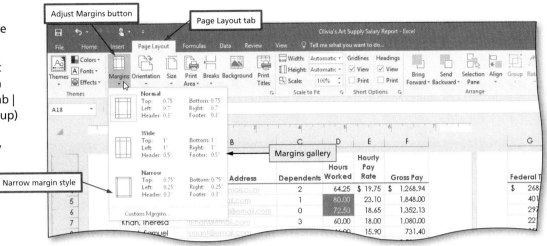

Figure 2–60

3

- Click Narrow in the Margins gallery to change the worksheet margins to the Narrow margin style.

- Click the center of the Header area above the worksheet title.

- Type `Jayne Smith` and then press the ENTER key. Type `Chief Financial Officer` to complete the worksheet header (Figure 2–61).

- If requested by your instructor, type your name instead of Jayne Smith.

- Select cell A6 to deselect the header.

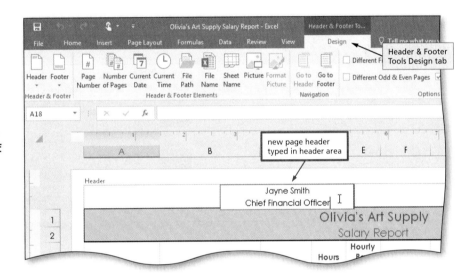

Figure 2–61

Q&A | What else can I place in a header?
You can add additional text, page number information, date and time information, the file path of the workbook, the file name of the workbook, the sheet name of the workbook, and pictures to a header.

4

- Display the Page Layout tab.

- Click the 'Change Page Orientation' button (Page Layout tab | Page Setup group) to display the Change Page Orientation gallery (Figure 2–62).

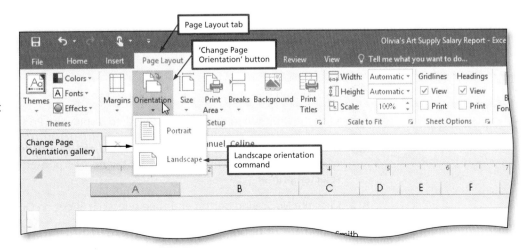

Figure 2–62

- Click Landscape in the Change Page Orientation gallery to change the worksheet's orientation to landscape (Figure 2–63).

Q&A Do I need to change the orientation every time I want to print the worksheet?

No. Once you change the orientation and save the workbook, Excel will save the orientation setting for that workbook until you change it. When you open a new workbook, Excel sets the orientation to portrait.

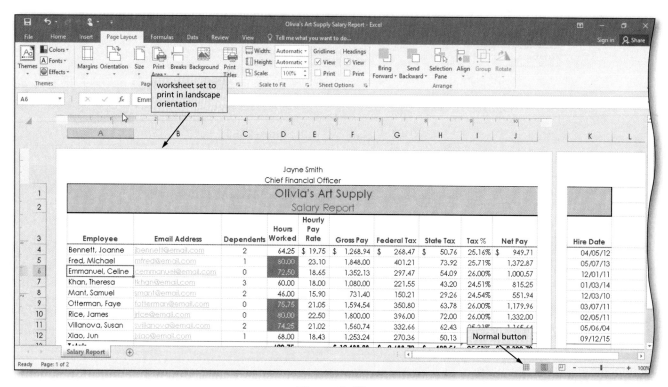

Figure 2–63

Other Ways

1. Click Page Setup Dialog Box Launcher (Page Layout tab | Page Setup group), click Page tab (Page Setup dialog box), click Portrait or Landscape, click OK button

---

To Print a Worksheet

Excel provides multiple options for printing a worksheet. In the following sections, you first print the worksheet and then print a section of the worksheet. The following steps print the worksheet.

1 Click File on the ribbon to open the Backstage view.

2 Click the Print tab in the Backstage view to display the Print gallery.

3 If necessary, click the Printer Status button in the Print gallery to display a list of available Printer options and then click the desired printer to change the currently selected printer.

4 Click the No Scaling button and then select 'Fit Sheet on One Page' to select it.

5 Click the Print button in the Print gallery to print the worksheet in landscape orientation on the currently selected printer.

6 When the printer stops, retrieve the hard copy (Figure 2–64).

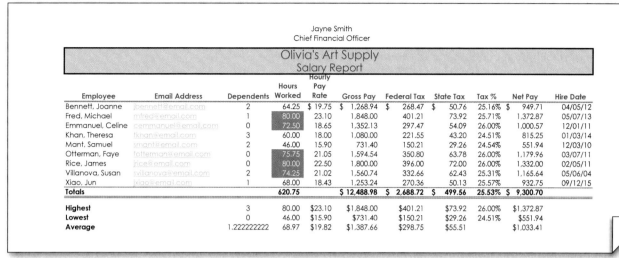

Figure 2–64

To Print a Section of the Worksheet

1 ENTER FORMULAS | 2 ENTER FUNCTIONS | 3 VERIFY FORMULAS
4 FORMAT WORKSHEET | 5 CHECK SPELLING | 6 PRINT WORKSHEET

You can print portions of the worksheet by selecting the range of cells to print and then clicking the Selection option button in the Print what area in the Print dialog box. *Why? To save paper, you only want to print the portion of the worksheet you need, instead of printing the entire worksheet.* The following steps print the range A3:F16.

- Select the range to print, cells A3:F16 in this case.
- Click File on the ribbon to open the Backstage view.
- Click the Print tab to display the Print gallery.
- Click 'Print Active Sheets' in the Settings area (Print tab | Print gallery) to display a list of options that determine what Excel should print (Figure 2–65).

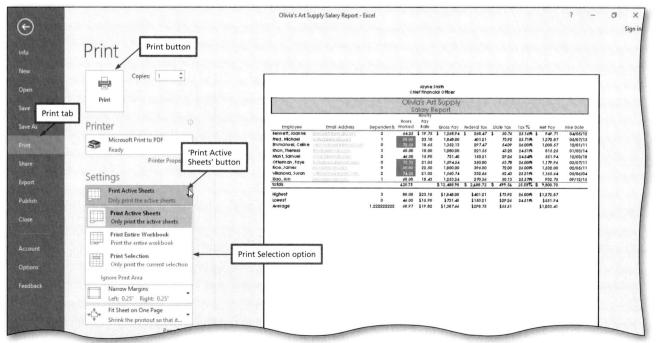

Figure 2–65

- Click Print Selection to instruct Excel to print only the selected range.

- Click the Print button in the Print gallery to print the selected range of the worksheet on the currently selected printer (Figure 2–66).

- Click the Normal button on the status bar to return to Normal view.

- Click anywhere in the worksheet, such as cell A18, to deselect the range A3:F16.

Q&A | What can I print?

Excel includes three options for selecting what to print (Figure 2–65). As shown in the previous steps, the Print Selection option instructs Excel to print the selected range. The 'Print Active Sheets' option instructs Excel to print the active worksheet (the worksheet currently on the screen) or selected worksheets. Finally, the 'Print Entire Workbook' option instructs Excel to print all of the worksheets in the workbook.

Jayne Smith
Chief Financial Officer

Employee	Email Address	Dependents	Hours Worked	Hourly Pay Rate	Gross Pay
Bennett, Joanne	jbennett@email.com	2	64.25	$ 19.75	$ 1,268.94
Fred, Michael	mfred@email.com	1	80.00	23.10	1,848.00
Emmanuel, Celine	cemmanuel@email.com	0	72.50	18.65	1,352.13
Khan, Theresa	tkhan@email.com	3	60.00	18.00	1,080.00
Mant, Samuel	smant@email.com	2	46.00	15.90	731.40
Otterman, Faye	fotterman@email.com	0	75.75	21.05	1,594.54
Rice, James	jrice@email.com	0	80.00	22.50	1,800.00
Villanova, Susan	svillanova@email.com	2	74.25	21.02	1,560.74
Xiao, Jun	jxiao@email.com	1	68.00	18.43	1,253.24
Totals			**620.75**		**$ 12,488.98**
Highest		3	80.00	$23.10	$1,848.00
Lowest		0	46.00	$15.90	$731.40
Average		1.222222222	68.97	$19.82	$1,387.66

Figure 2–66

Other Ways

1. Select range, click Print Area button (Page Layout tab | Page Setup group), click 'Set Print Area', click File tab to open Backstage view, click Print tab, click Print button

Displaying and Printing the Formulas Version of the Worksheet

BTW

Values versus Formulas

When completing class assignments, do not enter numbers in cells that require formulas. Most instructors will check both the values version and formulas version of your worksheets. The formulas version verifies that you entered formulas, rather than numbers, in formula-based cells.

Thus far, you have been working with the values version of the worksheet, which shows the results of the formulas you have entered, rather than the actual formulas. Excel also can display and print the formulas version of the worksheet, which shows the actual formulas you have entered, rather than the resulting values.

The formulas version is useful for debugging a worksheet. **Debugging** is the process of finding and correcting errors in the worksheet. Viewing and printing the formulas version instead of the values version makes it easier to see any mistakes in the formulas.

When you change from the values version to the formulas version, Excel increases the width of the columns so that the formulas do not overflow into adjacent cells, which makes the formulas version of the worksheet significantly wider than the values version. To fit the wide printout on one page, you can use landscape orientation, which already has been selected for the workbook, and the Fit to option in the Page tab in the Page Setup dialog box.

To Display the Formulas in the Worksheet and Fit the Printout on One Page

The following steps change the view of the worksheet from the values version to the formulas version of the worksheet and then print the formulas version on one page. *Why? Printing the formulas in the worksheet can help you verify that your formulas are correct and that the worksheet displays the correct calculations.*

1

- Press CTRL+ACCENT MARK (`) to display the worksheet with formulas.
- Click the right horizontal scroll arrow until column K appears (Figure 2–67).

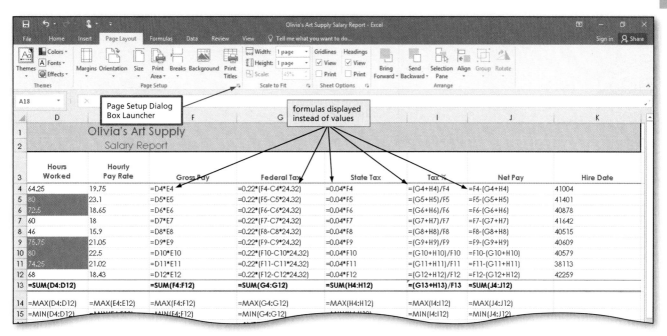

Figure 2–67

2

- Click the Page Setup Dialog Box Launcher (Page Layout tab | Page Setup group) to display the Page Setup dialog box (Figure 2–68).

- If necessary, click Landscape in the Orientation area in the Page tab to select it.

- If necessary, click the Fit to option button in the Scaling area to select it.

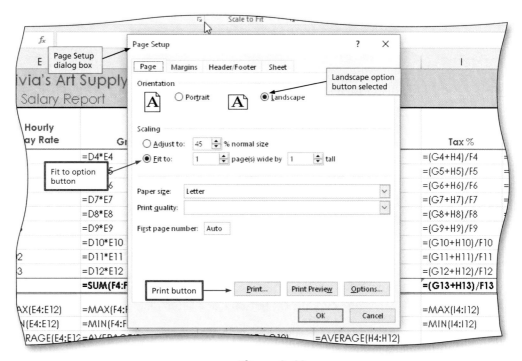

Figure 2–68

- Click the Print button (Page Setup dialog box) to open the Print tab in the Backstage view. In the Backstage view, select the Print Active Sheets option in the Settings area of the Print gallery (Figure 2–69).

- Click the Print button to print the worksheet.

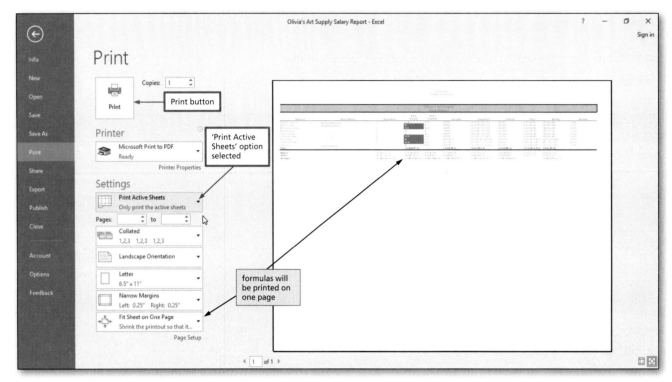

Figure 2–69

- After viewing and printing the formulas version, press CTRL+ACCENT MARK (`) to instruct Excel to display the values version.

- Click the left horizontal scroll arrow until column A appears.

To Change the Print Scaling Option Back to 100%

Depending on your printer, you may have to change the Print Scaling option back to 100% after using the Fit to option. Doing so will cause the worksheet to print at the default print scaling of 100%. The following steps reset the Print Scaling option so that future worksheets print at 100%, instead of being resized to print on one page.

1. If necessary, display the Page Layout tab and then click the Page Setup Dialog Box Launcher (Page Layout tab | Page Setup group) to display the Page Setup dialog box.

2. Click the Adjust to option button in the Scaling area to select the Adjust to setting.

3. If necessary, type 100 in the Adjust to box to adjust the print scaling to 100%.

4. Click the OK button (Page Setup dialog box) to set the print scaling to normal.

5 Display the Home tab.

6 Save the workbook again on the same storage location with the same file name.

7 If desired, sign out of your Microsoft account.

8 Exit Excel.

Q&A | What is the purpose of the Adjust to box in the Page Setup dialog box?
The Adjust to box allows you to specify the percentage of reduction or enlargement in the printout of a worksheet. The default percentage is 100%. When you click the Fit to option button, this percentage changes to the percentage required to fit the printout on one page.

Summary

In this module you have learned how to enter formulas, calculate an average, find the highest and lowest numbers in a range, verify formulas using Range Finder, add borders, align text, format numbers, change column widths and row heights, and add conditional formatting to a range of numbers. In addition, you learned how to use the spelling checker to identify misspelled words in a worksheet, print a section of a worksheet, and display and print the formulas version of the worksheet using the Fit to option.

What decisions will you need to make when creating workbooks in the future?

1. Determine the workbook structure.

   a) Determine the formulas and functions you will need for your workbook.

   b) Sketch a layout of your data and functions.

2. Create the worksheet.

   a) Enter the titles, subtitles, and headings.

   b) Enter the data, desired functions, and formulas.

3. Format the worksheet.

   a) Determine the theme for the worksheet.

   b) Format the titles, subtitles, and headings using styles.

   c) Format the totals, minimums, maximums, and averages.

   d) Format the numbers and text.

   e) Resize columns and rows.

CONSIDER THIS: PLAN AHEAD

Apply Your Knowledge

Reinforce the skills and apply the concepts you learned in this module.

Cost Analysis Worksheet

Note: To complete this assignment, you will be required to use the Data Files. Please contact your instructor for information about accessing the required files.

Instructions: Run Excel. Open the workbook Apply 2-1 Proximity Bus. You will enter and copy formulas and functions and apply formatting to the worksheet in order to analyze the costs associated with a bus company's fleet of vehicles, as shown in Figure 2–70.

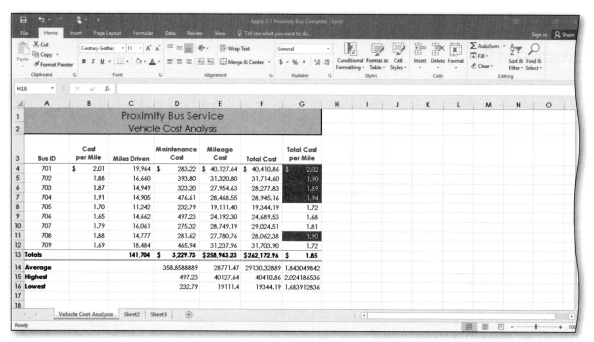

Figure 2–70

Perform the following tasks:

1. Use the following formulas in cells E4, F4, and G4:
   Mileage Cost (cell E4) = Cost per Mile * Miles Driven or = B4 * C4
   Total Cost (cell F4) = Maintenance Cost + Mileage Cost or = D4 + E4
   Total Cost per Mile (cell G4) = Total Cost / Miles Driven or = F4 / C4
   Use the fill handle to copy the three formulas in the range E4:G4 to the range E5:G12.

2. Determine totals for the miles driven, maintenance cost, mileage cost, and total cost in row 13. Copy the formula in cell G12 to G13 to assign the formula in cell G12 to G13 in the total line. If necessary, reapply the Total cell style to cell G13.

3. In the range D14:D16, determine the average value, highest value, and lowest value, respectively, for the values in the range D4:D12. Use the fill handle to copy the three functions to the range E14:G16.

4. Format the worksheet as follows:

   a. Change the workbook theme to Vapor Trail by using the Themes button (Page Layout tab | Themes group)

   b. Cell A1 — change to Title cell style

   c. Cell A2 — change to a font size of 16

   d. Cells A1:A2 — Red, Accent 1, Lighter 60% fill color and a thick outside borders

   e. Cells B4, D4:G4, and D13:G13 — accounting number format with two decimal places and fixed dollar signs by using the 'Accounting Number Format' button (Home tab | Number group)

 f. Cells B5:B12, and D5:G12 — comma style format with two decimal places by using the Comma Style button (Home tab | Number group)

 g. Cells C4:C13 — comma style format with no decimal places.

 h. Cells G4:G12 — apply conditional formatting so that cells with a value greater than 1.85 appear with a red background color and white font

5. If necessary increase the size of any columns that do not properly display data.

6. Switch to Page Layout view. Enter your name, course, laboratory assignment number, and any other information, as specified by your instructor, in the Header area.

7. Preview and print the worksheet in landscape orientation. Save the workbook using the file name, Apply 2-1 Proximity Bus Complete.

8. Use Range Finder to verify the formula in cell G13.

9. Print the range A3:D16. Press CTRL+ACCENT MARK (`) to change the display from the values version of the worksheet to the formulas version. Print the formulas version in landscape orientation on one page by using the Fit to option in the Page tab in the Page Setup dialog box. Press CTRL+ACCENT MARK (`) to change the display of the worksheet back to the values version. Close the workbook without saving it.

10. ✺ Besides adding a header to your document, can you think of anything else that could be added when printing the worksheet?

11. Submit the workbook as specified by your instructor.

Extend Your Knowledge

Extend the skills you learned in this module and experiment with new skills. You may need to use Help to complete the assignment.

Creating a Customer Tracking Worksheet for Jonee's Animal Supply

Note: To complete this assignment, you will be required to use the Data Files. Please contact your instructor for information about accessing the required files.

Instructions: Run Excel. Open the workbook Extend 2–1 Jonee's Animal Supply. You are to apply Flash Fill and four types of conditional formatting to cells in a worksheet (Figure 2–71).

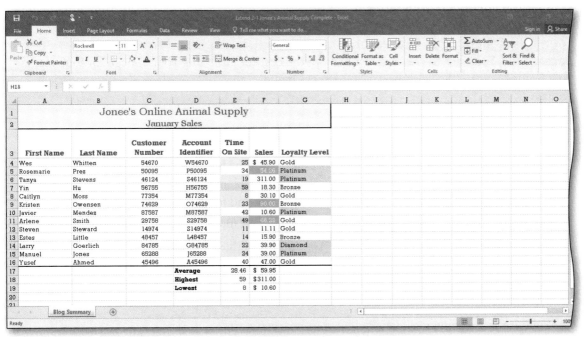

Figure 2–71

Continued >

Extend Your Knowledge *continued*

Perform the following tasks:

1. Add the account identifiers to the cells in the range D4:D16. The account identifier is determined by taking the first initial of the customer's last name followed by the entire customer number. For example, the account identifier for Wes Whitten is W54670. Continue entering two or three account identifiers, then use Flash Fill to complete the remaining cells. If necessary, add the thick bottom border back to cell D16.

2. Select the range E4:E16. Click the Conditional Formatting button (Home tab | Styles group) and then click New Rule on the Conditional Formatting menu. Select 'Format only top or bottom ranked values' in the Select a Rule Type area (New Formatting Rule dialog box).

3. If requested by your instructor, enter any value between 10 and 30 in the text box, (otherwise enter 20) in the Edit the Rule Description (New Formatting Rule dialog box) area, and then click the '% of the selected range' check box to select it.

4. Click the Format button, and choose a light purple background in the Fill sheet to assign this conditional format. Click the OK button in each dialog box and view the worksheet.

5. With range E4:E16 selected, apply a conditional format to the range that uses a yellow background color to highlight cells with scores that are below average. *Hint:* Explore some of the preset conditional rules to assist with formatting this range of cells.

6. With range F4:F16 selected, apply a conditional format to the range that uses a white font and green background to highlight cells that contain a value between 50 and 150.

7. With range G4:G16 selected, apply a conditional format to the range that uses a light gray background color to highlight cells that contain Platinum or Diamond. (*Hint:* You need to apply two separate formats, one for Platinum and one for Diamond.)

8. ✳ When might you want to look for values above the average in a worksheet?

9. Save the workbook using the file name, Extend 2–1 Jonee's Animal Supply Complete. Submit the revised workbook as specified by your instructor.

Expand Your World

Create a solution that uses cloud or web technologies by learning and investigating on your own from general guidance.

Four-Year College Cost Calculator

Instructions: You want to create an estimate of the cost for attending your college for four years. You decide to create the worksheet using Excel Online so that you can share it with your friends online.

Perform the following tasks:

1. Sign in to your Microsoft account on the web and run Excel Online.

2. Create a blank workbook. In the first worksheet, use row headings for each year of college (Freshman, Sophomore, Junior, and Senior). For the column headings, use your current expenses (such as car payment, rent, utilities, tuition, and food).

3. Enter expenses for each year based upon estimates you find by searching the web.

4. Calculate the total for each column. Also determine highest, lowest, and average values for each column.

5. Using the techniques taught in this module, create appropriate titles and format the worksheet accordingly.

6. Submit the assignment as specified by your instructor.

In the Labs

Design, create, modify, and/or use a workbook following the guidelines, concepts, and skills presented in this module. Labs 1 and 2, which increase in difficulty, require you to create solutions based on what you learned in the module; Lab 3 requires you to apply your creative thinking and problem-solving skills to design and implement a solution.

Lab 1: Insurance Premium Worksheet

Problem: You are a part-time assistant in the accounting department at Aylin Insurance, an Orlando-based insurance company. You have been asked to use Excel to generate a report that summarizes the existing balances on annual premiums, similar to the one shown in Figure 2–72. Include the three columns of customer data in Table 2-6 in the report, plus two additional columns to compute a monthly fee and a current balance for each customer. Assume no negative unpaid monthly balances.

Perform the following tasks:

1. Enter and format the worksheet title **Aylin Insurance** and worksheet subtitle **Premium Analysis** in cells A1 and A2. Change the theme of the worksheet to the Berlin theme. Apply the Title cell style to cells A1 and A2. Change the font size in cell A1 to 26 points, and change the font size in cell A2 to 18 points. Merge and center the worksheet title and subtitle across columns A through E. Draw a thick outside border around the range A1:A2.

2. Change the width of column A to 20.00 points. Change the widths of columns B through E to 14.00 points. Change the heights of row 3 to 36.00 points and row 14 to 25.50 points.

Table 2–6 Aylin Insurance Premium Data

Customer	Previous Balance	Payments
Albasco, Robin	1600.72	72.15
Deon, Jade	1518.62	382.3
Goodman, Brad	679.29	80.69
Hill, Raine	1060.42	107.6
Klonde, Albert	1178.83	125.63
Lang, Rose	1280.2	79.85
Moore, Jeffrey	1253.88	389.79
Piper, Taylor	477.11	278.52
Sothens, Mary	821.31	153.14

© 2015 Cengage Learning

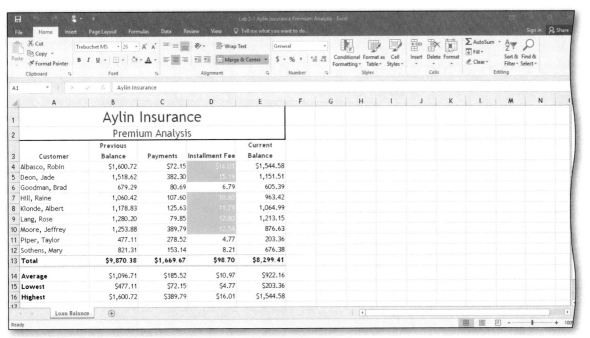

Figure 2–72

Continued >

In the Labs *continued*

3. Enter the column titles in row 3 and row titles in the range A13:A16, as shown in Figure 2–72. Center the column titles in the range A3:E3. Apply the Heading 4 cell style to the range A3:E3. Apply the Total cell style to the range A13:E13. Bold the titles in the range A13:A16. Change the font size in the range A3:E16 to 12 points.

4. Enter the data in Table 2-6 in the range A4:C12.

5. Use the following formulas to determine the installment fee in column D and the current balance in column E for the first customer. Copy the two formulas down through the remaining customers.

   a. Installment Fee (cell D4) = 1% * Previous Balance

   b. Current Balance (E4) = Previous Balance – Payments + Installment Fee

6. Determine the totals in row 13.

7. Determine the average, minimum, and maximum values in cells B14:B16 for the range B4:B12, and then copy the range B14:B16 to C14:E16.

8. Format the numbers as follows: (a) assign the currency style with a floating dollar sign to the cells containing numeric data in the ranges B4:E4 and B13:E16, and (b) assign a number style with two decimal places and a thousand's separator (currency with no dollar sign) to the range B5:E12.

9. Use conditional formatting to change the formatting to white font on an orange background in any cell in the range D4:D12 that contains a value greater than 10.

10. Change the worksheet name from Sheet1 to Loan Balance and the sheet tab color to the Orange standard color.

11. Change the worksheet header with your name, course number, and other information as specified by your instructor.

12. Use the spelling checker to check the spelling in the worksheet. Preview and then print the worksheet in landscape orientation. Save the workbook using the file name, Lab 2-1 Aylin Insurance Premium Analysis.

13. ✹ When you created the formula for the installment fee, you used 1%. What would you have to do if the rate changed today to 2% to update the formulas?

Lab 2: **Sales Summary Worksheet**

Problem: You have been asked to build a worksheet for International Moving Company that analyzes the financing needs for the company's first year in business. The company plans to begin operations in January with an initial investment of $750,000.00. The expected revenue and costs for the company's first year are shown in Table 2–7. The desired worksheet is shown in Figure 2–73. The initial investment is shown as the starting balance for January (cell B4). The amount of financing required by the company is shown as the lowest ending balance (cell F18).

Table 2–7 International Moving Company Financing Needs Data		
Month	**Incomes**	**Expenses**
January	1209081	1262911
February	1163811	1381881
March	1300660	1250143
April	1229207	1209498
May	1248369	1355232
June	1196118	1260888
July	1162970	1242599
August	1195824	1368955
September	1305669	1235604
October	1224741	1383254
November	1159644	1411768
December	1210000	1540000

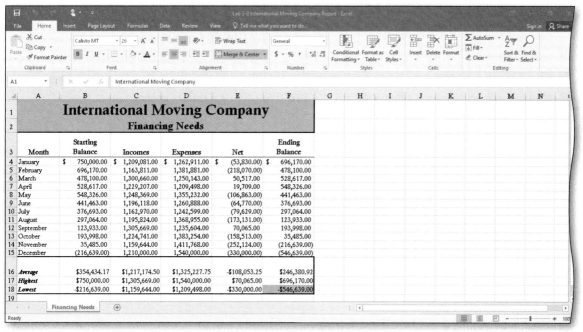

Figure 2–73

Perform the following tasks:

1. Apply the Slate theme to a new workbook.

2. Increase the width of column A to 12.00 and the width of columns B through F to 14.50.

3. Enter the worksheet title **International Moving Company** in cell A1 and the worksheet subtitle **Financing Needs** in cell A2. Enter the column titles in row 3, as shown in Figure 2–73. In row 3, use ALT+ENTER to start a new line in a cell.

4. Enter the financing needs data described in Table 2-7 in columns A, C, and D in rows 4 through 15. Enter the initial starting balance (cell B4) of 750000.00. Enter the row titles in the range A16:A18, as shown in Figure 2–73.

5. For the months of February through December, the starting balance is equal to the previous month's ending balance. Obtain the starting balance for February by setting the starting balance of February to the ending balance of January. Use a cell reference rather than typing in the data. Copy the formula for February to the remaining months.

6. Obtain the net amounts in column E by subtracting the expenses in column D from the incomes in column C. Enter the formula in cell E4 and copy it to the range E5:E15. Obtain the ending balance amounts in column F by adding the starting balance in column B to the net in column E. Enter the formula in cell F4 and copy it to the range F5:F15.

7. In the range B16:B18, use the AVERAGE, MAX, and MIN functions to determine the average value, highest value, and lowest value in the range B4:B15. Copy the range B16:B18 to the range C16:F18.

8. One at a time, merge and center the worksheet title and subtitle across columns A through F. Select cells A1 and A2 and change the background color to Tan, Accent 2 from the theme colors (column 6, row 1). Apply the Title cell style to cells A1 and A2. Change the worksheet title in cell A1 to 26-point. Bold both the title and subtitle. Draw a thick outside border around the range A1:A2.

9. Center the titles in row 3, columns A through F. Apply the Heading 2 cell style to the range A3:F3. Italicize and bold the row titles in the range A16:A18.

10. Draw a thick outside border around the range A16:F18. Change the background color for cell F18 to the same colors applied to the worksheet title in Step 8.

Continued >

In the Labs *continued*

11. Change the row heights of row 3 to 42.00 points and row 16 to 33.00 points.

12. Assign the accounting number format to the range B4:F4. Assign the comma style format to the range B5:F15. Assign a currency format with a floating dollar sign to the range B16:F18.

13. Rename the sheet tab as **Financing Needs**. Apply the Orange color from the standard colors (column 3) to the sheet tab.

14. Change the worksheet header with your name, course number, and other information as specified by your instructor.

15. Save the workbook using the file name, Lab 2-2 International Moving Company Report. Print the entire worksheet in landscape orientation. Next, print only the range A3:B15.

16. Display the formulas version by pressing CTRL+ACCENT MARK (`). Print the formulas version using the Fit to option in the Scaling area in the Page tab (Page Setup dialog box). After printing the worksheet, reset the Scaling option by selecting the Adjust to option in the Page tab (Page Setup dialog box) and changing the percent value to 100%. Change the display from the formulas version to the values version by pressing CTRL+ACCENT MARK (`). Do not save the workbook.

17. Submit the revised workbook as requested by your instructor.

18. ✳ In reviewing the worksheet you created, how do you think the company could obtain a positive result without increasing income or decreasing expenses?

Lab 3: **Consider This: Your Turn**

Apply your creative thinking and problem-solving skills to design and implement a solution.

Internet Service Summary

Instructions Part 1: You and your friends have decided to subscribe to a new Internet service provider. You would like to maximize services while keeping costs low. Research and find three Internet service providers in your area. If you cannot find three service providers in your area, you can research three service providers in another area of your choosing. For each company, find the best service package as well as the basic service package. Using the cost figures you find, calculate the cost per month for each service for a year. Include totals, minimum, maximum, and average values. Use the concepts and techniques presented in this module to create and format the worksheet.

Instructions Part 2: Which companies did you choose for your report? Which services offered the best deals that you would be willing to use?

3 Working with Large Worksheets, Charting, and What-If Analysis

Objectives

You will have mastered the material in this module when you can:

- Rotate text in a cell
- Create a series of month names
- Copy, paste, insert, and delete cells
- Format numbers using format symbols
- Enter and format the system date
- Use absolute and mixed cell references in a formula
- Use the IF function to perform a logical test
- Create and format sparkline charts
- Change sparkline chart types and styles
- Use the Format Painter button to format cells

- Create a clustered column chart on a separate chart sheet
- Use chart filters to display a subset of data in a chart
- Change the chart type and style
- Reorder sheet tabs
- Change the worksheet view
- Freeze and unfreeze rows and columns
- Answer what-if questions
- Goal seek to answer what-if questions
- Use the Smart Lookup Insight
- Understand accessibility features

Introduction

This module introduces you to techniques that will enhance your ability to create worksheets and draw charts. This module also covers other methods for entering values in cells, such as allowing Excel to automatically enter and format values based on a perceived pattern in the existing values. In addition, you will learn how to use absolute cell references and how to use the IF function to assign a value to a cell based on a logical test.

When you set up a worksheet, you should use cell references in formulas whenever possible, rather than constant values. The use of a cell reference allows you to change a value in multiple formulas by changing the value in a single cell. The cell references in a formula are called assumptions. **Assumptions** are values in cells that you can change to determine new values for formulas. This module emphasizes the use of assumptions and shows how to use assumptions to answer what-if questions, such as what happens to the six-month operating income if you decrease the Equipment

For an introduction to Windows and instructions about how to perform basic Windows tasks, read the Office and Windows module at the beginning of this book, where you can learn how to resize windows, change screen resolution, create folders, move and rename files, use Windows Help, and much more.

Repair and Maintenance expenses assumption by 1%. Being able to analyze the effect of changing values in a worksheet is an important skill in making business decisions.

Worksheets are normally much larger than those you created in the previous modules, often extending beyond the size of the Excel window. When you cannot view the entire worksheet on the screen at once, working with a large worksheet can be frustrating. This module introduces several Excel commands that allow you to control what is displayed on the screen so that you can focus on critical parts of a large worksheet. One command allows you to freeze rows and columns so that they remain visible, even when you scroll. Another command splits the worksheet into separate panes so that you can view different parts of a worksheet on the screen at once. Another changes the magnification to allow you to see more content, albeit at a smaller size. This is useful for reviewing the general layout of content on the worksheet.

From your work in Module 1, you know how easily you can create charts in Excel. This module covers additional charting techniques that allow you to convey meaning visually, such as by using sparkline charts or clustered column charts. This module also introduces the Accessibility checker.

For an introduction to Office and instructions about how to perform basic tasks in Office apps, read the Office and Windows module at the beginning of this book, where you can learn how to run an application, use the ribbon, save a file, open a file, print a file, exit an application, use Help, and much more.

Project — Financial Projection Worksheet with What-If Analysis and Chart

The project in this module uses Excel to create the worksheet and clustered column chart shown in Figures 3–1a and 3–1b. Kaitlyn's Ice Cream Shoppe operates kiosks at colleges and universities and serves both hard and soft serve ice cream. Each December and June, the chief executive officer projects monthly sales revenues, costs of goods sold, gross margin, expenses, and operating income for the upcoming six-month period, based on figures from the previous six months. The CEO requires an easy-to-read worksheet that shows financial projections for the upcoming six months to use for procuring partial financing and for determining staffing needs. The worksheet should allow for quick analysis, if projections for certain numbers change, such as the percentage of expenses

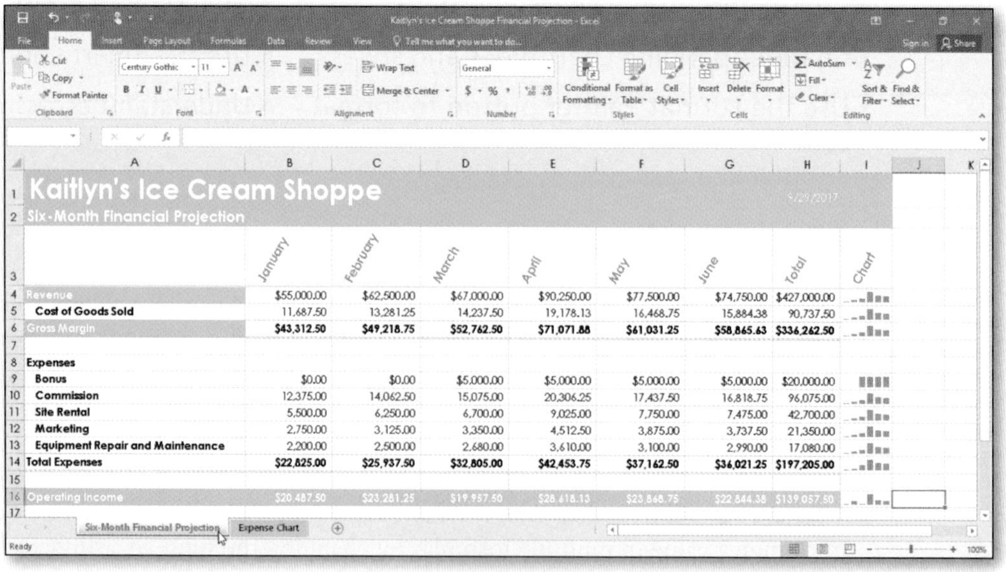

BTW
Excel Screen Resolution
If you are using a computer or mobile device to step through the project in this module and you want your screens to match the figures in this book, you should change your screen's resolution to 1366 x 768. For information about how to change a computer's resolution, refer to the Office and Windows module at the beginning of this book.

(a) Worksheet

Figure 3–1

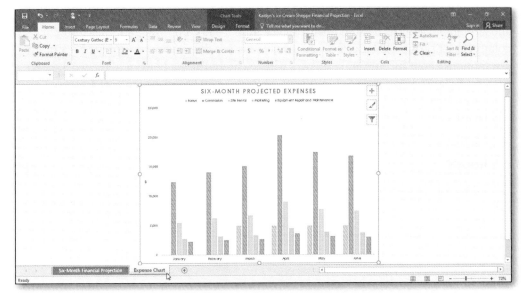

(b) Clustered Column Chart

Figure 3–1 (Continued)

allocated to commission or the cost of the kiosk rentals. In addition, you need to create a column chart that shows the breakdown of expenses for each month in the period.

The requirements document for the Kaitlyn's Ice Cream Shoppe Six-Month Financial Projection worksheet is shown in Figure 3–2. It includes the needs, source of data, summary of calculations, and chart requirements.

BTW

Touch Screen Differences

The Office and Windows interfaces may vary if you are using a touch screen. For this reason, you might notice that the function or appearance of your touch screen differs slightly from this module's presentation.

Worksheet Title	Kaitlyn's Ice Cream Shoppe Six-Month Financial Projection
Needs	• A wokseet that shows Kaitlyn's Ice Cream Shoppe projected monthly sales revenue, cost of goods sold, gross margin, expenses, and operating income for a six-month period. • A clustered column chart that shows the expected contribution of each expense category to total expenses.
Source of Data	Data supplied by the business owner includes projections of the monthly sales and expenses based on prior year figures (see Table 3–1). Remaining numbers in the worksheet are based on formulas.
Calculations	The following calculations are needed for each month: • Cost of Goods Sold = Revenue * (1 – Margin) • Gross Margin = Revenue – Cost of Goods Sold • Bonus expense = Predetermined bonus amount if Revenue exceeds the Revenue for Bonus, otherwise Bonus = 0 • Commission expense = Commission percentage × Revenue • Site Rental expense = Kiosk Rental Percentage × Revenue • Marketing expense = Marketing percentage × Revenue • Equipment Repair and Maintenance expense = Equipment Repair and Maintenance percentage × Revenue • Total expenses = sum of all expenses • Operating Income = Gross Margin – Total expenses
Chart Requirements	• Show sparkline charts for revenue and each of the items noted in the calculations area above. • Show a clustered column chart that shows the contributions of each month's expense categories to the total monthly expense figure.

Figure 3–2

Using a sketch of the worksheet can help you visualize its design. The sketch of the worksheet consists of titles, column and row headings, location of data values, calculations, and a rough idea of the desired formatting (Figure 3–3a). The sketch of the clustered column chart shows the expected expenses for each of the six months (Figure 3–3b). The assumptions about income and expenses will be entered at the bottom of the worksheet (Figure 3–3a). The projected monthly sales revenue will be entered in row 4 of the worksheet. The projected monthly sales revenue and the assumptions shown in Table 3–1 will be used to calculate the remaining numbers in the worksheet.

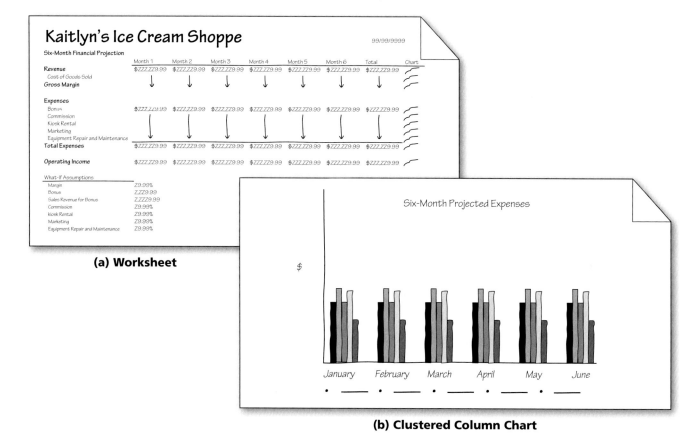

(a) Worksheet

(b) Clustered Column Chart

Figure 3–3

Table 3–1 Kaitlyn's Ice Cream Shoppe Six-Month Financial Projections Data and What-If Assumptions	
Projected Monthly Total Sales Revenues	
January	55,000.00
February	62,500.00
March	67,000.00
April	90,250.00
May	77,500.00
June	74,750.00
What-If Assumptions	
Margin	78.75%
Bonus	$3,500.00
Sales Revenue for Bonus	65,000.00
Commission	25.00%
Site Rental	10.00%
Marketing	5.00%
Equipment Repair and Maintenance	3.50%

With a solid understanding of the requirements document, an understanding of the necessary decisions, and a sketch of the worksheet, the next step is to use Excel to create the worksheet.

In this module, you will learn how to create and use the workbook shown in Figure 3–1. The following roadmap identifies general activities you will perform as you progress through this module:

1. ENTER the HEADINGS and DATA in the worksheet.
2. ENTER FORMULAS and FUNCTIONS in the worksheet.
3. CREATE SPARKLINE CHARTS in a range of cells.
4. FORMAT the WORKSHEET.
5. CREATE a COLUMN CHART on a separate chart sheet.
6. CHANGE VIEWS of the worksheet.
7. ASK WHAT-IF QUESTIONS.

BTW
Excel Help
At any time while using Excel, you can find answers to questions and display information about various topics through Excel Help. Used properly, this form of assistance can increase your productivity and reduce your frustrations by minimizing the time you spend learning how to use Excel. For instructions about Excel Help and exercises that will help you gain confidence in using it, read the Office and Windows module at the beginning of this book.

To Enter the Worksheet Titles and Apply a Theme

The worksheet contains two titles in cells A1 and A2. In the previous modules, titles were centered across the worksheet. With large worksheets that extend beyond the size of a window, it is best to leave titles left-aligned, as shown in the sketch of the worksheet in Figure 3–3a, so that the worksheet will print the title on the first page if the worksheet requires multiple pages. This allows the user to easily find the worksheet title when necessary. The following steps enter the worksheet titles and change the workbook theme to Savon.

1 Run Excel and create a blank workbook in the Excel window.

2 Select cell A1 and then type `Kaitlyn's Ice Cream Shoppe` as the worksheet title.

3 Select cell A2, type `Six-Month Financial Projection` as the worksheet subtitle, and then press the ENTER key to enter the worksheet subtitle.

4 Apply the Savon theme to the workbook.

BTW
The Ribbon and Screen Resolution
Excel may change how the groups and buttons within the groups appear on the ribbon, depending on the computer or mobile device's screen resolution. Thus, your ribbon may look different from the ones in this book if you are using a screen resolution other than 1366 x 768.

BTW
Rotating Text in a Cell
In Excel, you use the Alignment sheet in the Format Cells dialog box (shown in Figure 3–5) to position data in a cell by centering, left-aligning, or right-aligning; indenting; aligning at the top, bottom, or center; and rotating. If you enter 90 in the Degrees box in the Orientation area, the text will appear vertically and read from bottom to top in the cell.

Rotating Text and Using the Fill Handle to Create a Series

The data on the worksheet, including month names and the What-If Assumptions section, now can be added to the worksheet.

What should you take into account when planning a worksheet layout?
Using Excel, you can change text and number formatting in many ways, which affects the visual impact of the worksheet. Rotated text often provides a strong visual appeal. Rotated text also allows you to fit more text into a smaller column width. When laying out a worksheet, keep in mind the content you want to emphasize and the length of the cell titles relative to the numbers.

CONSIDER THIS

To Rotate Text in a Cell

The design of the worksheet calls specifically for data for the six months of the selling season. Because there always will be only six months of data in the worksheet, place the months across the top of the worksheet as column headings rather than as row headings. Place the income and expense categories in rows, as they are more numerous than the number of months. This layout allows you to easily navigate the worksheet. Ideally, a proper layout will create a worksheet that is longer than it is wide.

When you first enter text, its angle is zero degrees (0°), and it reads from left to right in a cell. Excel allows you to rotate text in a cell counterclockwise by entering a number between 1° and 90°. *Why? Rotating text is one method of making column headings visually distinct.* The following steps enter the month name, January, in cell B3 and format cell B3 by rotating the text.

- If necessary, click the Home tab and then select cell B3 because this cell will include the first month name in the series of month names.

- Type **January** as the cell entry and then click the Enter button.

- Click the Alignment Settings Dialog Box Launcher (Home tab | Alignment group) to display the Format Cells dialog box (Figure 3–4).

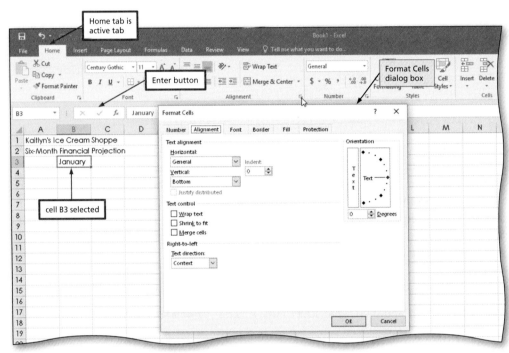

Figure 3–4

2

- Click the 60° point in the Orientation area (Format Cells dialog box) to move the indicator in the Orientation area to the 60° point and display a new orientation in the Degrees box (Figure 3–5).

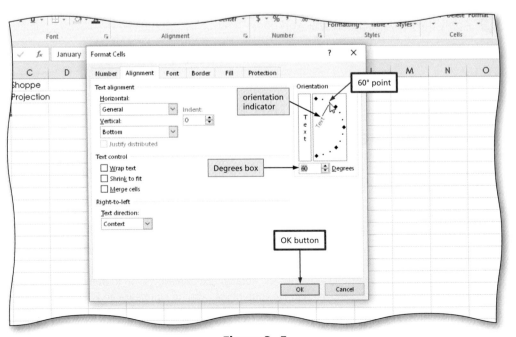

Figure 3–5

- Click the OK button
(Format Cells dialog
box) to rotate the
text in the active
cell and increase
the height of the
current row to best
fit the rotated text
(Figure 3–6).

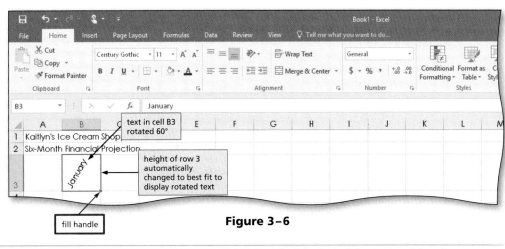

Figure 3–6

Other Ways

1. Right-click selected cell, click Format Cells on shortcut menu, click Alignment tab (Format Cells dialog box), click 60° point, click OK button

To Use the Fill Handle to Create a Series of Month Names

1 ENTER HEADINGS & DATA | 2 ENTER FORMULAS & FUNCTIONS | 3 CREATE SPARKLINE CHARTS
4 FORMAT WORKSHEET | 5 CREATE COLUMN CHART | 6 CHANGE VIEWS | 7 ASK WHAT-IF QUESTIONS

Why? *Once the first month in the series has been entered and formatted, you can complete the data series using the fill handle rather than typing and formatting all the entries.* The following steps use the fill handle and the entry in cell B3 to create a series of month names in cells C3:G3.

- Drag the fill handle
on the lower-right
corner of cell B3 to
the right to select
the range to fill,
C3:G3 in this case.
Do not release
the mouse button
(Figure 3–7).

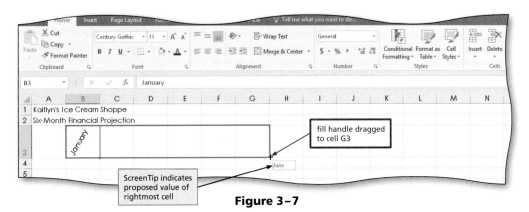

Figure 3–7

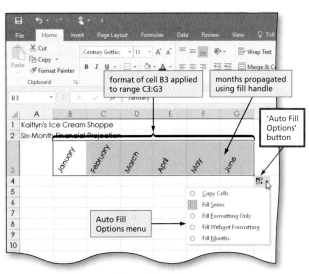

- Release the mouse button to create a month name series in
the selected range and copy the format of the selected cell to
the selected range.

- Click the 'Auto Fill Options' button below the lower-right
corner of the fill area to display the Auto Fill Options menu
(Figure 3–8).

Q&A

What if I do not want to copy the format of cell B3 during
the auto fill operation?

In addition to creating a series of values, dragging the
fill handle instructs Excel to copy the format of cell B3 to
the range C3:G3. With some fill operations, you may not
want to copy the formats of the source cell or range to the
destination cell or range. If this is the case, click the 'Auto
Fill Options' button after the range fills and then select the
desired option on the Auto Fill Options menu (Figure 3–8).

Figure 3–8

- Click the 'Auto Fill Options' button to hide the Auto Fill Options menu.

- Select cell H3, type **Total,** and then press the RIGHT ARROW key to enter a column heading.

- Type **Chart** in cell I3 and then press the RIGHT ARROW key.

Q&A
Why is the word, Total, formatted with a 60° rotation?
Excel tries to save you time by recognizing the format in adjacent cell G3 and applying it to cell H3. Such behavior also occurs when typing the column heading in cell I3.

Other Ways

1. Type text in cell, apply formatting, right-drag fill handle in direction to fill, click Fill Months on shortcut menu

2. Type text in cell, apply formatting, select range, click Fill button (Home tab | Editing group), click Series, click AutoFill (Series dialog box), click OK button

BTW
The Fill Handle
If you drag the fill handle up or to the left, Excel will decrement the series rather than increment the series. To copy a word, such as January or Monday, which Excel might interpret as the start of a series, hold down the CTRL key while you drag the fill handle to a destination area. If you drag the fill handle back into the middle of a cell, Excel erases the contents of the cell.

Using the Auto Fill Options Menu

As shown in Figure 3–8, Fill Series is the default option that Excel uses to fill an area, which means it fills the destination area with a series, using the same formatting as the source area. If you choose another option on the Auto Fill Options menu, Excel changes the contents of the destination range. Following the use of the fill handle, the 'Auto Fill Options' button remains active until you begin the next Excel operation. Table 3–2 summarizes the options on the Auto Fill Options menu.

Table 3–2 Options Available on the Auto Fill Options Menu

Auto Fill Option	Description
Copy Cells	Fill destination area with contents using format of source area. Do not create a series.
Fill Series	Fill destination area with series using format of source area. This option is the default.
Fill Formatting Only	Fill destination area using format of source area. No content is copied unless fill is series.
Fill Without Formatting	Fill destination area with contents, without applying the formatting of source area.
Fill Months	Fill destination area with series of months using format of source area. Same as Fill Series and shows as an option only if source area contains the name of a month.

You can create several different types of series using the fill handle. Table 3–3 illustrates several examples. Notice in examples 4 through 7, 9, and 11 that, if you use the fill handle to create a series of nonsequential numbers or months, you must enter the first item in the series in one cell and the second item in the series in an adjacent cell, and then select both cells and drag the fill handle through the destination area.

BTW
Custom Fill Sequences
You can create your own custom fill sequences for use with the fill handle. For example, if you often type the same list of products or names in Excel, you can create a custom fill sequence. You then can type the first product or name and then use the fill handle automatically to fill in the remaining products or names. To create a custom fill sequence, display the Excel Options dialog box by clicking Options in the Backstage view. Click the Advanced tab (Excel Options dialog box) and then click the 'Edit Custom Lists' button in the General section (Excel Options dialog box).

Table 3–3 Examples of Series Using the Fill Handle

Example	Contents of Cell(s) Copied Using the Fill Handle	Next Three Values of Extended Series
1	4:00	5:00, 6:00, 7:00
2	Qtr2	Qtr3, Qtr4, Qtr1
3	Quarter 1	Quarter 2, Quarter 3, Quarter 4
4	22-Jul, 22-Sep	22-Nov, 22-Jan, 22-Mar
5	2017, 2018	2019, 2020, 2021
6	1, 2	3, 4, 5
7	625, 575	525, 475, 425
8	Mon	Tue, Wed, Thu
9	Sunday, Tuesday	Thursday, Saturday, Monday
10	4th Section	5th Section, 6th Section, 7th Section
11	2205, 2208	2211, 2214, 2217

To Increase Column Widths

Why? In Module 2, you increased column widths after the values were entered into the worksheet. Sometimes, you may want to increase the column widths before you enter values and, if necessary, adjust them later. The following steps increase the column widths.

- Move the pointer to the boundary between column heading A and column heading B so that the pointer changes to a split double arrow in preparation of adjusting the column widths.

- Drag the pointer to the right until the ScreenTip displays the desired column width, Width: 38.00 (309 pixels) in this case. Do not release the mouse button (Figure 3–9).

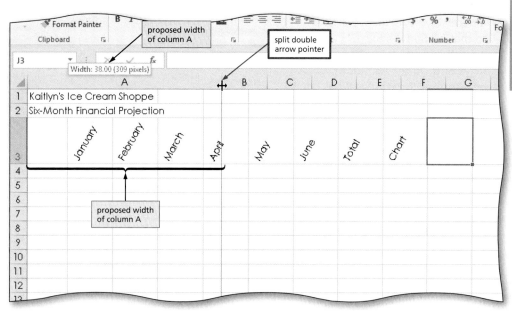

Figure 3–9

- Release the mouse button to change the width of the column.

- Click column heading B to select the column and then drag through column heading G to select the range in which to change the widths.

- Move the pointer to the boundary between column headings B and C in preparation of resizing column B and then drag the pointer to the right until the ScreenTip displays the desired width, Width: 14.50 (121 pixels) in this case. Do not lift your finger or release the mouse button (Figure 3–10).

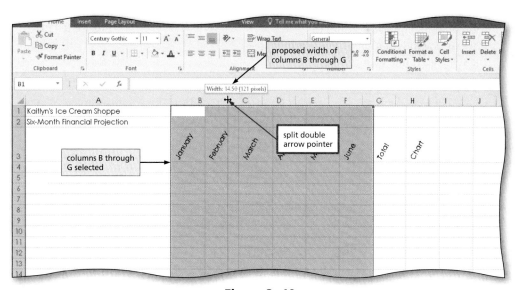

Figure 3–10

- Release the mouse button to change the width of the selected columns.

- If necessary, scroll the worksheet so that column H is visible and then use the technique described in Step 1 to increase the width of column H to 18.00 (149 pixels).

To Enter and Indent Row Titles

Excel allows you to indent text in cells. The following steps enter the row titles in column A and indent several of the row titles to create a visual hierarchy. **Why?** *You can create a hierarchy by indenting some of the row titles, like in an outline or table of contents.*

- If necessary, scroll the worksheet so that column A and row 4 are visible and then enter **Revenue** in cell A4, **Cost of Goods Sold** in cell A5, **Gross Margin** in cell A6, **Expenses** in cell A8, **Bonus** in cell A9, **Commission** in cell A10, **Site Rental** in cell A11, **Marketing** in cell A12, **Equipment Repair and Maintenance** in cell A13, **Total Expenses** in cell A14, and **Operating Income** in cell A16.

- Select cell A5 and then click the Increase Indent button (Home tab | Alignment group) to increase the indentation of the text in the selected cell.

- Select the range A9:A13 and then click the Increase Indent button (Home tab | Alignment group) to increase the indentation of the text in the selected range (Figure 3–11).

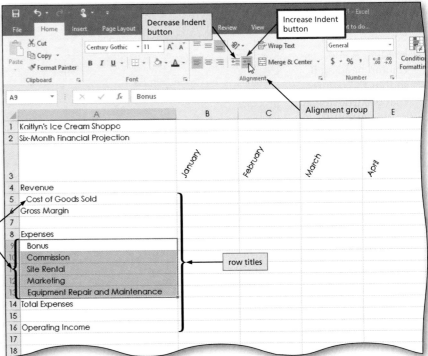

Figure 3–11

- Select cell A18 to finish entering the row titles and deselect the current cell.

Q&A

What happens when I click the Increase Indent button?

The Increase Indent button (Home tab | Alignment group) indents the contents of a cell two spaces to the right each time you click it. The Decrease Indent button decreases the indent by two spaces each time you click it.

Other Ways

1. Right-click range, click Format Cells on shortcut menu, click Alignment tab (Format Cells dialog box), click Left (Indent) in Horizontal list, type number of spaces to indent in Indent box, click OK button (Format Cells dialog box)

Copying a Range of Cells to a Nonadjacent Destination Area

The What-If Assumptions section should be placed in an area of the worksheet that is accessible yet does not impair the view of the main section of the worksheet. As shown in Figure 3–3a, the What-If Assumptions will be placed below the calculations in the worksheet. This will allow the reader to see the main section of the worksheet when first opening the workbook. Additionally, the row titles in the Expenses area are the same as the row titles in the What-If Assumptions table, with the exception of the two additional entries in cells A19 (Margin) and A21 (Sales Revenue for Bonus). Hence, the row titles in the What-If Assumptions table can be created by copying the range A9:A13 to the range A19:A23 and then inserting two rows for the additional entries in cells A19 and A21. You cannot use the fill handle to copy the range because the source area (range A9:A13) is not adjacent to the destination area (range A19:A23).

A more versatile method of copying a source area is to use the Copy button and Paste button (Home tab | Clipboard group). You can use these two buttons to copy a source area to an adjacent or nonadjacent destination area.

BTW

Fitting Entries in a Cell

An alternative to increasing column widths or row heights is to shrink the characters in a cell to fit the current width of the column. To shrink to fit, click Format Cells Alignment Dialog Box Button Launcher (Home tab | Alignment group) and then place a check mark in the 'Shrink to fit' check box in the Text control area (Format Cells dialog box).

To Copy a Range of Cells to a Nonadjacent Destination Area

1 ENTER HEADINGS & DATA | **2 ENTER FORMULAS & FUNCTIONS** | **3 CREATE SPARKLINE CHARTS**
4 FORMAT WORKSHEET | **5 CREATE COLUMN CHART** | **6 CHANGE VIEWS** | **7 ASK WHAT-IF QUESTIONS**

The Copy button copies the contents and format of the source area to the **Office Clipboard**, a temporary storage area in the computer's memory that allows you to collect text and graphics from any Office document and then paste them into almost any other type of document. The Paste button pastes a copy of the contents of the Office Clipboard in the destination area. *Why? Copying the range of cells rather than reentering the content assures consistency within the worksheet.* The following steps enter the What-If Assumptions row heading and then use the Copy and Paste buttons to copy the range A9:A13 to the nonadjacent range A19:A23.

- With cell A18 selected, type **What-If Assumptions** as the new row title and then click the Enter button.

- Select the range A9:A13 and then click the Copy button (Home tab | Clipboard group) to copy the values and formats of the selected range, A9:A13 in this case, to the Office Clipboard.

- Select cell A19, the top cell in the destination area (Figure 3–12).

Q&A
Why do I not select the entire destination area?
You are not required to select the entire destination area (A19:A23) because Excel only needs to know the upper-left cell of the destination area. In the case of a single column range, such as A19:A23, the top cell of the destination area (cell A19) also is the upper-left cell of the destination area.

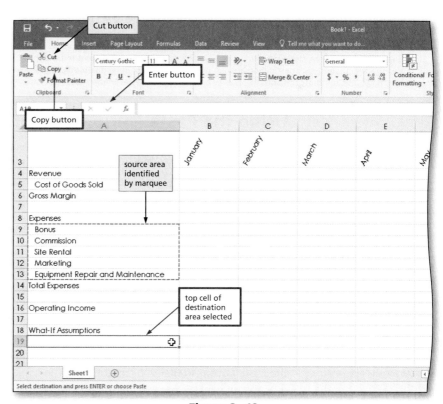

Figure 3–12

- Click the Paste button (Home tab | Clipboard group) to copy the values and formats of the last item placed on the Office Clipboard, range A9:A13, to the destination area, A19:A23. If necessary, scroll down to see the complete destination area (Figure 3–13).

Q&A

What if there was data in the destination area before I clicked the Paste button?

Any data contained in the destination area prior to the copy and paste is lost. When you complete a copy, the values and formats in the destination area are replaced with the values and formats of the source area. If you accidentally delete valuable data, click the Undo button on the Quick Access Toolbar or press CTRL+Z.

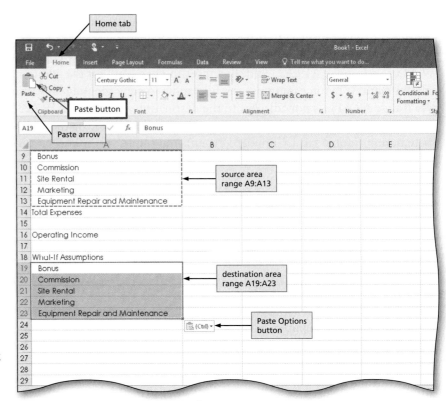

Figure 3–13

❸
- Press the ESC key to remove the marquee from the source area and disable the Paste button (Home tab | Clipboard group).

Other Ways

1. Right-click source area, click Copy on shortcut menu, right-click destination area, click Paste icon on shortcut menu

2. Select source area and point to border of range; while holding down CTRL key, drag source area to destination area

3. Select source area, press CTRL+C, select destination area, press CTRL+V

BTW

Copying and Pasting from Other Programs
If you need data in Excel that is stored in another program, copying and pasting likely will help you. You might need to experiment before you are successful, because Excel might attempt to copy formatting or other information that you did not intend to paste from the other program. Trying various Paste Option buttons will solve most of such problems.

BTW

Move It or Copy It
Contrary to popular belief, move and copy operations are not the same. When you move a cell, the data in the original location is cleared and the format of the cell is reset to the default. When you copy a cell, the data and format of the copy area remains intact. In short, you should copy cells to duplicate entries and move cells to rearrange entries.

Using the Paste Options Menu

After you click the Paste button, Excel displays the Paste Options button, as shown in Figure 3–13. If you click the Paste Options arrow and select an option in the Paste Options gallery, Excel modifies the most recent paste operation based on your selection. Table 3–4 summarizes the options available in the Paste Options gallery. When the Paste Options button is visible, you can use keyboard shortcuts to access the paste commands available in the Paste Options gallery. Additionally, you can use combinations of the options in the Paste Options gallery to customize your paste operation. That is, after clicking one of the icons in the Paste Options gallery, you can display the gallery again to further adjust your paste operation. The Paste button (Home tab | Clipboard group) includes an arrow that, when clicked, displays the same options as the Paste Options button.

An alternative to clicking the Paste button is to press the ENTER key. The ENTER key completes the paste operation, removes the marquee from the source area, and disables the Paste button so that you cannot paste the copied source area to other destination areas. The ENTER key was not used in the previous set of steps so that the capabilities of the Paste Options button could be discussed. The Paste Options button does not appear on the screen when you use the ENTER key to complete the paste operation.

Using Drag and Drop to Move or Copy Cells

You also can use the mouse to move or copy cells. First, you select the source area and point to the border of the cell or range. You know you are pointing to the

Table 3–4 Paste Gallery Commands

Paste Option Icon	Paste Option	Description
	Paste	Copy contents and format of source area. This option is the default.
	Formulas	Copy formulas from the source area, but not the contents and format.
	Formulas & Number Formatting	Copy formulas and format for numbers and formulas of source area, but not the contents.
	Keep Source Formatting	Copy contents, format, and styles of source area.
	No Borders	Copy contents and format of source area, but not any borders.
	Keep Source Column Widths	Copy contents and format of source area. Change destination column widths to source column widths.
	Transpose	Copy the contents and format of the source area, but transpose, or swap, the rows and columns.
	Values	Copy contents of source area but not the formatting for formulas.
	Values & Number Formatting	Copy contents and format of source area for numbers or formulas, but use format of destination area for text.
	Values & Source Formatting	Copy contents and formatting of source area but not the formula.
	Formatting	Copy format of source area but not the contents.
	Paste Link	Copy contents and format and link cells so that a change to the cells in source area updates the corresponding cells in destination area.
	Picture	Copy an image of the source area as a picture.
	Linked Picture	Copy an image of the source area as a picture so that a change to the cells in source area updates the picture in destination area.

border of the cell or range when the pointer changes to a four-headed arrow. To move the selected cell or cells, drag the selection to the destination area. To copy a selection, hold down the CTRL key while dragging the selection to the destination area. You know Excel is in Copy mode when a small plus sign appears next to the pointer. Be sure to release the mouse button before you release the CTRL key. Using the mouse to move or copy cells is called **drag and drop**.

Using Cut and Paste to Move Cells

Another way to move cells is to select them, click the Cut button (Home tab | Clipboard group) (Figure 3–12) to remove the cells from the worksheet and copy them to the Office Clipboard, select the destination area, and then click the Paste button (Home tab | Clipboard group) or press the ENTER key. You also can use the Cut command on the shortcut menu, instead of the Cut button on the ribbon.

Inserting and Deleting Cells in a Worksheet

At any time while the worksheet is on the screen, you can insert cells to enter new data or delete cells to remove unwanted data. You can insert or delete individual cells; a range of cells, rows, or columns; or entire worksheets.

BTW
Cutting
When you cut a cell or range of cells using the Cut command on a shortcut menu or Cut button (Home tab | Clipboard group), Excel copies the cells to the Office Clipboard; it does not remove the cells from the source area until you paste the cells in the destination area by either clicking the Paste button (Home tab | Clipboard group) or pressing the ENTER key. When you complete the paste, Excel clears the cell's or range of cell's entries and their formats from the source area.

To Insert a Row

Why? *According to the sketch of the worksheet in Figure 3–3a, two rows must be inserted in the What-If Assumptions table, one above Bonus for the Margin assumption and another between Bonus and Commission for the Sales Revenue for Bonus assumption.* The following steps insert the new rows into the worksheet.

- Right-click row heading 20, the row below where you want to insert a row, to display the shortcut menu and the mini toolbar (Figure 3–14).

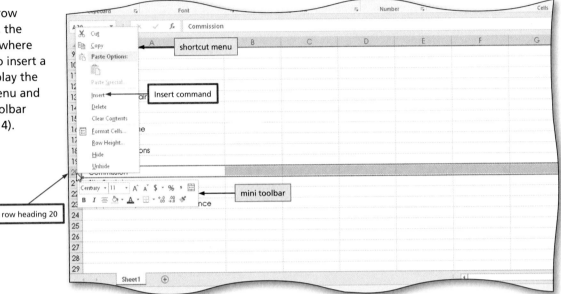

Figure 3–14

- Click Insert on the shortcut menu to insert a new row in the worksheet by shifting the selected row and all rows below it down one row.

- Select cell A20 in the new row and then type **Sales Revenue for Bonus** to enter a new row title (Figure 3–15).

Q&A

What is the resulting format of the new row?

The cells in the new row inherit the formats of the cells in the row above them. You can change this behavior by clicking the Insert Options button that appears below the inserted row. Following the insertion of a row, the Insert Options button allows you to select from the following options: (1) 'Format Same As Above', (2) 'Format Same As Below', and (3) Clear Formatting. The 'Format Same as Above' option is the default. The Insert Options button remains active until you begin the next Excel operation. Excel does not display the Insert Options button if the initial row does not contain any formatted data.

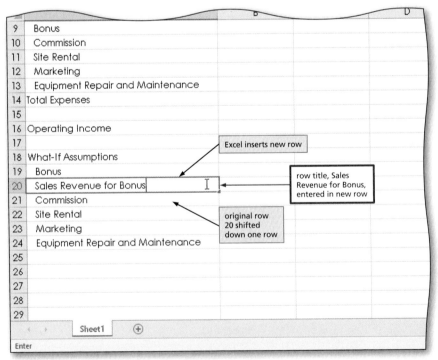

Figure 3–15

3

- Right-click row heading 19, the row below where you want to insert a row, to display the shortcut menu and the mini toolbar.

- Click Insert on the shortcut menu to insert a new row in the worksheet.

- Click the Insert Options button below row 19 (Figure 3–16).

- Click 'Format Same As Below' on the menu.

- Select cell A19 in the new row and then type **Margin** to enter a new row title.

Q&A

What would happen if cells in the shifted rows were included in formulas?

If the rows that shift down included cell references in formulas located in the worksheet, Excel would automatically adjust the cell references in the formulas to their new locations. Thus, in Step 2, if a formula in the worksheet referenced a cell in row 19 before the insert, then Excel would adjust the cell reference in the formula to row 20 after the insert.

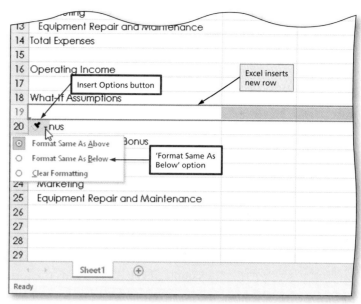

Figure 3–16

4

- Save the workbook on your hard drive, OneDrive, or other storage location using **Kaitlyn's Ice Cream Shoppe Financial Projection** as the file name.

Other Ways

1. Click Insert Cells arrow (Home tab | Cells group), click 'Insert Sheet Rows'
2. Press CTRL+SHIFT+PLUS SIGN, click Entire row (Insert dialog box), click OK button

---

Inserting Columns

You insert columns into a worksheet in the same way you insert rows. To insert columns, select one or more columns immediately to the right of where you want Excel to insert the new column or columns. Select the number of columns you want to insert, click the Insert arrow (Home tab | Cells group), and then click 'Insert Sheet Columns' in the Insert list; or right-click the selected column(s) and then click Insert on the shortcut menu. The Insert command on the shortcut menu requires that you select an entire column (or columns) to insert a column (or columns). Following the insertion of a column, Excel displays the Insert Options button, which allows you to modify the insertion in a fashion similar to that discussed earlier when inserting rows.

Inserting Single Cells or a Range of Cells

You can use the Insert command on the shortcut menu or the Insert Cells command on the Insert menu — produced by clicking the Insert button (Home tab | Cells group) — to insert a single cell or a range of cells. You should be aware that if you shift a single cell or a range of cells, however, it no longer lines up with its associated cells. To ensure that the values in the worksheet do not get out of order,

BTW

Inserting Multiple Rows
If you want to insert multiple rows, you have two choices. You can insert a single row by using the Insert command on the shortcut menu and then repeatedly press the F4 key to continue inserting rows. Alternatively, you can select a number of existing rows equal to the number of rows that you want to insert. For instance, if you want to insert five rows, select five existing rows in the worksheet, right-click the selected rows, and then click Insert on the shortcut menu.

BTW

Dragging Ranges
You can move and insert a selected cell or range between existing cells by holding down the SHIFT key while you drag the selection to the gridline where you want to insert the selected cell or range. You also can copy and insert by holding down the CTRL+SHIFT keys while you drag the selection to the desired gridline.

spreadsheet experts recommend that you insert only entire rows or entire columns. When you insert a single cell or a range of cells, Excel displays the Insert Options button so that you can change the format of the inserted cell, using options similar to those for inserting rows and columns.

Deleting Columns and Rows

The Delete button (Home tab | Cells group) or the Delete command on the shortcut menu removes cells (including the data and format) from the worksheet. Deleting cells is not the same as clearing cells. The Clear Contents command, described in Module 1, clears the data from the cells, but the cells remain in the worksheet. The Delete command removes the cells from the worksheet and shifts the remaining rows up (when you delete rows) or shifts the remaining columns to the left (when you delete columns). If formulas located in other cells reference cells in the deleted row or column, Excel does not adjust these cell references. Excel displays the error message **#REF!** in those cells to indicate a cell reference error. For example, if cell A7 contains the formula =A4+A5 and you delete row 5, Excel assigns the formula =A4+#REF! to cell A6 (originally cell A7) and displays the error message, #REF!, in cell A6. Excel also displays an Error Options button when you select the cell containing the error message, #REF!, which allows you to select options to determine the nature of the problem.

1 ENTER HEADINGS & DATA | 2 ENTER FORMULAS & FUNCTIONS | 3 CREATE SPARKLINE CHARTS

To Enter Numbers with Format Symbols

4 FORMAT WORKSHEET | 5 CREATE COLUMN CHART | 6 CHANGE VIEWS | 7 ASK WHAT-IF QUESTIONS

The next step in creating the Financial Projection worksheet is to enter the what-if assumptions values in the range B19:B25. The numbers in the table can be entered and then formatted using techniques from Modules 1 and 2, or each number can be entered with **format symbols**, which assign a format to numbers as they are entered. When a number is entered with a format symbol, Excel displays it with the assigned format. Valid format symbols include the dollar sign ($), comma (,), and percent sign (%).

If you enter a whole number, it appears without any decimal places. If you enter a number with one or more decimal places and a format symbol, Excel displays the number with two decimal places. Table 3–5 illustrates several examples of numbers entered with format symbols. The number in parentheses in column 4 indicates the number of decimal places.

Table 3–5 Numbers Entered with Format Symbols			
Format Symbol	**Typed in Formula Bar**	**Displays in Cell**	**Comparable Format**
,	374,149	374,149	Comma(0)
	5,833.6	5,833.60	Comma(2)
$	$58917	$58,917	Currency(0)
	$842.51	$842.51	Currency(2)
	$63,574.9	$63,574.90	Currency(2)
%	85%	85%	Percent(0)
	12.80%	12.80%	Percent(2)
	68.2242%	68.2242%	Percent(4)

Why? *In some cases, using a format symbol is the most efficient method for entering and formatting data.* The following step enters the numbers in the What-If Assumptions table with format symbols.

1

- Enter the following values, using format symbols to apply number formatting: **78.75%** in cell B19, **3,500.00** in cell B20, **65,000.00** in cell B21, **25.00%** in cell B22, **10.00%** in cell B23, **5.00%** in cell B24, and **3.50%** in cell B25 (Figure 3–17).

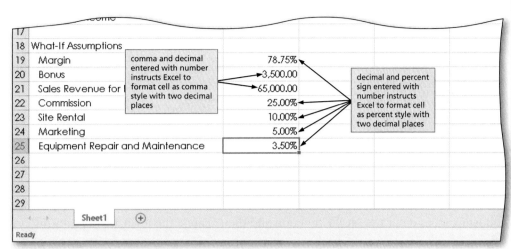

Figure 3–17

Other Ways

1. Right-click range, click Format Cells on shortcut menu, click Number tab (Format Cells dialog box), click category in Category list, select desired format, click OK button

2. Press CTRL+1, click Number tab (Format Cells dialog box), click category in Category list, select desired format, click OK button

To Enter the Projected Monthly Sales

The following steps enter the projected revenue, listed previously in Table 3–1, in row 4 and compute the projected six-month revenue in cell H4.

1 If necessary, display the Home tab.

2 Enter **55,000.00** in cell B4, **62,500.00** in cell C4, **67,000.00** in cell D4, **90,250.00** in cell E4, **77,500.00** in cell F4, and **74,750.00** in cell G4.

3 Select cell H4 and then click the Sum button (Home tab | Editing group) twice to create a sum in the selected cell (Figure 3–18).

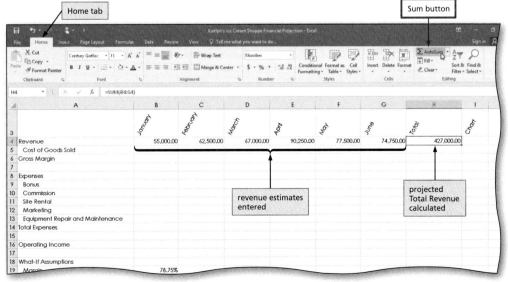

Figure 3–18

To Enter and Format the System Date

Why? *The sketch of the worksheet in Figure 3–3a includes a date stamp on the right side of the heading section. A date stamp shows the date a workbook, report, or other document was created or the time period it represents.* In business, a report often is meaningless without a date stamp. For example, if a printout of the worksheet in this module were distributed to the company's analysts, the date stamp would show when the six-month projections were made, as well as what time period the report represents.

A simple way to create a date stamp is to use the NOW function to enter the system date tracked by your computer in a cell in the worksheet. The **NOW function** is one of 24 date and time functions available in Excel. When assigned to a cell, the NOW function returns a number that corresponds to the system date and time beginning with December 31, 1899. For example, January 1, 1900 equals 1, January 2, 1900 equals 2, and so on. Noon equals .5. Thus, noon on January 1, 1900 equals 1.5 and 6:00 p.m. on January 1, 1900 equals 1.75. If the computer's system date is set to the current date, then the date stamp is equivalent to the current date. The following steps enter the NOW function and then change the format from mm/dd/yyyy hh:mm to mm/dd/yyyy.

1

- Select cell H1 and then click the Insert Function button in the formula bar to display the Insert Function dialog box.

- Click the 'Or select a category' arrow (Insert Function dialog box) and then select 'Date & Time' to populate the 'Select a function' list with data and time functions.

- Scroll down in the 'Select a function' list and then click NOW to select the required function (Figure 3–19).

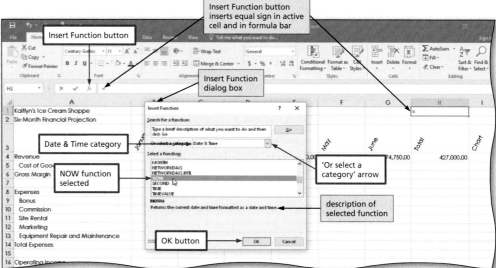

Figure 3–19

2

- Click the OK button (Insert Function dialog box) to close the Insert Function dialog box and display the Function Arguments dialog box (Figure 3–20).

 What is meant by 'Formula result = Volatile' in the Function Arguments dialog box?
The NOW function is an example of a volatile function. A **volatile function** is one where the number that the function returns is not constant but changes each time the worksheet is opened. As a result, any formula using the NOW function will have a variable result.

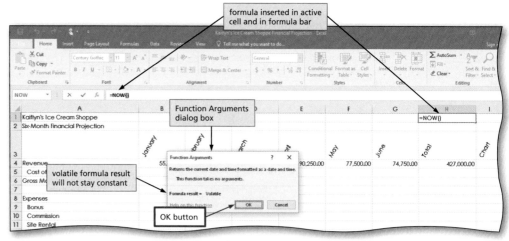

Figure 3–20

❸

- Click the OK button (Function Arguments dialog box) to display the system date and time in the selected cell, using the default date and time format, which is mm/dd/yyyy hh:mm.

Q&A What does the mm/dd/yyyy hh:mm format represent?
The mm/dd/yyyy hh:mm format can be explained as follows: the first mm is the month, dd is the day of the month, yyyy is the year, hh is the hour of the day, and the second mm is the minutes past the hour. Excel applies this date and time format to the result of the NOW function.

- Right-click cell H1 to display a shortcut menu and mini toolbar.

- Click Format Cells on the shortcut menu to display the Format Cells dialog box.

- If necessary, click the Number tab (Format Cells dialog box) to display the Number sheet.

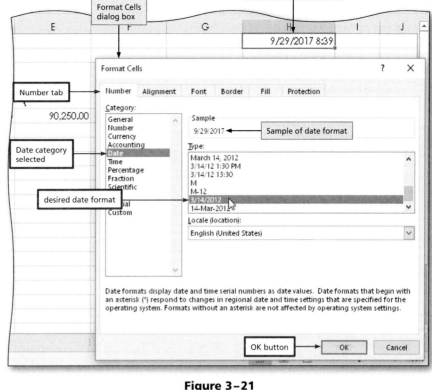

Figure 3–21

- Click Date in the Category list (Format Cells dialog box) to display the date format options in the Type list. Scroll down in the Type list and then click 3/14/2012 to display a sample of the data in the Sample area in the dialog box (Figure 3–21).

Q&A Why do the dates in the Type box show March 14, 2012 instead of the current date?
March 14, 2012 is just used as a sample date in this version of Office.

❹

- Click the OK button (Format Cells dialog box) to display the system date (the result of the NOW function) in the format mm/dd/yyyy.

- Double-click the border between columns H and I to change the width of the column to best fit (Figure 3–22).

 **Experiment**

- If instructed by your professor, select cell H2 and enter the place of your birth.

- Save the workbook again on the same storage location with the same file name.

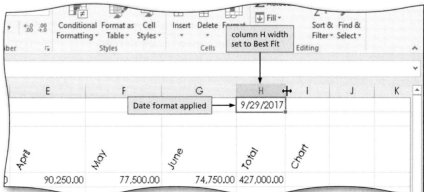

Figure 3–22

Q&A Why should I save the workbook again?
You have made several modifications to the workbook since you last saved it. Thus, you should save it again.

Other Ways

1. Click 'Date & Time' button (Formulas tab | Function Library group), click NOW
2. Press CTRL+SEMICOLON (this enters the date as a static value, meaning the date will not change when the workbook is opened at a later date)
3. Press CTRL+SHIFT+# to format date as day-month-year

CONSIDER THIS

When would you not want to use the system date?

Using the system date results in the date value being updated whenever the worksheet is opened. Think carefully about whether or not this is the result you want. If you want the date to reflect the current date, using the system date is appropriate. If you want to record when the worksheet was created, using a hard-coded date makes more sense. If both pieces of information may be important, consider two date entries in the worksheet: a fixed entry identifying the date the worksheet was created and the volatile system date.

Break Point: If you wish to take a break, this is a good place to do so. You can exit Excel now. To resume at a later time, run Excel, open the file called Kaitlyn's Ice Cream Shoppe Financial Projection, and continue following the steps from this location forward.

BTW

Absolute Referencing
Absolute referencing is one of the more difficult worksheet concepts to understand. One point to keep in mind is that the paste operation is the only operation affected by an absolute cell reference. An absolute cell reference instructs the paste operation to use the same cell reference as it copies a formula from one cell to another.

Absolute Versus Relative Addressing

The next sections describe the formulas and functions needed to complete the calculations in the worksheet.

As you learned in Modules 1 and 2, Excel modifies cell references when copying formulas. However, sometimes while copying formulas you do not want Excel to change a cell reference. To keep a cell reference constant when copying a formula or function (that is, the cell references do not change relative to where you are copying the formula), Excel uses a technique called **absolute cell referencing**. To specify an absolute cell reference in a formula, enter a dollar sign ($) before any column letters or row numbers you want to keep constant in formulas you plan to copy. For example, $B$4 is an absolute cell reference, whereas B4 is a relative cell reference. Both reference the same cell. The difference becomes apparent when they are copied to a destination area. A formula using the absolute cell reference $B$4 instructs Excel to keep the cell reference B4 constant (absolute) in the formula as it is copied to the destination area. A formula using the **relative cell reference** B4 instructs Excel to adjust the cell reference as it is copied to the destination area. A cell reference where one factor remains constant and the other one varies is called a **mixed cell reference**. A mixed cell reference includes a dollar sign before the column or the row, not before both. When planning formulas, be aware of when you might need to use absolute, relative, and mixed cell references. Table 3–6 provides some additional examples of each of these types of cell references.

Table 3–6 Examples of Absolute, Relative, and Mixed Cell References		
Cell Reference	**Type of Reference**	**Meaning**
$B$4	Absolute cell reference	Both column and row references remain the same when you copy this cell, because the cell references are absolute.
B4	Relative cell reference	Both column and row references are relative. When copied to another cell, both the column and row in the cell reference are adjusted to reflect the new location.
B$4	Mixed reference	This cell reference is mixed. The column reference changes when you copy this cell to another column because it is relative. The row reference does not change because it is absolute.
$B4	Mixed reference	This cell reference is mixed. The column reference does not change because it is absolute. The row reference changes when you copy this cell reference to another row because it is relative.

Figure 3–23 illustrates how the type of cell reference used affects the results of copying a formula to a new place in a worksheet. In Figure 3–23a, cells D6:D9 contain formulas. Each formula multiplies the content of cell A2 by 2; the difference between formulas lies in how cell A2 is referenced. Cells C6:C9 identify the type of reference: absolute, relative, or mixed.

Figure 3–23b shows the values that result from copying the formulas in cells D6:D9 to ranges E6:E9, F7:F10, and G11:G14. Figure 3–23c shows the formulas that result from copying the formulas. While all formulas initially multiplied the content of cell A2 by 2, the values and formulas in the destination ranges illustrate how Excel adjusts cell references according to how you reference those cells in original formulas.

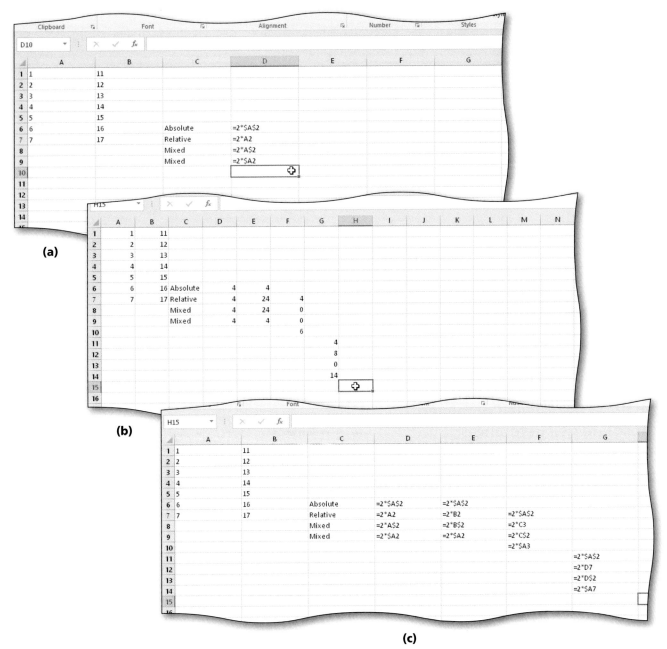

Figure 3–23

In the worksheet, you need to enter formulas that calculate the following values for January: cost of goods sold (cell B5), gross margin (cell B6), expenses (range B9:B13), total expenses (cell B14), and operating income (cell B16). The formulas are based on the projected monthly revenue in cell B4 and the assumptions in the range B19:B25.

The calculations for each column (month) are the same, except for the reference to the projected monthly revenue in row 4, which varies according to the month (B4 for January, C4 for February, and so on). Thus, the formulas for January can be entered in column B and then copied to columns C through G. Table 3–7 shows the formulas for determining the January cost of goods sold, gross margin, expenses, total expenses, and operating income in column B.

Table 3–7 Formulas for Determining Cost of Goods Sold, Gross Margin, Expenses, Total Expenses, and Operating Income for January

Cell	Row Title	Calculation	Formula
B5	Cost of Goods Sold	Revenue times (1 minus Margin %)	=B4 * (1 – B19)
B6	Gross Margin	Revenue minus Cost of Goods Sold	=B4 – B5
B9	Bonus	Bonus equals value in B20 or 0	=IF(B4 >= B21, B20, 0)
B10	Commission	Revenue times Commission %	=B4 * B22
B11	Site Rental	Revenue times Site Rental %	=B4 * B23
B12	Marketing	Revenue times Marketing %	=B4 * B24
B13	Equipment Repair and Maintenance	Revenue times Equipment Repair and Maintenance %	=B4 * B25
B14	Total Expenses	Sum of April Expenses	=SUM(B9:B13)
B16	Operating Income	Gross Margin minus Total Expenses	=B6 – B14

To Enter a Formula Containing Absolute Cell References

1 ENTER HEADINGS & DATA | 2 ENTER FORMULAS & FUNCTIONS | 3 CREATE SPARKLINE CHARTS
4 FORMAT WORKSHEET | 5 CREATE COLUMN CHART | 6 CHANGE VIEWS | 7 ASK WHAT-IF QUESTIONS

Why? *As the formulas are entered in column B for January, as shown in Table 3–7, and then copied to columns C through G (February through June) in the worksheet, Excel will adjust the cell references for each column.* After the copy, the February Commission expense in cell C10 would be =C4 * C22. While the cell reference C4 (February Revenue) is correct, the cell reference C22 references an empty cell. The formula for cell C10 should read =C4 * B22, rather than =C4 * C22, because B22 references the Commission % value in the What-If Assumptions table. In this instance, you must use an absolute cell reference to keep the cell reference in the formula the same, or constant, when it is copied. To enter an absolute cell reference, you can type the dollar sign ($) as part of the cell reference or enter it by pressing the F4 key with the insertion point in or to the right of the cell reference to change it to absolute. The following steps enter the cost of goods sold formula =B4 * (1 – B19) in cell B5 using Point mode.

1

• Click cell B5 to select the cell in which to enter the first formula.

• Type = (equal sign), select cell B4, type *(1-B19 to continue entering the formula, and then press the F4 key to change the cell reference from a relative cell reference to an absolute cell reference. Type) (closing parenthesis) to complete the formula (Figure 3–24).

Q&A

Is an absolute reference required in this formula?

No, a mixed cell reference also could have been used. The formula in cell B5 will be copied across columns, rather than down rows. So, the formula entered in cell B5 in Step 1 could have been entered as =B4*(1–$B19) using a mixed cell reference, rather than =B4*(1–$B$19), because when you copy a formula across columns, the row does not change. The key is to ensure that column B remains constant as you copy the formula across columns. To change the absolute cell reference to a mixed cell reference, continue to press the F4 key until you achieve the desired cell reference.

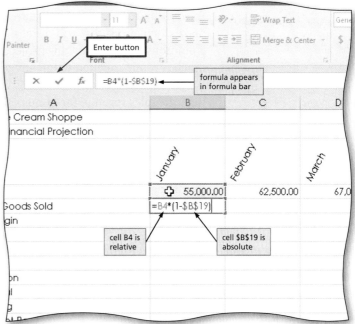

Figure 3–24

2

• Click the Enter button in the formula bar to display the result, 11687.5, instead of the formula in cell B5 (Figure 3–25).

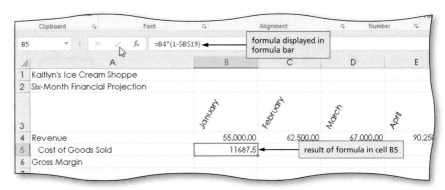

Figure 3–25

3

• Click cell B6 to select the cell in which to enter the next formula, type = (equal sign), click cell B4, type − (minus sign), and then click cell B5 to add a reference to the cell to the formula.

• Click the Enter button in the formula bar to display the result in the selected cell, in this case gross margin for January, 43,312.50, in cell B6 (Figure 3–26).

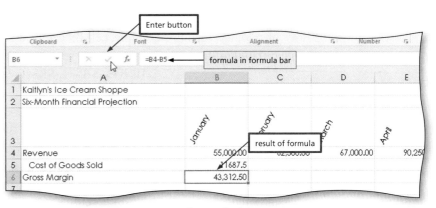

Figure 3–26

Making Decisions — The IF Function

In addition to calculations that are constant across all categories, you may need to make calculations that will differ depending on whether a particular condition or set of conditions are met. For this project, you need to vary compensation according to how much revenue is generated in any particular month. According to the requirements document in Figure 3–2, a bonus will be paid in any month where revenue is greater than the sales revenue for bonus value. If the projected January revenue in cell B4 is greater than or equal to the sales revenue for bonus in cell B21 (65,000.00), then the projected January bonus value in cell B9 is equal to the bonus value in cell B20 (3,500.00); otherwise, the value in cell B9 is equal to 0. One way to assign the projected January bonus value in cell B9 is to manually check to see if the projected revenue in cell B4 equals or exceeds the sales revenue for the bonus amount in cell B21 and, if so, then to enter 3,500.00 in cell B9. You can use this manual process for all six months by checking the values for the each month.

Because the data in the worksheet changes each time a report is prepared or the figures are adjusted, however, it is preferable to have Excel calculate the monthly bonus. To do so, cell B9 must include a formula or function that compares the projected revenue with the sales revenue for bonus value, and displays 3,500.00 or 0.00 (zero), depending on whether the projected January revenue in cell B4 is greater than, equal to, or less than the sales revenue for bonus value in cell B21. This decision-making process is a **logical test**. It can be represented in diagram form, as shown in Figure 3–27.

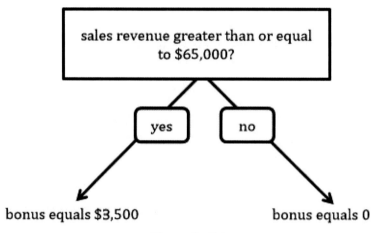

Figure 3–27

In Excel, you use the **IF function** when you want to assign a value to a cell based on a logical test. For example, cell B9 can be assigned the following IF function:

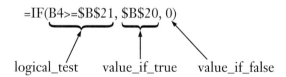

This IF function instructs Excel that if the projected January revenue in cell B4 is greater than or equal to the sales revenue for bonus value in cell B21, then Excel should display the bonus value found in cell B20 in cell B9. If the projected January revenue in cell B4 is not greater than or equal to the sales revenue for bonus value in cell B21, then Excel should display a 0 (zero) in cell B9.

The general form of the IF function is:

=IF(logical_test, value_if_true, value_if_false)

The argument, logical_test, is made up of two expressions and a comparison operator. Each expression can be a cell reference, a number, text, a function, or a formula. In this example, the logical test compares the projected revenue with the sales revenue for bonus, using the comparison operator greater than or equal to. Valid comparison operators, their meanings, and examples of their use in IF functions are shown in Table 3–8. The argument, value_if_true, is the value you want Excel to display in the cell when the logical test is true. The argument, value_if_false, is the value you want Excel to display in the cell when the logical test is false.

Table 3–8 Comparison Operators		
Comparison Operator	**Meaning**	**Example**
=	Equal to	=IF(A1=A2, "True", "False")
<	Less than	=IF(A1<A2, "True", "False")
>	Greater than	=IF(A1>A2, "True", "False")
>=	Greater than or equal to	=IF(A1>=A2, "True", "False")
<=	Less than or equal to	=IF(A1<=A2, "True", "False")
<>	Not equal to	=IF(A1<>A2, "True", "False")

To Enter an IF Function

1 ENTER HEADINGS & DATA | 2 ENTER FORMULAS & FUNCTIONS | 3 CREATE SPARKLINE CHARTS
4 FORMAT WORKSHEET | 5 CREATE COLUMN CHART | 6 CHANGE VIEWS | 7 ASK WHAT-IF QUESTIONS

Why? *Use an IF function to determine the value for a cell based on a logical test.* The following steps assign the IF function =IF(B4>=$B$21,$B$20,0) to cell B9. This IF function determines whether or not the worksheet assigns a bonus for January.

- Click cell B9 to select the cell for the next formula.

- Click the Insert Function button in the formula bar to display the Insert Function dialog box.

- Click the 'Or select a category' arrow (Insert Function dialog box) and then select Logical in the list to populate the 'Select a function' list with logic functions.

- Click IF in the 'Select a function' list to select the required function (Figure 3–28).

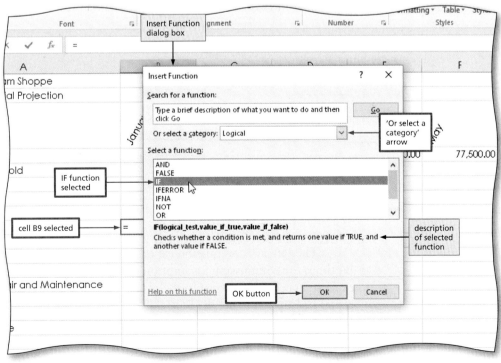

Figure 3–28

2

- Click the OK button (Insert Function dialog box) to display the Function Arguments dialog box.

- Type **b4>=b21** in the Logical_test box to enter a logical test for the IF function.

- Type **b20** in the Value_if_ true box to enter the result of the IF function if the logical test is true.

- Type **0** (zero) in the Value_if_ false box to enter the result of the IF function if the logical test is false (Figure 3–29).

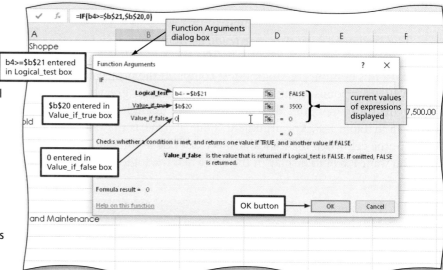

Figure 3–29

3

- Click the OK button (Function Arguments dialog box) to insert the IF function in the selected cell (Figure 3–30).

Q&A Why does cell B9 contain the value 0 (zero)?

The value that Excel displays in cell B9 depends on the values assigned to cells B4, B20, and B21. For example, if the value for January revenue in cell B4 is increased to 65,000.00 or higher, then the IF function in cell B9 will display 3,500.00. If you change the sales revenue for bonus in cell B21 from 65,000.00 to another number and the value in cell B4 is greater than or equal to the value in cell B21, it also will change the results in cell B9.

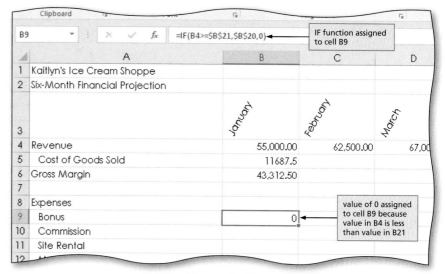

Figure 3–30

Other Ways

1. Click Logical button (Formulas tab | Function Library group), click IF

To Enter the Remaining Formulas for January

The January commission expense in cell B10 is equal to the revenue in cell B4 times the commission assumption in cell B22 (25.00%). The January site rental expense in cell B11 is equal to the projected January revenue in cell B4 times the site rental assumption in cell B23 (10.00%). Similar formulas determine the remaining January expenses in cells B12 and B13.

The total expenses value in cell B14 is equal to the sum of the expenses in the range B9:B13. The operating income in cell B16 is equal to the gross margin in cell B6 minus the total expenses in cell B14. Because the formulas are short, they are typed in the following steps, rather than entered using Point mode.

1 Select cell B10. Type =b4*b22 and then press the DOWN ARROW key to enter the formula in the selected cell. Type =b4*b23 and then press the DOWN ARROW key to enter the formula in cell B11. Type =b4*b24, press the DOWN ARROW key, type =b4*b25, and then press the DOWN ARROW key again.

2 With cell B14 selected, click the Sum button (Home tab | Editing group) twice to insert a SUM function in the selected cell. Select cell B16 to prepare to enter the next formula. Type =b6-b14 and then press the ENTER key to enter the formula in the selected cell.

3 Press CTRL+ACCENT MARK (`) to display the formulas version of the worksheet (Figure 3–31).

4 When you are finished viewing the formulas version, press CTRL+ACCENT MARK (`) again to return to the values version of the worksheet.

Q&A | Why should I view the formulas version of the worksheet?
Viewing the formulas version (Figure 3–31) of the worksheet allows you to check the formulas you entered in the range B5:B16. Recall that formulas were entered in lowercase. You can see that Excel converts all the formulas from lowercase to uppercase.

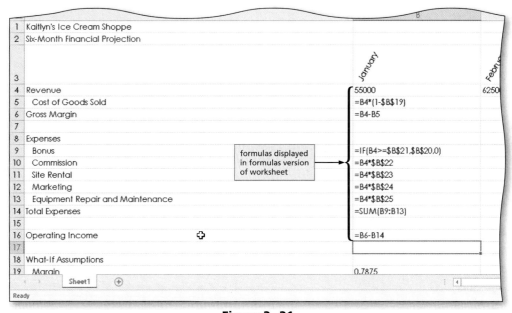

Figure 3–31

To Copy Formulas with Absolute Cell References Using the Fill Handle

1 ENTER HEADINGS & DATA | 2 ENTER FORMULAS & FUNCTIONS | **3 CREATE SPARKLINE CHARTS**
4 FORMAT WORKSHEET | 5 CREATE COLUMN CHART | 6 CHANGE VIEWS | 7 ASK WHAT-IF QUESTIONS

Why? *Using the fill handle ensures a quick, accurate copy of the formulas.* The following steps use the fill handle to copy the January formulas in column B to the other five months in columns C through G.

- Select the range
  B5:B16 and then
  point to the fill
  handle in the lower-
  right corner of the
  selected cell, B16 in
  this case, to display
  the crosshair pointer
  (Figure 3–32).

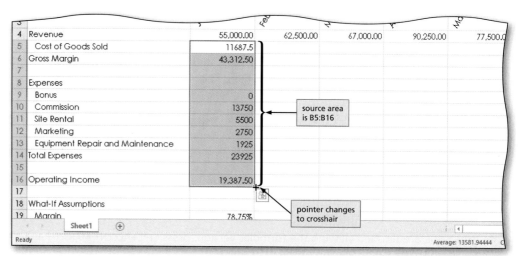

Figure 3–32

- Drag the fill handle
  to the right to copy
  the formulas from
  the source area,
  B5:B16 in this case,
  to the destination
  area, C5:G16 in this
  case, and display the
  calculated amounts
  (Figure 3–33).

Q&A

What happens
to the formulas
after performing
the copy operation?
Because the formulas
in the range B5:B16
use absolute cell
references, when
they are copied to the
range C5:G16, they still refer to the values
in the What-If Assumptions table.

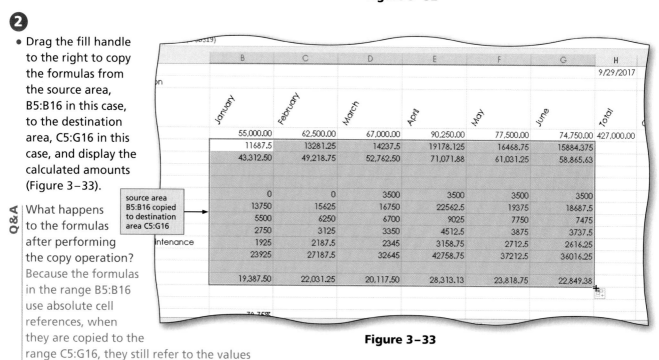

Figure 3–33

To Determine Row Totals in Nonadjacent Cells

The following steps determine the row totals in column H. To determine the
row totals using the Sum button, select only the cells in column H containing numbers
in adjacent cells to the left. If, for example, you select the range H5:H16, Excel will
display 0s as the sum of empty rows in cells H7, H8, and H15.

1 Select the range H5:H6. While holding down the CTRL key, select the range H9:H14
and cell H16, as shown in Figure 3–34.

2 Click the Sum button (Home tab | Editing group) to display the row totals in the
selected ranges (Figure 3–34).

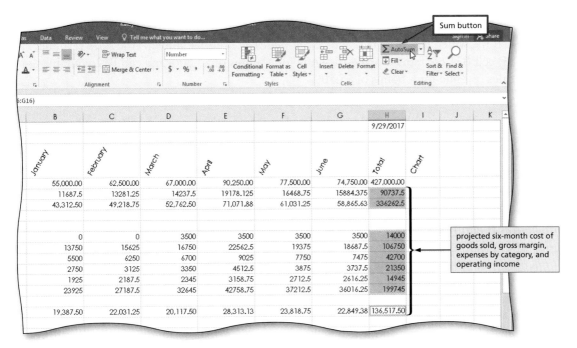

Figure 3–34

3 Save the workbook again on the same storage location with the same file name.

Nested Forms of the IF Function

A **nested IF function** is one in which the action to be taken for the true or false case includes yet another IF function. The second IF function is considered to be nested, or layered, within the first. You can use a nested IF function to add another condition to the decision-making process. Study the nested IF function below, which would add another level of bonus to the compensation at Kaitlyn's Ice Cream Shoppe. In this case, Kaitlyn's Ice Cream Shoppe assigns a bonus for sales of $65,000 and above. For months where sales make that level, additional bonus money is available for sales of $80,000 and above. In this case, three outcomes are possible, two of which involve paying a bonus. Figure 3–35 depicts a decision tree for this logical test.

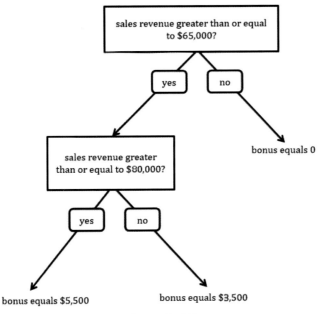

Figure 3–35

BTW

Using IFERROR
Similar to the IF function, the IFERROR function checks a formula for correctness. For example, =IFERROR(formula, "Error Message") examines the formula argument. If an error appears (such as #N/A), Excel displays the Error Message text in the cell instead of the Excel #N/A error.

Assume the following in this example: (1) the nested IF function is assigned to cell B9, which will display one of three values; (2) cell B4 contains the sales revenue; (3) cell B21 contains the sales revenue for a bonus of $3,500; and cell B22 contains the sales revenue for a bonus of $5,500.

=IF(B4>=B21, IF(B4>=B22,5500,3500),0)

The nested IF function instructs Excel to display one, and only one, of the following three values in cell B9: (1) 5,500, (2) 3,500, or (3) 0.

You can nest IF functions as deep as you want, but after you get beyond three IF functions, the logic becomes difficult to follow, and alternative solutions, such as the use of multiple cells and simple IF functions, should be considered.

Adding and Formatting Sparkline Charts

Sometimes you may want to condense a range of data into a small chart in order to show a trend or variation in the range, and Excel's standard charts may be too large or extensive for your needs. A sparkline chart provides a simple way to show trends and variations in a range of data within a single cell. Excel includes three types of sparkline charts: line, column, and win/loss. Because sparkline charts appear in a single cell, you can use them to convey succinct, eye-catching summaries of the data they represent.

To Add a Sparkline Chart to the Worksheet

1 ENTER HEADINGS & DATA | 2 ENTER FORMULAS & FUNCTIONS | 3 CREATE SPARKLINE CHARTS
4 FORMAT WORKSHEET | 5 CREATE COLUMN CHART | 6 CHANGE VIEWS | 7 ASK WHAT-IF QUESTIONS

Each row of monthly data, including those containing formulas, provides useful information that can be summarized by a line sparkline chart. **Why?** *A line sparkline chart is a good choice because it shows trends over the six-month period for each row of data.* The following steps add a line sparkline chart to cell I4 and then use the fill handle to create line sparkline charts in the range I5:I16 to represent the monthly data shown in rows 4 through 16.

- If necessary, scroll the worksheet so that both columns B and I and row 3 are visible on the screen.
- Select cell I4 to prepare to insert a sparkline chart in the cell.
- Display the Insert tab and then click the Line Sparkline button (Insert tab | Sparklines group) to display the Create Sparklines dialog box (Figure 3–36).

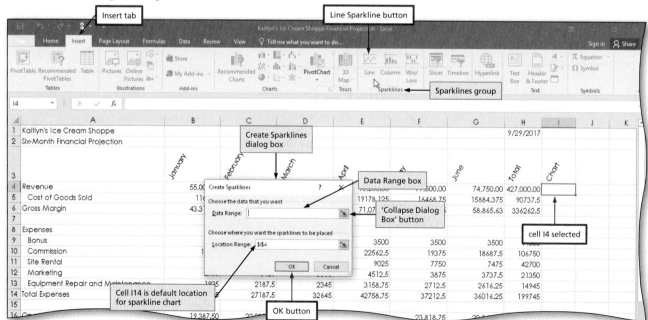

Figure 3–36

2

- Drag through the range B4:G4 to select the range. Do not release the mouse button (Figure 3–37).

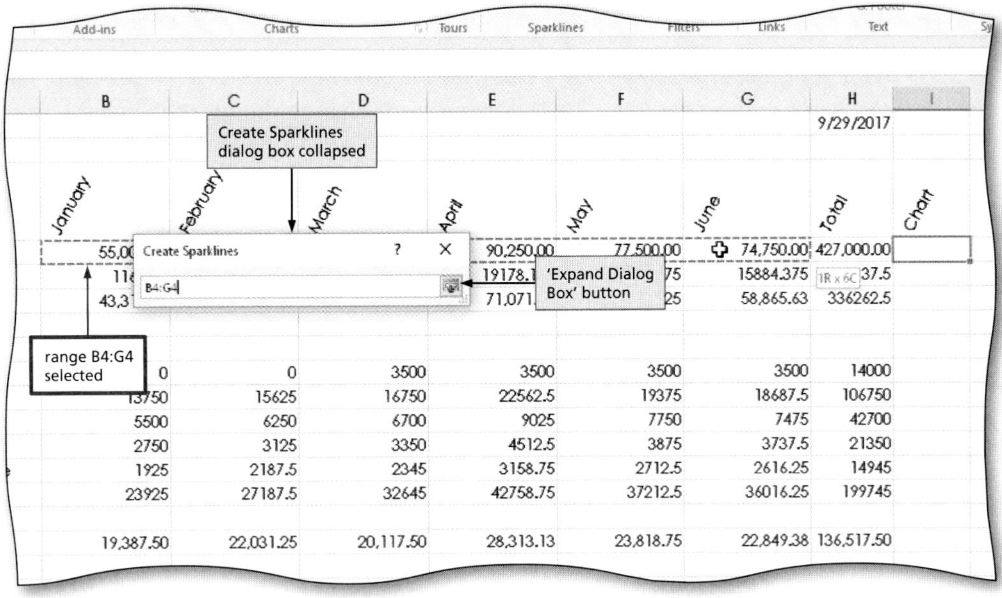

Q&A What happened to the Create Sparklines dialog box?

When a dialog box includes a 'Collapse Dialog Box' button (Figure 3–36), selecting cells or a range collapses the dialog box so that only the current text box is visible. This allows you to select your desired range without the dialog box getting in the way. Once the selection is made, the dialog box expands back to its original size. You also can click the 'Collapse Dialog Box' button to make your selection and then click the 'Expand Dialog Box' button (Figure 3–37) to expand the dialog box.

Figure 3–37

3

- Release the mouse button to insert the selected range, B4:G4 in this case, in the Data Range box.

- Click the OK button shown in Figure 3–36 (Create Sparklines dialog box) to insert a line sparkline chart in the selected cell and display the Sparkline Tools Design tab (Figure 3–38).

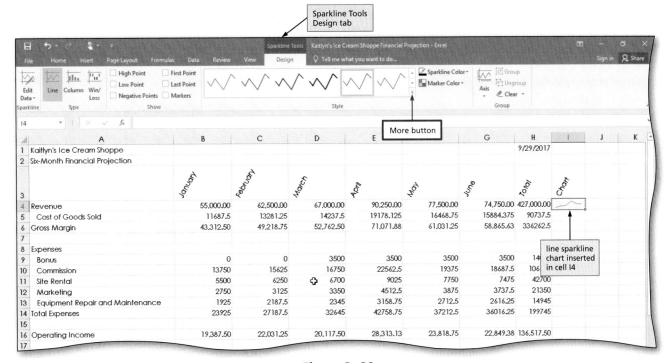

Figure 3–38

To Change the Sparkline Style and Copy the Sparkline Chart

Why? *The default style option may not provide the visual impact you seek. Changing the sparkline style allows you to alter how the sparkline chart appears.* The following steps change the sparkline chart style.

- Click the More button (Sparkline Tools Design tab | Style group) to display the Sparkline Style gallery (Figure 3–39).

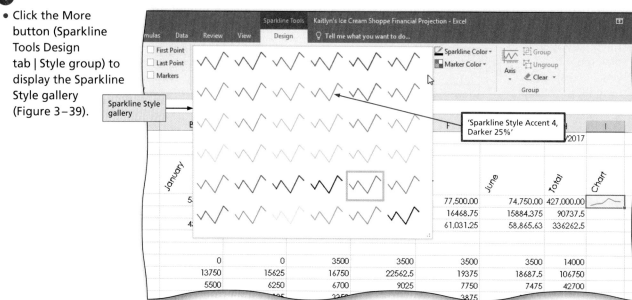

Figure 3–39

- Click 'Sparkline Style Accent 4, Darker 25%' in the Sparkline Style gallery to apply the style to the sparkline chart in the selected cell, I4 in this case.

- Point to the fill handle in cell I4 and then drag through cell I16 to copy the line sparkline chart.

- Select cell I18 (Figure 3–40).

Q&A Why do sparkline charts not appear in cells I7, I8, and I15? There is no data in the ranges B7:G7, B8:G8, and B15:G15, so Excel cannot draw sparkline charts. If you added data to cells in those ranges, Excel would then generate line sparkline charts for those rows, because the drag operation defined sparkline charts for cells I7, I8, and I15.

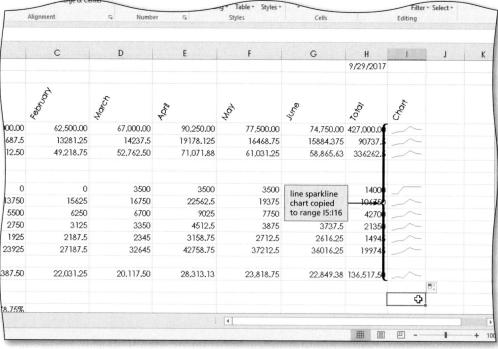

Figure 3–40

To Change the Sparkline Type

In addition to changing the sparkline chart style, you also can change the sparkline chart type. *Why? You may decide that a different chart type will better illustrate the characteristics of your data.* As shown in Figure 3–40, most of the sparkline charts look similar. Changing the sparkline chart type allows you to decide if a different chart type will better present your data to the reader. The following steps change the line sparkline charts to column sparkline charts.

- Select the range I4:I16 to select the sparkline charts.

- Click the Sparkline Tools Design tab to make it the active tab.

- Click the 'Convert to Column Sparkline' button (Sparkline Tools Design tab | Type group) to change the sparkline charts in the selected range to the column type (Figure 3–41).

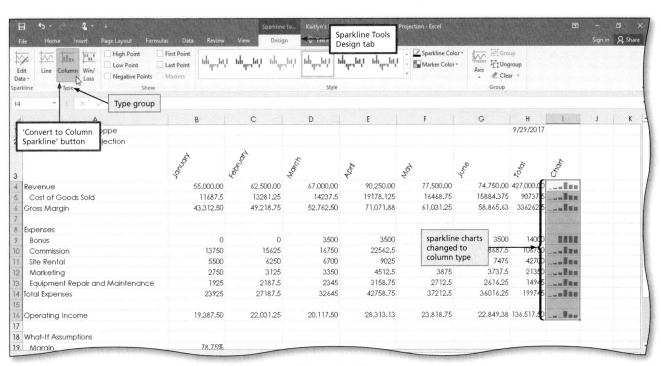

Figure 3–41

- Select cell I18.

- Save the workbook again on the same storage location with the same file name.

Formatting the Worksheet

The worksheet created thus far shows the financial projections for the six-month period, from January to June. Its appearance is uninteresting, however, even though some minimal formatting (formatting assumptions numbers, changing the column widths, formatting the date, and formatting the sparkline chart) was performed earlier. This section completes the formatting of the worksheet by making the numbers easier to read and emphasizing the titles, assumptions, categories, and totals, as shown in Figure 3–42.

BTW

**Customizing
Sparkline Charts**
You can customize sparkline charts in a number of ways on the Sparkline Tools Design tab. In the Show group (Sparkline Tools Design tab), you can specify values to show as markers on the chart, such as the highest value, lowest value, any negative numbers, the first point, and the last point. You can change the color of the sparkline and markers in the Style group (Sparkline Tools Design tab).

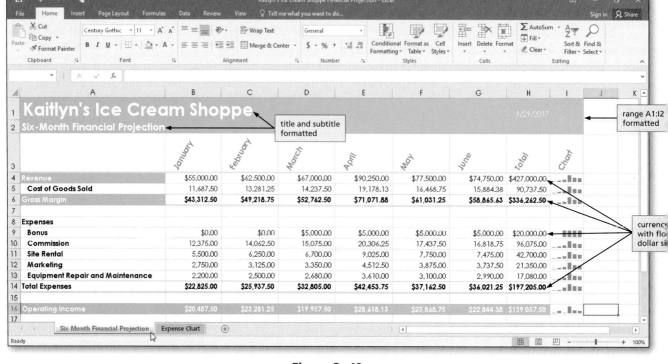

Figure 3–42

How should you format various elements of the worksheet?

A worksheet, such as the one presented in this module, should be formatted in the following manner: (1) format the numbers; (2) format the worksheet title, column titles, row titles, and total rows; and (3) format the assumptions table. Numbers in heading rows and total rows should be formatted with a currency symbol. Other dollar amounts should be formatted with a comma style. The assumptions table should be diminished in its formatting so that it does not distract from the main data and calculations in the worksheet. Assigning a smaller font size to the data in the assumptions table would set it apart from other data formatted with a larger font size.

To Assign Formats to Nonadjacent Ranges

1 ENTER HEADINGS & DATA | 2 ENTER FORMULAS & FUNCTIONS | 3 CREATE SPARKLINE CHARTS
4 FORMAT WORKSHEET | 5 CREATE COLUMN CHART | 6 CHANGE VIEWS | 7 ASK WHAT-IF QUESTIONS

The following steps assign formats to the numbers in rows 4 through 16. **Why?** *These formats increase the readability of the data.*

❶

- Select the range B4:H4 as the first range to format.

- While holding down the CTRL key, select the nonadjacent ranges B6:H6, B9:H9, B14:H14, and B16:H16, and then release the CTRL key to select nonadjacent ranges.

- Click the Number Format Dialog Box Launcher (Home tab | Number group) to display the Format Cells dialog box.

- Click Currency in the Category list (Format Cells dialog box), if necessary select 2 in the Decimal places box and then select $ in the Symbol list to ensure a dollar sign shows in the cells to be formatted, and select the black font color ($1,234.10) in the Negative numbers list to specify the desired currency style for the selected ranges (Figure 3–43).

Why was this particular style chosen for the negative numbers?

In accounting, negative numbers often are shown with parentheses surrounding the value rather than with a negative sign preceding the value. Although the data being used in this module contains no negative numbers, you still must select a negative number format. It is important to be consistent when selecting negative number formats if you are applying different formats in a column; otherwise, the decimal points may not line up.

Q&A

Why is the Format Cells dialog box used to create the format for the ranges in this step?

The requirements for this worksheet call for a floating dollar sign. You can use the Format Cells dialog box to assign a currency style with a floating dollar sign, instead of using the 'Accounting Number Format' button (Home tab | Number group), which assigns a fixed dollar sign.

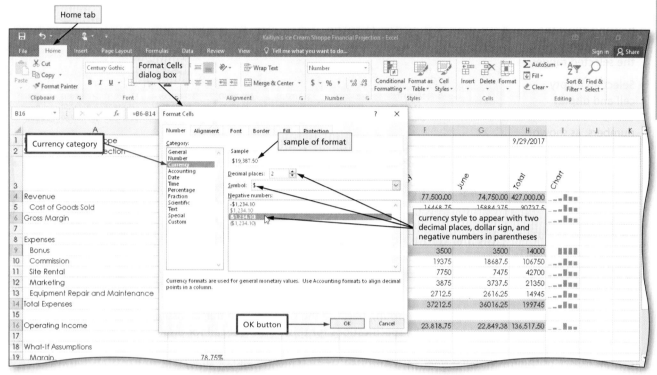

Figure 3–43

2

- Click the OK button (Format Cells dialog box) to close the Format Cells dialog box and apply the desired format to the selected ranges.

- Select the range B5:H5 as the next range to format.

- While holding down the CTRL key, select the range B10:H13, and then release the CTRL key to select nonadjacent ranges.

- Click the Number Format Dialog Box Launcher (Home tab | Number group) to display the Format Cells dialog box.

- Click Currency in the Category list (Format Cells dialog box), if necessary select 2 in the Decimal places box, select None in the Symbol list so that a dollar sign does not show in the cells to be formatted, and select the black font color (1,234.10) in the Negative numbers list (Figure 3–44).

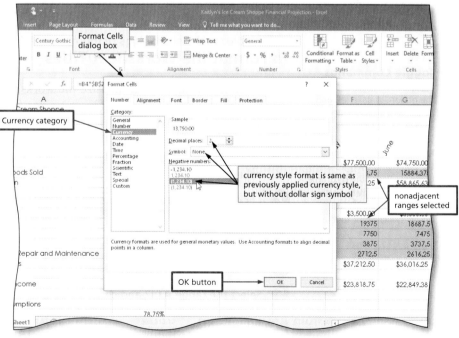

Figure 3–44

To Copy a Cell's Format Using the Format Painter Button

Why? *Using the format painter, you can format a cell quickly by copying a cell's format to another cell or a range of cells.* The following steps use the format painter to copy the format of cell A4 to cells A6 and the range A16:H16.

- If necessary, click cell A4 to select a source cell for the format to paint.

- Double-click the Format Painter button (Home tab | Clipboard group) and then move the pointer onto the worksheet to cause the pointer to change to a block plus sign with a paintbrush (Figure 3–48).

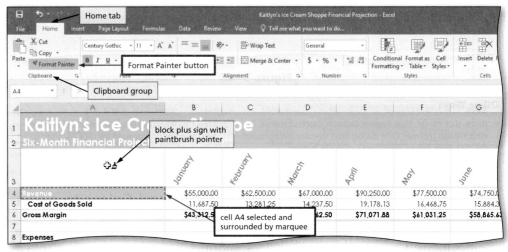

Figure 3–48

- Click cell A6 to assign the format of the source cell, A4 in this case, to the destination cell, A6 in this case.

- With the pointer still a block plus sign with a paintbrush, drag through the range A16:H16 to assign the format of the source cell, A4 in this case, to the destination range, A16:H16 in this case.

- Click the Format Painter button or press the ESC key to turn off the format painter.

- Apply the currency style to the range B16:H16 to cause the cells in the range to appear with a floating dollar sign and two decimal places (Figure 3–49).

Q&A Why does the currency style need to be reapplied to the range B16:H16?

Sometimes, the use of the format painter results in unintended outcomes. In this case, changing the background fill color and font color for the range B16:H16 resulted in the loss of the currency style because the format being copied did not include the currency style. Reapplying the currency style to the range results in the proper number style, fill color, and font color.

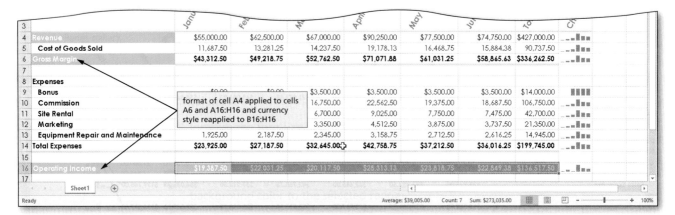

Figure 3–49

Other Ways

1. Click Copy button (Home tab | Clipboard group), select cell, click Paste arrow (Home tab | Clipboard group), click Formatting button in Paste gallery

2. Right-click cell, click Copy on shortcut menu, right-click cell, click Formatting icon on shortcut menu

Q&A Why is the Format Cells dialog box used to create the format for the ranges in this step?
The requirements for this worksheet call for a floating dollar sign. You can use the Format Cells dialog box to assign a currency style with a floating dollar sign, instead of using the 'Accounting Number Format' button (Home tab | Number group), which assigns a fixed dollar sign.

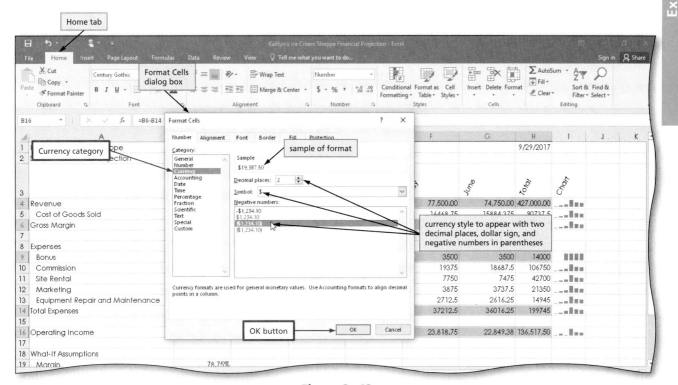

Figure 3–43

2

- Click the OK button (Format Cells dialog box) to close the Format Cells dialog box and apply the desired format to the selected ranges.

- Select the range B5:H5 as the next range to format.

- While holding down the CTRL key, select the range B10:H13, and then release the CTRL key to select nonadjacent ranges.

- Click the Number Format Dialog Box Launcher (Home tab | Number group) to display the Format Cells dialog box.

- Click Currency in the Category list (Format Cells dialog box), if necessary select 2 in the Decimal places box, select None in the Symbol list so that a dollar sign does not show in the cells to be formatted, and select the black font color (1,234.10) in the Negative numbers list (Figure 3–44).

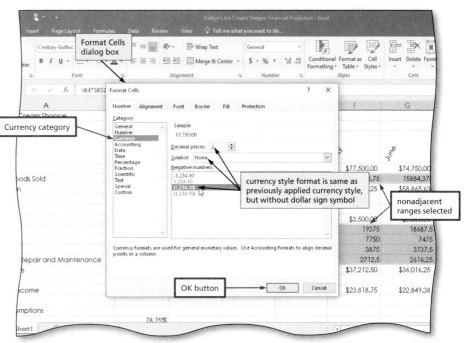

Figure 3–44

❸

- Click the OK button (Format Cells dialog box) to close the Format Cells dialog box and apply the desired format to the selected ranges.

- Select an empty cell and display the formatted numbers, as shown in Figure 3–45.

Q&A Why is the Format Cells dialog box used to create the style for the ranges in Steps 2 and 3? The Format Cells dialog box is used to assign the comma style instead of the Comma Style button (Home tab | Number group), because the Comma Style button assigns a format that displays a dash (–) when a cell has a value of 0. The specifications for this worksheet call for displaying a value of 0 as 0.00 (see cell B9 in Figure 3–45) rather than as a dash. To create a comma style using the Format Cells dialog box, you use a currency style with no dollar sign.

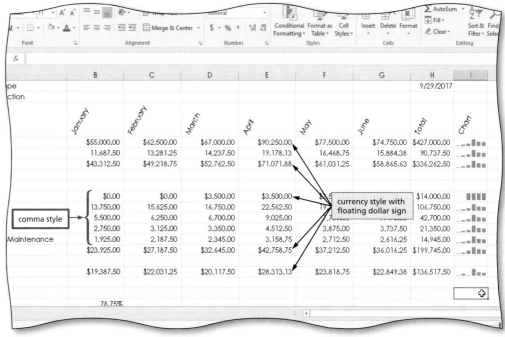

Figure 3–45

Other Ways

1. Right-click range, click Format Cells on shortcut menu, click Number tab (Format Cells dialog box), click category in Category list, select format, click OK button (Format Cells dialog box)

2. Press CTRL+1, click Number tab (Format Cells dialog box), click category in Category list, select format, click OK button (Format Cells dialog box)

To Format the Worksheet Titles

The following steps emphasize the worksheet titles in cells A1 and A2 by changing the font and font size. The steps also format all of the row headers in column A with a bold font style.

❶ Press CTRL+HOME to select cell A1 and then click the column A heading to select the column.

❷ Click the Bold button (Home tab | Font group) to bold all of the data in the selected column.

❸ Increase the font size in cell A1 to 28 point.

❹ Increase the font size in cell A2 to 16 point.

❺ Select the range A1:I2 and change the fill color to Green, Accent 4 to add a background color to the selected range.

❻ With A1:I2 selected, change the font color to White, Background 1.

❼ Click an empty cell to deselect the range (Figure 3–46).

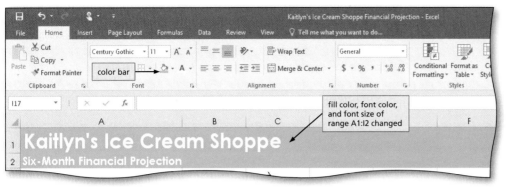

Figure 3–46

Other Ways

1. Right-click range, click Format Cells on shortcut menu, click Fill tab (Format Cells dialog box) to color background (or click Font tab to color font), click OK button

2. Press CTRL+1, click Fill tab (Format Cells dialog box) to color background (or click Font tab to color font), click OK button

To Assign Cell Styles to Nonadjacent Rows and Colors to a Cell

The following steps improve the appearance of the worksheet by formatting the headings in row 3 and the totals in rows 6, 14, and 16. Cell A4 also is formatted with a background color and font color.

① Select the range A3:I3 and apply the Heading 2 cell style.

② Select the range A6:H6 and while holding down the CTRL key, select the ranges A14:H14 and A16:H16.

③ Apply the Total cell style to the selected nonadjacent ranges.

④ Select cell A4 and click the Fill Color button (Home tab | Font group) to apply the last fill color used (Green, Accent 4) to the cell contents.

⑤ Click the Font Color button (Home tab | Font group) to apply the last font color used (White, Background 1) to the cell contents (Figure 3–47).

BTW
The Fill and Font Color Buttons
You may have noticed that the color bar at the bottom of the Fill Color and Font Color buttons (Home tab | Font group) (Figure 3–46) changes to the most recently selected color. To apply this same color to a cell background or text, select a cell and then click the Fill Color button to use the color as a background or click the Font Color button to use the color as a font color.

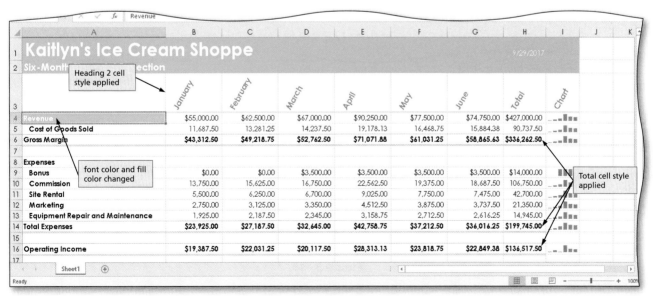

Figure 3–47

To Copy a Cell's Format Using the Format Painter Button

Why? *Using the format painter, you can format a cell quickly by copying a cell's format to another cell or a range of cells.* The following steps use the format painter to copy the format of cell A4 to cells A6 and the range A16:H16.

❶

- If necessary, click cell A4 to select a source cell for the format to paint.

- Double-click the Format Painter button (Home tab | Clipboard group) and then move the pointer onto the worksheet to cause the pointer to change to a block plus sign with a paintbrush (Figure 3–48).

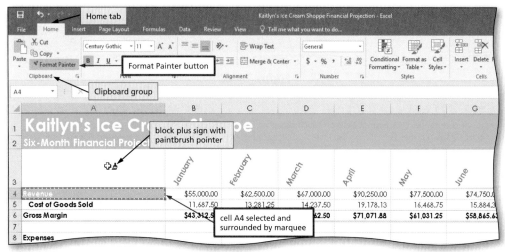

Figure 3–48

❷

- Click cell A6 to assign the format of the source cell, A4 in this case, to the destination cell, A6 in this case.

- With the pointer still a block plus sign with a paintbrush, drag through the range A16:H16 to assign the format of the source cell, A4 in this case, to the destination range, A16:H16 in this case.

- Click the Format Painter button or press the ESC key to turn off the format painter.

- Apply the currency style to the range B16:H16 to cause the cells in the range to appear with a floating dollar sign and two decimal places (Figure 3–49).

Q&A Why does the currency style need to be reapplied to the range B16:H16?
Sometimes, the use of the format painter results in unintended outcomes. In this case, changing the background fill color and font color for the range B16:H16 resulted in the loss of the currency style because the format being copied did not include the currency style. Reapplying the currency style to the range results in the proper number style, fill color, and font color.

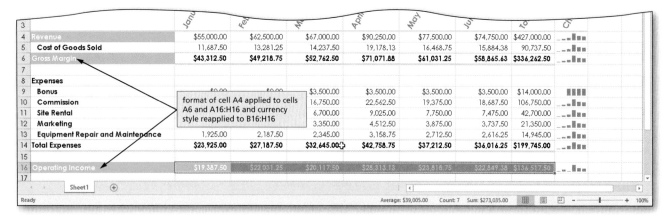

Figure 3–49

Other Ways

1. Click Copy button (Home tab | Clipboard group), select cell, click Paste arrow (Home tab | Clipboard group), click Formatting button in Paste gallery
2. Right-click cell, click Copy on shortcut menu, right-click cell, click Formatting icon on shortcut menu

To Format the What-If Assumptions Table

The following steps format the What-If Assumptions table, the final step in improving the appearance of the worksheet.

1 Select cell A18.

2 Change the font size to 8 pt.

3 Italicize and underline the text in cell A18.

4 Select the range A19:B25, and change the font size to 8 pt.

5 Select the range A18:B25 and then click the Fill Color button (Home tab | Font group) to apply the most recently used background color to the selected range.

6 Click the Font Color button (Home tab | Font group) to apply the most recently used font color to the selected range.

7 Deselect the range A18:B25 and display the What-If Assumptions table, as shown in Figure 3–50.

8 Save the workbook on the same storage location with the same file name.

Q&A | What happens when I click the Italic and Underline buttons?
When you assign the italic font style to a cell, Excel slants the characters slightly to the right, as shown in cell A18 in Figure 3–50. The underline format underlines only the characters in the cell, rather than the entire cell, as is the case when you assign a cell a bottom border.

BTW

Painting a Format to Nonadjacent Ranges
Double-click the Format Painter button (Home tab | Clipboard group) and then drag through the nonadjacent ranges to paint the formats to the ranges. Click the Format Painter button again to deactivate it.

BTW

Selecting Nonadjacent Ranges
One of the more difficult tasks to learn is selecting nonadjacent ranges. To complete this task, do not hold down the CTRL key when you select the first range because Excel will consider the current active cell to be the first selection, and you may not want the current active cell in the selection. Once the first range is selected, hold down the CTRL key and drag through the nonadjacent ranges. If a desired range is not visible in the window, use the scroll arrows to view the range. You need not hold down the CTRL key while you scroll.

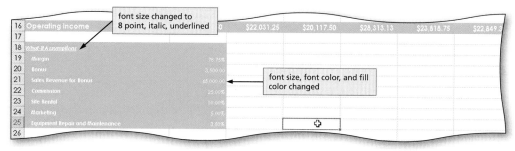

Figure 3–50

Break Point: If you wish to take a break, this is a good place to do so. You can exit Excel now. To resume at a later time, run Excel, open the file called Kaitlyn's Ice Cream Shoppe Financial Projection, and continue following the steps from this location forward.

Adding a Clustered Column Chart to the Workbook

The next step in the module is to create a clustered column chart on a separate sheet in the workbook, as shown in Figure 3–51. Use a clustered column chart to compare values side by side, broken down by category. Each column shows the value for a particular category, by month in this case.

The clustered column chart in Figure 3–51 shows the projected expense amounts, by category, for each of the six months. The clustered column chart allows the user to see how the various expense categories compare with each other each month, and across months.

Recall that charts can either be embedded in a worksheet or placed on a separate chart sheet. The clustered column chart will reside on its own sheet, because if placed on the worksheet, it would not be visible when the worksheet first opens and could be missed.

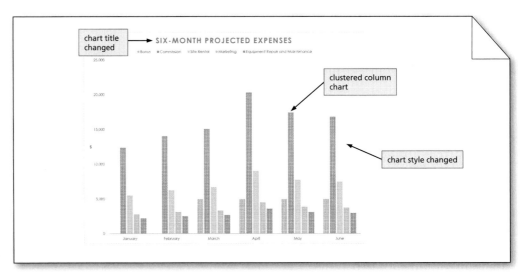

Figure 3–51

In this worksheet, the ranges to chart are the nonadjacent ranges B3:G3 (month names) and A9:G13 (monthly projected expenses, by category). The month names in the range B3:G3 will identify the major groups for the chart; these entries are called **category names**. The range A9:G13 contains the data that determines the individual columns in each month cluster, along with the names that identify each column; these entries are called the **data series**. Because six months of five expense categories are being charted, the chart will contain six clusters of five columns each, unless a category has the value of zero for a given month.

To Draw a Clustered Column Chart on a Separate Chart Sheet Using the Recommended Charts Feature

1 ENTER HEADINGS & DATA | 2 ENTER FORMULAS & FUNCTIONS | 3 CREATE SPARKLINE CHARTS
4 FORMAT WORKSHEET | 5 CREATE COLUMN CHART | 6 CHANGE VIEWS | 7 ASK WHAT-IF QUESTIONS

Why? *This Excel feature evaluates the selected data and makes suggestions regarding which chart types will provide the most suitable representation.* The following steps use the Recommended Charts feature to draw the clustered column chart on a separate chart sheet.

1

- Select the range A3:G3 to identify the range of the categories.

- Hold down the CTRL key and select the data range A9:G13.

- Display the Insert tab.

- Click the Recommended Charts button (Insert tab | Charts group) to display the Insert Chart dialog box with the Recommended Charts tab active (Figure 3–52).

Experiment

- Click the various recommended chart types, reading the description for each of its best use and examining the chart preview.

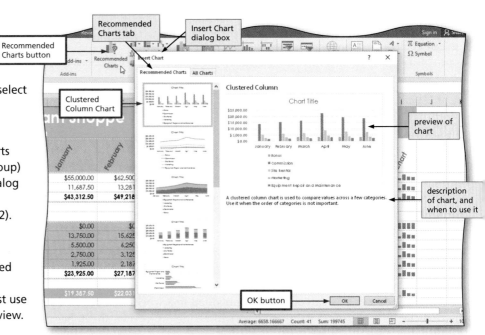

Figure 3–52

2

- Click the first Clustered Column recommended chart to select it and then click the OK button (Insert Chart dialog box).

- When Excel draws the chart, click the Move Chart button (Chart Tools Design tab | Location group) to display the Move Chart dialog box.

- Click New sheet (Move Chart dialog box) and then type **Expense Chart** in the New sheet text box to enter a sheet tab name for the chart sheet (Figure 3–53).

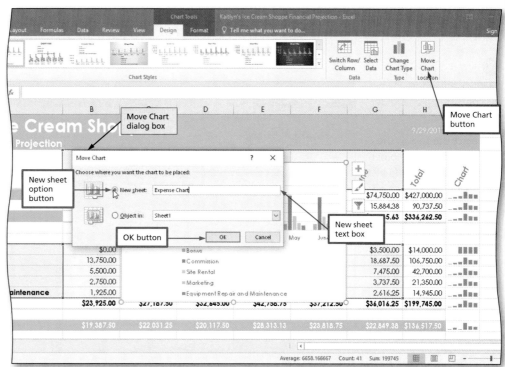

Figure 3–53

3

- Click the OK button (Move Chart dialog box) to move the chart to a new chart sheet with a new sheet tab name, Expense Chart (Figure 3–54).

Q&A Why do January and February have only four columns charted?
Both January and February have a value of $0 for the Bonus category. Values of zero are not charted in a column chart, so these two months have one fewer column than the other months.

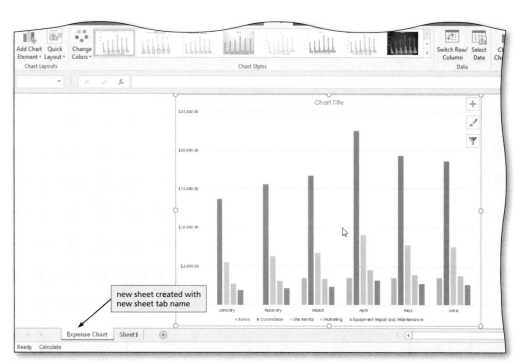

Figure 3–54

Other Ways

1. Select range to chart, PRESS F11

To Insert a Chart Title

The next step is to insert a chart title. *Why? A chart title identifies the chart content for the viewer.* Before you can format a chart item, such as the chart title, you must select it. The following step inserts a chart title.

- Click anywhere in the chart title placeholder to select it.

- Select the text in the chart title placeholder and then type **Six-Month Projected Expenses** to add a new chart title.

- Select the text in the new title and then display the Home tab.

- Click the Underline button (Home tab | Font group) to assign an underline format to the chart title (Figure 3–55).

- Click anywhere outside of the chart title to deselect it.

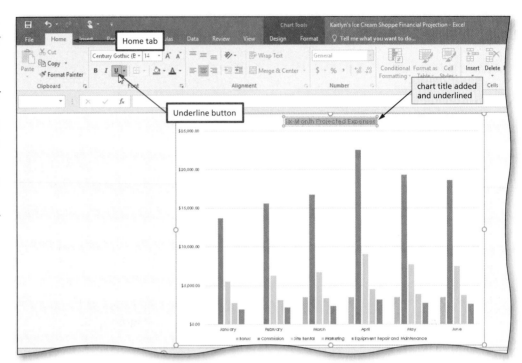

Figure 3–55

To Add Data Labels

The next step is to add data labels. *Why? Data labels can make a chart more easily understood. You can remove them if they do not accomplish that.* The following steps add data labels.

- Click the Chart Elements button (on the chart) to display the Chart Elements gallery. Point to Data Labels to display an arrow and then click the arrow to display the Data Labels fly-out menu (Figure 3–56).

🔎 **Experiment**

- If you are using a mouse, point to each option on the Data Labels fly-out menu to see a live preview of the data labels.

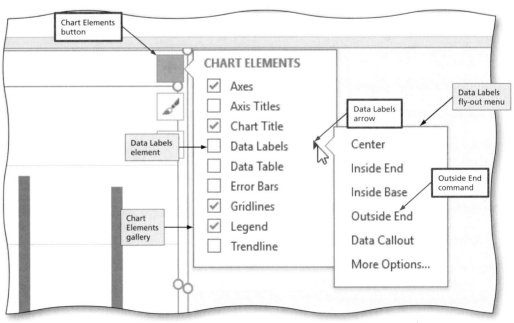

Figure 3–56

2

- Click Outside End on the Data Labels fly-out menu so that data labels are displayed outside the chart at the end of each column.

- Click the Chart Elements button to close the gallery (Figure 3–57).

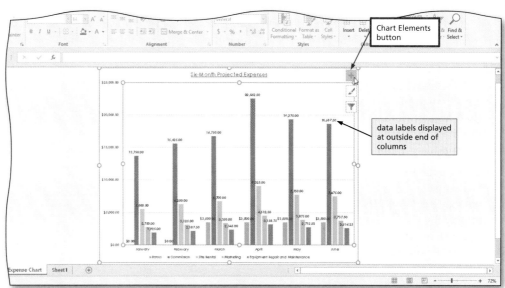

Figure 3–57

To Apply Chart Filters

1 ENTER HEADINGS & DATA | 2 ENTER FORMULAS & FUNCTIONS | 3 CREATE SPARKLINE CHARTS
4 FORMAT WORKSHEET | 5 CREATE COLUMN CHART | 6 CHANGE VIEWS | 7 ASK WHAT-IF QUESTIONS

Why? *With some data, you may find that certain data series or categories make it difficult to examine differences and patterns between other series or categories. Excel allows you to easily filter data series and categories to allow more in-depth examinations of subsets of data.* In this case, filters can be used to temporarily remove the compensation categories Bonus and Commission from the chart, to allow a comparison across the non-compensation expenses. The following steps apply filters to the clustered column chart.

1

- Click the Chart Filters button (on the chart) to display the Chart Filters gallery.

- In the Series section, click the Bonus and Commission check boxes to remove their check marks and then click the Apply button to filter these series from the chart (Figure 3–58).

 What happens when I remove the check marks from Bonus and Commission?
When you remove the check marks from Bonus and Commission, Excel filters the Bonus and Commission series out and redraws the chart without them.

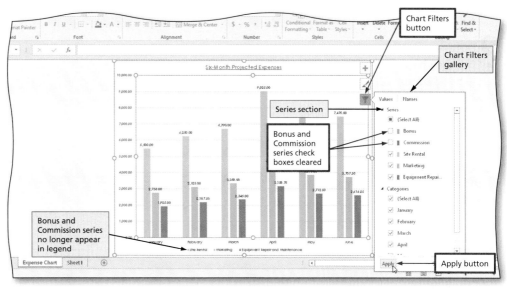

Figure 3–58

2

- Click the Chart Filters button to close the gallery.

To Add an Axis Title to the Chart

Why? Often the unit of measurement or categories for the charted data is not obvious. You can add an axis title, or titles for both axes, for clarity or completeness. The following steps add an axis title for the vertical axis.

- If necessary, click anywhere in the chart area outside the chart to select the chart.

- Click the Chart Elements button to display the Chart Elements gallery. Point to Axis Titles to display an arrow and then click the arrow to display the Axis Titles fly-out menu.

🔍 **Experiment**

- Point to each option on the fly-out menu to see a live preview of the axes' titles.

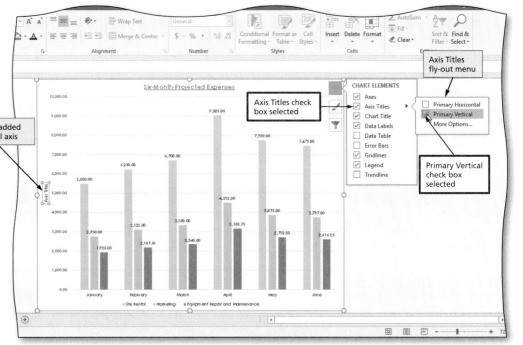

Figure 3–59

- Click Primary Vertical on the Axis Titles fly-out menu to add an axis title to the vertical axis (Figure 3–59).

②

- Click the Chart Elements button to remove the Chart Elements gallery from the window.

- Select the placeholder text in the vertical axis title and replace it with $ (a dollar sign).

- Right-click the axis title to display a shortcut menu (Figure 3–60).

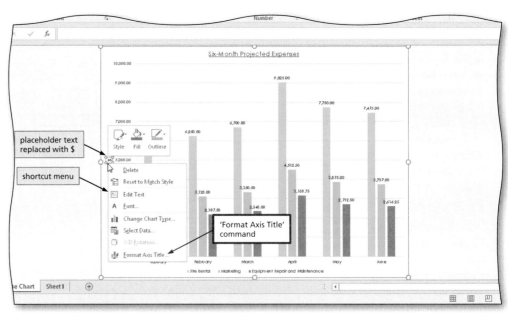

Figure 3–60

- Click 'Format Axis Title' on the shortcut menu to open the Format Axis Title task pane.

- If necessary, click the Title Options tab, click the 'Size & Properties' button, and then, if necessary, click the Alignment arrow to expand the Alignment section.

- Click the Text direction arrow to display the Text direction list (Figure 3–61).

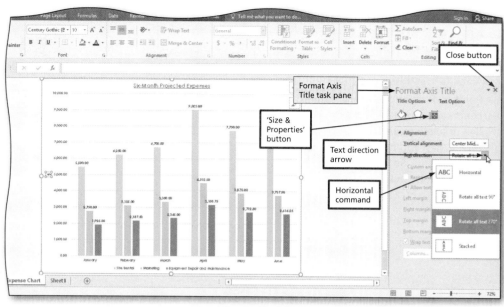

Figure 3–61

- Click Horizontal in the Text direction list to change the orientation of the vertical axis title.

- Click the Close button (shown in Figure 3–61) on the task pane to close the Format Axis Title task pane.

To Change the Chart Style

Why? You decide that a chart with a different look would better convey meaning to viewers. The following steps change the chart style.

- Click the More button (Chart Tools Design tab | Chart Styles group) (shown in Figure 3–61) to display the Chart Styles gallery (Figure 3–62).

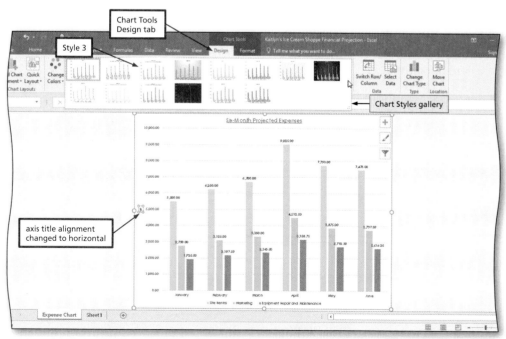

Figure 3–62

- Click Style 3 to apply a new style to the chart (Figure 3–63).

🔍 **Experiment**

- Point to the various chart styles to see a live preview of each one. When you have finished, click Style 3 to apply that style.

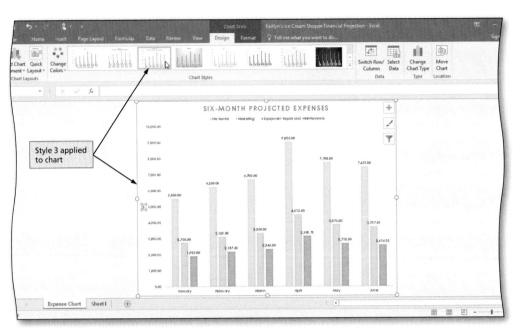

Figure 3–63

To Modify the Chart Axis Number Format

1 ENTER HEADINGS & DATA | 2 ENTER FORMULAS & FUNCTIONS | 3 CREATE SPARKLINE CHARTS
4 FORMAT WORKSHEET | 5 CREATE COLUMN CHART | 6 CHANGE VIEWS | 7 ASK WHAT-IF QUESTIONS

Why? *The two decimal places in the vertical chart axis numbers are not necessary and make the axis appear cluttered.* The following steps format the numbers in the chart axis to contain no decimal places.

- Right-click any value on the vertical axis to display the shortcut menu (Figure 3–64).

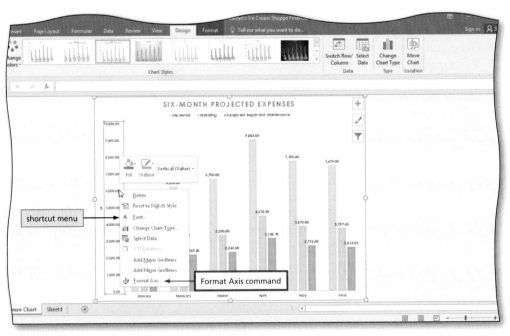

Figure 3–64

2

- Click Format Axis on the shortcut menu to open the Format Axis task pane.

- If necessary, click the Axis Options tab in the Format Axis task pane and then scroll until Number is visible. Click the Number arrow to expand the Number section and then scroll to review options related to formatting numbers.

- Change the number in the Decimal places text box to 0 (Figure 3–65).

3

- Close the Format Axis task pane.

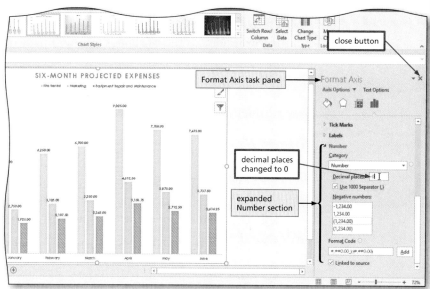

Figure 3–65

To Remove Filters and Data Labels

You decide that the data labels on the bars are distracting and add no value to the chart. You decide to remove the data labels and filters so that all expense data is once again visible. The following steps remove the data labels and the filters.

1 Click the Chart Elements button to display the Chart Elements gallery.

2 Click the Data Labels check box to remove the check mark for the data labels.

3 Click the Chart Elements button again to close the gallery.

4 Click the Chart Filters button to display the Chart Filters fly-out menu.

5 In the Series section, click Bonus and then Commission, click the Apply button to add the compensation data back into the chart, and then click the Chart Filters button again to close the menu (Figure 3–66).

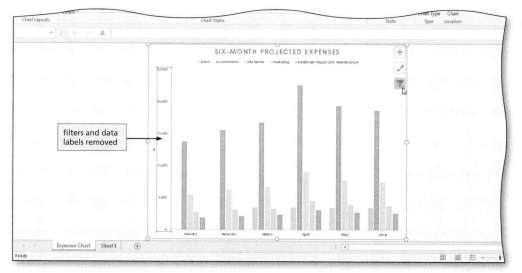

Figure 3–66

Organizing the Workbook

Once the content of the workbook is complete, you can address the organization of the workbook. If the workbook has multiple worksheets, place the worksheet on top that you want the reader to see first. Default sheet names in Excel are not descriptive. Renaming the sheets with descriptive names helps the reader find information that he or she is looking for. Modifying the sheet tabs through the use of color further distinguishes multiple sheets from each other.

To Rename and Color Sheet Tabs

The following steps rename the sheets and color the sheet tabs.

1 Change the color of the Expense Chart sheet tab to Green, Accent 4 (column 8, row 1).

2 Double-click the sheet tab labeled Sheet1 at the bottom of the screen.

3 Type `Six-Month Financial Projection` as the new sheet tab name and then press the ENTER key.

4 Change the sheet tab color of the Six-Month Financial Projection sheet to Blue, Accent 2 (column 6, row 1) and then select an empty cell (Figure 3–67).

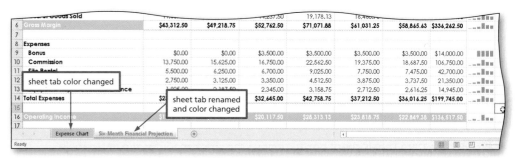

Figure 3–67

To Reorder the Sheet Tabs

1 ENTER HEADINGS & DATA | 2 ENTER FORMULAS & FUNCTIONS | 3 CREATE SPARKLINE CHARTS
4 FORMAT WORKSHEET | 5 CREATE COLUMN CHART | 6 CHANGE VIEWS | 7 ASK WHAT-IF QUESTIONS

Why? *You want the most important worksheets to appear first in a workbook, so you need to change the order of sheets.* The following step reorders the sheets so that the worksheet precedes the chart sheet in the workbook.

- Drag the Six-Month Financial Projection tab to the left so that it precedes the Expense Chart sheet tab to rearrange the sequence of the sheets (Figure 3–68).

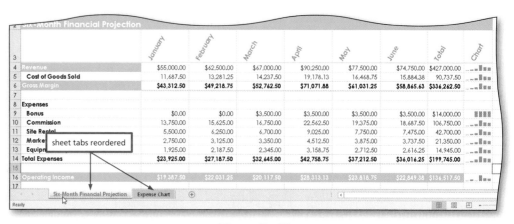

Figure 3–68

Other Ways

1. To move sheet, right-click sheet tab, click Move or Copy on shortcut menu, click OK button

To Check Spelling in Multiple Sheets

By default, the spelling checker reviews spelling only in the selected sheets. It will check all the cells in the selected sheets, unless you select a range of two or more cells. Before checking the spelling, the following steps select both worksheets in the workbook so that both are checked for any spelling errors.

1 With the Six-Month Financial Projection sheet active, press CTRL+HOME to select cell A1. Hold down the CTRL key and then click the Expense Chart tab to select both sheets.

2 Display the Review tab and then click the Spelling button (Review tab | Proofing group) to check spelling in the selected sheets.

3 Correct any errors and then click the OK button (Spelling dialog box or Microsoft Excel dialog box) when the spelling checker is finished.

BTW
Checking Spelling
Unless you first select a range of cells or an object before starting the spelling checker, Excel checks the entire selected worksheet, including all cell values, cell comments, embedded charts, text boxes, buttons, and headers and footers.

To Preview and Print the Worksheet

After checking the spelling, the next step is to preview and print the worksheets. As with spelling, Excel previews and prints only the selected sheets. In addition, because the worksheet is too wide to print in portrait orientation, the orientation must be changed to landscape. The following steps adjust the orientation and scale, preview the worksheets, and then print the worksheets.

1 If both sheets are not selected, hold down the CTRL key and then click the tab of the inactive sheet.

2 Click File on the ribbon to open the Backstage view.

3 Click the Print tab in the Backstage view to display the Print gallery.

4 Click the Portrait Orientation button in the Settings area and then select Landscape Orientation to select the desired orientation.

5 Click the No Scaling button in the Settings area and then select 'Fit Sheet on One Page' to cause the worksheets to print on one page.

6 Verify that the selected printer will print a hard copy of the document. If necessary, click the printer button to display a list of available printer options and then click the desired printer to change the currently selected printer.

7 Click the Print button in the Print gallery to print the worksheet in landscape orientation on the currently selected printer.

8 When the printer stops, retrieve the printed worksheets (shown in Figure 3–69a and Figure 3–69b).

9 Right-click the Six-Month Financial Projection tab, and then click Ungroup Sheets on the shortcut menu to deselect the Expense Chart tab.

10 Save the workbook again on the same storage location with the same file name.

BTW
Distributing a Workbook
Instead of printing and distributing a hard copy of a workbook, you can distribute the workbook electronically. Options include sending the workbook via email; posting it on cloud storage (such as OneDrive) and sharing the file with others; posting it on social media, a blog, or other website; and sharing a link associated with an online location of the workbook. You also can create and share a PDF or XPS image of the workbook, so that users can view the file in Acrobat Reader or XPS Viewer instead of in Excel.

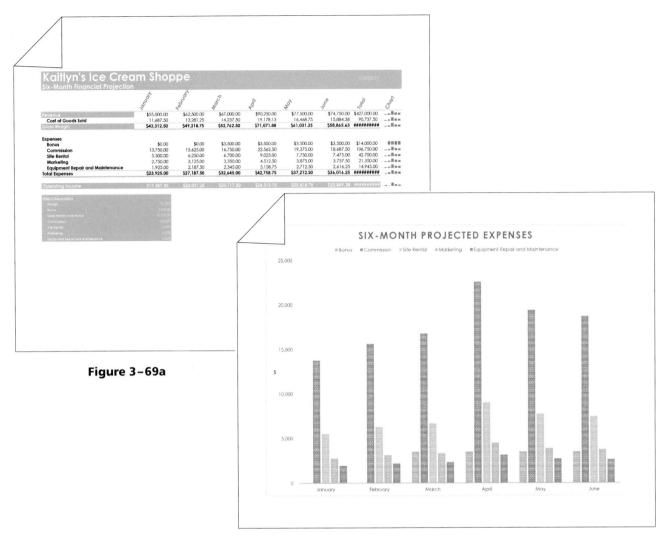

Figure 3–69a

Figure 3–69b

Changing the View of the Worksheet

With Excel, you easily can change the view of the worksheet. For example, you can magnify or shrink the worksheet on the screen. You also can view different parts of the worksheet at the same time by using panes.

To Shrink and Magnify the View of a Worksheet or Chart

1 ENTER HEADINGS & DATA | 2 ENTER FORMULAS & FUNCTIONS | 3 CREATE SPARKLINE CHARTS
4 FORMAT WORKSHEET | 5 CREATE COLUMN CHART | 6 CHANGE VIEWS | 7 ASK WHAT-IF QUESTIONS

You can magnify (zoom in) or shrink (zoom out) the appearance of a worksheet or chart by using the Zoom button (View tab | Zoom group). *Why? When you magnify a worksheet, Excel enlarges the view of the characters on the screen, but shows fewer columns and rows. Alternatively, when you shrink a worksheet, Excel is able to display more columns and rows.* Magnifying or shrinking a worksheet affects only the view; it does not change the window size or the size of the printout of the worksheet or chart. The following steps shrink and magnify the view of the worksheet.

1

- If cell A1 is not active, press CTRL+HOME.
- Display the View tab and then click the Zoom button (View tab | Zoom group) to display a list of magnifications in the Zoom dialog box (Figure 3–70).

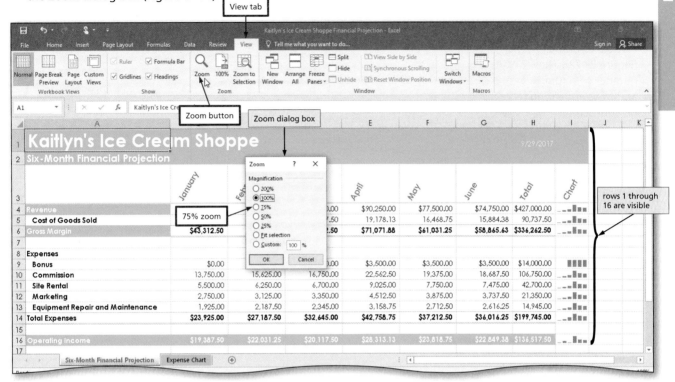

Figure 3–70

2

- Click 75% and then click the OK button (Zoom dialog box) to shrink the display of the worksheet (Figure 3–71). The number of columns and rows appearing on your screen may differ from Figure 3–71.

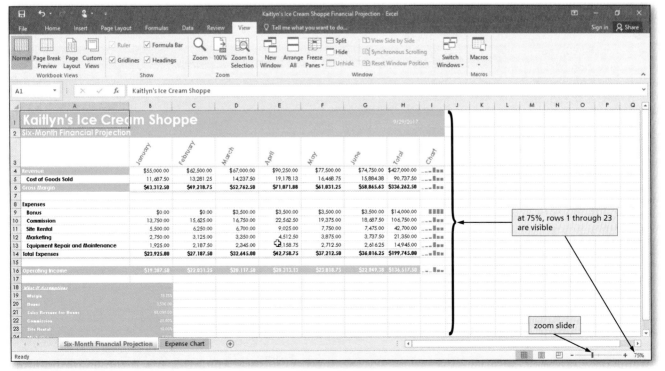

Figure 3–71

- Click the Zoom Out button on the status bar until the worksheet is displayed at 70% and all worksheet content is visible (Figure 3–72). The number of columns and rows appearing on your screen may differ from Figure 3–72.

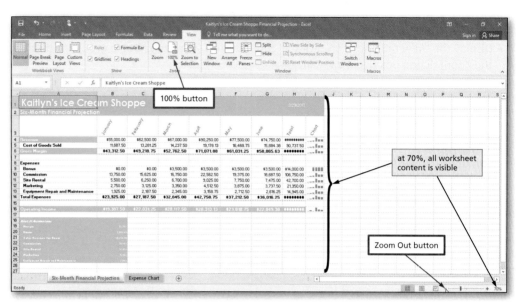

Figure 3–72

- Click the 100% button (View tab | Zoom group) to display the worksheet at 100%.

Other Ways

1. Drag zoom slider to increase or decrease zoom level

To Split a Window into Panes

1 ENTER HEADINGS & DATA | 2 ENTER FORMULAS & FUNCTIONS | 3 CREATE SPARKLINE CHARTS
4 FORMAT WORKSHEET | 5 CREATE COLUMN CHART | 6 CHANGE VIEWS | 7 ASK WHAT-IF QUESTIONS

When working with a large worksheet, you can split the window into two or four panes to view different parts of the worksheet at the same time. *Why? Splitting the Excel window into four panes at cell E8 allows you to view all four corners of the worksheet simultaneously.* The following steps split the Excel window into four panes.

- Select cell E8, the intersection of the four proposed panes, as the cell at which to split the window.
- If necessary, display the View tab (Figure 3–73).

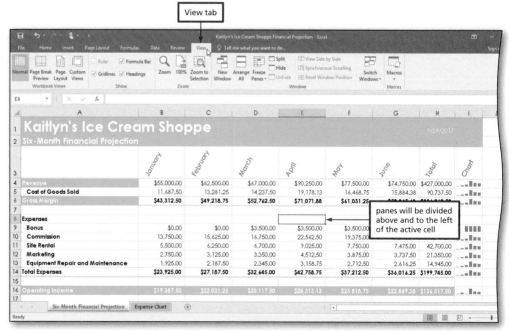

Figure 3–73

2

- Click the Split button (View tab | Window group) to divide the window into four panes.
- Use the scroll arrows to show the four corners of the worksheet at the same time (Figure 3–74).

Q&A

What is shown in the four panes?

The four panes in Figure 3–74 show the following: (1) range A1:D7 in the upper-left pane; (2) range E1:J7 in the upper-right pane; (3) range A17:D25 in the lower-left pane; and (4) range E17:J25 in the lower-right pane. The vertical split bar is the vertical bar running up and down the middle of the window. The horizontal split bar is the horizontal bar running across the middle of the window. If you use the scroll bars below the window, you will see that the panes split by the horizontal split bar scroll together horizontally. The panes split by the vertical split bar scroll together vertically when using the scroll bars to the right of the window. To resize the panes, drag either split bar to the desired location.

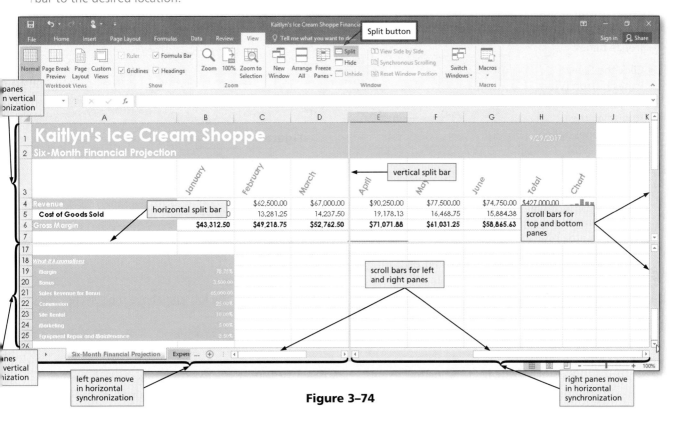

Figure 3–74

To Remove the Panes from the Window

The following step removes the panes from the window.

1 Click the Split button (View tab | Window group) to remove the four panes from the window.

Other Ways

1. Double-click intersection of horizontal and vertical split bars

To Freeze Worksheet Columns and Rows

1 ENTER HEADINGS & DATA | 2 ENTER FORMULAS & FUNCTIONS | 3 CREATE SPARKLINE CHARTS
4 FORMAT WORKSHEET | 5 CREATE COLUMN CHART | 6 CHANGE VIEWS | **7 ASK WHAT-IF QUESTIONS**

Why? *Freezing worksheet columns and rows is a useful technique for viewing large worksheets that extend beyond the window.* Normally, when you scroll down or to the right, the column content in the top rows and the row content in the leftmost columns no longer appear on the screen. When the content of these rows and/or columns helps to identify or define other content still visible on the worksheet, it can make it difficult to remember what the numbers in the visible cells represent. To alleviate this problem, Excel allows you to freeze columns and rows, so that their content, typically column or row titles, remains on the screen, no matter how far down or to the right you scroll. You also may wish to keep numbers visible that you need to see when making changes to content in another part of the worksheet, such as the revenue, cost of goods sold, and gross margin information in rows 4 through 6. The following steps use the Freeze Panes button (View tab | Window group) to freeze the worksheet title and column titles in row 3, and the row titles in column A.

- Scroll the worksheet until Excel displays row 3 as the first row and column A as the first column on the screen.

- Select cell B4 as the cell on which to freeze panes.

- Click the Freeze Panes button (View tab | Window group) to display the Freeze Panes gallery (Figure 3–75).

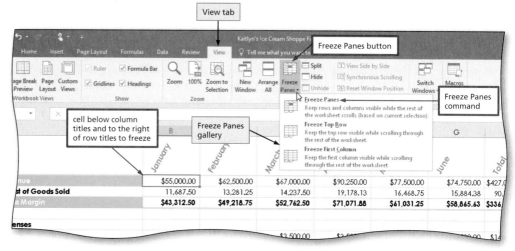

Figure 3–75

Why should I ensure that row 3 is the first row visible?

Before freezing the titles, it is important to align the first row that you want frozen with the top of the worksheet. For example, if you used the Freeze Panes button in cell B4 while displaying row 1, then Excel would freeze and display the worksheet title and subtitle, leaving only a few rows of data visible in the Six-Month Financial Projection area of the worksheet. To ensure that you can view as much data as possible, always scroll to a row that maximizes the view of your important data before freezing panes.

- Click Freeze Panes in the Freeze Panes gallery to freeze rows and columns to the left and above the selected cell, column A and row 3 in this case.

- Scroll down in the worksheet until row 9 is displayed directly below row 3 (Figure 3–76).

What happens after I click the Freeze Panes command?

Excel displays a thin, dark gray line on the right side of column A, indicating the split between the frozen row titles in column A and the rest of the worksheet. It also displays a thin, dark gray line below row 3, indicating the split between the frozen column titles in row 3 and the rest of the worksheet. Scrolling down or to the right in the worksheet will not scroll the content of row 3 or column A off the screen (Figure 3–76).

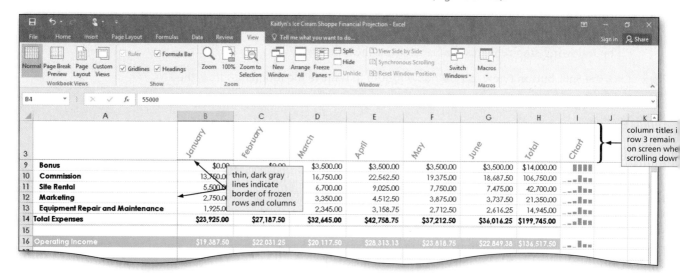

Figure 3–76

To Unfreeze the Worksheet Columns and Rows

Why? *Keep columns and rows frozen only as long as you need to view the worksheet in that configuration.* The following steps unfreeze the titles in column A and row 3 to allow you to work with the worksheet without frozen rows and columns, or to freeze the worksheet at a different location.

1 Press CTRL+HOME to select cell B4 and view the upper-left corner of the screen.

2 Click the Freeze Panes button (View tab | Window group) to display the Freeze Panes gallery.

3 Click Unfreeze Panes in the Freeze Panes gallery to unfreeze the frozen columns and rows.

4 Display the Home tab.

5 Save the workbook again on the same storage location with the same file name.

Q&A | Why does pressing CTRL+HOME select cell B4?
When the titles are frozen and you press CTRL+HOME, Excel selects the upper-leftmost cell of the unfrozen section of the worksheet. For example, in Step 1 of the previous steps, Excel selected cell B4. When the titles are unfrozen, pressing CTRL+HOME selects cell A1.

BTW
Freezing Titles
If you want to freeze only column headings, select the appropriate cell in column A before you click the Freeze Panes button (View tab | Window group). If you want to freeze only row titles, select the appropriate cell in row 1 before you click the Freeze Panes button. To freeze both column headings and row titles, select the cell that is the intersection of the column and row titles before you click the Freeze Panes button.

What-If Analysis

The automatic recalculation feature of Excel is a powerful tool that can be used to analyze worksheet data. Using Excel to scrutinize the impact of changing values in cells that are referenced by formulas in other cells is called **what-if analysis** or sensitivity analysis. When new data is entered, Excel not only recalculates all formulas in a worksheet but also redraws any associated charts.

In the workbook created in this module, many of the formulas are dependent on the assumptions in the range B19:B25. Thus, if you change any of the assumption values, Excel recalculates all formulas. Excel redraws the clustered column chart as well, because it is based on these numbers.

To Analyze Data in a Worksheet by Changing Values

1 ENTER HEADINGS & DATA | 2 ENTER FORMULAS & FUNCTIONS | 3 CREATE SPARKLINE CHARTS
4 FORMAT WORKSHEET | 5 CREATE COLUMN CHART | 6 CHANGE VIEWS | **7 ASK WHAT-IF QUESTIONS**

Why? *The effect of changing one or more values in the What-If Assumptions table — essentially posing what-if questions — allows you to review the results of different scenarios.* In this case, you are going to examine what would happen to the six-month operating income (cell H16) if the following changes were made in the What-If Assumptions table: Bonus $3,500.00 to $5,000.00; Commission 25.00% to 22.50%; Equipment Repair and Maintenance 3.50% to 4.00%. To answer a question like this, you need to change only the second, fourth, and seventh values in the What-If Assumptions table. The following step splits the screen, which allows you to view income and expense figures simultaneously, and then changes values in the worksheet to answer a what-if question. When a new value is entered, Excel recalculates the formulas in the worksheet and redraws the clustered column chart to reflect the new data.

- Scroll the worksheet so that row 4 is the first row visible on the worksheet.
- Click in cell A7 to select the row above which to split the window.
- Click the Split button (View tab | Window group) to split the window after row 6.
- Use the scroll arrows in the lower-right pane to scroll the window content until row 9 is the first row visible in the lower part of the screen, as shown in Figure 3–77.
- Enter **5,000** in cell B20, **22.50%** in cell B22, and **4.00%** in cell B25 (Figure 3–77), which causes the six-month operating income in cell H16 to increase from $136,517.50 to $139,057.50.
- Save the workbook again on the same storage location with the same file name.

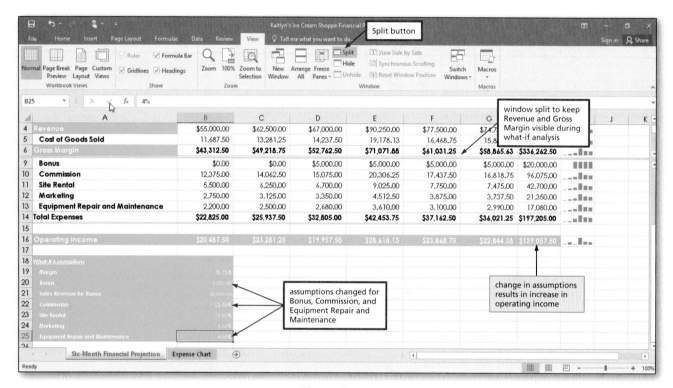

Figure 3–77

To Goal Seek

Why? *If you know the result you want a formula to produce, you can use goal seeking to determine the value of a cell on which the formula depends.* The previous step, which made changes to the What-If Assumptions table, resulted in an operating income that approaches but does not reach $145,000.00. The following steps use the Goal Seek command (Data tab | Forecast group) to determine what Site Rental percentage (cell B23), in conjunction with the earlier changes in assumptions, will yield a six-month operating income of $145,000 in cell H16, rather than the $139,057.50 calculated in the previous set of steps.

1

- If necessary, use the scroll arrows in the lower pane to ensure that you can view all of the What-If Assumptions table and the Operating Income figures.

- Select cell H16, the cell that contains the six-month operating income.

- Display the Data tab and then click the 'What-If Analysis' button (Data tab | Forecast group) to display the What-If Analysis menu (Figure 3–78).

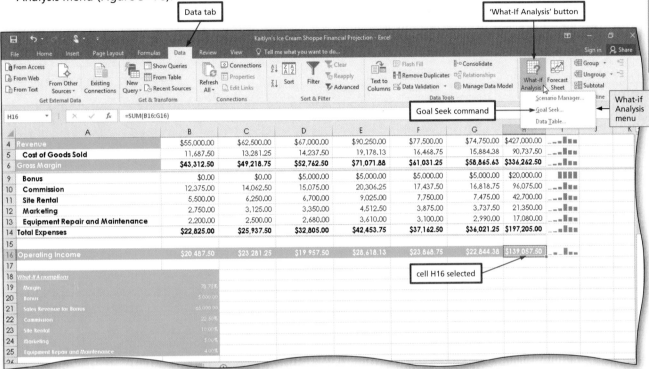

Figure 3–78

2

- Click Goal Seek to display the Goal Seek dialog box with the Set cell box set to the selected cell, H16 in this case.

- Click the To value text box, type **145,000** and then click the 'By changing cell' box to select the 'By changing cell' box.

- Click cell B23 on the worksheet to assign the current cell, B23 in this case, to the 'By changing cell' box (Figure 3–79).

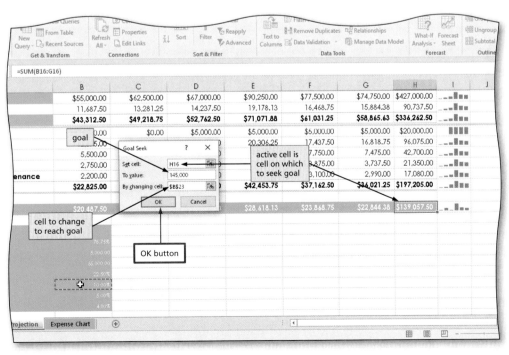

Figure 3–79

- Click the OK button (Goal Seek dialog box) to goal seek for the sought-after value in the To value text box, $145,000.00 in cell H16 in this case (Figure 3–80).

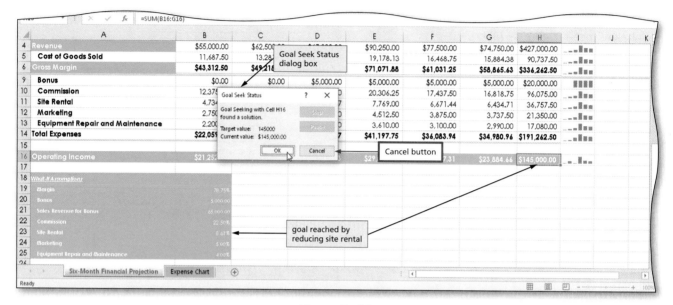

Figure 3–80

What happens when I click the OK button?

Excel changes cell H16 from $139,057.50 to the desired value of $145,000.00. More importantly, Excel changes the Site Rental assumption in cell B23 from 10.00% to 8.61% (Figure 3–80). Excel also displays the Goal Seek Status dialog box. If you click the OK button, Excel keeps the new values in the worksheet. If you click the Cancel button, Excel redisplays the original values.

- Click the Cancel button in the Goal Seek Status dialog box to redisplay the original values in the worksheet.

- Click the Split button (View tab | Window group) to remove the two panes from the window.

Goal Seeking

Goal seeking assumes you can change the value of only one cell referenced directly or indirectly to reach a specific goal for a value in another cell. In this example, to change the six-month operating income in cell H16 to $145,000.00, the Site Rental percentage in cell B23 must decrease by 1.39% from 10.00% to 8.61%.

You can see from this goal seeking example that the cell to change (cell B23) does not have to be referenced directly in the formula or function. For example, the six-month operating income in cell H16 is calculated by the function =SUM(B16:G16). Cell B23 is not referenced in this function. Instead, cell B23 is referenced in the formulas in row 11, on which the monthly operating incomes in row 16 are based. By tracing the formulas and functions, Excel can obtain the desired six-month operating income by varying the value for the Site Rental assumption.

Insights

The Insights feature in Excel uses the Bing search engine and other Internet resources to help you locate more information about the content in your workbooks. One common use of this feature is to look up the definition of a word. When looking up a definition, Excel uses contextual data so that it can return the most relevant information.

1 ENTER HEADINGS & DATA | 2 ENTER FORMULAS & FUNCTIONS | 3 CREATE SPARKLINE CHARTS

4 FORMAT WORKSHEET | 5 CREATE COLUMN CHART | 6 CHANGE VIEWS | 7 ASK WHAT-IF QUESTIONS

To Use the Smart Lookup Insight

Smart Lookup uses Bing and other Internet resources to find useful information about text in your spreadsheet and then displays that information in the Insights task pane. *Why? If you need additional information about some terminology in a workbook you are creating or viewing, Smart Lookup can provide that information.* The following steps use Smart Lookup to look up information about the text in cell A6.

- Select cell A6.

- Display the Review tab and then click Smart Lookup (Review tab | Insights group) to display the Insights task pane containing information about the text in the selected cell (Figure 3–81).

Q&A Why did I see a 'We value your privacy' message?
This message appears the first time you use the Smart Lookup insight. If you agree to the terms, click the Got it button to continue.

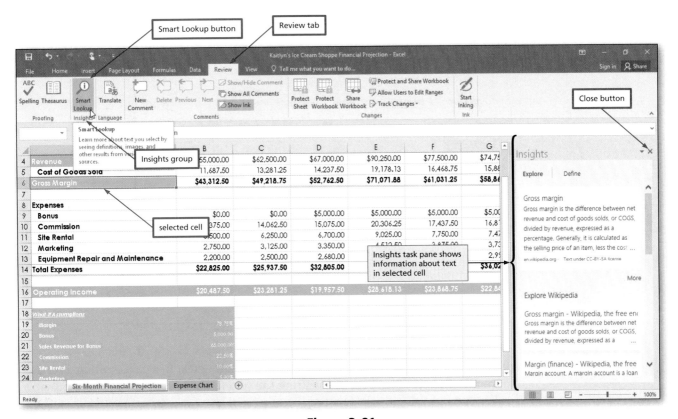

Figure 3–81

- Click the Close button on the Insights task pane to close the task pane.
- If desired, sign out of your Microsoft account.
- Exit Excel.

Accessibility Features

Excel provides a utility that can be used to check a workbook for potential issues related to **accessibility**. Accessibility refers to the practice of removing barriers that may prevent individuals with disabilities from interacting with your data or the app. To use the Check Accessibility command, click File on the ribbon to open the Backstage view, click the Info tab, click the 'Check for Issues' button, and then click Check Accessibility. Excel will check your workbook for content that could prove difficult for people with disabilities to read, either alone or with adaptive tools. The resulting report (Figure 3–82 shows an example) will identify issues and offer suggestions for addressing the reported issues.

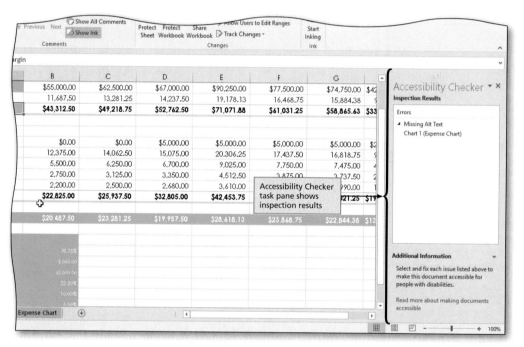

Figure 3–82

Summary

In this module, you learned how to use Excel to create a six-month financial projection workbook. Topics covered included rotating text in a cell, creating a series of month names, entering and formatting the system date, using absolute and mixed cell references, using the IF function, creating and changing sparkline charts, using the format painter, creating a clustered column chart, using chart filters, reordering sheet tabs, changing the worksheet view, freezing and unfreezing rows and columns, answering what-if questions, goal seeking, using Smart Lookup, and understanding accessibility features.

What decisions will you need to make when creating your next worksheet to evaluate and analyze data using what-if analysis?

Use these guidelines as you complete the assignments in this module and create your own worksheets for evaluating and analyzing data outside of this class.

1. Determine the workbook structure.

   a) Determine the data you will need for your worksheet.

   b) Determine the layout of your data on the worksheet.

   c) Determine the layout of the assumptions table on the worksheet.

   d) Determine the location and features of any charts.

2. Create the worksheet.

   a) Enter titles, subtitles, and headings.

   b) Enter data, functions, and formulas.

3. Format the worksheet.

   a) Format the titles, subtitles, and headings.

   b) Format the numbers as necessary.

   c) Format the text.

4. Create and use charts.

   a) Select data to chart.

   b) Select a chart type for selected data.

   c) Format the chart elements.

   d) Filter charts if necessary to view subsets of data.

5. Perform what-if analyses.

   a) Adjust values in the assumptions table to review scenarios of interest.

   b) Use Goal Seek to determine how to adjust a variable value to reach a particular goal or outcome.

Apply Your Knowledge

Reinforce the skills and apply the concepts you learned in this module.

Understanding Logical Tests and Absolute Cell Referencing

Note: To complete this assignment, you will be required to use the Data Files. Please contact your instructor for information about accessing the required files.

Instructions Part 1: For each of the following logical tests, indicate whether an IF function in Excel would return a value of True or False; given the following cell values: C2 = 88; H12 = 15; L3 = 24; M14 = 150; and G4 = 5.

1. C2 > H12   Returned value: _____

2. L3 = G4   Returned value: _____

3. M14 + 15 * H12 / 10 <= L3   Returned value: _____

4. M14 – G4 < H12 / C2   Returned value: _____

5. (C2 + H12) * 2 >= L3 – (C2 / 4) * 2   Returned value: _____

6. L3 + 300 > H12 * G4 + 10   Returned value: _____

7. G4 * M14 >= 2 * (H12 + 25)   Returned value: _____

8. H12 = 10 * (C2 / 8)   Returned value: _____

Instructions Part 2: Write cell L23 as a relative reference, absolute reference, mixed reference with the column varying, and mixed reference with the row varying.

_____   _____   _____   _____

Instructions Part 3: Run Excel. Open the workbook Apply 3-1 Absolute Cell References. You will re-create the numerical grid pictured in Figure 3–83.

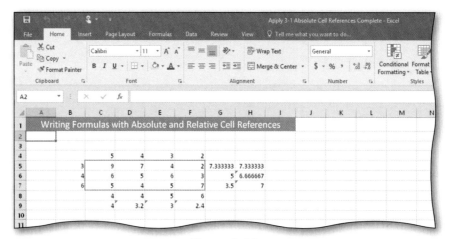

Figure 3–83

Perform the following tasks:

1. Enter a formula in cell C8 that divides the sum of cells C5 through C7 by cell C4. Write the formula so that when you copy it to cells D8:F8, Excel adjusts all the cell references according to the destination cells. Verify your formula by checking it against the values found in cells C8, D8, E8, and F8 in Figure 3–83.

2. Enter a formula in cell G5 that divides the sum of cells C5 through F5 by cell B5. Write the formula so that when you copy the formula to cells G6 and G7, Excel adjusts all the cell references according to the destination cells. Verify your formula by checking it against the values found in cells G5, G6, and G7 in Figure 3–83.

3. Enter a formula in cell C9 that divides the sum of cells C5 through C7 by cell C4. Write the formula using an absolute cell reference so that when you copy the formula to cells D9:F9, cell C4 remains absolute. Verify your formula by checking it against the values found in cells C9, D9, E9, and F9 in Figure 3–83.

4. Enter a formula in cell H5 that divides the sum of cells C5:F5 by cell B5. Write the formula using an absolute cell reference so that when you copy the formula to cells H6 and H7, cell B5 remains absolute. Verify your formula by checking it with the values found in cells H5, H6, and H7 in Figure 3–83.

5. Apply the worksheet name, Cell References, to the sheet tab and apply the Orange, Accent 2 Theme color to the sheet tab.

6. If requested by your instructor, add a dash followed by your name to the worksheet title in cell A1.

7. Save the workbook using the file name, Apply 3-1 Absolute Cell References Complete. Submit the revised workbook as specified by your instructor.

8. ✷ How would you rewrite the formula in cell H5 using relative and mixed cell references only, to come up with the same result as showing in Figure 3–83, and to produce the results currently showing in cells G6 and G7 in cells H6 and H7 when the formula in cell H5 is copied to those cells?

Extend Your Knowledge

Extend the skills you learned in this module and experiment with new skills. You may need to use Help to complete the assignment.

The Fill Handle and Nested IF Functions
Note: To complete this assignment, you will be required to use the Data Files. Please contact your instructor for information about accessing the required files.

Perform the following tasks:

Instructions Part 1:   Run Excel. Open the workbook Extend 3-1 Fill and IF. If necessary, make Fill the active sheet.

1. Use the fill handle on one column at a time to propagate the 12 series through row 14, as shown in Figure 3–84. (*Hint*: Search in Help to learn more about the fill handle and Auto Fill.) In cells O2:O13, indicate the actions used with the fill handle to propagate the series. For instance, in cell O2, enter **Drag**. For instances where you need to select something other than the cell in row 2 prior to using the fill handle, enter the selection and then the drag action, **A2:A3 Drag** for example.

2. Select cell D20. While holding down the CTRL key, one at a time drag the fill handle three cells to the right, to the left, up, and down to generate four series of numbers beginning with zero and incremented by one.

3. Select cell H20. Point to the cell border so that the pointer changes to a plus sign with four arrows. Drag the pointer down to cell H22 to move the contents of cell H20 to cell H22.

4. If necessary, select cell H22. Point to the cell border so that the pointer changes to a plus sign with four arrows. While holding down the CTRL key, drag the pointer to cell K22 to copy the contents of cell H22 to cell K22.

Continued >

Extend Your Knowledge *continued*

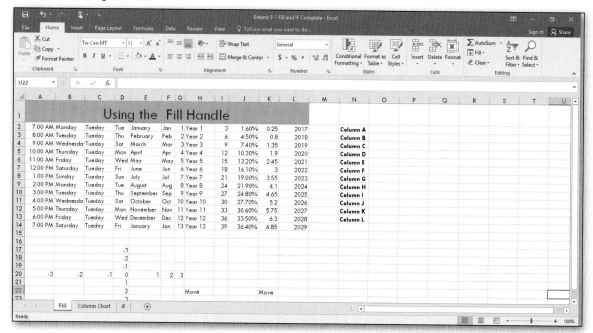

Figure 3–84

5. Select cell K20. Drag the fill handle in to the center of cell K20 until that the cell is shaded and the cell contents are deleted.

6. Select cell range H2:I14, and insert a 3-D column chart on a new sheet.

7. Change the chart title to Annual Breakdown.

8. Add a data table with no legend keys to the chart.

9. Apply the chart sheet name, Column Chart, to the sheet and move the sheet to follow the Fill sheet.

10. Save the workbook using the file name, Extend 3-1 Fill and IF Complete.

Instructions Part 2: Switch to the IF sheet in the Extend 3-1 Fill and IF Complete workbook.

1. Write an IF function in cell C2 that assigns a grade of 'Pass' if the score in cell B2 is 50 or above, and a grade of 'Fail' if the score in cell B2 is below 50. Copy this function to cells C3:C18.

2. Write a nested IF function in cell D2 that assigns a grade of A for scores between 80 and 100, a grade of B for scores between 65 and 79, a grade of C for scores between 50 and 64, and a grade of F for scores below 50. (*Hint*: Search in Help for nested IF when constructing your function.) Copy this function to cells D3:D18.

3. If requested by your instructor, change the student number in cell A3 on the IF sheet to your student number.

4. Save the workbook and submit the revised workbook as specified by your instructor.

5. ❂ Students who do not take a test receive a score of NS. How would you include a score of NS as a grade in each of Steps 1 and 2?

Expand Your World

Create a solution that uses cloud or web technologies by learning and investigating on your own from general guidance.

Analyzing and Graphing Development Indicators

Note: To complete this assignment, you will be required to use the Data Files. Please contact your instructor for information about accessing the required files.

Instructions: You are working as part of a group creating a report on historical education trends in the developing nation of Mali, comparing three related development indicators concerning school enrollment over time. Your task is to format the worksheet containing the historical data, chart the historical education indicators, and make the chart available to your group using OneDrive. Run Excel and then open the workbook, Expand 3-1 Education Indicators.

Perform the following tasks:
1. Save the workbook using the file name, Expand 3-1 Education Indicators Charted.
2. Format the worksheet using techniques you have learned to present the data in a visually appealing form.
3. Create charts that present the data for each of the three indicators. Think about what interested you in these indicators in the first place, and decide which chart types will best present the data. (*Hint:* If you are not sure which types to use, consider selecting the data and using the Recommended Chart button to narrow down and preview suitable choices.) Format the charts to best present the data in a clear, attractive format.
4. Give each worksheet a descriptive name and color the tabs using theme colors. Reorder the sheets so that the data table appears first, followed by the charts.
5. If requested by your instructor, export the file to OneDrive.
6. Submit the revised workbook as specified by your instructor.
7. ☀ Justify your choice of chart types in Step 3. Explain why you selected these types over other suitable choices.

In the Labs

Design, create, modify and/or use a workbook following the guidelines, concepts, and skills presented in this module. Labs 1 and 2, which increase in difficulty, require you to create solutions based on what you learned in the module; Lab 3 requires you to apply your creative thinking and problem-solving skills to design and implement a solution.

Lab 1: Eight-Year Financial Projection

Problem: Your supervisor in the finance department at August Online Technology has asked you to create a worksheet for the flagship product that will project the annual gross margin, total expenses, operating income, income taxes, and net income for the next eight years based on the assumptions in Table 3–9. The desired worksheet is shown in Figure 3–85.

Table 3–9 August Online Technology Financial Projection Assumptions	
Units Sold in Prior Year	235,411
Unit Cost	$150.00
Annual Sales Growth	3.25%
Annual Price Increase	3.00%
Margin	29.90%

Continued >

In the Labs *continued*

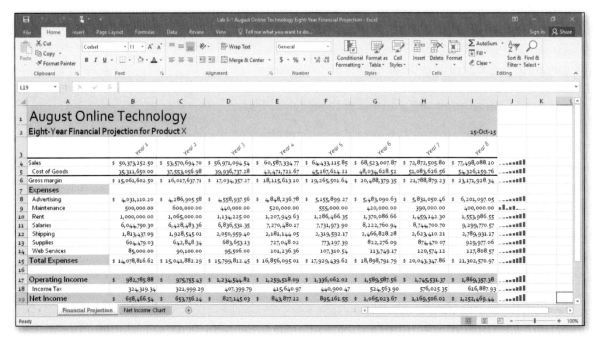

Figure 3–85

Perform the following tasks:

Instructions Part 1: Run Excel, open a blank workbook, and then create the worksheet.

1. Apply the Parallax theme to the worksheet.

2. Enter the worksheet title `August Online Technology` in cell A1 and the subtitle `Eight-Year Financial Projection for Product X` in cell A2. Format the worksheet title in cell A1 to 26-point and the worksheet subtitle in cell A2 to 16-point. Enter the system date in cell I2 using the NOW function. Format the date to the 14-Mar-12 style.

3. Change the following column widths: A = 24.00 characters; B through I = 14.00 characters. Change the heights of rows 7, 15, 17, 19, and 22 to 18.00 points.

4. Enter the eight column titles Year 1 through Year 8 in the range B3:I3 by entering Year 1 in cell B3 and then dragging cell B3's fill handle through the range C3:I3. Format cell B3 as follows:

   a. Increase the font size to 12.
   b. Center and italicize it.
   c. Angle its contents 45 degrees.

5. Use the Format Painter button to copy the format assigned to cell B3 to the range C3:I3.

6. Enter the row titles, as shown in Figure 3-85, in the range A4:A19. Change the font size in cells A7, A15, A17, and A19 to 14-point. Add thick bottom borders to the ranges A3:I3 and A5:I5. Use the Increase Indent button (Home tab | Alignment group) to increase the indent of the row titles in cell A5, the range A8:A14, and cell A18.

7. If requested by your instructor, change the entry in row 14 by inserting your surname prior to the text, Web Services.

8. Enter the table title `Assumptions` in cell A22. Enter the assumptions in Table 3–9 in the range A23:B27. Use format symbols when entering the numbers. Change the font size of the table title in cell A22 to 14-point and underline it.

9. Select the range B4:I19 and then click the Number Format Dialog Box Launcher (Home tab | Number group) to display the Format Cells dialog box. Use the Number category (Format Cells dialog box) to assign the appropriate style that displays numbers with two decimal places and negative numbers in black font and enclosed in parentheses to the range B4:I19.

10. Complete the following entries:

   a. Year 1 Sales (cell B4) = Units Sold in Prior Year * (Unit Cost / (1 – Margin))

   b. Year 2 Sales (cell C4) = Year 1 Sales * (1 + Annual Sales Growth) * (1 + Annual Price Increase). Copy cell C4 to the range D4:I4.

   c. Year 1 Cost of Goods (cell B5) = Year 1 Sales * (1 – Margin). Copy cell B5 to the range C5:I5.

   d. Gross Margin (cell B6) = Year 1 Sales – Year 1 Cost of Goods. Copy cell B6 to the range C6:I6.

   e. Year 1 Advertising (cell B8) = 1250 + 8% * Year 1 Sales. Copy cell B8 to the range C8:I8.

   f. Maintenance (row 9): Year 1 = 500,000; Year 2 = 600,000; Year 3 = 440,000; Year 4 = 520,000; Year 5 = 555,000; Year 6 = 420,000; Year 7 = 390,000; Year 8 = 400,000.

   g. Year 1 Rent (cell B10) = 1,000,000

   h. Year 2 Rent (cell C10) = Year 1 Rent + (6.5% * Year 1 Rent). Copy cell C10 to the range D10:I10.

   i. Year 1 Salaries (cell B11) = 12% * Year 1 Sales. Copy cell B11 to the range C11:I11.

   j. Year 1 Shipping (cell B12) = 3.6% * Year 1 Sales. Copy cell B12 to the range C12:I12.

   k. Year 1 Supplies (cell B13) = 1.2% * Year 1 Sales. Copy cell B13 to the range C13:I13.

   l. Year 1 Web Services (cell B14) = 85,000

   m. Year 2 Web Services (cell C14) = Year 1 Web Services + (6% * Year 1 Web Services). Copy cell C14 to the range D14:I14.

   n. Year 1 Total Expenses (cell B15) = SUM(B8:B14). Copy cell B15 to the range C15:I15.

   o. Year 1 Operating Income (cell B17) = Year 1 Gross Margin – Year 1 Total Expenses. Copy cell B17 to the range C17:I17.

   p. Year 1 Income Tax (cell B18): If Year 1 Operating Income is less than 0, then Year 1 Income Tax equals 0; otherwise Year 1 Income Tax equals 33% * Year 1 Operating Income. Copy cell B18 to the range C18:I18.

   q. Year 1 Net Income (cell B19) = Year 1 Operating Income – Year 1 Income Tax. Copy cell B19 to the range C19:I19.

   r. In cell J4, insert a column sparkline chart (Insert tab | Sparklines group) for cell range B4:I4.

   s. Insert column sparkline charts in cells J5, J6, J8:J15, and J17:J19 using ranges B5:I5, B6:I6, B8:I8 – B15:I15, and B17:I17 – B19:I19 respectively.

11. Apply the Currency number format with a dollar sign, two decimal places, and negative numbers in black with parentheses to the following ranges: B4:I4, B6:I6, B8:I8, B15:I15, B17:I17, and B19:I19. Apply the comma style format to the following ranges: B5:I5 and B9:I14. Apply the Number format with two decimal places and the 1000 separator to the range B18:I18.

12. Change the background colors, as shown in Figure 3–85. Use Blue, Accent 1, Lighter 40% for the background colors.

13. Save the workbook using the file name, Lab 3-1 August Online Technology Eight-Year Financial Projection.

14. Preview the worksheet. Use the Orientation button (Page Layout tab | Page Setup group) to fit the printout on one page in landscape orientation. Preview the formulas version (CTRL+`) of the worksheet in landscape orientation using the Fit to option. Press CTRL+` to instruct Excel to display the values version of the worksheet. Save the workbook again.

Continued >

In the Labs *continued*

Instructions Part 2: Create a chart to present the data, shown in Figure 3–86. If necessary, run Excel and open the workbook Lab 3-1 August Online Technology Eight-Year Financial Projection.

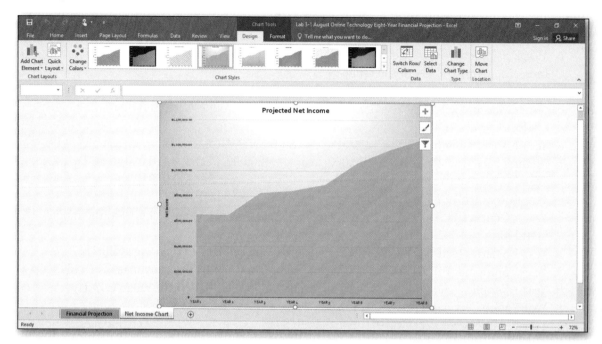

Figure 3–86

1. Use the nonadjacent ranges B3:I3 and B19:I19 to create a Stacked Area chart (*Hint:* use the Recommended Charts button). When the chart appears, click the Move Chart button to move the chart to a new sheet.

2. Change the chart title to `Projected Net Income`.

3. Use the Chart Elements button to add a vertical axis title. Edit the axis title text to read `Net Income`. Bold the axis title.

4. Change the Chart Style to Style 4 in the Chart Styles Gallery (Chart Tools Design tab | Chart Styles group). Use the 'Chart Quick Colors' button (Chart Tools Design tab | Chart Styles group) to change the color scheme to Monochromatic, Color 5.

5. Rename the sheet tabs Financial Projection and Net Income Chart. Rearrange the sheets so that the worksheet is leftmost and change the tab colors to those of your choosing.

6. Click the Financial Projection tab to return to the worksheet. Save the workbook using the same file name (Lab 3-1 August Online Technology Eight-Year Financial Projection) as defined in Part 1.

Instructions Part 3: Use Goal Seek to analyze three different sales scenarios. If necessary, open the workbook Lab 3-1 August Online Technology Eight-Year Financial Projection.

1. Divide the window into two panes between rows 6 and 7. Use the scroll bars to show both the top and bottom of the worksheet. Using the numbers in columns 2 and 3 of Table 3–10, analyze the effect of changing the annual sales growth (cell B25) and annual price increase (cell B26) on the net incomes in row 19. Record the answers for each case and submit the results in a form as requested by your instructor.

Case	Annual Sales Growth	Annual Price Increase
Table 3–10 August Online Technology Alternative Projections		
1	4.25%	2.00%
2	2.25%	3.00%
3	1.25%	4.00%

2. Close the workbook without saving it and then reopen it. Use the 'What-If Analysis' button (Data tab | Forecast group) to goal seek. Determine a margin that would result in a Year 8 net income of $1,500,000. Save the workbook with your needed changes as Lab 3-1 August Online Technology Eight-Year Financial Projection GS. Submit the workbook with the new values or the results of the goal seek as requested by your instructor.

3. ✹ How would you use what-if analysis tools to determine what Annual Sales Growth you would need to achieve in order to keep prices steady over the eight-year projection period?

Lab 2: **Updating a Weekly Payroll Worksheet**

Note: To complete this assignment, you will be required to use the Data Files. Please contact your instructor for information about accessing the required files.

Problem: PHM Reliable Catering is a company that provides catering services to both small and large businesses. You have been asked to update the weekly payroll report to reflect changes in personnel, to update certain mandatory deductions, and to add overtime computations. The final worksheet is shown in Figure 3–87. Run Excel. Open the workbook, Lab 3-2 PHM Reliable Catering Weekly Payroll Report.

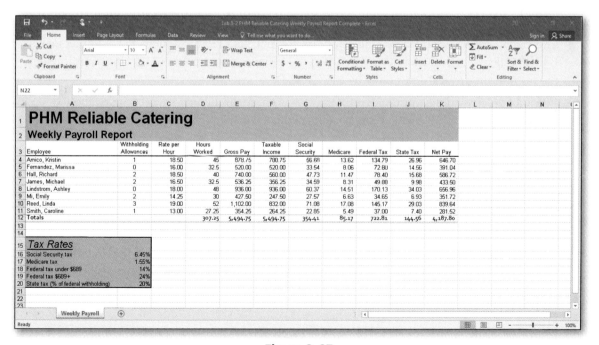

Figure 3–87

Continued >

In the Labs *continued*

Perform the following tasks:

1. Save the workbook using the file name, Lab 3-2 PHM Reliable Catering Weekly Payroll Report Complete.

2. Apply the Depth theme to the worksheet.

3. Delete rows 12 through 14 to remove the statistics below the Totals row.

4. Delete column B. Set column A width to 31.00 and columns B through K to 11.00. Select row 3 and set text to wrap in this row using the Wrap Text button (Home tab | Alignment group), and then set the row height to best fit.

5. Delete the record for the employee Evans, Timothy. Add two blank lines directly above the row for Mi, Emily, and add the information for the two new employees listed in Table 3–11.

Table 3–11 PHM Reliable Catering New Employee Data			
Employee	Withholding Allowances	Rate Per Hour	Hours Worked
James, Michael	2	16.50	32.5
Lindstrom, Ashley	0	18.00	48

6. If requested by your instructor, replace one of the employee's names with your name.

7. If necessary, use the fill handle in cell E6 to copy the gross pay formula to the rows of the two new employees.

8. Add the Tax Rates information shown in Figure 3–87 in cells A15:B20 to your worksheet.

9. Change the font size in cell A1 to 28-point. Change the font size in cell A2 to 18-point. Change the font in cell A15 to 18-point italic and underlined. Change the row height for rows 1, 2, and 15 to best fit.

10. Insert three columns to the right of the Gross Pay column. Add the column titles `Taxable Income`, `Social Security`, and `Medicare` in cells F3:H3. Center the contents of cells B3:K3. Calculate the Social Security and Medicare taxes in columns G and H by multiplying the tax rates in the Tax Rates table by the Gross Pay.

11. Federal tax calculations must take into account two tiers of income tax, which are applied to the taxable income. Calculate the taxable income, which is the Gross Pay — (number of withholding allowances × $90).

12. Calculate the federal tax withheld. If an employee has a taxable income of greater than or equal to $689, then the federal tax withheld equals $110.85 plus the federal tax rate found in cell B19 multiplied by the taxable income in excess of $689. If an employees taxable income is $689 or less, the federal tax withheld equals the taxable income multiplied by the federal tax rate found in cell B18. Use the IF function to calculate the federal tax in Column I.

13. State tax is calculated as a percentage of federal tax. Use the tax rate in the Tax Rates table to calculate state tax in column J.

14. Calculate Net Pay in column K, as Gross Pay — Social Security, Medicare, Federal Tax, and State Tax.

15. Use the background color Gold, Accent 5, Darker 25% for the ranges A1:K2 and A15:B20.

16. Center the range B4:B11. Apply the currency style with two decimal places, no dollar signs, and negative numbers in black and parentheses to the range C4:C11 and E4:K12.

17. Apply a Thick Bottom Border to the range A3:K3. Apply the Total cell style to the range A12:K12. Apply a Thick Outside Border to the range A15:B20.

18. Change the sheet tab name to Weekly Payroll and the tab color to match the color used as background color in cell A1.

19. Preview the worksheet. Fit the printout of the worksheet on one page in landscape orientation. Save the workbook again.

20. Submit the workbook as specified by your instructor.

Lab 3: **Consider This: Your Turn**

Apply your creative thinking and problem-solving skills to design and implement a solution.

Transportation Costs

Instructions Part 1: You are thinking about buying a new vehicle, and you want to make sure that you buy one that offers the highest fuel savings. You decide to research hybrid cars as well as gas-only cars. Your friends are also interested in your results. Together, you decide to research the fuel costs associated with various types of vehicles. Research the gas mileage for six vehicles: three should run only on gas, and the others should be hybrid vehicles, combining gas and battery power. After you find the gas mileage for each vehicle, you will use formulas to calculate the fuel cost for one month, one year, and three years. Assume that in a typical month, you will drive 500 miles. Develop a worksheet following the general layout in Table 3–12 that shows the fuel cost analysis. Use the formulas listed in Table 3–13 and the concepts and techniques presented in this module to create the worksheet. You will need to find the average price of gas for your market. Add a chart showing the cost comparisons as an embedded chart.

Table 3–12 Fuel Cost Analysis				
Vehicle	**Miles Per Gallon**	**Fuel Cost 1 Month**	**Fuel Cost 1 Year**	**Fuel Cost 3 Years**
Gas 1		Formula A	Formula B	Formula C
Gas 2		—	—	—
Gas 3		—	—	—
Hybrid 1		—	—	—
Hybrid 2		—	—	—
Hybrid 3		—	—	—
Assumptions				
Distance per Month	500			
Price of Gas				

Table 3–13 Fuel Cost Analysis Formulas
Formula A = (Distance per Month / Miles per Gallon)*Price of Gas
Formula B = ((Distance per Month / Miles per Gallon)*Price of Gas)*12
Formula C = ((Distance Per Month / Miles per Gallon)*Price of Gas)*36

Instructions Part 2: ✷ You made several decisions while creating the workbook for this assignment. Why did you select the chart type used to compare fuel costs? What other costs might you want to consider when making your purchase decision?

4 | Financial Functions, Data Tables, and Amortization Schedules

Objectives

You will have mastered the material in this module when you can:

- Assign a name to a cell and refer to the cell in a formula using the assigned name
- Determine the monthly payment of a loan using the financial function PMT
- Understand the financial functions PV (present value) and FV (future value)
- Create a data table to analyze data in a worksheet
- Create an amortization schedule
- Control the color and thickness of outlines and borders
- Add a pointer to a data table
- Analyze worksheet data by changing values
- Use range names and print sections of a worksheet
- Set print options
- Protect and unprotect cells in a worksheet
- Hide and unhide worksheets and workbooks
- Use the formula checking features of Excel

Introduction

Two of the more powerful aspects of Excel are its wide array of functions and its capability of organizing answers to what-if questions. In this module, you will learn about financial functions such as the PMT function, which allows you to determine a monthly payment for a loan, and the PV function, which allows you to determine the present value of an investment.

In earlier modules, you learned how to analyze data by using Excel's recalculation feature and goal seeking. This module introduces an additional what-if analysis tool, called a **data table**. You use a data table to automate data analyses and organize the results returned by Excel. Another important loan analysis tool is an amortization schedule. An **amortization schedule** shows the beginning and ending balances of a loan and the amount of payment that is applied to the principal and interest during each payment period.

In previous modules, you learned how to print in a variety of ways. In this module, you will learn additional methods of printing using range names and a print area.

Finally, this module introduces you to cell protection; hiding and unhiding worksheets and workbooks; and formula checking. **Cell protection** ensures that users do not inadvertently change values that are critical to the worksheet. Hiding portions of a workbook lets you show only the parts of the workbook that the user needs to see. The **formula checker** examines the formulas in a workbook in a manner similar to the way the spelling checker examines a workbook for misspelled words.

Project — Mortgage Payment Calculator with Data Table and Amortization Schedule

The project in this module follows proper design guidelines and uses Excel to create the worksheet shown in Figure 4–1. NCU, a credit union, provides mortgages (loans) for homes and other types of property. The credit union's chief financial officer has asked for a workbook that loan officers and customers can use to calculate mortgage payment information, review an amortization schedule, and compare mortgage payments for varying annual interest rates. To ensure that the loan officers and customers do not delete the formulas in the worksheet, she has asked that cells in the worksheet be protected so that they cannot be changed accidentally.

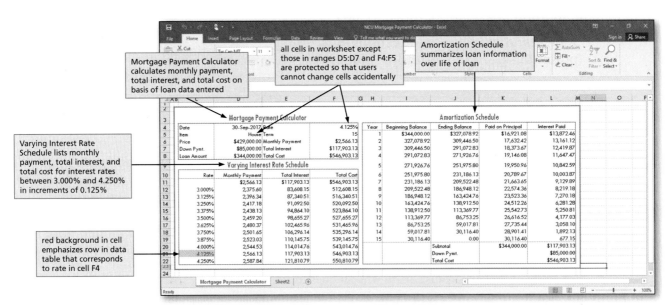

Figure 4–1

The requirements document for the NCU Mortgage Payment Calculator worksheet is shown in Figure 4–2. It includes the needs, source of data, summary of calculations, and special requirements.

Worksheet Title	NCU Mortgage Payment Calculator
Needs	An easy-to-read worksheet that 1. Determines the monthly payment, total interest, and total cost for a mortgage. 2. Shows a data table that answers what-if questions based on changing interest rates. 3. Highlights the rate in the data table that matches the actual interest rate. 4. Shows an amortization schedule that lists annual summaries of interest paid, principal paid, and balance on principal.
Source of data	Data supplied by the credit union includes interest rate and term of mortgage. Data supplied by the customer includes item to be purchased, price, down payment. All other data is calculated or created in Excel.
Calculations	1. The following calculations must be made for each mortgage: a. Mortgage Amount = Price − Down Payment b. Monthly Payment = PMT function c. Total Interest = 12 × Term × Monthly Payment − Loan Amount d. Total Cost = 12 × Term × Monthly Payment + Down Payment 2. The Amortization Schedule involves the following calculations: a. Beginning Balance = Loan Amount b. Ending Balance = PV function or zero c. Paid on Principal = Beginning Balance − Ending Balance d. Interest Paid = 12 × Monthly Payment − Paid on Principal or 0 e. Paid on Principal Subtotal = SUM function f. Interest Paid Subtotal = SUM function
Special Requirements	1. Assign names to the ranges of the three major worksheet components separately and together to allow the worksheet components to be printed separately or together easily. 2. Use locked cells and worksheet protection to prevent loan officers and customers from inadvertently making changes to formulas and functions contained in the worksheet.

Figure 4–2

In addition, using a sketch of the worksheet can help you visualize its design. The sketch of the worksheet consists of titles, column and cell headings, the location of data values, and a general idea of the desired formatting (Figure 4–3).

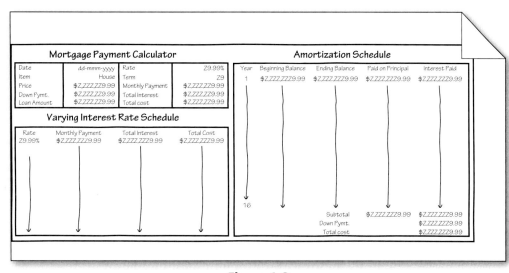

Figure 4–3

BTW
Good Worksheet Design
Consider creating worksheets with an eye towards reusing them in the future. Carefully design worksheets as if they will be on display and evaluated by your fellow workers. Smart worksheet design starts with visualizing the results you need. A well-designed worksheet often is used for many years.

As shown in the worksheet sketch in Figure 4–3, the three basic sections of the worksheet are the Mortgage Payment Calculator on the upper-left side, the Varying Interest Rate Schedule data table on the lower-left side, and the Amortization Schedule on the right side. The worksheet will be created in this order.

With a good understanding of the requirements document, an understanding of the necessary decisions, and a sketch of the worksheet, the next step is to use Excel to create the worksheet.

In this module, you will learn how to create and use the workbook shown in Figure 4–1. The following roadmap identifies general activities you will perform as you progress through this module:

1. CREATE the MORTGAGE PAYMENT CALCULATOR in the worksheet.
2. CREATE a DATA TABLE in the worksheet.
3. CREATE the AMORTIZATION SCHEDULE in the worksheet.
4. FORMAT the WORKSHEET.
5. CREATE PRINT AREAS in the worksheet.
6. PROTECT CELLS in the worksheet.
7. CHECK FORMULAS of the worksheet.

To Apply a Theme to the Worksheet

The following steps apply the Integral theme to the workbook.

1 Run Excel and create a blank workbook in the Excel window.

2 Apply the Integral theme to the workbook.

To Enter the Section and Row Titles and System Date

The next step is to enter the Mortgage Payment Calculator section title, row titles, and system date. The Mortgage Payment Calculator section title also will be changed to the Title cell style and vertically middle-aligned. The following steps enter the section title, row titles, and system date.

1 Select cell C3 and then type **Mortgage Payment Calculator** as the section title.

Q&A Why did I not begin creating the worksheet in cell A1?
Two rows at the top of the worksheet and two columns on the left of the worksheet will be left blank to provide a border around the worksheet.

2 Select the range C3:F3 and then click the 'Merge & Center' button (Home tab | Alignment group) to merge and center the section title in the selected range.

3 Click the Cell Styles button (Home tab | Styles group) and then click Title cell style in the Cell Styles gallery to apply the selected style to the active cell.

4 Click the Middle Align button (Home tab | Alignment group) to vertically center the text in the selected cell.

5 Select cell C4, type `Date` as the row title, and then press the TAB key to complete the entry in the cell and select the cell to the right.

6 With cell D4 selected, type `=NOW()` and then click the Enter button to add a function to the cell that displays today's date.

7 Right-click cell D4 to open a shortcut menu and then click Format Cells on the shortcut menu to display the Format Cells dialog box. Click the Number tab to display the Number sheet, click Date in the Category list, scroll down in the Type list, and then click 14–Mar-2012 to select a date format.

8 Click the OK button (Format Cells dialog box) to close the Format Cells dialog box.

9 Enter the following text in the indicated cells:

Cell	Text	Cell	Text
		E4	Rate
C5	Item	E5	Term
C6	Price	E6	Monthly Payment
C7	Down Pymt.	E7	Total Interest
C8	Loan Amount	E8	Total Cost

BTW
Touch Screen Differences
The Office and Windows interfaces may vary if you are using a touch screen. For this reason, you might notice that the function or appearance of your touch screen differs slightly from this module's presentation.

To Adjust the Column Widths and Row Heights

To make the worksheet easier to read, the width of columns A and B will be decreased and used as a separator between the left edge of the worksheet and the row headings. Using a column(s) as a separator between sections on a worksheet is a technique used by spreadsheet specialists. The width of columns C through F will be increased so that the intended values fit. The height of row 3, which contains the title, will be increased so that it stands out. The height of rows 1 and 2 will be decreased to act as visual separators for the top of the calculator.

1 Click column heading A and then drag through column heading B to select both columns. Position the pointer on the right boundary of column heading B and then drag to the left until the ScreenTip indicates Width: .92 (12 pixels) to change the width of both columns.

2 Position the pointer on the right boundary of column heading C and then drag to the right until the ScreenTip indicates Width: 12.00 (101 pixels) to change the column width.

3 Click column heading D to select it and then drag through column headings E and F to select multiple columns. Position the pointer on the right boundary of column heading F and then drag until the ScreenTip indicates Width: 16.00 (133 pixels) to change multiple column widths.

4 Click row heading 1 to select it and then drag through row heading 2 to select both rows. Position the pointer on the bottom boundary of row heading 2 and then drag until the ScreenTip indicates Height: 9.00 (12 pixels).

5 Select an empty cell to deselect the selected columns (Figure 4–4).

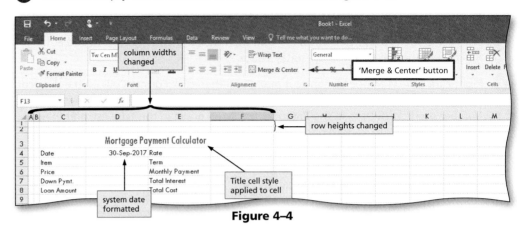

Figure 4–4

To Change the Sheet Tab Name

The following steps change the Sheet1 sheet tab name to a descriptive name and then save the workbook.

1 Double-click the Sheet1 tab and then enter **Mortgage Payment Calculator** as the sheet tab name.

2 Save the workbook on your hard drive, OneDrive, or other storage location using **NCU Mortgage Payment Calculator** as the file name.

Q&A Why should I save the workbook at this time?
You have performed many tasks while creating this workbook and do not want to risk losing work completed thus far.

BTW
Cell References in Formulas
Are you tired of writing formulas that are difficult to decipher because of cell references? The Name Manager can help add clarity to your formulas by allowing you to assign names to cells. You then can use the names, such as Rate, rather than the cell reference, such as D2, in the formulas you create. To access the Name Manager, click the Name Manager button (Formulas tab | Defined Names group).

Creating Cell Names

Worksheets often have column titles at the top of each column and row titles to the left of each row that describe the data within the worksheet. You can use these titles within formulas when you want to refer to the related data by name. A **cell name** often is created from column and row titles. You also can define descriptive names that are not column titles or row titles to represent cells, ranges of cells, formulas, or constants. Names are global to the workbook. That is, a name assigned to a cell or cell range on one worksheet in a workbook can be used on other worksheets in the same workbook to reference the named cell or range. Assigning names to a cell or range of cells allows you to select them quickly using the Name box (shown in Figure 4–7). Clicking the name will select the corresponding cell or range, and highlight the cell or range on the worksheet.

To Format Cells before Entering Values

While you usually format cells after you enter values, Excel also allows you to format cells before you enter the values. The following steps assign the currency style format with a floating dollar sign to the ranges D6:D8 and F6:F8 before the values are entered.

1 Select the range D6:D8 and, while holding down the CTRL key, select the nonadjacent range F6:F8.

2 Right-click one of the selected ranges to display a shortcut menu and then click Format Cells on the shortcut menu to display the Format Cells dialog box.

3 If necessary, click the Number tab (Format Cells dialog box) to display the Number sheet, select Currency in the Category list, and then select the second format, $1,234.10 (red font color), in the Negative numbers list.

4 Click the OK button (Format Cells dialog box) to assign the currency style format with a floating dollar sign to the selected ranges, D6:D8 and F6:F8 in this case.

Q&A

What will happen when I enter values in these cells?
As you enter numbers into these cells, Excel will display the numbers using the currency style format. You also could have selected the range C6:F8 rather than the nonadjacent ranges and assigned the currency style format to this range, which includes text. The currency style format has no impact on text in a cell.

To Enter the Loan Data

As shown in the Source of Data section of the requirements document in Figure 4–2, five items make up the loan data in the worksheet: the item to be purchased, the price of the item, the down payment, the interest rate, and the term (number of years) over which the loan is paid back. The following steps enter the loan data.

1 Select cell D5. Type **House** and then click the Enter button in the formula bar to enter text in the selected cell.

2 With cell D5 still active, click the Align Right button (Home tab | Alignment group) to right-align the text in the selected cell.

3 Select cell D6 and then enter **429000** for the price of the house.

4 Select cell D7 and then enter **85000** for the down payment.

5 Select cell F4 and then enter **4.125%** for the interest rate.

6 Click the Enter button in the formula bar to complete the entry of the interest rate, and then click the Increase Decimal button (Home tab | Number group) once to increase the number of decimal places to three.

7 Select cell F5 and then enter **15** for the number of years.

8 Click the Enter button in the formula bar to complete the entry of data in the worksheet (Figure 4–5).

BTW
When to Format
Excel lets you format cells (1) before you enter data; (2) when you enter data, through the use of format symbols; (3) incrementally after entering sections of data; and (4) after you enter all the data. Experienced users usually format a worksheet in increments as they build the worksheet, but occasions do exist when it makes sense to format cells before you enter any data.

BTW
Entering Percentages
When you format a cell to display percentages, Excel assumes that whatever you enter into that cell in the future will be a percentage. Thus, if you enter the number .5, Excel translates the value as 50%. A potential problem arises, however, when you start to enter numbers greater than or equal to one. For instance, if you enter the number 25, do you mean 25% or 2500%? If you want Excel to treat the number 25 as 25% instead of 2500% and Excel interprets the number 25 as 2500%, then click Options in the Backstage view. When the Excel Options dialog box appears, click Advanced in the left pane, and make sure the 'Enable automatic percent entry' check box in the right pane is selected.

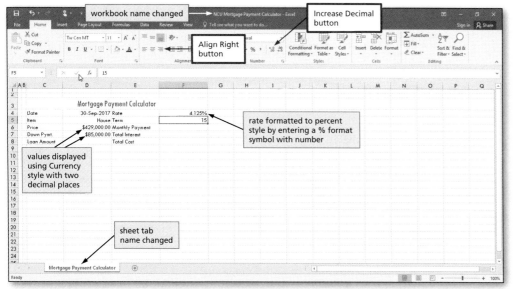

Figure 4–5

BTW
Entering Interest Rates
An alternative to requiring the user to enter an interest rate as a percentage, such as 4.125%, is to allow the user to enter the interest rate as a number without a percent sign (4.125) and then divide the interest rate by 1200, rather than 12.

Q&A Why are the entered values already formatted?

The values in cells D6 and D7 in Figure 4–5 are formatted using the currency style with two decimal places because this format was assigned to the cells prior to entering the values. Because the percent sign (%) was appended to 4.125 when it was entered in cell F4, Excel formats the interest rate using the percentage style with two decimal places (thus, the value appears as 4.13). Using the Increase Decimal button increased the number of visible decimal places to three.

To Create Names Based on Row Titles

1 CREATE MORTGAGE PAYMENT CALCULATOR | 2 CREATE DATA TABLE | 3 CREATE AMORTIZATION SCHEDULE
4 FORMAT WORKSHEET | 5 CREATE PRINT AREAS | 6 PROTECT CELLS | 7 CHECK FORMULAS

Why? Naming a cell that you plan to reference in a formula helps make the formula easier to read and remember. For example, the loan amount in cell D8 is equal to the price in cell D6 minus the down payment in cell D7. According to what you learned in earlier modules, you can enter the loan amount formula in cell D8 as =D6 – D7. By naming cells D6 and D7 using the corresponding row titles in cells C6 and C7, however, you can enter the loan amount formula as =Price – Down_Pymt., which is clearer and easier to understand than =D6 – D7. In addition to assigning a name to a single cell, you can follow the same steps to assign a name to a range of cells. The following steps assign the row titles in the range C6:C8 to their adjacent cell in column D and assign the row titles in the range E4:E8 to their adjacent cell in column F.

- Select the range C6:D8.

- Display the Formulas tab.

- Click the 'Create from Selection' button (Formulas tab | Defined Names group) to display the Create Names from Selection dialog box (Figure 4–6).

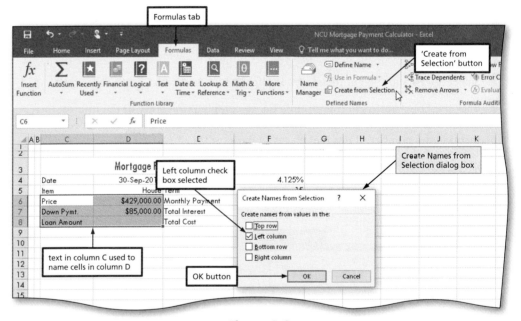

Figure 4–6

2

- Click the OK button (Create Names from Selection dialog box) to name the cells selected in the right column of the selection, D6:D8 in this case.

- Select the range E4:F8 and then click the 'Create from Selection' button (Formulas tab | Defined Names group) to display the Create Names from Selection dialog box.

- Click the OK button (Create Names from Selection dialog box) to assign names to the cells selected in the right column of the selection, F4:F8 in this case.

Q&A Are names absolute or relative cell references?

Names are absolute cell references. This is important to remember if you plan to copy formulas that contain names rather than cell references.

• Deselect the selected range and then click the Name box arrow in the formula bar to view the created names (Figure 4–7).

Q&A

Is a cell name valid when it contains a period, as with the Down_Pymt. cell name?
Yes. Periods and underscore characters are allowed in cell names. A cell name may not begin with a period or an underscore, however.

Are there any limitations on cell names?
Names may not be longer than 255 characters.

What if I make a mistake creating a cell name?
Click the Name Manager button (Formulas tab | Defined Names group) to display the Name Manager dialog box. Select the range to edit or delete, and then click the appropriate button to edit or delete the selected range.

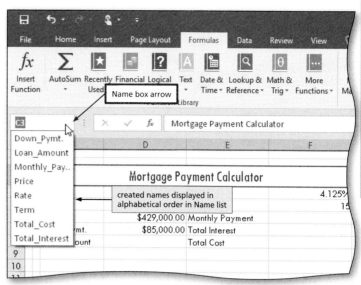

Figure 4–7

Other Ways

1. Select cell or range, type name in Name box, press ENTER key
2. Select cell or range, click Define Name button (Formulas tab | Defined Names group), type name, click OK button (New Name dialog box)
3. Select cell or range, click Name Manager button (Formulas tab | Defined Names group), click New (Name Manager dialog box), type name, click OK button (New Name dialog box), click Close button (Name Manager dialog box)
4. Select range, press CTRL+SHIFT+F3

What do you do if a cell you want to name does not have a text item in an adjacent cell?
If you want to assign a name that does not appear as a text item in an adjacent cell, use the Define Name button (Formulas tab | Defined Names group) or select the cell or range and then type the name in the Name box in the formula bar.

CONSIDER THIS

What do I need to consider when naming cells, and how can I use named cells?
You can use the assigned names in formulas to reference cells in the ranges D6:D8 or F4:F8. Excel is not case sensitive with respect to names of cells. You can enter the cell names in formulas in either uppercase or lowercase letters. To use a name that consists of two or more words in a formula, you should replace any space with the underscore character (_), as this is a commonly used standard for creating cell names. For example, the name, Down Pymt., can be written as down_pymt. or Down_Pymt. when you want to reference the adjacent cell D7. The Name Manager dialog box appears when you click the Name Manager button. The Name Manager dialog box allows you to create new names and edit or delete existing names.

CONSIDER THIS

To Enter the Loan Amount Formula Using Names

1 CREATE MORTGAGE PAYMENT CALCULATOR | 2 CREATE DATA TABLE | 3 CREATE AMORTIZATION SCHEDULE
4 FORMAT WORKSHEET | 5 CREATE PRINT AREAS | 6 PROTECT CELLS | 7 CHECK FORMULAS

Why? *Once you have created names, you can use them instead of cell references in formulas.* To determine the loan amount, enter the formula =Price – Down_Pymt. in cell D8. The following steps enter the formula using names.

1

- Select cell D8.

- Type **=p** and then scroll down the Formula AutoComplete list until you see the Price entry (Figure 4–8).

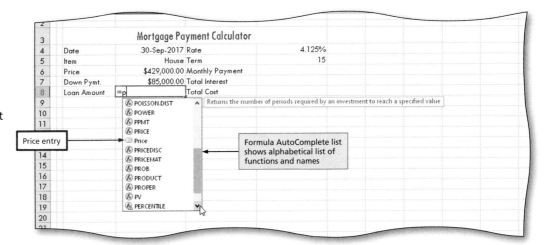

Figure 4–8

2

- Double-click Price to enter it in cell D8.

- Type **–d**.

- Double-click Down_Pymt. in the Formula AutoComplete list to select it and display the formula in both cell D8 and the formula bar using the cell names instead of the cell references (Figure 4–9).

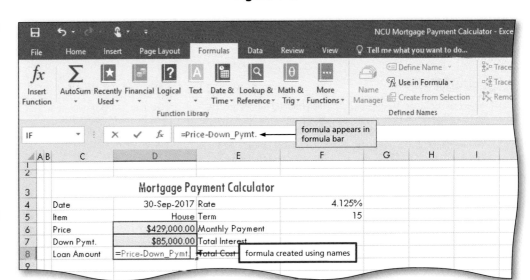

Figure 4–9

3

- Click the Enter button to assign the formula to the selected cell, =Price – Down_Pymt. to cell D8 (Figure 4–10).

Q&A What happens if I enter my formula using Point mode instead of using names?

If you enter a formula using Point mode and click a cell that has an assigned name, Excel will insert the name of the cell rather than the cell reference.

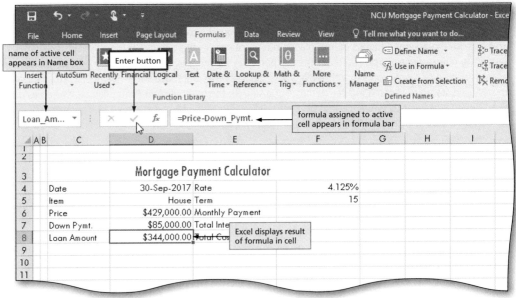

Figure 4–10

The PMT Function

You can use Excel's PMT function to determine the monthly payment. The **PMT function** calculates the payment for a loan based on constant payments and a constant interest rate. The PMT function has three arguments: rate, periods, and loan amount. Its general form is as follows:

=PMT (rate, periods, loan amount)

where rate is the interest rate per payment period, periods is the number of payments over the life of the loan, and loan amount is the amount of the loan.

In the worksheet shown in Figure 4–10, Excel displays the annual interest rate in cell F4. Financial institutions, however, usually calculate interest on a monthly basis. The rate value in the PMT function is, therefore, Rate / 12 (cell F4 divided by 12), rather than just Rate (cell F4). The periods (or number of payments) in the PMT function is 12 * Term (12 times cell F5) because each year includes 12 months, or 12 payments.

Excel considers the value returned by the PMT function to be a debit and, therefore, returns a negative number as the monthly payment. To display the monthly payment as a positive number, begin the function with a negative sign instead of an equal sign. The PMT function for cell F6 is:

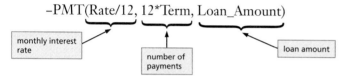

–PMT(Rate/12, 12*Term, Loan_Amount)

monthly interest rate

number of payments

loan amount

To Enter the PMT Function

1 CREATE MORTGAGE PAYMENT CALCULATOR | 2 CREATE DATA TABLE | 3 CREATE AMORTIZATION SCHEDULE
4 FORMAT WORKSHEET | 5 CREATE PRINT AREAS | 6 PROTECT CELLS | 7 CHECK FORMULAS

Why? *The next step in building the mortgage payment calculator is to determine the monthly payment for the mortgage.* The following steps use the keyboard, rather than Point mode or the Insert Function dialog box, to enter the PMT function to determine the monthly payment in cell F6.

- Select cell F6.

- Type the function `–pmt(Rate/12, 12*Term, Loan_Amount` in cell F6, which also displays in the formula bar (Figure 4–11).

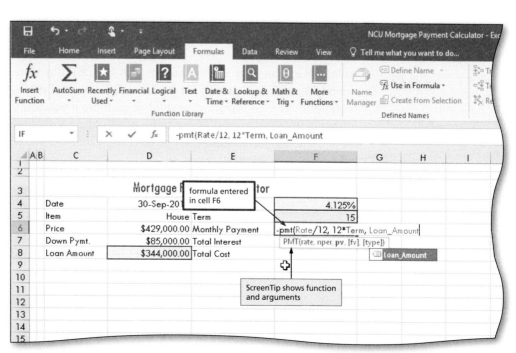

Figure 4–11

What happens as I begin to enter the function?
The ScreenTip shows the general form of the PMT function (after you type the opening parenthesis). The arguments in brackets in the ScreenTip are optional and not required for the computation required in this project. The Formula AutoComplete list (Figure 4–8) shows functions and cell names that match the letters that you type on the keyboard. You can type the complete cell name, such as Loan_Amount, or double-click the cell name in the list. When you have completed entering the function and click the Enter button or press the ENTER key, Excel will add the closing parenthesis to the function. Excel also may scroll the worksheet to the right in order to accommodate the ScreenTip.

2

• Click the Enter button in the formula bar to complete the function (Figure 4–12).

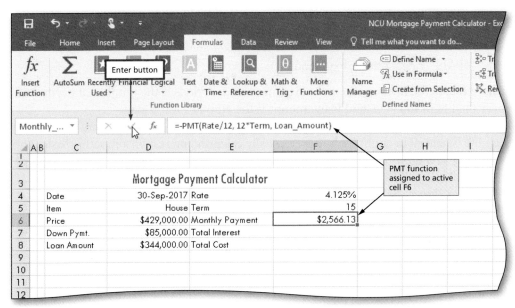

Figure 4–12

Other Ways

1. Click Financial button (Formulas tab | Function Library group), select PMT function, enter arguments, click OK button

2. Click Insert Function button in formula bar, select Financial category, select PMT function, click OK button, enter arguments, click OK button (Function Arguments dialog box)

Other Financial Functions

In addition to the PMT function, Excel provides more than 50 financial functions to help you solve the most complex finance problems. These functions save you from entering long, complicated formulas to obtain needed results. For example, the **FV function** returns the future value of an investment based on scheduled payments and an unchanging interest rate. The FV function requires the following arguments: the interest rate per period, the number of periods, and the payment made each period (which cannot change). For example if you want to invest $200 per month for five years at an annual interest rate of 6%, the FV function will calculate how much money you will have at the end of five years. Table 4–1 summarizes three of the more frequently used financial functions.

Table 4–1 Frequently Used Financial Functions

Function	Description
FV (rate, periods, payment)	Returns the future value of an investment based on periodic, constant payments and a constant interest rate.
PMT (rate, periods, loan amount)	Calculates the payment for a loan based on the loan amount, constant payments, and a constant interest rate.
PV (rate, periods, payment)	Returns the present value of an investment. The present value is the total amount that a series of future payments now is worth.

To Determine the Total Interest and Total Cost

The next step is to determine the total interest the borrower will pay on the loan (the lending institution's gross profit on the loan) and the total cost the borrower will pay for the item being purchased. The total interest (cell F7) is equal to the number of payments times the monthly payment, minus the loan amount:

$$=12*Term*Monthly\_Payment-Loan\_Amount$$

The total cost of the item to be purchased (cell F8) is equal to the price plus the total interest:

$$=Price+Total\_Interest$$

The following steps enter formulas to determine the total interest and total cost using names.

1 Select cell F7, use the keyboard to enter the formula `=12 * term * monthly_ payment - loan_amount` to determine the total interest, and then click the Enter button.

2 Select cell F8 and then use the keyboard to enter the formula `=price + total_ interest` to determine the total cost.

3 Select an empty cell to deselect cell F8 (Figure 4–13).

4 Save the workbook again on the same storage location with the same file name.

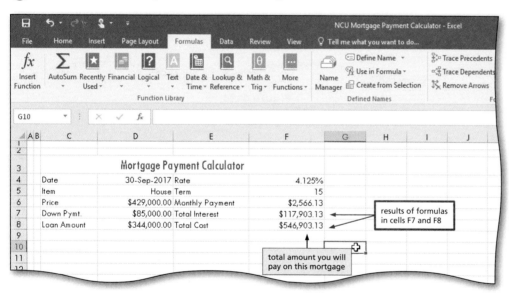

Figure 4–13

BTW

Range Finder
Remember to check all your formulas carefully. You can double-click a cell containing a formula and Excel will use Range Finder to highlight the cells that provide data for that formula. While Range Finder is active, you can drag the outlines from one cell to another to change the cells referenced in the formula, provided the cells have not been named.

BTW

Testing a Worksheet
It is good practice to test the formulas in a worksheet repeatedly until you are confident they are correct. Use data that tests the limits of the formulas. For example, you should enter negative numbers, zero, and large positive numbers when test ing formulas.

To Enter New Loan Data

Assume you want to purchase a condominium for $185,900.00. You have $45,000 for a down payment and you want the loan for a term of 10 years. NCU currently is charging 3.625% interest for a 10–year loan. The following steps enter the new loan data.

1 Enter `Condominium` in cell D5.

2 Enter `185900` in cell D6.

3 Enter `45000` in cell D7.

4 Enter `3.625%` in cell F4.

5 Enter 10 in cell F5, and then select an empty cell to recalculate the loan information in cells D8, F6, F7, and F8 (Figure 4–14).

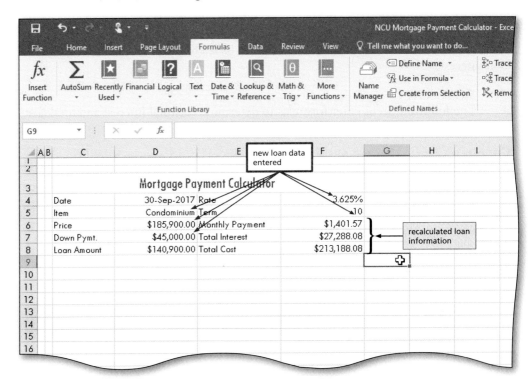

Figure 4–14

To Enter the Original Loan Data

The following steps reenter the original loan data.

1 Enter `House` in cell D5.

2 Enter `429000` in cell D6.

3 Enter `85000` in cell D7.

4 Enter `4.125` in cell F4.

5 Enter 15 in cell F5 and then select cell C10 to complete the entry of the original loan data.

BTW
Expanding Data Tables
The data table created in this module is relatively small. You can continue the series of percentages to the bottom of the worksheet and insert additional formulas in columns to create as large of a data table as you want.

Q&A What is happening on the worksheet as I enter the original data?
Excel instantaneously recalculates all formulas in the worksheet each time you enter a value. Once you have re-entered all the initial data, Excel displays the original loan information, as shown in Figure 4–13.

Can the Undo button on the Quick Access Toolbar be used to change back to the original data?
Yes. The Undo button must be clicked five times, once for each data item. You also can click the Undo arrow and drag through the first five entries in the Undo list.

Using a Data Table to Analyze Worksheet Data

BTW
Data Tables
Data tables have one purpose: to organize the answers to what-if questions. You can create two kinds of data tables. The first type involves changing one input value to see the resulting effect on one or more formulas. The second type involves changing two input values to see the resulting effect on one formula.

You already have seen that if you change a value in a cell, Excel immediately recalculates any formulas that reference the cell directly or indirectly. But what if you want to compare the results of the formula for several different values? Writing down or trying to remember all the answers to the what-if questions would be unwieldy. If you use a data table, however, Excel will organize the answers in the worksheet for you.

A **data table** is a range of cells that shows answers generated by formulas in which different values have been substituted. Data tables must be built in an unused area of the worksheet (in this case, the range C9:F22). Figure 4–15a illustrates the content needed for the Data Table command. With a **one-input data table**, you can vary the value in one cell (in this worksheet, cell F4, the interest rate). Excel then calculates the results of one or more formulas and fills the data table with the results, as shown in Figure 4–15b.

The interest rates that will be used to analyze the loan formulas in this project range from 3.000% to 4.250%, increasing in increments of 0.125%. The one-input data table shown in Figure 4–15b illustrates the impact of varying the interest rate on three formulas: the monthly payment (cell F6), total interest paid (cell F7), and the total cost of the item to be purchased (cell F8). The series of interest rates in column C are called input values.

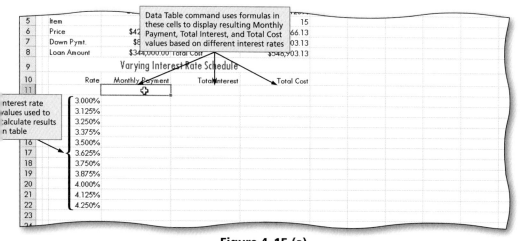

Figure 4–15 (a)

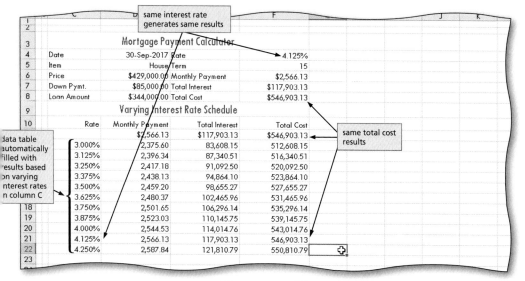

Figure 4–15 (b)

Can you use a data table when you need to vary the values in two cells rather than one?
An alternative to a one-input table is a two-input data table. A **two-input data table** allows you to vary the values in two cells. For example, you can use a two-input data table to see how your monthly mortgage payment will be affected by changing both the interest rate and the term of the loan.

To Enter the Data Table Title and Column Titles

The first step in constructing the data table shown in Figure 4–15b is to enter the data table section title and column titles in the range C9:F10 and adjust the heights of rows 9 and 10.

1 Select cell C9 and then type `Varying Interest Rate Schedule` as the data table section title.

2 Select cell C3 and then click the Format Painter button (Home tab | Clipboard group) to copy the format of the cell. Click cell C9 to apply the copied format to the cell.

3 Type `Rate` In cell C10, `Monthly Payment` in cell D10, `Total Interest` in cell E10, and `Total Cost` in cell F10 to create headers for the data table. Select the range C10:F10 and right-align the column titles.

4 Position the pointer on the bottom boundary of row heading 9 and then drag up until the ScreenTip indicates Height: 20.25 (27 pixels).

5 Position the pointer on the bottom boundary of row heading 10 and then drag down until the ScreenTip indicates Height: 17.25 (23 pixels).

6 Click cell C12 to deselect the range C10:F10 (Figure 4–16).

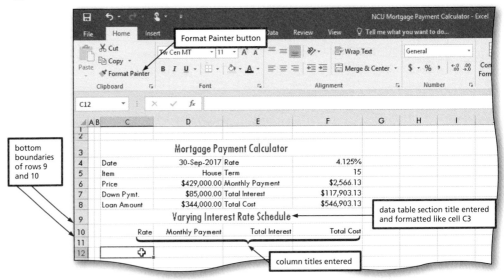

Figure 4–16

To Create a Percentage Series Using the Fill Handle

1 CREATE MORTGAGE PAYMENT CALCULATOR | 2 CREATE DATA TABLE | 3 CREATE AMORTIZATION SCHEDULE
4 FORMAT WORKSHEET | 5 CREATE PRINT AREAS | 6 PROTECT CELLS | 7 CHECK FORMULAS

Why? *These percentages will serve as the input data for the data table.* The following steps create the percentage series in column C using the fill handle.

1

- With cell C12 selected, type **3.0%** as the first number in the series.

- Select cell C13 and then type **3.125%** as the second number in the series.

- Select the range C12:C13.

- Drag the fill handle through cell C22 to create the border of the fill area as indicated by the shaded border (Figure 4–17). Do not lift your finger or release the mouse button.

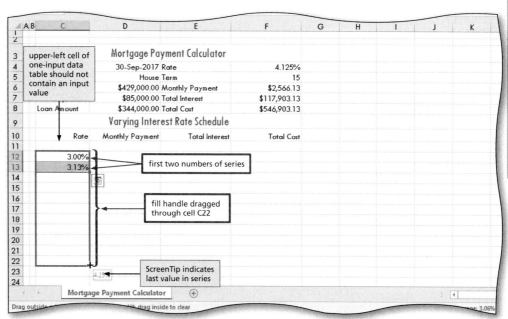

Figure 4–17

2

- Lift your finger or release the mouse button to generate the percentage series, in this case from 3.00% to 4.25%.

- Click the Increase Decimal button (Home tab | Number group) to increase the number of decimal places shown to 3.

- Click cell D11 to deselect the selected range, C12:C22 in this case (Figure 4–18).

Q&A

What is the purpose of the percentages in column C?

The percentages in column C represent different annual interest rates, which will be used when calculating the data table. The series begins in cell C12, not cell C11, because the cell immediately to the upper-left of the formulas in a one-input data table should not include an input value.

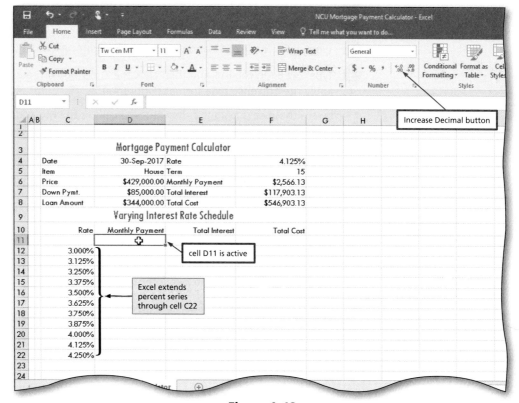

Figure 4–18

Other Ways

1. Right-drag fill handle in direction to fill, click Fill Series on shortcut menu

To Enter the Formulas in the Data Table

The next step in creating the data table is to enter the three formulas at the top of the table in cells D11, E11, and F11. The three formulas are the same as the monthly payment formula in cell F6, the total interest formula in cell F7, and the total cost formula in cell F8. The number of formulas you place at the top of a one-input data table depends on the purpose of the table. Some one-input data tables will have only one formula, while others might have several. In this case, three formulas are affected when the interest rate changes.

Excel provides four ways to enter these formulas in the data table: (1) retype the formulas in cells D11, E11, and F11; (2) copy cells F6, F7, and F8 to cells D11, E11, and F11, respectively; (3) enter the formulas **=monthly payment** in cell D11, **=total interest** in cell E11, and **=total cost** in cell F11; or (4) enter the formulas **=F6** in cell D11, **=F7** in cell E11, and **=F8** in cell F11.

The best alternative to define the formulas in the data table is the fourth alternative, which involves using the cell references preceded by an equal sign. This method is best because (1) it is easier to enter; (2) if you change any of the formulas in the range F6:F8, the formulas at the top of the data table are immediately updated; and (3) Excel automatically will assign the format of the cell reference (currency style format) to the cell. Using the third alternative, which involves using cell names, is nearly as good an alternative, but Excel will not assign formatting to the cells when you use cell names. The following steps enter the formulas of the data table in row 11.

1 With cell D11 active, type **=f6** and then press the RIGHT ARROW key to enter the first parameter of the function to be used in the data table.

2 Type **=f7** in cell E11 and then press the RIGHT ARROW key.

3 Type **=f8** in cell F11 and then click the Enter button to assign the formulas and apply the Currency style format (Figure 4–19).

Q&A

Why are these cells assigned the values of cells in the Mortgage Payment Calculator area of the worksheet?

It is important to understand that the entries in the top row of the data table (row 11) refer to the formulas that the loan officer and customer want to evaluate using the series of percentages in column C. Furthermore, recall that when you assign a formula to a cell, Excel applies the format of the first cell reference in the formula to the cell. Thus, Excel applies the currency style format to cells D11, E11, and F11 because that is the format of cells F6, F7, and F8.

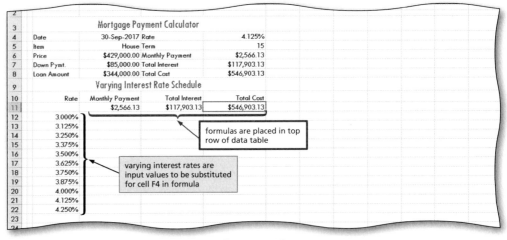

Figure 4–19

To Define a Range as a Data Table

After creating the interest rate series in column C and entering the formulas in row 11, the next step is to define the range C11:F22 as a data table. Cell F4 is the input cell for the data table, which means cell F4 is the cell in which values from column C in the data table are substituted in the formulas in row 11. *Why?* You want *Excel to generate the monthly payment, monthly interest, and total cost for the various interest rates.*

❶

- Select the range C11:F22 as the range in which to create the data table.

- Display the Data tab and then click the 'What-If Analysis' button (Data tab | Forecast group) to display the What-If Analysis menu (Figure 4–20).

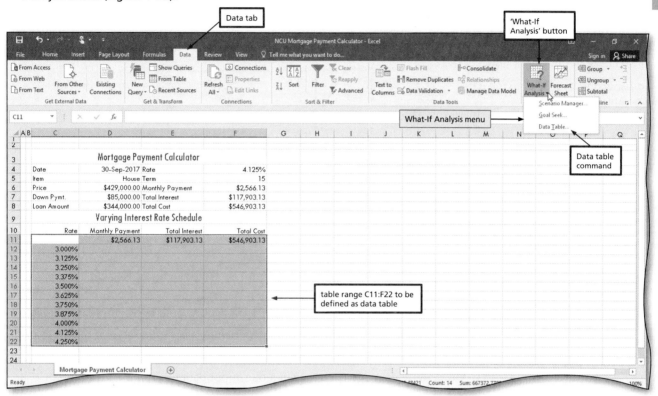

Figure 4–20

❷

- Click Data Table on the What-If Analysis menu to display the Data Table dialog box.

- Click the 'Column input cell' box (Data Table dialog box) and then click cell F4 in the Mortgage Payment Calculator section of the spreadsheet to select the input cell for the data table (Figure 4–21).

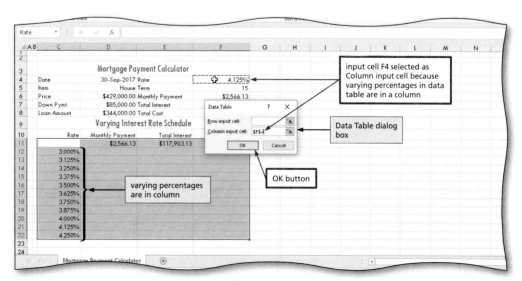

Figure 4–21

Q&A What is the purpose of clicking cell F4?
The purpose of clicking cell F4 is to select it for the Column input cell. A marquee surrounds the selected cell F4, indicating it will be the input cell in which values from column C in the data table are substituted in the formulas in row 11. $F$4 now appears in the 'Column input cell' box in the Data Table dialog box.

- Click the OK button (Data Table dialog box) to create the data table.

- Apply the currency style with no currency symbol and the second format in the Negative numbers list to the range D12:F22.

- Deselect the selected range, D11:F22 in this case (Figure 4–22).

Q&A How does Excel create the data table?
Excel calculates the results of the three formulas in row 11 for each interest rate in column C and immediately fills columns D, E, and F of the data table. The resulting values for each interest rate are displayed in the corresponding rows.

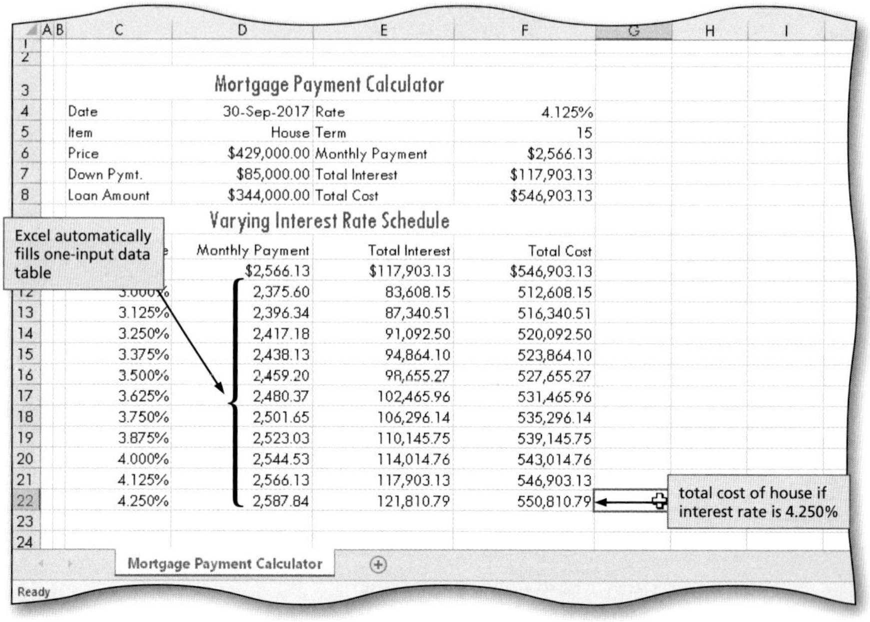

Figure 4–22

More about Data Tables

The following list details important points you should know about data tables:

1. The formula(s) you are analyzing must include a cell reference to the input cell.

2. You can have as many active data tables in a worksheet as you want.

3. While only one value can vary in a one-input data table, the data table can analyze as many formulas as you want.

4. To include additional formulas in a one-input data table, enter them in adjacent cells in the same row as the current formulas (row 11 in Figure 4–22) and then define the entire new range as a data table by using the Data Table command on the What-If Analysis menu.

5. You delete a data table as you would delete any other item on a worksheet. That is, select the data table and then press the DELETE key.

Break Point: If you wish to take a break, this is a good place to do so. You can exit Excel now. To resume at a later time, run Excel, open the file called NCU Mortgage Payment Calculator, and continue following the steps from this location forward.

BTW
Amortization Schedules
Hundreds of websites offer amortization schedules. To find these websites, use a search engine, such as Google, and search using the keywords, amortization schedule.

Creating an Amortization Schedule

The next step in this project is to create the Amortization Schedule section on the right side of Figure 4–23. An amortization schedule shows the beginning and ending balances of a loan and the amount of payment that applies to the principal and interest for each year over the life of the loan. For example, if a customer wanted to pay off the loan after six years, the Amortization Schedule section would tell the loan officer what the payoff would be (cell J10 in Figure 4–23). The Amortization Schedule section shown in Figure 4–23 will work only for loans of up to 15 years; however, you could extend the table to any number of years. The Amortization Schedule section also contains summaries in rows 20, 21, and 22. These summaries should agree exactly with the corresponding amounts in the Mortgage Payment Calculator section in the range C3:F8.

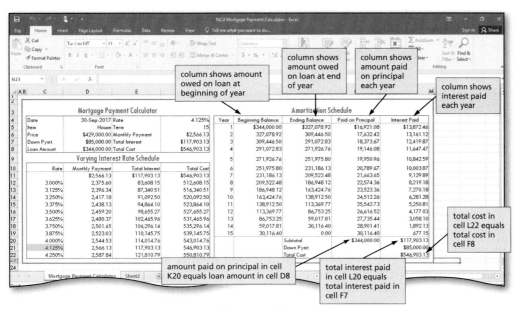

Figure 4–23

To Change Column Widths and Enter Titles

The first step in creating the Amortization Schedule section is to adjust the column widths and enter the section title and column titles. The following steps adjust column widths and enter column titles for the Amortization Schedule section.

1 Position the pointer on the right boundary of column heading G and then drag to the left until the ScreenTip shows Width: .92 (12 pixels) to change the column width.

2 Position the pointer on the right boundary of column heading H and then drag to the left until the ScreenTip shows Width: 6.00 (53 pixels) to change the column width.

3 Drag through column headings I through L to select them. Position the pointer on the right boundary of column heading L and then drag to the right until the ScreenTip shows Width: 16.00 (133 pixels) to change the column widths.

4 Select cell H3. Type **Amortization Schedule** and then press the ENTER key to enter the section title.

5 Select cell C3, click the Format Painter button (Home tab | Clipboard group) to activate the format painter, and then click cell H3 to copy the format of cell C3.

6 Click the 'Merge & Center' button (Home tab | Alignment group) to split the selected cell, cell H3 in this case. Select the range H3:L3 and then click the 'Merge & Center' button (Home tab | Alignment group) to merge and center the section title over the selected range.

7 Enter the following column headings in row 4: **Year** in cell H4, **Beginning Balance** in cell I4, **Ending Balance** in cell J4, **Paid on Principal** in cell K4, and **Interest Paid** in cell L4. Select the range H4:L4 and then click the Center button (Home tab | Alignment group) to center the column headings.

BTW
Column Borders
In this module, columns A and G are used as column borders to divide sections of the worksheet from one another, as well as from the row headings. A column border is an unused column with a significantly reduced width. You also can use row borders to separate sections of a worksheet.

8 Select cell H5 to display the centered section title and column headings (Figure 4–24).

Q&A Why was cell H3 split, or unmerged, in Step 6?

After using the format painter, Excel attempted to merge and center the text in cell H3 because the source of the format, cell C3, is merged and centered across four columns. The Amortization Schedule section, however, includes five columns. Splitting cell H3 changed cell H3 back to being one column instead of including four columns. Next, the section heading was merged and centered across five columns as required by the design of the worksheet.

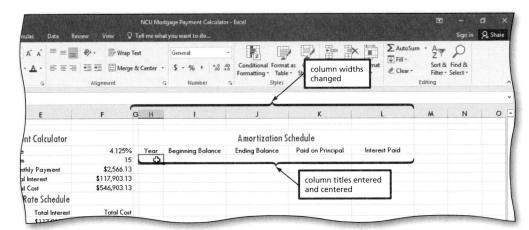

Figure 4–24

To Create a Series of Integers Using the Fill Handle

The next step is to use the fill handle to create a series of numbers that represent the years during the life of the loan. The series begins with 1 (year 1) and ends with 15 (year 15). The following steps create a series of years in the range H5:H19.

1 With cell H5 active, type **1** as the initial year. Select cell H6 and then type **2** to represent the next year.

2 Select the range H5:H6 and then drag the fill handle through cell H19 to complete the creation of a series of integers, 1 through 15 in the range H5:H19 in this case (Figure 4–25).

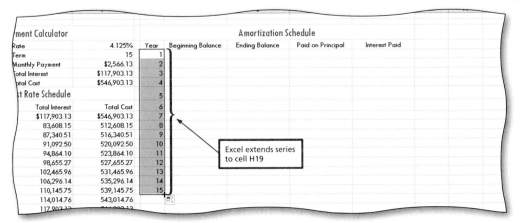

Figure 4–25

Q&A

Why is year 5 of the amortization schedule larger than the other rows in the amortization schedule?

The design of the worksheet called for a large font size for the varying interest rate schedule section of the worksheet, which is in row 9 of the worksheet. To accommodate the larger font size, the height of row 9 was increased. Year 5 of the worksheet is in the taller row 9 and, therefore, is taller than the other years in the amortization schedule.

Formulas in the Amortization Schedule

Four formulas form the basis of the amortization schedule. These formulas are found in row 5. Later, these formulas will be copied through row 19. The formulas are summarized in Table 4–2.

Table 4–2 Formulas for the Amortization Schedule

Cell	Column Heading	Formula	Example
I5	Beginning Balance	=D8	The beginning balance (the balance at the end of a year) is the initial loan amount in cell D8.
J5	Ending Balance	=IF(H5<=$F$5, PV($F$4/12, 12*($F$5–H5), –$F$6), 0)	The ending balance (the balance at the end of a year) is equal to the present value of the payments paid over the remaining life of the loan. (This formula is fully explained in the following text.)
K5	Paid on Principal	=I5–J5	The amount paid on the principal at the end of the year is equal to the beginning balance (cell I5) minus the ending balance (cell J5).
L5	Interest Paid	=IF(I5>0, 12*$F$6–K5, 0)	The interest paid during the year is equal to 12 times the monthly payment (cell F6) minus the amount paid on the principal (cell K5).

Of the four formulas in Table 4–2, perhaps the most difficult to understand is the PV function that will be assigned to cell J5. The **PV function** returns the present value of an annuity. An **annuity** is a series of fixed payments (such as the monthly payment in cell F6) made at the end of each of a fixed number of periods (months) at a fixed interest rate. You can use the PV function to determine the amount the borrower still owes on the loan at the end of each year. The PV function has three arguments: rate, number of periods, and payment amount per period. Its general form is as follows:

$$=PV(rate, period, payment)$$

where rate is the interest rate per payment period, period is the number of payments remaining in the life of the loan, and payment is the amount of the monthly payment.

The PV function is used to determine the ending balance after the first year (cell J5) by using a term equal to the number of months for which the borrower still must make payments. For example, if the loan is for 15 years (180 months), then the borrower still owes 168 payments after the first year (180 months–12 months). The number of payments outstanding can be determined from the formula 12*($F$5–H5) or 12*(15–1), which equals 168. Recall that column H contains integers that represent the years of the loan. After the second year, the number of payments remaining is 156, and so on.

If you assign the PV function as shown in Table 4–2 to cell J5 and then copy it to the range J6:J19, the ending balances for each year will be displayed properly. However, if the loan is for fewer than 15 years, any ending balances for the years beyond the term of the loan are invalid. For example, if a loan is taken out for 5 years, then the rows representing years 6 through 15 in the amortization schedule should be zero. The PV function, however, will display negative numbers for those years even though the loan already has been paid off.

To avoid displaying negative ending balances, the worksheet should include a formula that assigns the PV function to the range I5:I19 as long as the corresponding year in column H is less than or equal to the number of years in the term (cell F5). If the corresponding year in column H is greater than the number of years in cell F5, then the ending balance for that year and the remaining years should be zero. The following IF function causes either the value of the PV function or zero to be displayed in cell J5, depending on whether the corresponding value in column H is greater than — or less than or equal to — the number of years in cell F5. Recall that the dollar signs within the cell references indicate the cell references are absolute and, therefore, will not change as you copy the function downward.

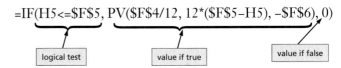

=IF(H5<=$F$5, PV($F$4/12, 12*($F$5–H5), –$F$6), 0)

logical test · value if true · value if false

In the preceding formula, the logical test determines if the year in column H is less than or equal to the term of the loan in cell F5. If the logical test is true, then the IF function assigns the PV function to the cell. If the logical test is false, then the IF function assigns zero (0) to the cell. You also could use two double-quote symbols (" ") to indicate to Excel to leave the cell blank if the logical test is false.

The PV function in the IF function includes absolute cell references (cell references with dollar signs) to ensure that the references to cells in column F do not change when the IF function later is copied down the column.

To Enter the Formulas in the Amortization Schedule

1 CREATE MORTGAGE PAYMENT CALCULATOR | 2 CREATE DATA TABLE | **3 CREATE AMORTIZATION SCHEDULE**
4 FORMAT WORKSHEET | 5 CREATE PRINT AREAS | 6 PROTECT CELLS | 7 CHECK FORMULAS

Why? *Creating an amortization schedule allows you to see the costs of a mortgage and the balance still owed for any year in the term of the loan. This information can be very helpful when making financial decisions.* The following steps enter the four formulas shown in Table 4–2 into row 5. Row 5 represents year 1 of the loan.

- Select cell I5 and then enter =d8 as the beginning balance of the loan.

- Select cell J5 and then type
=if(h5<=f5, pv(f4/12, 12* (f5–h5), –f6), 0) as the entry (Figure 4–26).

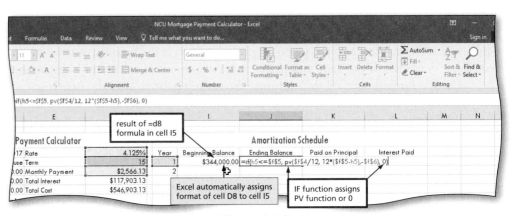

Figure 4–26

2

- Click the Enter button in the formula bar to insert the formula in the selected cell (Figure 4–27).

Q&A What happens when the Enter button is clicked?

Excel evaluates the IF function in cell J5 and displays the result of the PV function (327078.9227), because the value in cell H5 (1) is less than the term of the loan in cell F5 (15). With cell J5 active, Excel also displays the formula in the formula bar. If the borrower wanted to pay off the loan after one year, the cost would be $327,078.92.

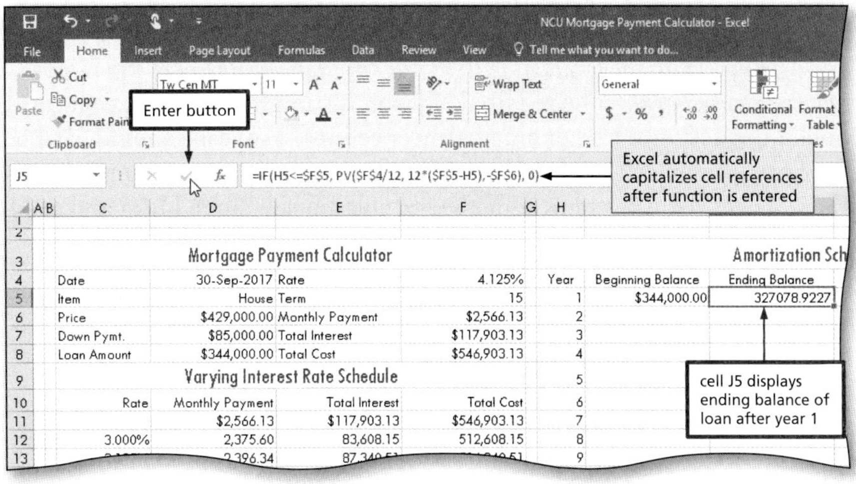

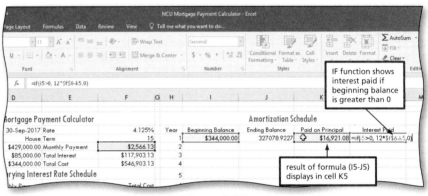

Figure 4–27

3

- Select cell K5. Enter the formula =i5 – j5 and then press the RIGHT ARROW key to complete the entry and select cell L5.

- Enter the formula =if(i5 > 0, 12 * f6 – k5, 0) in cell L5 (Figure 4–28).

Figure 4–28

4

- Click the Enter button in the formula bar to complete the entry of the formula (Figure 4–29).

Q&A Why are some of the cells in the range I5:L5 not formatted?

When you enter a formula in a cell, Excel assigns the cell the same format as the first cell reference in the formula. For example, when you enter =d8 in cell I5, Excel assigns the format in cell D8 to cell I5. The same applies to cell K5. Although this method of formatting also works for most functions, it does not work for the IF function. Thus, the results of the IF functions in cells J5 and L5 are formatted using the general style format, which is the default format when you open a new workbook.

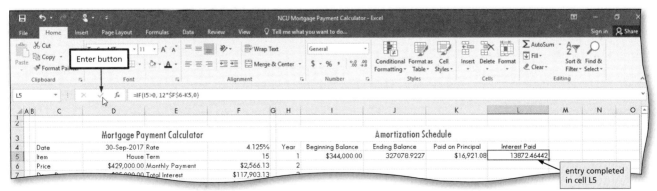

Figure 4–29

To Copy the Formulas to Fill the Amortization Schedule

Why? *With the formulas entered into the first row, the next step is to copy them to the remaining rows in the amortization schedule.* The required copying is straightforward, except for the beginning balance column. To obtain the next year's beginning balance (cell I6), last year's ending balance (cell J5) must be used. After cell J5 (last year's ending balance) is copied to cell I6 (next year's beginning balance), then I6 can be copied to the range I7:I19. The following steps copy the formulas in the range J5:L5 and cell I6 through to the remainder of the amortization schedule.

- Select the range J5:L5 and then drag the fill handle down through row 19 to copy the formulas through the amortization schedule, J6:L19 in this case (Figure 4–30).

Q&A

Why do some of the numbers seem incorrect?
Many of the numbers are incorrect because the cells in column I — except for cell I5 — do not yet contain values.

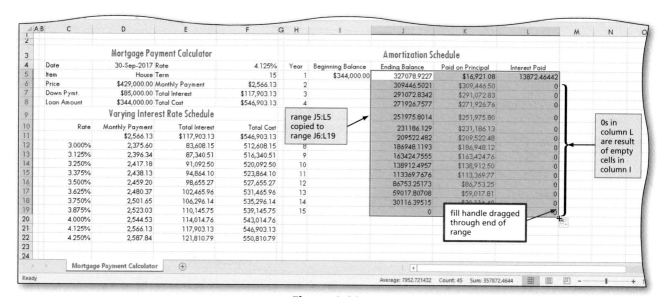

Figure 4–30

- Select cell I6, type =j5 as the cell entry, and then click the Enter button in the formula bar to display the ending balance (327078.9227) for year 1 as the beginning balance for year 2 (Figure 4–31).

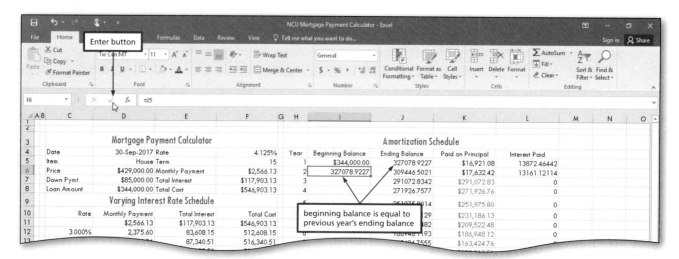

Figure 4–31

- With cell I6 active, drag the fill handle down through row 19 to copy the formula in cell I6 (=J5) to the range I7:I19 (Figure 4–32).

Q&A

What happens after the fill operation is complete?

Because the cell reference J5 is relative, Excel adjusts the row portion of the cell reference as it is copied downward. Thus, each new beginning balance in column I is equal to the ending balance of the previous year.

E	F	G	H	I	J	K	L	M	N	O
Calculator					Amortization Schedule					
	4.125%		Year	Beginning Balance	Ending Balance	Paid on Principal	Interest Paid			
	15		1	$344,000.00	327078.9227	$16,921.08	13872.46442			
Payment	$2,566.13		2	327078.9227	309446.5021	$17,632.42	13161.12114			
terest	$117,903.13		3	309446.5021	291072.8342	$18,373.67	12419.87378			
Cost	$546,903.13		4	291072.8342	271926.7577	$19,146.08	11647.4652			
ate Schedule			5	271926.7577	251975.8014	$19,950.96	10842.58543			
Total Interest	Total Cost		6	251975.8014	231186.129	$20,789.67	10003.8694			
$117,903.13	$546,903.13		7	231186.129	209522.482	$21,663.65	9129.894684	Paid on Principal and Interest Paid values now are correct		
83,608.15	cell copied through range I6 to I19		8	209522.482	186948.1193	$22,574.36	8219.179042			
87,340.51			9	186948.1193	163424.7555	$23,523.36	7270.177927			
91,092.50	520,092.50		10	163424.7555	138912.4957	$24,512.26	6281.28186			
94,864.10	523,864.10		11	138912.4957	113369.7676	$25,542.73	5250.813702			
98,655.27	527,655.27		12	113369.7676	86753.25173	$26,616.52	4177.025807			
102,465.96	531,465.96		13	86753.25173	59017.80708	$27,735.44	3058.097064			
106,296.14	535,296.14		14	59017.80708	30116.39515	$28,901.41	1892.129799			
110,145.75	539,145.75		15	30116.39515	0	$30,116.40	677.1465667			
114,014.76	543,014.76									
117,903.13	546,903.13									
121,810.79	550,810.79									

fill handle dragged through destination range

Figure 4–32

Other Ways

1. Select cells containing formulas to copy, click Copy (Home tab | Clipboard group), select destination cell or range, click Paste (Home tab | Clipboard group)

To Enter the Total Formulas in the Amortization Schedule

The next step is to determine the amortization schedule totals in rows 20 through 22. These totals should agree with the corresponding totals in the Mortgage Payment Calculator section (range F7:F8). The following steps enter the total formulas in the amortization schedule.

1 Select cell J20 and then enter **Subtotal** as the row title.

2 Select the range K20:L20 and then click the Sum button (Home tab | Editing group) to sum the selected range.

3 Select cell J21 and then enter **Down Pymt.** as the row title.

4 Select cell L21 and then enter **=d7** to copy the down payment to the selected cell.

5 Select cell J22 and then enter **Total Cost** as the row title.

6 Select cell L22, type `=K20 + L20 + L21` as the total cost, and then click the Enter button in the formula bar to complete the amortization schedule totals (Figure 4–33).

Q&A

What was accomplished in the previous steps?

The formula assigned to cell L22 (=K20+L20+L21) sums the total amount paid on the principal (cell K20), the total interest paid (cell L20), and the down payment (cell L21). Excel assigns cell K20 the same format as cell K5 because cell K5 is the first cell reference in =SUM(K5:K19). Furthermore, because cell K20 was selected first when the range K20:L20 was selected to determine the sum, Excel assigned cell L20 the same format it assigned to cell K20. Finally, cell L21 was assigned the currency style format, because cell L21 was assigned the formula =d7, and cell D7 has a currency style format. For the same reason, the value in cell L22 appears with the currency style format.

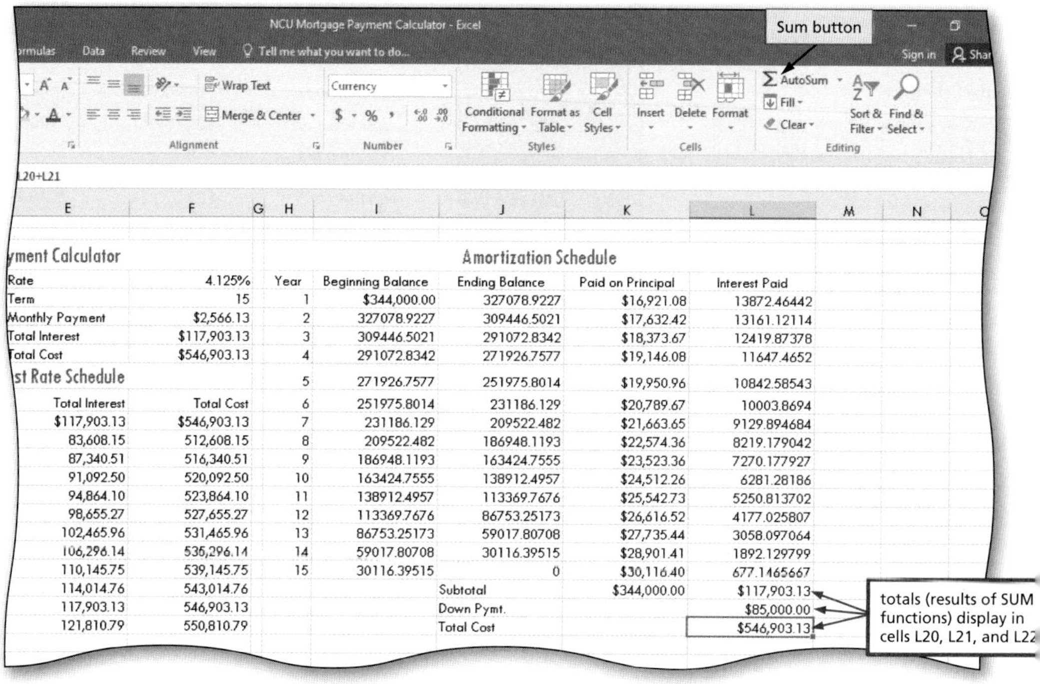

Figure 4–33

To Format the Numbers in the Amortization Schedule

The next step in creating the amortization schedule is to format it so that it is easier to read. When the beginning balance formula (=d8) was entered earlier into cell I5, Excel copied the currency style format along with the value from cell D8 to cell I5. The following steps copy the currency style format from cell I5 to the range J5:L5. The comma style format then will be assigned to the range I6:L19.

1 Select cell I5 and then click the Format Painter button (Home tab | Clipboard group) to turn on the format painter. Drag through the range J5:L5 to assign the currency style format to the cells.

2 Select the range I6:L19 and then right-click the selected range to display a shortcut menu. Click Format Cells on the shortcut menu to display the Format Cells dialog box and then, if necessary, click the Number tab (Format Cells dialog box) to display the Number sheet.

3 Select Currency in the Category list to select a currency format, select None in the Symbol list to choose no currency symbol, and then click the second format, 1,234.10, in the Negative numbers list to create a currency format.

4 Click the OK button (Format Cells dialog box) to apply the currency format to the selected range.

5 Deselect the range I6:L19 and display the numbers in the amortization schedule, as shown in Figure 4–34.

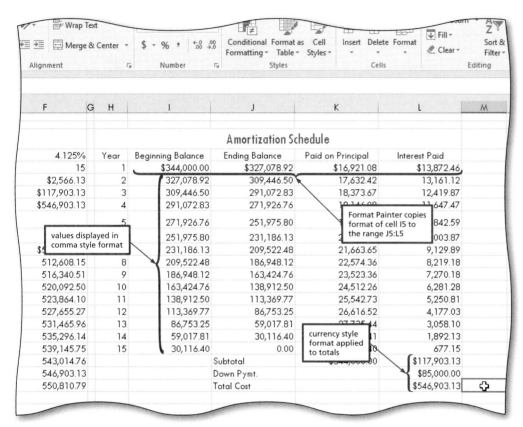

Figure 4–34

BTW
Round-Off Errors
If you manually add the numbers in column L (range L5:L19) and compare it to the sum in cell L20, you will notice that the total interest paid is $0.01 off. This round-off error is due to the fact that some of the numbers involved in the computations have additional decimal places that do not appear in the cells. You can use the ROUND function on the formula entered into cell L5 to ensure the total is exactly correct. For information on the ROUND function, click the Insert Function button in the formula bar, click 'Math & Trig' in the 'Or select a category' list, scroll down in the 'Select a function' list, and then click ROUND.

BTW
Undoing Formats
If you began assigning formats to a range and then realize you made a mistake and want to start over, select the range, click the Cell Styles button (Home tab | Styles group), and then click Normal in the Cell Styles gallery.

Formatting the Worksheet

Previous modules introduced you to outlining a range using cell borders or cell background colors to differentiate portions of a worksheet. The Borders button (Home tab | Font group), however, offers only a limited selection of border thicknesses. To control the color and thickness, Excel requires that you use the Border sheet in the Format Cells dialog box.

To Add Custom Borders to a Range

1 CREATE MORTGAGE PAYMENT CALCULATOR | 2 CREATE DATA TABLE | 3 CREATE AMORTIZATION SCHEDULE
4 FORMAT WORKSHEET | 5 CREATE PRINT AREAS | 6 PROTECT CELLS | 7 CHECK FORMULAS

Why? *Borders can be used to distinguish the different functional parts of a worksheet.* The following steps add a medium blue border to the Mortgage Payment Calculator section. To subdivide the row titles and numbers further, light borders also are added within the section, as shown in Figure 4–1.

- Select the range C4:F8 and then right-click to display a shortcut menu and mini toolbar (Figure 4–35).

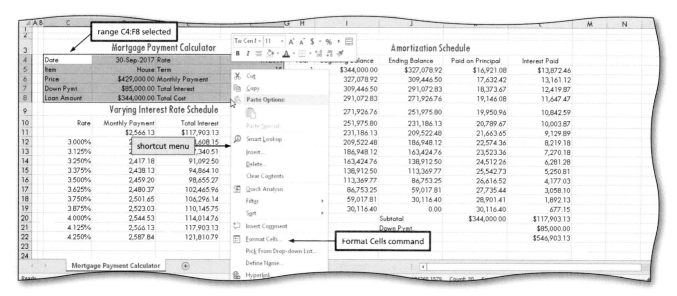

Figure 4–35

2

- Click Format Cells on the shortcut menu to display the Format Cells dialog box.

- Display the Border tab (Format Cells dialog box).

- Click the Color arrow to display the Colors palette and then select the Blue, Accent 2 color (column 6, row 1) in the Theme Colors area.

- Click the medium border in the Style area (column 2, row 5) to select the line style for the border.

- Click the Outline button in the Presets area to preview the outline border in the Border area (Figure 4–36).

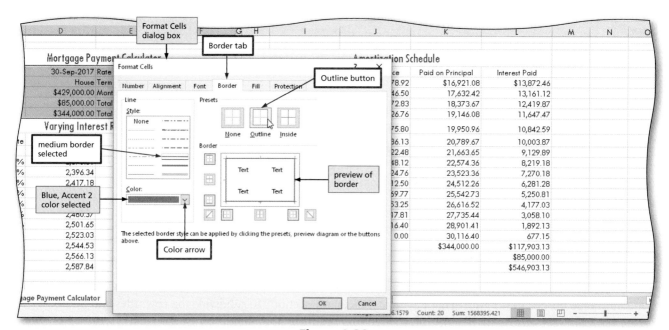

Figure 4–36

3

- Click the light border in the Style area (column 1, row 7) and then click the Vertical Line button in the Border area to preview the blue vertical border in the Border area (Figure 4–37).

Q&A How do I create a border?
As shown in Figure 4–37, you can add a variety of borders with different colors to a cell or range of cells. It is important that you select border characteristics in the order specified in the steps; that is, (1) choose the border color, (2) choose the border line style, and then (3) choose the border type. This order first defines the border characteristics and then applies those characteristics. If you do these steps in any other order, you may not end up with the borders you intended.

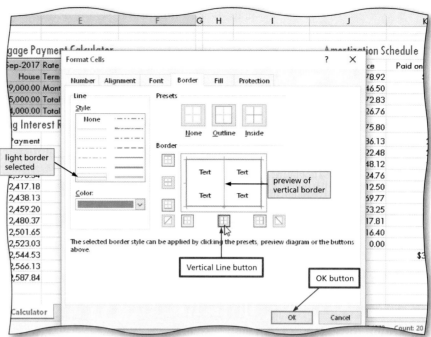

Figure 4–37

4

- Click the OK button to add a blue outline with vertical borders to the right side of each column in the selected range, C4:F8 in this case (Figure 4–38).

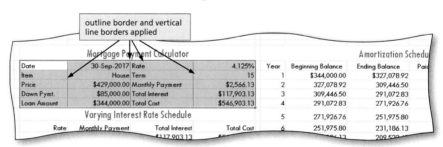

Figure 4–38

Other Ways

1. Click More Borders button arrow (Home tab | Font group), click More Borders, select border options, click OK

2. Click Format button (Home tab | Cells group), click Format Cells, click Border tab, select border options, click OK

To Add Borders to the Varying Interest Rate Schedule

The following steps add the same borders you applied to the Mortgage Payment Calculator to the Varying Interest Rate Schedule.

1 Select the range C10:F22. Right-click the selected range to display a shortcut menu and then click Format Cells on the shortcut menu to display the Format Cells dialog box.

2 If necessary, click the Border tab (Format Cells dialog box) to display the Border sheet. Click the Color arrow to display the Colors palette and then click Blue, Accent 2 (column 6, row 1) in the Theme Colors area to change the border color.

3 Click the medium border in the Style area (column 2, row 5). Click the Outline button in the Presets area to preview the border in the Border area.

④ Click the light border in the Style area (column 1, row 7). Click the Vertical Line button in the Border area to preview the border in the Border area.

⑤ Click the OK button (Format Cells dialog box) to apply custom borders to the selected range.

⑥ Select the range C10:F10 and then use the Format Cells dialog box to apply a blue, light bottom border to the selected range.

⑦ Deselect the range to display the worksheet, as shown in Figure 4–39.

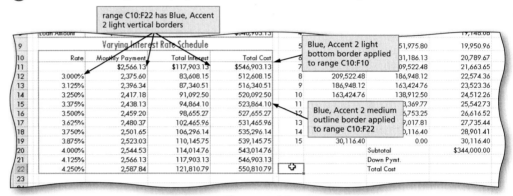

Figure 4–39

To Add Borders to the Amortization Schedule

The following steps add the borders to the Amortization Schedule.

① Select the range H4:L22, and then display the Format Cells dialog box.

② Apply a Blue, Accent 2, medium border style using the Outline preset.

③ Change the border style to light (column 1, row 7) and then click the Vertical Line button in the Border area to preview the border in the Border area.

④ Click the OK button to apply custom borders to the selected range.

⑤ Select the range H5:L19 and then use the Format Cells dialog box to apply a blue, light upper border and a blue, light bottom border to the selected range.

⑥ Deselect the range to display the worksheet, as shown in Figure 4–40.

Figure 4–40

To Use Borders and Fill Color to Visually Define and Group the Financial Tools

The following steps add a border and fill color to the entire group of financial tools on the worksheet.

1 Change the height of row 23 to 9.0 (12 pixels).

2 Change the width of column M to .92 (12 pixels).

3 Select the range B2:M23.

4 Add a Dark Green, Accent 5, (column 9, row 1) heavy style (column 2, row 6) Outline border to the selected range.

5 With the range B2:M23 still selected, click the Fill Color arrow (Home tab | Font group) and apply a fill color of White, Background 1 (column 1, row 1) to the selected range. Deselect the range (Figure 4–41).

6 Save the workbook again on the same storage location with the same file name.

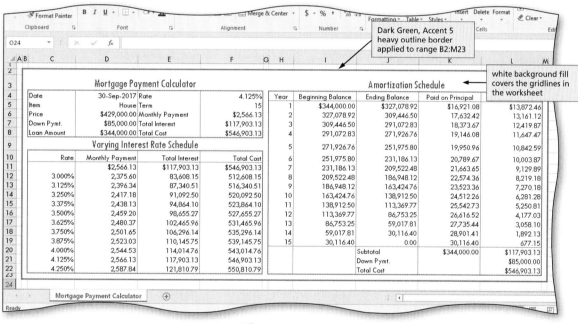

Figure 4–41

Highlighting Cells in the Data Table Using Conditional Formatting

If the interest rate in cell F4 is between 3.000% and 4.250% and its decimal portion is a multiple of 0.125 (such as 4.125%), then one of the rows in the data table agrees exactly with the monthly payment, interest paid, and total cost in the range F6:F8. For example, in Figure 4–41 row 21 (4.125%) in the data table agrees with the results in the range F6:F8, because the interest rate in cell C21 is the same as the interest rate in cell F4. Analysts often look for the row in the data table that agrees with the input cell results. You can use conditional formatting to highlight a row, or a single cell in the row.

BTW

Conditional Formatting
You can add as many conditional formats to a range as you like. After adding the first condition, click the Conditional Formatting button (Home tab | Styles group) and then click New Rule to add more conditions. If more than one condition is true for a cell, then Excel applies the formats of each condition, beginning with the first.

To Add a Pointer to the Data Table Using Conditional Formatting

Why? *To make the row with the active interest rate stand out, you can add formatting that serves as a pointer to that row.* To add a pointer, you can use conditional formatting to highlight the cell in column C that agrees with the input cell (cell F4). The following steps apply conditional formatting to column C in the data table.

1

- Select the range C12:C22 and then click the Conditional Formatting button (Home tab | Styles group) to display the Conditional Formatting gallery.

- Point to 'Highlight Cells Rules' to display the submenu (Figure 4–42).

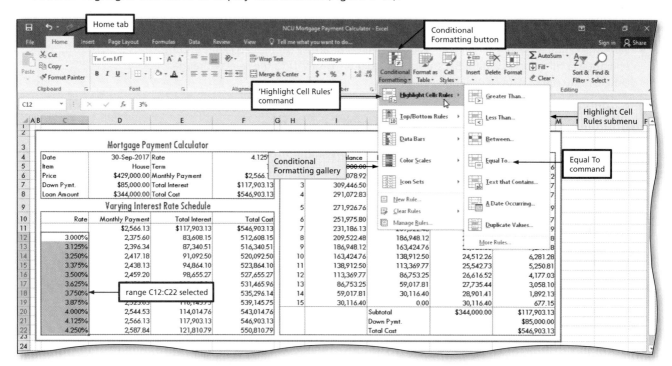

Figure 4–42

2

- Click Equal To on the Highlight Cells Rules submenu to display the Equal To dialog box.

- Type **=$F$4** in the 'Format cells that are EQUAL TO:' box (Equal To dialog box) (Figure 4–43).

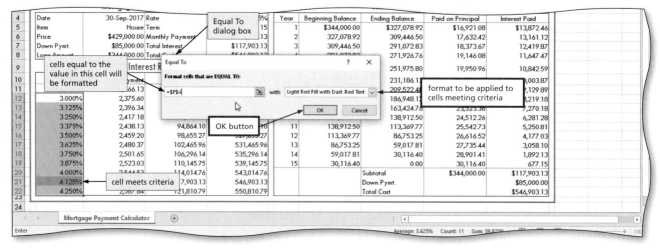

Figure 4–43

❸

- Click the OK button to apply the conditional formatting rule.

- Deselect the range (Figure 4–44).

Q&A

How does Excel apply the conditional formatting?
Cell C21 in the data table, which contains the value, 4.125%, appears with a red background and dark red text, because the value 4.125% is the same as the interest rate value in cell F4.

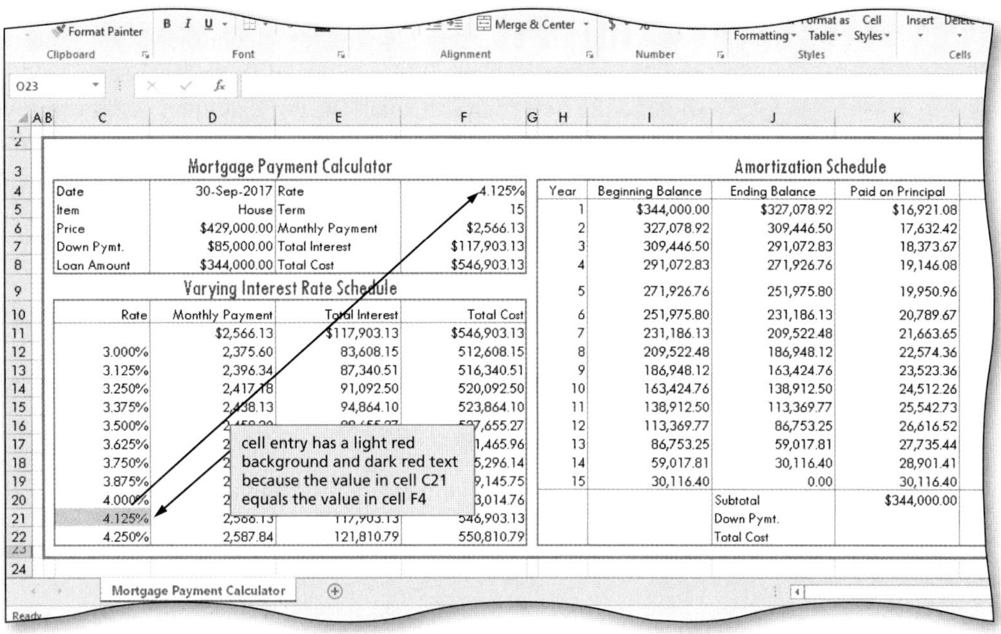

Figure 4–44

❹

- Select cell F4 and then enter **4.000** as the interest rate (Figure 4–45).

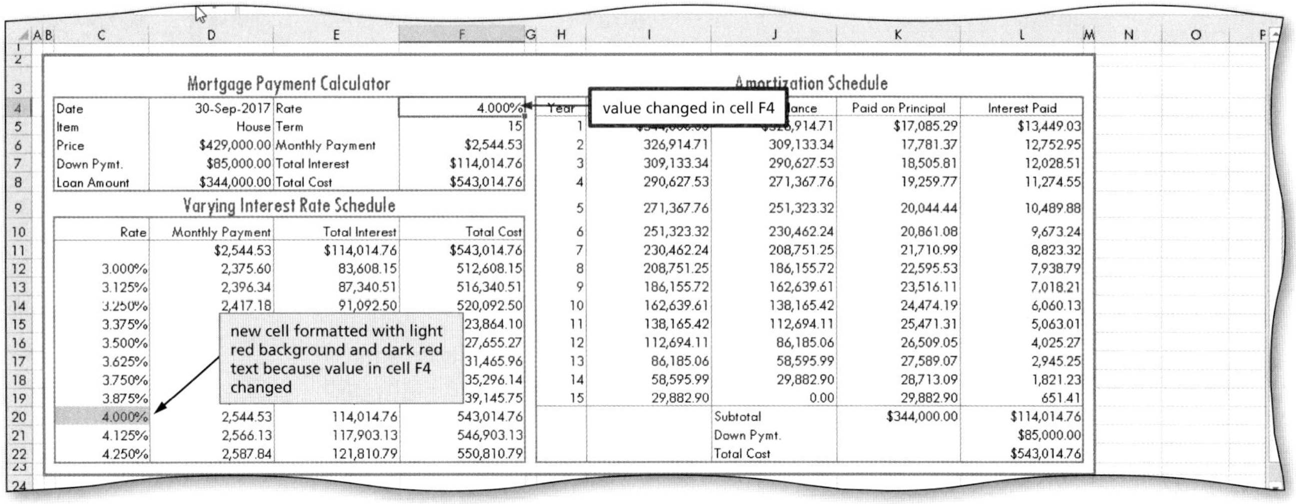

Figure 4–45

❺

- Enter **4.125** in cell F4 to return the Mortgage Payment Calculator, Varying Interest Rate Schedule, and Amortization Schedule sections to their original states.

Q&A

What happened when I changed the interest rate from 4.125% to 4.000%?
The cell containing the new rate received a red background and dark red text, while the original cell (cell C21) reverted to its original formatting (Figure 4–45). The red background and dark red text serve as a pointer in the data table to indicate which row agrees with the input cell (cell F4). When the loan officer using this worksheet enters a new percentage in cell F4, the pointer will move or disappear. The formatting will disappear if the interest rate in cell F4 falls outside the range of the data table or does not appear in the data table, for example, if the interest rate is 5.000% or 4.100%.

To Enter New Loan Data

With the Mortgage Payment Calculator, Varying Interest Rate Schedule, and Amortization Schedule sections of the worksheet complete, you can use them to generate new loan information. For example, assume you want to purchase land for $125,000.00. You have $30,000.00 for a down payment and want a seven-year loan. NCU currently is charging 3.625% interest for a seven-year loan on land. The following steps enter the new loan data.

1 Enter **Land** in cell D5.

2 Enter **125000** in cell D6.

3 Enter **30000** in cell D7.

4 Enter **3.625** in cell F4.

5 Enter **7** in cell F5 and then press the DOWN ARROW key to calculate the loan data.

6 Click on an empty cell to display the worksheet, as shown in Figure 4–46.

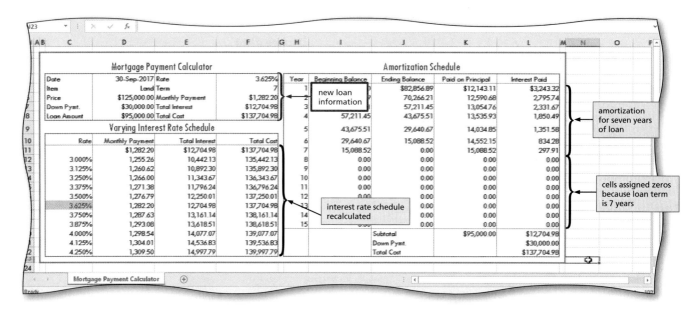

Figure 4–46

To Enter the Original Loan Data

The following steps reenter the original loan data.

1 Enter **House** in cell D5.

2 Enter **429000** in cell D6.

3 Enter **85000** in cell D7.

4 Enter **4.125** in cell F4.

5 Enter **15** in cell F5.

Printing Sections of the Worksheet

In Module 2, you learned how to print a section of a worksheet by first selecting it and then using the Selection option in the Print dialog box. If you find yourself continually selecting the same range in a worksheet to print, you can set a specific range to print each time you print the worksheet. When you set a range to print, Excel will continue to print only that range until you clear it.

To Set Up a Worksheet to Print

1 CREATE MORTGAGE PAYMENT CALCULATOR | 2 CREATE DATA TABLE | 3 CREATE AMORTIZATION SCHEDULE
4 FORMAT WORKSHEET | 5 CREATE PRINT AREAS | 6 PROTECT CELLS | 7 CHECK FORMULAS

Why? *Specifying print options allows you to conserve paper and toner and to customize the layout of your worksheet on the printed page.* This section describes print options available in the Page and Sheet tabs in the Page Setup dialog box (Figure 4–47). These print options affect the way the worksheet will appear in the printed copy or when previewed. One important print option is the capability of printing in black and white, even when your printer is a color printer. Printing in black and white not only speeds up the printing process but also saves ink. The following steps ensure any printed copy fits on one page and prints in black and white.

- Display the Page Layout tab and then click the Page Setup Dialog Box Launcher (Page Layout tab | Page Setup group) to display the Page Setup dialog box.

- If necessary, click the Page tab (Page Setup dialog box) to display the Page sheet and then click Fit to in the Scaling area to set the worksheet to print on one page (Figure 4–47).

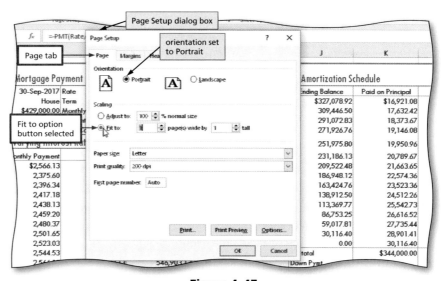

Figure 4–47

- Click the Sheet tab (Page Setup dialog box) and then click 'Black and white' in the Print area to select the check box (Figure 4–48).

- Click the OK button (Page Setup dialog box) to close the dialog box.

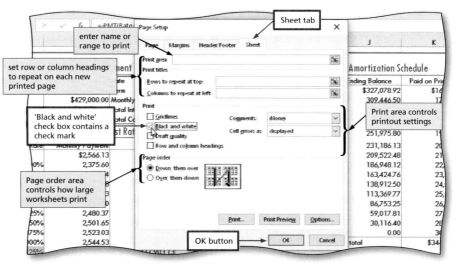

Figure 4–48

Other Ways

1. Click File tab, click Print tab, click Page Setup link, select options

To Set the Print Area

Why? *If you do not need to print the entire worksheet, setting the print area allows you easily to specify the section you want to print.* The following steps print only the Mortgage Payment Calculator section by setting the print area to the range C3:F8.

- Select the range C3:F8 and then click the Print Area button (Page Layout tab | Page Setup group) to display the Print Area menu (Figure 4–49).

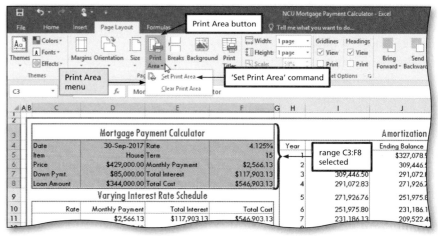

Figure 4–49

- Click 'Set Print Area' on the Print Area menu to set the range of the worksheet that Excel should print.

- Click File on the ribbon to open the Backstage view and then click the Print tab to display the Print gallery.

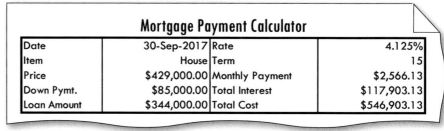

Figure 4–50

- Click the Print button in the Print gallery to print the selected area (Figure 4–50).

- Click the Print Area button (Page Layout tab | Page Setup group) to display the Print Area menu and then click the 'Clear Print Area' command to reset the print area to the entire worksheet.

Q&A

What happens when I set a print area?

When you set a print area, Excel will print the specified range, rather than the entire worksheet. If you save the workbook with the print area set, then Excel will remember the settings the next time you open the workbook and continue to print only the specified range. Clicking 'Clear Print Area' on the Print Area menu, as described in Step 3, will revert the settings so that the entire workbook will print.

To Name and Print Sections of a Worksheet

Why? *If you regularly are going to print a particular section of a worksheet, naming the section allows you to specify that section whenever you need to print it.* With some spreadsheet apps, you will want to print several different areas of a worksheet, depending on the request. Rather than using the 'Set Print Area' command or manually selecting the range each time you want to print, you can name the ranges using the Name box in the formula bar. You then can use one of the names to select an area before using the 'Set Print Area' command or Print Selection option. The following steps name the Mortgage Payment Calculator, the Varying Interest Rate Schedule, the Amortization Schedule sections, as well as the entire worksheet, and then print each section.

1

- Click the Page Setup Dialog Box Launcher (Page Layout tab | Page Setup group) to display the Page Setup dialog box, click the Sheet tab and then click 'Black and white' to remove the check mark and ensure that Excel prints in color on color printers.

- Click the OK button to close the Page Setup dialog box.

- If necessary, select the range C3:F8, click the Name box in the formula bar, and then type **Mortgage_Payment** to name the range (Figure 4–51). *Hint:* Remember to include the underscore between Mortgage and Payment.

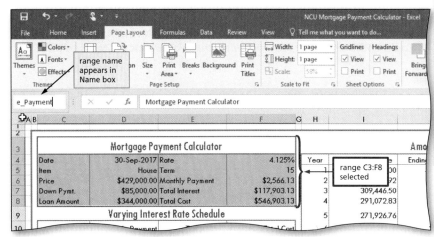

Figure 4–51

2

- Press the ENTER key to create the range name.

- Select the range C9:F22, click the Name box in the formula bar, type **Interest_Schedule** as the name of the range, and then press the ENTER key to create a range name.

- Select the range H3:L22, click the Name box in the formula bar, type **Amortization_Schedule** as the name of the range, and then press the ENTER key to create a range name.

- Select the range B2:M23, click the Name box in the formula bar, type **Financial_Tools** as the name of the range, and then press the ENTER key to create a range name.

- Select an empty cell and then click the Name box arrow in the formula bar to display the Name box list with the new range names (Figure 4–52).

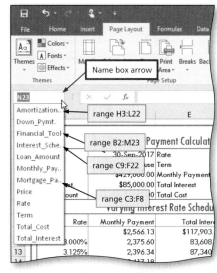

Figure 4–52

3

- Click Mortgage_Payment in the Name list to select the range associated with the name, C3:F8 in this case.

- Click File on the ribbon to open the Backstage view and then click the Print tab in the Backstage view to display the Print gallery.

- Click the 'Print Active Sheets' button in the Settings area and then click Print Selection to select the desired item to print (Figure 4–53).

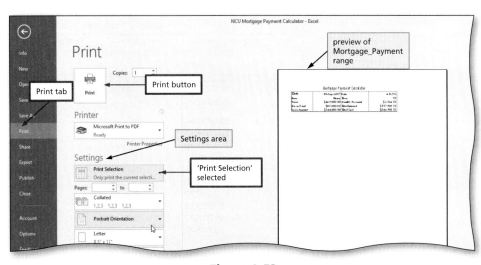

Figure 4–53

4

- Click the Print button in the Print gallery to print the selected named range, Mortgage_Payment in this case.

- One at a time, use the Name box to select the names Interest_Schedule, Amortization_Schedule, and Financial_ Tools, and then print them following the instructions in Step 3 to print the remaining named ranges (Figure 4–54).

5

- Save the workbook again on the same storage location with the same file name.

Mortgage_Payment
range printout

Mortgage Payment Calculator

Date	30-Sep-2017	Rate	4.125%
Item	House	Term	15
Price	$429,000.00	Monthly Payment	$2,566.13
Down Pymt.	$85,000.00	Total Interest	$117,903.13
Loan Amount	$344,000.00	Total Cost	$546,903.13

Figure 4–54a

Interest_Schedule range printout

Varying Interest Rate Schedule

Rate	Monthly Payment	Total Interest	Total Cost
	$2,566.13	$117,903.13	$546,903.13
3.000%	2,375.60	83,608.15	512,608.15
3.125%	2,396.34	87,340.51	516,340.51
3.250%	2,417.18	91,092.50	520,092.50
3.375%	2,438.13	94,864.10	523,864.10
3.500%	2,459.20	98,655.27	527,655.27
3.625%	2,480.37	102,465.96	531,465.96
3.750%	2,501.65	106,296.14	535,296.14
3.875%	2,523.03	110,145.75	539,145.75
4.000%	2,544.53	114,014.76	543,014.76
4.125%	2,566.13	117,903.13	546,903.13
4.250%	2,587.84	121,810.79	550,810.79

Figure 4–54b

Amortization_Schedule
range printout

Amortization Schedule

Year	Beginning Balance	Ending Balance	Paid on Principal	Interest Paid
1	$344,000.00	$327,078.92	$16,921.08	$13,872.46
2	327,078.92	309,446.50	17,632.42	13,161.12
3	309,446.50	291,072.83	18,373.67	12,419.87
4	291,072.83	271,926.76	19,146.08	11,647.47
5	271,926.76	251,975.80	19,950.96	10,842.59
6	251,975.80	231,186.13	20,789.67	10,003.87
7	231,186.13	209,522.48	21,663.65	9,129.89
8	209,522.48	186,948.12	22,574.36	8,219.18
9	186,948.12	163,424.76	23,523.36	7,270.18
10	163,424.76	138,912.50	24,512.26	6,281.28
11	138,912.50	113,369.77	25,542.73	5,250.81
12	113,369.77	86,753.25	26,616.52	4,177.03
13	86,753.25	59,017.81	27,735.44	3,058.10
14	59,017.81	30,116.40	28,901.41	1,892.13
15	30,116.40	0.00	30,116.40	677.15
		Subtotal	$344,000.00	$117,903.13
		Down Pymt.		$85,000.00
		Total Cost		$546,903.13

Figure 4–54c

Q&A

Why does the Financial_Tools range print on one page? Recall that the Fit to option was selected earlier (Figure 4–47). This selection ensures that each of the printouts fits across the page in portrait orientation.

| Financial_Tools range printout | | | | | | | | | |

Mortgage Payment Calculator | | | | | **Amortization Schedule** | | | |

Date	30-Sep-2017	Rate		4.125%	Year	Beginning Balance	Ending Balance	Paid on Principal	Interest Paid
Item	House	Term		15	1	$344,000.00	$327,078.92	$16,921.08	$13,872.46
Price	$429,000.00	Monthly Payment		$2,566.13	2	327,078.92	309,446.50	17,632.42	13,161.12
Down Pymt.	$85,000.00	Total Interest		$117,903.13	3	309,446.50	291,072.83	18,373.67	12,419.87
Loan Amount	$344,000.00	Total Cost		$546,903.13	4	291,072.83	271,926.76	19,146.08	11,647.47
Varying Interest Rate Schedule					5	271,926.76	251,975.80	19,950.96	10,842.59
	Rate	Monthly Payment	Total Interest	Total Cost	6	251,975.80	231,186.13	20,789.67	10,003.87
		$2,566.13	$117,903.13	$546,903.13	7	231,186.13	209,522.48	21,663.65	9,129.89
	3.000%	2,375.60	83,608.15	512,608.15	8	209,522.48	186,948.12	22,574.36	8,219.18
	3.125%	2,396.34	87,340.51	516,340.51	9	186,948.12	163,424.76	23,523.36	7,270.18
	3.250%	2,417.18	91,092.50	520,092.50	10	163,424.76	138,912.50	24,512.26	6,281.28
	3.375%	2,438.13	94,864.10	523,864.10	11	138,912.50	113,369.77	25,542.73	5,250.81
	3.500%	2,459.20	98,655.27	527,655.27	12	113,369.77	86,753.25	26,616.52	4,177.03
	3.625%	2,480.37	102,465.96	531,465.96	13	86,753.25	59,017.81	27,735.44	3,058.10
	3.750%	2,501.65	106,296.14	535,296.14	14	59,017.81	30,116.40	28,901.41	1,892.13
	3.875%	2,523.03	110,145.75	539,145.75	15	30,116.40	0.00	30,116.40	677.15
	4.000%	2,544.53	114,014.76	543,014.76			Subtotal	$344,000.00	$117,903.13
	4.125%	2,566.13	117,903.13	546,903.13			Down Pymt.		$85,000.00
	4.250%	2,587.84	121,810.79	550,810.79			Total Cost		$546,903.13

Figure 4–54d

Other Ways

1. Select cell or range, click Define Name button (Formulas tab | Defined Names group), type name, click OK button (New Name dialog box)

2. Select cell or range, click Name Manager button (Formulas tab | Defined Names group), click New button, type name, click OK button (New Name dialog box), click Close button (Name Manager dialog box)

3. Select cell or range, press CTRL+F3

Break Point: If you wish to take a break, this is a good place to do so. You can exit Excel now. To resume at a later time, run Excel, open the file called NCU Mortgage Payment Calculator, and continue following the steps from this location forward.

Protecting and Hiding Worksheets and Workbooks

When building a worksheet for novice users, you should protect the cells in the worksheet that you do not want changed, such as cells that contain text or formulas. Doing so prevents users from making changes to text and formulas in cells.

When you create a new worksheet, all the cells are assigned a locked status, but the lock is not engaged, which leaves cells unprotected. **Unprotected cells** are cells whose values you can change at any time. **Protected cells** are cells that you cannot change.

CONSIDER THIS

How do you determine which cells to protect in a worksheet?

Deciding which cells to protect often depends upon the audience for your worksheet. In general, the highest level of security would be to protect all cells except those that require an entry by the user of the worksheet. This level of protection might be recommended for novice users, clients, or customers. A lesser safeguard would be to protect any cells containing formulas, so that users of the worksheet cannot modify the formulas. Finally, if you are creating a worksheet for your boss or a trusted team member, you might want to leave the cells unprotected, in case he or she needs to edit the worksheet. In any case, you should protect cells only after the worksheet has been tested fully and the correct results appear. Protecting a worksheet is a two-step process:

1. Select the cells you want to leave unprotected and then change their cell protection settings to an unlocked status.

2. Protect the entire worksheet.

At first glance, these steps may appear to be backwards. However, once you protect the entire worksheet, you cannot change anything, including the locked status of individual cells.

To Protect a Worksheet

Why? Protecting a worksheet allows you to determine which cells a user can modify. In the Mortgage Payment Calculator worksheet, the user should be able to make changes to only five cells: the item in cell D5, the price in cell D6, the down payment in cell D7, the interest rate in cell F4, and the term in cell F5 (Figure 4–55). These cells must remain unprotected so that the user can enter data. The remaining cells in the worksheet can be protected so that the user cannot change them. The following steps protect the NCU Mortgage Payment Calculator worksheet.

- Select the range D5:D7 and then while holding down the CTRL key, select the nonadjacent range F4:F5.

- Right-click one of the selected ranges to display a shortcut menu and mini toolbar (Figure 4–55).

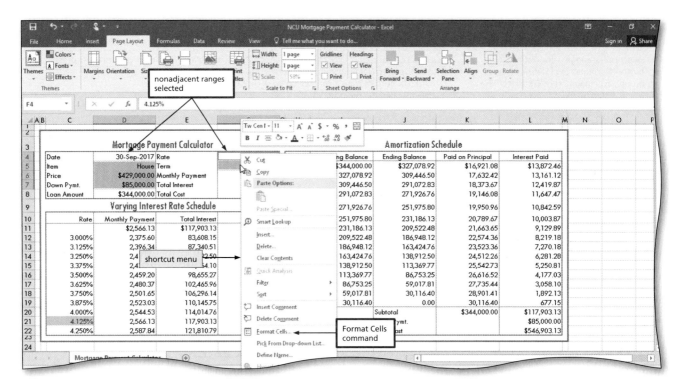

Figure 4–55

❷

- Click Format Cells on the shortcut menu to display the Format Cells dialog box.

- Click the Protection tab (Format Cells dialog box) and then click Locked to remove the check mark (Figure 4–56).

Q&A What happens when I remove the check mark from Locked check box?

Removing the check mark from Locked check box allows users to modify the selected cells (D5:D7 and F4:F5) after the Protect Sheet command is invoked.

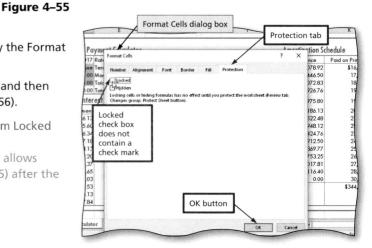

Figure 4–56

- Click the OK button to close the Format Cells dialog box.

- Deselect the ranges, and display the Review tab (Figure 4–57).

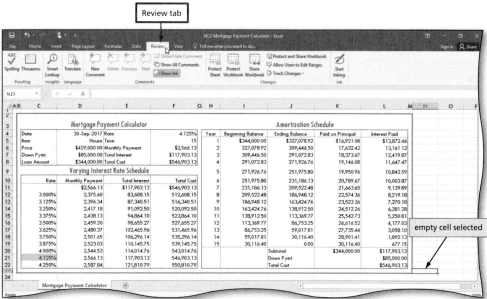

Figure 4–57

- Click the Protect Sheet button (Review tab | Changes group) to display the Protect Sheet dialog box.

- Verify that the 'Protect worksheet and contents of locked cells' check box (at the top of the Protect Sheet dialog box) and the first two check boxes in the list contain check marks so that the user of the worksheet can select both locked and unlocked cells (Figure 4–58).

Q&A What do the three checked settings mean?

With all three check boxes selected, the worksheet (except for the cells left unlocked) is protected from modification. The two check boxes in the list allow users to select any cell on the worksheet, but they only can change unlocked cells.

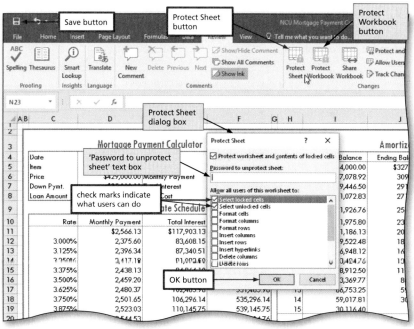

Figure 4–58

- Click the OK button (Protect Sheet dialog box) to close the Protect Sheet dialog box.

- Save the workbook again on the same storage location with the same file name.

Other Ways

1. Click Format Cells Dialog Box Launcher (Home tab | Font, Alignment, or Number group), click Protection tab, remove check mark from Locked check box, click OK button

2. Click File tab, click Info tab, click Protect Workbook, click Protect Current Sheet, select options, click OK

More about Worksheet Protection

Now all of the cells in the worksheet, except for the ranges D5:D7 and F4:F5, are protected. The Protect Sheet dialog box, shown in Figure 4–58, enables you to protect the worksheet using a password. You can create a password when you want to prevent others from changing the worksheet from protected to unprotected. The additional settings in the list in the Protect Sheet dialog box also give you the option to modify the protection so that the user can make certain changes, such as formatting cells or inserting hyperlinks.

If you want to protect more than one worksheet in a workbook, either select each worksheet before you begin the protection process or click the Protect Workbook button, shown in Figure 4–58. If you want to unlock cells for specific users, you can use the 'Allow Users to Edit Ranges' button (Review tab | Changes group).

When this protected worksheet is made available to users, they will be able to enter data in only the unprotected cells. If they try to change any protected cell, such as the monthly payment in cell F6, Excel will display a dialog box with an error message, as shown in Figure 4–59. You can eliminate this error message by removing the check mark from the 'Select unlocked cells' check box in the Protect Sheet dialog box (Figure 4–58). With the check mark removed, users cannot select a locked cell.

To unprotect the worksheet so that you can change all cells in the worksheet, click the Unprotect Sheet button (Review tab | Changes group).

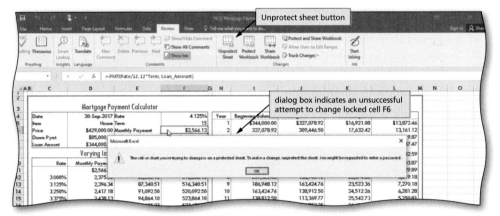

Figure 4–59

To Hide and Unhide a Worksheet

1 CREATE MORTGAGE PAYMENT CALCULATOR | 2 CREATE DATA TABLE | 3 CREATE AMORTIZATION SCHEDULE
4 FORMAT WORKSHEET | 5 CREATE PRINT AREAS | 6 PROTECT CELLS | 7 CHECK FORMULAS

Why? *You can hide rows, columns, and worksheets that contain sensitive data. Afterwards, when you need to access these hidden rows, columns, and worksheets, you can unhide them.* The following steps hide and then unhide a worksheet.

- Click the New sheet button to insert a new worksheet in the workbook.

- Right-click the Mortgage Payment Calculator sheet tab to display a shortcut menu (Figure 4–60).

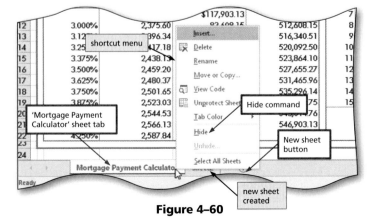

Figure 4–60

Q&A Why insert a new worksheet?
Workbooks must contain at least one visible worksheet. In order to hide the Mortgage Payment Calculator worksheet, there must be another visible worksheet in the workbook.

Why does the Unhide command on the shortcut menu appear dimmed?
The Unhide command appears dimmed when it is unavailable; because no worksheets are hidden, the command is unavailable.

②

- Click Hide on the shortcut menu to hide the Mortgage Payment Calculator worksheet.

- Right-click any sheet tab to display a shortcut menu.

- Click Unhide on the shortcut menu to display the Unhide dialog box.

- If necessary, click Mortgage Payment Calculator in the Unhide sheet list (Unhide dialog box) to select the worksheet to unhide (Figure 4–61).

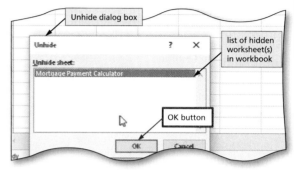

Figure 4–61

 Q&A Why should I hide a worksheet?
Hiding worksheets in a workbook is a common approach when working with complex workbooks that contain one worksheet with the results users need to see and one or more worksheets with essential data that, while important to the functionality of the workbook, is unimportant to users of the workbook. Thus, these data worksheets often are hidden from view. Although the worksheets are hidden, the data and formulas on the hidden worksheets remain available for use by other worksheets in the workbook. This same logic applies to hidden rows and columns.

③

- Click the OK button (Unhide dialog box) to reveal the hidden worksheet.

To Hide and Unhide a Workbook

1 CREATE MORTGAGE PAYMENT CALCULATOR | 2 CREATE DATA TABLE | 3 CREATE AMORTIZATION SCHEDULE
4 FORMAT WORKSHEET | 5 CREATE PRINT AREAS | 6 PROTECT CELLS | 7 CHECK FORMULAS

In addition to hiding worksheets, you also can hide an entire workbook. *Why? This feature is useful when you have several workbooks open simultaneously and want the user to be able to view only one of them. Also, some users hide the entire workbook when the computer is unattended and they do not want others to be able to see the workbook.* The following steps hide and unhide a workbook.

①

- Display the View tab (Figure 4–62).

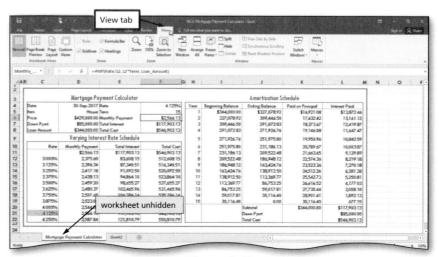

Figure 4–62

- Click the Hide Window button (View tab | Window group) to hide the NCU Mortgage Payment Calculator workbook.

- Click the Unhide Window button (View tab | Window group) to display the Unhide dialog box.

- If necessary, click NCU Mortgage Payment Calculator in the Unhide workbook list (Unhide dialog box) to select a workbook to unhide (Figure 4–63).

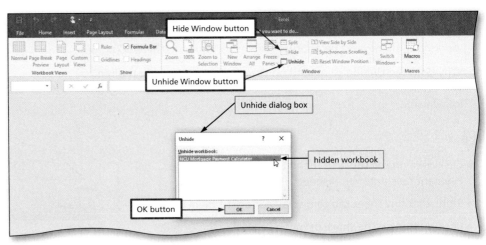

Figure 4–63

- Click the OK button (Unhide dialog box) to unhide the selected hidden workbook and display the workbook in the same state as it was in when it was hidden.

Formula Checking

Similar to the spelling checker, Excel has a formula checker that checks formulas in a worksheet for rule violations. You invoke the formula checker by clicking the Error Checking button (Formulas tab | Formula Auditing group). Each time Excel encounters a cell containing a formula that violates one of its rules, it displays a dialog box containing information about the formula and a suggestion about how to fix the formula. Table 4–3 lists Excel's error checking rules. You can choose which rules you want Excel to use by enabling and disabling them in the Formulas pane in the Excel Options dialog box shown in Figure 4–64.

Table 4–3 Error Checking Rules

Rule	Description
Cells containing formulas that result in an error	The cell contains a formula that does not use the expected syntax, arguments, or data types.
Inconsistent calculated column formula in tables	The cell contains formulas or values that are inconsistent with the column formula or tables.
Cells containing years represented as 2 digits	The cell contains a text date with a two-digit year that can be misinterpreted as the wrong century.
Numbers formatted as text or preceded by an apostrophe	The cell contains numbers stored as text.
Formulas inconsistent with other formulas in the region	The cell contains a formula that does not match the pattern of the formulas around it.
Formulas which omit cells in a region	The cell contains a formula that does not include a correct cell or range reference.
Unlocked cells containing formulas	The cell with a formula is unlocked in a protected worksheet.
Formulas referring to empty cells	The cells referenced in a formula are empty.
Data entered in a table is invalid	The cell has a data validation error.

To Enable Background Formula Checking

1 CREATE MORTGAGE PAYMENT CALCULATOR | 2 CREATE DATA TABLE | 3 CREATE AMORTIZATION SCHEDULE
4 FORMAT WORKSHEET | 5 CREATE PRINT AREAS | 6 PROTECT CELLS | **7 CHECK FORMULAS**

Through the Excel Options dialog box, you can enable background formula checking. *Why? You want Excel to continually review the workbook for errors in formulas as you create or manipulate data, formulas, and functions.* The following steps enable background formula checking.

- Click File on the ribbon to open the Backstage view and then click the Options tab to display the Excel Options dialog box.

- Click Formulas in the left pane (Excel Options dialog box) to display options related to formula calculation, performance, and error handling in the right pane.

- Click any check box in the 'Error checking rules' area that does not contain a check mark so that all error checking rules are enabled (Figure 4–64). As you add check marks, click the 'Reset Ignored Errors' button to reset error checking.

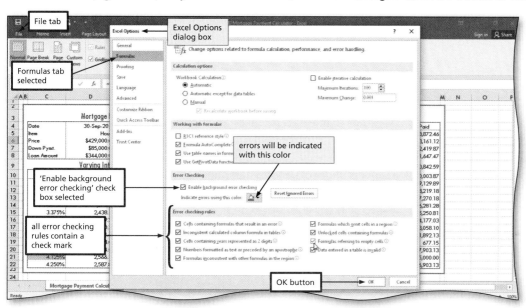

Figure 4–64

- Click the OK button (Excel Options dialog box) to close the Excel Options dialog box.

- If desired, sign out of your Microsoft account.

- Exit Excel.

More about Background Formula Checking

When background formula checking is enabled and a formula fails to pass one of the rules, Excel adds a small green triangle to the upper-left corner of the cell.

Assume, for example, that background formula checking is enabled and that cell F6, which contains the PMT function in the NCU Mortgage Payment Calculator workbook, is unlocked. Because one of the error checking rules, shown in Table 4–3, stipulates that a cell containing a formula must be locked, Excel displays a green triangle in the upper-left corner of cell F6.

When you select the cell with the green triangle, a Trace Error button appears next to the cell. If you click the Trace Error button, Excel displays the Trace Error menu (Figure 4–65). The first item in the menu identifies the error (Unprotected

BTW

Distributing a Workbook
Instead of printing and distributing a hard copy of a workbook, you can distribute the workbook electronically. Options include sending the workbook via email; posting it on cloud storage (such as OneDrive) and sharing the file with others; posting it on social media, a blog, or other website; and sharing a link associated with an online location of the workbook. You also can create and share a PDF or XPS image of the workbook, so that users can view the file in Acrobat Reader or XPS Viewer instead of in Excel.

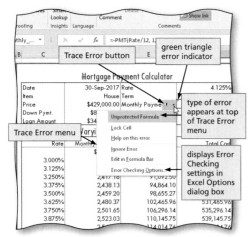

Figure 4–65

Formula). The remainder of the menu lists commands from which you can choose. The first command locks the cell. Invoking the Lock Cell command fixes the problem so that the formula no longer violates the rule. Selecting the 'Error Checking Options' command displays the Excel Options dialog box with the Formulas tab active, as shown in Figure 4–64.

The background formula checker can become annoying when you are creating worksheets that may violate the formula rules until referenced cells contain data. You often can end up with green triangles in cells throughout your worksheet. If this is the case, then disable background formula checking by removing the check mark from the 'Enable background error checking' check box (Figure 4–64) and use the Error Checking button (Formulas tab | Formula Auditing group) to check your worksheet once you have finished creating it. Use background formula checking or the Error Checking button during the testing phase to ensure the formulas in your workbook do not violate the rules listed in Table 4–3.

Summary

In this module, you learned how to use names, rather than cell references, to enter formulas; use financial functions, such as the PMT and PV functions; analyze data by creating a data table and amortization schedule; set print options and print sections of a worksheet using names and the Set Print Area command; protect a worksheet or workbook; hide and unhide worksheets and workbooks; and check for errors.

CONSIDER THIS: PLAN AHEAD

What decisions will you need to make when creating your next financial decision-making worksheet?
Use these guidelines as you complete the assignments in this module and create your own worksheets for evaluating financial scenarios.

1. Determine the worksheet structure.
    a) Determine the data you will need.
    b) Determine the layout of your data.
    c) Determine the layout of the financial calculator.
    d) Determine the layout of any data tables.

2. Create the worksheet.
    a) Enter titles, subtitles, and headings.
    b) Enter data, functions, and formulas.
    c) Assign names to cells and cell ranges.
    d) Create data tables.

3. Format the worksheet.
    a) Format the titles, subtitles, and headings.
    b) Format the numbers as necessary.
    c) Format the text.

4. Perform what-if analyses.
    a) Adjust values in the assumptions table to review scenarios of interest.

5. Secure the cell contents.
    a) Lock and unlock cells as necessary.
    b) Protect the worksheet.

Apply Your Knowledge

Reinforce the skills and apply the concepts you learned in this module.

Loan Payment Calculator

Note: To complete this assignment, you will be required to use the Data Files. Please contact your instructor for information about accessing the Data Files.

Instructions: Run Excel. Open the workbook Apply 4–1 Loan Payment Calculator. You will re-create the Loan Payment Calculator pictured in Figure 4–66. You will be instructed to print several times in this assignment. If requested or allowed by your instructor, consider saving paper by printing to a PDF file.

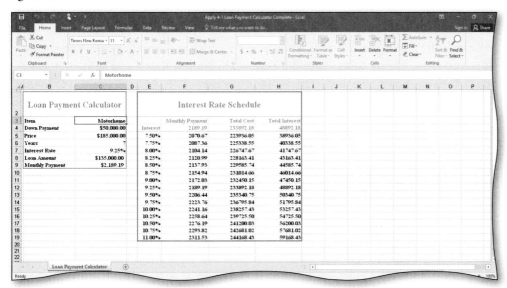

Figure 4–66

Perform the following tasks:

1. Select the range B4:C9. Use the 'Create from Selection' button (Formulas tab | Defined Names group) to create names for cells in the range C4:C9 using the row titles in the range B4:B9.

2. Enter the formulas shown in Table 4–4.

Cell	Formula
Table 4–4 Loan Payment Calculator and Interest Rate Schedule Formulas	
C8	=Price–Down_Payment
C9	=-PMT(Interest_Rate/12, 12*Years, Loan_Amount)
F4	=Monthly_Payment
G4	=12*Monthly_Payment*Years+Down_Payment
H4	=G4–Price

3. Use the Data Table button in the What-If Analysis gallery (Data tab | Forecast group) to define the range E4:H19 as a one-input data table. Use the Interest Rate in the Loan Payment Calculator as the column input cell.

4. Use the Page Setup dialog box to select the Fit to and 'Black and white' options. Select the range B2:C9 and then use the 'Set Print Area' command to set a print area. Use the Print button in the Print gallery in the Backstage view to print the worksheet. Use the 'Clear Print Area' command to clear the print area.

Continued >

Apply Your Knowledge *continued*

5. Name the following ranges: B2:C9 – **Calculator**; E2:H19 – **Rate_Schedule**; and B2:H19 – **All_Sections**. Print each range by selecting the name in the Name box and using the Print Selection option on the Print tab in the Backstage view.

6. Unlock the range C3:C7. Protect the worksheet so that the user can select only unlocked cells.

7. Press CTRL+` and then print the formulas version in landscape orientation. Press CTRL+` again to return to the values version.

8. Hide and then unhide the Loan Payment Calculator worksheet. Hide and then unhide the workbook. Delete the extra worksheet you made so that you could hide the Loan Payment Calculator worksheet. Unprotect the worksheet and then hide columns E through H. Select columns D and I and reveal the hidden columns. Hide rows 11 through 19. Print the worksheet. Select rows 10 and 20 and unhide rows 11 through 19. Protect the worksheet.

9. Determine the monthly payment and print the worksheet for each data set: (a) Item = **Home**; Down Payment = **$50,000.00**; Price = **$244,900.00**; Years = **15**; Interest Rate = **4.125%**; (b) Item = **Debt Consolidation Loan**; Down Payment = **$0.00**; Price = **$25,000.00**; Years = **5**; Interest Rate = **11.75%**. Set the values in cells C3:C7 back to the Motorhome values after completing the above calculations.

10. If requested by your instructor, add your initials to cell E3. You will need to unprotect the worksheet and unlock the cell to do so. Make sure to lock the cell and protect the worksheet after adding your initials.

11. Save the workbook using the file name, Apply 4–1 Loan Payment Calculator Complete. Submit the revised workbook as specified by your instructor.

12. ✳ How would you revise the Interest Rate Schedule to be more informative to the user?

Extend Your Knowledge

Extend the skills you learned in this module and experiment with new skills. You may need to use Help to complete the assignment.

Retirement Planning

Note: To complete this assignment, you will be required to use the Data Files. Please contact your instructor for information about accessing the Data Files.

Instructions: Run Excel. Open the workbook Extend 4–1 403B Planning Sheet. The data file contains a financial calculator for a 403(b) retirement plan. You will create a two-input data table that will help employees understand the impact that the amount they invest and the rate of return will have on their retirement earnings (Figure 4-67). Recall from the module that a two-input data table allows for two variables (amount invested and rate of return, in this case) in a formula.

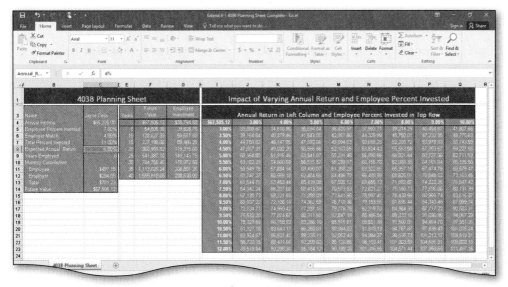

Figure 4–67

Perform the following tasks:

1. Type **Impact of Varying Annual Return and Employee Percent Invested** in cell I1. Type **Annual Return in Left Column and Employee Percent Invested in Top Row** in cell I3.

2. Save the workbook using the file name, Extend 4–1 403B Planning Sheet Complete.

3. Change the width of column H to 0.67 (8 pixels). Merge and center the titles in cells I1 and I3 over columns I through Q. Format the titles using the Title cell style for both the title and subtitle, a font size of 18 for the title, and a font size of 14 for the subtitle. Change the column widths of columns I through Q to 13.00 (96 pixels). Format cells I1 and I3 to match the fill and font color in cell B1.

4. For a two-input data table, the formula you are analyzing must be assigned to the upper-left cell in the range of the data table. Because cell C14 contains the future value formula to be analyzed, enter **=c14** in cell I4.

5. Use the fill handle to create two lists of percentages: (a) 3.00% through 12.00% in increments of 0.50% in the range I5:I23 and (b) 3.00% through 10.00% in increments of 1.00% in the range J4:Q4.

6. Use the Data Table button in the What-If Analysis gallery (Data tab | Forecast group) to define the range I4:Q23 as a two-input data table. Enter **C8** in the 'Row input cell' box and **C5** in the 'Column input cell' box (Data Table dialog box). Click the OK button to populate the table.

7. Format the two-input data table using a white font color and the fill color used in cells B3:G12. Bold ranges I4:Q4 and I5:I23. Format cells J5:Q23 to match the number format used in cells F5:G12. Place a light border around the range I3:Q23, light borders between columns in that same range, and a bottom border on the range I4:Q4.

8. Protect the worksheet so that the user can select only unlocked cells (C3:C6 and C8:C9).

9. If necessary, change the print orientation to landscape. Print the worksheet using the Fit to option. Print the formulas version of the worksheet.

10. If requested by your instructor, change the name in cell C3 to your name.

11. Save your changes to the workbook and submit the revised workbook as specified by your instructor.

12. ✷ How could you improve the design of the worksheet to make the impact of various combinations of Employee Investment and Expected Annual Return more easily identified?

Expand Your World

Create a solution that uses cloud or web technologies by learning and investigating on your own from general guidance.

Down Payment Options for a Home

Note: To complete this assignment, you will be required to use the Data Files. Please contact your instructor for information about accessing the Data Files.

Instructions: You are planning to buy a home as soon as you can save enough to make a 20% down payment. Your task is to create a calculator that you can use to determine possible savings options, and to share this calculator with family using OneDrive. Run Excel and open the workbook, Expand 4–1 Down Payment Calculator.

Perform the following tasks:

1. Save the file using the file name Expand 4–1 Down Payment Calculator Complete.

2. Identify a home for sale in your local housing market that you would consider buying. Use the asking price for that home as the current value of the house, or use an online tool such as Zillow.com to find the current estimated value of the home. Enter this value in your Down Payment Calculator, and calculate the needed down payment.

3. Determine the amount you consider reasonable as a monthly savings toward a down payment, and enter this in your down payment calculator.

4. Use the Future Value function to calculate how much you could save, using the rate of return and years to save in the worksheet. Remember to use a minus sign before the function so that the calculation will appear positive.

5. Create a two-input data table that calculates the future value of savings. You can decide which two inputs you would like to use for your data table.

6. Format the worksheet using techniques you have learned to present the worksheet content in a visually appealing form.

7. If requested by your instructor, save the file on OneDrive.

8. Use Excel Online to create two charts showing the relationship between the future value of savings and the two inputs from your data table.

9. Submit the workbook as specified by your instructor.

10. ✳ Why did you select the two inputs used in your data table? How useful are they for evaluating down payment savings options?

In the Labs

Design, create, modify and/or use a workbook following the guidelines, concepts, and skills presented in this module. Labs 1 and 2, which increase in difficulty, require you to create solutions based on what you learned in the module; Lab 3 requires you to apply your creative thinking and problem-solving skills to design and implement a solution.

Lab 1: **Analyzing Education Savings**

Problem: You have been asked by the employee relations and resource department to develop an education planning worksheet that will allow each current employee to see the effect (dollar accumulation) of investing a percentage of his or her monthly salary in a 529(c) Education Savings plan over a period of years (Figure 4–68). Employees can contribute up to $15,000 per year per child to plans. The employee relations and resource department wants a one-input data table to show the future value of the investment for different years. The final worksheet is shown in Figure 4–68.

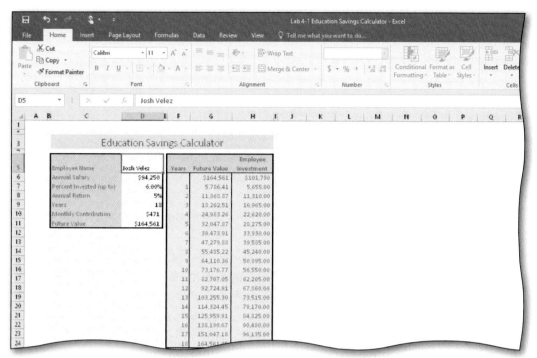

Figure 4–68

Perform the following tasks:

1. Run Excel. Apply the Retrospect theme to the worksheet. Change the column widths to the following: A and F = 6.57 (51 pixels); B, E, and I = 0.75 (9 pixels); C = 22.14 (160 pixels); D, G, and H = 12.71 (94 pixels). Change the heights of rows 2, 4, and 25 to 8.25 (11 pixels).

2. In cell C3, enter **Education Savings Calculator** as the worksheet title. Merge and center cell C3 across columns C through H. Apply the Title cell style to cell C3. Change the background color of C3 to Olive Green, Text 2, Lighter 80% and change its font color to Brown, Accent 3, Darker 25%.

3. Enter **Employee Name** in cell C5, **Annual Salary** in cell C6, **Percent Invested (up to)** in cell C7, **Annual Return** in cell C8, **Years** in cell C9, **Monthly Contribution** in cell C10, and **Future Value** in cell C11. Add the data in Table 4–5 to column D. Use the currency and percent style formats to format the numbers in the range D6:D8.

Table 4–5 Education Savings Employee Data	
Row Title	**Data**
Employee Name	Josh Velez
Annual Salary	$94,250
Percent Invested	6.00%
Annual Return	5%
Years	18

4. Use the Create from Selection button (Formulas tab | Defined Names group) to assign the row titles in column C (range C6:C11) as cell names for the adjacent cells in column D. Use these newly created names to assign formulas to cells in the range D10:D11.

Continued >

a. Employee Monthly Contribution (cell D10) = IF(Percent_Invested__up_to * Annual_Salary < 15000, Percent_Invested__up_to * Annual_Salary / 12, 15000 / 12)

b. Future Value (cell D11) = –FV(Annual_Return/12, Years*12, Monthly_Contribution)

The Future Value function (FV) returns to the cell the future value of the investment. The future value of an investment is its value at some point in the future based on a series of payments of equal amounts made over a number of periods while earning a constant rate of return.

c. If necessary, use the Format Painter button (Home tab | Clipboard group) to assign the currency style format in cell D6 to the range D10:D11.

5. Add the background color Orange, Accent 1, Lighter 60%, and the font color Olive Green, Text 2 to cells C5:C11, and a medium outside border to the range C5:D11, as shown in Figure 4–68.

6. Use the concepts and techniques developed in this module to add the data table in Figure 4–68 to the range F5:H24 as follows:

a. Enter and format the table column titles in row 5 as shown in Figure 4–68.

b. Use the fill handle to create the series of years beginning with 1 and ending with 18 in increments of 1 in column F, beginning in cell F7.

c. In cell G6, enter =D11 as the formula. In cell H6, enter =12 * D10 * D9 as the formula (recall that using cell references in the formulas means Excel will copy the formats).

d. Use the Data Table command to define the range F6:H24 as a one-input data table. Use cell D9 as the column input cell.

e. Format the numbers in the range G7:H24 using the comma style format. Add the background color Orange, Accent 1, Lighter 60%, the font color Olive Green, Text 2, and a light bottom border to cells F5:H5. Add light vertical borders to cells F6:H24, and a medium outside border to the range F5:H24, as shown in Figure 4–68.

7. Add a fill pattern with the pattern color Tan, Accent 5, Lighter 60% and the pattern style 12.5% Gray to the range B2:I25. *Hint:* Look on the Fill sheet in the Format Cells dialog box. Change the sheet tab name to **Education Savings Calculator** and color to Orange, Accent 1, Lighter 60%, as shown in Figure 4–68.

8. Remove gridlines by removing the check mark from the View Gridlines check box (Page Layout tab | Sheet Options group).

9. If requested by your instructor, change the Employee Name in cell D5 to your name.

10. Unlock the cells in the range D5:D9. Protect the worksheet. Allow users to select only unlocked cells.

11. Save the workbook using the file name, Lab 4–1 Education Savings Calculator. Submit the workbook as requested by your instructor.

Lab 2: **Consumer Debt Analysis and Interest Comparison Table**

Problem: As part of an ongoing program to educate incoming students about the financial realities of credit cards, you have been asked to create a consumer debt analysis worksheet including an interest comparison table, as shown in Figure 4–69. This worksheet, which will be distributed during freshman orientation as part of the electronic orientation package, also should demonstrate the goal-seeking capabilities of Excel.

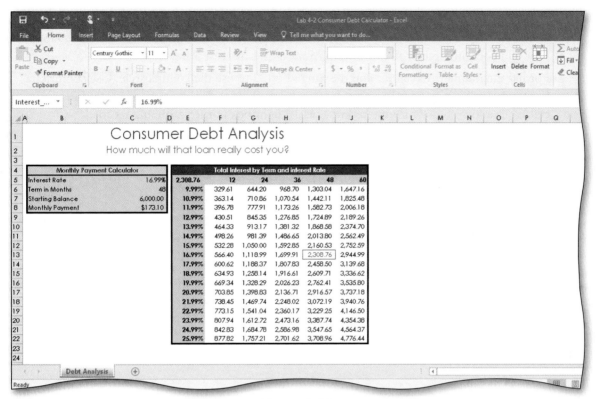

Figure 4–69

Perform the following tasks:

1. Run Excel. Apply the Ion Boardroom theme to a new worksheet. Change the width of columns A and D to .85 (11 pixels), columns B:C to 21.25 (175 pixels), and columns E:J to 9.50 (81 pixels).

2. Enter the worksheet title, **Consumer Debt Analysis**, in cell B1, apply the Title cell style, change its font size to 28–point and font color to Plum, Accent 1. Enter the worksheet subtitle, **How much will that loan really cost you?**, in cell B2, and apply the Title cell style, and change its font color to Plum, Accent 1. One at a time, merge and center cells B1 and B2 across columns B through J.

3. Type **Monthly Payment Calculator** in cell B4, and merge and center the range B4:C4. Type **Total Interest by Term and Interest Rate** in cell E4, and then merge and center the range E4:J4. Bold the text in cells B4 and E4. Type **Interest Rate** in cell B5, **Term in Months** in cell B6, **Starting Balance** in cell B7, and **Monthly Payment** in cell B8. Create the series shown in E6:E22 (enter **9.99%** in cell E6, **10.99%** in cell E7, and then use the Fill Handle to fill the remaining percentages through cell E22) and F5:J5 (enter **12**, **24**, **36**, **48**, and **60** in the cells, respectively). Use the Create from Selection button (Formulas tab | Defined Names group) to assign the row titles in the ranges B5:B8 to the adjacent cells in ranges C5:C8.

4. Enter **16.99%** in cell C5, **48** in cell C6, and **6000** in cell C7. Apply the comma style format to cell C7. Determine the monthly payment amount by entering the PMT function in cell C8. (*Hint:* Unlike the module project, in this example the term is expressed in months, not years. The interest rate remains an annual rate, however. Adjust your use of the function accordingly.)

5. Enter a formula for total interest paid in cell E5. Total interest is determined by calculating the total of all monthly payments for the term, and then subtracting the starting balance from that total.

Continued >

In the Labs *continued*

6. Create the interest comparison table in the range E5:J22 by creating a two-input data table. Row and column inputs will be Term in Months and Interest Rate, respectively.

7. Format the numbers in cell E5 and the range F6:J22 to use the comma style. Use conditional formatting to format the cell in the two-input data table that is equal to the Total Interest in cell E5 to a font color of Plum, Accent 1, and a light box border of Plum, Accent 1.

8. Change the colors and draw the borders as shown in Figure 4–69. Change the sheet tab name to Debt Analysis and the tab color to Plum, Accent 1.

9. If requested by your instructor, add the word, for, at the end of the title in cell B1, followed by your initials.

10. Unlock the cells in the ranges C5:C7. Protect the worksheet so that users can select any cell in the worksheet, but can change only the unlocked cells.

11. Remove gridlines by removing the check mark from the View Gridlines check box (Page Layout tab | Sheet Options group).

12. Save the workbook using the file name, Lab 4–2 Consumer Debt Calculator.

13. Submit the assignment as requested by your instructor.

14. ✳ How would you adjust your calculations if you wanted to make payments every two weeks rather than every month? How much would you save on the debt assuming an interest rate of 12.99%?

Lab 3: **Consider This: Your Turn**

Apply your creative thinking and problem-solving skills to design and implement a solution.

Determining the Break-Even Point

Part 1:   You have been hired by Alison Chang, owner of a small start-up company, to create a data table that analyzes the break-even point for a new product she is developing. She would like you to analyze the break-even point for prices ranging from $12.99 to $17.99 per unit, in $0.50 increments. You can calculate the number of units she must sell to break even (break-even point) if you know the fixed expenses, the price per unit, and the expense (cost) per unit. The following formula determines the break-even point:

Break-Even Point = Fixed Expenses / (Price per Unit – Expense per Unit)

Assume Fixed Expenses = $7,000; Price per Unit = $14.99; and Expense per Unit = $8.00.

Use the concepts and techniques presented in this module to determine the break-even point and then create the data table. Use the Price per Unit as the input cell and the break-even value as the result. Protect the worksheet so that only cells with data can be selected. Submit your assignment in the format specified by your instructor.

You can calculate additional break-even points by using a two-way table and varying Fixed Expenses or Expense per Unit in addition to Price per Unit. Which of the following provides the owner with a wider range of break-even points: varying Fixed Expenses between $6500 and $7000 in increments of $250 or varying Expense per Unit between $7.60 and $8.00 in increments of $0.20?

Part 2: ✳ You made several decisions while creating the worksheet for this assignment. How did you set up the worksheet? How did you decide how to create the data table? What additional break-even points did you calculate, and why?

5 | Working with Multiple Worksheets and Workbooks

Objectives

You will have mastered the material in this module when you can:

- Format a consolidated worksheet
- Fill using a linear series
- Use date, time, and rounding functions
- Apply a custom format code
- Create a new cell style
- Copy a worksheet
- Drill to add data to multiple worksheets at the same time
- Select and deselect sheet combinations

- Enter formulas that use 3-D cell references
- Use the Paste gallery
- Format a 3-D pie chart with an exploded slice and lead lines
- Save individual worksheets as separate workbook files
- View and hide multiple workbooks
- Consolidate data by linking separate workbooks

Introduction

Typically, an organization will need to store data unique to various areas, departments, locations, or regions. If you enter each department's data, for example, on a different worksheet in a single workbook, you can use the sheet tabs at the bottom of the Excel window to move from worksheet to worksheet or department to department. Note, however, that many business applications require data from several worksheets to be summarized on one worksheet. To facilitate this summarization, you can create a cumulative worksheet, entering formulas and functions that reference cells from the other worksheets. The process of summarizing data gathered from multiple worksheets onto one worksheet is called **consolidation**.

Another important concept presented in this module is the use of custom format codes and cell styles. Custom format codes allow you to specify, in detail, how a cell entry will appear. For example, you can create a custom format code to indicate how positive numbers, negative numbers, zeros, and text are displayed in a cell. Custom cell styles store specific font formatting for repeated use.

As you learn how to work with multiple worksheets and workbooks, you also will learn about Excel's many formatting features for pie charts, such as exploding slices and adding lead lines.

Project — Consolidated Expenses Worksheet

The project in the module follows proper design guidelines and uses Excel to create the worksheets shown in Figure 5–1. Twelve-Tone Concert Venues manages three different small venues for concerts and shows, each with seating for approximately one thousand people. The management wants to project consolidated expenses for the next two years, along with separate worksheets for each venue. The first worksheet shows the actual expenses for 2017, the projected percentage change, and the resulting expenses for 2018 and 2019. The 2017 expenses — consolidated from the three venues — will be highlighted in a 3-D pie chart. These expenses do not include talent expenses as that is handled by booking and ticket agencies.

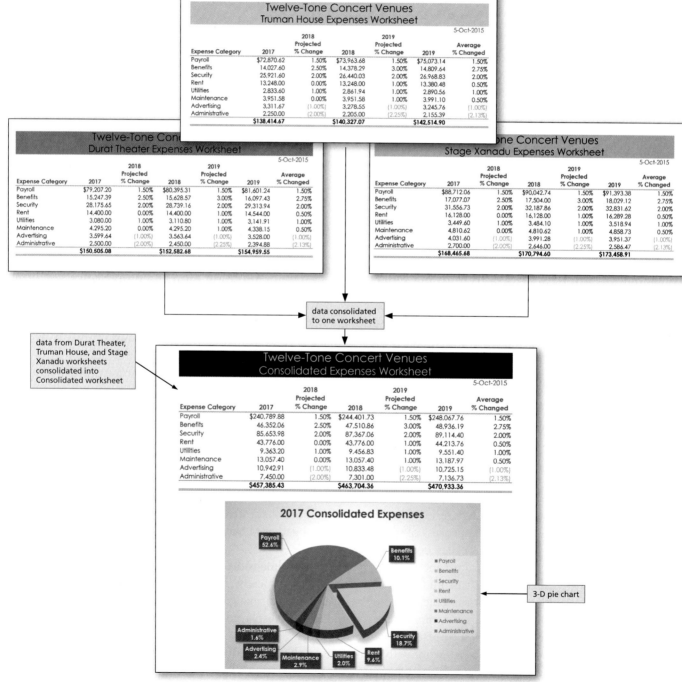

Figure 5–1

The requirements document for the Concert Venues Consolidated Workbook is shown in Table 5–1. It includes the needs, source of data, summary of calculations, and other facts about its development.

Table 5–1 Requirements Document

Worksheet Title	Twelve-Tone Concert Venues
Needs	The needs are as follows: 1. Create a workbook containing three worksheets (one for each of the three venues), one worksheet to consolidate the expenses, and a pie chart. 2. Each worksheet should be identical in structure and allow for display of the current expenses and projected expenses for the next two years. 3. The worksheets should print with a common header and footer. 4. The chart should show the 2017 consolidated expenses and draw attention to the largest expense after payroll.
Source of Data	Twelve-Tone Concert Venues will provide the data for each of the three venues. Projection assumptions also will be provided by Twelve-Tone Concert Venues.
Calculations	The following formulas should be included: a. 2018 Expenses = 2017 Expenses + (2017 Expenses * 2018 % Change) b. 2019 Expenses = 2018 Expenses + (2018 Expenses * 2019 % Change) c. Average % Change = (2018 % Change + 2019 % Change) / 2 d. Use the SUM function to determine totals Note: Use dummy data in the consolidated worksheet to verify the formulas. Round the percentages. Format other numbers using standard accounting rules, which require a dollar sign only on the first and last numbers in a currency column.
Other Tasks	Investigate a method the company can use to consolidate data from multiple workbooks into a new workbook.

In addition, using a sketch of the worksheet can help you visualize its design. The sketch of the consolidated worksheet (the first of the four worksheets in this workbook) consists of titles, column and row headings, the location of data values, and a general idea of the desired formatting, as shown in Figure 5–2.

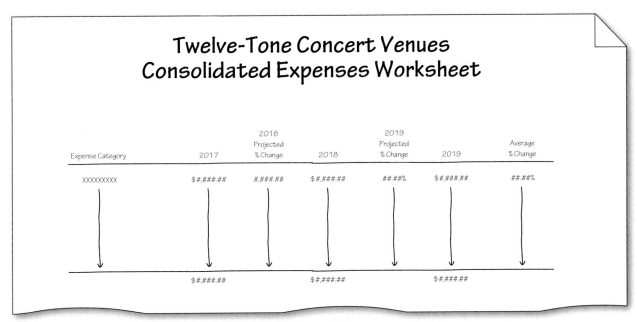

Figure 5–2

The following roadmap identifies general activities you will perform as you progress through this module:

1. Create and FORMAT the consolidated WORKSHEET.
2. FILL using a LINEAR SERIES.
3. USE DATE and ROUND FUNCTIONS.
4. APPLY a CUSTOM FORMAT CODE.
5. CREATE CELL STYLES.
6. Add and POPULATE WORKSHEETS.
7. INSERT a 3-D Pie CHART.
8. LINK WORKBOOKS.

BTW
The Ribbon and Screen Resolution
Excel may change how the groups and buttons within the groups appear on the ribbon, depending on the computer's screen resolution. Thus, your ribbon may look different from the ones in this book if you are using a screen resolution other than 1366 × 768.

Creating the Consolidated Worksheet

The first step in creating the workbook is to create the first worksheet shown in Figure 5–1. This worksheet eventually will contain consolidated data with titles, column and row headings, formulas, and formatting. It also represents the format used on each of the individual locations, which will be copied to the three other worksheets. You will create sample data first, to verify formats and formulas.

To Apply a Theme

1 FORMAT WORKSHEET	2 FILL LINEAR SERIES	3 USE DATE & ROUND FUNCTIONS	4 APPLY CUSTOM FORMAT CODE
5 CREATE CELL STYLES	6 POPULATE WORKSHEETS	7 INSERT CHART	8 LINK WORKBOOKS

The following steps apply a theme to the worksheet.

1 Run Excel and create a blank workbook in the Excel window. Maximize the Excel window and the worksheet, if necessary.

2 Zoom to approximately 120%.

3 Display the Page Layout tab, click the Themes button (Page Layout tab | Themes group), and then scroll to display the Mesh theme (Figure 5–3).

4 Click the Mesh theme to apply it to the workbook.

Q&A What is the best way to zoom?
You can use the Zoom In and Zoom Out buttons on the taskbar, or drag the Zoom slider. Some users like using CTRL+WHEEL to zoom. The View tab also has some useful zoom tools.

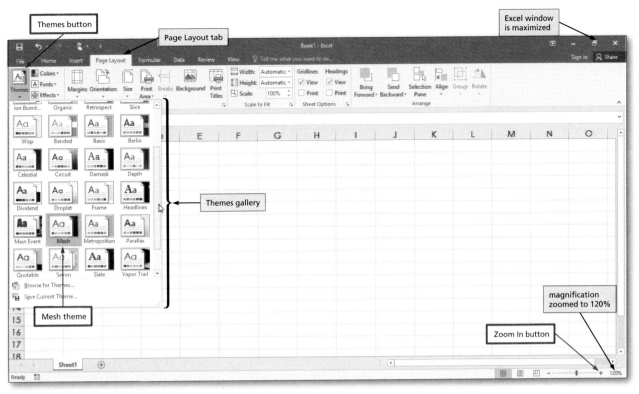

Figure 5–3

To Format the Worksheet

The following steps format the cells in the consolidated worksheet. The row heights and column widths need to be changed to accommodate the data in the worksheet.

1 Drag the bottom boundary of row heading 4 down until the row height is 51.00 (68 pixels) to change the row height.

2 Drag the right boundary of column heading A to the right until the column width is 18.00 (149 pixels) to change the column width.

3 Click the heading for column B and then SHIFT+CLICK the heading for column G to select all the columns in the range.

4 Drag the right boundary of column heading G to 12.00 (101 pixels) to change the width of multiple columns.

5 Click cell A1 to deselect the columns (Figure 5–4).

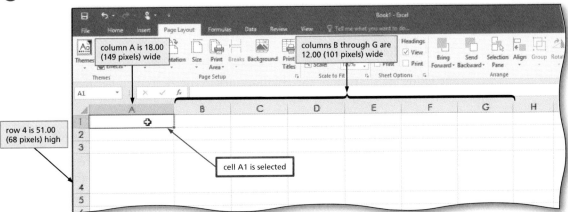

Figure 5–4

To Enter the Title, Subtitle, and Row Titles

The following steps enter the titles in cells A1 and A2 and the row titles in column A.

1 In cell A1, type `Twelve-Tone Concert Venues` and then click cell A2 (or press the DOWN ARROW key) to enter the worksheet title.

2 In cell A2, type `Consolidated Expenses Worksheet` and then press the DOWN ARROW key twice to select cell A4.

3 In cell A4, type `Expense Category` and then click cell A5 (or press the DOWN ARROW key) to enter the column heading.

4 Enter the following row titles beginning in cell A5: `Payroll, Benefits, Security, Rent, Utilities, Maintenance, Advertising,` and `Administrative`.

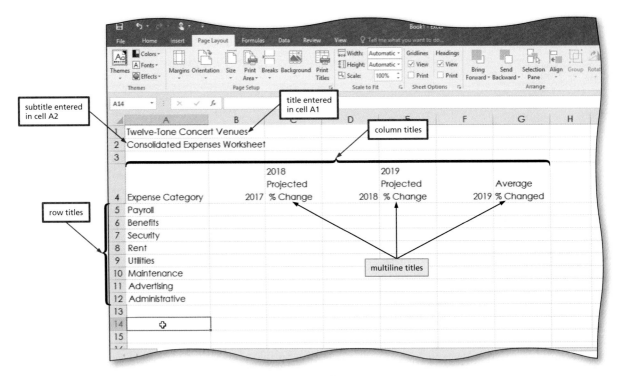

Figure 5–5

To Enter Column Titles

The following steps enter the column titles in row 4. Remember that multi-line titles are created by pressing ALT+ENTER to move to a new line within a cell.

1 Select cell B4. Type `2017` and then select cell C4 to enter the column heading.

2 Enter the following column titles beginning in row 4, as shown in Figure 5–5, pressing ALT+ENTER to move to a new line within a multi-line cell: `2018 Projected % Change, 2018, 2019 Projected % Change, 2019,` and `Average % Changed`.

Fill Series

In previous modules, you used the fill handle to create a numerical series. By entering the first two numbers in a series, Excel determined the increment amount, and filled the cells accordingly. There are other kinds of series, however, including a **date series** (Jan, Feb, Mar, etc.), an **auto fill series** (1, 1, 1, etc.), a **linear series** (1, 2, 3, etc. or 2, 4, 6, etc.), and a **growth series** that multiplies values by a constant factor. For these precise series, you can use the Fill button and the Series dialog box.

BTW
Touch Screen Differences
The Office and Windows interfaces may vary if you are using a touch screen. For this reason, you might notice that the function or appearance of your touch screen differs slightly from this module's presentation.

To Create Linear Series

1 FORMAT WORKSHEET | 2 FILL LINEAR SERIES | 3 USE DATE & ROUND FUNCTIONS | 4 APPLY CUSTOM FORMAT CODE
5 CREATE CELL STYLES | 6 POPULATE WORKSHEETS | 7 INSERT CHART | 8 LINK WORKBOOKS

While creating the consolidated worksheet in this module, sample data is used for the 2017 expenditures, the 2018 projected % change, and the 2019 projected % change values. *Why? Entering sample data creates placeholder content and assists in the layout of the consolidated worksheet.*

You will use the fill handle to create a series of integers in column B. Normally you would enter the first two numbers in a series so that Excel can determine the increment amount; however, if your series is incremented by 1, you do not have to enter two numbers. You can CTRL+drag the fill handle to increment by 1 across cells.

If you want to increment by a different value, you can use the Series dialog box. In the Series dialog box, you can choose to increment by any step value, including positive and negative decimals, again by entering only a single value. The following steps create sample data in the consolidated worksheet.

1
- Select cell B5.
- Type 1 and then click the Enter button in the formula bar to enter the first value in the series.
- CTRL+drag the fill handle down through cell B12 to create a fill series incremented by 1 (Figure 5–6).

Q&A
How do I use the fill handle, if I am using a touch screen?
Press and hold the selected cell to display the mini toolbar, tap AutoFill on the mini toolbar, and then drag the AutoFill icon.

What would happen if I did not use the CTRL key?
If you drag without the CTRL key, the cells would be filled with the number, 1.

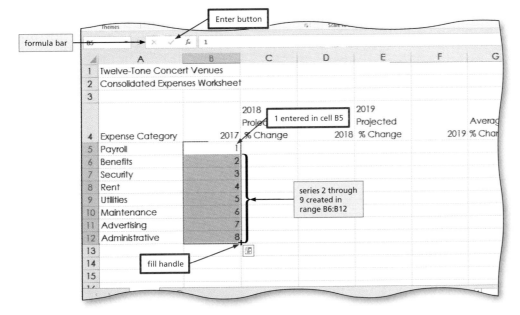

Figure 5–6

2

- Select cell C5 and then type **2%** to enter a percentage in this column.

- Display the Home tab.

- Select the range C5:C12 and then click the Fill button (Home tab | Editing group) to display the Fill gallery (Figure 5–7).

 How are the directional commands in the Fill gallery used?

Those commands are alternatives to using the fill handle. Select an empty cell or cells adjacent to the cell that contains the data that you want to use. You then can fill the selection using the Fill button and the appropriate directional command.

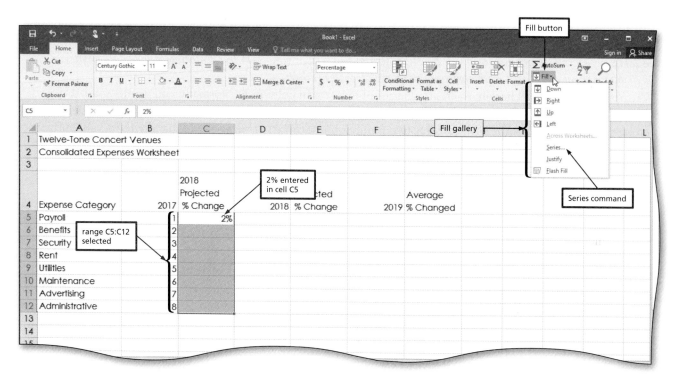

Figure 5–7

3

- Click Series to display the Series dialog box.

- Type **.021** in the Step value box to increment by a decimal number (Figure 5–8).

 Why am I using an increment of .021?

You are generating random placeholder numbers. You can use any increment step; however, since this column will eventually be percentages, a decimal may be appropriate.

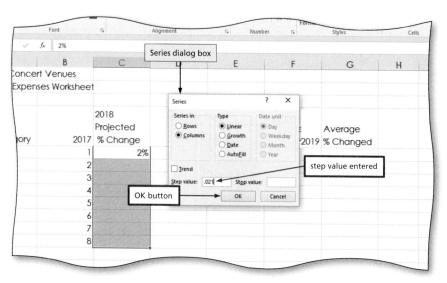

Figure 5–8

4

- Click the OK button (Series dialog box) to fill the series.

- Click the Increase Decimal button (Home tab | Number group) twice, to display two decimal places.

- Repeat Steps 2, 3, and 4 to create a linear series beginning with 3% and incrementing by .01 in the range E5:E12.

- Click an empty cell to remove the selection (Figure 5–9).

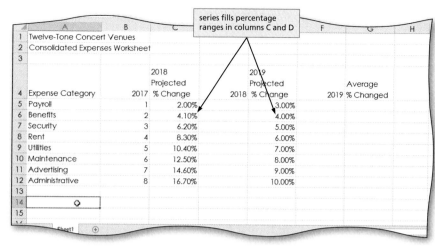

Figure 5–9

Other Ways

1. To increment by 1, enter first number; select original cell and blank adjacent cell, drag fill handle through range

Date, Time, and Round Functions

Entering dates in Excel can be as easy as typing the parts of the date separated by slashes, such as 6/14/2017. However, when you want a date that automatically updates, or you want to access part of the current date for a variety of reasons, Excel has many date and time functions, including those shown in Table 5–2. Use Excel Help to search for more information about these and other date and time functions.

BTW
Creating Customized Formats
Each format symbol within the format code has special meaning. Table 5–2 summarizes the more frequently used format symbols and their meanings.

Table 5–2 Functions Related to Date and Time

	Function	Definition	Syntax	Example	Sample Result
Date Functions	DATE	Returns the formatted date based on the month, day, and year	DATE(year, month, day)	=DATE(117,6,14)	6/14/2017
	DATEVALUE	Converts a date that is stored as text to a serial number for calculations	DATEVALUE(date_text)	=DATEVALUE("6/14/2017")	42900
	DAY	Returns the day value from a serial date	DAY(serial_number)	=DAY(42900)	14
	MONTH	Returns the month value from a serial date	MONTH(serial_number)	=MONTH(42900)	6
	TODAY	Returns the current date	TODAY()	=TODAY()	6/14/2017
	WEEKDAY	Returns the day of the week from a serial date, with a second option for starting the week on Sunday (1) or Monday (2)	WEEKDAY(serial_number,return_type)	=WEEKDAY(42900,1)	4 (Wednesday)
	YEAR	Returns the year value from a serial date	YEAR(serial_number)	=YEAR(42900)	2017
Time Functions	HOUR	Returns the hour value from a serial date	HOUR(serial_number)	=HOUR(0.33605324)	8
	MINUTE	Returns the minute value from a serial date	MINUTES(serial_number)	=MINUTE(0.33605324)	3
	SECOND	Returns the second value from a serial date	SECOND(serial_number)	=SECOND(0.33605324)	55
	TIME	Returns the formatted date based on the hour, minute, and second	TIME(hour, minute, second)	=TIME(8,3,55)	8:03 AM
	TIMEVALUE	Converts a time that is stored as text to a serial number for calculations	TIMEVALUE(time_text)	=TIMEVALUE("8:03:55 am")	0.33605324
Other Functions	NOW	Returns both date and time	NOW()	=NOW()	6/14/2017 8:03

BTW

Creating a Growth Series
You can create a growth series by doing the following: enter an initial value in the first cell, select the first cell and the range to fill, click the Fill button (Home tab | Editing group), click Series on the Fill menu, click Growth in the Type area (Series dialog box), and then enter a constant factor in the Step value box.

BTW

Updating the TODAY function
If the TODAY function does not update the date when you expect it to, you might need to change the settings that control when the worksheet recalculates. On the File tab, click Options, and then in the Formulas category under Calculation options, make sure that Automatic is selected.

BTW

Copying
To copy the contents of a cell to the cell directly below it, click in the target cell and press CTRL+D.

Excel stores the date and time as a **serial number** representing the number of days since January 1900, followed by a fractional portion of a 24-hour day. For example, June 14, 2017, is stored internally as 42900. The time, for example 3:00 p.m., is stored internally as .625. Therefore the entire date and time would be stored as 42900.625. When you format a serial number, you can use the Short Date, Long Date, or Time formats (Format Cells dialog box). If, however, you have generated the serial number from a function such as MONTH, DAY, or YEAR, you must use the Number format because the return value is an integer; formatting it with a date or time format would produce an incorrect date.

If you are performing math with dates and times, your answer will result in a serial number. For example, if you wanted to calculate elapsed time from 9:00 a.m. to 3:30 p.m., subtraction would result in a serial number, 0.2708. You then would need to format the number with the TIME format (h:mm), which would result in 6:30 or 6 hours and 30 minutes (Figure 5–10).

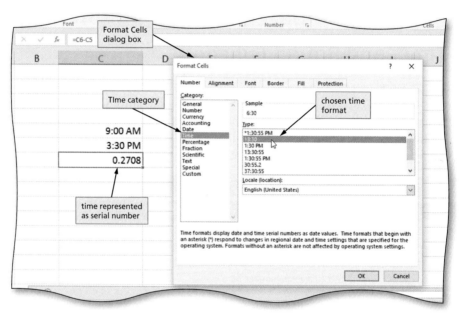

Figure 5–10

Another set of useful functions have to do with rounding. Rounding numbers off, especially for dollars and cents, prevents formulas from creating awkward answers with long decimal notations. Table 5–3 displays some of the more popular round functions.

Table 5–3 Rounding Functions				
Function	**Definition**	**Syntax**	**Example**	**Sample Result**
ROUND	Rounds a number to a specified number of decimal places	ROUND(number, num_digits)	=ROUND(833.77,0)	834
ROUNDDOWN	Rounds a number down, toward zero	ROUNDDOWN(number, num_digits)	=ROUNDDOWN(833.77,0)	833
ROUNDUP	Rounds a number up, away from zero	ROUNDUP(number, num_digits)	=ROUNDUP(833.77,0)	834
MROUND	Returns a number rounded to the desired multiple	MROUND(number, multiple)	=MROUND(833.77,5)	835

When should you use the ROUND function?

When you multiply or divide decimal numbers, the answer may contain more decimal places than the format allows. If this happens, you run the risk of the column totals being off by a penny or so; resulting values of calculations could include fractions of a penny beyond the two decimal places that currency formats usually display. For example, as shown in the worksheet sketch in Figure 5–2, columns C, E, and G use the currency and comma style formats with two decimal places; however, the formulas used to calculate values for these columns result in several additional decimal places that Excel maintains for computation purposes. For this reason, it is recommended that you use the ROUND function on formulas that potentially can result in more decimal places than the applied format displays in a given cell.

To Use the TODAY Function

1 FORMAT WORKSHEET | 2 FILL LINEAR SERIES | 3 USE DATE & ROUND FUNCTIONS | 4 APPLY CUSTOM FORMAT CODE
5 CREATE CELL STYLES | 6 POPULATE WORKSHEETS | 7 INSERT CHART | 8 LINK WORKBOOKS

Recall that you have used the NOW function to access the system date and time. You also can use the **TODAY function**, which returns only the date. Both functions are designed to update each time the worksheet is opened. The function takes no arguments but accesses the internal clock on your computer and displays the current date. As with the NOW function, you can format the date in a variety of styles.

The TODAY function also is useful for calculating intervals. For example, if you want to calculate an age, you can subtract the birth year from the TODAY function to find that person's age as of this year's birthday. The following steps use the TODAY function to enter the system date into the worksheet. *Why? The TODAY function will update each time the worksheet is opened.*

1

- Select cell G3, type
  `=today()`, and then click
  the Enter button to enter the
  system date (Figure 5–11).

Q&A

Should I use lowercase or
uppercase on functions?
Either one will work. To
delineate functions in the text
passages of this book, they are
displayed in all caps.

Figure 5–11

2

- Right-click cell G3 and then
  click Format Cells on the
  shortcut menu.

- If necessary, click Date in the
  Category list (Format Cells
  dialog box).

- Click 14-Mar-12 in the Type
  list to format the date
  (Figure 5–12).

Q&A

Why change the format of the
date?
The date might be displayed as
a series of number signs if the
date, as initially formatted by
Excel, does not fit in the width
of the cell.

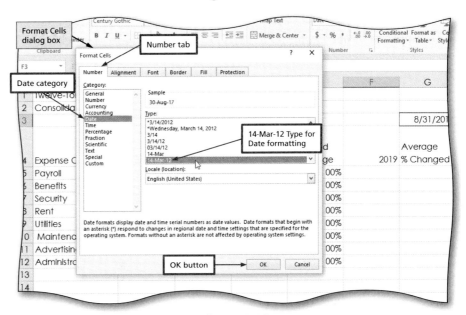

Figure 5–12

- Click the OK button (Format Cells dialog box) to close the dialog box.
- Click an empty cell to deselect the previous cell.

Other Ways

1. Select cell, click Date & Time button (Formulas tab | Function Library group), click TODAY, click OK button (Function Arguments dialog box)

To Enter Formulas Using the ROUND Function

1 FORMAT WORKSHEET | 2 FILL LINEAR SERIES | 3 USE DATE & ROUND FUNCTIONS | **4 APPLY CUSTOM FORMAT CODE**
5 CREATE CELL STYLES | 6 POPULATE WORKSHEETS | 7 INSERT CHART | 8 LINK WORKBOOKS

The **ROUND function** in Excel is used to round numbers to a specified number of decimal places. The general form of the ROUND function is

=ROUND (number, number of digits)

where the number argument can be a number, a cell reference that contains a number, or a formula that results in a number; and the number of digits argument can be any positive or negative number used to determine the number of places to which the number will be rounded. Positive numbers round to the right of the decimal point; for example, 18.257 formatted for 1 decimal place would display 18.3. Negative numbers round to the left of the decimal point; for example, 18.257 formatted for -1 decimal place would display 20.

The following is true about the ROUND function:

- If the number of digits argument is greater than 0 (zero), then the number is rounded to the specified number of digits to the right of the decimal point.
- If the number of digits argument is equal to 0 (zero), then the number is rounded to the nearest integer.
- If the number of digits argument is less than 0 (zero), then the number is rounded to the specified number of digits to the left of the decimal point.

The following steps enter the formulas for the first expenditure, Payroll, in cells D5, F5, and G5. (See Table 5–4.)

Table 5–4 Formulas for cells D5, F5, and G5

Cell	Description	Formula	Entry
D5	2018 Expense	ROUND(2017 Expense + 2017 Expense * 2018 % Change, 2)	=ROUND(B5 + B5 * C5, 2)
F5	2019 Expense	ROUND(2018 Expense + 2018 Expense * 2019 % Change, 2)	=ROUND(D5 + D5 * E5, 2)
G5	Average % Change	ROUND((2018 % Change + 2019 % Change) / 2, 4)	=ROUND((C5 + E5) / 2, 4)

The projected expenses will be rounded to two decimal places, while the average will be rounded to four decimal places. *Why? Because the averages are very small at this point in the process, using four decimal digits provides the most representative results.*

- Select cell D5, type
  =round(b5+b5*c5,2),
  and then click the Enter button in the formula bar to display the resulting value (Figure 5–13).

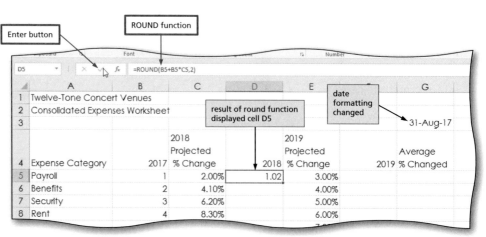

Figure 5–13

2

- Drag the fill handle on cell D5 down to copy the formula to cells D6:D12.

- Select cell F5, type =round(d5+d5*e5,2), and then click the Enter button to display the resulting value (Figure 5–14).

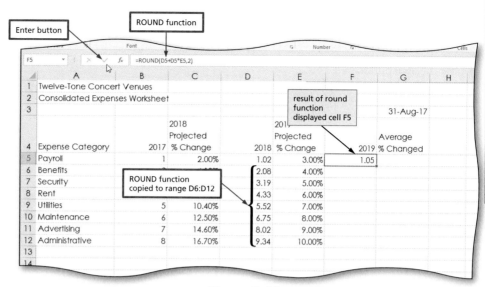

Figure 5–14

3

- Select cell G5, type =round((c5+e5)/2,4), and then click the Enter button to display the resulting value (Figure 5–15).

Q&A Do I need to use two sets of parentheses in the function?

Yes, the outer set of parentheses are for the function and the inner set is to force Excel to add the two values before dividing to calculate the average.

Recall that Excel follows the order of operations and performs multiplication and division before addition and subtraction, unless you use parentheses.

	A	B	C	D	E	F	G
1	Twelve-Tone Concert Venues						
2	Consolidated Expenses Worksheet						
3							Aug-17
4	Expense Category	2017	2018 Projected % Change		2019 Projected 2018 % Change		Average 2019 % Changed
5	Payroll	1	2.00%	1.02	3.00%	1.05	0.025
6	Benefits	2	4.10%	2.08	4.00%		
7	Security	3	6.20%	3.19	5.00%		
8	Rent	4	8.30%	4.33	6.00%		
9	Utilities	5	10.40%	5.52	7.00%		
10	Maintenance	6	12.50%	6.75	8.00%		
11	Advertising	7	14.60%	8.02	9.00%		

Enter button / ROUND function / =ROUND((C5+E5)/2,4) / result of round function displayed cell G5

Figure 5–15

4

- Select cells F5:G5.

- Drag the fill handle down through cells F12:G12 to copy both formulas down to the selected range (Figure 5–16).

Q&A Are the values in column G supposed to display all four decimal places?

Yes, because you entered a 4 at the end of the function, Excel rounds to four decimal places; however, a default setting in Excel is to ignore zeroes at the end of decimal places, because they are not significant. You will change that default setting later in the module.

	2018 Projected % Change		2019 Projected 2018 % Change		Average 2019 % Changed	
Concert Venues						31-Aug-17
Consolidated Expenses Worksheet						
Expense Category	2017	% Change		% Change		% Changed
Payroll	1	2.00%	1.02	3.00%	1.05	0.025
Benefits	2	4.10%		4.00%	2.16	0.0405
Security	3	6.20%		5.00%	3.35	0.056
Rent	4	8.30%		6.00%	4.59	0.0715
Utilities	5	10.40%	5.52	7.00%	5.91	0.087
Maintenance	6	12.50%	6.75	8.00%	7.29	0.1025
Advertising	7	14.60%	8.02	9.00%	8.74	0.118
Administrative	8	16.70%	9.34	10.00%	10.27	0.1335

ROUND functions copied to range F6:G12

Figure 5–16

5

- Select cell B13.

- Click the Sum button (Home tab | Editing group), select the range B5:B12, and then click the Enter button to sum the column (Figure 5–17).

- If the Trace Error button is displayed, click it, and then click Ignore Error on the Trace Error menu to ignore an error that Excel mistakenly reported.

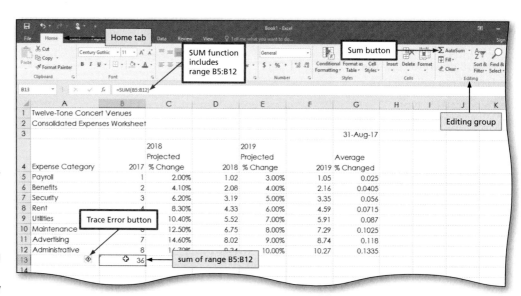

Figure 5–17

 Why did Excel report an error?
When you use the SUM function, Excel assumes that all contiguous numbers should be summed, in this case the range, B4:B12. When you changed the range to B5:B12, Excel flagged this as a potential error, due to the exclusion of cell B4, which also included a numeric value.

6

- Select cell D13, click the Sum button (Home tab | Editing group), select the range D5:D12, and then click the Enter button to sum the column.

- In cell F13, calculate the sum for the range F5:F12.

- Click an empty cell to deselect the previous cell (Figure 5–18).

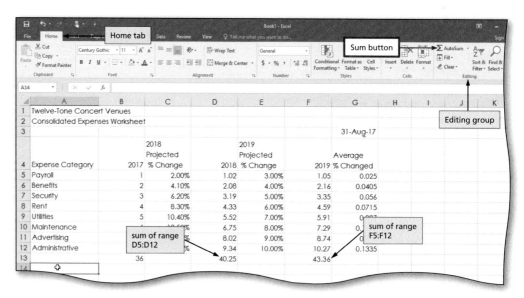

Figure 5–18

7

- Save the workbook on your hard drive, OneDrive, or other storage location using Concert Venues Consolidated as the file name.

Other Ways

1. Select cell, click Math & Trig button (Formulas tab | Function Library group), click ROUND, enter formula in Number box (Formula Arguments dialog box), enter number of digits in Num_digits box, click OK button

Break Point: If you wish to take a break, this is a good place to do so. You can exit Excel. To resume at a later time, run Excel, open the file called Concert Venues Consolidated, and continue following the steps from this location forward.

To Format the Title and Subtitle

The following steps format the worksheet title and subtitle to change the font size, to center both titles across columns A through G, to change the background color, and to change the font color. You will choose colors from the Mesh theme.

1 Select the range A1:A2, click the Cell Styles button (Home tab | Styles group), and then click the Title style to apply the style to the range. Recall that pointing to a style will cause Excel to display the name of the style in a ScreenTip.

2 Select cell A1 and change the font size to 20.

3 Select the range A1:G1 and then click the 'Merge & Center' button (Home tab | Alignment group) to merge and center the text in the selected range.

4 Select cell A2 and change the font size to 18.

5 Select the range A2:G2 and then click the 'Merge & Center' button (Home tab | Alignment group) to merge and center the text in the selected range.

6 Select the range A1:A2, click the Fill Color arrow (Home tab | Font group), and then click 'Black, Text 1' in the Fill Color gallery to change the fill color.

7 Click the Font Color arrow (Home tab | Font group) and then click 'Orange, Accent 6, Lighter 60%' (column 10, row 3) in the Font Color gallery to change the font color.

To Format the Column Titles and Total Row

The following steps center and underline the column titles, and create borders on the total row.

1 Select the range B4:G4 and then click the Center button (Home tab | Alignment group) to center the text in the cells.

2 CTRL+click cell A4 to add it to the selected range, and then use the Cell Styles button (Home tab | Styles group) to apply the Heading 3 cell style.

3 Select the range A13:G13 and then assign the Total cell style to the range.

4 Click an empty cell to deselect the range (Figure 5–19).

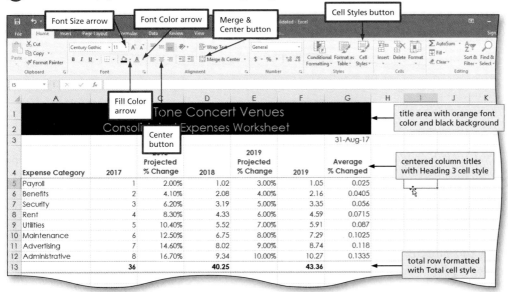

Figure 5–19

To Format with a Floating Dollar Sign

The consolidated worksheet for this module contains floating dollar signs in the first row of numbers and in the totals. The following steps use the Format Cells dialog box to assign a currency style with a floating dollar sign and two decimal places to the appropriate cells. Recall that a floating dollar sign always appears immediately to the left of the first significant digit in the cell, while the Accounting Number Format button (Home tab | Number group) creates a fixed dollar sign.

1 Select cell B5. While holding down the CTRL key, select the nonadjacent cells D5, F5, B13, D13, and F13. Right-click any selected cell to display the shortcut menu.

2 Click Format Cells on the shortcut menu to display the Format Cells dialog box. If necessary, click the Number tab (Format Cells dialog box) to display the Number sheet.

3 Click Currency in the Category list. If necessary, click the Symbol button and then click $ in the list.

4 Click the red ($1,234.10) in the Negative numbers list to select a currency format that displays negative numbers in red with parentheses and a floating dollar sign.

5 Click the OK button (Format Cells dialog box) to assign the Currency style.

6 Click an empty cell to deselect the previous cells (Figure 5–20).

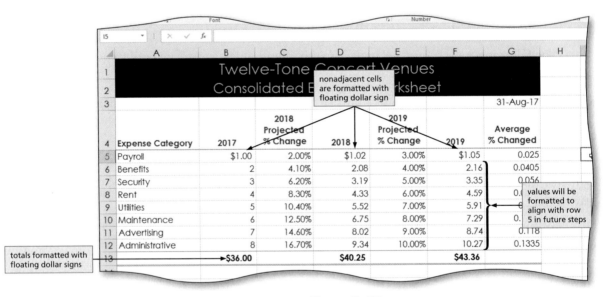

Figure 5–20

Format Codes

BTW

Selecting a Range of Cells
You can select any range of cells with entries surrounded by blank cells by clicking a cell in the range and pressing CTRL+SHIFT+* (asterisk).

Excel assigns an internal **format code** to every format style listed in the Format Cells dialog box. These format codes do not print, but act as a template, with placeholders to define how you want to apply unique formatting. Table 5–5 provides a list of some of the format code symbols and how they can be combined into a new format code. To view the entire list of format codes that are provided with Excel, select Custom in the Category list (Format Cells dialog box).

Table 5–5 Format Symbols in Format Codes

Format Symbol	Example of Symbol in Code	Description
# (number sign)	###.##	Serves as a digit placeholder. If the value in a cell has more digits to the right of the decimal point than number signs in the format, Excel rounds the number. All digits to the left of the decimal point are displayed.
0 (zero)	0.00	Works like a number sign (#), except that if the number is less than 1, Excel displays a 0 in the ones' place.
. (period)	#0.00	Ensures Excel will display a decimal point in the number. The placement of zeros determines how many digits appear to the left and right of the decimal point.
% (percent)	0.00%	Displays numbers as percentages of 100. Excel multiplies the value of the cell by 100 and displays a percent sign after the number.
, (comma)	#,##0.00	Displays a comma as a thousands' separator.
( )	#0.00;(#0.00)	Displays parentheses around negative numbers.
$, +, or −	$#,##0.00; ($#,##0.00)	Displays a floating sign ($, +, or −).
* (asterisk)	$*##0.00	Displays a fixed sign ($, +, or −) to the left, followed by spaces until the first significant digit.
[color]	#.##;[Red]#.##	Displays the characters in the cell in the designated color. In the example, positive numbers appear in the default color, and negative numbers appear in red.
" " (quotation marks)	$0.00 "Surplus"; $-0.00 "Shortage"	Displays text along with numbers entered in a cell.
_ (underscore)	#,##0.00_)	Adds a space. When followed by a parentheses, positive numbers will align correctly with parenthetical negative numbers.

BTW
Sample Data
As you develop more sophisticated workbooks, it will become increasingly important that you create good test data to ensure your workbooks are free of errors. The more you test a workbook, the more confident you will be in the results generated. Always take the time to select sample data that tests the limits of the formulas.

Before you create custom format codes or modify existing codes, you should understand their makeup. A format code can have up to four sections: the desired format for positive numbers, the desired format for negative numbers, how zeros should be treated, and any desired format for text. Each section is separated by a semicolon. For example, the following format code would produce results similar to the sample values shown.

$$\$* \#,\#\#0.00;\ [\text{Magenta}]\$(\#,\#\#0.00);\ * \text{“-”??};\ \text{“The answer is “@}$$

| $ 15.75 | $(1,238.99) | − | The answer is yes |

A format code need not have all four sections. For most applications, a format code will have a positive section and possibly a negative section. If you omit the zero formatting section, zero values will use the positive number formatting.

BTW
Summing a Row or Column
You can reference an entire column or an entire row in a function argument by listing only the column or only the row. For example, = sum(a:a) sums all the values in all the cells in column A, and = sum(1:1) sums all the values in all the cells in row 1. You can verify this by entering = sum(a:a) in cell C1 and then begin entering numbers in a few of the cells in column A. Excel will respond by showing the sum of the numbers in cell C1.

1 FORMAT WORKSHEET | 2 FILL LINEAR SERIES | 3 USE DATE & ROUND FUNCTIONS | 4 APPLY CUSTOM FORMAT CODE

To Create a Custom Format Code

5 CREATE CELL STYLES | 6 POPULATE WORKSHEETS | 7 INSERT CHART | 8 LINK WORKBOOKS

The following steps create and assign a custom format code to the ranges that contain percentages. **Why?** *A workbook may call for a visual presentation of data that cannot be accomplished with Excel's existing format codes.* In this case, the format code will display percentages with two decimal places to the right of the decimal point and also display negative percentages in magenta with parentheses.

1

- CTRL+drag to select the ranges C5:C12, E5:E12, and G5:G12, right-click any of the selected ranges to display the shortcut menu, and then click Format Cells to display the Format Cells dialog box.

- If necessary, click the Number tab (Format Cells dialog box) and then click Custom in the Category list.

- Delete the word General in the Type box (Format Cells dialog box) and then type `0.00%; [Magenta] (0.00%)` to enter a custom format code (Figure 5–21).

Q&A | What does the custom format mean?
The custom format has been modified to show percentages with two decimal places and to show negative percentages in magenta with parentheses. A zero value will display as 0.00%. In the Sample area, Excel displays a sample of the custom format assigned to the first number in the selected ranges.

2

- Click the OK button (Format Cells dialog box) to display the numbers using the custom format code (Figure 5–22).

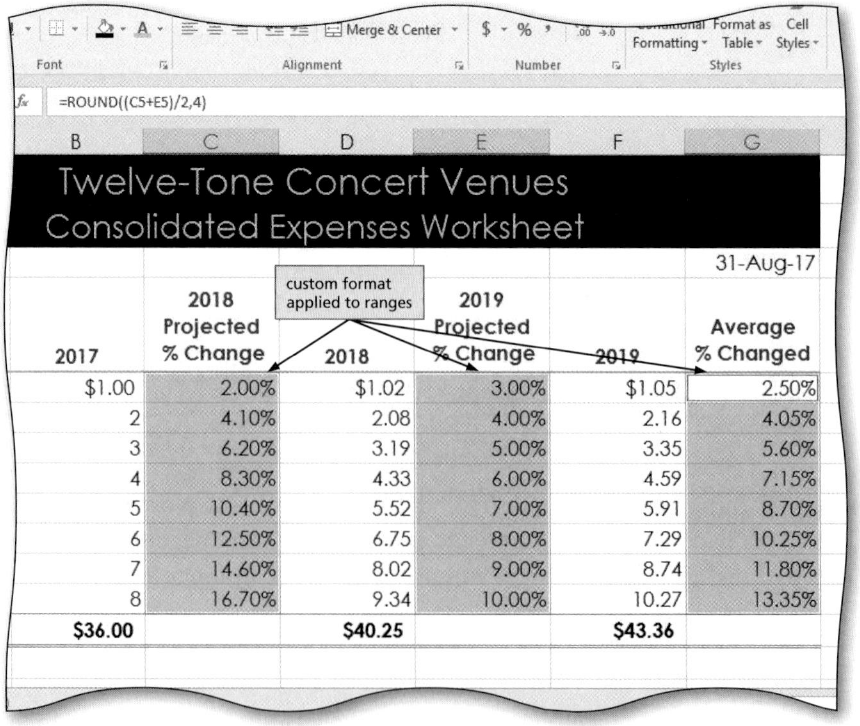

Q&A | Can I reuse the custom format code?
Yes. When you create a new custom format code, Excel adds it to the bottom of the Type list on the Number sheet (Format Cells dialog box) to make it available for future use.

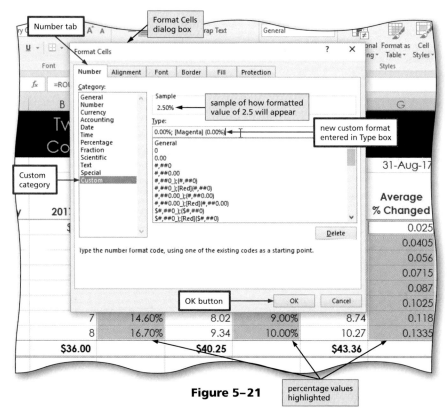

Figure 5–21

Figure 5–22

Other Ways

1. Select range or ranges, click Number Format Dialog Box Launcher (Home tab | Number group), click Custom in Category list (Format Cells dialog box | Number tab), enter format code in Type box, click OK button

To Format with the Comma Style

The following steps format the numbers other than the first row or totals with the comma style.

1 Select the ranges B6:B12, D6:D12, and F6:F12.

2 Click the Comma Style button (Home tab | Number group) to display the numbers in the selected ranges using the comma style.

3 Select an empty cell to deselect the range.

Q&A Why is the comma style used for numbers that are not large enough to display commas?
The comma style allows the values in the cells to align properly with the values in row 5, which are formatted with the currency style with floating dollar signs and parentheses for negative numbers.

Creating a Cell Style

Recall that a cell style is a group of built-in format specifications, such as font, font style, color, size, alignment, borders, and shading. A cell style also may contain information regarding nonvisual characteristics, such as cell protection. Earlier you used the Title cell style to format the worksheet headings. Now you will learn how to create a custom cell style. In addition to those styles listed in the Cell Styles gallery, Excel makes several cell styles available with all workbooks and themes, such as currency, comma, and percent, listed in the Number group (Home tab).

BTW
Accuracy
The result of an arithmetic operation, such as multiplication or division, is accurate to the factor with the least number of decimal places.

Tips to remember when creating a new style

• When you are creating a cell style, pay close attention to the Style Includes area of the Style dialog box (Figure 5–24). A style affects the format of a cell or range of cells only if the corresponding check box is selected. For example, if the Font check box is not selected in the Style dialog box, then the cell maintains the font format it had before the style was assigned.

• If you assign two different styles to a cell or range of cells, Excel adds the second style to the first, rather than replacing it. If the two cell styles include different settings for an attribute, such as fill color, then Excel applies the setting for the second style.

• You can merge styles from another workbook into the active workbook by using the Merge Styles command in the Cell Styles gallery (Home tab | Styles group). Before you use the Merge Styles command, however, you must open the workbook that contains the desired styles.

• The six check boxes in the Style dialog box are identical to the six tabs in the Format Cells dialog box (Figure 5–24).

CONSIDER THIS

Once created, new cell styles appear at the top of the Cell Styles gallery, and are saved for the current workbook. By right-clicking the style in the Cell Styles gallery, you can delete, modify, or duplicate the style. Create a new style in a workbook or merge styles when you plan to use a group of format specifications over and over.

It is easy to confuse cell styles and format codes. While they overlap slightly in some areas, cell styles have more to do with words, fonts and borders, while format codes have more to do with values, decimal places, and special characters.

BTW
Normal Style
The Normal style is the format style that Excel initially assigns to all cells in a workbook. If you change the Normal style, Excel applies the new format specifications to all cells that are not assigned another style.

To Create a New Cell Style

The following steps create a new style called 4-Digit Year by modifying the existing Normal style. *Why?* *Creating a new style allows you to group a number of cell formats together for ease, reuse, and consistency of application.* The **Normal style** is the default style that is applied to all cells when you start Excel. The Normal style includes characteristics such as font, border, alignment, and other settings. You will create a new style to include a date and alignment format, along with other characteristics of the Normal style. The new style will use dark orange text and be centered within the cell.

- Click the Cell Styles button (Home tab | Styles group) to display the Cell Styles gallery (Figure 5–23).

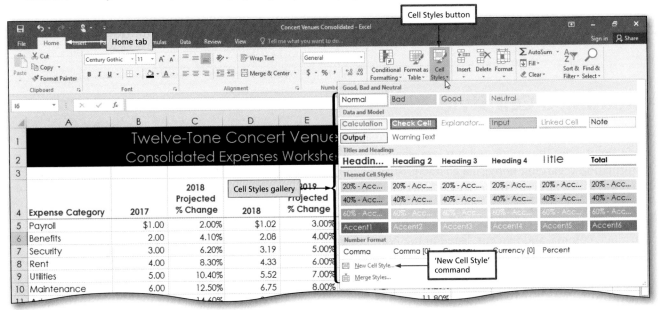

Figure 5–23

- Click 'New Cell Style' in the Cell Styles gallery to display the Style dialog box.

- In the Style name text box, type `4-Digit Year` to name the new style (Figure 5–24).

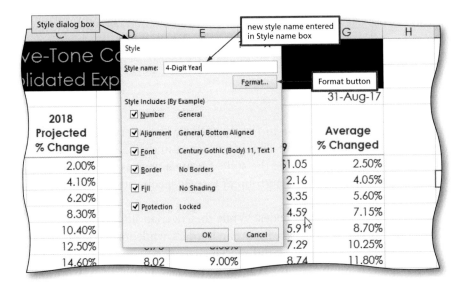

Figure 5–24

3

- Click the Format button (Style dialog box) to display the Format Cells dialog box.

- If necessary, click the Number tab (Format Cells dialog box), click Date in the Category list, and then click '14-Mar-2012' in the Type list to define the new style as a date style (Figure 5–25).

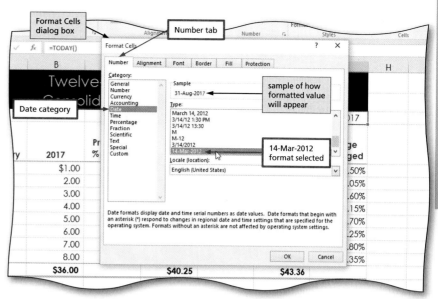

Figure 5–25

4

- Click the Alignment tab (Format Cells dialog box) to display the Alignment sheet. Click the Horizontal button, and then click Center to define the alignment of the new style (Figure 5–26).

Q&A What is the difference between the text alignment options here and the ones on the Home tab? Many of them are the same; however, in this dialog box, you can make adjustments that are more precise. Keep in mind that you cannot use the buttons on the Home tab when you are creating a new style.

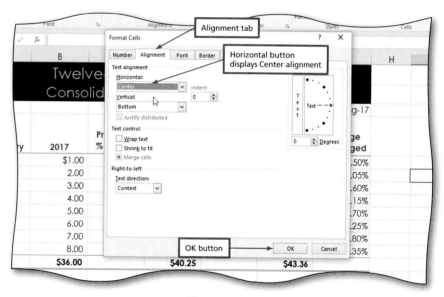

Figure 5–26

5

- Click the Font tab (Format Cells dialog box) and then click the Color button to display the Color gallery (Figure 5–27).

Q&A What are superscript and subscript on the Font sheet? A **superscript** is a small number placed above the normal text line to indicate exponentiation. A **subscript** is a small number placed below the normal text line such as those used in scientific and chemical notations.

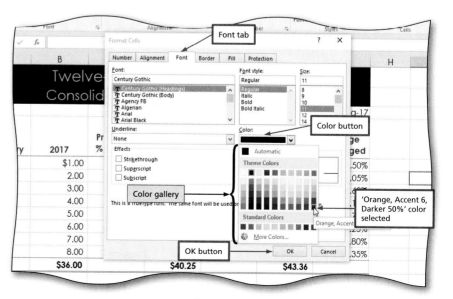

Figure 5–27

- Click 'Orange, Accent 6 Darker 50%' (column 10, row 6) to set the new color.

- Click the OK button (Format Cells dialog box) to close the Format Cells dialog box.

- Click Border, Fill, and Protection to clear the check boxes (Style dialog box), indicating that the new style does not use these characteristics (Figure 5–28).

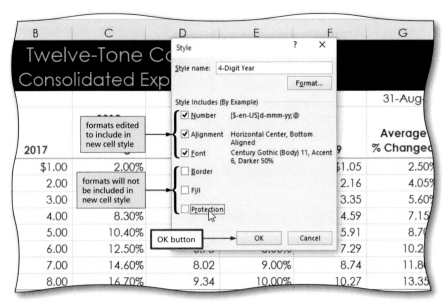

- Click the OK button (Style dialog box) to create the new style.

Figure 5–28

To Apply a New Style

1 FORMAT WORKSHEET | 2 FILL LINEAR SERIES | 3 USE DATE & ROUND FUNCTIONS | 4 APPLY CUSTOM FORMAT CODE
5 CREATE CELL STYLES | 6 POPULATE WORKSHEETS | 7 INSERT CHART | 8 LINK WORKBOOKS

In earlier steps, cell G3 was assigned the system date using the TODAY function. The following steps assign cell G3 the new 4-Digit Year style, which centers the content of the cell and assigns it the date format dd-mmm-yyyy in orange. *Why? Using a style ensures a consistent application of formatting instructions.*

1

- Select cell G3 and then click the Cell Styles button (Home tab | Styles group) to display the Cell Styles gallery (Figure 5–29).

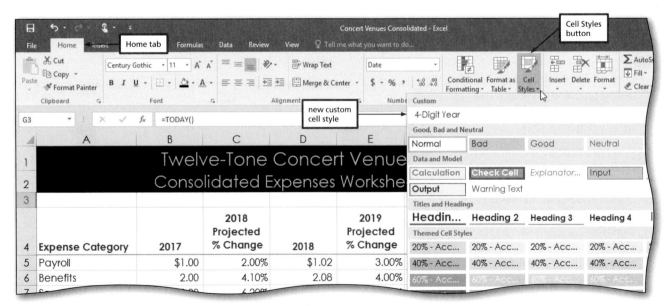

Figure 5–29

2

- Click the 4-Digit Year style to assign the new style to the selected cell (Figure 5–30).

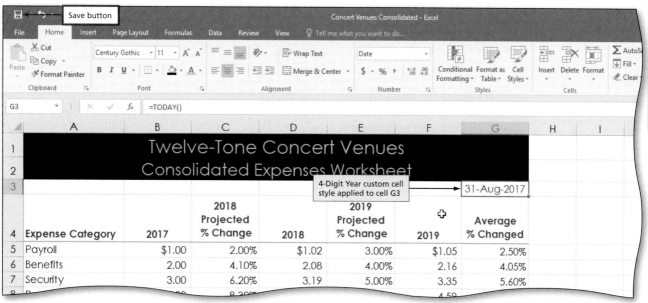

Figure 5–30

To Use the Spelling Checker

The formatting is complete. The following steps use the spelling checker to check the spelling in the worksheet, and then save the consolidated worksheet.

1 Select cell B2, click the Review tab, and then click the Spelling button (Review tab | Proofing group) to check the spelling in the workbook. Correct any misspelled words.

2 Click the Save button on the Quick Access Toolbar to save the workbook.

Break Point: If you wish to take a break, this is a good place to do so. You can exit Excel. To resume at a later time, run Excel, open the file called Concert Venues Consolidated, and continue following the steps from this location forward.

Working with Multiple Worksheets

A workbook contains one worksheet by default. You can add more worksheets, limited only by the amount of memory in your computer. When working with multiple worksheets, you should name and color the sheet tabs so that you can identify them easily. With the consolidated worksheet complete, the next steps are to insert and populate worksheets in the workbook, by copying the data from the consolidated worksheet to the location worksheets, and adjusting the formatting and values. You will learn three different ways to copy data across worksheets.

BTW
Default Number of Worksheets
An alternative to adding worksheets is to change the default number of worksheets before you open a new workbook. To change the default number of worksheets in a blank workbook, click Options in the Backstage view and then change the number in the 'Include this many sheets' box in the 'When creating new workbooks' area (Excel Options dialog box).

How do I determine how many worksheets to add to a workbook?

Excel provides three basic choices when you consider how to organize data. Use a single worksheet when the data is tightly related. In this case, you may want to analyze the data in a table and use columnar data, such as department, region, or quarter, to identify groups. Use multiple worksheets when data is related but can stand alone on its own. For example, each region, department, or quarter may contain enough detailed information that you may want to analyze the data in separate worksheets. Use multiple workbooks when data is loosely coupled, or when it comes from multiple sources.

To Add a Worksheet to a Workbook

In a previous module, you learned that you could add a worksheet to a workbook by clicking the New sheet button at the bottom of the workbook. The Concert Venues Consolidated workbook requires four worksheets — one for each of the three venue sites and one for the consolidated totals. The following step adds the first new worksheet.

1 Click the New sheet button at the bottom of the window to add a new worksheet to the workbook.

To Copy and Paste from One Worksheet to Another

1 FORMAT WORKSHEET | 2 FILL LINEAR SERIES | 3 USE DATE & ROUND FUNCTIONS | 4 APPLY CUSTOM FORMAT CODE
5 CREATE CELL STYLES | 6 POPULATE WORKSHEETS | 7 INSERT CHART | 8 LINK WORKBOOKS

With two worksheets in the workbook, the next step is to copy the contents of Sheet1 to Sheet2. *Why? When the desired content of the new worksheet mirrors or closely follows that of an existing worksheet, copying the existing content minimizes the chances of introducing errors.* Sheet1 eventually will be used as the Consolidated worksheet with consolidated data. Sheet2 will be used for one of the three venue site worksheets.

In the process of copying, you must first select the populated cells. You can press CTRL+A to select the rectangular range that contains populated cells. You can press CTRL+A twice to select all of the rows and columns in the worksheet, you can drag around the cells to create a selection, or you can click the Select All button located just below the Name box at the intersection of the row and column headings. The manner in which you select all of the data depends on where you are in the worksheet and your personal preference of using the mouse versus the keyboard. The following steps copy the content of one worksheet to another using the Select All button.

1

- Click the Sheet1 sheet tab to display the worksheet.

- Click the Select All button to select the entire worksheet.

- Click the Copy button (Home tab | Clipboard group) to copy the contents of the worksheet (Figure 5–31).

Can I use the shortcut keys, CTRL+C and CTRL+V, to copy and paste?

Yes. In addition, you can use the shortcut menu to copy and paste.

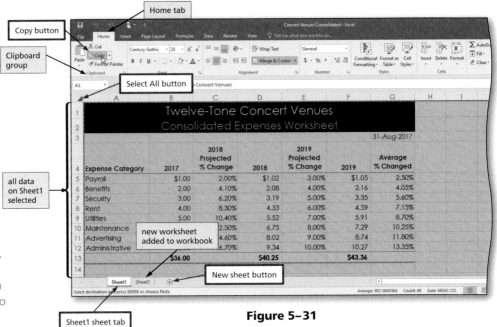

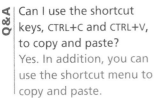

Figure 5–31

- Click the Sheet2 sheet tab at the bottom of the worksheet to display Sheet2.

- Press the ENTER key to copy the data from the Office Clipboard to the selected sheet.

- Zoom to approximately 120% (Figure 5–32).

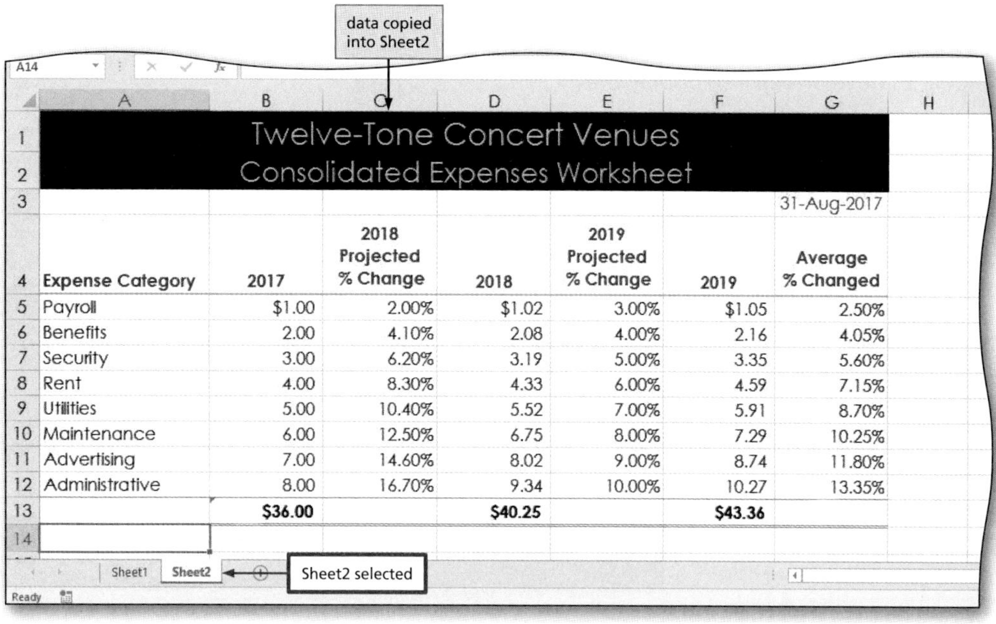

Q&A Can I use the Paste button (Home tab | Clipboard group) to paste the data?
Yes. Recall that if you complete a paste operation using the ENTER key however, the marquee disappears and the Office Clipboard is cleared, as it no longer contains the copied data following the action.

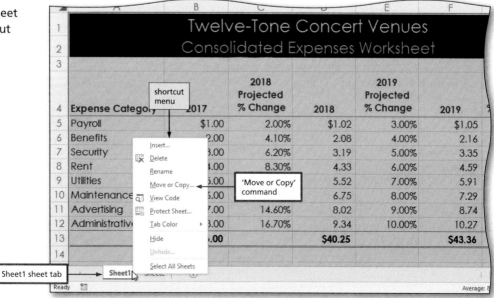

Figure 5–32

Other Ways

1. Select cells, press CTRL+C, select destination cell press CTRL+V
2. Select cells, press CTRL+C, select destination cell, press ENTER
3. Right-click selected cells, click Copy, right-click destination cell, click appropriate Paste button

To Copy a Worksheet Using a Shortcut Menu

1 FORMAT WORKSHEET | 2 FILL LINEAR SERIES | 3 USE DATE & ROUND FUNCTIONS | 4 APPLY CUSTOM FORMAT CODE
5 CREATE CELL STYLES | 6 POPULATE WORKSHEETS | **7 INSERT CHART** | **8 LINK WORKBOOKS**

The following steps create a worksheet using the shortcut menu that appears when you right-click a sheet tab. **Why?** *The shortcut menu and resulting dialog box allow you more flexibility in exactly where and how to move and copy.*

- Right-click the Sheet1 sheet tab to display the shortcut menu (Figure 5–33).

Figure 5–33

2

- Click 'Move or Copy' to display the Move or Copy dialog box.

- In the Before sheet list (Move or Copy dialog box), click '(move to end)' and then click to place a check mark in the 'Create a copy' check box (Figure 5–34).

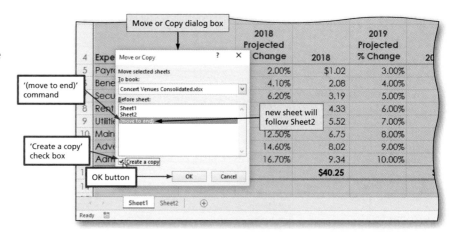

Figure 5–34

3

- Click the OK button to add a copy of the Sheet1 worksheet to the workbook (Figure 5–35).

Q&A

Why is it named Sheet1 (2) instead of Sheet3?
Excel indicates that it is a copy by referring to the original sheet.

	Twelve-Tone Concert Venues						
	Consolidated Expenses Worksheet						
							31-Aug-2017
	Expense Category	2017	2018 Projected % Change	2018	2019 Projected % Change	2019	Average % Changed
5	Payroll	$1.00	2.00%	$1.02	3.00%	$1.05	2.50%
6	Benefits	2.00	4.10%	2.08	4.00%	2.16	4.05%
7	Security	3.00	6.20%	3.19	5.00%	3.35	5.60%
8	Rent	4.00	8.30%	4.33	6.00%	4.59	7.15%
9	Utilities	5.00	10.40%	5.52	7.00%	5.91	8.70%
10	Maintenance	6.00	12.50%	6.75	8.00%	7.29	10.25%
11	Advertising	7.00	14.60%	8.02	9.00%	8.74	11.80%
12	Administrative	8.00	16.70%	9.34	10.00%	10.27	13.35%
13		$36.00		$40.25		$43.36	

Figure 5–35

To Copy a Worksheet Using the CTRL Key

1 FORMAT WORKSHEET | 2 FILL LINEAR SERIES | 3 USE DATE & ROUND FUNCTIONS | 4 APPLY CUSTOM FORMAT CODE
5 CREATE CELL STYLES | 6 POPULATE WORKSHEETS | **7 INSERT CHART** | 8 LINK WORKBOOKS

Another way to create a copy of a worksheet is by pressing the CTRL key while you drag the sheet tab. *Why? Using the CTRL key is faster than selecting and copying, then pasting.* As you drag, Excel will display a small triangular arrow to show the destination location of your copy. The following steps create a third copy, for a total of four worksheets in the workbook.

1

- Select Sheet1.

- CTRL+drag the Sheet1 sheet tab to a location to the right of the other sheet tabs. Do not release the drag (Figure 5–36).

2

- Release the drag to create the worksheet copy named Sheet1 (3).

Figure 5–36

To Drill an Entry through Worksheets

The next step is to replace the sample numbers for the 2018 and 2019 projected percentage change. The percentage changes are identical on all four sheets. For example, the 2018 % change for payroll in cell D6 is 1.50% on all four sheets.

To speed data entry, Excel allows you to enter a number in the same cell through all selected worksheets. This technique is referred to as **drilling an entry**. *Why drill an entry? In cases where multiple worksheets have the same layout and the same calculations performed on data, drilling entries of data or formulas ensures consistency across the worksheets.* When you drill, all affected sheets must be selected. Table 5–6 contains the new figures for cells C5:C12 and E5:E12.

Table 5–6 Projected % Change Values for 2018 and 2019				
Category	**Cell**	**2018 Projected % Change**	**Cell**	**2019 Projected % Change**
Payroll	C5	1.5	E5	1.5
Benefits	C6	2.5	E6	3
Security	C7	2	E7	2
Rent	C8	0	E8	1
Utilities	C9	1	E9	1
Maintenance	C10	0	E10	1
Advertising	C11	–1	E11	–1
Administrative	C12	–2	E12	–2.25

The following steps select all sheets, drill the 2018 and 2019 projected percentage change entries from Table 5–6 through all four worksheets, and then ungroup the selection.

1

- Right-click Sheet1 and then click 'Select All Sheets' on the shortcut menu.

- Select cell C5. Type **1.5** and then press the DOWN ARROW key to change sample data in the selected cell to the actual value.

- Enter the 15 remaining 2018 and 2019 values from Table 5–6 to the appropriate cells to display the actual percentages (Figure 5–37).

Q&A   What is the benefit of drilling data through worksheets?

In these steps, 16 new numbers were entered on one worksheet. By drilling the entries through the other worksheets, 64 new numbers now appear, 16 on each of the worksheets. Excel's capability of drilling data through selected worksheets is an efficient way to enter data that is common among worksheets.

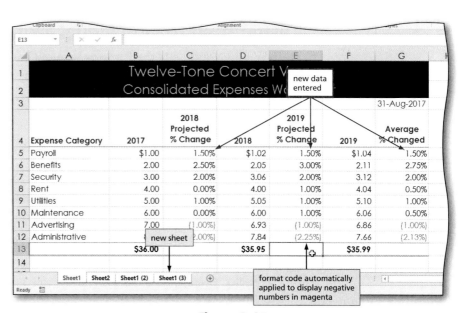

Figure 5–37

● Right-click Sheet1 and then click Ungroup Sheets on the shortcut menu.

● One at a time, click the Sheet2 sheet tab, the Sheet1 (2) sheet tab, and the Sheet1 (3) sheet tab to verify that all four worksheets are identical.

BTW
Deleting Worksheets
Recall from Module 4 that you can delete a worksheet by right-clicking the sheet tab of the worksheet you want to delete, and then clicking Delete on the shortcut menu.

Selecting and Deselecting Sheets

Beginning Excel users sometimes have difficulty trying to select and deselect sheets. Table 5–7 summarizes how to select and deselect multiple sheets using a mouse and keyboard.

Table 5–7 Summary of How to Select and Deselect Sheets	
Task	**How to Carry Out the Task**
Select individual sheet	Click sheet tab.
Select all sheets	Right-click any sheet tab, click 'Select All Sheets' on shortcut menu.
Select adjacent sheets	Select the first sheet by clicking its tab, and then hold down the SHIFT key and click the sheet tab at the other end of the list of adjacent sheet tabs.
Select nonadjacent sheets	Select the first sheet by clicking its tab, then hold down the CTRL key and click the sheet tabs of the remaining sheets you want to select.
Deselect all sheets	Right-click any sheet tab, click Ungroup Sheets on shortcut menu or click the individual sheet tab that you wish to select.
Deselect one of many sheets	CTRL+click the sheet tab you want to deselect.

BTW
Selecting Multiple Worksheets
When multiple worksheets are selected, the Excel title bar reflects the selection by adding the notation, [Group]. All of the sheet tabs also are highlighted.

Customizing the Individual Worksheets

With the outline of the Concert Venues Consolidated workbook created, you will modify the individual worksheets by changing the worksheet name, sheet tab color, and worksheet subtitle. You also will change the color of the title area and enter the 2017 Expenses in column B.

To Modify the Durat Theater Worksheet

The following steps modify the Durat Theater worksheet (Sheet2).

1 Double-click the Sheet2 sheet tab to select it. Type **Durat Theater** and then press the ENTER key to change the worksheet name.

2 Right-click the Durat Theater sheet tab, point to Tab Color on the shortcut menu, and then click 'Orange, Accent 6' (column 10, row 1) in the Theme Colors area to change the sheet tab color.

3 Double-click cell A2. Drag through the word, Consolidated, to select the text, and then type **Durat Theater** to change the worksheet subtitle.

4 Select the range A1:A2. Click the Fill Color arrow (Home tab | Font group) and then click 'Orange, Accent 6' (column 10, row 1) in the Theme Colors area (Fill Color gallery) to change the fill color of the selected range.

5 Click the Font Color arrow (Home tab | Font group) and then click Automatic in the Font Color gallery to change the font color of the selected range.

6 Enter the following data in the indicated cells:

Cell	Data for Durat Theater	Cell	Data for Durat Theater
B5	79207.20	B9	3080.00
B6	15247.39	B10	4295.20
B7	28175.65	B11	3599.64
B8	14400.00	B12	2500.00

7 Click an empty cell to deselect the previous cell (Figure 5–38).

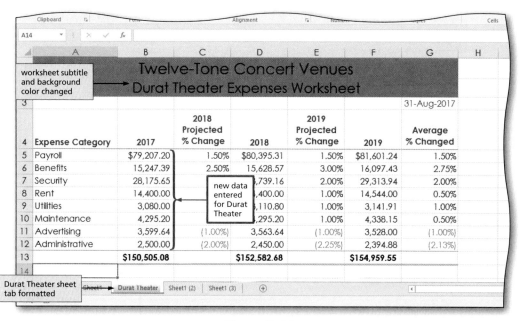

Figure 5–38

To Modify the Truman House Sheet

The following steps modify the Truman House Theater worksheet Sheet1 (2)

1 Double-click the Sheet1 (2) sheet tab to select it. Type **Truman House** and then press the ENTER key to change the worksheet name.

2 Right-click the Truman House sheet tab, point to Tab Color on the shortcut menu, and then click 'Gray - 50%, Accent 1, Lighter 60%' (column 5, row 3) in the Theme Colors area to change the sheet tab color.

3 Double-click cell A2. Drag through the word, Consolidated, to select the text, and then type **Truman House** to change the worksheet subtitle.

4 Select the range A1:A2. Click the Fill Color arrow (Home tab | Font group) and then click 'Gray - 50%, Accent 1, Lighter 60%' (column 5, row 3) in the Theme Colors area (Fill Color gallery) to change the fill color of the selected range.

5 Click the Font Color arrow (Home tab | Font group) and then click Automatic in the Font Color gallery to change the font color of the selected range.

6 Enter the following data in the indicated cells:

Cell	Data for Truman House Theater	Cell	Data for Truman House Theater
B5	72870.62	B9	2833.60
B6	14027.60	B10	3951.58
B7	25921.60	B11	3311.67
B8	13248.00	B12	2250.00

7 Click an empty cell to deselect the previous cell (Figure 5–39).

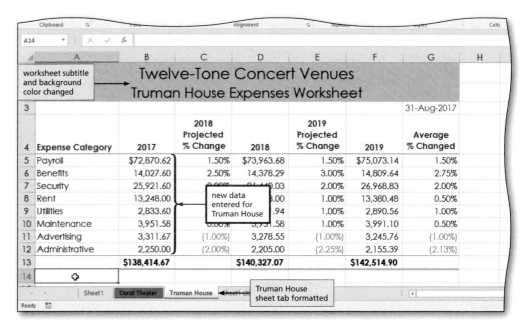

Figure 5–39

To Modify the Stage Xanadu Worksheet

The following steps modify the Stage Xanadu worksheet Sheet1 (3).

1 Double-click the Sheet1 (3) sheet tab to select it. Type **Stage Xanadu** and then press the ENTER key to change the worksheet name.

2 Right-click the Stage Xanadu sheet tab, point to Tab Color on the shortcut menu, and then click Light Blue in the Standard Colors area to change the sheet tab color.

3 Double-click cell A2. Drag through the word, Consolidated, to select the text, and then type **Stage Xanadu** to change the worksheet subtitle.

④ Select the range A1:A2. Click the Fill Color arrow (Home tab | Font group) and then click Light Blue in the Standard Colors area (Fill Color gallery) to change the fill color of the selected range.

⑤ Click the Font Color arrow (Home tab | Font group) and then click Automatic in the Font Color gallery to change the font color of the selected range.

⑥ Enter the following data in the indicated cells:

Cell	Data for Stage Xanadu	Cell	Data for Stage Xanadu
B5	88712.06	B9	3449.60
B6	17077.07	B10	4810.62
B7	31556.73	B11	4031.60
B8	16128.00	B12	2700.00

⑦ Click an empty cell to deselect the previous cell (Figure 5–40).

⑧ Click the Save button on the Quick Access Toolbar.

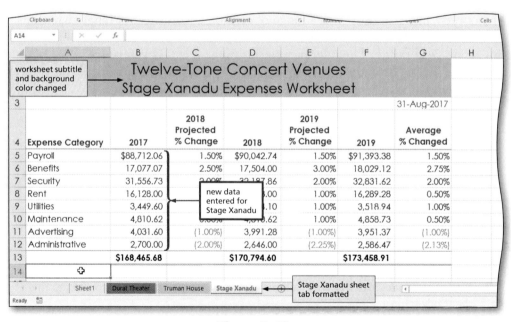

Figure 5–40

Referencing Cells Across Worksheets

With the three location worksheets complete, you now can consolidate the data. Because this consolidation worksheet contains totals of the data, you need to reference cell data from other worksheets.

BTW
Drilling an Entry
Besides drilling a number down through a workbook, you can drill a format, a function, or a formula down through a workbook.

BTW
Importing Data
Expenses, such as those entered into the range B5:B12, often are maintained in another workbook, file, or database. If the expenses are maintained elsewhere, ways exist to link to a workbook or to import data from a file or database into a workbook. Linking to a workbook is discussed later in this module. To see a list of typical sources of outside data, click the `Get Data From Other Sources' button (Data tab | Get External Data group).

BTW
3-D References
If you are summing numbers on noncontiguous sheets, hold down the CTRL key rather than the shift key when selecting the sheets.

To reference cells in other worksheets within a single workbook, you use the worksheet name, which serves as the **worksheet reference**, combined with the cell reference. The worksheet reference must be enclosed within single quotation marks (') when the worksheet name contains a non-alphabetical character such as a space. Excel requires an exclamation point (!) as a delimiter between the worksheet reference and the cell reference. Therefore, the reference to cell B5 on the Durat Theater worksheet would be entered as

= 'Durat Theater'!B5

These worksheet and cell references can be used in formulas, such as

= 'Durat Theater'!B5 + 'Truman House'!B5 + 'Stage Xanadu'!B5

A worksheet reference such as 'Durat Theater' always is absolute, meaning that the worksheet reference remains constant if you were to copy the formula to other locations.

Worksheet references also can be used in functions and range references such as

= SUM('Durat Theater:Stage Xanadu'!B5)

The SUM argument ('Durat Theater:Stage Xanadu'!B5) instructs Excel to sum cell B5 on each of the three worksheets (Durat Theater, Truman House, and Stage Xanadu). The colon (:) delimiter between the first worksheet name and the last worksheet name instructs Excel to include these worksheets and all worksheets in between, just as it does with a range of cells on a worksheet. A range that spans two or more worksheets in a workbook, such as 'Durat Theater:Stage Xanadu'!C6, is called a **3-D range**. The reference to this range is a **3-D reference**. A 3-D reference is also absolute. You can paste the 3-D reference to other cells on the worksheet.

To Modify the Consolidated Worksheet

The following steps change the worksheet name from Sheet1 to Consolidated and then color the sheet tab.

1 Double-click the Sheet1 sheet tab. Type `Consolidated` and then press the ENTER key to rename the tab.

2 Right-click the Consolidated sheet tab, point to Tab Color on the shortcut menu, and then click 'Black, Text 1' (row 1, column 2) in the Theme Colors area to change the sheet tab color.

To Enter a 3-D Reference

1 FORMAT WORKSHEET | 2 FILL LINEAR SERIES | 3 USE DATE & ROUND FUNCTIONS | 4 APPLY CUSTOM FORMAT CODE
5 CREATE CELL STYLES | 6 POPULATE WORKSHEETS | **7 INSERT CHART** | **8 LINK WORKBOOKS**

To consolidate the payroll expenses, the following steps create 3-D references in cells B5, D5, and F5 on the Consolidated worksheet. **Why?** *Using 3-D references is the most efficient method of referencing cells that reside in the same location on different worksheets.* You can enter a worksheet reference in a cell by typing the worksheet reference or by clicking the appropriate sheet tab while in Point mode. When you click the sheet tab, Excel activates the worksheet and automatically adds the worksheet name and an exclamation point after the insertion point in the formula bar. Then, click the desired cell or drag through the cells you want to reference on the sheet.

If the range of cells to be referenced is located on several worksheets (as when selecting a 3-D range), click the first sheet tab and then select the cell(s). Finally, SHIFT+click the last sheet tab you want to reference. Excel will include the cell(s) on the first worksheet, on the last worksheet, and those on any worksheets in between.

1

- Select cell B5 and then click the Sum button (Home tab | Editing group) to display the SUM function (Figure 5–41).

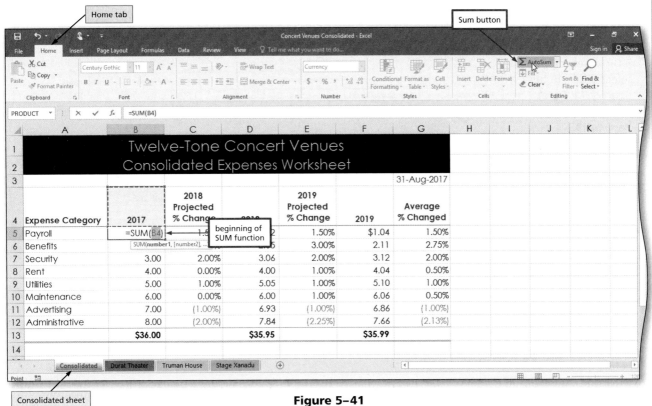

Figure 5–41

2

- Click the Durat Theater tab and then click cell B5 to select the first portion of the argument for the SUM function.

- SHIFT+click the Stage Xanadu tab to select the ending range of the argument for the SUM function (Figure 5–42).

Q&A

Could I just type the 3-D reference?
Yes, however the Point mode is used in this step, which prevents any errors in typing the reference.

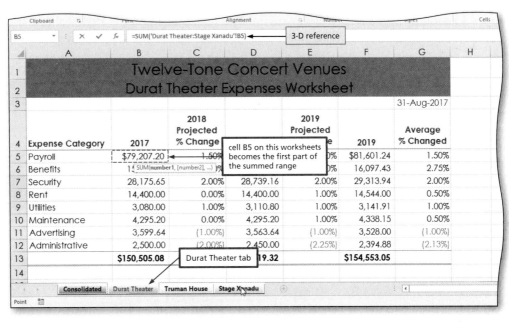

Figure 5–42

③

- Click the Enter button in the formula bar to enter the SUM function with the 3-D references in the selected cell, in this case =SUM('Durat Theater:Stage Xanadu'!B5) (Figure 5–43).

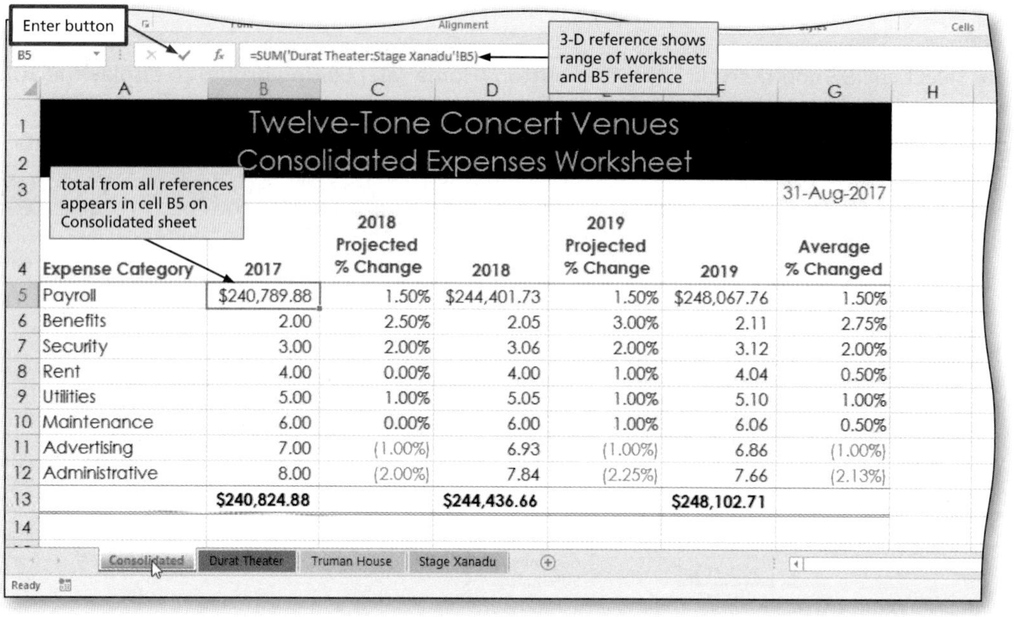

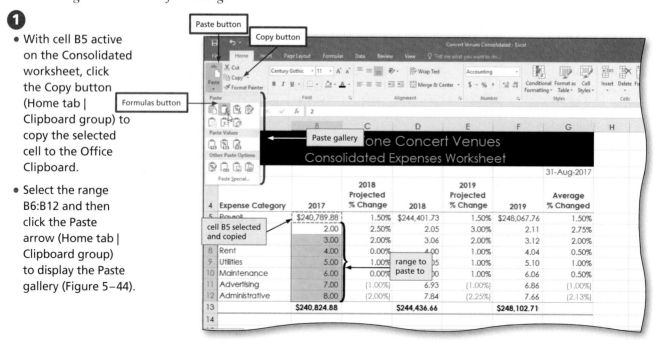

Q&A

Should each worksheet name in the function have individual sets of single quotes?
No, in a 3-D reference that uses a range, Excel requires a single quote before the first worksheet name in the range and an ending single quote after the last worksheet name.

Figure 5–43

To Use the Paste Gallery

In earlier modules, you learned about the Paste Options button, which allows you to choose different ways to paste and copy formulas, values, and functions. The Paste gallery, which displays when you click the Paste arrow (Home tab | Clipboard group), offers many of the same choices, and depending on the type of pasting, many others. When copying a formula that includes a 3-D reference, it is advisable to choose the Formulas button from the Paste gallery to copy without formatting. Using other paste methods such as the fill handle, ENTER key, or Paste button could result in changing the formatting of the destination cells.

The following steps copy and paste the 3-D reference using the Paste gallery. *Why? Using the Paste gallery will not change the destination formatting.*

①

- With cell B5 active on the Consolidated worksheet, click the Copy button (Home tab | Clipboard group) to copy the selected cell to the Office Clipboard.

- Select the range B6:B12 and then click the Paste arrow (Home tab | Clipboard group) to display the Paste gallery (Figure 5–44).

Figure 5–44

2

- Click the Formulas button (column 2, row 1) in the Paste gallery to copy the SUM function to the desired range, replicating the 3-D references.

- Press the ESC key to clear the marquee (Figure 5–45).

- Deselect the previous range.

- Click the Save button on the Quick Access Toolbar to save the workbook.

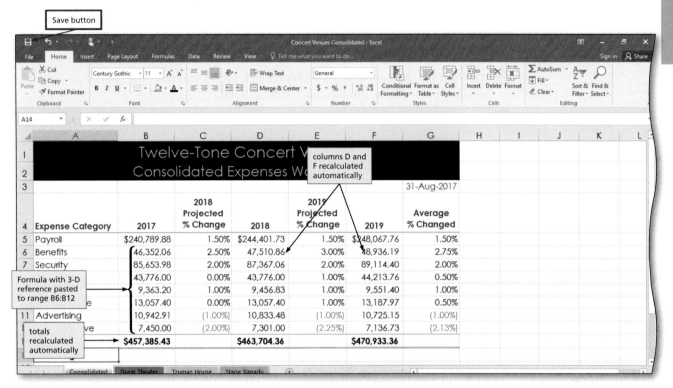

Figure 5–45

Other Ways

1. Right-click selected cell(s), click Copy, right-click destination cell(s), click appropriate Paste button

---

Break Point: If you wish to take a break, this is a good place to do so. You can exit Excel. To resume at a later time, run Excel, open the file called Concert Venues Consolidated, and continue following the steps from this location forward.

Formatting Pie Charts

In Module 1, you created a pie chart. Pie charts show the contribution of each piece of data to the whole, or total, of the data. You can format a pie chart in many ways including resizing, moving, rotating, adding data labels and leader lines, adding a decorative background, and exploding a slice.

As outlined in the requirements document in Table 5–1, the worksheet should include a pie chart to represent graphically the 2017 expenses totals for all three venues. The pie chart resides at the bottom of the consolidated worksheet, so it will print on the same page.

BTW

Y-Rotation and Perspective
The Y-Rotation arrows tilt the chart toward the back or front, allowing you to control the elevation of the chart. You can tilt the chart toward or away from you in order to enhance the view of the chart. The Perspective value makes close slices appear larger and those further away appear smaller.

To Insert a 3-D Pie Chart on a Worksheet

The following steps insert the 3-D pie chart on the Consolidated worksheet.

1 Select the range A5:B12 to identify the category names and data for the pie chart.

2 Display the Insert tab, click the 'Insert Pie or Doughnut Chart' button (Insert tab | Charts group), and then click 3-D Pie in the Insert Pie or Doughnut Chart gallery to create the desired chart type.

3 Click the chart title, select the text, and then type `2017 Consolidated Expenses` to change the chart title.

4 Deselect the chart title, click the Chart Styles button to display the Chart styles gallery, and then apply Style 3 to the chart (Figure 5–46).

5 Click an empty cell or click the Chart Styles button to close the Chart Styles gallery.

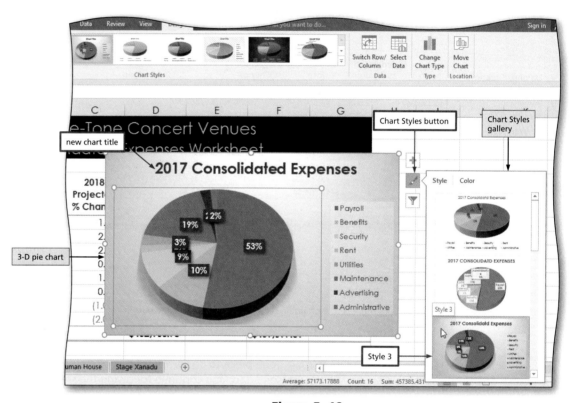

Figure 5–46

To Move a Chart on the Same Worksheet

1 FORMAT WORKSHEET | 2 FILL LINEAR SERIES | 3 USE DATE & ROUND FUNCTIONS | 4 APPLY CUSTOM FORMAT CODE
5 CREATE CELL STYLES | 6 POPULATE WORKSHEETS | 7 INSERT CHART | 8 LINK WORKBOOKS

The following step moves the chart to the space below the data that was used to create the chart. *Why? By default, Excel places charts in the center of the worksheet. You need to move it in order to uncover the data on the worksheet.*

• Point to the border of the chart. When the pointer changes to a four-headed arrow, drag the chart below the worksheet numbers to the desired location (in this case, approximately cell A15) (Figure 5–47).

Experiment

- Point to each of the styles in the Chart Styles group (Design tab) and watch the chart change to reflect each style.

Q&A

Could I use the Move Chart button (Chart Tools Design tab | Location group) to move the chart?
No. That button moves the chart from sheet to sheet rather than to a new location on the same worksheet.

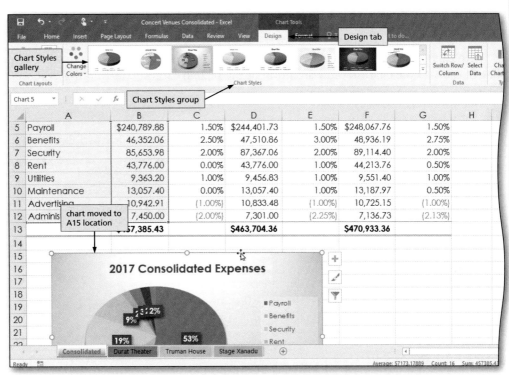

Figure 5–47

To Resize a Chart

1 FORMAT WORKSHEET | 2 FILL LINEAR SERIES | 3 USE DATE & ROUND FUNCTIONS | 4 APPLY CUSTOM FORMAT CODE
5 CREATE CELL STYLES | 6 POPULATE WORKSHEETS | 7 INSERT CHART | **8 LINK WORKBOOKS**

The following step resizes the chart to make it larger and more legible. *Why? The chart as created by Excel may not be the optimal size for your worksheet needs.*

1

- If necessary, scroll down until you can see both the bottom of the chart and row 34.

- SHIFT+drag the lower-right resizing handle of the chart until the chart is the desired size (in this case, approximately to cell G34).

- If necessary, zoom out until you can see the entire chart (Figure 5–48).

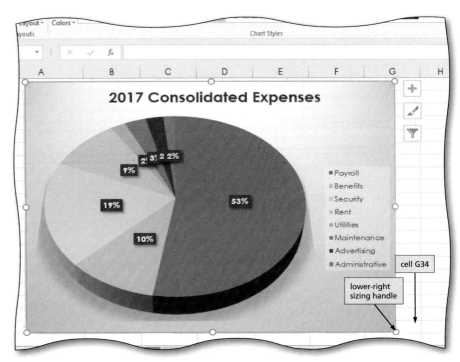

Figure 5–48

To Explode a Slice

In this chart, the Payroll slice dominates because it is so large. The following steps explode the next-largest slice of the 3-D pie chart to draw attention to the second-largest contributing expense. *Why? Exploding, or offsetting, a slice in a chart emphasizes it.*

- Click the Security slice (19%) twice to select it. (Do not double-click.)
- Right-click the selected slice to display the shortcut menu (Figure 5–49).

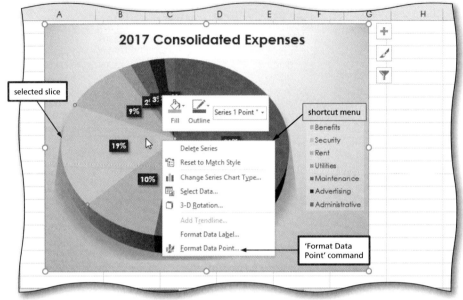

Figure 5–49

- Click 'Format Data Point' on the shortcut menu to open the Format Data Point task pane.
- Drag the Point Explosion slider to the right until the Point Explosion box reads 20% to edit the offset distance for the slice (Figure 5–50).

Experiment

- Select different slices and use the Point Explosion slider to offset additional slices and note how the size of the chart changes as you offset additional slices. When done, reset the slices so that the Security slice is the only slice offset, set to 20%.

Q&A | Should I offset more slices?
You can offset as many slices as you want, but remember that the reason for offsetting a slice is to emphasize it. Offsetting multiple slices tends to reduce the impact on the reader and reduces the overall size of the pie chart.

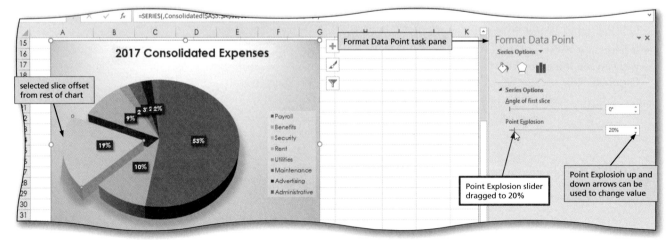

Figure 5–50

Other Ways

1. Click slice twice, drag away from other slices

To Rotate the 3-D Pie Chart

When Excel initially draws a pie chart, it always positions the chart so that one of the dividing lines between two slices is a straight line pointing to 12 o'clock (or 0°). As shown in Figure 5–50, that line that currently divides the Administrative and Payroll slices. This line defines the rotation angle of the 3-D pie chart. Excel allows you to control the rotation angle, elevation, perspective, height, and angle of the axes. The following steps rotate the 3-D pie chart. *Why? With a three-dimensional chart, you can change the view to better show the section of the chart you are trying to emphasize.*

1

- Right-click the chart to display the shortcut menu, and then click '3-D Rotation' on the shortcut menu to open the Format Chart Area task pane.

- In the X Rotation box (Format Chart Area dialog box), type **220** to rotate the chart (Figure 5–51).

Q&A | What happens if I click the X Rotation up arrow?
Excel will rotate the chart 10° in a clockwise direction each time you click the X Rotation up arrow.

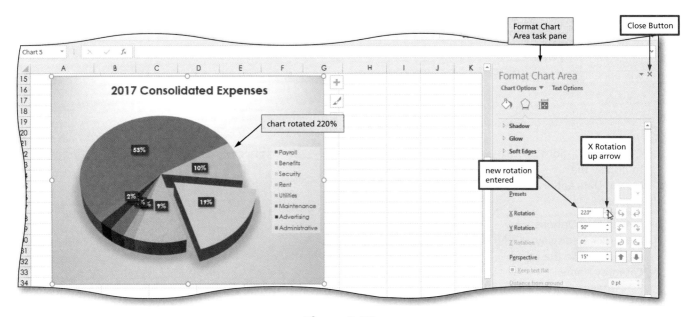

Figure 5–51

2

- Click the Close button (Format Chart Area task pane) to close the task pane.

Other Ways

1. Click Chart Elements arrow (Chart Tools Format tab | Current Selection group), click Plot Area, click Format Selection button (Chart Tools Format tab | Current Selection group), click Effects button (Format Plot Area dialog box), click up or down arrow in X Rotation box

---

To Format Data Labels

The following steps format the data labels using the Format Data Labels task pane. You will choose the elements to include in the data label, set the position, choose number formatting and create leader lines. *Why? A **leader line** connects a data label with its data point helping you identify individual slices.*

1

- Click the Chart Elements button to display the Chart Elements gallery. Point to Data Labels and then click the Data Labels arrow to display the Data Labels submenu (Figure 5–52).

Q&A How does the Legend check box affect the pie chart? If you uncheck the Legend check box, Excel will remove the legend from the chart. If you point to Legend, an arrow will appear. Clicking the arrow displays a list for legend placement.

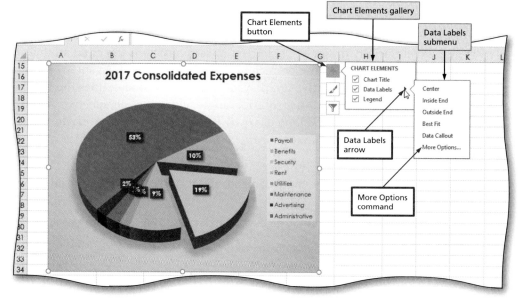

Figure 5–52

2

- Click More Options to display the Format Data Labels task pane.

- In the Label Options area, click to display check marks in the Category Name, Percentage, and 'Show Leader Lines' check boxes. Click to remove check marks in any other check boxes, if necessary (Figure 5–53).

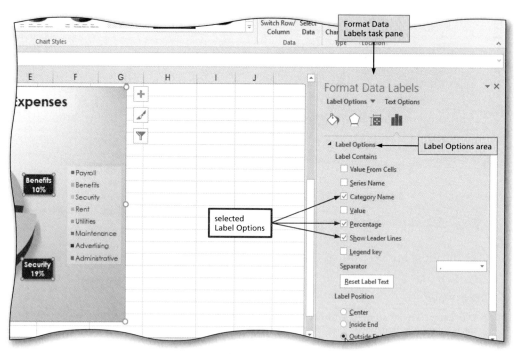

Figure 5–53

 3

- In the Label Position area, click Outside End.

- Scroll down in the task pane and click Number to display the Number settings.

- Scroll as necessary to click the Category button and then click Percentage to choose the number style.

- Select any text in the Decimal places text box and then type   1   to format the percentage with one decimal place (Figure 5–54).

Q&A

Why did my chart change immediately?
The options in the Format Data Labels task pane use live preview to show you what it will look like.

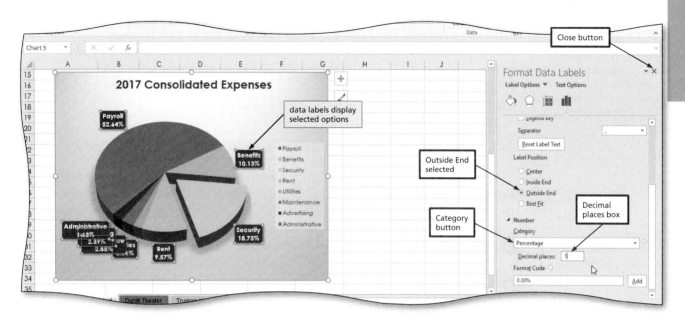

Figure 5–54

4

- Click the Close button on the Format Data Labels task pane to close it.

- One at a time, drag each data label out slightly from the chart to make the leader lines visible (Figure 5–55).

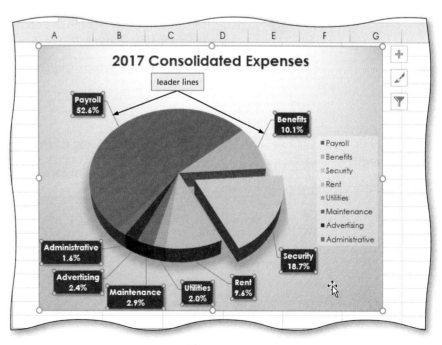

Figure 5–55

Other Ways

1. Click Chart Elements arrow (Chart Tools Format tab | Current Selection group), click Series 1 Data Labels, click Format Selection button (Chart Tools Format tab | Current Selection group), choose settings (Format Data Labels dialog box)

Printing Multiple Worksheets

Before printing a workbook with multiple worksheets, you should consider the page setup, which defines the appearance and format of a printed worksheet. You can add a header, which appears at the top of every printed page, and a footer, which appears at the bottom of every printed page. You also can change the margins to increase or decrease the white space surrounding the printed worksheet or chart. As you modify the page setup, remember that Excel does not copy page setup characteristics to other worksheets. Thus, even if you assigned page setup characteristics to the Consolidated worksheet before copying it to each location's worksheet, the page setup characteristics would not be copied to the new worksheet. You must select all worksheets before changing the page setup.

To Change Margins and Center the Printout Horizontally

The following steps select all of the worksheets and then use the Page Setup dialog box to change the margins and center the printout of each location's worksheet horizontally.

1 Right-click the Consolidated sheet tab and then click 'Select All Sheets' on the shortcut menu.

2 Display the Page Layout tab and then click the 'Page Setup Dialog Box Launcher' (Page Layout tab | Page Setup group) to display the Page Setup dialog box.

3 If necessary, click the Page tab (Page Setup dialog box) and then click Landscape to set the page orientation to landscape.

4 Click the Margins tab. Enter .5 in both the Left box and Right box to change the left and right margins.

5 Click the Horizontally check box in the Center on page area to center the worksheet on the printed page horizontally (Figure 5–56).

6 Click the OK button (Page Setup dialog box) to close the Page Setup dialog box.

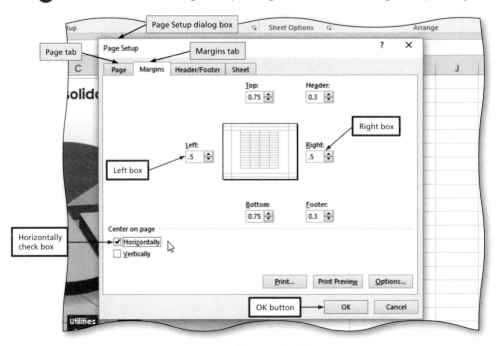

Figure 5–56

To Add a Header

The following steps use Page Layout view to change the headers on the worksheets.

1 With all of the worksheets still selected, click the Page Layout button on the status bar to display the first worksheet in Page Layout view.

2 If necessary, scroll the worksheet up until the Header area is displayed. Click the left header box and then type **Shelly Cashman** (or your name) to enter a page header in the left header box.

If requested by your instructor, add your student ID number to the left header box, below the name entry.

3 Click the center header box and then type **Twelve-Tone Concert Venues** to enter the title.

4 Click the right header box and then click the Current Date button (Header & Footer Tools Design tab | Header & Footer Elements group) to insert the current date (Figure 5–57).

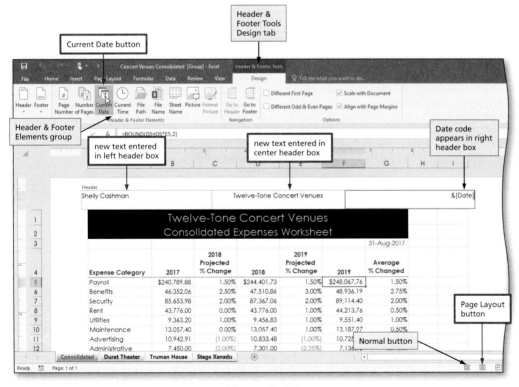

Figure 5–57

To Add a Footer

The following steps change the footers on the worksheets.

1 Scroll the workbook down to view the footer area.

2 Click the middle footer box to select it and then click the Sheet Name button (Header & Footer Tools Design tab | Header & Footer Elements group) to insert the sheet name that appears on the sheet tab as part of the footer.

❸ While in the same box, type **Page** as text in the footer. Press the SPACEBAR and then click the Page Number button (Header & Footer Tools Design tab | Header & Footer Elements group) to insert the page number in the footer (Figure 5–58).

◄ | My chart runs over into a new page. What should I do?
Q&A | Verify that your margin settings match those in Figure 5–56. If the problem remains, | change the bottom margin to .5 inches.

ⓟ Experiment

- Click the left footer box, and then click other buttons in the Header & Footer Elements group on the Header & Footer Tools Design tab. When finished, delete the contents of the left footer box.

❹ Click anywhere on the worksheet to deselect the page footer.

❺ Click the Normal button on the status bar to return to Normal view.

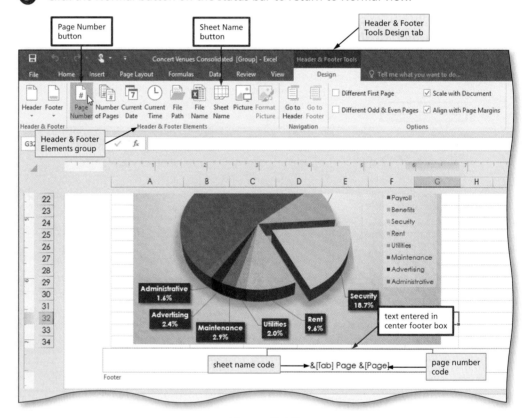

Figure 5–58

To Preview and Print All Worksheets in a Workbook

The following steps print all four worksheets in the workbook.

❶ If necessary, right-click any sheet tab and then click 'Select All Sheets' on the shortcut menu.

❷ Ready the printer.

❸ Open the Backstage view. Click the Print tab (Backstage view) to display the Print gallery.

❹ Click the Next Page and Previous Page buttons below the preview to preview the other pages.

5 Click the Print button to print the workbook as shown in Figure 5–59.

6 Right-click the selected tabs and click Ungroup Sheets on the shortcut menu to deselect the four sheets.

7 Save the workbook.

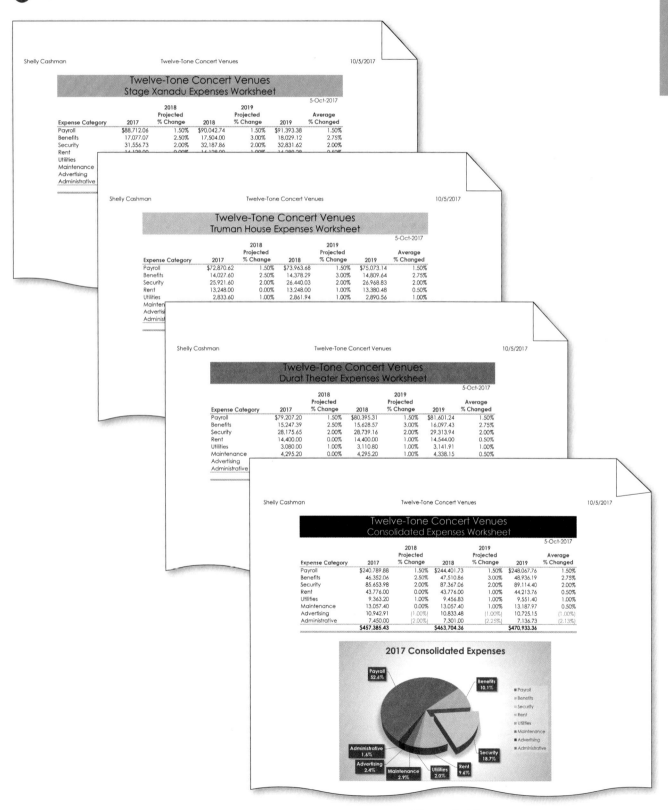

Figure 5–59

TO PRINT NONADJACENT SHEETS IN A WORKBOOK

If you wanted to print nonadjacent sheets in a workbook, you would perform the following steps.

1. With the first sheet active, hold down the CTRL key, and then click the nonadjacent sheet tab.

2. Display the Print gallery in the Backstage view and then click the Print button to print the nonadjacent worksheets.

3 SHIFT+click the first sheet tab to deselect the nonadjacent sheet.

Creating Separate Files From Worksheets

Sometimes you may want to save individual worksheets as their own separate workbooks. For example, you may want to reveal only the data in an individual worksheet to certain customers or clients, or individual departments or franchises may want a copy of their own data. Keep in mind that any 3-D references will not work in the newly saved workbook. Saving, moving, or copying a worksheet to a new workbook sometimes is called splitting or breaking out the worksheets.

To Create a Separate File from a Worksheet

The following steps create a new workbook from each location worksheet. *Why? Each individual venue would like to receive a file with its own projections for the next two years.* None of the three location worksheets contains a 3-D reference.

1

- Right-click the Durat Theater sheet tab and then click 'Move or Copy' on the shortcut menu to display the Move or Copy dialog box

- Click the To book button (Move or Copy dialog box) to display the choices (Figure 5–60).

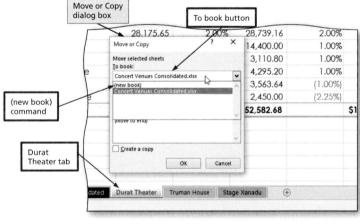

Figure 5–60

2

- Click (new book) in the list to create a new workbook.

- Click the 'Create a copy' check box to ensure it displays a check mark (Figure 5–61).

Q&A

What if I do not check the check box?
In that case, Excel would remove the worksheet from the current workbook in a move function. The Consolidated sheet no longer would display values from the moved worksheet, breaking the 3-D reference.

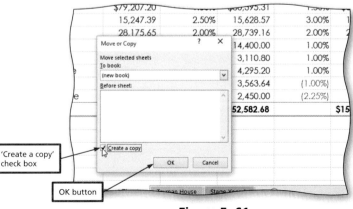

Figure 5–61

- Click the OK button to create the new workbook.

- Save the new file with the name Durat Theater Projected Expenses in the same folder as the Concert Venues Consolidated file.

4

- Repeat Steps 1 through 3 to save the Truman House and Stage Xanadu worksheets as separate workbooks in the same location. Use the new file names, Truman House Projected Expenses and Stage Xanadu Projected Expenses.

- Close each workbook, including the Concert Venues Consolidated workbook.

Consolidating Data by Linking Separate Workbooks

Earlier in this module, the data from three worksheets was consolidated into a fourth worksheet in the same workbook using 3-D references; however, sometimes the data you need is not in the same workbook. In those cases, it is necessary to consolidate data from separate workbooks, which is also referred to as **linking**. A **link** is a reference to a cell, or range of cells, in another workbook. The consolidated main workbook that contains the links to the separate workbooks is called the **dependent workbook**. The separate, individual workbooks from which you need data are called the **source workbooks**.

You can create a link, using the point mode if both the source workbook and dependent workbook(s) are open. If the source workbook is not open, you have to type the entire drive path, folder, worksheet name, and cell reference into the formula bar. This is known as an **absolute path**. You must include single quotes (') surrounding the drive, folder, workbook name, and worksheet name. You must surround the workbook name with brackets ([ ]). You must include an exclamation point (!) as a delimiter between the sheet name and cell reference. For example, you might type the following:

'C:\My Documents\[Venue Expenses.xlsx]Durat Theater'!D5

drive   folder   workbook name   worksheet   cell reference name

BTW
Consolidation
You also can consolidate data across different workbooks using the Consolidate button (Data tab | Data Tools group), rather than by entering formulas. For more information on the consolidate button, type **Consolidate** in the Search box in the Excel Help dialog box, and then click the 'Consolidate data from multiple worksheets in a single worksheet' link in the Results list.

Moving Linked Workbooks

Special care should be taken when moving linked workbooks. You should move all of the workbooks together. If you move the dependent workbook without the source workbook(s), all links become absolute—even if you used the point mode to reference them. In addition, if you happen to move the dependent workbook to another computer, without the source workbook(s), the link is broken.

Excel may offer to update or enable your links when you open the dependent workbook independent of the source workbook(s). After moving workbooks, it is best to open the source workbooks first.

BTW
Circular References
A circular reference is a formula that depends on its own value. The most common type is a formula that contains a reference to the same cell in which the formula resides.

The remainder of this module demonstrates how to search for workbooks and how to link separate workbooks, creating a 2018 Consolidated Expenses Worksheet.

What happens if I update data in one or more of the linked workbooks?

If the source workbooks are open, Excel automatically reads the data in the source workbooks and recalculates formulas in the dependent workbook. Any value changes in the open source workbooks will update in the dependent workbook.

If the source workbooks are not open, then Excel displays a security warning in a pane below the ribbon. If you click the Enable Content button in the warning pane, Excel reads the data in the source workbooks and recalculates the formulas in the dependent workbook, but it does not open the source workbooks.

To Open a Data File and Save it to a New Location

The 2018 Consolidated Expenses workbook is located in the Data Files. Please contact your instructor for information about accessing the Data Files. The file contains headings and formatting and is ready for linking. In the following steps, you will open the workbook and save it to the same location as the files created in the previous steps. For a more complete explanation of opening and saving files, see the Office and Windows module at the beginning of this book. If the Data Files are saved in the same location as your previously saved solution files, you can omit these steps.

1 Run Excel, if necessary, and open the file named 2018 Consolidated Expenses.

2 Display the Backstage view and then click the Save As tab to open the Save As dialog box.

3 Navigate to the location of your previously saved files, and then click the Save button (Save As dialog box) to save the file in a new location.

4 Close the file without exiting Excel.

To Search For and Open Workbooks

1 FORMAT WORKSHEET | 2 FILL LINEAR SERIES | 3 USE DATE & ROUND FUNCTIONS | 4 APPLY CUSTOM FORMAT CODE
5 CREATE CELL STYLES | 6 POPULATE WORKSHEETS | 7 INSERT CHART | **8 LINK WORKBOOKS**

Excel has a powerful search tool that you can use to locate workbooks (or any file) stored on the hard drive, using the Search box in the Open dialog box. ***Why search for workbooks?*** *The search tool can be used when you cannot remember exactly the name of the file or its location.* In this example, the search text, Expenses, will be used to locate the necessary workbooks. The following steps locate and open the four workbooks of interest.

1

- Display the Backstage view and then click the Open tab to display the Open gallery.

- Click Browse in the left pane and then navigate to the location of your previously saved solution files.

- Type **expenses** in the Search box as the search text.

- One at a time, CTRL+click each of the workbooks that have the word Expenses in the title (Figure 5–62).

Q&A Why did the search results include the Concert Venues Consolidated file?

The word, expenses, is in one of the cells in that file. Excel searches through both the file names and file contents.

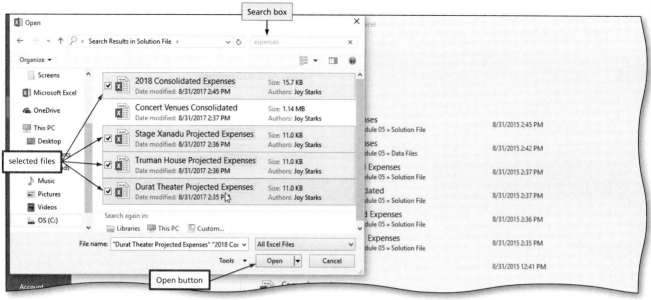

Figure 5–62

2
- Click the Open button (Open dialog box) to open the selected workbooks.

To Switch to a Different Open Workbook

1 FORMAT WORKSHEET | 2 FILL LINEAR SERIES | 3 USE DATE & ROUND FUNCTIONS | 4 APPLY CUSTOM FORMAT CODE
5 CREATE CELL STYLES | 6 POPULATE WORKSHEETS | 7 INSERT CHART | **8 LINK WORKBOOKS**

The following steps switch to a different open workbook. *Why? You may want to change quickly to another workbook to verify data.*

1
- Display the View tab and then click the Switch Windows button (View tab | Window group) to display the names of the open workbooks (Figure 5–63).

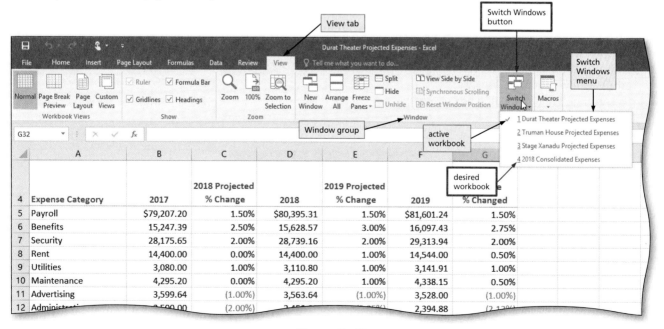

Figure 5–63

2

- Click the name of the desired workbook, in this case, 2018 Consolidated Expenses (Figure 5–64).

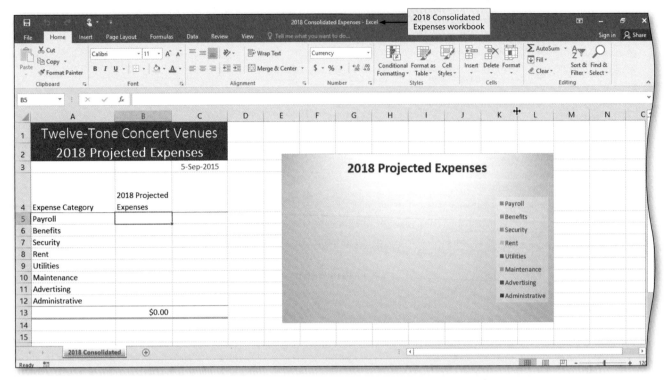

Figure 5–64

Other Ways

1. Point to Excel app button (Windows 10 taskbar), click desired live preview

To Arrange Multiple Workbooks

1 FORMAT WORKSHEET | 2 FILL LINEAR SERIES | 3 USE DATE & ROUND FUNCTIONS | 4 APPLY CUSTOM FORMAT CODE
5 CREATE CELL STYLES | 6 POPULATE WORKSHEETS | 7 INSERT CHART | **8 LINK WORKBOOKS**

The following steps arrange the multiple open workbooks on the screen so that each one appears in its own window. *Why? Viewing multiple workbooks gives you a chance to check for loosely related data and verify formats.*

1

- Click the Arrange All button (View tab | Window group) to display the Arrange Windows dialog box.

- Click Vertical (Arrange Windows dialog box) to arrange the windows vertically, and then, if necessary, click the 'Windows of active workbook' check box to clear it (Figure 5–65).

Q&A How can I arrange workbooks in the Excel window?

Multiple opened workbooks can be arranged in four ways as shown in the Arrange Windows dialog box. You can modify any of the arranged workbooks after first clicking within its window to activate it. To return to showing one workbook, double-click its title bar.

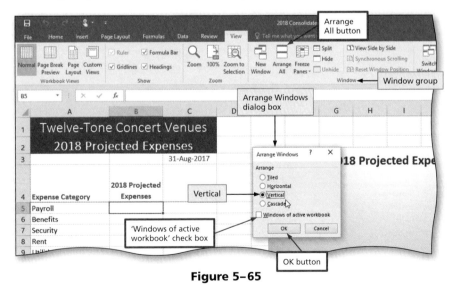

Figure 5–65

2

- Click the OK button (Arrange Windows dialog box) to display the opened workbooks arranged vertically (Figure 5–66).

Q&A Why do the windows display horizontally across the screen, yet the screens were set to Vertical?
The chosen effect determines the change on an individual window, not the group of windows. When you select Vertical, each individual window appears vertically as tall as possible. If you choose Horizontal, the windows appear as wide as possible.

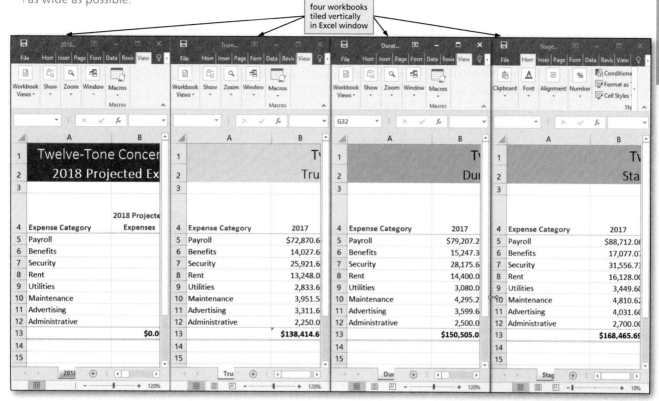

Figure 5–66

To Hide Workbooks

1 FORMAT WORKSHEET | 2 FILL LINEAR SERIES | 3 USE DATE & ROUND FUNCTIONS | 4 APPLY CUSTOM FORMAT CODE
5 CREATE CELL STYLES | 6 POPULATE WORKSHEETS | 7 INSERT CHART | **8 LINK WORKBOOKS**

The following step hides all open workbooks except one. *Why? Hiding is the best way to remove any tiling or arrangement.*

1

- Double-click the title bar of the desired workbook to hide the other opened workbooks. In this case, double-click the 2018 Consolidated Expenses title bar to maximize the window.

- Select cell B5 (Figure 5–67).

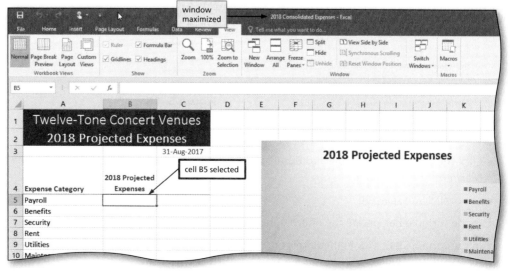

Figure 5–67

To Consolidate Data by Linking Workbooks

1 FORMAT WORKSHEET | 2 FILL LINEAR SERIES | 3 USE DATE & ROUND FUNCTIONS | 4 APPLY CUSTOM FORMAT CODE
5 CREATE CELL STYLES | 6 POPULATE WORKSHEETS | 7 INSERT CHART | **8 LINK WORKBOOKS**

The following steps consolidate the data from the three location workbooks into the 2018 Consolidated Expenses workbook. *Why link workbooks? When set up correctly, linking workbooks provides the user with a simple method of consolidating and updating linked data in the original workbook and any workbook with links to the updated data.*

- Click the Sum button (Home tab | Editing group) to begin a SUM function entry in cell B5.

- Display the View tab and then click the Switch Windows button (View tab | Window group) to display the Switch Windows menu (Figure 5–68).

Q&A

Does the workbook have to be open to link to it?
Yes, the workbook needs to be open if you want to use point mode. Otherwise, you would have to type the absolute or relative link.

Could I drill cell references in the formula?
No, drilling only applies to selected worksheets within a single workbook, not multiple open workbooks.

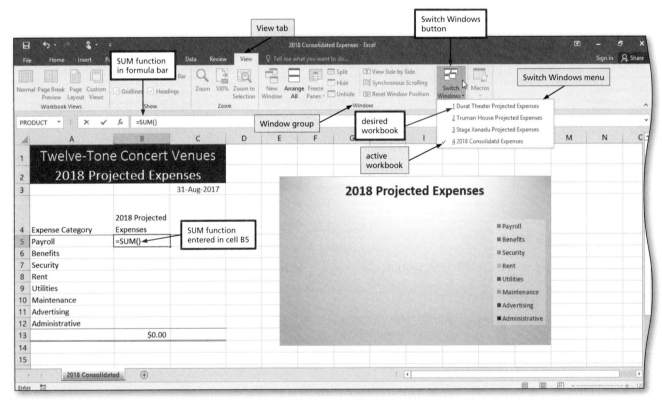

Figure 5–68

- Click the Durat Theater Projected Expenses worksheet name on the Switch Windows menu to select the workbook. Maximize the workbook.

- Click cell D5 to select it.

- In the formula bar, delete the dollar signs ($) so that the reference is not absolute.

- In the formula bar, click immediately after D5 and then press the COMMA key (Figure 5–69).

Q&A Why do I have to remove the dollar signs ($)?
Linked cell references are absolute ($B$5). You must edit the formula and change these to relative cell references because you plan to copy the SUM function in a later step. If the cell references were left as absolute, then the copied function always would refer to cell B5 in the three workbooks no matter where you copy the SUM function.

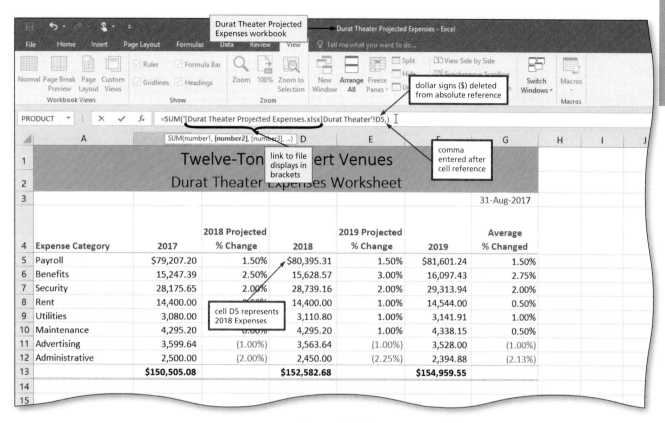

Figure 5–69

3

- Click the Switch Windows button (View tab | Window group) and then click the Truman House Projected Expenses workbook to display the workbook. Maximize the workbook

- Select cell D5 as the next argument in the SUM function.

- If necessary, click the Expand Formula Bar arrow (Formula bar) to display the entire formula. Delete the dollar signs ($) in the reference. Click immediately after D5 in the formula bar and then press the COMMA key.

- Click the Switch Windows button (View tab | Window group), and then click the Stage Xanadu Projected Expenses workbook. Maximize the workbook.

- Select cell D5 as the final argument in the SUM function.

- In the formula bar, delete the dollar signs ($) in the reference.

- Click the Enter button in the formula bar to complete the SUM function and return to the 2018 Consolidated Expenses workbook (Figure 5–70).

Q&A What if I make a mistake while editing the formula?
If you are still editing, click the Cancel button on the Formula bar, and start again. If you have entered the formula already, click the Undo button. Note that Excel formula error messages do not always indicate the exact location of the error.

Why did the pie chart start filling in?
Excel offers a live preview called **cell animation** that updates as you insert new data. The data file had the pie chart set up to reference the appropriate cells in column B.

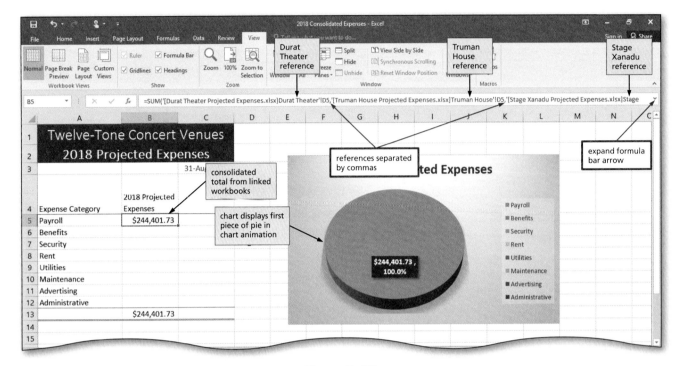

Figure 5–70

 4

- With cell B5 active in the 2018 Consolidated Expenses workbook, drag the cell's fill handle down through cell B12 to copy the formula to the range.

- Apply the comma format to cells B6:B12 to remove the floating dollar signs.

- Format the chart as necessary, exploding the Security slice, editing labels, and adding leader lines as shown in Figure 5–71.

Q&A I cannot access the Chart Elements button. What should I do?
Click the Chart Elements arrow (Chart Tools Format tab | Current Selection group) and then choose the area you wish to format. Click the Format Selection button (Chart Tools Format tab | Current Selection group). The same dialog box or task pane will open.

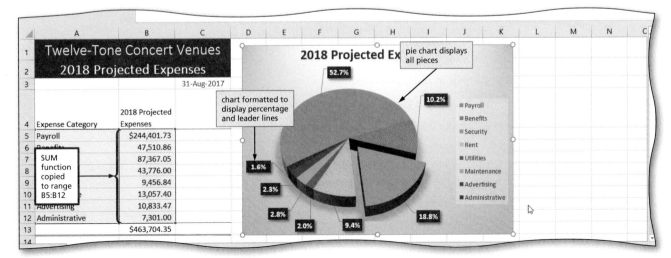

Figure 5–71

5

- Click the Save button on the Quick Access Toolbar to save the workbook.

- If Excel displays a dialog box, click the OK button (Microsoft Excel dialog box) to save the workbook.

To Close All Workbooks at One Time

To close all four workbooks at one time and exit Excel, complete the following steps.

1 Right-click the Excel app button on the taskbar and then click 'Close all windows' on the shortcut menu to close all open workbooks and exit Excel.

2 If a dialog box appears, click the Save button to save any changes made to the files since the last save.

Summary

In this module, you learned how to create and use a consolidated worksheet. After using the Fill button to create a series, you used the TODAY and ROUND functions to format data. You created a custom format code for a 4-digit year and a custom cell style that used specialized percentage styles for both positive and negative numbers. You learned how to work with multiple worksheets including several ways to copy worksheet data to a new worksheet, and drill an entry through those new worksheets. As you created the consolidated worksheet, you entered a 3-D reference and used the Paste gallery to replicate that reference. You added a pie chart to the consolidated worksheet complete with an exploded slice and formatted data labels with leader lines. You printed the multiple worksheets. Finally, you learned how to break out or split the worksheets into separate workbooks and consolidate the data to a new workbook by linking. With multiple workbooks open, you switched to different worksheets, arranged them in the Excel window, and hid them.

What decisions will you need to make when creating your next workbook to evaluate and analyze data using consolidated worksheets?

Use these guidelines as you complete the assignments in this module and create your own worksheets for evaluating and analyzing data outside of this class.

1. Determine the workbook structure.

    a) Determine how many worksheets and/or workbooks you will need.

    b) Determine the data you will need for your worksheets.

    c) Determine the layout of your data on the consolidated worksheet.

2. Create and format the consolidated worksheet.

    a) Enter titles, subtitles, and headings.

    b) Enter placeholder data, functions, and formulas.

3. Format the worksheet.

    a) Format the titles, subtitles, and headings.

    b) Format the numbers as necessary.

    c) Create and use custom format codes and styles.

4. Create the additional worksheets.

    a) Determine the best method for adding additional worksheets, based on the data in the consolidated worksheet.

b) Add the new worksheets to the workbook.

c) Add data and formatting to the new worksheets.

d) Create 3-D references where necessary to replace placeholders in the consolidated sheet with calculated values.

5. Create and use charts.

a) Select the data to chart.

b) Select a chart type for selected data.

c) Format the chart elements.

6. Consolidate workbooks.

a) Create separate workbooks from worksheets if necessary.

b) Link multiple workbooks to facilitate easy updating of data across workbooks.

Apply Your Knowledge

Reinforce the skills and apply the concepts you learned in this module.

Consolidating Payroll Worksheets

Note: To complete this assignment, you will be required to use the Data Files. Please contact your instructor for information about accessing the Data Files.

Instructions: Run Excel. Open the workbook Apply 5–1 Annual Payroll. Follow the steps below to consolidate the payroll figures for a small company. At the conclusion of the instructions, the Annual Totals sheet should resemble the worksheet shown in Figure 5–72.

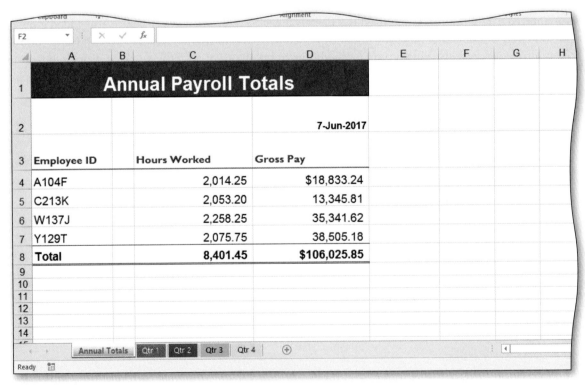

Figure 5–72

Perform the following tasks:

1. One by one, click each of the tabs and review the quarterly totals and formats. Change each tab color to match the background color of cell A1 on the corresponding worksheet.

2. Right-click the Annual Totals tab and then click Select All Sheets on the shortcut menu. Perform the following steps.

  a. Insert the date in cell D2 using the TODAY function. Create the 4-Digit Year cell style created earlier in this module. Change the font color to black, if necessary. Right-justify the new style. Apply the cell style to cell D2.

  b. Format the column headings in the range A3:D3 using Heading 3 cell style. Format the range A8:D8 with the Total cell style.

  c. Select the range C5:D7 and format it with the comma style (Home tab | Number group).

  d. Use the SUM function to total columns C and D.

  e. Switch to Page Layout view. Add a worksheet header with file name in the center of the header, and the date in the right header. Add the sheet name and page number to the center of the footer.

  f. If requested by your instructor, add a dash followed by your name to the worksheet left header.

  g. Click outside the header area. Click the 'Page Setup Dialog Box Launcher' (Page Layout tab, Page Setup group) to display the Page Setup dialog box. Center all worksheets horizontally on the page (Margins tab). Close the Page Setup dialog box. Return to Normal view.

3. Click the Qtr 1 sheet tab to select it. SHIFT+click the Q4 sheet tab to select all four quarters without the Annual Totals worksheet. Perform the following steps.

  a. Select cell D4. Use the ROUND function with two decimal places to calculate the gross pay by multiplying B4 by C4.

  b. Use the fill handle to replicate the function to cells D5:D7.

  c. Select the range, C4:C8 and format it with the comma style (Home tab | Number group).

  d. CTRL+click cells D4 and D8 to select them. Format the cells using the currency format (Format Cells dialog box), with a floating dollar sign and parentheses for negative numbers.

4. To consolidate the worksheets, click the Annual Totals sheet tab to select only the Annual Totals worksheet. To create a SUM function with a 3-D reference, select cell C4, and then click the Sum button (Home tab | Editing group). Click the Qtr 1 sheet tab to display the worksheet, and then click cell C4 to select the first portion of the argument for the SUM function. SHIFT+click the Qtr 4 sheet tab to select the ending range of the argument for the SUM function. Click the Enter button in the formula bar to enter the SUM function with the 3-D references in the selected cell.

5. On the Annual Totals sheet, copy the function in cell C4. Paste to the range C5:C7 using the Formulas button in the Paste gallery.

6. Repeat steps 4 and 5 to create a 3-D reference in cell D4 and copy it to the range D5:D7.

7. Preview the five worksheets and print them if instructed to do so.

8. Click the Annual Totals sheet tab to select the sheet. Save the workbook as Apply 5 – 1 Annual Payroll Complete. Submit the workbook as requested by your instructor.

9. ✻ What would have been the effect if you had consolidated the workbook before rounding the gross pays for each quarter? If you then rounded all of the numbers, would the answers have been the same? Why or why not?

Continued >

Extend Your Knowledge

Extend the skills you learned in this module and experiment with new skills. You may need to use Help to complete the assignment.

Creating and Editing Custom Format Codes

Note: To complete this assignment, you will be required to use the Data Files. Please contact your instructor for information about accessing the Data Files.

Instructions: Run Excel. Open the workbook Extend 5-1 Custom Format Codes, shown in Figure 5–73a. For each of the entries in the Custom Formats Codes worksheet, you will either create a new custom format code or edit the code already applied to the cell entry. When completed, the worksheet should appear as shown in Figure 5–73b. You should not change the entries in the cells, just the formatting code applied to the entries.

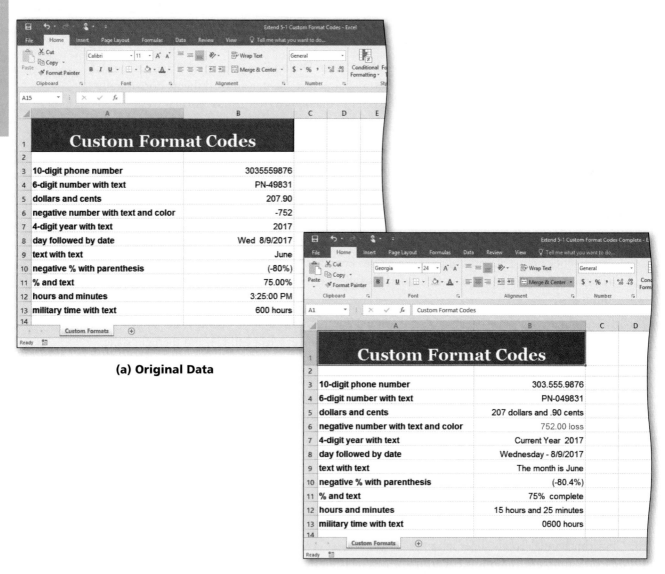

(a) Original Data

(b) Data with Custom Format codes

Figure 5–73

Perform the following tasks:

1. Save the workbook as Extend 5-1 Custom Format Codes Complete.

2. Select cell B3. Display the Format Cells dialog box, and note that the General format has been applied to this cell. Create a custom format code that will display the 10-digit number entered in cell B3 in the format shown in Figure 5 – 73b.

3. Select cell B4. Display the Format Cells dialog box, and note that a Custom Format code has been applied to this cell. Edit this custom format code to display the 6-digit number with text in cell B4 in the format shown in Figure 5 – 73b.

4. For each of the remaining cells in the range B5:B13, edit or create a custom format code to produce formatted cell contents that match Figure 5 – 73b.

5. Add a header to the worksheet that contains the file name (center) and page number (right).

6. If requested by your instructor, enter your phone number in cell B3 in place of the existing 10-digit number.

7. Save your changes to the workbook and submit the revised workbook as specified by your instructor.

8. ✳ For many of the entries, several custom formats can produce the result shown in Figure 5 – 73b. What criteria would you use to determine which custom format to use in instances where more than one format would produce the result in Figure 5 – 73b?

Expand Your World

Create a solution that uses cloud and web technologies by learning and investigating on your own from general guidance.

Consolidating and Charting Weather Data in a Workbook

Instructions: You have to gather and analyze weather data from four cities for a group environmental studies project. You decide to use Excel to create the charts and store the data.

Perform the following tasks:

1. Run Excel. Open a blank workbook, and save it with the file name, Expand 5 – 1 Weather Charts.

2. Search online for average monthly weather statistics by city and state. Choose four different locations or use ones suggested by your instructor. Copy the weather statistics, such as precipitation and temperature to your workbook. Create a separate worksheet for each city. Format the worksheets using techniques you have used in this module.

3. Create a master worksheet that consolidates all city data into a single table.

4. For each city, create a chart. Use a type indicative of your data. Use the city name as the title. Move all four charts to a single new worksheet.

5. Save the workbook and submit it as specified by your instructor.

6. ✳ How did you choose your chart type? How could you make the charts more meaningful? Would you include data labels and leader lines? What kind of chart would you use for the consolidated worksheet?

In the Labs

Design, create, modify, and/or use a workbook following the guidelines, concepts, and skills presented in this module. Labs 1 and 2, which increase in difficulty, require you to create solutions based on what you learned in the module; Lab 3 requires you to apply your creative thinking and problem-solving skills to design and implement a solution.

Lab 1: Using a Master Sheet to Create a Multiple-Sheet Workbook

Note: To complete this assignment, you will be required to use the Data Files. Please contact your instructor for information about accessing the Data Files.

Problem: You are part of a task force assessing the classroom capacities of the middle schools in your district. You have been charged with creating a master worksheet for the district and separate worksheets for each of the two middle schools. The middle school worksheets should be based on the district worksheet. Once the worksheets have been created, the middle school data can be entered into the appropriate worksheets, and the district worksheet will reflect district-wide information. The district worksheet appears as shown in Figure 5–74.

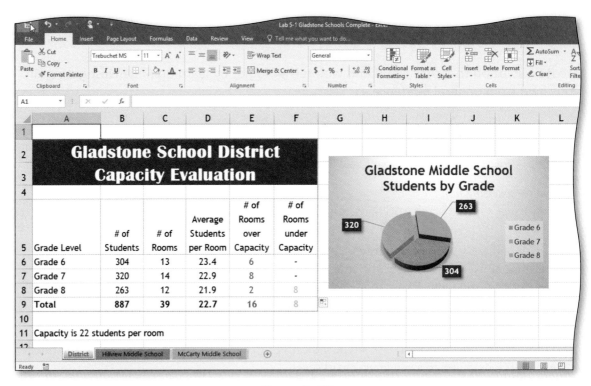

Figure 5–74

Perform the following tasks:

1. Run Excel. Open the workbook Lab 5–1 Gladstone Schools from the Data Files. Save the workbook using the file name Lab 5–1 Gladstone Schools Complete.

2. Add two worksheets to the workbook after Sheet1 and then paste the contents of Sheet1 to the two empty worksheets.

3. From left to right, rename the sheet tabs District, Hillview Middle School, and McCarty Middle School. Color the tabs as shown in Figure 5–74. On each of the school worksheets,

change the title in cell B2 to match the sheet tab name. On each worksheet, fill the range A2:F3 to match the color of its sheet tab. Enter the data in Table 5–8 into the school worksheets.

Table 5–8 Middle School Classroom Capacity Figures

School	Grade	# of Students	# of Rooms	# of Rooms over Capacity	# of Rooms under Capacity
Hillview Middle School	6	180	8	2	0
	7	188	8	8	0
	8	145	7	0	7
McCarty Middle School	6	124	5	4	0
	7	132	6	0	0
	8	118	5	2	1

4. On the two school worksheets, calculate Average Students per Room in column D and totals in row 9.

5. On the District worksheet, use the SUM function, 3-D references, and copy-and-paste capabilities of Excel to populate the ranges B6:C8 and E6:F8. First, compute the sum in cells B6:C6 and E6:F6, and then copy the ranges B6:D6 and E6:F6 through ranges B7:C8 and E7:F8 respectively. Finally, calculate average students per room for the district for each grade level, and for the district as a whole.

6. Select the range E6:E9 on the District worksheet. Select all the worksheets and then use the Format Cells dialog box to apply a custom format of [Red]#,###;;"-".

7. Select the range F6:F9 on the District worksheet. Select all the worksheets and then use the Format Cells dialog box to apply a custom format that will format all nonzero numbers similar to the format applied in Step 6 but with green for nonzero entries.

8. Use the Cell Styles button (Home tab | Styles group) to create a new cell style named My Title. Use the Format button (Styles dialog box) to create a format. Use the Font sheet (Format Cells dialog box) to select the Britannic Bold font, a font size of 22, and a white font color. Check only the Alignment and Font check boxes in the Style dialog box.

9. Select cells A2:A3 on the District worksheet. Select all the worksheets. Apply the My Title style to the cell.

10. Using Figure 5–74 as a guide, add borders to the worksheets. The borders should be the same on all worksheets.

11. Select the District worksheet. Create a 3-D pie chart using the range A6:B8. Edit the title to match Figure 5–74. Apply the Chart Style 3 to the chart.

12. Move the chart to the right of the data. Right-click the pie to display the shortcut menu and then click 'Format Data Series' to open the Format Data Series task pane. Set the Pie Explosion to 10% to offset all of the slices.

13. Select the chart area and display the Format Chart Area task pane. Set the X rotation to 100°.

14. Use the Chart Elements button to display the Data Labels submenu. Click More Options. Select only the Value and 'Show Leader Lines' options. Choose the Outside End label position and adjust the labels as necessary to display the leader lines.

15. If requested by your instructor, enter the text **Prepared by** followed by your name in the header, on the left side.

16. Save the workbook. Submit the revised workbook as specified by your instructor.

17. ☀ Did you calculate an average in cell D9 using the data in column D or the data in row 9? Explain the reasoning for your choice.

In the Labs *continued*

Lab 2: **Consolidating Data by Linking Workbooks**

Note: To complete this assignment, you will be required to use the Data Files. Please contact your instructor for information about accessing the Data Files.

Problem: The Apply Your Knowledge exercise in this module calls for consolidating the payroll data from four worksheets to a fifth worksheet in the same workbook. This exercise takes the same data, this time stored in four separate workbooks, and then consolidates the total sales and total commission by linking to a fifth workbook.

Part 1: *Perform the following tasks:*
1. If necessary, copy the following five files from the Data Files to the location at which you save your solution files. Lab 5 – 2 Commission Annual, Lab 5 – 2 Commission Quarter 1, Lab 5 – 2 Commission Quarter 2, Lab 5 – 2 Commission Quarter 3, and Lab 5 – 2 Commission Quarter 4. Run Excel. Using the Search box with the term, commission, open the five files.

2. Use the Switch Windows button (View tab | Window group) to make Lab 5 – 2 Commission Annual the active workbook. Save the workbook in the same location, using the file name, Lab 5 – 2 Commission Annual Complete.

3. Select cell C9. Click the Sum button (Home tab | Editing group) and then switch to the Lab 5 – 2 Commission Quarter 1 workbook. When the workbook is displayed, click cell D9, change the absolute cell reference $D$9 in the formula bar to the relative cell reference by deleting the dollar signs. Click immediately after D9 in the formula bar and then press the COMMA key.

4. Switch to the Lab 5 – 2 Commission Quarter 2 workbook. When the workbook is displayed, click cell D9, change the absolute cell reference $D$9 to D9, click immediately after D9 in the formula bar, and then press the COMMA key.

5. Repeat Step 3 for the Quarter 3 and Quarter 4 workbooks. After adding the Quarter 4 workbook reference, press the ENTER key rather than the COMMA key to sum the four quarter sales figures. The annual total sales for employee DK52 should be $221,500.00 as shown in Figure 5–75.

6. With the workbook Lab 5 – 2 Commission Annual Complete window active, select cell C9 and drag the fill handle through D9 to display total commission for employee DK52.

7. Select cells D9 and C9. Drag the fill handle through cell D13 to display the total sales and total commission for all employees, and as annual totals. When the Auto Fill Options button is displayed next to cell D14, click the Auto Fill Options button and then click 'Fill Without Formatting'.

8. Save and close all workbooks. Submit the solution as specified by your instructor.

Part 2:   *Perform the following tasks to update the total sales for Quarter 3 and Quarter 4.*

1. If necessary, run Excel and open Lab 5–2 Commission Quarter 3. Change the quarterly sales for employee LM33 in row 10 from 34,000.00 to 39,500.00. Save and close the workbook.

2. Open Lab 5–2 Commission Quarter 4. Change the Quarterly Sales for employee TZ98 in row 12 from 32,000.00 to 29,000.00. Save and close the workbook.

3. Open Lab 5–2 Commission Annual Complete workbook saved earlier in Part 1 of this exercise. If Excel displays a security warning, click the Enable Content button. Save the workbook using the file name, Lab 5–2 Commission Annual Complete Revised. Click the Edit Links button (Data tab | Connections group). Select each file in the Edit Links dialog box and then click the Update Values button (Edit Links dialog box) to instruct Excel to apply the current values in the four source workbooks to the consolidated workbook (Figure 5–75).

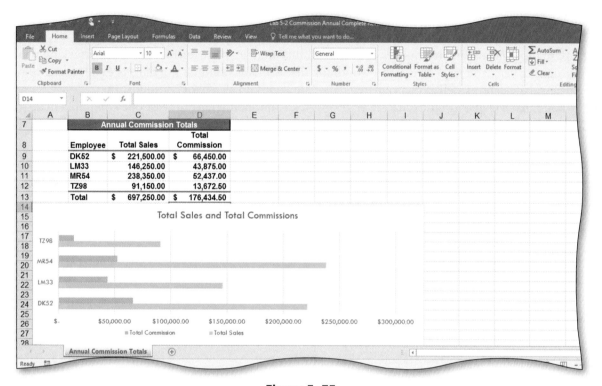

Figure 5–75

4. If requested by your instructor, enter the text **Prepared by** followed by your name in the header, on the left side.

5. Create a chart based on the data in cells you have B8:D12, using the recommended chart feature. Format the chart using techniques learned in this module and others. Move the chart below the sales and commission information. Resize the chart to a size that you think best suits the content and formatting.

6. Save the workbook. Submit the revised workbook as specified by your instructor.

7. ☀ Assess the relative strengths and weaknesses of the two approaches to building a consolidated worksheet, from four separate quarterly workbooks as used in this exercise, and using internal worksheets as you did in the Apply Your Knowledge exercise.

In the Labs *continued*

Lab 3: **Consider This: Your Turn**

Apply your creative thinking and problem-solving skills to design and implement a solution.

Tracking Fitness Data

Note: To complete this assignment, you will be required to use the Data Files. Please contact your instructor for information about accessing the Data Files.

Part 1: You have just started a new running regimen. You decide to track your progress so that you can evaluate your workouts. You decide to use Excel to track information about time, distance, and frequency of your runs. You plan to record the data for each run and to consolidate data on a weekly basis so that you can see how you are progressing from week to week.

Use the concepts and techniques presented in this module to create a workbook for tracking your running data. You want to create a workbook that contains multiple worksheets to allow you to review daily data, as well as consolidated data. Use your knowledge of consolidation to design a workbook that will allow you to analyze your progress. You should have at least one computed field, such as average miles per run, in your worksheets. You should include at least one chart presenting fitness data. Submit your assignment in the format specified by the instructor.

Part 2: ✳ This exercise had you create a chart presenting fitness data. List two other ways you could chart the data in Excel. What are the strengths and weaknesses of each of the three chart types for the data you are presenting?

6 Creating, Sorting, and Querying a Table

Objectives

You will have mastered the material in this module when you can:

- Create and manipulate a table
- Delete duplicate records
- Add calculated columns to a table with structured references
- Use the VLOOKUP function to look up a value in a table
- Use icon sets with conditional formatting
- Insert a total row
- Sort a table on one field or multiple fields
- Sort, query, and search a table using AutoFilter

- Remove filters
- Create criteria and extract ranges
- Apply database and statistical functions
- Use the MATCH and INDEX functions to find a value in a table
- Display automatic subtotals
- Use outline features to group, hide, and unhide data
- Create a treemap chart

Introduction

A **table**, also called a **database**, is an organized collection of data. For example, a list of friends, a group of students registered for a class, an inventory list, a club membership roster, or an instructor's grade book — all can be arranged as tables in a worksheet. In these cases, the data related to each person or item is called a **record**, and the individual data items that make up a record are called **fields**. For example, in a table of clients, each client would have a separate record; each record might include several fields, such as name, address, phone number, current balance, billing rate, and status. A record also can include fields that contain references, formulas, and functions.

You can use a worksheet's row-and-column structure to organize and store a table. Each row of a worksheet can store a record, and each column can store one field for each record. Additionally, a row of column headings at the top of the worksheet can store field names that identify each field.

After you enter a table onto a worksheet, you can use Excel to (1) add and delete records, (2) change the values of fields in records, (3) sort the records so that Excel presents them in a different order, (4) determine subtotals for numeric fields, (5) display records that meet comparison criteria, and (6) analyze data using database functions. This module illustrates all six of these table capabilities.

Project — Coffee Craft Daily Services

The project in this module follows proper design guidelines and uses Excel to create the worksheet shown in Figures 6–1a and 6–1b, and the chart (Figure 6–1c). The Coffee Craft company repairs industrial coffee makers, brewers, and espresso machines for restaurants, hotels, coffee shops, and QSRs (Quick Service Restaurants). The company has asked for a workbook that lists their daily service calls and then summarizes key information about technicians and their performance. The data in the workbook should be easy to summarize, sort, edit, and query.

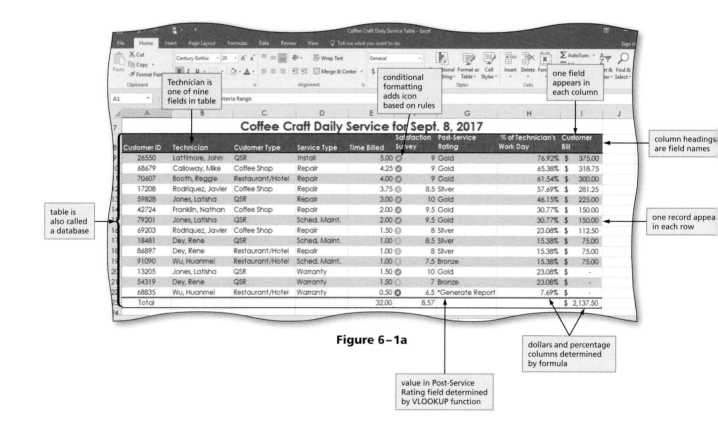

Figure 6–1a

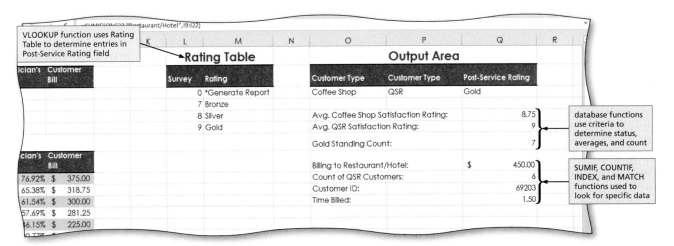

Figure 6–1b

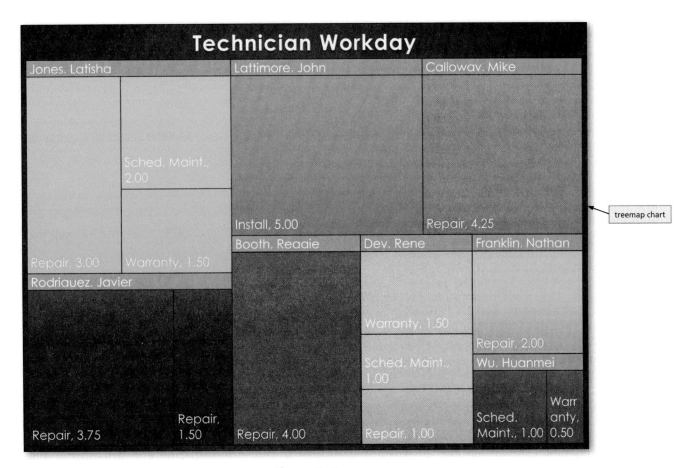

Figure 6–1c

Figure 6–2 shows a sample requirements document for the Coffee Craft Daily Service Table. It includes the needs, source of data, calculations, special requirements, and other facts about its development.

Worksheet Title	Coffee Craft Daily Services Table
Needs	• A worksheet table that lists daily service calls with the customer ID, technician, customer type, service type, and time billed. • The worksheet also should assign a Gold, Silver, or Bronze standing based on the Satisfaction Survey number. Low ratings should present a message, *Generate Report. • The worksheet should calculate the % of Technician's Work Day and also the Customer Bill. • The worksheet should be easy for management to sort, search, filter, and total.
Source of Data	Data supplied by the business owner includes the information in bullet 1 above (see Table 6-1). Remaining numbers in the worksheet are based on calculations.

Calculations	The following calculations are needed:
	• the % of Technician's Work Day = Time billed/6.5
	• Customer Bill = Time Billed * 75, only for non-warranty work (IF function)
	• Standing that is determined as follows:
	  ○ Gold = a high score of 9 to 10
	  ○ Silver = an adequate score of 8 to 8.99
	  ○ Bronze = a low score of 7 to 7.99
	  ○ *Generate Report = an unacceptable score below 7
	• Average Coffee Shop Satisfaction Rating = DAVERAGE function
	• Average QSR Satisfaction Rating = DAVERAGE function
	• Gold Standing Count = DCOUNT function
	• Total of bills to Restaurants/Hotels = SUMIF function
	• Count of QSR customers = COUNTIF function
	• Look up Time Billed by Customer ID

Other Requirements	• Provide a way to search, sort, and select data based on certain criteria. • Provide an area to ascertain statistics about technicians, such as averages, counts, and totals based on specific factors. • A criteria area will be created above the table to store criteria for use in a query. An extract area will be created below the table to display records that meet the criteria. • Provide a hierarchical and visual chart to display all of the technicians and their work day.

Figure 6–2

Table 6–1 describes the field names, columns, types of data, and descriptions that you can refer to when creating the table.

Table 6–1 Column Information for Coffee Craft Daily Service Table			
Column Headings (Field Names)	Column in Worksheet	Type of Data	Description
Customer ID	A	Numeric	6-digit whole number, previously assigned by service provider
Technician	B	Text	Last name, first name
Customer Type	C	Text	Coffee Shop, Restaurant/Hotel, or QSR
Service Type	D	Text	Repair, Sched. Maint., or Warranty
Time Billed	E	Numeric	Time measured in decimal hours with two decimal places
Satisfaction Survey	F	Numeric	Decimal number with one decimal place, calculated by service provider
Post-Service Rating	G	Text calculation (VLOOKUP function)	Standing of Gold, Silver, Bronze, or *Generate Report based on Satisfaction Survey
% of Technician's Work Day	H	Percentage calculation (Time Billed / 6.5)	Billed time displayed as a percentage of 6.5 hour work day (8 hours minus allowance for travel)
Customer Bill	I	Numeric calculation (Time Billed * 75)	Customer billing at $75 per hour for non-warranty work

Using a sketch of the worksheet can help you visualize its design. The sketch of the service call table consists of the title, column headings, location of data values, and an idea of the desired formatting (Figure 6–3a). (The sketch does not show the criteria area above the table and the extract area below the table.) The general layout of the rating table, output area, and required statistics and query are shown in Figure 6–3b.

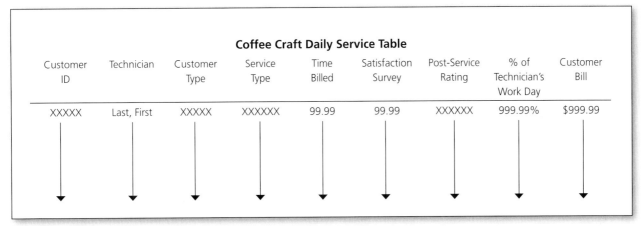

Coffee Craft Daily Service Table

Customer ID	Technician	Customer Type	Service Type	Time Billed	Satisfaction Survey	Post-Service Rating	% of Technician's Work Day	Customer Bill
XXXXX	Last, First	XXXXX	XXXXXX	99.99	99.99	XXXXXX	999.99%	$999.99

(a) Data Table

Rating Table		Output Area		
Survey	**Rating**	**Customer Type**	**Customer Type**	**Post-Service Rating**
0	*Generate Report	Coffee Shop	QSR	Gold
7	Bronze			
8	Silver	Average Coffee Shop Satisfaction Rating:		99.99
9	Gold	Average QSR Satisfaction Rating:		99.99
		Gold Standing Count:		99
		Billing to Restaurant/Hotel:		$ 999,999
		Count of QSR Customers:		99
		Customer ID:		99999
		Time Billed:		99.99

(b) Rating Table and Output Area
Figure 6–3

With a good understanding of the requirements document, a clear list of the necessary decisions, and a sketch of the worksheet, the next step is to use Excel to create the worksheet.

The following roadmap identifies general activities you will perform as you progress through this module:

1. CREATE and format a TABLE.
2. Use LOOKUP TABLES in the worksheet.
3. Insert CALCULATED FIELDS using structured references.

4. Apply CONDITIONAL FORMATTING and icon sets.

5. SORT TABLES.

6. QUERY a TABLE.

7. Extract records with CRITERIA RANGES.

8. Use DATABASE functions and CONDITIONAL FUNCTIONS.

9. Display automatic SUBTOTALS, outline, and TREEMAP chart.

To Open and Save a File

The following steps open a file and save it with a new name. To complete these steps, you will be required to use the Data Files. Please contact your instructor for information about accessing the Data Files.

1 Run Excel and open the Data File named Coffee Craft Daily Service Data.

2 If the Excel window is not maximized, click the Maximize button on its title bar to maximize the window.

3 Click the Themes button (Page Layout tab | Themes group) and then click the Vapor Trail theme.

4 Save the workbook on your hard drive, OneDrive, or other storage location using Coffee Craft Daily Service Table as the file name.

5 If necessary, click cell A1 (Figure 6–4).

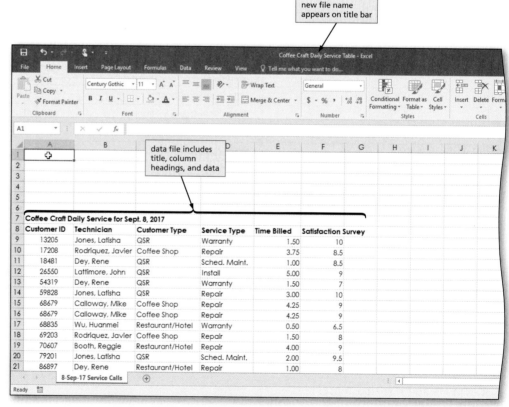

Figure 6–4

Table Guidelines

When you create a table in Excel, you should follow some basic guidelines, as listed in Table 6–2.

Table 6–2 Guidelines for Creating a Table in Excel
Table Size and Workbook Location
1. Do not enter more than one table per worksheet.
2. Maintain at least one blank row between a table and other worksheet entries.
3. A table can have a maximum of 16,384 fields and 1,048,576 records on a worksheet.
Column Headings (Field Names)
1. Place column headings (field names) in the first row of the table.
2. Do not use blank rows or rows with repeating characters, such as dashes or underscores, to separate the column headings (field names) from the data.
3. Apply a different format to the column headings than to the data. For example, bold the column headings and format the data below the column headings using a regular style. Most table styles follow these guidelines.
4. Column headings (field names) can be up to 32,767 characters in length. The column headings should be meaningful.
Contents of Table
1. Each cell in any given column should have similar data. For example, Customer Type entries should use the company standard wording for the types of customers, such as QSR for Quick Service Restaurant.
2. Format the data to improve readability, but do not vary the format of the data within the cells of a column.

BTW
The Ribbon and Screen Resolution
Excel may change how the groups and buttons within the groups appear on the ribbon, depending on the computer's screen resolution. Thus, your ribbon may look different from the ones in this book if you are using a screen resolution other than 1366 x 768.

Creating a Table

When you create a table in Excel, you can manage and analyze the data in that table, independently from the rest of the data on the worksheet. The advantages of creating a table include:

- Automatic expansion of the table to accommodate data
- Header row remains visible while scrolling
- Automatic reformatting
- Integrated filter and sort functionality
- Automatic fill and calculated fields
- Easy access to structured references
- Automatic adjustment of associated charts and ranges

BTW
Touch Screen Differences
The Office and Windows interfaces may vary if you are using a touch screen. For this reason, you might notice that the function or appearance of your touch screen differs slightly from this module's presentation.

How should you format a table?
Format a table so that the records are distinguished easily. The data in the worksheet should start several rows from the top in order to leave room for a criteria area. Using banded rows (background colors varying between rows) to format the table provides greater readability. Some columns require calculations that can be created by using the column headings or cell references within formulas. In some cases, calculated columns in tables require looking up values outside of the table. You can use Excel's special lookup functions in such cases. Totals also can be added to the table for averages, sums, and other types of calculations.

CONSIDER THIS

To Format a Range as a Table

The easiest way to create a table is to apply a table style. *Why? Excel automatically creates the table when applying a table style to a range.* You can create a table before or after entering column headings and data. The following steps format a range as a table.

- Zoom to 120% and then scroll down until cell A7 is at the top of the workspace.

- Select the range A8:F22.

- Click the 'Format as Table' button (Home tab | Styles group) to display the Format as Table gallery (Figure 6–5).

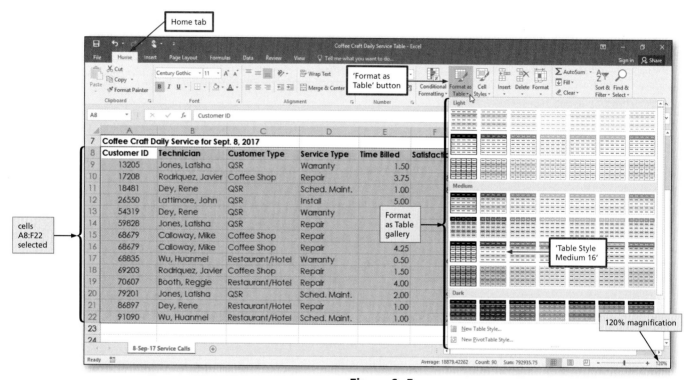

Figure 6–5

- Click 'Table Style Medium 16' in the Format as Table gallery to display the Format As Table dialog box.

- If necessary, click the 'My table has headers' check box to select the option to format the table with headers (Figure 6–6).

Q&A What is a header?
A table header is the column heading that appears above the data. In this case, you want to create the table and include the column headings.

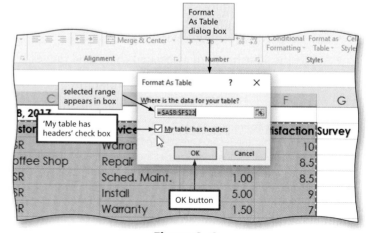

Figure 6–6

❸

- Click the OK button (Format As Table dialog box) to create a table from the selected range.

- Click outside the table to deselect it (Figure 6–7).

Q&A

◁ What are the buttons with the arrows beside the column headings?

The buttons are part of the AutoFilter that you will learn about later in the module.

data range becomes table

each column heading displays filter button

| H13 | ▼ | : | × | ✓ | *fx* | | | |

◢	A	B	C	D	E	F
7	**Coffee Craft Daily Service for Sept. 8, 2017**					
8	**Customer ID** 🔽	**Technician** 🔽	**Customer Type** 🔽	**Service Type** 🔽	**Time Billed** 🔽	**Satisfaction Surv**
9	13205	Jones, Latisha	QSR	Warranty	1.50	
10	17208	Rodriquez, Javier	Coffee Shop	Repair	3.75	
11	18481	Dey, Rene	QSR	Sched. Maint.	1.00	
12	26550	Lattimore, John	QSR	Install	5.00	
13	54319	Dey, Rene	QSR	Warranty	1.50	
14	59828	Jones, Latisha	QSR	Repair	3.00	
15	68679	Calloway, Mike	Coffee Shop	Repair	4.25	
16	68679	Calloway, Mike	Coffee Shop	Repair	4.25	
17	68835	Wu, Huanmei	Restaurant/Hotel	Warranty	0.50	
18	69203	Rodriquez, Javier	Coffee Shop	Repair	1.50	
19	70607	Booth, Reggie	Restaurant/Hotel	Repair	4.00	
20	79201	Jones, Latisha	QSR	Sched. Maint.	2.00	
21	86897	Dey, Rene	Restaurant/Hotel	Repair	1.00	
22	91090	Wu, Huanmei	Restaurant/Hotel	Sched. Maint.	1.00	

Figure 6–7

Other Ways

1. Select range, click Table button (Insert tab | Tables group), click OK button, choose table style (Table Tools Design tab | Table Styles group)

To Wrap Text

The following steps wrap the text in cell F8 to make the heading easier to read.

❶ Change the width of column F to 11.

❷ Select cell F8, and then click the Wrap Text button (Home tab | Alignment group) (Figure 6–8).

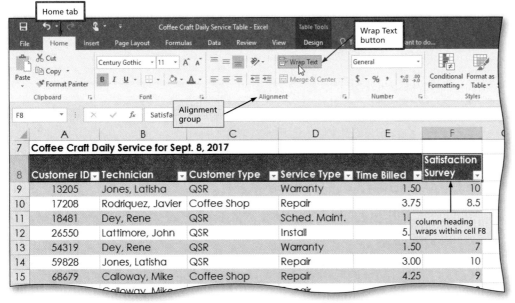

Home tab

Wrap Text button

Alignment group

◢	A	B	C	D	E	F	C
7	**Coffee Craft Daily Service for Sept. 8, 2017**						
8	**Customer ID** 🔽	**Technician** 🔽	**Customer Type** 🔽	**Service Type** 🔽	**Time Billed** 🔽	**Satisfaction Survey** 🔽	
9	13205	Jones, Latisha	QSR	Warranty	1.50	10	
10	17208	Rodriquez, Javier	Coffee Shop	Repair	3.75	8.5	
11	18481	Dey, Rene	QSR	Sched. Maint.	1.		
12	26550	Lattimore, John	QSR	Install	5.		
13	54319	Dey, Rene	QSR	Warranty	1.50	7	
14	59828	Jones, Latisha	QSR	Repair	3.00	10	
15	68679	Calloway, Mike	Coffee Shop	Repair	4.25	9	

column heading wraps within cell F8

Figure 6–8

BTW

Ranges to Tables

If you select a range before clicking the 'Format as Table' button (Home tab | Styles group), Excel will fill in the range for you in the Format As Table dialog box.

BTW

Banded Columns

Banded columns offer alternating colors every other column. You also can include a different color for the first and/or last column in a table. The style that you choose for a table must have these colors defined in the style. The style used in this module does not include special formatting for banded columns or the first and last columns.

To Name the Table

1 CREATE TABLE | 2 LOOKUP TABLES | 3 CALCULATED FIELDS | 4 CONDITIONAL FORMATTING | 5 SORT TABLES
6 QUERY TABLES | 7 CRITERIA RANGES | 8 DATABASE & CONDITIONAL FUNCTIONS | 9 SUBTOTALS & TREEMAP

The following step gives a name to the table. *Why? Referring to the table by name rather than by range reference will save time.*

- Click anywhere in the table and then display the Table Tools Design tab.

- Click the Table Name text box (Table Tools Design tab | Properties group).

- Type **Service_Calls** and then press the ENTER key to name the table (Figure 6–9).

Q&A

Why should I use an underscore in the table name?

Excel does not allow spaces in table names. Excel also requires that table names begin with a letter or underscore.

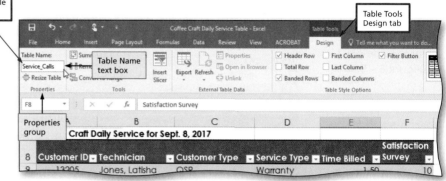

Figure 6–9

Other Ways

1. Select range, click Name Manager button (Formulas tab | Defined Names group), click New button (Name Manager dialog box), enter name (New Name dialog box), click OK button, click Close button

---

To Remove Duplicates

1 CREATE TABLE | 2 LOOKUP TABLES | 3 CALCULATED FIELDS | 4 CONDITIONAL FORMATTING | 5 SORT TABLES
6 QUERY TABLES | 7 CRITERIA RANGES | 8 DATABASE & CONDITIONAL FUNCTIONS | 9 SUBTOTALS & TREEMAP

Duplicate entries may appear in tables. *Why? Duplicates sometimes happen when data is entered incorrectly, by more than one person, or from more than one source.* The following steps remove duplicate records in the table. In this particular table, the service call for customer 68679 was entered twice by mistake.

- Click anywhere in the table.

- Click the Remove Duplicates button (Table Tools Design tab | Tools group) to display the Remove Duplicates dialog box.

- Click the Select All button (Remove Duplicates dialog box) to select all columns (Figure 6–10).

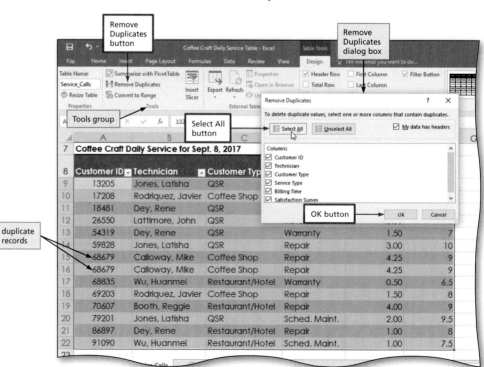

Figure 6–10

2

- Click the OK button (Remove Duplicates dialog box) to remove duplicate records from the table (Figure 6–11).

Q&A
Did Excel reformat the table?
Yes. The Banded Rows check box (Table Tools Design tab | Table Style Options group) is checked automatically when you selected the table format. **Row banding** causes

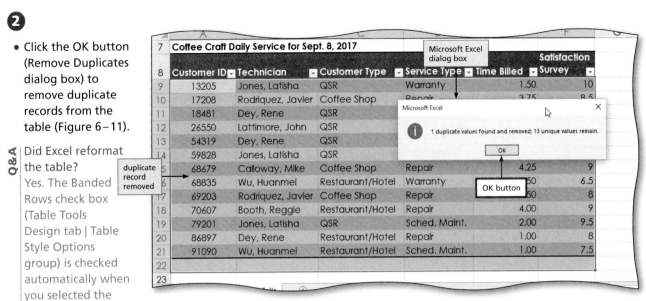

adjacent rows to have different formatting; each row in the table is distinguishable from surrounding rows.

Figure 6–11

3

- Click the OK button (Microsoft Excel dialog box) to finish the process.

 Experiment

- Examine the table to verify removal of the duplicate record for customer 68679.

Other Ways

1. Select range, click Remove Duplicates button (Data tab | Data Tools group)

To Enter a New Record into a Table

1 CREATE TABLE | 2 LOOKUP TABLES | 3 CALCULATED FIELDS | 4 CONDITIONAL FORMATTING | 5 SORT TABLES
6 QUERY TABLES | 7 CRITERIA RANGES | 8 DATABASE & CONDITIONAL FUNCTIONS | 9 SUBTOTALS & TREEMAP

The following step enters a new service call record into the table. You will insert the information just below the table. **Why?** *Data entered in rows or columns adjacent to the table becomes part of the table.* Excel will format the new table data automatically.

1

- Select cell A22.

- Type the new entries below.

 Experiment

- As you enter the data, notice that Excel tries to complete your fields based on previous common entries.

A22	42724
B22	Franklin, Nathan
C22	Coffee Shop
D22	Repair
E22	2.00
F22	9.5

If requested by your instructor, enter your name as the technician in cell B22.

row 22 displays new data

- If necessary, click outside the table to deselect it (Figure 6–12).

12	26550			Install		9
13	54319	Dey, Rene	QSR	Warranty	1.50	7
14	59828	Jones, Latisha	QSR	Repair	3.00	10
15	68679	Calloway, Mike	Coffee Shop	Repair	4.25	9
16	68835	Wu, Huanmei	Restaurant/Hotel	Warranty	0.50	6.5
17	69203	Rodriquez, Javier	Coffee Shop	Repair	1.50	8
18	70607	Booth, Reggie	Restaurant/Hotel	Repair	4.00	9
19	79201	Jones, Latisha	QSR	Sched. Maint.	2.00	9.5
20	86897	Dey, Rene	Restaurant/Hotel	Repair	1.00	8
21	91090	Wu, Huanmei	Restaurant/Hotel	Sched. Maint.	1.00	7.5
22	42724	Franklin, Nathan	Coffee Shop	Repair	2.00	9.5
23						

Figure 6–12

Other Ways

1. Drag table sizing handle down to add new row, enter data

To Add New Columns to the Table

When you add a new column heading in a column adjacent to the current column headings in the table, Excel automatically adds the adjacent column to the table's range and copies the font format of the existing table heading to the new column heading. The following steps insert column headings for three new columns in the table.

1 Change the column width of column G to 16.00. Click cell G8. Type **Post-Service Rating** and then click the Enter button to enter the heading. Click the Wrap Text button (Home tab | Alignment group) to wrap the text.

2 Change the column width of column H to 16.50. Click cell H8. Type **% of Technician's Work Day** and then click the Enter button to enter the heading. Wrap the text in the cell.

3 Change the column width of column I to 11.00. Click cell I8. Type **Customer Bill** and then click the Enter button to enter the heading. Wrap the text in the cell (Figure 6–13).

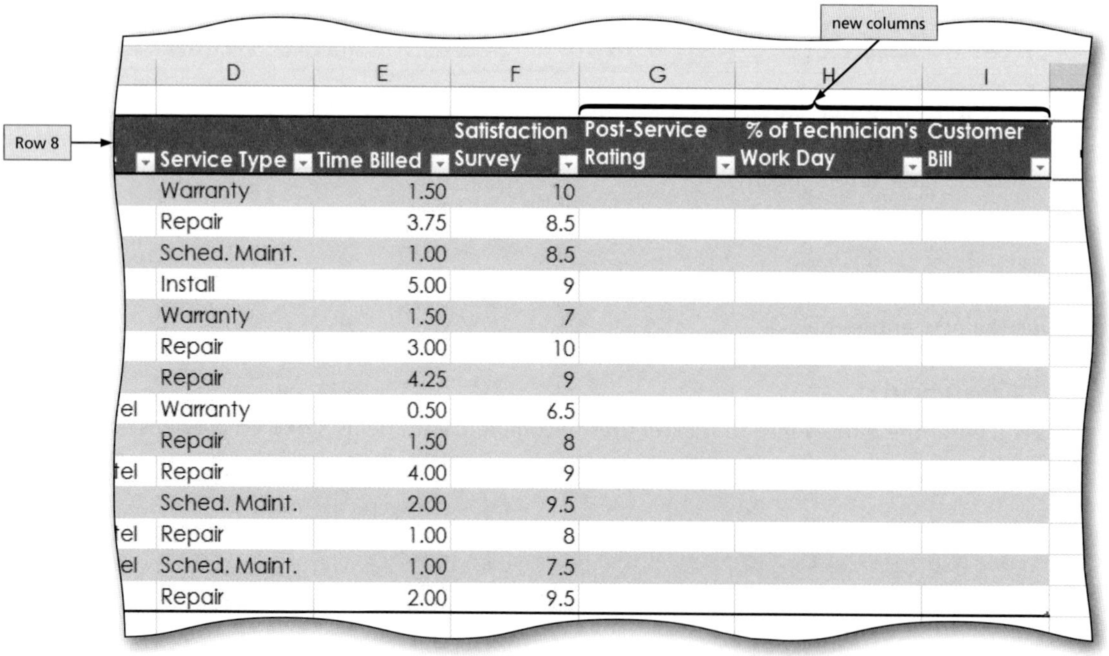

new columns

Row 8

	D	E	F	G	H	I
	Service Type	Time Billed	Satisfaction Survey	Post-Service Rating	% of Technician's Work Day	Customer Bill
	Warranty	1.50	10			
	Repair	3.75	8.5			
	Sched. Maint.	1.00	8.5			
	Install	5.00	9			
	Warranty	1.50	7			
	Repair	3.00	10			
	Repair	4.25	9			
el	Warranty	0.50	6.5			
	Repair	1.50	8			
tel	Repair	4.00	9			
	Sched. Maint.	2.00	9.5			
tel	Repair	1.00	8			
el	Sched. Maint.	1.00	7.5			
	Repair	2.00	9.5			

Figure 6–13

To Center Across Selection

The following steps center the title in cell A7 across a selection using the Format Cells dialog box. In earlier modules, recall you used the 'Merge & Center' button (Home tab | Alignment group) to center text across a range. *Why? This earlier technique centered the title, but it removed access to individual cells, because the cells were merged.* The Center Across Selection format centers text across multiple cells but does not merge the selected cell range into one cell.

- Select the range A7:I7. Right-click the selected range to display the shortcut menu (Figure 6–14).

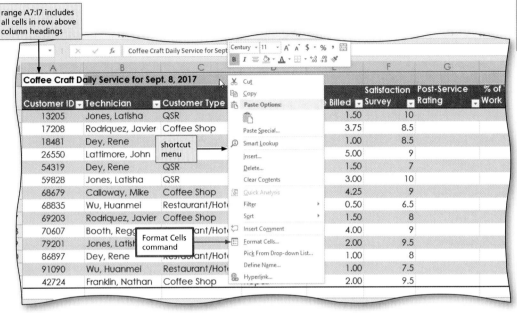

Figure 6–14

- Click Format Cells on the shortcut menu to display the Format Cells dialog box.

- Click the Alignment tab (Format Cells dialog box) and then click the Horizontal button in the Text alignment area to display a list of horizontal alignments (Figure 6–15).

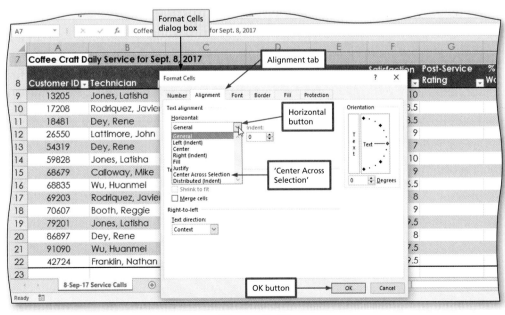

Figure 6–15

- Click 'Center Across Selection' in the Horizontal list (Format Cells dialog box) to select the option to center the title across the selection.

- Click the OK button (Format Cells dialog box) to apply the settings.

- Click the Cell Styles button (Home tab | Styles group), and then apply the Title style to cell A7. Bold the cell, and then change the font size to 20 (Figure 6–16).

Figure 6–16

④

- Click the Save button on the Quick Access Toolbar to save the workbook again.

Using a Lookup Table

The entries in the Satisfaction Survey column give the user a numerical evaluation of the customer feedback for each technician. Some people, however, prefer simple ratings or letter grades, which, when used properly, group the technicians in the same way sports teams award their medals or instructors group student grades. Excel contains functions that allow you to assign such rankings based on a range of values that are stored in a separate area on the worksheet. This range is sometimes called a **table array** or a **lookup table**.

The two most widely used lookup functions are HLOOKUP and VLOOKUP. Both functions find a value in a lookup table and return a corresponding value from the table to the cell containing the function. The **HLOOKUP function** is used when the table direction for a field of data is horizontal, or across the worksheet. The **VLOOKUP function** is used when a table direction is vertical, or down the worksheet. The VLOOKUP function is used more often because most tables are vertical, as is the table in this module.

The Rating column in this project rates each technician with a value of gold, silver, or bronze for the service call. As shown in Table 6–3, any technician receiving an average score of 9 or more receives a gold rating. A technician with a score of 8 or more receives

BTW

Other Database Functions

For a complete list of the database functions available for use with a table, click the Insert Function button in the formula bar. When Excel displays the Insert Function dialog box, select Database in the 'Or select a category' list. The 'Select a function' box displays the database functions. If you click a database function name, Excel displays a description of the function.

Table 6–3 How the Ratings Are Determined	
Survey	**Rating**
0 to 6.99	*Generate Report
7 to 7.99	Bronze
8 to 8.99	Silver
9 and higher	Gold

a silver rating. A technician with a score of 7 or more receives a bronze rating. An average score of less than 7 will cause the table to relay a message that the office should generate a report and get back in touch with the customer to help remedy the situation.

To facilitate the display of each technician's rating, you will use the VLOOKUP function. The general form of the VLOOKUP function is

=VLOOKUP(lookup_value, table_array, col_index_num)

The three arguments of the VLOOKUP function represent the data that the function needs to do its job. The first argument is the **lookup value**, which is the data, or the location of the data, that you wish to look up. In the case of the service call table, that data is located in column F, the Satisfaction Survey. You only need to enter the first occurrence of the data, cell F9; because it is a relative reference in a table, Excel will fill in the rest.

The second argument is the location of the lookup table (represented as table_array in the syntax of the function). The location is a contiguous set of rows and columns with the numeric rating in the left column and the corresponding rating, letter grade, or text value in the other columns. The left column values in a table array are called **table arguments**, and they must be in sequence from lowest to highest. In this project, the table arguments are 0, 7, 8, and 9 — the lowest value in each rating. One or more columns to the right of the table arguments are the return values. The **return value** is the answer you want to appear as a result of the VLOOKUP function. In the service call table, the return value will be *Generate Report, Bronze, Silver, or Gold.

The third argument of the function is the **column index number** (represented as col_index_num in the syntax of the function), which represents the column location of the return value within the table array. In this project, that is column 2.

A fourth, optional argument allows you to enter a logical value that specifies whether you want VLOOKUP to find an exact match or an approximate match.

To Create a Table Array Area

Before using the VLOOKUP function, you must create the table array. The following steps create a table array in the range L1:M7.

1 Change the width of column M to 16.5.

2 Click cell L1. Type `Rating Table` as the table array title and then click the Enter button on the formula bar.

3 Apply the Title style and bold formatting to cell L1.

4 Select the range L1:M1. Right-click the selection and then click Format Cells on the shortcut menu to display the Format Cells dialog box. On the Alignment tab (Format Cells dialog box), click the Horizontal button, and then click 'Center Across Selection'. Click the OK button to apply the settings.

5 In cell L2, type `Survey` to enter the column heading.

6 In cell M2, type `Rating` to enter the column heading.

7 Select cell I8. Click the Format Painter button (Home tab | Clipboard group) and then drag through cells L2:M2 to copy the format of the selected cell to the column headings.

8 Enter the data shown below (Figure 6–17).

Cell	Data	Cell	Data
L3	0	M3	*Generate Report
L4	7	M4	Bronze
L5	8	M5	Silver
L6	9	M6	Gold

Q&A

Why do the table arguments contain single digits instead of a range?
You only have to enter the least value for each argument. Excel will evaluate all values in the range.

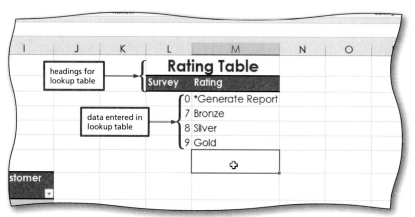

Figure 6–17

To Use the VLOOKUP Function

1 CREATE TABLE | 2 LOOKUP TABLES | 3 CALCULATED FIELDS | 4 CONDITIONAL FORMATTING | 5 SORT TABLES
6 QUERY TABLES | 7 CRITERIA RANGES | 8 DATABASE & CONDITIONAL FUNCTIONS | 9 SUBTOTALS & TREEMAP

The following steps use the VLOOKUP function and the table array to determine the Post-Service Rating for each technician. *Why? Using the VLOOKUP function with a table allows Excel to display the ratings, rather than the user typing them in individually.*

1

- Click cell G9. Type
  `=vlookup(f9,`
  `$L$3:$M$6,2)`
  as the cell entry
  (Figure 6–18).

Q&A

Why should I use absolute cell references in the function?
You need to use absolute cell references, indicated by the dollar signs, so that Excel will not adjust the table array location when it creates the calculated column in the next step. If Excel adjusted the cell references, you would see unexpected results in column G.

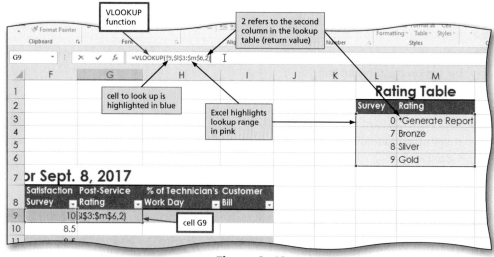

Figure 6–18

• Click the Enter button to create a calculated column for the selected field, the Post-Service Rating field in this case.

• Scroll the worksheet to show the completed table (Figure 6–19).

Q&A

What happens when you click the Enter button?
Because cell G9 is the first record in a table, Excel continues the calculated column by replicating the VLOOKUP function through row 22.

How does the VLOOKUP function determine the ratings?
The LOOKUP function is not searching for a table argument that matches the lookup value exactly. The VLOOKUP function begins the search at the top of the table and works downward. As soon as it finds the first table argument greater than the lookup value, it stops, and the function returns the previous row's corresponding value from column M.

	Service Type	Time Billed	Satisfaction Survey	Post-Service Rating	% of Technician's Cu... Work Day	Bill
	Warranty	1.50	10	Gold		
	Repair	3.75	8.5	Silver		
	Sched. Maint.	1.00	8.5	Silver		
	Install	5.00	9	Gold		
	Warranty	1.50	7	Bronze		
	Repair	3.00	10	Gold		
	Repair	4.25	9	Gold		
el	Warranty	0.50	6.5	*Generate Report		
	Repair	1.50	8	Silver		
tel	Repair	4.00	9	Gold		
	Sched. Maint.	2.00	9.5	Gold		
tel	Repair	1.00	8	Silver		
tel	Sched. Maint.	1.00	7.5	Bronze		
	Repair	2.00	9.5	Gold		

Excel fills in column with data from lookup table

Figure 6–19

Other Ways

1. Click Insert Function box in formula bar, click 'Or select a category' button, click 'Lookup & Reference', click VLOOKUP in 'Select a function' list, enter arguments

2. Click 'Lookup & Reference' button (Formulas tab | Function Library group), click VLOOKUP, enter arguments

Adding Calculated Fields to the Table

A **calculated field** or **computational field** is a field (column) in a table that contains a formula, function, cell reference, structured reference, or condition. When you create a calculated field, Excel automatically fills in the column without the use of a fill or copy command; you do not have to use the fill handle to replicate formulas in a calculated field.

Table 6–4 contains the three calculated fields used in this project. You created the first one in the previous steps.

Table 6–4 Calculated Fields		
Column Heading	**Column**	**Calculated Field**
Post-Service Rating	G	Uses the VLOOKUP function to determine a rating based upon the Satisfaction Survey (column F).
% of Technician's Work Day	H	Divide the Time Billed by 6.5 hours
Customer Bill	I	Multiply the Time Billed by 75

To Create Calculated Fields

1 CREATE TABLE | 2 LOOKUP TABLES | 3 CALCULATED FIELDS | 4 CONDITIONAL FORMATTING | 5 SORT TABLES
6 QUERY TABLES | 7 CRITERIA RANGES | 8 DATABASE & CONDITIONAL FUNCTIONS | 9 SUBTOTALS & TREEMAP

Another advantage of using a table is in how you type formulas in a calculated field. Rather than using normal cell references, Excel allows you to type a structured reference. A **structured reference** uses some combination of the table name (such as Service_Calls), the column heading (such as Time Billed), or any named or special rows, rather than the usual column letter and row number references (such as F10). Named rows use a

sign before the row name (such as #Totals). If the column heading contains any spaces between words, its name must be enclosed in brackets (such as [Satisfaction Survey] for column F).

Using structured references has several advantages. *Why? Excel updates structured references automatically when any column heading changes or when you add new data to the table. Using this notation also makes formulas easier to read.* If you have multiple tables, you can include the table name in the structured reference, making it easier to locate data in large workbooks. The following steps enter structured references for the last two columns of data in the table.

- Click cell H9 to select it.

- Click the Percent Style button (Home tab | Number group) and then click the Increase Decimal button (Home tab | Number group) twice so that data is formatted with two decimal places.

- Type   = [to display the list of available fields in the table (Figure 6–20).

Q&A

What is the purpose of the [(left bracket)?

The [begins a structured reference and causes Excel to display the list of table fields (column headings).

Figure 6–20

- Double-click Time Billed to select the field to use for the structured reference.

- Type   ] / 6 . 5 to complete the formula and then click the Enter button to create the calculated column (Figure 6–21).

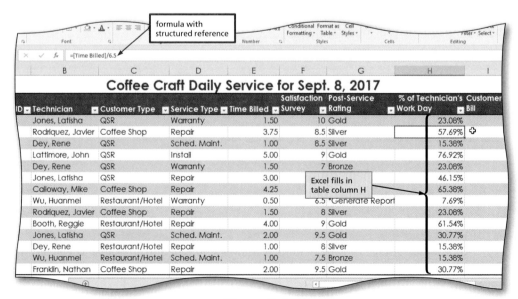

Figure 6–21

Q&A

Do I have to set the formatting before I enter the structured reference formula?

No, you do not have to; however, applying formatting before entering the formula prompts Excel to generate the calculated column with your desired formatting. Otherwise, you would have to format the column manually after it generates.

Why am I dividing by 6.5?

The company uses a 6.5-hour workday, allowing some time for technician travel.

❸

- Click cell I9 to select it.

- Click the 'Accounting Number Format' button (Home tab | Number group) so that data in the selected column is displayed as a dollar amount with two decimal places.

- Type =if(d9= "Warranty",0, [Time Billed]* 75) and then click the Enter button to create a calculated column (Figure 6–22).

IF function includes structured reference

Warranty work values appear as hyphen representing a zero charge

`=IF(D10="Warranty",0,[Time Billed]*75)`

Coffee Craft Daily Service for Sept. 8, 2017

Technician	Customer Type	Service Type	Time Billed	Satisfaction Survey	Post-Service Rating	% of Technician's Work Day	Customer Bill
Jones, Latisha	QSR	Warranty	1.50	10	Gold	23.08%	$
Rodriquez, Javier	Coffee Shop	Repair	3.75	8.5	Silver	57.69%	$ 281.25
Dey, Rene	QSR	Sched. Maint.	1.00	8.5	Silver	15.38%	$ 75.00
Lattimore, John	QSR	Install	5.00	9	Gold	76.92%	$ 375.00
Dey, Rene	QSR	Warranty	1.50	7	Bronze	23.08%	$ -
Jones, Latisha	QSR	Repair	3.00	10	Gold	46.15%	$ 225.00
Calloway, Mike	Coffee Shop	Repair	4.25	9	Gold	65.38%	$ 318.75
Wu, Huanmei	Restaurant/Hotel	Warranty	0.50	6.5	*General	7.69%	$ -
Rodriquez, Javier	Coffee Shop	Repair	1.50	8	Silver	23.08%	$ 112.50
Booth, Reggie	Restaurant/Hotel	Repair	4.00	9	Gold	61.54%	$ 300.00
Jones, Latisha	QSR	Sched. Maint.	2.00	9.5	Gold	30.77%	$ 150.00
Dey, Rene	Restaurant/Hotel	Repair	1.00	8	Silver	15.38%	$ 75.00
Wu, Huanmei	Restaurant/Hotel	Sched. Maint.	1.00	7.5	Bronze	15.38%	$ 75.00
Franklin, Nathan	Coffee Shop	Repair	2.00	9.5	Gold	30.77%	$ 150.00

Excel fills in calculated column

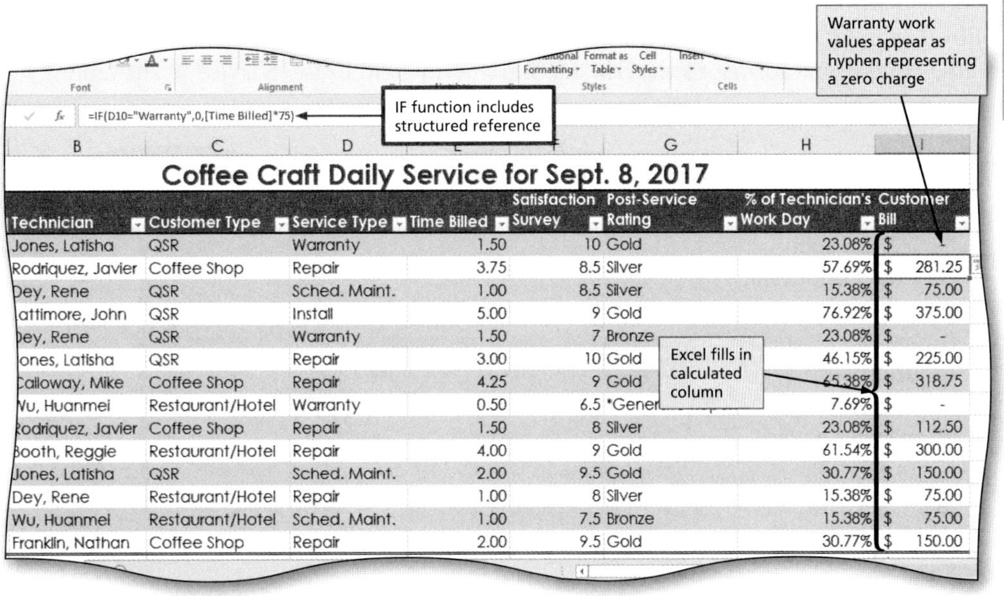

Figure 6–22

Q&A

What does the IF function do in the formula?

The IF function looks for service calls related to warranty (the condition in the function); in those cases the customer is billed zero (the first argument). The company charges other customers $75 per hour for repair services (the second argument in the function).

Conditional Formatting

Conditional formatting allows you to create rules that change the formatting of a cell based on its value. For example, you might want negative values to appear highlighted in red. Excel includes five preset types of conditional formats: highlight, top and bottom rules, data bars, color scales, and icon sets, as well as the ability to create your own conditional formats. You can combine different types of formats on any cell or range. For example, based on a cell's value, you can format it to include both an icon and a specific background color. You also can apply multiple conditional formatting rules to a cell or range.

The Conditional Formatting Rules Manager dialog box allows you to view all of the rules for the current selection or for an entire worksheet and change the order in which the rules are applied to a cell or range. In addition, you can stop applying subsequent rules after one rule is found to be true. For example, if the first rule specifies that a negative value should appear in red, then you may not want to apply any other conditional formats to the cell.

To Add a Conditional Formatting Rule with an Icon Set

The Post-Service Rating field provides succinct feedback to the user about performance of the technician on each service call. Another method to present the information visually is to display an icon next to the Satisfaction Survey number. Conditional formatting provides a variety of icons, including traffic signals, circles, flags, bars, and arrows. Icon sets include sets of three, four, or five icons. *Why? You choose an icon set depending on how many ways you want to group your data.* In the case of the ratings for the technicians, you will use three different icons. Once you choose an icon set, you define rules for each of the conditions. The following steps add a conditional format to the Satisfaction Survey field in the Service_Calls table.

- Select the range F9:F22 and then click the Conditional Formatting button (Home tab | Styles group) to display the Conditional Formatting gallery (Figure 6–23).

🄿 **Experiment**

- Point to each item in the Conditional Formatting gallery and then point to various items in the sub galleries to watch how the table changes.

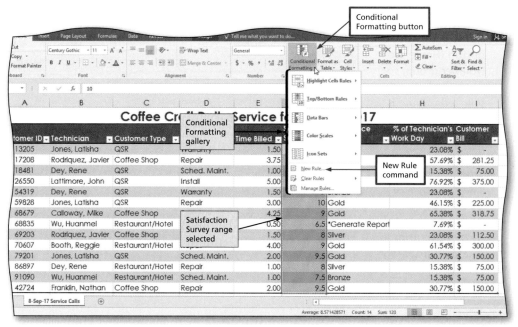

Figure 6–23

- Click New Rule in the Conditional Formatting gallery to display the New Formatting Rule dialog box.

- Click the Format Style button (New Formatting Rule dialog box) to display the Format Style list (Figure 6–24).

Q&A

What do the color scale formats do? You can choose between two or three values and apply different color backgrounds. Excel graduates the shading from one value to the next.

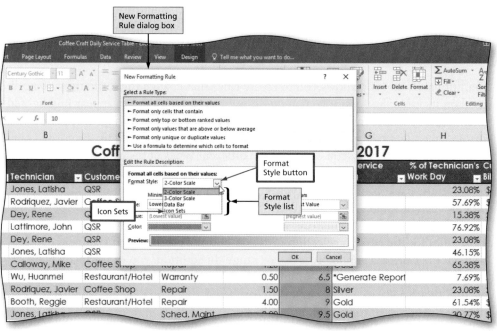

Figure 6–24

3

- Click Icon Sets in the Format Style list (New Formatting Rule dialog box) to display the Icon Style area.

- Click the Icon Style button to display the Icon Style list and then scroll as necessary to display the '3 Symbols (Circled)' icon style in the list (Figure 6–25).

🔍 **Experiment**

- Click a variety of icon styles in the Icon Styles list to view the options for each style.

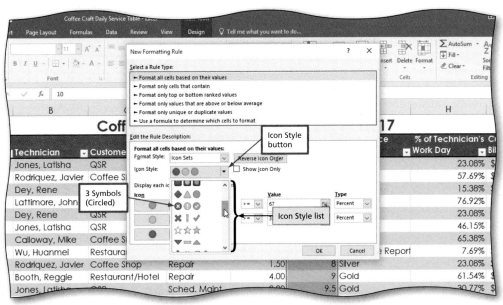

Figure 6–25

4

- Click the '3 Symbols (Circled)' icon style in the Icon Style list (New Formatting Rule dialog box) to select an icon style that includes three different circles.

- Click the first Type button and then click Number in the list to select a numeric value.

- Click the second Type button and then click Number in the list to select a numeric value.

- Type 9 in the first Value box. Type 7 in the second Value box and then press the TAB key to complete the conditions (Figure 6–26).

Q&A Why do the numbers next to each icon change as I type?
Excel automatically updates this area as you change the conditions. Use this area as an easy-to-read status of the conditions that you are creating.

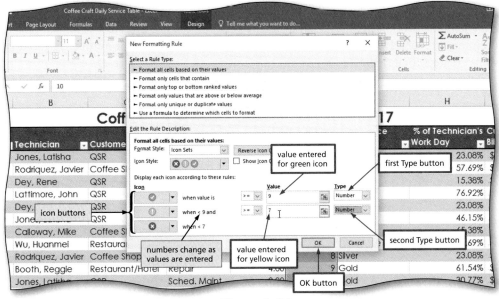

Figure 6–26

- Click the OK button (New Formatting Rule dialog box) to display icons in each row of the table in the Satisfaction Survey field (Figure 6–27).

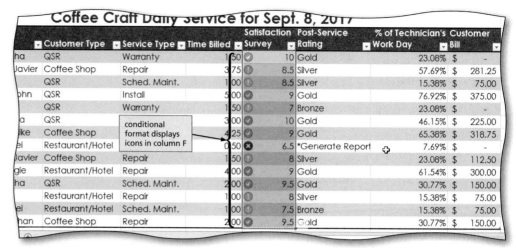

Figure 6–27

Working with Tables in Excel

When a table is active, the Table Tools Design tab on the ribbon provides powerful commands that allow you to alter the appearance and contents of a table quickly. For example, you quickly can add and remove header and total rows in a table. You also can change the style of the first or last column. Other commands that you will learn in later modules include inserting slices, exporting tables, and summarizing the data with a PivotTable.

To Insert a Total Row

1 CREATE TABLE | 2 LOOKUP TABLES | 3 CALCULATED FIELDS | 4 CONDITIONAL FORMATTING | 5 SORT TABLES
6 QUERY TABLES | 7 CRITERIA RANGES | 8 DATABASE & CONDITIONAL FUNCTIONS | 9 SUBTOTALS & TREEMAP

The Total Row check box (Table Tools Design tab | Table Style Options group) inserts a total row at the bottom of the table, summing the values in the last column. *Why? The default setting creates a total in the last column; however, total rows display a button beside each cell to create other totals and functions.* If the values are nonnumeric, then Excel counts the number of records and puts that number in the total row. The following steps create a total row.

- Click anywhere in the table and then display the Table Tools Design tab (Figure 6–28).

ⓟ Experiment

- Select a variety of combinations of check boxes in the Table Style Options group on the Table Tools Design tab to see their effect on the table. When finished, make sure that the check boxes are set as shown in Figure 6–28.

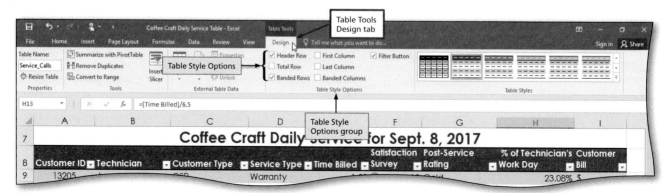

Figure 6–28

- Click the Total Row check box (Table Tools Design tab | Table Style Options group) to display the total row and display the sum in the last column of the table, cell I23 in this case.

- Select cell E23 in the total row and then click the button on the right side of the cell to display a list of available functions (Figure 6–29).

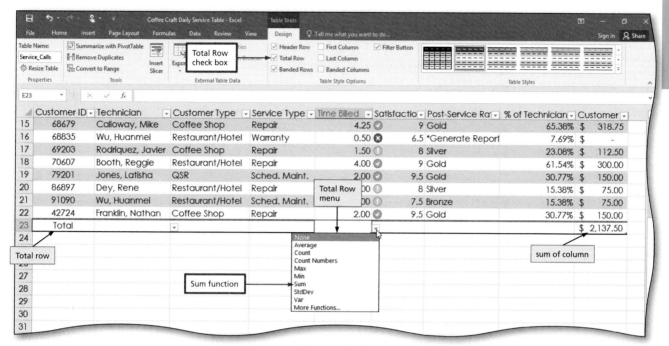

Figure 6–29

- Click Sum in the list to select the Sum function for the selected cell in the total row, thus totaling the billable hours for the day.

- Repeat the process to create an average in cell F23, thus averaging the satisfaction surveys. Format the cell by decreasing the decimals to two decimal places (Figure 6–30).

Experiment

- Choose other cells in the total row and experiment with the different kinds of statistical functions, such as using the MAX function in cell H23 or the COUNT function in cell D23.

Figure 6–30

- Click the Save button on the Quick Access Toolbar to save the workbook again.

Other Ways

1. Right-click table, point to Table on shortcut menu, click Totals Row on submenu

Break Point: If you wish to take a break, this is a good place to do so. You can exit Excel. To resume at a later time, run Excel, open the file called Coffee Craft Daily Service Table, and continue following the steps from this location forward.

BTW
**Distributing a
Workbook**
Instead of printing and
distributing a hard copy of a
workbook, you can distribute
the workbook electronically.
Options include sending the
workbook via email; posting
it on cloud storage (such as
OneDrive) and sharing the
file with others; posting it
on social media, a blog, or
other website; and sharing a
link associated with an online
location of the workbook.
You also can create and
share a PDF or XPS image of
the workbook, so that users
can view the file in Acrobat
Reader or XPS Viewer instead
of in Excel.

To Print the Table

When a table is selected and you display the Print tab in the Backstage view, an option in the Settings area allows you to print the contents of just the active, or selected, table. The following steps print the table in landscape orientation using the Fit Sheet on One Page option.

1 If necessary, click anywhere in the table to make it active, and then click File on the ribbon to open the Backstage view.

2 Click the Print tab to display the Print gallery.

3 Click the 'Print Active Sheets' button in the Settings area to display a list of printing options.

4 Click the 'Print Selected Table' command to choose to print only the selected table.

5 In the Settings area, select the options to print the table in landscape orientation. Use the Fit Sheet on One Page option (Figure 6–31).

6 Click the Print button to print the table.

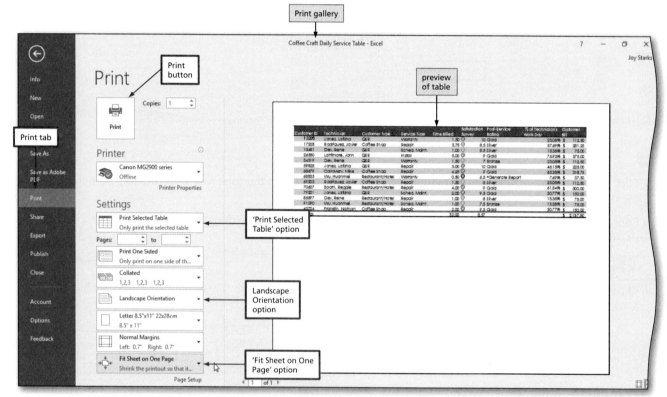

Figure 6–31

Sorting a table

The data in a table is easier to work with and more meaningful if the records appear sequentially based on one or more fields. Arranging records in a specific sequence is called **sorting**. Data is in **ascending order** if it is sorted from lowest to highest, earliest to most recent, or alphabetically from A to Z. Data is in **descending order** if it is sorted from highest to lowest, most recent to earliest, or alphabetically from Z to A.

The field or fields you select to sort are called **sort keys**. When you sort a table, all of the records in each row move together; so even if the selected cell is in the last name column, for example, the first name and all data in the row will be moved when the table is sorted by last name.

You can sort data in a table by using one of the following techniques:

- Select a cell in the field on which to sort, click the 'Sort & Filter' button (Home tab | Editing group), and then click one of the sorting options on the Sort & Filter menu.

- With the table active, click the filter button in the column on which to sort and then click one of the sorting options in the table.

- Use the Sort button (Data tab | Sort & Filter group).

- Use the 'Sort A to Z' or 'Sort Z to A' button (Data tab | Sort & Filter group).

- Right-click anywhere in a table and then point to Sort on the shortcut menu to display the Sort submenu.

BTW
Sorting Dates
When you use AutoFilter to sort date fields, the filter menu will list commands such as 'Sort Newest to Oldest' and 'Sort Oldest to Newest'.

Which field is best for sorting?

Ideally, the user of the worksheet should be able to sort the table on any field using a variety of methods and sort using multiple fields at the same time. Depending on what you want to show, you may sort by a name field or list value, by a numeric field, or by date. You also can sort a table in ascending or descending order.

CONSIDER THIS

To Sort Ascending

1 CREATE TABLE | 2 LOOKUP TABLES | 3 CALCULATED FIELDS | 4 CONDITIONAL FORMATTING | 5 SORT TABLES
6 QUERY TABLES | 7 CRITERIA RANGES | 8 DATABASE & CONDITIONAL FUNCTIONS | 9 SUBTOTALS & TREEMAP

The following steps sort the table in ascending order by the Technician field using the 'Sort & Filter' button (Home tab | Editing group). **Why?** *Names commonly display in alphabetical order.*

- Scroll to display the entire table. If necessary, display the Home tab.

- Click cell B9 and then click the 'Sort & Filter' button (Home tab | Editing group) to display the Sort & Filter menu (Figure 6–32).

Q&A What if the column I choose includes numeric or date data?

If the column you choose includes numeric data, then the Sort & Filter menu shows the 'Sort Smallest to Largest' and 'Sort Largest to Smallest' commands. If the column you choose includes date data, then the Sort & Filter menu shows the 'Sort Oldest to Newest' and 'Sort Newest to Oldest' commands.

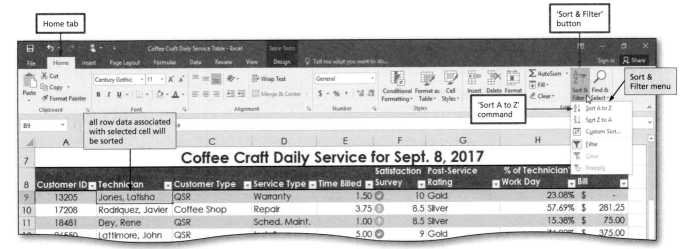

Figure 6–32

2

- Click 'Sort A to Z' to sort the table in ascending order by the selected field, Technician in this case (Figure 6–33).

🔍 **Experiment**

- Select other fields in the table and use the same procedure to sort on the fields you choose. When you are finished, remove any sorting, select cell A9, and repeat the two steps above.

Q&A
Can I undo the sort?
Yes, you can click the Undo button (Quick Access Toolbar) or press CTRL+Z; however, if you close your file, the original order will be lost. If you want to undo a sort, it is a good practice to do so before continuing with other commands.

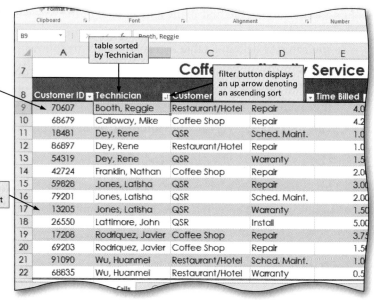

Figure 6–33

Other Ways

1. Select field in table, click 'Sort A to Z' button (Data tab | Sort & Filter group)

2. Click filter button of field on which to sort, click 'Sort A to Z'

3. Right-click column to sort, point to Sort on shortcut menu, click 'Sort A to Z'

To Sort Descending

1 CREATE TABLE | 2 LOOKUP TABLES | 3 CALCULATED FIELDS | 4 CONDITIONAL FORMATTING | 5 SORT TABLES
6 QUERY TABLES | 7 CRITERIA RANGES | 8 DATABASE & CONDITIONAL FUNCTIONS | 9 SUBTOTALS & TREEMAP

The following step sorts the records in descending order by Time Billed using the 'Sort Largest to Smallest' button on the Data tab. **Why?** *Sometimes it is more convenient to use the Data tab and sort with a single click.*

1

- Click cell E9 to position the sort in the Time Billed column.

- Display the Data tab.

- Click the 'Sort Largest to Smallest' button (Data tab | Sort & Filter group) to sort the table in descending sequence by the selected field, Time Billed, in this case (Figure 6–34).

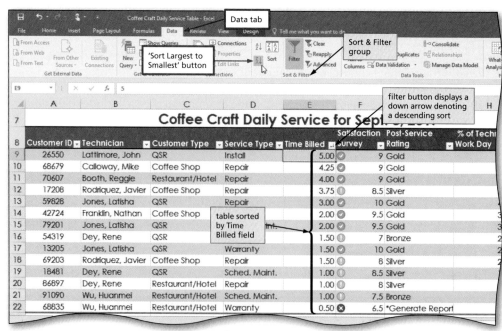

Figure 6–34

Other Ways

1. Select field in table, click 'Sort and Filter' button (Home tab | Editing group), click 'Sort Largest to Smallest'

2. Click filter button of field on which to sort, click 'Sort Largest to Smallest'

3. Right-click column to sort, point to Sort on shortcut menu, click 'Sort Largest to Smallest'

To Custom Sort a Table

While Excel allows you to sort on a maximum of 256 fields in a single sort operation, in these steps you will use the Custom Sort command to sort the Coffee Craft Daily Service Table using three fields. You will sort by Satisfaction Survey within Service Type within Customer Type. *Why? That phrase means that the records within the table first are arranged by Customer Type (Coffee Shop, QSR, or Restaurant/Hotel). Then, within Customer Type, the records are arranged alphabetically by Service Type (Repair, Sched. Maint., Warranty). Finally, within Service Type, the records are arranged from largest to smallest by the Satisfaction Survey number.* In this case, Customer Type is the major sort key, Service Type is the intermediate sort key, and Satisfaction Survey is the minor sort key. You can sort any field in ascending or descending order, depending on how you want the data to look. The following steps sort the Service_ Calls table on multiple fields.

1

- Display the Home tab.
- With a cell in the table active, click the 'Sort & Filter' button (Home tab | Editing group) to display the Sort & Filter menu.
- Click Custom Sort on the Sort & Filter menu to display the Sort dialog box.
- Click the 'Column Sort by' button (Sort dialog box) to display the field names in the table (Figure 6–35).

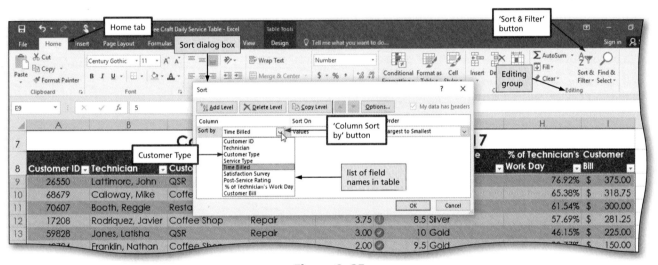

Figure 6–35

2

- Click Customer Type to select the first sort level, or major sort key.
- If necessary, click the Sort on button (Sort dialog box) and then click Values in the Sort On list.
- If necessary, click the Order button and then click 'A to Z' to sort the field alphabetically (Figure 6–36).

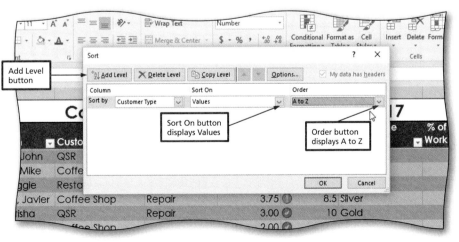

Figure 6–36

- Click the Add Level button (Sort dialog box) to add a second sort level.
- Click the Then by button and then click Service Type in the Then by list to select an intermediate sort key.
- If necessary, select Values in the Sort On list.
- If necessary, select 'A to Z' in the Order list to sort the field alphabetically (Figure 6–37).

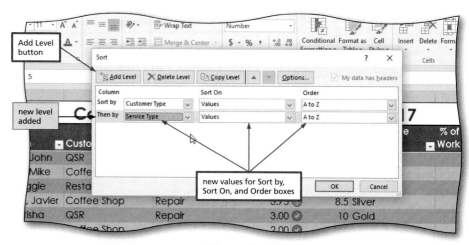

Figure 6–37

- Click the Add Level button to add a new sort level.
- Click the second Then by button and then click Satisfaction Survey to select a minor sort key.
- If necessary, select Values in the Sort On list. Select 'Largest to Smallest' in the Order list to specify that the field should be sorted in reverse order (Figure 6–38).

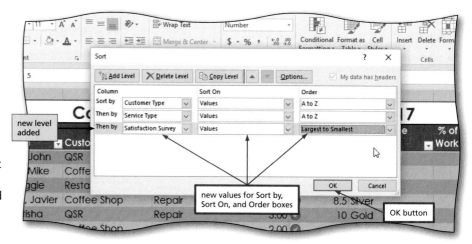

Figure 6–38

- Click the OK button to sort the table, in this case by Satisfaction Survey (descending) within Service Type (ascending) within Customer Type (ascending) (Figure 6–39).

Q&A What should I do if I make a sorting error?
If you make a mistake in a sort operation, you can return the records to their original order by clicking the Undo button on the Quick Access Toolbar or by pressing CTRL+Z. You can undo all steps back to when you originally opened the file — even if you have saved multiple times. Once you close the file however, there is no way to undo a sorting error.

Figure 6–39

Querying a Table Using AutoFilter

When you first create a table, Excel automatically enables AutoFilter, a tool used to sort, query, and filter the records in a table. While using AutoFilter, filter buttons appear to the right of the column headings. Clicking a button displays the filter menu for the column with various commands and a list of all items in the field (shown in Figure 6–40).

The sort commands work the same way as the sort buttons that you learned about earlier. The filter commands let you choose to display only those records that meet specified criteria such as color, number, or text. In this context, **criteria** means a logical rule by which data is tested and chosen. For example, you can filter the table to display a specific name or item by typing it in a Search box. The name you selected acts as the criteria for filtering the table, which results in Excel displaying only those records that match the criteria. The selected check boxes indicate which items will appear in the table. By default, all of the items are selected. If you deselect an item from the filter menu, it is called the filter criterion. Excel will not display any record that contains the unchecked item.

As with the previous sort techniques, you can include more than one column when you filter, by clicking a second filter button and making choices. The process of filtering activity based on one or more filter criteria is called a **query**. After you filter data, you can copy, find, edit, format, chart, or print the filtered data without rearranging or moving it.

BTW

Scrolling Tables
When you scroll down in a table to display more rows, the column headings remain on the screen in a manner similar to using the Freeze Panes command (View tab | Window group).

To Sort a Table Using AutoFilter

1 CREATE TABLE | 2 LOOKUP TABLES | 3 CALCULATED FIELDS | 4 CONDITIONAL FORMATTING | 5 SORT TABLES
6 QUERY TABLES | 7 CRITERIA RANGES | 8 DATABASE & CONDITIONAL FUNCTIONS | 9 SUBTOTALS & TREEMAP

The following steps sort the table by Customer Bill using the 'Sort Largest to Smallest' command on the filter menu. *Why? Using the filter menu sometimes is easier than other sort methods; you do not have to leave the table area and move to the ribbon to perform the sort.*

- Click the filter button in the Customer Bill column to display the filter menu (Figure 6–40).

🔎 **Experiment**

- Click various filter buttons. Notice that the filter menu is context sensitive, which means it changes depending on what you are trying to filter. When you are finished, again click the Filter button in the Customer Bill column.

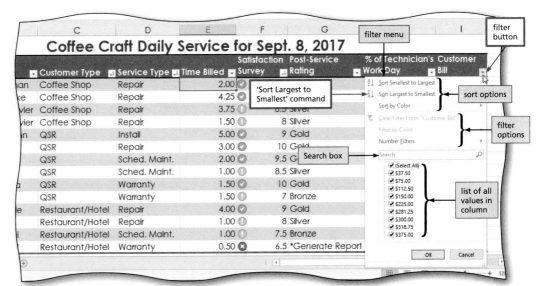

Figure 6–40

2

- Click 'Sort Largest to Smallest' on the filter menu to sort the table in descending sequence by the selected field (Figure 6–41).

Q&A

Does performing a new sort overwrite the previous sort?

Yes. A new sort undoes the previous sort, even if it is a custom sort or a sort based on multiple sort keys.

table is sorted by Customer Bill

Coffee Craft Daily Service for Sept. 8, 2017

	Customer Type	Service Type	Time Billed	Satisfaction Survey	Post-Service Rating	% of Technician's Work Day	Customer Bill
ohn	QSR	Install	5.00	9	Gold	76.92%	$ 375.00
ike	Coffee Shop	Repair	4.25	9	Gold	65.38%	$ 318.75
e	Restaurant/Hotel	Repair	4.00	9	Gold	61.54%	$ 300.00
vier	Coffee Shop	Repair	3.75	8.5	Silver	57.69%	$ 281.25
a	QSR	Repair	3.00	10	Gold	46.15%	$ 225.00
an	Coffee Shop	Repair	2.00	9.5	Gold	30.77%	$ 150.00
b	QSR	Sched. Maint.	2.00	9.5	Gold	30.77%	$ 150.00
vier	Coffee Shop	Repair	1.50	8	Silver	23.08%	$ 112.50
	QSR	Sched. Maint.	1.00	8.5	Silver	15.38%	$ 75.00
	Restaurant/Hotel	Repair	1.00	8	Silver	15.38%	$ 75.00
ei	Restaurant/Hotel	Sched. Maint.	1.00	7.5	Bronze	15.38%	$ 75.00
na	QSR	Warranty	1.50	10	Gold	23.08%	$ -
	QSR	Warranty	1.50	7	Bronze	23.08%	$ -
ei	Restaurant/Hotel	Warranty	0.50	6.5	*Generate Report	7.69%	$ -

Figure 6–41

To Query a Table Using AutoFilter

1 CREATE TABLE | 2 LOOKUP TABLES | 3 CALCULATED FIELDS | 4 CONDITIONAL FORMATTING | 5 SORT TABLES
6 QUERY TABLES | **7 CRITERIA RANGES** | 8 DATABASE & CONDITIONAL FUNCTIONS | 9 SUBTOTALS & TREEMAP

The following steps query the Coffee Craft Daily Service Table using AutoFilter. **Why?** *The AutoFilter will cause the table to display only specific records, which may be helpful in very large tables.* In this case, using the check boxes on the filter menu, you will choose those records with a Service Type not equal to Warranty and whose Post-Service Rating is equal to Gold.

1

- Click the filter button in cell D8 to display the filter menu for the Service Type column.

- Click Warranty in the filter menu to remove the check mark and cause Excel to hide all warranty service calls (Figure 6–42).

Q&A

What else appears on the filter menu?

Below the Text Filters command is a

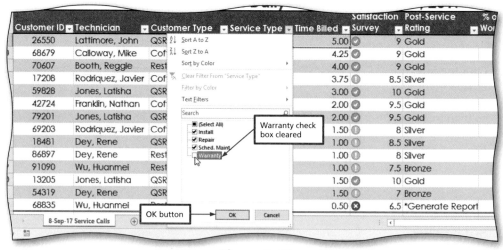

Figure 6–42

list of all of the values that occur in the selected column. A check mark in the top item, (Select All), indicates that all values for this field are displayed in the table.

2

- Click the OK button to apply the AutoFilter criterion.

- Click the filter button in cell G8 to display the filter menu for the selected column.

- Click to remove the check marks beside Bronze and Silver, so that only the Gold check box contains a check mark (Figure 6–43).

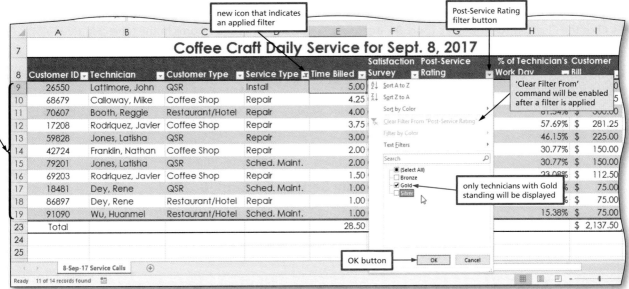

Figure 6–43

3

- Click the OK button to apply the AutoFilter criterion (Figure 6–44).

Q&A

Are both filters now applied to the table?
Yes. When you select a second filter criterion, Excel adds it to the first; hence, each record must pass two tests to appear as part of the final subset of the table.

Did the filter remove the previous sort?
No. Notice in Figure 6–44 that the records still are sorted in descending order by Customer Bill.

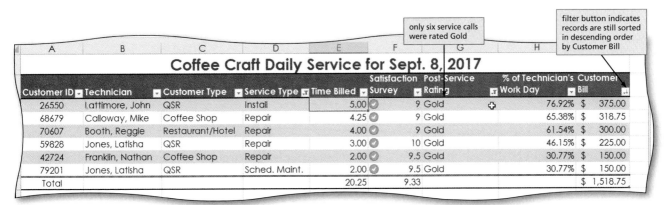

Figure 6–44

Other Ways

1. Click filter button, enter desired data in Search box (filter menu), click OK button

To Remove Filters

You can remove a filter from a specific column or remove all of the filters in a table at once. Each filter menu has a 'Clear Filter From' command that removes the column filter (shown in Figure 6–43). The Clear button (Data tab | Sort & Filter group) removes all of the filters. The following step removes all filters at once, to show all records in the table. **Why?** *The filters, or query, hid some of the records in the previous steps.*

- Click anywhere in the table and display the Data tab.
- Click the Clear button (Data tab | Sort & Filter group) to display all of the records in the table (Figure 6–45).

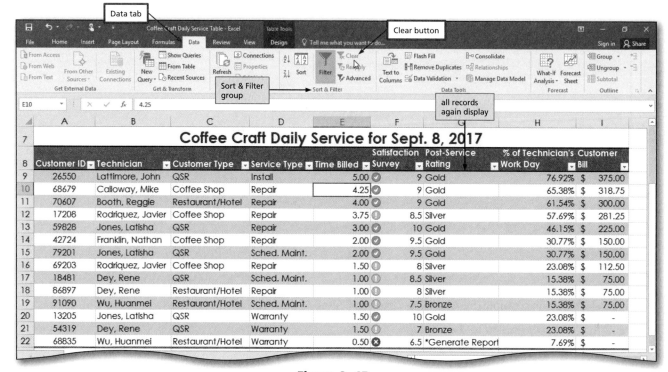

Figure 6–45

Other Ways

1. Click desired filter button, click (Select All) on filter menu

2. Right-click filtered column, point to Filter on shortcut menu, click 'Clear Filter From' command

To Search a Table Using AutoFilter

1 CREATE TABLE | 2 LOOKUP TABLES | 3 CALCULATED FIELDS | 4 CONDITIONAL FORMATTING | 5 SORT TABLES
6 QUERY TABLES | 7 CRITERIA RANGES | 8 DATABASE & CONDITIONAL FUNCTIONS | 9 SUBTOTALS & TREEMAP

Using AutoFilter, you can search for specific records by entering data in the Search box. The data you enter is called the **search string**. For example, in a student table, you might want to search for a specific student ID number that might be difficult to locate in a large set of records. If an exact match exists, the value appears in the filter menu; then, if you click the OK button, the entire record appears in the table. Table searches are not case sensitive.

Alternately, you can search for similar or related data. In the Search box, you can type **?** (question mark) to represent any single character. For example in a quiz table, if you wanted to find answer1, answer2, and answer3, you could type **answer?** as the search string. Another way to search includes using an * (asterisk) to represent a series of characters. For example, in an inventory table, to find all of the items that relate to drive, you could type ***drive*** in the Search box. The filter would display results such as flash drives, CD-R drive, and drivers. The ? and * are called **wildcard characters**.

The following steps search for a specific record in a table using the filter menu. *Why? When tables are large, searching for individual records using the filter menu is quick and easy.*

- Click the filter button in the Technician column to display the filter menu.
- Click the Search box, and then type **jones** as the search string (Figure 6–46).

Q&A

Is this search the same as using the Find command?

No. This command searches for data within the table only and then displays all records that match the search string. Three records matching the search appear in Figure 6–47. The Find command looks over the entire worksheet and highlights one cell.

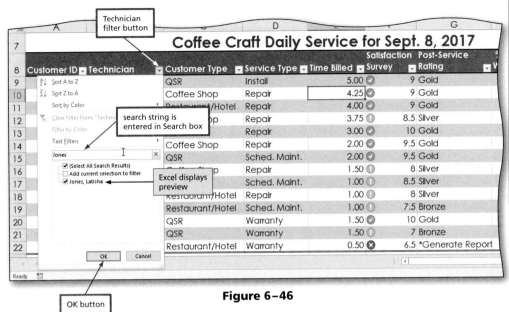

Figure 6–46

❷

- Click the OK button to perform the search (Figure 6–47).

 Experiment

- Search other columns for different kinds of data. Note that the total row reflects only the records displayed by the filter.

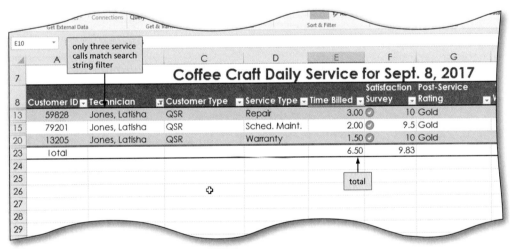

Figure 6–47

❸

- Click the Clear button (Data tab | Sort & Filter group) to display all of the records in the table.

To Enter Custom Criteria Using AutoFilter

1 CREATE TABLE | 2 LOOKUP TABLES | 3 CALCULATED FIELDS | 4 CONDITIONAL FORMATTING | 5 SORT TABLES
6 QUERY TABLES | **7 CRITERIA RANGES** | 8 DATABASE & CONDITIONAL FUNCTIONS | 9 SUBTOTALS & TREEMAP

Another way to query a table is to use the Custom Filter command. The Custom Filter command allows you to enter custom criteria, such as multiple options or ranges of numbers. *Why? Not all queries are exact numbers; many times a range of numbers is required.* The following steps enter custom criteria to display records that represent service calls whose Satisfaction Survey number is between 7 and 9, inclusive; that is, the number is greater than or equal to 7 and less than or equal to 9 ($7 \leq$ Satisfaction Survey ≤ 9).

- Click the filter button in cell F8 to display the filter menu for the Satisfaction Survey column.

- Point to Number Filters to display the Number Filters submenu (Figure 6–48).

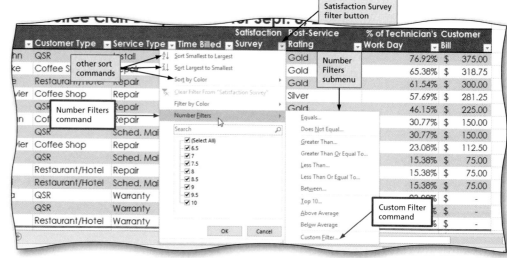

Figure 6–48

2

- Click Custom Filter on the Number Filters submenu to display the Custom AutoFilter dialog box.

- Click the first Satisfaction Survey button (Custom AutoFilter dialog box), click 'is greater than or equal to' in the list, and then type 7 in the first value box.

- Click the second Satisfaction Survey button. Scroll as necessary, and then click 'is less than or equal to' in the list. Type 9 in the second value box (Figure 6–49).

Q&A How are the And and Or option buttons used?
You can click options button to select the appropriate operator. The AND operator indicates that both parts of the criteria must be true; the OR operator indicates that only one of the two must be true.

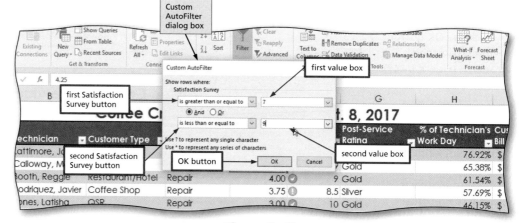

Figure 6–49

3

- Click the OK button (Custom AutoFilter dialog box) to display records in the table that match the custom AutoFilter criteria, in this case, service calls in which the Satisfaction Survey number is between 7 and 9, inclusive (Figure 6–50).

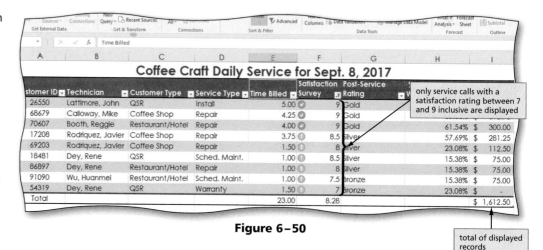

Figure 6–50

4

- Click the Clear button (Data tab | Sort & Filter group) to display all of the records in the table.

More about AutoFilters

Other important points regarding AutoFilter include the following:

- When you query a table to display some records and hide others, Excel displays a filter icon on the filter buttons used to establish the filter. Excel also displays the row headings of the selected records in blue.

- Excel does not sort hidden records.

- If the filter buttons do not appear, then you must manually enable AutoFilter by clicking the Filter button (Data tab | Sort & Filter group).

- To remove a filter criterion for a single piece of data in a field, click the Select All check box on the filter menu for that field.

- When you create a formula in the total row of a table, the formula automatically recalculates the values even when you filter the list. For example, the results shown in the Total row in Figure 6–50 update automatically if you apply a filter to the table.

- You can filter and sort a column by color or conditional formatting using the 'Sort by Color' and 'Filter by Color' commands on the filter menu (shown in Figure 6–48).

To Turn Off AutoFilter

You can turn off and on the AutoFilter feature by hiding or showing the filter buttons. *Why? Sometimes you may want to view the table without the distraction of the buttons.* The following steps hide and then redisplay the AutoFilter.

❶

- Click the Filter button (Data tab | Sort & Filter group) to hide the filter buttons in the table (Figure 6–51).

❷

- Click the Filter button (Data tab | Sort & Filter group) again to display the filter buttons in the table.

❸

- Click the Save button on the Quick Access Toolbar to save the workbook.

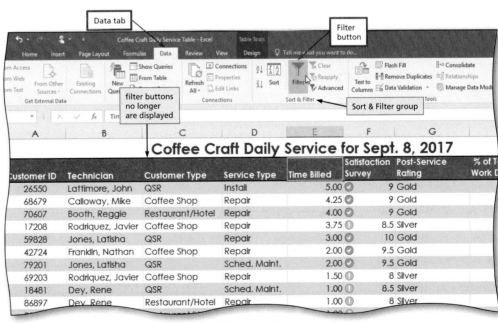

Figure 6–51

Other Ways

1. Click 'Sort & Filter' button (Home tab | Editing group), click Filter command in 'Sort & Filter' list

2. CTRL+SHIFT+L

Using Criteria and Extract Ranges

Another advanced filter technique called a criteria range manipulates records that pass comparison criteria. A **criteria range** is a location separate from the table used to list specific search specifications. Like a custom filter, a criteria range compares entered data with a list or table, based on column headings. Using a criteria range sometimes is faster than entering criteria through the AutoFilter system because once the range is established, you do not have to access any menus or dialog boxes to perform the query. You also can create an **extract range** in which Excel copies the records that meet the comparison criteria in the criteria range to another part of the worksheet.

CONSIDER THIS

Does Excel provide another way to pull data out of a table?

Yes. You can create a criteria area and extract area on the worksheet. The criteria area can be used to enter rules regarding which records to extract, without having to change the AutoFilter settings. For example, the criteria area might ask for all full-time students with a grade of A from the table. The extract area can be used to store the records that meet the criteria. Extracting records allows you to pull data from a table so that you can analyze or manipulate the data further. For example, you may want to know which customers are delinquent on their payments. Extracting records that meet this criterion allows you then to use the records to create a mailing to such customers.

To Create a Criteria Range

When creating a criteria range, it is important to place it away from the table itself. Commonly, criteria ranges are located directly above the table. That way, if the table grows downward or to the right in the future, the criteria range will not interfere. It also is a good practice to copy the necessary column headings rather than type them, to prevent errors. The following steps create a criteria range and copy the column headings.

1 Select the range A7:I8 and then press CTRL+C to copy the range.

2 Select cell A1 and then press the ENTER key to paste the clipboard contents.

3 Change the title to `Criteria Range` in cell A1.

4 If necessary, use the format painter to copy the formatting and wrap column headings to match the table headings.

5 Select the range A2:I3, click the Name box, type `Criteria` as the range name, and then press the ENTER key (Figure 6–52).

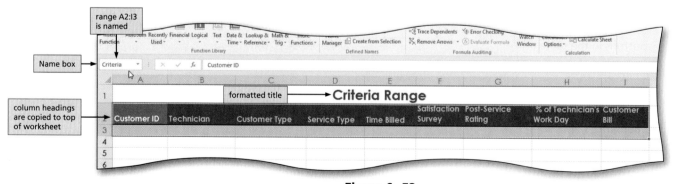

Figure 6–52

To Query Using a Criteria Range

The following steps use the criteria range and the Advanced Filter dialog box to query the table and display only the records that pass the test: Service Type = Repair AND Time Billed > 2 AND Satisfaction Survey >= 8. The criteria data is entered directly below the criteria range headings. *Why? Because the Advanced Filter dialog box searches for a match using column headings and adjacent rows.*

1

- In cell D3, enter the criteria **Repair**, in cell E3 type **>2**, and in cell F3 type **>=8** (Figure 6–53).

Figure 6–53

2

- Click the table to make it active.

- Click the Advanced button (Data tab | Sort & Filter group) to display the Advanced Filter dialog box (Figure 6–54).

Q&A What are the default values in the Advanced Filter dialog box?

In the Action area, the 'Filter the list, in-place' option button is the default selection. Excel automatically selects the table (range $A$8:$I$23) in the List range box. Excel also automatically selects the criteria range ($A$2:$I$3) in the Criteria range box, because the name Criteria was assigned to the range A2:I3 earlier.

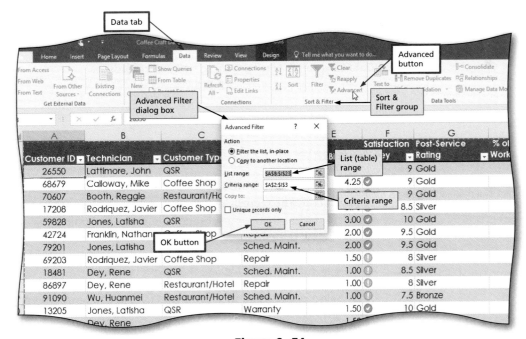

Figure 6–54

3

- Click the OK button (Advanced Filter dialog box) to hide all records that do not meet the comparison criteria. If necessary, scroll up to display the criteria range (Figure 6–55).

◄ **Q&A** What is the main difference between using the AutoFilter query technique and using the Advanced Filter dialog box with a criteria range?

Like the AutoFilter query technique, the Advanced Filter command displays a subset of the table. The primary difference between the two is that the Advanced Filter command allows you to create more complex comparison criteria, because the criteria range can be as many rows long as necessary, allowing for many sets of comparison criteria.

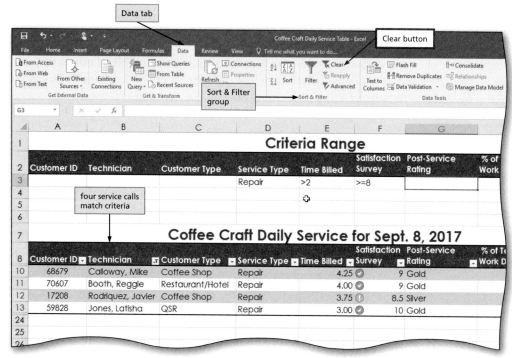

Figure 6–55

4

- Click the Clear button (Data tab | Sort & Filter group) to show all records.

BTW
AND and OR Queries
If you want to create a query that includes searches on two fields, you enter the data across the same row in the criteria range. If you want to search for one piece of data OR another, enter the second piece of data on the next row.

To Create an Extract Range

In the previous steps, you filtered data in place within the table itself; however, you can copy the records that meet the criteria to another part of the worksheet, rather than displaying them as a subset of the table. The following steps create an extract range below the table.

1 Select the range A7:I8 and then press CTRL+C to copy the range.

2 Select cell A25 and then press the ENTER key to paste the contents.

3 Change the title to **Extract Area** in cell A25.

4 Select the range A26:I45, click the Name box, type **Extract** as the range name, and then press the ENTER key.

◄ **Q&A** Why am I including so many rows in the extraction range?

The table has many records; you want to make sure you have enough room for any search that the company might desire.

5 If necessary, use the format painter to copy the formatting and wrap column headings to match the table headings (Figure 6–56).

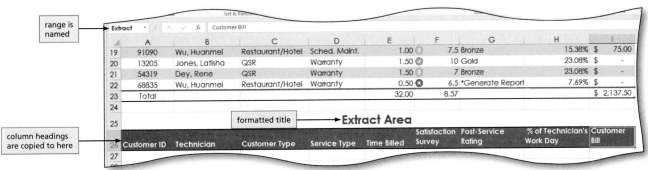

Figure 6–56

To Extract Records

1 CREATE TABLE | 2 LOOKUP TABLES | 3 CALCULATED FIELDS | 4 CONDITIONAL FORMATTING | 5 SORT TABLES
6 QUERY TABLES | 7 CRITERIA RANGES | **8 DATABASE & CONDITIONAL FUNCTIONS** | 9 SUBTOTALS & TREEMAP

The following steps extract records that meet the previous criteria, using the Advanced Filter dialog box. *Why? The Advanced Filter dialog box allows you to use the complex criteria from a criteria range on the worksheet and send the results to a third location, leaving the table undisturbed.*

1

- Click the table to make it active.

- Click the Advanced button (Data tab | Sort & Filter group) to display the Advanced Filter dialog box.

- Click 'Copy to another location' in the Action area (Advanced Filter dialog box) to cause the records that meet the criteria to be copied to a different location on the worksheet (Figure 6–57).

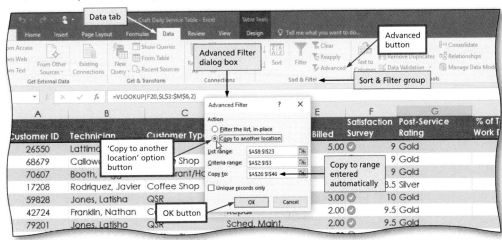

Figure 6–57

2

- Click the OK button to copy any records that meet the comparison criteria in the criteria range from the table to the extract range. Scroll to display the entire extraction area (Figure 6–58).

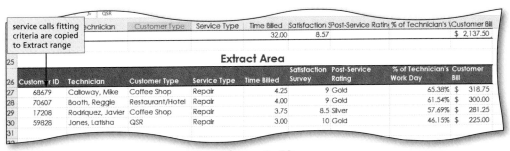

Figure 6–58

Q&A What happens to the rows in the extract range if I perform another advanced filter operation?

Each time you use the Advanced Filter dialog box with the 'Copy to another location' option, Excel clears cells below the field names in the extract range before it copies a new set of records that pass the new test.

3

- Click the Save button on the Quick Access Toolbar to save the workbook again.

Break Point: If you wish to take a break, this is a good place to do so. You can exit Excel. To resume at a later time, run Excel, open the file called Coffee Craft Daily Service Table, and continue following the steps from this location forward.

More about the Criteria Range

BTW

Keeping Data in Order

If you want to perform various sorts, but need to have a way to return to the original order, you might consider adding a column that numbers the entries before sorting.

The comparison criteria in the criteria range determine the records that will pass the test when the Advanced Filter dialog box is used. As you have seen, multiple entries in a single data row of the criteria range create an AND condition. The following examples describe different comparison criteria.

- If the criteria range contains a blank row, it means that no comparison criteria have been defined. Thus, all records in the table pass the test and will be displayed.
- If you want an OR operator in the same field, your criteria range must contain two (or more) data rows. Enter the criteria data on separate rows. Records that pass either (or any) comparison criterion will be displayed.
- If you want an AND operator in the same field name, you must add a column in the criteria range and duplicate the column heading.
- If you want an OR operator on two different fields, your criteria range must contain two (or more) data rows. Enter the criteria for each field on a separate row. Records will display that pass either (or any) comparison criterion.
- When the comparison criteria below different field names are in the same row, then records pass the test only if they pass all the comparison criteria, an AND condition. If the comparison criteria for the field names are in different rows, then the records must pass only one of the tests, an OR condition.

BTW

Using Quotation Marks

Many of the database functions require a field name as one of the arguments. If your field name is text, rather than a cell reference, number, or range, the argument must be enclosed in quotation marks.

Using Database Functions

BTW

Functions and Ranges

When using a function such as DAVERAGE or DCOUNT, Excel automatically adjusts the first argument if the table grows or shrinks. With functions such as SUMIF and COUNTIF, you have to correct the function argument to reflect the new range if the range grows or shrinks.

Excel includes 12 database functions that allow you to evaluate numeric data in a table. These functions each begin with the letter D for data table, to differentiate them from their worksheet counterparts. As the name implies, the **DAVERAGE function** calculates the average of numbers in a table field that pass a test. The general form of the DAVERAGE function is

=DAVERAGE(table range, "field name", criteria range)

Another often-used table function is the DCOUNT function. The **DCOUNT function** counts the number of numeric entries in a table field that pass a test. The general form of the DCOUNT function is

=DCOUNT(table range, "field name", criteria range)

In both functions, table range is the location of the table, field name is the name of the field in the table, and criteria range is the comparison criteria or test to pass. Note that Excel requires that you surround field names with quotation marks unless you previously named the field.

Other database functions that are similar to the functions described in previous modules include the DMAX, DMIN, and DSUM functions. See Excel Help for a complete list of database functions.

To Create an Output Area

The following steps set up an output area in preparation for using the database functions. Cells O2:Q3 will be used as criteria. Cells O5:O11 will be labels for the output.

① Change the width of columns O, P, and Q to 18.00.

② Select cell O1 and then type **Output Area** to enter a criteria area title. Center the title across the selection O1:Q1. If necessary, copy the formatting from cell L1 to cell O1.

③ In cell O2, type **Customer Type**. In cell P2, type **Customer Type**. In cell Q2, type **Post-Service Rating** to create the column headings. Use the format painter to copy the formatting from cell L2 to cells O2:Q2.

④ Enter other labels as shown below (Figure 6–59).

Cell	Text
O3	Coffee Shop
P3	QSR
Q3	Gold
O5	Avg. Coffee Shop Satisfaction Rating:
O6	Avg. QSR Satisfaction Rating:
O7	Gold Standing Count:
O8	Billing to Restaurant/Hotel:
O9	Count of QSR Customers:
O10	Customer ID:
O11	Time Billed:

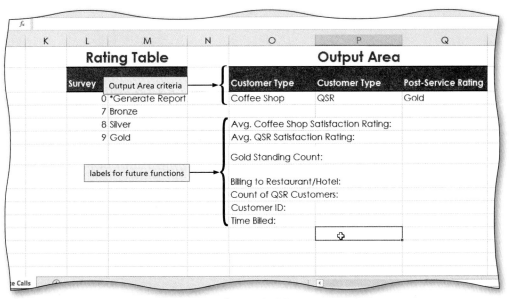

Figure 6–59

To Use the DAVERAGE and DCOUNT Database Functions

The following steps use the DAVERAGE function to find the average Coffee Shop Satisfaction rating. You will use the DCOUNT function to count the number of service calls that have a Gold rating. *Why? The DAVERAGE and DCOUNT functions allow you to enter a range to average, and criteria with which to filter the table.* The DAVERAGE function requires a numeric field from the table range; therefore, you will use "Satisfaction Survey" as the second argument. Field names used as numeric arguments in these functions should be surrounded with quotation marks, unless previously named.

- Select cell Q5 and then type `=daverage (a8:i22, "Satisfaction Survey",o2:o3)` to enter a database function (Figure 6–60).

Q&A My function does not wrap as shown in the figure. Did I do something wrong?
No, it depends on how far to the right you are scrolled. If there is not enough room on the screen, Excel will wrap long cell entries.

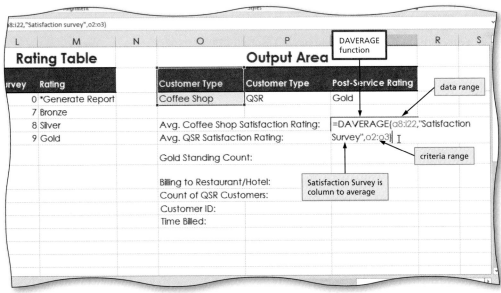

Figure 6–60

- Click the Enter button to finish the function and display the answer.

- Select cell Q6 and then type `=daverage (a8:i22, "Satisfaction Survey",p2:p3)` to enter a second database function (Figure 6–61).

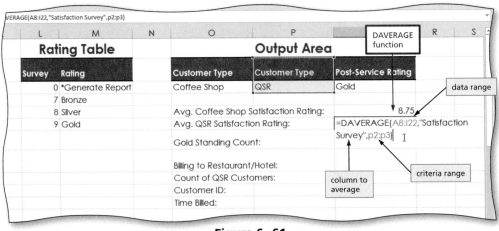

Figure 6–61

Q&A Why do the two DAVERAGE functions, which both use the Satisfaction Survey field, generate different answers?
The criteria range differentiates the two entries. The range O2:O3 averages the satisfaction survey results for Coffee Shop customers. The range P2:P3 averages the survey results related to QSR customers.

3

- Click the Enter button to finish the function.

- Select cell Q7 and then type **=dcount(a8:i22, "Satisfaction Survey",q2:q3)** to enter a database function.

- Click the Enter button to finish the function (Figure 6–62).

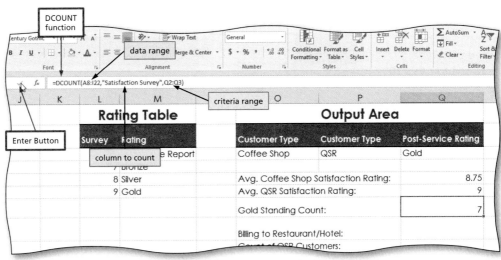

Figure 6–62

Q&A | What is the DCOUNT function actually counting?
The DCOUNT function is counting the number of Gold ratings in the table, as referenced by the Q2:Q3 criteria.

Other Ways

1. Click Insert Function box in formula bar, click 'Or select a category' button, click 'Database', click DAVERAGE or DCOUNT in 'Select a function' list, enter arguments

---

Using the Sumif, Countif, Match, and Index Functions

Four other functions are useful when querying a table and analyzing its data. The SUMIF and COUNTIF functions sum values in a range, or count values in a range, only if they meet a criteria. The MATCH function returns the position number of an item in a range or table. For example, if you search for a specific student name, the MATCH function might find it in position 3 (or the third column in the table). You then can use that number with other functions, cell references, or searches. The INDEX function returns the value of a cell at the intersection of a particular row position and column position within a table or range. For example, you might want to know the age of the fifth student in a table, where ages are stored in the second column. Using the numbers 5 and 2 would eliminate the need to know the exact cell reference because the positions are relative to the table or range. Unlike the database functions, the range for these functions need not be a table.

To Use the SUMIF Function

1 CREATE TABLE | 2 LOOKUP TABLES | 3 CALCULATED FIELDS | 4 CONDITIONAL FORMATTING | 5 SORT TABLES
6 QUERY TABLES | 7 CRITERIA RANGES | **8 DATABASE & CONDITIONAL FUNCTIONS** | **9 SUBTOTALS & TREEMAP**

The following step uses the SUMIF function to ascertain the sum of the billings to Restaurants and Hotels. *Why? The SUMIF function allows you to sum a range based on criteria.* The general format of the SUMIF function is

=SUMIF(criteria_range, data, sum_range)

The first argument is the criteria range, or the range you want to search. The second argument is the desired piece of data in that range; it must be enclosed in quotes if the data is alphanumeric. The third argument is the location of the values you want summed. In this case, you are searching column C for "Restaurant/Hotel", and then summing Column I.

1

- Click cell Q8 and then type `=sumif(c9:c22, "Restaurant/ Hotel",i9:i22)` and then press the ENTER key to enter a function.

- Apply the accounting number format style to cell (Figure 6–63).

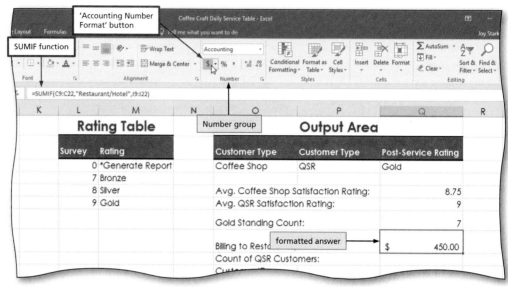

Figure 6–63

Other Ways

1. Click Insert Function box in formula bar, click 'Or select a category' button, click 'Math & Trig', click SUMIF in 'Select a function' list, enter arguments

2. Click 'Math & Trig' button (Formulas tab | Function Library group), click SUMIF, enter arguments

To Use the COUNTIF Functions

1 CREATE TABLE | 2 LOOKUP TABLES | 3 CALCULATED FIELDS | 4 CONDITIONAL FORMATTING | 5 SORT TABLES
6 QUERY TABLES | 7 CRITERIA RANGES | 8 DATABASE & CONDITIONAL FUNCTIONS | 9 SUBTOTALS & TREEMAP

The following step uses the COUNTIF to ascertain the number of QSR customers. **Why?** In large tables, counting the number of records that match certain conditions provides useful data for analysis. The general format of the COUNTIF function is

$$=COUNTIF(count\_range, data)$$

The first argument is the range containing the cells with which to compare the data in the second argument. Again, if the data is text rather than numbers, the data must be enclosed in quotes. In this case, you are counting the number of QSR service calls in Column C.

- In cell Q9, type `=countif (c9:c22,"QSR")`, and then click the Enter button to enter the function (Figure 6–64).

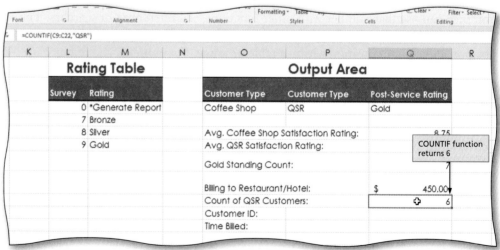

Figure 6–64

Other Ways

1. Click Insert Function box in formula bar, click 'Or select a category' button, click 'Statistical', click COUNTIF in 'Select a function' list, enter arguments

2. Click 'More Functions' button (Formulas tab | Function Library group), point to 'Statistical', click COUNTIF, enter arguments

To Use the MATCH and INDEX Functions

The MATCH function can be used to find the position number using the general format

=MATCH(lookup_value, lookup_array, match_type)

The first argument is the cell reference for the search data. The second argument is the range to search. The range must be a group of cells in a row or column. The third argument specifies the type of search: –1 for matches less than the lookup value, 0 (zero) for an exact match, and 1 for matches higher than the lookup value.

The INDEX function finds a value in a table or range based on a relative row and column. The general format is

=INDEX(range, row, column)

When used together, the MATCH and INDEX function provide the ability to look up a particular value in a table based on criteria. Because the MATCH function returns the row location in this case, you can use it as the second argument in the INDEX function. For example, to find the Time Billed for a specific customer in the table, the format would be

=INDEX(A9:I22, MATCH(Q10, A9:A22, 0), 5).

Within the INDEX function, A9:I22 is the table range, the MATCH function becomes the row, and 5 refers to column E, the time billed data. That final argument must be an integer rather than an alphabetic reference to the column. Within the MATCH function, Q10 is the location of the customer number you wish to search for, followed by the range of customer numbers in A9:A22, followed by a designation of 0 for an exact match. Sometimes called nesting, the inner function is performed first.

The following steps assume you want to look up the Time Billed for any given customer by using the customer number. *Why? The table is not sorted by customer number; this method makes it easier for the company to find the time billed for a specific customer.*

1

- Click cell Q10 and then type 69203 to enter a lookup value.

- In cell Q11, type =index(a9:i22, match(q10, a9:a22, 0), 5), and then press the ENTER key to enter a function.

- Display the data with two decimal places (Figure 6–65).

2

- Click the Save button on the Quick Access Toolbar to save the workbook again.

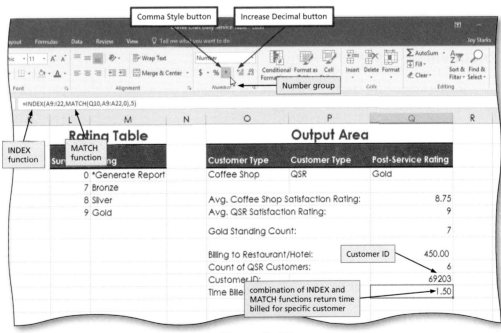

Figure 6–65

Other Ways

1. Click Insert Function box in formula bar, click 'Or select a category' button, click 'Lookup & Reference', click MATCH or INDEX in 'Select a function' list, enter arguments

2. Click 'Lookup & Reference' button (Formulas tab | Function Library group), click MATCH or INDEX, enter arguments

Summarizing Data

Another way to summarize data is by using subtotals. A subtotal is the sum of a subset of data while a grand total sums all of the data in a row or column. You can create sub totals automatically, as long as the data is sorted. For subtotals, the field on which you sort is called the **control field**. For example, if you choose the Customer type field as your control field, all of the Coffee Shop, QSR, and Restaurants/Hotel entries will be together within the data range. You then might request subtotals for the Time Billed and Customer Bill fields. Excel calculates and displays the subtotal each time the Customer Type field changes. A grand total displays at the bottom of the range. The most common subtotal uses the SUM function, although you can use other functions. If you change the control field, Excel updates the subtotal automatically. Note that the subtotal feature cannot be used with the table feature, only with normal ranges of data.

The Subtotal command displays outline symbols beside the rows or above the columns of the data you wish to group. The **outline symbols** include plus and minus signs for showing and hiding portions of the spreadsheet, as well as brackets identifying the groups. For example, you might want to minimize the display of technicians who have a bronze rating and show only those with silver and gold ratings. Outlining is extremely useful for making large tables more manageable in size and appearance.

To Sort the Data

Subtotals can only be performed on sorted data. The following step sorts the table by Customer Type.

 Click the filter button in cell C8 and then click the 'Sort A to Z' command to sort the Customer Type data.

To Convert a Table to a Range

1 CREATE TABLE | 2 LOOKUP TABLES | 3 CALCULATED FIELDS | 4 CONDITIONAL FORMATTING | 5 SORT TABLES
6 QUERY TABLES | 7 CRITERIA RANGES | 8 DATABASE & CONDITIONAL FUNCTIONS | 9 SUBTOTALS & TREEMAP

In preparation for creating subtotals, the following steps convert the table back to a range. *Why? The Subtotal command is not available for tables.*

- Right-click anywhere in the table and then point to Table on the shortcut menu to display the Table submenu (Figure 6–66).

- Click 'Convert to Range' (Table submenu) to display a Microsoft Excel dialog box.

- Click the Yes button (Microsoft Excel dialog box) to convert the table to a range.

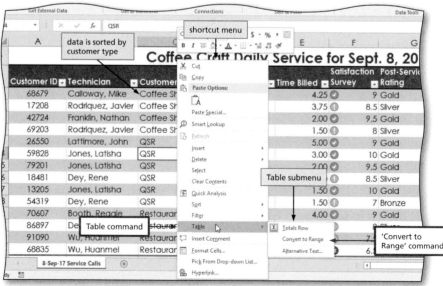

Figure 6–66

Other Ways

1. Click 'Convert to Range' button (Table Tools Design tab | Tools group), click Yes button (Microsoft Excel dialog box)

To Display Subtotals

The following steps display subtotals for the Time Billed and Customer Bill based on Customer Type. *Why? Subtotals are useful pieces of data for comparisons and analysis.*

1

- Click in one of the numeric fields you wish to subtotal (in this case, column I).

- Click the Subtotal button (Data tab | Outline group) to display the Subtotal dialog box.

- Click the 'At each change in' button (Subtotal dialog box) and then click Customer Type to select the control field.

- If necessary, click the Use function button and then select Sum in the Use function list.

- In the 'Add subtotal to' list (Subtotal dialog box), click Time Billed and Customer Bill to select values to subtotal. Clear any other check boxes (Figure 6–67).

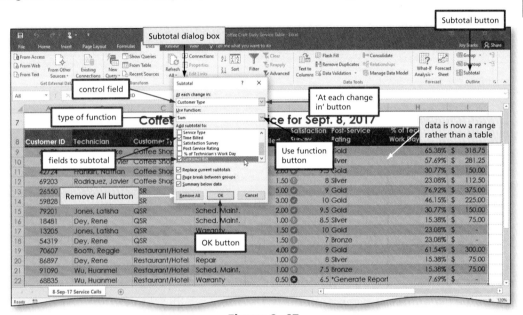

Figure 6–67

2

- Click the OK button to add subtotals to the range. Deselect the range.

- Zoom to 100% magnification.

- Scroll so that cell A8 is at the top of the worksheet, so that you can see the entire subtotal and outline area (Figure 6–68).

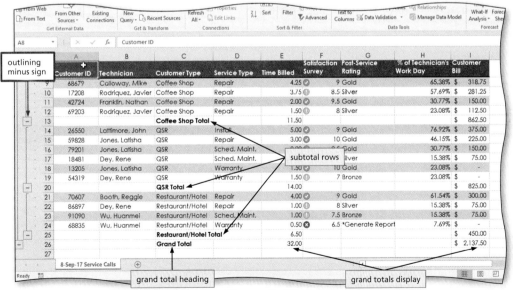

Figure 6–68

Q&A What changes does Excel make to the worksheet?
Excel adds three subtotal rows — one subtotal for each different Customer Type — and one grand total row for the entire table. The names for each subtotal row come from the sorted controls field and appear in bold. Thus, the text, Coffee Shop Total, in cell C13 identifies the row that contains subtotals for Time Billed and Customer Bill for the Coffee Shop customer type. Excel also displays the outlining feature.

To Use the Outline Feature

Excel turns on the outline feature automatically when you create subtotals. The following steps use the outline feature of Excel. *Why? The outline feature allows you to hide and show data and totals.*

- Click the second outlining column header to collapse the outline and hide the data (Figure 6–69).

Experiment

- One at a time, click each of the plus signs (+) in column two on the left side of the window to display detail records for each Customer Type.

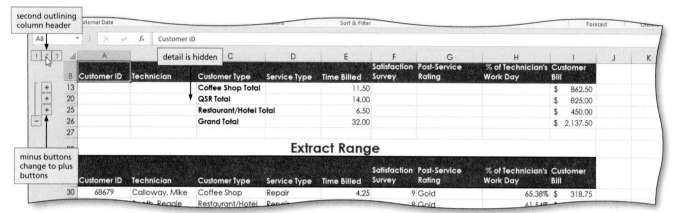

Figure 6–69

- Save the file with a new name, Coffee Craft Daily Service with Subtotals.

To Remove Automatic Subtotals

The following step removes the subtotals. *Why? In order to prepare the data for a chart, you want to remove subtotals.*

- Click the Subtotal button (Data tab | Outline group) to display the Subtotal dialog box.

- Click the Remove All button (Subtotal dialog box) to remove all subtotals (Figure 6–70).

- Close the file without quitting Excel. If you are prompted to save the file, click the No button (Microsoft Excel dialog box).

Figure 6–70

Treemap Charts

A **treemap chart** provides a hierarchical, visual view of data, making it easy to spot patterns and trends. Instead of hierarchical levels, treemap charts use rectangles to represent each branch and sub branch (or data category) by size, enabling users to display categories by color and proximity and to compare proportions. One of the fields in a treemap chart must be numeric, in order to generate the size of each rectangle. As with other types of charts, you can format fonts, colors, shape, and text effects, as well as add data fields and adjust data labels. Treemap charts compare values and proportions among large amounts of data that might be difficult to show with other types of charts.

To Create a Treemap Chart

1 CREATE TABLE | 2 LOOKUP TABLES | 3 CALCULATED FIELDS | 4 CONDITIONAL FORMATTING | 5 SORT TABLES
6 QUERY TABLES | 7 CRITERIA RANGES | 8 DATABASE & CONDITIONAL FUNCTIONS | **9 SUBTOTALS & TREEMAP**

The following steps create a treemap chart to compare technicians. ***Why?*** *The company would like to see how the technicians are spending their day using the Technician as the branch and the Repair Type as the sub branch. The Time billed will be reflected by the size of the rectangles.*

- Open the file named Coffee Craft Daily Service Table.

- If necessary, click the Filter button (Data tab | Sort & Filter group) to display the filter buttons. Sort the data in ascending order by Technician.

- Drag to select cells B8: E22 to select them.

- Display the Insert tab and then click the 'Insert Hierarchy Chart' button to display the gallery (Figure 6–71).

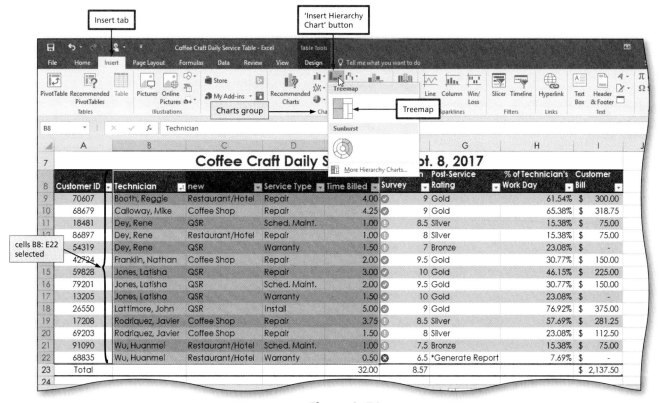

Figure 6–71

Do I have to use the table file rather than the file with subtotals?

Recall that you removed the table formatting in the file with subtotals. It is easier to start with the data stored as a table.

2

- Click Treemap (Insert Hierarchy Chart gallery) to insert the chart.

- Click the sixth chart style (Chart Tools Design tab | Chart Styles group) to select the style.

- Click the Chart Elements button located to the right of the chart and then click the Legend check box to remove the check mark (Figure 6–72).

 Experiment

- Point to each rectangle in the chart to see a ScreenTip showing from which data points the rectangle was created.

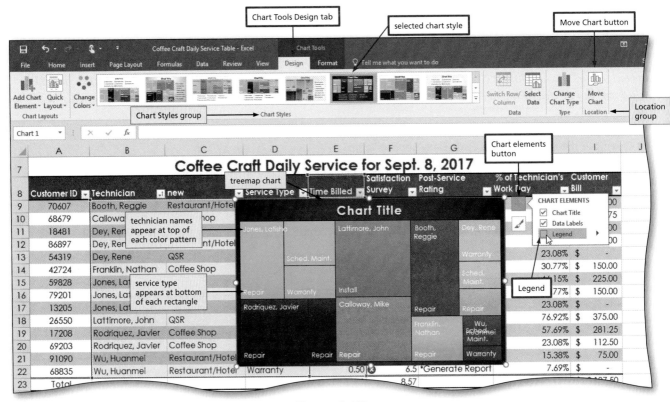

Figure 6–72

Other Ways

1. Select data, click the Recommended Charts button (Insert tab | Charts group), click All Charts tab (Recommended Charts dialog box), click Treemap, click OK button

To Move the Chart and Edit Fonts

The following steps move the chart to its own named worksheet and then edit the chart title and data label fonts.

1 Click the Move Chart button (Chart Tools Design tab | Location group) and then click New sheet in the Move Chart dialog box.

2 Type **Technician Treemap** in the New sheet text box (Move Chart dialog box) and then click the OK button.

3 Right-click the Chart Title and then click Edit Text on the shortcut menu. On the Home tab, change the font size to 24. Type **Technician Workday** to change the title.

4 Click any of the data labels in the chart. Change the font size to 14 (Figure 6–73).

Q&A How is the data presented in this chart?
The treemap allows you to compare each technician's day with other technicians: how much time they spent (size of color block) and how many service calls they completed during that time (number of subdivisions within each color block).

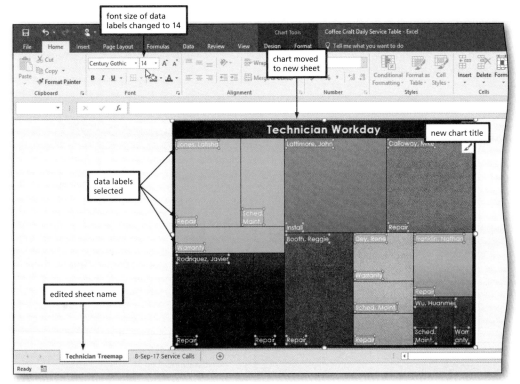

Figure 6–73

To Edit Treemap Settings

1 CREATE TABLE | 2 LOOKUP TABLES | 3 CALCULATED FIELDS | 4 CONDITIONAL FORMATTING | 5 SORT TABLES
6 QUERY TABLES | 7 CRITERIA RANGES | 8 DATABASE & CONDITIONAL FUNCTIONS | **9 SUBTOTALS & TREEMAP**

The following steps format the chart with settings that are unique to treemaps. *Why? Changing some of the settings will make the branches stand out and make the chart more user-friendly.*

1

• Right-click any of the rectangles to display the shortcut menu. Do not right-click a data label (Figure 6–74).

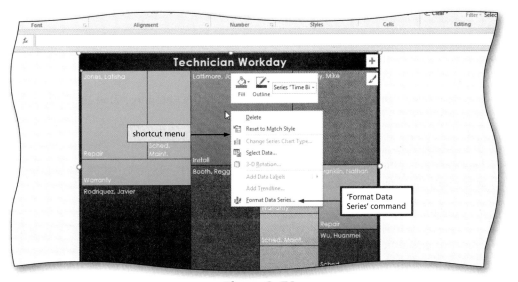

Figure 6–74

2

- Click 'Format Data Series' on the shortcut menu to display the Format Data Series task pane.
- Click Banner in the Label Options area (Figure 6–75).

 Experiment

- Click each of the label options and watch the chart change. When you are finished experimenting, click Banner.

Q&A What other choices can I make in the Format Data Series task pane?
On the Effects tab, you can add shadows, a glow, or other special effects. On the Fill & Line tab, you can change the color of the fill and the borders for each rectangle.

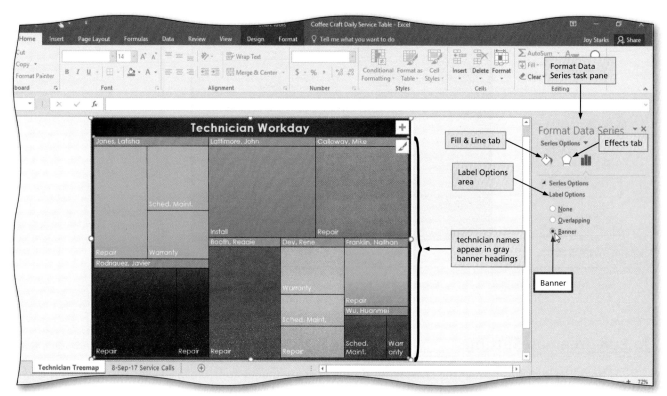

Figure 6–75

3

- Right-click any of the data labels, and then click 'Format Data Labels' on the shortcut menu to display the Format Data Labels task pane.
- Click to display a check mark in the Value check box. The Category Name check box should contain a check mark already (Figure 6–76).

 Experiment

- Click various combinations of the check marks and watch the chart change. When you are finished experimenting, select only Category Name and Value.

Q&A Why did the task pane display only three choices of labels?
You selected four fields in the data. The first field displays in the banner. The Series Name is the name of the numeric field, in this case Time Billed. Category represents the Service Type. Value is the numeric data, which also dictates the size of the rectangle.

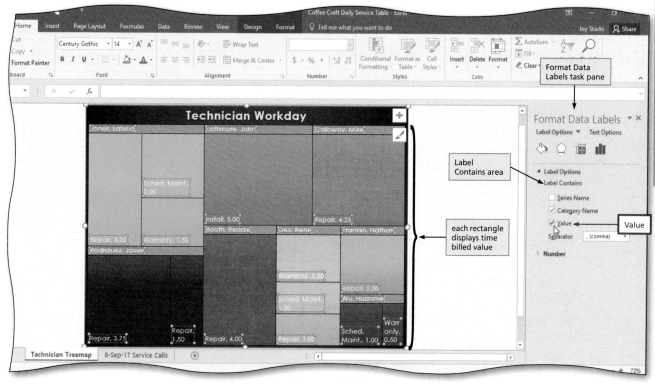

Figure 6–76

4 Save the file with the name `Coffee Craft Daily Service with Treemap` as the file name.

5 Click the Close button on the right side of the title bar to close the file and exit Excel.

6 If the Microsoft Office Excel dialog box is displayed, click the Don't Save button.

Summary

In this module, you learned how to create, sort, format, and filter a table (also called a database). You created calculated fields using structured references. Using conditional formatting, you applied an icon set to a field in the table. As you queried the table, you used AutoFilters with customized criteria. In a separate area of the worksheet, you created criteria and extract ranges to quickly search for and display specific data. You also created an output area using database functions such as SUMIF, COUNTIF, MATCH, and INDEX. After converting the table back to a range, you summarized data with subtotals. Finally, you created a treemap chart to display the technician workday in a visual format.

CONSIDER THIS

What decisions will you need to make when creating your next worksheet with a table to create, sort, and query?

Use these guidelines as you complete the assignments in this module and create your own worksheets for evaluating and analyzing data outside of this class.

1. Enter data for the table.

    a) Use columns for fields of data.

    b) Put each record on a separate row.

    c) Create user-friendly column headings.

    d) Format the range as a table.

    e) Format individual columns as necessary.

2. Create other fields.

    a) Use calculated fields with structured references.

    b) To apply rankings or settings, use a lookup table.

    c) To apply conditional formatting, consider icon sets or color groupings.

    d) Use total rows.

3. Sort the table.

    a) Sort ascending, descending, or combinations using tools on the Home tab and the Data tab.

4. Employ table AutoFilters for quick searches and sorts.

5. Create criteria and extract ranges to simplify queries.

6. Use functions.

    a) Use DAVERAGE and DCOUNT for database functions analyzing table data.

    b) Use SUMIF, COUNTIF, MATCH, and INDEX to find answers based on conditions.

7. Summarize data with subtotals and use outlining.

8. Create a treemap chart.

Apply Your Knowledge

Reinforce the skills and apply the concepts you learned in this module.

Creating a Table with Conditional Formatting

Note: To complete this assignment, you will be required to use the Data Files. Please contact your instructor for information about accessing the Data Files.

Instructions: The Dean's office has provided a list of student scholarship recipients and their current grade point averages. You are to create a table to include letter grades and summary data as shown in Figure 6–77. The conditional formatting is based on a green circle for 3.0 GPA or above, yellow for 2.0 or above, and red for students below 2.0 that are in danger of losing their scholarships.

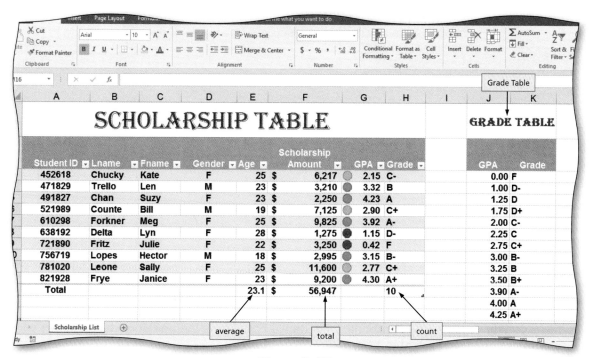

Figure 6–77

Perform the following tasks:

1. Run Excel and open the file named Apply 6–1 Scholarship Table. Save the file on your storage device with the name, Apply 6–1 Scholarship Table Complete.

2. Select the range, A2:G13. Click the 'Format as Table' button (Home tab | Styles group) and then click 'Table Style Medium 7' in the Format as Table gallery. When Excel displays the Format As Table dialog box, if necessary, click the 'My table has headers' check box to select the option to format the table with headers.

3. Name the table, Scholarships, by using the Table Name text box (Table Tools Design tab | Properties group).

4. Remove duplicates in the table by clicking the Remove Duplicates button (Table Tools Design tab | Tools group). When Excel displays the Remove Duplicates dialog box, click the Select All button and then click the OK button.

5. If requested to do so by your instructor, add your name as a scholarship winner and fill in the corresponding fields of data.

6. Insert a new column in the table (column H), with the column heading, Grade.

Continued >

Apply Your Knowledge *continued*

7. Change the row height of row 1 to 39. Click cell A1. Apply the Title cell formatting, the Algerian font, and a font size of 28. Center the title across the selection, A1:H1, using the Format Cells dialog box.

8. Add dollar signs with no decimal places to the scholarship amounts and format column widths as necessary. Wrap the text in cell F2. Format the GPA figures to have two decimal places.

9. To create the lookup table, enter the data from Table 6–5, beginning with Grade Table in cell J1. Format cell J1 with the Algerian font at size 14. Use the format painter to copy the table column heading format to cells J2 and K2. Right-align the GPA amounts and format with two decimal places. Left-align the grades.

Table 6–5 Scholarship Grade Table	
Grade Table	
GPA	**Grade**
0.00	F
1.00	D–
1.25	D
1.75	D+
2.00	C–
2.25	C
2.75	C+
3.00	B-
3.25	B
3.50	B+
3.90	A-
4.00	A
4.25	A+

10. In cell H3, type = **vlookup(g3, j3:k15, 2)** to enter the calculated column in the main table.

11. To apply conditional formatting:

a. Select the range G3:G12, click the Conditional Formatting button (Home tab | Styles group), and then click New Rule to display the New Formatting Rule dialog box.

b. Click the Format Style button (New Formatting Rule dialog box) to display the Format Style list.

c. Click Icon Sets in the Format Style list (New Formatting Rule dialog box) to display the Icon area.

d. Click the Icon Style button and then click '3 Traffic Lights (Unrimmed)' in the Icon Style list (New Formatting Rule dialog box) to select an icon style that includes three different colored circles.

e. Click the first Type button and then click Number in the list to select a numeric value. Click the second Type button and then click Number in the list to select a numeric value.

f. Type **3** in the first Value box, type **2** in the second Value box, and then press the TAB key to complete the conditions.

g. Click the OK button (New Formatting Rule dialog box) to display icons in each row of the table.

12. Display the total row by clicking the Total Row check box (Table Tools Design tab | Table Style Options group). Average the Age column, and sum the Scholarship Amount column.

13. Save the file again.

14. Use the Sort button on the Data tab to sort in ascending order by last name.

15. Use the 'Sort & Filter' button on the Home tab to sort in descending order by scholarship amount.

16. Use the Sort command on the filter menu to sort by grade point, with the highest grade point first.

17. Submit the workbook in the format specified by your instructor.

18. ✳ What other kind of criteria, filter, or output might be helpful if the table were larger? When might you use some of the database and statistical functions on this kind of data? Why?

Extend Your Knowledge

Extend the skills you learned in this module and experiment with new skills. You may need to use Help to complete the assignment.

Using Functions

Note: To complete this assignment, you will be required to use the Data Files. Please contact your instructor for information about accessing the Data Files.

Instructions: Run Excel. Open the workbook Extend 6–1 Business Analyst Table. You have been asked to summarize the data in a variety of ways as shown in Figure 6–78. Complete the following tasks to summarize the data.

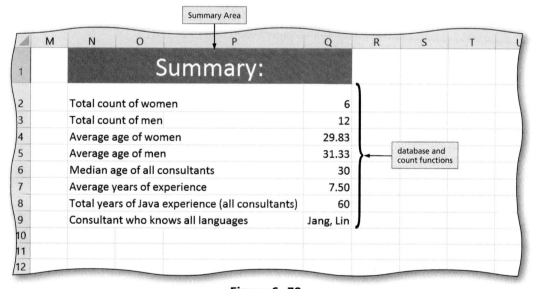

Figure 6–78

Perform the following tasks:

1. Save the workbook using the file name, Extend 6–1 Business Analyst Table Complete.

2. Create a new column called Count in column L. Use the COUNTIF function in cell L11 to count all of the Y entries in the row — indicating the number of languages in which the consultant is proficient.

3. If requested to do so by your instructor, insert your name and programming language experience as an additional row in the table.

4. Name the table, BA_Table.

Continued >

Extend Your Knowledge *continued*

5. Beside the table, create Summary title and row headings as shown in Figure 6–78.

6. Use the COUNTIF function for males and females. Use the AVERAGEIF function for the average ages. (*Hint*: Use Help to learn about the AVERAGEIF function.)

7. Use the MEDIAN function to find the median age of all consultants. (*Hint*: If necessary, use Help to learn about the MEDIAN function.)

8. Use the AVERAGE function to average the years of experience.

9. Use the SUMIF function to find the total years of Java experience in the company.

10. Use the MATCH function wrapped inside the INDEX function, as you did in the module, to find the one technician who is proficient in all seven languages.

11. Round off the averages to two decimal places, if necessary.

12. Save the file again and submit the assignment as requested by your instructor.

13. ✳ Which functions used structured references? Why?

Expand Your World

Create a solution that uses cloud and web technologies by learning and investigating on your own from general guidance.

Converting Files

Problem: You would like to place your Excel table on the web in a user-friendly format. You decide to investigate a Web 2.0 tool that will help you convert your table to HTML.

Instructions:

1. Run Excel and open any completed exercise from this module.

2. Drag through the table and column headings to select them. Press CTRL+C to copy the table cells.

3. Run a browser and navigate to http://tableizer.journalistopia.com/ (Figure 6–79).

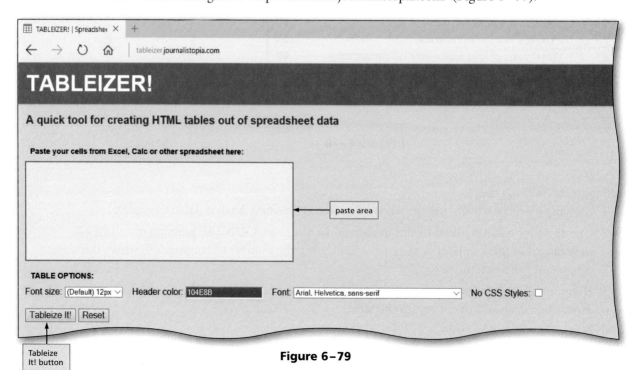

Figure 6–79

4. Click inside the gray paste area, and then press CTRL+V to paste the cells.

5. Click the Tableize It! button and wait a few seconds.

6. If you want to create an HTML page, copy the HTML code generated by Tableizer into a text editor such as Notepad. Save the Notepad file with the file name, MyTable.html. Display the file in a browser.

7. ✳ Many websites use tables to compare products, services, and pricing plans. Research HTML tables and web accessibility. What kinds of issues do screen readers have with HTML tables? Is it the best way to present information on the web?

In the Labs

Design, create, modify, and/or use a workbook following the guidelines, concepts, and skills presented in this module. Labs 1 and 2, which increase in difficulty, require you to create solutions based on what you learned in the module; Lab 3 requires you to apply your creative thinking and problem-solving skills to design and implement a solution.

Lab 1: **Creating Structured References, a Lookup Table, and a Treemap**

Problem: The City Market wants an easier way to keep track of the shelf life of fresh vegetables. You will format and summarize the data as shown in Figure 6–80a, and create the treemap shown in Figure 6–80b.

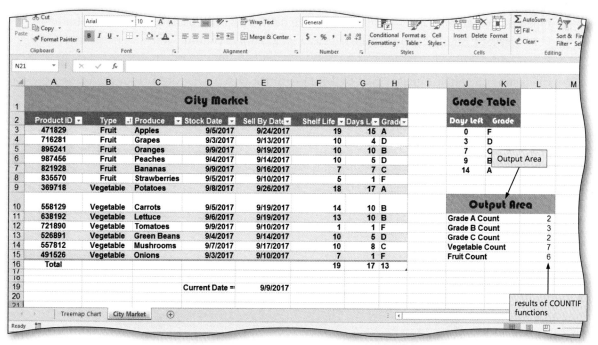

(a) Table and Analysis

Continued >

In the Labs *continued*

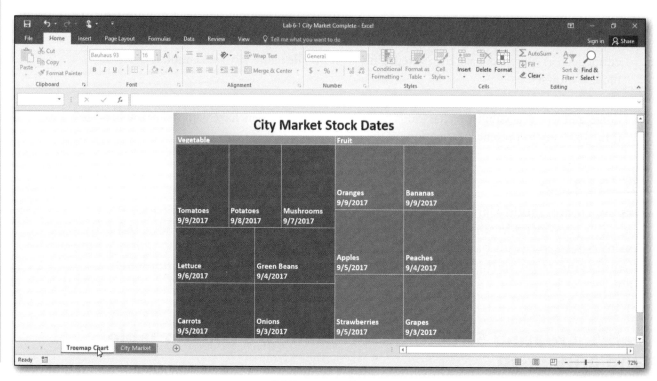

(b) Treemap Chart
Figure 6–80

Perform the following tasks:

1. Open the workbook Lab 6–1 City Market. Save the workbook using the file name, Lab 6–1 City Market Complete. Format the data as a table. Adjust column widths as necessary.

2. Create three new calculated columns, Shelf Life, Days Left, and Grade. The formula for calculating the Shelf Life is = [Sell By Date] – [Stock Date]. The formula for calculating the Days Left is = [Sell By Date] – currentDate. (*Hint:* currentDate is a named cell, E19.)

3. The Grade column will require you to create a lookup table area, shown in Table 6–6. Type the heading, **Grade Table** in cell J1 and fill in the column headings and data below that, as shown in Table 6–6. The calculation for the Grade column will use the VLOOKUP function. Recall that in a table, the first argument of the VLOOKUP function references the first cell in the column that you want to look up (such as G3). The second argument is the range of the lookup table with absolute references (such as $J$3:$K$7). The third argument is the column number of the rating within the lookup table (such as 2).

Table 6–6 Grade Table

Grade Table	
Days Left	**Grade**
0	F
3	D
7	C
9	B
14	A

4. Create an output area, as shown in Figure 6–80a, using several COUNTIF functions to total the grades, fruits, and vegetables. Recall that the first argument of the COUNTIF function is the range of data (for instance, the grade ratings in H3:H15, or the type of produce in B3:B15) and the second argument is the desired data (such as "A" or "Vegetable").

5. To create the treemap:

   a. Sort the table by Type and then select the range B2:F15.

   b. Select the Treemap chart and apply the second chart style.

   c. Remove the legend.

   d. Move the Chart to a new worksheet, named, Treemap Chart.

   e. Change the font size of the chart title to 32 and type `City Market Stock Dates` as the new title. Change the font size of the data labels to 18.

   f. Apply the Banner label option to the data series.

   g. Display the Category name and Value data labels, and separate the labels by placing Value on a new line.

6. If requested to do so by your instructor, on the City Market tab, add one more item to the Output Area to display the count of your favorite fruit or vegetable. (*Hint:* If you use the correct function and arguments, the count should equal 1.)

7. Save the file again and submit the assignment as requested by your instructor.

8. ✺ If you were to add a criteria range, or filtering technique, to the worksheet, for what kinds of data and conditions would you search? Why? What criteria would be most important to the owner of the City Market?

Lab 2: **Creating and Querying a Table**

Note: To complete this assignment, you will be required to use the Data Files. Please contact your instructor for information about accessing the Data Files.

Problem: Vacation Rentals would like the answers to the questions listed below about rental units. Run Excel. Open the workbook Lab 6–2 Rental Units Data. Save the workbook using the file name, Lab 6–2 Rental Units Table Complete.

Perform the following tasks:

1. Format the data as a table using your choice of Table styles. Adjust column widths and wrap text in the headings as necessary. Remove any duplicates from the table. Name the table Rental_ Units.

2. Create a heading in cell A7 that says Vacation Rentals. Center the title across the selection, A7:L7. Format the heading.

3. Copy the headings from the table to create both a criteria range (above) and an extract area (below) the table. Name the ranges.

Continued >

In the Labs *continued*

4. Fill in the comparison criteria to select records from the list to solve each of the problems in the following steps. So that you better understand what is required for this assignment, the answer is given for the first problem.

   a. Select records of units with at least 2 bedrooms and a pool. The criteria displays in Figure 6–81a. The extracted records display in Figure 6–81b.

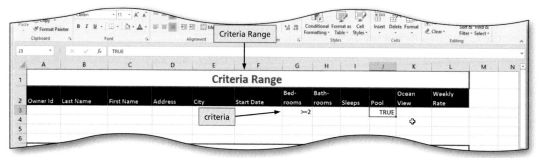

Figure 6–81a

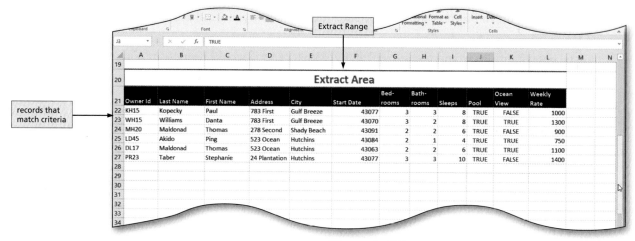

Figure 6–81b

   b. Select records that are located in the city of Gulf Breeze and have an ocean view.

   c. Select records that have only 1 bathroom.

   d. Select rental locations that are available in November and are less than $1000 per week.

   e. Select all locations owned by Thomas Maldonad.

   f. Select locations that can sleep 6 or 8 and are located on First street.

5. Save the file again and submit the assignment as requested by your instructor.

6. ✹ Do you think a treemap chart would work with the data in this exercises? Why or why not? What fields would you include?

Lab 3: **Consider This: Your Turn**

Apply your creative thinking and problem-solving skills to design and implement a solution.

Querying an Inventory

Part 1:   A local company would like to be able to search their inventory in an easy manner. They have given you sample data shown in Table 6–7.

Table 6–7 Inventory Data				
Inventory Number	**Description**	**Manufacturer**	**List Price**	**Quantity in Stock**
AX1D1	projector	Aldus	$595.00	2
CD7XL	coder	Boles	$195.00	4
R562W	stylus	Indirection	$49.00	14
TP45L	touch pad	Gladstone	$180.00	2
BC30W	card reader	Boles	$199.00	11
MX550	scanner/fax	Menem	$295.00	2
QR123	bar code scanner	Boles	$375.00	5

Create the criteria range, the table, and the extract range with formatted headings and data.

Save the worksheet. Perform the following extractions.

    a) all inventory items with more than 10 in stock

    b) all inventory items from the manufacturer, Boles

    c) all inventory items under $100

    d) all inventory items with 5 or less in stock and a list price of less than $300

Part 2:   ✸ Do you think small companies without extensive database experience might use tables such as this every day? What would be some advantages and disadvantages? What calculated fields might you add to the table?

7 Creating Templates, Importing Data, and Working with SmartArt, Images, and Screenshots

Objectives

You will have mastered the material in this module when you can:

- Create and use a template
- Import data from a text file, an Access database, a webpage, and a Word document
- Use text functions
- Paste values and paste text
- Transpose data while pasting it
- Convert text to columns
- Replicate formulas

- Use the Quick Analysis gallery
- Find and replace data
- Insert and format a bar chart
- Insert and modify a SmartArt graphic
- Add pictures to a SmartArt Graphic
- Apply text effects
- Include a hyperlinked screenshot

Introduction

In today's business environment, you often find that you need to create multiple worksheets or workbooks that follow the same basic format. A **template** is a special-purpose workbook you can create and use as a pattern for new, similar workbooks or worksheets. A template usually consists of a general format (worksheet title, column and row titles, and numeric formatting) and formulas that are common to all the worksheets. Templates can be saved to a common storage location so that everyone in a company can use them to create standardized documents.

Another important concept to understand is Excel's capability to use and analyze data from a wide variety of sources. In this module, you will learn how to **import**, or bring in, data from various external sources into an Excel worksheet and then analyze that data. Excel allows you to import data from a number of types of sources, including text files, webpages, database tables, data stored in Word documents, and XML files.

Finally, a chart, graphic, image, or screenshot often conveys information or an idea better than words or numbers. You can insert and modify graphics, images, and screenshots to enhance the visual appeal of an Excel workbook and illustrate its contents. Many of the skills you learn when working with graphics in Excel will be similar when working in other Office programs, such as Word, Publisher, or PowerPoint.

Project — Home Security Systems

Home Security Systems (HSS) is a retail and online outlet for hardware used in securing homes and small businesses. The company owner has requested that the in-store and online sales results for the last two years be compared among its four stores. One of the stores provides the requested data in a plain text format (Figure 7–1a) rather than in an Excel workbook. To make use of that data in Excel, the data must be imported before it can be formatted and manipulated. The same is true of formats in which the other locations store data, such as Microsoft Access tables (Figure 7–1b), webpages (Figure 7–1c), or Microsoft Word documents (Figure 7–1d). Excel provides the tools necessary to import and manipulate the data from these sources into a single worksheet (Figure 7–1e). Using the data from the worksheet, you will create a bar chart to summarize total sales by category (Figure 7–1f). Finally, you will add SmartArt graphics that include images (Figure 7–1g) and a hyperlinked screenshot to support your work (Figure 7–1h).

Figure 7–2 illustrates the requirements document for the HSS Sales Analysis workbook. It includes the needs, sources of data, calculations, charts, and other facts about the workbook's development.

In addition, using a sketch of the main worksheet can help you visualize its design. The sketch of the worksheet consists of titles, column and cell headings, the location of data values, and a general idea of the desired formatting in the worksheet. The data will include 2016 and 2017 data, with a summary on the right (Figure 7–3a). Figure 7–3b displays a basic sketch of the requested graph, a bar chart, showing the 2017 totals by category.

With a good understanding of the requirements document, an understanding of the necessary decisions, and a sketch of the worksheet and graph, the next step is to use Excel to create the workbook.

The following roadmap identifies general activities you will perform as you progress through this module:

1. CREATE a TEMPLATE with sample data and formulas.
2. USE a TEMPLATE to create a new workbook.
3. IMPORT and format outside DATA into an Excel workbook.
4. USE the QUICK ANALYSIS gallery to create totals and charts easily.
5. FIND and REPLACE data.
6. INSERT and format a BAR CHART.
7. CREATE and format a SMARTART graphic to display pictures and text.
8. ADD a hyperlinked SCREENSHOT.

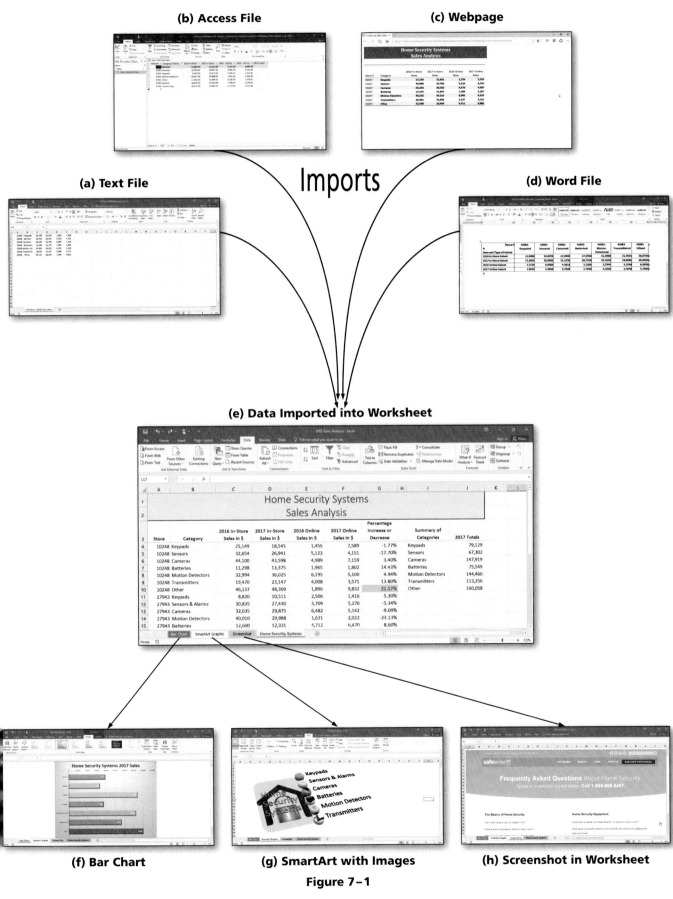

(b) Access File

(c) Webpage

(a) Text File

Imports

(d) Word File

(e) Data Imported into Worksheet

(f) Bar Chart

(g) SmartArt with Images

(h) Screenshot in Worksheet

Figure 7–1

Worksheet Title	Home Security Systems Sales Analysis
Needs	• A template with headings, sample data, and formulas than can be used to create similar worksheets • A workbook, made from the template, containing a worksheet that combines sales data from the four stores • A chart that compares the 2017 total sales for each category of products that the store sells
Source of Data	The four sales managers will submit data from their respective stores as follows: • Store 10248 saves data in a text file. • Store 27943 uses an Access database. • Store 33607 maintains web data. • Store 42681 uses Word to store data in a table.
Calculations	Include the following formula in the template for each line item in the inventory: • =((D4+F4)/(C4+E4))-1 This formula takes the total of 2017 in-store and online sales minus the total of 2016 in-store and online sales to arrive at a percentage, and then subtracts 1 to arrive at just the increase or decrease. Include the following two functions to help summarize the data: • IF(COUNTIF($B$4:B4,B4)=1,B4," ") This formula will find the unique categories in column B. It includes the COUNTIF function that will return true if a match occurs. If no match is made, the value will be false; then, the IF function will display the value from column B. • =SUMIF($B$4:$B$100,I4,$D$4:$D$100)+SUMIF($B$4:$B$100,I4,$F$4:$F$100) This function will add the 2017 in-store and online sales on a category basis. It adds the value in column D plus the value in column F, if cell I4 matches the value from column B. The function will look through row 100 as the maximum number of records.
Chart Requirements	Create a bar chart to compare the categories for sales in 2017. Include the chart on a separate worksheet.
Other Requirements	• Investigate a SmartArt graphic to include the pictures given to you by the company, to be included on a separate worksheet. • On a separate worksheet, include a screenshot of the website they recommend for questions about home security systems (http://safewise.com/home-security-faq).

Figure 7–2

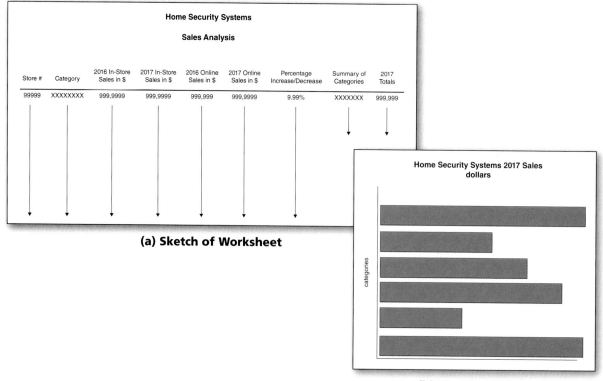

(a) Sketch of Worksheet

(b) Sketch of Chart

Figure 7–3

Creating Templates

The first step in building the project in this module is to create and save a template that contains the titles, column and row headings, formulas, and formats. After the template is saved, it can be used every time a similar workbook is developed. Because templates help speed and simplify their work, many Excel users create a template for each project on which they work. Templates can be simple — possibly using a special font or worksheet title; or they can be more complex — perhaps using specific formulas and format styles, such as the template for the HSS Sales Analysis workbook.

What factors should you keep in mind when building a template?

A template usually contains data and formatting that will appear in every workbook created from that template. Because the template will be used to create a number of other worksheets, make sure you consider the layout, cell formatting, and contents of the workbook as you design the template. Set row heights and column widths. Use placeholders for data when possible and use dummy data to verify formulas. Format the cells in the template.

Creating a template, such as the one shown in Figure 7–4, follows the same basic steps used to create a workbook. The only difference between developing a workbook and a template is the file type used when saving the template.

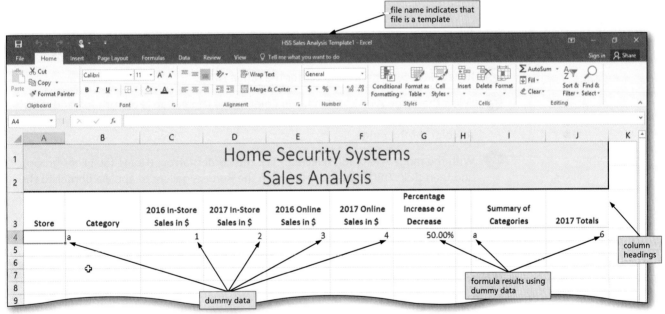

Figure 7–4

To Open a Blank Workbook and Format the Rows and Columns

The following steps open a blank workbook and set the row height and column widths.

1 Run Excel.

2 Click the Blank workbook thumbnail on the Excel start screen to create a blank workbook and display it in the Excel window.

3 If the Excel window is not maximized, click the Maximize button on its title bar to maximize the window.

4 CTRL+click rows 1 and 2 to select them. Using the row heading area, drag the bottom boundary of row 2 down, until the ScreenTip displays 'Height 28.50 (38 pixels)' to change the height of the rows. For row 3, drag the bottom boundary down until the ScreenTip displays Height 45.75 (61 pixels) to change the height of the row.

5 Set the column widths as follows: A = 9.00 (68 pixels), B = 17.00 (124 pixels), C = 14.00 (103 pixels), D = 14.00 (103 pixels), E = 14.00 (103 pixels), F = 14.00 (103 pixels), G = 14.00 (103 pixels), H = 3.00 (26 pixels), I = 17.00 (124 pixels), and J = 14.00 (103 pixels).

To Enter Titles in the Template

The following steps enter and format the titles in cells A1 and A2.

1 In cell A1, type **Home Security Systems** to enter the worksheet title.

2 In cell A2, type **Sales Analysis** to enter the worksheet subtitle.

3 Display the Page Layout tab. Click the Theme Colors button (Page Layout tab | Themes group) and then click Blue Green in the Colors gallery to apply the Blue Green colors to the worksheet.

4 Select the range A1:A2. Click the Cell Styles button (Home tab | Styles group) and then apply the Title cell style to the range. Change the font size to 24.

5 Select the range A1:J1. Click the 'Merge & Center' button (Home tab | Alignment group) to merge and center the selected cells.

6 Repeat Step 5 to merge and center the range A2:J2.

7 Select the range A1:A2, click the Fill Color arrow (Home tab | Font group), and then click 'Aqua, Accent 2, Lighter 60%' (column 6, row 3) in the Fill Color gallery to set the fill color for the range.

8 With the range A1:A2 still selected, click the Borders arrow (Home tab | Font group), and then click 'Thick Outside Borders' in the Borders gallery to apply a border to the range.

9 Select cell A3 and zoom to 130% (Figure 7–5).

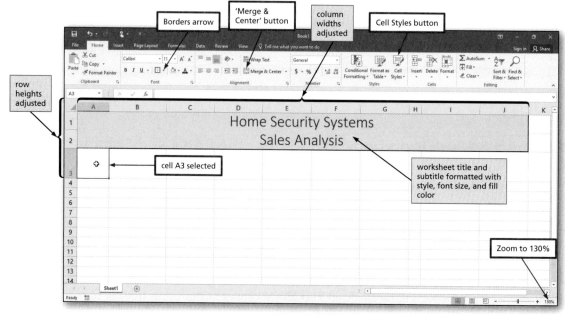

Figure 7–5

To Enter Column Titles in the Template

The following steps enter and format the column titles in row 3.

1 Select cells A3:J3 and then click the Wrap Text button (Home tab | Alignment group) to apply the formatting. Click the Center button (Home tab | Alignment group) and then apply the Heading 3 cell style to the range.

2 Type the following column titles into the appropriate cells (Figure 7–6).

A3	Store
B3	Category
C3	2016 In-Store Sales in $
D3	2017 In-Store Sales in $
E3	2016 Online Sales in $
F3	2017 Online Sales in $
G3	Percentage Increase or Decrease
H3	<blank>
I3	Summary of Categories
J3	2017 Totals

Figure 7–6

To Enter Sample Data in the Template

When a template is created, sample data or dummy data is used in place of actual data to verify the formulas in the template. Selecting simple text, such as a, b, or c, and numbers, such as 1, 2, and 3, allows you to check quickly to see if the formulas are generating the proper results. In templates with more complex formulas, you may want to use numbers that test the extreme boundaries of valid data, such as the lowest or highest possible number, or a maximum number of records.

The following steps enter sample data in the template.

1 Select cell B4. Type **a** to enter the first piece of sample data.

2 Select cell C4. Type **1** to enter the first number in the series.

③ Enter the other dummy data as shown in Figure 7–7.

④ Select the range C4:F4. Apply the comma style with no decimal places to the selected range.

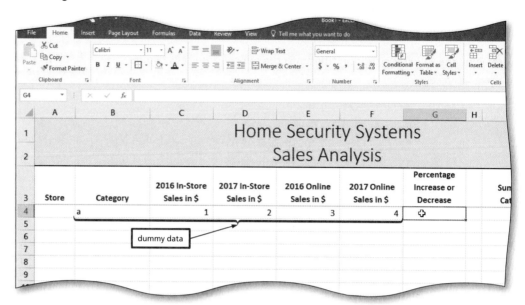

Figure 7–7

To Enter Formulas and Functions in the Template

The following steps enter formulas and functions to summarize data in the template, as described in the requirements document. The percentage formula adds the 2017 in-store and online sales and divides that by the 2016 sales. It subtracts 1 to include only the increase or decrease. The summary of categories uses a function to look for unique values in future imported data. The 2017 totals add any imported values from columns D and F that match the unique category identified in column I.

① Select cell G4. Type `=((d4+f4)/(c4+e4))-1` as the formula for calculating the percentage increase or decrease from 2016 to 2017 and then click the Enter button.

② Format cell G4 with a percent sign and two decimal places.

③ Select cell I4. Type = `if(countif($b$4:b4,b4)=1,b4,"")` to enter a function that displays a value from the Category list if it is unique. Click the Enter button.

④ Select cell J4. Type `=sumif($b$4:$b$100,i4,$d$4:$d$100) + sumif($b$4:$b$100,i4,$f$4:$f$100)`   to enter a function that adds columns d and f, if the value returned in cell I4 matches the data in the Category list in column B. The function will look through row 100 as the maximum number of records. Click the Enter button.

⑤ Format cell J4 with a comma and no decimal places.

⑥ Change the sheet tab name to Home Security Systems to provide a descriptive name for the worksheet.

⑦ Change the sheet tab color to Aqua, Accent 2 to format the tab (Figure 7–8).

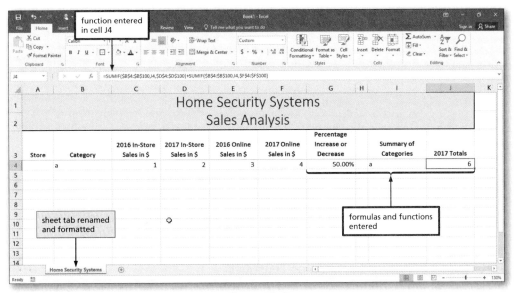

Figure 7–8

---

1 CREATE TEMPLATE | 2 USE TEMPLATE | 3 IMPORT DATA | 4 USE QUICK ANALYSIS
5 FIND & REPLACE | 6 INSERT BAR CHART | 7 CREATE SMARTART | 8 ADD SCREENSHOT

To Save the Template

Saving a template is similar to saving a workbook, except that the file type, Excel Template, is selected in the 'Save as type' box (Save As dialog box). Excel saves the file with the extension, .xltx, to denote its template status. Saving in that format prevents users from accidentally saving over the template file and causes Excel to open new workbooks based on the template with the proper format. In business situations, it is a good idea to save the template in the default Templates folder location. **Why?** *Company templates saved in the Templates folder appear with other templates when users need to find them.* In lab situations, however, you should save templates on your personal storage device. The following steps save the template using the file name, HSS Sales Analysis Template on your storage device.

- Click cell A4 to position the current cell.

- Click the Save button on the Quick Access Toolbar to display the Save As gallery and then click the Browse button to display the Save As dialog box.

- Type **HSS Sales Analysis Template** in the File name box to enter a name for the file.

- Click the 'Save as type' arrow and then click Excel Template in the list to specify that this workbook should be saved as a template.

- Navigate to your storage device and desired folder, if any (Figure 7–9).

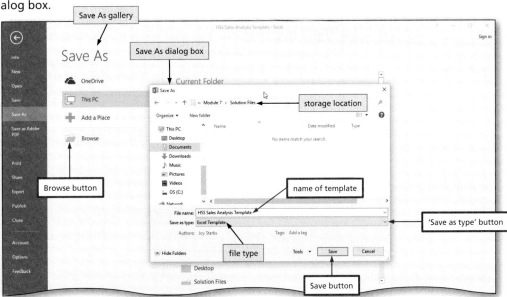

Figure 7–9

Q&A | Why does Excel change the folder location when the Excel Template file type is chosen?
When the Excel Template file type is chosen in the 'Save as type' box, Excel automatically changes the location to the Templates folder created when Office 2016 was installed. In a production environment — that is, when you are creating a template for a business, a school, or an application — the template typically would be saved in the Templates folder, not on your personal storage device.

- Click the Save button (Save As dialog box) to save the template in the selected folder on the selected save location with the entered file name.

- Exit Excel.

Other Ways

1. Press CTRL+S, click Browse button (Save As gallery), type file name (Save As dialog box), select Excel Template in 'Save as type' box, select drive or folder, click Save button

TO CHANGE THE DEFAULT LOCATION OF TEMPLATES

If you wanted to change the default location where templates are stored, you would perform the following steps. Once this option is set, all templates you save will appear automatically under Personal in the New gallery.

1. Click File on the ribbon to open the Backstage view.

2. Click Options to display the Excel Options dialog box.

3. Click Save in the left pane (Excel Options dialog box) and then in the Save workbooks area, enter the path to the personal templates location in the 'Default personal templates location' box. This path typically is C:\Users\ UserName\Documents\Custom Office Templates\.

4. Click the OK button (Excel Options dialog box).

TO SET THE READ-ONLY ATTRIBUTE

Once a template is created, you may want to change the file's attribute, or classification, to read-only. With a **read-only file**, you can open and access the file normally, but you cannot make permanent changes to it. That way, users will be forced to save changes to the template with a new file name, keeping the original template intact and unchanged for the next user.

While you can view system properties in Excel 2016, you cannot change the read-only attribute from within Excel. Setting the read-only attribute is a function of the operating system. If you wanted to set the read-only property of the template, you would perform the following steps.

1. Click the File Explorer app button on the taskbar. Navigate to your storage location.

2. Right-click the template file name to display the shortcut menu.

3. Click Properties on the shortcut menu to display the Properties dialog box.

4. If necessary, click the General tab (Properties dialog box) to display the General sheet.

5. Verify that the file is the one you previously saved on your storage device by looking at the Location information.

6. Click to place a check mark in the Read-only check box in the Attributes area.

7. Click the OK button (Properties dialog box) to close the dialog box and apply the read-only attribute.

Break Point: If you wish to take a break, this is a good place to do so. To resume at a later time, continue following the steps from this location forward.

To Open a Template and Save It as a Workbook

As with other Office apps, you can open an Excel template in one of several ways:

- If you use the Open gallery in the Backstage view, you will open the template file itself for editing.

- If you have stored the template in the default template storage location, you can click the New tab in the Backstage view and then click Personal. Clicking the template file in the Personal gallery will open a new file based on the template.

- If you stored the template in another location, you must double-click the file in the File Explorer window to create a new file based on the template.

When you open a file based on a template, Excel names the new workbook using the template name with an appended digit 1 (e.g., Monthly Budget Template1). **Why?** *Adding a 1 to the file name delineates it from the template; it is similar to what Excel does when you first run Excel and it assigns the name Book1 to the new workbook.* You can save the file with a new file name if you want.

The following steps open a file based on the template. You then will save it in the .xlsx format with a new file name in order to proceed with data entry.

- Click the File Explorer app button on the taskbar to run the File Explorer app.

- Navigate to your storage location (Figure 7–10).

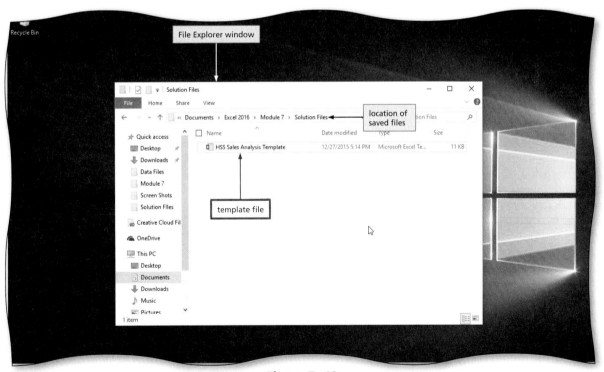

Figure 7–10

- Double-click the file named HSS Sales Analysis Template to open a new file based on the template (Figure 7–11).

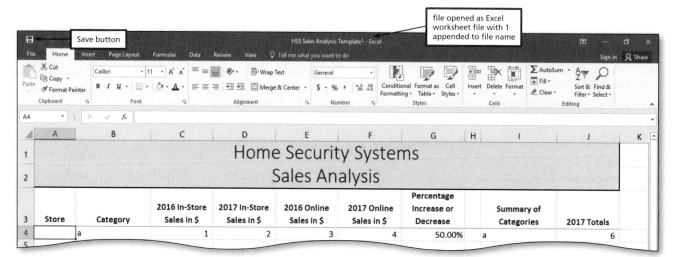

Figure 7–11

- Click the Save button (Quick Access Toolbar) to display the Save As gallery in the Backstage view.

- Click the Browse button to display the Save As dialog box.

- Type **HSS Sales Analysis** in the File name box (Save As dialog box) and then navigate to your storage location (Figure 7–12).

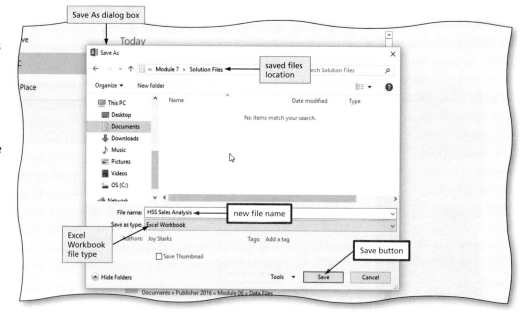

Figure 7–12

Q&A Should I change the file type?

No. Excel automatically selects Excel Workbook as the file type when you attempt to save a file based on a template.

- Click the Save button (Save As dialog box) to save the file with the new file name.

Importing Data

Data may come from a variety of sources and in a range of formats. Even though many users keep data in databases, such as Microsoft Access, it is common to receive text files with fields of data separated by commas. More and more companies are creating HTML files and posting data on the web. Word documents, especially those including tables of data, often are used in business as a source of data for workbooks. **XML (Extensible Markup Language)**, a popular format for data exchange, is a set of encoding rules that formats data to be readable by both humans and devices. Excel allows you to import data made available in all of those formats and more. Importing data into Excel can create a link that can be used to update data whenever the original file changes.

How should you plan for importing data?

Before importing data, become familiar with the layout of the data, so that you can anticipate how each data element will be arranged in the worksheet. In some cases, the data will need to be transposed, meaning that the rows and columns need to be switched. You also might need to format the data, move it, or convert it from or to a table.

In the following sections, you will import data from four different stores and in four different formats. You will look for data inconsistencies, format the data as necessary, and replicate the formulas to create the consolidated worksheet shown as a printout in Figure 7–13.

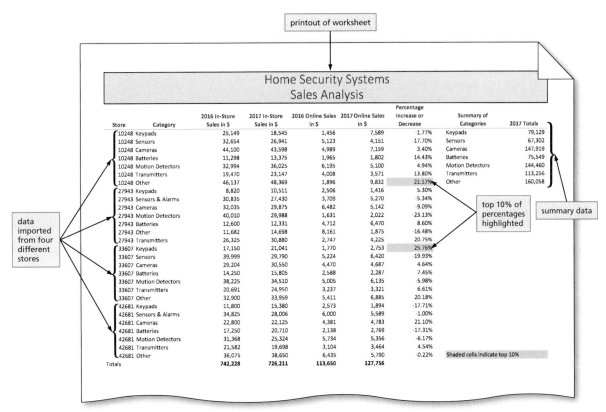

Figure 7–13

Text Files

A **text file** contains data with little or no formatting. Many programs, including Excel, offer an option to import data from a text file. Text files may have a file extension such as .txt, .csv, .asc, or .cdl, among others. Companies sometimes generate these text files from input fields via proprietary business applications.

In text files, commas, tabs, or other characters often separate the fields. Alternately, the text file may have fields of equal length in columnar format. Each record usually exists on a separate line. A **delimited file** contains data fields separated by a selected character, such as a comma. Such a file is called a **comma-delimited text file**. A **fixed-width file** contains data fields of equal length with spaces between the fields. In the case of a fixed-width file, a special character need not separate the data fields. During the import process, Excel provides a preview to help identify the type of text file being imported.

To Import Data from a Text File

1 CREATE TEMPLATE | 2 USE TEMPLATE | 3 IMPORT DATA | 4 USE QUICK ANALYSIS
5 FIND & REPLACE | 6 INSERT BAR CHART | 7 CREATE SMARTART | 8 ADD SCREENSHOT

The following steps import a comma-delimited text file into the HSS Sales Analysis workbook using the Text Import Wizard. *Why? The wizard helps you make sure the data is imported correctly.* To complete these steps, you will be required to use the Data Files. Please contact your instructor for information about accessing the Data Files. The text file contains data about sales for Store #10248 (shown in Figure 7–1a).

- With the HSS Sales Analysis workbook active, if necessary, select cell A4.
- Click Data on the ribbon to display the Data tab.
- Click the 'Get Data From Text' button (Data tab | Get External Data group) to display the Import Text File dialog box.
- If necessary, navigate to the location of the Data Files to display the files (Figure 7–14).

Q&A Why can I not find the 'Get Data From Text' button?
If any add-in or accessory programs have been installed in Excel, Excel may display a 'Get External Data' button on the Data tab that combines several types of data. Click the button to display a menu containing the 'Get Data From Text' button.

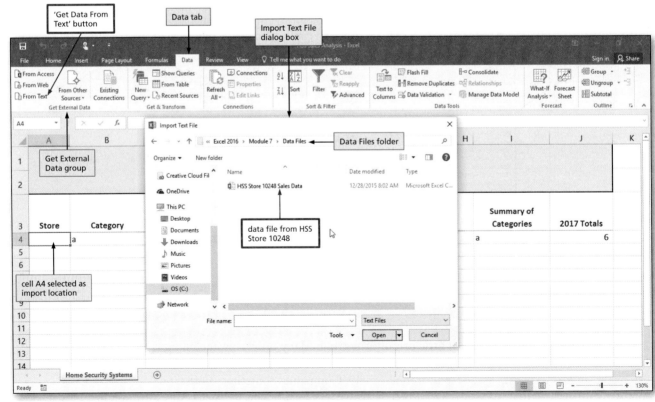

Figure 7–14

2

- Double-click the file name 'HSS Store 10248 Sales Data' to start the Text Import Wizard and display the Text Import Wizard - Step 1 of 3 dialog box (Figure 7–15).

Q&A

What is the purpose of the Text Import Wizard?

The Text Import Wizard provides step-by-step instructions for importing data from a text file into an Excel worksheet. The Preview box shows that the text file contains one record per line and the fields are separated by commas. The Delimited option button is selected in the Original data type area.

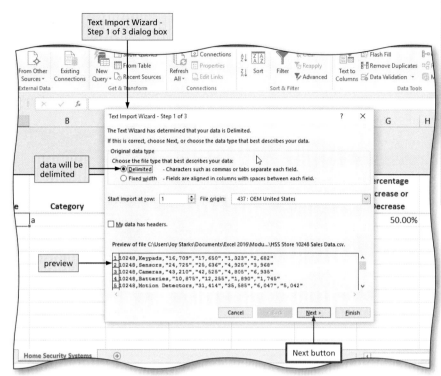

Figure 7–15

3

- Click the Next button (Text Import Wizard - Step 1 of 3 dialog box) to display the Text Import Wizard - Step 2 of 3 dialog box.

- Click Tab to remove the check mark.

- Click Comma to place a check mark in the Comma check box and to display the data fields correctly in the Data preview area (Figure 7–16).

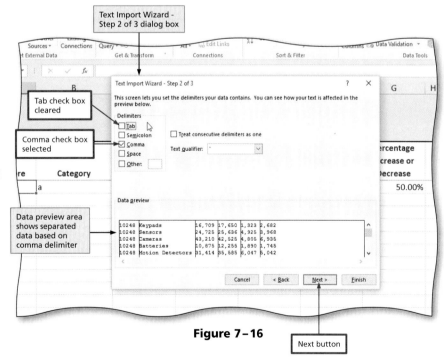

Figure 7–16

4

- Click the Next button (Text Import Wizard - Step 2 of 3 dialog box) to display the Text Import Wizard - Step 3 of 3 dialog box (Figure 7–17).

 What is the purpose of the Advanced button?
When clicked, the Advanced button displays settings related to numerical data such as decimals and thousands separators.

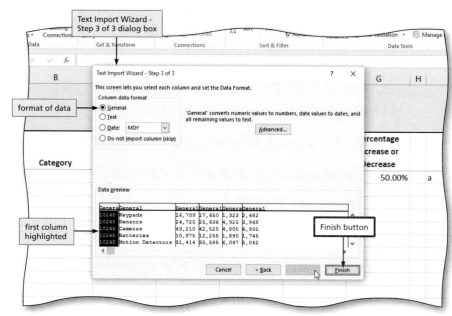

Figure 7–17

5

- Click the Finish button (Text Import Wizard - Step 3 of 3 dialog box) to complete the Text Import Wizard and display the Import Data dialog box (Figure 7–18).

 What is shown in the Import Data dialog box when importing text?
The Import Data dialog box allows you to choose in which cell to import the text and to specify properties of the imported text.

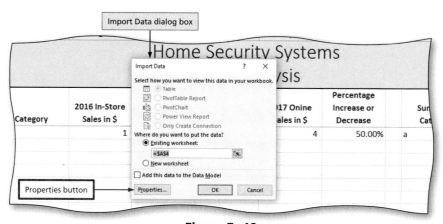

Figure 7–18

6

- Click the Properties button (Import Data dialog box) to display the External Data Range Properties dialog box.
- Click 'Adjust column width' to remove the check mark.
- Click the 'Overwrite existing cells with new data, clear unused cells' option button to select it (Figure 7–19).

 What are the Refresh control options?
The Refresh control options allow you to receive updated data from the text file based on a manual refresh, a specific time interval, or every time the workbook is opened, thus linking the text file to the current workbook.

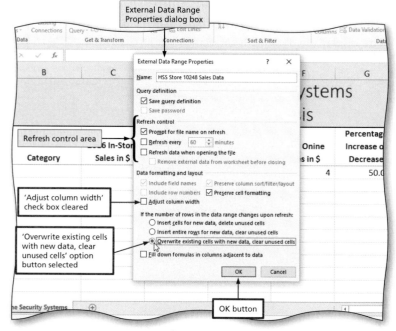

Figure 7–19

7

- Click the OK button (External Data Range Properties dialog box) to accept the settings and display the Import Data dialog box again.

- Click the OK button (Import Data dialog box) to import the data from the text file into the worksheet beginning at cell A4 (Figure 7–20).

- Select cell C4 and then display the Home tab.

- Click the Format Painter button (Home tab | Clipboard group) and then drag through the range C5:F10 to copy the formatting to the range (Figure 7–20).

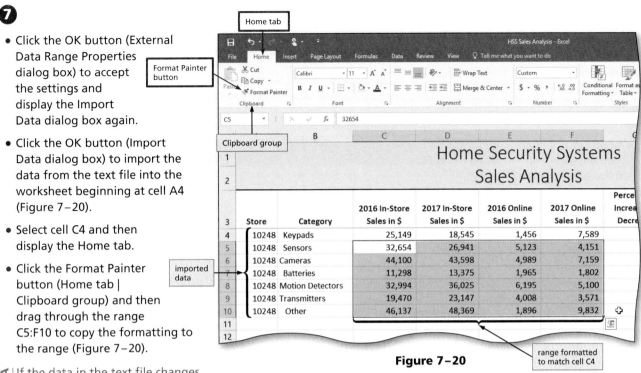

Figure 7–20

Q&A If the data in the text file changes, how do I manually refresh it?
After the text file is imported, Excel can refresh, or update, the data whenever the original text file changes using the Refresh All button (Data tab | Connections group).

Text Formatting

Sometimes data imported from various sources will have some input inconsistencies and will need to be reformatted. It is important to check imported data closely and make corrections as necessary, without changing any values. Excel has a series of text functions to help you convert numbers to text, correct inconsistencies in capitalization, and trim off excess spaces, as well as functions to retain only parts of a cell contents or join pieces of text together. Table 7–1 displays some of the available text functions.

Table 7–1 Text Functions

Function	Purpose	Syntax	Example	Result
TEXT	Converts a numeric value to text and lets you specify the display formatting by using special format strings (Once converted, you cannot use it in calculations.)	TEXT(value, format_text)	=TEXT(42.5, "$0.00")	$42.50
TRIM	Removes all spaces from text except for single spaces between words	TRIM(text)	TRIM(" Roy S. Lyle ")	Roy S. Lyle
RIGHT	Returns the rightmost characters from a text value	RIGHT(text,[num_chars])	RIGHT("Joyce",1)	e
LEFT	Returns the leftmost characters from a text value	LEFT(text,[num_chars])	LEFT ("Joyce",2)	Jo
MID	Returns a specific number of characters starting at a specified position	MID(text, start_num, num_chars)	MID("Joyce",2,3)	oyc
UPPER	Converts text to uppercase	UPPER(text)	UPPER("Joyce")	JOYCE
LOWER	Converts text to lowercase	LOWER(text)	LOWER("Joyce")	joyce
CONCATENATE	Joins several text items into one text item	CONCATENATE(text1, [text2], ...)	CONCATENATE ("Mari","lyn")	Marilyn

To Use the Trim Function

The following steps trim extra spaces from the category data you imported. *Why? You notice that the data was stored with extra spaces, making it impossible to align the words in the column.* In a separate part of the workspace, you will use the TRIM function that will remove all spaces from text except for single spaces between words. You then will paste the trimmed values to replace the originals.

1

• Select cell B12, type **=trim(b4)** and then click the Enter button to trim the spaces from the data in cell B4 and display it in cell B12 (Figure 7–21).

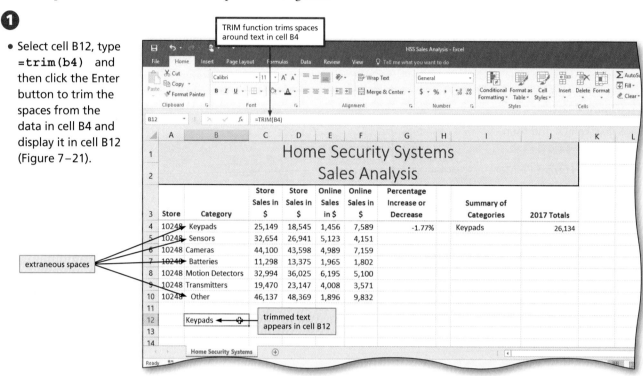

Figure 7–21

2

• Drag the fill handle of cell B12 down through cell B18 to display the trimmed data for all categories.

• Do not deselect (Figure 7–22).

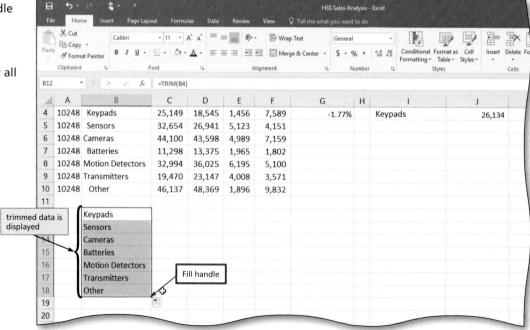

Figure 7–22

To Paste Values Only

The following steps cut the data from cells B12 through B18 and paste only the trimmed values back to cells B4 through B10. **Why?** *If you simply paste the contents of the clipboard using* CTRL+V, *you will retain the trim function notation. You want only the trimmed values.* To paste values, you will use Paste Options.

- With the range B12:B18 still selected, press CTRL+C to copy the data.

- Right-click cell B4 to display the shortcut menu (Figure 7–23).

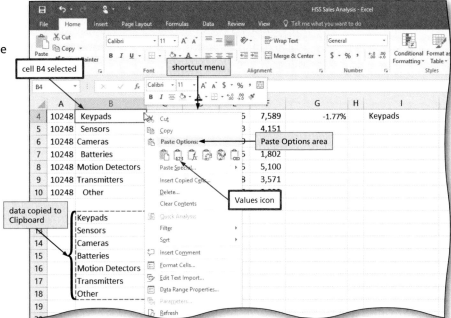

Figure 7–23

- In the Paste Options area, click the Values icon to paste only the values.

- Delete the data in the B12:B18 because you have already pasted it to the correct location and no longer need it (Figure 7–24).

Experiment

- Click various cells in the range B4:B10 to verify that the values were posted, rather than the trim function.

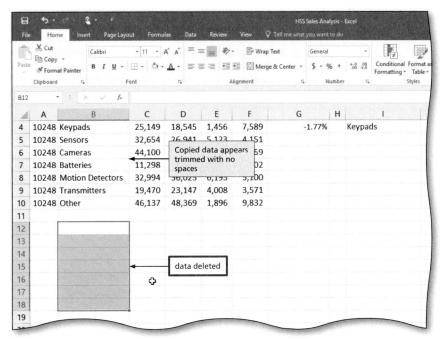

Figure 7–24

Access Files

Data from Microsoft Access files are stored in tabular format. Each row is a record; columns indicate fields. When you import Access files, you commonly import an entire table, which includes column headings. Sometimes you may need to make a query of the data. A **query** is a way to qualify the data to import by specifying a matching condition or asking a question of a database. For example, a query can identify only those records that pass a certain test, such as records containing numeric fields greater than a specific amount or records containing text fields matching a specific value. When Excel imports a database table, the data is placed in an Excel table.

To Import Data from an Access Table

1 CREATE TEMPLATE | 2 USE TEMPLATE | 3 IMPORT DATA | 4 USE QUICK ANALYSIS
5 FIND & REPLACE | 6 INSERT BAR CHART | 7 CREATE SMARTART | 8 ADD SCREENSHOT

The following steps import an entire table from an Access database into an Excel table and then reformat the data to match the existing worksheet. *Why? A table inserted in the middle of a longer list like this one would be confusing. The table needs to be converted to a range; the cells then should be reformatted after Excel imports the data.* To complete these steps, you will be required to use the Data Files. Please contact your instructor for information about accessing the Data Files. The table in the Access database contains data about sales revenue for Store #27943 (shown in Figure 7–1b).

- Select cell A11 so that the Access table is imported starting in cell A11.

- Click the 'Get Data From Access' button (Data tab | Get External Data group) to display the Select Data Source dialog box.

- Navigate to the location of the Data Files (Figure 7–25).

Q&A

What if the database contains more than one table?
If more than one table is in the database, then Excel allows you to choose which table to import.

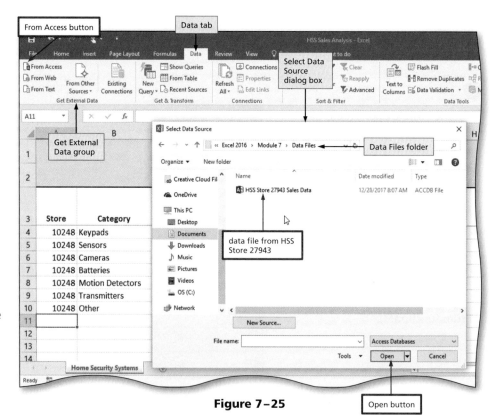

Figure 7–25

2

- Click the file 'HSS Store 27943 Sales Data' to select the file.

- Click the Open button (Select Data Source dialog box) to display the Import Data dialog box (Figure 7–26).

Q&A What is shown in the Import Data dialog box when importing from an Access database?
The Import Data dialog box allows you to choose whether to import the data into a table, a PivotTable Report, a PivotChart and associated PivotTable Report, or only create a connection to the data. You also can choose to import the data to an existing worksheet or a new worksheet.

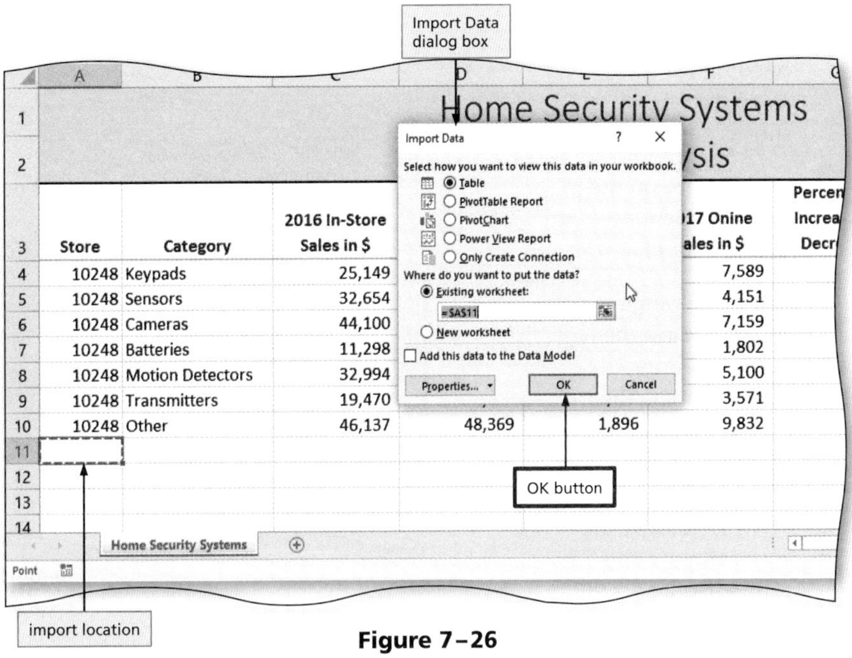

Import Data dialog box

Home Security Systems

Analysis

	Store	Category	2016 In-Store Sales in $		2017 Onine ales in $	Percen Increa Decr
4	10248	Keypads	25,149		7,589	
5	10248	Sensors	32,654		4,151	
6	10248	Cameras	44,100		7,159	
7	10248	Batteries	11,298		1,802	
8	10248	Motion Detectors	32,994		5,100	
9	10248	Transmitters	19,470		3,571	
10	10248	Other	46,137	48,369	1,896	9,832

Import Data dialog box contents:
? ✕
Select how you want to view this data in your workbook.
○ Table
○ PivotTable Report
○ PivotChart
○ Power View Report
○ Only Create Connection
Where do you want to put the data?
● Existing worksheet:
=$A$11
○ New worksheet
☐ Add this data to the Data Model
Properties... OK Cancel

OK button

import location

Figure 7–26

3

- Click the OK button (Import Data dialog box) to import the table data in the database beginning at cell A11.

- Scroll as necessary to display rows 11-18 (Figure 7–27).

Q&A What happened to the layout of the worksheet when Excel imported the data?
Excel created a table using the data from the database. The names of the fields in the Access database appear in row 11. The table is formatted with the default table style for the worksheet's theme.

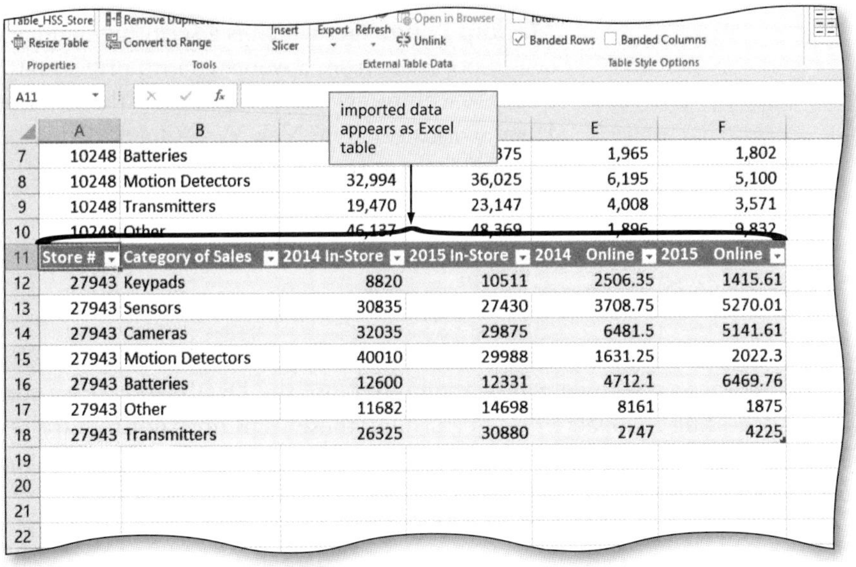

Table_HSS_Store Remove Dupl... Insert Export Refresh Open in Browser Total... Banded Rows ☐ Banded Columns
Resize Table Convert to Range Slicer Unlink Banded Rows Banded Columns
Properties Tools External Table Data Table Style Options

A11

	A	B			E	F
7	10248	Batteries	375		1,965	1,802
8	10248	Motion Detectors	32,994	36,025	6,195	5,100
9	10248	Transmitters	19,470	23,147	4,008	3,571
10	10248	Other	46,137	48,369	1,896	9,832
11	Store #	Category of Sales	2014 In-Store	2015 In-Store	2014 Online	2015 Online
12	27943	Keypads	8820	10511	2506.35	1415.61
13	27943	Sensors	30835	27430	3708.75	5270.01
14	27943	Cameras	32035	29875	6481.5	5141.61
15	27943	Motion Detectors	40010	29988	1631.25	2022.3
16	27943	Batteries	12600	12331	4712.1	6469.76
17	27943	Other	11682	14698	8161	1875
18	27943	Transmitters	26325	30880	2747	4225
19						
20						
21						
22						

imported data appears as Excel table

Figure 7–27

To Format the Access Data

The following steps convert the Access data table to a range and format it. Recall that you have converted tables to ranges in a previous module.

1 Right-click cell A11 and then point to Table on the shortcut menu.

2 Click 'Convert to Range' on the Table submenu to display a Microsoft Excel dialog box.

3 Click the OK button (Microsoft Excel dialog box) to convert the table to a range.

4 Right-click the row heading for row 11 to display the shortcut menu.

5 Click Delete on the shortcut menu to delete row 11.

6 Select the range A10:F10. Click the Format Painter button (Home tab | Clipboard group) and then drag though the range A11:F17 to copy the formatting to the range (Figure 7–28).

	A		C	D	E	F
7	10248 B		11,298	13,375	1,965	1,802
8	10248	Motion Detectors	32,994	36,025	6,195	5,100
9	10248	Transmitters	19,470	23,147	4,008	3,571
10	10248	Other	46,137	48,369	1,896	9,832
11	27943	Keypads	8,820	10,511	2,506	1,416
12	27943	Sensors	30,835	27,430	3,709	5,270
13	27943	Cameras	32,035	29,875	6,482	5,142
14	27943	Motion Detectors	40,010	29,988	1,631	2,022
15	27943	Batteries	12,600	12,331	4,712	6,470
16	27943	Other	11,682	14,698	8,161	1,875
17	27943	Transmitters	26,325	30,880	2,747	4,225

imported data converted to range and column headings removed

data formatted to match range A10:F10

Figure 7–28

Web Data

Webpages use a file format called HTML. **HTML** stands for **Hypertext Markup Language**, which is a scripting language that browsers can interpret. Excel can import data from a webpage into preformatted areas of the worksheet using a web query. A **web query** selects data from the Internet or from an HTML file to add to the Excel worksheet. The New Web Query dialog box includes options to specify which parts of the webpage to import and how much of the HTML formatting to keep.

To Import Data from a Webpage

1 CREATE TEMPLATE | 2 USE TEMPLATE | 3 IMPORT DATA | 4 USE QUICK ANALYSIS
5 FIND & REPLACE | 6 INSERT BAR CHART | 7 CREATE SMARTART | 8 ADD SCREENSHOT

The following steps create a new web query and then import data from a webpage into the worksheet. To complete these steps, you will be required to use the Data Files. Please contact your instructor for information about accessing the Data Files. Performing these steps does not require being connected to the Internet. *Why? In this case, the webpage (shown in Figure 7–1c) is stored with the Data Files; normally you would have to be connected to the Internet.*

1

- Select cell A18 to specify the destination location and then display the Data tab.

- Click the 'Get Data From Web' button (Data tab | Get External Data group) to display the New Web Query dialog box.

- In the address bar, type the drive letter followed by a COLON (:), the path location of the Data Files, followed by the name of the desired file. Separate the name of each folder with a SLASH (/). For example, type `c:/users/username/documents/cis 101/data files/HSS Store 33607 Sales Data.htm` to insert the file name. Your file path will differ.

- Click the Go button (New Web Query dialog box) to display the webpage in the preview area.

- Resize the New Web Query dialog box as necessary (Figure 7–29).

Q&A Could I navigate to the file and double-click?

No, double-clicking the file would open it in a browser, rather than creating a query. You must type in the location, just as you would for a URL. Contact your instructor for the exact path and location.

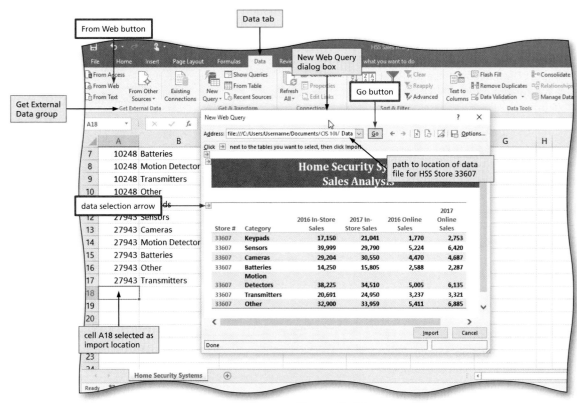

Figure 7–29

❷

- Click the data selection arrow button near the data in the HTML table to select it (Figure 7–30).

 Why did Excel add file:/// at the beginning of the address in the address bar?

Excel appends file:/// to the beginning of the address to indicate that the address points to a file saved on disk rather than a file on the web.

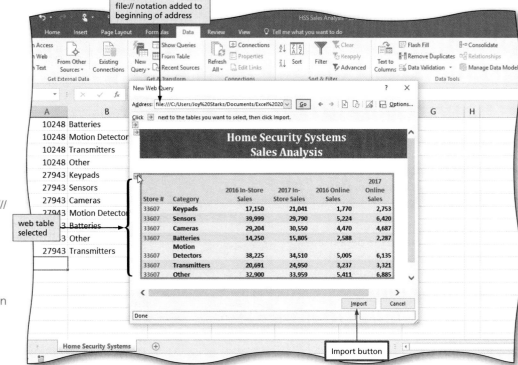

Figure 7–30

- Click the Import button (New Web Query dialog box) to display the Import Data dialog box and a marquee around cell A18 (Figure 7–31).

Q&A Can I change the location of the imported data?
Yes. By default, the cell that is active when the web query is performed will become the upper-left cell of the imported range. To import the data to a different location, change the location in the Existing worksheet box (Import Data dialog box).

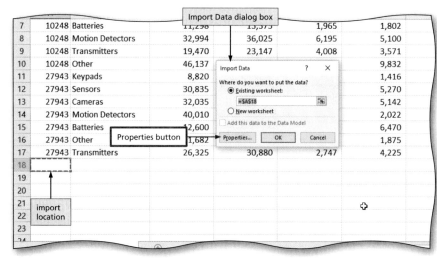

Figure 7–31

- Click the Properties button (Import Data dialog box) to display the External Data Range Properties dialog box.

- Click 'Adjust column width' to remove the check mark (Figure 7–32).

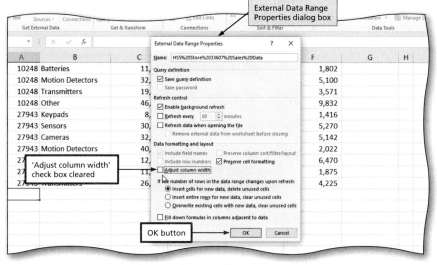

Figure 7–32

- Click the OK button (External Data Range Properties dialog box) to close the dialog box.

- Click the OK button (Import Data dialog box) to import the data from the webpage into the worksheet beginning at cell A18 (Figure 7–33).

Q&A Why do the column headings appear in row 18?
Because the column headings appeared in the webpage, they are imported with the other data and are displayed in row 18. The extra column headings must be deleted.

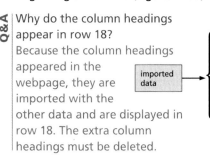

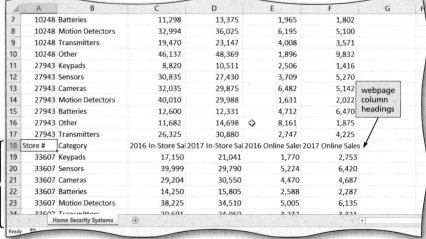

Figure 7–33

- Delete row 18 to remove the imported headings.

- Use the format painter to copy the format of cells A17:F17 to the range A18:F24 (Figure 7–34).

Q&A

Why should I use a web query instead of copying and pasting from a webpage?

Using a web query has advantages over other methods of importing data from a webpage. For example, copying data from webpages to the Office Clipboard and then pasting it into Excel does not maintain all of the webpage formatting. In addition, copying only the desired data from a webpage can be tedious. Finally, copying and pasting does not create a link to the webpage for future updating.

	27943	Cameras		29,875	3,142
14	27943	Motion Detectors	40,010	29,988	1,631	2,022
15	27943	Batteries	12,600	12,331	4,712	6,470
16	27943	Other	11,682	14,698	8,161	1,875
17	27943	Transmitters	26,325	30,880	2,747	4,225
18	33607	Keypads	17,150	21,041	1,770	2,753
19	33607	Sensors	39,999	29,790	5,224	6,420
20	33607	Cameras	29,204	30,550	4,470	4,687
21	33607	Batteries	14,250	15,805	2,588	2,287
22	33607	Motion Detectors	38,225	34,510	5,005	6,135
23	33607	Transmitters	20,691	24,950	3,237	3,321
24	33607	Other	32,900	33,959	5,411	6,885
25					
26					

Home Security Systems ⊕

Ready

range A18:F24 formatted to match range A17:F17

Average: 19384.7

Figure 7–34

Using Word Data

A Word document often contains data stored in a table. While you could save your Word data in a text format such as .txt and import it as you did earlier, you can copy and paste directly from Word to Excel. A few things should be taken into consideration, however. On some occasions, Word data requires some manipulation once you paste it into Excel. For example, the Word data may be easier to work with if the rows and columns were switched, and, thus, you will need to transpose the data. In other situations, you may find that Excel did not paste the data into separate columns, and, thus, you will need to split the data or convert the text into columns. Finally, some text to column conversions need extra space or columns when the data is split, requiring you to move other data out of the way. An example of each will occur in the following sections, as you copy, paste, transpose, move, and split data from Word to Excel.

To Paste Text without Formatting

1 CREATE TEMPLATE | 2 USE TEMPLATE | 3 IMPORT DATA | 4 USE QUICK ANALYSIS
5 FIND & REPLACE | 6 INSERT BAR CHART | 7 CREATE SMARTART | 8 ADD SCREENSHOT

The Word document that contains data from Store # 42681 (Figure 7–1d) includes a Word table with rows and columns. The following steps copy and paste that data from Word into Excel. *Why? The manipulations that you will need to make on the Word data are performed more easily in Excel.* The Paste Special command allows you to choose to paste text only without any kind of formatting from the source or the destination locations; it also provides options for pasting HTML, pictures, and hyperlinks. To complete these steps, you will be required to use the Data Files. Please contact your instructor for information about accessing the Data Files.

- Scroll as necessary to select cell A34.

- Run Word and then open the Word document named, HSS Store 42681 Sales Data, from the Data Files.

- In the Word document, drag through all of the cells in the second through last columns in the table to select the table cells.

- Press CTRL+C to copy the contents of the table to the Office Clipboard (Figure 7–35).

Q&A

Why did I select cell A34 in Excel?

You will paste the data to that location, out of the way, in order to manipulate it.

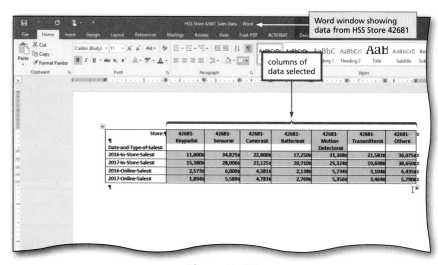

Figure 7–35

2

- Exit Word and, if necessary, click the Excel app button on the taskbar to make Excel the active window.

- With cell A34 active, click the Paste arrow (Home tab | Clipboard group) to display the Paste gallery (Figure 7–36).

Q&A Could I use the 'Keep Source Formatting' or 'Match Destination Formatting' buttons in the Paste gallery?
No. Both of those paste options include formatting information that you do not want to use while importing the data.

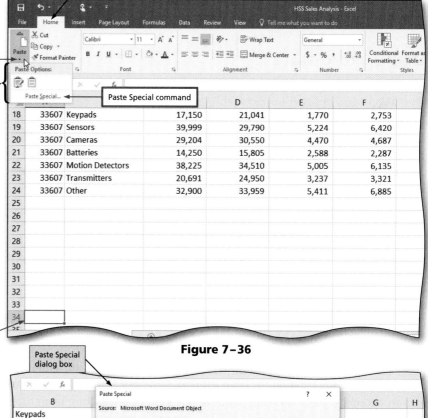

Figure 7–36

3

- Click the Paste Special command in the Paste gallery to display the Paste Special dialog box.

- Click Text in the As list (Figure 7–37).

Q&A Why do I select the Text format in the As list?
The Text format brings in only text that has not been processed, formatted, or manipulated, also known as **raw data**. Importing raw data provides greater flexibility to manipulate the text in Excel.

Figure 7–37

4

- Click the OK button (Paste Special dialog box) to paste the contents of the Office Clipboard as raw data.

- Scroll as necessary to display the data, but do not select any other cells (Figure 7–38).

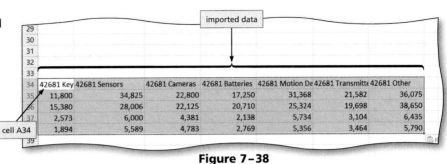

Figure 7–38

1 CREATE TEMPLATE | 2 USE TEMPLATE | 3 IMPORT DATA | 4 USE QUICK ANALYSIS
5 FIND & REPLACE | 6 INSERT BAR CHART | 7 CREATE SMARTART | 8 ADD SCREENSHOT

To Transpose Columns and Rows

Recall that the Paste gallery may display many different kinds of paste options, depending upon the data on the Office Clipboard and the paste location. When you copy and paste within Excel (rather than across apps), the Paste gallery displays many more options for pasting, such as pasting only the formulas, pasting only the values, pasting as a picture, and pasting transposed data, among others. The Transpose option in the Paste gallery automatically flips the rows and columns during the paste. In other words, the row headings become column headings or vice versa. All pasted data is switched as well. The following steps copy the data and paste it, transposed. **Why?** *The original Word data had category titles across the top; the spreadsheet template expects titles down the left side.*

- With the range A34:G38 still selected, press CTRL+C to copy the selection to the Office Clipboard.

- Scroll as necessary, and then select cell A25 to prepare for pasting the data to that location.

- Click the Paste arrow (Home tab | Clipboard group) to display the Paste gallery (Figure 7–39).

Experiment

- Using live preview, point to each of the paste options in the Paste gallery to see how the pasted format changes.

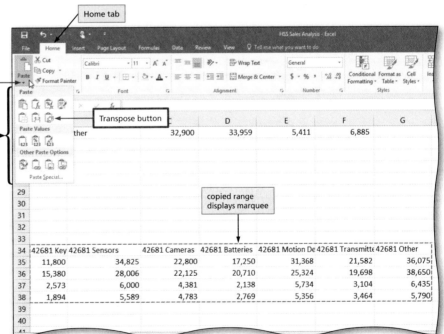

Figure 7–39

Q&A Why do I have to copy the data to the clipboard again?
The Transpose paste command is available only when Excel recognizes the cell format. You cannot transpose directly from copied Word tables.

2

- Click the Transpose button in the Paste gallery to transpose and paste the copied cells to the range beginning with cell A25 (Figure 7–40).

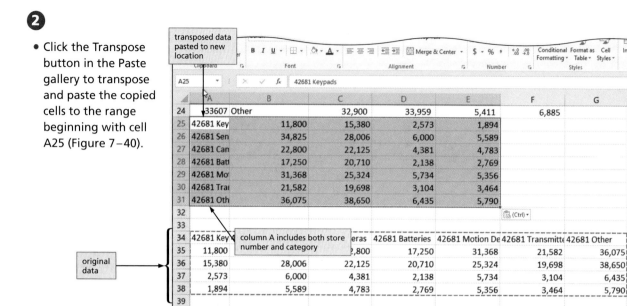

Figure 7–40

To Delete, Cut, Paste, and Format Data

The following steps delete the original Word data from range A34:G38 because you no longer need it. The steps also move some of the transposed data to make room for splitting column A into two columns.

1 Delete the data in the range A34:G38.

2 Select the range B25:E31 and then press CTRL+X to cut the data.

3 Select cell C25 and then press CTRL+V to paste the data.

4 Use the format painter to copy the formatting of cell C24 to the range C25:F31 (Figure 7–41).

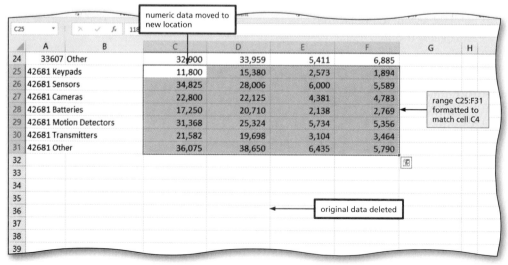

Figure 7–41

To Convert Text to Columns

Column A of the imported data from Store #42681 includes both the store and category in the same cell. The following steps split the data. *Why? The data must be separated using Excel's 'Text to Columns' command so that the category information is in column B.* You have two choices when splitting the column. You can have Excel split the data based on a specific character, such as a space or comma; or, you can have Excel split the data based on a certain number of characters or fixed width. In this case, because the data from HSS includes multiple spaces, it is better to use a fixed width to separate the store number from the inventory category.

1

- Select the range A25:A31 to prepare for converting the text to columns.

- Display the Data tab.

- Click the 'Text to Columns' button (Data tab | Data Tools group) to display the Convert Text to Columns Wizard - Step 1 of 3 dialog box.

- Click the Fixed width option button (Figure 7–42).

Q&A What other tasks can be accomplished using the Convert Text to Columns Wizard?
With the Delimited option, you can split the data into separate columns by specifying a break at a specific character.

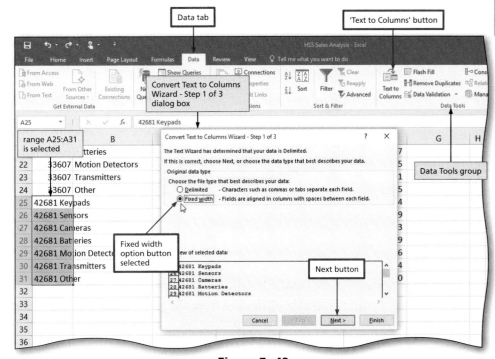

Figure 7–42

2

- Click the Next button (Convert Text to Columns Wizard - Step 1 of 3 dialog box) to accept a fixed width column and to display the Convert Text to Columns Wizard - Step 2 of 3 dialog box.

- In the Data preview area, drag the arrow line to the right one space to specify the width for the first column (Figure 7–43).

 **Experiment**

- Click the Next button to view options related to formatting or skipping parts of the data before splitting it. Do not make any changes.

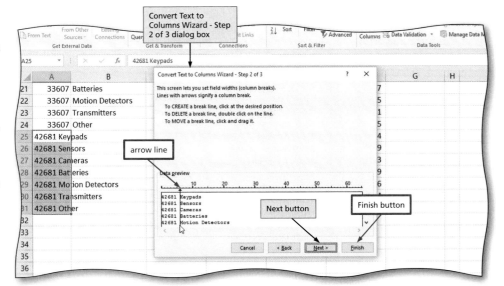

Figure 7–43

- Click the Finish button (Convert Text to Columns Wizard dialog box) to close the dialog box and separate the data in column A into two columns (Figure 7–44).

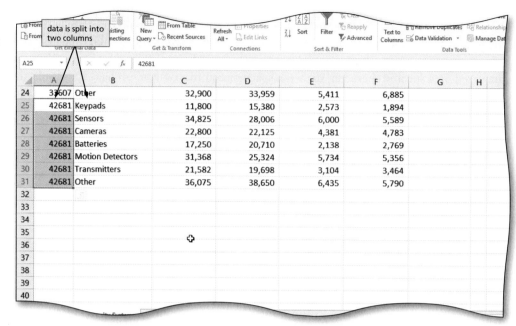

Figure 7–44

To Replicate Formulas

1 CREATE TEMPLATE | 2 USE TEMPLATE | 3 IMPORT DATA | 4 USE QUICK ANALYSIS
5 FIND & REPLACE | 6 INSERT BAR CHART | 7 CREATE SMARTART | 8 ADD SCREENSHOT

When you opened the workbook derived from the template, it contained a worksheet title, headings for each column, and a formula to calculate the percentage increase or decrease from 2016 to 2017. The formula and functions in cells G4, I4, and J4 must be copied or filled to complete the calculations. Some spreadsheet specialists refer to copying formulas as **replication**. You often replicate formulas after completing an import. *Why? Usually, the total number of records to be imported is unknown when you first begin a workbook.* The following steps use the fill handle to replicate the formulas.

- Select the location of the formula you wish to replicate (in this case, cell G4).

- Drag the fill handle down through the end of the data (in this case, row 31) to replicate the formula (Figure 7–45).

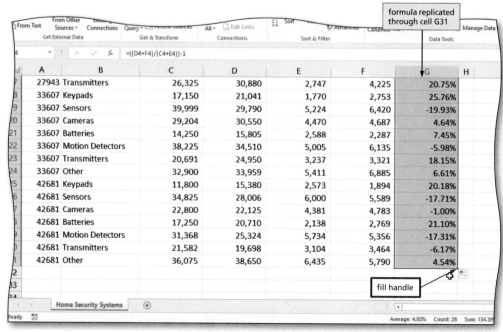

Figure 7–45

2

- Select cells I4:J4.

- Drag the fill handle down through row 10 to replicate the formulas and functions (Figure 7–46).

Why did I stop the replication of the summary at row 10?

Only seven categories are used for the stores; however, you can replicate further if more categories are added. If you were to copy the formulas to row 11, you would see that cell I11 remains blank and cell J11 does not display a value.

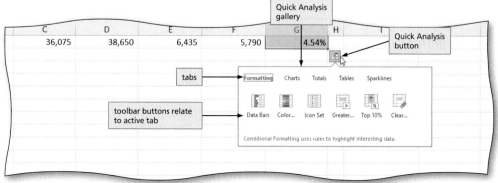

functions replicated through cell J10

Home Security Systems
Sales Analysis

7 In-Store ales in $	2016 Online Sales in $	2017 Onine Sales in $	Percentage Increase or Decrease	Summary of Categories	2017 Totals
18,545	1,456	7,589	-1.77%	Keypads	79,129
26,941	5,123	4,151	-17.70%	Sensors	133,597
43,598	4,989	7,159	3.40%	Cameras	147,919
13,375	1,965	1,802	14.43%	Batteries	75,549
36,025	6,195	5,100	4.94%	Motion Detectors	144,460
23,147	4,008	3,571	13.80%	Transmitters	113,256
48,369	1,896	9,832	21.17%	Other	160,058
10,511	2,506	1,416	5.30%		
27,430	3,709	5,270	5.34%		

Figure 7–46

3

- Click the Save button (Quick Access Toolbar) to save the workbook with the same name in the same location.

Break Point: If you wish to take a break, this is a good place to do so. You can exit Excel now. To resume at a later time, run Excel, open the file called HSS Sales Analysis, and continue following the steps from this location forward.

Using the Quick Analysis Gallery

Recall that in a previous module you used the status bar shortcut menu to provide an easy analysis of selected data. Another tool for analyzing data quickly is the Quick Analysis gallery. Quick Analysis first appears as a button below and to the right of selected data. When clicked, Excel displays the Quick Analysis gallery (Figure 7–47).

Each tab at the top of the gallery displays its own set of buttons to help you complete a task easily. For example, notice in Figure 7–47 that the Formatting tab displays conditional formatting options. The tabs always apply to the previously selected area of the worksheet. In addition, the Quick Analysis gallery uses live preview — in other words, you can preview how the feature will affect your data by pointing to the button in the gallery.

C	D	E	F	G	H	I
36,075	38,650	6,435	5,790	4.54%		

Quick Analysis gallery

Quick Analysis button

tabs

Formatting   Charts   Totals   Tables   Sparklines

toolbar buttons relate to active tab

Data Bars   Color...   Icon Set   Greater...   Top 10%   Clear...

Conditional Formatting uses rules to highlight interesting data.

Figure 7–47

To Format Using the Quick Analysis Gallery

The following steps use the Quick Analysis gallery to format the top 10% of column G, the percentage increase or decrease in sales. *Why? The company executives want to see the stores and products with the highest increase in sales.* Formatting using the Quick Analysis gallery is much faster than using the ribbon to apply conditional formatting.

- Select the range you want to analyze, in this case G4:G31.

- Click the Quick Analysis button to display the Quick Analysis gallery.

- If necessary, click the Formatting tab to display the Quick Analysis gallery related to formatting (Figure 7–48).

🔎 **Experiment**

- Point to each of the buttons on the Quick Analysis gallery to display a live preview.

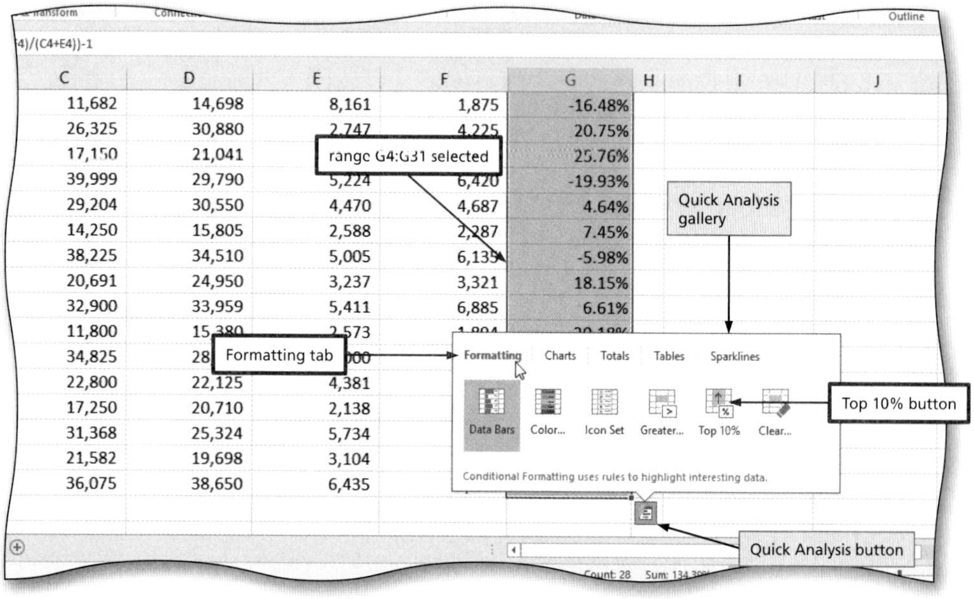

Figure 7–48

- Click the Top 10% button (Quick Analysis gallery).

- Click outside the selection and scroll as necessary to display the cells highlighted by the conditional formatting (Figure 7–49).

Q&A Why did Excel highlight the numbers in pink? The default value for conditional formatting is pink.

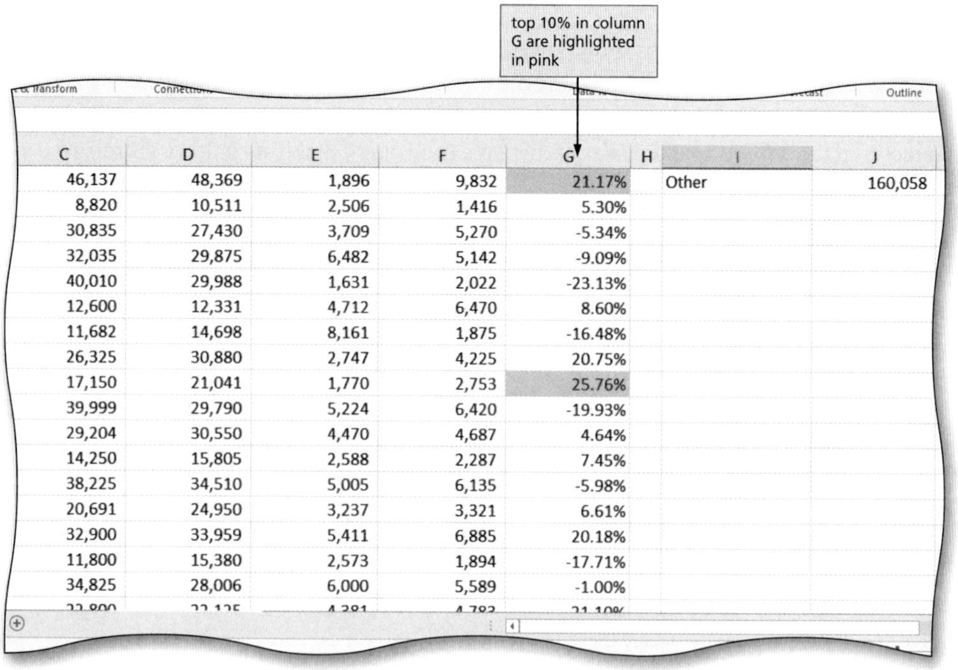

Figure 7–49

3

- Click cell I32. Type **Shaded cells indicate top 10%** and then press the ENTER key to create a legend for the formatting.

- Drag through cells I32:J32 and display the Home tab.

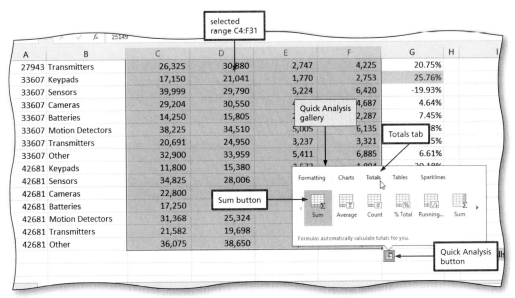

				6.61%	
11,800	15,380	2,573	1,894	20.18%	
34,825	28,006	6,000	5,589	-17.71%	
22,800	22,125	4,381	4,783	-1.00%	formatted legend in cell I32
17,250	20,710	2,138	2,769	21.10%	
31,368	25,324	5,734	5,356	-17.31%	
21,582	19,698	3,104	3,464	-6.17%	
36,075	38,650	6,435	5,790	4.54%	

Shaded cells indicate top 10%

Figure 7–50

- Click the Fill Color arrow (Home tab | Font Group) and then More Colors to display the Colors dialog box. Double-click a pink color to format the cell.

- Click outside the selection to view the formatting (Figure 7–50).

  If instructed to do so, select cell I33, type **Prepared by** and then type your name.

Q&A

How would I clear the formatting?

You can highlight the cell or cells, click the Quick Analysis button, click the Formatting tab, and then click the Clear button (Quick Analysis gallery).

To Total Data Using the Quick Analysis Gallery

1 CREATE TEMPLATE | 2 USE TEMPLATE | 3 IMPORT DATA | 4 USE QUICK ANALYSIS
5 FIND & REPLACE | 6 INSERT BAR CHART | 7 CREATE SMARTART | 8 ADD SCREENSHOT

The following steps use the Quick Analysis gallery to total the sales data from the four stores. *Why? Companies routinely want to examine grand totals for all stores.*

1

- Select the range you want to analyze, in this case C4:F31.

- Click the Quick Analysis button to display the Quick Analysis gallery and then click the Totals tab to display the Quick Analysis gallery related to totals (Figure 7–51).

Experiment

- Point to each of the buttons on the Totals tab to display a live preview.

selected range C4:F31

A	B	C	D	E	F	G	H
27943	Transmitters	26,325	30,880	2,747	4,225	20.75%	
33607	Keypads	17,150	21,041	1,770	2,753	25.76%	
33607	Sensors	39,999	29,790	5,224	6,420	-19.93%	
33607	Cameras	29,204	30,550		4,687	4.64%	
33607	Batteries	14,250	15,805		2,287	7.45%	
33607	Motion Detectors	38,225	34,510	5,005	6,135	8%	
33607	Transmitters	20,691	24,950	3,237	3,321	5%	
33607	Other	32,900	33,959	5,411	6,885	6.61%	
42681	Keypads	11,800	15,380				
42681	Sensors	34,825	28,006				
42681	Cameras	22,800					
42681	Batteries	17,250					
42681	Motion Detectors	31,368	25,324				
42681	Transmitters	21,582	19,698				
42681	Other	36,075	38,650				

25149

Quick Analysis gallery

Totals tab

Formatting   Charts   Totals   Tables   Sparklines

Sum button

Sum   Average   Count   % Total   Running...   Sum

Formulas automatically calculate totals for you.

Quick Analysis button

Figure 7–51

- Click the Sum button (Quick Analysis gallery).

- Select cell A32 and then type **Totals** to enter a row heading.

- Replicate cell G31 down to G32 to indicate the total percentage increase or decrease (Figure 7–52).

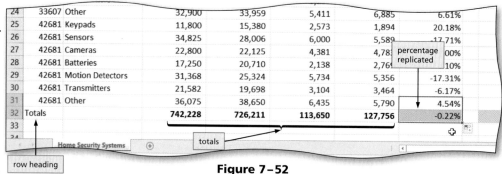

Figure 7–52

Using the Find and Replace Commands

To locate a specific piece of data in a worksheet, you can use the Find command on the Find & Select menu. The data you search for sometimes is called the **search string**. To locate and replace the data, you can use the Replace command on the Find & Select menu. If you have a cell range selected, the Find and Replace commands search only the range; otherwise, the Find and Replace commands begin at cell A1, regardless of the location of the active cell. The Find and Replace commands are not available for charts.

Selecting either the Find or Replace command displays the Find and Replace dialog box. The Find and Replace dialog box has two variations. One version displays minimal options, while the other version displays all of the available options. When you select the Find or Replace command, Excel displays the dialog box variation that was used the last time either command was selected.

To Find Data

The following steps show how to locate the search string, Batteries. The Find and Replace dialog box that displays all the options will be used to customize the search by using the Match case and 'Match entire cell contents' options. **Why?** *Match case means that the search is case sensitive and the cell contents must match the data exactly the way it is typed. 'Match entire cell contents' means that the data cannot be part of another word or phrase and must be unique in the cell.*

- If necessary, display the Home tab.

- Click the 'Find & Select' button (Home tab | Editing group) to display the Find & Select menu (Figure 7–53).

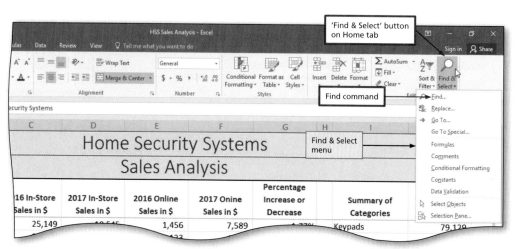

Figure 7–53

● Click Find on the Find & Select menu to display the Find and Replace dialog box.

● Click the Options button (Find and Replace dialog box) to expand the dialog box so that it appears as shown in Figure 7–54.

● Type **Batteries** in the Find what box to enter the search string.

● Click Match case and then click 'Match entire cell contents' to place check marks in those check boxes (Figure 7–54).

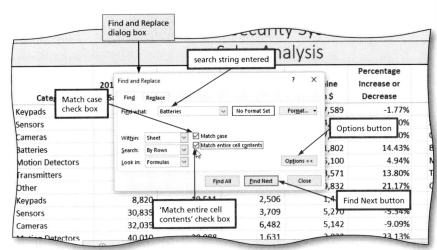

Figure 7–54

Q&A | Why does the appearance of the Options button change?
The two less than signs pointing to the left on the Options button indicate that the more comprehensive Find and Replace dialog box is active.

● Click the Find Next button (Find and Replace dialog box) to cause Excel to begin the search and locate an occurrence of the search string (Figure 7–55).

Q&A | What if Excel does not find any occurrences of the search string?
If the Find command does not find the string for which you are searching, Excel displays a dialog box indicating it searched the selected worksheets and cannot find the search string.

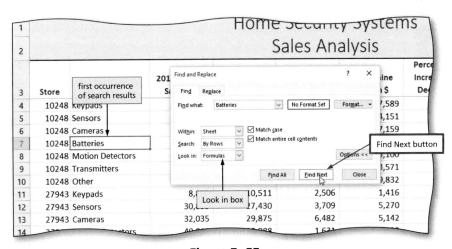

Figure 7–55

● Continue clicking the Find Next button (Find and Replace dialog box) to find the string, Batteries, in three other cells on the worksheet.

● Click the Close button (Find and Replace dialog box) to stop searching and close the Find and Replace dialog box.

Q&A | What happens if you continue clicking the Find Next button?
Excel will cycle through the cells again. You have to watch the row and column references to determine if you have found them all.

Why did Excel not find the word Batteries in cell I7?
The default value in the Look in box (shown in Figure 7–55) was to search for formulas, which includes cells with entered text, but does not include the result of functions such as the one from the template, replicated in cell I7.

Other Ways

1. Press CTRL+F, enter search string, click Find Next button (Find and Replace dialog box)

Working with the Find and Replace Dialog Box

The Format button in the Find and Replace dialog box allows you to fine-tune the search by adding formats, such as bold, font style, and font size, to the search string. The Within box options include Sheet and Workbook. The Search box indicates whether Excel will search vertically through rows or horizontally across columns. The Look in box allows you to select Formulas, Values, or Comments. If you select Formulas, Excel will look in all cells except those containing functions or comments. If you select Values, Excel will look for the search string in cells that do not contain formulas, such as text or functions. If you select Comments, Excel will look only in comments.

If you select the Match case check box, Excel will locate only cells in which the string is in the same case. For example, when matching the case, accessories is not the same as Accessories. If you select the 'Match entire cell contents' check box, Excel will locate only the cells that contain the search string and no other characters. For example, Excel will find a cell entry of Other, but not Others.

To Find and Replace

1 CREATE TEMPLATE | 2 USE TEMPLATE | 3 IMPORT DATA | 4 USE QUICK ANALYSIS
5 FIND & REPLACE | 6 INSERT BAR CHART | 7 CREATE SMARTART | 8 ADD SCREENSHOT

The Replace command replaces the found search string with new data. You can use it to find and replace one occurrence at a time, or you can use the Replace All button to replace the data in all locations at once. The following steps show how to use the Replace All button. **Why?** *You want to replace the string, Sensors, with the string, Sensors & Alarms.*

- Click the Find & Select button (Home tab | Editing group) to display the Find & Select menu.

- Click Replace on the Find & Select menu to display the Find and Replace dialog box.

- Type **Sensors** in the Find what box and then type **Sensors & Alarms** in the Replace with box to specify the text to find and to replace.

- If necessary, click Match case and then click 'Match entire cell contents' to place check marks in those check boxes (Figure 7–56).

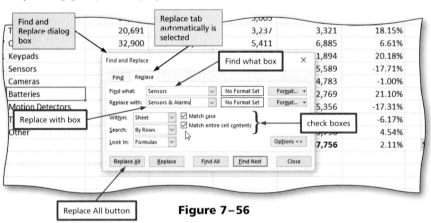

Figure 7–56

- Click the Replace All button (Find and Replace dialog box) to replace the string (Figure 7–57).

Q&A

What happens when Excel replaces the string?

Excel replaces the string, Sensors, with the replacement string, Sensors & Alarms, throughout the entire worksheet. If other worksheets contain matching cells, Excel replaces those cells as well. Excel displays the Microsoft Excel dialog box indicating four replacements were made.

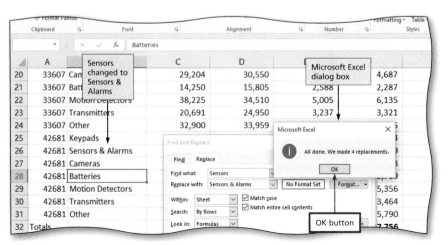

Figure 7–57

❸

- Click the OK button (Microsoft Excel dialog box).

- Click the Close button (Find and Replace dialog box).

◀ Q&A | Why did Excel change the function value in cell I5?
Even though this cell is a function and therefore would not be changed because of the Formula designation in the Find and Replace dialog box, cell I5 searches column B. So, when Excel changed column B, the function itself changed cell I5.

Other Ways

1. Press CTRL+H, enter search string, enter replace string, click Replace All button (Find and Replace dialog box)

Inserting a Bar Chart

The requirements document shown in Figure 7–2 specifies that the workbook should include a bar chart, sometimes called a bar graph. A bar chart uses parallel, horizontal bars of varying lengths to measure and compare categories of data or amounts, such as sales, counts, or rates. The bars can be all one color, or each bar may be a different color.

CONSIDER THIS ❋

When should you use a bar chart?
You should use a bar graph when you want to compare different groups of data. Because bar charts plot numerical data in rectangular blocks against a scale, viewers can develop a clear mental image of comparisons by distinguishing the relative lengths of the bars. You also can use a bar graph to display numerical data when you want to present distributions of data. Bar charts tend to be better than column charts for positive numbers, larger numbers of categories, and longer data labels.

If you are comparing more than one piece of data per category, the chart becomes a clustered bar chart. The only differences between a bar chart and a column chart are in orientation and the amount of room for data labels. Longer data labels display better using bar charts. If you have any negative values, the bars appear pointing left; columns would appear pointing down. You will create the bar chart shown in Figure 7–58 by using the Quick Analysis gallery and formatting the data, axes, and title.

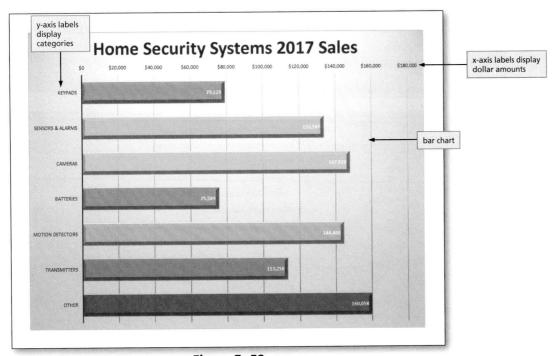

Figure 7–58

To Insert a Chart Using the Quick Analysis Gallery

The following steps insert a chart using the Quick Analysis gallery. *Why? The Quick Analysis gallery is near the data and provides an easy way to access charts.*

- Select the range I4:J10 to select the data to include in the chart.
- Click the Quick Analysis button to display the Quick Analysis gallery.
- Click the Charts tab to display the buttons related to working with charts on the toolbar (Figure 7–59).

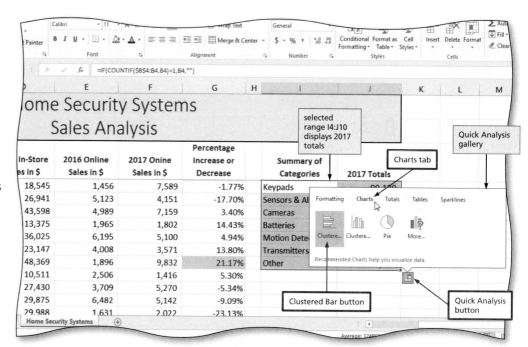

Figure 7–59

- Click the Clustered Bar button (Quick Analysis gallery) to insert the chart (Figure 7–60).

Q&A

Why are only three charts displayed?
Excel lists the charts that it recommends for your data. You can click the More button (Quick Analysis gallery) to open the Insert Chart dialog box and choose another style. (The cone chart shape is no longer available in Excel 2016.)

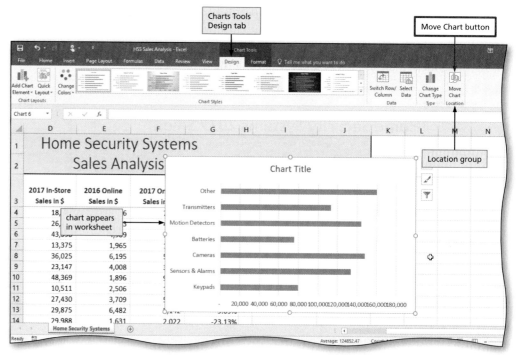

Figure 7–60

- Click the Move Chart button (Chart Tools Design tab | Location group) to display the Move Chart dialog box.

- Click the New sheet option button and then type **Bar Chart** as the sheet name in the New sheet text box (Figure 7–61).

- Click the OK button (Move Chart dialog box) to move the chart to the new sheet.

- Change the sheet tab color to blue.

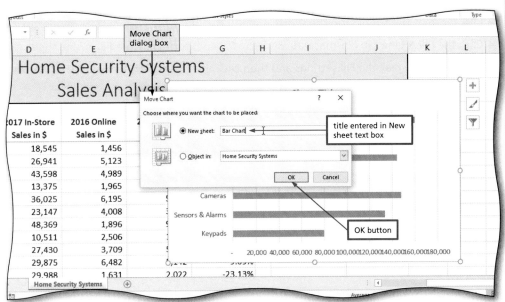

Figure 7–61

To Format the Chart

1 CREATE TEMPLATE | 2 USE TEMPLATE | 3 IMPORT DATA | 4 USE QUICK ANALYSIS
5 FIND & REPLACE | 6 INSERT BAR CHART | **7 CREATE SMARTART** | 8 ADD SCREENSHOT

The following steps change the style of the chart; change the color, order, and bevel of the category bars; and then edit the number format of the x-axis or horizontal labels. *Why? You always should customize the chart with formatting that applies to the data and the concept you are trying to portray.* You also will reverse the order of the categories to display the longest bar across the bottom.

- Click the Style 3 button (Chart Tools Design tab | Chart Styles group) to change the style of the chart.

- Right-click any of the data bars on the chart to display the shortcut menu (Figure 7–62).

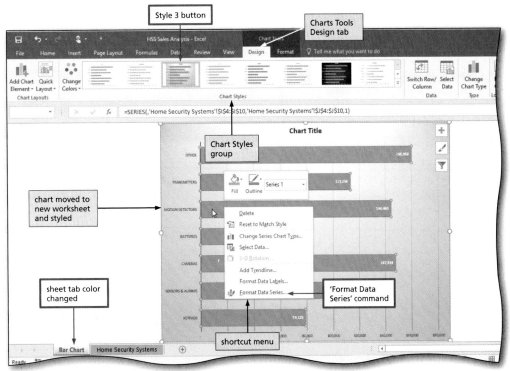

Figure 7–62

- Click 'Format Data Series' on the shortcut menu to display the Format Data Series task pane.
- Click the Fill & Line tab (Format Data Series task pane) to display the Fill & Line sheet.
- If necessary, display the Fill settings and then click the 'Vary colors by point' check box to display the bars in various colors (Figure 7–63).

Experiment

- Click the Series Options tab (Format Data Series task pane) to view the settings. Notice that you can set the Series Overlap (for clustered charts) and the Gap Width (the interval between bars).

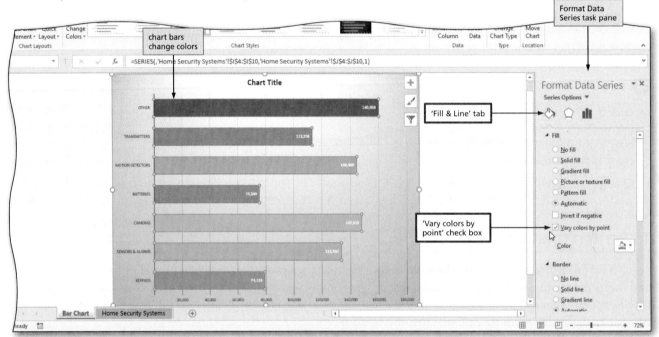

Figure 7–63

- Click the Effects tab to display the Effects sheet. If necessary, display the 3-D Format settings (Figure 7–64).

Q&A
What kinds of effects can I change on the Effects sheet? You can change the shadow, glow, edges, bevel, and 3-D format of the bars.

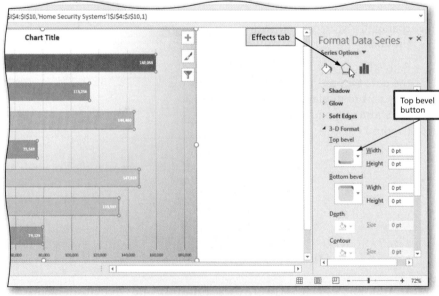

Figure 7–64

4

- Click the Top bevel button to display the Top bevel gallery (Figure 7–65).

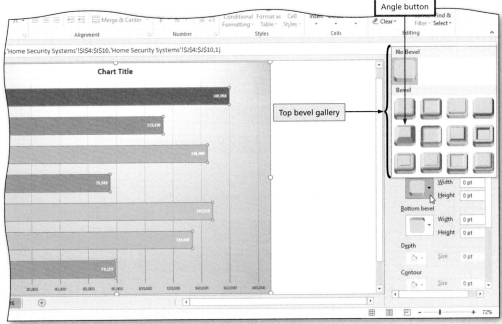

Figure 7–65

5

- Click the Angle button (Top bevel gallery) to apply an angle bevel to the bars in the chart.

- Right-click the y-axis or vertical category labels and then click Format Axis on the shortcut menu to display the Format Axis task pane.

- If necessary, click the Axis Options tab (Format Axis task pane) to display the sheet.

- In the Axis position area, click the 'Categories in reverse order' check box (Figure 7–66).

Q&A

What other options can I set using the Format Axis task pane?

You can change how tick marks, labels, and numbers display. On the Size & Properties tab, you can set the alignment, text direction, and margins of the axes. The Fill & Line tab and the Effects tab are similar to the Format Data Series task pane that you used earlier.

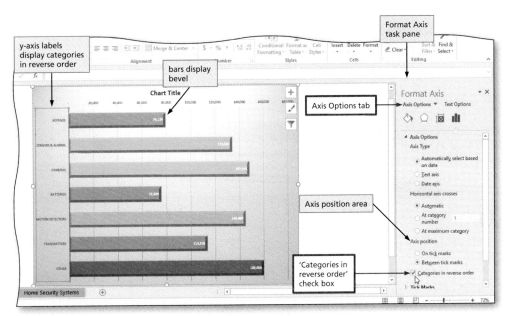

Figure 7–66

6

- Right-click the x-axis or horizontal labels across the top of the chart and then click Format Axis on the shortcut menu to display the Format Axis task pane.

- If necessary, click the Axis Options tab (Format Axis task pane) to display the sheet.

- Scroll down as necessary in the Format Axis task pane and then click Number to display the settings related to numbers (Figure 7–67).

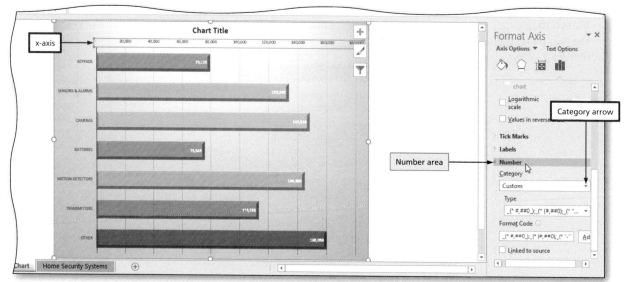

Figure 7–67

7

- Click the Category arrow to display its menu and then click Currency in the list (Figure 7–68).

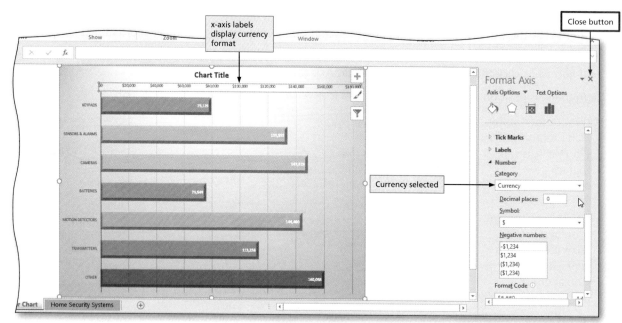

Figure 7–68

8

- Close the task pane.

To Format the Chart Title

The following steps format the chart title.

1 Click the chart title and then press CTRL+A to select all of the text.

2 Display the Home tab and change the font size to 32.

3 Type **Home Security Systems 2017 Sales** to change the title (Figure 7–69).

4 Click the Save button (Quick Access Toolbar) to save the workbook with the same name in the same location.

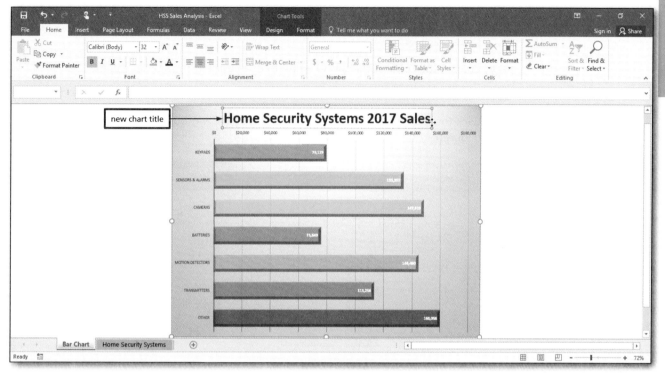

Figure 7–69

Break Point: If you wish to take a break, this is a good place to do so. You can exit Excel now. To resume at a later time, run Excel, open the file called HSS Sales Analysis, and continue following the steps from this location forward.

Working with SmartArt Graphics

A **SmartArt graphic** is a customizable diagram that you use to pictorially present lists, processes, and relationships. For example, you can use a SmartArt graphic to illustrate the manufacturing process to produce an item. Excel includes nine types of SmartArt graphics: List, Process, Cycle, Hierarchy, Relationship, Matrix, Pyramid, Picture, and Office.com. Each type of graphic includes several layouts, or templates, from which to choose. After selecting a SmartArt graphic type and layout, you customize the graphic to meet your needs and present your information and ideas in a compelling manner.

How do you choose the type of SmartArt graphics to add?

Consider what you want to illustrate in the SmartArt graphic. For example, if you are showing nonsequential or grouped blocks of information, select a SmartArt graphic in the List category. To show progression or sequential steps in a process or task, select a Process diagram. After inserting a SmartArt graphic, increase its visual appeal by formatting the graphic, for example, with 3-D effects and coordinated colors.

CONSIDER THIS

In the following sections, you will create a SmartArt graphic with shapes, pictures, and text. You then will add a style to the SmartArt graphic.

To Create a New Sheet

In preparation for inserting a SmartArt graphic, the following steps create a new sheet and hide gridlines.

1 Click the New sheet button to create a third sheet in the workbook.

2 Rename the worksheet `SmartArt Graphic` to provide a descriptive name for the worksheet.

3 Change the color of the tab to white to distinguish it from other sheets.

4 Click View on the ribbon to display the View tab.

5 Click the View Gridlines check box (View tab | Show group) to turn off gridlines (Figure 7–70).

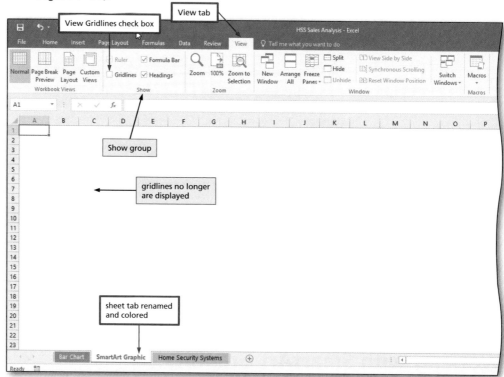

Figure 7–70

To Insert a SmartArt Graphic

1 CREATE TEMPLATE | 2 USE TEMPLATE | 3 IMPORT DATA | 4 USE QUICK ANALYSIS
5 FIND & REPLACE | 6 INSERT BAR CHART | 7 CREATE SMARTART | 8 ADD SCREENSHOT

To illustrate the categories of products sold by HSS, you decide to use a SmartArt graphic. *Why? A SmartArt graphic with pictures can be used in marketing and promotional material for the company.* The following steps insert a SmartArt graphic named Accented Picture.

1

- Display the Insert tab.

- Click the 'Insert a SmartArt Graphic' button (Insert tab | Illustrations group) to display the Choose a SmartArt Graphic dialog box.

- Click the desired type of SmartArt in the left pane; in this case, click Picture to display the available SmartArt layouts in the middle pane (Choose a SmartArt Graphic dialog box).

- Click the desired layout in the gallery, in this case, the Accented Picture layout, to see a preview of the chart in the preview area (Figure 7–71).

Q&A What do the middle and right panes of the dialog box display?

The middle pane of the dialog box (the layout gallery) displays available types of picture charts, and the right pane (the preview area) displays a preview of the selected SmartArt graphic.

Experiment

- Click the various SmartArt graphics to see a preview of each in the preview area. When you are finished, click Accented Picture in the middle pane.

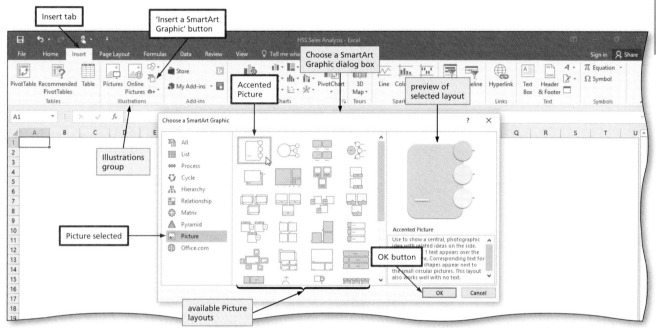

Figure 7–71

2

- Click the OK button (Choose a SmartArt Graphic dialog box) to insert an Accented Picture SmartArt graphic in the worksheet (Figure 7–72).

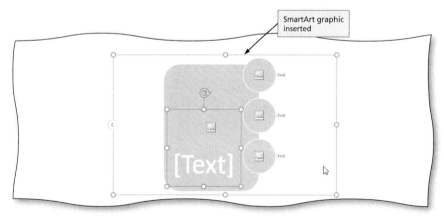

Figure 7–72

To Color and Resize the SmartArt Graphic

1 CREATE TEMPLATE | 2 USE TEMPLATE | 3 IMPORT DATA | 4 USE QUICK ANALYSIS
5 FIND & REPLACE | 6 INSERT BAR CHART | **7 CREATE SMARTART** | **8 ADD SCREENSHOT**

The following steps change the color of the SmartArt graphic and then resize it. *Why? You want the graphic to appear visually pleasing and as large as possible in the given space.*

1

- Click the Change Colors button (SmartArt Tools Design tab | SmartArt Styles group) to display the Change Colors gallery (Figure 7–73).

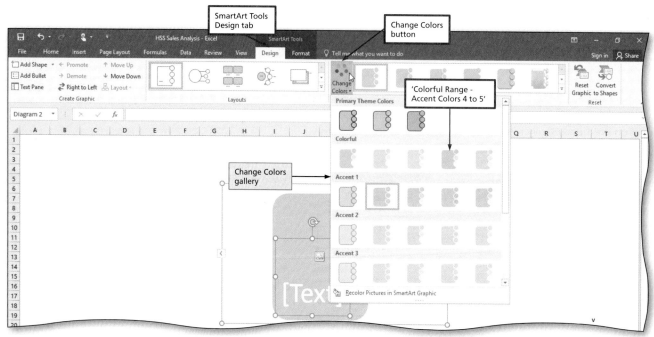

Figure 7–73

2

- Click 'Colorful Range - Accent Colors 4 to 5' in the gallery to change the color.
- Drag the sizing handles to resize the SmartArt graphic to fill the screen, approximately rows 1 through 23 and columns F through Q (Figure 7–74).

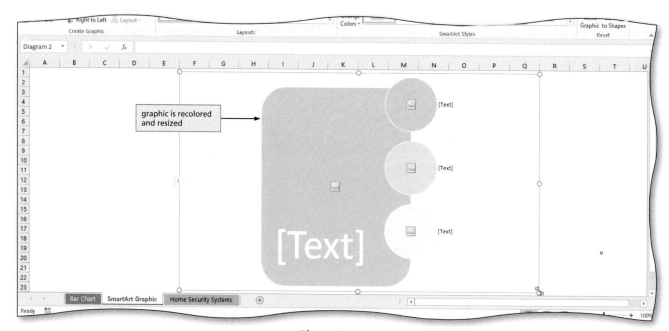

Figure 7–74

 Experiment

- Click the SmartArt Tools Format tab and look at the various groups, buttons, and galleries available to format SmartArt graphics.

To Add Shapes to a SmartArt Graphic

Many SmartArt graphics include more than one shape, such as a picture, text box, or combinations, grouped in levels. Level 1 is considered the largest object or main level. Level 2 is a sublevel and may display one to three shapes when first created. You can add a shape or text box to each level. You also can **demote** or **promote** a shape, which means you can move the shape to a lower level or an upper level, respectively.

The default Accented Picture SmartArt graphic layout includes a large shape for level 1 and three smaller shapes at level 2. The following step adds three new shapes to the SmartArt graphic. *Why? You decide to show six categories in the SmartArt graphic.*

1

• Click the Add Shape button (SmartArt Tools Design tab | Create Graphic group) three times to add three more level 2 shapes (Figure 7–75).

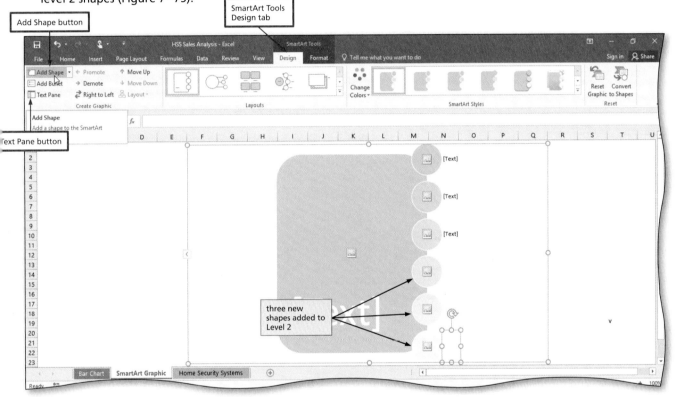

Figure 7–75

Q&A

Why does Excel change the layout of the chart?
When you add a new shape to a SmartArt graphic, Excel rearranges the shapes in the graphic to fit in the same area. As shown in Figure 7–75, Excel reduces the size of each circle and the font size of the text to accommodate the added circles.

Other Ways

1. Right-click SmartArt graphic, point to Add Shape on shortcut menu, click 'Add Shape After' or 'Add Shape Before' on Add Shape submenu

To Add Text to a SmartArt Graphic

The following steps add text to the SmartArt graphic. You can type text directly in the text boxes of the SmartArt graphic, or you can display a Text Pane and add text to the shape through the Text Pane. The Text Pane displays a bulleted outline corresponding to each of the shapes in the SmartArt graphic. *Why? You may find it easier to enter text in the Text Pane because you do not have to select any object to replace the default text.*

- If the Text Pane does not appear, click the Text Pane button (SmartArt Tools Design tab | Create Graphic group) to display the Text Pane.

- Click the first bulleted item in the Text Pane and then type **Home Security Systems** to replace the default text (Figure 7–76).

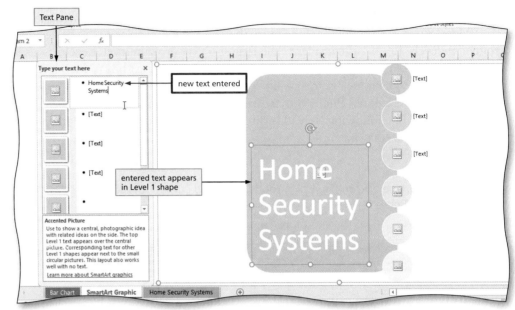

Figure 7–76

- Enter text in the other boxes as shown in Figure 7–77.

Q&A Did Excel resize my font?
Yes. Excel resizes all of the level 2 fonts to autofit the text in the graphic. Thus, it is important to resize the graphic before adding text.

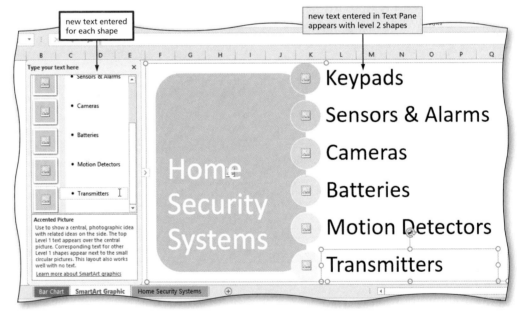

Figure 7–77

Other Ways

1. Click left arrow on edge of SmartArt graphic border to open Text Pane, insert text

2. Click individual text box in SmartArt graphic, type text

To Add Pictures to a SmartArt Graphic

1 CREATE TEMPLATE | 2 USE TEMPLATE | 3 IMPORT DATA | 4 USE QUICK ANALYSIS
5 FIND & REPLACE | 6 INSERT BAR CHART | 7 CREATE SMARTART | 8 ADD SCREENSHOT

The following steps add pictures to the SmartArt graphic. **Why?** *The CEO wants to highlight the kinds of products the company sells.* Other times, you may want to locate images or clip art from the web, also called online pictures. Excel 2016 uses a Bing Image Search to help you locate images licensed under Creative Commons. The resulting images may or may not be royalty and copyright free. You must read the specific license for any image you plan to use, even for educational purposes. In this module, you will add pictures from the Data Files. Please contact your instructor for information about accessing the Data Files.

1

- Scroll to the top of the Text Pane and then click the first Insert Picture icon to display the Insert Pictures dialog box (Figure 7–78).

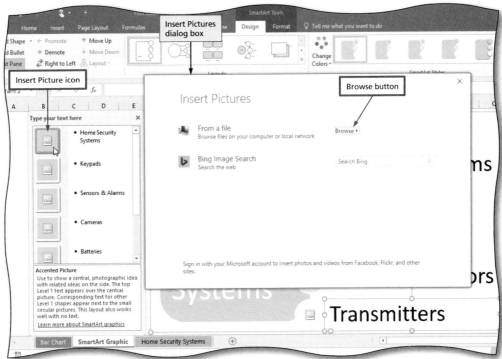

Figure 7–78

2

- Click the Browse button to display the Insert Picture dialog box and then browse to the Data Files (Figure 7–79).

 Why do the files in my dialog box appear differently? Your system may display a different view. If you want to match the display in Figure 7–79, click the 'Change your view' arrow and then click Large Icons.

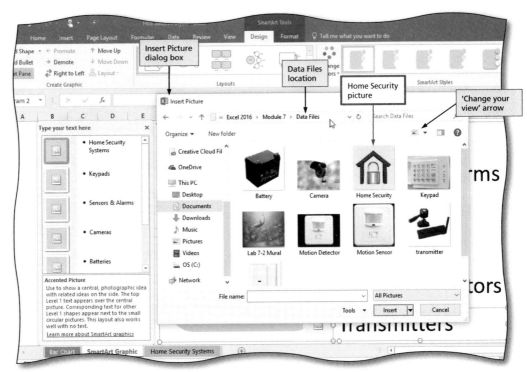

Figure 7–79

- Double-click the file named Home Security to place it in the SmartArt graphic (Figure 7–80).

Q&A Do I need to use a special type of picture file or format?
Excel accepts a wide variety of formats including .png, .gif, .bmp, .jpg, and .tif, among others. Excel will resize the graphic as necessary to fit the space in the SmartArt graphic.

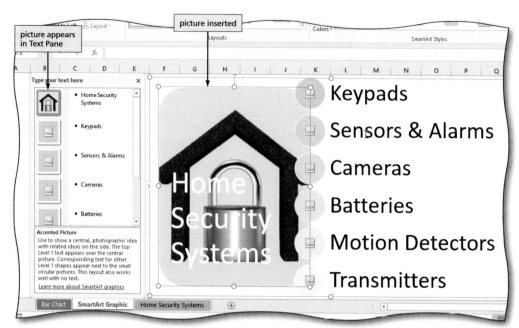

Figure 7–80

- One at a time, click each of the Insert Picture icons in the Text Pane to insert the appropriate picture from the Data Files: Keypad, Window Sensor, Camera, Battery, Motion Detector, and Transmitter (Figure 7–81).

Q&A Could I also use the Insert Picture icon in the shape?
Yes, as with the text, you can add a picture from either the Text Pane or the shape itself.

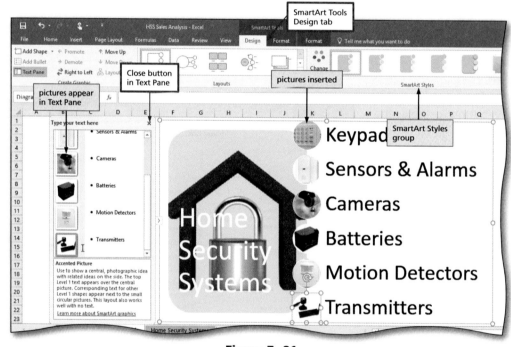

Figure 7–81

- Click the Close button in the Text Pane to close it.

Other Ways

1. Click Insert Picture icon in SmartArt graphic, select location (Insert Pictures dialog box), double-click picture

To Format Text Effects

The following steps format the text, Home Security Systems, with an outline text effect. *Why? Outlining, also called stroking the letters, will make them easier to read with the picture background.* You also will move the text box.

1

- Select the text, Home Security Systems.

- Right-click the text and then click Format Text Effects on the shortcut menu to display the Format Shape task pane.

- If necessary, click the 'Text Fill & Outline' tab (Format Shape task pane) and then click Text Outline to display the choices.

- In the Text Outline area, click the Solid line option button and then click the Outline color arrow to display the color gallery (Figure 7–82).

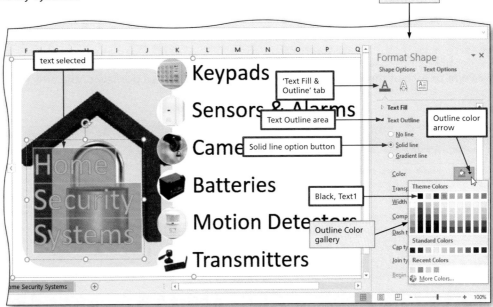

Figure 7–82

2

- Click 'Black, Text 1' in the Outline color gallery to add an outline to the text.

- Click outside of the SmartArt graphic to remove the selection and then drag the text box up as shown in Figure 7–83.

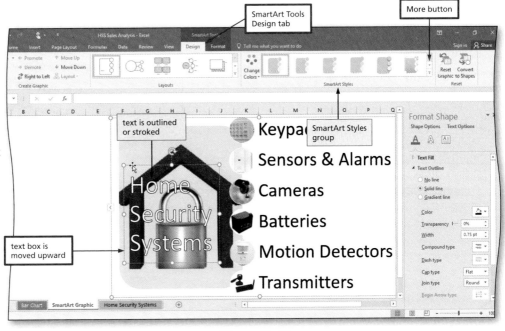

Figure 7–83

3

- Close the Format Shape task pane.

Other Ways
1. Click Text Outline button (SmartArt Tools Format tab | WordArt Styles group), select color (Text Outline gallery)

To Add a Style to a SmartArt Graphic

Excel allows you to change the style of your SmartArt graphic. *Why? The SmartArt styles create different special effects for added emphasis or flair.* The following steps change the style of the SmartArt graphic.

- If necessary, display the SmartArt Tools Design tab.
- Click the More button (SmartArt Tools Design tab | SmartArt Styles group) to display the SmartArt Styles gallery (Figure 7–84).

🔎 Experiment

- Point to each of the SmartArt styles in the gallery to see a live preview of the effect on the worksheet.

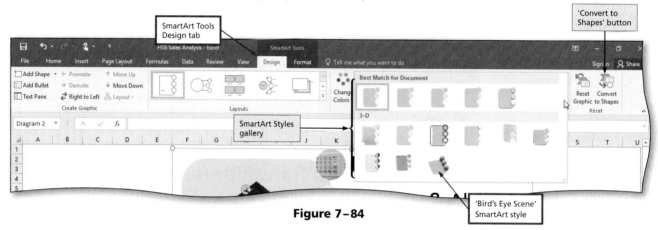

Figure 7–84

- Click the 'Bird's Eye Scene' style to apply it to the SmartArt graphic (Figure 7–85).

Q&A | What does the 'Convert to Shapes' button do?
Clicking the 'Convert to Shapes' button (SmartArt Tools Design tab | Reset group) converts the SmartArt graphic to individual shapes that can be resized, moved, or deleted independently of the others.

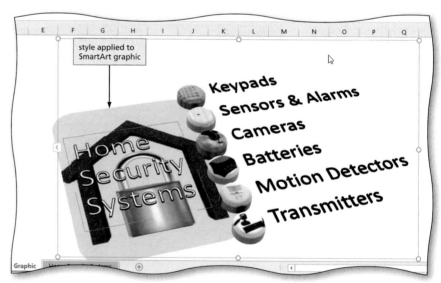

Figure 7–85

- Click the Save button (Quick Access Toolbar) to save the workbook with the same name in the same location.

TO INSERT AN INDIVIDUAL IMAGE INTO A WORKBOOK

If you wanted to insert an individual image into your workbook, you would perform the following steps.

1. Select the cell at which you wish the image to display.
2. Display the Insert tab.
3. Click the From File button (Insert tab | Illustrations group) to display the Insert Picture dialog box.
4. Navigate to the location of the picture to insert and then double-click the file to insert the picture in the worksheet.
5. Resize the picture as necessary.
6. To format the picture, display the Picture Tools Format tab.
7. Click the Picture Styles More button (Picture Tools Format tab | Picture Styles group) to display the Picture Styles gallery.
8. Click the desired picture style to apply the style to the image.

Break Point: If you wish to take a break, this is a good place to do so. You can exit Excel now. To resume at a later time, run Excel, open the file called HSS Sales Analysis, and continue following the steps from this location forward.

Using Screenshots on a Worksheet

Excel allows you to take a screenshot of any open window and add it to a workbook. Using the screenshot feature, you can capture whole windows or only part of a window. For example, if your company has a webpage, you can take a screenshot of the page and insert it into a workbook before presenting the workbook at a meeting. In addition, you can capture a screen clipping to include in your Excel workbook. A **screen clipping** is a portion of the screen, usually of one object or a section of a window. You first will create a new worksheet in the workbook to hold the screenshot and then insert a screenshot of a webpage.

To Create Another New Sheet

In preparation for inserting the screenshot, the following steps create another new sheet.

1 Click the New sheet button to create a fourth sheet in the workbook.

2 Rename the worksheet `Screenshot` to provide a descriptive name for the worksheet.

3 Change the color of the tab to orange and hide the gridlines on the worksheet.

4 If necessary, click cell A1 to make it the active cell (Figure 7–86).

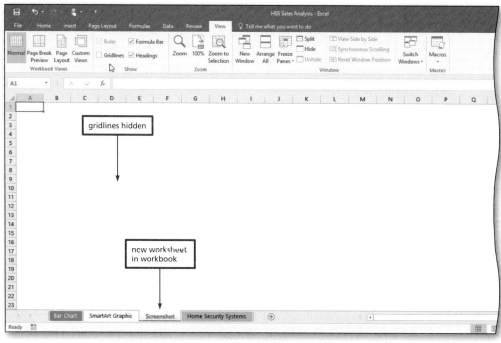

Figure 7–86

To Insert a Screenshot on a Worksheet

1 CREATE TEMPLATE | 2 USE TEMPLATE | 3 IMPORT DATA | 4 USE QUICK ANALYSIS
5 FIND & REPLACE | 6 INSERT BAR CHART | 7 CREATE SMARTART | **8 ADD SCREENSHOT**

The staff at HSS often shares helpful home security websites with customers. The following steps add a screenshot to a worksheet. *Why? In anticipation of an upcoming meeting where the sales analysis will be reviewed, the CEO requests a screenshot of a popular website that answers typical home security questions.*

- Run Internet Explorer or a similar browser.
- Type `http://safewise.com/home-security-faq` in the address bar and then press the ENTER key to display the webpage (Figure 7–87).

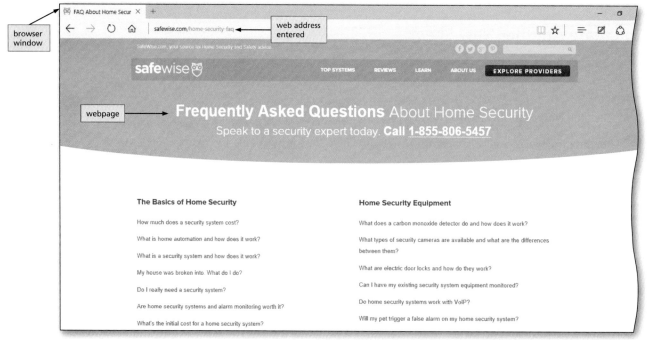

Figure 7–87

- Click the Excel app button on the taskbar to return to Excel.
- Display the Insert tab.
- Click the 'Take a Screenshot' button (Insert tab | Illustrations group) to display the Take a Screenshot menu (Figure 7–88).

Q&A My browser window is not displayed in the gallery. Did I do something wrong?
If Excel cannot link to your browser, you may have to insert a screen clipping instead of a screenshot. To do so, click Screen Clipping (Take a Screenshot gallery), navigate to the desired window, and then draw a rectangle over the portion of the screen you want to insert into the Excel workbook. Note that this process inserts a picture rather than a hyperlinked screenshot and displays the Picture Tools Format tab.

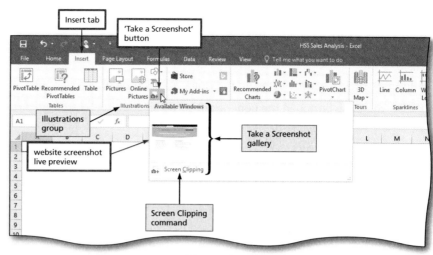

Figure 7–88

- Click the 'Frequently Asked Questions About Home Security' live preview to start the process of inserting a screenshot (Figure 7–89).

Q&A Should I include the hyperlink?
If you plan to present your workbook to an audience and wish to view the updated website in a browser, you should insert the screenshot with a hyperlink. Inserting the hyperlink also gives you access to the link at a later time, without retyping it.

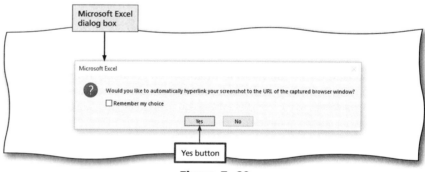

Figure 7–89

- Click the Yes button (Microsoft Excel dialog box) to insert the screenshot with a hyperlink (Figure 7–90).

 **Experiment**

- Scroll to view the entire screenshot. Note that the screenshot displays only the part of the webpage displayed in the browser.

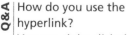 How do you use the hyperlink?
You can right-click the screenshot and then click Open Hyperlink on the shortcut menu. Clicking Open Hyperlink opens a browser and displays the website.

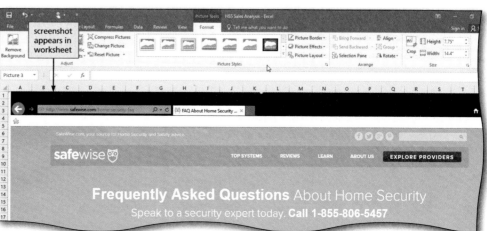

Figure 7–90

- Right-click the browser app button on the taskbar and then click Close window on the shortcut menu to exit the browser.
- In Excel, click the Save button on the Quick Access Toolbar.
- Click the Close button in the upper-right corner of the title bar to exit Excel.

Summary

In this module, you have learned how to create a template that can be used every time a similar workbook is developed. Starting from the template, you gathered external data by importing a text file, an Access database, a Word document, and a website. You formatted the data and transposed it when necessary. You replicated the formulas and functions, and then used Quick Analysis to display specific formatting. Then, you created a bar chart, formatting the bars with a style, color, and bevel. After reversing the order of the categories, you edited the number format of the horizontal labels. While creating a SmartArt graphic, you inserted pictures relevant to the spreadsheet and formatted the SmartArt with text and styles. Finally, you inserted a hyperlinked screenshot in the workbook.

CONSIDER THIS: PLAN AHEAD

What decisions will you need to make when creating your next workbook based on a template to analyze data including a chart, SmartArt graphic, and screenshot?
Use these guidelines as you complete the assignments in this module and create your own worksheets for evaluating and analyzing data outside of this class.

1. Create a template.

    a) Format rows and columns.

    b) Enter titles and headings.

    c) Enter sample or dummy data.

    d) Enter formulas and functions.

    e) Save as a template file type.

2. Create a new workbook based on the template and import data.

    a) Open a template file and save it as a workbook file.

    b) Import data corresponding to type of data.

    c) Format imported data.

    d) Paste special and transpose data when necessary.

3. Format using the Quick Analysis gallery.

    a) Apply formatting or totals using the Quick Analysis gallery.

4. Create new sheets for each part of your analysis workbook.

5. Use SmartArt graphics to illustrate data.

    a) Gather appropriate pictures.

    b) Use text effects to enhance graphic.

6. Use screenshots to aid in presenting analysis.

    a) Hyperlink screenshots from the web, if necessary.

Apply Your Knowledge

Reinforce the skills and apply the concepts you learned in this module.

Using a Template to Create a Consolidated Workbook

Note: To complete these steps, you will be required to use the Data Files. Please contact your instructor for information about accessing the Data Files.

Instructions: You will create the 2016-2017 consolidated workbook and SmartArt graphic for Prototype Labs shown in Figure 7–91.

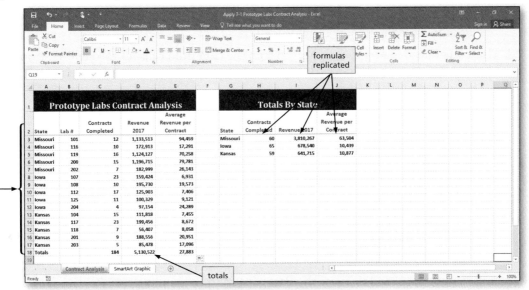

a) Imported Data in Worksheet

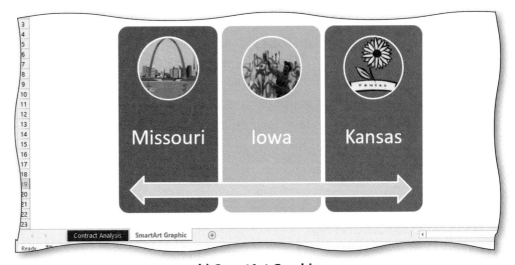

b) SmartArt Graphic

Figure 7–91

Perform the following tasks:

1. Open a File Explorer window and double-click the file named Apply 7-1 Prototype Labs Template from the Data Files. Save the template as a workbook using the file name, Apply 7-1 Prototype Labs Contract Analysis.

2. Add a second sheet to the workbook, named SmartArt Graphic. Color the tab white.

Continued >

Apply Your Knowledge *continued*

3. To import a text file:

   a. With the Contract Analysis worksheet active, select cell A3. Import the text file named, Apply 7-1 Prototype Labs Missouri from the Data Files.

   b. In the wizard dialog boxes, choose the Delimited format with commas.

   c. When Excel displays the Import Data dialog box, click the Properties button to display the External Data Range Properties dialog box. Remove the check mark in the 'Adjust column width' check box (External Data Range Properties dialog box). Click the 'Overwrite existing cells with new data, clear unused cells' option button to select it.

   d. Click the OK button to close the External Data Range Properties dialog box. Click the OK button to close the Import Data dialog box.

4. Use a separate area of the worksheet to trim the data from cells A3 through A7. Copy the trimmed data back to the range. Delete the data you no longer need.

5. To import an Access table:

   a. Select cell A8. Import the Access file named, Apply 7-1 Prototype Labs Iowa, from the Data Files.

   b. Convert the table to a range.

   c. Delete the headings in row 8. Use the format painter to copy the formatting from cells A7:D7 to the range A8:D12.

6. To paste data from Word:

   a. Select cell A20. Run Word and open the file named, Apply 7-1 Prototype Labs Kansas. In the Word table, copy the data in columns 2 through 6.

   b. Return to Excel and then use the Paste Special command to paste the data as text.

   c. Copy the Excel range, A20:E22. Click cell A13 and transpose the data while pasting it.

   d. Delete the original imported data in cells A20:E22.

   e. Cut the data in cells B13:C17 and paste it to cell C13 to move it one column to the right.

   f. Select cells A13:A17. Click the 'Text to Columns' button (Data tab | Data Tools group). In the wizard dialog boxes, choose the Delimited format with commas.

   g. Use the format painter to copy the formatting from cells A12:D12 to the range A13:D17.

7. Use the fill handle to replicate cells H3:J3 to H4:J5.

8. Enter the word, `Totals`, in cell A18. Use the Quick Analysis gallery to sum the range C3:D17.

9. Replicate the formula in cell E3 down through cell E18.

10. Insert your name and course number in cell A21.

11. Go to the SmartArt Graphic sheet. Remove the gridlines. Insert the Continuous Picture list SmartArt graphic. Resize the SmartArt graphic as necessary.

12. One at a time, replace the word, Text, with the words, Missouri, Iowa, and Kansas, respectively.

13. Change the color scheme to 'Colorful - Accent Colors' in the Change Colors gallery.

14. One at a time, click the picture icon in each part of the graphic, and search the web for a graphic related to the state. Make sure you review the license to ensure you can comply with any copyright restrictions.

15. Save the file again.

16. Submit the publication in the format specified by your instructor.

17. ✳ In what format do you think most companies submit data? Why? If the data changes, how do the consolidated workbooks with imported data adjust? Do all the formats lend themselves to recalculating? Why or why not?

Extend Your Knowledge

Extend the skills you learned in this module and experiment with new skills. You may need to use Help to complete the assignment.

Inserting a SmartArt Organization Chart and Image on a Worksheet

Note: To complete these steps, you will be required to use the Data Files. Please contact your instructor for information about accessing the Data Files.

Instructions: Run Excel. Open the workbook Extend 7-1 Highsmith Investment from the Data Files and then save the workbook as Extend 7-1 Highsmith Investment Complete. You will add a SmartArt graphic and an image to the workbook and then format both graphics as shown in Figure 7–92.

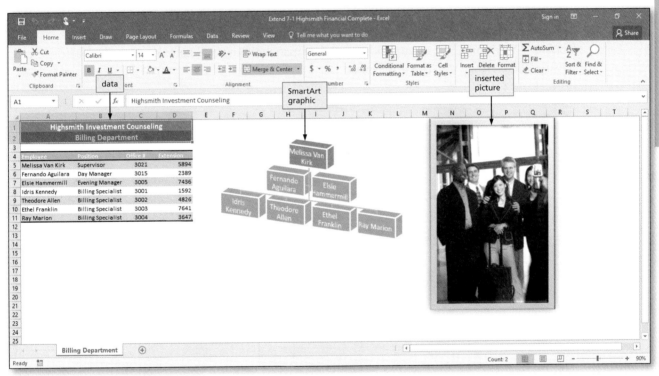

Figure 7–92

Perform the following tasks:

1. Insert a SmartArt graphic using the Hierarchy type and the Organization Chart layout.

2. Select the shape in the second row of the chart and then add a shape.

3. Add a shape in the third row. If necessary, promote the shape to be level with the other three.

4. Display the Text Pane and drag its border to the right side of the chart. Use cutting and pasting techniques to insert the names from column A into the graphic, as shown in Figure 7–92. Insert your name in place of the Evening Manager.

5. Change the color scheme of the hierarchy chart to Gradient Loop - Accent 2 in the Change Colors gallery.

6. Use the SmartArt Styles gallery to change the style to Brick Scene.

7. Move the SmartArt Graphic to the right of the data.

8. Use Help to read about formatting pictures. Insert an online picture related to the search term, people, similar to the one shown in Figure 7–92. Format the picture using a Picture style (Picture Tools Format tab | Picture Styles group) with a wide gray border.

Continued >

Extend Your Knowledge *continued*

9. Move and resize the picture so that it fits beside the SmartArt graphic.

10. Add your name and course number to the worksheet.

11. Save the workbook. Submit the assignment as requested by your instructor.

12. ✳ When do you think a company would use a spreadsheet like this? What formatting and changes might make it even more useful?

Expand Your World

Create a solution that uses cloud and web technologies by learning and investigating on your own from general guidance.

Using Web Data

Problem: You would like to import some web statistics about your state. You decide to retrieve U.S. census data from the web (Figure 7–93).

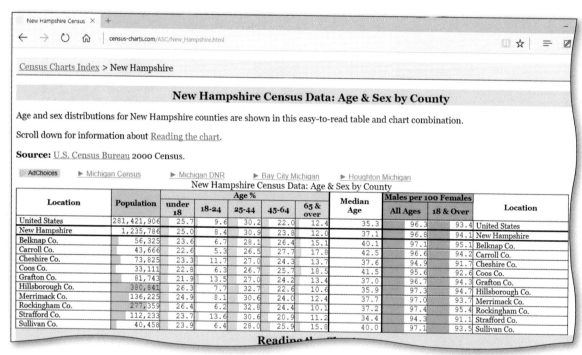

New Hampshire Census ✕ +

census-charts.com/ASC/New_Hampshire.html

Census Charts Index > New Hampshire

New Hampshire Census Data: Age & Sex by County

Age and sex distributions for New Hampshire counties are shown in this easy-to-read table and chart combination.

Scroll down for information about Reading the chart.

Source: U.S. Census Bureau 2000 Census.

▶ AdChoices   ▶ Michigan Census   ▶ Michigan DNR   ▶ Bay City Michigan   ▶ Houghton Michigan

New Hampshire Census Data: Age & Sex by County

Location	Population	under 18	18-24	25-44	45-64	65 & over	Median Age	All Ages	18 & Over	Location
				Age %				Males per 100 Females		
United States	281,421,906	25.7	9.6	30.2	22.0	12.4	35.3	96.3	93.4	United States
New Hampshire	1,235,786	25.0	8.4	30.9	23.8	12.0	37.1	96.8	94.1	New Hampshire
Belknap Co.	56,325	23.6	6.7	28.1	26.4	15.1	40.1	97.1	95.1	Belknap Co.
Carroll Co.	43,666	22.6	5.3	26.5	27.7	17.8	42.5	96.6	94.2	Carroll Co.
Cheshire Co.	73,825	23.3	11.7	27.0	24.3	13.7	37.6	94.9	91.7	Cheshire Co.
Coos Co.	33,111	22.8	6.3	26.7	25.7	18.5	41.5	95.6	92.6	Coos Co.
Grafton Co.	81,743	21.9	13.5	27.0	24.2	13.4	37.0	96.7	94.3	Grafton Co.
Hillsborough Co.	380,841	26.3	7.7	32.7	22.6	10.6	35.9	97.3	94.7	Hillsborough Co.
Merrimack Co.	136,225	24.9	8.1	30.6	24.0	12.4	37.7	97.0	93.7	Merrimack Co.
Rockingham Co.	277,359	26.4	6.2	32.8	24.4	10.1	37.2	97.4	95.4	Rockingham Co.
Strafford Co.	112,233	23.7	13.6	30.6	20.9	11.2	34.4	94.3	91.1	Strafford Co.
Sullivan Co.	40,458	23.9	6.4	28.0	25.9	15.8	40.0	97.1	93.5	Sullivan Co.

Reading the chart

Figure 7–93

Instructions:

1. Run a browser and navigate to http://www.census-charts.com/.

2. In the Data by State and County area, click 'Age and Sex' and then click your state.

3. When the website presents the data, copy the URL address.

4. Run Excel and open a blank workbook.

5. Hide the grid lines and rename the sheet Screenshot. Use the 'Take a Screenshot' button (Insert tab | Illustrations group) to insert a screenshot of your data. Close the browser.

6. Add a new sheet to the workbook, named Web Data.

7. Select cell B2. Click the 'Get Data From Web' button (Data tab | Get External Data group). Paste the URL into the address text box in the New Web Query dialog box. Click the Go button (New Web Query dialog box).

8. When the webpage appears, double-click its title bar to maximize the window. Click the table selection arrows to select the table with the numeric data. Click the Import button (New Web Query dialog box).

9. When Excel displays the Import Data dialog box, click the OK button.

10. When Excel displays the data, format the title and column headings, as well as the column widths. Save the file and submit it in the format specified by your instructor.

11. ✻ What kinds of analysis could you perform in Excel on the data you downloaded from the census website? What would make the data more meaningful and useful? Why?

In the Labs

Design, create, modify, and/or use a workbook following the guidelines, concepts, and skills presented in this module. Labs 1 and 2, which increase in difficulty, require you to create solutions based on what you learned in the module; Lab 3 requires you to apply your creative thinking and problem-solving skills to design and implement a solution.

Lab 1: Using the Quick Analysis Gallery and Formatting a Bar Chart

Note: To complete these steps, you will be required to use the Data Files. Please contact your instructor for information about accessing the Data Files.

Problem: Custom Fragrances has prepared an annual sales analysis but would like to show the data in a more visual way, along with grand totals (Figure 7–94).

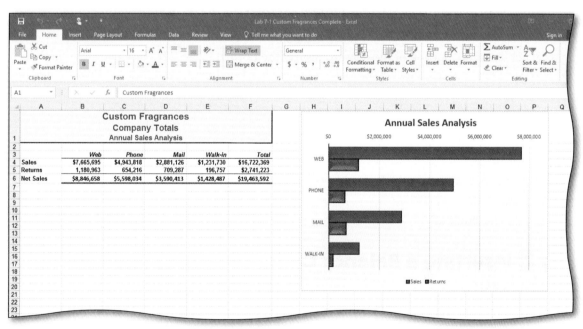

Figure 7–94

Instructions Part 1: Perform the following tasks:

1. Open the workbook, Lab 7–1 Custom Fragrances from the Data Files. Save the file with file name Lab 7–1 Custom Fragrances Complete.

2. In cell A6, type **Net Sales** to enter a row heading.

Continued >

In the Labs *continued*

3. Select the range B4:E5. Click the Quick Analysis button, click Totals, and then click Sum. Use a Cell Style to create a double-underline below the totals.

4. In cell F3, type `Total` to enter a column heading. Copy the formatting from cell E3 to F3.

5. Select the range B4:E6. Click the Quick Analysis button, click Totals, and then click the second Sum button to create row totals. Copy other formatting as necessary.

6. Drag through the range A3:E5. Use the Quick Analysis gallery to insert a Clustered Bar Chart. Move the Chart beside the data.

7. Format the chart as follows:

   a. With the chart selected, click the Change Colors button (Chart Tools Design tab | Chart Styles group), and then click Color 4 in the gallery.

   b. Change the chart style to Style 3 (Chart Tools Design tab | Chart Styles group).

   c. Click any of the data labels (the numbers on the bars themselves), and press the DELETE key to delete the data labels.

   d. Right-click the y-axes or vertical labels. Click Format Axis on the shortcut menu. In the Axis position area, reverse the order of the categories.

   e. With the task pane still displayed, click any of the data bars that represent Sales to display the Format Data Series task pane. On the Fill & Line tab, add a black, solid line border to the series. On the Effects tab, click the 3-D format area, and then click the Top bevel button. In the gallery, click the Soft Round style.

   f. Repeat step 7e for the data bars representing the Returns.

   g. Click the x-axis or horizontal labels at the top of the chart to display the Format Axis task pane. Click the Axis Options tab (Format Axis task pane) and expand Axis Options. To narrow the range in the chart area and thus make the bars seem larger, in the Bounds area, type `8000000` in the Maximum text box. In the Units area, type `2000000` in the Major text box.

   h. Click an empty portion of the chart to display the Format Chart Area task pane. On the Fill & Line tab, if necessary, click Border, and then click Gradient Line. Click the Preset gradients button and then click 'Light Gradient - Accent 3' in the gallery. Close the task pane.

   i. Change the chart title to Annual Sales Analysis.

8. Add your name and course number to the worksheet.

9. Save the file again.

10. Submit the publication in the format specified by your instructor.

11. ☀ Would a different style of chart create a more effective visual representation of the data? Why do you think so?

Lab 2: Inserting a Balance Chart and Image on a Worksheet

Note: To complete these steps, you will be required to use the Data Files. Please contact your instructor for information about accessing the Data Files.

Problem: The Joy of Art, a local company, is considering having a mural painted on the side of its building. You have been asked to create a worksheet with a high-level overview of the pros and cons regarding the mural. The finished worksheet should look like Figure 7–95.

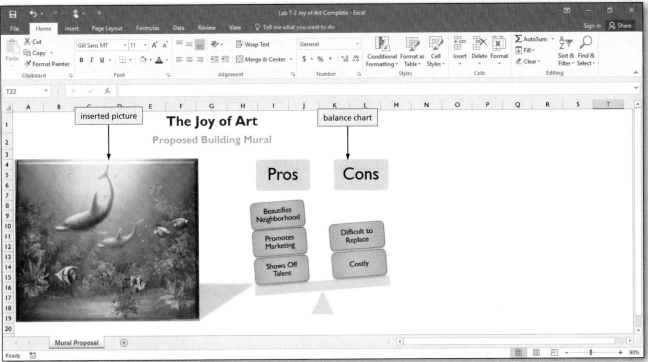

Figure 7–95

Perform the following tasks:

1. Run Excel. Open the workbook Lab 7–2 Joy of Art from the Data Files. Save it as Lab 7–2 Joy of Art Complete.

2. Insert the Lab 7–2 Mural image file from the Data Files in the worksheet.

3. Move and resize the image so that its upper-left corner is aligned with the upper-left corner of cell A4 and the lower-right corner of the image is aligned with the lower-right corner of cell F19.

4. Format the image as follows:

   a. Click the Picture Effects button (Picture Tools Format tab | Picture Styles group), click Shadow, and then click 'Perspective Diagonal Upper Right'.

   b. Click the Picture Effects button (Picture Tools Format tab | Picture Styles group), click Bevel, and then click Art Deco.

5. Insert a SmartArt graphic using the Relationship type and the Balance layout.

6. Move and resize the SmartArt graphic so that its upper-left corner is aligned with the upper-left corner of H4 and the lower-right corner of the graphic is aligned with the lower-right corner of cell M19.

7. Use the Text Pane to enter three Pros: Shows Off Talent, Promotes Marketing, and Beautifies Neighborhood; and two Cons: Costly and Difficult to Replace. Make certain that the Pros column appears on the left of the chart. Be sure to delete the unused shape on the right side of the balance chart. The upper-left shape in the chart should read Pros, and the upper-right shape in the chart should read Cons. Note that the direction of the tilt of the balance changes when more pros than cons are entered in the chart.

8. Format the Balance SmartArt as follows:

   a. Change the color scheme to 'Colored Fill - Accent 3' in the Change Colors gallery.

   b. Apply the Subtle Effect SmartArt style.

Continued >

In the Labs *continued*

9. Add your name to cell N1.

10. Save the workbook. Submit the assignment as requested by your instructor.

11. ✳ In what other kinds of situations might you use a balance chart, other than for pros and cons? Would a table listing the pros and cons be as effective? Why or why not?

Lab 3: **Consider This: Your Turn**

Apply your creative thinking and problem-solving skills to design and implement a solution.

Create a Cover Sheet

Part 1: You are competing to design a cover sheet for an academic department at your school to include in their workbooks when they send out statistics. Run a browser and view the webpage for your chosen department at your school. Create a workbook and turn off the viewing of gridlines for the first sheet. Insert a screenshot of the department webpage and size it appropriately. Insert a SmartArt list to highlight three or four of the best qualities of your department. Use text effects to enhance the text. Change the colors to match more closely your school colors. Choose an appropriate SmartArt style. Below the SmartArt graphic, add a screen clipping of the school's logo. Finally, next to the logo add your name and format it so that it appears as a title. Below your name, in a smaller font, insert the name of your department.

Part 2: ✳ How did you decide on which SmartArt layout and style to use?

8 | Working with Trendlines, PivotTables, PivotCharts, and Slicers

Objectives

You will have mastered the material in this module when you can:

- Analyze worksheet data using a trendline

- Create a PivotTable report

- Format a PivotTable report

- Apply filters to a PivotTable report

- Create a PivotChart report

- Format a PivotChart report

- Apply filters to a PivotChart report

- Analyze worksheet data using PivotTable and PivotChart reports

- Create calculated fields

- Create slicers to filter PivotTable and PivotChart reports

- Format slicers

- Analyze PivotTable and PivotChart reports using slicers

Introduction

In both academic and business environments, people are presented with large amounts of data that needs to be analyzed and interpreted. Data increasingly is available from a wide variety of sources and gathered with ease. Analysis of data and interpretation of the results are important skills to acquire. Learning how to ask questions that identify patterns in data is a skill that can provide businesses and individuals with information that can be used to make decisions about business situations.

Project — LinkMe Internet Service Provider

LinkMe ISP (Internet Service Provider) is a company that sells five different types of Internet connection service plans: Basic, Basic Plus, Hi-Speed, Deluxe 150, and T3. They keep records on sales regions, including city, suburban, and rural sales. They also keep track of online sales versus other venues such as retail outlets, trade shows, and telemarketing.

The owner of LinkMe ISP is interested in reviewing sales figures for the past six years. She also has requested that you compare the last two years of sales figures for the different service types, by region and by venue. In this module, you will learn how to use the trendline charting feature in Excel to examine data for trends. You also will analyze sales data for LinkMe ISP using PivotTable and PivotChart reports. The results of this analysis are shown in Figure 8–1.

A **trendline** (Figure 8–1a) is a visual way to show how two variables relate to each other. Trendlines often are used to represent changes in one set of data over time, but also can compare changes in one set of data with changes in another. Excel can overlay a trendline on certain types of charts.

In addition to trendlines, PivotTable reports and PivotChart reports provide methods to manipulate and visualize data. A PivotTable report (Figure 8–1b) is an interactive view of worksheet data that gives users the ability to summarize the data by selecting and grouping categories. When using a PivotTable report, you can change selected categories quickly, without needing to manipulate the worksheet itself. You can examine and analyze several complex organizations of the data and may spot relationships you might not otherwise see. For example, you can look at total sales for each region, broken down by service type, and then look at the quarterly sales for certain subgroupings, without having to do complex reorganization of the data.

A PivotChart report (Figure 8–1c) is an interactive chart that allows users to change the data groupings. For example, if LinkMe ISP wanted to view a pie chart showing percentages of total sales for each service type, a PivotChart could show that percentage categorized by city versus rural sales, without having to rebuild the chart from scratch for each view. PivotChart reports are visual representations of PivotTables. When you create a PivotChart report, Excel creates and associates a PivotTable with that PivotChart.

Slicers (Figure 8–1d) are graphic objects that you click to filter the data in PivotTables and PivotCharts. Each slicer button clearly identifies its purpose (the applied filter), making it easy to interpret the data displayed in the PivotTable report.

Using trendlines, PivotTables, PivotCharts, and slicers, a user with little knowledge of formulas, functions, and ranges can complete powerful what-if analyses on a set of data.

Figure 8–2 illustrates the requirements document for the LinkMe ISP Sales Analysis worksheet. It includes the needs, source of data, calculations, and other facts about the worksheet's development.

The following roadmap identifies general activities you will perform as you progress through this module:

1. CREATE the LINE CHART and TRENDLINE.

2. CREATE the PIVOTTABLE.

3. CHANGE the LAYOUT and VIEW of the PivotTable

4. FILTER the PIVOTTABLE.

5. FORMAT the PIVOTTABLE.

6. CREATE the PIVOTCHART.

7. CHANGE the PIVOTCHART VIEW and CONTENTS.

8. ADD SLICERS.

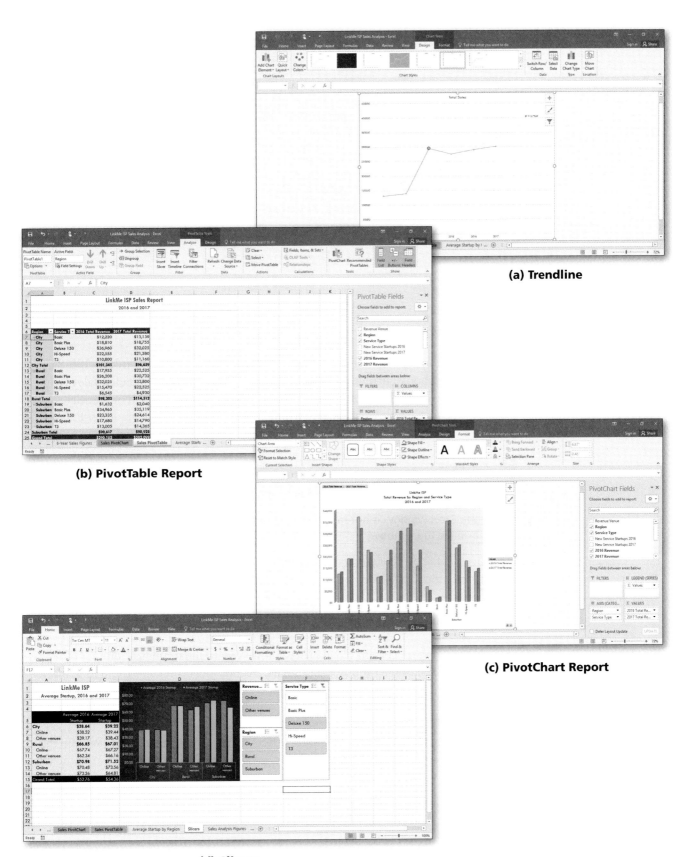

(a) Trendline

(b) PivotTable Report

(c) PivotChart Report

(d) Slicers

Figure 8–1

Worksheet Title	LinkMe ISP Sales Analysis
Needs	Evaluate different sets of sales data analysis: 1. Total Sales data for 2012–2017. Provide a visual representation of revenue over the past 6 years, and a forecast for the next 2 years based on the current trend. 2. Sales data for 2016 and 2017 for all venues, with details identifying region, service type, and number of start-ups sold. For this data, use PivotTables and PivotCharts to look for patterns and anomalies in the data, based on different breakouts. Some breakouts of interest include Total Sales and Average Sales for Region and Service type, by Revenue Venue. 3. Set up slicers to facilitate easy examination of various subgroupings for users with little or no Excel experience.
Source of Data	Data is available in the workbook LinkMe ISP Sales Data.xlsx.
Calculations	In addition to total sales for the various groupings, produce comparisons of average sales for those groupings. Finally, create calculations of the value of the average sales for various combinations.

Figure 8–2

To Run Excel and Open a Workbook

The following steps run Excel and open a workbook named LinkMe ISP Sales Data. The workbook currently has two worksheets, one showing detailed sales figures, named Sales Analysis Figures, and one summarizing the data, named 6-Year Sales Figures. To complete these steps, you will be required to use the Data Files. Please contact your instructor for information about accessing the Data Files.

1 Run Excel.

2 Open the file named LinkMe ISP Sales Data from the Data Files.

3 If the Excel window is not maximized, click the Maximize button on its title bar to maximize the window.

4 Save the file on your storage device with the name, LinkMe ISP Sales Analysis.

Adding a Trendline to a Chart

Using a trendline on certain Excel charts allows you to illustrate how one set of data is changing in relation to another set of data. Trends most often are thought about in terms of how a value changes over time, but trends also can describe the relationship between two variables, such as height and weight. In Excel, you add a trendline to most types of charts, such as unstacked 2-D area, bar, column, line, inventory, scatter (X, Y), and bubble charts, among others. Chart types that do not examine the relationship between two variables, such as pie and doughnut charts that examine the contribution of different parts to a whole, cannot include trendlines.

How do you determine which trends to analyze?

Before you add a trendline to a chart, you need to determine which data series to analyze. If the chart uses only one data series, Excel uses it automatically. If the chart involves more than one data series, you select the one you want to use as a trendline. You then can analyze current or future trends.

To analyze a current trend, make sure you have enough data available for the period you want to analyze. For example, two years of annual sales totals might not provide enough data to analyze sales performance. Five years of annual sales totals or two years of monthly sales totals are more likely to present a trend.

To analyze a future trend, you use a trendline to project data beyond the values or scope of the data set. This process is called forecasting. **Forecasting** helps predict data values that are outside of a data set. For example, if a data set is for a 10-year period and the data shows a trend in that 10-year period, Excel can predict values beyond that period or estimate what the values may have been before that period.

When you add a trendline to a chart, you can set the number of periods to forecast forward or backward in time. For example, if you have six years of sales data, you can forecast two periods forward to show the trend for eight years: six years of current data and two years of projected data. You also can display information about the trendline on the chart itself to help guide your analysis. For example, you can display the equation used to calculate the trend and show the **R-squared value**, which is a number from 0 to 1 that measures the strength of the trend. An R-squared value of 1 means the estimated values in the trendline correspond exactly to the actual data.

To Create a 2-D Line Chart

1 CREATE LINE CHART & TRENDLINE | **2 CREATE PIVOTTABLE** | **3 CHANGE LAYOUT & VIEW** | **4 FILTER PIVOTTABLE**
5 FORMAT PIVOTTABLE | **6 CREATE PIVOTCHART** | **7 CHANGE PIVOTCHART VIEW & CONTENTS** | **8 ADD SLICERS**

Why? *Line charts are suited to charting a variable, in this case sales, over a number of time periods.* The following steps create a 2-D line chart of the LinkMe ISP sales data. You will add a trendline to the chart later in the module.

- If necessary, click the '6-Year Sales Figures' sheet tab.

- Select cells A4:G5 to select the range to be charted (Figure 8–3).

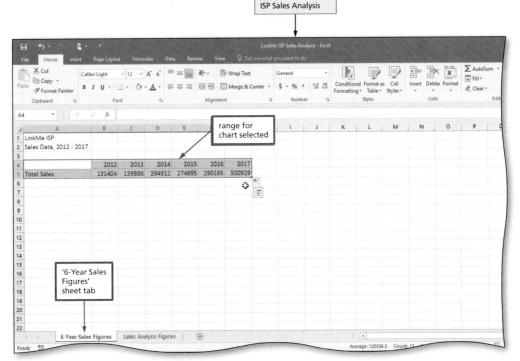

Figure 8–3

- Click Insert on the ribbon to display the Insert tab.
- Click the 'Insert Line or Area Chart' button (Insert tab | Charts group) to display the Insert Line and Area Chart gallery (Figure 8–4).

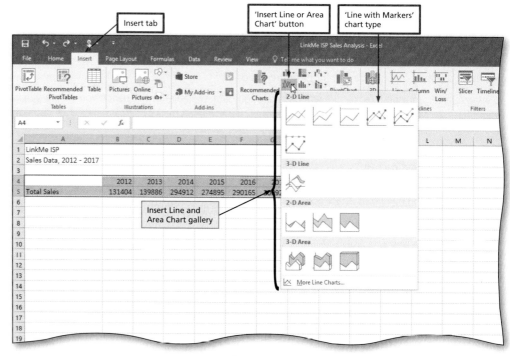

Figure 8–4

- Click 'Line with Markers' in the 2-D Line area to insert a 2-D line chart with data markers (Figure 8–5).

Q&A What are data markers?
A data marker is the symbol in a chart that represents a single value from a worksheet cell. In this case, the data markers are circles that represent the six sales figures.

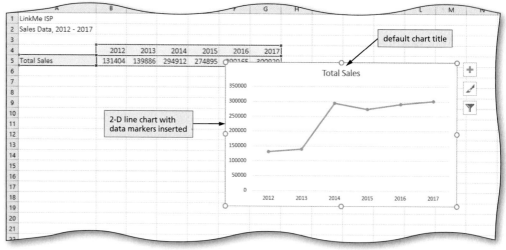

Figure 8–5

Why do the selected cells appear with colored fill?
Excel uses colors to identify chart elements when preparing to create a chart. In this case, the red cell is the chart title, the purple cells are the x-axis or category values (in this case, years), and the blue cells are the data or values.

- If necessary, display the Chart Tools Design tab.
- Click the Move Chart button (Chart Tools Design tab | Location group) to display the Move Chart dialog box.
- Click New sheet (Move Chart dialog box) to select the option button.
- Double-click the default text in the New sheet text box to select the text, and then type **Trendline Chart** to enter a name for the new worksheet (Figure 8–6).

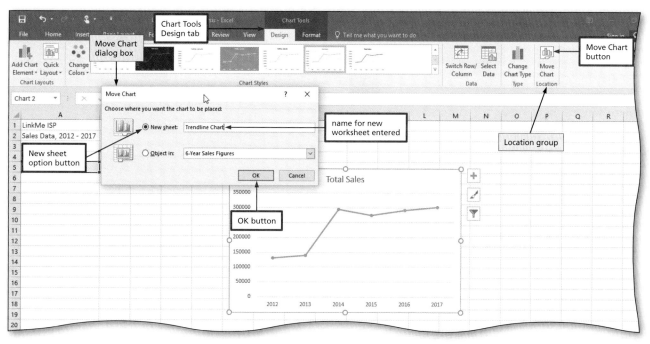

Figure 8–6

5

- Click the OK button (Move Chart dialog box) to move the chart to a new worksheet.

- Click the chart title and select the text.

- Type **LinkMe ISP Sales 2012 – 2017** to enter the new chart title.

- Click outside of the chart area to deselect the chart (Figure 8–7).

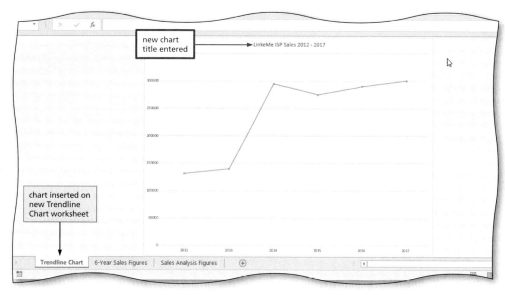

Figure 8–7

Other Ways

1. Click Quick Analysis button, click Charts tab, click Line button

To Add a Trendline to a Chart

1 CREATE LINE CHART & TRENDLINE | 2 CREATE PIVOTTABLE | 3 CHANGE LAYOUT & VIEW | 4 FILTER PIVOTTABLE
5 FORMAT PIVOTTABLE | 6 CREATE PIVOTCHART | 7 CHANGE PIVOTCHART VIEW & CONTENTS | 8 ADD SLICERS

The following steps add a trendline to the LinkMe ISP Total Sales 2012 – 2017 chart. *Why? You add a trendline to a chart to analyze current and/or future trends. A trendline must be added to an existing chart.* The chart will predict the total sales two years beyond the data set in the six-year sales figures worksheet.

- Click the chart to select it and display the Chart Tools Design tab if necessary.

- Click the 'Add Chart Element' button (Chart Tools Design tab | Chart Layouts group) to display the Add Chart Element menu.

- Point to Trendline to display the Trendline gallery (Figure 8–8).

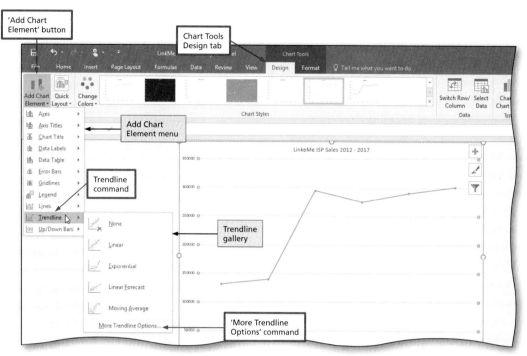

Figure 8–8

- Click 'More Trendline Options' (Trendline gallery) to display the Format Trendline task pane.

- If necessary, click the Trendline Options tab.

- If necessary, click Linear in the Trendline Options area to select a linear trendline type (Figure 8–9).

Q&A

Why should I select the Linear option button in this case?
The 2-D line chart you created is a basic line chart, so it is appropriate to apply a linear trendline, which shows values that are increasing or decreasing at a steady rate.

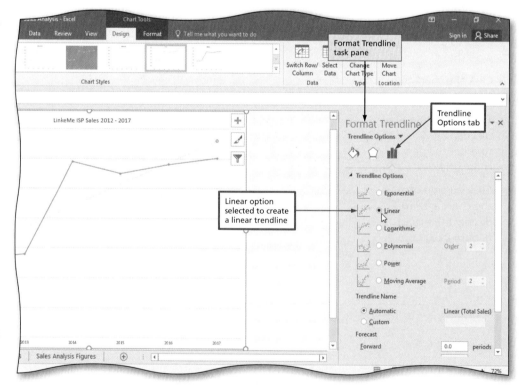

Figure 8–9

❸

- If necessary, scroll down in the Format Trendline task pane until the Forecast area is visible.

- Select the Forward text box and type **2.0** to add a trendline to the chart with a two-period forward forecast.

Q&A What does it mean to enter a two-period forward forecast?
A two-period forward forecast estimates the values for the two time periods that follow the data you used to create the line chart. In this case, it will estimate total sales for the next two years.

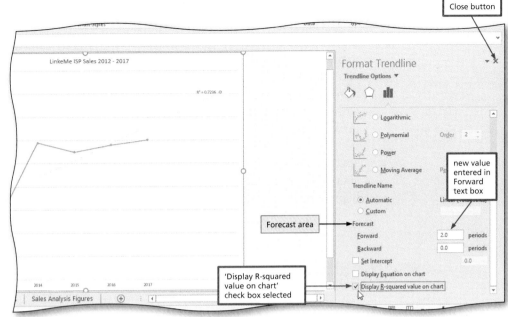

Figure 8–10

- Click the 'Display R-squared value on chart' check box to display the R-squared value on the chart (Figure 8–10).

Q&A What is the R-squared value?
The R-squared value is a measure of how well the trendline describes the relationship between total sales and time. The closer the value is to 1, the more accurate the trendline.

❹

- Click the Close button (Format Trendline task pane) to add the trendline with the selected options.

- Display the Page Layout tab.

- Use the Themes button (Page Layout tab | Themes group) to apply the Integral theme to the workbook (Figure 8–11).

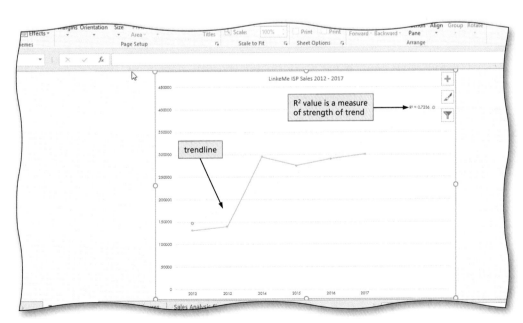

Figure 8–11

Other Ways

1. Right-click graphed line, click Add Trendline on shortcut menu

More about Trendlines

It is important to take note of the axes when looking at trendlines. Charts with trendlines often are reformatted to start the vertical axis at a number other than zero, particularly when the values on the vertical axis are high. When interpreting a trendline, you should look at the vertical axis to see if it starts at zero. If it does not, be aware that trends represented by the trendline may appear exaggerated. Figure 8–12 shows a chart with a trendline that uses the same data as the chart in Figure 8–11. The difference between the two charts is in the vertical axis, which starts at zero in Figure 8–11 and at 100,000 in Figure 8–12. The difference between the projected values for 2018 and 2019 appears much larger in Figure 8–12 where the axis starts at 100,000. When looking at charts, always check the axes to be sure that the differences shown in the chart are not being visually overstated.

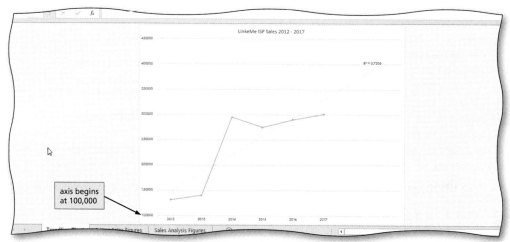

Figure 8–12

To Change the Format of a Data Point

1 CREATE LINE CHART & TRENDLINE | 2 CREATE PIVOTTABLE | 3 CHANGE LAYOUT & VIEW | 4 FILTER PIVOTTABLE
5 FORMAT PIVOTTABLE | 6 CREATE PIVOTCHART | 7 CHANGE PIVOTCHART VIEW & CONTENTS | 8 ADD SLICERS

The following steps change the format of the 2014 data point. **Why?** *When graphing data, you may want to call visual attention to a particular data point or points.*

1

- Click the 2014 data point twice to select the single point. Do not double-click.

- Right-click the selected data point to display the shortcut menu (Figure 8–13).

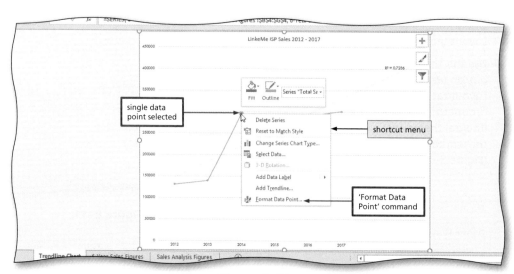

Figure 8–13

2

- Click 'Format Data Point' on the shortcut menu to display the Format Data Point task pane.

- Click the 'Fill & Line' tab (Format Data Point task pane) to display the Fill & Line options.

- Click Marker, and then if necessary, click Marker Options to expand the section.

- Select the contents of the Size box, and then type 12 as the new size.

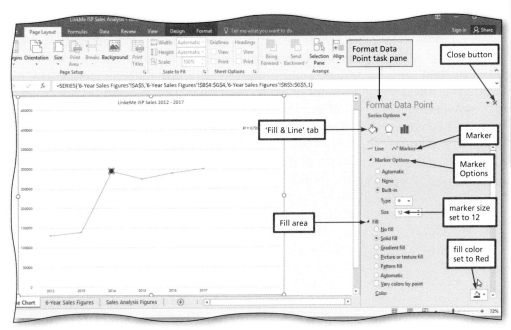

Figure 8–14

- If necessary, click Fill to expand the Fill section.

- Click the Color button and then click Red in the Standard Colors area to change the color of the data point to red (Figure 8–14).

3

- Click the Close button (Format Data Point task pane) and then click away from the data point to view the change (Figure 8–15).

4

- Click the Save button (Quick Access Toolbar) to save the workbook with the same name in the same location.

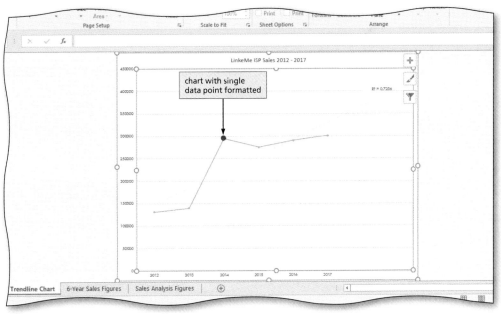

Figure 8–15

Break Point: If you wish to take a break, this is a good place to do so. Exit Excel. To resume at a later time, run Excel and open the file named LinkMe ISP Sales Analysis, and then continue following the steps from this location forward.

Creating and Formatting PivotTable Reports

A PivotTable report, also called a PivotTable, is an interactive tool that summarizes worksheet data. It uses filter buttons in the cells and a task pane to change the way the data is presented, without changing any of the original data. Normally, when working with data tables or lists of data, each different reorganization of the data requires a new table or list. In contrast, you can reorganize data and examine summaries in a PivotTable report with a few clicks. PivotTable reports allow you to view different summaries of the data quickly and easily, using just a single table.

When creating a PivotTable report, you can use categories in the data to summarize different groups or totals. PivotTables use two types of fields: data, which contains values that the PivotTable will summarize, and category, which describes the data by categorizing it. Category fields typically correspond to columns in the original data, and data fields correspond to summary values across categories. You can change row and column groupings quickly to summarize the data in different ways to ask new questions. Reorganizing the table reveals different levels of detail and allows you to analyze specific subgroups.

One PivotTable created in this project is shown in Figure 8–16. It summarizes the LinkMe ISP data to show the total sales and average sales in 2016 and 2017 for each region by service type (Basic, Basic Plus, Hi-Speed, Deluxe 150, and T3). The filter button in cell A6 filters the results by region, and the filter button in cell B6 filters the results by service type. Columns C and D show the values for the total sales in 2016 and 2017, and columns E and F show the values for the average sales in 2016 and 2017.

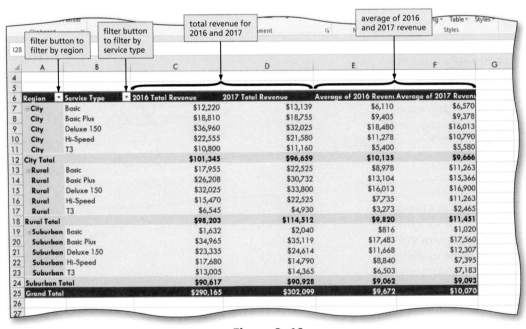

Figure 8–16

How do you determine which fields to use in a PivotTable?

You can create PivotTable and PivotChart reports in almost any configuration of your existing data. To use this powerful tool effectively, you need to create these reports with various questions in mind. Look at the categories you can use to describe your data and think about how the various categories can interact. Common questions relate to how the data changes over time, and how the data varies in geographical locations, such as states or regions, different functional groups within an organization, different product groupings, and demographic groupings, such as age and gender.

You can create PivotTable reports either on the same worksheet as the data to be analyzed or on a new worksheet in the same workbook.

To Create a Blank PivotTable

1 CREATE LINE CHART & TRENDLINE | 2 CREATE PIVOTTABLE | 3 CHANGE LAYOUT & VIEW | 4 FILTER PIVOTTABLE
5 FORMAT PIVOTTABLE | 6 CREATE PIVOTCHART | 7 CHANGE PIVOTCHART VIEW & CONTENTS | 8 ADD SLICERS

The following steps create a blank PivotTable report using the ribbon. *Why? Creating a blank PivotTable allows the user to create a framework within which to use the available data.* When you create a PivotTable, each column heading from your original data will represent a field of data accessible via the PivotTable Fields task pane.

1

- Click the 'Sales Analysis Figures' sheet tab to make the worksheet active.
- Click cell B3 to select a cell containing data for the PivotTable.
- Display the Insert tab.

🔎 **Experiment**

- Click the Recommended PivotTables button to view the various ways the data might be represented in tabular form. Click the Cancel button (Recommend PivotTables dialog box) to continue.

- Click the PivotTable button (Insert tab | Tables group) to display the Create PivotTable dialog box (Figure 8–17).

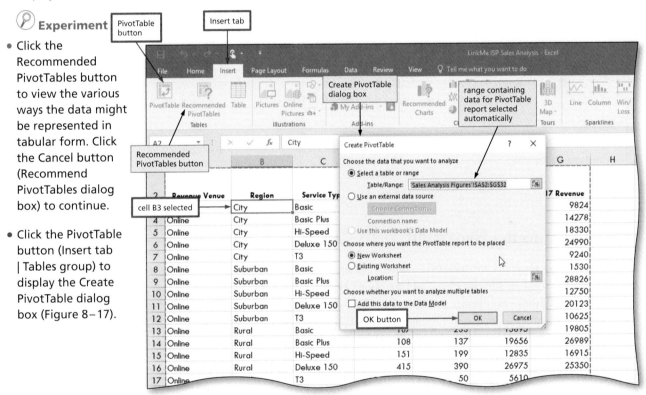

Figure 8–17

2

- Click the OK button (Create PivotTable dialog box) to create a blank PivotTable report on a new worksheet and display the PivotTable Fields task pane (Figure 8–18).

Q&A

Why is the PivotTable blank?
When you create a PivotTable, you first insert the structure. The resulting PivotTable is blank until you add content to it, which you do in the next set of steps.

My PivotTable Fields task pane just disappeared. What happened?
If you click outside of the PivotTable, the task pane no longer will be displayed. To redisplay the pane, click in the PivotTable.

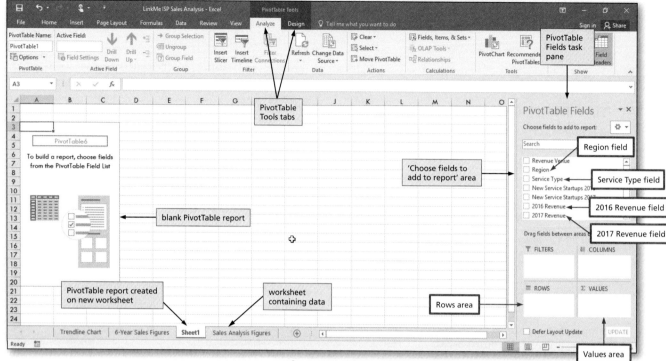

Figure 8–18

Other Ways

1. Click cell in range, click Recommended PivotTables (Insert tab | Tables group), click Blank PivotTable button (Recommended PivotTables dialog box)

To Add Data to the PivotTable

1 CREATE LINE CHART & TRENDLINE | 2 CREATE PIVOTTABLE | 3 CHANGE LAYOUT & VIEW | 4 FILTER PIVOTTABLE
5 FORMAT PIVOTTABLE | 6 CREATE PIVOTCHART | 7 CHANGE PIVOTCHART VIEW & CONTENTS | 8 ADD SLICERS

Why? *Once the blank PivotTable is created, it needs to be populated using any or all of the fields in the PivotTable Fields task pane.* You can add data by selecting check boxes in the PivotTable Fields task pane or by dragging fields from the Choose fields area to the one of the four boxed areas in the lower part of the task pane. Once you add a field, it becomes a button in the task pane, with its own button menu. Table 8–1 describes the four areas in the PivotTable Fields task pane and their common usage.

Table 8–1 Field Areas in the PivotTable Fields Task Pane	
Areas	**Use**
FILTERS	Fields added to the Filters area create a report filter and filter button in the PivotTable, representing a subset that meets a selection criterion.
COLUMNS	Normally, Excel creates a field in the Columns area when multiple fields are dragged to the Values area. Fields directly added to the Columns fields should contain summary numeric data
ROWS	Fields added to the Rows area become rows in the PivotTable. Subsequent fields added to the Rows area become subsets of the first field.
VALUES	Fields added to the Values area must contain numeric data from the source data

The following step adds data to the PivotTable. The rows will show the Service Type and within that the region. As you add the 2016 Total Revenue and 2017 Total Revenue fields to the Values area, Excel will create columns.

1

- Drag the Service Type field from the 'Choose fields to add to report' area to the Rows area to add the field to a row in the PivotTable.

- Click the Region check box in the 'Choose fields to add to report' area to add the Region field to the Rows area below the Service Type field.

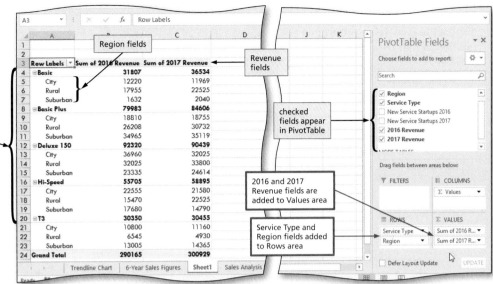

Figure 8–19

Q&A How did the Region field end up in the Rows area?

Excel places a checked field in the group it determines is correct for that field. You can drag the field to a different group if you choose.

- Drag the 2016 Revenue field to the Values area to add the field to column B of the PivotTable.

- Drag the 2017 Revenue field to the Values area to add the field to column C of the PivotTable (Figure 8–19).

Q&A What is shown in the PivotTable?

Excel displays the Service Type and Region fields as rows in the PivotTable. The 2016 Sales and 2017 Sales display as columns.

Other Ways

1. Click check box for each field name (PivotTable Fields task pane)

To Change the Layout of a PivotTable

1 CREATE LINE CHART & TRENDLINE | 2 CREATE PIVOTTABLE | 3 CHANGE LAYOUT & VIEW | **4 FILTER PIVOTTABLE**
5 FORMAT PIVOTTABLE | 6 CREATE PIVOTCHART | 7 CHANGE PIVOTCHART VIEW & CONTENTS | 8 ADD SLICERS

You can display a PivotTable in one of three layouts. By default, PivotTable reports are presented in a compact layout. ***Why change the layout?*** *When using multiple row labels, a different layout can make identifying the groups and subgroups easier for the reader.* The following steps change the layout of the PivotTable report to the tabular layout and then add item labels to all rows.

1

- If necessary, display the PivotTable Tools Design tab.

- Click the Report Layout button (PivotTable Tools Design tab | Layout group) to display the Report Layout menu (Figure 8–20).

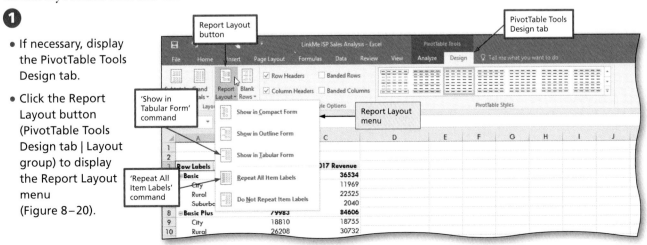

Figure 8–20

2

- Click 'Show in Tabular Form' to display the PivotTable report in a tabular format (Figure 8–21).

Experiment

- Click all the layout options to review the differences in the layout. When done, click 'Show in Tabular Form' once again.

	A	B	C	D
3	Service Type	Region	Sum of 2016 Revenue	Sum of 2017 Revenue
4	Basic	City	12220	11969
5		Rural	17955	22525
6		Suburban	1632	2040
7	Basic Total		31807	36534
8	Basic Plus	City	18810	18755
9		Rural	26208	30732
10		Suburban	34965	35119
11	Basic Plus Total		79983	84606
12	Deluxe 150	City	36960	32025
13		Rural	32025	33800
14		Suburban	23335	24614
15	Deluxe 150 Total		92320	90439
16	Hi-Speed	City	22555	21580
17		Rural	15470	22525
18		Suburban	17680	14790
19	Hi-Speed Total		55705	58895
20	T3	City	10800	11160
21		Rural	6545	4930
22		Suburban	13005	14365
23	T3 Total		30350	30455
24	Grand Total		290165	300929

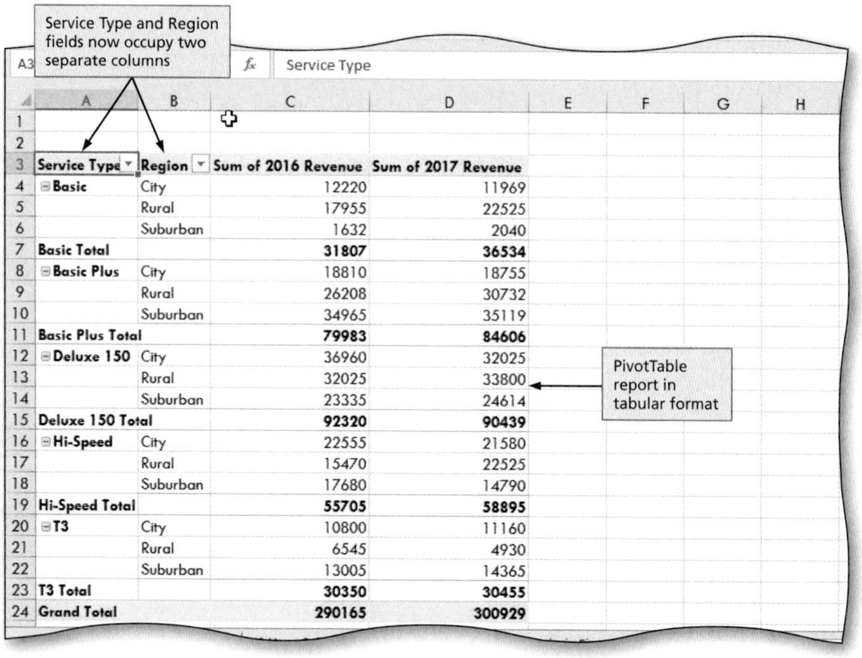

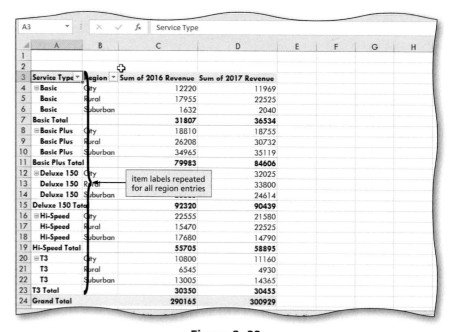

Figure 8–21

3

- Click the Report Layout button (PivotTable Tools Design tab | Layout group) again, and then click 'Repeat All Item Labels' to display Service Type labels for all Region entries (Figure 8–22).

	A	B	C	D
3	Service Type	Region	Sum of 2016 Revenue	Sum of 2017 Revenue
4	Basic	City	12220	11969
5	Basic	Rural	17955	22525
6	Basic	Suburban	1632	2040
7	Basic Total		31807	36534
8	Basic Plus	City	18810	18755
9	Basic Plus	Rural	26208	30732
10	Basic Plus	Suburban	34965	35119
11	Basic Plus Total		79983	84606
12	Deluxe 150	City		32025
13	Deluxe 150	Rural		33800
14	Deluxe 150	Suburban		24614
15	Deluxe 150 Total		92320	90439
16	Hi-Speed	City	22555	21580
17	Hi-Speed	Rural	15470	22525
18	Hi-Speed	Suburban	17680	14790
19	Hi-Speed Total		55705	58895
20	T3	City	10800	11160
21	T3	Rural	6545	4930
22	T3	Suburban	13005	14365
23	T3 Total		30350	30455
24	Grand Total		290165	300929

Figure 8–22

To Change the View of a PivotTable Report

1 CREATE LINE CHART & TRENDLINE | 2 CREATE PIVOTTABLE | 3 CHANGE LAYOUT & VIEW | 4 FILTER PIVOTTABLE
5 FORMAT PIVOTTABLE | 6 CREATE PIVOTCHART | 7 CHANGE PIVOTCHART VIEW & CONTENTS | 8 ADD SLICERS

If you use the sort and summary features in Excel, comparing the revenue for each service type and region would require many steps. With PivotTable reports, this comparison is accomplished quickly. The PivotTable report in the LinkMe ISP Sales Analysis workbook currently shows the sum of the sales revenue for each year by service type and then region (Figure 8–22). ***Why change the view of a PivotTable report?*** *You can change the view of this data depending on what you want to analyze.* The following step changes the view of the PivotTable to show the total revenue by region for each service type.

- In the Rows area (PivotTable task pane), drag the Service Type button below the Region button to group total sales by Region (rather than by Service Type) (Figure 8–23).

Experiment

- Drag other fields to the Rows area and rearrange it to see how the data in the PivotTable changes. When you are finished, remove all fields in the Rows area but Region and Service Type as shown in Figure 8–23.

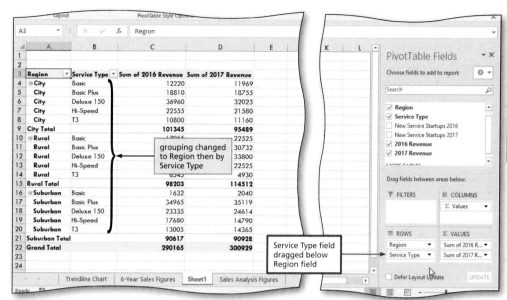

Figure 8–23

Other Ways

1. Click Service Type arrow, click Move Down on menu

To Filter a PivotTable Report Using a Report Filter

1 CREATE LINE CHART & TRENDLINE | 2 CREATE PIVOTTABLE | 3 CHANGE LAYOUT & VIEW | 4 FILTER PIVOTTABLE
5 FORMAT PIVOTTABLE | 6 CREATE PIVOTCHART | 7 CHANGE PIVOTCHART VIEW & CONTENTS | 8 ADD SLICERS

Why? In a PivotTable report, you can add detail by further categorizing the data to focus on a particular subgroup or subgroups. You can use the Revenue Venue field to view sales in a particular venue by service type and region. Viewing a PivotTable report for a subset of data that meets a selection criterion is known as filtering. The following steps add a report filter to change the view of the PivotTable and then filter the PivotTable by Revenue Venue.

- Drag the Revenue Venue field from the 'Choose field to add to report' area (PivotTable Fields task pane) to the Filters area to create a report filter in the PivotTable (Figure 8–24).

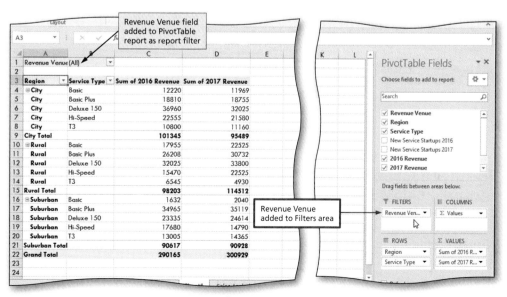

Figure 8–24

2

- Click the filter button in cell B1 to display the filter menu for column B, Revenue Venue in this case.

- Click Online on the filter menu to select the Online criterion (Figure 8–25).

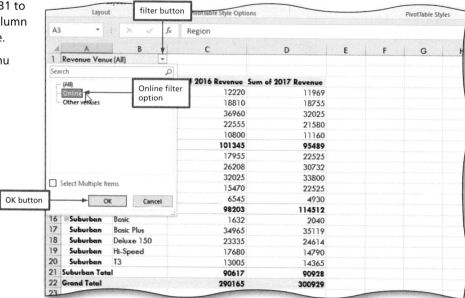

Figure 8–25

3

- Click the OK button to display totals for online sales only (Figure 8–26).

 Q&A What is shown now in the PivotTable report?
Now the PivotTable shows total sales for each region and service type for online sales only.

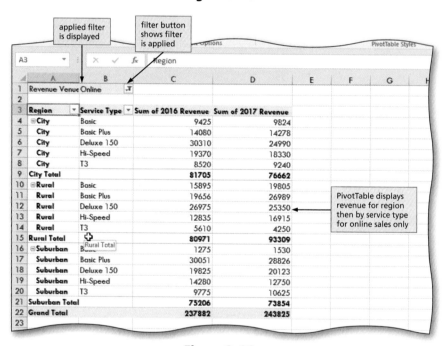

Figure 8–26

To Filter a PivotTable Report Using Multiple Selection Criteria

1 CREATE LINE CHART & TRENDLINE | 2 CREATE PIVOTTABLE | 3 CHANGE LAYOUT & VIEW | 4 FILTER PIVOTTABLE | 5 FORMAT PIVOTTABLE | 6 CREATE PIVOTCHART | 7 CHANGE PIVOTCHART VIEW & CONTENTS | 8 ADD SLICERS

Why? *You may need to identify a subset that is defined by more than one filter criterion.* The following steps change the filter field and select multiple criteria on which to filter.

1

- Drag the Service Type button from the Rows area to the Filters area.

- Drag the Revenue Venue button from the Filters area to the Rows area below Region (Figure 8–27).

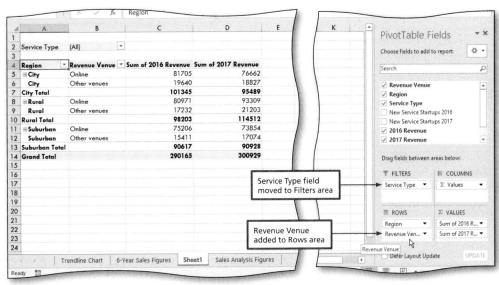

Figure 8–27

2

- Click the filter button in cell B2 to display the filter menu for the Service Type field.

- Click the 'Select Multiple Items' check box to prepare to select multiple criteria.

- Click to remove the check mark in each of the Basic, Hi-Speed, and T3 check boxes to deselect these criteria (Figure 8–28).

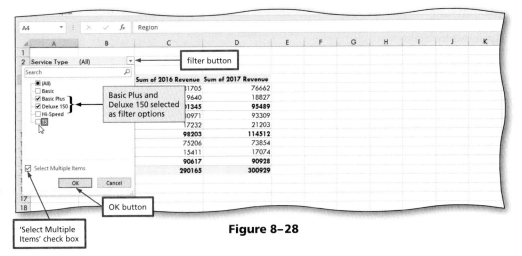

Figure 8–28

3

- Click the OK button to display sales totals for Basic Plus and Deluxe 150 service types (Figure 8–29).

Q&A How do I know which criteria have been selected? With a filter, you need to click the filter button to see which criteria have been selected.

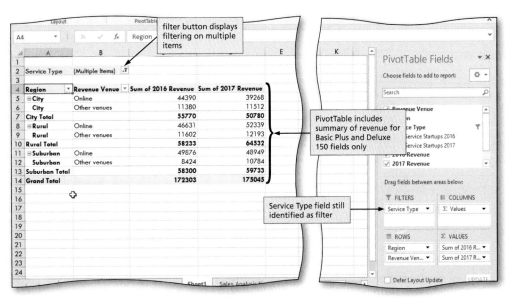

Figure 8–29

To Remove a Report Filter from a PivotTable Report

Why? *When you no longer need to display filtered data in a PivotTable, you can remove the filter easily.* The following step removes the Service Type report filter from the PivotTable report.

- Click the filter button in cell B2 and then click the (All) check box to include all service type criteria in the PivotTable report.

- Click the OK button.

- Drag the Service Type button out of the Filters area (PivotTable Fields task pane) to remove the field from the PivotTable report (Figure 8–30).

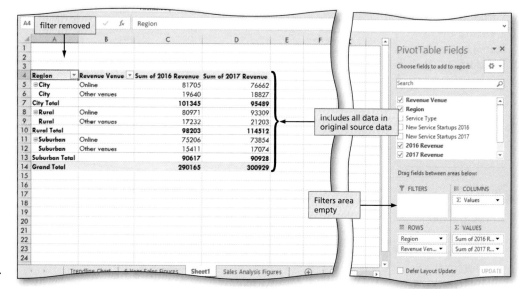

Figure 8–30

Q&A Should I drag it to a specific location?

No. You can drag it out of the box to any blank area on the worksheet.

To Remove and Add Data to the PivotTable Report

The following steps remove the Revenue Venue field from the Rows area and add the Service Type field.

1 In the PivotTable Fields task pane, drag the Revenue Venue button out of the Rows area to remove the field from the report.

2 Click the Service Type check box in the 'Choose fields to add to report' area to add the Service Type field to the Rows area below the Region field.

To Filter a PivotTable Report Using the Row Label Filter

Report filters are added to the PivotTable report by adding a field to the Filters area of the PivotTable Fields task pane. **Why use a Row Label filter?** *In a PivotTable report, you may want to look at a subset of data based on fields that are already in use.* When the field of interest is already part of the PivotTable and included in the Rows area of the PivotTable Fields task pane, you can use row label filters to view a subset of the data. Like other filter buttons, row label filters display within the column heading. When you click the filter button, Excel displays a menu of available fields. The following steps use a row label filter for Service Type to restrict data in the PivotTable to the Basic Plus and Deluxe 150 service types.

- Click the filter button in cell B4 to display the filter menu for the Service Type field (Figure 8–31).

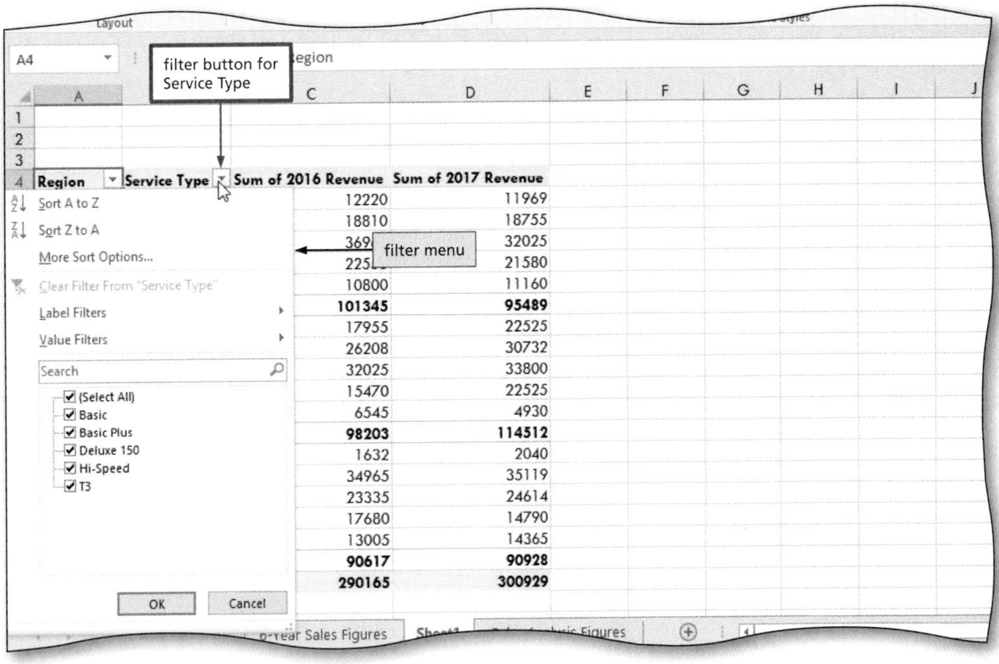

Q&A I do not have a filter button in cell B4. How do I access the filter?

The filter buttons may be hidden. Click the Field Headers button (PivotTable Tools Analyze tab | Show group) to turn on the field headers and make the filter buttons visible.

Why does cell B4 not appear selected when I use the filter button?

Filtering happens independently of cell selection. You do not need to select the cell in which the filter button is located in order to use the filter. In Figure 8–31, for example, the filter button for Service Type has been clicked while cell A4 is the active or selected cell.

Figure 8–31

- Click the Basic, Hi-Speed, and T3 check boxes on the filter menu to leave only the Basic Plus and Deluxe 150 service plans selected (Figure 8–32).

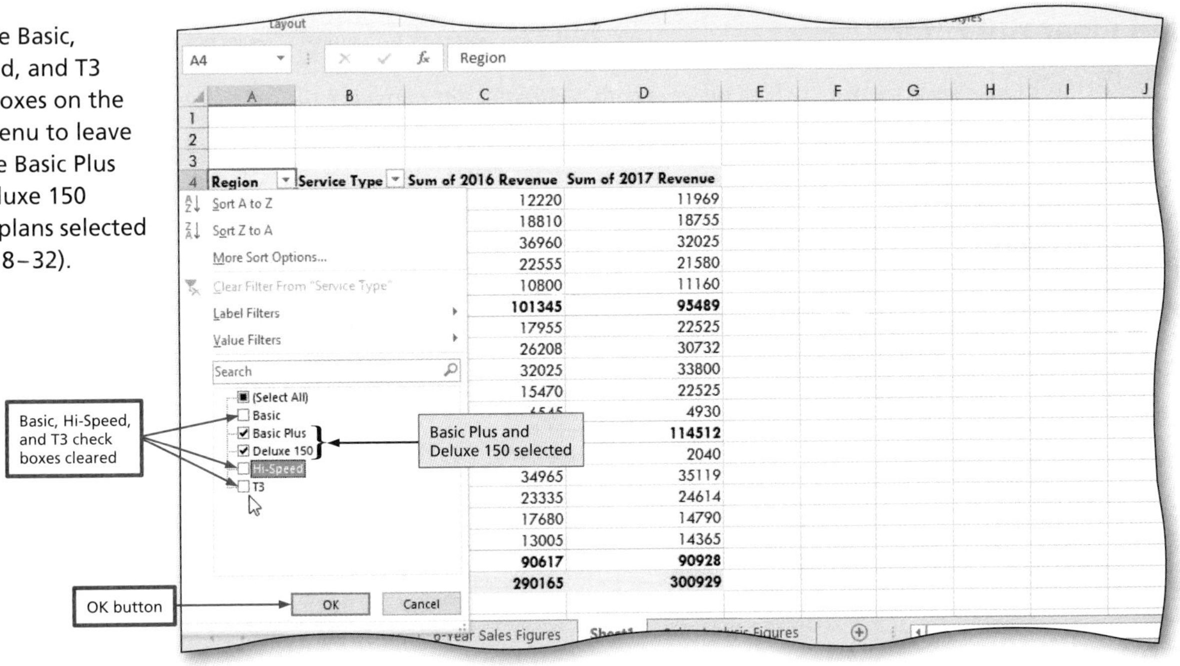

Figure 8–32

- Click the OK button to display totals for Basic Plus and Deluxe 150 service types only, categorized by region (Figure 8–33).

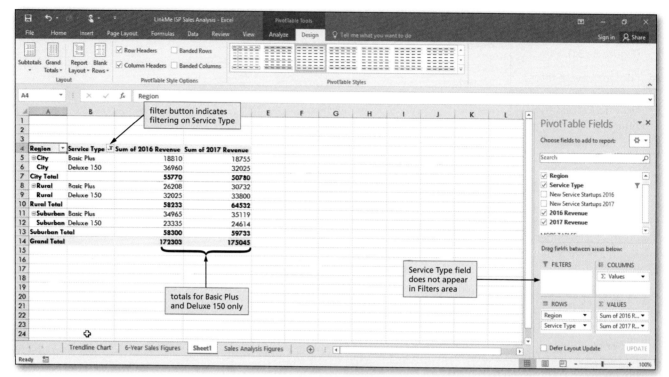

Figure 8–33

To Clear the Filter

1 CREATE LINE CHART & TRENDLINE | 2 CREATE PIVOTTABLE | 3 CHANGE LAYOUT & VIEW | 4 FILTER PIVOTTABLE
5 FORMAT PIVOTTABLE | 6 CREATE PIVOTCHART | 7 CHANGE PIVOTCHART VIEW & CONTENTS | 8 ADD SLICERS

Why? *Once you have reviewed the subset of data, you may want to remove the criteria using the Row Label filter to display all records.* The following steps clear the filter in order to display all records.

- Click the filter button in cell B4 again to display the filter menu for the Service Type field (Figure 8–34).

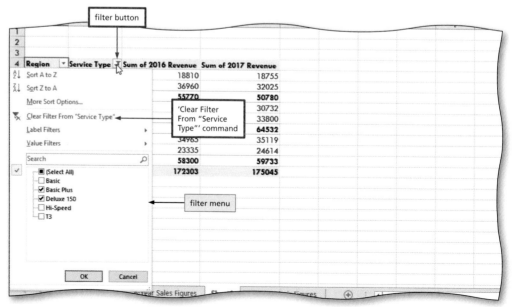

Figure 8–34

2

- Click 'Clear Filter From "Service Type"' on the filter menu to display totals for all service types in all regions (Figure 8–35).

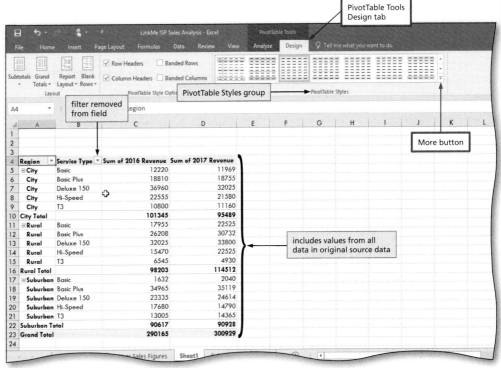

Figure 8–35

Other Ways

1. Click filter button, click (Select All) check box on filter menu, click OK button

Formatting PivotTable Reports

You can use several formatting options to enhance the appearance of PivotTable reports and make the content easier to read. Excel includes a number of preset PivotTable report styles to simplify this task. These styles function in a similar fashion to Excel's table styles. Care should be taken when formatting PivotTable reports, however, because formatting techniques that work for regular tables of data do not behave in the same fashion in PivotTable reports. PivotTable report formatting requires the use of PivotTable styles and field settings.

How do you choose a particular PivotTable style?

When you plan PivotTables and PivotCharts, consider what information you want to display in each report. As you are developing a report, review the galleries of PivotTable and PivotChart styles to find the best one to display your data. For example, some PivotTable styles include banded rows and columns, which can make it easier to scan and interpret the report.

CONSIDER THIS

To Format a PivotTable Report

1 CREATE LINE CHART & TRENDLINE | 2 CREATE PIVOTTABLE | 3 CHANGE LAYOUT & VIEW | 4 FILTER PIVOTTABLE
5 FORMAT PIVOTTABLE | 6 CREATE PIVOTCHART | 7 CHANGE PIVOTCHART VIEW & CONTENTS | 8 ADD SLICERS

Why? *PivotTable reports benefit from formatting to enhance their readability.* The following steps format a PivotTable report by applying a PivotTable style and specifying number formats for the fields.

1

- Name the Sheet1 tab, Sales PivotTable and set the color to Turquoise, Accent 1.

- Click cell A7 to select a cell in the PivotTable.

- Click the More button in the PivotTable Styles gallery (PivotTable Tools Design tab | PivotTable Styles group) to expand the gallery.

- Scroll down until the Dark section of the gallery is visible.

- Point to 'Pivot Style Dark 9' (PivotTable Styles gallery) to display a preview of the style in the PivotTable (Figure 8–36).

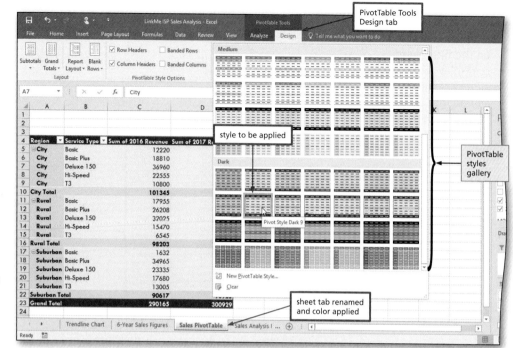

Figure 8–36

2

- Click 'Pivot Style Dark 9' in the PivotTable Styles gallery to apply the style to the PivotTable report.

- Right-click cell C6 and then click Number Format on the shortcut menu to display the Format Cells dialog box.

- Click Currency in the Category list (Format Cells dialog box) to select the Currency number format.

- Type 0 in the Decimal places box to specify no decimal places (Figure 8–37).

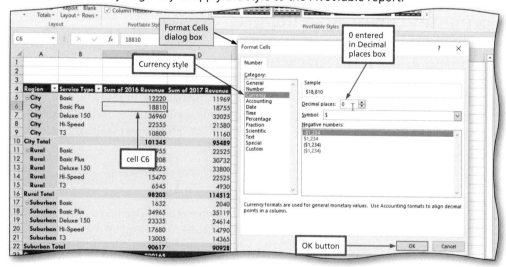

Figure 8–37

3

- Click the OK button to apply the Currency style to all 2016 revenue values in the PivotTable report.

Q&A

Why does the number format change apply to all Revenue values?

In a PivotTable, when you format a single cell using Number Format, that formatting is applied to the entire set of values to which that single cell belongs.

Can I use the formatting options on the Home tab?

Yes, but you would have to highlight all of the cells first and then apply the formatting. The Number Format command is easier.

4

- Select cell D6 and then repeat Step 3 to apply the Currency style to all 2017 revenue values.

- Click cell E24 to deselect the PivotTable report.

- Click the Save button on the Quick Access Toolbar to save the workbook (Figure 8–38).

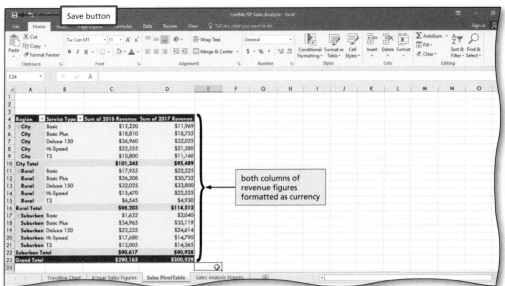

Figure 8–38

Break Point: If you wish to take a break, this is a good place to do so. Exit Excel. To resume at a later time, run Excel and open the file named LinkMe ISP Sales Analysis, and then continue following the steps from this location forward.

Summary Functions

In PivotTable reports, you easily can change the function used to summarize data in the original table. For example, in Figure 8–38, the data is totalled for 2016 and 2017 using a SUM function. You can change that to other summary functions. Summary functions can be inserted in one of three ways: by using the shortcut menu of a cell in the PivotTable, by using the field button menu in the Values area (PivotTable Fields task pane), or by using the Field Settings button (PivotTable Tools Analyze tab | Active Field group).

Table 8–2 lists the summary functions Excel provides for analysis of data in PivotTable reports. These functions also apply to PivotChart Reports.

Table 8–2 Summary Functions for PivotTable Report and PivotChart Report Data Analysis	
Summary Function	**Description**
Sum	Sum of the values (default function for numeric source data)
Count	Number of data values
Average	Average of the values
Max	Largest value
Min	Smallest value
Product	Product of the values
Count Numbers	Number of data values that contain numeric data
StdDev.s	Estimate of the standard deviation of all of the data to be summarized, used when data is a sample of a larger population of interest
StdDev.p	Standard deviation of all of the data to be summarized, used when data is the entire population of interest
Var.s	Estimate of the variance of all of the data to be summarized, used when data is a sample of a larger population of interest
Var.p	Variance of the data to be summarized, used when data is the entire population of interest

To Switch Summary Functions

Why? *The default summary function in a PivotTable is the SUM function.* For some comparisons, using a different summary function will yield more useful measures. In addition to analyzing the total revenue by region and service type, you are interested in looking at average sales. Currently, the PivotTable report for LinkMe ISP displays the total sales for each region by service type. Average sales by service type and by region might be a better measure for comparing the revenue. The following steps switch summary functions in a PivotTable using the shortcut menu.

- Right-click cell C5 to display the shortcut menu and then point to 'Summarize Values By' to display the Summarize Values By submenu (Figure 8–39).

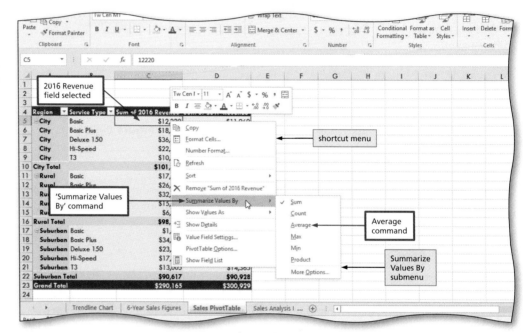

Figure 8–39

- Click Average on the Summarize Values By submenu to change the summary function from Sum to Average (Figure 8–40).

Q&A

Why did the column title in cell C4 change?

When you change a summary function, the column heading automatically updates to reflect the new summary function chosen.

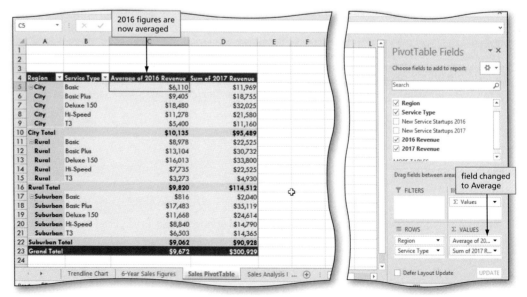

Figure 8–40

- Repeat Steps 1 and 2 to change the summary function used in column D from Sum to Average (Figure 8–41).

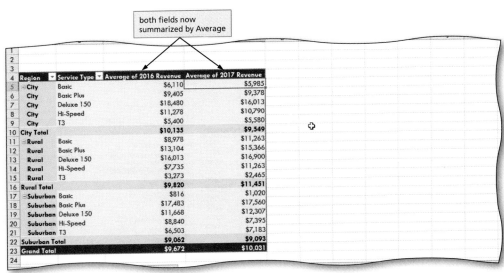

Figure 8–41

1 CREATE LINE CHART & TRENDLINE | 2 CREATE PIVOTTABLE | 3 CHANGE LAYOUT & VIEW | 4 FILTER PIVOTTABLE
5 FORMAT PIVOTTABLE | 6 CREATE PIVOTCHART | 7 CHANGE PIVOTCHART VIEW & CONTENTS | 8 ADD SLICERS

To Insert a New Summary Function

Why? *In addition to changing summary functions, you may need to add new fields to analyze additional or more complex questions.* You have been asked to review and compare both total and average sales for 2016 and 2017. You will need to add value fields and change the summary function to meet this request. The following steps add a second value calculation for each of the two years and use these fields to add a summary function in the PivotTable report. This time, you will use the menu displayed when you click the value field button to access the Value Field Settings dialog box.

- In the PivotTable Fields task pane, drag the 2016 Revenue field to the Values area above the 'Average of 2016 Sales' button to add the field to the PivotTable.

- In the Values area, click the 'Sum of 2016 Revenue' button to display the Sum of 2016 Sales menu (Figure 8–42).

Q&A
Why did I place the new field above the other items in the Values area?
Dragging the new field to a location above the other fields will place the data in a new column before the others in the PivotTable report, in this case in column C.

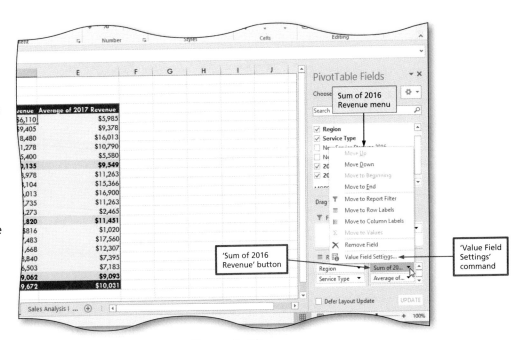

Figure 8–42

- Click 'Value Field Settings' to display the Value Field Settings dialog box.

- In the Custom Name text box (Value Field Settings dialog box), type `2016 Total Revenue` to change the field name (Figure 8–43).

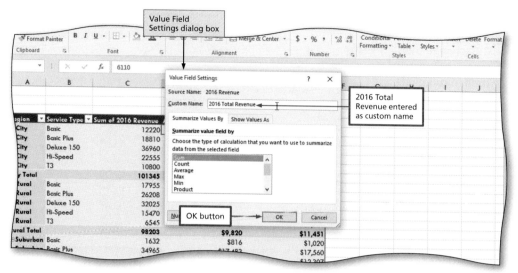

Figure 8–43

- Click the OK button (Value Field Settings dialog box) to apply the custom name.

- In the PivotTable Fields task pane, drag the 2017 Revenue field to the Values area, and place it between the '2016 Total Revenue' button and the 'Average of 2016 Revenue' button.

- In the Values area, click the 'Sum of 2017 Revenue' button to display its menu, and then click 'Value Field Settings' to display the Value Field Settings dialog box.

- In the Custom Name text box, type `2017 Total Revenue` and then click the OK button (Value Field Settings dialog box) to rename the field.

- Using the buttons in the Values area, rename the other two fields to customize the column headings in cells E4 and F4 as shown in Figure 8–44.

- Format the values in columns C and then D to the Currency category, 0 decimal places, and the $ symbol (Figure 8–44).

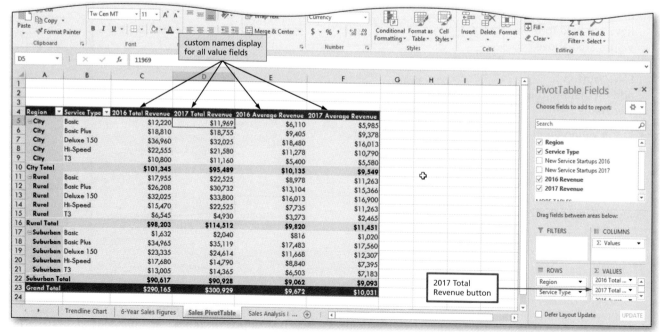

Figure 8–44

To Customize the Field Headers and Field List

The following steps hide the PivotTable Fields task pane, hide the field headers, and then turn off column autofitting. **Why?** *Customizing the display of the field headers and field list can provide a less-cluttered worksheet.*

1

- Display the PivotTable Tools Analyze tab.
- Click the Field List button (PivotTable Tools Analyze tab | Show group) to hide the PivotTable Fields task pane.
- Click the Field Headers button (PivotTable Tools Analyze tab | Show group) to hide the field headers (Figure 8–45).

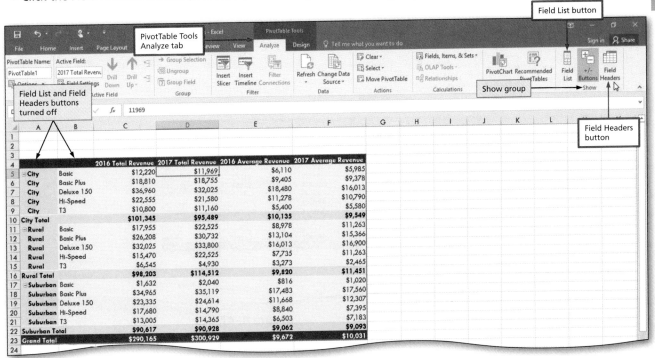

Figure 8–45

How can I display the PivotTable Fields task pane and field headers after hiding them?
The Field List and Field Headers buttons (PivotTable Tools Analyze tab | Show group) are toggle buttons—clicking them again turns the display back on.

2

- Click the PivotTable Options button (PivotTable Tools Analyze tab | PivotTable group) to display the PivotTable Options dialog box.
- Click the 'Autofit column widths on update' check box to remove the check mark (Figure 8–46).

3

- Click the OK button (PivotTable Options dialog box) to turn off the autofitting of column widths.

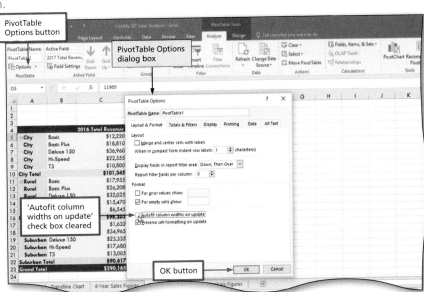

Figure 8–46

To Expand and Collapse Categories

The Expand and Collapse buttons expand and collapse across categories, reducing the amount of detail visible in the report without removing the field from the report. *Why customize the display of these buttons? In some instances, the report may be more visually appealing without the Expand or Collapse buttons in the report.* The following steps expand and collapse categories using the buttons and shortcut menus, and then suppress the display of the Expand and Collapse buttons in the report.

- Click the Collapse button in cell A5 to collapse the City information (Figure 8–47).

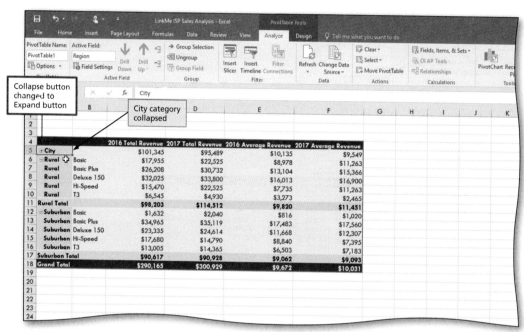

Figure 8–47

- Right-click cell A12 to display the shortcut menu and then point to Expand/Collapse to display the Expand/Collapse submenu (Figure 8–48).

Q&A

Which method should I use to expand and collapse?
Either way is fine. Sometimes the Collapse button is not visible, in which case you would have to use the shortcut menu.

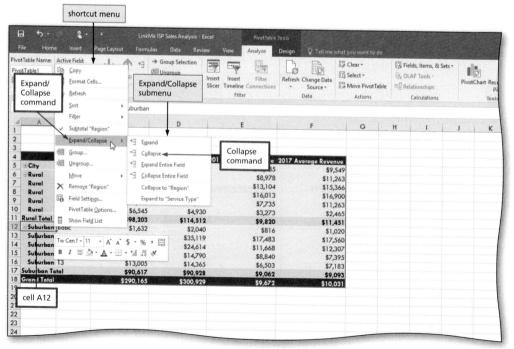

Figure 8–48

3

- Click Collapse on the Expand/Collapse submenu to collapse the Suburban data.
- Click the '+/– Buttons' button (PivotTable Tools Analyze tab | Show group) to hide the Expand and Collapse buttons in the PivotTable (Figure 8–49).

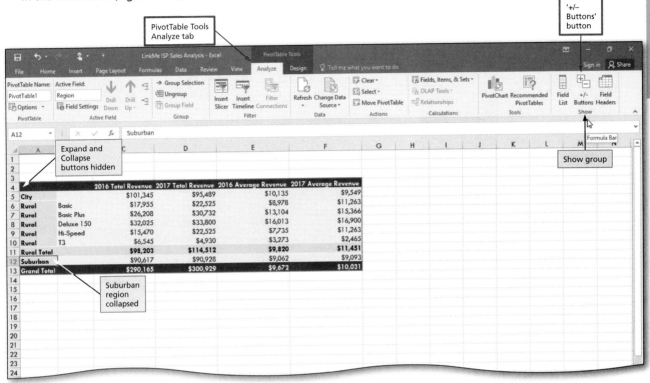

Figure 8–49

4

- Right-click cell A5 and then point to Expand/Collapse on the shortcut menu to display the Expand/Collapse submenu.
- Click 'Expand Entire Field' on the Expand/Collapse submenu to redisplay all data (shown in Figure 8–50).

To Create a Title

The following steps insert two blank rows and create a title for the PivotTable. You must insert new rows because Excel requires the two rows above the PivotTable to be reserved for extra filters.

1 Insert two blank rows above row 1 for the title and subtitle.

2 In cell A1, enter the title `LinkMe ISP Sales Report` and then enter the subtitle `2016 and 2017` in cell A2.

3 Merge and center the text in cell A1 across A1:F1.

4 Merge and center the text in cell A2 across A2:F2.

5 Apply the Title style to cell A1 and bold the cell.

6 Apply the Heading 2 style to cell A2 (Figure 8–50).

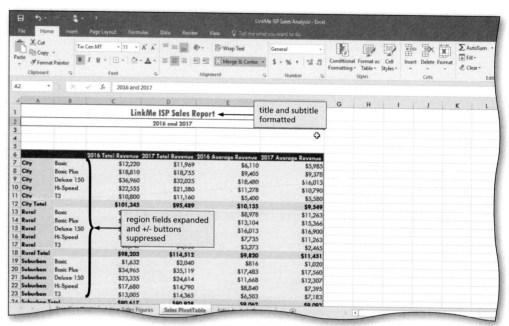

Figure 8–50

To Update a PivotTable

1 CREATE LINE CHART & TRENDLINE | 2 CREATE PIVOTTABLE | 3 CHANGE LAYOUT & VIEW | 4 FILTER PIVOTTABLE
5 FORMAT PIVOTTABLE | 6 CREATE PIVOTCHART | 7 CHANGE PIVOTCHART VIEW & CONTENTS | 8 ADD SLICERS

When you update cell contents in Excel, you also update related tables, formula calculations, and charts. *Why does this not work for PivotTables? PivotTables do not update automatically when you change the underlying data for the PivotTable report. You must update the PivotTable manually to recalculate summary data in the PivotTable report.* Two figures in the original data worksheet are incorrect: the New Service Startups 2017 and the 2017 Revenue for Basic City service sold in Other Venues. The following steps correct the typographical errors in the underlying worksheet, and then update the PivotTable report.

- Click the 'Sales Analysis Figures' sheet tab to make it the active worksheet.

- Click cell E18 and then type 51 as the new value.

- Click cell G18, type 3315, and then press the ENTER key to change the contents of the cell (Figure 8–51).

Q&A
What data will this change in the PivotTable?
The changed value is for sales of Basic City Service sold in Other Venues. This change will be reflected in cells D7 and F7 in the Sales PivotTable worksheet when the update is performed.

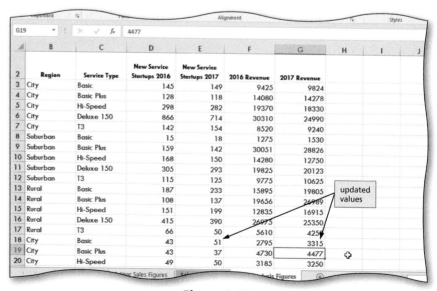

Figure 8–51

②

- Click the Sales PivotTable sheet tab to make it the active worksheet.

- If necessary, click inside the PivotTable report to make it active.

- Display the PivotTable Tools Analyze tab on the ribbon.

- Click the Refresh button (PivotTable Tools Analyze tab | Data group) to update the PivotTable report to reflect the change to the underlying data.

- Click the Save button on the Quick Access Toolbar to save the workbook (Figure 8–52).

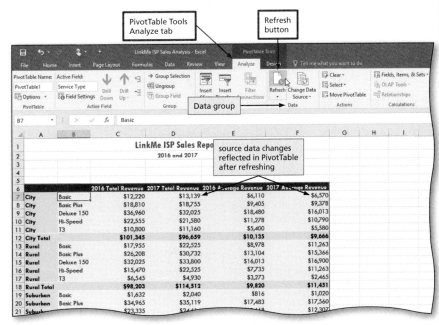

Figure 8–52

Q&A

Do I always have to refresh the data?

Yes. The contents of a PivotTable are not refreshed when the data from which they are created changes. This means you must refresh the PivotTable manually when underlying data changes.

If I add rows or columns to the data, will refreshing update the PivotTable?

If your data is in a data table, yes. Otherwise, you will have to create a new PivotTable.

Break Point: If you wish to take a break, this is a good place to do so. Exit Excel. To resume at a later time, run Excel and open the file named LinkMe ISP Sales Analysis, and then continue following the steps from this location forward.

Creating and Formatting PivotChart Reports

A PivotChart report, also called a PivotChart, is an interactive chart that allows users to change, with just a few clicks, the groupings that graphically present the data in chart form. As a visual representations of PivotTables, each PivotChart Report must be associated or connected with a PivotTable report. Most users create a PivotChart from an existing PivotTable; however, you can create a new PivotTable and PivotChart at the same time. If you create the PivotChart first, Excel will create the PivotTable automatically.

To Create a PivotChart Report from an Existing PivotTable Report

1 CREATE LINE CHART & TRENDLINE | 2 CREATE PIVOTTABLE | 3 CHANGE LAYOUT & VIEW | 4 FILTER PIVOTTABLE
5 FORMAT PIVOTTABLE | 6 CREATE PIVOTCHART | **7 CHANGE PIVOTCHART VIEW & CONTENTS** | 8 ADD SLICERS

If you already have created a PivotTable report, you can create a PivotChart report for that PivotTable using the PivotChart button (PivotTable Tools Analyze tab | Tools group). The following steps create a 3-D clustered column PivotChart report from the existing PivotTable report. *Why? The PivotChart will show the two-year data for revenue side by side.*

- If necessary, click cell A7 to select it in the PivotTable report.

- Click the Field List button (PivotTable Tools Analyze tab | Show group) to display the PivotTable Fields task pane.

- Click the PivotChart button (PivotTable Tools Analyze tab | Tools group) to display the Insert Chart dialog box.

- Click '3-D Clustered Column' in the Column Chart gallery to select the chart type (Figure 8–53).

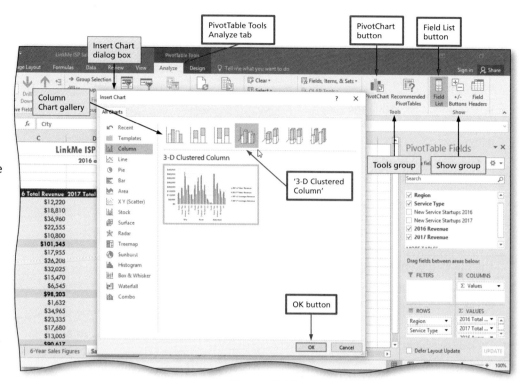

Figure 8–53

- Click the OK button (Insert Chart dialog box) to add the chart to the Sales PivotTable worksheet (Figure 8–54).

Q&A
My chart does not display field buttons across the top. Did I do something wrong?
No. It may be that they are just turned off. Click the Field Buttons button (PivotChart Tools Analyze tab | Show/ Hide Group) to turn them on.

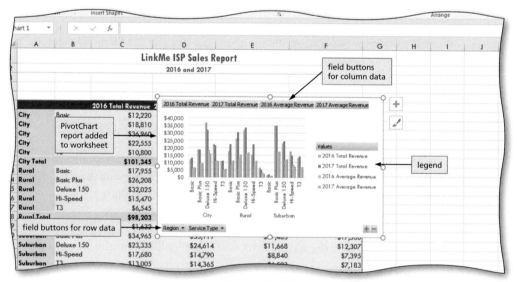

Figure 8–54

Other Ways

1. Click Insert PivotChart button (Insert tab | Charts group), select chart type (Insert Chart dialog box), click OK button

To Move the PivotChart Report

By default, a PivotChart report will be created on the same page as the associated PivotTable report. The following steps move the PivotChart report to a separate worksheet and then change the tab color to match that of the PivotTable report tab.

1 Display the PivotChart Tools Design tab.

2 With the 3-D Clustered Column chart selected, use the Move Chart button (PivotChart Tools Design tab | Location group) to move the chart to a new worksheet named Sales PivotChart.

3 Set the tab color to Turquoise, Accent 1 (shown in Figure 8–55).

To Remove Fields

The following step deletes the average Sales Data from the PivotTable and PivotChart Reports. Because the PivotTable and PivotChart are connected, removing the fields from one worksheet automatically removes the fields from the other.

1 In the PivotChart Fields task pane, drag 2016 Average Revenue and 2017 Average Revenue out of the Values area to remove the average sales data from the PivotChart report and PivotTable report (Figure 8–55).

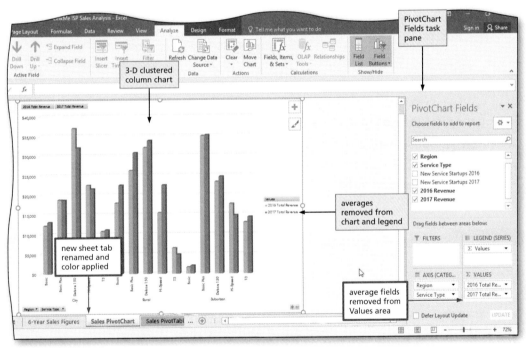

Figure 8–55

To Change the PivotChart Type and Format the Chart

1 CREATE LINE CHART & TRENDLINE | 2 CREATE PIVOTTABLE | 3 CHANGE LAYOUT & VIEW | 4 FILTER PIVOTTABLE
5 FORMAT PIVOTTABLE | 6 CREATE PIVOTCHART | **7 CHANGE PIVOTCHART VIEW & CONTENTS** | 8 ADD SLICERS

Why? Selecting a chart type instead of using the default type provides variety for the reader. The default chart type for a PivotChart is a clustered column chart, however PivotCharts can support most chart types, except scatter (X, Y), stock, and bubble. The following steps change the PivotChart type to 3-D cylinder, add a title to the PivotChart report, and apply formatting options to the chart.

1

- Click one of the lighter blue '2016 Total Revenue' columns to select the data series.

- Right-click to display the shortcut menu (Figure 8–56).

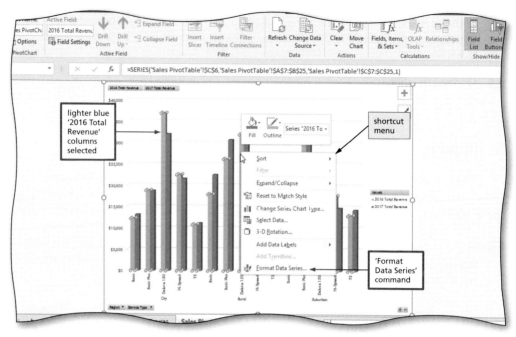

Figure 8–56

2

- Click 'Format Data Series' on the shortcut menu to open the Format Data Series task pane.

- In the Column shape section (Series Options tab), click Cylinder (Figure 8–57).

◁ Q&A I cannot see a difference. What changed?

The lighter blue data columns now display a rounded top. It will be more obvious later in the module and when printed.

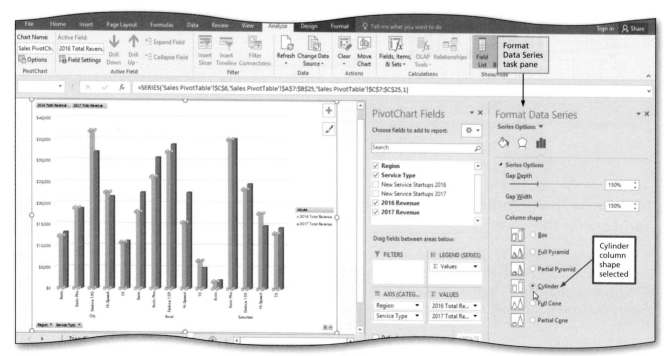

Figure 8–57

3

- Repeat the process to change the 2017 Total Revenue column to a cylinder and then close the Format Data Series task pane.

- Click the Chart Elements button to display the menu and then click to place a check mark in the Chart Title check box.

- Select the chart title and then type **LinkMe ISP** as the first line in the chart title. Press the ENTER key to move to a new line.

- Type **Total Revenue by Region and Service Type** as the second line in the chart title and then press the ENTER key to move to a new line.

- Type **2016 and 2017** as the third line in the chart title.

- Select all of the text in the title and change the font color to black (Figure 8–58).

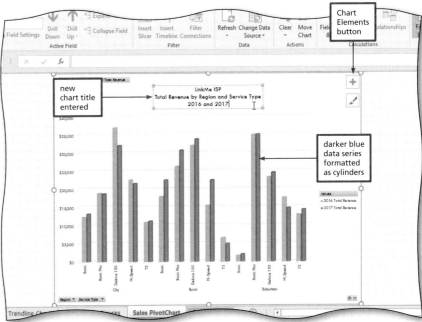

Figure 8–58

4

- Display the PivotChart Tools Format tab.

- Click the Chart Elements arrow (PivotChart Tools Format tab | Current Selection group) to display the Chart Elements menu (Figure 8–59).

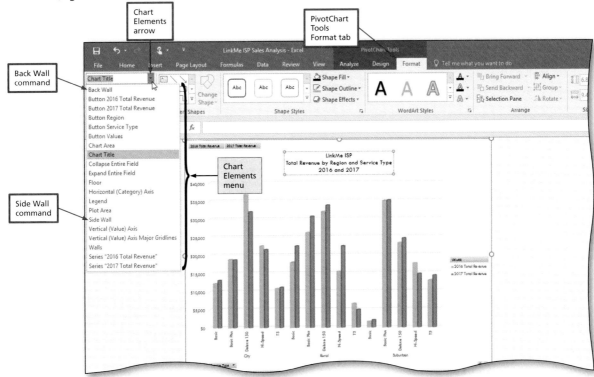

Figure 8–59

5

- Click Back Wall on the Chart Elements menu to select the back wall of the chart.

- Click the Shape Fill arrow (PivotChart Tools Format tab | Shape Styles group) to display the Shape Fill gallery.

- Point to Gradient in the Shape Fill gallery to display the Gradient submenu (Figure 8–60).

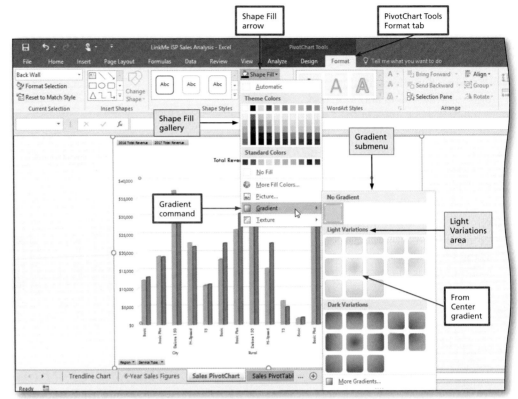

Figure 8–60

6

- Click From Center in the Light Variations area to apply a gradient fill to the back wall of the chart (Figure 8–61).

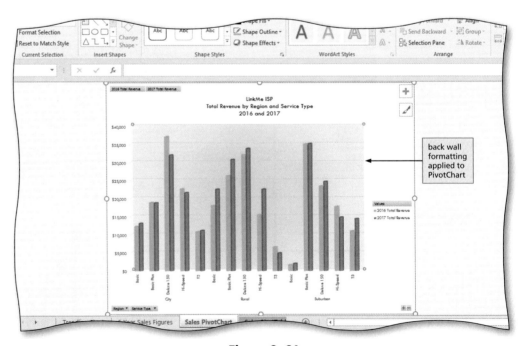

Figure 8–61

7

- Repeat Steps 5 and 6 after selecting Side Wall on the Chart Elements menu (Figure 8–62).

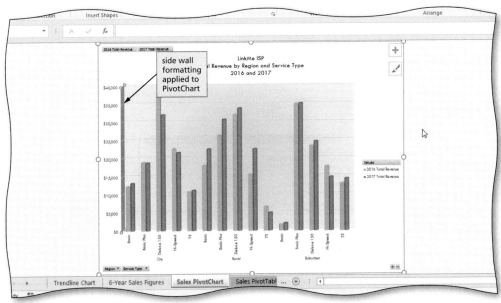

Figure 8–62

To Change the View of a PivotChart Report

1 CREATE LINE CHART & TRENDLINE | 2 CREATE PIVOTTABLE | 3 CHANGE LAYOUT & VIEW | 4 FILTER PIVOTTABLE
5 FORMAT PIVOTTABLE | 6 CREATE PIVOTCHART | **7 CHANGE PIVOTCHART VIEW & CONTENTS** | **8 ADD SLICERS**

Why change the view of a PivotChart? *Changing the view of the PivotChart lets you analyze different relationships graphically.* As with regular charts, when the source data is changed, any charts built upon that data update to reflect those changes. Unique to PivotCharts, however, is that the reverse is also true. Changes made to the view of the PivotChart are reflected automatically in the view of the PivotTable. The following steps change the view of the PivotChart report that causes a corresponding change in the view of its associated PivotTable report.

1

- Display the PivotChart Tools Analyze tab.

- If necessary, click the Field List button (PivotChart Tools Analyze tab | Show /Hide group) to display the PivotChart Fields task pane.

- Click the Region check box in the 'Choose fields to add to report' area to deselect the Region field.

- Place a check mark in the Revenue Venue check box to select the field and add it to the Axis area (Figure 8–63).

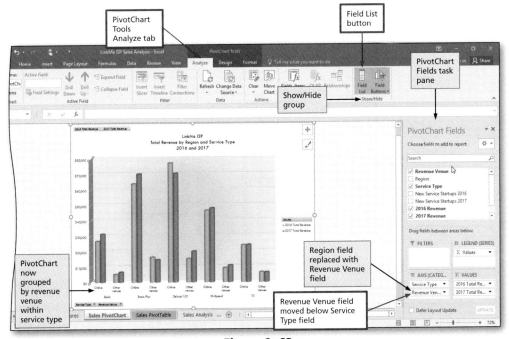

Figure 8–63

- Click the Sales
  PivotTable sheet tab
  to view the changes
  in the corresponding
  PivotTable report.

- If necessary, click
  the Field List button
  (PivotTable Tools
  Analyze tab | Show
  group) to display the
  Pivot Table Fields task
  pane (Figure 8–64).

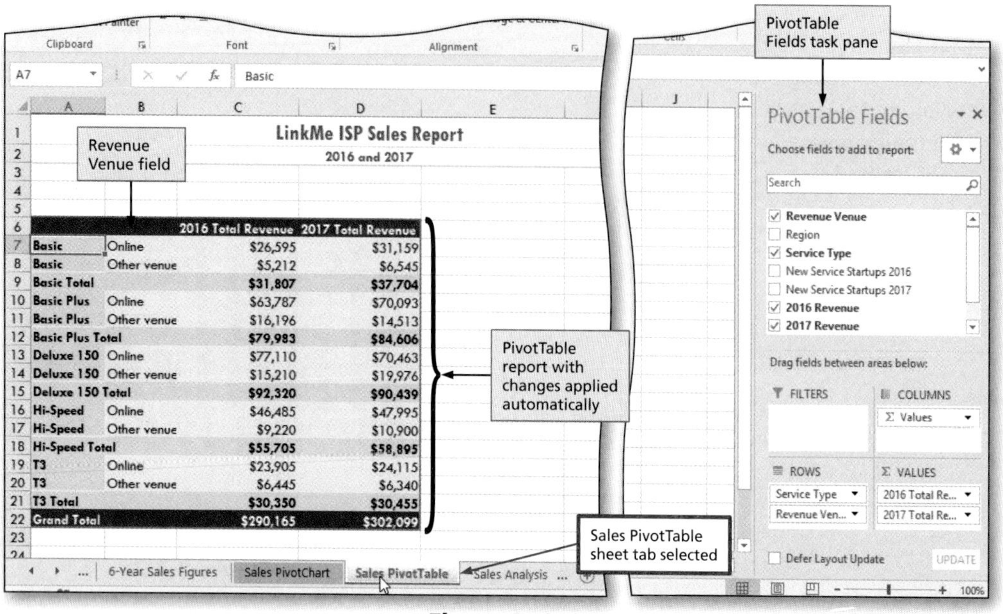

Q&A What usually
happens when
the view of the
PivotChart report
changes?
Changes to the
PivotChart are
reflected automatically in the PivotTable. Changes to category (x-axis) fields, such as Revenue Venue, are made to
row fields in the PivotTable. Changes to series (y-axis) fields appear as changes to column fields in the PivotTable.

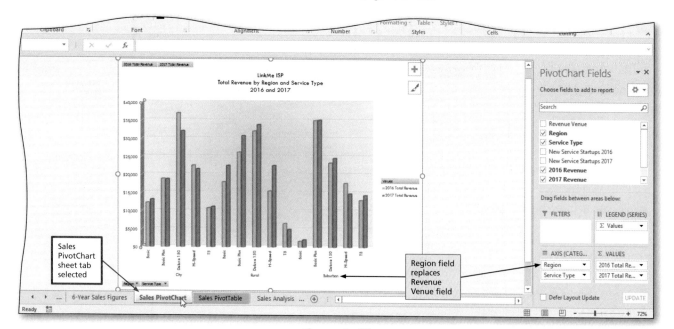

Figure 8–64

- In the PivotTable task pane remove the Revenue Venue field from the Rows area and replace it with the Region field.

- If necessary, change the order of the row labels to display the data first by Region and then by Service type.

- Click the Sales PivotChart sheet tab to make it the active tab (Figure 8–65).

Figure 8–65

4

- Click the Save button on the Quick Access Toolbar to save the workbook.

To Create a PivotChart and PivotTable Directly from Data

The requirements document included a request to create a second PivotChart and PivotTable that examine the average sale amount, controlling for different variables. *Why? Creating a second PivotChart and PivotTable offers a platform for pursuing multiple inquiries of the data simultaneously.* The following steps create a PivotChart report and an associated PivotTable report directly from the available data.

- Click the 'Sales Analysis Figures' sheet tab to display the worksheet.

- Click cell A3 to select a cell displaying revenue data and then display the Insert tab.

- Click the PivotChart arrow (Insert tab | Charts group) to display the PivotChart menu (Figure 8–66).

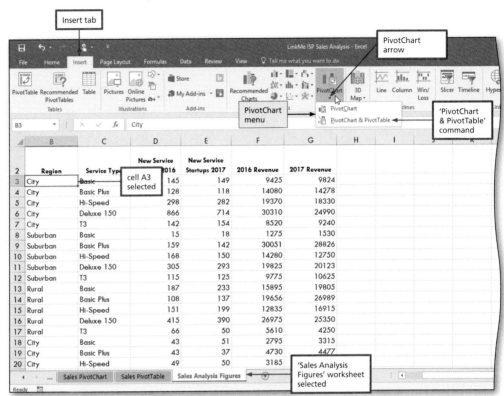

Figure 8–66

2

- Click 'PivotChart & PivotTable' on the PivotChart menu to display the Create PivotTable dialog box.

- If necessary, click New Worksheet (Create PivotTable dialog box) (Figure 8–67).

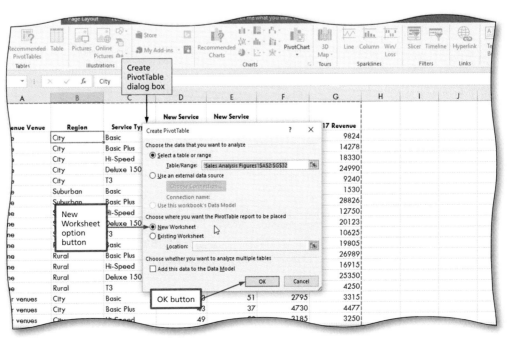

Figure 8–67

- Click the OK button to add a new worksheet containing a blank PivotTable and blank PivotChart (Figure 8–68).

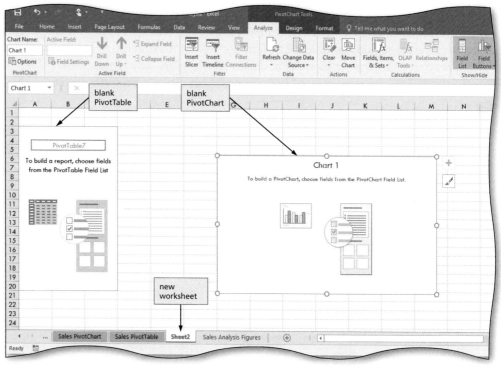

Figure 8–68

- Use the PivotChart Fields task pane to add the Region and Revenue Venue fields to the Axis area.

- Add the 2016 Revenue and 2017 Revenue fields to the Values area in the PivotChart Fields task pane (Figure 8–69).

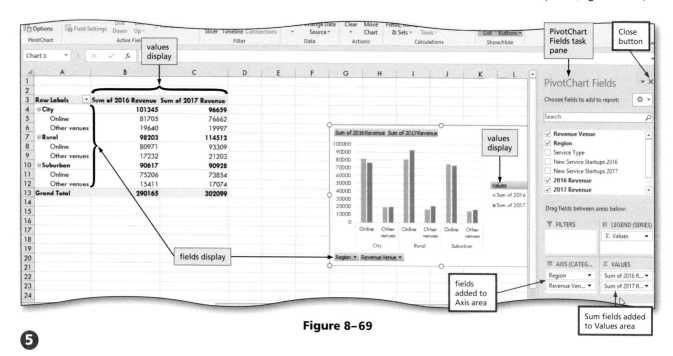

Figure 8–69

5

- Close the PivotChart Fields task pane.

- Rename the new worksheet as Average Startup by Region.

To Create a Calculated Field to a PivotTable Report

The following steps create calculated fields to use in the PivotTable and PivotChart reports. *Why? You would like to review the average start-up sales by region and venue for 2016 and 2017, but this information currently is not part of the data set with which you are working.* You will need to calculate the values you need through the use of a calculated field. A **calculated field** is a field with values not entered as data but determined by computation involving data in other fields. In this case, Average 2016 Startup and Average 2017 Startup will be new calculated fields, based on dividing the existing values of the 2016 Revenue and 2017 Revenue by the New Service Startups 2016 and 2017 respectively.

- If necessary, click the PivotTable to make it active and display the PivotTable Tools Analyze tab.

- Click the 'Fields, Items, & Sets' button (PivotTable Tools Analyze tab | Calculations group) to display the Fields, Items, & Sets menu (Figure 8–70).

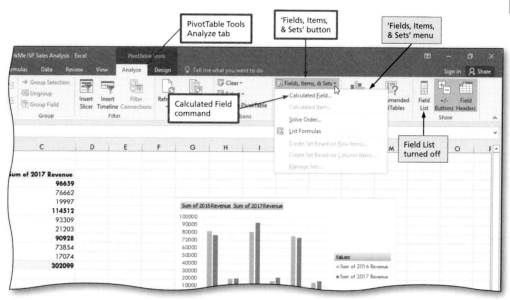

Figure 8–70

- Click Calculated Field to display the Insert Calculated Field dialog box.

- In the Name box, type **Average 2016 Startup**.

- In the Formula text box, delete the value to the right of the equal sign, in this case, 0.

- In the Fields list, double-click the 2016 Revenue field to insert it in the Formula text box.

- Type / (slash), and then double-click the 'New Service Startups 2016' field to complete the formula, which should read = '2016 Revenue' / 'New Service Startups 2016' (Figure 8–71).

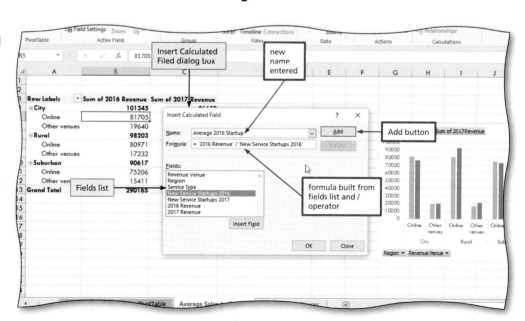

Figure 8–71

3

- Click the Add button (Insert Calculated Field dialog box) to add the calculated field to the Fields list.

- Repeat Step 2 to create a calculated field named Average 2017 Startup, calculated using 2017 Revenue divided by New Service Startups 2017 (Figure 8–72).

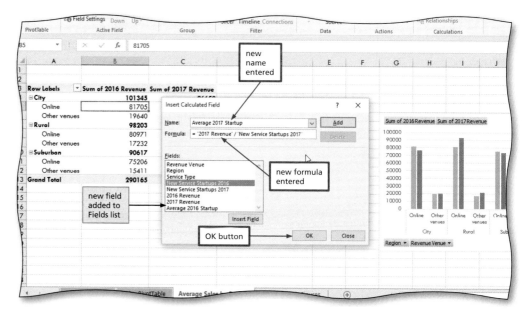

Figure 8–72

4

- Click the Add button (Insert Calculated Field dialog box) and then click the OK button to close the dialog box (Figure 8–73).

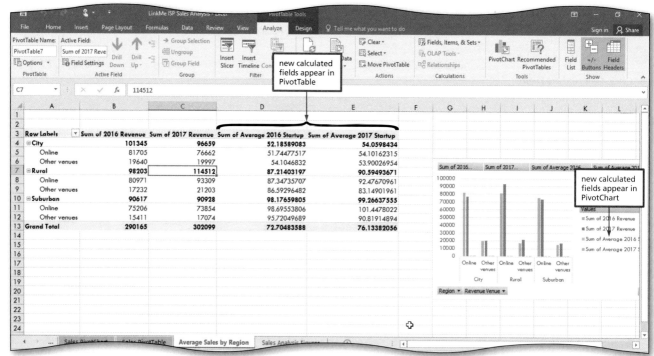

Figure 8–73

To Format the PivotTable

Now that you have added a calculated field, you can format the PivotTable and PivotChart so they look professional and are easy to interpret. The following steps format the PivotTable report.

1 If necessary, click the Field List button (PivotTable Tools Analyze tab | Show group) to display the PivotTable Fields task pane and then click to remove the check mark in the 2016 Revenue check box and the 2017 Revenue check box to remove these fields.

2 If necessary, click cell A3 to select it. Display the PivotTable Tools Design tab and then apply 'Pivot Style Medium 12' to the PivotTable.

3 Insert two blank rows above the PivotTable. In cell A1, enter the title **LinkMe ISP**. In cell A2, enter the subtitle **Average Startup, 2016 and 2017**.

4 Merge and center the text across A1:C1 and A2:C2. Apply the Title style to cell A1 and bold the text. Apply the Heading 2 style to cell A2.

5 Change the field name in cell B5 to Average 2016 Startup. Change the field name in cell C5 to Average 2017 Startup. If Excel displays a message about the field name already existing, place a space in front of the field name.

6 Apply the currency number format with 2 decimal places and the $ symbol to the Average 2016 Startup and Average 2017 Startup fields.

7 Change the column widths for columns B and C to 12.00, and change the width for column D to 50.

8 Wrap and center the field names in cells B5 and C5.

9 Use the Field List button, the '+/– Buttons' button, and the Field Headers button (PivotTable Tools Analyze tab | Show group) to hide the field list, the Expand/Collapse buttons, and the field headers (Figure 8–74).

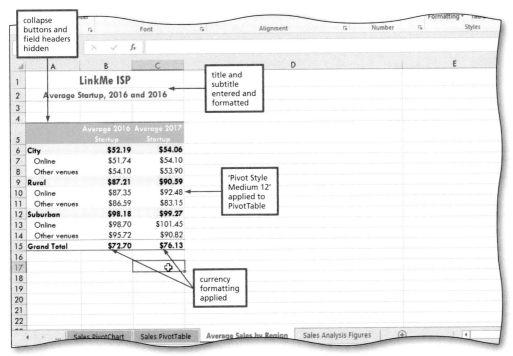

Figure 8–74

To Format the PivotChart

The following steps format the PivotChart report.

1 If necessary, click in the PivotChart report to select it. Move and resize the PivotChart report so that it fills the range D1:D15.

2 Apply Style 12 in the Chart Styles gallery (PivotChart Tools Design tab | Chart Styles group).

3 Use the 'Chart Quick Colors' button (PivotChart Tools Design tab | Chart Styles group) to change the colors to Color 3 in the Colorful area.

4 Use the 'Add Chart Element' button (PivotChart Tools Design tab | Chart Layouts group) to position the legend at the top of the PivotChart report.

5 Click the Field Buttons button (PivotChart Tools Analyze tab | Show/Hide group) to hide the field buttons.

6 Save the workbook (Figure 8–75).

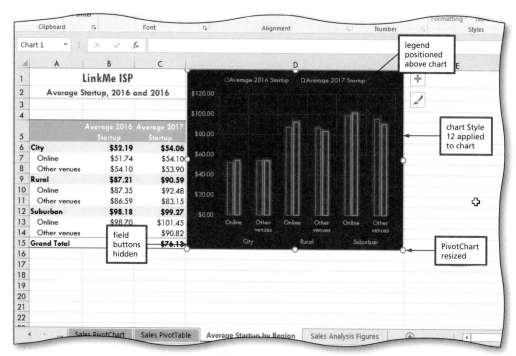

Figure 8–75

Working with Slicers

One of the strengths of PivotTables is that you can ask questions of the data by using filters. Being able to identify and examine subgroups is a useful analytical tool; however, when using filters and autofilters, the user cannot always tell which subgroups the filters and autofilters have selected, without clicking filter buttons to see the subgroups selected. Slicers are buttons you click to filter the data in PivotTables and PivotCharts, making the data easier to interpret. With Slicers, the subgroups are immediately identifiable and can be changed with a click of a button or buttons.

Why would you use slicers rather than row, column, or report filters?

One effective way to analyze PivotTable data is to use slicers to filter the data in more than one field. Slicers let you refine the display of data in a PivotTable. They offer the following advantages over filtering directly in a PivotTable:

- In a PivotTable, you use the filter button to specify how to filter the data, which involves a few steps. After you create a slicer, you can perform this same filtering task in one step.

- You can filter only one PivotTable at a time, whereas you can connect slicers to more than one PivotTable to filter data.

- Excel treats slicers as graphic objects, which means you can move, resize, and format them as you can any other graphic object. As graphic objects, they invite interaction.

The owner of LinkMe ISP has asked you to set up a PivotChart and PivotTable with a user-friendly way for anyone to explore the average start-up sales data. You can use slicers to complete this task efficiently.

To Copy a PivotTable and PivotChart

To create a canvas for exploratory analysis of revenue data, you first need to create a new PivotTable and a PivotChart. The following steps copy an existing PivotTable and PivotChart to a new worksheet, format the PivotTable, and rename the worksheet.

1 Create a copy of the Average Startup by Region worksheet and then move the copy so that it precedes the Sales Analysis Figures worksheet.

2 Rename the new worksheet, Slicers.

3 Apply chart Style 8 to the PivotChart to format the PivotChart.

4 Apply the Pivot Style Medium 20 style to the PivotTable.

5 Set the column widths of columns E to 17.00 and column F to 19.00.

6 If necessary, turn off the display of field headers and +/– buttons (Figure 8–76).

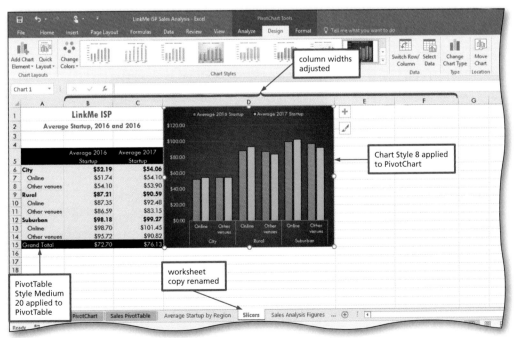

Figure 8–76

To Add Slicers to the Worksheet

The following steps add a slicer that provides an easier way to filter the new PivotTable and PivotChart. *Why?* *To analyze sales data for specific subgroups, you can use slicers instead of PivotTable filters.*

- If necessary, click to make the PivotChart active and display the PivotChart Tools Analyze tab.

- Click the Insert Slicer button (PivotChart Tools Analyze tab | Filter group) to display the Insert Slicers dialog box.

- Click to place check marks in the Revenue Venue, Region, and Service Type check boxes (Figure 8–77).

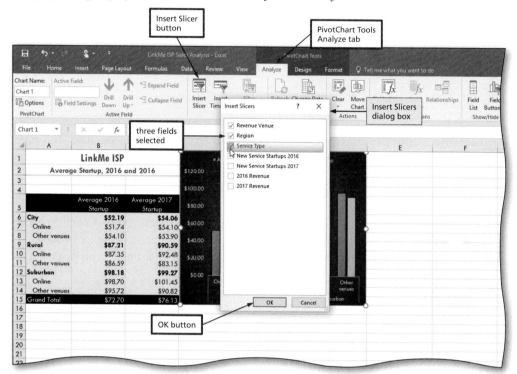

Figure 8–77

- Click the OK button (Insert Slicers dialog box) to display the selected slicers on the worksheet (Figure 8–78).

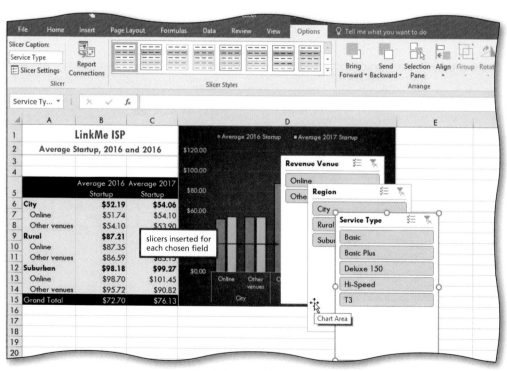

Figure 8–78

To Format Slicers

The following steps move the slicers to the right of the PivotChart and then format them. *Why? The slicers need to be moved and formatted so that they do not obscure the PivotTable or PivotChart and are easy to read and use.*

1

- Click the title bar of the Revenue Venue slicer and then drag the slicer to column E. Use the sizing handles to adjust the length of the slicer so that it ends at the bottom of row 6, and fits the width of the slicer so that it ends at the right edge of column E.

- Click and drag the Service Type slicer to column F. Use the sizing handles to adjust the length of the slicer so that it ends at the bottom of row 15 and the width so that it fits in column F.

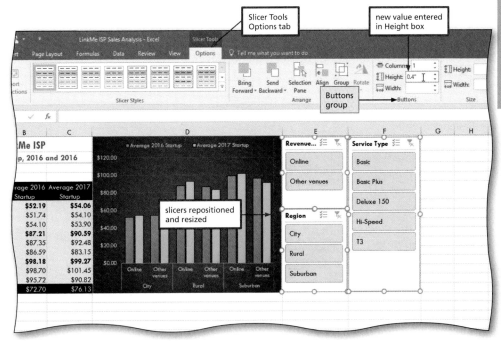

Figure 8–79

- Click and then drag the Region slicer to column E, just below the Revenue Venue slicer. Use the sizing handles to change the length of the slicer so that it ends at the bottom of row 15 and the width so that it fits in column E.

- Hold down the CTRL key and then, one at a time, click each of the slicer title bars to select all three.

- Select the text in the Height box (Slicer Tools Options tab | Buttons group), type **.4,** and then press the ENTER key to set the button height (Figure 8–79).

2

- Click the 'Slicer Style Light 5' Slicer style (Slicer Tools Options tab | Slicer Styles group) to apply it to the slicers (Figure 8–80).

3

- Click any cell to deselect the slicers.

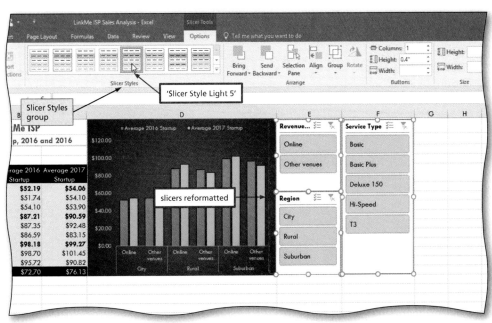

Figure 8–80

To Use the Slicers

Why use slicers? Slicers provide you with a visual means of filtering data. You do not need knowledge of Excel to use slicers. Instead, you click the subgroups of interest. Slicers based on row label fields provide the same results as filters in a PivotTable. They narrow the table down to a visible subgroup or subgroups. Clicking a slicer displays only that slicer's data. You can select multiple fields by using the Multi-Select button in the slicer title bar or by using CTRL+click to add a button (in the same slicer) to the display. The following steps use slicers to review average sales for different combinations of Region and Revenue Venue.

- Click Online in the Revenue Venue slicer to display the data for online sales in the PivotTable and PivotChart calculations.

- Hold down the CTRL key and then click City in the Region slicer to remove the City data and show the rural and suburban areas only (Figure 8–81).

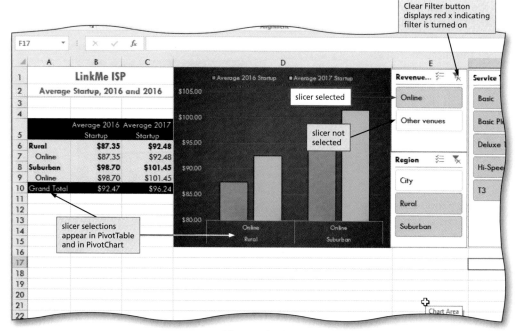

Figure 8–81

- Click Other venues in the Revenue Venue slicer to see the data for other venues from the rural and suburban areas only (Figure 8–82).

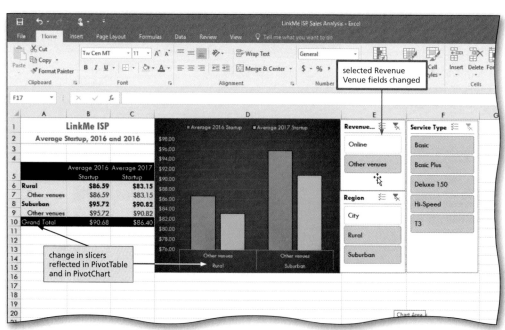

Figure 8–82

To Use the Slicers to Review Data Not in the PivotTable

You can look for possible explanations of patterns by using slicers to analyze data other than that which displays in the PivotTable. ***Why?*** *Slicers based on fields not included in the PivotTable provide the same results as report filters.* Slicers regroup and narrow the PivotTable content to groups not visible in the PivotTable. The following steps use slicers to review data not currently visible in the PivotTable.

- Click the Clear Filter button on the Revenue slicer and on the Region slicer to remove the filters and return the PivotTable and PivotChart to their unfiltered states.

- Click the Deluxe 150 button in the Service Type slicer to see the aggregate data for the average start-up prices for customers who chose the Deluxe 150 service, broken down by Revenue Venue and Region (Figure 8–83).

Experiment

- Click different service types and combinations of service types to see how the aggregate data changes.

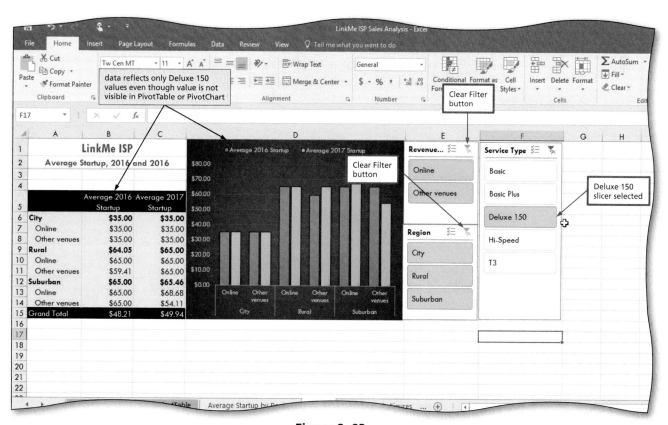

Figure 8–83

- If necessary, click the Deluxe 150 button in the Service Type slicer to select it, click the Multi-Select button in the slicer header, and then click the T3 button in the Service type slicer to view the aggregate data, broken down by Revenue Venue and Region (Figure 8–84).

Q&A

How can I save a particular PivotTable setup?

PivotTables are dynamic by nature. To save a particular configuration, make a copy of the worksheet, and use the Protect Sheet command (Review tab | Changes group) to keep changes from being made to the worksheet copy. You can continue to use the PivotTable on the original worksheet to analyze the data.

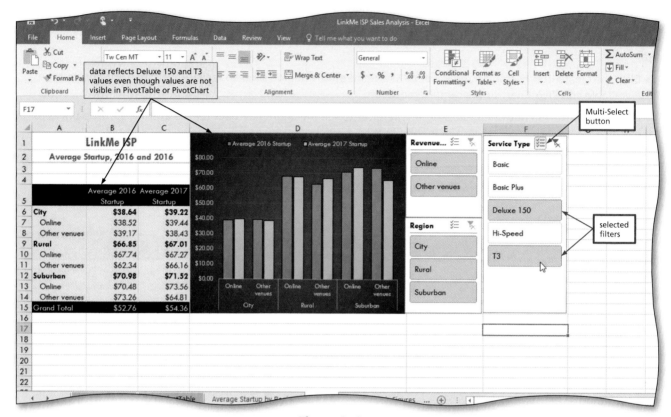

Figure 8–84

❸

If instructed to do so, enter your name and course number in cell F17 and F18 respectively.

• Save the workbook and exit Excel. If the Microsoft Office Excel dialog box is displayed, click the Don't Save button.

Summary

In this module, you learned how to create a 2-D line chart and add a trendline to extend the trend to two more time periods. You added an R-squared (R^2) value to the trendline to measure the strength of the trend and formatted a data point. You created and formatted a PivotTable report based on raw data. Using the PivotTable Fields task pane, you added row fields and columns to the PivotTable. You created calculated fields in the PivotTable using summary functions. To see the power of the PivotTable, you inserted, deleted, and organized fields to view the data in different ways. You created and formatted a PivotChart Report from a PivotTable, filtering and analyzing data. You then created both a PivotTable and PivotChart from scratch and added a calculated field. Finally, you created slicers to make manipulating PivotTables and PivotCharts easier.

What decisions will you need to make when creating your next worksheet to analyze data using trendlines, PivotCharts, and PivotTables?

Use these guidelines as you complete the assignments in this module and create your own worksheets for evaluating and analyzing data outside of this class.

1. Identify trend(s) to analyze with a trendline.

    a) Determine data to use.

    b) Determine time period to use.

    c) Determine type and format of trendline.

2. Identify questions to ask of your data.

    a) Determine which variables to combine in a PivotTable or PivotChart.

3. Create and format PivotTables and PivotCharts.

    a) Add all fields to the field list.

    b) Use formatting features for PivotTables and PivotCharts.

4. Manipulate PivotTables and PivotCharts to analyze data.

    a) Select fields to include in PivotTables and PivotCharts.

    b) Use filters to review subsets of data.

    c) Use calculated fields and summary statistics to look at different measures of data.

    d) Create and use slicers to look at subsets of data.

CONSIDER THIS: PLAN AHEAD

Apply Your Knowledge

Reinforce the skills and apply the concepts you learned in this module.

Creating a PivotTable

Note: To complete these steps, you will be required to use the Data Files. Please contact your instructor for information about accessing the Data Files.

Instructions: Run Excel. Open the document Apply 8-1 Totes & Bags from the Data Files and then save the workbook as Apply 8-1 Totes & Bags Complete. The owner of Totes & Bags wants you to create a PivotTable from the current inventory and then manipulate it to display different totals. Figure 8–85 shows the completed Inventory PivotTable worksheet.

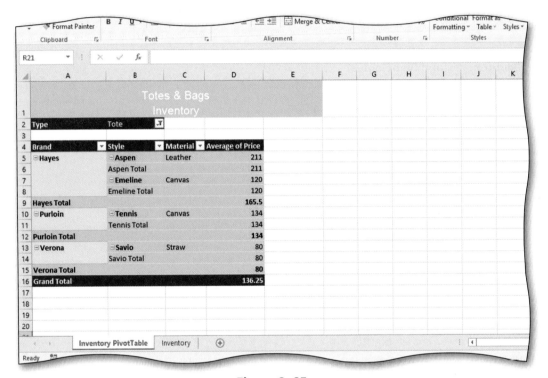

Figure 8–85

Perform the following tasks:

1. Select cell A3 and then click the PivotTable button (Insert tab | Tables group) to display the Create PivotTable dialog box. Make sure New Worksheet is selected and then click the OK button.

2. Drag the Brand field from the 'Choose fields to add to report' area to the Rows area to add the Brand field to the PivotTable. Repeat this step for the Style, Material, and Type fields.

3. Drag the Price field from the 'Choose fields to add to report' area to the Values area to add the sum of the Price field to the PivotTable.

4. Change the summary calculation for Price from Sum to Average by clicking the 'Sum of Price' button in the Values area of the PivotTable Fields task pane, click Value Field Settings, and then choose Average in the Value Field Settings dialog box.

5. Click the Report Layout button (PivotTable Tools Design tab | Layout group) to display the Report Layout menu. Change the PivotTable report layout to tabular. Widen the columns as necessary to read the column headings.

6. If instructed to do so, enter the brand names in column G and the averages in column H, or write them down.

7. Click the filter button in cell A3 to display the filter menu. Select only Kipling Leathers and Donna and then click the OK button. If instructed to do so, enter the averages for those two brands and the overall average in a blank area of the worksheet, or write them down.

8. Remove the Brand filter so that all data is displayed.

9. If necessary, click the Field List button (PivotTable Tools Analyze tab | Show group) to display the PivotTable Fields task pane. Drag the Type button in the Rows area to the Filters area in the PivotTable Fields task pane to create a new filter.

10. In the filter area above the PivotTable, click the filter button for the Type field, click Tote, and then click the OK button. If instructed to do so, enter the averages for the brands and the overall total in a blank area of the worksheet, or write them down.

11. Click cell A4, click the PivotTable Styles More button (PivotTable Tools Design tab | PivotTable Styles group), and then click 'Pivot Style Dark 2' to apply the style to the PivotTable.

12. Add a blank line at the top of the worksheet. Copy the heading from the Inventory worksheet and change the height of the row as necessary.

13. If requested by your instructor, in cell A20, type **List compiled by**, followed by your name.

14. Name the worksheet Inventory PivotTable. Save the workbook with the PivotTable, and then close the workbook.

15. Submit the revised document in the format specified by your instructor.

16. ✴ List two changes you would make to the PivotTable report to make it more easily interpreted by the user, and explain why you would make these changes. These changes could be to formatting, layout, or both.

Extend Your Knowledge

Extend the skills you learned in this module and experiment with new skills. You may need to use Help to complete the assignment.

Grouping Content in PivotTables

Note: To complete these steps, you will be required to use the Data Files. Please contact your instructor for information about accessing the Data Files.

Instructions: Run Excel. Open the workbook Extend 8-1 Mervin's Barbecue from the Data Files and then save the workbook using the file name, Extend 8-1 Mervin's Barbecue Complete. Create a PivotTable and PivotChart for Mervin's Barbecue that analyzes a year's worth of sales data. Figure 8–86 shows the completed Income Review worksheet.

Extend Your Knowledge *continued*

Figure 8–86

Perform the following tasks:

1. Use Help to learn about using dates in a PivotTable and PivotChart and using the Grouping dialog box.

2. Create a PivotTable based on the data in the Sales Data worksheet. Use Date as the Rows field and use Sales as the Values field. Note that Excel breaks the date fields down into months and days. Name the new worksheet containing the PivotTable, Income Review. Change the PivotTable style to 'Pivot Style Medium 17'. Add a title and subtitle to the PivotTable, as shown in Figure 8–86. Merge and center the titles across columns A and B. Format cell A1 using the Title cell style and A2 using the Heading 2 cell style. Change the font color in both cells to black, if necessary. Insert two blank rows for future filters.

3. Format the Sales data using the Number Format command to format the values to be currency with no decimal places.

4. Use the Group Field command (PivotTable Tools Analyze tab | Group group) to group the daily sales figures by months and quarters. Display the Expand and Collapse buttons.

5. Create a PivotChart, and locate it on the same worksheet as the PivotTable. Use the 3-D Clustered Column chart type, and set up the chart to have no legend. Hide the Expand and Collapse buttons in the PivotChart. Right-click in the chart area, choose '3-D Rotation' on the shortcut menu, and set X rotation to 100° and Y rotation to 50°. Change chart colors to Color 17. Edit the chart title to match the PivotTable title and resize the PivotChart as shown in Figure 8–86.

6. If requested by your instructor, add a worksheet header with your name and course number.

7. Preview and then print the PivotTable worksheet in landscape orientation.

8. Save the workbook with the new page setup characteristics.

9. Submit the revised document in the format specified by your instructor.

10. ✷ What other chart type would you use to present this data for the user? Why would you choose that particular chart type?

Expand Your World

Create a solution that uses cloud and web technologies by learning and investigating on your own from general guidance.

Creating Charts for a School District

Note: To complete these steps, you will be required to use the Data Files. Please contact your instructor for information about accessing the Data Files.

Problem: You volunteer with the Northville school district. The district would like to make available for parents some summary results from the latest round of statewide testing of the students in 4th, 7th, 10th, and 12th grade. Data has been compiled for the three testing areas, Math, Science, and English, for each of the eight schools in the district. The data includes both the average score for each grade and school combination and the test goal the various grades were charged with meeting. Assume for computation purposes that the class sizes for the schools across grades are within one or two students of each other, allowing calculation of goal averages without weighting. You have been tasked with creating a PivotTable for the school district for use on the publicly available portion of their OneDrive. The school district would like a PivotTable that would allow parents to visit OneDrive and, using slicers, examine the data for any school/grade combinations that are of interest to them. In addition to the PivotTable, you need to create brief instructions for visitors on how to use slicers to view combinations of grade and school.

Instructions:

1. Open the workbook Expand 8-1 Northville School District from the Data Files and then save the workbook using the file name, Expand 8-1 Northville School District Complete.

2. Create a PivotTable for the data provided. Set up the PivotTable to allow users to compare average scores and goals by school and/or grade.

3. Format the PivotTable and slicers to provide the user with a visually pleasing, easy-to-use product. You will need to decide which PivotTable elements to display, and how to display them. You also will need to make decisions about how to format various elements, taking into account color, size, default text, etc. (*Hint:* If the filter button menu does not produce the desired results, you may need to use the shortcut menu to move the grades up or down.) As you create the slicers, select multiple fields by using the Multi-Select button in the slicer title bar.

4. Write a brief instruction guide for users. You can place this guide in a group of merged cells, or you can insert a text box on the worksheet (visit Help to learn about text boxes and how to use them). You will need to make formatting decisions to ensure that the instructions are

Expand Your World *continued*

readable and fit on the worksheet with the PivotTable and slicers. Remember when setting up this worksheet that if you have content on your worksheet that you need available to set up the table, but the user does not need to see to use the PivotTable, you can hide specific rows/columns/worksheets without affecting the performance of the workbook contents. This can free up space on the worksheet for the content that needs to be visible.

5. If requested by your instructor, add a line at the bottom of your guide identifying you as the author of the guide.

6. Save the workbook on OneDrive, and test its performance. Make any changes necessary. Submit the revised document in the format specified by your instructor.

7. ☀ Evaluate the strengths and weaknesses of this method of making information available to parents. List three concerns, and suggest how you might begin to address them.

In the Labs

Design, create, modify, and/or use a workbook following the guidelines, concepts, and skills presented in this module. Labs 1 and 2, which increase in difficulty, require you to create solutions based on what you learned in the module; Lab 3 requires you to apply your creative thinking and problem-solving skills to design and implement a solution.

Lab 1: Creating a PivotTable, PivotChart, and Trendline

Note: To complete these steps, you will be required to use the Data Files. Please contact your instructor for information about accessing the Data Files.

Problem: You work for Altar Holdings and help the financial director prepare and analyze revenue and expense reports. He has asked you to create two PivotTables and corresponding PivotCharts based on sales data. One PivotTable and PivotChart summarize the sales by Supplier (Figure 8–87a). The other PivotTable and PivotChart summarize the Digital Products sales by month for the top supplier (Figure 8–87b).

Perform the following tasks:
1. Open the workbook Lab 8-1 Altar Holdings from the Data Files and then save the workbook using the file name, Lab 8-1 Altar Holdings Complete.

2. Using the data in the Sales Results worksheet, create the PivotTable and associated PivotChart shown in Figure 8–87a in a separate worksheet in the workbook. Name the worksheet Sales by Supplier.

3. Change the contents of cell A4 to Supplier and cell B3 to Store. Apply the 'Pivot Style Dark 21' style to the PivotTable. Format the values as currency values with a dollar sign and no decimal places. Apply the chart Style 14 to the PivotChart. Resize the PivotChart to cover the range A18:G35 and then hide the field buttons.

4. Create a second PivotTable and associated PivotChart, as shown in Figure 8–87b, in a separate worksheet in the workbook. Name the worksheet Digital Product Sales by Month.

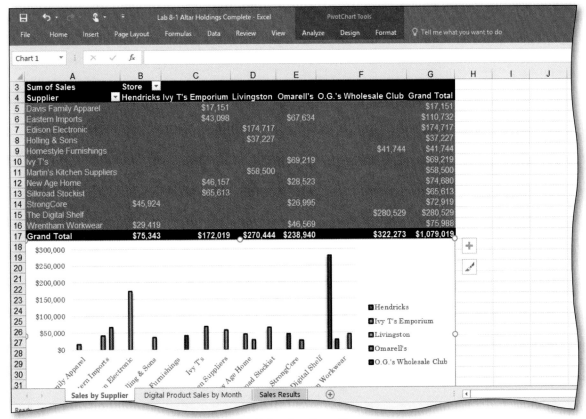

(a) Sales by Supplier

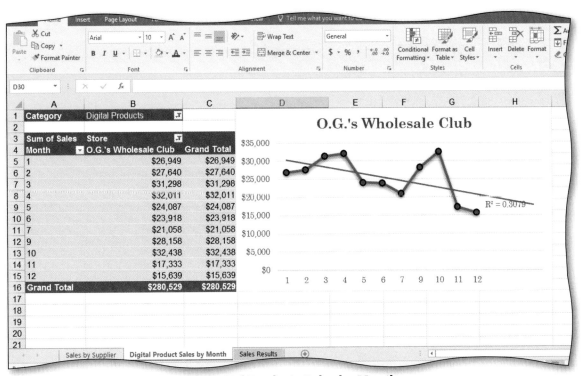

(b) Digital Products Sales by Month

Figure 8–87

In the Labs *continued*

5. Change the contents of cell A4 to Month and cell B3 to Store. Apply the 'Pivot Style Dark 4' style to the PivotTable. Format the values as currency values with a dollar sign and no decimal places.

6. Filter the category by Digital Products. Filter the store to O.G.'s Wholesale Club.

7. Change the chart type to Line and then add a linear trendline that forecasts the trend for three more months. Add the R-squared value to the trendline. Apply the chart Style 15 to the PivotChart and then hide the field buttons. Delete the legend. Resize the chart to the range D1:H16.

8. If requested by your instructor, add the text, Contact number, followed by your phone number to cell B66 of the Sales Results worksheet.

9. Save the workbook. Submit the revised document in the format specified by your instructor.

10. ✹ How helpful is the monthly breakdown when analyzing sales of various products?

Lab 2: Manipulating PivotTables and PivotCharts with Slicers

Note: To complete these steps, you will be required to use the Data Files. Please contact your instructor for information about accessing the Data Files.

Problem: The office manager at Evans Law Firm has asked you to analyze the current week's billing worksheet using PivotTables and PivotCharts. She wants you to create them for three scenarios: (a) the payment amount totals for hours billed, (b) the averages of the hours per region, and (c) the cost of the miscellaneous hours if they had been billable. The PivotTables and PivotCharts should appear as shown in Figure 8–88.

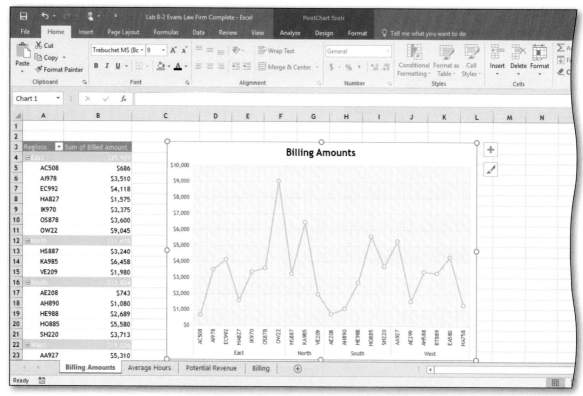

(a) Total Billed Amounts and Hours by Region

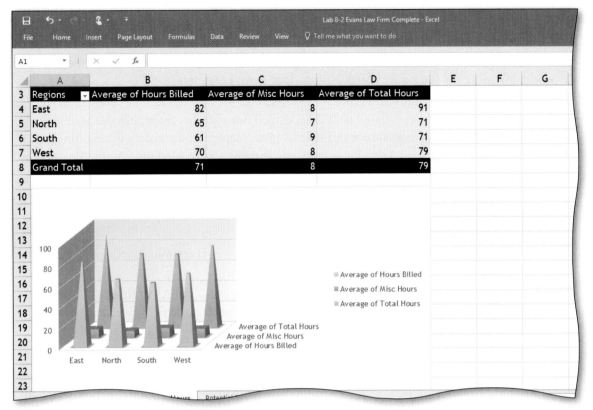

(b) Average Hours by Region

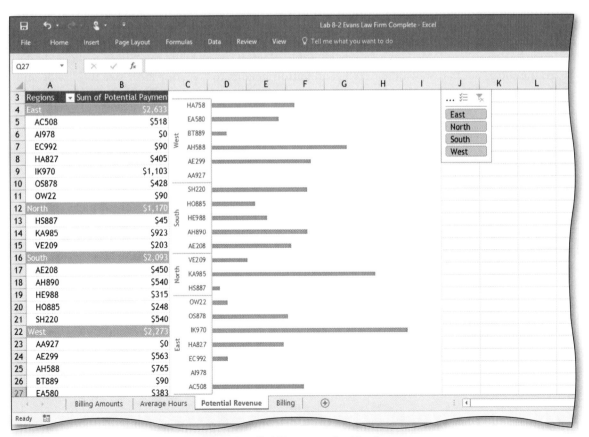

(c) Potential Revenue by Region

Figure 8–88

In the Labs *continued*

Perform the following tasks:

1. Run Excel. Open the workbook Lab 8-2 Evans Law Firm from the Data Files and then save the workbook using the file name, Lab 8-2 Evans Law Firm Complete.

2. Create the PivotTable shown in Figure 8–88a based on the data in the range A4:F26 in the Billing worksheet. Add a calculated field called Billed Amount that multiplies the hours billed by 45. Create the PivotChart shown in Figure 8–88a. Name the worksheet Billing Amounts. Change the contents of cell A3 to Regions. Apply the Pivot Style Medium 2 to the PivotTable. Format the Billed Amount values as currency values with a dollar sign and no decimal places. Apply the chart Style 6 to the PivotChart.

3. On a new worksheet create the PivotTable and Partial Pyramids PivotChart shown on the Average Hours worksheet in Figure 8–88b.

   a. To create the Partial Pyramids PivotChart, begin with a 3-D column chart. Format each data series with the Partial Pyramid option.

   b. Change the calculations to averages. Change the contents of cell A3 to Regions. Apply the 'Pivot Style Medium 17' style to the PivotTable. Format all value fields as number with no decimal places.

   c. Apply the chart Style 11 to the PivotChart. Change the fill of the back wall and wide wall to the Gradient style, 'Linear Diagonal – Top Left to Bottom Right'.

4. Create the PivotTable shown in Figure 8–88c. Add a calculated field called Potential Payment that multiplies the miscellaneous hours by 45. Create the PivotChart shown in Figure 8–88c. Name the worksheet Potential Revenue. Change cell A3 to Regions. Apply the 'Pivot Style Medium 5' style to the PivotTable. Format the Potential Payment values as currency values with a dollar sign and no decimal places. Apply the chart Style 2 to the PivotChart and change colors to Monochromatic Color 8. Remove the legend and chart title. Hide all field buttons, and close the PivotTable Fields task pane. Add a Region slicer. Apply the 'Slicer Style Light 4' to the slicer. Set button widths to 0.8" and button heights to 0.2". Set slicer size to 1" wide and 1.37" high. Position the slicer as shown in Figure 8–88c.

5. If requested by your instructor, add a worksheet header with your name and course number.

6. Select all three PivotTable sheets. With the three sheets selected, preview and then print the sheets. Save the workbook with the new page setup characteristics. Submit the revised document in the format specified by your instructor.

7. ✹ In this exercise, you have to scroll to see all parts of the PivotTable. Did you find this a hindrance when working on the PivotTables and PivotCharts? How could you address this when setting up your PivotTables and PivotCharts?

Lab 3: **Consider This: Your Turn**

Apply your creative thinking and problem-solving skills to design and implement a solution.

Budget Analysis

Note: To complete these steps, you will be required to use the Data Files. Please contact your instructor for information about accessing the Data Files.

Part 1: You have created a table that shows your household income and expenses. You would now like to create charts to help you analyze your budget. Part of this includes identifying a trend in your spending habits. Open the workbook Lab 8-3 Budget Analysis from the Data Files and then save the workbook using the file name, Lab 8-3 Household Budget Analysis Complete.

Create a chart using the expenses from the budget. Create a second chart using the cash flow data from the budget. Add a trendline to the chart that shows trends for the next four months. Submit your assignment in the format specified by your instructor.

Part 2: In Part 1, you made choices about which type(s) of chart(s) to use to present budget data. What was the rationale behind those selections? How did the data in the Household Expenses pose a special challenge? How might you address that challenge?

9 Formula Auditing, Data Validation, and Complex Problem Solving

Objectives

You will have mastered the material in this module when you can:

- Use formula auditing techniques to analyze a worksheet
- Trace precedents and dependents
- Use error checking to identify and correct errors
- Add data validation rules to cells
- Enable the Solver add-in
- Use trial and error to solve a problem on a worksheet

- Use goal seeking to solve a problem
- Circle invalid data on a worksheet
- Use Solver to solve a complex problem
- Use the Scenario Manager to record and save sets of what-if assumptions
- Create a Scenario Summary report
- Create a Scenario PivotTable report

Introduction

Excel offers many tools that can be used to solve complex problems. In previous modules, simple what-if analyses have shown the effect of changing one value on another value of interest. This module introduces you to auditing the formulas in a worksheet, validating data, and solving complex problems. **Formula auditing** allows you to examine formulas to determine which cells are referenced by those formulas and examine cells to determine which formulas are built upon those cells. Auditing the formulas in a worksheet can give insight into how a worksheet is structured and how cells are related to each other. Formula auditing is especially helpful when presented with a workbook created by someone else.

Data validation allows you to set cells so that the values they accept are restricted in terms of type and range of data. This feature can be set up to display prompts and error messages when users select a cell or enter invalid data. You also can use data validation to circle cells containing data that does not meet the criteria you specified.

When trying to solve some problems, you can make an educated guess if you are familiar with the data and the structure of the workbook. This process is called **trial and error**. For simpler problems, you may find a solution using this process. For more complex problems, you might need to use software, such as Excel, to find a satisfactory solution.

One of the tools that Excel provides to solve complex problems is Solver, which allows you to specify up to 200 cells that can be adjusted to find a solution to a problem. Solver also lets you place limits or constraints on allowable values for some or all of those cells. A **constraint** is a limitation on the possible values that a cell can contain. Solver will try many possible solutions to find one that solves the problem subject to the constraints placed on the data.

Project — Life Coach Services Scheduling Analysis

In this module, you will learn how to use the Life Coach Services Analysis workbook shown in Figure 9–1. Life Coach Services provides three types of coaching services to their clients: business coaching, individual coaching, and mentoring. The company employs three coaches who can provide all or some of the specific coaching services offered. The three coaches have different schedule capacities for a 40-hour work week. Paula schedules in 30-minute intervals and is able to see two clients per hour. Frank and Kristen schedule in 60-minute intervals and are able to see one client per hour. Additionally, Paula cannot take on mentoring clients and Frank cannot serve business clients. Service types that cannot be scheduled for a specific coach are shaded in gray.

The Scheduling Plan worksheet, shown in Figure 9–1a, was created to determine the most cost-effective way of scheduling coaching time to meet the needs of existing clients. The worksheet includes the details of the scheduling requirements for the three coaches, taking into account their schedule capacities as well as labor and material costs per client. A second worksheet, on the Costs tab, details the material costs and prices for the three different types of service.

The details of the first solution determined by Solver are shown in Figure 9–1b. Solver was given the goal of minimizing the total costs (cell E14) while also accommodating the following constraints: the number of clients assigned to each coach (range B7:D9) cannot be negative or fractional, the total number of clients of each type (range E7:E9) must equal the totals shown in the scheduling constraints area, and the total hours for any individual coach (range B11:D11) must not exceed the value shown in cell B18. Applying these constraints, Solver calculated the optimal distribution of coaching services among the coaches, shown in the range B7:D9, necessary to achieve the goal of minimizing the total costs (and maximizing total profit). Solver modified the values for each service type (rows 7 through 9) that resulted in changes in the total hours and costs per coach (rows 11 through 14) and minimized the total cost to Life Coach Services. However, if you applied a different set of scheduling constraints, Solver would determine a new solution. When Solver finishes solving a problem, you can create an Answer Report. An Answer Report (Figure 9–1c) summarizes the answer found by Solver, by identifying which constraints were in place and which values in the worksheet were manipulated in order to solve the problem within the constraints.

Excel's Scenario Manager is a what-if analysis tool that allows you to record and save different sets, or scenarios, of what-if assumptions for the same worksheet. In this case, you will use Scenario Manager to manage the two sets of Solver data for the Scheduling Plan worksheet. The Scenario Manager also allows you to create reports that summarize the scenarios on your worksheet. Both the Scenario Summary report (Figure 9–1d) and the Scenario PivotTable (Figure 9–1e) concisely present the differences among different scheduling scenarios. Like any PivotTable, the Scenario PivotTable allows you to interact with the data easily.

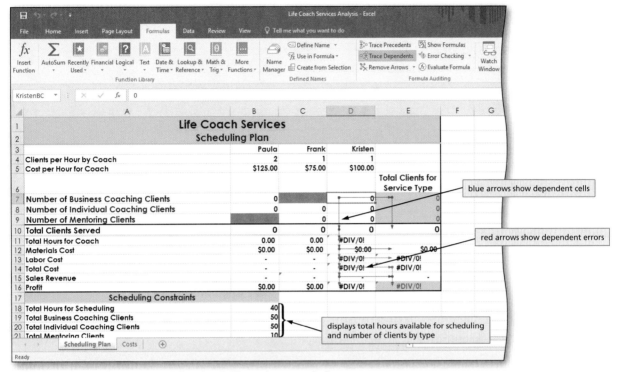

(a) Scheduling Plan Worksheet

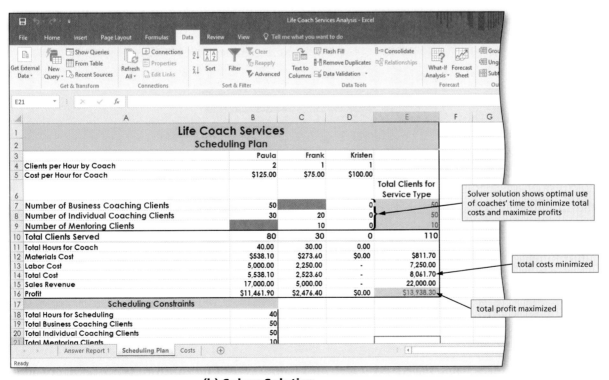

(b) Solver Solution

Figure 9–1 (Continued)

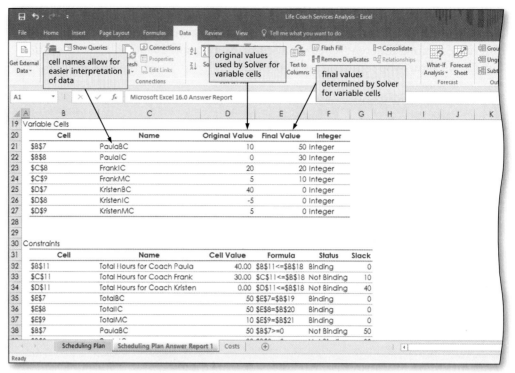

(c) Scheduling Plan Answer Report

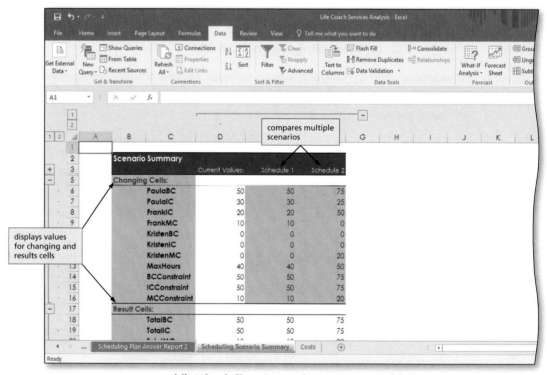

(d) Scheduling Scenario Summary Table

Figure 9–1 (Continued)

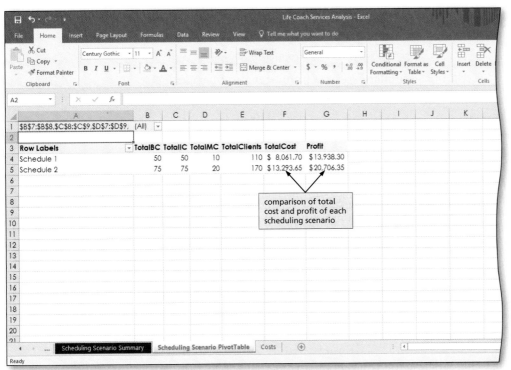

(e) Scheduling Scenario PivotTable

Figure 9–1

Figure 9–2 illustrates the requirements document for the Life Coach Services Analysis workbook. It includes the needs, source of data, and other facts about its development.

Worksheet Title	Life Coach Services Analysis
Needs	Evaluate two different sets of scheduling data to determine the optimal scheduling distribution to minimize total cost. Data include: • Three coaches, two of whom can coach only two types of clients • Three types of clients: business, individual, and mentoring • Labor and materials costs per coach Constraints include: • The numbers of coaching clients must be nonnegative integer values • The total number of clients for each type of service must equal the totals shown within the scheduling constraints area • Do not exceed the total hours for any individual coach
Source of Data	Cost and price information is available in the Life Coach Services workbook on the Costs worksheet.
Calculations	All formulas are set up in the workbook. The worksheets in the workbook should be reviewed to familiarize yourself with the calculations.
Other Requirements	None

Figure 9–2

With a good understanding of the requirements document and an understanding of the necessary decisions, the next step is to use Excel to create the workbook. In this module, you will learn how to create the Life Coach Services Analysis workbook shown in Figure 9–1.

The following roadmap identifies general activities you will perform as you progress through this module:

1. ANALYZE the WORKBOOK FORMULAS in the existing workbook.

2. SET DATA VALIDATION RULES to restrict cell contents.

3. CUSTOMIZE Excel ADD-INS to enable the Solver tool.

4. SOLVE COMPLEX PROBLEMS using what-if analysis tools.

5. CREATE AND EVALUATE SCENARIOS using Scenario Manager.

6. PRODUCE summary REPORTS from Scenario Manager.

To Run Excel and Open a Workbook

The following steps run Excel and open a workbook named Life Coach Services. The workbook currently contains two worksheets. The Scheduling Plan tab shows the overall scheduling plan and scheduling constraints for the coaches and services, while the Costs tab summarizes the related costs for each of the coaching services. To complete these steps, you will be required to use the Data Files. Please contact your instructor for information about accessing the Data Files.

1 Run Excel.

2 Open the file named Life Coach Services from the Data Files.

3 If the Excel window is not maximized, click the Maximize button on its title bar to maximize the window.

4 Save the workbook on your hard drive, OneDrive, or other storage location using Life Coach Services Analysis as the file name (Figure 9–3).

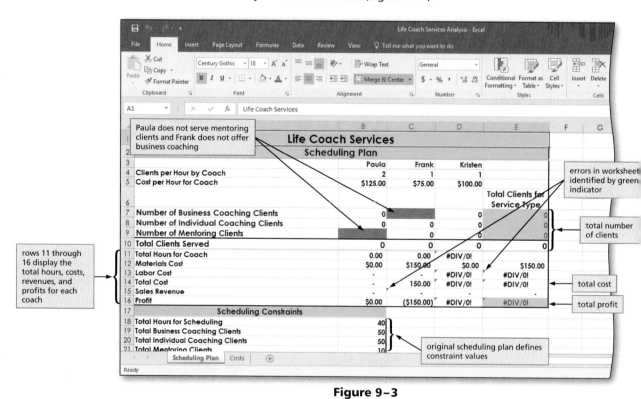

Figure 9–3

About the Scheduling Plan Worksheet

The Scheduling Plan worksheet shown in Figure 9–3 provides information about three coaches and three types of services. Rows 4 and 5 contain the hourly capacity and cost for each of the three coaches. The range B7:D9 will show the optimal combination of clients served by each coach that minimizes the total cost to Life Coach Services, which is the problem that needs to be solved in this module.

The gray cells indicate that a particular coach cannot provide a certain type of service. The total hours, costs, revenues, and profits for each coach (rows 11 to 16) are based on the numbers of clients shown in the range B7:D9. As the numbers of clients change, the values in the range B10:D16 are updated. Your goal is to determine the best distribution of clients, without exceeding the maximum number of hours per coach (cell B18), while minimizing total cost to the company (cell E14).

The current worksheet displays the scheduling constraints for the first scenario in the range B18:B21. As outlined in the requirements document in Figure 9–2, a second set of constraints also must be analyzed. Thus the information in the range B18:B21 will be modified to reflect the constraints associated with the different scenario.

Formula Auditing

Errors can be introduced into a worksheet when using formulas. Formula auditing is the process of reviewing formulas for errors. Errors may be obvious, with results that indicate that a formula is incorrect. For example, in Figure 9–3, cells D11, D13, E13, D14, E14, D16, and E16 display error codes. These errors are flagged by both the error code #DIV/0! and the error indicator, a green triangle, in the upper-left corner of those cells. Errors also may be less obvious, introduced through formulas that, while technically correct, result in unintended results in the worksheet. Error indicators with no accompanying error code, such as that found in cell C15, should be examined for these less-obvious errors. A complex worksheet should be reviewed to correct obvious errors *and* to correct formulas that do not produce error indicators but still do not produce the intended results.

Excel provides formula auditing tools, found in the Formula Auditing group on the Formulas tab, that can be used to review the formulas in a worksheet. Some tools, such as the Error Checking command, deal with identified errors. Other auditing tools provide visual cues to identify how cells in a worksheet are related to each other. Tracer arrows are drawn from one cell to another, identifying cells that are related to other cells through their use in a formula. A tracer arrow can be drawn from a cell that appears in a formula in another cell or from a cell that contains a formula with cell references. Red tracer arrows indicate that one of the referenced cells contains an error.

A cell containing a formula that references other cells is said to have precedents. Each cell referenced in the formula is a **precedent** of the cell containing the formula. For example, in the formula C24 = C23/$B$1, cells C23 and B1 are precedents of cell C24. Cells C23 and B1 also can have precedents, and these cells also would be precedents of cell C24. Tracing precedents can highlight where a formula may be incorrect.

BTW
Tracing Precedents and Dependents
When all levels of precedents or dependents have been identified, Excel will sound a beep if you try to trace another level.

To Trace Precedents

1 ANALYZE WORKBOOK FORMULAS | **2 SET DATA VALIDATION RULES** | **3 CUSTOMIZE ADD-INS**
4 SOLVE COMPLEX PROBLEMS | **5 CREATE & EVALUATE SCENARIOS** | **6 PRODUCE REPORTS**

Why? *Tracing precedents in Excel allows you to identify upon which cells a particular cell is based, not only directly by the formula in the cell but indirectly via precedents for the precedent cells.* The following steps trace the precedent cells for cell E12, which displays the Total Materials Cost for accommodating the scheduling needs.

- If necessary, make Scheduling Plan the active sheet.

- Display the Formulas tab and then select cell E12.

- Click the Trace Precedents button (Formulas tab | Formula Auditing group) to draw a tracer arrow across precedents of the selected cell (Figure 9–4).

Q&A How do I interpret the precedent arrows?

The arrow in Figure 9–4 terminates with an arrowhead on the traced cell, in this case cell E12. The heavy blue line that runs through the range of cells B12:D12 indicates that all cells in the range are precedents of the traced cell, E12.

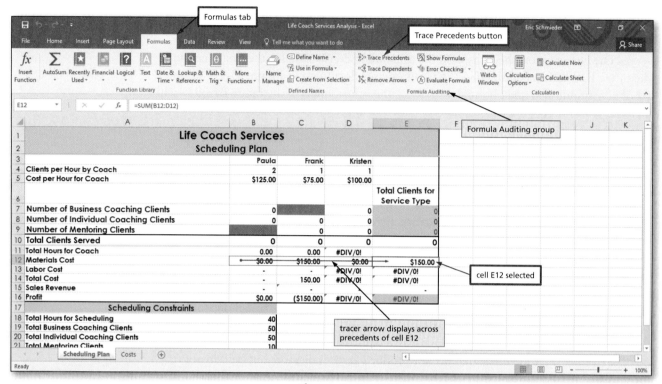

Figure 9–4

2

- Click the Trace Precedents button (Formulas tab | Formula Auditing group) again to draw arrows indicating precedents of cells B12:D12 (Figure 9–5).

Q&A How do I interpret the new precedent arrows?

The new arrows in Figure 9–5 have arrowheads on traced cells and dots on cells that are direct precedents of the cells with arrowheads. For instance, cell B12 has a tracer arrow to it with a blue line

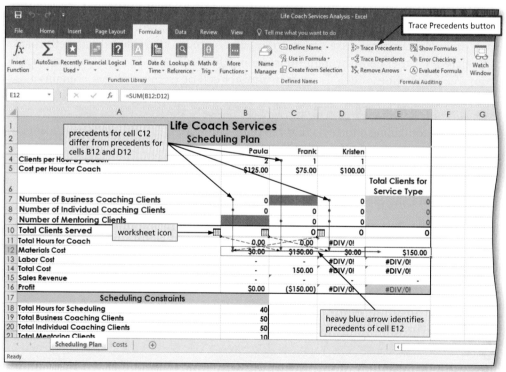

Figure 9–5

appearing in the range B7:B11 and dots in cell B7 and B8. This indicates that the cells containing dots, cells B7 and B8, are precedents of cell B12, while the other cells, without dots, are not. In addition, there is a black dashed line connecting cell B12 to a worksheet icon that indicates that precedent cells exist on another worksheet.

To Review Precedents on a Different Worksheet

Why? *Precedents also can be located on different worksheets in the same workbook or in different workbooks.* In Figure 9–5, the dashed precedent arrows and worksheet icons identify precedents on another worksheet. Cell C12, which has precedents on a different worksheet, displays a value of $150.00 in material costs, although no clients have been assigned to Frank. This is inconsistent with the surrounding cell values that accurately display no initial material costs for Paula and Kristen. The following steps review the precedents for cell C12.

1

- Click cell C12 to display the formula in the formula bar (Figure 9–6).

Q&A I am having difficulty selecting cell C12. Is this cell locked?
When precedent or dependent arrows are drawn through a cell, the area that you can click in the cell to select it is reduced. Click near the boundaries of the cell in order to select it.

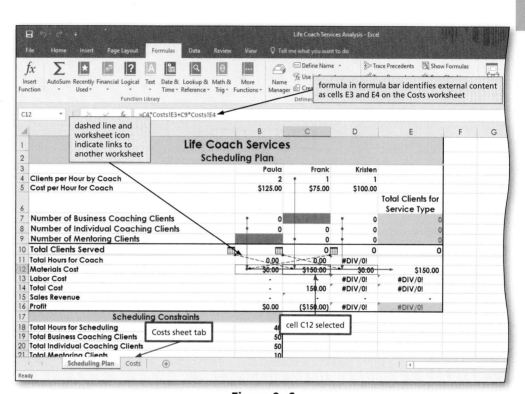

Figure 9–6

2

- Review the formula in the formula bar to identify the location of the precedent cell or cells, in this case cells E3 and E4 on the Costs worksheet.

- Display the Costs worksheet.

- Review the precedent cells to determine if the reference to them in the formula is correct as written (Figure 9–7).

Q&A Are the cells referenced in the formula in cell C12 in the Scheduling Plan worksheet correct?
The formula in cell C12 should calculate the material costs for Frank. However, the formula contains multiple errors. In the Costs worksheet, the formula incorrectly references the Price per Session values (cells E3 and E4) instead of the Material Cost per Session values (cells C3 and C4). In the Scheduling Plan worksheet, the formula incorrectly references the Clients per Hour by Coach that Frank can serve (cell C4) instead than the Number of Individual Coaching Clients served by Frank (cell C8).

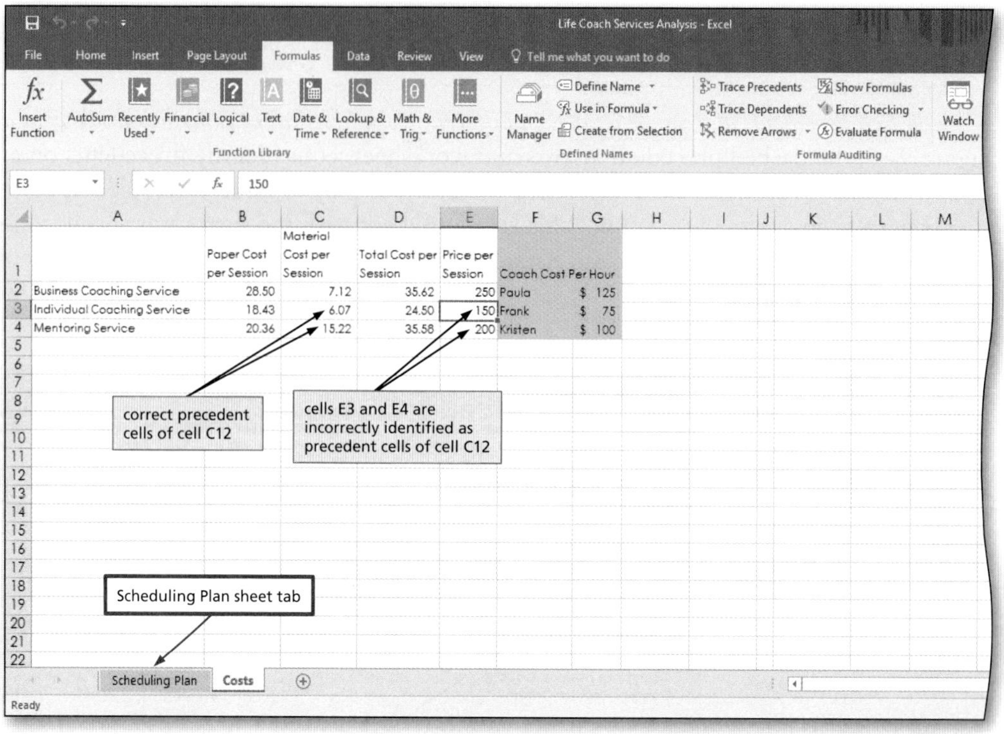

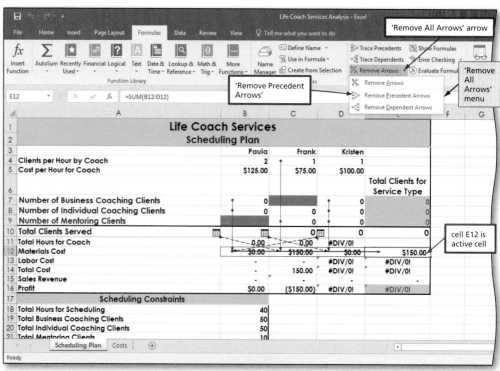

Figure 9–7

To Remove the Precedent Arrows

1 ANALYZE WORKBOOK FORMULAS │ 2 SET DATA VALIDATION RULES │ 3 CUSTOMIZE ADD-INS
4 SOLVE COMPLEX PROBLEMS │ 5 CREATE & EVALUATE SCENARIOS │ 6 PRODUCE REPORTS

Why? *Reducing visual clutter makes the worksheet easier to edit.* After reviewing the precedents of cell E12, you determine that the formula in cell C12 needs to be changed to calculate the total material cost correctly for Frank. The following steps remove the precedent arrows level by level and then correct the formula in cell C12.

- Display the Scheduling Plan worksheet and then select cell E12.

- Click the 'Remove All Arrows' arrow (Formulas tab | Formula Auditing group) to display the 'Remove All Arrows' menu (Figure 9–8).

Figure 9–8

❷

- Click 'Remove Precedent Arrows' on the 'Remove All Arrows' menu to remove precedent arrows linking to the Costs sheet.

- Click the 'Remove All Arrows' button (Formulas tab | Formula Auditing group) to remove the remaining tracer arrows.

- Edit the formula in cell C12 to read =C8*Costs!C3+ C9*Costs!C4 to correct the error.

- Click the Enter button to accept the change (Figure 9–9).

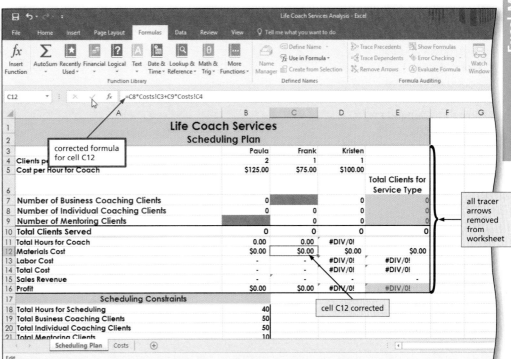

Figure 9–9

TO REVIEW PRECEDENTS ON A DIFFERENT WORKSHEET USING THE GO TO COMMAND

You can use precedent arrows to navigate directly to precedents on a different worksheet or different workbook. If you choose to use this feature, you would use the following steps:

1. Double-click on the dashed precedent arrow to display the Go To dialog box.

2. Select the cell reference to navigate to from the Go to list (Go To dialog box).

3. Click the OK button (Go To dialog box) to navigate to the selected cell reference.

To Trace Dependents

1 ANALYZE WORKBOOK FORMULAS | 2 SET DATA VALIDATION RULES | 3 CUSTOMIZE ADD-INS
4 SOLVE COMPLEX PROBLEMS | 5 CREATE & EVALUATE SCENARIOS | 6 PRODUCE REPORTS

Why? Identifying dependents highlights where changes will occur in the worksheet as a result of changing the value in the cell you are identifying as a referenced cell. A cell that references another cell is said to be a **dependent** of that referenced cell. If cell A3 contained the formula =B2/B4, cell A3 would be a dependent of cells B2 and B4. Changing the value in cell B2 or cell B4 also changes the result in the dependent cell A3. The following steps trace the dependents of cell D7, which will display the optimal number of business coaching clients for Kristen.

1

• Select cell D7.

• Click the Trace Dependents button (Formulas tab | Formula Auditing group) to draw arrows to dependent cells D10, D12, D15, and E7 (Figure 9–10).

Q&A What is the meaning of the dependent arrows?

As shown in Figure 9–10, the arrowheads indicate which cells directly depend on the selected cell. In this case, cell D7 is explicitly referenced in formulas in cells D10, D12, D15, and E7.

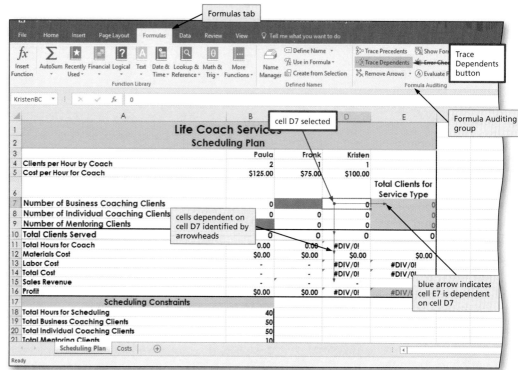

Figure 9–10

2

• Click the Trace Dependents button three more times to draw arrows indicating the indirectly dependent cells — those cells which depend on cells that directly or indirectly depend on the selected cell — of cell D7 (Figure 9–11).

Q&A How do I know when I have identified all remaining dependents?

If no additional dependents are present when you click the Trace Dependents button, Excel does not draw additional arrows but plays an error tone.

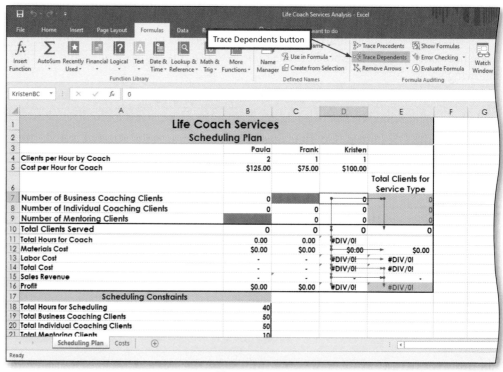

Figure 9–11

To Remove the Dependent Arrows

Why? *Tracing dependents identified the cells that depend on cell D7, which will help to correct the #DIV/0! errors in the worksheet. Once dependent cells are identified, you may want to remove the arrows to clear the worksheet of extraneous content.* The following step clears the dependent arrows from the worksheet.

1

- Click the 'Remove All Arrows' button (Formulas tab | Formula Auditing group) to remove all of the dependent arrows (Figure 9–12).

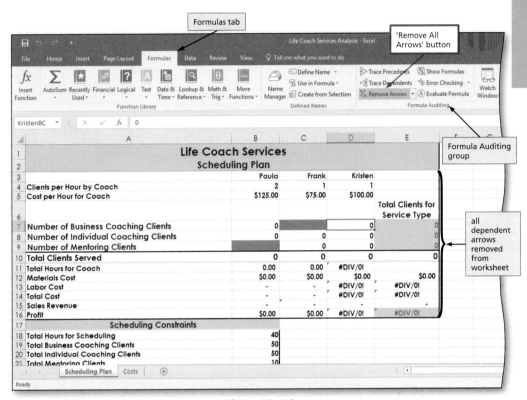

Figure 9–12

To Use Error Checking to Correct Errors

Why use error checking? *Excel can provide assistance in determining the source of errors in the worksheet.* Cells D11, D13:E14, and D16:E16 all contain error codes. Their contents indicate that these cells are in error because the formulas they contain attempt to divide a number by zero. For example, cell E16 contains references to cells E14 and E15. Cell E14 refers to the range B14:D14. The cells in the range B14:D14 also contain references to other cells. The source of the error in cell E16 could be in any of the directly or indirectly referenced cells. To identify the source, it is important to review all precedents to the cell containing the error. The following steps use error checking features to find the source of these errors and correct them.

1

- Select cell E16.

- Click the Trace Precedents button (Formulas tab | Formula Auditing group) six times to identify all precedents of cell E16.

- Click cell D5 to display the formula with reference to a cell on the Costs worksheet (Figure 9–13).

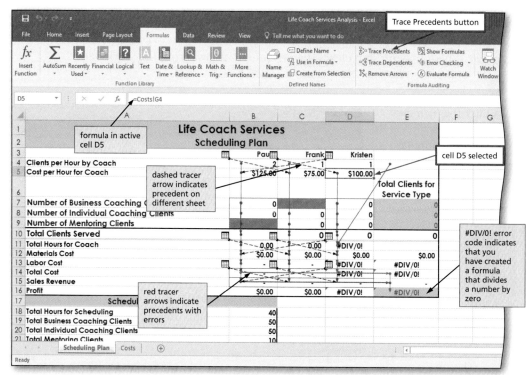

Figure 9–13

2

- Make Costs the active worksheet.

- Review cell G4 (Costs worksheet) to determine if the reference to it in the formula in cell D5 of the Scheduling Plan worksheet is correct (Figure 9–14).

Q&A
Is cell G4 (Costs worksheet) the correct reference for the formula in cell D5 (Scheduling worksheet)?
Cell G4 is the Coach Cost Per Hour for Kristen and contains the value 100. Cell D5 on the Scheduling Plan worksheet represents the cost per hour for Kristen. Thus cell G4 is the correct reference for cell D5.

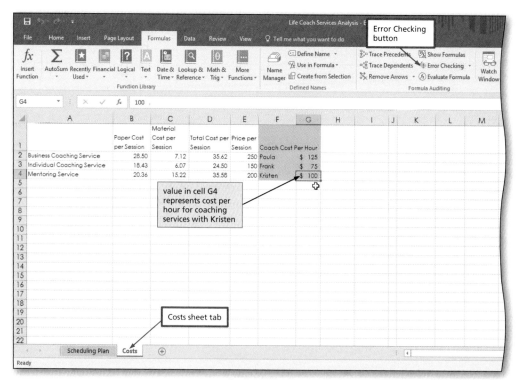

Figure 9–14

- Make Scheduling Plan the active worksheet and then select cell E16.
- Click the Error Checking button (Formulas tab | Formula Auditing group) to display the Error Checking dialog box (Figure 9–15).

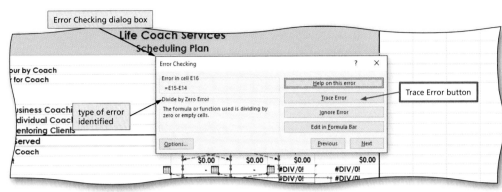

Figure 9–15

- Click the Trace Error button (Error Checking dialog box) to highlight the precedents of the active cell, which also contain error codes (Figure 9–16).

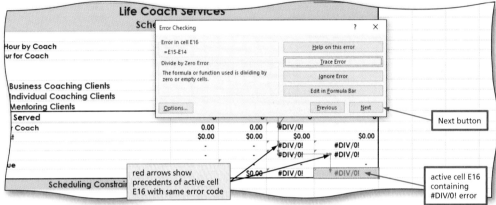

Figure 9–16

- Click the Next button (Error Checking dialog box) to move to the next error in the workbook, found in cell D11 in this case (Figure 9–17).

Experiment
- Drag the Error Checking dialog box to view empty cell E4, referenced in the formula in cell D11.

Q&A
What happens when I click the Next button?
Excel will move to the next cell in which it finds an error code or an error indicator.

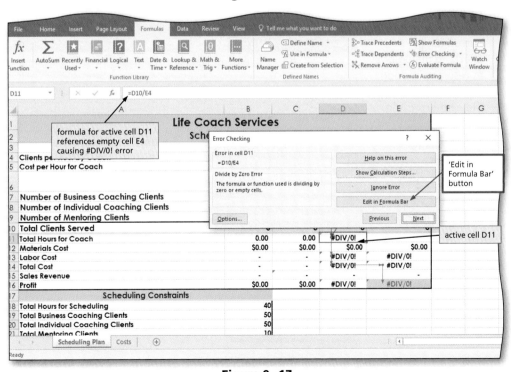

Figure 9–17

Excel moves forward or backward through the workbook, row by row, when you click the Next or Previous button. Clicking the Next button does not move to a precedent or dependent cell. In this case, clicking the Next button displayed the first error in the workbook, because the workbook contains no errors after cell E16.

6

- Click the 'Edit in Formula Bar' button (Error Checking dialog box) and edit cell D11 to read =D10/D4.

- Click the Enter button in the formula bar to complete the edit of the cell and to correct the remaining #DIV/0! errors (Figure 9–18).

Q&A
Why did correcting one error in cell D11 correct all the #DIV/0! errors in the worksheet?
The other cells containing #DIV/0! errors were directly or indirectly dependent on the value in cell D11, thus correcting the error in cell D11 provided a valid value for use in the other formulas.

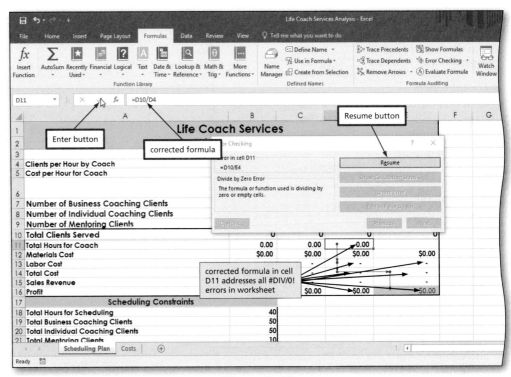

Figure 9–18

7

- Click the Resume button (Error Checking dialog box) to resume checking errors, in this case the next error is in cell C15.

- Review the formula in cell C15.

- Click cell D15 and review the formula in the formula bar for accuracy.

- Click cell B15 and review the formula (Figure 9–19).

Q&A
Why did Excel jump to cell C15 when I clicked the Resume button?
Clicking the Resume button selects the next cell containing an error if the error in the previously selected cell is corrected. If the error was not corrected, the selected cell would not change.

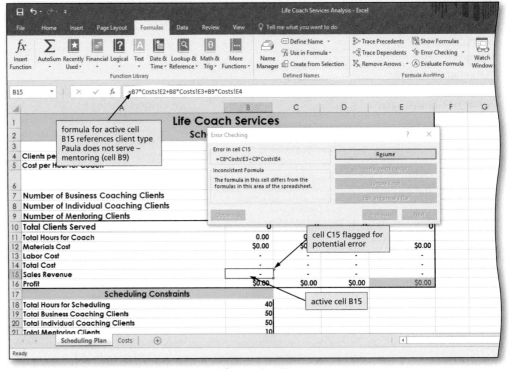

Figure 9–19

Are the formulas in cells B15, C15, and D15 accurate?
Although all three formulas produce accurate results, the formula in cell C15 is flagged as a potential error because it is inconsistent with the other two. The formula in cell C15 references only the types of clients Frank serves. For greater accuracy, the formula in cell B15 should reference only the types of clients that Paula serves.

8

- Edit the formula in cell B15 to read `=B7*Costs!E2+ B8*Costs!E3` (Figure 9–20).

- Click the Resume button (Error Checking dialog box) to complete the edit.

Q&A Why did the error flag in cell C15 disappear after editing the formula in cell B15?
The formula in cell C15 was originally flagged as a potential error because the formula was inconsistent with the cells on either side of it. Once the formula in cell B15 was edited, Excel no longer expects consistency because none of the cells in the range B15:D15 contain formulas that are consistent with each other, so the error flag is removed.

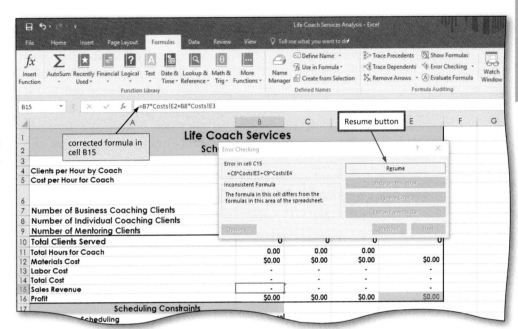

Figure 9–20

9

- Click the OK button in the Microsoft Excel dialog box to close the open dialog boxes.

- If necessary, click the 'Remove All Arrows' button (Formulas tab | Formula Auditing group) to remove all of the dependent arrows (Figure 9–21).

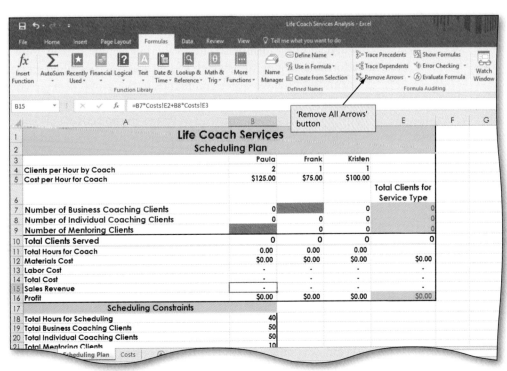

Figure 9–21

BTW
Setting Iterative Calculation Options
In certain situations, you will want Excel to recalculate a formula that contains a circular reference, to enable Excel to converge upon an acceptable solution. Changing the iterative calculation option allows Excel to recalculate a formula a specified number of times after the initial circular reference error message is dismissed. To allow Excel to recalculate a formula, display the Excel Options dialog box and then click the Formulas tab. In the Calculation options area, click to select the 'Enable iterative calculation' check box. You can specify the maximum number of iterations and maximum amount of change between iterations. Be aware that turning on this option will slow down the worksheet due to the additional computations.

More about the Formula Auditing Group

In the previous steps, you used some of the buttons in the Formula Auditing group on the Formulas tab to identify and correct errors in your worksheet. You already have used the Trace Precedents, Trace Dependents, and 'Remove All Arrows' buttons to gain insight into the structure of the worksheet. You also have used the Error Checking button to check for errors throughout the worksheet. When Error Checking is clicked, Excel highlights each error in the worksheet in sequence and displays options for correcting the error. When you select a cell containing an error and then click the Error Checking arrow, you have two additional options. The Trace Error command uses red arrows to highlight the precedents of the selected cell, which may help you identify the source of the error. The second option, Circular References, is available only when the error in the cell is a circular reference. A **circular reference** occurs when one of the defining values in a cell is itself. For example, if you type =B2/A2 in cell B2, you have created a circular reference. Excel displays an error message when you create a circular reference and provides you with access to the appropriate Help topic. In complex worksheets with multiple precedent levels, these errors are not uncommon.

Table 9–1 lists common error codes identified in Excel.

Table 9–1 Common Excel Error Codes	
Error Code	**Description**
#DIV/0!	Indicates that a formula divides a number by zero
#N/A!	Indicates that a formula cannot locate a referenced value
#NAME?	Indicates use of an invalid function name
#NULL!	Indicates that a formula incorrectly contains a space between two or more cell references
#NUM!	Indicates that a formula contains invalid numeric values
#REF!	Indicates that a cell reference in a formula is not valid; it may be pointing to an empty cell, for instance
#VALUE!	Indicates that a calculation includes nonnumeric data

The Formula Auditing group contains three other commands you can use when auditing formulas. The Evaluate Formula button allows you to move through a formula step by step, which can be a useful tool when working with long, complex formulas. The two other commands in the group provide you with options for viewing the worksheet and keeping an eye on cells of interest. The Show Formulas button displays the formulas instead of values in the active worksheet. The Watch Window button opens a separate window that displays values and formulas for specific cells that you choose to monitor.

Using the Watch Window

The Watch Window (Figure 9–22a) allows you to keep an eye on cells that you have identified as being related; this allows you to observe changes to the cells even when viewing a different worksheet or workbook. For example, if you were watching cell E12, which displays total material costs, and you changed the value in cell C3 on the Costs worksheet, the Watch Window would display the updated value of cell E12 on the Scheduling Plan worksheet. You add cells to the Watch Window using the Add Watch button in the Watch Window and the Add Watch dialog box (Figure 9–22b). The Watch Window continues to show the values of watched cells even as you navigate the worksheet and the cells no longer are in view. Similarly, if you change the view to another worksheet or workbook, the Watch Window allows you to continue to monitor the cell values.

Excel Module 9

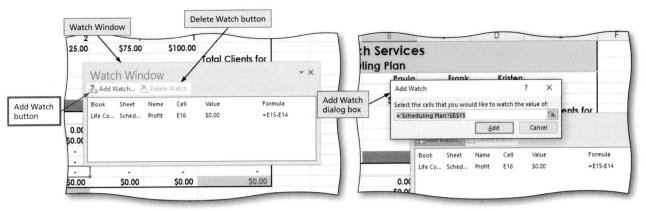

(a) Watch Window   (b) Add Watch Dialog Box

Figure 9–22

To Open the Watch Window

If you wanted to open the Watch Window, you would perform the following steps:

1. If necessary, display the Formulas tab.
2. Click the Watch Window button (Formulas tab | Formula Auditing group) to open the Watch Window (Figure 9–22a).
3. If necessary, move the Watch Window to a location where it does not obscure cells you want to observe to make it easier to select the cells you want to add.

To Add Cells to the Watch Window

If you wanted to add cells to the Watch Window, you would perform the following steps:

1. Click the Add Watch button on the Watch Window toolbar to display the Add Watch dialog box (Figure 9–22b).
2. Select the cell or cells to be watched.
3. Click the Add button (Add Watch dialog box) to add the selected cells to the Watch Window.

To Delete Cells from the Watch Window

If you wanted to delete cells from the Watch Window, you would perform the following steps:

1. In the Watch Window dialog box, select the cell you want to stop watching.
2. Click the Delete Watch button in the Watch Window to delete the selected cell from the Watch Window.

Data Validation

When calculating formulas, some values used in calculations might not have any useful meaning for the problem at hand. For example, cells B7 and D7 in the Scheduling Plan worksheet display the number of business coaching clients served. Because you cannot serve a negative number of clients, only values greater than or equal to zero should be entered in cells B7 and D7. In other words, only values greater than or equal to zero are valid in cells B7 and D7. Excel provides you with tools to restrict the values that can be placed in cells to valid values. You can place restrictions on values, provide a message to the user when a cell with restrictions is selected, and create an error message that is displayed when an invalid value is entered.

Excel's data validation rules apply only when you enter data into the cell manually. Excel does not check the validation rules if a cell is calculated by a formula or set in a way other than by direct input by the user.

The types of data validation criteria you can use include specific values, whole numbers, a value in a list (such as a text value), dates, and custom values. When using the custom validation type, you can use a formula that evaluates to either true or false. If the value is false, users may not enter data in the cell. Suppose, for example, you have a cell that contains an employee's salary. If the salary is zero, which indicates the employee no longer is with the company, you may want to prohibit a user from entering a percentage in another cell that contains the employee's raise for the year.

To Add Data Validation to Cells

1 ANALYZE WORKBOOK FORMULAS | 2 SET DATA VALIDATION RULES | 3 CUSTOMIZE ADD-INS
4 SOLVE COMPLEX PROBLEMS | 5 CREATE & EVALUATE SCENARIOS | 6 PRODUCE REPORTS

Why add data validation? In the Scheduling Plan worksheet, the numbers of each type of client served by each coach must be nonnegative whole numbers. The cells that need to be restricted are cells B7:B8, C8:C9, and D7:D9 because they display the number of each type of client. You can use data validation to apply these conditions and restrictions to the cells. The following steps add data validation to cells in the ranges B7:B8, C8:C9, and D7:D9.

- Display the Data tab and then select cells B7 and D7.

- Click the Data Validation button (Data tab | Data Tools group) to display the Data Validation dialog box.

- Click the Allow arrow (Data Validation dialog box) and then click Whole number in the Allow list to select it as the validation criteria type.

- Click the Data arrow and then click 'greater than or equal to' in the Data list to select it.

- Type 0 in the Minimum box to specify that the values in the selected cells must be whole numbers greater than or equal to zero (Figure 9–23).

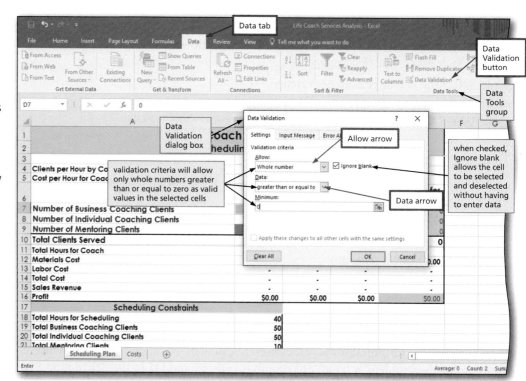

Figure 9–23

Q&A How else can I validate data?

Excel allows several types of validation to be set in the Settings sheet (Data Validation dialog box) shown in Figure 9–23. Each selection in this sheet changes the type of value that Excel allows a user to enter in the cell. In the Allow list, the Any value selection allows you to enter any value but still allows you to specify an input message for the cell. The Whole number, Decimal, Date, and Time selections permit only values of those types to be entered in the cell. The List selection allows you to specify a range that contains a list of valid values for the cell. The Text length selection allows only a certain length of text string to be entered in the cell. The Custom selection allows you to specify a formula that validates the data entered by the user.

②

- Click the Input Message tab (Data Validation dialog box) to display the Input Message sheet.

- Type **Number of Business Clients** in the Title text box to enter a title for the message displayed when cell B7 or D7 is selected.

- Type **Enter the number of business coaching clients to be served by this coach. The number must be a whole number that is greater than or equal to zero.** in the Input message text box to enter the text for the message (Figure 9–24).

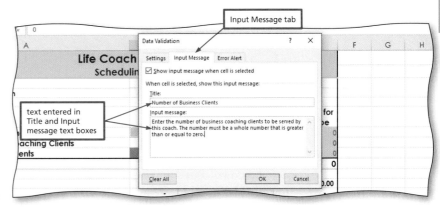

Figure 9–24

③

- Click the Error Alert tab (Data Validation dialog box) to display the Error Alert sheet.

- If necessary, Click the Style arrow and then click Stop to select the Stop error style.

- Type **Input Error** in the Title text box to enter a title for the error message displayed if invalid data is entered in cell B7 or D7.

- Type **You must enter a whole number that is greater than or equal to zero.** in the Error message text box to enter the text for the error message (Figure 9–25).

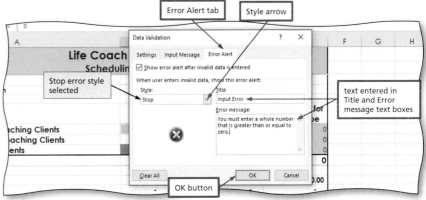

Figure 9–25

Q&A What is a Stop error style?

You can select one of three types of error styles. Stop prevents users from entering invalid data in a cell. Warning displays a message that the data is invalid and lets users accept the invalid entry, edit it, or remove it. Information displays a message that the data is invalid but still allows users to enter it.

④

- Click the OK button (Data Validation dialog box) to accept the data validation settings for cells B7 and D7.

⑤

- Repeat Steps 1 through 4 two more times, once for individual clients in cells B8:D8 and once for mentoring clients in cells C9:D9. Use the same settings in the Settings sheet for the values that can be entered in the cells. When creating the title for the input message for cells B8:D8, use **Number of Individual Clients**. Similarly, use the title **Number of Mentoring Clients** for cells C9:D9. Make the appropriate changes for the text in the input messages and error alerts.

- Click cell E21 to make it the active cell.

- Save the workbook again on the same storage location with the same file name.

Q&A What is the result of these validation rules?

When a user selects one of the cells in the ranges B7:B8, C8:C9, or D7:D9, Excel displays the input message defined in Figure 9–24. When the user enters a value that either is less than zero or is not a whole number in cells in the ranges B7:B8, C8:C9, and D7:D9, Excel displays the error message defined in Figure 9–25 and forces the user to change the value to a valid number before deselecting the cell. The validation rules will be tested later in the module.

Break Point: If you wish to take a break, this is a good place to do so. You can exit Excel now. To resume at a later time, run Excel, open the file called Life Coach Services Analysis, and continue following the steps from this location forward.

Customizing Excel Add-Ins

Excel provides optional commands and features through the inclusion of add-ins. An add-in is an accessory program that adds functionality to Excel. Although some add-ins are built into Excel, including the Solver add-in used in this module, others may be downloaded and installed as needed. In any case, add-ins for Excel must be installed before they are available for use.

Add-ins are managed through the Add-ins tab accessible through the Excel Options dialog box. Once activated, the add-in and related commands are accessible through the ribbon, often in custom tabs or groups. The Solver and Analysis ToolPak add-ins are represented by buttons in the Analyze group on the Data tab. Euro Currency Tools, another built-in add-in for Excel, appears as commands in the Solutions group on the Formulas tab.

The Solver Add-In

The Solver add-in is a tool you use to generate the best possible solution for complex problems from a wide range of possibilities. Solver works to optimize a specific cell, called an objective cell, by maximizing, minimizing, or setting it to a specific value. For example, you may want to minimize total cost (cell E14) or maximize profit (cell E16). Because of the number of precedents to these cell values, it can be difficult to determine which values should change. When you decrease the number of business coaching clients for one coach, you have to increase the number assigned to another coach to ensure that all clients are being served. This change not only has an impact on costs and resulting profit but also impacts the number of hours required of the individual coaches. Solver takes into account all of the various constraints when determining the best solution. In the scheduling plan problem, constraints include the number of hours an individual coach can work in a week (cell B18) and the number of clients in each category of coaching service (B19:B21). The countless options make it difficult to identify the best solution to the problem using other methods of what-if analysis such as trial and error or Goal Seek.

To Enable the Solver Add-In

1 ANALYZE WORKBOOK FORMULAS | 2 SET DATA VALIDATION RULES | 3 CUSTOMIZE ADD-INS
4 SOLVE COMPLEX PROBLEMS | 5 CREATE & EVALUATE SCENARIOS | 6 PRODUCE REPORTS

Many of the advanced features of Excel, such as the Solver add-in, are hidden until the user adds the feature to the user interface. *Why? Excel is a powerful application with many features that the average user does not need to access on a regular basis. These features are hidden to keep the interface from becoming too overwhelming.* The following steps will add the Solver add-in to Excel and verify the additional features on the Data tab of the ribbon.

1

- Display the Backstage view.

- Click the Options tab to display the Excel Options dialog box (Figure 9–26).

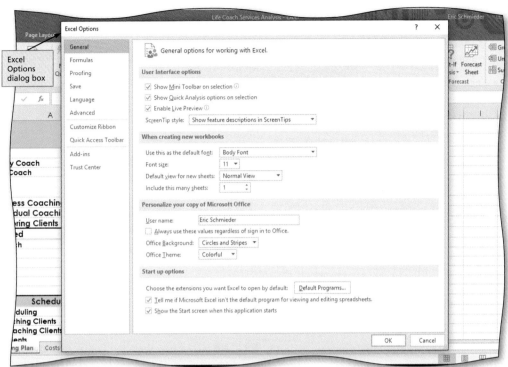

Figure 9–26

2

- Click the Add-ins tab to display the View and manage Microsoft Office Add-ins (Figure 9–27).

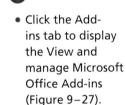

Why is my list of add-ins different? Depending on the applications installed and enabled for use in Excel, the list of active, inactive, and available add-ins may be different.

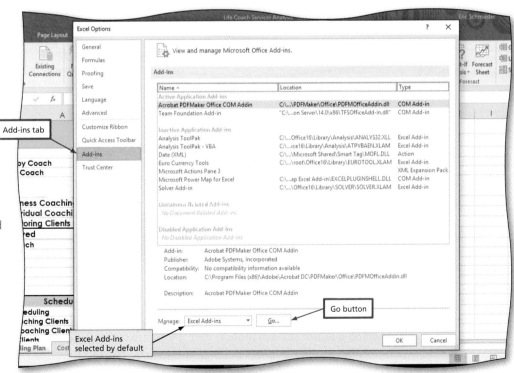

Figure 9–27

3

- If necessary, click Excel Add-ins in the Manage list to select it as the add-in type.
- Click Go to display the Add-ins dialog box (Figure 9–28).

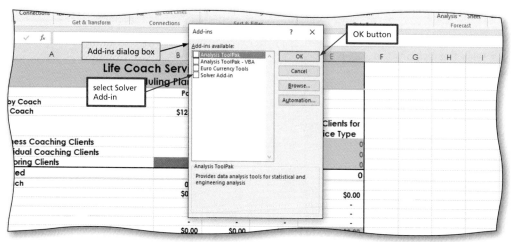

Figure 9–28

4

- Click to select the Solver Add-in item in the Add-ins available list (Add-ins dialog box).
- Click OK to close the Add-ins dialog box.
- If necessary, display the Data tab to verify the addition of the Analyze group and Solver button (Figure 9–29).

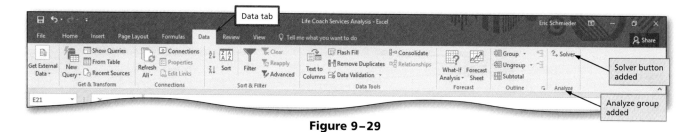

Figure 9–29

Solving Complex Problems

BTW
Copying Validation Rules
You can copy validation rules from one cell to other cells using the Paste Special command. Select the cell that contains the validation rules you want to copy and then click Copy. Select the cell or cells to which you want to apply the validation rules, click the Paste button arrow, and then click Paste Special. Click Validation in the Paste area and then click the OK button (Paste Special dialog box).

In the Life Coach Services Analysis workbook, the problem of determining how to schedule client services to minimize total cost within the constraints provided is not straightforward, due to the number of variables involved. Remember from the requirements document that these constraints include the number of hours each individual coach can work in a week (cell B18), the number of clients that need to be served in each category (cells B19:B21), and the types of clients each coach serves.

You can attempt to solve the problem manually, through trial and error, or you can use an Excel tool to automate some or all of the solution. To solve the problem manually, you could try adjusting values in the ranges B7:B8, C8:C9, and D7:D9 until the goal for the schedule is met. Remember that Life Coach Services wants to identify the best distribution of clients to coaches that will minimize their total costs. Because so many possible combinations could meet the criteria, you could hold one or more of the cells affected by constraints constant and make adjustments to the other cells to attempt to meet the rest of the criteria. For example, you could assign all ten of the mentoring clients to Kristen (cell D9) and reassign a corresponding number of individual coaching clients to Frank (cell C8) to see how that one change affects the total costs.

How should you approach solving a complex problem?

When considering an approach to a complex problem in Excel, start with the least complex method of attempting to solve the problem. In general, the following methods can be useful in the order shown:

1. **Use trial and error** to modify the values in the worksheet. Use a commonsense approach, and keep in mind the range of acceptable answers to your problem. For example, the number of coaching clients should not be a negative number.

2. **Use Excel's Goal Seek feature** to have Excel automatically modify a cell's value in a worksheet in an attempt to reach a certain goal in a dependent cell.

3. **Use Excel's Solver feature** to provide Excel with all of the known rules, or constraints, of your problem as well as the goal you are seeking. Allow Solver to attempt as many different solutions to your problem as possible.

To Use Trial and Error to Attempt to Solve a Complex Problem

1 ANALYZE WORKBOOK FORMULAS | 2 SET DATA VALIDATION RULES | 3 CUSTOMIZE ADD-INS
4 SOLVE COMPLEX PROBLEMS | **5 CREATE & EVALUATE SCENARIOS** | **6 PRODUCE REPORTS**

Trial and error is not making blind guesses. Trial and error is a process of making incremental changes in order to observe the impact on the desired result. *Why use trial and error? With an understanding of how the worksheet is set up and how the various values interact, you can make informed and incremental changes, or trials, based on how each decision affects the worksheet.* In the first trial for the Life Coach Services workbook, you will set up the schedule so that all the services are delivered by Kristen, the one coach that can deliver all three types of services, and then make some adjustments based on the results. The following steps illustrate the process of using trial and error to attempt to solve a complex problem.

- Click cell D7 to make it the active cell and display the Number of Business Clients input message.

- Type **47.5** and then press the ENTER key to enter the number of business coaching clients for Kristen and display the Input Error dialog box (Figure 9–30).

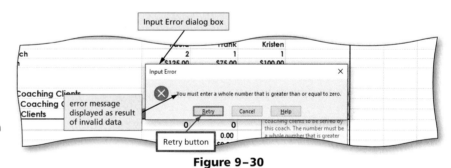

Figure 9–30

Q&A Why does the Input Error dialog box appear after entering 47.5 in cell D7?

You set a data validation rule in cell D7 that accepts only whole numbers greater than or equal to zero. Because 47.5 is not a whole number, Excel displays the Input Error dialog box with the title and error message you specified when you set the data validation rule.

- Click the Retry button (Input Error dialog box) to return to cell D7.

- Enter **50** in cell D7 as the number of business clients to schedule with Kristen and then press the ENTER key.

- Enter **50** in cell D8 as the number of individual clients to schedule with Kristen and then press the ENTER key.

- Enter **10** in cell D9 as the number of mentoring clients to schedule with Kristen and then press the ENTER key (Figure 9–31).

Q&A Do the values entered in Step 2 solve the scheduling problem for Kristen?

No. Each coach must be scheduled for 40 hours or less, as indicated by cell B18. The values entered in Step 2 mean that Kristen will spend 110 hours to deliver the scheduled services, as shown in cell D11.

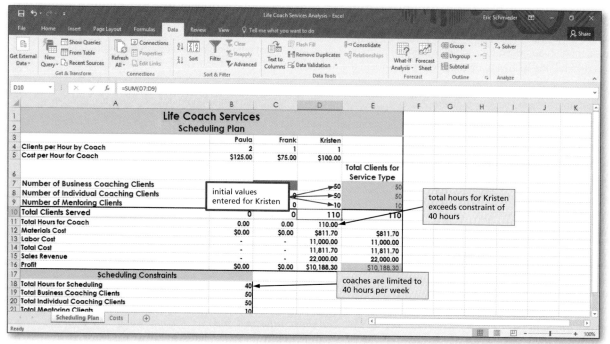

Figure 9–31

3

- Click cell D7 to make it the active cell.

- Type **40** and then press the ENTER key to reduce the number of business coaching clients for Kristen.

- Click cell B7 to make it the active cell. Type **10** and then press the ENTER key to enter the number of business coaching clients to be served by Paula.

- Click an empty cell, in this case cell A6, to view the results (Figure 9–32).

Q&A

Do the values entered in Step 3 solve the scheduling problem for Kristen?

No. The values entered in Step 3 mean that Kristen still needs to allocate 100 hours for coaching clients in her schedule, which is greater than the 40-hour constraint (B18).

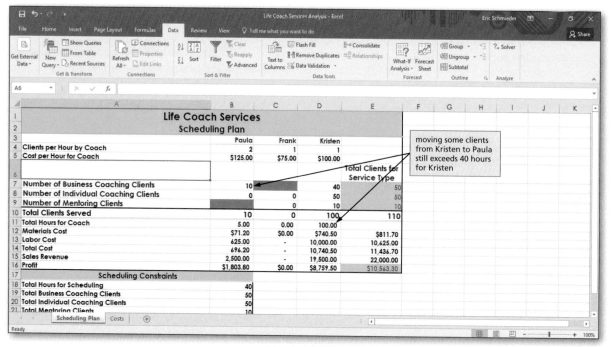

Figure 9–32

4

- Click cell C8 to make it the active cell.

- Enter **20** as the number of individual coaching clients for Frank.

- Enter **30** in cell D8 to reduce the number of individual coaching clients for Kristen.

- Enter **5** in cell C9 as the number of mentoring clients for Frank.

- Enter **5** in cell D9 and then press the ENTER key to reduce the number of mentoring clients for Kristen (Figure 9–33).

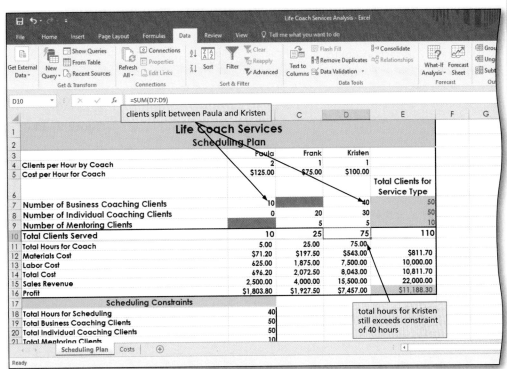

Figure 9–33

Q&A Do the values entered in Step 4 solve the scheduling problem for all the coaches?

No. The scheduled time for Kristen still exceeds the 40-hour scheduling constraint.

What are some problems with using trial and error?

While trial and error can be used on simple problems, it has many limitations when used to solve complex problems. The Scheduling Plan worksheet has seven cells (B7, B8, C8, C9, D7, D8, and D9) that can be adjusted to solve the problem. Endless combinations of values could be entered in those seven cells to try to come up with a solution. Using trial and error, it is difficult to determine if a solution you reach satisfies the goal of minimizing the total cost.

To Use Goal Seek to Attempt to Solve a Complex Problem

1 ANALYZE WORKBOOK FORMULAS | 2 SET DATA VALIDATION RULES | 3 CUSTOMIZE ADD-INS
4 SOLVE COMPLEX PROBLEMS | 5 CREATE & EVALUATE SCENARIOS | 6 PRODUCE REPORTS

The previous set of steps illustrates a situation where Goal Seek may help you to solve a complex problem. The total hours for Kristen, as shown in cell D11, needs to be less than or equal to 40 hours. The formula in cell D11 is =D10/ D4, where D10 is the sum of cells D7:D9. Therefore, D11 depends on cells D7:D9 and cell D4. With Goal Seek, you can manipulate one of these precedent cells to find a solution for cell D11 that meets the 40-hour constraint. Goal seeking will change the value of one cell until the specified goal is met in another cell. You decide to have Goal Seek manipulate cell D8, because Paula is not currently scheduled for individual coaching. Any reduction in Kristen's individual clients would produce an equal increase in Paula's individual clients. In using Goal Seek, you hope that the problem of scheduling the other client types has already been solved.

The following steps use Goal Seek to change the number of individual clients for Kristen to keep the total hours for Kristen at less than or equal to 40.

①

- If necessary, display the Data tab.
- Click the 'What-If Analysis' button (Data tab | Forecast group) to display the What-If Analysis menu (Figure 9–34).

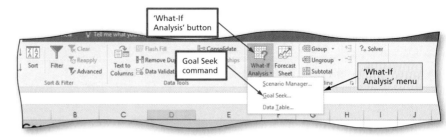

Figure 9–34

②

- Click Goal Seek on the What-If Analysis menu to display the Goal Seek dialog box.
- Type **$D$11** in the Set cell text box (Goal Seek dialog box) to specify which cell should contain the goal value.
- Type **40** in the To value text box as the goal value.
- If necessary, move the Goal Seek dialog box so that cell D8 is visible on the worksheet, click the 'By changing cell' text box, and then click cell D8 to enter its reference in the 'By changing cell' text box (Figure 9–35).

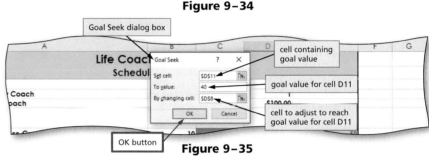

Figure 9–35

③

- Click the OK button (Goal Seek dialog box) to seek the goal of 40 hours in cell D11 and display the Goal Seek Status dialog box, which indicates that goal seeking found a solution (Figure 9–36).

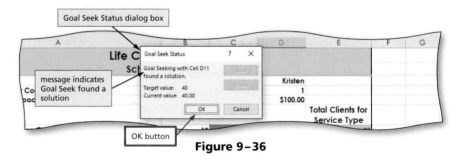

Figure 9–36

④

- Click the OK button (Goal Seek Status dialog box) to close the dialog box and display the updated worksheet.
- Click cell E21 to deselect any other cell (Figure 9–37).

Q&A How can the number of individual coaching clients (cell D8) contain a negative number when data validation rules allow only numbers greater than or equal to zero? Data validation rules are applied only to data that is entered into a cell. Entries that are the result of calculations will not produce a data validation error.

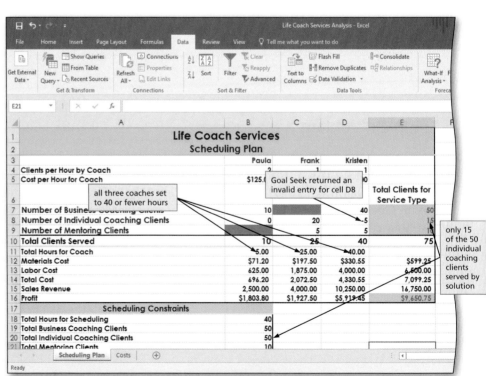

Figure 9–37

To Circle Invalid Data

Why? *The 'Circle Invalid Data' command checks for invalid data entered as the result of a formula or automated tool, such as Goal Seek.* The previous set of steps illustrates how the data validation rules apply only to data directly entered into a cell, not to the results of actions such as Goal Seek. In this case, Goal Seek found a solution that satisfied the criteria specified for the goal, but that solution violated the conditions specified for data validation. It is good practice to check your worksheet for invalid data periodically through use of the 'Circle Invalid Data' command. The following steps check for and circle any invalid data on the Scheduling Plan worksheet.

1

- Click the Data Validation arrow (Data tab | Data Tools group) to display the Data Validation menu (Figure 9–38).

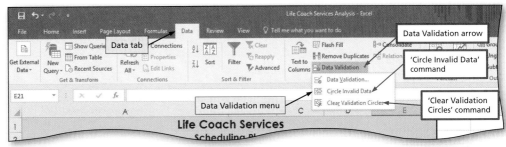

Figure 9–38

2

- Click 'Circle Invalid Data' on the Data Validation menu to place a red validation circle around any invalid data, in this case cell D8 (Figure 9–39).

Q&A
Now that I have identified invalid data, what do I do with that information?
Once you identify invalid data in a worksheet, you should determine how to correct the data.

What are some limitations of using goal seeking?
Goal seeking allows you to manipulate only one cell in order to reach a goal. In this example, to change the total number of hours scheduled for Kristen to 40, the number of individual coaching clients is changed to –5. Goal Seek can produce a result that is acceptable mathematically, but not logically, as is the case here.

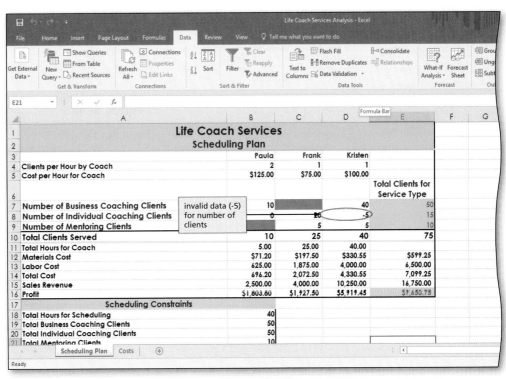

Figure 9–39

To Clear Validation Circles

Why? Once the invalid data has been identified, it is easier to work when the worksheet is clear of extraneous marks. The following step clears the validation circles.

- Click the Data Validation arrow (Data tab | Data Tools group) to display the Data Validation menu.

- Click 'Clear Validation Circles' on the Data Validation menu to remove the red validation circle.

- Select cell E21 to deselect any other cell and then save the workbook (Figure 9–40).

Q&A Has the scheduling problem been solved? No. Although each coach's schedule is meeting the 40-hour constraint, not enough individual clients are being served. (And there is the issue of the invalid data.) But even if all the scheduling constraints were met, you still would have no way of knowing whether the goal to minimize cost (cell E14) has been achieved.

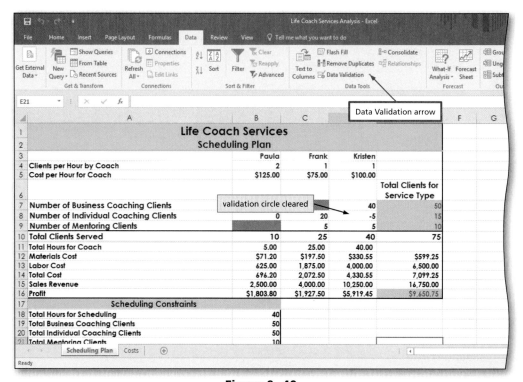

Figure 9–40

Using Solver to Solve Complex Problems

BTW
Solver Requirements
Regardless of the technique Solver uses to solve a problem, it requires three different types of input from the user: the objective, or the result you need for the target cell; variable cells, the values that can change; and constraints, the conditions that the solution has to meet.

Solver allows you to solve complex problems where a number of variables can be changed in a worksheet in order to meet a goal in a particular cell. Unlike Goal Seek, Solver is not restricted to changing one cell at a time and can efficiently evaluate many combinations for a solution.

The technique Solver uses to solve a problem depends on the model that the user selects as best representing the data. For the current scheduling problem, you will use LP Simplex, a technique in Solver associated with linear programming. **Linear programming** is a complex mathematical process used to solve problems that include multiple variables and the minimizing or maximizing of result values. Solver essentially tries as many possible combinations of solutions as it can. On each attempt to solve the problem, Solver checks to see if it has found a solution. The other two techniques are beyond the scope of this book.

In order for Solver to solve the scheduling problem, Solver must modify data until an optimum value is reached for the selected cell. The cells modified by Solver are called **decision variable cells**, also known as changing cells or adjustable cells. In this case, these are cells in the ranges B7:B8, C8:C9, and D7:D9. The cell that Solver is working to optimize, either by finding its maximum or its minimum value, is known as the **objective cell**, or target cell. In this case, Solver is trying to minimize the total cost of providing coaching services, which makes cell E14 the objective or target cell.

Solver will attempt to minimize the value of cell E14 by varying the values in the decision variable, or changing, cells, within the constraints set by Life Coach Services. Figure 9–41a displays the result of using Solver on the Scheduling Plan worksheet.

Constraints are the requirements that have been placed on certain values in the problem and are listed in the requirements document. For example, one constraint is that no coach should be scheduled for more than 40 hours. Other constraints include the types of clients that each coach is certified to work with and the number of each type of client served by Life Coach Services.

When Solver reaches a solution to a problem, it generates an Answer Report. An Answer Report is a worksheet summarizing a Solver calculation. It shows the answer for the target cell, the values used in the changing cells to arrive at that answer, and the constraints that were applied to the calculation. Figure 9–41b shows a Solver Answer Report. By creating an Answer Report, you satisfy the requirement to document the results of the scheduling calculation.

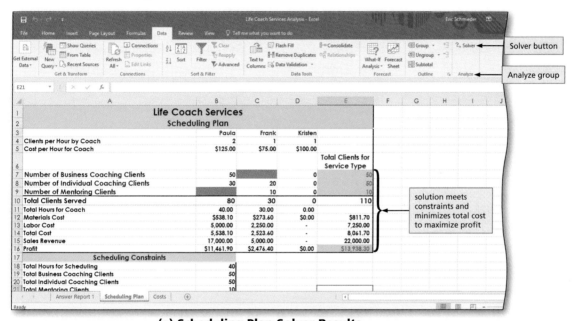

(a) Scheduling Plan Solver Results

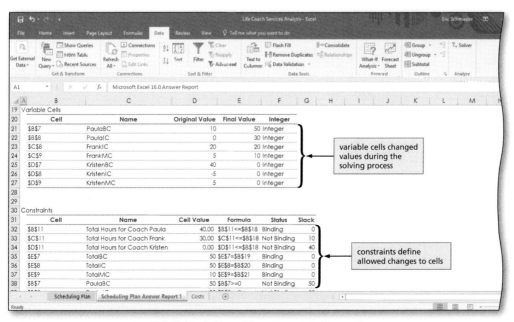

(b) Scheduling Plan Answer Report

Figure 9–41

Note: If the Solver button does not appear on the Data tab, then you must complete the steps earlier in this module to enable the Solver add-in.

To Use Solver to Find the Optimal Solution to a Complex Problem

1 ANALYZE WORKBOOK FORMULAS | 2 SET DATA VALIDATION RULES | 3 CUSTOMIZE ADD-INS
4 SOLVE COMPLEX PROBLEMS | 5 CREATE & EVALUATE SCENARIOS | 6 PRODUCE REPORTS

To solve the scheduling problem for Life Coach Services, you set Solver the goal of minimizing the total cost of the coaching services, shown in cell E14, within the constraints set in the Requirements Document. To accomplish this goal, Solver can modify the number of clients of each type served by each coach (represented by the ranges B7:B8, C8:C9, and D7:D9). *Why use Solver? Solver allows Excel to evaluate multiple combinations of values for changing variables to find an optimal solution to a complex problem.* The constraints are summarized in Table 9–2. The following steps use Solver to find the optimal solution to the scheduling problem in the Scheduling Plan worksheet within the given constraints.

Table 9–2 Constraints for Solver		
Cell or Range	**Operator**	**Constraint**
$B$7:$B$8	>=	0
$B$7:$B$8	int	integer
$C$8:$C$9	>=	0
$C$8:$C$9	int	integer
$D$7:$D$9	>=	0
$D$7:$D$9	int	integer
$E$7	=	$B$19
$E$8	=	$B$20
$E$9	=	$B$21
$B$11	<=	$B$18
$C$11	<=	$B$18
$D$11	<=	$B$18

- Click the Solver button (Data tab | Analyze group) to display the Solver Parameters dialog box.
- Click the Collapse Dialog button in the Set Objective text box to collapse the Solver Parameters dialog box.
- Click cell E14 to set the target cell.
- Click the Expand Dialog button on the right side of the collapsed Solver Parameters dialog box to expand the dialog box (Figure 9–42).

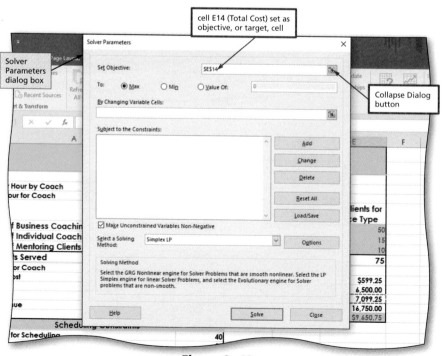

Figure 9–42

2

- Click Min in the To area to specify that the value of the target cell should be as small as possible.

- Click the Collapse Dialog button in the 'By Changing Variable Cells' box to collapse the Solver Parameters dialog box.

- Select the range B7:B8, hold down the CTRL key, and then select the ranges C8:C9 and D7:D9.

- Click the Expand Dialog button on the right side of the collapsed Solver Parameters dialog box to expand the dialog box (Figure 9–43).

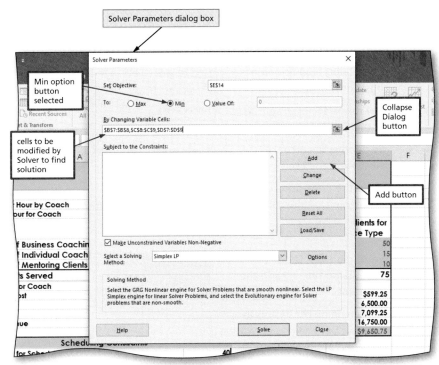

Figure 9–43

3

- Click the Add button to display the Add Constraint dialog box.

- If necessary, move the Add Constraint dialog box so that the range B7:B8 is visible.

- Select the range B7:B8 to set the value of the Cell Reference text box.

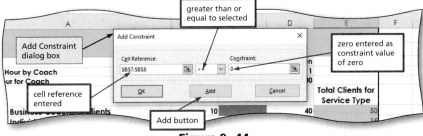

Figure 9–44

- Click the middle arrow and then select >= in the list.

- Type 0 in the Constraint text box to set the constraint on the cells in the range B7:B8 to be greater than or equal to zero (Figure 9–44).

Q&A

How do I use the Constraint text box?

When adding constraints, as shown in Figure 9–44, you first enter a cell reference followed by an operator. If the operator is <=, >=, or =, then you enter the constraint value in the Constraint text box. The constraint can be a value or a cell reference. Other valid operators are int, for an integer value; bin, for cells that contain only one of two values, such as yes/no or true/false; or dif, for an "all different" constraint where no two values are the same.

What do the entries in the Add Constraint dialog box in Figure 9–44 mean?

The entries limit the number of clients served by Paula (cells B7:B8) to a number greater than or equal to zero.

4

- Click the Add button (Add Constraint dialog box) to add a second constraint.

- Select the range B7:B8 to set the value of the Cell Reference box.

- Click the middle box arrow and then select int in the list to set a constraint on the cells in the range B7:B8 to be assigned only integer values (Figure 9–45).

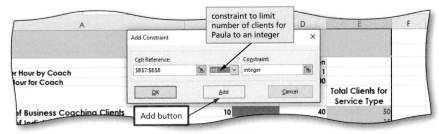

Figure 9–45

- Click the Add button (Add Constraint dialog box) to add a third constraint.

- Select the range C8:C9 to set the value of the Cell Reference box.

- Click the middle box arrow and then select >= in the list.

- Type 0 in the Constraint box to set the constraint on the cells in the range C8:C9 to be greater than or equal to zero (Figure 9–46).

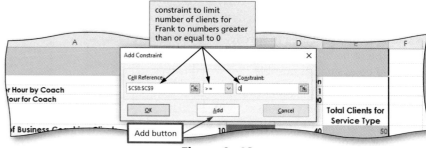

Figure 9–46

- Click the Add button (Add Constraint dialog box) to add the next constraint.

- Enter the remaining constraints as shown in Table 9–2, beginning with the constraints for the range C8:C9.

- After entering the last constraint, click the OK button (Add Constraint dialog box) to close the dialog box and display the Solver Parameters dialog box (Figure 9–47).

Q&A What should I do if a constraint does not match the ones shown in Figure 9–47?
Select the constraint, click the Change button (Solver Parameters dialog box), and then enter the constraints as shown in the table.

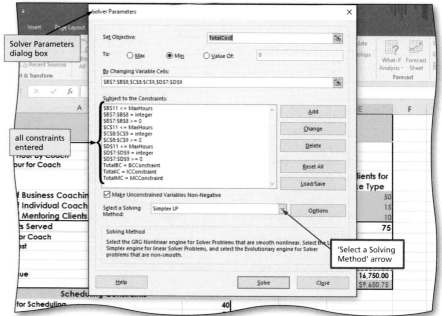

Figure 9–47

7

- If necessary, click Simplex LP in the 'Select a Solving Method' list to select the linear progression method (Figure 9–48).

Q&A What does Simplex LP mean?
LP stands for linear progression, and Simplex refers to the basic problem-solving method used to solve linear problems. Linear problems are ones in which a "straight-line" approach of cause and effect can seek to determine a goal value by modifying values that impact the goal. For example, a decrease in costs results in an increase in profits.

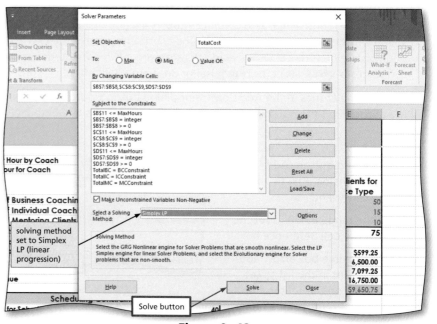

Figure 9–48

- Click the Solve button (Solver Parameters dialog box) to display the Solver Results dialog box, indicating that Solver found a solution to the problem.

- Click Answer in the Reports list to select the type of report to generate (Figure 9–49).

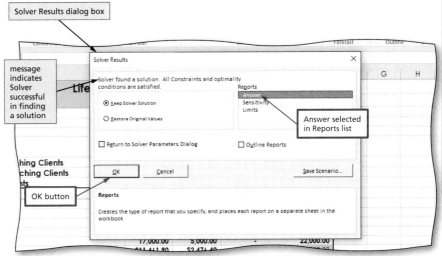

Figure 9–49

- Click the OK button (Solver Results dialog box) to display the values found by Solver and the newly recalculated totals (Figure 9–50).

Q&A What is the result of using Solver?

Solver found a solution to the scheduling problem, shown in Figure 9–50, that meets the constraints and minimizes the total cost of the coaching services. This solution has Paula being assigned 80 clients, Frank being assigned 30 clients, and Kristen not being scheduled with any clients. Paula was assigned so many clients because she can see two clients per hour, so her labor cost is the lowest of all three coaches at $62.50 per client. The other two coaches only see one client per hour and therefore have a higher per client cost.

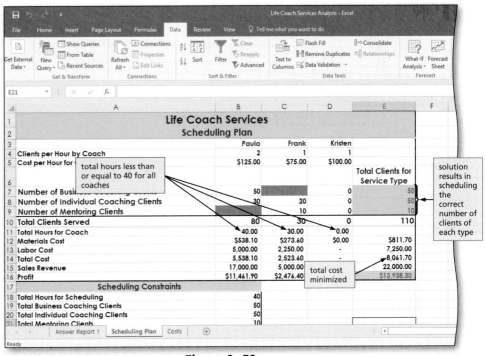

Figure 9–50

To View the Solver Answer Report

1 ANALYZE WORKBOOK FORMULAS | 2 SET DATA VALIDATION RULES | 3 CUSTOMIZE ADD-INS
4 SOLVE COMPLEX PROBLEMS | 5 CREATE & EVALUATE SCENARIOS | 6 PRODUCE REPORTS

Solver generates the requested Answer Report on a separate worksheet after it finds a solution. The Answer Report summarizes the problem that you have presented to Solver. It shows the original and final values of the target, or objective, cell along with the original and final values of the changing cells (decision variable cells) that Solver modified to find the answer. Additionally, it lists all of the constraints that you entered.

Why view the Answer Report generated by Solver? The Answer Report documents that a particular problem has been solved correctly. Because it lists all of the relevant information in a concise format, you can use the Answer Report to make certain that you have entered all of the constraints and allowed Solver to modify all the necessary values to solve the problem. You also can use the report to reconstruct the Solver model in the future.

The following steps view the Solver Answer Report.

1

- Click the Answer Report 1 sheet tab to display the Solver Answer Report (Figure 9–51).

  If requested by your instructor, add the name of your hometown in cell A3, following the content already in that cell.

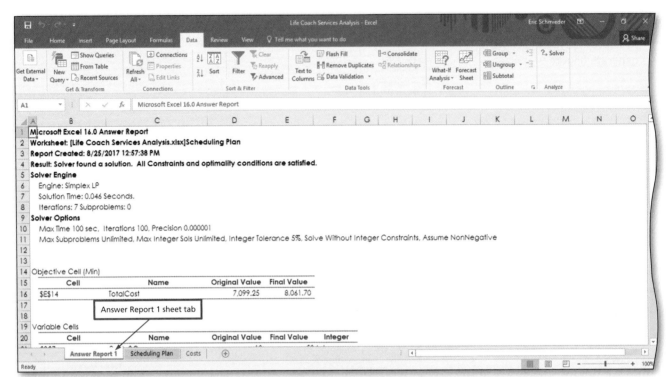

Figure 9–51

2

- Drag the Answer Report 1 sheet tab to the right of the Scheduling Plan sheet tab to move the worksheet in the workbook.

- Double-click the Answer Report 1 sheet tab to select the name.

- Type `Scheduling Plan Answer Report 1` and then press the ENTER key to rename the worksheet.

- Change the color of the sheet tab to 'Red, Accent 5' (column 9, row 1).

- Scroll down to view the remaining cells of the Answer Report (Figure 9–52).

- Save the workbook again on the same storage location with the same file name.

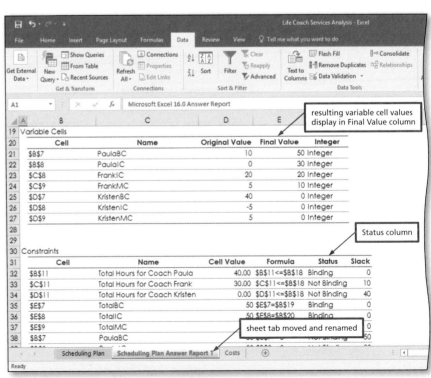

Figure 9–52

Working with Solver Options

When you selected the Simplex LP method of solving the production problem
in the Solver Parameters dialog box, you selected a linear programming method that
assumes the problem follows a cause and effect relationship, by which changes to one
value have a direct impact on another value. After choosing the Solver method, you
can select various options to further configure the inner workings of Solver. Note that
Excel saves the most recently used Solver parameters and options. Discussion of many
of these parameters is beyond the scope of this book. Table 9–3 presents some of the
more commonly used Solver options.

BTW
Viewing Other
Solutions
If you want to view solutions
other than the one Solver
identifies as optimal, select
the Show Iteration Results
check box in the Solver
Parameters dialog box. After
each iteration, the Show Trial
Solution dialog box will be
displayed and you will have
the option of saving that
scenario and then stopping
Solver or continuing on to
the next solution.

Table 9–3 Commonly Used Solver Parameters	
Parameter	**Meaning**
Max Time	The total time that Solver should spend trying different solutions, expressed in seconds
Iterations	The number of possible answer combinations that Solver should try
Constraint Precision	Instructs Solver in how close it must come to the target value in order to consider the problem to be solved. For example, if the target value is 100 and and you set tolerance to 5%, then generating a solution with a target value of 95 is acceptable
Use Automatic Scaling	Selected by default, automatic scaling specifies that Solver should internally rescale values of variables, restraints, and the objective to reduce the effect of outlying values.

When using Solver, three issues must be kept in mind. First, some problems
do not have solutions. The constraints may be constructed in such a way that Solver
cannot find an answer that satisfies all of the constraints. Second, sometimes multiple
answers solve the same problem. Solver does not indicate when this is the case, and you
will have to use your own judgment to determine if you should seek another solution.
As long as you are confident that you have given Solver all of the constraints for a
problem, however, all answers should be equally valid. Finally, if Solver fails to find a
solution, more time or more iterations may be required to solve the problem.

Break Point: If you wish to take a break, this is a good place to do so. You can now exit Excel. To resume at a later time, run
Excel, open the file called Life Coach Services Analysis, and continue following the steps from this location forward.

Using Scenarios and Scenario Manager to Analyze Data

Scenarios are named combinations of values, or what-if assumptions, that are
assigned to variables in a model. In this project, you will create different scheduling
plans—scenarios—based on different assumptions. For example, you have created a
scheduling plan that required distributing 50 business coaching clients, 50 individual
coaching clients, and 10 mentoring clients among three coaches while not exceeding
40 hours for any coach. Changing the number of clients in any or all of the categories

BTW
Naming Cell Ranges
Naming ranges for use with input variables is helpful when dealing with multiple input variables. Assign names to all the input variables before creating your first scenario. Named ranges will make scenario reports easier to understand and interpret.

would create a new scenario. Each set of values in these examples represents a what-if assumption. You use the Scenario Manager to keep track of various scenarios, and produce a report detailing the what-if assumptions and results for each scenario.

The primary uses of the Scenario Manager are to:

1. Create different scenarios with multiple sets of changing cells;
2. Build summary worksheets that contain the different scenarios; and
3. View the results of each scenario on your worksheet.

You will use the Scenario Manager for each of these three applications. After you create the scenarios, you will instruct Excel to build the summary worksheets, including a Scenario Summary worksheet and a Scenario PivotTable worksheet.

To Save the Current Data as a Scenario

1 ANALYZE WORKBOOK FORMULAS | 2 SET DATA VALIDATION RULES | 3 CUSTOMIZE ADD-INS
4 SOLVE COMPLEX PROBLEMS | 5 CREATE & EVALUATE SCENARIOS | 6 PRODUCE REPORTS

Why? *The current data on the Scheduling Plan worksheet consists of constraints and the values that correctly solve the scheduling problem.* These values can be saved as a scenario named Schedule 1 that can be accessed later or compared with other scenarios. The following steps save the current data for the Schedule 1 scenario using the Scenario Manager dialog box.

- Make Scheduling Plan the active sheet.
- Click the 'What-If Analysis' button (Data tab | Forecast group) to display the What-If Analysis menu (Figure 9–53).

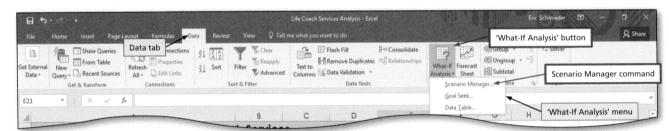

Figure 9–53

- Click Scenario Manager on the What-If Analysis menu to display the Scenario Manager dialog box, which indicates that no scenarios are defined (Figure 9–54).

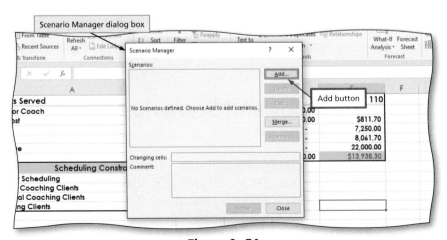

Figure 9–54

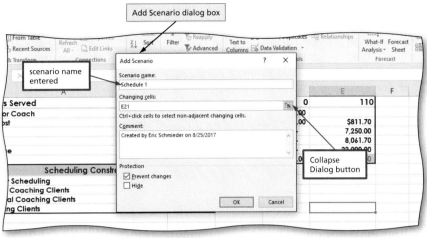

3

- Click the Add button (Scenario Manager dialog box) to open the Add Scenario dialog box.

- Type **Schedule 1** in the Scenario name text box (Add Scenario dialog box) to provide a name for the scenario (Figure 9–55).

Figure 9–55

4

- Click the Collapse Dialog button (Add Scenario dialog box) to collapse the dialog box.

- Select the range B7:B8, type , (comma), select the ranges C8:C9, type , (comma), select D7:D9, type , (comma), and then select B18:B21 to enter the ranges in the Changing cells box (Figure 9–56).

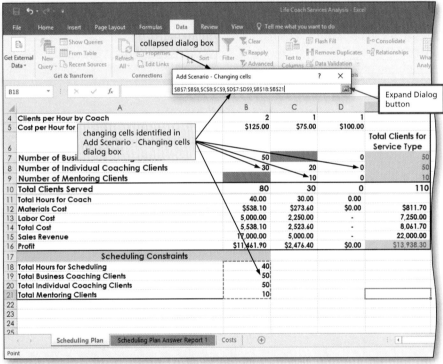

Figure 9–56

5

- Click the Expand Dialog button (Add Scenario dialog box) to display the Edit Scenario dialog box (Figure 9–57).

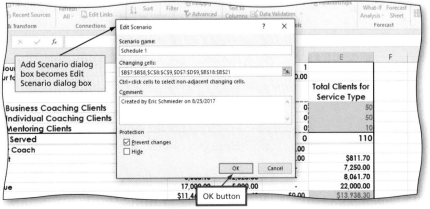

Figure 9–57

- Click the OK button (Edit Scenario dialog box) to accept the settings and display the Scenario Values dialog box (Figure 9–58).

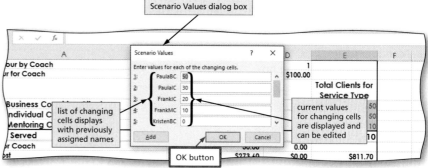

Figure 9–58

- Click the OK button (Scenario Values dialog box) to display the Scenario Manager dialog box with the Schedule 1 scenario selected in the Scenarios list (Figure 9–59).

Q&A

What can I do with the scenario?
After the scenario has been saved, you can recall it at any time using the Scenario Manager. In Figure 9–58, the values of the changing cells in the Scenario Values dialog box default to the current values in the worksheet. By changing the text boxes next to the cell names, you can save the scenario using values different from the current values.

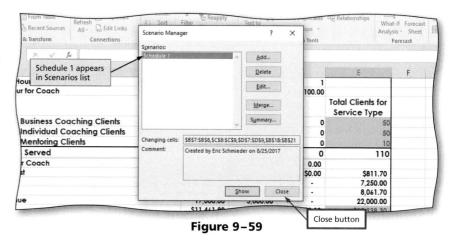

Figure 9–59

8

- Click the Close button (Scenario Manager dialog box) to save the Schedule 1 scenario in the workbook.

Adding Data for a New Scenario

BTW

Baseline Scenarios
For each model, it is helpful to define a baseline scenario that represents the starting assumptions. Even if the results of the baseline scenario do not figure prominently in the final analysis, they represent the starting point and should be saved.

After saving the Schedule 1 scenario, you will enter the data for the Schedule 2 scenario directly in the worksheet and then use Solver to solve the Schedule 2 scenario in the same way that you solved the Schedule 1 scenario. Because both scenarios are based on the same model, you do not need to reenter the constraints into the Scenario Manager. The Answer Report meets the requirement that you create supporting documentation for your answer.

To Add the Data for a New Scenario

The constraints for the Schedule 2 scenario require that 75 business coaching clients, 75 individual coaching clients, and 20 mentoring clients be served without exceeding 50 hours for any coach. These values must be entered into the appropriate cells before you can use Solver. The following steps add the data for a new scenario.

1 Click cell B18 and then type **50** as the maximum hours for scheduling.

2 Click cell B19 and then type **75** as the number of business coaching clients.

3 Click cell B20 and then type **75** as the number of individual coaching clients.

4 Click cell B21, type **20** as the number of mentoring clients, and then click cell E21 to deselect cell B21 (Figure 9–60).

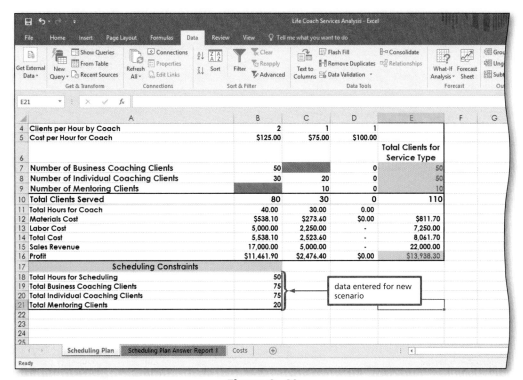

Figure 9–60

To Use Solver to Find a New Solution

1 ANALYZE WORKBOOK FORMULAS | 2 SET DATA VALIDATION RULES | 3 CUSTOMIZE ADD-INS
4 SOLVE COMPLEX PROBLEMS | 5 CREATE & EVALUATE SCENARIOS | 6 PRODUCE REPORTS

Why? *After entering the new values, the total number of clients shown in the range E7:E9 no longer satisfies the scheduling constraints for the Schedule 2 scenario.* You now must use Solver to determine if a solution exists for the constraints of Schedule 2. The following steps use Solver to seek a solution.

1

• Click the Solver button (Data tab | Analyze group) to display the Solver Parameters dialog box with the objective cell, changing cells, and constraints used with the previous scenario (Figure 9–61).

Q&A Why am I not updating the constraints?

When you set up the constraints in Solver for Schedule 1, you used cell references rather than actual values for the number of each type of client. Entering the new values in cells B18:B21 automatically updated the constraints.

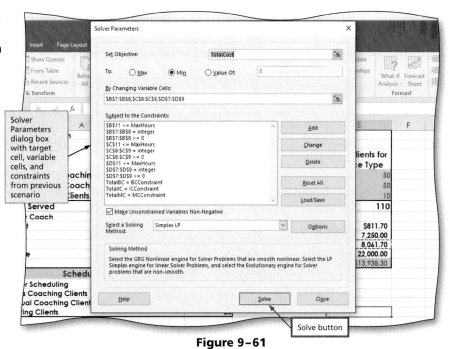

Figure 9–61

- Click the Solve button (Solver Parameters dialog box) to solve the problem using Solver and display the Solver Results dialog box.

- Click Answer in the Reports list to select a report type (Figure 9–62).

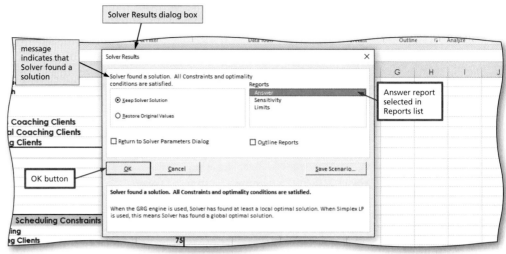

Figure 9–62

- Click the OK button (Solver Results dialog box) to display the solution found by Solver (Figure 9–63).

Q&A

What did Solver accomplish?

As shown in Figure 9–63, Solver found a solution that satisfies all of the constraints and minimizes the total cost. In this new scenario, total cost will be $13,293.65.

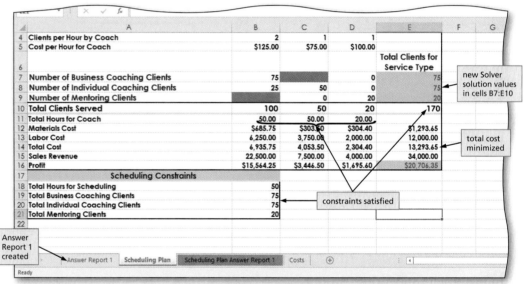

Figure 9–63

To View the Solver Answer Report for the Schedule 2 Solution

1 ANALYZE WORKBOOK FORMULAS | 2 SET DATA VALIDATION RULES | 3 CUSTOMIZE ADD-INS
4 SOLVE COMPLEX PROBLEMS | 5 CREATE & EVALUATE SCENARIOS | **6 PRODUCE REPORTS**

Why? *Viewing the answer report allows you to compare the results of the Schedule 1 and Schedule 2 solutions.* The next step views the Answer Report for the Schedule 2 solution.

- Drag the Answer Report 1 sheet tab to the right of the Scheduling Plan Answer Report 1 sheet tab to move the worksheet.

- Rename the Answer Report 1 worksheet as `Scheduling Plan Answer Report 2`.

- Change the sheet tab color to 'Red, Accent 6' (column 10, row 1).

- Scroll down to view the remaining cells of the Schedule 2 Answer Report (Figure 9–64).

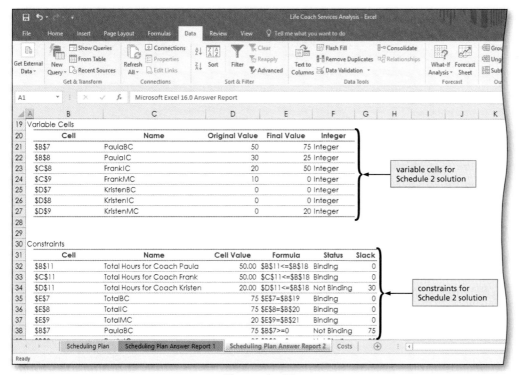

Figure 9–64

To Save the Second Solver Solution as a Scenario

1 ANALYZE WORKBOOK FORMULAS | 2 SET DATA VALIDATION RULES | 3 CUSTOMIZE ADD-INS
4 SOLVE COMPLEX PROBLEMS | 5 CREATE & EVALUATE SCENARIOS | 6 PRODUCE REPORTS

Why? *With a second scenario created, you can begin to take advantage of the Scenario Manager.* The Scenario Manager allows you to compare multiple scenarios side by side. In order to use the Scenario Manager for this, you first must save the second Solver solution as a scenario. The following steps save the second Solver solution as a scenario.

- Make Scheduling Plan the active worksheet.

- Click the 'What-If Analysis' button (Data tab | Forecast group) to display the What-If Analysis menu (Figure 9–65).

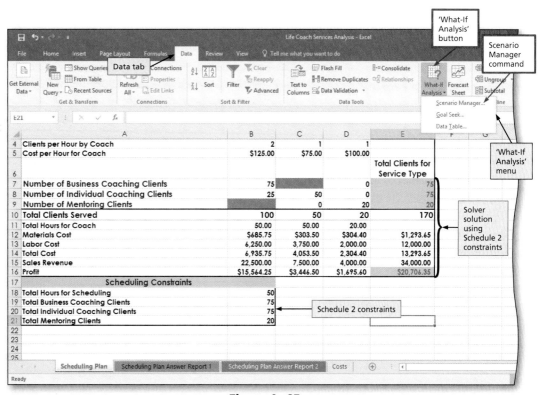

Figure 9–65

2

- Click Scenario Manager on the What-If Analysis menu to display the Scenario Manager dialog box (Figure 9–66).

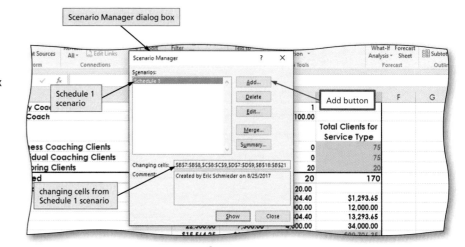

Figure 9–66

3

- Click the Add button (Scenario Manager dialog box) to display the Add Scenario dialog box.

- Type **Schedule 2** in the Scenario name text box to name the new scenario (Figure 9–67).

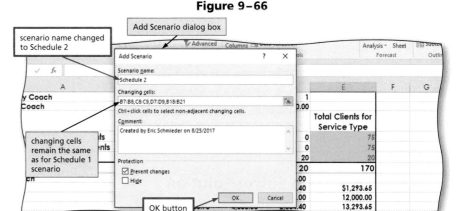

Figure 9–67

4

- Click the OK button (Add Scenario dialog box) to display the Scenario Values dialog box with the current values from the worksheet (Figure 9–68).

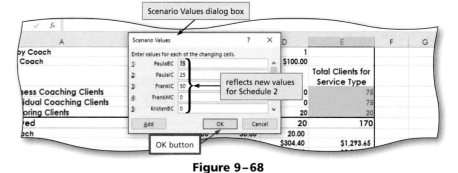

Figure 9–68

5

- Click the OK button (Scenario Values dialog box) to display the updated Scenarios list in the Scenario Manager dialog box (Figure 9–69).

6

- Click the Close button (Scenario Manager dialog box) to save the Schedule 2 scenario and close the dialog box.

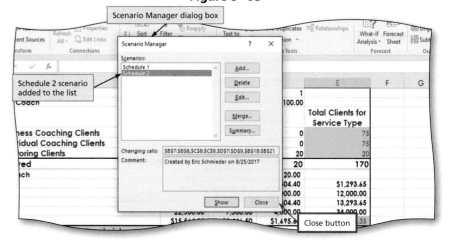

Figure 9–69

To Show a Saved Scenario

Why? *You can display and review any scenario in the workbook by using the Show button in the Scenario Manager dialog box.* The following steps display the Schedule 1 scenario created earlier.

- Click the 'What-If Analysis' button (Data tab | Forecast group) to display the What-If Analysis menu.

- Click Scenario Manager on the What-If Analysis menu to display the Scenario Manager dialog box.

- Click the scenario of interest, Schedule 1 in this case, to select it (Figure 9–70).

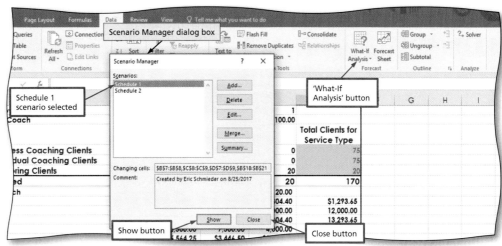

Figure 9–70

- Click the Show button (Scenario Manager dialog box) to display the data for the selected scenario in the worksheet.

- Click the Close button (Scenario Manager dialog box) to close the dialog box (Figure 9–71).

Q&A

Do I have to use the Scenario Manager to switch between scenarios?

Once you have viewed two or more scenarios consecutively, you can use the Undo and Redo commands to switch between them as an alternative to using the Scenario Manager.

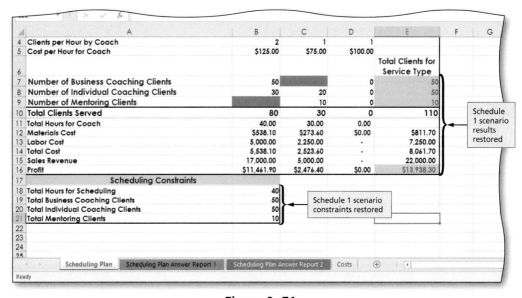

Figure 9–71

Summarizing Scenarios

You can create a Scenario Summary worksheet or a Scenario PivotTable worksheet to review and analyze various what-if scenarios when making decisions. A Scenario Summary worksheet, generated by the Scenario Manager, is a worksheet in outline format (Figure 9–72a) that you can print and manipulate just like any other worksheet. Module 6 presented skills that you can use to manipulate outline features for information presentation.

BTW
**Scenario Summary
Details**
Clicking the show detail
button on the Scenario
Summary worksheet will
display any information
entered in the Comments
box of the Scenario Manager
dialog box, along with
creation and modification
information.

The Scenario PivotTable worksheet (Figure 9–72b) generated by the Scenario Manager also is a worksheet that you can print and manipulate like other worksheets. PivotTables summarize large amounts of data, and can be rearranged and regrouped to show the data in various forms. Module 8 presented skills that can be used to analyze summary data using PivotTables. The Scenario PivotTable worksheet allows you to compare the results of multiple scenarios.

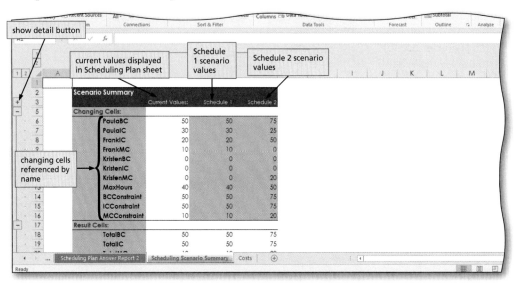

(a) Scheduling Scenario Summary

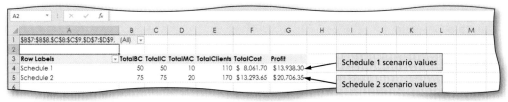

(b) Scheduling Scenario PivotTable

Figure 9–72

To Create a Scenario Summary Worksheet

1 ANALYZE WORKBOOK FORMULAS | 2 SET DATA VALIDATION RULES | 3 CUSTOMIZE ADD-INS
4 SOLVE COMPLEX PROBLEMS | 5 CREATE & EVALUATE SCENARIOS | 6 PRODUCE REPORTS

Why? A Scenario Summary worksheet is a useful decision-making tool. The Scenario Summary worksheet in Figure 9–72a shows the number of each type of coaching service scheduled and total cost of the scheduled services for the current worksheet values and the Schedule 1 and Schedule 2 scenarios. The optimal number of each type of service to be scheduled for each coach, as calculated by Solver, is shown for both scheduling plans. The following steps create a Scenario Summary worksheet.

- Click the 'What-If Analysis' button (Data tab | Forecast group) to display the What-If Analysis menu.

- Click Scenario Manager on the What-If Analysis menu to display the Scenario Manager dialog box (Figure 9–73).

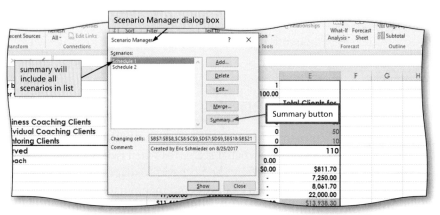

Figure 9–73

- Click the Summary button (Scenario Manager dialog box) to display the Scenario Summary dialog box.

- Click the Collapse Dialog button (Scenario Summary dialog box) and then select the cells E7:E10, E14, and E16. (You can use CTRL+click to select multiple cells or add commas in between selecting each range or cell.)

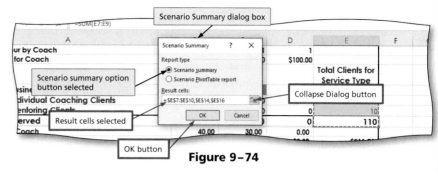

Figure 9–74

- Click the Expand Dialog button to return to the Scenario Summary dialog box (Figure 9–74).

- Click the OK button (Scenario Summary dialog box) to generate a Scenario Summary report.

- Rename the Scenario Summary worksheet as **Scheduling Scenario Summary** to provide a descriptive name for the sheet.

- Change the sheet tab color to 'Gray-80%, Text 2' (column 4, row 1).

- Drag the Scheduling Scenario Summary sheet tab to the right of the Scheduling Plan Answer Report 2 sheet tab to reposition the worksheet in the workbook (Figure 9–75).

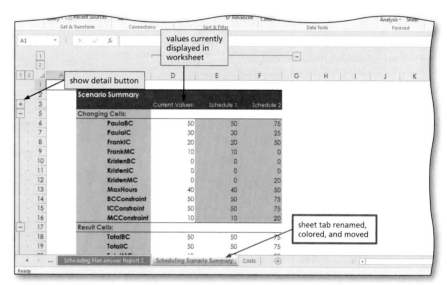

Figure 9–75

Q&A | What is shown in the Scheduling Scenario Summary worksheet?

The Scheduling Scenario Summary worksheet shows the current values in the Scheduling Plan worksheet next to the results of any scenarios you have created. In Figure 9–75, current values are shown in column D, and scenarios Schedule 1 and Schedule 2 are shown side by side (in columns E and F) allowing you to compare results and determine the best available option.

Working with an Outlined Worksheet

Excel automatically outlines the Scheduling Scenario Summary worksheet. The symbols for expanding and collapsing the rows appear above and to the left of the worksheet. You can hide or display levels of detail by using the hide detail and show detail symbols. You can also use the row- and column-level show detail buttons to collapse or expand rows and columns.

The outline feature is especially useful when working with very large worksheets. With smaller worksheets, the feature may not provide any real benefits. You can remove an outline by clicking the Ungroup arrow (Data tab | Outline group) and then clicking Clear Outline on the Ungroup menu.

EX 544 **Excel Module 9** Formula Auditing, Data Validation, and Complex Problem Solving

1 ANALYZE WORKBOOK FORMULAS | 2 SET DATA VALIDATION RULES | 3 CUSTOMIZE ADD-INS
4 SOLVE COMPLEX PROBLEMS | 5 CREATE & EVALUATE SCENARIOS | **6 PRODUCE REPORTS**

To Create a Scenario PivotTable Worksheet

Excel also can create a Scenario PivotTable report worksheet to help analyze and compare the results of multiple scenarios. *Why create a Scenario PivotTable report worksheet? A Scenario PivotTable report worksheet gives you the ability to summarize the scenario data and reorganize the rows and columns to obtain different views of the summarized data.* The Scenario PivotTable summarizes the Schedule 1 and Schedule 2 scenarios and displays the result cells for the two scenarios for easy comparison. The following steps create the Scenario PivotTable worksheet.

1

- Click the Scheduling Plan sheet tab to make Scheduling Plan the active worksheet. You may have to scroll through the sheet tabs to locate the worksheet.

- Click the 'What-If Analysis' button (Data tab | Forecast group) to display the What-If Analysis menu.

- Click Scenario Manager on the What-If Analysis menu to display the Scenario Manager dialog box (Figure 9–76).

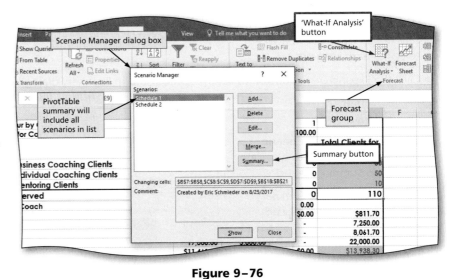

Figure 9–76

2

- Click the Summary button (Scenario Manager dialog box) to display the Scenario Summary dialog box.

- Click 'Scenario PivotTable report' in the Report type area (Scenario Summary dialog box) (Figure 9–77).

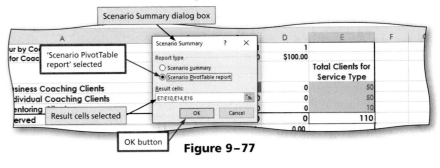

Figure 9–77

3

- Click the OK button to create the Scenario PivotTable (Figure 9–78).

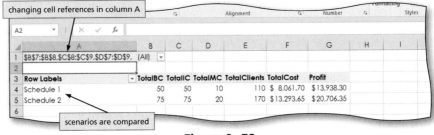

Figure 9–78

4

- Rename the Scenario PivotTable worksheet as `Scheduling Scenario PivotTable` to provide a descriptive name for the worksheet.

- Change the sheet tab color for the Scheduling Scenario PivotTable worksheet to 'Dark Teal, Accent 1' (column 5, row 1).

- Drag the Scheduling Scenario PivotTable sheet tab to the right of the Scheduling Scenario Summary sheet tab to reposition the worksheet in the workbook.

- Format cells F4:G5 using the Accounting number format.

- Click cell A2 to deselect any other cell.

- If necessary, close the PivotTable Fields task pane (Figure 9–79).

How can I use the PivotTable?
After creating the PivotTable, you can treat it like any other worksheet. Thus, you can print or chart a PivotTable. If you update the data in one of the scenarios, click the Refresh All button (Data tab | Connections group) to update the PivotTable. Note that if you merely change values on a scenario worksheet, it is not the same as changing the scenario. If you want to change the data in a scenario, you must enter the new data using the Scenario Manager.

❺

- Save the workbook and exit Excel.

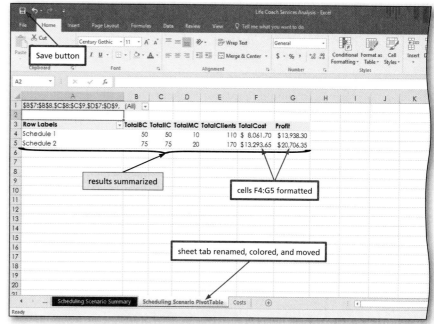

Figure 9–79

Summary

In this module, you learned how to analyze a worksheet using formula auditing techniques and tracer arrows. You established data validation rules, and informed users about the validation rules. You solved a complex problem with Excel, including using trial and error, goal seeking, and Solver. You used the Scenario Manager to manage different problems on the same worksheet, and then summarized the results of the scenarios with a Scenario Summary worksheet and a Scenario PivotTable worksheet.

CONSIDER THIS: PLAN AHEAD

What decisions will you need to make when creating your next worksheet to solve a complex problem?
Use these guidelines as you complete the assignments in this module and create your own worksheets for evaluating and analyzing data outside of this class.

1. Review and analyze workbook structure and organization.
   a) Review all formulas.
   b) Use precedent and dependent tracing to determine dependencies.
   c) Use formula auditing tools to correct formula errors.
2. Establish data validation rules.
   a) Identify changing cells.
   b) Determine data restrictions to address using data validation.
3. Configure useful add-ins.
   a) Identify missing add-ins.
   b) Use Excel Options to enable necessary add-ins.
   c) Verify inclusion on the ribbon.
4. Determine strategies for problem solving.
   a) Use trial and error to modify input or changing values.
   b) Use Goal Seek.
   c) Use Solver to address multiple constraints and changing cells.
5. Create and store scenarios.
   a) Use the Scenario Manager to keep track of multiple scenarios.
   b) Use a Scenario Summary worksheet to present and compare multiple scenarios.
   c) Use a Scenario PivotTable report to manipulate and interpret scenario results.

Apply Your Knowledge

Reinforce the skills and apply the concepts you learned in this module.

Calculating Vehicles for a Shipment

Note: To complete this assignment, you will be required to use the Data Files. Please contact your instructor for information about accessing the Data Files.

Instructions: Run Excel. Open the workbook Apply 9-1 American Auto Imports LLC from the Data Files and then save the workbook as Apply 9-1 American Auto Imports LLC Complete.

American Auto Imports LLC ships automobiles from various European nations for resale in North America. Vehicles are shipped to the North American distribution hub in standard shipping containers with a maximum capacity of 800 cubic feet. Use Solver to find the optimal mix of vehicles so that each shipment includes at least one of each type of vehicle and no more than four of Vehicle 2. Maximize total profit for the shipment. Figure 9–80 shows the completed Costs and Shipping worksheet.

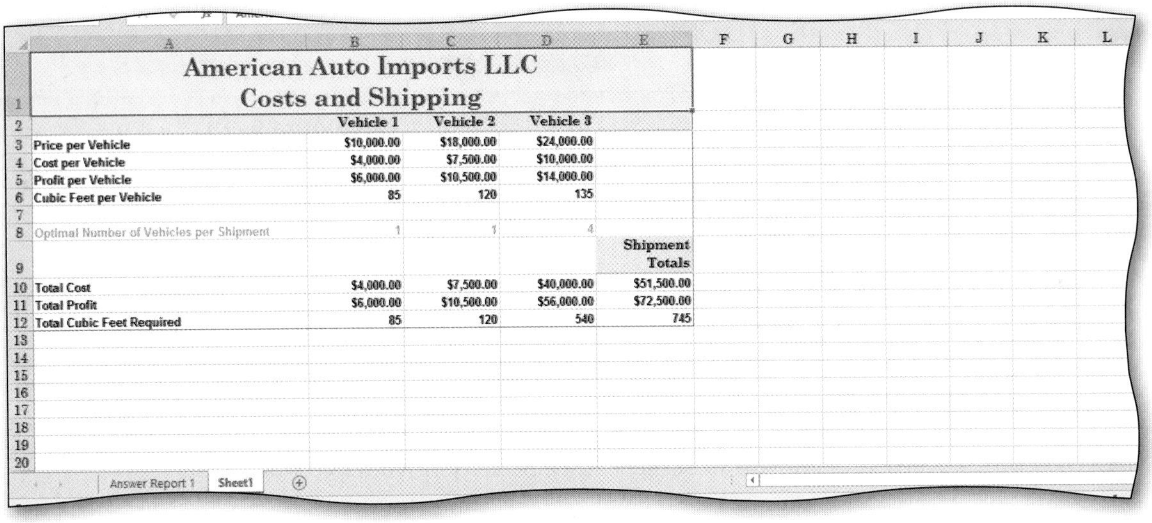

	A	B	C	D	E
1	American Auto Imports LLC				
2	Costs and Shipping	Vehicle 1	Vehicle 2	Vehicle 3	
3	Price per Vehicle	$10,000.00	$18,000.00	$24,000.00	
4	Cost per Vehicle	$4,000.00	$7,500.00	$10,000.00	
5	Profit per Vehicle	$6,000.00	$10,500.00	$14,000.00	
6	Cubic Feet per Vehicle	85	120	135	
7					
8	Optimal Number of Vehicles per Shipment	1	1	4	
9					Shipment Totals
10	Total Cost	$4,000.00	$7,500.00	$40,000.00	$51,500.00
11	Total Profit	$6,000.00	$10,500.00	$56,000.00	$72,500.00
12	Total Cubic Feet Required	85	120	540	745

Answer Report 1 | Sheet1

Figure 9–80

Perform the following tasks:

1. Use Solver to find a solution to the problem so that the Total Profit on the shipment (cell E11) is maximized. Allow Solver to change cells B8, C8, and D8. The results in cells B8, C8, and D8 should be integer values. Add constraints to Solver to limit the number of vehicles to no more than four of Vehicle 2 and to include at least one of each vehicle type. The Total Cubic Feet Required (cell E12) should be limited to no more than 800 to accommodate the maximum volume constraint. Use the Simplex LP option in Solver. Solver should find the answer as shown in Figure 9–80.

2. Instruct Solver to create the Answer Report for your solution.

3. Trace precedents for cell E12 by clicking the Trace Precedents button (Formulas tab | Formula Auditing group) two times. Remove the precedent arrows. Trace dependents for cell C8 by clicking the Trace Dependents button (Formulas tab | Formula Auditing group) two times. Remove the dependent arrows.

4. Use the Watch Window to monitor cells E10:E12. Change values in the range B8:D8 and view changes in the Watch Window. Close the Watch Window.

5. If requested by your instructor, add the month and year of your birth to the end of the first line in cell A1.

6. Save the workbook. Submit the revised workbook in the format specified by your instructor.

7. ❋ How would you adjust the constraints to further investigate maximizing total profit? Which constraints would you change and why?

Extend Your Knowledge

Extend the skills you learned in this module and experiment with new skills. You may need to use Help to complete the assignment.

Working with Data Validation Rules

Note: To complete this assignment, you will be required to use the Data Files. Please contact your instructor for information about accessing the Data Files.

Instructions: Run Excel. Open the workbook Extend 9-1 Travel League Registration and then save the workbook as Extend 9-1 Travel League Registration Complete.

You have been asked to create data validation rules in an Excel worksheet that calculates registration fees for a travel league program that runs three leagues: baseball/softball, football, and soccer. These leagues are popular and space is limited, so players are restricted to one league per year. Registration fees vary according to the league. The league provides some add-on services such as equipment and private coaching. They also offer a discount for registrations paid in full when registering. Figure 9–81 shows the completed League Registration worksheet.

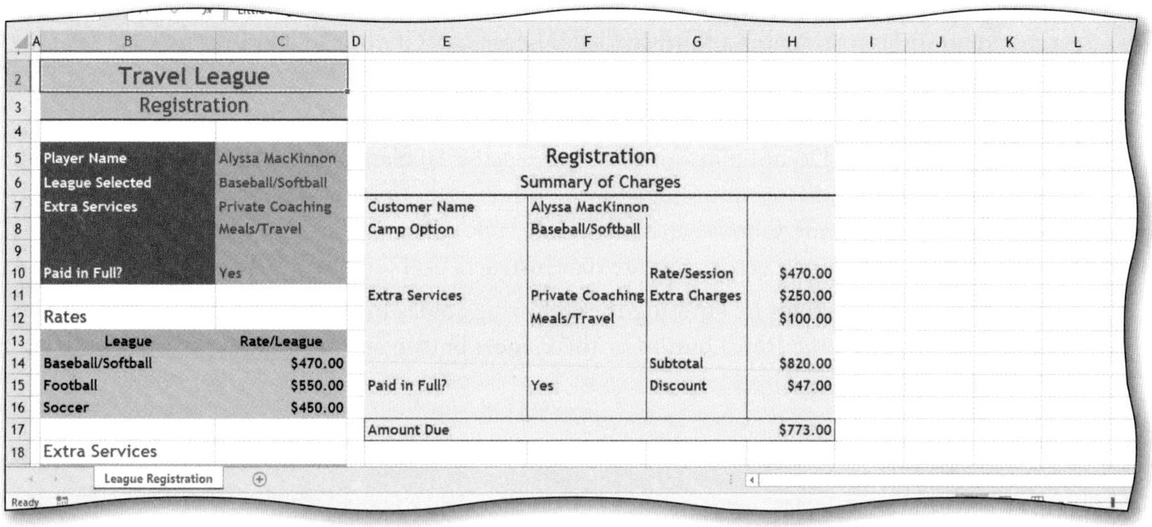

Figure 9–81

Perform the following tasks:

1. In cell C5 on the League Registration worksheet, enter a data validation rule that allows users to enter any value. Use the following:

   Input message title: Player Name

   Input message: Please enter the player's full name.

   Error alert title: Input Error

   Error message: Enter player name.

   Error alert style: Stop

2. In cell C6, enter a data validation rule that requires users to select a league from a list. Allow users to select the data from a list of leagues, which is contained in the range B14:B16. Do not allow users to leave cell C6 blank. Use the following for data validation:

   Input message title: Which League?

   Input message: Click the arrow to select the desired league.

   Error alert title: Invalid League

   Error message: Select Baseball/Softball, Football, or Soccer from the list.

   Error alert style: Stop

Continued >

Extend Your Knowledge *continued*

3. In cell C7, enter another data validation rule that allows users to select a valid entry from a list of extra services, which are included in cells B20:B22. These are optional services, so you can allow users to leave cell C7 blank. For the input message, use an appropriate title and display text that reminds users to enter the first extra service the customer needs. Choose a style of error alert considering that if users enter a service, they must select one of the three services in the list. Enter an appropriate error alert title and an error message that instructs users to select a service from the list.

4. In cell C8, enter a data validation rule that uses the custom formula =AND(C8<>C7,C8<>C9) as its validation criteria to verify that the value entered in cell C8 is not the same as the value in cell C7 or C9. For the input message, use an appropriate title and display text that reminds users to enter a second service if desired. Choose a style of error alert considering that if users enter a second service, they must enter one of the three services not already entered. Enter an appropriate error alert title and an error message.

5. In cell C9, enter a data validation rule that uses a custom formula similar to the one you entered for cell C8. This formula, however, should verify that the value entered in cell C9 is not the same as the value in cell C7 or C8. For the input message, use an appropriate title and display text that reminds users to enter a third service if necessary. Choose an appropriate style of error, error alert title, and error message.

6. In cell C10, enter a data validation rule that instructs users to enter Yes if paying at time of registration, No if not. Do not allow users to leave cell C10 blank. Use Payment as the input message title and enter an input message that reminds users to enter Yes if paying at time of registration, and No if not. Choose an appropriate style of error alert. Use Invalid Entry as the error alert title and enter an error message that instructs users to enter Yes or No.

7. Test the data validation rules by entering the following values in the specified cells. If an error message appears, Click the Retry button or the Cancel button and then enter valid data.
   C5: Alyssa MacKinnon
   C6: Baseball/Softball
   C7: Private Coaching
   C8: Meals/Travel
   C9:
   C10: Yes

8. If requested by your instructor, enter the following text in cell E20: **Registered by <yourname>**, substituting your initials for <yourname>.

9. Save the workbook. Submit the revised workbook in the format specified by your instructor.

10. ✸ The range C7:C9 used two different approaches to prompting users for information, selecting from a list or typing information based on a screen prompt. Which do you think is more effective, and why? List a weakness of the approach you feel is more effective.

Expand Your World

Create a solution that uses cloud and web technologies by learning and investigating on your own from general guidance.

Add-ins for Excel Online

Problem: You use Excel Online through your OneDrive account and understand that there are limitations to the online versions of the Office apps compared to the desktop applications, but are interested in what add-ins may improve your overall productivity with Excel Online.

Instructions:

1. Sign into OneDrive and create a new workbook using Excel Online.

2. Explore the Office Add-ins collection available from the Insert tab of the ribbon in the new workbook.

3. Browse options in the Education and Productivity categories of the Store as well as those in another category of your choice.

4. Create a document that summarizes the features of an add-in from each of the three categories.

5. Save the document. Submit the document as specified by your instructor.

6. ✻ Compare the add-ins available in Excel 2016 to those available for Excel Online. What are the strengths and weaknesses of each? Which would you recommend, and why?

In the Labs

Design, create, modify, and/or use a workbook following the guidelines, concepts, and skills presented in this module. Labs 1 and 2, which increase in difficulty, require you to create solutions based on what you learned in the module; Lab 3 requires you to apply your creative thinking and problem-solving skills to design and implement a solution.

Lab 1: **Reaching Monthly Budget Goals**

Note: To complete this assignment, you will be required to use the Data Files. Please contact your instructor for information about accessing the Data Files.

Problem: You want to select the best payback options for a car loan you will be getting. You have created a data table to examine the effects of interest rates from 3.5% to 6.5% for a loan. You want to use Goal Seek to determine how many months it will take to pay off a loan of $22,000.00 with an interest rate of 5.9% using different monthly payment goals.

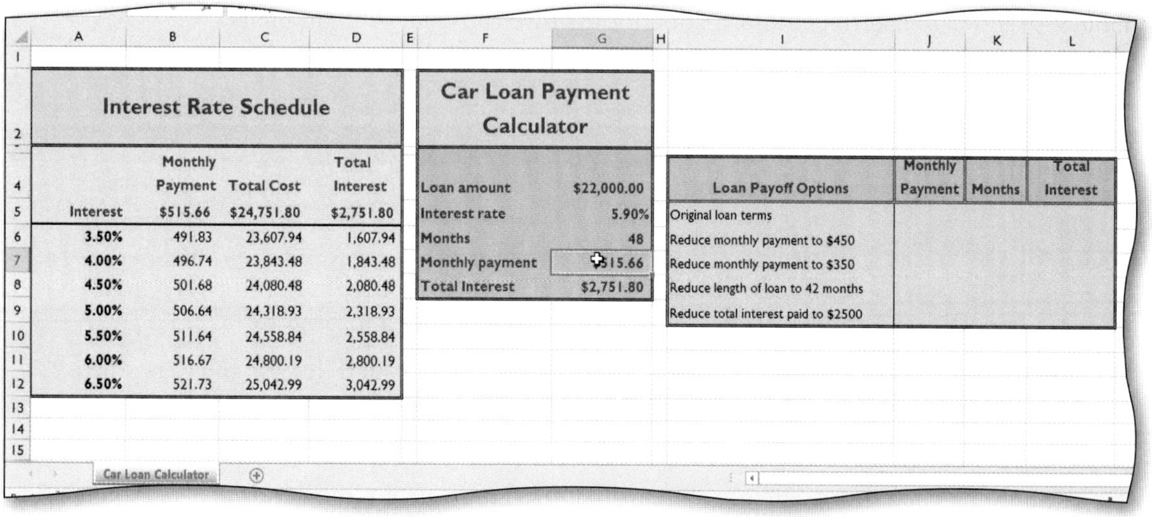

Figure 9–82

Perform the following tasks:

1. Open the workbook Lab 9-1 Car Loan from the Data Files and then save the workbook as Lab 9-1 Car Loan Complete (Figure 9–82).

2. Enter a loan amount of 22,000 (cell G4), interest rate of 5.9% (cell G5), and months of 48 (cell G6) in the payment calculator portion of the workbook.

Continued >

In the Labs *continued*

3. Enter the Monthly Payment, Months, and Total Interest Paid values from the Car Loan Payment Calculator in the Original loan terms row of the Loan Payoff Options table found in the range I4:L9.

4. Select cell G7. Use Goal Seek (Data tab | Forecast group) to determine how many months you will need to pay off the loan if you pay $450.00 per month by setting cell G7 to the value 450 and changing cell G6. Update the Loan Payoff Options table with the results of this Goal Seek.

5. Use Goal Seek to determine how many months you would need to pay off the loan if you pay $350.00 per month. Update the Loan Payoff Options table with the results of this Goal Seek.

6. Reduce the loan term to 42 months and record the monthly payment and total interest paid in the Loan Payoff Options table.

7. If requested by your instructor, enter your name in cell I2.

8. Save the workbook. Submit the revised workbook as specified by your instructor.

9. ✺ Use Goal Seek to determine the Monthly Payment and Months for the final option in the Loan Payoff Options table, reducing the total interest paid to $2500. Which variable did you choose to change? What other variable could you change to reach a total interest of $2,500?

Lab 2: **Finding the Optimal Product Mix**

Note: To complete this assignment, you will be required to use the Data Files. Please contact your instructor for information about accessing the Data Files.

Problem: Michaels Chocolates sells chocolates in single bars, 6-packs, and 12-packs to convenience and grocery stores. They are expanding to a national chain big box store where they have purchased 45 square feet of shelf space. They want to optimize the use of that shelf space to ensure that they showcase all three configurations of their product while maximizing profit as best they can. Table 9–4 shows the pertinent information for the three product configurations.

Table 9–4 Michaels Chocolates Information			
Item	**Profit per Item**	**Square Feet per Item**	**Display Constraints**
Single bars	0.08	0.0625	50 maximum
6-packs	0.45	0.4	30 minimum
12-packs	0.88	0.75	30 minimum

Perform the following tasks:

1. Open the workbook Lab 9-2 Michaels Chocolates from the Data Files and then save the workbook with the file name, Lab 9-2 Michaels Chocolates Complete.

2. Enter the data in Table 9–4 into the worksheet.

3. Use Solver to determine the mix of items that maximizes profit, subject to the constraints shown in Table 9–4. Use the Simplex LP option in Solver. Instruct Solver to create an Answer Report if it can find a solution to the problem. Save the scenario as Maximize Profit 1. (Hint: use the Save Scenario button in the Solver Results dialog box.) Rename the Answer Report containing the scenario as Maximize Profit 1. Figure 9–83 shows the values Solver should find.

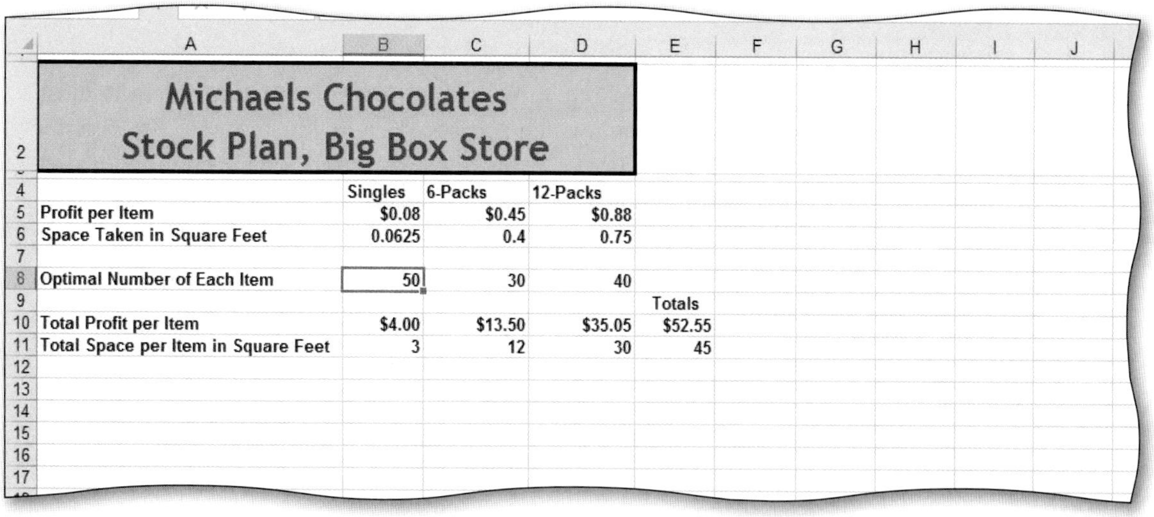

	A	B	C	D	E
		Singles	6-Packs	12-Packs	
4					
5	Profit per Item	$0.08	$0.45	$0.88	
6	Space Taken in Square Feet	0.0625	0.4	0.75	
7					
8	Optimal Number of Each Item	50	30	40	
9					Totals
10	Total Profit per Item	$4.00	$13.50	$35.05	$52.55
11	Total Space per Item in Square Feet	3	12	30	45

Figure 9–83

4. If the company decides to set the maximum number of 12-packs at 30, how would this affect the mix of items? Use Solver to determine the new mix. Instruct Solver to create an Answer Report if it can find a solution to the problem. Save the scenario as Maximize Profit 2, and rename the Answer Report containing the scenario as Maximize Profit 2.

5. Create a Scenario Summary showing the two scenarios you saved in the Scenario Manager.

6. If requested by your instructor, change the name of the store in cell A2 from Big Box Store to <streetname> Store, where <streetname> is the name of the street you lived on in high school.

7. Save the workbook. Submit the workbook as specified by your instructor.

8. ✳ What changes would you suggest to the company to maximize profit, other than raising prices? How could you use scenarios to make your point?

Lab 3: **Consider This: Your Turn**

Apply your creative thinking and problem-solving skills to design and implement a solution.

Using Solver to Plan Professional Development Programs

Part 1:   You have started a new position at a progressive technology company that uses a professional development skill point model in its annual review process. You have been asked to create a worksheet that managers could use with their employees to determine an optimal training plan for professional development. The managers are interested in being able to review combinations of courses for an employee and to vary the length of training. The managers will provide you with a list of courses, and the number of skill points per 15 minutes of coursework, for each entry on the list, for technicians and developers.

You have explained that this is a complex problem-solving exercise, and that the best approach is to build a simple workbook to test first. Your goal is to create a test workbook that reflects the structure needed to solve this problem. For test data, use four professional development

Continued >

In the Labs *continued*

activities and fictitious skills points per 15-minute block, or unit. You will want to solve for how many units of different types, or the same type, of coursework would give the individual the most benefit, subject to constraints. You can constrain which courses the individual can elect to register and how many units of each course he or she does. As indicated, you need to take an individual's position into account. You will have different skill points for technicians and developers for each unit of each course.

Part 2: In addition to type and length of course, what other information would you consider building into a more complex model? What are the challenges associated with introducing the information you are suggesting?

0 | Data Analysis with Power Tools and Creating Macros

Objectives

You will have mastered the material in this module when you can:

- Explain Excel's power tools
- Customize the ribbon and enable data analysis
- Use the Get & Transform data commands
- Create a query using Query Editor
- Build a PivotTable using Power Pivot
- Explain data modelling
- Create a measure
- View cube functions

- Use Power View
- Create tiles in a Power View report
- Use 3D Maps
- Save a tour as an animation
- Explain Power BI
- Create hyperlinks
- Use the macro recorder to create a macro
- Execute a macro

Introduction

Excel has a wide range of interlinked power tools — Get & Transform, Power Pivot, Power View, 3D Maps, and Power BI (Business Intelligence) — to analyze business data, whether you need to export data for business intelligence, pivot or manipulate data to find trends, create data models, or show data more visually.

Table 10–1 describes the five power tools available with Excel 2016. In this module, you only will touch on each of the power tools. The topic is vast and would require a lot of time and data modelling experience to explore all of the features associated with each tool. Power Pivot and Power View are not available in all versions of Excel. While you may have limited access to these tools, you will be able to work through the majority of the steps in this module.

Table 10–1 Power Tools	
Tool	**Purpose**
Get & Transform (formerly called Power Query)	The Get & Transform commands enable you to extract, connect, refine, and transform large amounts of data into an accessible Excel file. You can use Get & Transform to exert greater control over columns, formulas, and filtering tools, and also to modify data types and extract PivotTables.
Power Pivot	Power Pivot enables you to import and compare large amounts of data from multiple sources to build analytical relationships. You can use Power Pivot to create and model data tables, feed data to other Power Tools, and use data analysis expressions. Power Pivot is not available with all versions of Excel.
Power View	Power View is an interactive visualization tool used to provide a drag-and-drop interface for rapid model building. You can use Power View to connect to different data models within the same workbook, create new relationships among current data, and introduce key performance indicators (KPIs) based on those relationships. Power View can group (or smart group) data automatically to create advanced pie charts, maps, data cards, and other data visualizations.
3D Maps (formerly called Power Map)	3D Maps let you plot and visualize geographic or temporal data on a three-dimensional map. With filtering, you can compare how different factors affect your data. You can use a 3D Map to build custom regions, capture screenshots, and build cinematic time tours or animations through your data.
Power BI	Power BI, or Power Business Intelligence, is an Excel-based cloud tool that combines the other Power Tools with some additional features to enable you to find and visualize data, share, and collaborate. Power BI includes a wide range of forecasting tools, a drag-and-drop canvas, dashboards, report generation, and data modelling. Currently Power BI is available only to businesses, Office 365 subscribers, or as a download.

In addition to using Excel's power tools, you will create hyperlinks to move quickly to other parts of the workbook, animations, and external websites. You also will record a macro to automate a task.

Project — Business Decisions Demographics

The project in this module follows proper design guidelines and uses Excel to create the workbook shown in Figures 10 – 1 and 10 – 2. Business Decisions is a data analytics firm that specializes in examining raw data, looking for patterns, correlations, and other associations to help companies and organizations make better business decisions. Business Decisions has a new client who wants to open a business offering high-end replacement windows in South Carolina, but who first needs to understand the demographics of various communities who could support her business. Making use of data from the U.S. Census Bureau, Business Decisions plans to present several forms of visual data to its client using Excel's power tools.

Figure 10–1a shows the opening worksheet that includes a picture and hyperlinks to the other pages. Figure 10–1b queries the external data to display the top 15 most populous counties. Figure 10–1c lists the cities, along with the number of housing units and total area from a different data table.

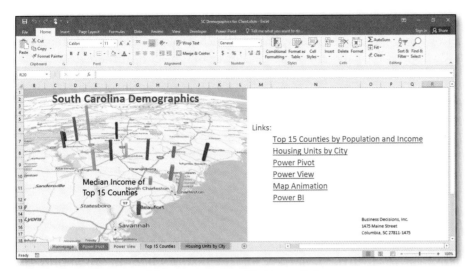

(a) Homepage with Hyperlinks

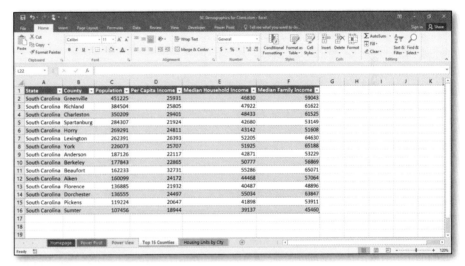

(b) Top 15 Most Populous Counties

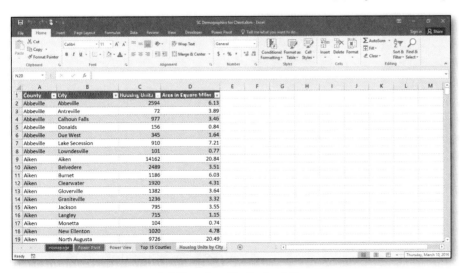

(c) Housing Units by City

Figure 10–1

Figure 10–2a displays a PivotTable that merges the two data sources to display the number of housing units per county. Figure 10–2b displays a Power View report. Figure 10–2c displays the data represented in Power BI. Power BI (pronounced bee-eye) or Business Intelligence is a powerful web-based tool to visualize and share data. Finally, the data then will be transformed into an interactive map. The 3D Maps window is shown in Figure 10–2d.

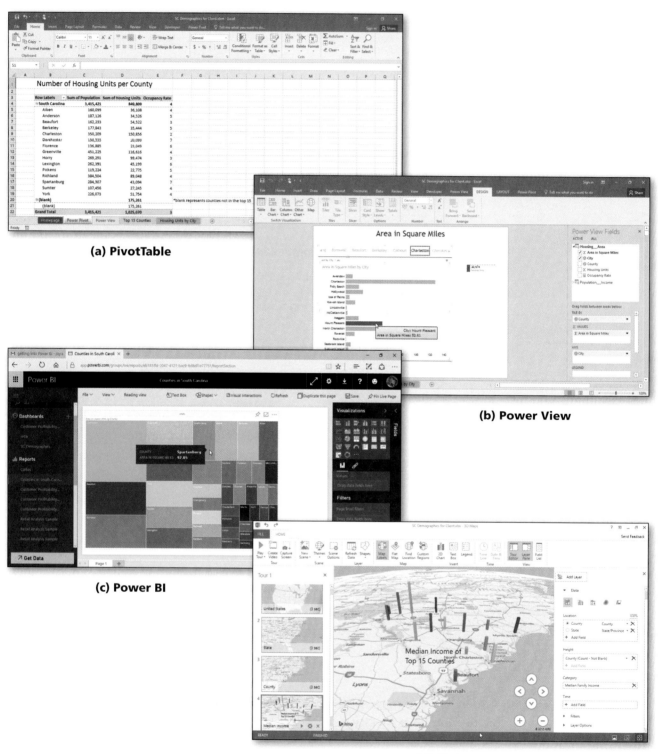

(a) PivotTable

(b) Power View

(c) Power BI

(d) 3D Map

Figure 10–2

Figure 10–3 illustrates the requirements document for the Business Decisions Demographics workbook. It includes the needs, source of data, and other facts about its development.

Worksheet Title	Demographic Analysis for Proposed Car Dealership
Needs	Business Decisions would like to present a variety of data visualizations to the client, including: 1. Top 15 most populous counties in order from most to least. 2. A list of all of the incorporated cities in the state, along with the number of housing units in each, and the total area represented in square miles. 3. A Power Pivot report combining the data sources to show the relationship between city, population, and housing units. 4. A Power View report showing the square miles and housing units for individual cities. 5. An animated map showing the counties with the highest median household income. 6. An attractive opening worksheet with hyperlinks to each of the above items, 1 through 5, and a hyperlink to the Power BI website.
Source of Data	Data is available in two external sources, downloaded from the U.S. Census Bureau: SC Housing Units by City and SC Population & Income by County.
Calculations	Average occupancy rate for each county that is calculated by taking the population of the county divided by the number of housing units. This calculation will appear in the Power Pivot report.

Figure 10–3

Workflow

Recall that in previous modules you imported data from a variety of sources including an Access database, Word table, a comma-delimited text file, and a table from the web. The workflow to create connections for use with the power tools is similar:

- Connect to the data — make connections to data in the cloud, in a service, or from local sources. You can work with the connected data by creating a permanent connection from your workbook to that data source, ensuring that the data you work with is always up-to-date.
- Transform the data — shape the data locally to meet your needs; the original source remains unchanged.
- Combine data from various sources— create a data model from multiple data sources and get a unique view into the data.
- Share the data —save, share, or use transformed data for reports and presentations.

The following roadmap identifies general activities you will perform as you progress through this module:

1. ENABLE DATA ANALYSIS and customize the ribbon.
2. GET and TRANSFORM data.
3. USE POWER PIVOT.
4. USE POWER VIEW.
5. USE 3D MAP.
6. CREATE a home page with HYPERLINKS.
7. RECORD, save, and execute MACROS.

To Create a Workbook in a New Folder

The following steps run Excel and open a blank workbook. Then, after changing the color scheme, you will use the Save As dialog box to create a new folder and save the workbook on your storage device.

1 Run Excel.

2 Click the Blank workbook from the template gallery.

3 If necessary, maximize the Excel window.

4 Set the color scheme to Orange Red.

5 Display the Backstage view, click the Save As tab, and then click Browse to open the Save As dialog box.

6 Browse to your storage device and then click the New folder button. Name the new folder Module 10.

7 Double-click the new folder, Module 10, to open it.

8 In the File name box, type `SC Demographics for Client` as the file name.

9 Click the Save button (Save As dialog box) to save the file in the new folder.

To Copy Data Files

Sometimes data sources move to different locations. You probably have noticed while surfing the web that some webpages no longer exist or have been redirected. On your computer, you may have links that no longer work after moving a file to a different folder. Anytime your workbook is connected to data, there is a chance that the data file might be moved. Therefore, if you are using local data — that is the data stored on your computer — it is a good idea to store the workbook and any connected data sources in the same folder location.

The following steps copy two files from the Data Files to your storage location (the new folder you just created). See the Office 2016 and Windows 10 Module for more information about this process. If you already have downloaded the Data Files to the same storage location that you are using to create and save files in this module, you can skip these steps.

To complete these steps, you will be required to use the Data Files. Please contact your instructor for information about accessing the Data Files.

1 Click the File Explorer button on the Windows taskbar to open a File Explorer window.

2 Navigate to the location of the Data Files for this module.

3 Select both the 'SC Housing Units by City' file and the 'SC Population & Income by County' file, and then copy and paste the files in to the new folder you just created.

4 Close the File Explorer window.

To Enable Data Analysis

1 ENABLE DATA ANALYSIS | 2 GET & TRANSFORM | 3 USE POWER PIVOT | 4 USE POWER VIEW
5 USE 3D MAPS | 6 CREATE HYPERLINKS | 7 RECORD MACROS

The following steps verify that Data Analysis has been enabled in the version of Excel that you are running. *Why? Data analysis commands are required in order to use the power tools.*

1

- Display the Backstage view and then click the Options tab to open the Excel Options dialog box.

- In the left pane of the dialog box, click Advanced to display the Advanced Options.

- Scroll to the Data area.

- If necessary, click to display a check mark in the 'Enable Data Analysis add-ins: Power Pivot, Power View, and Power Map' check box (Figure 10–4).

Q&A I do not see the Enable option. What should I do?
You may have a version of Excel that does not support data analysis and the power tools. Continue with the steps and contact your instructor.

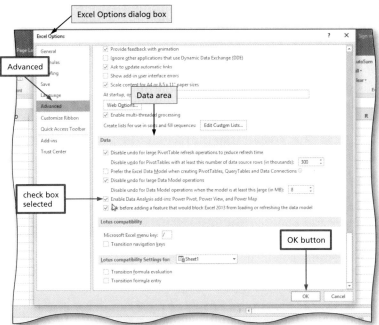

Figure 10–4

2

- Click the OK button (Excel Options dialog box) to close the dialog box and enable the data analysis tools.

Q&A Should I see a change in Excel?
No. Changing the setting assures that you will not see an error message when you try to use the power tools later in the module.

TO ADD IN POWER MAP

If you could not enable data analysis in the previous steps, you may need to add Power Map to your version of Excel in order to run 3D Maps. Recall from a previous module that you used the Add-ins option to add Solver to Excel. The following steps add in Power Map.

1. Display the Backstage view and then click the Options tab to open the Excel Options dialog box.

2. In the left pane of the dialog box, click Add-ins to display the Add-ins Options.

3. Near the bottom of the dialog box, click the Manage arrow and then click COM Add-ins.

4. Click the Go button to open the COM Add-ins dialog box.

5. Click to display a check mark in the Microsoft Power Map for Excel check box. If you have check boxes for Power View or Power Pivot, select those as well.

6. Click the OK button (COM Add-ins dialog box).

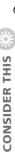
CONSIDER THIS

What should I keep in mind when customizing the ribbon?

- Customize the ribbon when you need to access new features of Excel, or when you regularly need to access commands that are not part of the ribbon already.

- If the new command will be used at various times, with different tabs, consider adding the command or button to the Quick Access Toolbar.

- If you need to add a single command to the ribbon, choose a tab with plenty of room to hold the new command and its new group.

- If you need to add several commands, consider creating a new tab on the ribbon.

- If you are using a computer in a lab situation, reset the ribbon when you are done.

To Customize the Ribbon

The following steps customize the ribbon. *Why? Due to space constraints on the ribbon and the advanced nature of the power tools, some of the commands do not display automatically.* You will enable the Power Pivot tab on the ribbon, add the 'Insert a Power View' button to the Insert tab, and then enable the Developer tab that you will use later in the module.

The Power Pivot tool is not available in all versions of Excel. If you do not see the Power Pivot tab in the following steps, contact your instructor or IT administrator to see if your version of Excel can run Power Pivot; you may have to use an Add-in process.

1

- Right-click a blank area of the ribbon to display the shortcut menu (Figure 10–5).

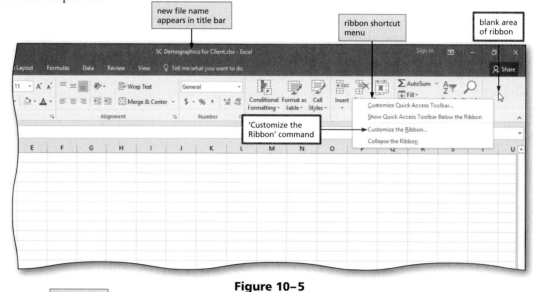

Figure 10–5

2

- Click 'Customize the Ribbon' on the shortcut menu to display the Excel Options dialog box.

- In the Main Tabs area, scroll as necessary, and then click to display a check mark in both the Developer and the Power Pivot check boxes, if necessary (Figure 10–6).

Q&A I do not see Power Pivot. What should I do?

Contact your instructor to see if your version of Excel can run Power Pivot. If not, you can still continue with these steps and use the Developer ribbon.

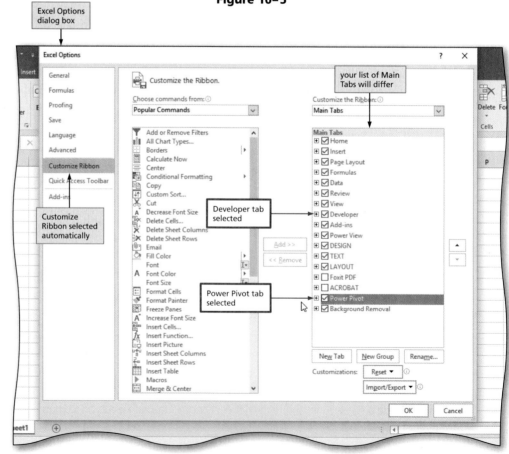

Figure 10–6

3

- In the Main Tabs area, click Insert (not the check box) to select the Insert tab.
- Click the New Group button to insert a new group on the selected tab (in this case, the Insert tab) (Figure 10–7).

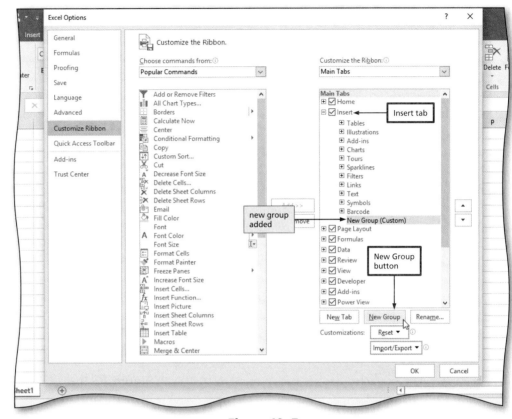

Figure 10–7

4

- Click the 'Choose commands from' button to display the menu (Figure 10–8).

Can I add a command directly to a tab?
No. You only can add commands to new groups.

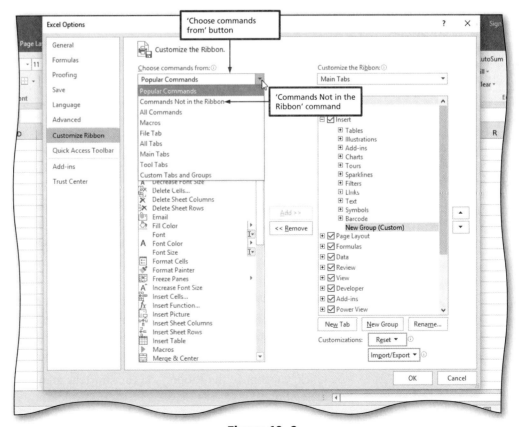

Figure 10–8

- Click 'Commands Not in the Ribbon' to display only those commands.

- Scroll down and click 'Insert a Power View Report' to select it.

- Click the Add button to add the command to the new group (Figure 10–9).

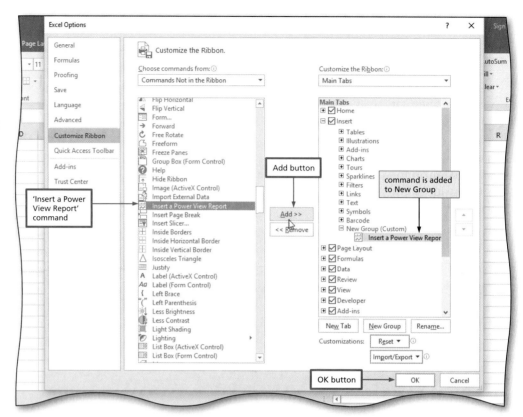

Figure 10–9

- Click the OK button (Excel Options dialog box) to display the customization on the ribbon (Figure 10–10).

Experiment

- Click the Insert tab and look at the new group and new button. Click the Home tab.

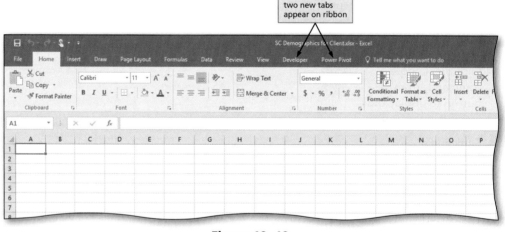

Figure 10–10

Other Ways

1. Display Backstage view, click Options, click Customize Ribbon (Excel Options dialog box), click appropriate check box in Main Tabs list, add necessary commands, click OK button

TO RENAME A NEW GROUP

If you wanted to rename a new group to customize the ribbon further, you would perform the following steps.

1. Right-click a blank area of the ribbon to display the shortcut menu.

2. Click 'Customize the Ribbon' on the shortcut menu to display the Excel Options dialog box.

3. In the Main Tabs area, navigate to and then click 'New Group (Custom)' to select it.

4. Click the Rename button to display the Rename dialog box.

5. Choose an appropriate symbol and enter a display name.

6. Click the OK button (Rename dialog box).

7. Click the OK button (Excel Options dialog box).

Get & Transform

Formerly called Power Query, the Get & Transform commands located on the Data tab allow you to extract, connect, clean, and transform large amounts of data into an accessible Excel table. Importing data in this fashion is different from the way you imported data in previous modules. The Get & Transform commands allow you to edit, as well as query or transform, imported data without making a permanent change to the data. Excel uses a dedicated window named Query Editor to facilitate and display data transformations. Recall that you queried tables in a previous module by searching for and limiting the display of certain data. When you use the Query Editor, you are provided with many more tools to group rows, replace values, remove duplicates, and edit columns, among others. The resulting query table then becomes a displayed subset of the actual data.

BTW

Getting Data from Access Databases
When you click the New Query button (Data Tab | Get & Transform group) and choose an Access database, the Navigator window appears so you can select which table (or tables) you want to use in your query. When you select a table, a preview of its data is shown in the right pane of the Navigator window.

To Get Data

1 ENABLE DATA ANALYSIS | 2 GET & TRANSFORM | 3 USE POWER PIVOT | 4 USE POWER VIEW
5 USE 3D MAPS | 6 CREATE HYPERLINKS | 7 RECORD MACROS

The following steps connect to a table with data provided by the U.S. Census Bureau from the 2010 Census from the state of South Carolina. The table is located in the Data Files. *Why? Connecting with the U.S. Census Bureau website is somewhat cumbersome and requires many steps.* You will use the New Query button (Data tab | Get & Transform group) to connect to the data. When you bring the data into Excel, you are working with a local copy; you will not change the original data source in any way. Should the data source be updated externally however, you easily can refresh your local copy. The local data becomes a table, also called a query.

To complete these steps, you will be required to use the Data Files. Please contact your instructor for information about accessing the Data Files.

1

- Display the Data tab.

- Click the New Query button (Data tab | Get & Transform group) to display the New Query menu.

- Point to the From File command to display the From File submenu (Figure 10–11).

 Experiment

- Point to the other commands on the New Query menu and look at the various sources from which you can get data. When you are done, point to From File again.

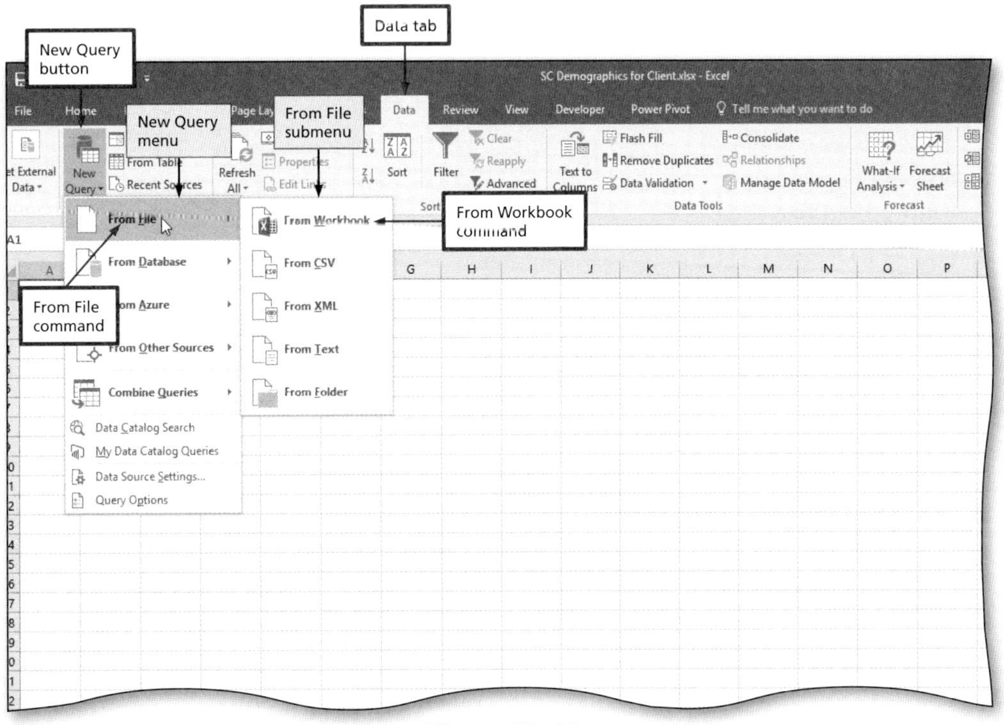

Figure 10–11

2

- Click From Workbook on the From File submenu to display the Import Data dialog box.

- If necessary, navigate to the Module 10 folder to display the files (Figure 10–12).

Q&A Could I have clicked From Web and navigated to the Census data?
Yes; however, you would have had to perform many additional steps to drill down to the desired data for this project.

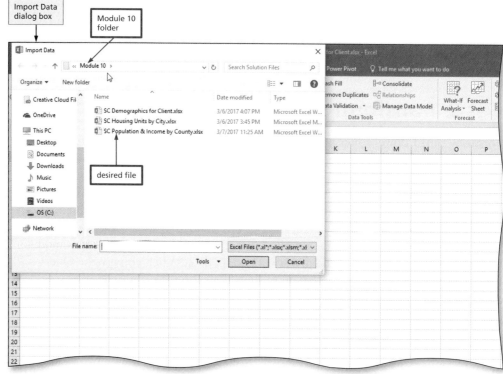

Figure 10–12

 3

- Double-click the file named 'SC Population & Income by County' to display the Navigator dialog box.

- Click the table named Population & Income to preview the data (Figure 10–13).

Q&A Could I have used the Get External Data button on the Data tab, as I did in a previous module?
No. Using that command imports the data without the ability to query and transform the data using the power tools.

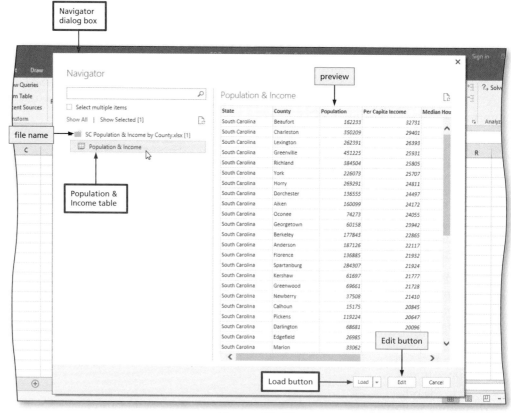

Figure 10–13

What does the Edit button do?
If you know that you want to edit the data before creating the query, you can click the Edit button to display the Query Editor window.

4

- Click the Load button (Navigator dialog box) to import the data (Figure 10–14).

Q&A How is the data displayed?
Excel shows 46 rows of data for the counties in South Carolina in a table format.

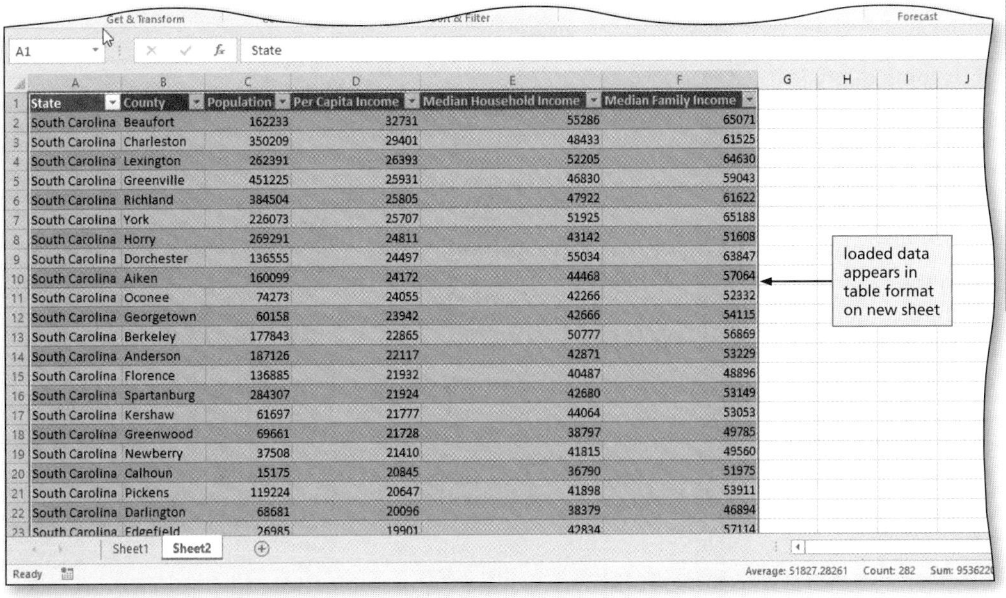

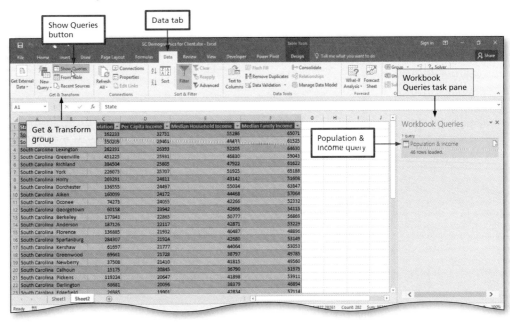

loaded data appears in table format on new sheet

Figure 10–14

To Transform the Data

1 ENABLE DATA ANALYSIS | 2 GET & TRANSFORM | 3 USE POWER PIVOT | 4 USE POWER VIEW
5 USE 3D MAPS | 6 CREATE HYPERLINKS | 7 RECORD MACROS

When you get data using a Get & Transform command, Excel provides advanced editing and querying techniques to use with that data. The Worksheet Queries task pane shows all of the files connected to your workbook. In the following steps you will use the Query Editor to sort the data and only display the top 15 most populous counties. *Why? The client wants you to narrow down the counties to the places with the most people.*

1

- If necessary, display the Data tab.

- If necessary, click the Show Queries button (Data tab | Get & Transform group) to display the Worksheet Queries task pane (Figure 10–15).

 Experiment

- Point to the Population & Income query in the Worksheet Queries task pane to display information about the file.

Figure 10–15

Show Queries button

Data tab

Get & Transform group

Workbook Queries task pane

Population & Income query

- Double-click the Population & Income query in the Worksheet Queries task pane to display the Query Editor window.

- In the third column, click the Population column filter button to display the filter menu (Figure 10–16).

Q&A Is the Query Editor a separate app?
Query Editor is like an app within an app. The Query Editor window has its own ribbon, tabs, and groups and is navigated independently from Excel. The Query Settings task pane allows you to make changes to the data and keeps track of each change, in order.

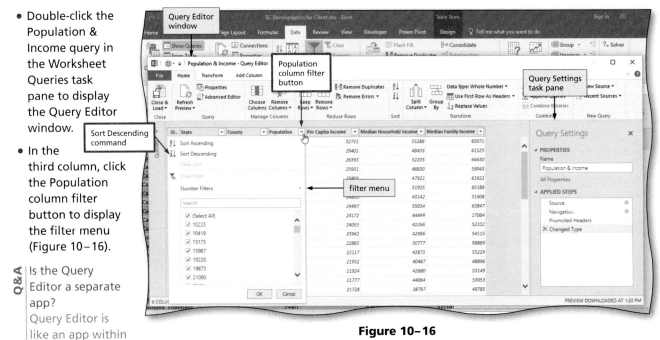

Figure 10–16

- On the filter menu, click Sort Descending to sort the data in order by population with the most populous county first (Figure 10–17).

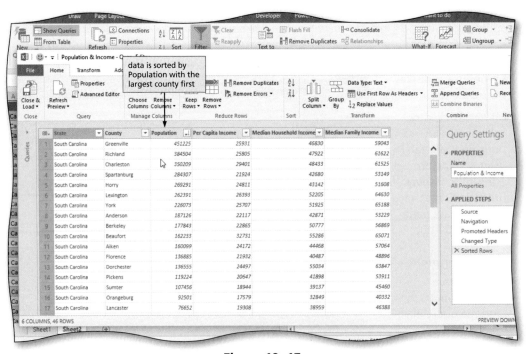

Figure 10–17

- Click the Keep Rows button (Home tab | Reduce Rows group) to display the menu (Figure 10–18).

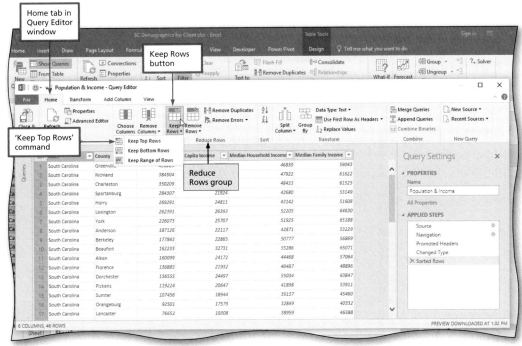

Figure 10–18

❺

- Click the 'Keep Top Rows' command to display the Keep Top Rows dialog box.

- Type **15** in the Number of rows text box (Figure 10–19).

Q&A Could I have just deleted the rows in the main Excel window?
You could have; however, that would permanently delete the local copy of the data. Using the Query Editor, you can restore the data if you need it later.

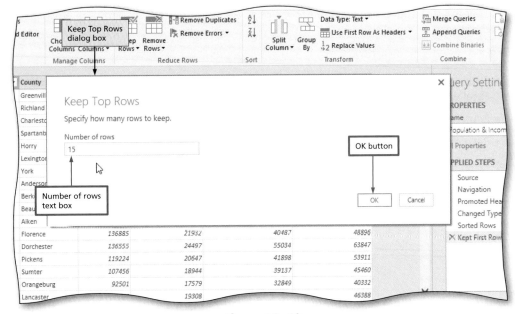

Figure 10–19

• Click the OK button (Keep Top Rows dialog box) to return to the Query Editor window (Figure 10–20).

Q&A What happens if my source data moves?

If you suspect that your source data has moved, display the Query Editor window and then click the Refresh Preview button (Query Editor window | Home tab | Query group). If an error message appears, click the 'Go To Error' button, click the Edit Details button, and then navigate to the new location of the file.

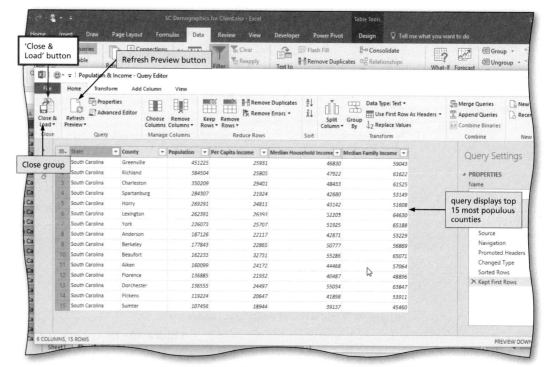

Figure 10–20

• Click the Close & Load button (Home tab | Close group) to load the transformed data into the worksheet in the Excel window.

• Rename the sheet tab with the name Top 15 Counties.

• Recolor the sheet tab with the color Light Green.

Q&A What is the new tab on the ribbon?

It is the Query Tools Query tab (shown in Figure 10–22), which allows you to make additional queries easily.

To Get Another Data Source

The following steps add a second data source to the workbook.

1 In the Excel window, click the New Query button (Data tab | Get & Transform group), point to From File to display the From File submenu, and then click From Workbook to display the Import Data dialog box.

2 If necessary, navigate to the Module 10 folder to display the files.

3 Click the file named 'SC Housing Units by City' to select it and then click the Open button to display the Navigator dialog box.

4 Click the 'Housing & Area' table to preview the data.

5 Click the Load button (Navigator dialog box) to import the data (Figure 10–21).

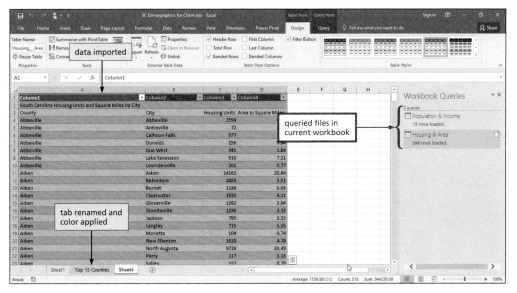

Figure 10–21

To Edit Using the Query Tab

1 ENABLE DATA ANALYSIS | 2 GET & TRANSFORM | 3 USE POWER PIVOT | 4 USE POWER VIEW

5 USE 3D MAPS | 6 CREATE HYPERLINKS | 7 RECORD MACROS

The following steps edit the query to remove a heading from the imported data and to convert the second row into column headings. This time you will use the Query Tools Query tab to access the Query Editor window. *Why? Depending on where you in the process of getting and transforming your data, the Query Tool Query tab may be more convenient than using the Worksheet Queries task pane.* You also will save the file again.

1

- Display the Query Tools Query tab.

- Click the Edit button (Query Tools Query tab | Edit group) to display the Query Editor window.

- In the Query Editor window, click the Remove Rows button (Home tab | Reduce Rows group) to display the Remove Rows menu (Figure 10-22).

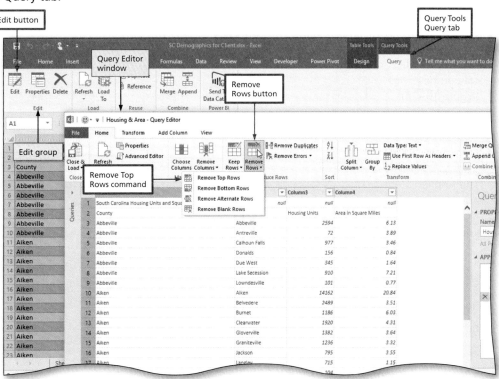

Figure 10–22

2

- Click Remove Top Rows to display the Remove Top Rows dialog box.

- Type 1 in the Number of rows text box (Figure 10–23).

Q&A Why am I removing the first row?
The first row is the title of the imported worksheet; it is not part of the data itself.

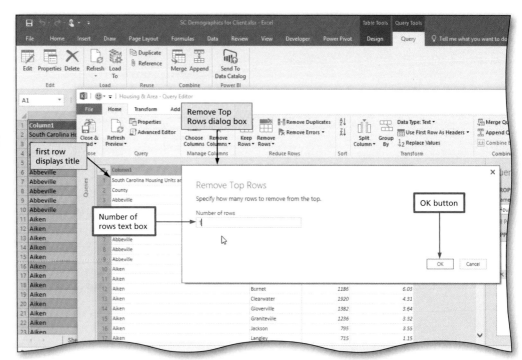

Figure 10–23

3

- Click the OK button (Remove Top Rows dialog box) to remove the first row.

- Click the 'Use First Row As Headers' button (Home tab | Transform group) to use the imported table's column headings (Figure 10–24).

Q&A What is the Applied Steps area in the Query Settings task pane?
The Applied Steps area displays each manipulation that you performed on the data, in order. You can click a step to return to that view of the data or delete the step.

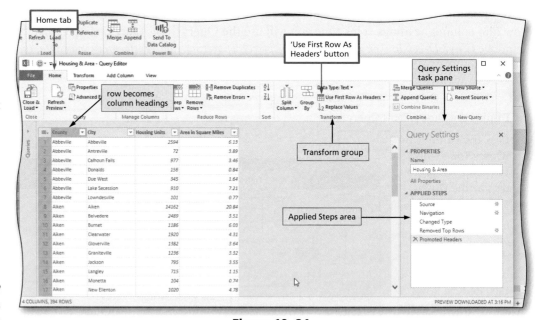

Figure 10–24

4

- Click the Close & Load button (Home tab | Close group) to load the transformed data into the worksheet.

- Rename the sheet tab with the name Housing Units by City.

- Recolor the sheet tab with the color Light Blue.

- Save the file.

Break Point: If you wish to take a break, this is a good place to do so. Exit Excel. To resume at a later time, run Excel, open the file named SC Demographics for Client, and then continue following the steps from this location forward.

Power Pivot

Power Pivot is a tool that extends the analytical functionality of PivotTables in Excel. It includes the capability to include data from multiple data sources into one PivotTable. Valued as a Business Intelligence (BI) tool by the business community, Power Pivot especially is helpful when analyzing large, complex sets of related tables. Using Power Pivot, you can import some or all of the tables from a relational database into Excel in order to analyze the data using PivotTables and the enhanced features.

Data Models

Power Pivot, along with the other power tools, provides a data modelling tool to help you explore, analyze, and manage your data. **Data modelling** is the process of creating a model, simulation, or small-scale representation of data and the relationships among pieces of data. Data modelling often includes multiple ways to view the same data and ensure that all data and processes are identified. A **data model** documents the processes and events to capture and translate complex data into easy-to-understand information. It is an approach for integrating data from multiple tables, effectively building a relational database inside Excel. A **relational database** is any collection of data that can be accessed or reassembled without having to reorganize the tables.

CONSIDER THIS

Are data models unique to Power Pivot?

No. You used the concept of a data model when you created PivotTable and PivotChart reports; a field list is a visual representation of a data model. The difference between Power Pivot and a PivotTable is that you can create a more sophisticated data model using Power Pivot. When importing relational data, the creation of a data model occurs automatically when you select multiple tables. However, if the tables are from different sources, they may have to be added to the data model manually.

To Add a Query to a Data Model

1 ENABLE DATA ANALYSIS | 2 GET & TRANSFORM | 3 USE POWER PIVOT | **4 USE POWER VIEW**
5 USE 3D MAPS | **6 CREATE HYPERLINKS** | **7 RECORD MACROS**

The following steps add a query to the data model. *Why? You cannot create the Power Pivot PivotTable unless both queries are added to the data model.* You will use the Add to Data Model command. If you do not have Power Pivot, simply read these steps.

- If necessary, display the Housing Units by City worksheet and then click in the table to make it active.

- Click Power Pivot on the ribbon to display the Power Pivot tab (Figure 10–25).

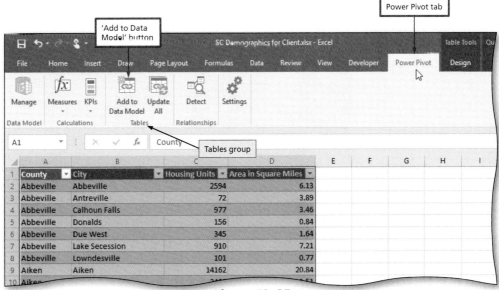

Figure 10–25

- Click the 'Add to Data Model' button (Power Pivot tab | Tables group) to add the data on the current worksheet to the data model (Figure 10–26).

Q&A What window is displayed?
Excel displays the maximized Power Pivot for Excel window that contains tabs and groups used when working with multiple tables from multiple sources.

Figure 10–26

- Close the Power Pivot for Excel window to return to the regular Excel window.

To Add Another Query to the Data Model

The following steps add another query to the data model. If you do not have Power Pivot, skip these steps.

① Click the Top 15 Counties tab to display the worksheet.

② Click any cell in the data.

③ Click the 'Add to Data Model' button (Power Pivot tab | Tables group) to add a second query to the data model (Figure 10–27).

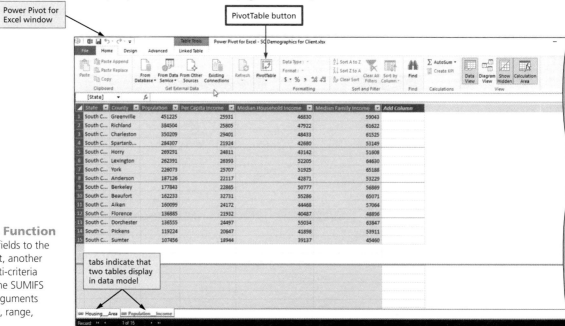

BTW
The SUMIFS Function
Besides adding fields to the PivotTable report, another way to find multi-criteria sums is to use the SUMIFS function with arguments of range, critera, range, criteria, etc.

Figure 10–27

To Build a PivotTable Using Power Pivot

The following steps create a PivotTable using Power Pivot, based on the two queries. *Why? Using Power Pivot provides you with the most flexibility and functionality when building a PivotTable.* If you do not have access to Power Pivot, you can create a regular PivotTable report.

- With the Power Pivot for Excel window still open, click the PivotTable button to display the Create PivotTable dialog box.

- If necessary, click the New Worksheet option button to select it (Figure 10–28).

Q&A Can I make a PivotTable without Power Pivot?
Yes. Click the PivotTable button (Insert tab | Tables group). In the Create PivotTable dialog box, click to display a check mark in the 'Add this data to the Data Model' check box.

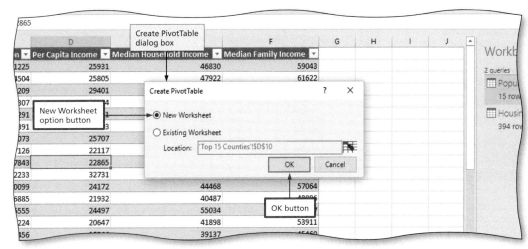

Figure 10–28

- Click the OK button to create a PivotTable on a new sheet and to display the PivotTable Fields task pane (Figure 10–29).

Q&A Why do I not see both of my tables?
In the PivotTable Fields task pane, click the All tab. If you see a More Tables link, click the Yes button (Create a New Table dialog box).
You later can delete any unused worksheets that might be created by this process.

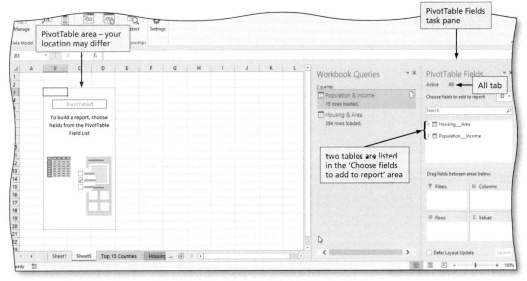

Figure 10–29

3

- In the Choose fields to add to the report area, click Population_Income (PivotTable Fields task pane) to display the fields from the query table.

- Click the check boxes beside the State field and the County field to add the fields to the Rows area.

- Click the Population check box to add the field to the Values area (Figure 10–30).

Q&A Why do the query tables use an underscore in their name?

Database structures rarely allow spaces in the names of files or fields. Excel wants to make sure the data can be used in many kinds of databases.

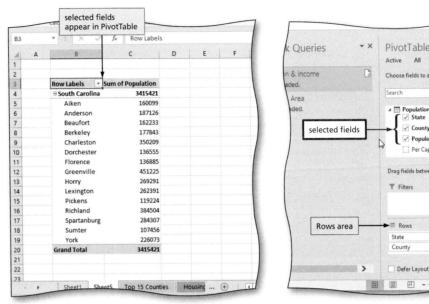

Figure 10–30

4

- Scroll up in the 'Choose fields to add to the report' area and then click Housing_Area (PivotTable Fields task pane) to display the fields from the query table (Figure 10–31).

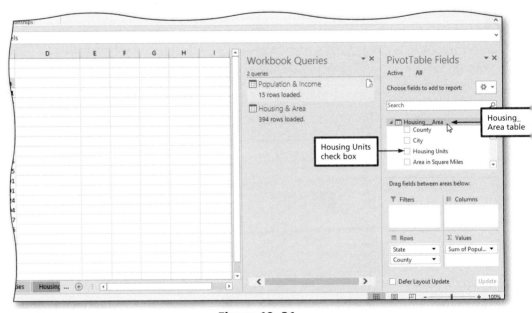

Figure 10–31

5

- Click the Housing Units check box to add the field to the Values area (Figure 10–32).

Q&A
Why do all of the counties have the same number of housing units?
The PivotTable does not associate the housing units with the counties automatically. You will create that relationship in the next series of steps.

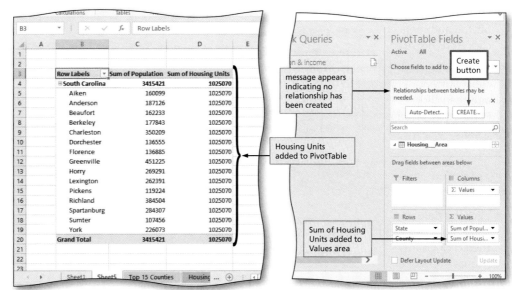

Figure 10–32

To Create a Relationship

1 ENABLE DATA ANALYSIS | 2 GET & TRANSFORM | 3 USE POWER PIVOT | 4 USE POWER VIEW
5 USE 3D MAPS | 6 CREATE HYPERLINKS | 7 RECORD MACROS

A **relationship** is a field or column that two data sources have in common. For example, a payroll file and a human resource file might each have a field named employee_number. Sometimes that field is named identically in the two files and has the same number of rows; other times the name is different. One file might use the field name last_name and another file might call it LastName. Those two fields would have to be manually associated.

When the number of rows are different, the relationship is said to be **one-to-many**. For example, both a client file and an employee file might have a field named salesperson. In the employee file, there is only one record for each salesperson; however, in the client file, several clients might be assigned to the same salesperson.

The following steps create a relationship using the County field. *Why? Both query tables have a column named County, although it is a one-to-many relationship. The Population_Income query has one line of data for each county. The Housing_Units query table has many cities listed for each county.*

1

- Click the Create button in the PivotTable Fields task pane to display the Create Relationship dialog box (Figure 10–33).

Q&A
I do not have a Create button or it did not work. What should I do?
Click the Relation-ships button (Data tab | Data Tools) to display the Manage Relationships dialog box. Click the New button.

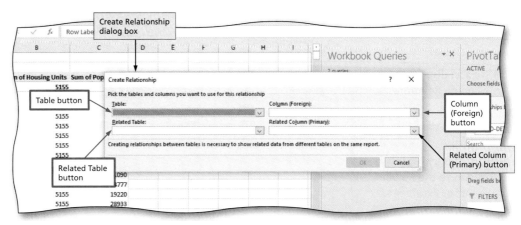

Figure 10–33

- Click the Table button and then click Housing_Area.
- Click the Related Table button and then click Population_Income (Figure 10–34).

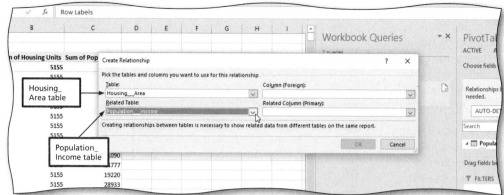

Figure 10–34

- Click the Column (Foreign) button and then click County (Figure 10–35).

Q&A Why is it called a foreign column? Foreign, or foreign key, refers to a *field* in one *table* that uniquely identifies a row in a different table. Even though the names may be the same, the field is foreign to the second table. For most Excel purposes, it does not matter which table you use for the foreign versus primary key.

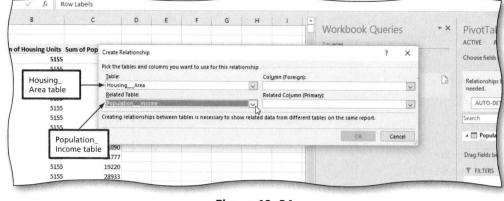

Figure 10–35

- Click the OK button (Create Relationship dialog box) to create the relationship between the tables and adjust the numbers in the PivotTable.

- If Excel displays the Manage Relationships dialog box, click the Close button.

- If necessary, minimize the Power Pivot for Excel window to return to the regular Excel window (Figure 10–36).

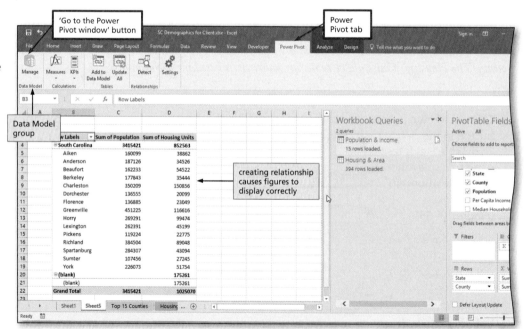

Figure 10–36

Other Ways

1. Click Detect Relationships button (Power Pivot tab | Relationship group), select relationships

To View Relationships

The following steps graphically display the relationship that you created in the previous steps using the Power Pivot window. *Why? Sometimes looking at a picture makes the concept clearer.* If you do not have Power Pivot, simply read these steps.

- Click the 'Go to the Power Pivot window' button (Power Pivot tab | Data Model group) to make the Power Pivot for Excel window active.

- Click the Diagram View button (Home tab | View group) to see a visual display.

- Resize each of the table views to display all of the data, and then drag the tables slightly to see the relationship of one-to-many (Figure 10–37).

- Click the Data View button (Home tab | View group) to return to the Data View.

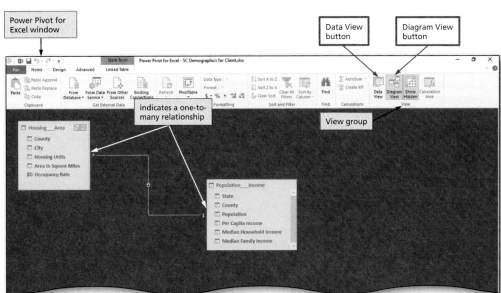

Figure 10–37

To Manage Relationships

You can set up multiple relationships using Power Pivot. You may need to add, edit, or delete relationships at some point. To do this, you would use the Manage Relationships command in the Power Pivot window, as shown in the following steps.

1. Click the 'Go to the Power Pivot window' button (Power Pivot tab | Data Model group) to make the Power Pivot for Excel window active.

2. Display the Design tab and then click the Manage Relationships button in the Power Pivot for Excel window (Design tab | Relationships group) to display the Manage Relationships dialog box.

3. Use the Create, Edit, or Delete button to make changes to the selected relationship and then click the Close button (Manage Relationships dialog box) to close the dialog box.

4. Minimize the Power Pivot for Excel window.

To Create a Measure

A **measure** is a calculated named field in Power Pivot. Measures use a special set of functions and commands called data analysis expressions or DAX. Measures have several advantages over simple formulas and other calculated fields. *Why? With measures, you can create aggregate formulas that use one or multiple rows from multiple sources, which will adjust as you rearrange the pivot. You can format measures as you create them for global formatting benefits. Measures become fields in pivot field lists and can be used in multiple reports and across multiple worksheets. In regular PivotTables, you cannot create calculated fields using multiple data sources.*

The following steps create a measure to calculate the average number of people in each household. If you do not have Power Pivot, simply read these steps.

- If necessary, minimize the Power Pivot for Excel window.

- Click any cell in the PivotTable and then click the Measures button (Power Pivot tab | Calculations group) to display the menu (Figure 10–38).

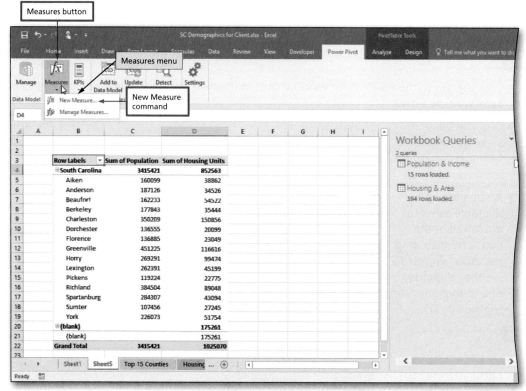

Figure 10–38

- Click New Measure in the Measures menu to display the Measure dialog box.

- In the Measure name text box, select any default text and then type `Occupancy Rate` to name the column.

- In the Description text box, select any default text and then type `number of people per housing unit` to create a description.

- In the Formula box following the equal sign, type [(left bracket) to prompt Excel to display the available fields that exist in the PivotTable (Figure 10–39).

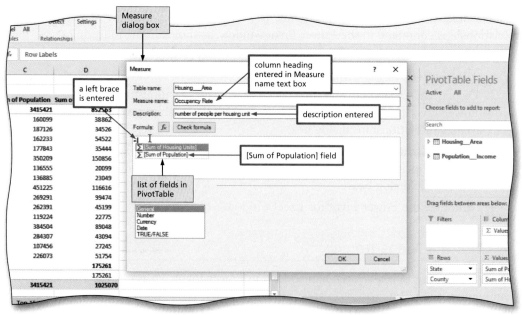

Figure 10–39

3

- Double-click the [Sum of Population] field to insert it into the formula.

- Type   /[to enter the division symbol and to display again the available fields.

- Double-click the [Sum of Housing Units] field to insert it into the formula.

- In the Category box, click Number.

- Click the Format button and then click Whole Number to choose the format (Figure 10–40).

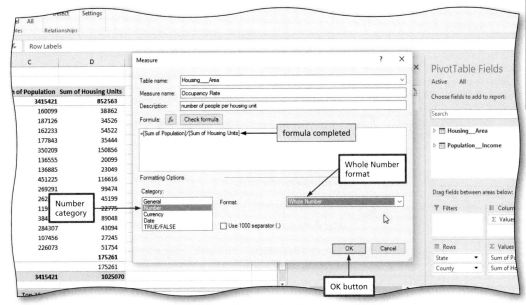

Figure 10–40

4

- Click the OK button (Measure dialog box) to create the measure and display the new column (Figure 10–41).

Q&A Could I obtain the same result by creating a calculated field in the PivotTable?
No. The Calculated Field option is unavailable to PivotTable data with multiple data sources.

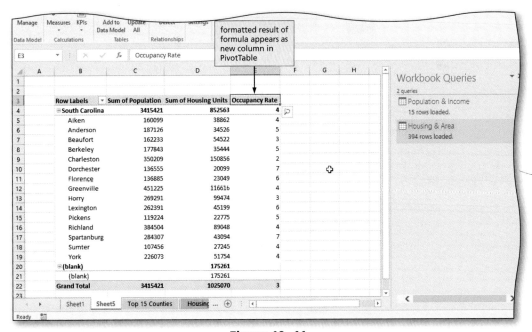

Figure 10–41

To Finish Formatting the PivotTable

The following steps format the other columns of numbers, insert a heading for the page, add a footnote, and save the file.

1 Right-click any number in the 'Sum of Population' column and then click Number Format on the shortcut menu to display the Format Cells dialog box.

2 In the Category area (Format Cells dialog box), click Number. Change the decimal places to 0 and then click to select the 'Use 1000 Separator' check box.

3 Click the OK button (Format Cells dialog box) to return to the PivotTable.

4 Repeat Steps 1 and 2 for the numbers in the Sum of Housing Units column.

5 Click cell A1. If necessary, change the font color to black. Change the font size to 20. Type **Number of Housing Units per County** and then press the ENTER key to complete the text.

6 Drag through cells A1 through E1 and then click the Merge & Center button (Home tab | Alignment group) to merge and center the title.

7 Click cell F20. Type ***blank represents counties not in the top 15** to create a footnote.

8 Rename the worksheet tab with the name, Power Pivot.

9 Recolor the worksheet tab with the color, Blue.

10 Save the file again (Figure 10–42).

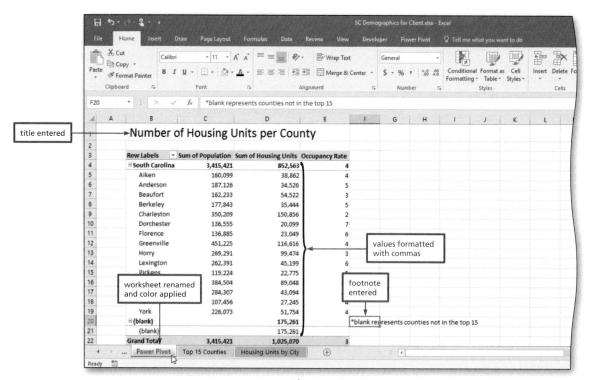

Figure 10–42

Cube Functions

Normally if you want to reference a piece of data, you use a cell reference such as B4. If the data in that cell changes, your reference will reflect that change as well. And when you want to replicate a formula containing a reference that should not change, you use an absolute reference, such as $B$4. In PivotTables, however, neither of those cell references work. The data is prone to change dramatically, from numeric to text, from field to field, or even to blank. Formula or other references to that data immediately become invalid or display errors when the data is pivoted.

The solution to that problem is to use cube functions. **Cube functions** are a set of advanced analytic functions that you can use with multidimensional data, also called **data cubes**. A Power Pivot report is considered a data cube because of its 3-D cube-like structure. With a cube function, you can reference any piece of data in the PivotTable to use in formulas or in other functions, or merely to display the data in other places in the workbook. The cube function will adjust automatically if you change the way your data pivots.

Table 10–2 lists the cube functions.

BTW
The AVERAGEIFS Function
Like its single-criteria counterpart AVERAGEIF, the AVERAGEIFS function averages all arguments that meet multiple criteria.

Table 10–2 Cube Functions

Function	Return Value	Purpose
CUBEKPIMEMBER	Returns the name of a key performance indicator (KPI)	Produces a quantifiable measure such as net income
CUBEMEMBER	Returns a member or tuple from the cube	Validates that the member or tuple exists in the cube
CUBEMEMBERPROPERTY	Returns the value of a member property from the cube	Validates that a member name exists within the cube and to return the specified property for this member
CUBERANKEDMEMBER	Returns the nth, or ranked, member in a set	Returns one or more elements in a set, such as the top salesperson or the top 10 athletes
CUBESET	Defines a set of members by sending an expression to the cube	Identifies sets for use in other cube functions
CUBESETCOUNT	Returns the number of items in a set	Finds how many entries are in a set
CUBEVALUE	Returns an aggregated value from the cube	Displays values from the cube

The cube functions use a variety of arguments in their construction. Recall than an argument refers to any piece of information that the function needs in order to do its job. Arguments are placed in parentheses following the function name. Arguments are separated by commas. Table 10–3 lists some of the arguments used in the construction of cube functions.

For example, the following CUBEMEMBER function includes a reference to the connection or data model, and then the name of the table followed by the name of the value. The function would return the calculated sum from the PivotTable.

```
=CUBEMEMBER("ThisWorkbookDataModel","[Measures].[Sum
                  of Housing Units]"
```

The reference to "ThisWorkbookDataModel" and the reference to Measures are standard references called constants; they should be entered exactly as written above. The reference to Sum of Housing Units is a variable and would be changed to match the field name in the PivotTable.

BTW
The GETPIVOTDATA Function
Another way to extract data stored in a PivotTable is to use the GETPIVOTDATA function. The function takes at least two arguments: the name of the data field and a reference to any cell in the PivotTable report. It returns the sum of that field. An optional third argument allows you to enter a search term. The GETPIVOTDATA function also can search calculated fields.

Table 10–3 Cube Function Arguments	
Argument	**Definition**
Caption or property	An alternate text to display in the cell that is perhaps more user-friendly than the database, field or row name
Connection	Names the table, query, or data model
Key performance indicator (KPI)	A quantifiable measurement, such as net profit, used to monitor performance
Measures	A pivot calculation such as sum, average, minimum, or maximum
Member expression	Uses database field-like references to the data rather than cell references
Rank	An integer to represent which piece of data to return in an ordered list
Set	A string to represent a set of values that has been defined or returned by another cube function
Sort by	A field name to sort by when a function returns a set of values
Sort order	An integer to represent how the data should be ordered when a function returns a set of values
Tuple	A row of values in a relational database

To View Cube Functions

1 ENABLE DATA ANALYSIS | 2 GET & TRANSFORM | 3 USE POWER PIVOT | 4 USE POWER VIEW
5 USE 3D MAPS | 6 CREATE HYPERLINKS | 7 RECORD MACROS

The following steps use the Convert to Formulas command. *Why? The command converts the cells in a Power Pivot report or a PivotTable report to cube references, allowing you to see the functions behind the scenes.*

- Click cell E3 in the PivotTable.

- Display the PivotTable Tools Analyze tab.

- Click the OLAP Tools button (PivotTable Tools Analyze tab | Calculations group) to display the menu (Figure 10–43).

Q&A

What does OLAP stand for?
OLAP stands for Online Analytical Processing that is an advanced analytic tool to assist users in data warehousing and data mining, especially with multidimensional data such as a PivotTable with two outside sources.

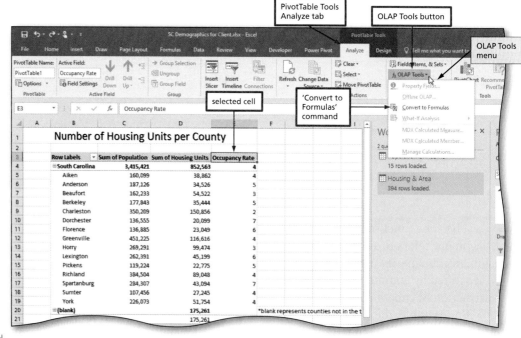

Figure 10–43

2

- Click Convert to Formulas on the OLAP Tools menu to view the cube function in the formula bar (Figure 10–44).

 Experiment

- Click various cells in the table, including the row and column headings, while watching the formula bar. Note the various cube functions that make up the PivotTable.

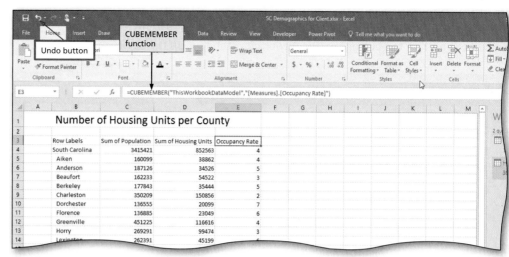

Figure 10–44

3

- Click the Undo button on the Quick Access Toolbar, to hide the cube functions and display the PivotTable.

- If necessary, close the Power Pivot window and return to the Excel window.

Power View

Power View is another of the interactive visualization power tools. Power View uses a drag-and-drop interface to create a variety of charts, maps, data cards, and other data visualizations. A unique feature of a Power View report is the use of tiles and filters. A **tile** is a button on a Power View navigation strip that is used to group data. A Power View filter is a way to focus on a particular piece of data by clicking on it, similar to a PivotTable slicer. Power View supports multiple views of the data, tiles, and filters in the same view or report.

To Start Power View

1 ENABLE DATA ANALYSIS | 2 GET & TRANSFORM | 3 USE POWER PIVOT | 4 USE POWER VIEW
5 USE 3D MAPS | 6 CREATE HYPERLINKS | 7 RECORD MACROS

Earlier in this module, you added the Insert a Power View Report button to the Insert tab. The following steps use the new button to start Power View. Power View will display two new tabs on the ribbon. *Why? Power View uses many tools and needs its own ribbons to display the buttons and menus.* The Power View tab helps you add objects to the view. Once you add data to the view, the Design tab appears with access to charts many formatting tools. If you could not enable the data analysis features earlier in this module, you may not have access to Power View.

1

- Display the tab containing the New Group you added earlier in the module (in this case, the Insert tab).

- Click the 'Insert a Power View Report' button (Insert tab | New Group group) to open Power View and to display the Power View tab.

- Close the Workbook Queries task pane, if necessary (Figure 10–45).

 Q&A

My Power View button did not work. What should I do?
See your instructor regarding access to Power View. If you do not have access, read through these steps and study the figures.

Does the order of the worksheet tabs matter?
No. Your order may vary depending on how you minimized or closed other windows.

Experiment

- Point to each of the buttons on the Power View tab to view the associated ScreenTip.

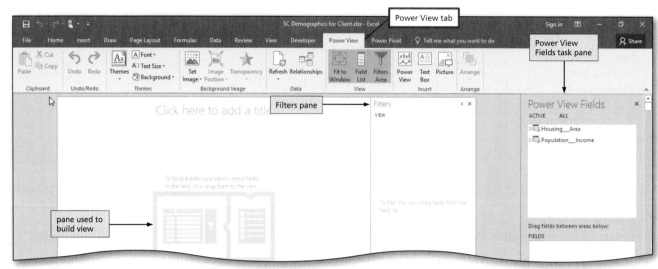

Figure 10–45

To Create a Power View Report with Tiles

1 ENABLE DATA ANALYSIS | 2 GET & TRANSFORM | 3 USE POWER PIVOT | 4 USE POWER VIEW
5 USE 3D MAPS | 6 CREATE HYPERLINKS | 7 RECORD MACROS

The following steps add data to the Power View data visualization area to create a Power View report that shows city and square miles data by county. You will create a tile for each county. *Why? Using a tile for each county will help you navigate the large amount of data and reduce the need to scroll. When you click a tile, only data related to that field value is displayed.* If you do not have Power View, simply read these steps.

1

- In the Power View Fields task pane, click the triangle beside the Housing_Area table to display the fields.
- Click the check boxes for County, City, and 'Area in Square Miles' to display them in the report (Figure 10–46).

Experiment

- Scroll in the report to see more of the data.

Figure 10–46

②

- If necessary, display the Design tab.

- Click the Tiles button (Design tab | Tiles group) to tile the data.

- Near the light blue line at the bottom of the table itself, rather than the tiles, drag the lower-right corner of the table to fill approximately two-thirds of the pane.

- In the Power View Fields task pane, click to remove the check mark in the County check box, as you no longer need the field in the report table (Figure 10–47).

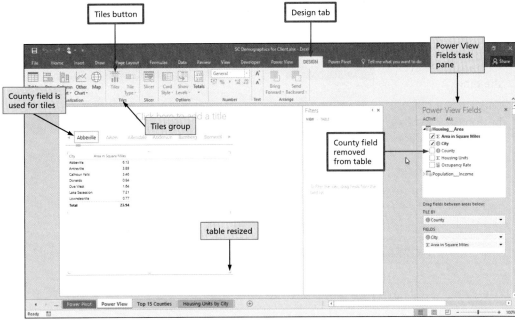

Figure 10–47

Q&A My table will not resize. What did I do wrong?

Try resizing the tiles area or resize using the upper-right sizing handle.

③

- In the Power View Fields task pane, drag the Housing Units field to the report pane to create a second table to the right of the first one (Figure 10–48).

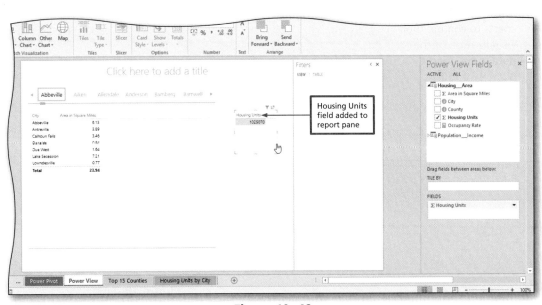

Figure 10–48

To Switch Visualizations

The following steps convert the left table to a bar chart visualization and convert the right table to a card visualization. *Why? Different kinds of visualizations add variety and aid in reading the data.* If you do not have Power View, simply read these steps.

- Click any item in the left table to select the table.

- Click the Bar Chart button (Design tab | Switch Visualization group) to display the bar chart choices (Figure 10–49).

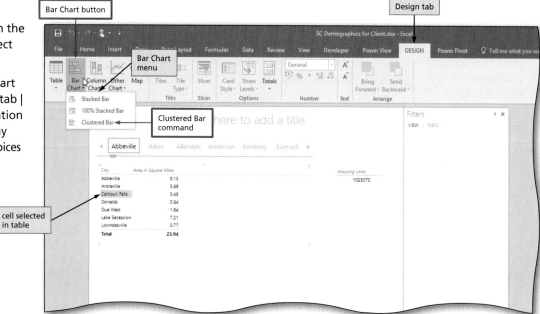

Figure 10–49

- Click Clustered Bar in the list of bar charts to change the visualization of the data in the report (Figure 10–50).

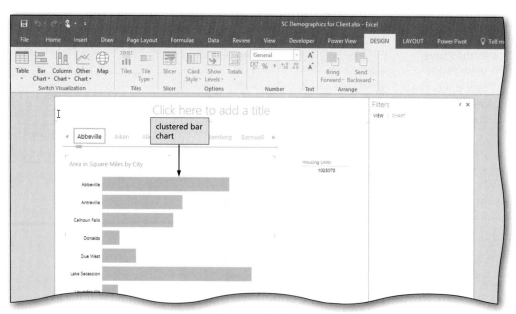

Figure 10–50

- Click the Housing Units data in the table to select the table.

- Click the Table button (Design tab | Switch Visualization group) and then click Card in the list to display the data in the Card format.

To Format the Power View Report

The following steps format the Power View report. *Why? Adding a theme and title enhance the report and improves comprehension.* You also will format the numbers. If you do not have Power View, simply read these steps.

- Display the Power View tab.

- Click the Themes button (Power View tab | Themes group) to display the Power View themes.

- Scroll to display more themes (Figure 10–51).

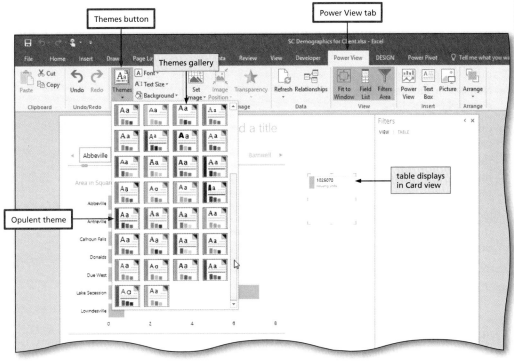

Figure 10–51

- Click the Opulent theme to change the colors in the Power Pivot report.

- In the report pane, click the title area. Type **Area in Square Miles** to enter the title text (Figure 10–52).

Q&A

Could I add a background to the report?

Yes. You can use the Background button (Power View tab | Themes group) to add a colored background; or you can insert a picture in the background using the Set Image button (Power View tab | Background Image group).

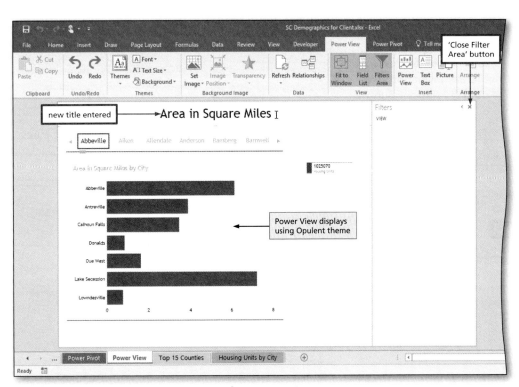

Figure 10–52

- Click the data in the Housing Units table card on the right side of the pane.

- Display the Design tab.

- Click the Comma Style button (Design tab | Number group) to add commas to the data.

- Click the Decrease Decimal button (Design tab | Number group) twice to remove the decimal places.

- On the Filters pane, click the 'Close Filter Area' button to remove it from the display (Figure 10–53).

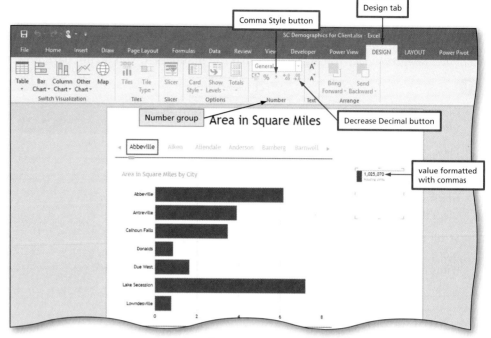

Figure 10–53

To Highlight Data in the Visualization

1 ENABLE DATA ANALYSIS | 2 GET & TRANSFORM | 3 USE POWER PIVOT | 4 USE POWER VIEW
5 USE 3D MAPS | 6 CREATE HYPERLINKS | 7 RECORD MACROS

The following steps use the tiles and filters to highlight specific data items. *Why? Sometimes when presenting data, you may want to focus in on a piece of data (in this case, one city in one county).* You also will save the file. If you do not have Power View, simply read these steps.

- Above the bar chart, click the right-arrow in the tile navigation strip until Charleston county is displayed.

- Click the Charleston tile.

- In the bar chart, click Mount Pleasant to display the data for that specific city (Figure 10–54).

- Save the file again.

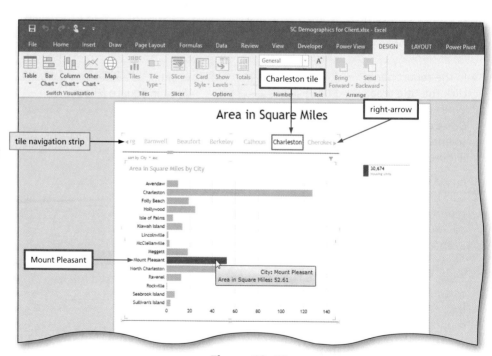

Figure 10–54

Break Point: If you wish to take a break, this is a good place to do so. Exit Excel. To resume at a later time, run Excel, open the file named SC Demographics for Client, and then continue following the steps from this location forward.

3D Maps

The 3D Maps power tool, formerly called Power Map, helps show your data in relation to a geographical area on a map. You can create a single map, or several maps, that become an animation focusing in on your data. The animation is called a tour, and each map is called a scene. If you are going to create a tour, you should plan out each scene and decide what data you want to display in each one.

The 3D Maps command opens a new window that uses a lot of your computer's resources. It is a good idea to close any apps other than Excel while working with 3D Maps.

To Open the 3D Maps Window

1 ENABLE DATA ANALYSIS | 2 GET & TRANSFORM | 3 USE POWER PIVOT | 4 USE POWER VIEW
5 USE 3D MAPS | 6 CREATE HYPERLINKS | 7 RECORD MACROS

The following steps open the 3D Maps window. *Why? The 3D Maps windows has the tools to create a map or tour.*

1

- Click the Housing Units by City sheet tab and click anywhere within the data.

- Display the Insert tab (Figure 10–55).

Q&A Do I have to be in a specific worksheet to access 3D Maps?
No. 3D Maps can be accessed from any worksheet or window. Excel will add a note to the current worksheet explaining that a map is associated with it, however.

Figure 10–55

2

- Click the 3D Map button (Insert tab | Tours group) to open the 3D Maps window (Figure 10–56).

Q&A I do not see two tables in my field list. What should I do?
It is possible that the second table was not added to the data model. Minimize the 3D Map window and return to the main Excel window. Click the sheet tab of the missing data and click any cell in the table. Click the 3D Map arrow (Insert tab | Tours group) and then click 'Add the Selected Data to 3D Maps' on the menu.

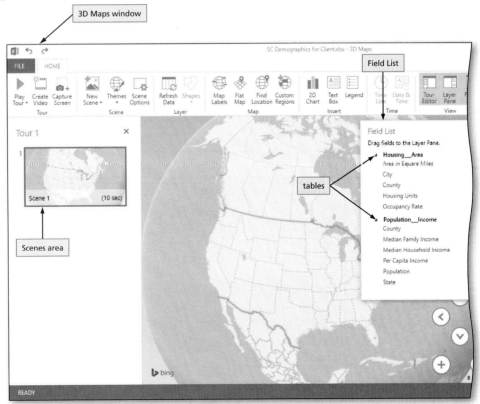

Figure 10–56

To Create Scenes

If you want to create more than just a single static map, you must add scenes to the tour. The following steps add three scenes to the tour. *Why? The first scene will focus in on the state, the second one will focus on the counties with map labels, and the third will display the population for each of the 15 most populous counties.*

- In the 3D Maps window, click the New Scene button (Home tab | Scene group) to add a new scene to the tour.

- In the Field List, drag the State field from the Population_Income table to the Location area in the Layer pane to focus in on the state.

- If the map does not zoom to South Carolina, click the Select One button and then click State/Province in the list.

- Click the Map Labels button (Home tab | Map group) to display state labels on the map (Figure 10–57).

Q&A Does the map have its own worksheet tab?
No. You can save the tour as an animation, but the only way to revisit your map is to use the 3D Map button (Insert tab | Tours group).

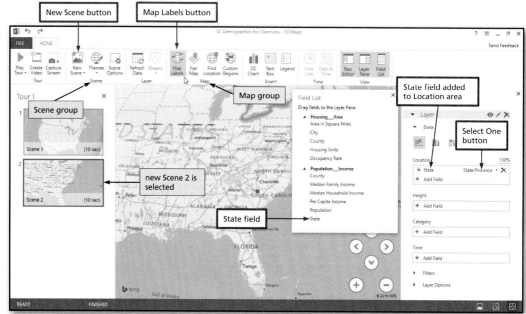

Figure 10–57

- Click the New Scene button (Home tab | Scene group) to add a Scene 3 to the tour.

- In the Field List, drag the County field from the Population_Income table to the Location area in the Layer pane to change the map. If necessary, click the Select One button and then click County in the list.

- Click the Zoom in button several times to zoom in on the state of South Carolina.

- If necessary, drag in the map to better position the state and adjust the Field List (Figure 10–58).

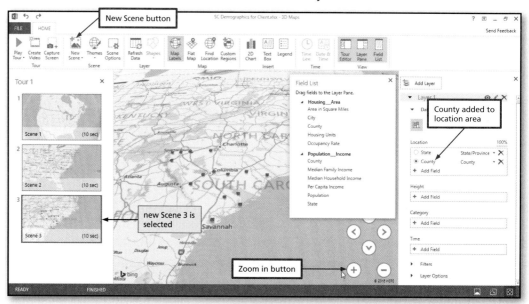

Figure 10–58

❸

- Click the New Scene button (Home tab | Scene group) to add a Scene 4 to the tour.

- In the Field List, drag the Median Family Income field to the Category area in the Layer pane to change the map.

- In the Field List, drag the County field from the Housing_Area table, to the Height area in the Layer pane (Figure 10–59).

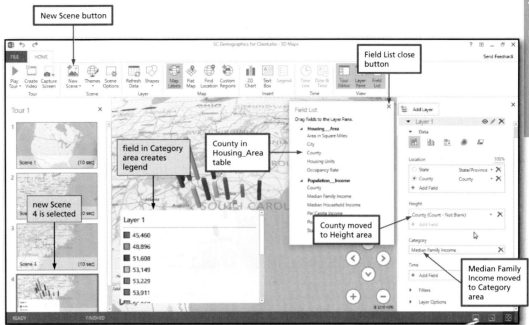

Figure 10–59

❹

- Close the Field List.

- Right-click the Layer 1 legend and then click Remove.

- In the map, click the Tilt down button three times and click the Zoom in button several times.

- Drag in the map to better position the state.

- Point to any of the data bars to display the data card (Figure 10–60).

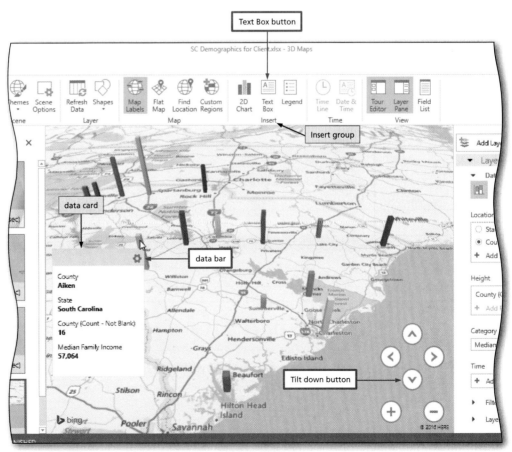

Figure 10–60

- Click the Text Box button (Home tab | Insert group) to display the Add Text Box dialog box.

- Change the font size to 24.

- In the Title text box, type Median Income of Top 15 Counties to enter the title (Figure 10–61).

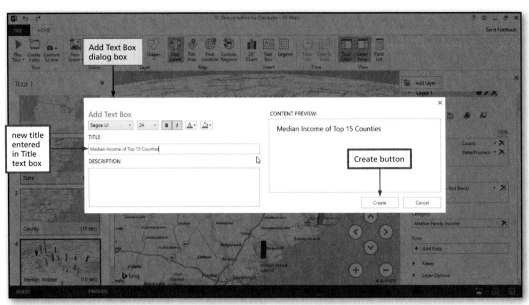

Figure 10–61

6

- Click the Create button (Add Text Box dialog box) to create a text box title for the map.

- Drag the text box to the lower left portion of the map and resize it as necessary (Figure 10–62).

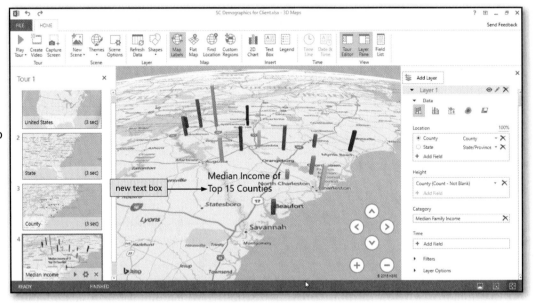

Figure 10–62

To Format Scene Options

1 ENABLE DATA ANALYSIS | 2 GET & TRANSFORM | 3 USE POWER PIVOT | 4 USE POWER VIEW
5 USE 3D MAPS | 6 CREATE HYPERLINKS | 7 RECORD MACROS

The following steps format scene options. *Why? To make the animation smoother, you will change the duration of each scene and then select a scene effect.*

1

- Click Scene 1 in the Tour pane.

- Click the Scene Options button (Home tab | Scene group) to display the Scene Options dialog box.

- Select the text in the Scene duration box and then type **3** to change the scene to a length of three seconds.

- In the Scene Name text box type **United States** to change the name.

- Click the Effect button to display the list of effects (Figure 10–63).

- Click Push In to select the effect.

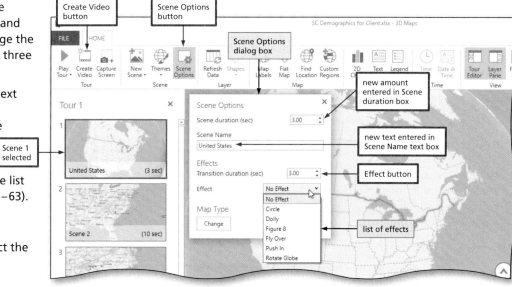

Figure 10–63

- Repeat Steps 1 and 2 for scene 2. Use the name State.

- Repeat Steps 1 and 2 for scene 3. Use the name County.

- Repeat Steps 1 and 2 for scene 4. Use the name Median Income.

To Finish the Animation Steps

1 ENABLE DATA ANALYSIS | 2 GET & TRANSFORM | 3 USE POWER PIVOT | 4 USE POWER VIEW
5 USE 3D MAPS | **6 CREATE HYPERLINKS** | **7 RECORD MACROS**

The following steps play the tour, save a copy of the tour, and take a screen shot of the final map. *Why? You will paste the screen shot to Sheet1 in preparation for creating a home page for the workbook.* You also will save the file.

- Click the Play Tour button (Home tab | Tour group) to play the animation. When the animation is finished, click the "Go back to Edit view." button in the lower left corner of the animation window to return to the 3D Maps window.

- Adjust any of the maps as necessary.

- Click the Create Video button (Home tab | Tour group) to display the Create Video dialog box.

- Click the 'Computers & Tablets' option button (Figure 10–64).

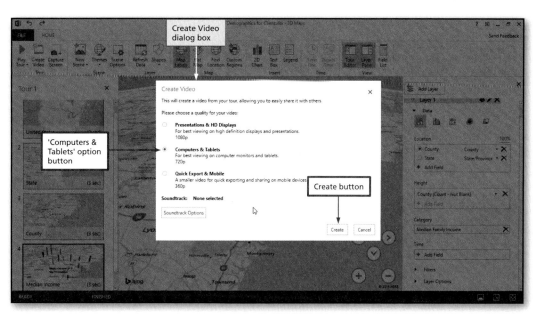

Figure 10–64

- Click the Create button (Create Video dialog box) to display the Save Movie dialog box.

- Type `County Income in South Carolina` in the File name box and then navigate to your storage device and the Module 10 folder that you created earlier in the module (Figure 10–65).

- Click the Save button to save the video. When Excel has finished saving the video, click the Close button, if necessary.

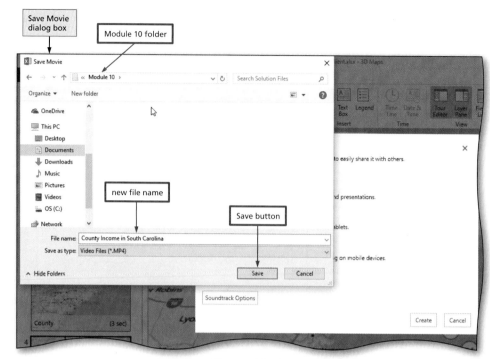

Figure 10–65

Q&A Can I play the video?

Yes, if you wish to view the video, navigate to the storage location, right-click the file, and then click Open or Play on the shortcut menu. When the video is finished, click the Close button in the video window.

To Capture a Screen

1 ENABLE DATA ANALYSIS | 2 GET & TRANSFORM | 3 USE POWER PIVOT | 4 USE POWER VIEW
5 USE 3D MAPS | 6 CREATE HYPERLINKS | 7 RECORD MACROS

The following steps capture a screen. *Why? A screen capture is a picture that can be used in other places in the workbook and in other applications because it is stored on the clipboard.*

- If necessary, click the Close button of any open dialog boxes.

- If necessary, select Scene 4 and then click the Capture Screen button (Home tab | Tour group) to place a copy of the map on the clipboard (Figure 10–66).

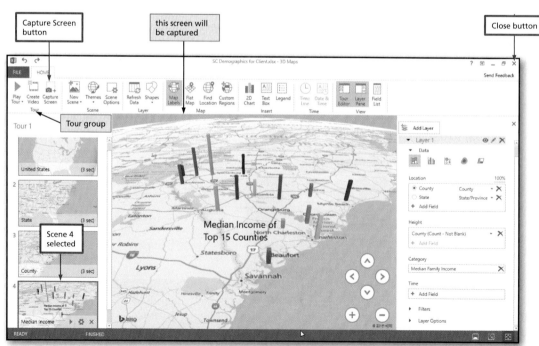

Figure 10–66

2

- Close the 3D Maps window and navigate to Sheet1 in the workbook.

- Click the Paste button (Home tab | Clipboard group) to paste the map to Sheet1 (Figure 10–67).

3

- Save the file.

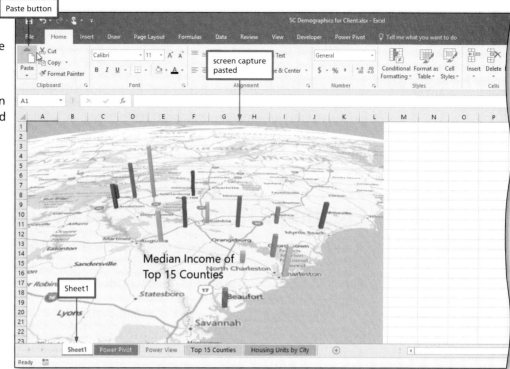

Figure 10–67

Power BI

Microsoft's Power BI is a business intelligence tool to visualize and share data. It is a web-based tool designed to help business users gain insights from their data. Power BI can generate reports with a wide variety of tools including the Excel power tools. Currently, Power BI is free for businesses; otherwise, you are required to have an Office 365 subscription to publish to Power BI.

In Power BI, a dashboard is the file management system where you can upload many different types of files. You can create multiple dashboards. Files in the dashboard are then used to create reports. Figure 10–68 displays a treemap chart using

BTW
Power BI Website
Microsoft's Power BI website has many samples, blogs, and a guided learning tutorial about how to use Power BI. Visit powerbi.microsoft.com for more information.

Figure 10–68

the South Carolina demographic information. Notice the tools in the Visualizations task pane are similar to those in the various Power Tool task panes. The Navigation pane is on the left.

Power BI is integrated into Excel in several ways. For example, on the Query Tools Query tab, which appears on the ribbon after you have used the Get & Transform tools to perform a query on your data, there is a Send to Data Catalog button (for version of Excel with data analysis enabled) that automatically loads the data in the query and opens Power BI. Data Catalogs can be shared with everyone within a business. After saving your file to OneDrive, you can publish the entire spreadsheet to Power BI by clicking Publish in the Backstage view.

Creating a Home Page with Hyperlinks

Some Excel users create a home page or introductory worksheet to help with navigation, especially when novice users of Excel may need to interact with complex workbooks. A home page should display a title, links to other worksheets or pertinent materials, and perhaps a graphic.

A **hyperlink**, or hypertext, is a computer link or reference to another location. A hyperlink can link to a page on the web, to an email address, to a location on a storage device, or another location within a workbook. Users click links to navigate or browse to the location. In Excel, hyperlinks can be created using cell data or linked to a graphic.

To Create a Home Page

1 ENABLE DATA ANALYSIS | 2 GET & TRANSFORM | 3 USE POWER PIVOT | 4 USE POWER VIEW
5 USE 3D MAPS | 6 CREATE HYPERLINKS | **7 RECORD MACROS**

Earlier you copied a screen shot of the 3D map and pasted it to Sheet1. The following steps insert a title for the home page using a text box. **Why?** *A text box can be placed in front of a graphic; if you try to type in a cell, the text will appear behind the graphic.*

- Display the Insert tab.

- Click the Text Box button (Insert tab | Text group) and then draw a text box across the top of the graphic. Do not cover up any of the data bars on the map.

- Change the font size to 28 and the font color to purple. Set the text to bold. Click the Center button (Home tab | Alignment group).

- Type South Carolina Demographics to enter the text (Figure 10–69).

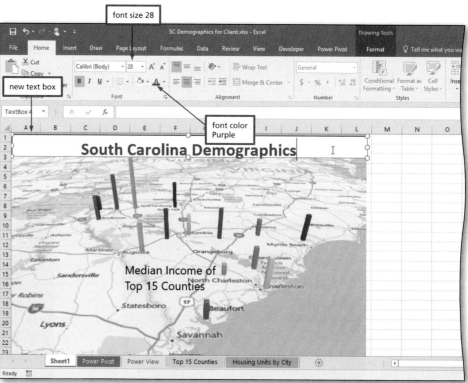

Figure 10–69

2

- Display the Drawing Tools Format tab.

- Click the Shape Fill arrow (Drawing Tools Format tab | Shape Styles group) and then click No Fill in the Shape Fill gallery.

- Click the Shape Outline arrow (Drawing Tools Format tab | Shape Styles group) and then click No Outline in the Shape Outline gallery.

- Click outside the textbox to display the results (Figure 10–70).

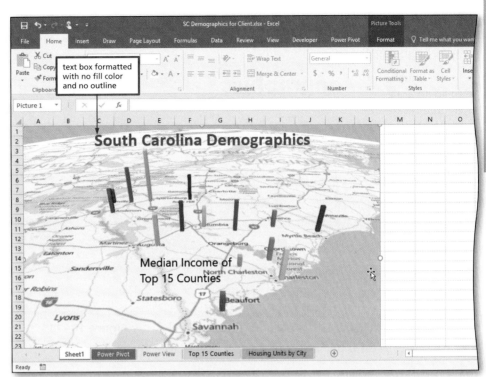

Figure 10–70

To Insert a Hyperlink

1 ENABLE DATA ANALYSIS | 2 GET & TRANSFORM | 3 USE POWER PIVOT | 4 USE POWER VIEW
5 USE 3D MAPS | 6 CREATE HYPERLINKS | **7 RECORD MACROS**

To create a hyperlink in Excel, you select the cell or graphic and then decide from among four type of hyperlinks: links to places in the workbook, links to files or webpages, a link to create a new file, or links to email addresses. Table 10–4 displays the text and hyperlinks that you will enter on the home page of the SC Demographics for Client workbook.

Table 10–4 Homepage Text and Hyperlinks			
Cell	**Text**	**Hyperlink location**	**Hyperlink**
M6	Links:	<none>	<none>
N7	Top 15 Counties by Population and Income	Place in current document	Top 15 Counties
N8	Housing Units by City	Place in current document	Housing Units by City
N9	Power Pivot	Place in current document	Power Pivot
N10	Power View	Place in current document	Power View
N11	Map Animation	Existing file	County Income in South Carolina.mp4
N12	Power BI	Eternal webpage	http://powerbi.microsoft.com

The following steps create hyperlinks on the home page. *Why? Creating links to other tabs, files, and websites will help users navigate through the workbook.*

①

- Enter the text from Table 10–4 into the appropriate cells.

- In the column heading area, double-click the border between columns N and O to widen column N.

- Zoom to 150% (Figure 10–71).

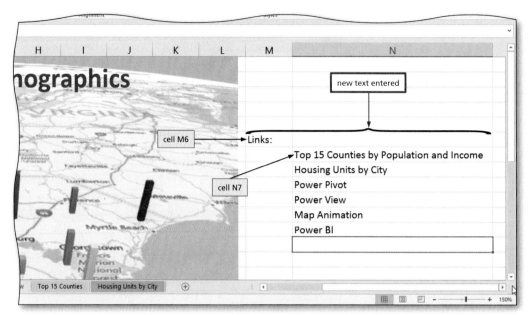

Figure 10–71

②

- Display the Insert tab.

- Select the cell you wish to make a hyperlink (in this case, cell N7) and then click the 'Add a Hyperlink' button (Insert tab | Links group) to display the Insert Hyperlink dialog box.

- In the Link to area, click the 'Place in This Document' button to identify the type of hyperlink.

- In the 'Or select a place in this document' area, click 'Top 15 Counties' (Figure 10–72).

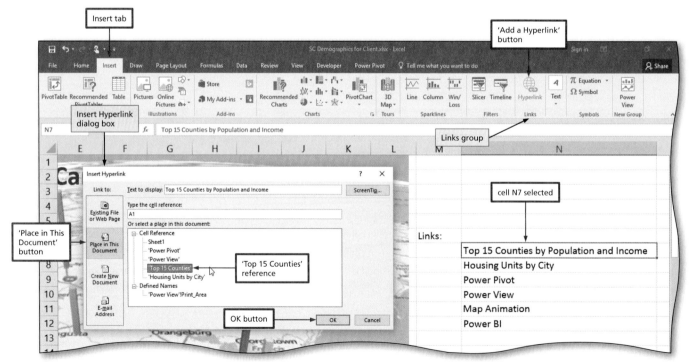

Figure 10–72

3

- Click the OK button (Insert Hyperlink dialog box) to assign the hyperlink.

- Repeat the process for cells N8, N9, and N10, referring to Table 10–4 as necessary.

- Click cell N11 to select it (Figure 10–73).

Q&A

How can I tell if a cell is hyperlinked?
Excel will underline a hyperlink and, when a user hovers over a hyperlink, the pointer will appear as a hand.

How do I edit a hyperlink if I make a mistake?
Right-click the hyperlink to display the shortcut menu and then click Edit Hyperlink to display the Edit Hyperlink dialog box.

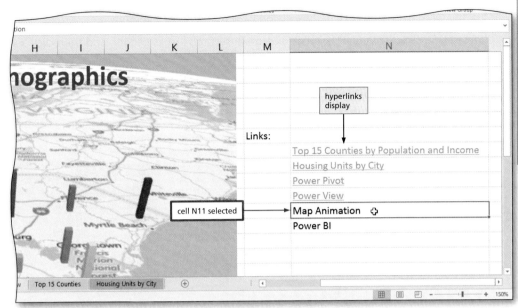

Figure 10–73

4

- Click the 'Add a Hyperlink' button (Insert tab | Links group) again and then click the 'Existing File or Web Page' button to identify the type of hyperlink.

- If necessary, click Current Folder in the Look in area.

- Click 'County Income in South Carolina. mp4' to select the file (Figure 10–74).

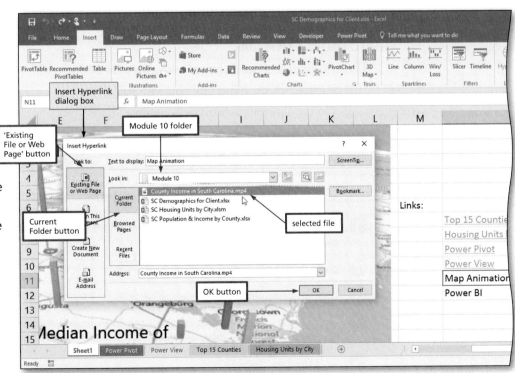

Figure 10–74

- Click the OK button (Insert Hyperlink dialog box) to apply the hyperlink.

- Click cell N12, click the 'Add a Hyperlink' button (Insert tab | Links group), and then click 'Existing File or Web Page' to identify the last hyperlink.

- In the Address box, type `http://powerbi.microsoft.com` to enter the webpage address (Figure 10–75).

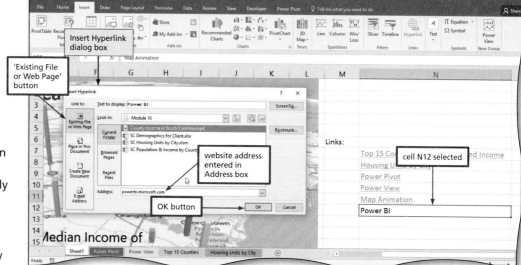

⑥

- Click the OK button (Insert Hyperlink dialog box) to apply the hyperlink.

- One at a time, click each of the hyperlinks to verify its functionality.

- Save the file.

Figure 10–75

Other Ways

1. Right-click cell, click Hyperlink, enter settings and hyperlink address (Insert Hyperlink dialog box), click OK button

2. Press CTRL+K, enter settings and hyperlink address (Insert Hyperlink dialog box), click OK button

BTW
Distributing a Workbook
Instead of printing and distributing a hard copy of a workbook, you can distribute the workbook electronically. Options include sending the workbook via email; posting it on cloud storage (such as OneDrive) and sharing the file with others; posting it on a social networking site, blog, or other website; and sharing a link associated with an online location of the workbook. You also can create and share a PDF or XPS image of the workbook, so that users can view the file in Acrobat Reader or XPS Viewer instead of in Excel.

TO DELETE A HYPERLINK

If you wanted to delete a hyperlink you would perform the following steps.

1. Right-click the hyperlink you wish to delete.

2. On the shortcut menu, click Remove Hyperlink.

To Format the Home Page

The following steps format the home page.

① On Sheet1, drag to select cells M6 through N12. Change the font color to purple and change the font size to 20.

② Zoom to 100%.

③ Turn off gridlines.

④ Change the name of the worksheet tab to Homepage. Change the color to purple (shown in Figure 10–75).

⑤ Save the file.

Break Point: If you wish to take a break, this is a good place to do so. Exit Excel. To resume at a later time, run Excel, open the file named SC Demographics for Client, and then continue following the steps from this location forward.

Macros

A **macro** is a set of commands and instructions grouped together to allow a user to accomplish a task automatically. Because Excel does not have a command or button for every possible worksheet task, you can create a macro to group together commonly used combinations of tasks, which then can be reused later. People also use macros to record commonly used text, to ensure consistency in calculations and formatting, as well as to manipulate nonnumeric data. In this module, you will learn how to create a macro using the macro recorder. After recording a macro, you can play it back, or execute it, as often as you want to repeat the steps you recorded with the macro recorder.

Three steps must be taken in preparation for working with macros in Excel. First, you must display the Developer tab (which you did earlier in the module). Second, a security setting in Excel must be modified to enable macros whenever you use Excel. Finally, Excel requires that a workbook which includes macros be saved as an Excel Macro-Enabled Workbook file type; the file extension is xlsm.

BTW
Naming Macros
If you use an uppercase letter when naming a macro, the user will have to use the SHIFT key when executing the macro.

BTW
Enabling Macros
Excel remembers your decision about enabling macros. If you have enabled macros in a worksheet, Excel will not ask you about enabling them the next time you open the worksheet, but will open the worksheet with macros enabled.

Should you customize applications with macros?

Casual Microsoft Office users do not know that customization is available. Creating special macros, events, or buttons on the ribbon can really help a user to be more productive. Creating a macro for repeating tasks also saves time and reduces errors. If you understand how to do so, customization is an excellent productivity tool.

To Enable Macros

1 ENABLE DATA ANALYSIS | 2 GET & TRANSFORM | 3 USE POWER PIVOT | 4 USE POWER VIEW
5 USE 3D MAPS | 6 CREATE HYPERLINKS | **7 RECORD MACROS**

The following steps enable macros in the workbook. *Why? Enabling macros allows the workbook to open with executable macros.*

1

- Click the Developer tab to make it the active tab.

- Click the Macro Security button (Developer tab | Code group) to display the Trust Center dialog box.

- Click 'Enable all macros' to select the option button (Figure 10–76).

2

- Click the OK button (Trust Center dialog box) to close the dialog box and enable macros.

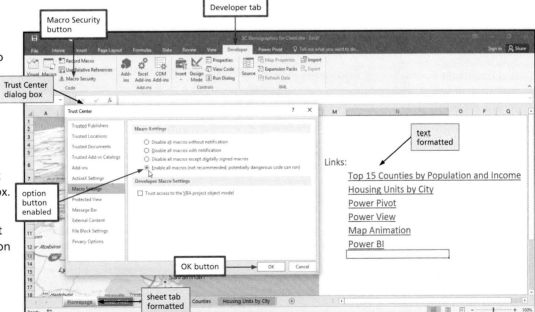

Figure 10–76

BTW
Storing Macros
In the Record Macro dialog box, you can select the location to store the macro in the `Store macro in' box. If you want a macro to be available to use in any workbook whenever you use Excel, select Personal Macro Workbook in the Store macro in list. This selection causes the macro to be stored in the Personal Macro Workbook, which is part of Excel. If you click New Workbook in the Store macro in list, then Excel stores the macro in a new workbook. Most macros created with the macro recorder are workbook-specific and thus are stored in the active workbook.

BTW
Shortcut Keys
Macro shortcut keys take precedence over Excel's existing shortcut keys. If you assign an existing shortcut key to a macro, it no longer will work for its original purpose. For instance, assigning CTRL+C to a macro means that you no longer will be able to use that shortcut key to copy content.

Recording Macros

A macro is created by recording a set of steps as they are performed. The steps and their order should be determined and rehearsed before creating the macro. When you create a macro, you assign a name to it. A macro name can be up to 255 characters long; it can contain numbers, letters, and underscores, but it cannot contain spaces or other punctuation. The name is used later to identify the macro when you want to execute it. Executing a macro causes Excel to perform each of the recorded steps in order.

Entering a cell reference always directs the macro to that specific cell. Navigating to a cell using keyboard navigation, however, requires the use of relative cell addressing. If you will be using keyboard navigation, you must ensure that the Use Relative References button (Developer tab | Code group) is selected so that the macro works properly. For example, suppose you record a macro in cell C1 that moves to cell C4 and enters text. If the Use Relative References button is not selected, the macro will always move to C4 and enter text; C4 would be considered an absolute reference. If the Use Relative References button is selected while recording, the macro will move three cells to the right of the current position and enter text (which will not always be cell C4).

You can copy macros to other workbooks by copying the macro code. You will learn more about coding in the next module.

To Record a Macro

1 ENABLE DATA ANALYSIS | 2 GET & TRANSFORM | 3 USE POWER PIVOT | 4 USE POWER VIEW
5 USE 3D MAPS | 6 CREATE HYPERLINKS | 7 RECORD MACROS

The following steps record a macro named Address_Block, with the shortcut key CTRL+M to execute the macro. **Why?** *The company wants to be able to use the shortcut to display company information.*

- Select cell O15.

- Click the 'Use Relative References' button (Developer tab | Code group) to indicate relative references.

- Click the Record Macro button (Developer tab | Code group) to display the Record Macro dialog box.

- When the Record Macro dialog box is displayed, type **Address_Block** in the Macro name text box.

- Type **m** in the Shortcut key text box to set the shortcut key for the macro to CTRL+M.

- In the Description text box, type **This macro prints the name of the company and the address in a block of three cells.** to enter the text (Figure 10–77).

Q&A Where are macros stored?

In this module, the macro will be stored in the current workbook. If you want a macro to be available in any workbook, you would click the 'Store macro in' button and then select Personal Macro Workbook.

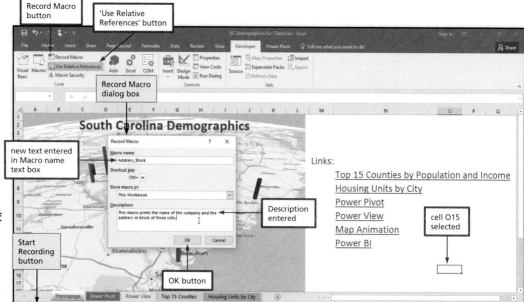

Figure 10–77

2

- Click the OK button (Record Macro dialog box) to begin recording the macro and to change the Record Macro button to the Stop Recording button (Figure 10–78).

Q&A What will be included in the macro?

Any task you perform in Excel will be part of the macro. When you are finished recording the macro, clicking the Stop Recording button on the ribbon or on the status bar ends the recording.

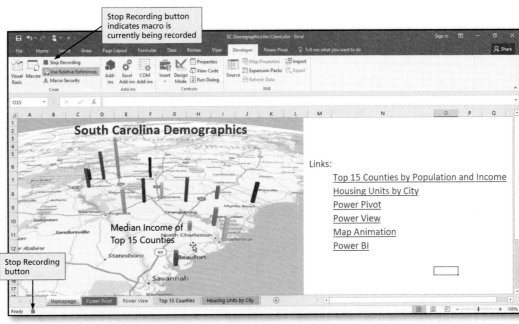

Figure 10–78

What is the purpose of the Record Macro button on the status bar?

You can use the Record Macro button on the status bar to start or stop recording a macro. When you are not recording a macro, this button is displayed as the Record Macro button. If you click it to begin recording a macro, the button changes to become the Stop Recording button.

3

- Type **Business Decisions, Inc.** and press the DOWN ARROW key.

- Type **1475 Maine Street** and press the DOWN ARROW key.

- Type **Columbia, SC 27811-1475** and press the DOWN ARROW key to complete the text (Figure 10–79).

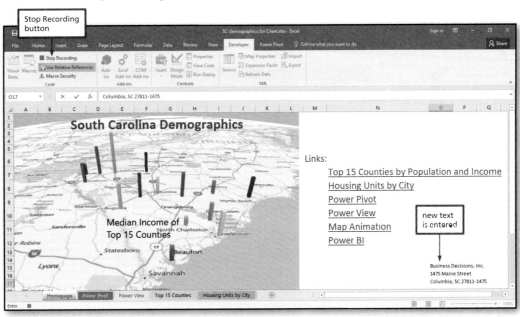

Figure 10–79

4

- Click the Stop Recording button (Developer tab | Code group) to stop recording the worksheet activities.

Q&A What if I make a mistake while recording the macro?

If you make a mistake while recording a macro, delete the macro and record it again. You delete a macro by clicking the View Macros button (Developer tab | Code group), clicking the name of the macro in the Macro dialog box, and then clicking the Delete button. You then can record the macro again with the same macro name.

Other Ways

1. Click Record Macro button on status bar, enter macro information (Record Macro dialog box), click OK button, enter steps, click Stop Recording button on status bar

To Execute a Macro

The following steps execute or playback the macro on the other worksheet pages. **Why?** *The company wants their name and address on each sheet.* You will use the shortcut key to execute the macro on the Power Pivot worksheet. You will use the View Macros button to execute the macro for the Top 15 Counties worksheet.

- Click the Power Pivot sheet tab and then click cell L19.

- Press **CTRL+M** to execute the macro with the shortcut key (Figure 10–80).

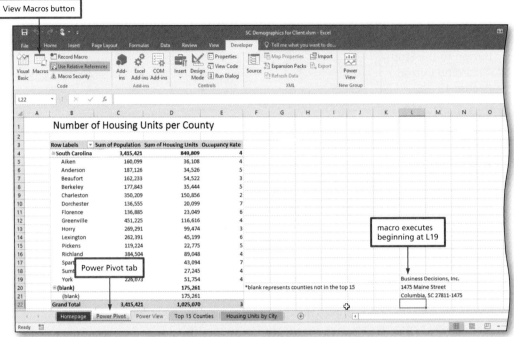

Figure 10–80

- Click the 'Top 15 Counties' sheet tab and then click cell L19.

- Click the View Macros button (Developer tab | Code group) to display the Macro dialog box (Figure 10–81).

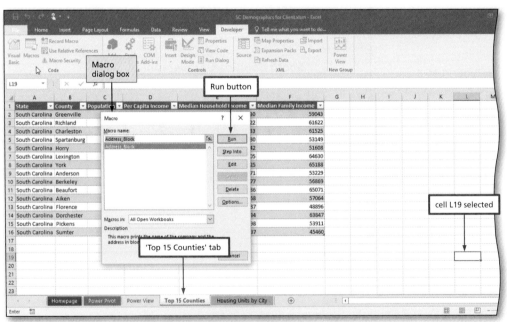

Figure 10–81

- Click the Run
button (Macros
dialog box)
to execute
the macro
(Figure 10–82).

- Repeat the
process for the
Housing Units
by City tab.
Because the
Power View
worksheet is a
chart, it has no
specific cells.
Do not apply the macro on that worksheet.

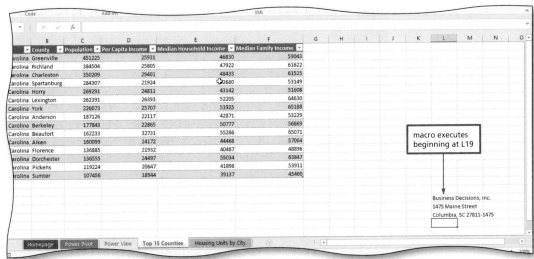

Figure 10–82

Other Ways

1. Press ALT+F8, select macro, click Run button (Macro dialog box)

TO CREATE A MACRO BUTTON ON THE QUICK ACCESS TOOLBAR

If you wanted to create a button on the Quick Access Toolbar to run the macro, you
would perform the following steps.

1. Right-click anywhere on the Quick Access Toolbar to display the shortcut menu.
2. Click 'Customize Quick Access Toolbar' on the shortcut menu to display the
Customize the Quick Access Toolbar options in the Excel Options dialog box.
3. Click the 'Choose commands from' arrow in the right pane to display a list of
commands to add to the Quick Access Toolbar.
4. Click Macros in the Choose commands from list to display a list of macros.
5. Click the name of the macro in the Macros list to select it.
6. Click the Add button (Excel Options dialog box) to add the macro to the
Customize Quick Access Toolbar list.
7. Click the OK button (Excel Options dialog box) to close the dialog box.

BTW

Starting Macros
Before recording a macro, you
should select your starting cell.
If you select it after you begin
recording the macro, the macro
always will start in that particular
cell, which may limit the macro's
usefulness.

To Save a Workbook as a Macro-Enabled Workbook

1 ENABLE DATA ANALYSIS | 2 GET & TRANSFORM | 3 USE POWER PIVOT | 4 USE POWER VIEW
5 USE 3D MAPS | 6 CREATE HYPERLINKS | **7 RECORD MACROS**

The following steps save the workbook as a macro-enabled workbook. *Why? Workbooks with macro must be
saved as macro-enabled.*

- Display the Backstage view, click the Save As tab, click the Browse button, and then navigate to your storage
location.

- Click the 'Save as type' button (Save As dialog box) and then click 'Excel Macro-Enabled Workbook' to select the file format (Figure 10–83).

- Click the Save button (Save As dialog box) to save the workbook as an Excel Macro-Enabled Workbook file.

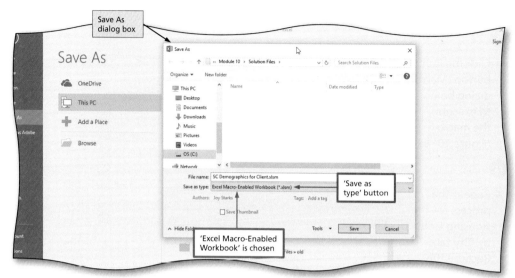

Figure 10–83

To Reset the Ribbon

1 ENABLE DATA ANALYSIS | 2 GET & TRANSFORM | 3 USE POWER PIVOT | 4 USE POWER VIEW
5 USE 3D MAPS | 6 CREATE HYPERLINKS | **7 RECORD MACROS**

It is a good idea to reset the ribbon when you are finished using the customized tools. *Why? Other Excel users may not expect to see new tabs and new button groups, especially in lab situations.* The following steps reset the ribbon, removing all customization, and then exit Excel.

- Right-click a blank area of the ribbon and then click 'Customize the Ribbon' on the shortcut menu to display the Excel Options dialog box.

- Click the Reset button to display its menu (Figure 10–84).

- Click 'Reset all customizations' in the Reset menu.

- When Excel displays a Microsoft Office dialog box asking if you want to delete all customizations, click the Yes button.

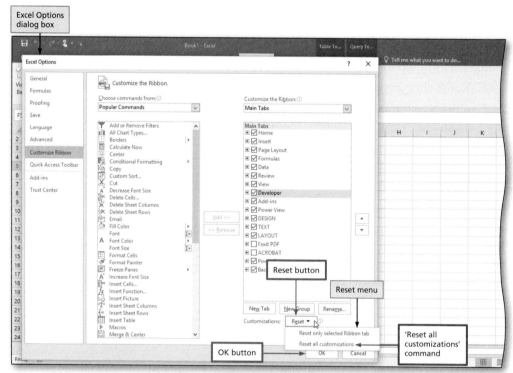

Figure 10–84

- Click the OK button to close the Excel Options dialog box.

- Exit Excel. If the Microsoft Office Excel dialog box is displayed, click the Don't Save button.

Summary

In this module, you learned how to use Excel's power tools. You learned how to enable data analysis in workbooks and customize the ribbon to display different tabs and all groups. You imported data by using the Get & Transform commands to create query tables. You used the Query Editor window to make changes to the data before using it as a table. Using Power Pivot, you added tables to the data model, created a PivotTable with relationships, and used a measure to create a calculated column. You also viewed the cube functions in Power Pivot.

You used Power View to create a report with tiles. You learned how to switch visualizations and highlight data in the Power View report. After opening the 3D Maps window, you create scenes with different map views, map labels, and displayed data related to geography. You created a tour animation and saved it.

You learned that Power BI is a tool that is used to create visualizations of your data to share in the cloud.

Finally, you created a home page with a captured screen shot and hyperlinks to the other tabs and webpages. You recorded a reusable macro with the company information.

What decisions will you need to make when using Power Tools, creating hyperlinks and recording macros?

Use these guidelines as you complete the assignments in this module and create your own worksheets for evaluating and analyzing data outside of this class.

1. Select your data carefully. Make sure it is in a tabular format. If the original data could possibly move, copy the data in a new folder and create your spreadsheet in that folder.

2. Choose the kind of visualization you wish to create.

3. If you want to create a PivotTable from multiple sources of data, use Power Pivot.

4. If you want to create a chart with multiple data sources, or to use interactive tiles or data card visualizations, use Power View.

5. If you have data that is geographic in nature, use 3D Maps.

6. Design a user interface to access your data more conveniently. Include hyperlinks, macro instructions, screen captures, and graphics.

7. Determine any actions you want to automate and create a macro. The steps and their order should be determined and rehearsed before creating the macro.

8. Test the user interface. The final step in creating a user interface is to verify that the interface behaves as designed and as a user expects.

CONSIDER THIS: PLAN AHEAD

Apply Your Knowledge

Reinforce the skills and apply the concepts you learned in this module.

Creating a Power View Report

Note: To complete this assignment, you will be required to use the Data Files. Please contact your instructor for information about accessing the Data Files. This assignment also requires access to Power View.

Instructions: Run Excel. Open a blank workbook and then save the workbook as Apply 10 – 1 Peppers Complete. The owner of a local restaurant wants you to create a Power View report that they eventually will upload to their website. The report should describe the peppers they use in various dishes on the menu as shown in Figure 10 – 85. They have provided you with a database file that has two tables in it.

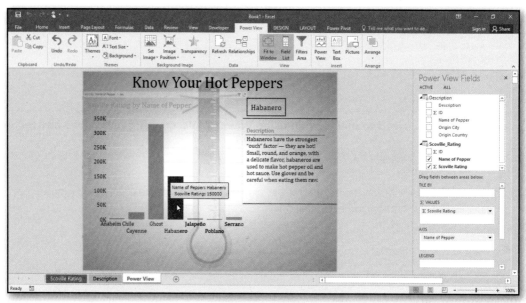

Figure 10 – 85

Perform the following tasks:
1. Open a File Explorer window. Copy and paste the Apply 10 – 1 Peppers.accdb data file from the Data Files for Module 10 to the location where you stored the Apply 10 – 1 Peppers Complete Excel file.

2. If necessary, customize the ribbon as described in the module to include a new group with the Insert a Power View Report command.

3. In the Excel window, set the color scheme to Aspect.

4. Click the New Query button (Data tab | Get & Transform group), point to From Database, and then click From Microsoft Access Database. Navigate to your storage location and double-click the Apply 10 – 1 Peppers file.

5. When the Navigator dialog box is displayed, load the Description table. Change the table style to Table Style Medium 5 (Table Tools Design tab | Table Styles group). Rename the sheet tab, Description, and color the tab Green.

6. Change the column width of column C, Description, to 35. Wrap the text. Change the row height of rows 2 through 8 to 115. You may need to zoom out while changing the row height.

7. Repeat Steps 4 and 5 to load the Scoville Rating table. Use Table Style Medium 3. Rename the sheet tab, Scoville Rating, and color the tab Red.

8. Click the 'Insert a Power View Report' button that you added to the ribbon, which will open a new worksheet, labelled Power View or Power View1.

9. If necessary, in the Power View Fields task pane, click the triangle next to the Scoville_Rating table to view the fields. If necessary, click the Name of Pepper and Scoville Rating check boxes to add them to the table. Remove the check mark in the ID check box, if necessary.

10. Click the Column Chart button (Design tab | Switch Visualization group) and then click Clustered Column. Resize the chart to cover approximately 2/3 of the report area.

11. In the Power View Fields task pane, click the All tab if necessary, and then click the triangle next to the Description table. Drag the Description field to an area beside the table, creating a second visualization. Drag the Name of Pepper field to the Tile By area.

12. To create the relationship between the two tables, click the Relationships button (Power View tab | Data group). When Excel displays the Manage Relationships dialog box, click the New button and link the two tables by the common field Name of Pepper. Resize the tables as shown in Figure 10–85. *Hint:* you may need to resize the inner table in the second visualization to wrap the text correctly.

13. Display the Power View tab. Use the Themes group to change the theme to NewsPrint, the font to Cambria, the Text Size to 150%, and the Background to Light1 Center Gradient. Edit the title as shown in Figure 10–85.

14. Use the Background Image group to set the image to the Apply 10–1 Thermometer.png file in the Data Files. Change the Transparency to 80%.

15. Click one of the bars in the column chart to verify that the tables are synchronized.

16. If instructed to do so, insert a text box with your name and course number in the lower-right corner of the Power View report.

17. Delete Sheet1 in the workbook. Save the file again.

18. Display the Backstage view and then click Print. Change the print settings to landscape and fit the Power View report to the paper size. Print the report.

19. Submit the revised workbook and the report printout in the format specified by your instructor.

20. Reset the ribbon customization and close Excel.

21. ☀ How might you use the other fields in the Description table? Would they be appropriate for the Power View? Why or why not?

Extend Your Knowledge

Extend the skills you learned in this module and experiment with new skills. You may need to use Help to complete the assignment.

Creating a Macro, Editing a Macro, and Assigning It to a Button

Note: To complete this assignment, you will be required to use the Data Files. Please contact your instructor for information about accessing the Data Files.

Instructions: Run Excel. Open the workbook Extend 10–1 Avia Salon from the Data Files for Students and then save the workbook as an Excel Macro-Enabled Workbook file type using the file name, Extend 10–1 Avia Salon Complete.

Continued >

Extend Your Knowledge *continued*

In the following steps, you will create a macro to add a column to a worksheet, assign the macro to a button on the Quick Access Toolbar, and then execute the macro. Figure 10–86 shows the completed worksheet.

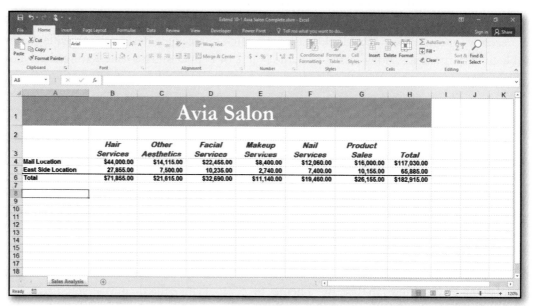

Figure 10–86

Perform the following tasks:

1. If the Developer tab is not displayed on the ribbon, display the Backstage view, click Options in the left pane to display the Excel Options dialog box, click Customize Ribbon, click the Developer check box in the Customize the Ribbon area, and then click the OK button.

2. Create a macro that adds a column before the Product Sales column by doing the following:

   a. Click the Record Macro button (Developer tab | Code group).

   b. When the Record Macro dialog box appears, name the macro, AddColumn, assign the keyboard shortcut CTRL+N. Store the macro in this workbook, enter your name in the Description box, and then click the OK button (Record Macro dialog box) to start the macro recording process.

   c. Select cell C3, click the Insert Cells arrow (Home tab | Cells group), and then click the 'Insert Sheet Columns' command from the Insert Cells menu.

   d. Select cell C6, sum the cell range C4:C5, set the column width to 15, and then click the Stop Recording button (Developer tab | Code group).

3. In the newly added column, enter **Nail Services** in cell C3, **12060** in cell C4, and **7400** in cell C5.

4. Click the View Macros button (Developer tab | Code group) to display the Macro dialog box. Run the AddColumn macro to add a column. Enter the following data: **Makeup Services**, **8400**, and **2740**.

5. Right-click anywhere on the Quick Access Toolbar and then click 'Customize Quick Access Toolbar' on the shortcut menu. When the Excel Options dialog box is displayed, click the 'Choose commands from' arrow and click Macros. Click AddColumn, click the Add button, and then click the OK button to add a Macro button to the Quick Access Toolbar.

6. While still in column C, run the macro as follows:

   a. Click the AddColumn button on the Quick Access Toolbar and then enter `Facial Services`, `22455`, and `10235` for the column values.

   b. Press CTRL+SHIFT+N and then enter `Other Aesthetics`, `14115`, and `7500` for the column values.

7. If requested by your instructor, add the following text to the end of the text in cell A1: `(EST. <year of birth>)`, replacing <year of birth> with your year of birth.

8. Right-click the AddColumn button on the Quick Access Toolbar and then click 'Remove from Quick Access Toolbar' on the shortcut menu.

9. Use Help to learn how to access the VBA window. In the VBA window, click File on the menu bar and then click print to print the AddColumn macro.

10. Save the workbook. Submit the revised workbook and the macro printout in the format specified by your instructor.

11. ✳ How would using the 'Use Relative References' button when recording your macro change how you insert columns using the AddColumn macro?

Expand Your World

Create a solution that uses cloud and web technologies by learning and investigating on your own from general guidance.

Creating a Power BI Treemap

Note: To complete these steps, you will be required to use the file you created in this module, named SC Demographics for Client. If you did not create this file, see your instructor for ways to complete this assignment. You must be connected to the Internet to perform these steps. If you are working in a lab situation, your IT administrator must have turned on access to Power BI. If you are working from home, you will need access to your Office 365 account.

Problem: You decide to create a Power Bi visualization to share with others via the web (Figure 10–87).

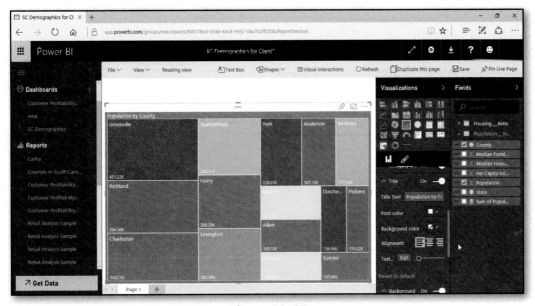

Figure 10–87

Continued >

Expand Your World *continued*

Instructions:

1. Open a browser and navigate to https://powerbi.microsoft.com. If you have an Office 365 account, Sign in. If not, see your instructor for login assistance.

2. In the upper-left corner, click the 'Show the navigation pane' button, if necessary. (If the 'Show the navigation pane' button is unavailable, click the Get button (local files) to display the Get Data > Files window.)

3. Click the plus sign next to Dashboards in the My Workspace pane on left side of the screen. Type **SC Demographics** to name a new dashboard and then press the ENTER key.

4. Click the Get Data button at the bottom of the navigation pane. Follow the instructions to import a local file. Navigate to your storage location and double-click the SC Demographics for Client.xlsx that you created in this module.

5. Double-click the file to open a blank report.

6. If necessary, click Edit report on the toolbar to open the Visualizations task pane and the Fields task pane.

7. In the Visualizations task pane, click the Treemap icon.

8. In the Fields task pane, open the Population_Income table and click the County and Populations check boxes. Resize the treemap chart as necessary.

9. In the Visualizations task pane, click the Format tab. Turn on Data labels. Set the background color to gray and the title font color to white.

10. If instructed to do so, enter your name in the Title Text box (Visualizations task pane).

11. Delete the Power View tab.

12. Save the file. Send a link to your instructor. Close Power BI.

13. ✳ How was creating a treemap visualization in Power BI different than creating it in Excel. In Power BI, what advantages do you have with regard to sharing the report?

In the Labs

Design, create, modify, and/or use a workbook following the guidelines, concepts, and skills presented in this module. Labs 1 and 2, which increase in difficulty, require you to create solutions based on what you learned in the module; Lab 3 requires you to apply your creative thinking and problem-solving skills to design and implement a solution.

Lab 1: Creating a 3D Map and Home Page

Note: To complete this assignment, you will be required to use the Data Files. Please contact your instructor for information about accessing the Data Files.

Problem: The State of Alaska wants a visual report displaying the number of visitors to its top 10 National Parks in a recent year. They also would like to be able to access the National Park Service website within the report. You decide to create a workbook with a home page and 3D Map.

Perform the following tasks:

1. Run Excel and open a blank workbook. Save the file on your storage location with the name, Lab 10–1 National Parks in Alaska Complete.

2. Using File Explorer, copy the Data File named Lab 10–1 National Parks in Alaska and paste it to your storage location.

3. Click the New Query button (Data tab | Get & Transform group) and choose to import from a workbook. Using the Import Data dialog box, navigate to your storage location and import the Lab 10–1 National Parks in Alaska file.

4. When Excel displays the Navigator dialog box, click the Top 10 Parks table and then click the Edit button.

5. Using the Query Editor window, remove the first row, which is a title. Make the next row the header row. Close and load the query.

6. Widen columns as necessary to view all of the data. Add commas to the visitor figures.

7. Click the 3D Map button (Insert tab | Tours group) to open the 3D Maps window.

8. For Scene 1:

   a. Remove any locations in the Layer Pane.

   b. Zoom out and reposition the map to show the entire United States.

9. Create Scene 2.

   a. In the Location area (Layer Pane), click the Add Field button and then click State in the field list.

   b. Create a text box with the word, Alaska.

10. Create Scene 3.

    a. Remove the text box and turn on Map Labels.

    b. In the Location area (Layer Pane), click the Add Field button (Layer Pane) and then click National Park in the field list. Click the Select One button and then click Other in the list.

    c. In the Height area (Layer Pane), click the Add Field button and then click Visitors in 2015.

    d. In the Category area (Layer Pane), click the Add Field button and then click National Park. Right-click the Legend and then click Remove.

    e. Zoom in as close as possible, while keeping all of the data bars on the map.

    f. For each data bar, right-click the data bar and then click Add Annotation. In the Add Annotation dialog box, click the National Park option button, click the Custom option button, and then edit the title field to display only the name of the park. Choose a position for the annotation (left or right), and how high on the bar you want the annotation to display. As you add annotations, try not to overlap.

11. For Scenes 1 and 2, change the scene options to a duration of 3 seconds and use the Fly Over Effect. For Scene 3, change the scene option to a duration of 3 seconds and use the Push In effect.

12. Play the tour (Figure 10–88) and then make any adjustments necessary. Capture a screenshot of scene 3. Create a video of the tour with the name Alaska State Parks.

13. Close the 3D Maps window and return to the Excel window. Save the file.

14. Navigate to Sheet1 in the workbook. Rename the worksheet Homepage. Paste the screen capture.

15. In cell M3, type `Links:` to enter a heading.

16. Navigate to the Top 15 Parks worksheet and copy the range, B2:B11. Paste the range to cell M5 on the home page.

17. Open a browser and navigate to http://www.nps.gov/state/ak/index.htm. Scroll down to Bering Land Bridge National Preserve. Right-click the heading and then click Copy link on the shortcut menu.

Continued >

In the Labs *continued*

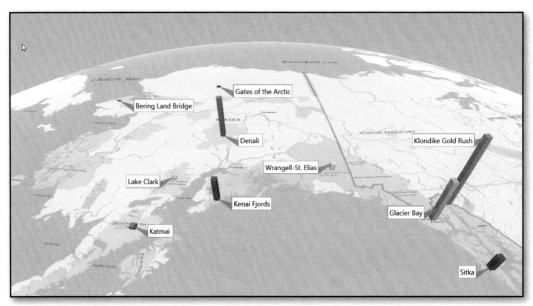

Figure 10–88

18. Return to the workbook. Right-click cell M5 and then click Hyperlink on the shortcut menu. Paste the web address in the Address box. Click the OK button.

19. Repeat Steps 17 and 18 for each of the other nine parks.

20. In cell M15, type **Map Animation**. Hyperlink the cell to the stored video you created.

21. If instructed to do so, enter your name and course number on the home page.

22. Save the file. See your instructor for ways to submit this file.

23. ✳ Would you use Excel for a presentation? What are the advantages and disadvantages of using visualizations in Excel versus apps like PowerPoint or Prezi?

Lab 2: Using Power Pivot

Note: To complete this assignment, you will be required to use the Data Files. Please contact your instructor for information about accessing the Data Files. You also will need access to Power Pivot.

Problem: The Resident Life office at your school has a list of approved dormitories, resident halls, and apartments, both on- and off-campus. They have asked you to merge two data files related to locations and occupancy. You create the PivotTable shown in Figure 10–89.

Perform the following tasks:
1. Run Excel and open a blank workbook. If necessary, customize the ribbon as described in the module to include the Power Pivot tab. Save the file on your storage location with the file name Lab 10–2 Residences Complete.

2. Using File Explorer, copy the Data Files named Lab 10–2 Residence Halls and Lab 10–2 Locations, and paste them to your storage location.

3. Use the commands in the Get & Transform group on the Data tab to import two query tables: Lab 10–2 Residence Halls and Lab 10–2 Locations. Use the Query Editor window as necessary to format the data.

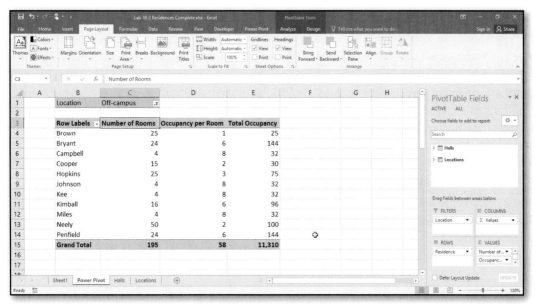

Figure 10–89

4. In the Excel workbook, format the two tables and rename the sheet tabs. Name the tabs, Halls and Locations.

5. If you have access to Power Pivot, use the Power Pivot tab to add each worksheet to the data model. Use the Power Pivot for Excel window to create a PivotTable on a new worksheet. If you do not have access to Power Pivot, create a PivotTable using the Insert tab.

6. In the Excel window, access the PivotTable Fields task pane. Place check marks in the Residence, # of Rooms, and Max Occupancy check boxes from the Halls table and a check mark in the Location check box from the Locations table. Create a relationship as necessary.

7. Double click the column headings and rename them Number of Rooms and Occupancy per Room.

8. In the PivotTable Fields task pane, drag the Location field to the Filters area.

9. If you have access to Power Pivot, click the Measures button and then click New Measure on the menu. Name the new measure, Total Occupancy, and use the LEFT BRACKET key ([ ) to help you multiply the Number of Rooms times the Occupancy per Room.

10. Format the PivotTable as necessary. Name the sheet tab, Power Pivot. Delete the Sheet1 tab.

11. Click the filter button in cell C1, click the All tab if necessary, and then click Off-campus to display only the off campus housing choices as shown in Figure 10–89.

12. If instructed to do so, create a home page with a picture of your school, and your name and course number.

13. Save the workbook. Remove the ribbon customization. Submit the revised document in the format specified by your instructor.

14. ✸ What other measure might you create with this data? How would the Residence Life office use this data to manage room assignments?

Continued >

In the Labs *continued*

Lab 3: Creating a Tourist Map

Part 1: You decide to create a map of tourist sites for your upcoming trip to New York City. Create a workbook named Lab 10–3 NYC Highlights. In column A, enter the name of five tourist destinations in New York City, such as the 911 Memorial, the Statue of Liberty, the Empire State Building, etc. Use the web to find the address for those locations. For each location, enter the street address, city, and state into your spreadsheet. Convert the data to a table. Edit the column headings and adjust the column widths, as necessary. Access 3D Maps and add the appropriate fields to the location area. Zoom in. Create a flat map with map labels and data cards that display the name of the destination and the address. Post a screen capture to your social media.

Part 2: ⚙ What kind of industries might use the 3D Maps tool on a regular basis? Why might 3D Maps be the tool of choice over map-specific apps? How could you use the 3D Maps tool in presentations?

11 | User Interfaces, Visual Basic for Applications (VBA), and Collaboration Features in Excel

Objectives

You will have mastered the material in this module when you can:

- Add and configure worksheet form controls such as command buttons, option buttons, and check boxes
- Record user input to another location on the worksheet
- Understand Visual Basic for Applications (VBA) code and explain event-driven programs
- Explain sharing and collaboration techniques
- Use passwords to assign protected and unprotected status to a worksheet

- Compare and merge workbooks
- Review a digital signature on a workbook
- Insert, edit, delete, and review comments in a workbook
- Manage tracked changes in a shared workbook
- Format a worksheet background
- Enhance charts and sparklines
- Save a custom view of a worksheet

Introduction

This module introduces you to user interface design using form controls and ActiveX controls in a worksheet, the Visual Basic for Applications (VBA) programming environment, sharing and collaboration features of worksheets and workbooks, the use of comments in Excel, and the process of tracking changes in shared workbooks.

With Excel, you can design a user-friendly interface that permits users to easily enter information into the workbook, regardless of their experience with the app.

Form controls include interface elements such as option buttons, check boxes, and group boxes. ActiveX controls, including the text box and command button controls used in this module, provide the same core functionality as the form controls, but allow you, as the designer, greater power to customize the appearance of the control. The VBA programming environment is used to program the functionality of the ActiveX controls.

When working on a team, the sharing features of Excel make it easy to provide team members access to worksheet data, protect information as necessary, and track changes made throughout the workbook. Distributing a workbook through OneDrive, Office 365, or SharePoint maintains ownership of the file while providing all members of the team access to the most current version of the data at all times. Commenting features of Excel encourage feedback on specific content within the worksheet.

Additional collaboration tools permit users to view multiple versions of the same workbook side by side for comparison or to compare and merge copies of the same workbook after editing by individual team members.

Project — Global Pharmaceutical Company Sales Analysis

The project in this module follows proper design guidelines and uses Excel to create the workbooks shown in Figure 11–1. Global Pharmaceutical Company (GPC) develops and markets generic drugs to hospitals and health clinics worldwide. Because GPC's reach is global, there are members of the sales team located in offices throughout the world. The head of sales wants to use advanced features of Excel to share information about GPC's prospective clients and projected revenue among the sales team. The GPC Sales Analysis workbook consists of three worksheets — Prospect Recorder, Sales Data Analysis, and a hidden Prospect List. The GPC Events workbook consists of two worksheets — Event Expenses and Prior Years. Multiple copies of both workbooks exist with changes made by multiple users.

The Prospect Recorder worksheet (Figure 11–1a) in the GPC Sales Analysis workbook provides a framework for recording information about sales prospects. You will add form controls and ActiveX controls to finish the interface development. You will then create VBA code to add functionality to the command button controls added to the worksheet. The functionality added through the VBA programming environment will present a series of dialog boxes instructing the salesperson to enter the prospect's contact information, and then will copy the prospect's information into the hidden Prospect List worksheet.

The Sales Data Analysis worksheet (Figure 11–1b) in the GPC Sales Analysis workbook provides production details for 2017 and 2018 related to the three production lines (production facilities are located in Brazil, India, and Mexico) and four product types (generic versions of antihistamine, antihypertensive, anti-inflammatory, and antithyroid drugs). You will add comments and track changes made by other users of the shared workbook.

The Event Expenses worksheet (Figure 11–1c) in the GPC Events workbook contains estimated costs for three sales events throughout the year 2018. Colleagues Noah and Serenity have made changes to their individual shared copies of the workbook that you will merge into a single workbook file. You will add a watermark to this worksheet.

The Prior Years worksheet (Figure 11–1d) in the GPC Events workbook contains attendance figures for prior events (2011 through 2017) and a chart representing the data. You will add a background to this worksheet. You will add finishing touches to the existing chart and add sparklines for each event. You will also create a custom view for the worksheet and prepare the workbook for distribution to users of older versions of Excel.

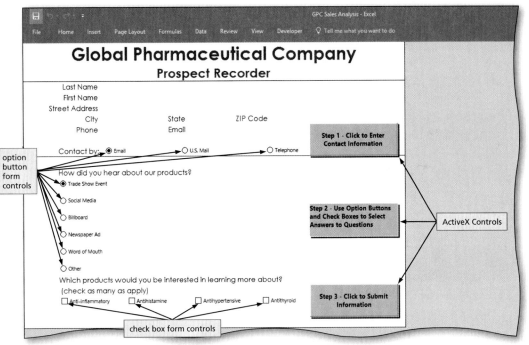

(a) Prospect Recorder Form

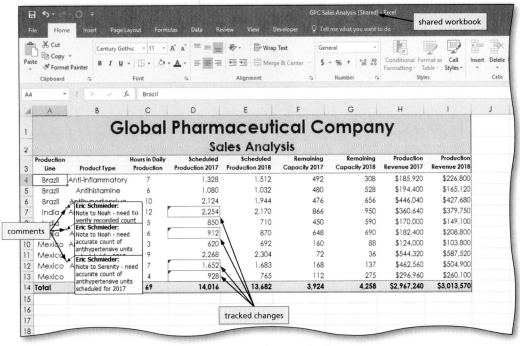

(b) GPC Sales Analysis

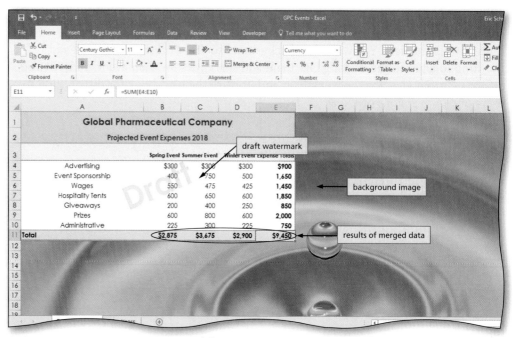

(c) Event Expenses

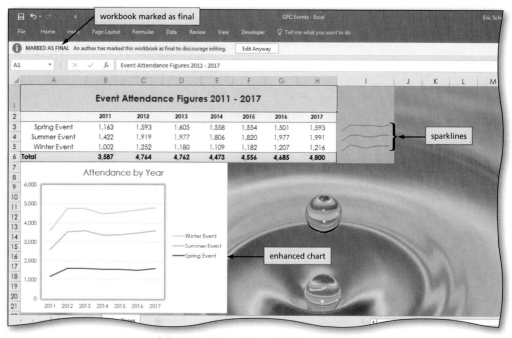

(d) Prior Years Event Attendance

Figure 11–1

The requirements document for Global Pharmaceutical Company Sales Analysis and Events workbooks is shown in Figure 11–2. It includes the needs, source of data, calculations, and other facts about the worksheets' development.

Worksheet Titles	Prospect Recorder, Sales Data Analysis, Event Expenses, and Prior Years
Needs	Global Pharmaceutical Company (GPC) develops and markets four types of generic drugs (antihistamine, antihypertensive, anti-inflammatory, and antithyroid) to hospitals and health clinics worldwide through three production facilities in Brazil, India, and Mexico.
	The company would like a workbook to record information about sales prospects and maintain current information regarding scheduled production and sales. Additionally, a second workbook is needed to maintain current data on the upcoming 2018 sales events and consolidate historic attendance information on events held from 2011 through 2017.
	Several copies of each workbook exist. The information required of the prospects has been structured in a hidden Prospect List worksheet, but the sales manager wants a form created to make data entry easier. Changes have been made to sales analysis data in a shared copy of the workbook and those changes need to be reviewed and accepted or rejected. Finally, three copies of the shared events workbook exist with different cost values for the events. These values need to be merged into a single workbook and visual enhancements to the worksheets are desired for presentation purposes.
Source of Data	Updated values for 2018 event costs are included in the GPC Events Noah and GPC Events Serenity workbooks. Changes have been made and tracked in the GPC Sales Analysis Changed workbook.
Calculations	All formulas are set up in the workbook. The worksheets in the workbook should be reviewed to familiarize yourself with the calculations.
Other Requirements	None.

Figure 11–2 Requirements Document

The following roadmap identifies general activities you will perform as you progress through this module:

1. DESIGN the USER INTERFACE.
2. RECORD USER INPUT to another location using the user interface.
3. WRITE the Visual Basic for Applications (VBA) CODE.
4. TEST the USER INTERFACE.
5. SHARE AND COLLABORATE on a workbook.
6. USE COMMENTS for review discussion.
7. TRACK CHANGES made to the workbook.
8. FINALIZE the WORKBOOK.

To Run Excel and Open a Workbook

The following steps run Excel and open a workbook named GPC Sales Analysis. To complete these steps, you will be required to use the Data Files. Please contact your instructor for information about accessing the Data Files.

1 Run Excel.

2 Open the file named GPC Sales from the Data Files.

3 If the Excel window is not maximized, click the Maximize button on its title bar to maximize the window.

4 Save the workbook on your hard drive, OneDrive, or other storage location as a macro-enabled workbook (.xlsm format) using GPC Sales Analysis as the file name (Figure 11–3).

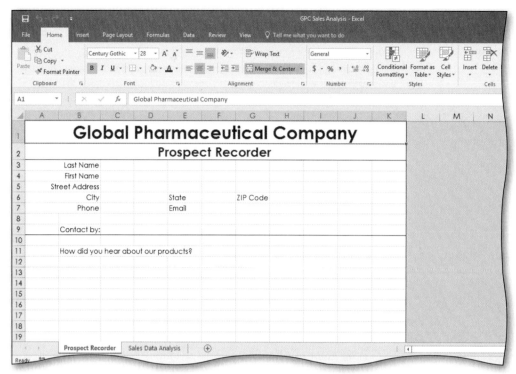

Figure 11–3

Designing the User Interface

The GPC sales team is using Excel to maintain information on prospects and their product interests. The head of sales has requested a simple user interface that can be used by salespeople to record details about prospects in the workbook. You will create a method of entering data for people with little or no knowledge of Excel, who might not know which cells to select or how to navigate the worksheet. Figure 11–4 shows the approach that will be used to create the user interface and how the Prospect Recorder worksheet will look when complete.

When a user clicks the 'Click to Enter Contact Information' command button, it will trigger Excel to display a series of input dialog boxes to capture contact information. The remaining data (the prospect's preferred method of communication, how they heard about GPC's products, and their specific product interest) will be entered using check boxes and option buttons to help reduce input errors that can be caused by mistyped data. Multiple check boxes can be selected for product interests. Unlike check boxes, option buttons restrict users to one selection per group, in this case to one preferred method of contact and one source of information. Because all of the data entry will use controls and input dialog boxes, you can protect the workbook to restrict the user's interaction with the worksheet to those controls and dialog boxes.

Planning Controls into the Worksheet Design

Two types of controls are used to create the user interface: form controls and ActiveX controls. Form controls and ActiveX controls look identical in the controls gallery. They do have functional differences, however, that can help determine which one is the best choice for an object.

User Interfaces, Visual Basic for Applications (VBA), and Collaboration Features in Excel   **Excel Module 11**   **EX** 623

Excel Module 11

Step 1 — Create the User Interface

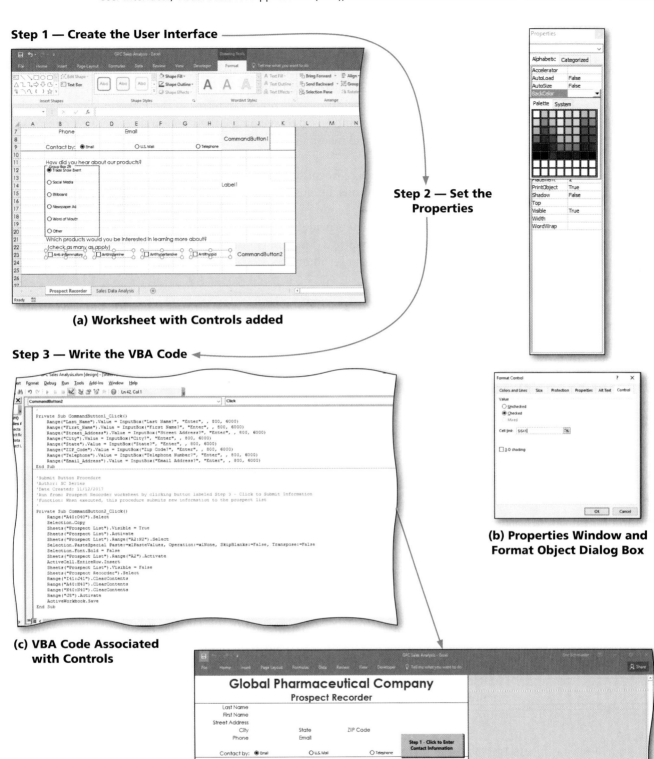

(a) Worksheet with Controls added

Step 2 — Set the Properties

(b) Properties Window and Format Object Dialog Box

Step 3 — Write the VBA Code

(c) VBA Code Associated with Controls

(d) Final Product

Figure 11–4

Form controls require no knowledge of VBA to use. You can assign an Excel macro directly to a form control, allowing the macro to be run with a click. Form controls also allow you to reference cells easily and use Excel functions and expressions to manipulate data. You can customize their appearance at a rudimentary level.

ActiveX controls provide great flexibility in terms of their design. They have extensive properties that can be used to customize their appearance. ActiveX controls cannot be assigned an Excel macro directly. The macro code must be part of the VBA code for the control.

To create the Prospect Recorder interface, you will use form controls for the check box and option buttons, because of their ease of use and ability to use Excel functions with no additional code. You will use ActiveX controls for the command button and label controls to provide a more visually appealing interface than would be possible just using form controls. Figure 11-5 displays the gallery of controls available to use when constructing a user interface.

Figure 11–5

The option button controls will be used with the INDEX function to record the single selections for two entries: the prospect's preferred method of contact and how prospects heard about the products. When selected, the control will return a number indicating which option button was selected. The INDEX function matches that selection to a list and returns the entry in the list. This allows the workbook to contain entries such as Email, U.S. Mail, and Telephone, rather than values that the control returns such as 1, 2, and 3. The INDEX function will make use of the named ranges, Contact_Method and Information_Source, that will be created in the Prospect Recorder worksheet. These named ranges will be placed in column W to keep them out of sight but still on the same worksheet as the user interface.

Finally, the user interface will record input in two places. It will temporarily record user input in row 40 of the Prospect Recorder worksheet, which is out of sight when the user interface is visible. Once the user input is recorded in row 40, an ActiveX control will copy the input to a hidden worksheet, Prospect List. When testing the interface, you will verify the data recorded in the hidden worksheet.

To Display the Developer Tab

As discussed in Module 10 when creating macros, the Developer tab provides access to various VBA controls. Before you can work with VBA, you need to prepare the workbook by providing access to the necessary tools. The following steps display the Developer tab on the ribbon.

User Interfaces, Visual Basic for Applications (VBA), and Collaboration Features in Excel   **Excel Module 11**   **EX** 625

Excel Module 11

1 Display the Backstage view.

2 Click Options in the left pane to display the Excel Options dialog box.

3 Click Customize Ribbon in the left pane (Excel Options dialog box) to display the Customize the Ribbon tools.

4 Click the Developer check box in the Main Tabs list to select the Developer tab for display on the ribbon.

5 Click the OK button (Excel Options dialog box) to close the dialog box.

To Add Form Controls to a Worksheet

1 DESIGN USER INTERFACE | 2 RECORD USER INPUT | 3 WRITE VBA CODE | 4 TEST USER INTERFACE
5 SHARE & COLLABORATE | 6 USE COMMENTS | 7 TRACK CHANGES | 8 FINALIZE WORKBOOK

Why? You will use form controls not only to ensure consistent data entry but also to make the final interface one *that someone unfamiliar with Excel will be able to use easily.* The following steps create the form controls. Do not be concerned about the exact placement of controls on the form. The option buttons and check boxes will be aligned later in the module.

- If necessary, display the Prospect Recorder worksheet.

- Display the Developer tab and then click the Insert Controls button (Developer tab | Controls group) to display the Controls gallery (Figure 11–6).

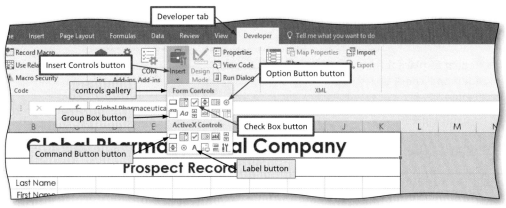

Figure 11–6

2

- Click the Option Button button in the Form Controls area (column 6, row 1) in the Controls gallery.

- Drag the pointer to place the option button control in cell C9 (approximately), as shown in Figure 11–7.

- Repeat to place eight additional option buttons (Figure 11–7).

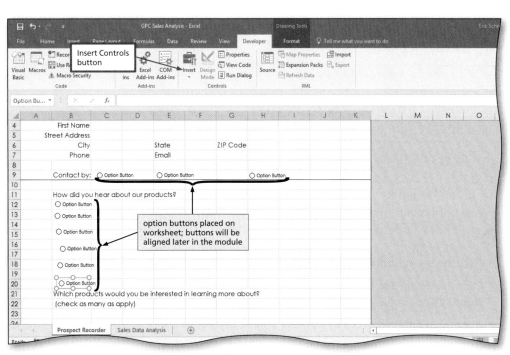

Figure 11–7

Why does my option button have more label text showing than in the figure?
The amount of text visible is determined by the size of the control. Dragging through a larger space on the worksheet will result in more label text being displayed. You can adjust the amount of visible label text by resizing the control.

❸

- Click the Insert Controls button (Developer tab | Controls group) to display the Controls gallery, as shown in Figure 11–6.

- Click the Check Box button in the Form Controls area (column 3, row 1) in the Controls gallery.

- Drag so that the check box control is displayed in cell B24 (approximately), as shown in Figure 11–8.

- Repeat to place three additional check boxes (Figure 11–8).

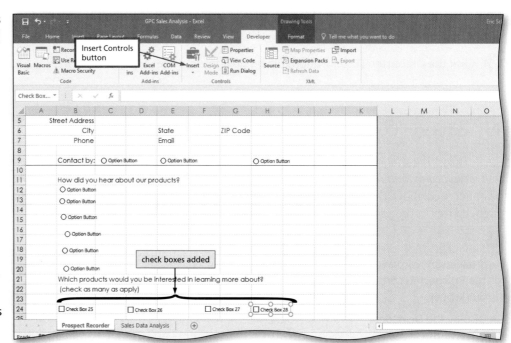

Figure 11–8

 What if I placed a control incorrectly?
If you want to reposition a control, right-click the control to select it and then drag it to its new location. You can delete a control by right-clicking the control and selecting Cut on the shortcut menu.

The check box is not the size I need it to be. What can I do?
Check boxes are resized easily. The check boxes here will be resized after the captions are changed later in this module.

Other Ways

1. Select control, click Copy button (Home tab | Clipboard group), click Paste button (Home tab | Clipboard group)
2. Right-click control, click Copy on shortcut menu, right-click worksheet, click Paste on shortcut menu
3. Select control, press CTRL+C to copy, press CTRL+V to paste

To Group Option Buttons in the User Interface

1 DESIGN USER INTERFACE | 2 RECORD USER INPUT | 3 WRITE VBA CODE | 4 TEST USER INTERFACE
5 SHARE & COLLABORATE | 6 USE COMMENTS | 7 TRACK CHANGES | 8 FINALIZE WORKBOOK

Why? *With form controls, only one of the option buttons on the entire form can be selected unless the option buttons are grouped. When grouped, only one option button per group can be selected.* Use the group box form control to group one set of the option buttons together. The following step first creates the group box form control, and then groups option buttons inside it.

❶

- Click the Insert Controls button (Developer tab | Controls group) to display the Controls gallery.

- Click the Group Box button in the Form Controls area (column 1, row 2) in the Controls gallery, as shown in Figure 11–6.

- Drag the pointer from cell B12 to C20, approximately, so that the group box control encloses the six 'How did you hear' option buttons (Figure 11–9).

Q&A

How accurately do I have to draw the group box?
The option button controls need to be completely enclosed in the group box control in order for it to work correctly.

Why did I not add a group box control around the Contact by option buttons?
Group boxes are used to logically collect option buttons in order to limit the selection of options to only one choice from the group. Any option buttons not contained within a group box are treated as a group contained by the form, so the Contact by option buttons are grouped by default. Without the addition of one group box on the form, the user would only be able to select one option button out of the nine option buttons.

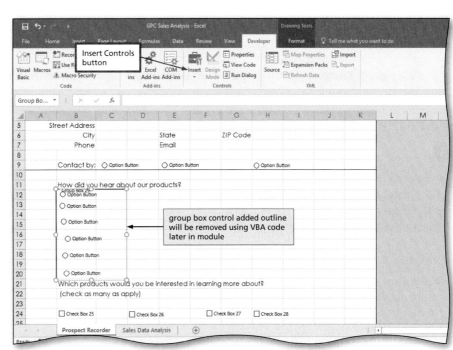

Figure 11–9

To Add a Label Control to the Worksheet

1 DESIGN USER INTERFACE | 2 RECORD USER INPUT | 3 WRITE VBA CODE | 4 TEST USER INTERFACE
5 SHARE & COLLABORATE | 6 USE COMMENTS | 7 TRACK CHANGES | 8 FINALIZE WORKBOOK

A total of 13 option buttons and check box controls have been added to the form so far. Adding a label can guide the user on the use of these controls within the process of entering the prospect information. *Why? A label control can be used to impart information in a user interface.* The following step adds a label control to the worksheet.

- Click cell I14.
- Click the Insert Controls button (Developer tab | Controls group) to display the Controls gallery.
- Click the Label button in the ActiveX Controls area (column 3, row 2) of the Controls gallery as shown in Figure 11–6.
- Using the selected cell I14 as a guide, drag the pointer (a crosshair) from the upper-left corner of cell I14 to the lower-right corner of cell J15 to insert the label control (Figure 11–10).

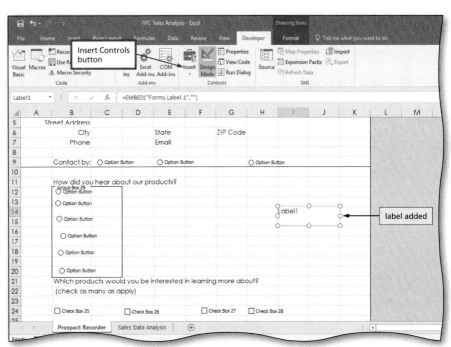

Figure 11–10

To Add a Command Button Control to the Worksheet

The use of command buttons gives the user control over the execution of each step of the process when entering data into the form. ***Why?*** *A command button control can have Visual Basic code associated with it that accomplishes more complex actions than a macro or a form button can accommodate.* The following steps add two command button controls to the worksheet.

- Click the Insert Controls button (Developer tab | Controls group) to display the Controls gallery.

- Click the Command Button button in the ActiveX Controls area (column 1, row 1) of the Controls gallery.

- Drag the pointer (a crosshair) from the upper-left corner of cell I7 to the lower-right corner of cell J9, as shown in Figure 11–11.

2

- Repeat Step 1 to add a second command button in the location shown in Figure 11–11.

- Save the workbook again on the same storage location with the same file name (Figure 11–11).

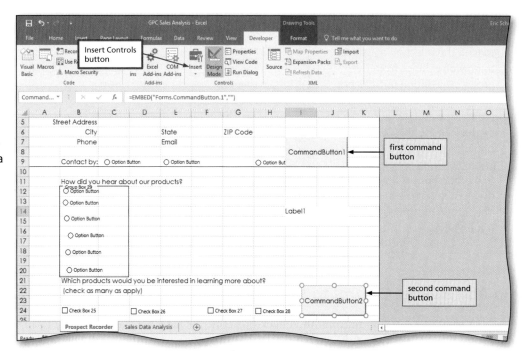

Figure 11–11

Setting Form Control Properties

Each form control in the Controls gallery has many properties, or characteristics, that can be set to determine the form control's appearance and behavior. You set these properties using the Format Control dialog box, which can be accessed by right-clicking the form control and selecting Format Control from the shortcut menu, or by selecting the control and clicking the Control Properties button (Developer tab | Controls group) on the ribbon.

The next step is to set the properties for the 13 form controls in the user interface. The group box, while technically a form control, will not be formatted here. This will be formatted using VBA later in the module. The three ActiveX controls also will be formatted later in the module. The form control properties will be set as follows:

BTW

Adding Alternative Text for Accessibility
Alternative text is used to assist users with disabilities. To set alternative text on form controls, right-click the control, click Format Control on the shortcut menu, and then enter the desired alternative text on the Alt Text tab of the Format Control dialog box.

- **Option buttons** — Set the captions to match those in Figure 11–4d. Resize the controls so that the entire caption shows. Align and horizontally distribute the Contact by controls. Align and vertically distribute the option buttons inside the group box.

- **Group box** — Hide the group box border.

- **Check boxes** — Set the captions to match those in Figure 11–4d. Resize the controls so that the entire caption shows. Align and horizontally distribute the check box controls.

To Format the Form Controls

Why? *The option button controls must be formatted to identify their purpose for the user. Other formatting options can be used to make the controls and the worksheet upon which they are found easier and more pleasant to use.* The following steps change the text associated with the option button controls, resize the controls, and align and distribute the controls.

- Right-click the first option button control in the Contact by area to display the shortcut menu (Figure 11–12).

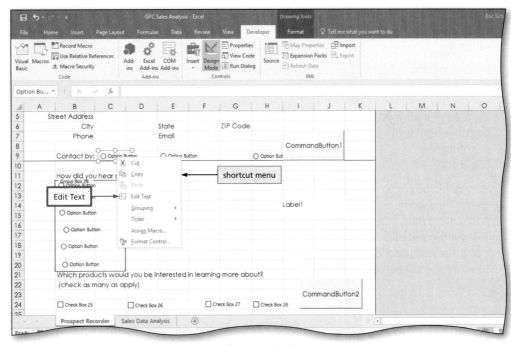

Figure 11–12

- Click Edit Text on the shortcut menu to edit the control text.

- Delete the text in the control and type **Email** to replace the text.

- Resize the control so that it just encloses the new text (Figure 11–13).

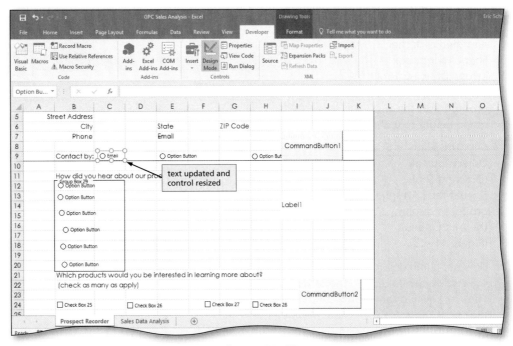

Figure 11–13

- Repeat Steps 1 and 2 to resize and rename the other two contact controls, naming them as shown in Figure 11–14.

- If necessary, click the Telephone control to select it.

- Hold down the ALT key and then drag the control until the right edge is aligned with the right edge of column H (Figure 11–14).

Q&A
Why did I hold down the ALT key while positioning the Telephone control?
Using the ALT key aligns the controls to the grid making it easier to place items on the form.

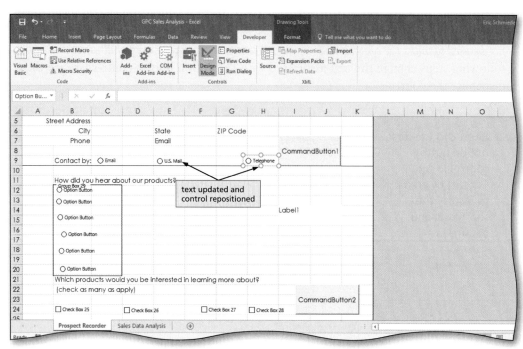

Figure 11–14

- Hold down the CTRL key and then click the other two controls to select all three option button controls.

- Display the Drawing Tools Format tab and then click the Shape Height box arrow (Drawing Tools Format tab | Size group) to set the shape height to 0.2".

- Click the Align Objects button (Drawing Tools Format tab | Arrange group) to display the Align menu (Figure 11–15).

Q&A
Why did I hold down the CTRL key while clicking the other two controls?
The CTRL key adds additional controls to the selection so that formatting and alignment options can be adjusted on the set of controls rather than individually.

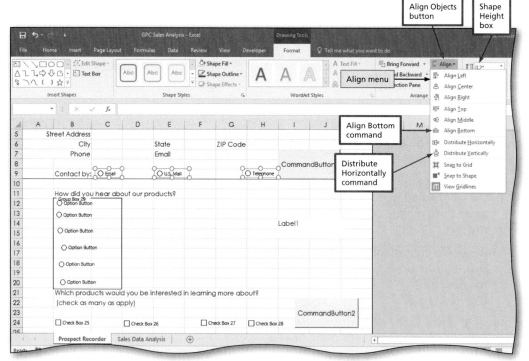

Figure 11–15

5

- Click Align Bottom on the Arrange menu to align the three controls along their bottom borders.

- Click the Align Objects button again (Drawing Tools Format tab | Arrange group) to display the alignment options.

- Click Distribute Horizontally on the Arrange menu to space the three controls evenly between columns C and H.

- Make C8 the active cell to deselect the option buttons and then click to select the Email option button (Figure 11–16).

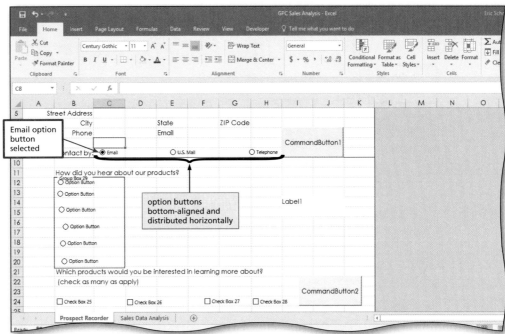

Figure 11–16

Q&A

How can I make the controls more visible?

You can format the controls with borders and fill colors to make them stand out from the background. From the shortcut menu, you can select Format Control and then use the Color and Lines tab in the Format Control dialog box to apply colors and patterns.

Can I make the controls a specific size?

The size of controls can also be set using the Format Control command on the shortcut menu.

To Format the Controls in the Group Box

The following steps format the option buttons in the group box control.

1 Right-click each of the six option buttons in the group box in turn and edit the text to match the text in Figure 11–17.

2 Move the top option button so that its upper-left corner aligns with the upper-left corner of cell B12, and then move the bottom option button so that its lower-left corner aligns with the lower-left corner of cell B20.

3 Select all six controls, and using the Shape Height and Shape Width boxes (Drawing Tools Format tab | Size group), set the control height to 0.2" and the shape width to 1.1".

4 With the six controls still selected, using the Align Objects button (Drawing Tools Format tab | Arrange group), apply the Align Left and Distribute Vertically formats to the group.

5 Make A10 the active cell to deselect the option buttons, and then click to select the Trade Show Event option button (Figure 11–17).

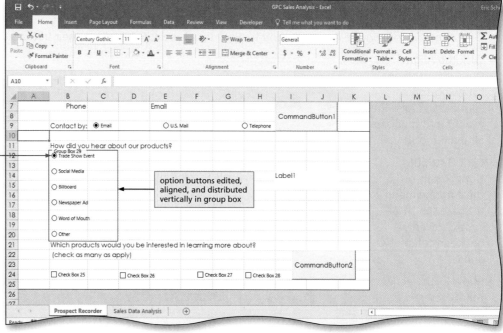

Figure 11–17

To Format the Check Box Controls

The check box controls are formatted in the same fashion as the option button controls. The following steps format and align the check box controls.

1 Select each of the four check box buttons , and in turn, type the following: **Anti-inflammatory, Antihistamine, Antihypertensive,** and **Antithyroid.**

2 Move the leftmost check box button so that its upper-left corner aligns with the upper-left corner of cell B23, and move the rightmost check box button so that its upper-right corner aligns with the upper-right corner of cell H23.

3 Select all four controls and then using the Shape Height and Shape Width boxes (Drawing Tools Format tab | Size group), set the control height to 0.2" and the shape width to 1.2".

4 If necessary select all four controls and then using the Align Objects button (Drawing Tools Format tab | Arrange group), apply the Align Top and Distribute Horizontally formats to the group (Figure 11–18).

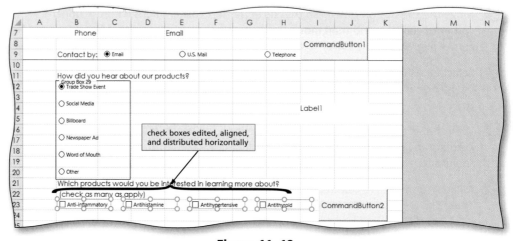

Figure 11–18

Setting ActiveX Control Properties

Like with form controls, each ActiveX control in the Controls gallery has many properties that determine the control's appearance and behavior. You set these properties in Design mode, which is entered by using the Design Mode button in the Controls group on the Developer tab on the ribbon. This will open the Properties dialog box where the control properties can be set or edited.

The user interface contains three ActiveX controls: two command buttons and a text box. The color, font, and effects for these controls will be modified by applying property values.

To Format the ActiveX Controls

1 DESIGN USER INTERFACE | **2** RECORD USER INPUT | **3** WRITE VBA CODE | **4** TEST USER INTERFACE
5 SHARE & COLLABORATE | **6** USE COMMENTS | **7** TRACK CHANGES | **8** FINALIZE WORKBOOK

Why? *Format the command button and label controls to provide instructions to the user and to make them visually prominent. Adding color, font formatting, shadow properties, and detailed captions to the ActiveX controls draw a user's attention.* The following steps set the properties using the Properties window.

- Select the two command button controls and the label control.

- Display the Developer tab and then click the Control Properties button (Developer tab | Controls group) to open the Properties window.

- Click the BackColor property to display the BackColor arrow.

- Click the BackColor arrow to display the BackColor options.

- Click the Palette tab to display the color options (Figure 11–19)

Q&A Why does the Properties window look different from other dialog boxes in Excel?
The Properties window is part of the VBA interface and is used to manage ActiveX controls in Excel.

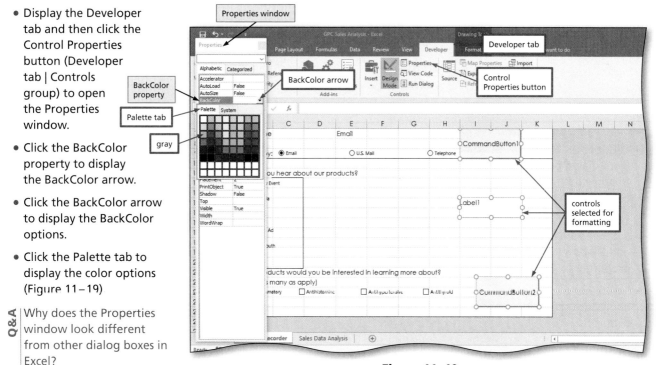

Figure 11–19

❷

- Click gray (column 1, row 3) to add a gray background to the command buttons.
- Click the Font property to display the ellipsis button.
- Click the ellipsis button to display the Font dialog box.
- Select Segoe UI in the Font list, Bold in the Font style list, and 10 in the Size list to change the font on the command buttons and in the label (Figure 11–20).

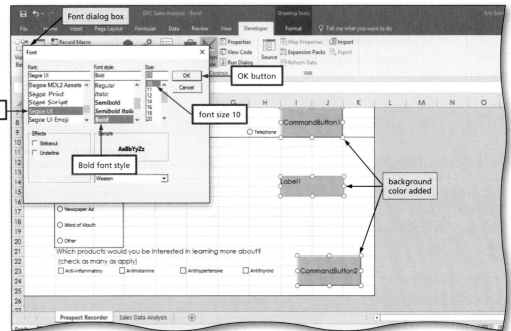

Figure 11–20

❸

- Click the OK button (Font dialog box) to apply this font to the text in the controls.
- Set the WordWrap and Shadow properties to True.
- Set Height to 50.25 and Width to 140.25 (Figure 11–21).

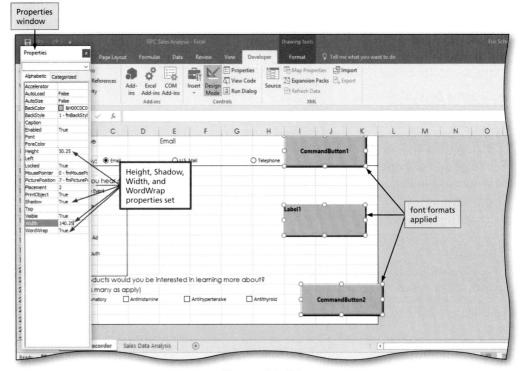

Figure 11–21

- Select the command button controls individually and then enter the text shown in Figure 11–22 into the Caption property for each command button.

- Select the label control and then enter the text shown in the figure into the Caption property (Figure 11–22).

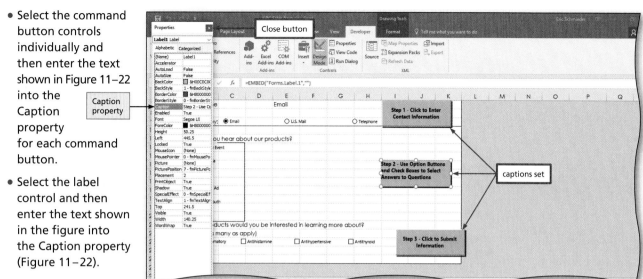

Figure 11–22

- Close the Properties window.

- Select the command buttons and the label and use the Align Objects button (Drawing Tools Format tab | Arrange group) to apply the Align Right and Distribute Vertically formats to the group.

- With the three controls still selected, use the arrow keys to move the controls as a group to the locations shown in Figure 11–23.

- Save the workbook again on the same storage location with the same file name (Figure 11–23).

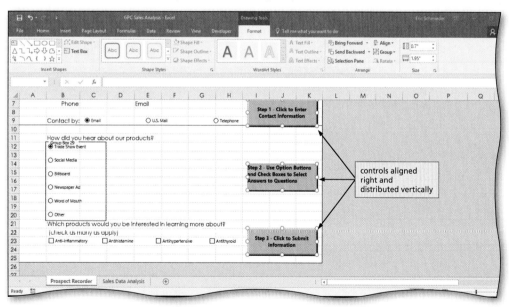

Figure 11–23

Recording User Input

Once you have added the controls to the worksheet, consider where the information will be stored within the workbook, so that it will be accessible to Excel and experienced users, but not distracting to users entering data in the form. For this project, you will temporarily store input in row 40 of the worksheet before copying that information into the Prospects List worksheet for long-term retention. To prepare for the user input you will name the cells for each of fields directly entered by the user and use INDEX functions to look up values selected with the option button controls.

To Assign Names to Ranges and Cells

The following steps assign names to ranges and cells and enter necessary references. The lists of cell names and references are found in Tables 11–1 and 11–2.

1 Select the range W11:W13 and then assign the name Contact_Method to the range. Assign the name Information_Source to the range W3:W8.

2 Select the range A39:H40 and use the 'Create from Selection' button (Formulas tab | Defined Names group) to assign the names in cells A39:H39 to the cells A40:H40. Using Table 11–1 as a guide, verify that the names have been assigned to the correct cells.

3 Enter the cell references listed in Table 11–2 into the appropriate cells.

Table 11–1 Cell Names

Cell	Name
A40	Last_Name
B40	First_Name
C40	Street_Address
D40	City
E40	State
F40	Zip_Code
G40	Telephone
H40	Email_Address

Table 11–2 Cell References

Cell	Reference
C3	=A40
C4	=B40
C5	=C40
C6	=D40
F6	=E40
H6	=F40
C7	=G40
F7	=H40

To Record User Input for Controls

1 DESIGN USER INTERFACE | 2 RECORD USER INPUT | 3 WRITE VBA CODE | 4 TEST USER INTERFACE
5 SHARE & COLLABORATE | 6 USE COMMENTS | 7 TRACK CHANGES | 8 FINALIZE WORKBOOK

The option button controls you added to the form will be used with the INDEX function to record the user's selections for two data points: the prospect's preferred method of contact and how the prospect heard about GPC's products. When a user selects one of the Contact by options, Excel interprets that input as a number (1, 2, or 3, reflecting which option button was selected) and then records that number in cell I41. You will enter an INDEX function in cell I40 that matches that number to a list, found in the named range in column W. By using the INDEX function, Excel will record the user's selections as Email, U.S. Mail, and Telephone, rather than the numerical values (1, 2, or 3) returned by the control. *Why? User input has to be changed from a numerical value to one that salespeople can understand.* The following steps record the user's Contact by option to another place on the worksheet.

 1

- Right-click the Email option button control to display the shortcut menu.

- Click Format Control to display the Format Control dialog box.

- If necessary, click the Control tab (Format Control dialog box) to display the Control sheet.

- Type **$I$41** in the Cell link box (Format Control dialog box) to link the option button output to cell I41 (Figure 11–24).

Q&A Why did I link only one of the option buttons to cell I41?
Option buttons work collectively as a group with a single identity assigned to the set of options. The specific value of the selected option button will be assigned to the output cell I41.

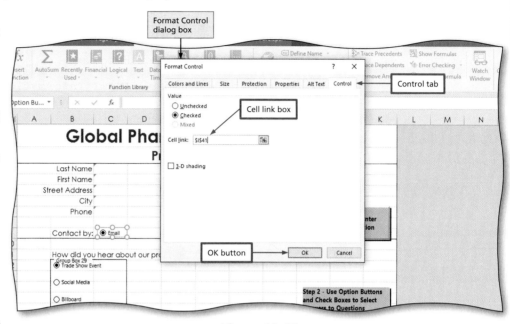

Figure 11–24

 2

- Click the OK button (Format Control dialog box) to close the dialog box.

- Scroll down and then click cell I40 to make it the active cell.

- Type **=INDEX (Contact_ Method,$I$41)** to record text from named range Contact_Method rather than numbers in cell I40 (Figure 11–25).

- Click the Enter button.

Q&A How does the INDEX function work here?
In this instance, the INDEX function looks at the value in cell I41, which identifies which option button was selected, and returns the entry associated with that value from the named range, Contact_Method. The named range contact is found in column W in this worksheet.

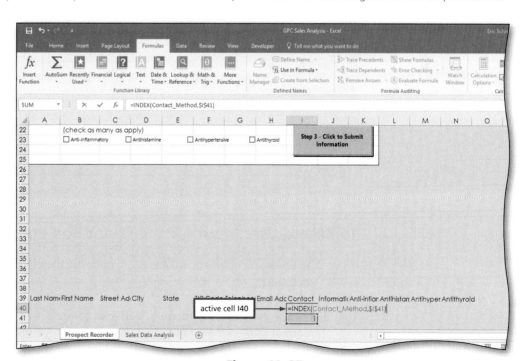

Figure 11–25

To Record User Input for the Group Box Controls

The following steps record the user response to the 'How did you hear about our products?' question in another place on the worksheet.

1 Right-click the Trade Show Event option button control and then click Format Control on the shortcut menu. If necessary, click the Control tab.

2 Type $J$41 in the Cell link box (Format Control dialog box).

3 Click the OK button (Format Control dialog box).

4 Make cell J40 the active cell. Enter =INDEX(Information_Source,$J$41) to return text from the named range Information_Source rather than numbers in row 40 (Figure 11–26).

5 Click the Enter button.

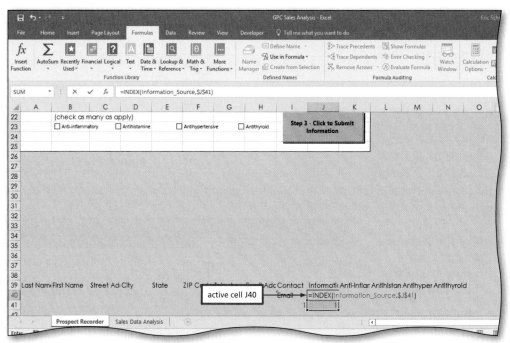

Figure 11–26

To Record User Input for the Check Box Controls

The following steps record the user input for the check boxes at another place on the worksheet.

1 Right-click the Anti-inflammatory check box control. Use the shortcut menu to display the Format Control dialog box.

2 Type $K$40 in the Cell link box (Format Control dialog box, Control tab).

3 Click the OK button (Format Control dialog box).

4 Repeat Steps 1 through 3 for each of the remaining three check box controls, using cells $L$40, $M$40, and $N$40 for the cell links.

5 Save the workbook again on the same storage location with the same file name.

Q&A Why do I have to link each check box control to a specific cell?
Unlike option buttons that work in groups, check box controls can each be either checked or unchecked representing TRUE or FALSE values.

Writing Code for a Command Button

Using the Controls gallery to insert a command button control into a worksheet places the object only. To have the button take action when a user clicks it, you must write VBA code that tells Excel what to do after the command button is clicked.

The next step is to write the procedure that will execute when the user clicks the 'Step 1 - Click to Enter Contact Information' button. A **procedure** is the code executed in response to an event. In VBA, procedures are blocks of code that begin with the words Private Sub and end with the line End Sub. You will enter code in the Visual Basic Editor, which is accessed from the Developer tab on the ribbon. The Visual Basic Editor is like an app within an app. The Visual Basic Editor window has its own ribbon, tabs, and groups and is navigated independently from Excel.

The Visual Basic Editor is a full-screen editor, which allows you to enter a procedure by typing the lines of VBA code as if you were using word processing software. At the end of each line, you press the ENTER key or use the DOWN ARROW key to move to the next line. If you make a mistake in a line of code, also called a statement, you can use the arrow keys and the DELETE or BACKSPACE key to correct it. You also can move the insertion point to previous lines to make corrections. As an app inside an app, the code entered in the Visual Basic Editor is saved with the macro-enabled Excel workbook. Saving from either the Visual Basic Editor or Excel will save the macro-enabled workbook and related VBA code.

When you trigger the event that executes a procedure, such as clicking a button, Excel steps through the Visual Basic statements one at a time, beginning at the top of the procedure. The statements should reflect the steps you want Excel to take, in the exact order in which they should occur. An **event-driven program** includes procedures that are executed when specific actions are taken by the user or other events occur.

After you determine what you want the procedure to do, write the VBA code on paper, creating a table similar to Table 11–3. Test the code before you enter it in the Visual Basic Editor, by stepping through the instructions one at a time yourself. As you do so, think about how the procedure affects the worksheet.

BTW

Printing VBA Code
Some people find it easier to review and edit code by working with a printout. To print out VBA code while using the Visual Basic Editor, click File on the menu bar and then click Print on the file menu.

BTW

Copying Macros Between Workbooks
Macros consist of VBA code that can be edited or copied between workbooks using the Visual Basic Editor. To copy macros between workbooks, open the workbook containing the existing macro and the destination workbook. Open the Visual Basic Editor. In the Project pane, drag the module that you want to copy to the destination workbook.

Should you document your code? Yes. Use comments to document each procedure. This will help you remember the purpose of the code or help somebody else understand the code. In Table 11–3, the first six lines are comments. Comments begin with the word Rem (short for Remark) or an apostrophe ('). Comments have no effect on the execution of a procedure; they simply provide information about the procedure, such as name, creation date, and function. Comments can be placed at the beginning before the Private Sub statement, in between lines of code, or at the end of a line of code, as long as each comment begins with an apostrophe ('). It is good practice to place comments containing overall documentation and information at the beginning, before the Sub statement.

CONSIDER THIS

To Enter the Command Button Procedures Using the Visual Basic Editor

Why? *To enter a procedure, you use the Visual Basic Editor.* Each command button has a separate function. The first button displays a series of dialog boxes that collect information about the prospect and enter it into appropriate locations on the worksheet. The second button copies the information to the hidden Prospect List worksheet. To activate the Visual Basic Editor, Excel must be in Design mode. The following steps activate the Visual Basic Editor and create the procedure for the two command buttons.

- If necessary, display the Developer tab and then click the Design Mode button (Developer tab | Controls group) to make Design Mode active.
- Click the Step 1 button on the worksheet to select the button.
- Click the View Code button (Developer tab | Controls group) to display the Microsoft Visual Basic for Applications editor and then, if necessary, maximize the window.
- Click the Object arrow at the top of the window and then select CommandButton1 from the list.
- Enter the VBA code shown in Table 11–3 (Figure 11–27).

Table 11–3 Enter Prospect Contact Information Button Procedure
'Enter Prospect Contact Information Button Procedure
'Author: SC Series
'Date Created: 11/12/2017
'Run from: Prospect Recorder worksheet by clicking button labeled Step 1 - Click to Enter Contact Information
'Function: When executed, this procedure enters contact information for the prospect
'
Private Sub CommandButton1_Click()
Range("Last_Name").Value = InputBox("Last Name?", "Enter", , 800, 6000)
Range("First_Name").Value = InputBox("First Name?", "Enter", , 800, 6000)
Range("Street_Address").Value = InputBox("Street Address?", "Enter", , 800, 6000)
Range("City").Value = InputBox("City?", "Enter", , 800, 6000)
Range("State").Value = InputBox("State?", "Enter", , 800, 6000)
Range("ZIP_Code").Value = InputBox("Zip Code?", "Enter", , 800, 6000)
Range("Telephone").Value = InputBox("Telephone Number?", "Enter", , 800, 6000)
Range("Email_Address").Value = InputBox("Email Address?", "Enter", , 800, 6000)
End Sub

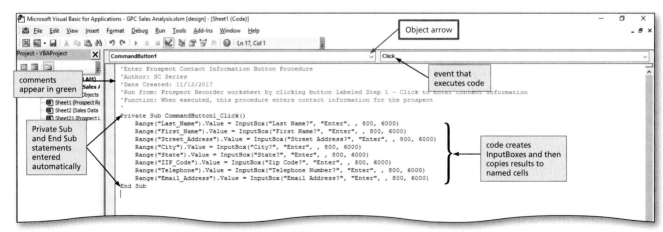

Figure 11–27

- Click the Object arrow and then click CommandButton2 in the list.
- Enter the VBA code shown in Table 11–4 (Figure 11–28).
- If requested by your instructor, enter your place of birth following the Author entry.

Table 11–4 Submit Button Procedure

'Submit Button Procedure

'Author: SC Series

'Date Created: 11/12/2017

'Run from: Prospect Recorder worksheet by clicking button labeled Step 3 - Click to Submit Information

'Function: When executed, this procedure submits new information to the prospect list

'

Private Sub CommandButton2_Click()

    Range("A40:O40").Select

    Selection.Copy

    Sheets("Prospect List").Visible = True

    Sheets("Prospect List").Activate

    Sheets("Prospect List").Range("A2:N2").Select

    Selection.PasteSpecial Paste:=xlPasteValues, Operation:=xlNone, SkipBlanks:=False, Transpose:=False

    Selection.Font.Bold = False

    Sheets("Prospect List").Range("A2").Activate

    ActiveCell.EntireRow.Insert

    Sheets("Prospect List").Visible = False

    Sheets("Prospect Recorder").Select

    Range("I41:J41").ClearContents

    Range("A40:H40").ClearContents

    Range("K40:N40").ClearContents

    Range("J8").Activate

    ActiveWorkbook.Save

End Sub

Figure 11–28

• Verify your code by comparing it with the content of Tables 11–3 and 11–4.

To Remove the Outline from the Group Control

1 DESIGN USER INTERFACE | 2 RECORD USER INPUT | 3 WRITE VBA CODE | **4 TEST USER INTERFACE**
5 SHARE & COLLABORATE | 6 USE COMMENTS | 7 TRACK CHANGES | 8 FINALIZE WORKBOOK

Why? *Removing the outline from the group control will result in a more visually pleasing user interface.* Removing the outline requires a line of VBA code. You will enter this in the Immediate window in the Visual Basic Editor. The Immediate window often is used for debugging and executing statements during design. As its name suggests, code entered in this window is executed immediately upon exiting the Visual Basic Editor. The following step removes the outline from the group control.

• Press CTRL+G to open the Immediate window.

• Type **activesheet. groupboxes.visible = false** and then press the ENTER key to remove the box from around the group control (Figure 11–29).

• Close the Visual Basic Editor window.

• Save the workbook again on the same storage location with the same file name.

Figure 11–29

Break Point: If you wish to take a break, this is a good place to do so. You can now exit Excel. To resume at a later time, run Excel, open the file called GPC Sales Analysis, and continue following the steps from this location forward.

Sharing and Collaboration

If others need to edit a workbook or suggest changes, Excel provides three ways to collaborate. In addition, Excel offers several methods to protect your privacy or hide data that you may not want to share with others. Before distributing your workbook to others, you should consider what type of hidden information might be in your document. In previous modules, you have learned to hide rows and columns, protect cells, protect worksheets, and protect workbooks. Other types of information may be hidden in a workbook. Excel provides a tool called the Document Inspector to inspect and report such information. You then easily can remove the hidden information or choose to leave the information in the document.

When distributing a workbook, you also should consider whether the intended recipients have the most recent version of Excel. If this is not the case, Excel allows you to save a workbook for use in previous versions of Excel, such as Excel 97-2003. When you save a workbook in the Excel 97-2003 Workbook file format, Excel will invoke the Compatibility Checker, which notifies you if any of the content of your workbook cannot be saved in that format. Additionally, the Compatibility Checker will inform you if any content will not appear the same in the new format, such as cell or chart formatting.

To Prepare and Protect the Worksheet

Why? You are removing the ribbon from view and protecting the worksheet to restrict what the user can do in this worksheet. The following steps prepare and protect the worksheet, and then save the workbook.

1

- If necessary, click the Design Mode button (Developer tab | Controls group) to exit Design mode.

- Display the Backstage view.

- Click Options to display the Excel Options dialog box.

- Click the Advanced tab (Excel Options dialog box) to display the advanced options.

- Scroll to the 'Display options for this worksheet' area in the right pane and then, if necessary, click the 'Show page breaks' and 'Show a zero in cells that have zero value' check boxes to remove the check marks (Figure 11–30).

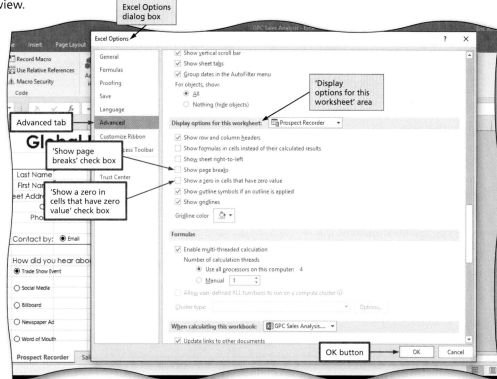

Figure 11–30

2

- Click the OK button to close the dialog box.

- Display the View tab.

- Click the View Gridlines, Formula Bar, and View Headings check boxes (View tab | Show group) to remove the check marks (Figure 11–31).

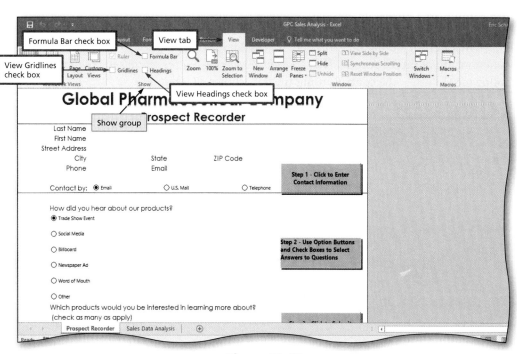

Figure 11–31

③

- Click the 'Collapse the Ribbon' button on the ribbon to collapse the ribbon.
- Display the Review tab and then click the Protect Sheet button (Review tab | Changes group) to display the Protect Sheet dialog box.
- Type **Prospect17** in the 'Password to unprotect sheet' text box and then click the OK button (Protect Sheet dialog box) to display the Confirm Password dialog box.
- Type **Prospect17** in the 'Reenter password to proceed' text box and then click the OK button (Confirm Password dialog box) to close the dialog boxes.
- Press the F5 key to display the Go To dialog box.
- Type **J8** in the Reference text box (Go To dialog box) and then click the OK button (Go To dialog box) to make cell J8 the active cell and close the dialog box.
- Save the workbook again on the same storage location with the same file name (Figure 11–32).

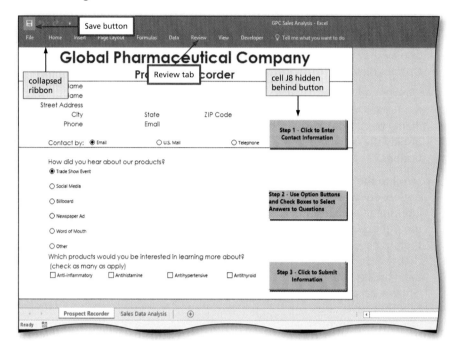

Figure 11–32

Q&A

Do any rules apply to passwords?
Yes. Passwords in Excel can contain, in any combination, letters, numbers, spaces, and symbols, and can be up to 15 characters long. Passwords are case sensitive. If you decide to password-protect a worksheet, make sure you save the password in a secure place. If you lose the password, you will not be able to open or gain access to the password-protected worksheet.

To Test the Controls in the Worksheet

1 DESIGN USER INTERFACE | 2 RECORD USER INPUT | 3 WRITE VBA CODE | 4 TEST USER INTERFACE
5 SHARE & COLLABORATE | 6 USE COMMENTS | 7 TRACK CHANGES | 8 FINALIZE WORKBOOK

Before distributing the workbook for use, it is good practice to test the controls and verify the proper functionality of the VBA code. *Why? The final step is to test the controls in the Prospect Recorder worksheet.* The following steps test the controls using the data shown in Table 11–5.

Table 11–5 Prospect Records

Field	Record 1	Record 2
Last Name	Derringer	Shum
First Name	Kevin	Laurie
Address	572 Birch Street	31 Windsor Road
City	Clayton	Parkville
State	NC	MD
Zip Code	27520	21234
Phone	555-555-1212	555-555-1313
Email	kderringer@scseries.com	lshum@scseries.com
Contact Preference	Telephone	Email
Information Source	Social Media	Trade Show Event
Interest(s)	Antihypertensive	Anti-inflammatory & Antithyroid

1

- For each of the records in Table 11–5, use the command buttons to enter the data, follow the prompts, and then submit the data.

- Unhide the Prospect List worksheet (right-click the Prospect Recorder worksheet tab, click Unhide, and then click OK), and confirm that the records were copied correctly (Figure 11–33).

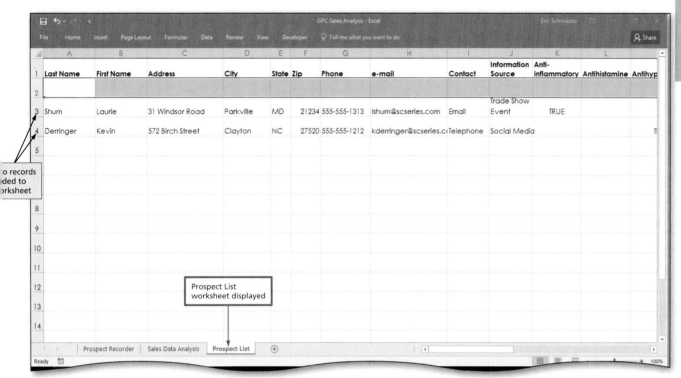

Figure 11–33

2

- Hide the Prospect List worksheet.

Collaborating with Others

Collaborating means working together on a document in cooperation with other Excel users. Excel provides three ways to collaborate.

The first option is to distribute the workbook to others, physically on storage media, through email using the Share gallery in the Backstage view, or via OneDrive. In the Share gallery, the document can be embedded as part of the email message, which allows users to view the spreadsheet upon opening the email message, or the file can be sent as an email attachment, which allows recipients of the email message to open the file if Excel is installed on their computer or mobile device.

A second option is to collaborate by sharing the workbook using the Sharing feature in Excel. Sharing involves more than simply giving another user a copy of a file; it allows multiple people to work independently on the same workbook at the same time if they are in a networked environment. Sharing a workbook puts restrictions on the types of edits a user can make, which provides a degree of control over the editing process that distributing the workbook does not. If users are not in a networked environment, workbook sharing allows them to work on the workbook in turn, while keeping track of who was responsible for each edit.

BTW
Passwords and Workbook Sharing
Excel keeps a change history of 30 days by default for a shared workbook. You can use passwords with a shared workbook to protect the change history. Use the Protect Shared Workbook button (Review tab | Changes group). The workbook cannot be shared at the time the password is added.

A third option is to collaborate interactively with other people through discussion threads or online meetings. SharePoint Services with Microsoft Office 2016 allows people at different sites to share and exchange files.

Sharing can be turned on for a workbook using the Share Workbook button on the Review tab. When workbook sharing is enabled, a number of Excel features — merging cells, deleting worksheets, changing or removing passwords, using scenarios, creating data tables, modifying macros, using data validation, and creating PivotTables — are disabled for the workbook. For this reason, limit the number of occasions when a workbook is shared; further, sharing should be used only for the purpose of reviewing and modifying the contents of worksheet data.

To Distribute a Workbook via OneDrive

1 DESIGN USER INTERFACE | 2 RECORD USER INPUT | 3 WRITE VBA CODE | 4 TEST USER INTERFACE
5 SHARE & COLLABORATE | 6 USE COMMENTS | 7 TRACK CHANGES | 8 FINALIZE WORKBOOK

You can use OneDrive to distribute workbooks instead of sending them as attachments to email messages. Just as with sharing via email, colleagues can make changes, and then save the workbook on OneDrive for review. Saving workbooks for distribution on OneDrive does not differ from using OneDrive to save your own files, although you do need to make the workbook available to others by saving it in an accessible location. **Why?** *You may need to have a workbook reviewed by someone who does not share network access with you.* You can send a shared workbook using OneDrive. When the recipient sends the edited workbook back to you for review, his or her changes will be tagged just as they would be if the recipient opened the workbook on the network. The following steps save the workbook and send it by OneDrive.

- Display the Backstage view.

- Click the Share tab to display the Share gallery.

- If necessary, click the 'Share with People' button to display the 'Share with People' options in the right pane (Figure 11–34).

Q&A Why do I have a 'Save to Cloud' button instead of the 'Share with People' button?
Your file is saved on the local computer or USB file storage location and must be saved to a OneDrive location for sharing. Click the 'Save to Cloud' button and navigate to a storage location on your OneDrive before proceeding to Step 2.

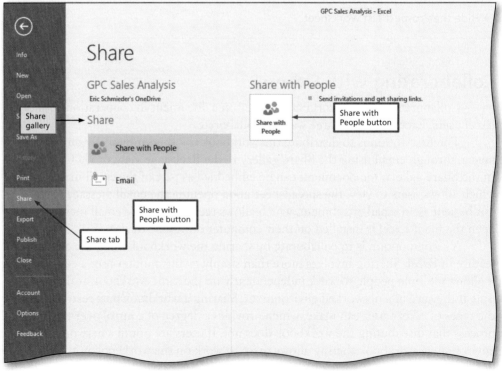

Figure 11–34

- Click the 'Share with People' button in the right pane to display the Share task pane for sending invitations and getting sharing links.

- Enter a recipient's email address in the Invite people text box (Figure 11–35).

- Verify that Can edit is selected.

- Add a brief message to the recipient and then click the Share button to send the message with a link to the shared workbook.

- Close the Share task pane.

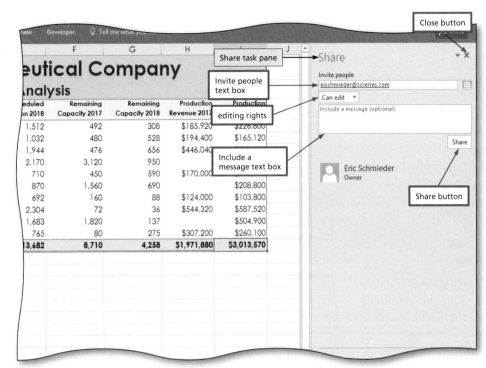

Figure 11–35

Q&A A Sharing Information dialog box was displayed after I clicked the Share button. Why?
To prevent automated programs from sharing spam documents, OneDrive may request completion of an additional authentication step.

To Share and Collaborate on a Workbook

1 DESIGN USER INTERFACE | 2 RECORD USER INPUT | 3 WRITE VBA CODE | 4 TEST USER INTERFACE
5 SHARE & COLLABORATE | 6 USE COMMENTS | 7 TRACK CHANGES | 8 FINALIZE WORKBOOK

Working together in the same workbook at the same time can improve efficiency in networked team environments. *Why? Sharing a workbook can provide you with a timely, interactive editing process with colleagues.* The following steps turn on sharing for the GPC Sales Analysis workbook and then allow collaboration with another user in a networked environment to make changes to the workbook.

- If necessary, display the Sales Data Analysis worksheet.

- Display the View tab and then click the 'Pin the ribbon' button on the ribbon to keep the ribbon open.

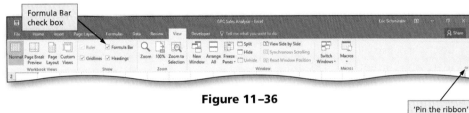

Figure 11–36

- Click the Formula Bar check box (View tab | Show group) to redisplay the formula bar (Figure 11–36).

- Display the Review tab and then click the Share Workbook button (Review tab | Changes group) to display the Share Workbook dialog box.

- Click the 'Allow changes by more than one user at the same time' check box to insert a check mark (Figure 11–37).

- Click the OK button (Share Workbook dialog box) to share the workbook with other users.

- When Excel displays the Microsoft Excel dialog box, click the OK button to save and then share the workbook.

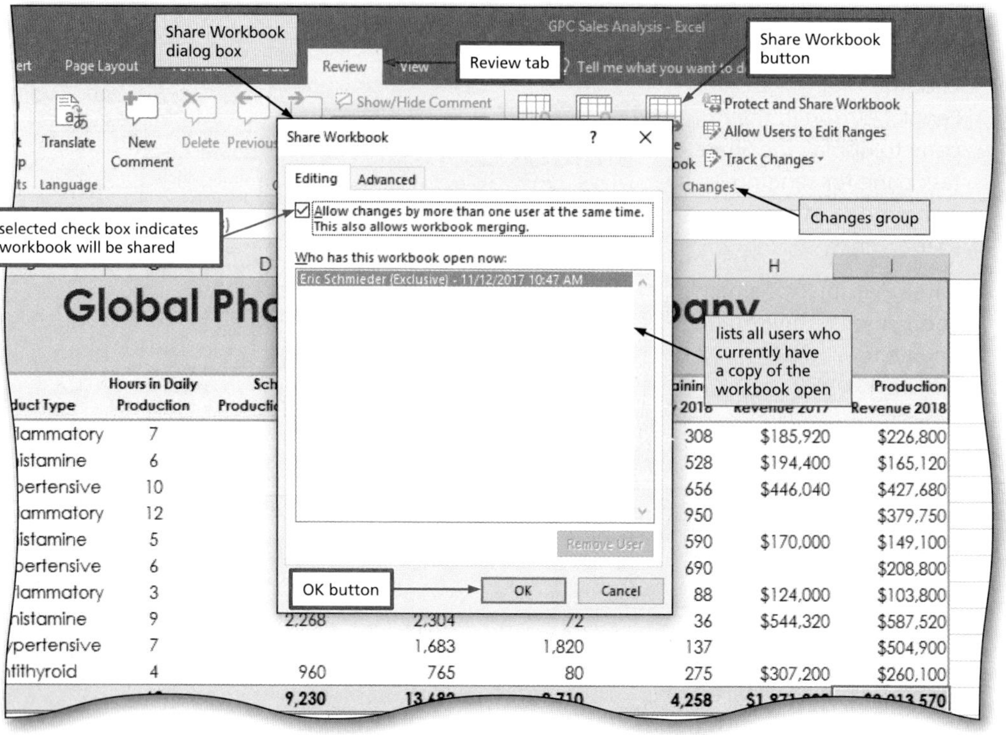

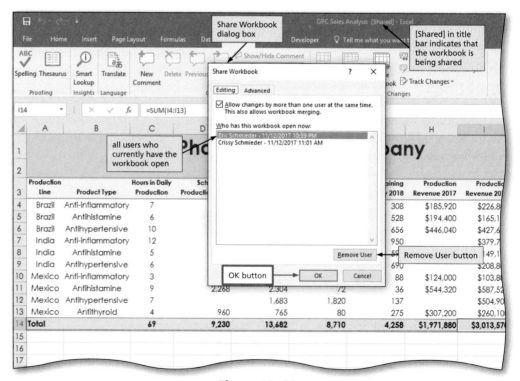

Figure 11–37

- If possible, have a classmate open a second copy of the workbook.

- With a second copy of the workbook open, click the Share Workbook button (Review tab | Changes group) to display the Share Workbook dialog box, which lists all users who currently have the workbook open (Figure 11–38).

Figure 11–38

4

- Click the OK button (Share Workbook dialog box) to close the dialog box.

- Ask the second workbook user to click cell D7, enter 2254 as the new value, and then save the workbook.

User Interfaces, Visual Basic for Applications (VBA), and Collaboration Features in Excel **Excel Module 11** **EX 649**

Excel Module 11

- In your copy of the workbook, click the Save button on the Quick Access Toolbar to display the Microsoft Excel dialog box indicating that the workbook has been updated with changes saved by another user (Figure 11–39).

Q&A Must I save the workbook before I am notified of another user's changes?

Yes. Until the workbook is saved, Excel provides no indication that another user has changed the shared workbook. To prohibit another user from saving additional updates to the workbook, click the user name in the Share Workbook dialog box and then click the Remove User button.

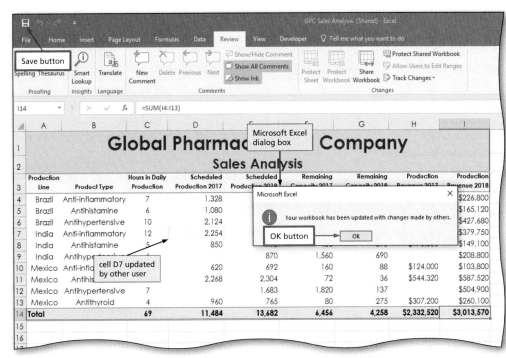

Figure 11–39

5

- Click the OK button (Microsoft Excel dialog box) to close the dialog box.

- Point to the triangle in cell D7 to display the comment that identifies the other user's changes (Figure 11–40).

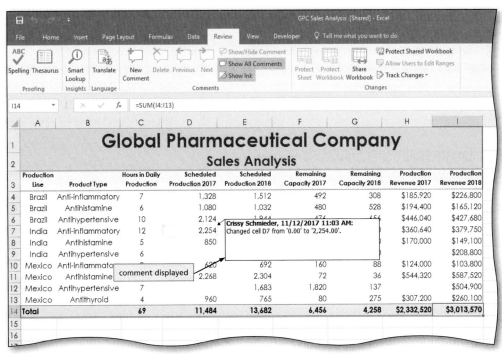

Figure 11–40

- Ask the second user of the workbook to close the workbook.

- Click the Share Workbook button (Review tab | Changes group) to display the Share Workbook dialog box.

- Click the 'Allow changes by more than one user at the same time' check box to remove the check mark (Figure 11–41).

- Click the OK button (Share Workbook dialog box) to stop sharing the workbook.

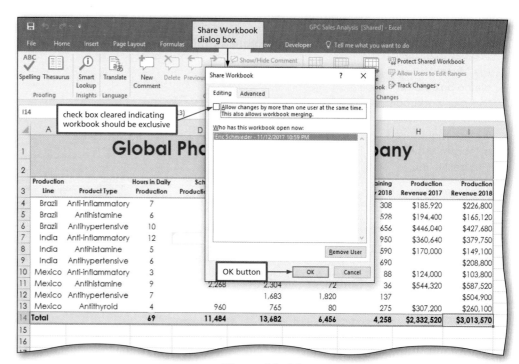

Figure 11–41

- If Excel displays the Microsoft Excel dialog box asking whether the workbook should be removed from shared use, click the Yes button.

- If desired, save the workbook in the same storage location where you save your files.

Q&A
How long are changes kept?

The changes made to a workbook are called the change history. When a workbook is shared, Excel keeps the changes made for 30 days unless you set the change history to store changes for a different number of days. To alter the length of time the change history will be kept, select the Advanced tab in the Share Workbook dialog box, and set 'Keep change history for' to the desired interval.

To Unprotect a Password-Protected Worksheet

1 DESIGN USER INTERFACE | 2 RECORD USER INPUT | 3 WRITE VBA CODE | 4 TEST USER INTERFACE
5 SHARE & COLLABORATE | 6 USE COMMENTS | 7 TRACK CHANGES | 8 FINALIZE WORKBOOK

The Prospect Recorder worksheet in the GPC Sales Analysis workbook is protected, which restricts the changes you can make to the worksheet to unlocked cells only. You cannot make changes to locked cells or modify the worksheet itself. *Why unprotect the worksheet? You will unprotect the worksheet to allow changes to locked cells and the worksheet itself.* Recall from Module 4 that a password ensures that users cannot unprotect the worksheet simply by clicking the Unprotect button. The password for the worksheet is Prospect17. The following steps unprotect the password-protected Prospect Recorder worksheet.

- Display the Prospect Recorder worksheet.

- If necessary, display the Review tab, and then click the Unprotect Sheet button (Review tab | Changes group) to display the Unprotect Sheet dialog box.

- When the Unprotect Sheet dialog box appears, type **Prospect17** in the Password text box (Figure 11–42).

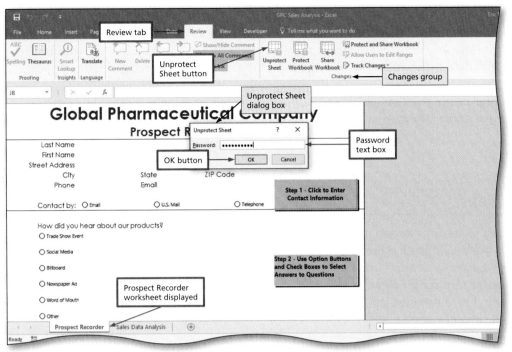

Figure 11–42

- Click the OK button (Unprotect Sheet dialog box) to unprotect the Prospect Recorder worksheet.

- Save and close the GPC Sales Analysis workbook.

Q&A Can I work with the entire worksheet now?
Yes. With the worksheet unprotected, you can modify the contents of cells, regardless of whether they are locked or unlocked. Cells must both be locked and the worksheet protected to restrict what users can do to cell contents.

Comparing and Merging Workbooks

Excel provides you with two methods to use when working with multiple versions of a workbook. You can open multiple copies of the same workbook and move through the workbooks in a synchronized manner so that the same area of each workbook is always in view. For example, as a user scrolls down a worksheet, Excel automatically updates the view of the second worksheet to show the same rows as the first worksheet. This functionality allows for a side-by-side visual comparison of two workbooks.

In the case of multiple copies of a workbook, Excel provides the capability to merge multiple copies into a single workbook. This feature requires you to do some preparation. To merge the changes from one or more workbooks into another, all workbooks must satisfy the following requirements:

- The original workbook must be shared before making copies, and each workbook must be a copy of the same workbook.

- When copies of the workbook are made, track changes or sharing must be enabled, so that the change history of the workbook is kept.

- Clicking the Share Workbook button on the Review tab displays a dialog box with a tab for recording the number of days to record the change history. Shared workbooks must be merged within that time period.

- If the workbooks have been assigned passwords, all workbooks involved in the merge must have the same password.

- Each copy of the workbook must have a different file name.

BTW
Merging and the Change History
If there are any concerns about how long it will take to get all copies of a workbook back, err on the side of caution and set a high number of days for recording the change history.

When all of the copies of the workbook are available on your hard disk, USB drive, OneDrive, or other storage medium, you can use the 'Compare and Merge Workbooks' command to merge the workbooks. When Excel merges the workbooks, both data and comments are merged, so that if comments are recorded, they appear one after another in a given cell's comment box. If Excel cannot merge the workbooks, information from one workbook still can be incorporated into another by copying and pasting the information from one workbook to another.

To Compare Workbooks

1 DESIGN USER INTERFACE | 2 RECORD USER INPUT | 3 WRITE VBA CODE | 4 TEST USER INTERFACE
5 SHARE & COLLABORATE | 6 USE COMMENTS | 7 TRACK CHANGES | 8 FINALIZE WORKBOOK

Global Pharmaceutical Company plans to participate in three sales events in 2018. Proposed event expenditures are saved in a workbook that has been shared and copied to two other members of the staff for review. Because two different users — Serenity and Noah — modified the separate workbooks, the workbooks must be merged. *Why compare workbooks? Before merging the workbooks, they can be compared visually to note the changes made by different users.* The following steps open the GPC Events and GPC Events Noah workbooks and compare the workbooks side by side.

- Open the file GPC Events from the Data Files.
- If the file opens in a maximized state, click the workbook's Restore Down button to resize the window.
- Open the file GPC Events Noah from the Data Files.
- If the file opens in a maximized state, click the workbook's Restore Down button to resize the window.
- Display the View tab and then click the 'View Side by Side' button (View tab | Window group) to display the workbooks side by side (Figure 11–43).
- Use the scroll bar in the active window to scroll the GPC Events worksheet.

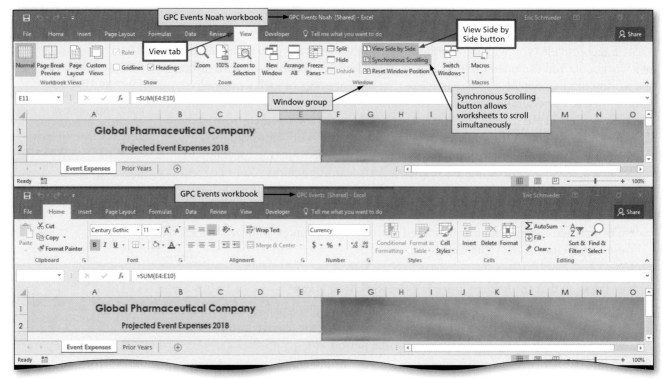

Figure 11–43

User Interfaces, Visual Basic for Applications (VBA), and Collaboration Features in Excel **Excel Module 11** **EX 653**

Excel Module 11

How should the workbooks be arranged after clicking the 'View Side by Side' button?
Depending on how previous Excel windows were arranged on your computer, the workbooks may appear next to each other left-to-right, or with one window above the other. To change how the windows are positioned, drag one workbook window to the desired screen edge to dock it. Dock the second workbook window on the opposite edge.

What happens when I scroll the worksheet?
Because the Synchronous Scrolling button is selected, both worksheets scroll at the same time so that you can make a visual comparison of the workbooks.

❷

- Click the 'View Side by Side' button (View tab | Window group) again to display the windows separately and turn off synchronous scrolling.

- Close the GPC Events Noah workbook.

- If Excel displays a Microsoft Excel dialog box, click the Don't Save button.

- Click the Maximize button in the GPC Events window to maximize the window.

To Merge Workbooks

1 DESIGN USER INTERFACE | 2 RECORD USER INPUT | 3 WRITE VBA CODE | 4 TEST USER INTERFACE
5 SHARE & COLLABORATE | 6 USE COMMENTS | 7 TRACK CHANGES | 8 FINALIZE WORKBOOK

Why? When multiple users have made changes to copies of a workbook, merging can be more efficient and accurate than copying changes over to a single workbook. After the initial review, the next step is to merge the two workbooks changed by Serenity and Noah into the original GPC Events workbook. All three of the workbooks are shared. The following steps merge the workbooks containing changes from Serenity and Noah with the original workbook, GPC Events.

❶

- Save the GPC Events workbook as GPC Events Merged in the same storage location where you save your files.

- Click the 'Customize Quick Access Toolbar' arrow next to the Quick Access Toolbar and then click More Commands on the Customize Quick Access Toolbar menu to display the Excel Options dialog box.

- Select All Commands in the 'Choose commands from' list.

- Scroll to and click the 'Compare and Merge Workbooks' command in the All Commands list.

- Click the Add button (Excel Options dialog box) to add the 'Compare and Merge Workbooks' command to the Customize Quick Access Toolbar list on the right of the dialog box (Figure 11–44).

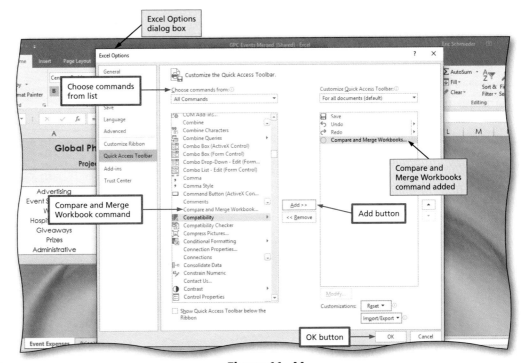

How do I undo changes from a merge?
Merged changes cannot be undone. Make sure you make a copy of your files before you perform the merge.

Figure 11–44

②

- Click the OK button to add the 'Compare and Merge Workbooks' button to the Quick Access Toolbar.

- Click the 'Compare and Merge Workbooks' button on the Quick Access Toolbar to display the Select Files to Merge Into Current Workbook dialog box.

- If necessary, navigate to the location of your data files.

- Click 'GPC Events Noah', hold down the SHIFT key, and then click 'GPC Events Serenity' to select both files (Figure 11–45).

Q&A Why is my 'Compare and Merge Workbooks' button gray?
The workbook must be shared before you can use the 'Compare and Merge Workbooks' button. Check to make sure your workbook is shared.

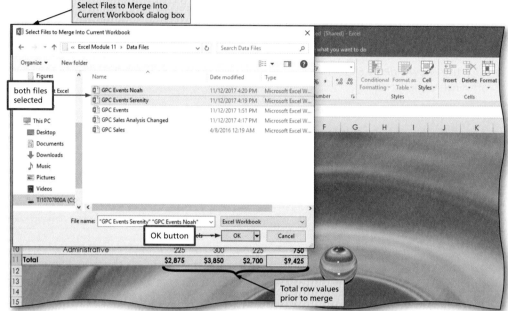

Figure 11–45

③

- Click the OK button (Select Files to Merge Into Current Workbook dialog box) to merge the workbooks (Figure 11–46).

Q&A What is the result of the merge?
The workbooks have been merged, and the GPC Events worksheet reflects the changes from Serenity and Noah. If Serenity and Noah had changed a common cell with different values, Excel would have displayed a prompt, asking which change to keep in the merged workbook.

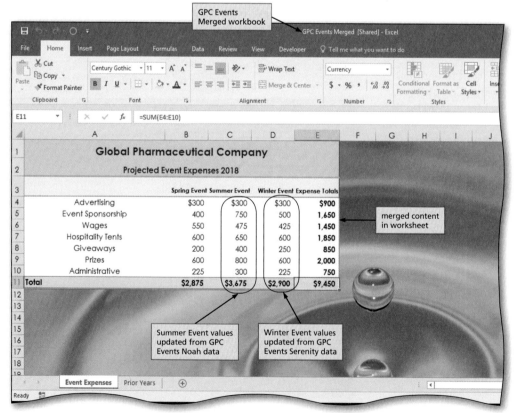

Figure 11–46

To Turn Off Workbook Sharing

Now that the three copies of the shared workbook have been merged into a single file, workbook sharing is no longer necessary. *Why? Turn off workbook sharing once the workbooks have been merged to have access to all of Excel's features.* The following steps turn off workbook sharing so that the data can be manipulated.

- Display the Review tab and then click the Share Workbook button (Review tab | Changes group) to display the Share Workbook dialog box.

- Click the 'Allow changes by more than one user at the same time' check box to remove the check mark (Figure 11–47).

- Click the OK button (Share Workbook dialog box) to turn off workbook sharing.

- If Excel displays the Microsoft Excel dialog box, Click the Yes button.

- Save and close the GPC Events Merged workbook.

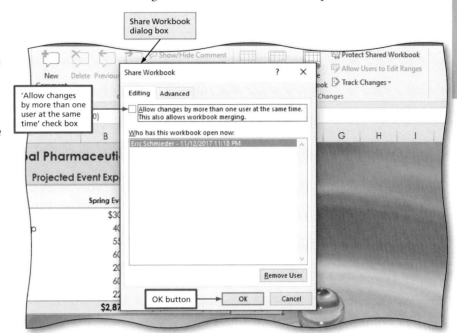

Figure 11–47

Digital Signatures

Some users prefer to attach a digital signature to verify the authenticity of a document. A **digital signature** is an electronic, encrypted, and secure stamp of authentication on a document. This signature confirms that the file originated from the signer (file developer) and that it has not been altered.

A digital signature may be visible or invisible. In either case, the digital signature references a digital certificate. A **digital certificate** is an attachment to a file or email message that vouches for its authenticity, provides secure encryption, or supplies a verifiable signature. Many users who receive files containing macros enable the macros based on whether they are digitally signed by a developer on the user's list of trusted sources.

You can obtain a digital certificate from a commercial **certificate authority** (CA), from your network administrator, or you can create a digital signature yourself. A digital certificate you create yourself is not issued by a formal certification authority. Thus, signed macros using such a certificate are referred to as **self-signed projects**. Certificates you create yourself are considered unauthenticated and still will generate a warning when opened if the security level is set to very high, high, or medium. Many users, however, consider self-signed projects safer to open than those with no certificates at all.

To Add a Signature Box and Digital Signature to a Workbook

After adding a digital signature, Excel will display the digital signature whenever the document is opened. If you wanted to add a digital signature to an Excel workbook, you would perform the following steps.

1. Open the GPC Sales Analysis workbook and, if necessary, unprotect the Prospect Recorder worksheet using the password, Prospect17.

2. Click the Insert tab and then click the 'Add a Signature Line' button in the Text group.

3. Enter your name in the Suggested signer text box (Signature Setup dialog box) and then click the OK button to add the signature box to the workbook.

4. Right-click the signature box and then click Sign on the shortcut menu to display the Sign dialog box. To sign a Microsoft Office document you need a digital ID. If necessary, you will be prompted to get one from a Microsoft Partner.

5. In the Sign dialog box, enter your name in the signature box or click the Select Image link to select a file that contains an image of your signature.

6. Click the Sign button (Sign dialog box) to digitally sign the document.

To Review a Digital Signature on a Workbook

BTW

Copying Comments
You can copy comments from one cell to other cells using the Paste Special command. Select the cell that contains the comment you need to copy, click the Copy button (Home tab | Clipboard group), select the cell or cells to which you want to apply the comment, click the Paste arrow, and then click Paste Special. In the Paste Special dialog box, in the Paste list, select Comments, and then click the OK button.

Excel will display the digital signature whenever the document is opened. When you open a digitally signed document, Excel displays a message announcing the signature on the status bar while the file opens. After the file is opened, Excel displays a certification icon on the status bar. You can click the icon to find out who digitally signed the document. The word, Signed, also appears on the title bar in parentheses, indicating the document is signed digitally. If you wanted to review a digital signature on an Excel workbook, you would perform the following steps.

1. Display the Backstage view. If necessary, click the Info tab and then click View Signatures to open the Signatures task pane.

2. Select a name from the Valid signature list (Signature task pane), click the arrow to display the shortcut menu, and then click Signature Details to display the certificate.

3. When you are finished reviewing the certificate, click the Close button (Signature Details dialog box) and then close the workbook.

Gathering Feedback Using Comments

Comments are the electronic version of sticky notes or annotations in the margin. They can request additional information or clarification of existing information. Comments can provide direction to the reader about how to interpret content or describe what type of content to add. You can add a comment to any cell in a worksheet. Once added, you can edit, format, move, copy, or resize comments. You can choose to show comments in a worksheet, to display only a comment indicator, or to hide comments. Comments work well when multiple people are collaborating on a worksheet. Comments added by each user are identified by a name in the comment, set by the user.

Depending on the nature of the comments, you may decide to delete some or all comments after reading them and making edits to the worksheet, if appropriate.

To Add Comments to a Worksheet

Why? *Comments in Excel can be used to remind the user of material that needs to be added or updated.* The Sales Analysis worksheet in the GPC Sales Analysis workbook has some missing data. The following steps add comments to the worksheet in cells A7, A9, and A12.

- If necessary, open the GPC Sales Analysis workbook and then click the Enable Content button in the yellow Security Warning bar below the ribbon.

- If necessary, display the Sales Data Analysis worksheet.

- Display the Review tab and, if necessary, click the 'Show All Comments' button (Review tab | Comments group) to toggle the option off and hide all comments in the workbook.

- Right-click cell A7 to display the shortcut menu (Figure 11–48).

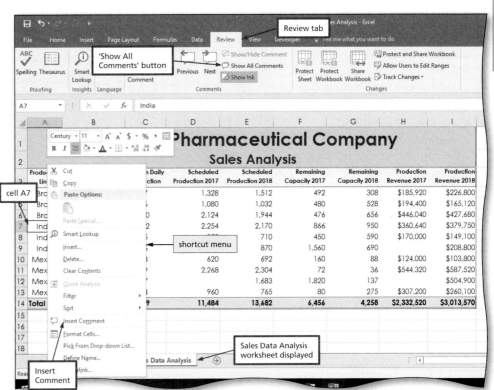

Figure 11–48

- Click Insert Comment on the shortcut menu to open a comment box next to the selected cell and display a comment indicator in the cell.

- Enter the text `Note to Noah - need count of anti-inflammatory units scheduled for 2017 production in India.` in the comment box (Figure 11–49).

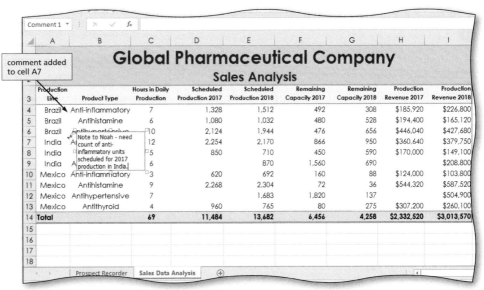

Figure 11–49

- Click outside the comment box to close the comment box and display only the red comment indicator in cell A7.

- Enter a comment in cell A9 with the text `Note to Noah - need accurate count of antihypertensive units scheduled for 2017 production in India.`

- Click outside the comment box to close the comment box and display only the red comment indicator in cell A9.

- Enter a comment in cell A12 with the text `Note to Serenity - need accurate count of antihypertensive units scheduled for 2017 production in Mexico.`

- Click outside the comment box to close the comment box and display only the red comment indicator in cell A12 (Figure 11–50).

Q&A My comment boxes do not close when I click outside the comment box. Why?
The Show All Comments option must be active. To turn it off and display only the red comment indicators, click the Show All Comments button (Review tab | Comments group).

Global Pharmaceutical Company
Sales Analysis

Production Line	Product Type	Hours in Daily Production	Scheduled Production 2017	Scheduled Production 2018	Remaining Capacity 2017	Remaining Capacity 2018	Production Revenue 2017	Re
Brazil	Anti-inflammatory	7	1,328	1,512	492	308	$185,920	
Brazil	Antihistamine	6	1,080	1,032	480	528	$194,400	
Brazil	Antihypertensive	10	2,124	1,944	476	656	$446,040	
India	Anti-inflamm...	10	2,254	2,170	866	950	$360,640	
India	Antihista...		850	710	450	590	$170,000	
India	Antihyper...			870	1,560	690		
Mexico	Anti-inflamm...		620	692	160	88	$124,000	
Mexico	Antihistamine	9	2,268	2,304	72	36	$544,320	
Mexico	Antihypertensive	7		1,683	1,820	137		
Mexico	Antithyroid	4	960	765	80	275	$307,200	
Total		**69**	**11,484**	**13,682**	**6,456**	**4,258**	**$2,332,520**	

comment indicators in cells A7, A9, and A12

Prospect Recorder | Sales Data Analysis

Figure 11–50

Other Ways

1. Click Insert a Comment (Review tab | Comments group)   2. SHIFT+F2

To Display All Comments on a Worksheet

1 DESIGN USER INTERFACE | 2 RECORD USER INPUT | 3 WRITE VBA CODE | 4 TEST USER INTERFACE
5 SHARE & COLLABORATE | 6 USE COMMENTS | 7 TRACK CHANGES | 8 FINALIZE WORKBOOK

Why? *While editing the worksheet, you may find it helpful to have comments visible.* The comments currently are hidden. The following step makes all comments visible.

- If necessary, display the Review tab and then click the 'Show All Comments' button (Review tab | Comments group) to show all comments in the workbook (Figure 11–51).

- Click the 'Show All Comments' button again to hide all comments in the workbook.

Q&A Can I quickly read a hidden comment in a worksheet?
Point to a comment indicator to display the related comment.

Can I print comments?
Yes. You can print comments where they appear on the worksheet by displaying all comments and then printing the sheet. You can print a list of comments separately using the Sheet tab in the Page Setup dialog box. To do so, click the Page Setup Dialog Box Launcher (Page Layout tab | Page Setup group), click the Sheet tab (Page Setup dialog box), click the Comments arrow, and then click 'At end of sheet' in the Comments list.

What is the Show Ink button and should it be selected?
Comments can be added to worksheets using ink annotations from tablet or touch screen users. If the Show Ink button is turned off, these annotations will not be visible. No ink annotations are recorded in this worksheet, so the button has no impact on which comments are displayed.

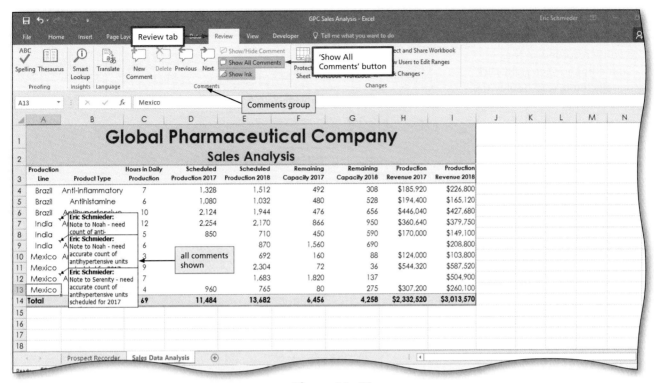

Figure 11–51

To Edit Comments on a Worksheet

1 DESIGN USER INTERFACE | 2 RECORD USER INPUT | 3 WRITE VBA CODE | 4 TEST USER INTERFACE
5 SHARE & COLLABORATE | 6 USE COMMENTS | **7 TRACK CHANGES** | 8 FINALIZE WORKBOOK

You want to alert Noah to the need for verification of a recorded value related to the initial comment in cell A7. **Why?** *After adding comments to a worksheet, you may need to edit them to add or change information or you may want to change the appearance of a particular comment to make it stand out from other comments.* The following steps edit and format the comment in cell A7.

- Click cell A7 to make active the cell containing the comment to format.

- Click the Edit Comment button (Review tab | Comments group) to open the comment for editing.

- Change the comment by typing the words, **to verify recorded**, between the words, need and count, so that the text reads as follows: Note to Noah - need to verify recorded count of anti-inflammatory units scheduled for 2017 production in India (Figure 11–52).

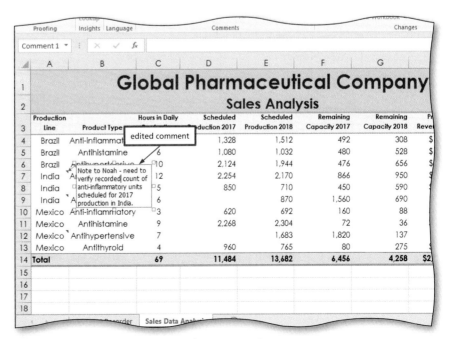

Figure 11–52

2

- Select the words you just added, to verify recorded, in the comment, and then right-click the selected text to display the shortcut menu.

- Click Format Comment on the shortcut menu to display the Format Comment dialog box.

- Change the Color to Red (column 1, row 3) and change the Font style to Bold for the selected text (Figure 11–53).

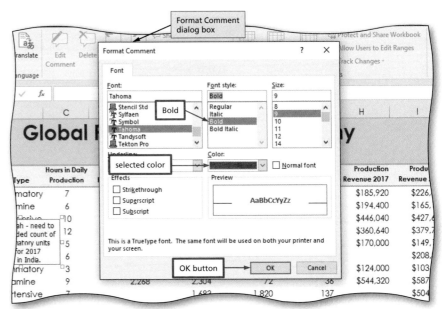

Figure 11–53

3

- Click the OK button (Format Comment dialog box) to apply the selected formatting to the comment text. Use the sizing handles to resize the comment box as necessary so that all the text is visible (Figure 11–54).

- Click cell A4 to deselect and hide the comment.

- Save the workbook again on the same storage location with the same file name.

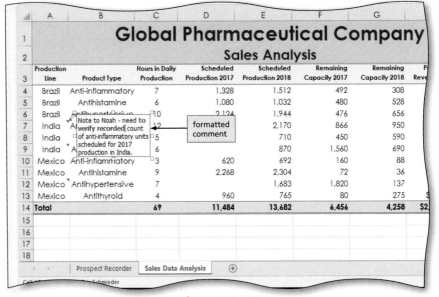

Figure 11–54

Break Point: If you wish to take a break, this is a good place to do so. You can now exit Excel. To resume at a later time, run Excel, open the file called GPC Sales Analysis, and continue following the steps from this location forward.

Tracking Changes on a Workbook

When a workbook is shared with other users, changes made and saved by the other users are visible only when you attempt to save changes. When Excel recognizes that another user has modified a shared workbook, Excel displays a dialog box indicating that the workbook has been updated with changes saved by other users; you then can review and accept or reject their work. If both you and another user change the same cell, Excel displays a Resolve Conflicts dialog box when the workbook is saved. The dialog box lists the conflicting changes and provides options to choose which change to accept in the workbook.

Tracking changes means that Excel, through the Track Changes command, will display the edited cells with a comment indicating who made the change, when the change was made, and what the original value was of the cell that was changed. If either tracking or sharing is enabled, Excel enables the other by default.

To Turn On Track Changes

1 DESIGN USER INTERFACE | 2 RECORD USER INPUT | 3 WRITE VBA CODE | 4 TEST USER INTERFACE
5 SHARE & COLLABORATE | 6 USE COMMENTS | **7 TRACK CHANGES** | **8 FINALIZE WORKBOOK**

Multiple users may make changes to the workbook and you want to ensure that a history of changes is recorded for review. **Why?** *Tracking changes when working collaboratively keeps a record of the changes that others make to a workbook.* The following steps turn on track changes.

- If necessary, display the Review tab and then click the Track Changes button (Review tab | Changes group) to display the Track Changes menu (Figure 11–55).

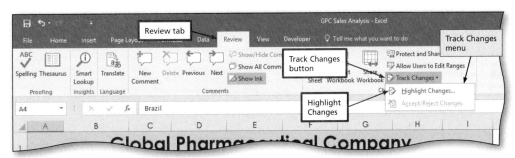

Figure 11–55

- Click Highlight Changes on the Track Changes menu to display the Highlight Changes dialog box.
- Click the 'Track changes while editing. This also shares your workbook.' check box to insert a check mark.
- If necessary, click all of the check boxes in the Highlight which changes area to clear them (Figure 11–56).

Q&A

What is the purpose of clearing the check marks?

Clicking the 'Track changes while editing. This also shares your workbook.' check box enables track changes and shares the workbook. The When, Who, and Where check boxes play no role when you first enable track changes.

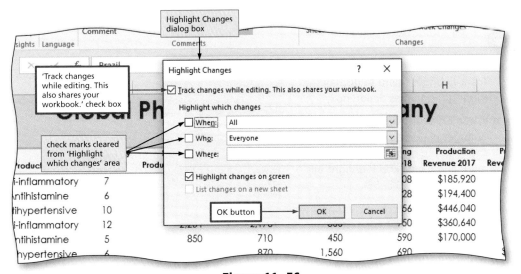

Figure 11–56

- Click the OK button (Highlight Changes dialog box) to close the dialog box.
- If a Microsoft Excel dialog box appears, click the OK button (Microsoft Excel dialog box) to save, share, and track changes in the workbook.

Reviewing Tracked Changes

Instead of writing suggestions and changes on a printed copy and sending it to the person in charge of a workbook, Excel's track changes feature allows users to enter suggested changes directly in the workbook. The owner of the workbook then looks through each change and makes a decision about whether to accept it.

To Open a Workbook and Review Tracked Changes

1 DESIGN USER INTERFACE | 2 RECORD USER INPUT | 3 WRITE VBA CODE | 4 TEST USER INTERFACE
5 SHARE & COLLABORATE | 6 USE COMMENTS | 7 TRACK CHANGES | 8 FINALIZE WORKBOOK

After others have reviewed a workbook, it usually is returned to the owner. When track changes is enabled for a workbook, the file, when returned to the owner, will contain other users' changes, corrections, and comments. *Why review tracked changes? The owner of the workbook then can review those changes and make decisions about whether to accept the changes.* A workbook named GPC Sales Analysis Changed, which includes tracked changes from other users to the GPC Sales Analysis workbook, is saved in the Data Files. The following steps use this workbook to review tracked changes.

- With Excel active, open the file GPC Sales Analysis Changed from the Data Files and then save it as GPC Sales Analysis Reviewed in the same storage location where you save your files.

- If necessary, click the Enable Editing button on the Protected View bar to open the workbook for editing and display the Sales Data Analysis worksheet.

- Display the Review tab and then click the Track Changes button (Review tab | Changes group) to display the Track Changes menu (Figure 11–57).

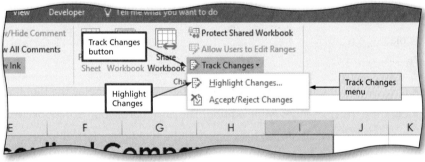

Figure 11–57

- Click Highlight Changes on the Track Changes menu to display the Highlight Changes dialog box.

- When Excel displays the Highlight Changes dialog box, click the When check box to remove the check mark and have Excel highlight all changes (Figure 11–58).

Q&A

What is the purpose of clearing the When check mark?

Clearing the check mark from the When check box indicates to Excel that all changes in the change history should be available for review. Excel can track three categories of changes in the change history. The When check box allows you to specify the time period from which you want to review changes. The Who check box allows you to specify which individual users changes you want to review. The Where check box allows you to specify a range of cells to check for changes.

Why would I select the When, Who, and Where check boxes?
You would select these check boxes when you want to highlight only some changes, such as those made since you last saved or those made by everyone except you.

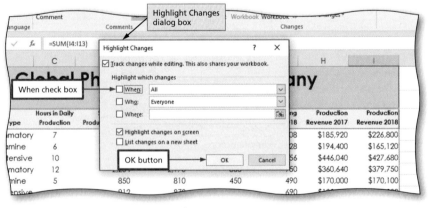

Figure 11–58

3

- Click the OK button (Highlight Changes dialog box) to close the dialog box.

- Point to cell D9 to display a comment box with information about the change made to the cell D9 (Figure 11–59).

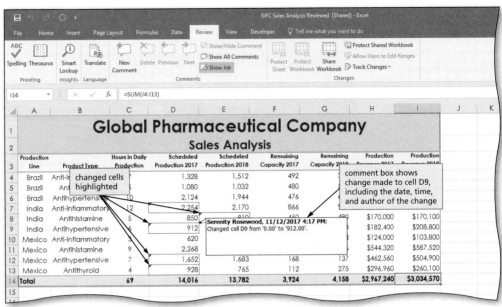

Figure 11–59

4

- Click the Track Changes button (Review tab | Changes group) to display the Track Changes menu.

- Click 'Accept/Reject Changes' on the Track Changes menu to display the 'Select Changes to Accept or Reject' dialog box.

- If necessary, clear all the check boxes in the Which changes area, indicating that all changes in the change history file should be reviewed (Figure 11–60).

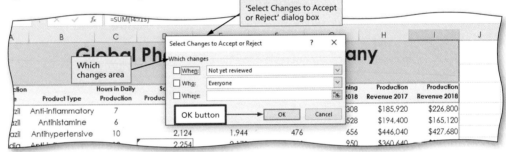

Figure 11–60

- Click the OK button ('Select Changes to Accept or Reject' dialog box) to display the first tracked change (Figure 11–61).

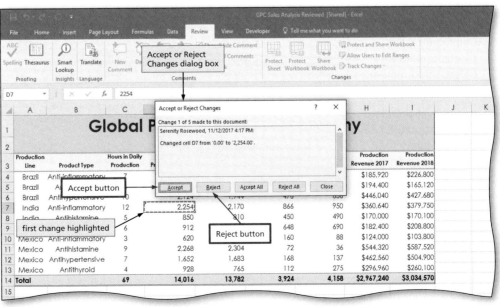

Figure 11–61

6

- Click the Accept button (Accept or Reject Changes dialog box) to accept the change to cell D7 and display the second tracked change.

- Click the Reject button (Accept or Reject Changes dialog box) to reject the change to cell E8 and display the next tracked change.

- As Excel displays each change in the Accept or Reject Changes dialog box, read the details of the change, and then click the Accept button until the dialog box closes.

- Click the 'Show All Comments' button (Review tab | Comments group) to display all comments in the worksheet (Figure 11–62).

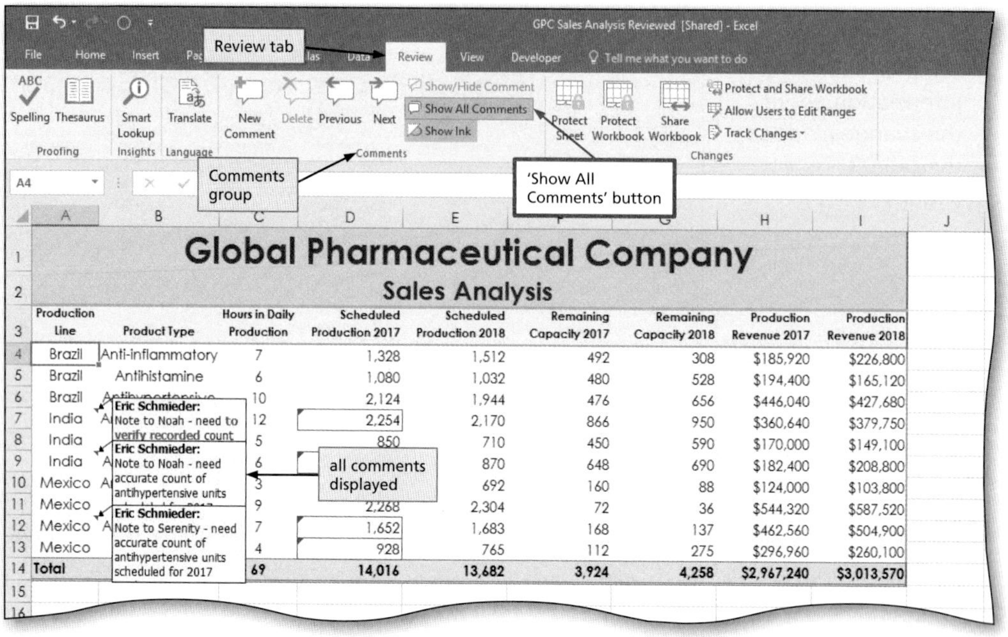

Q&A Could I click the Accept All button to accept all remaining changes?
Yes, though when you click the Accept All button, you cannot review the details of each change.

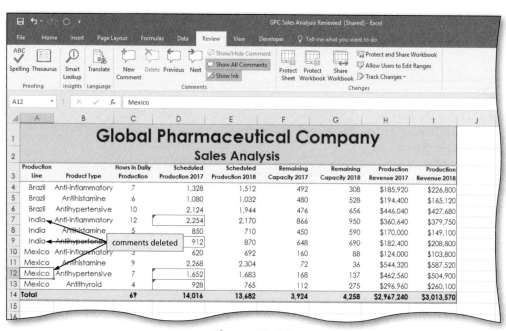

Figure 11–62

7

- Right-click cell A7 and then click Delete Comment on the shortcut menu to delete the comment.

- Right-click cell A9 and then click Delete Comment on the shortcut menu to delete the comment.

- Right-click cell A12 and then click Delete Comment on the shortcut menu to delete the comment (Figure 11–63).

Figure 11–63

Other Ways

1. Click Delete Comment button (Review tab | Comments group)

To Turn Off Track Changes

Why? *When workbook sharing is enabled, Excel denies access to a number of features. Turning off track changes, which also turns off sharing and saves the workbook, provides access to those features again.* The workbook is saved as an **exclusive workbook**, one that is not shared and can be opened only by a single user. The following steps turn off track changes and make the workbook exclusive.

- Click the Track Changes button (Review tab | Changes group) to display the Track Changes menu.

- Click Highlight Changes on the Track Changes menu to display the Highlight Changes dialog box.

- Click the 'Track changes while editing' check box to remove the check mark (Figure 11–64).

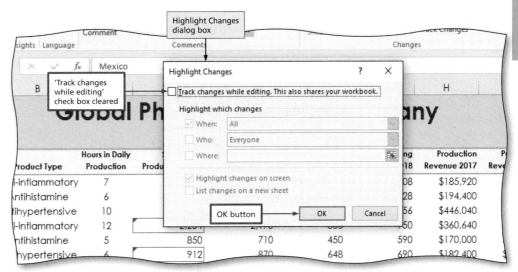

Figure 11–64

- Click the OK button (Highlight Changes dialog box) to turn off track changes, close the dialog box, and display the Microsoft Excel dialog box asking if the workbook should be made exclusive (Figure 11–65).

Q&A What is the change history, and how can it be protected?

Excel keeps a change history with each shared workbook. In the case of a shared workbook in which changes should be tracked, Excel provides a way for users to make data entry changes but does not allow them to modify the change history. To protect the change history associated with a shared workbook, click the Protect and Share Workbook button (Review tab | Changes group). When Excel displays the Protect Shared Workbook dialog box, click 'Sharing with track changes' to select it and then click the OK button. After a shared workbook is protected, no one can unprotect or change it except the owner.

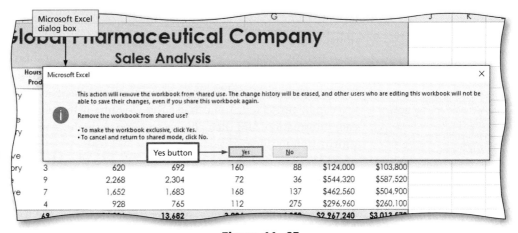

Figure 11–65

- Click the Yes button to make the workbook exclusive.

- Save changes and close the GPC Sales Analysis Reviewed workbook.

What happens when track changes is disabled?

When track changes is disabled, sharing is disabled as well. At the same time, Excel erases the change history. The workbook is saved automatically, as an exclusive workbook, which is not shared and can be opened only by a single user.

How do I know that the workbook is an exclusive workbook?

The text, Shared, is no longer displayed on the title bar.

Finalizing a Workbook

Once a workbook functions in the manner to which it was designed, final touches can be added to the worksheets to make them more attractive and easy to use. Excel provides several ways of finalizing a workbook that include enhancing existing objects and data, preparing custom views for multiple users, protecting your privacy, and saving the workbook in other formats. As you finalize the workbook, you should consider enhancements to charts and data that can make the information more visually appealing or easy to interpret.

For example, to improve the appearance of the Prior Years worksheet, you will add a watermark identifying the content on the Event Expenses worksheet as draft, to ensure that the salespeople understand that the details are subject to change. A **watermark** is semi-transparent text overlaid on the worksheet that is used to convey something about the state of the worksheet, such as Draft or Confidential status. You will also add a background to the Prior Years worksheet. Worksheet backgrounds place an image behind the data in cells of a worksheet.

When preparing the workbook for distribution, consider establishing a custom view so that the content will display in your preferred way when you access the workbook after others have used it. Regional settings in Excel allow for support of global users.

Before distributing your workbook to others, you should consider what hidden information might be in your workbook. As you learned in previous modules, rows and columns can be hidden from view, as can worksheets and workbooks. Cells also can be protected. You can use the Document Inspector to inspect and report such information, and then choose to remove the hidden information or leave the information in the workbook.

Also before distributing a workbook, you should consider whether the intended recipients have the most recent version of Excel. If this is not the case, Excel allows you to save a workbook for use in previous versions of Excel, such as Excel 97-2003. When you save a workbook in the Excel 97-2003 Workbook file format, Excel will invoke the Compatibility Checker, which notifies you if any of the content of the workbook cannot be saved in that format. Additionally, the Compatibility Checker will inform you if any content will appear differently in the Excel 97-2003 Workbook format, such as cell or chart formatting.

To Add a Watermark to a Worksheet

1 DESIGN USER INTERFACE | 2 RECORD USER INPUT | 3 WRITE VBA CODE | 4 TEST USER INTERFACE
5 SHARE & COLLABORATE | 6 USE COMMENTS | 7 TRACK CHANGES | **8 FINALIZE WORKBOOK**

Why? A watermark can be used to provide a reminder to the user. In this case, it will remind the users that the worksheet contains draft content. Excel does not have a watermark function, but you can use WordArt to mimic one. The following steps add a watermark to the Event Expenses worksheet.

1

- Reopen the GPC Events Merged workbook from the storage location where your files are saved and then make Event Expenses the active worksheet. If necessary, turn off workbook sharing.

- Display the Insert tab and then click the Insert WordArt button (Insert tab | Text group) to display the Insert WordArt gallery (Figure 11–66).

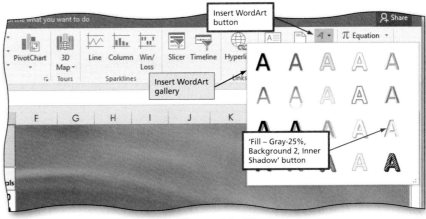

Figure 11–66

2

- Click 'Fill - Gray-25%, Background 2, Inner Shadow' (column 5, row 3 of the Insert WordArt gallery) to insert a new WordArt object.

- If necessary, select the text in the WordArt object and then type **Draft** as the watermark text.

- Point to the border of the WordArt object, and when the pointer changes to a four-headed arrow, drag the WordArt object to the center of the worksheet content, as shown in Figure 11–67.

- With the WordArt text selected, right-click the WordArt object to display a shortcut menu (Figure 11–67).

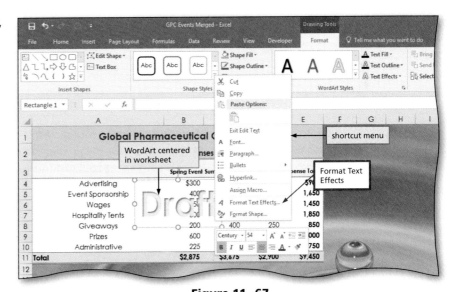

Figure 11–67

3

- Click 'Format Text Effects' on the shortcut menu to open the Format Shape task pane.

- If necessary, click the Text Options tab (Format Shape task pane) to display the sheet.

- Click the 'Text Fill & Outline' tab (Format Shape task pane) and then expand the Text Fill section.

- Set the Transparency slider to 80% to change the transparency of the Word Art (Figure 11–68).

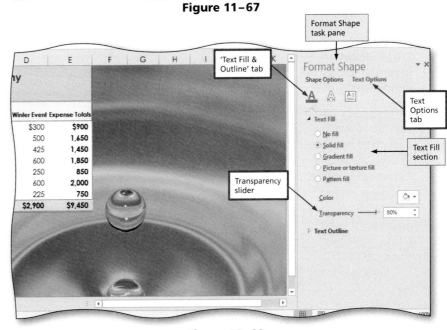

Figure 11–68

- Click the Close button in the Format Shape task pane to close it.

- With the WordArt object still selected, drag the rotation handle until the orientation of the WordArt object appears as shown in Figure 11–69.

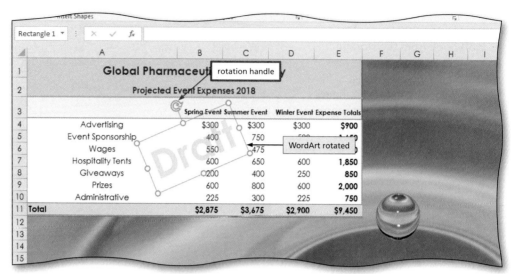

Figure 11–69

To Format a Worksheet Background

1 DESIGN USER INTERFACE | 2 RECORD USER INPUT | 3 WRITE VBA CODE | 4 TEST USER INTERFACE
5 SHARE & COLLABORATE | 6 USE COMMENTS | 7 TRACK CHANGES | **8 FINALIZE WORKBOOK**

Excel allows an image to be used as a worksheet background. *Why? Worksheet backgrounds can provide visual appeal to a worksheet, allowing for a corporate logo or other identifying image to serve as the background for an entire worksheet.* The following steps add an image as a worksheet background to the Prior Years worksheet.

- Display the Prior Years worksheet.

- Display the Page Layout tab and then click the Background button (Page Layout tab | Page Setup group) to display the Insert Pictures dialog box (Figure 11–70).

Q&A — Why do I have additional locations listed in my Insert Pictures dialog box?
If you are logged in to your Microsoft account, you will have additional, cloud-based locations listed.

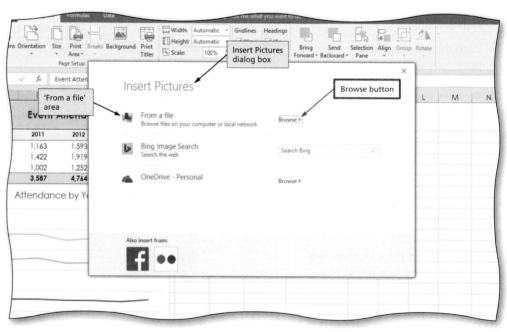

Figure 11–70

- Click the Browse
  button in the
  From a file area to
  display the Sheet
  Background dialog
  box.

- Navigate to the
  location of the Data
  Files, and then select
  the waterdroplet
  image file
  (Figure 11–71).

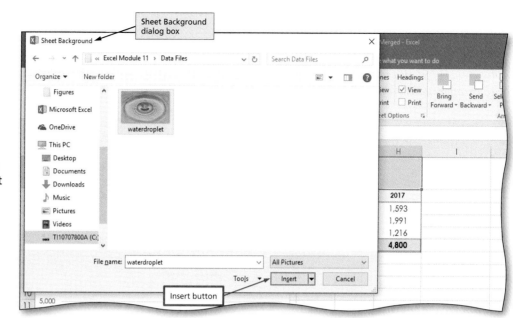

Figure 11–71

- Click the Insert button (Sheet Background dialog box) to display the image as the worksheet background.

- If gridlines are displayed, click the View Gridlines check box (Page Layout tab | Sheet Options group) to remove the check mark and turn off gridlines (Figure 11–72).

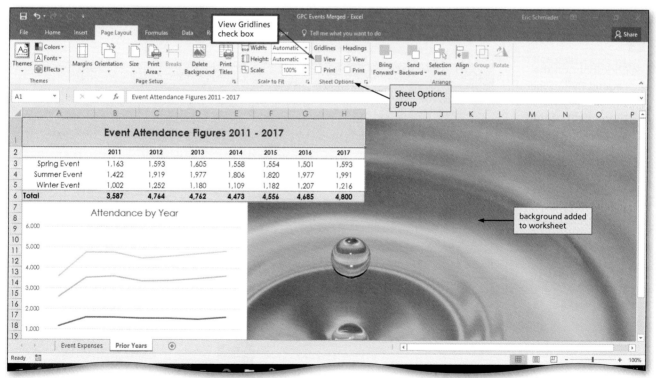

Figure 11–72

To Add a Legend to a Chart

Adding a legend to the chart will improve the readability of the chart by identifying which event each line represents. *Why? With line charts containing multiple lines, a legend is necessary for the reader to be able to understand the chart information.* The following steps add a legend to the chart.

- Click anywhere in the Attendance by Year chart to select it.
- Click the Chart Elements button to display the Chart Elements gallery. Point to Legend to display an arrow and then click the arrow to display the Legend fly-out menu (Figure 11–73).

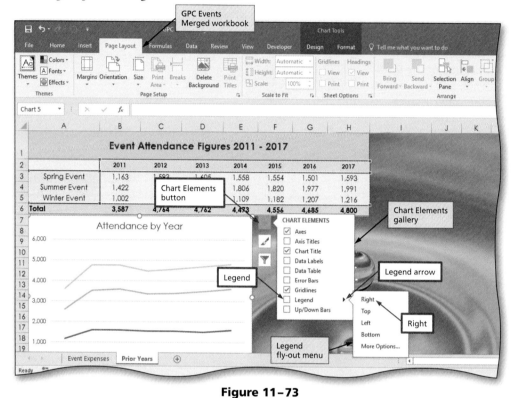

Figure 11–73

2

- Click Right on the Legend fly-out menu to add a legend to the right of the chart.
- Click the Chart Elements button to close the gallery (Figure 11–74).

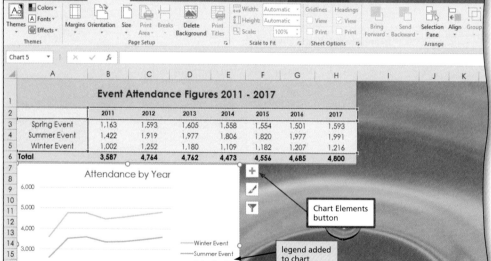
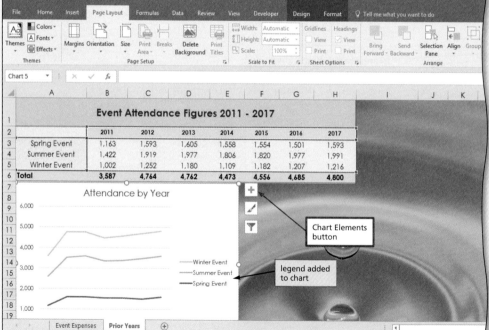

Figure 11–74

To Add a Shadow to a Chart Element

Adding a shadow to the plot area separates it from the other chart elements and improves the visual appeal of the chart. *Why? Shadows and other design features can add depth and a more professional look to your charts.* The following steps add a shadow to the plot area of the chart.

- Click anywhere in the plot area to select it.

- Right-click the plot area to display a shortcut menu (Figure 11–75).

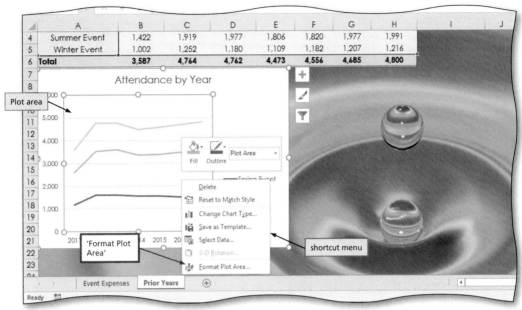

Figure 11–75

- Click 'Format Plot Area' on the shortcut menu to open the Format Plot Area task pane.

- If necessary, click the Effects tab (Format Plot Area task pane) and then expand the Shadow settings.

- Click the Presets/ Shadow button to display the Shadow gallery (Figure 11–76).

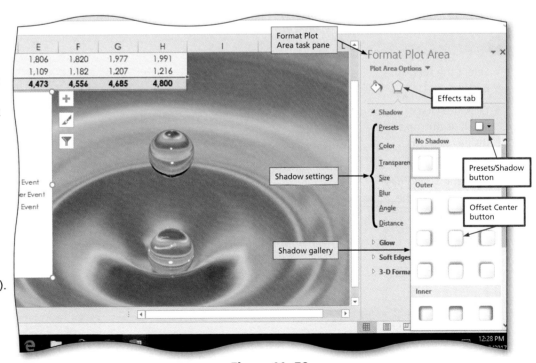

Figure 11–76

- Click the Offset Center button (Outer area) to apply a shadow effect to the plot area of the chart.
- Close the Format Plot Area task pane and then deselect the plot area (Figure 11–77).

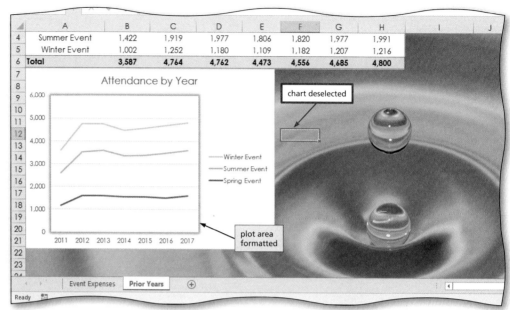

Figure 11–77

To Add a Sparklines Using the Quick Analysis Gallery

1 DESIGN USER INTERFACE | 2 RECORD USER INPUT | 3 WRITE VBA CODE | 4 TEST USER INTERFACE | 5 SHARE & COLLABORATE | 6 USE COMMENTS | 7 TRACK CHANGES | 8 FINALIZE WORKBOOK

Why? *Sparklines are charts that are inserted immediately beside the data that creates them, allowing for easy comparison of numerical and graphical data.* The following steps add sparkline charts for attendance figures.

- Select the range B3:H5.
- Click the Quick Analysis button to display the Quick Analysis gallery.
- Click the Sparklines tab to display the Quick Analysis gallery related to sparklines (Figure 11–78).

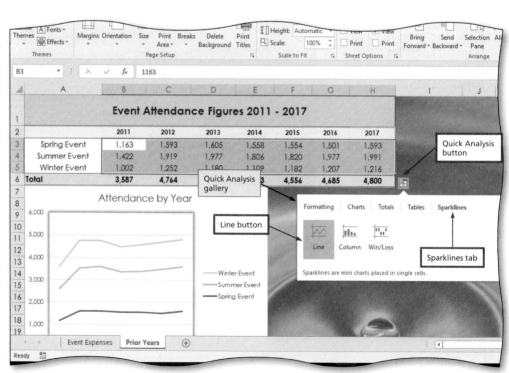

Figure 11–78

- Click the Line button (Quick Analysis gallery) to insert sparklines in cells I3:I5.

- Apply the Tan, Accent 2 (column 6, row 1) fill color (Home tab | Font group) to the range I1:I6.

- Make cell A1 the active cell to deselect the range (Figure 11–79).

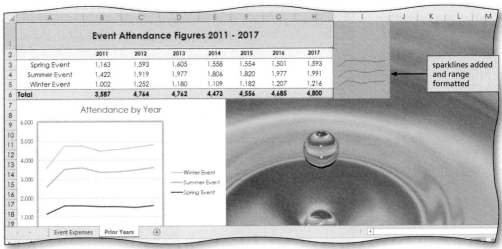

Figure 11–79

Saving Custom Views

Custom views allow certain layout and printing characteristics of a workbook to be saved and then used later. When a custom view of a workbook is saved, Excel stores information about the workbook's current window size and print settings. Before saving a custom view, make sure the workbook reflects the desired layout and print settings.

The Custom Views button on the View tab is used to save, delete, and display custom views. When a user saves a custom view, Excel also stores the name of the current worksheet. When a user displays a custom view by clicking the Show button in the Custom Views dialog box, Excel switches to the worksheet that was active in the workbook when the custom view was saved.

BTW

Save a Chart as a Template
Chart objects can be saved as templates for reuse. To save a chart as a template, right-click the chart, click Save as Template on the shortcut menu, enter a file name for the template in the Save Chart Template dialog box, and then click Save.

To Save a Custom View of a Workbook

1 DESIGN USER INTERFACE | 2 RECORD USER INPUT | 3 WRITE VBA CODE | 4 TEST USER INTERFACE
5 SHARE & COLLABORATE | 6 USE COMMENTS | 7 TRACK CHANGES | **8 FINALIZE WORKBOOK**

Why? *If a workbook requires that you customize certain layout and printing settings to use it effectively, using a custom view allows you to save those settings with the workbook. Whenever the workbook is opened, it will be opened with those settings active.* The following steps create and save a custom view of the GPC Events workbook.

- Click View on the ribbon to display the View tab.

- Click the Zoom button (View tab | Zoom group) to display the Zoom dialog box.

- Click the 75% option button (Zoom dialog box) to select 75% magnification (Figure 11–80).

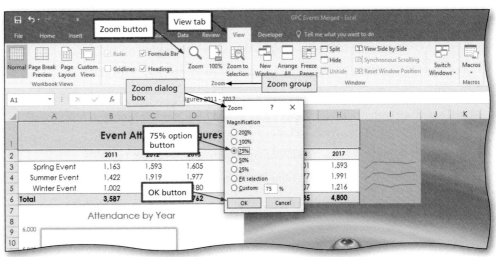

Figure 11–80

2

• Click the OK button (Zoom dialog box) to set the zoom to 75%.

• Click the Custom Views button (View tab | Workbook Views group) to display the Custom Views dialog box (Figure 11–81).

Q&A Why does my Custom Views dialog box contain a list of views?
The views listed will reflect the authors of any open documents as well as any users signed in to Windows.

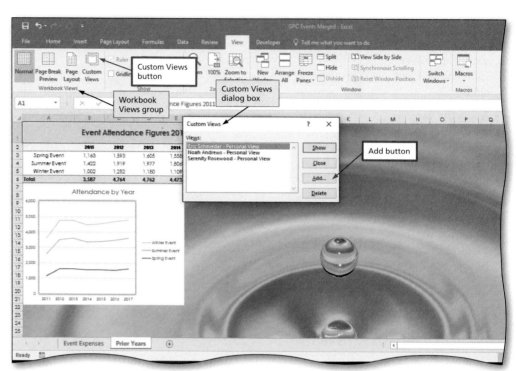

Figure 11–81

3

• Click the Add button (Custom Views dialog box) to display the Add View dialog box.

• Type **Event Attendance** in the Name text box to provide a name for the custom view (Figure 11–82).

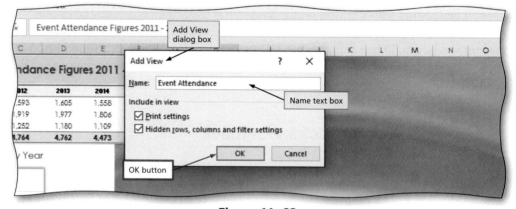

Figure 11–82

4

• Click the OK button (Add View dialog box) to close the dialog box.

• Click the 100% button (View tab | Zoom group) to set the zoom to 100%.

• Click the Custom Views button (View tab | Workbook Views group) to display the Custom Views dialog box.

• Click Event Attendance in the Views list and then click the Show button (Custom Views dialog box) to display the Event Attendance view, which includes a zoom to 75%.

• Click the 100% button (View tab | Zoom group) to set the zoom to 100%.

• Save the workbook again on the same storage location with the same file name.

Q&A Can I delete a custom view?
Yes. To delete custom views, use the Delete button in the Custom Views dialog box shown in Figure 11–81.

Internationalization Features

Excel provides internationalization features you can use when creating workbooks. Use of these features should be determined based on the intended audience of the workbook. For instance, if you are creating a workbook that will be used in European countries where decimal notation differs from that used in North America, consider setting up the workbook to use the European notation by creating custom number formats or changing the symbol used with the Currency or Accounting number formats.

By default, workbooks use formatting consistent with the country or region selected when installing Windows. Situations exist where a workbook will need to contain text or number formatting consistent with a different country or region. Several options are available for applying international formats to content.

Displaying International Symbols

You can format a cell or range of cells with international currency symbols using the Format Cells dialog box. Both the Accounting and Currency number categories provide a selection of symbols for use when formatting monetary cell entries. You also can select from the more commonly used currency symbols when applying the accounting number format by clicking the 'Accounting Number Format' arrow (Home tab | Number group) and selecting the desired currency from the list.

You can use the Symbol button (Insert tab | Symbols group) to enter international characters and monetary symbols as cell entries. To insert a character, click the Symbol button to display the Symbol dialog box, select the font you are using from the Font list, and then scroll until you see the symbol of interest. Select the symbol and then click the Insert button (Symbol dialog box) to insert the symbol at the location of the insertion point in your worksheet.

Displaying Data in Multiple International Formats

Data formatting varies from country to country and region to region globally, including the use of different characters to separate decimal places and differing date formats. If preparing a workbook for use in another region, consider changing the location setting in Windows to the region of your audience. Use the Windows search box to search for Region to access the settings and format options for a specific region.

Collaborating with Users Who Do Not Use Excel 2016

It is not unusual to collaborate with others who are using different software versions, or different software entirely, to do their work. You even can find different versions of software being used within the same company. When collaborating with others, you should make decisions about how to save and distribute files after considering how your colleagues will be using the workbooks you create. In instances where people are working with earlier versions of software or different software, you need to provide workbooks in formats that they can use.

Before sharing a workbook with others, you can mark the workbook as being final. When another user of your workbook opens the workbook, he or she will be notified that you have marked the workbook as final. The workbook can still be edited, but only if the user clicks a button to indicate that he or she wants to edit the workbook.

To Save a Workbook in an Earlier Version of Excel and Mark as Final

Why? *You occasionally need to save a workbook for use in previous versions of Excel. Each version of Excel includes varying features, so you can use the Compatibility Checker to determine if the features used in your workbook are compatible with earlier versions of Excel.* The following steps check the compatibility of the workbook while saving the workbook in the Excel 97-2003 Workbook file format.

1

- Display the Backstage view, click the Save As tab, and then navigate to the location where you store your files.

- Click the 'Save as type' arrow (Save As dialog box) and then click 'Excel 97-2003 Workbook' to select the file format (Figure 11–83).

Q&A Would saving the file using the same name overwrite the original version of the workbook?
No. It is not necessary to save the workbook with a new file name. The 'Excel 97-2003' version of the workbook will have a file extension of .xls, while the original has a file extension of .xlsx.

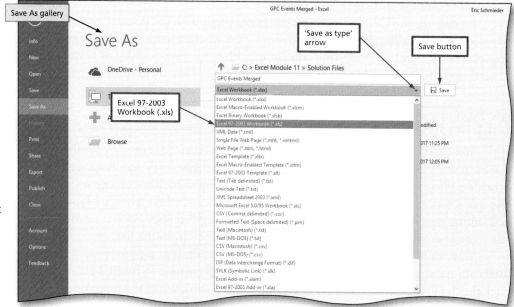

Figure 11–83

2

- Click the Save button (Save As dialog box) to display the Microsoft Excel - Compatibility Checker dialog box.

- Resize the dialog box so that it displays all the issues (Figure 11–84).

Q&A What is shown in the Microsoft Excel - Compatibility Checker dialog box?
The Summary states that some of the chart elements and the sparklines used on the Prior Years worksheet are not compatible with previous versions of Excel. While the workbook still will be saved in the Excel 97-2003 file format, the sparklines will not be saved. In addition, some cell formatting is unique to Excel 2016. These formats will be converted to the nearest approximation in the earlier version of Excel.

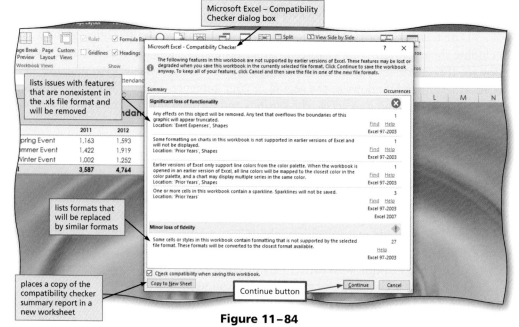

Figure 11–84

3

- Click the Continue button (Microsoft Excel - Compatibility Checker dialog box) to save the workbook in the Excel 97-2003 Workbook file format.

- Display the Backstage view.

- Click the Protect Workbook button in the Info gallery to display the Protect Workbook menu (Figure 11–85).

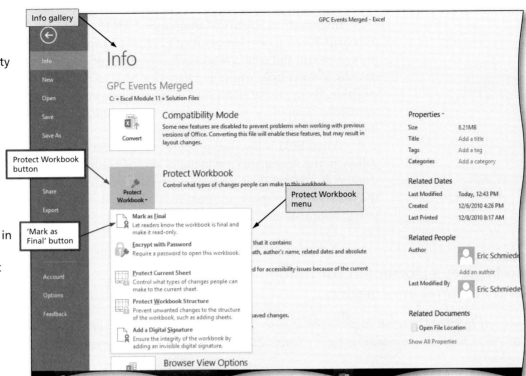

Figure 11–85

4

- Click 'Mark as Final' on the Protect Workbook menu to display the Microsoft Excel dialog box.

- Click the OK button (Microsoft Excel dialog box) to indicate you want to mark the workbook as final.

- If necessary, click the Continue button on the Microsoft Excel - Compatibility Checker dialog box.

- Click the OK button to close the Microsoft Excel dialog box and mark the workbook as final (Figure 11–86).

- Close the workbook.

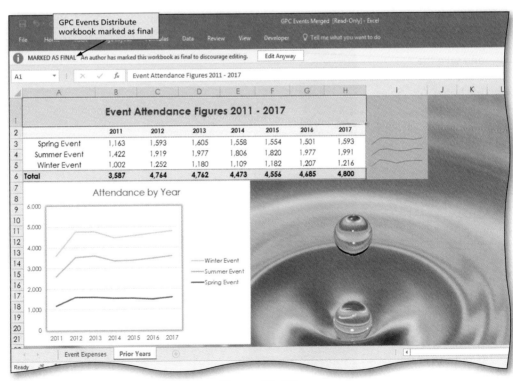

Figure 11–86

Q&A I have saved the workbook in .xls format, but the sparklines are still showing. Why?
Although the .xls format does not support newer features such as sparklines, Excel 2016 does. If you close the file and reopen the workbook saved in the older format, the sparklines will be missing.

Information Rights Management

Information Rights Management (IRM) is a feature of Excel that allows you to restrict access to workbooks. With IRM, you can restrict who can view, modify, print, forward, and copy a workbook. The types of restrictions include a variety of options. For example, expiration dates for reading or modifying a workbook are available. Before using IRM, your computer first must be configured with IRM, as should the computers or mobile devices of anyone attempting to use a document that includes IRM features.

When IRM is installed properly, the Protect Workbook menu in the Info gallery in the Backstage view includes several commands for limiting access to the workbook. You can limit who can access the workbook and who can make changes to the workbook. For more information about IRM, search Excel Help using the search string, information rights management.

To Inspect a Document for Hidden and Personal Information

1 DESIGN USER INTERFACE | 2 RECORD USER INPUT | 3 WRITE VBA CODE | 4 TEST USER INTERFACE
5 SHARE & COLLABORATE | 6 USE COMMENTS | 7 TRACK CHANGES | **8 FINALIZE WORKBOOK**

Why? *The Document Inspector should be used before sharing a workbook publicly or when you suspect extraneous information remains in hidden rows and columns, hidden worksheets, document properties, headers and footers, or worksheet comments.*

The following steps make a copy of the GPC Sales Analysis workbook and then inspect the copy for hidden and personal information.

- If necessary, reopen GPC Sales Analysis and save the workbook with the file name, GPC Sales Distribute.

- If necessary, turn off workbook sharing.

- If necessary, make Sales Data Analysis the active worksheet.

- Display the Backstage view.

- Click the 'Check for Issues' button (Info gallery) to display the Check for Issues menu (Figure 11–87).

Q&A Why did I save this workbook with a different file name?

When preparing a workbook for distribution, you may decide to use the Document Inspector to make changes to the document. Saving the workbook with a different file name ensures that you will have a copy of the workbook with all of the original information intact for your records.

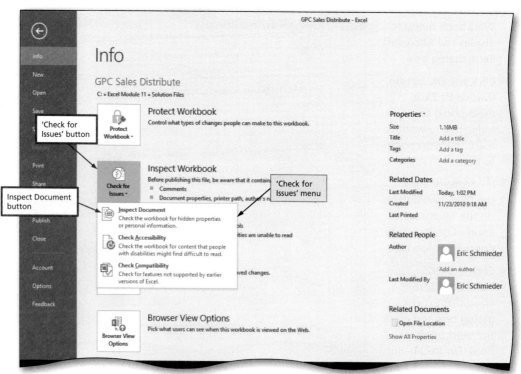

Figure 11–87

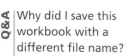

2

- Click Inspect Document (Check for Issues menu) to display the Document Inspector dialog box (Figure 11–88).

Q&A What is shown in the Document Inspector dialog box?
The Document Inspector dialog box allows you to choose which types of content to inspect. Typically you would leave all of the items selected, unless you are comfortable with some types of content not being inspected.

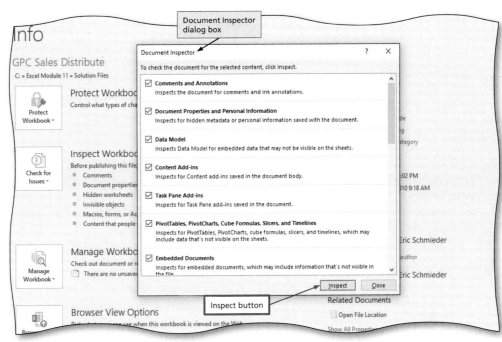

Figure 11–88

3

- Click the Inspect button (Document Inspector dialog box) to run the Document Inspector and display its results (Figure 11–89).

Q&A What did the Document Inspector find?
The Document Inspector found the hidden Prospect List worksheet, comments, and personal information (Figure 11–89), including document properties, author information, related dates, absolute path

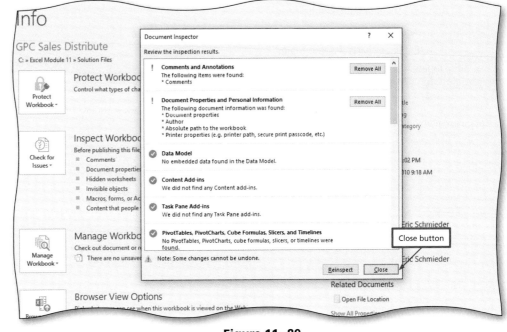

Figure 11–89

to the workbook, and printer properties. The Remove All button in the dialog box allows you quickly to remove the items found if needed. In many instances, you may want to take notes of the results and then investigate and remedy each one separately. In this workbook, all of these items found by the Document Inspector are expected and do not need to be remedied.

4

- Click the Close button (Document Inspector dialog box) to close the dialog box.
- Save the workbook and exit Excel.

Summary

In this module, you developed a custom form for recording information, using form controls, ActiveX controls, and VBA code. You shared workbooks on OneDrive and in a network environment. You compared and merged worksheet data from shared workbooks, used comments to provide feedback, and tracked changes made by other users. You added finishing touches to worksheets, learned about internationalization, and prepared workbooks for distribution.

CONSIDER THIS

What decisions will you need to make when using Excel to collect information or collaborate with others?

Use these guidelines as you complete the assignments in this module and create your own worksheets for creating Excel forms and collaborating with others outside of this class.

1. Determine the purpose and needs of the form data.

    a. Design a user interface with controls appropriate to the data being entered.

    b. Set control properties to give meaning and limitations to each control's use.

    c. Write the Visual Basic code associated with the user's actions, such as clicking a button.

    d. Test the user interface to prove that it behaves as expected.

2. Determine the audience, purpose, and options available for the collaboration.

3. Evaluate changes made by colleagues.

    a. With a single distributed workbook, use Track Changes and Accept/Reject changes.

    b. With multiple workbooks, use Compare and Merge and then Accept/Reject changes.

4. Add worksheet enhancements.

    a. Add watermarks and worksheet backgrounds as appropriate.

    b. Enhance charts if appropriate.

5. Prepare workbook(s) for distribution.

Apply Your Knowledge

Reinforce the skills and apply the concepts you learned in this module.

Working with Comments and Tracked Changes

Note: To complete this assignment, you will be required to use the Data Files. Please contact your instructor for information about accessing the Data Files.

Instructions: Run Excel. Open the workbook Apply 11–1 Travel Expenses from the Data Files and then save the workbook using the file name, Apply 11–1 Travel Expenses Complete.

Figure 11–90 shows the initial workbook. You need to make changes based on comments, create a worksheet showing the history of tracked changes, and accept or reject tracked changes.

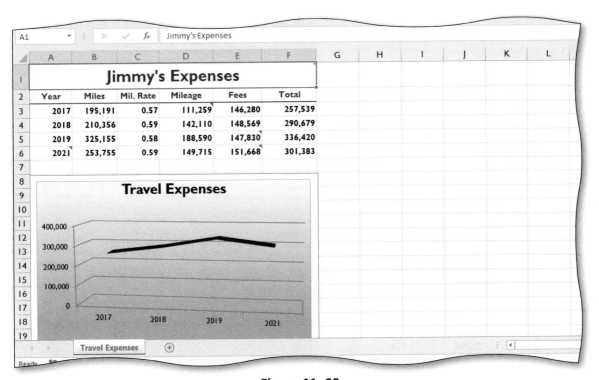

Figure 11–90

Perform the following tasks:

1. If necessary, share the workbook. Click the Track Changes button (Review tab | Changes group) and then click Highlight Changes. Clear the three check boxes in the 'Highlight which changes' area. Click the 'List changes on a new sheet' check box, and then click the OK button.

2. Make the Travel Expenses worksheet active, click the Track Changes button (Review tab | Changes group) and then click 'Accept/Reject Changes'. Clear the When check box and then click the OK button. Accept the change to cell B6. Reject the other change.

3. Click the 'Show All Comments' button (Review tab | Comments group). Make the changes as indicated in the comments. Delete the comments.

4. If requested by your instructor, add a comment to cell A2 noting your date of birth.

Continued >

Apply Your Knowledge *continued*

5. Save your changes to the workbook and then submit the revised workbook as specified by your instructor.
6. You can review changes made to the worksheet either by generating the History worksheet or by reviewing the comments added to the worksheet by the Highlight Changes command. Which method of reviewing changes do you prefer, and why?

Extend Your Knowledge

Extend the skills you learned in this module and experiment with new skills. You may need to use Help to complete the assignment.

Consolidating Worksheets by Category

Note: To complete this assignment, you will be required to use the Data Files. Please contact your instructor for information about accessing the Data Files.

Instructions: Run Excel. Open the workbook Extend 11–1 N&S Art Supplies from the Data Files and then save the workbook using the file name, Extend 11– 1 N&S Art Supplies Complete. Modify the workbook so that it consolidates data from existing worksheets. The data in the worksheets have the same column and row labels (Figure 11–91).

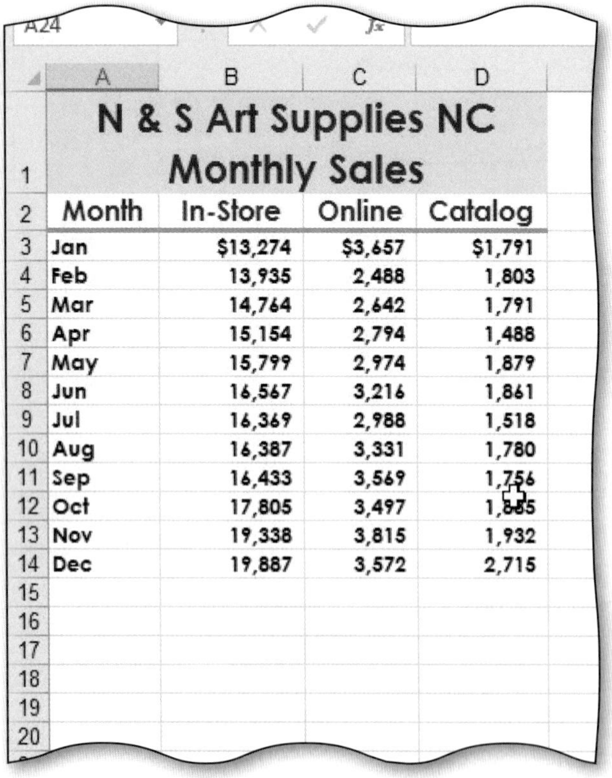

N & S Art Supplies NC Monthly Sales

Month	In-Store	Online	Catalog
Jan	$13,274	$3,657	$1,791
Feb	13,935	2,488	1,803
Mar	14,764	2,642	1,791
Apr	15,154	2,794	1,488
May	15,799	2,974	1,879
Jun	16,567	3,216	1,861
Jul	16,369	2,988	1,518
Aug	16,387	3,331	1,780
Sep	16,433	3,569	1,756
Oct	17,805	3,497	1,885
Nov	19,338	3,815	1,932
Dec	19,887	3,572	2,715

(a) N & S Art Supplies NC worksheet

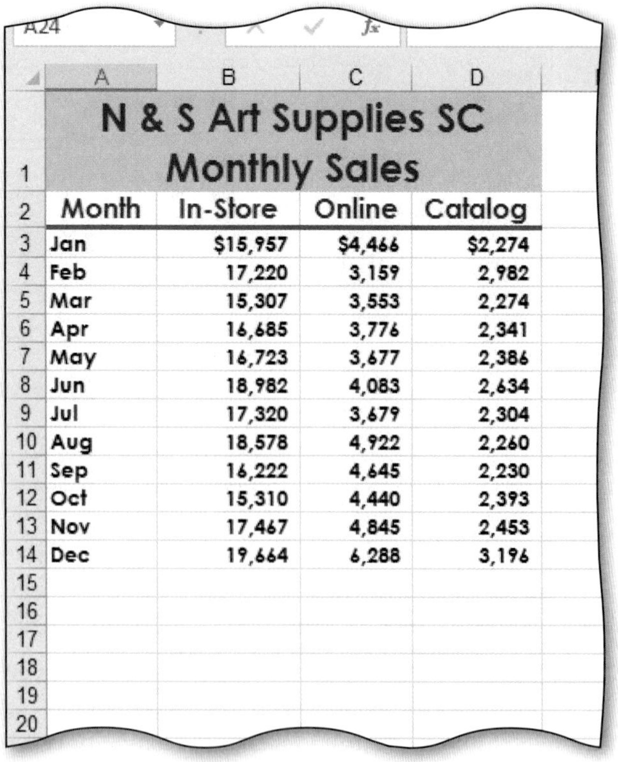

N & S Art Supplies SC Monthly Sales

Month	In-Store	Online	Catalog
Jan	$15,957	$4,466	$2,274
Feb	17,220	3,159	2,982
Mar	15,307	3,553	2,274
Apr	16,685	3,776	2,341
May	16,723	3,677	2,386
Jun	18,982	4,083	2,634
Jul	17,320	3,679	2,304
Aug	18,578	4,922	2,260
Sep	16,222	4,645	2,230
Oct	15,310	4,440	2,393
Nov	17,467	4,845	2,453
Dec	19,664	6,288	3,196

(b) N & S Art Supplies SC worksheet

Figure 11–91

Perform the following tasks:

1. Select the N&S Art Supplies NC worksheet. Select the range A2:D14, and then name the range NC.

2. Select the N&S Art Supplies SC worksheet. Select the range A2:D14, and then name the range SC.

3. Insert a blank worksheet. Name the worksheet Consolidated and color the tab blue. Copy the range A1:D1 from the N&S Art Supplies NC worksheet and then paste it to the range A1:D1 on the Consolidated worksheet. Change the background color of the range to Light Blue from the Standard Colors area in the background color palette. Edit the text in cell A1 to N&S Art Supplies Consolidated Monthly Sales.

4. Select cell A2. Click the Consolidate button (Data tab | Data Tools group). In the Consolidate dialog box, type NC in the Reference text box and then click the Add button (Consolidate dialog box). Type SC in the Reference text box, and then click the Add button. Click the Top row and Left column check boxes to insert check marks. Click the OK button (Consolidate dialog box) to consolidate the worksheets. If necessary, type Month in cell A2. Use Paste Special to copy the formatting and column widths for the ranges A2:D14 from either state worksheet to the consolidated worksheet.

5. If requested by your instructor, change NC to the abbreviation for the state in which you were born.

6. Save the workbook. Submit the revised workbook in the format specified by your instructor.

7. ✳ How does consolidation differ from copying and pasting content from one worksheet to another? How does it differ from using Compare and Merge?

Expand Your World

Create a solution that uses cloud and web technologies by learning and investigating on your own from general guidance.

Preparing Surveys

Problem: You have been asked to create a survey related to either education or employment to illustrate how to use form controls and ActiveX controls in Excel to create a survey and record responses.

Instructions:

1. Run a browser and navigate to http://zoho.com/survey. Search the website for a survey template in either education or employment that you can create in Excel with form controls. Select a template that contains at least 10 questions. Record the web address of the survey template and print a copy.

2. Run Excel and open a blank workbook. Using the skills you learned in this module, create a survey that includes the questions from the survey you found on zoho.com. You should use more than one type of control in creating your survey.

3. Write a VBA procedure to collect the entered data each time the survey is completed and store it on a separate, hidden worksheet.

Continued >

Expand Your World *continued*

4. Use worksheet protection and formatting to set up your survey so that a user can answer questions but not gain access to the hidden worksheet or areas on the current worksheet outside of the survey.

5. Save the file as Expand 11–1 Survey Complete and submit it in the format specified by your instructor.

6. ✳ Did you use ActiveX controls, form controls, or a combination of both in your survey? Explain why you chose one type of control over the other and give one benefit of using the other type of control.

In the Labs

Design, create, modify, and/or use a workbook following the guidelines, concepts, and skills presented in this module. Labs 1 and 2, which increase in difficulty, require you to create solutions based on what you learned in the module; Lab 3 requires you to apply your creative thinking and problem-solving skills to design and implement a solution.

Lab 1: **Merging Workbooks**

Note: To complete this assignment, you will be required to use the Data Files. Please contact your instructor for information about accessing the Data Files.

Problem: As the college-wide tutoring coordinator, you have created a workbook using the time sheets from the tutors and have shared the workbook with the tutoring center managers who made their own copies. They have sent their copies back with their changes to the timesheet data for the various tutors from the Fine Arts, Sciences, and Technology departments of Eastbrook Cole University. Damon, Addyson, and Carlee are the tutoring center managers for the three departments. You now need to merge their changes into one workbook. The result of the merge is shown in Figure 11–92.

Perform the following tasks:

1. Open the workbook Lab 11–1 ECU Tutoring from the Data Files, and then save the workbook as Lab 11–1 ECU Tutoring Complete.

2. If necessary, add the 'Compare and Merge Workbooks' button to the Quick Access Toolbar. Use the 'Compare and Merge Workbooks' button to merge the workbooks Lab 11–1 ECU Tutoring Addyson, Lab 11–1 ECU Tutoring Carlee, and Lab 11–1 ECU Tutoring Damon into Lab 11–1 ECU Tutoring Complete.

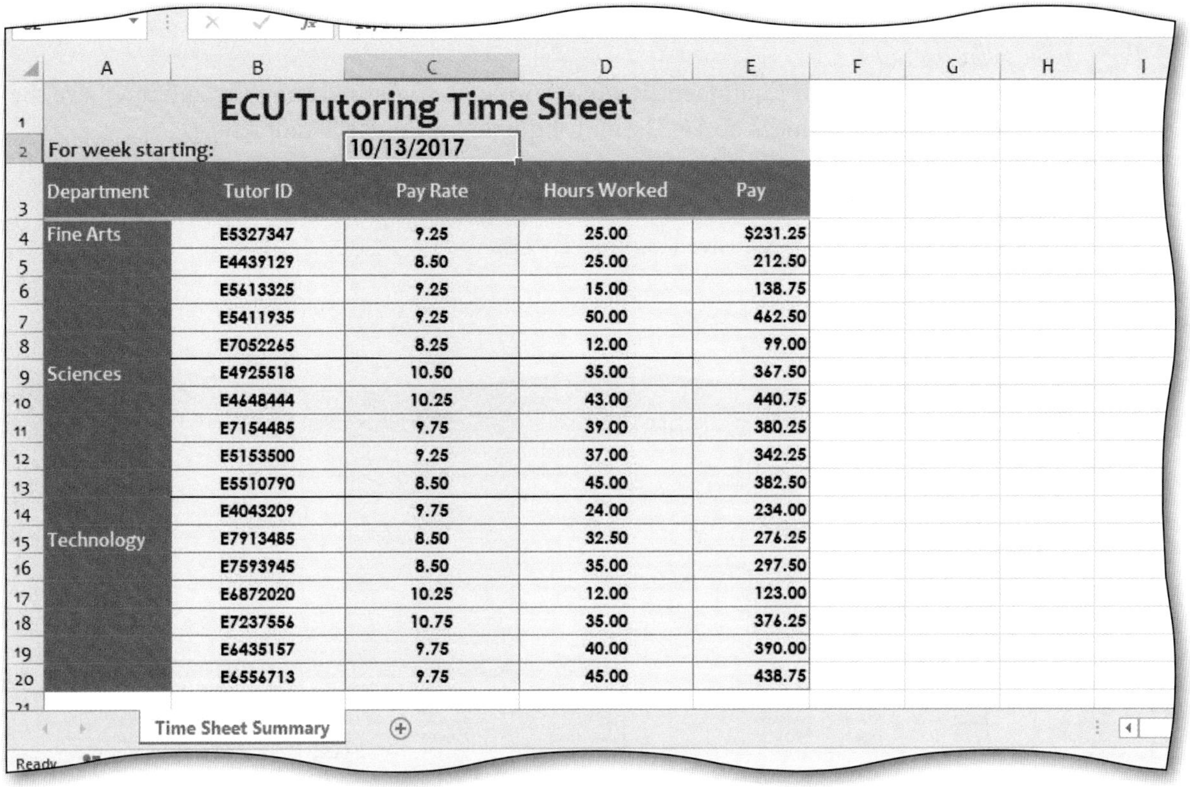

Figure 11–92

3. In the Lab 11–1 ECU Tutoring Complete workbook, use 'Accept/Reject Changes' on the Track Changes menu to accept all changes except for those in cells D7 and D10, which should be rejected. (*Hint:* Clear the When check box.)

4. Turn off sharing so that the workbook is exclusive.

5. If requested by your instructor, add a comment to cell A3 with your date of birth.

6. Save the workbook and submit the assignment in the format requested by your instructor.

7. ✸ What do you see as the disadvantages of merging and accepting/rejecting changes as compared with using comments exclusively for updating content?

Lab 2: **Merging Sales Data and Working with Charts and Backgrounds**

Note: To complete this assignment, you will be required to use the Data Files. Please contact your instructor for information about accessing the Data Files.

Problem: You work for Smith Equipment Rentals. You have been asked to merge revenue data from the three sectors where the equipment is rented. After you have merged the data, you will save a version in a previous version of Excel for sharing with your supervisor, who has Excel 2003.

Continued >

In the Labs *continued*

Perform the following tasks:

1. Open the Lab 11–2 Smith Equipment Rentals workbook from the Data Files and then save the workbook with the file name, Lab 11–2 Smith Equipment Rentals Complete.

2. Merge the workbooks Lab 11–2 Smith Equipment Rentals Sector 2 and Lab 11–2 Smith Equipment Rentals Sector 3 into Lab 11–2 Smith Equipment Rentals Complete. Turn off sharing so the workbook is exclusive (Figure 11–93).

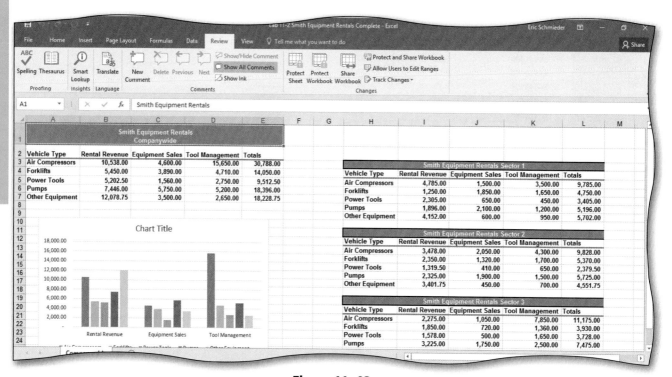

Figure 11–93

3. Enhance the chart by adding an appropriate chart title and a shadow to the plot area.

4. Add sparklines to the range F3:F7 representing the data in B3:E7.

5. Add a worksheet background that reflects the company's products and services. [*Hint:* Click the Background button (Page Layout tab | Page Setup group) and then use the search term, equipment, in the Bing Image Search text box in the Insert Pictures dialog box. Remember that although the Bing Image Search finds images licensed under Creative Commons, the resulting images may or may not be royalty and copyright free. You must read the specific license for any image you plan to use, even for educational purposes.]

6. Make any additional formatting changes to the page that you think are necessary now that the worksheet contains a background image.

7. If requested by your instructor, add a comment to cell A27 containing the name of your hometown.

8. Save the workbook.

9. Save a copy of the workbook using the file name, Lab 11–2 Smith Equipment Rentals Complete 2003, and the file type of Excel 97-2003 Workbook. After reviewing the Compatibility Checker results, click the Continue button (Compatibility Checker dialog box) to save the workbook.

10. Submit the assignment as specified by your instructor.

11. ✳ What formatting changes did you make to the worksheet to accommodate the image you used as a background?

Lab 3: **Consider This: Your Turn**

Apply your creative thinking and problem solving skills to design and implement a solution.

Using Commenting and Track Changes to Evaluate Report Differences

Part 1:   Open the workbook Lab 11–3 On Time Delivery on the Data Files and then save the workbook with the file name, Lab 11–3 On Time Delivery Complete. You have two reports for 2 years of On Time Delivery staffing that contain discrepancies in actual recorded hours by position. You have been charged with identifying discrepancies and then gathering information to better understand these discrepancies. Use the collaborative features of Excel to design a strategy for gathering information and presenting it. Use position titles rather than names for any comments or requests that are to be directed to a particular person. You should prepare a workbook or workbooks containing the collaborative content needed to gather information. In the workbook (or workbooks), insert a new sheet named Instructions. Insert a text box on this sheet and use it to describe how you would use your workbook(s) to gather and present the information requested. Save the workbook(s). Submit the assignment as requested by your instructor.

Part 2: ✳ Identify an alternative approach in Excel to this task, and explain why you chose the method you did over this alternative.

Index